International Business Transactions

Vol. I – Transactional Law Documents

International Business Transactions

Vol. I – Transactional Law Documents

edited by

Professor Dr. Frank Emmert, LL.M., FCIArb

3rd rev. ed., 2020

Copyright Acknowledgments:
Documents contained in this book are reproduced with permission from the following institutions:

Hague Conference on Private International Law
Organization of American States (OAS)
European Union (EU)
United Nations Commission on International Trade Law (UNCITRAL)
International Institute for the Unification of Private Law (UNIDROIT)
National Conference of Commissioners on Uniform State Laws
American Law Institute
International Chamber of Commerce (ICC)
League of Nations
United Nations (UN)
International Civil Aviation Organization (ICAO)
United Nations Conference on Trade and Development (UNCTAD)
International Underwriting Association (IUA)
Lloyd's Market Association
American Institute of Marine Underwriters (AIMU)

In the text of the various materials, "[...]" indicates deletions by the editor;
"[text in brackets]" indicates editorial additions or changes.

Although great care has been taken to include the precise language of the different documents and to have an accurate list of signatories at the end of the different conventions, the editor cannot accept any liability for mistakes in this volume. When in doubt, users are advised to double-check the wording of documents and to obtain the latest status list of signatory countries from the respective organizations that administer the documents.

Published by

Council on International Law and Politics
8409 Bay Colony Drive
Indianapolis, Indiana 46234
http://www.cilpnet.com

Publications Coordinator: Salma Taman
Cover design: Salma Taman

Cover art: Frank Emmert, for more information see http://www.TheIMACGallery.com
and on Instagram frank.emmert

Font Arial

ISBN: 978-1-950137-99-2

for S.T. ~ always and forever

TABLE OF CONTENTS

Vol. I – Transactional Law Documents

Part One: The General Framework for International Business Transactions

Part Two: The Documentary Sale 1 of 4 – Sales Contracts

Part Three: The Documentary Sale 2 of 4 – Payment and Financing Contracts

Part Four: The Documentary Sale 3 of 4 – Shipping Contracts

Part Five: The Documentary Sale 4 of 4 – Insurance Contracts

Volume II – Dispute Settlement Documents

Part Six: Enforcement of International Contracts and Agreements

A. Transnational Litigation

B. International Commercial Mediation and Arbitration

Part One: The General Framework for International Business Transactions

1) 1969 Vienna Convention on the Law of Treaties[1]

The States Parties to the present Convention,

Considering the fundamental role of treaties in the history of international relations,

Recognizing the ever-increasing importance of treaties as a source of international law and as a means of developing peaceful cooperation among nations, whatever their constitutional and social systems,

Noting that the principles of free consent and of good faith and the *pacta sunt servanda* rule are universally recognized,

Affirming that disputes concerning treaties, like other international disputes, should be settled by peaceful means and in conformity with the principles of justice and international law,

Recalling the determination of the peoples of the United Nations to establish conditions under which justice and respect for the obligations arising from treaties can be maintained,

Having in mind the principles of international law embodied in the Charter of the United Nations, such as the principles of the equal rights and self-determination of peoples, of the sovereign equality and independence of all States, of non-interference in the domestic affairs of States, of the prohibition of the threat or use of force and of universal respect for, and observance of, human rights and fundamental freedoms for all,

Believing that the codification and progressive development of the law of treaties achieved in the present Convention will promote the purposes of the United Nations set forth in the Charter, namely, the maintenance of international peace and security, the development of friendly relations and the achievement of cooperation among nations,

Affirming that the rules of customary international law will continue to govern questions not regulated by the provisions of the present Convention,

Have agreed as follows:

Part I. Introduction

Article 1 Scope of the Present Convention

The present Convention applies to treaties between States.

Article 2 Use of Terms

1. For the purposes of the present Convention:

(a) 'treaty' means an international agreement concluded between States in written form and governed by international law, whether embodied in a single instrument or in two or more related instruments and whatever its particular designation;

(b) 'ratification', 'acceptance', 'approval' and 'accession' mean in each case the international act so named whereby a State establishes on the international plane its consent to be bound by a treaty;

(c) 'full powers' means a document emanating from the competent authority of a State designating a person or persons to represent the State for negotiating, adopting or authenticating the text of a treaty, for expressing the consent of the State to be bound by a treaty, or for accomplishing any other act with respect to a treaty;

---

1 ©United Nations 1969. Vienna, 23 May 1969; in force since 27 January 1980; 1155 UNTS 331.

(d) 'reservation' means a unilateral statement, however phrased or named, made by a State, when signing, ratifying, accepting, approving or acceding to a treaty, whereby it purports to exclude or to modify the legal effect of certain provisions of the treaty in their application to that State;

(e) 'negotiating State' means a State which took part in the drawing up and adoption of the text of the treaty;

(f) 'contracting State' means a State which has consented to be bound by the treaty, whether or not the treaty has entered into force;

(g) 'party' means a State which has consented to be bound by the treaty and for which the treaty is in force;

(h) 'third State' means a State not a party to the treaty;

(i) 'international organization' means an intergovernmental organization.

2. The provisions of paragraph 1 regarding the use of terms in the present Convention are without prejudice to the use of those terms or to the meanings which may be given to them in the internal law of any State.

Article 3 International Agreements Not Within the Scope of the Present Convention

The fact that the present Convention does not apply to international agreements concluded between States and other subjects of international law or between such other subjects of international law, or to international agreements not in written form, shall not affect:

(a) the legal force of such agreements;

(b) the application to them of any of the rules set forth in the present Convention to which they would be subject under international law independently of the Convention;

(c) the application of the Convention to the relations of States as between themselves under international agreements to which other subjects of international law are also parties.

Article 4 Non-Retroactivity of the Present Convention

Without prejudice to the application of any rules set forth in the present Convention to which treaties would be subject under international law independently of the Convention, the Convention applies only to treaties which are concluded by States after the entry into force of the present Convention with regard to such States.

Article 5 Treaties Constituting International Organizations and Treaties Adopted Within an International Organization

The present Convention applies to any treaty which is the constituent instrument of an international organization and to any treaty adopted within an international organization without prejudice to any relevant rules of the organization.

Part II. Conclusion and Entry into Force of Treaties

SECTION 1. CONCLUSION OF TREATIES

Article 6 Capacity of States to Conclude Treaties

Every State possesses capacity to conclude treaties.

Article 7 Full Powers

1. A person is considered as representing a State for the purpose of adopting or authenticating the text of a treaty or for the purpose of expressing the consent of the State to be bound by a treaty if:

(a) he produces appropriate full powers; or

(b) it appears from the practice of the States concerned or from other circumstances that their intention was to consider that person as representing the State for such purposes and to dispense with full powers.

2. In virtue of their functions and without having to produce full powers, the following are considered as representing their State:

(a) Heads of State, Heads of Government and Ministers for Foreign Affairs, for the purpose of performing all acts relating to the conclusion of a treaty;

(b) heads of diplomatic missions, for the purpose of adopting the text of a treaty between the accrediting State and the State to which they are accredited;

(c) representatives accredited by States to an international conference or to an international organization or one of its organs, for the purpose of adopting the text of a treaty in that conference, organization or organ.

Article 8 Subsequent Confirmation of an Act Performed Without Authorization

An act relating to the conclusion of a treaty performed by a person who cannot be considered under article 7 as authorized to represent a State for that purpose is without legal effect unless afterwards confirmed by that State.

Article 9 Adoption of the Text

1. The adoption of the text of a treaty takes place by the consent of all the States participating in its drawing up except as provided in paragraph 2.

2. The adoption of the text of a treaty at an international conference takes place by the vote of two-thirds of the States present and voting, unless by the same majority they shall decide to apply a different rule.

Article 10 Authentication of the Text

The text of a treaty is established as authentic and definitive:

(a) by such procedure as may be provided for in the text or agreed upon by the States participating in its drawing up; or

(b) failing such procedure, by the signature, signature ad referendum or initialling by the representatives of those States of the text of the treaty or of the Final Act of a conference incorporating the text.

Article 11 Means of Expressing Consent to Be Bound by a Treaty

The consent of a State to be bound by a treaty may be expressed by signature, exchange of instruments constituting a treaty, ratification, acceptance, approval or accession, or by any other means if so agreed.

Article 12 Consent to Be Bound by a Treaty Expressed by Signature

1. The consent of a State to be bound by a treaty is expressed by the signature of its representative when:

(a) the treaty provides that signature shall have that effect;

(b) it is otherwise established that the negotiating States were agreed that signature should have that effect; or

(c) the intention of the State to give that effect to the signature appears from the full powers of its representative or was expressed during the negotiation.

2. For the purposes of paragraph 1:

(a) the initialling of a text constitutes a signature of the treaty when it is established that the negotiating States so agreed;

(b) the signature ad referendum of a treaty by a representative, if confirmed by his State, constitutes a full signature of the treaty.

Article 13 Consent to Be Bound by a Treaty Expressed by an Exchange of Instruments Constituting a Treaty

The consent of States to be bound by a treaty constituted by instruments exchanged between them is expressed by that exchange when:

(a) the instruments provide that their exchange shall have that effect; or

(b) it is otherwise established that those States were agreed that the exchange of instruments should have that effect.

Article 14 Consent to Be Bound by a Treaty Expressed by Ratification, Acceptance or Approval

1. The consent of a State to be bound by a treaty is expressed by ratification when:

(a) the treaty provides for such consent to be expressed by means of ratification;

(b) it is otherwise established that the negotiating States were agreed that ratification should be required;

(c) the representative of the State has signed the treaty subject to ratification; or

(d) the intention of the State to sign the treaty subject to ratification appears from the full powers of its representative or was expressed during the negotiation.

2. The consent of a State to be bound by a treaty is expressed by acceptance or approval under conditions similar to those which apply to ratification.

Article 15 Consent to Be Bound by a Treaty Expressed by Accession

The consent of a State to be bound by a treaty is expressed by accession when:

(a) the treaty provides that such consent may be expressed by that State by means of accession;

(b) it is otherwise established that the negotiating States were agreed that such consent may be expressed by that State by means of accession; or

(c) all the parties have subsequently agreed that such consent may be expressed by that State by means of accession.

Article 16 Exchange or Deposit of Instruments of Ratification, Acceptance, Approval or Accession

Unless the treaty otherwise provides, instruments of ratification, acceptance, approval or accession establish the consent of a State to be bound by a treaty upon:

(a) their exchange between the contracting States;

(b) their deposit with the depositary; or

(c) their notification to the contracting States or to the depositary, if so agreed.

Article 17 Consent to Be Bound by Part of a Treaty and Choice of Differing Provisions

1. Without prejudice to articles 19 to 23, the consent of a State to be bound by part of a treaty is effective only if the treaty so permits or the other contracting States so agree.

2. The consent of a State to be bound by a treaty which permits a choice between differing provisions is effective only if it is made clear to which of the provisions the consent relates.

Article 18 Obligation Not to Defeat the Object and Purpose of a Treaty Prior to its Entry into Force

A State is obliged to refrain from acts which would defeat the object and purpose of a treaty when:

(a) it has signed the treaty or has exchanged instruments constituting the treaty subject to ratification, acceptance or approval, until it shall have made its intention clear not to become a party to the treaty; or

(b) it has expressed its consent to be bound by the treaty, pending the entry into force of the treaty and provided that such entry into force is not unduly delayed.

SECTION 2. RESERVATIONS

Article 19 Formulation of Reservations

A State may, when signing, ratifying, accepting, approving or acceding to a treaty, formulate a reservation unless:

(a) the reservation is prohibited by the treaty;

(b) the treaty provides that only specified reservations, which do not include the reservation in question, may be made; or

(c) in cases not falling under sub-paragraphs (a) and (b), the reservation is incompatible with the object and purpose of the treaty.

Article 20 Acceptance of and Objection to Reservations

1. A reservation expressly authorized by a treaty does not require any subsequent acceptance by the other contracting States unless the treaty so provides.

2. When it appears from the limited number of the negotiating States and the object and purpose of a treaty that the application of the treaty in its entirety between all the parties is an essential condition of the consent of each one to be bound by the treaty, a reservation requires acceptance by all the parties.

3. When a treaty is a constituent instrument of an international organization and unless it otherwise provides, a reservation requires the acceptance of the competent organ of that organization.

4. In cases not falling under the preceding paragraphs and unless the treaty otherwise provides:

(a) acceptance by another contracting State of a reservation constitutes the reserving State a party to the treaty in relation to that other State if or when the treaty is in force for those States;

(b) an objection by another contracting State to a reservation does not preclude the entry into force of the treaty as between the objecting and reserving States unless a contrary intention is definitely expressed by the objecting State;

(c) an act expressing a State's consent to be bound by the treaty and containing a reservation is effective as soon as at least one other contracting State has accepted the reservation.

5. For the purposes of paragraphs 2 and 4 and unless the treaty otherwise provides, a reservation is considered to have been accepted by a State if it shall have raised no objection

to the reservation by the end of a period of twelve months after it was notified of the reservation or by the date on which it expressed its consent to be bound by the treaty, whichever is later.

Article 21 Legal Effects of Reservations and of Objections to Reservations

1. A reservation established with regard to another party in accordance with articles 19, 20 and 23:

(a) modifies for the reserving State in its relations with that other party the provisions of the treaty to which the reservation relates to the extent of the reservation; and

(b) modifies those provisions to the same extent for that other party in its relations with the reserving State.

2. The reservation does not modify the provisions of the treaty for the other parties to the treaty inter se.

3. When a State objecting to a reservation has not opposed the entry into force of the treaty between itself and the reserving State, the provisions to which the reservation relates do not apply as between the two States to the extent of the reservation.

Article 22 Withdrawal of Reservations and of Objections to Reservations

1. Unless the treaty otherwise provides, a reservation may be withdrawn at any time and the consent of a State which has accepted the reservation is not required for its withdrawal.

2. Unless the treaty otherwise provides, an objection to a reservation may be withdrawn at any time.

3. Unless the treaty otherwise provides, or it is otherwise agreed:

(a) the withdrawal of a reservation becomes operative in relation to another contracting State only when notice of it has been received by that State;

(b) the withdrawal of an objection to a reservation becomes operative only when notice of it has been received by the State which formulated the reservation.

Article 23 Procedure Regarding Reservations

1. A reservation, an express acceptance of a reservation and an objection to a reservation must be formulated in writing and communicated to the contracting States and other States entitled to become parties to the treaty.

2. If formulated when signing the treaty subject to ratification, acceptance or approval, a reservation must be formally confirmed by the reserving State when expressing its consent to be bound by the treaty. In such a case the reservation shall be considered as having been made on the date of its confirmation.

3. An express acceptance of, or an objection to, a reservation made previously to confirmation of the reservation does not itself require confirmation.

4. The withdrawal of a reservation or of an objection to a reservation must be formulated in writing.

SECTION 3. ENTRY INTO FORCE AND PROVISIONAL APPLICATION OF TREATIES

Article 24 Entry into Force

1. A treaty enters into force in such manner and upon such date as it may provide or as the negotiating States may agree.

2. Failing any such provision or agreement, a treaty enters into force as soon as consent to be bound by the treaty has been established for all the negotiating States.

3. When the consent of a State to be bound by a treaty is established on a date after the treaty has come into force, the treaty enters into force for that State on that date, unless the treaty otherwise provides.

4. The provisions of a treaty regulating the authentication of its text, the establishment of the consent of States to be bound by the treaty, the manner or date of its entry into force, reservations, the functions of the depositary and other matters arising necessarily before the entry into force of the treaty apply from the time of the adoption of its text.

Article 25 Provisional Application

1. A treaty or a part of a treaty is applied provisionally pending its entry into force if:

(a) the treaty itself so provides; or

(b) the negotiating States have in some other manner so agreed.

2. Unless the treaty otherwise provides or the negotiating States have otherwise agreed, the provisional application of a treaty or a part of a treaty with respect to a State shall be terminated if that State notifies the other States between which the treaty is being applied provisionally of its intention not to become a party to the treaty.

Part III. Observance, Application and Interpretation of Treaties

SECTION 1. OBSERVANCE OF TREATIES

Article 26 Pacta sunt servanda

Every treaty in force is binding upon the parties to it and must be performed by them in good faith.

Article 27 Internal Law and Observance of Treaties

A party may not invoke the provisions of its internal law as justification for its failure to perform a treaty. This rule is without prejudice to article 46.

SECTION 2. APPLICATION OF TREATIES

Article 28 Non-Retroactivity of Treaties

Unless a different intention appears from the treaty or is otherwise established, its provisions do not bind a party in relation to any act or fact which took place or any situation which ceased to exist before the date of the entry into force of the treaty with respect to that party.

Article 29 Territorial Scope of Treaties

Unless a different intention appears from the treaty or is otherwise established, a treaty is binding upon each party in respect of its entire territory.

Article 30 Application of Successive Treaties Relating to the Same Subject-Matter

1. Subject to Article 103 of the Charter of the United Nations, the rights and obligations of States parties to successive treaties relating to the same subject-matter shall be determined in accordance with the following paragraphs.

2. When a treaty specifies that it is subject to, or that it is not to be considered as incompatible with, an earlier or later treaty, the provisions of that other treaty prevail.

3. When all the parties to the earlier treaty are parties also to the later treaty but the earlier treaty is not terminated or suspended in operation under article 59, the earlier treaty applies only to the extent that its provisions are compatible with those of the latter treaty.

4. When the parties to the later treaty do not include all the parties to the earlier one:

(a) as between States parties to both treaties the same rule applies as in paragraph 3;

(b) as between a State party to both treaties and a State party to only one of the treaties, the treaty to which both States are parties governs their mutual rights and obligations.

5. Paragraph 4 is without prejudice to article 41, or to any question of the termination or suspension of the operation of a treaty under article 60 or to any question of responsibility which may arise for a State from the conclusion or application of a treaty, the provisions of which are incompatible with its obligations towards another State under another treaty.

SECTION 3. INTERPRETATION OF TREATIES

Article 31 General Rule of Interpretation

1. A treaty shall be interpreted in good faith in accordance with the ordinary meaning to be given to the terms of the treaty in their context and in the light of its object and purpose.

2. The context for the purpose of the interpretation of a treaty shall comprise, in addition to the text, including its preamble and annexes:

(a) any agreement relating to the treaty which was made between all the parties in connexion with the conclusion of the treaty;

(b) any instrument which was made by one or more parties in connexion with the conclusion of the treaty and accepted by the other parties as an instrument related to the treaty.

3. There shall be taken into account, together with the context:

(a) any subsequent agreement between the parties regarding the interpretation of the treaty or the application of its provisions;

(b) any subsequent practice in the application of the treaty which establishes the agreement of the parties regarding its interpretation;

(c) any relevant rules of international law applicable in the relations between the parties.

4. A special meaning shall be given to a term if it is established that the parties so intended.

Article 32 Supplementary Means of Interpretation

Recourse may be had to supplementary means of interpretation, including the preparatory work of the treaty and the circumstances of its conclusion, in order to confirm the meaning resulting from the application of article 31, or to determine the meaning when the interpretation according to article 31:

(a) leaves the meaning ambiguous or obscure; or

(b) leads to a result which is manifestly absurd or unreasonable.

Article 33 Interpretation of Treaties Authenticated in Two or More Languages

1. When a treaty has been authenticated in two or more languages, the text is equally authoritative in each language, unless the treaty provides or the parties agree that, in case of divergence, a particular text shall prevail.

2. A version of the treaty in a language other than one of those in which the text was authenticated shall be considered an authentic text only if the treaty so provides or the parties so agree.

3. The terms of the treaty are presumed to have the same meaning in each authentic text.

4. Except where a particular text prevails in accordance with paragraph 1, when a comparison of the authentic texts discloses a difference of meaning which the application of articles 31 and 32 does not remove, the meaning which best reconciles the texts, having regard to the object and purpose of the treaty, shall be adopted.

SECTION 4. TREATIES AND THIRD STATES

Article 34 General Rule Regarding Third States

A treaty does not create either obligations or rights for a third State without its consent.

Article 35 Treaties Providing for Obligations for Third States

An obligation arises for a third State from a provision of a treaty if the parties to the treaty intend the provision to be the means of establishing the obligation and the third State expressly accepts that obligation in writing.

Article 36 Treaties Providing for Rights for Third States

1. A right arises for a third State from a provision of a treaty if the parties to the treaty intend the provision to accord that right either to the third State, or to a group of States to which it belongs, or to all States, and the third State assents thereto. Its assent shall be presumed so long as the contrary is not indicated, unless the treaty otherwise provides.

2. A State exercising a right in accordance with paragraph 1 shall comply with the conditions for its exercise provided for in the treaty or established in conformity with the treaty.

Article 37 Revocation or Modification of Obligations or Rights of Third States

1. When an obligation has arisen for a third State in conformity with article 35, the obligation may be revoked or modified only with the consent of the parties to the treaty and of the third State, unless it is established that they had otherwise agreed.

2. When a right has arisen for a third State in conformity with article 36, the right may not be revoked or modified by the parties if it is established that the right was intended not to be revocable or subject to modification without the consent of the third State.

Article 38 Rules in a Treaty Becoming Binding on Third States Through International Custom

Nothing in articles 34 to 37 precludes a rule set forth in a treaty from becoming binding upon a third State as a customary rule of international law, recognized as such.

Part IV. Amendment and Modification of Treaties

Article 39 General Rule Regarding the Amendment of Treaties

A treaty may be amended by agreement between the parties. The rules laid down in Part II apply to such an agreement except in so far as the treaty may otherwise provide.

Article 40 Amendment of Multilateral Treaties

1. Unless the treaty otherwise provides, the amendment of multilateral treaties shall be governed by the following paragraphs.

2. Any proposal to amend a multilateral treaty as between all the parties must be notified to all the contracting States, each one of which shall have the right to take part in:

(a) the decision as to the action to be taken in regard to such proposal;

(b) the negotiation and conclusion of any agreement for the amendment of the treaty.

3. Every State entitled to become a party to the treaty shall also be entitled to become a party to the treaty as amended.

4. The amending agreement does not bind any State already a party to the treaty which does not become a party to the amending agreement; article 30, paragraph 4(b), applies in relation to such State.

5. Any State which becomes a party to the treaty after the entry into force of the amending agreement shall, failing an expression of a different intention by that State:

(a) be considered as a party to the treaty as amended; and

(b) be considered as a party to the unamended treaty in relation to any party to the treaty not bound by the amending agreement.

Article 41 Agreements to Modify Multilateral Treaties Between Certain of the Parties Only

1. Two or more of the parties to a multilateral treaty may conclude an agreement to modify the treaty as between themselves alone if:

(a) the possibility of such a modification is provided for by the treaty; or

(b) the modification in question is not prohibited by the treaty and:

  (i) does not affect the enjoyment by the other parties of their rights under the treaty or the performance of their obligations;

  (ii) does not relate to a provision, derogation from which is incompatible with the effective execution of the object and purpose of the treaty as a whole.

2. Unless in a case falling under paragraph 1(a) the treaty otherwise provides, the parties in question shall notify the other parties of their intention to conclude the agreement and of the modification to the treaty for which it provides.

Part V. Invalidity, Termination and Suspension of the Operation of Treaties

SECTION 1. GENERAL PROVISIONS

Article 42 Validity and Continuance in Force of Treaties

1. The validity of a treaty or of the consent of a State to be bound by a treaty may be impeached only through the application of the present Convention.

2. The termination of a treaty, its denunciation or the withdrawal of a party, may take place only as a result of the application of the provisions of the treaty or of the present Convention. The same rule applies to suspension of the operation of a treaty.

Article 43 Obligations Imposed by International Law Independently of a Treaty

The invalidity, termination or denunciation of a treaty, the withdrawal of a party from it, or the suspension of its operation, as a result of the application of the present Convention or of the provisions of the treaty, shall not in any way impair the duty of any State to fulfil any obligation embodied in the treaty to which it would be subject under international law independently of the treaty.

Article 44 Separability of Treaty Provisions

1. A right of a party, provided for in a treaty or arising under article 56, to denounce, withdraw from or suspend the operation of the treaty may be exercised only with respect to the whole treaty unless the treaty otherwise provides or the parties otherwise agree.

2. A ground for invalidating, terminating, withdrawing from or suspending the operation of a treaty recognized in the present Convention may be invoked only with respect to the whole treaty except as provided in the following paragraphs or in article 60.

3. If the ground relates solely to particular clauses, it may be invoked only with respect to those clauses where:

(a) the said clauses are separable from the remainder of the treaty with regard to their application;

(b) it appears from the treaty or is otherwise established that acceptance of those clauses was not an essential basis of the consent of the other party or parties to be bound by the treaty as a whole; and

(c) continued performance of the remainder of the treaty would not be unjust.

4. In cases falling under articles 49 and 50 the State entitled to invoke the fraud or corruption may do so with respect either to the whole treaty or, subject to paragraph 3, to the particular clauses alone.

5. In cases falling under articles 51, 52 and 53, no separation of the provisions of the treaty is permitted.

Article 45 Loss of a Right to Invoke a Ground for Invalidating, Terminating, Withdrawing from or Suspending the Operation of a Treaty

A State may no longer invoke a ground for invalidating, terminating, withdrawing from or suspending the operation of a treaty under articles 46 to 50 or articles 60 and 62 if, after becoming aware of the facts:

(a) it shall have expressly agreed that the treaty is valid or remains in force or continues in operation, as the case may be; or

(b) it must by reason of its conduct be considered as having acquiesced in the validity of the treaty or in its maintenance in force or in operation, as the case may be.

SECTION 2. INVALIDITY OF TREATIES

Article 46 Provisions of Internal Law Regarding Competence to Conclude Treaties

1. A State may not invoke the fact that its consent to be bound by a treaty has been expressed in violation of a provision of its internal law regarding competence to conclude treaties as invalidating its consent unless that violation was manifest and concerned a rule of its internal law of fundamental importance.

2. A violation is manifest if it would be objectively evident to any State conducting itself in the matter in accordance with normal practice and in good faith.

Article 47 Specific Restrictions on Authority to Express the Consent of a State

If the authority of a representative to express the consent of a State to be bound by a particular treaty has been made subject to a specific restriction, his omission to observe that restriction may not be invoked as invalidating the consent expressed by him unless the restriction was notified to the other negotiating States prior to his expressing such consent.

Article 48 Error

1. A State may invoke an error in a treaty as invalidating its consent to be bound by the treaty if the error relates to a fact or situation which was assumed by that State to exist at the time when the treaty was concluded and formed an essential basis of its consent to be bound by the treaty.

2. Paragraph 1 shall not apply if the State in question contributed by its own conduct to the error or if the circumstances were such as to put that State on notice of a possible error.

3. An error relating only to the wording of the text of a treaty does not affect its validity; article 79 then applies.

Article 49 Fraud

If a State has been induced to conclude a treaty by the fraudulent conduct of another negotiating State, the State may invoke the fraud as invalidating its consent to be bound by the treaty.

Article 50 Corruption of a Representative of a State

If the expression of a State's consent to be bound by a treaty has been procured through the corruption of its representative directly or indirectly by another negotiating State, the State may invoke such corruption as invalidating its consent to be bound by the treaty.

Article 51 Coercion of a Representative of a State

The expression of a State's consent to be bound by a treaty which has been procured by the coercion of its representative through acts or threats directed against him shall be without any legal effect.

Article 52 Coercion of a State by the Threat or Use of Force

A treaty is void if its conclusion has been procured by the threat or use of force in violation of the principles of international law embodied in the Charter of the United Nations.

Article 53 Treaties Conflicting with a Peremptory Norm of General International Law (jus cogens)

A treaty is void if, at the time of its conclusion, it conflicts with a peremptory norm of general international law. For the purposes of the present Convention, a peremptory norm of general international law is a norm accepted and recognized by the international community of States as a whole as a norm from which no derogation is permitted and which can be modified only by a subsequent norm of general international law having the same character.

SECTION 3. TERMINATION AND SUSPENSION OF THE OPERATION OF TREATIES

Article 54 Termination of or Withdrawal from a Treaty under its Provisions or by Consent of the Parties

The termination of a treaty or the withdrawal of a party may take place:

(a) in conformity with the provisions of the treaty; or

(b) at any time by consent of all the parties after consultation with the other contracting States.

Article 55 Reduction of the Parties to a Multilateral Treaty below the Number Necessary for its Entry into Force

Unless the treaty otherwise provides, a multilateral treaty does not terminate by reason only of the fact that the number of the parties falls below the number necessary for its entry into force.

Article 56 Denunciation of or Withdrawal from a Treaty Containing No Provision Regarding Termination, Denunciation or Withdrawal

1. A treaty which contains no provision regarding its termination and which does not provide for denunciation or withdrawal is not subject to denunciation or withdrawal unless:

(a) it is established that the parties intended to admit the possibility of denunciation or withdrawal; or

(b) a right of denunciation or withdrawal may be implied by the nature of the treaty.

2. A party shall give not less than twelve months' notice of its intention to denounce or withdraw from a treaty under paragraph 1.

Article 57 Suspension of the Operation of a Treaty under its Provisions or by Consent of the Parties

The operation of a treaty in regard to all the parties or to a particular party may be suspended:

(a) in conformity with the provisions of the treaty; or

(b) at any time by consent of all the parties after consultation with the other contracting States.

Article 58 Suspension of the Operation of a Multilateral Treaty by Agreement Between Certain of the Parties Only

1. Two or more parties to a multilateral treaty may conclude an agreement to suspend the operation of provisions of the treaty, temporarily and as between themselves alone, if:

(a) the possibility of such a suspension is provided for by the treaty; or

(b) the suspension in question is not prohibited by the treaty and:

(i) does not affect the enjoyment by the other parties of their rights under the treaty or the performance of their obligations;

(ii) is not incompatible with the object and purpose of the treaty.

2. Unless in a case falling under paragraph 1(a) the treaty otherwise provides, the parties in question shall notify the other parties of their intention to conclude the agreement and of those provisions of the treaty the operation of which they intend to suspend.

Article 59 Termination or Suspension of the Operation of a Treaty Implied by Conclusion of a Later Treaty

1. A treaty shall be considered as terminated if all the parties to it conclude a later treaty relating to the same subject-matter and:

(a) it appears from the later treaty or is otherwise established that the parties intended that the matter should be governed by that treaty; or

(b) the provisions of the later treaty are so far incompatible with those of the earlier one that the two treaties are not capable of being applied at the same time.

2. The earlier treaty shall be considered as only suspended in operation if it appears from the later treaty or is otherwise established that such was the intention of the parties.

Article 60 Termination or Suspension of the Operation of a Treaty as a Consequence of its Breach

1. A material breach of a bilateral treaty by one of the parties entitles the other to invoke the breach as a ground for terminating the treaty or suspending its operation in whole or in part.

2. A material breach of a multilateral treaty by one of the parties entitles:

(a) the other parties by unanimous agreement to suspend the operation of the treaty in whole or in part or to terminate it either:

(i) in the relations between themselves and the defaulting State, or

(ii) as between all the parties;

(b) a party specially affected by the breach to invoke it as a ground for suspending the operation of the treaty in whole or in part in the relations between itself and the defaulting State;

(c) any party other than the defaulting State to invoke the breach as a ground for suspending the operation of the treaty in whole or in part with respect to itself if the treaty is of such a character that a material breach of its provisions by one party radically changes the position of every party with respect to the further performance of its obligations under the treaty.

3. A material breach of a treaty, for the purposes of this article, consists in:

(a) a repudiation of the treaty not sanctioned by the present Convention; or

(b) the violation of a provision essential to the accomplishment of the object or purpose of the treaty.

4. The foregoing paragraphs are without prejudice to any provision in the treaty applicable in the event of a breach.

5. Paragraphs 1 to 3 do not apply to provisions relating to the protection of the human person contained in treaties of a humanitarian character, in particular to provisions prohibiting any form of reprisals against persons protected by such treaties.

Article 61 Supervening Impossibility of Performance

1. A party may invoke the impossibility of performing a treaty as a ground for terminating or withdrawing from it if the impossibility results from the permanent disappearance or destruction of an object indispensable for the execution of the treaty. If the impossibility is temporary, it may be invoked only as a ground for suspending the operation of the treaty.

2. Impossibility of performance may not be invoked by a party as a ground for terminating, withdrawing from or suspending the operation of a treaty if the impossibility is the result of a breach by that party either of an obligation under the treaty or of any other international obligation owed to any other party to the treaty.

Article 62 Fundamental Change of Circumstances

1. A fundamental change of circumstances which has occurred with regard to those existing at the time of the conclusion of a treaty, and which was not foreseen by the parties, may not be invoked as a ground for terminating or withdrawing from the treaty unless:

(a) the existence of those circumstances constituted an essential basis of the consent of the parties to be bound by the treaty; and

(b) the effect of the change is radically to transform the extent of obligations still to be performed under the treaty.

2. A fundamental change of circumstances may not be invoked as a ground for terminating or withdrawing from a treaty:

(a) if the treaty establishes a boundary; or

(b) if the fundamental change is the result of a breach by the party invoking it either of an obligation under the treaty or of any other international obligation owed to any other party to the treaty.

3. If, under the foregoing paragraphs, a party may invoke a fundamental change of circumstances as a ground for terminating or withdrawing from a treaty it may also invoke the change as a ground for suspending the operation of the treaty.

Article 63 Severance of Diplomatic or Consular Relations

The severance of diplomatic or consular relations between parties to a treaty does not affect the legal relations established between them by the treaty except in so far as the existence of diplomatic or consular relations is indispensable for the application of the treaty.

Article 64 Emergence of a New Peremptory Norm of General International Law (ius cogens)

If a new peremptory norm of general international law emerges, any existing treaty which is in conflict with that norm becomes void and terminates.

SECTION 4. PROCEDURE

Article 65 Procedure to Be Followed with Respect to Invalidity, Termination, Withdrawal from or Suspension of the Operation of a Treaty

1. A party which, under the provisions of the present Convention, invokes either a defect in its consent to be bound by a treaty or a ground for impeaching the validity of a treaty, terminating it, withdrawing from it or suspending its operation, must notify the other parties of its claim. The notification shall indicate the measure proposed to be taken with respect to the treaty and the reasons therefor.

2. If, after the expiry of a period which, except in cases of special urgency, shall not be less than three months after the receipt of the notification, no party has raised any objection, the party making the notification may carry out in the manner provided in article 67 the measure which it has proposed.

3. If, however, objection has been raised by any other party, the parties shall seek a solution through the means indicated in article 33 of the Charter of the United Nations.

4. Nothing in the foregoing paragraphs shall affect the rights or obligations of the parties under any provisions in force binding the parties with regard to the settlement of disputes.

5. Without prejudice to article 45, the fact that a State has not previously made the notification prescribed in paragraph 1 shall not prevent it from making such notification in answer to another party claiming performance of the treaty or alleging its violation.

Article 66 Procedures for Judicial Settlement, Arbitration and Conciliation

If, under paragraph 3 of article 65, no solution has been reached within a period of 12 months following the date on which the objection was raised, the following procedures shall be followed:

(a) any one of the parties to a dispute concerning the application or the interpretation of articles 53 or 64 may, by a written application, submit it to the International Court of Justice for a decision unless the parties by common consent agree to submit the dispute to arbitration;

(b) any one of the parties to a dispute concerning the application or the interpretation of any of the other articles in Part V of the present Convention may set in motion the procedure specified in the Annexe to the Convention by submitting a request to that effect to the Secretary-General of the United Nations.

Article 67 Instruments for Declaring Invalid, Terminating, Withdrawing from or Suspending the Operation of a Treaty

1. The notification provided for under article 65 paragraph 1 must be made in writing.

2. Any act declaring invalid, terminating, withdrawing from or suspending the operation of a treaty pursuant to the provisions of the treaty or of paragraphs 2 or 3 of article 65 shall be carried out through an instrument communicated to the other parties. If the instrument is not signed by the Head of State, Head of Government or Minister for Foreign Affairs, the representative of the State communicating it may be called upon to produce full powers.

Article 68 Revocation of Notifications and Instruments Provided for in Articles 65 and 67

A notification or instrument provided for in articles 65 or 67 may be revoked at any time before it takes effect.

SECTION 5. CONSEQUENCES OF THE INVALIDITY, TERMINATION OR SUSPENSION OF THE OPERATION OF A TREATY

Article 69 Consequences of the Invalidity of a Treaty

1. A treaty the invalidity of which is established under the present Convention is void. The provisions of a void treaty have no legal force.

2. If acts have nevertheless been performed in reliance on such a treaty:

(a) each party may require any other party to establish as far as possible in their mutual relations the position that would have existed if the acts had not been performed;

(b) acts performed in good faith before the invalidity was invoked are not rendered unlawful by reason only of the invalidity of the treaty.

3. In cases falling under articles 49, 50, 51 or 52, paragraph 2 does not apply with respect to the party to which the fraud, the act of corruption or the coercion is imputable.

4. In the case of the invalidity of a particular State's consent to be bound by a multilateral treaty, the foregoing rules apply in the relations between that State and the parties to the treaty.

Article 70 Consequences of the Termination of a Treaty

1. Unless the treaty otherwise provides or the parties otherwise agree, the termination of a treaty under its provisions or in accordance with the present Convention:

(a) releases the parties from any obligation further to perform the treaty;

(b) does not affect any right, obligation or legal situation of the parties created through the execution of the treaty prior to its termination.

2. If a State denounces or withdraws from a multilateral treaty, paragraph 1 applies in the relations between that State and each of the other parties to the treaty from the date when such denunciation or withdrawal takes effect.

Article 71 Consequences of the Invalidity of a Treaty Which Conflicts with a Peremptory Norm of General International Law

1. In the case of a treaty which is void under article 53 the parties shall:

(a) eliminate as far as possible the consequences of any act performed in reliance on any provision which conflicts with the peremptory norm of general international law; and

(b) bring their mutual relations into conformity with the peremptory norm of general international law.

2. In the case of a treaty which becomes void and terminates under article 64, the termination of the treaty:

(a) releases the parties from any obligation further to perform the treaty;

(b) does not affect any right, obligation or legal situation of the parties created through the execution of the treaty prior to its termination; provided that those rights, obligations or situations may thereafter be maintained only to the extent that their maintenance is not in itself in conflict with the new peremptory norm of general international law.

Article 72 Consequences of the Suspension of the Operation of a Treaty

1. Unless the treaty otherwise provides or the parties otherwise agree, the suspension of the operation of a treaty under its provisions or in accordance with the present Convention:

(a) releases the parties between which the operation of the treaty is suspended from the obligation to perform the treaty in their mutual relations during the period of the suspension;

(b) does not otherwise affect the legal relations between the parties established by the treaty.

2. During the period of the suspension the parties shall refrain from acts tending to obstruct the resumption of the operation of the treaty.

Part VI. Miscellaneous Provisions

Article 73 Cases of State Succession, State Responsibility and Outbreak of Hostilities

The provisions of the present Convention shall not prejudge any question that may arise in regard to a treaty from a succession of States or from the international responsibility of a State or from the outbreak of hostilities between States.

Article 74 Diplomatic and Consular Relations and the Conclusion of Treaties

The severance or absence of diplomatic or consular relations between two or more States does not prevent the conclusion of treaties between those States. The conclusion of a treaty does not in itself affect the situation in regard to diplomatic or consular relations.

Article 75 Case of an Aggressor State

The provisions of the present Convention are without prejudice to any obligation in relation to a treaty which may arise for an aggressor State in consequence of measures taken in conformity with the Charter of the United Nations with reference to that State's aggression.

Part VII. Depositaries, Notifications, Corrections and Registration

Article 76 Depositaries of Treaties

1. The designation of the depositary of a treaty may be made by the negotiating States, either in the treaty itself or in some other manner. The depositary may be one or more States, an international organization or the chief administrative officer of the organization.

2. The functions of the depositary of a treaty are international in character and the depositary is under an obligation to act impartially in their performance. In particular, the fact that a treaty has not entered into force between certain of the parties or that a difference has appeared between a State and a depositary with regard to the performance of the latter's functions shall not affect that obligation.

Article 77 Functions of Depositaries

1. The functions of a depositary, unless otherwise provided in the treaty or agreed by the contracting States, comprise in particular:

(a) keeping custody of the original text of the treaty and of any full powers delivered to the depositary;

(b) preparing certified copies of the original text and preparing any further text of the treaty in such additional languages as may be required by the treaty and transmitting them to the parties and to the States entitled to become parties to the treaty;

(c) receiving any signatures to the treaty and receiving and keeping custody of any instruments, notifications and communications relating to it;

(d) examining whether the signature or any instrument, notification or communication relating to the treaty is in due and proper form and, if need be, bringing the matter to the attention of the State in question;

(e) informing the parties and the States entitled to become parties to the treaty of acts, notifications and communications relating to the treaty;

(f) informing the States entitled to become parties to the treaty when the number of signatures or of instruments of ratification, acceptance, approval or accession required for the entry into force of the treaty has been received or deposited;

(g) registering the treaty with the Secretariat of the United Nations;

(h) performing the functions specified in other provisions of the present Convention.

2. In the event of any difference appearing between a State and the depositary as to the performance of the latter's functions, the depositary shall bring the question to the attention of the signatory States and the contracting States or, where appropriate, of the competent organ of the international organization concerned.

Article 78 Notifications and Communications

Except as the treaty or the present Convention otherwise provide, any notification or communication to be made by any State under the present Convention shall:

(a) if there is no depositary, be transmitted direct to the States for which it is intended, or if there is a depositary, to the latter;

(b) be considered as having been made by the State in question only upon its receipt by the State to which it was transmitted or, as the case may be, upon its receipt by the depositary;

(c) if transmitted to a depositary, be considered as received by the State for which it was intended only when the latter State has been informed by the depositary in accordance with article 77, paragraph 1(e).

Article 79 Correction of Errors in Texts or in Certified Copies of Treaties

1. Where, after the authentication of the text of a treaty, the signatory States and the contracting States are agreed that it contains an error, the error shall, unless they decide upon some other means of correction, be corrected:

(a) by having the appropriate correction made in the text and causing the correction to be initialled by duly authorized representatives;

(b) by executing or exchanging an instrument or instruments setting out the correction which it has been agreed to make; or

(c) by executing a corrected text of the whole treaty by the same procedure as in the case of the original text.

2. Where the treaty is one for which there is a depositary, the latter shall notify the signatory States and the contracting States of the error and of the proposal to correct it and shall specify an appropriate time-limit within which objection to the proposed correction may be raised. If, on the expiry of the time-limit:

(a) no objection has been raised, the depositary shall make and initial the correction in the text and shall execute a procès-verbal of the rectification of the text and communicate a copy of it to the parties and to the States entitled to become parties to the treaty;

(b) an objection has been raised, the depositary shall communicate the objection to the signatory States and to the contracting States.

3. The rules in paragraphs 1 and 2 apply also where the text has been authenticated in two or more languages and it appears that there is a lack of concordance which the signatory States and the contracting States agree should be corrected.

4. The corrected text replaces the defective text ab initio, unless the signatory States and the contracting States otherwise decide.

5. The correction of the text of a treaty that has been registered shall be notified to the Secretariat of the United Nations.

6. Where an error is discovered in a certified copy of a treaty, the depositary shall execute a procès-verbal specifying the rectification and communicate a copy of it to the signatory States and to the contracting Slates.

Article 80 Registration and Publication of Treaties

1. Treaties shall, after their entry into force, be transmitted to the Secretariat of the United Nations for registration or filing and recording, as the case may be, and for publication.

2. The designation of a depositary shall constitute authorization for it to perform the acts specified in the preceding paragraph.

Part VIII. Final Provisions

Article 81 Signature

The present Convention shall be open for signature by all States Members of the United Nations or of any of the specialized agencies or of the International Atomic Energy Agency or parties to the Statute of the International Court of Justice, and by any other State invited by the General Assembly of the United Nations to become a party to the Convention, as follows: until 30 November 1969, at the Federal Ministry for Foreign Affairs of the Republic of Austria, and subsequently, until 30 April 1970, at United Nations Headquarters, New York.

Article 82 Ratification

The present Convention is subject to ratification. The instruments of ratification shall be deposited with the Secretary-General of the United Nations.

Article 83 Accession

The present Convention shall remain open for accession by any State belonging to any of the categories mentioned in article 81. The instruments of accession shall be deposited with the Secretary-General of the United Nations.

Article 84 Entry into Force

1. The present Convention shall enter into force on the thirtieth day following the date of deposit of the thirty-fifth instrument of ratification or accession.

2. For each State ratifying or acceding to the Convention after the deposit of the thirty- fifth instrument of ratification or accession, the Convention shall enter into force on the thirtieth day after deposit by such State of its instrument of ratification or accession.

Article 85 Authentic Texts

The original of the present Convention, of which the Chinese, English, French, Russian and Spanish texts are equally authentic, shall be deposited with the Secretary-General of the United Nations.

IN WITNESS WHEREOF the undersigned Plenipotentiaries, being duly authorized thereto by their respective Governments, have signed the present Convention.

DONE at Vienna, this twenty-third day of May, one thousand nine hundred and sixty-nine.

Part Two: The Documentary Sale 1 of 4 -- Sales Contracts

2) 1955 Hague Convention on the Law Applicable to International Sale of Goods[1]

Article 1 [Scope of Application]

This Convention shall apply to international sales of goods.

It shall not apply to sales of securities, to sales of ships and of registered boats or aircraft, or to sales upon judicial order or by way of execution. It shall apply to sales based on documents.

For the purposes of this Convention, contracts to deliver goods to be manufactured or produced shall be placed on the same footing as sales provided the party who assumes delivery is to furnish the necessary raw materials for their manufacture or production.

The mere declaration of the parties, relative to the application of a law or the competence of a judge or arbitrator, shall not be sufficient to confer upon a sale the international character provided for in the first paragraph of this Article.

Article 2 [Priority of Party Choice of Law]

A sale shall be governed by the domestic law of the country designated by the contracting parties.

Such designation must be contained in an express clause, or unambiguously result from the provisions of the contract.

Conditions affecting the consent of the parties to the law declared applicable shall be determined by such law.

Article 3 [Default in the Absence of Party Choice of Law]

In default of a law declared applicable by the parties under the conditions provided in the preceding Article, a sale shall be governed by the domestic law of the country in which the vendor has his habitual residence at the time when he receives the order. If the order is received by an establishment of the vendor, the sale shall be governed by the domestic law of the country in which the establishment is situated.

Nevertheless, a sale shall be governed by the domestic law of the country in which the purchaser has his habitual residence, or in which he has the establishment that has given the order, if the order has been received in such country, whether by the vendor or by his representative, agent or commercial traveller.

In case of a sale at an exchange or at a public auction, the sale shall be governed by the domestic law of the country in which the exchange is situated or the auction takes place.

Article 4 [Law Applicable to Inspection of Goods]

In the absence of an express clause to the contrary, the domestic law of the country in which inspection of goods delivered pursuant to a sale is to take place shall apply in respect of the form in which and the periods within which the inspection must take place, the notifications concerning the inspection and the measures to be taken in case of refusal of the goods.

---

1 ©1955, Hague Conference on Private International Law.

Article 5 [Matters Excluded]

This Convention shall not apply to:

1. The capacity of the parties;
2. The form of the contract;
3. The transfer of ownership, provided that the various obligations of the parties, and especially those relating to risks, shall be subject to the law applicable to the sale pursuant to this Convention;
4. The effects of the sale as regards all persons other than the parties.

Article 6 [Public Policy Exception]

In each of the Contracting States, the application of the law determined by this convention may be excluded on a ground of public policy.

Article 7 [Application in Domestic Law]

The contracting States have agreed to incorporate the provisions of Articles 1-6 of this Convention in the national law of their respective countries.

Articles 8 - 12 [Omitted]

Entry into Force: 1 September 1964

Ratifications: Denmark (1964), Finland (1964), France (1964), Italy (1964), Niger (1971), Norway (1964), Sweden (1964), Switzerland (1972)

3) 1986 Hague Convention on the Law Applicable to Contracts for the International Sale of Goods[1]

The States Parties to the present Convention,

DESIRING to unify the choice of law rules relating to contracts for the international sale of goods,

BEARING IN MIND the *United Nations Convention on Contracts for the International Sale of Goods*, concluded at Vienna on 11 April 1980,

HAVE AGREED upon the following provisions:

Chapter I - Scope of the Convention

Article 1

This Convention determines the law applicable to contracts of sale of goods -

a) between parties having their places of business in different States;

b) in all other cases involving a choice between the laws of different States, unless such a choice arises solely from a stipulation by the parties as to the applicable law, even if accompanied by a choice of court or arbitration.

Article 2

The Convention does not apply to -

a) sales by way of execution or otherwise by authority of law;

b) sales of stocks, shares, investment securities, negotiable instruments or money; it does, however, apply to the sale of goods based on documents;

c) sales of goods bought for personal, family or household use; it does, however, apply if the seller at the time of the conclusion of the contract neither knew nor ought to have known that the goods were bought for any such use.

Article 3

For the purposes of the Convention, "goods" includes -

a) ships, vessels, boats, hovercraft and aircraft;

b) electricity.

Article 4

(1) Contracts for the supply of goods to be manufactured or produced are to be considered contracts of sale unless the party who orders the goods undertakes to supply a substantial part of the materials necessary for such manufacture or production.

(2) Contracts in which the preponderant part of the obligations of the party who furnishes goods consists of the supply of labour or other services are not to be considered contracts of sale.

Article 5

The Convention does not determine the law applicable to -

a) the capacity of the parties or the consequences of nullity or invalidity of the contract resulting from the incapacity of a party;

---

1 ©1986, Hague Conference on Private International Law.

b) the question whether an agent is able to bind a principal, or an organ to bind a company or body corporate or unincorporate;

c) the transfer of ownership; nevertheless, the issues specifically mentioned in Article 12 are governed by the law applicable to the contract under the Convention;

d) the effect of the sale in respect of any person other than the parties;

e) agreements on arbitration or on choice of court, even if such an agreement is embodied in the contract of sale.

Article 6

The law determined under the Convention applies whether or not it is the law of a Contracting State.

Chapter II - Applicable Law

Section 1 - Determination of the Applicable Law

Article 7

(1) A contract of sale is governed by the law chosen by the parties. The parties' agreement on this choice must be express or be clearly demonstrated by the terms of the contract and the conduct of the parties, viewed in their entirety. Such a choice may be limited to a part of the contract.

(2) The parties may at any time agree to subject the contract in whole or in part to a law other than that which previously governed it, whether or not the law previously governing the contract was chosen by the parties. Any change by the parties of the applicable law made after the conclusion of the contract does not prejudice its formal validity or the rights of third parties.

Article 8

(1) To the extent that the law applicable to a contract of sale has not been chosen by the parties in accordance with Article 7, the contract is governed by the law of the State where the seller has his place of business at the time of conclusion of the contract.

(2) However, the contract is governed by the law of the State where the buyer has his place of business at the time of conclusion of the contract, if -

a) negotiations were conducted, and the contract concluded by and in the presence of the parties, in that State; or

b) the contract provides expressly that the seller must perform his obligation to deliver the goods in that State; or

c) the contract was concluded on terms determined mainly by the buyer and in response to an invitation directed by the buyer to persons invited to bid (a call for tenders).

(3) By way of exception, where, in the light of the circumstances as a whole, for instance any business relations between the parties, the contract is manifestly more closely connected with a law which is not the law which would otherwise be applicable to the contract under paragraphs 1 or 2 of this Article, the contract is governed by that other law.

(4) Paragraph 3 does not apply if, at the time of the conclusion of the contract, the seller and the buyer have their places of business in States having made the reservation under Article 21, paragraph 1, sub-paragraph b).

(5) Paragraph 3 does not apply in respect of issues regulated in the United Nations Convention on Contracts for the International Sale of Goods (Vienna, 11 April 1980) where, at the time of the conclusion of the contract, the seller and the buyer have their places of business in different States both of which are Parties to that Convention.

Article 9

A sale by auction or on a commodity or other exchange is governed by the law chosen by the parties in accordance with Article 7 to the extent to which the law of the State where the auction takes place or the exchange is located does not prohibit such choice. Failing a choice by the parties, or to the extent that such choice is prohibited, the law of the State where the auction takes place or the exchange is located shall apply.

Article 10

(1) Issues concerning the existence and material validity of the consent of the parties as to the choice of the applicable law are determined, where the choice satisfies the requirements of Article 7, by the law chosen. If under that law the choice is invalid, the law governing the contract is determined under Article 8.

(2) The existence and material validity of a contract of sale, or of any term thereof, are determined by the law which under the Convention would govern the contract or term if it were valid.

(3) Nevertheless, to establish that he did not consent to the choice of law, to the contract itself, or to any term thereof, a party may rely on the law of the State where he has his place of business, if in the circumstances it is not reasonable to determine that issue under the law specified in the preceding paragraphs.

Article 11

(1) A contract of sale concluded between persons who are in the same State is formally valid if it satisfies the requirements either of the law which governs it under the Convention or of the law of the State where it is concluded.

(2) A contract of sale concluded between persons who are in different States is formally valid if it satisfies the requirements either of the law which governs it under the Convention or of the law of one of those States.

(3) Where the contract is concluded by an agent, the State in which the agent acts is the relevant State for the purposes of the preceding paragraphs.

(4) An act intended to have legal effect relating to an existing or contemplated contract of sale is formally valid if it satisfies the requirements either of the law which under the Convention governs or would govern the contract, or of the law of the State where the act was done.

(5) The Convention does not apply to the formal validity of a contract of sale where one of the parties to the contract has, at the time of its conclusion, his place of business in a State which has made the reservation provided for in Article 21, paragraph 1, sub-paragraph c).

Section 2 - Scope of the Applicable Law

Article 12

The law applicable to a contract of sale by virtue of Articles 7, 8 or 9 governs in particular -

a) interpretation of the contract;

b) the rights and obligations of the parties and performance of the contract;

c) the time at which the buyer becomes entitled to the products, fruits and income deriving from the goods;

d) the time from which the buyer bears the risk with respect to the goods;

e) the validity and effect as between the parties of clauses reserving title to the goods;

f) the consequences of non-performance of the contract, including the categories of loss for which compensation may be recovered, but without prejudice to the procedural law of the forum;

g) the various ways of extinguishing obligations, as well as prescription and limitation of actions;

h) the consequences of nullity or invalidity of the contract.

Article 13

In the absence of an express clause to the contrary, the law of the State where inspection of the goods takes place applies to the modalities and procedural requirements for such inspection.

Chapter III - General Provisions

Article 14

(1) If a party has more than one place of business, the relevant place of business is that which has the closest relationship to the contract and its performance, having regard to the circumstances known to or contemplated by the parties at any time before or at the conclusion of the contract.

(2) If a party does not have a place of business, reference is to be made to his habitual residence.

Article 15

In the Convention "law" means the law in force in a State other than its choice of law rules.

Article 16

In the interpretation of the Convention, regard is to be had to its international character and to the need to promote uniformity in its application.

Article 17

The Convention does not prevent the application of those provisions of the law of the forum that must be applied irrespective of the law that otherwise governs the contract.

Article 18

The application of a law determined by the Convention may be refused only where such application would be manifestly incompatible with public policy (ordre public).

Article 19

For the purpose of identifying the law applicable under the Convention, where a State comprises several territorial units each of which has its own system of law or its own rules of law in respect of contracts for the sale of goods, any reference to the law of that State is to be construed as referring to the law in force in the territorial unit in question.

Article 20

A State within which different territorial units have their own systems of law or their own rules of law in respect of contracts of sale is not bound to apply the Convention to conflicts between the laws in force in such units.

Article 21

(1) Any State may, at the time of signature, ratification, acceptance, approval or accession make any of the following reservations -

a) that it will not apply the Convention in the cases covered by sub-paragraph b) of Article 1;

b) that it will not apply paragraph 3 of Article 8, except where neither party to the contract has his place of business in a State which has made a reservation provided for under this sub-paragraph;

c) that, for cases where its legislation requires contracts of sale to be concluded in or evidenced by writing, it will not apply the Convention to the formal validity of the contract, where any party has his place of business in its territory at the time of conclusion of the contract;

d) that it will not apply sub-paragraph g) of Article 12 in so far as that sub-paragraph relates to prescription and limitation of actions.

(2) No other reservation shall be permitted.

(3) Any Contracting State may at any time withdraw a reservation which it has made; the reservation shall cease to have effect on the first day of the month following the expiration of three months after notification of the withdrawal.

Article 22

(1) This Convention does not prevail over any convention or other international agreement which has been or may be entered into and which contains provisions determining the law applicable to contracts of sale, provided that such instrument applies only if the seller and buyer have their places of business in States Parties to that instrument.

(2) This Convention does not prevail over any international convention to which a Contracting State is, or becomes, a Party, regulating the choice of law in regard to any particular category of contracts of sale within the scope of this Convention.

Article 23

This Convention does not prejudice the application -

a) of the United Nations Convention on Contracts for the International Sale of Goods (Vienna, 11 April 1980);

b) of the Convention on the Limitation Period in the International Sale of Goods (New York, 14 June 1974), or the Protocol amending that Convention (Vienna, 11 April 1980).

Article 24

The Convention applies in a Contracting State to contracts of sale concluded after its entry into force for that State.

Chapter IV - Final Clauses

Article 25

(1) The Convention is open for signature by all States.

(2) The Convention is subject to ratification, acceptance or approval by the signatory States.

(3) The Convention is open for accession by all States which are not signatory States as from the date it is open for signature.

(4) Instruments of ratification, acceptance, approval and accession shall be deposited with the Ministry of Foreign Affairs of the Kingdom of the Netherlands, depositary of the Convention. [...]

Article 27

(1) The Convention shall enter into force on the first day of the month following the expiration of three months after the deposit of the fifth instrument of ratification, acceptance, approval or accession referred to in Article 25. [...]

Article 28

For each State Party to the Convention on the law applicable to international sales of goods, done at The Hague on 15 June 1955, which has consented to be bound by this Convention and for which this Convention is in force, this Convention shall replace the said Convention of 1955.

Article 29

Any State which becomes a Party to this Convention after the entry into force of an instrument revising it shall be considered to be a Party to the Convention as revised.

Article 30

(1) A State Party to this Convention may denounce it by a notification in writing addressed to the depositary.

(2) The denunciation takes effect on the first day of the month following the expiration of three months after the notification is received by the depositary. Where a longer period for the denunciation to take effect is specified in the notification, the denunciation takes effect upon the expiration of such longer period after the notification is received by the depositary.

Article 31

The depositary shall notify the States Members of the Hague Conference on Private International Law and the States which have signed, ratified, accepted, approved or acceded in accordance with Article 25, of the following -

a) the signatures and ratifications, acceptances, approvals and accessions referred to in Article 25;

b) the date on which the Convention enters into force in accordance with Article 27;

c) the declarations referred to in Article 26;

d) the reservations and the withdrawals of reservations referred to in Article 21;

e) the denunciations referred to in Article 30.

In witness whereof the undersigned, being duly authorised thereto, have signed this Convention.

Done at The Hague, on the 22nd day of December, 1986, in the English and French languages, both texts being equally authentic, in a single copy which shall be deposited in the archives of the Government of the Kingdom of the Netherlands, and of which a certified copy shall be sent, through diplomatic channels, to each of the States Members of the Hague Conference on Private International Law as of the date of its Extraordinary Session of October 1985, and to each State which participated in that Session.

Entry into force: requires at least 5 ratifications

Ratifications to date: Argentina (1991), Moldova (1997)

4) 2015 Hague Principles on Choice of Law in International Commercial Contracts[1]

Introduction

I.1 When parties enter into a contract that has connections with more than one State, the question of which set of legal rules governs the transaction necessarily arises. The answer to this question is obviously important to a court or arbitral tribunal that must resolve a dispute between the parties but it is also important for the parties themselves, in planning the transaction and performing the contract, to know the set of rules that governs their obligations.

I.2 Determination of the law applicable to a contract without taking into account the expressed will of the parties to the contract can lead to unhelpful uncertainty because of differences between solutions from State to State. For this reason, among others, the concept of "party autonomy" to determine the applicable law has developed and thrived.

I.3 Party autonomy, which refers to the power of parties to a contract to choose the law that governs that contract, enhances certainty and predictability within the parties' primary contractual arrangement and recognises that parties to a contract may be in the best position to determine which set of legal principles is most suitable for their transaction. Many States have reached this conclusion and, as a result, giving effect to party autonomy is the predominant view today. However, this concept is not yet applied everywhere.

I.4 The Hague Conference on Private International Law ("the Hague Conference") believes that the advantages of party autonomy are significant and encourages the spread of this concept to States that have not yet adopted it, or have done so with significant restrictions, as well as the continued development and refinement of the concept where it is already accepted.

I.5 Accordingly, the Hague Conference has promulgated the Hague Principles on Choice of Law in International Commercial Contracts ("the Principles"). The Principles can be seen both as an illustration of how a comprehensive choice of law regime for giving effect to party autonomy may be constructed and as a guide to "best practices" in establishing and refining such a regime.

Choice of Law Agreements

I.6 The parties' choice of law must be distinguished from the terms of the parties' primary contractual arrangement ("main contract"). The main contract could be, for example, a sales contract, services contract or loan contract. Parties may either choose the applicable law in their main contract or by making a separate agreement on choice of law (hereinafter each referred to as a "choice of law agreement").

I.7 Choice of law agreements should also be distinguished from "jurisdiction clauses" (or agreements), "forum selection clauses" (or agreements) or "choice of court clauses" (or agreements), all of which are synonyms for the parties' agreement on the forum (usually a court) that will decide their dispute. Choice of law agreements should also be distinguished from "arbitration clauses" (or agreements), that denote the parties' agreement to submit their dispute to an arbitral tribunal. While these clauses or agreements (collectively referred to as "dispute resolution agreements") are often combined in practice with choice of law agreements, they serve different purposes. The Principles deal only with choice of law agreements and not with dispute resolution agreements or other matters commonly considered to be procedural issues.

---

1 ©2015, Hague Conference on Private International Law.

Nature of the Principles

I.8 As their title suggests, the Principles do not constitute a formally binding instrument such as a Convention that States are obliged to directly apply or incorporate into their domestic law. Nor is this instrument a model law that States are encouraged to enact. Rather, it is a non-binding set of principles, which the Hague Conference encourages States to incorporate into their domestic choice of law regimes in a manner appropriate for the circumstances of each State. In this way, the Principles can guide the reform of domestic law on choice of law and operate alongside existing instruments on the subject (see Rome I Regulation and Mexico City Convention both of which embrace and apply the concept of party autonomy).

I.9 As a non-binding instrument, the Principles differ from other instruments developed by the Hague Conference. While the Hague Conference does not exclude the possibility of developing a binding instrument in the future, it considers that an advisory set of non- binding principles is more appropriate at the present time in promoting the acceptance of the principle of party autonomy for choice of law in international contracts and the development of well-crafted legal regimes that apply that principle in a balanced and workable manner. As the Principles influence law reform, they should encourage continuing harmonisation among States in their treatment of this topic and, perhaps, bring about circumstances in which a binding instrument would be appropriate.

I.10 While the promulgation of non-binding principles is novel for the Hague Conference, such instruments are relatively common. Indeed, the Principles add to a growing number of non-binding instruments of other organisations that have achieved success in developing and harmonising law. See, e.g., the influence of the UNIDROIT Principles and the PECL on the development of contract law.

Purpose and Scope of the Principles

I.11 The overarching aim of the Principles is to reinforce party autonomy and to ensure that the law chosen by the parties has the widest scope of application, subject to clearly defined limits (Preamble, para. 1).

I.12 In order for the Principles to apply, two criteria must be satisfied. First, the contract in question must be "international". A contract is "international" within the meaning given to that term in the Principles unless the parties have their establishments in the same State and the relationship of the parties and all other relevant elements, regardless of the chosen law, are connected only with that State (see Art. 1(2)). The second criterion is that each party to the contract must be acting in the exercise of its trade or profession (see Art. 1(1)). The Principles expressly exclude from their scope certain specific categories of contracts in which the bargaining power of one party – a consumer or employee – is presumptively weaker (see Art. 1(1)).

I.13 While the aim of the Principles is to promote the acceptance of party autonomy for choice of law, the principles also provide for limitations on that autonomy. The most important limitations to party autonomy, and thus the application of the parties' chosen law, are contained in Article 11. Article 11 addresses limitations resulting from overriding mandatory rules and public policy (ordre public). The purpose of those limitations is to ensure that, in certain circumstances, the parties' choice of law does not have the effect of excluding certain rules and policies that are of fundamental importance to States.

I.14 The Principles provide rules only for situations in which the parties have made a choice of law (express or tacit) by agreement. The Principles do not provide rules for determining the applicable law in the absence of party choice. The reasons for this exclusion are twofold. First, the goal of the Principles is to further party autonomy rather than provide a comprehensive body of principles for determining the law applicable to international commercial contracts. Secondly, a consensus with respect to the rules that determine the applicable law in the absence of choice is currently lacking. The limitation of the scope of the Principles does not, however, preclude the Hague Conference from developing rules at a later date for the determination of the law applicable to contracts in the absence of a choice of law agreement.

Content of the Principles

I.15 The Preamble and 12 articles comprising the instrument may be considered to be an international code of current best practice with respect to the recognition of party autonomy in choice of law in international commercial contracts, with certain innovative provisions as appropriate.

I.16 Some provisions reflect an approach that is the subject of wide, international consensus. These include the fundamental ability of the parties to choose the applicable law (Preamble, para. 1 and Art. 2(1)) and appropriate limitations on the application of the parties' chosen law (see Art. 11). It is to be expected that a State that adopts a regime that supports party autonomy would necessarily adopt rules consistent with these provisions.

I.17 Other provisions reflect the view of the Hague Conference as to best practice and provide helpful clarifications for those States that accept party autonomy. These include provisions addressing the ability of parties to choose different laws to apply to different parts of their contract (see Art. 2(2)), to tacitly choose the applicable law (see Art. 4) and to modify their choice of law (see Art. 2(3)), as well as the lack of a required connection between the chosen law and the transaction or the parties (see Art. 2(4)). Also, in line with many national regimes and regional instruments, Article 7 provides for the separate treatment of the validity of a choice of law agreement from the validity of the main contract; and Article 9 describes the scope of the applicable law. Other best practice provisions provide guidance as to how to determine the scope of the application of the chosen law in the context of a triangular relationship of assignment (see Art. 10) and how to deal with parties that have establishments in more than one State (see Art. 12). Such best practice provisions provide important advice to States in adopting or modernising a regime that supports party autonomy. However, the Hague Conference recognises that a State can have a well-functioning party autonomy regime that does not accept all of these best practices.

I.18 Certain provisions of the Principles reflect novel solutions. One of the salient features is found in Article 3, which allows the parties to choose not only the law of a State but also "rules of law", emanating from non-State sources, within certain parameters. Historically, choice of norms or "rules of law" has typically been contemplated only in an arbitral context. Where a dispute is subject to litigation before a State court, private international law regimes have traditionally required that the parties' choice of law agreement designate a State system of law. Some regimes have allowed parties to incorporate by reference in their contract "rules of law" or trade usages. Incorporation by reference, however, is different from allowing parties to choose "rules of law" as the law applicable to their contract.

I.19 Other innovative provisions are contained in Articles 5, 6 and 8. Article 5 provides a substantive rule of private international law that no particular form is required for a choice of law agreement to be valid, unless otherwise agreed by the parties. Article 6 provides, inter alia, a solution to the vexed problem of the "battle of forms" or, more specifically, the outcome when both parties make choices of law via the exchange of "standard terms". Article 8 provides for the exclusion of renvoi but, unlike many other instruments, allows the parties to expressly agree otherwise.

Envisaged Users of the Principles

I.20 The envisaged users of the Principles include lawmakers, courts and arbitral tribunals, and parties and their legal advisors.

a. For lawmakers (whether legislators or courts), the Principles constitute a model that can be used to create new, or supplement and further develop, existing rules on choice of law

(Preamble, paras 2-3). Because of their non-binding nature, lawmakers at a national, regional, supranational or international level can implement the Principles in whole or in part. Lawmakers also retain the possibility of making policy decisions where the Principles defer to the law of the forum (see Arts 3, 11(2) and 11(4)).

b. For courts and arbitral tribunals, the Principles provide guidance as to how to approach questions concerning the validity and effects of a choice of law agreement, and resolve choice of law disputes within the prevailing legal framework (Preamble, paras 3-4). The Principles may be useful, in particular, for addressing novel situations.

c. For parties and their legal advisors, the Principles provide guidance as to the law or "rules of law" that the parties may legitimately be able to choose, and the relevant parameters and considerations when making a choice of law, including important issues as to the validity and effects of their choice, and the drafting of an enforceable choice of law agreement.

I.21 Users of the Principles are encouraged to read the articles in conjunction with the Preamble and Commentary. The Commentary accompanies each article and serves as an explanatory and interpretative tool. The Commentary includes many practical examples illustrating the application of the Principles. The structure and length of each commentary and illustration varies depending on the level of detail required to understand each article. The Commentary also includes comparative references to regional, supranational, or international instruments and to drafting history, where such references assist with interpretation. Users may also wish to consult the bibliography and materials accessible on the Hague Conference website.

Preamble

This instrument sets forth general principles concerning choice of law in international commercial contracts. They affirm the principle of party autonomy with limited exceptions.

They may be used as a model for national, regional, supranational or international instruments.

They may be used to interpret, supplement and develop rules of private international law.

They may be applied by courts and by arbitral tribunals.

Article 1 - Scope of the Principles

1. These Principles apply to choice of law in international contracts where each party is acting in the exercise of its trade or profession. They do not apply to consumer or employment contracts.

2. For the purposes of these Principles, a contract is international unless each party has its establishment in the same State and the relationship of the parties and all other relevant elements, regardless of the chosen law, are connected only with that State.

3. These Principles do not address the law governing -

a) the capacity of natural persons;

b) arbitration agreements and agreements on choice of court;

c) companies or other collective bodies and trusts;

d) insolvency;

e) the proprietary effects of contracts;

f) the issue of whether an agent is able to bind a principal to a third party.

Article 2 - Freedom of Choice

1. A contract is governed by the law chosen by the parties.

2. The parties may choose -

a) the law applicable to the whole contract or to only part of it; and

b) different laws for different parts of the contract.

3. The choice may be made or modified at any time. A choice or modification made after the contract has been concluded shall not prejudice its formal validity or the rights of third parties.

4. No connection is required between the law chosen and the parties or their transaction.

Article 3 - Rules of Law

The law chosen by the parties may be rules of law that are generally accepted on an international, supranational or regional level as a neutral and balanced set of rules, unless the law of the forum provides otherwise.

Article 4 - Express and Tacit Choice

A choice of law, or any modification of a choice of law, must be made expressly or appear clearly from the provisions of the contract or the circumstances. An agreement between the parties to confer jurisdiction on a court or an arbitral tribunal to determine disputes under the contract is not in itself equivalent to a choice of law.

Article 5 - Formal Validity of the Choice of Law

A choice of law is not subject to any requirement as to form unless otherwise agreed by the parties.

Article 6 - Agreement on the Choice of Law and Battle of Forms

1. Subject to paragraph 2 -

a) whether the parties have agreed to a choice of law is determined by the law that was purportedly agreed to;

b) if the parties have used standard terms designating two different laws and under both of these laws the same standard terms prevail, the law designated in the prevailing terms applies; if under these laws different standard terms prevail, or if under one or both of these laws no standard terms prevail, there is no choice of law.

2. The law of the State in which a party has its establishment determines whether that party has consented to the choice of law if, under the circumstances, it would not be reasonable to make that determination under the law specified in paragraph 1.

Article 7 - Severability

A choice of law cannot be contested solely on the ground that the contract to which it applies is not valid.

Article 8 - Exclusion of Renvoi

A choice of law does not refer to rules of private international law of the law chosen by the parties unless the parties expressly provide otherwise.

Article 9 - Scope of the Chosen Law

1. The law chosen by the parties shall govern all aspects of the contract between the parties, including but not limited to -

a) interpretation;

b) rights and obligations arising from the contract;

c) performance and the consequences of non-performance, including the assessment of damages;

d) the various ways of extinguishing obligations, and prescription and limitation periods;

e) validity and the consequences of invalidity of the contract;

f) burden of proof and legal presumptions;

g) pre-contractual obligations.

2. Paragraph 1 e) does not preclude the application of any other governing law supporting the formal validity of the contract.

Article 10 - Assignment

In the case of contractual assignment of a creditor's rights against a debtor arising from a contract between the debtor and creditor -

a) if the parties to the contract of assignment have chosen the law governing that contract, the law chosen governs mutual rights and obligations of the creditor and the assignee arising from their contract;

b) if the parties to the contract between the debtor and creditor have chosen the law governing that contract, the law chosen governs -

i) whether the assignment can be invoked against the debtor;

ii) the rights of the assignee against the debtor; and

iii) whether the obligations of the debtor have been discharged.

Article 11 - Overriding Mandatory Rules and Public Policy (Ordre Public)

1. These Principles shall not prevent a court from applying overriding mandatory provisions of the law of the forum which apply irrespective of the law chosen by the parties.

2. The law of the forum determines when a court may or must apply or take into account overriding mandatory provisions of another law.

3. A court may exclude application of a provision of the law chosen by the parties only if and to the extent that the result of such application would be manifestly incompatible with fundamental notions of public policy (ordre public) of the forum.

4. The law of the forum determines when a court may or must apply or take into account the public policy (ordre public) of a State the law of which would be applicable in the absence of a choice of law.

5. These Principles shall not prevent an arbitral tribunal from applying or taking into account public policy (ordre public), or from applying or taking into account overriding mandatory provisions of a law other than the law chosen by the parties, if the arbitral tribunal is required or entitled to do so.

Article 12 - Establishment

If a party has more than one establishment, the relevant establishment for the purpose of these Principles is the one which has the closest relationship to the contract at the time of its conclusion.

5) 1978 HAGUE CONVENTION ON THE LAW APPLICABLE TO AGENCY[1]

THE STATES SIGNATORIES TO THE PRESENT CONVENTION,

DESIRING to establish common provisions concerning the law applicable to agency,

HAVE RESOLVED to conclude a Convention to this effect, and have agreed upon the following provisions --

Chapter I - Scope of the Convention

Article 1

The present Convention determines the law applicable to relationships of an international character arising where a person, the agent, has the authority to act, acts or purports to act on behalf of another person, the principal, in dealing with a third party.

It shall extend to cases where the function of the agent is to receive and communicate proposals or to conduct negotiations on behalf of other persons.

The Convention shall apply whether the agent acts in his own name or in that of the principal and whether he acts regularly or occasionally.

Article 2

This Convention shall not apply to -

a) the capacity of the parties;

b) requirements as to form;

c) agency by operation of law in family law, in matrimonial property regimes, or in the law of succession;

d) agency by virtue of a decision of a judicial or quasi-judicial authority or subject to the direct control of such an authority;

e) representation in connection with proceedings of a judicial character;

f) the agency of a shipmaster acting in the exercise of his functions as such.

Article 3

For the purposes of this Convention -

a) an organ, officer or partner of a corporation, association, partnership or other entity, whether or not possessing legal personality, shall not be regarded as the agent of that entity in so far as, in the exercise of his functions as such, he acts by virtue of an authority conferred by law or by the constitutive documents of that entity;

b) a trustee shall not be regarded as an agent of the trust, of the person who has created the trust, or of the beneficiaries.

Article 4

The law specified in this Convention shall apply whether or not it is the law of a Contracting State.

Chapter II - Relations Between Principal and Agent

Article 5

The internal law chosen by the principal and the agent shall govern the agency relationship between them.

This choice must be express or must be such that it may be inferred with reasonable certainty from the terms of the agreement between the parties and the circumstances of the case.

Article 6

In so far as it has not been chosen in accordance with Article 5, the applicable law shall be the internal law of the State where, at the time of formation of the agency relationship, the agent has his business establishment or, if he has none, his habitual residence.

However, the internal law of the State where the agent is primarily to act shall apply if the principal has his business establishment or, if he has none, his habitual residence in that State.

Where the principal or the agent has more than one business establishment, this Article refers to the establishment with which the agency relationship is most closely connected.

Article 7

Where the creation of the agency relationship is not the sole purpose of the agreement, the law specified in Articles 5 and 6 shall apply only if -

a) the creation of this relationship is the principal purpose of the agreement, or

b) the agency relationship is severable.

Article 8

The law applicable under Articles 5 and 6 shall govern the formation and validity of the agency relationship, the obligations of the parties, the conditions of performance, the consequences of non-performance, and the extinction of those obligations.

This law shall apply in particular to -

a) the existence and extent of the authority of the agent, its modification or termination, and the consequences of the fact that the agent has exceeded or misused his authority;

b) the right of the agent to appoint a substitute agent, a sub-agent or an additional agent;

c) the right of the agent to enter into a contract on behalf of the principal where there is a potential conflict of interest between himself and the principal;

d) non-competition clauses and *del credere* clauses;

e) clientele allowances (*l'indemnité de clientèle*);

f) the categories of damage for which compensation may be recovered.

Article 9

Whatever law may be applicable to the agency relationship, in regard to the manner of performance the law of the place of performance shall be taken into consideration.

Article 10

This Chapter shall not apply where the agreement creating the agency relationship is a contract of employment.

Chapter III - Relations with the Third Party

Article 11

As between the principal and the third party, the existence and extent of the agent's authority and the effects of the agent's exercise or purported exercise of his authority shall be governed by the internal law of the State in which the agent had his business establishment at the time of his relevant acts.

However, the internal law of the State in which the agent has acted shall apply if -

a) the principal has his business establishment or, if he has none, his habitual residence in that State, and the agent has acted in the name of the principal; or

b) the third party has his business establishment or, if he has none, his habitual residence in that State; or

c) the agent has acted at an exchange or auction; or

d) the agent has no business establishment.

Where a party has more than one business establishment, this Article refers to the establishment with which the relevant acts of the agent are most closely connected.

Article 12

For the purposes of Article 11, first paragraph, where an agent acting under a contract of employment with his principal has no personal business establishment, he shall be deemed to have his establishment at the business establishment of the principal to which he is attached.

Article 13

For the purposes of Article 11, second paragraph, where an agent in one State has communicated with the third party in another, by message, telegram, telex, telephone, or other similar means, the agent shall be deemed to have acted in that respect at the place of his business establishment or, if he has none, of his habitual residence.

Article 14

Notwithstanding Article 11, where a written specification by the principal or by the third party of the law applicable to questions falling within Article 11 has been expressly accepted by the other party, the law so specified shall apply to such questions.

Article 15

The law applicable under this Chapter shall also govern the relationship between the agent and the third party arising from the fact that the agent has acted in the exercise of his authority, has exceeded his authority, or has acted without authority.

Chapter IV - General Provisions

Article 16

In the application of this Convention, effect may be given to the mandatory rules of any State with which the situation has a significant connection, if and in so far as, under the law of that State, those rules must be applied whatever the law specified by its choice of law rules.

Article 17

The application of a law specified by this Convention may be refused only where such application would be manifestly incompatible with public policy (*ordre public*).

Article 18 [Reservations]

Any Contracting State may, at the time of signature, ratification, acceptance, approval or accession, reserve the right not to apply this Convention to -

(1) the agency of a bank or group of banks in the course of banking transactions;

(2) agency in matters of insurance;

(3) the acts of a public servant acting in the exercise of his functions as such on behalf of a private person.

No other reservation shall be permitted.

Any Contracting State may also, when notifying an extension of the Convention in accordance with Article 25, make one or more of these reservations, with its effect limited to all or some of the territories mentioned in the extension.

Any Contracting State may at any time withdraw a reservation which it has made; the reservation shall cease to have effect on the first day of the third calendar month after notification of the withdrawal.

Article 19

Where a State comprises several territorial units each of which has its own rules of law in respect of agency, each territorial unit shall be considered as a State for the purposes of identifying the law applicable under this Convention.

Article 20

A State within which different territorial units have their own rules of law in respect of agency shall not be bound to apply this Convention where a State with a unified system of law would not be bound to apply the law of another State by virtue of this Convention.

Article 21

If a Contracting State has two or more territorial units which have their own rules of law in respect of agency, it may, at the time of signature, ratification, acceptance, approval or accession, declare that this Convention shall extend to all its territorial units or to one or more of them, and may modify its declaration by submitting another declaration at any time.

These declarations shall be notified to the Ministry of Foreign Affairs of the Kingdom of the Netherlands, and shall state expressly the territorial units to which the Convention applies.

Article 22

The Convention shall not affect any other international instrument containing provisions on matters governed by this Convention to which a Contracting State is, or becomes, a Party.

Chapter V - Final Clauses [...]

In witness whereof the undersigned, being duly authorised thereto, have signed this Convention.

Done at The Hague, on the 14th day of March, 1978, in the English and French languages, both texts being equally authentic, in a single copy which shall be deposited in the archives of the Government of the Kingdom of the Netherlands and of which a certified copy shall be sent, through diplomatic channels, to each of the States Members of the Hague Conference on Private International Law at the date of its Thirteenth Session.

Entry into force: 1 May 1992

Ratifications and binding effect as of June 2020: Argentina (1992), France (1992), Netherlands (1992), Portugal (1992)

6) 1994 Inter-American Convention on the Law Applicable to International Contracts ("Mexico Convention")[1]

The States Parties to this Convention,

REAFFIRMING their desire to continue the progressive development and codification of private international law among member States of the Organization of American States;

REASSERTING the advisability of harmonizing solutions to international trade issues;

BEARING in mind that the economic interdependence of States has fostered regional integration and that in order to stimulate the process it is necessary to facilitate international contracts by removing differences in the legal framework for them,

HAVE AGREED to approve the following Convention:

Chapter I - Scope of Application

Article 1

This Convention shall determine the law applicable to international contracts.

It shall be understood that a contract is international if the parties thereto have their habitual residence or establishments in different States Parties or if the contract has objective ties with more than one State Party.

This Convention shall apply to contracts entered into or contracts to which States or State agencies or entities are party, unless the parties to the contract expressly exclude it. However, any State Party may, at the time it signs, ratifies or accedes to this Convention, declare that the latter shall not apply to all or certain categories of contracts to which the State or State agencies and entities are party.

Any State Party may, at the time it ratifies or accedes to this Convention, declare the categories of contract to which this Convention will not apply.

Article 2

The law designated by the Convention shall be applied even if said law is that of a State that is not a party.

Article 3

The provisions of this Convention shall be applied, with necessary and possible adaptations, to the new modalities of contracts used as a consequence of the development of international trade.

Article 4

For purposes of interpretation and application of this Convention, its international nature and the need to promote uniformity in its application shall be taken into account.

Article 5

This Convention does not determine the law applicable to:

a) questions arising from the marital status of natural persons, the capacity of the parties, or the consequences of nullity or invalidity of the contract as a result of the lack of capacity of one of the parties;

---

1 ©1994, Organization of American States, Washington DC.

b) contractual obligations intended for successional questions, testamentary questions, marital arrangements or those deriving from family relationships;

c) obligations deriving from securities;

d) obligations deriving from securities transactions;

e) the agreements of the parties concerning arbitration or selection of forum;

f) questions of company law, including the existence, capacity, function and dissolution of commercial companies and juridical persons in general.

Article 6

The provisions of this Convention shall not be applicable to contracts which have autonomous regulations in international conventional law in force among the States Parties to this Convention.

Chapter 2 - Determination of Applicable Law

Article 7

The contract shall be governed by the law chosen by the parties. The parties' agreement on this selection must be express or, in the event that there is no express agreement, must be evident from the parties' behavior and from the clauses of the contract, considered as a whole. Said selection may relate to the entire contract or to a part of same.

Selection of a certain forum by the parties does not necessarily entail selection of the applicable law.

Article 8

The parties may at any time agree that the contract shall, in whole or in part, be subject to a law other than that to which it was previously subject, whether or not that law was chosen by the parties. Nevertheless, that modification shall not affect the formal validity of the original contract nor the rights of third parties.

Article 9

If the parties have not selected the applicable law, or if their selection proves ineffective, the contract shall be governed by the law of the State with which it has the closest ties.

The Court will take into account all objective and subjective elements of the contract to determine the law of the State with which it has the closest ties. It shall also take into account the general principles of international commercial law recognized by international organizations.

Nevertheless, if a part of the contract were separable from the rest and if it had a closer tie with another State, the law of that State could, exceptionally, apply to that part of the contract.

Article 10

In addition to the provisions in the foregoing articles, the guidelines, customs, and principles of international commercial law as well as commercial usage and practices generally accepted shall apply in order to discharge the requirements of justice and equity in the particular case.

Article 11

Notwithstanding the provisions of the preceding articles, the provisions of the law of the forum shall necessarily be applied when they are mandatory requirements.

It shall be up to the forum to decide when it applies the mandatory provisions of the law of another State with which the contract has close ties.

Chapter 3 - Existence and Validity of the Contract

Article 12

The existence and the validity of the contract or of any of its provisions, and the substantive validity of the consent of the parties concerning the selection of the applicable law, shall be governed by the appropriate rules in accordance with Chapter 2 of this Convention.

Nevertheless, to establish that one of the parties has not duly consented, the judge shall determine the applicable law, taking into account the habitual residence or principal place of business.

Article 13

A contract between parties in the same State shall be valid as to form if it meets the requirements laid down in the law governing said contract pursuant to this Convention or with those of the law of the State in which the contract is valid or with the law of the place where the contract is performed.

If the persons concerned are in different States at the time of its conclusion, the contract shall be valid as to form if it meets the requirements of the law governing it as to substance, or those of the law of one of the States in which it is concluded or with the law of the place where the contract is performed.

Chapter 4 - Scope of the Applicable Law

Article 14

The law applicable to the contract in virtue of Chapter 2 of this Convention shall govern principally:

a) its interpretation;

b) the rights and obligations of the parties;

c) the performance of the obligations established by the contract and the consequences of nonperformance of the contract, including assessment of injury to the extent that this may determine payment of compensation;

d) the various ways in which the obligations can be performed, and prescription and lapsing of actions;

e) the consequences of nullity or invalidity of the contract.

Article 15

The provisions of Article 10 shall be taken into account when deciding whether an agent can obligate its principal or an agency, a company or a juridical person.

Article 16

The law of the State where international contracts are to be registered or published shall govern all matters concerning publicity in respect of same.

Article 17

For the purposes of this Convention, “law” shall be understood to mean the law current in a State, excluding rules concerning conflict of laws.

Article 18

Application of the law designated by this Convention may only be excluded when it is manifestly contrary to the public order of the forum.

Chapter 5 - General Provisions

Article 19

In a State Party, the provisions of this Convention shall apply to contracts concluded subsequent to its entry into force in that State.

Article 20

This Convention shall not affect the application of other international conventions to which a State Party to this Convention is or becomes a party, insofar as they are pertinent, or those concluded within the context of integration movements.

Article 21

When signing, ratifying or acceding to this Convention, States may formulate reservations that apply to one or more specific provisions and which are not incompatible with the effect and purpose of this Convention.

A State Party may at any time withdraw a reservation it has formulated. The effect of such reservation shall cease on the first day of the third calendar month following the date of notification of withdrawal.

Article 22

In the case of a State which has two or more systems of law applicable in different territorial units with respect to matters covered by the Convention:

a) any reference to the laws of the State shall be construed as a reference to the laws in the territorial unit in question;

b) any reference to habitual residence or place of business in that State shall be construed as a reference to habitual residence or place of business in a territorial unit of that State.

Article 23

A State within which different territorial units have their own systems of law in regard to matters covered by this Convention shall not be obliged to apply this Convention to conflicts between the legal systems in force in such units.

Article 24

If a State has two or more territorial units in which different systems of law apply in relation to the matters dealt with in this Convention, it may, at the time of signature, ratification or accession, declare that this Convention shall extend to all its territorial units or to only one or more of them.

Such declaration may be modified by subsequent declarations, which shall expressly indicate the territorial unit or units to which the Convention applies. Such subsequent declarations shall be transmitted to the General Secretariat of the Organization of American States, and shall take effect ninety days after the date of their receipt.

Chapter 6 - Final Clauses

Article 25

This Convention shall be open to signature by the member States of the Organization of American States.

Article 26

This Convention shall be subject to ratification. The instruments of ratification shall be deposited with the General Secretariat of the Organization of American States.

Article 27

This Convention shall remain open for accession by any other State after it has entered into force. The instruments of accession shall be deposited with the General Secretariat of the Organization of American States.

Article 28

This Convention shall enter into force for the ratifying States on the thirtieth day following the date of deposit of the second instrument of ratification.

For each State ratifying or acceding to the Convention after the deposit of the second instrument of ratification, the Convention shall enter into force on the thirtieth day after deposit by such State of its instrument of ratification or accession.

Article 29

This Convention shall remain in force indefinitely, but any of the States Parties may denounce it. The instrument of denunciation shall be deposited with the General Secretariat of the Organization of American States. After one year from the date of deposit of the instrument of denunciation, the Convention shall no longer be in force for the denouncing State.

Article 30

The original instrument of this Convention, the English, French, Portuguese and Spanish texts of which are equally authentic, shall be deposited with the General Secretariat of the Organization of American States, which shall forward an authenticated copy of its text to the Secretariat of the United Nations for registration and publication in accordance with Article 102 of its Charter. The General Secretariat of the Organization of American States shall notify the Member States of the Organization and the States that have acceded to the Convention of the signatures, deposits of instruments of ratification, accession and denunciation, as well as of reservations, if any, and of their withdrawal.

IN WITNESS WHEREOF the undersigned Plenipotentiaries, being duly authorized thereto by their respective Governments, do hereby sign the present Convention.

DONE AT MEXICO, D.F., MEXICO, this seventeenth day of March, one thousand nine hundred and ninety-four.

Entry into force: 15 December 1996

Ratifications and binding effect: Venezuela (1996), Mexico (1996)

7) EU REGULATION 593/2008 ON THE LAW APPLICABLE TO CONTRACTUAL OBLIGATIONS ("ROME I")[1]

THE EUROPEAN PARLIAMENT AND THE COUNCIL OF THE EUROPEAN UNION,

HAVING REGARD to the Treaty establishing the European Community, and in particular Article 61(c) and the second indent of Article 67(5) thereof, [...]

ACTING IN ACCORDANCE with the procedure laid down in Article 251 of the Treaty,

Whereas:

(1) The Community has set itself the objective of maintaining and developing an area of freedom, security and justice. For the progressive establishment of such an area, the Community is to adopt measures relating to judicial cooperation in civil matters with a cross-border impact to the extent necessary for the proper functioning of the internal market.

(2) According to Article 65, point (b) of the Treaty, these measures are to include those promoting the compatibility of the rules applicable in the Member States concerning the conflict of laws and of jurisdiction.

(3) The European Council meeting in Tampere on 15 and 16 October 1999 endorsed the principle of mutual recognition of judgments and other decisions of judicial authorities as the cornerstone of judicial cooperation in civil matters and invited the Council and the Commission to adopt a programme of measures to implement that principle.

(4) On 30 November 2000 the Council adopted a joint Commission and Council programme of measures for implementation of the principle of mutual recognition of decisions in civil and commercial matters. The programme identifies measures relating to the harmonisation of conflict-of-law rules as those facilitating the mutual recognition of judgments.

(5) The Hague Programme, adopted by the European Council on 5 November 2004, called for work to be pursued actively on the conflict-of-law rules regarding contractual obligations (Rome I).

(6) The proper functioning of the internal market creates a need, in order to improve the predictability of the outcome of litigation, certainty as to the law applicable and the free movement of judgments, for the conflict-of-law rules in the Member States to designate the same national law irrespective of the country of the court in which an action is brought.

(7) The substantive scope and the provisions of this Regulation should be consistent with Council Regulation 44/2001 [...] on jurisdiction and the recognition and enforcement of judgments in civil and commercial matters (Brussels I)[2] and Regulation 864/2007 [...] on the law applicable to non-contractual obligations (Rome II).[3]

(8) Family relationships should cover parentage, marriage, affinity and collateral relatives. The reference in Article 1(2) to relationships having comparable effects to marriage and other family relationships should be interpreted in accordance with the law of the Member State in which the court is seised.

(9) Obligations under bills of exchange, cheques and promissory notes and other negotiable instruments should also cover bills of lading to the extent that the obligations under the bill of lading arise out of its negotiable character.

---

1 OJ 2008 L 177.

2 The current version of this Regulation can be found on p. II - 92.

3 See below, p. I - 67.

(10) Obligations arising out of dealings prior to the conclusion of the contract are covered by Article 12 of Regulation 864/2007. Such obligations should therefore be excluded from the scope of this Regulation.

(11) The parties' freedom to choose the applicable law should be one of the cornerstones of the system of conflict-of-law rules in matters of contractual obligations.

(12) An agreement between the parties to confer on one or more courts or tribunals of a Member State exclusive jurisdiction to determine disputes under the contract should be one of the factors to be taken into account in determining whether a choice of law has been clearly demonstrated.

(13) This Regulation does not preclude parties from incorporating by reference into their contract a non-State body of law or an international convention.

(14) Should the Community adopt, in an appropriate legal instrument, rules of substantive contract law, including standard terms and conditions, such instrument may provide that the parties may choose to apply those rules.

(15) Where a choice of law is made and all other elements relevant to the situation are located in a country other than the country whose law has been chosen, the choice of law should not prejudice the application of provisions of the law of that country which cannot be derogated from by agreement. This rule should apply whether or not the choice of law was accompanied by a choice of court or tribunal. Whereas no substantial change is intended as compared with Article 3(3) of the 1980 Convention on the Law Applicable to Contractual Obligations (the Rome Convention), the wording of this Regulation is aligned as far as possible with Article 14 of Regulation 864/2007.

(16) To contribute to the general objective of this Regulation, legal certainty in the European judicial area, the conflict-of-law rules should be highly foreseeable. The courts should, however, retain a degree of discretion to determine the law that is most closely connected to the situation.

(17) As far as the applicable law in the absence of choice is concerned, the concept of 'provision of services' and 'sale of goods' should be interpreted in the same way as when applying Article 5 of Regulation 44/2001 in so far as sale of goods and provision of services are covered by that Regulation. Although franchise and distribution contracts are contracts for services, they are the subject of specific rules.

(18) As far as the applicable law in the absence of choice is concerned, multilateral systems should be those in which trading is conducted, such as regulated markets and multilateral trading facilities as referred to in Article 4 of Directive 2004/39 [...] on markets in financial instruments, regardless of whether or not they rely on a central counter-party.

(19) Where there has been no choice of law, the applicable law should be determined in accordance with the rule specified for the particular type of contract. Where the contract cannot be categorised as being one of the specified types or where its elements fall within more than one of the specified types, it should be governed by the law of the country where the party required to effect the characteristic performance of the contract has his habitual residence. In the case of a contract consisting of a bundle of rights and obligations capable of being categorised as falling within more than one of the specified types of contract, the characteristic performance of the contract should be determined having regard to its centre of gravity.

(20) Where the contract is manifestly more closely connected with a country other than that indicated in Article 4(1) or (2), an escape clause should provide that the law of that other country is to apply. In order to determine that country, account should be taken, *inter alia*, of whether the contract in question has a very close relationship with another contract or contracts.

(21) In the absence of choice, where the applicable law cannot be determined either on the basis of the fact that the contract can be categorised as one of the specified types or as being the law of the country of habitual residence of the party required to effect the characteristic performance of the contract, the contract should be governed by the law of the country with which it is most closely connected. In order to determine that country, account should be taken, *inter alia*, of whether the contract in question has a very close relationship with another contract or contracts.

(22) As regards the interpretation of contracts for the carriage of goods, no change in substance is intended with respect to Article 4(4), third sentence, of the Rome Convention. Consequently, single-voyage charter parties and other contracts the main purpose of which is the carriage of goods should be treated as contracts for the carriage of goods. For the purposes of this Regulation, the term 'consignor' should refer to any person who enters into a contract of carriage with the carrier and the term 'the carrier' should refer to the party to the contract who undertakes to carry the goods, whether or not he performs the carriage himself.

(23) As regards contracts concluded with parties regarded as being weaker, those parties should be protected by conflict-of-law rules that are more favourable to their interests than the general rules.

(24) With more specific reference to consumer contracts, the conflict-of-law rule should make it possible to cut the cost of settling disputes concerning what are commonly relatively small claims and to take account of the development of distance-selling techniques. Consistency with Regulation 44/2001 requires both that there be a reference to the concept of directed activity as a condition for applying the consumer protection rule and that the concept be interpreted harmoniously in Regulation 44/2001 and this Regulation, bearing in mind that a joint declaration by the Council and the Commission on Article 15 of Regulation 44/2001 states that 'for Article 15(1)(c) to be applicable it is not sufficient for an undertaking to target its activities at the Member State of the consumer's residence, or at a number of Member States including that Member State; a contract must also be concluded within the framework of its activities'. The declaration also states that 'the mere fact that an Internet site is accessible is not sufficient for Article 15 to be applicable, although a factor will be that this Internet site solicits the conclusion of distance contracts and that a contract has actually been concluded at a distance, by whatever means. In this respect, the language or currency which a website uses does not constitute a relevant factor.'.

(25) Consumers should be protected by such rules of the country of their habitual residence that cannot be derogated from by agreement, provided that the consumer contract has been concluded as a result of the professional pursuing his commercial or professional activities in that particular country. The same protection should be guaranteed if the professional, while not pursuing his commercial or professional activities in the country where the consumer has his habitual residence, directs his activities by any means to that country or to several countries, including that country, and the contract is concluded as a result of such activities.

(26) For the purposes of this Regulation, financial services such as investment services and activities and ancillary services provided by a professional to a consumer, as referred to in sections A and B of Annex I to Directive 2004/39, and contracts for the sale of units in collective investment undertakings, whether or not covered by Council Directive 85/611 [...] on the coordination of laws, regulations and administrative provisions relating to undertakings for collective investment in transferable securities (UCITS), should be subject to Article 6 of this Regulation. Consequently, when a reference is made to terms and conditions governing the issuance or offer to the public of transferable securities or to the subscription and redemption of units in collective investment undertakings, that reference should include all aspects binding the issuer or the offeror to the consumer, but should not include those aspects involving the provision of financial services.

(27) Various exceptions should be made to the general conflict-of-law rule for consumer contracts. Under one such exception the general rule should not apply to contracts relating to rights *in rem* in immovable property or tenancies of such property unless the contract relates to the right to use immovable property on a timeshare basis within the meaning of Directive 94/47 [...] on the protection of purchasers in respect of certain aspects of contracts relating to the purchase of the right to use immovable properties on a timeshare basis.

(28) It is important to ensure that rights and obligations which constitute a financial instrument are not covered by the general rule applicable to consumer contracts, as that could lead to different laws being applicable to each of the instruments issued, therefore changing their nature and preventing their fungible trading and offering. Likewise, whenever such instruments are issued or offered, the contractual relationship established between the issuer or the offeror and the consumer should not necessarily be subject to the mandatory application of the law of the country of habitual residence of the consumer, as there is a need to ensure uniformity in the terms and conditions of an issuance or an offer. The same rationale should apply with regard to the multilateral systems covered by Article 4(1)(h), in respect of which it should be ensured that the law of the country of habitual residence of the consumer will not interfere with the rules applicable to contracts concluded within those systems or with the operator of such systems.

(29) For the purposes of this Regulation, references to rights and obligations constituting the terms and conditions governing the issuance, offers to the public or public take-over bids of transferable securities and references to the subscription and redemption of units in collective investment undertakings should include the terms governing, *inter alia*, the allocation of securities or units, rights in the event of over-subscription, withdrawal rights and similar matters in the context of the offer as well as those matters referred to in Articles 10, 11, 12 and 13, thus ensuring that all relevant contractual aspects of an offer binding the issuer or the offeror to the consumer are governed by a single law.

(30) For the purposes of this Regulation, financial instruments and transferable securities are those instruments referred to in Article 4 of Directive 2004/39.

(31) Nothing in this Regulation should prejudice the operation of a formal arrangement designated as a system under Article 2(a) of Directive 98/26 [...] on settlement finality in payment and securities settlement systems.

(32) Owing to the particular nature of contracts of carriage and insurance contracts, specific provisions should ensure an adequate level of protection of passengers and policy holders. Therefore, Article 6 should not apply in the context of those particular contracts.

(33) Where an insurance contract not covering a large risk covers more than one risk, at least one of which is situated in a Member State and at least one of which is situated in a third country, the special rules on insurance contracts in this Regulation should apply only to the risk or risks situated in the relevant Member State or Member States.

(34) The rule on individual employment contracts should not prejudice the application of the overriding mandatory provisions of the country to which a worker is posted in accordance with Directive 96/71 of the European Parliament and of the Council of 16 December 1996 concerning the posting of workers in the framework of the provision of services.

(35) Employees should not be deprived of the protection afforded to them by provisions which cannot be derogated from by agreement or which can only be derogated from to their benefit.

(36) As regards individual employment contracts, work carried out in another country should be regarded as temporary if the employee is expected to resume working in the country of origin after carrying out his tasks abroad. The conclusion of a new contract of employment with the original employer or an employer belonging to the same group of companies as the original

employer should not preclude the employee from being regarded as carrying out his work in another country temporarily.

(37) Considerations of public interest justify giving the courts of the Member States the possibility, in exceptional circumstances, of applying exceptions based on public policy and overriding mandatory provisions. The concept of 'overriding mandatory provisions' should be distinguished from the expression 'provisions which cannot be derogated from by agreement' and should be construed more restrictively.

(38) In the context of voluntary assignment, the term 'relationship' should make it clear that Article 14(1) also applies to the property aspects of an assignment, as between assignor and assignee, in legal orders where such aspects are treated separately from the aspects under the law of obligations. However, the term 'relationship' should not be understood as relating to any relationship that may exist between assignor and assignee. In particular, it should not cover preliminary questions as regards a voluntary assignment or a contractual subrogation. The term should be strictly limited to the aspects which are directly relevant to the voluntary assignment or contractual subrogation in question.

(39) For the sake of legal certainty there should be a clear definition of habitual residence, in particular for companies and other bodies, corporate or unincorporated. Unlike Article 60(1) of Regulation 44/2001, which establishes three criteria, the conflict-of-law rule should proceed on the basis of a single criterion; otherwise, the parties would be unable to foresee the law applicable to their situation.

(40) A situation where conflict-of-law rules are dispersed among several instruments and where there are differences between those rules should be avoided. This Regulation, however, should not exclude the possibility of inclusion of conflict-of-law rules relating to contractual obligations in provisions of Community law with regard to particular matters. This Regulation should not prejudice the application of other instruments laying down provisions designed to contribute to the proper functioning of the internal market in so far as they cannot be applied in conjunction with the law designated by the rules of this Regulation. The application of provisions of the applicable law designated by the rules of this Regulation should not restrict the free movement of goods and services as regulated by Community instruments, such as Directive 2000/31 [...] on certain legal aspects of information society services, in particular electronic commerce, in the Internal Market (Directive on electronic commerce).

(41) Respect for international commitments entered into by the Member States means that this Regulation should not affect international conventions to which one or more Member States are parties at the time when this Regulation is adopted. To make the rules more accessible, the Commission should publish the list of the relevant conventions in the *Official Journal of the European Union* on the basis of information supplied by the Member States.

(42) The Commission will make a proposal to the European Parliament and to the Council concerning the procedures and conditions according to which Member States would be entitled to negotiate and conclude, on their own behalf, agreements with third countries in individual and exceptional cases, concerning sectoral matters and containing provisions on the law applicable to contractual obligations.

(43) Since the objective of this Regulation cannot be sufficiently achieved by the Member States and can therefore, by reason of the scale and effects of this Regulation, be better achieved at Community level, the Community may adopt measures, in accordance with the principle of subsidiarity as set out in Article 5 of the Treaty. In accordance with the principle of proportionality, as set out in that Article, this Regulation does not go beyond what is necessary to attain its objective.

(44) [...].

(46) In accordance with Articles 1 and 2 of the Protocol on the position of Denmark, annexed to the Treaty on European Union and to the Treaty establishing the European Community, Denmark is not taking part in the adoption of this Regulation and is not bound by it or subject to its application,

HAVE ADOPTED THIS REGULATION:

Chapter I Scope

Article 1 Material Scope

1. This Regulation shall apply, in situations involving a conflict of laws, to contractual obligations in civil and commercial matters.

It shall not apply, in particular, to revenue, customs or administrative matters.

2. The following shall be excluded from the scope of this Regulation:

(a) questions involving the status or legal capacity of natural persons, without prejudice to Article 13;

(b) obligations arising out of family relationships and relationships deemed by the law applicable to such relationships to have comparable effects, including maintenance obligations;

(c) obligations arising out of matrimonial property regimes, property regimes of relationships deemed by the law applicable to such relationships to have comparable effects to marriage, and wills and succession;

(d) obligations arising under bills of exchange, cheques and promissory notes and other negotiable instruments to the extent that the obligations under such other negotiable instruments arise out of their negotiable character;

(e) arbitration agreements and agreements on the choice of court;

(f) questions governed by the law of companies and other bodies, corporate or unincorporated, such as the creation, by registration or otherwise, legal capacity, internal organisation or winding-up of companies and other bodies, corporate or unincorporated, and the personal liability of officers and members as such for the obligations of the company or body;

(g) the question whether an agent is able to bind a principal, or an organ to bind a company or other body corporate or unincorporated, in relation to a third party;

(h) the constitution of trusts and the relationship between settlors, trustees and beneficiaries;

(i) obligations arising out of dealings prior to the conclusion of a contract;

(j) insurance contracts arising out of operations carried out by organisations other than undertakings referred to in Article 2 of Directive 2002/83 [...] concerning life assurance the object of which is to provide benefits for employed or self-employed persons belonging to an undertaking or group of undertakings, or to a trade or group of trades, in the event of death or survival or of discontinuance or curtailment of activity, or of sickness related to work or accidents at work.

3. This Regulation shall not apply to evidence and procedure, without prejudice to Article 18.

4. In this Regulation, the term 'Member State' shall mean Member States to which this Regulation applies. However, in Article 3(4) and Article 7 the term shall mean all the Member States.

Article 2 Universal Application

Any law specified by this Regulation shall be applied whether or not it is the law of a Member State.

Chapter II Uniform Rules

Article 3 Freedom of Choice

1. A contract shall be governed by the law chosen by the parties. The choice shall be made expressly or clearly demonstrated by the terms of the contract or the circumstances of the case. By their choice the parties can select the law applicable to the whole or to part only of the contract.

2. The parties may at any time agree to subject the contract to a law other than that which previously governed it, whether as a result of an earlier choice made under this Article or of other provisions of this Regulation. Any change in the law to be applied that is made after the conclusion of the contract shall not prejudice its formal validity under Article 11 or adversely affect the rights of third parties.

3. Where all other elements relevant to the situation at the time of the choice are located in a country other than the country whose law has been chosen, the choice of the parties shall not prejudice the application of provisions of the law of that other country which cannot be derogated from by agreement.

4. Where all other elements relevant to the situation at the time of the choice are located in one or more Member States, the parties' choice of applicable law other than that of a Member State shall not prejudice the application of provisions of Community law, where appropriate as implemented in the Member State of the forum, which cannot be derogated from by agreement.

5. The existence and validity of the consent of the parties as to the choice of the applicable law shall be determined in accordance with the provisions of Articles 10, 11 and 13.

Article 4 Applicable Law in the Absence of Choice

1. To the extent that the law applicable to the contract has not been chosen in accordance with Article 3 and without prejudice to Articles 5 to 8, the law governing the contract shall be determined as follows:

(a) a contract for the sale of goods shall be governed by the law of the country where the seller has his habitual residence;

(b) a contract for the provision of services shall be governed by the law of the country where the service provider has his habitual residence;

(c) a contract relating to a right *in rem* in immovable property or to a tenancy of immovable property shall be governed by the law of the country where the property is situated;

(d) notwithstanding point (c), a tenancy of immovable property concluded for temporary private use for a period of no more than six consecutive months shall be governed by the law of the country where the landlord has his habitual residence, provided that the tenant is a natural person and has his habitual residence in the same country;

(e) a franchise contract shall be governed by the law of the country where the franchisee has his habitual residence;

(f) a distribution contract shall be governed by the law of the country where the distributor has his habitual residence;

(g) a contract for the sale of goods by auction shall be governed by the law of the country where the auction takes place, if such a place can be determined;

(h) a contract concluded within a multilateral system which brings together or facilitates the bringing together of multiple third-party buying and selling interests in financial instruments, as defined by Article 4(1), point (17) of Directive 2004/39, in accordance with non-discretionary rules and governed by a single law, shall be governed by that law.

2. Where the contract is not covered by paragraph 1 or where the elements of the contract would be covered by more than one of points (a) to (h) of paragraph 1, the contract shall be governed by the law of the country where the party required to effect the characteristic performance of the contract has his habitual residence.

3. Where it is clear from all the circumstances of the case that the contract is manifestly more closely connected with a country other than that indicated in paragraphs 1 or 2, the law of that other country shall apply.

4. Where the law applicable cannot be determined pursuant to paragraphs 1 or 2, the contract shall be governed by the law of the country with which it is most closely connected.

Article 5 Contracts of Carriage

1. To the extent that the law applicable to a contract for the carriage of goods has not been chosen in accordance with Article 3, the law applicable shall be the law of the country of habitual residence of the carrier, provided that the place of receipt or the place of delivery or the habitual residence of the consignor is also situated in that country. If those requirements are not met, the law of the country where the place of delivery as agreed by the parties is situated shall apply.

2. To the extent that the law applicable to a contract for the carriage of passengers has not been chosen by the parties in accordance with the second subparagraph, the law applicable shall be the law of the country where the passenger has his habitual residence, provided that either the place of departure or the place of destination is situated in that country. If these requirements are not met, the law of the country where the carrier has his habitual residence shall apply.

The parties may choose as the law applicable to a contract for the carriage of passengers in accordance with Article 3 only the law of the country where:

(a) the passenger has his habitual residence; or

(b) the carrier has his habitual residence; or

(c) the carrier has his place of central administration; or

(d) the place of departure is situated; or

(e) the place of destination is situated.

3. Where it is clear from all the circumstances of the case that the contract, in the absence of a choice of law, is manifestly more closely connected with a country other than that indicated in paragraphs 1 or 2, the law of that other country shall apply.

Article 6 Consumer Contracts

1. Without prejudice to Articles 5 and 7, a contract concluded by a natural person for a purpose which can be regarded as being outside his trade or profession (the consumer) with another person acting in the exercise of his trade or profession (the professional) shall be governed by the law of the country where the consumer has his habitual residence, provided that the professional:

(a) pursues his commercial or professional activities in the country where the consumer has his habitual residence, or

(b) by any means, directs such activities to that country or to several countries including that country, and the contract falls within the scope of such activities.

2. Notwithstanding paragraph 1, the parties may choose the law applicable to a contract which fulfils the requirements of paragraph 1, in accordance with Article 3. Such a choice may not, however, have the result of depriving the consumer of the protection afforded to him by provisions that cannot be derogated from by agreement by virtue of the law which, in the absence of choice, would have been applicable on the basis of paragraph 1.

3. If the requirements in points (a) or (b) of paragraph 1 are not fulfilled, the law applicable to a contract between a consumer and a professional shall be determined pursuant to Articles 3 and 4.

4. Paragraphs 1 and 2 shall not apply to:

(a) a contract for the supply of services where the services are to be supplied to the consumer exclusively in a country other than that in which he has his habitual residence;

(b) a contract of carriage other than a contract relating to package travel within the meaning of Council Directive 90/314 of 13 June 1990 on package travel, package holidays and package tours;

(c) a contract relating to a right *in rem* in immovable property or a tenancy of immovable property other than a contract relating to the right to use immovable properties on a time-share basis within the meaning of Directive 94/47;

(d) rights and obligations which constitute a financial instrument and rights and obligations constituting the terms and conditions governing the issuance or offer to the public and public take-over bids of transferable securities, and the subscription and redemption of units in collective investment undertakings in so far as these activities do not constitute provision of a financial service;

(e) a contract concluded within the type of system falling within the scope of Article 4(1)(h).

Article 7 Insurance Contracts

1. This Article shall apply to contracts referred to in paragraph 2, whether or not the risk covered is situated in a Member State, and to all other insurance contracts covering risks situated inside the territory of the Member States. It shall not apply to reinsurance contracts.

2. An insurance contract covering a large risk as defined in Article 5(d) of the First Council Directive 73/239 of 24 July 1973 on the coordination of laws, regulations and administrative provisions relating to the taking-up and pursuit of the business of direct insurance other than life assurance shall be governed by the law chosen by the parties in accordance with Article 3 of this Regulation.

To the extent that the applicable law has not been chosen by the parties, the insurance contract shall be governed by the law of the country where the insurer has his habitual residence. Where it is clear from all the circumstances of the case that the contract is manifestly more closely connected with another country, the law of that other country shall apply.

3. In the case of an insurance contract other than a contract falling within paragraph 2, only the following laws may be chosen by the parties in accordance with Article 3:

(a) the law of any Member State where the risk is situated at the time of conclusion of the contract;

(b) the law of the country where the policy holder has his habitual residence;

(c) in the case of life assurance, the law of the Member State of which the policy holder is a national;

(d) for insurance contracts covering risks limited to events occurring in one Member State other than the Member State where the risk is situated, the law of that Member State;

(e) where the policy holder of a contract falling under this paragraph pursues a commercial or industrial activity or a liberal profession and the insurance contract covers two or more risks which relate to those activities and are situated in different Member States, the law of any of the Member States concerned or the law of the country of habitual residence of the policy holder.

Where, in the cases set out in points (a), (b) or (e), the Member States referred to grant greater freedom of choice of the law applicable to the insurance contract, the parties may take advantage of that freedom.

To the extent that the law applicable has not been chosen by the parties in accordance with this paragraph, such a contract shall be governed by the law of the Member State in which the risk is situated at the time of conclusion of the contract.

4. The following additional rules shall apply to insurance contracts covering risks for which a Member State imposes an obligation to take out insurance:

(a) the insurance contract shall not satisfy the obligation to take out insurance unless it complies with the specific provisions relating to that insurance laid down by the Member State that imposes the obligation. Where the law of the Member State in which the risk is situated and the law of the Member State imposing the obligation to take out insurance contradict each other, the latter shall prevail;

(b) by way of derogation from paragraphs 2 and 3, a Member State may lay down that the insurance contract shall be governed by the law of the Member State that imposes the obligation to take out insurance.

5. For the purposes of paragraph 3, third subparagraph, and paragraph 4, where the contract covers risks situated in more than one Member State, the contract shall be considered as constituting several contracts each relating to only one Member State.

6. For the purposes of this Article, the country in which the risk is situated shall be determined in accordance with Article 2(d) of the Second Council Directive 88/357 of 22 June 1988 on the coordination of laws, regulations and administrative provisions relating to direct insurance other than life assurance and laying down provisions to facilitate the effective exercise of freedom to provide services and, in the case of life assurance, the country in which the risk is situated shall be the country of the commitment within the meaning of Article 1(1) (g) of Directive 2002/83.

Article 8 Individual Employment Contracts

1. An individual employment contract shall be governed by the law chosen by the parties in accordance with Article 3. Such a choice of law may not, however, have the result of depriving the employee of the protection afforded to him by provisions that cannot be derogated from by agreement under the law that, in the absence of choice, would have been applicable pursuant to paragraphs 2, 3 and 4 of this Article.

2. To the extent that the law applicable to the individual employment contract has not been chosen by the parties, the contract shall be governed by the law of the country in which or, failing that, from which the employee habitually carries out his work in performance of the contract. The country where the work is habitually carried out shall not be deemed to have changed if he is temporarily employed in another country.

3. Where the law applicable cannot be determined pursuant to paragraph 2, the contract shall be governed by the law of the country where the place of business through which the employee was engaged is situated.

4. Where it appears from the circumstances as a whole that the contract is more closely connected with a country other than that indicated in paragraphs 2 or 3, the law of that other country shall apply.

Article 9 Overriding Mandatory Provisions

1. Overriding mandatory provisions are provisions the respect for which is regarded as crucial by a country for safeguarding its public interests, such as its political, social or economic organi-

sation, to such an extent that they are applicable to any situation falling within their scope, irrespective of the law otherwise applicable to the contract under this Regulation.

2. Nothing in this Regulation shall restrict the application of the overriding mandatory provisions of the law of the forum.

3. Effect may be given to the overriding mandatory provisions of the law of the country where the obligations arising out of the contract have to be or have been performed, in so far as those overriding mandatory provisions render the performance of the contract unlawful. In considering whether to give effect to those provisions, regard shall be had to their nature and purpose and to the consequences of their application or non-application.

Article 10 Consent and Material Validity

1. The existence and validity of a contract, or of any term of a contract, shall be determined by the law which would govern it under this Regulation if the contract or term were valid.

2. Nevertheless, a party, in order to establish that he did not consent, may rely upon the law of the country in which he has his habitual residence if it appears from the circumstances that it would not be reasonable to determine the effect of his conduct in accordance with the law specified in paragraph 1.

Article 11 Formal Validity

1. A contract concluded between persons who, or whose agents, are in the same country at the time of its conclusion is formally valid if it satisfies the formal requirements of the law which governs it in substance under this Regulation or of the law of the country where it is concluded.

2. A contract concluded between persons who, or whose agents, are in different countries at the time of its conclusion is formally valid if it satisfies the formal requirements of the law which governs it in substance under this Regulation, or of the law of either of the countries where either of the parties or their agent is present at the time of conclusion, or of the law of the country where either of the parties had his habitual residence at that time.

3. A unilateral act intended to have legal effect relating to an existing or contemplated contract is formally valid if it satisfies the formal requirements of the law which governs or would govern the contract in substance under this Regulation, or of the law of the country where the act was done, or of the law of the country where the person by whom it was done had his habitual residence at that time.

4. Paragraphs 1, 2 and 3 of this Article shall not apply to contracts that fall within the scope of Article 6. The form of such contracts shall be governed by the law of the country where the consumer has his habitual residence.

5. Notwithstanding paragraphs 1 to 4, a contract the subject matter of which is a right *in rem* in immovable property or a tenancy of immovable property shall be subject to the requirements of form of the law of the country where the property is situated if by that law:

(a) those requirements are imposed irrespective of the country where the contract is concluded and irrespective of the law governing the contract; and

(b) those requirements cannot be derogated from by agreement.

Article 12 Scope of the Law Applicable

1. The law applicable to a contract by virtue of this Regulation shall govern in particular:

(a) interpretation;

(b) performance;

(c) within the limits of the powers conferred on the court by its procedural law, the consequences of a total or partial breach of obligations, including the assessment of damages in so far as it is governed by rules of law;

(d) the various ways of extinguishing obligations, and prescription and limitation of actions;

(e) the consequences of nullity of the contract.

2. In relation to the manner of performance and the steps to be taken in the event of defective performance, regard shall be had to the law of the country in which performance takes place.

Article 13 Incapacity

In a contract concluded between persons who are in the same country, a natural person who would have capacity under the law of that country may invoke his incapacity resulting from the law of another country, only if the other party to the contract was aware of that incapacity at the time of the conclusion of the contract or was not aware thereof as a result of negligence.

Article 14 Voluntary Assignment and Contractual Subrogation

1. The relationship between assignor and assignee under a voluntary assignment or contractual subrogation of a claim against another person (the debtor) shall be governed by the law that applies to the contract between the assignor and assignee under this Regulation.

2. The law governing the assigned or subrogated claim shall determine its assignability, the relationship between the assignee and the debtor, the conditions under which the assignment or subrogation can be invoked against the debtor and whether the debtor's obligations have been discharged.

3. The concept of assignment in this Article includes outright transfers of claims, transfers of claims by way of security and pledges or other security rights over claims.

Article 15 Legal Subrogation

Where a person (the creditor) has a contractual claim against another (the debtor) and a third person has a duty to satisfy the creditor, or has in fact satisfied the creditor in discharge of that duty, the law which governs the third person's duty to satisfy the creditor shall determine whether and to what extent the third person is entitled to exercise against the debtor the rights which the creditor had against the debtor under the law governing their relationship.

Article 16 Multiple Liability

If a creditor has a claim against several debtors who are liable for the same claim, and one of the debtors has already satisfied the claim in whole or in part, the law governing the debtor's obligation towards the creditor also governs the debtor's right to claim recourse from the other debtors. The other debtors may rely on the defences they had against the creditor to the extent allowed by the law governing their obligations towards the creditor.

Article 17 Set-Off

Where the right to set-off is not agreed by the parties, set-off shall be governed by the law applicable to the claim against which the right to set-off is asserted.

Article 18 Burden of Proof

1. The law governing a contractual obligation under this Regulation shall apply to the extent that, in matters of contractual obligations, it contains rules which raise presumptions of law or determine the burden of proof.

2. A contract or an act intended to have legal effect may be proved by any mode of proof recognised by the law of the forum or by any of the laws referred to in Article 11 under which that contract or act is formally valid, provided that such mode of proof can be administered by the forum.

Chapter III Other Provisions

Article 19 Habitual Residence

1. For the purposes of this Regulation, the habitual residence of companies and other bodies, corporate or unincorporated, shall be the place of central administration.

The habitual residence of a natural person acting in the course of his business activity shall be his principal place of business.

2. Where the contract is concluded in the course of the operations of a branch, agency or any other establishment, or if, under the contract, performance is the responsibility of such a branch, agency or establishment, the place where the branch, agency or any other establishment is located shall be treated as the place of habitual residence.

3. For the purposes of determining the habitual residence, the relevant point in time shall be the time of the conclusion of the contract.

Article 20 Exclusion of Renvoi

The application of the law of any country specified by this Regulation means the application of the rules of law in force in that country other than its rules of private international law, unless provided otherwise in this Regulation.

Article 21 Public Policy of the Forum

The application of a provision of the law of any country specified by this Regulation may be refused only if such application is manifestly incompatible with the public policy (*ordre public*) of the forum.

Article 22 States with More Than One Legal System

1. Where a State comprises several territorial units, each of which has its own rules of law in respect of contractual obligations, each territorial unit shall be considered as a country for the purposes of identifying the law applicable under this Regulation.

2. A Member State where different territorial units have their own rules of law in respect of contractual obligations shall not be required to apply this Regulation to conflicts solely between the laws of such units.

Article 23 Relationship with Other Provisions of Community Law

With the exception of Article 7, this Regulation shall not prejudice the application of provisions of Community law which, in relation to particular matters, lay down conflict-of-law rules relating to contractual obligations.

Article 24 Relationship with the Rome Convention

1. This Regulation shall replace the Rome Convention in the Member States, [...].

2. In so far as this Regulation replaces the provisions of the Rome Convention, any reference to that Convention shall be understood as a reference to this Regulation.

Article 25 Relationship with Existing International Conventions

1. This Regulation shall not prejudice the application of international conventions to which one or more Member States are parties at the time when this Regulation is adopted and which lay down conflict-of-law rules relating to contractual obligations.

2. However, this Regulation shall, as between Member States, take precedence over conventions concluded exclusively between two or more of them in so far as such conventions concern matters governed by this Regulation.

Article 26 List of Conventions

1. By 17 June 2009, Member States shall notify the Commission of the conventions referred to in Article 25(1). After that date, Member States shall notify the Commission of all denunciations of such conventions.

2. Within six months of receipt of the notifications referred to in paragraph 1, the Commission shall publish in the *Official Journal of the European Union*:

(a) a list of the conventions referred to in paragraph 1;

(b) the denunciations referred to in paragraph 1.

Article 27 Review Clause

1. By 17 June 2013, the Commission shall submit to the European Parliament, the Council and the European Economic and Social Committee a report on the application of this Regulation. If appropriate, the report shall be accompanied by proposals to amend this Regulation. The report shall include:

(a) a study on the law applicable to insurance contracts and an assessment of the impact of the provisions to be introduced, if any; and

(b) an evaluation on the application of Article 6, in particular as regards the coherence of Community law in the field of consumer protection.

2. By 17 June 2010, the Commission shall submit to the European Parliament, the Council and the European Economic and Social Committee a report on the question of the effectiveness of an assignment or subrogation of a claim against third parties and the priority of the assigned or subrogated claim over a right of another person. The report shall be accompanied, if appropriate, by a proposal to amend this Regulation and an assessment of the impact of the provisions to be introduced.

Article 28 Application in Time

This Regulation shall apply to contracts concluded after 17 December 2009.

Chapter IV Final Provisions

Article 29 Entry Into Force and Application

This Regulation shall enter into force on the 20th day following its publication in the *Official Journal of the European Union*.

It shall apply from 17 December 2009 except for Article 26 which shall apply from 17 June 2009.

This Regulation shall be binding in its entirety and directly applicable in the Member States in accordance with the Treaty establishing the European Community.

Done at Strasbourg, 17 June 2008.

8) EU Regulation 864/2007 on the Law Applicable to Non-Contractual Obligations ("Rome II")[1]

THE EUROPEAN PARLIAMENT AND THE COUNCIL OF THE EUROPEAN UNION,

Having regard to the Treaty establishing the European Community, and in particular Articles 61(c) and 67 thereof, [...]

Whereas:

(1) The Community has set itself the objective of maintaining and developing an area of freedom, security and justice. For the progressive establishment of such an area, the Community is to adopt measures relating to judicial cooperation in civil matters with a cross-border impact to the extent necessary for the proper functioning of the internal market.

(2) According to Article 65(b) of the Treaty, these measures are to include those promoting the compatibility of the rules applicable in the Member States concerning the conflict of laws and of jurisdiction.

(3) The European Council meeting in Tampere on 15 and 16 October 1999 endorsed the principle of mutual recognition of judgments and other decisions of judicial authorities as the cornerstone of judicial cooperation in civil matters and invited the Council and the Commission to adopt a programme of measures to implement the principle of mutual recognition.

(4) On 30 November 2000, the Council adopted a joint Commission and Council programme of measures for implementation of the principle of mutual recognition of decisions in civil and commercial matters. The programme identifies measures relating to the harmonisation of conflict-of-law rules as those facilitating the mutual recognition of judgments.

(5) The Hague Programme, adopted by the European Council on 5 November 2004, called for work to be pursued actively on the rules of conflict of laws regarding non-contractual obligations (Rome II).

(6) The proper functioning of the internal market creates a need, in order to improve the predictability of the outcome of litigation, certainty as to the law applicable and the free movement of judgments, for the conflict-of-law rules in the Member States to designate the same national law irrespective of the country of the court in which an action is brought.

(7) The substantive scope and the provisions of this Regulation should be consistent with [EU Regulation 1215/2012 on jurisdiction and the recognition and enforcement of judgments in civil and commercial matters [Brussels I *bis*, see p. II - 92] and the instruments dealing with the law applicable to contractual obligations.

(8) This Regulation should apply irrespective of the nature of the court or tribunal seised.

(9) Claims arising out of *acta iure imperii* should include claims against officials who act on behalf of the State and liability for acts of public authorities, including liability of publicly appointed office- holders. Therefore, these matters should be excluded from the scope of this Regulation.

(10) Family relationships should cover parentage, marriage, affinity and collateral relatives. The reference in Article 1(2) to relationships having comparable effects to marriage and other family relationships should be interpreted in accordance with the law of the Member State in which the court is seised.

(11) The concept of a non-contractual obligation varies from one Member State to another. Therefore for the purposes of this Regulation non-contractual obligation should be understood

---

1 OJ 2007 L 199, pp. 40-49.

as an autonomous concept. The conflict-of-law rules set out in this Regulation should also cover non-contractual obligations arising out of strict liability.

(12) The law applicable should also govern the question of the capacity to incur liability in tort/delict.

(13) Uniform rules applied irrespective of the law they designate may avert the risk of distortions of competition between Community litigants.

(14) The requirement of legal certainty and the need to do justice in individual cases are essential elements of an area of justice. This Regulation provides for the connecting factors which are the most appropriate to achieve these objectives. Therefore, this Regulation provides for a general rule but also for specific rules and, in certain provisions, for an 'escape clause' which allows a departure from these rules where it is clear from all the circumstances of the case that the tort/delict is manifestly more closely connected with another country. This set of rules thus creates a flexible framework of conflict-of-law rules. Equally, it enables the court seised to treat individual cases in an appropriate manner.

(15) The principle of the *lex loci delicti commissi* is the basic solution for non-contractual obligations in virtually all the Member States, but the practical application of the principle where the component factors of the case are spread over several countries varies. This situation engenders uncertainty as to the law applicable.

(16) Uniform rules should enhance the foreseeability of court decisions and ensure a reasonable balance between the interests of the person claimed to be liable and the person who has sustained damage. A connection with the country where the direct damage occurred (lex loci damni) strikes a fair balance between the interests of the person claimed to be liable and the person sustaining the damage, and also reflects the modern approach to civil liability and the development of systems of strict liability.

(17) The law applicable should be determined on the basis of where the damage occurs, regardless of the country or countries in which the indirect consequences could occur. Accordingly, in cases of personal injury or damage to property, the country in which the damage occurs should be the country where the injury was sustained or the property was damaged respectively.

(18) The general rule in this Regulation should be the *lex loci damni* provided for in Article 4(1). Article 4(2) should be seen as an exception to this general principle, creating a special connection where the parties have their habitual residence in the same country. Article 4(3) should be understood as an 'escape clause' from Article 4(1) and (2), where it is clear from all the circumstances of the case that the tort/delict is manifestly more closely connected with another country.

(19) Specific rules should be laid down for special torts/delicts where the general rule does not allow a reasonable balance to be struck between the interests at stake.

(20) The conflict-of-law rule in matters of product liability should meet the objectives of fairly spreading the risks inherent in a modern high-technology society, protecting consumers' health, stimulating innovation, securing undistorted competition and facilitating trade. Creation of a cascade system of connecting factors, together with a foreseeability clause, is a balanced solution in regard to these objectives. The first element to be taken into account is the law of the country in which the person sustaining the damage had his or her habitual residence when the damage occurred, if the product was marketed in that country. The other elements of the cascade are triggered if the product was not marketed in that country, without prejudice to Article 4(2) and to the possibility of a manifestly closer connection to another country.

(21) The special rule in Article 6 is not an exception to the general rule in Article 4(1) but rather a clarification of it. In matters of unfair competition, the conflict-of-law rule should protect compe-

titors, consumers and the general public and ensure that the market economy functions properly. The connection to the law of the country where competitive relations or the collective interests of consumers are, or are likely to be, affected generally satisfies these objectives.

(22) The non-contractual obligations arising out of restrictions of competition in Article 6(3) should cover infringements of both national and Community competition law. The law applicable to such non-contractual obligations should be the law of the country where the market is, or is likely to be, affected. In cases where the market is, or is likely to be, affected in more than one country, the claimant should be able in certain circumstances to choose to base his or her claim on the law of the court seised.

(23) For the purposes of this Regulation, the concept of restriction of competition should cover prohibitions on agreements between undertakings, decisions by associations of undertakings and concerted practices which have as their object or effect the prevention, restriction or distortion of competition within a Member State or within the internal market, as well as prohibitions on the abuse of a dominant position within a Member State or within the internal market, where such agreements, decisions, concerted practices or abuses are prohibited by Articles 81 and 82 of the Treaty or by the law of a Member State.

(24) 'Environmental damage' should be understood as meaning adverse change in a natural resource, such as water, land or air, impairment of a function performed by that resource for the benefit of another natural resource or the public, or impairment of the variability among living organisms.

(25) Regarding environmental damage, Article 174 of the Treaty, which provides that there should be a high level of protection based on the precautionary principle and the principle that preventive action should be taken, the principle of priority for corrective action at source and the principle that the polluter pays, fully justifies the use of the principle of discriminating in favour of the person sustaining the damage. The question of when the person seeking compensation can make the choice of the law applicable should be determined in accordance with the law of the Member State in which the court is seised.

(26) Regarding infringements of intellectual property rights, the universally acknowledged principle of the lex loci protectionis should be preserved. For the purposes of this Regulation, the term 'intellectual property rights' should be interpreted as meaning, for instance, copyright, related rights, the sui generis right for the protection of databases and industrial property rights.

(27) The exact concept of industrial action, such as strike action or lock-out, varies from one Member State to another and is governed by each Member State's internal rules. Therefore, this Regulation assumes as a general principle that the law of the country where the industrial action was taken should apply, with the aim of protecting the rights and obligations of workers and employers.

(28) The special rule on industrial action in Article 9 is without prejudice to the conditions relating to the exercise of such action in accordance with national law and without prejudice to the legal status of trade unions or of the representative organisations of workers as provided for in the law of the Member States.

(29) Provision should be made for special rules where damage is caused by an act other than a tort/delict, such as unjust enrichment, negotiorum gestio and culpa in contrahendo.

(30) Culpa in contrahendo for the purposes of this Regulation is an autonomous concept and should not necessarily be interpreted within the meaning of national law. It should include the violation of the duty of disclosure and the breakdown of contractual negotiations. Article 12 covers only non-contractual obligations presenting a direct link with the dealings prior to the conclusion of a contract. This means that if, while a contract is being negotiated, a person suffers personal injury, Article 4 or other relevant provisions of this Regulation should apply.

(31) To respect the principle of party autonomy and to enhance legal certainty, the parties should be allowed to make a choice as to the law applicable to a non-contractual obligation. This choice should be expressed or demonstrated with reasonable certainty by the circumstances of the case. Where establishing the existence of the agreement, the court has to respect the intentions of the parties. Protection should be given to weaker parties by imposing certain conditions on the choice.

(32) Considerations of public interest justify giving the courts of the Member States the possibility, in exceptional circumstances, of applying exceptions based on public policy and overriding mandatory provisions. In particular, the application of a provision of the law designated by this Regulation which would have the effect of causing non-compensatory exemplary or punitive damages of an excessive nature to be awarded may, depending on the circumstances of the case and the legal order of the Member State of the court seised, be regarded as being contrary to the public policy (ordre public) of the forum.

(33) According to the current national rules on compensation awarded to victims of road traffic accidents, when quantifying damages for personal injury in cases in which the accident takes place in a State other than that of the habitual residence of the victim, the court seised should take into account all the relevant actual circumstances of the specific victim, including in particular the actual losses and costs of after-care and medical attention.

(34) In order to strike a reasonable balance between the parties, account must be taken, in so far as appropriate, of the rules of safety and conduct in operation in the country in which the harmful act was committed, even where the non-contractual obligation is governed by the law of another country. The term 'rules of safety and conduct' should be interpreted as referring to all regulations having any relation to safety and conduct, including, for example, road safety rules in the case of an accident.

(35) A situation where conflict-of-law rules are dispersed among several instruments and where there are differences between those rules should be avoided. This Regulation, however, does not exclude the possibility of inclusion of conflict-of-law rules relating to non-contractual obligations in provisions of Community law with regard to particular matters.

This Regulation should not prejudice the application of other instruments laying down provisions designed to contribute to the proper functioning of the internal market in so far as they cannot be applied in conjunction with the law designated by the rules of this Regulation. The application of provisions of the applicable law designated by the rules of this Regulation should not restrict the free movement of goods and services as regulated by Community instruments, such as Directive 2000/31 [...] on Certain Legal Aspects of Information Society Services, in Particular Electronic Commerce, in the Internal Market (Directive on Electronic Commerce).[1]

(36) Respect for international commitments entered into by the Member States means that this Regulation should not affect international conventions to which one or more Member States are parties at the time this Regulation is adopted. To make the rules more accessible, the Commission should publish the list of the relevant conventions in the Official Journal of the European Union on the basis of information supplied by the Member States.

(37) The Commission will make a proposal to the European Parliament and the Council concerning the procedures and conditions according to which Member States would be entitled to negotiate and conclude on their own behalf agreements with third countries in individual and exceptional cases, concerning sectoral matters, containing provisions on the law applicable to non-contractual obligations.

---

1 OJ 2000 L 178, pp. 1-16.

(38) Since the objective of this Regulation cannot be sufficiently achieved by the Member States, and can therefore, by reason of the scale and effects of this Regulation, be better achieved at Community level, the Community may adopt measures, in accordance with the principle of subsidiarity set out in Article 5 of the Treaty. In accordance with the principle of proportionality set out in that Article, this Regulation does not go beyond what is necessary to attain that objective.

(39) [...]

(40) In accordance with Articles 1 and 2 of the Protocol on the position of Denmark, annexed to the Treaty on European Union and to the Treaty establishing the European Community, Denmark does not take part in the adoption of this Regulation, and is not bound by it or subject to its application,

HAVE ADOPTED THIS REGULATION:

CHAPTER I – SCOPE

Article 1 Scope

1. This Regulation shall apply, in situations involving a conflict of laws, to non-contractual obligations in civil and commercial matters. It shall not apply, in particular, to revenue, customs or administrative matters or to the liability of the State for acts and omissions in the exercise of State authority (acta iure imperii).

2. The following shall be excluded from the scope of this Regulation:

(a) non-contractual obligations arising out of family relationships and relationships deemed by the law applicable to such relationships to have comparable effects including maintenance obligations;

(b) non-contractual obligations arising out of matrimonial property regimes, property regimes of relationships deemed by the law applicable to such relationships to have comparable effects to marriage, and wills and succession;

(c) non-contractual obligations arising under bills of exchange, cheques and promissory notes and other negotiable instruments to the extent that the obligations under such other negotiable instruments arise out of their negotiable character;

(d) non-contractual obligations arising out of the law of companies and other bodies corporate or unincorporated regarding matters such as the creation, by registration or otherwise, legal capacity, internal organisation or winding-up of companies and other bodies corporate or unincorporated, the personal liability of officers and members as such for the obligations of the company or body and the personal liability of auditors to a company or to its members in the statutory audits of accounting documents;

(e) non-contractual obligations arising out of the relations between the settlors, trustees and beneficiaries of a trust created voluntarily;

(f) non-contractual obligations arising out of nuclear damage;

(g) non-contractual obligations arising out of violations of privacy and rights relating to personality, including defamation.

3. This Regulation shall not apply to evidence and procedure, without prejudice to Articles 21 and 22.

4. For the purposes of this Regulation, 'Member State' shall mean any Member State other than Denmark.

Article 2 Non-Contractual Obligations

1. For the purposes of this Regulation, damage shall cover any consequence arising out of tort/delict, unjust enrichment, negotiorum gestio or culpa in contrahendo.

2. This Regulation shall apply also to non-contractual obligations that are likely to arise.

3. Any reference in this Regulation to:

(a) an event giving rise to damage shall include events giving rise to damage that are likely to occur; and

(b) damage shall include damage that is likely to occur.

Article 3 Universal Application

Any law specified by this Regulation shall be applied whether or not it is the law of a Member State.

CHAPTER II – TORTS/DELICTS

Article 4 General Rule

1. Unless otherwise provided for in this Regulation, the law applicable to a non-contractual obligation arising out of a tort/delict shall be the law of the country in which the damage occurs irrespective of the country in which the event giving rise to the damage occurred and irrespective of the country or countries in which the indirect consequences of that event occur.

2. However, where the person claimed to be liable and the person sustaining damage both have their habitual residence in the same country at the time when the damage occurs, the law of that country shall apply.

3. Where it is clear from all the circumstances of the case that the tort/delict is manifestly more closely connected with a country other than that indicated in paragraphs 1 or 2, the law of that other country shall apply. A manifestly closer connection with another country might be based in particular on a pre-existing relationship between the parties, such as a contract, that is closely connected with the tort/delict in question.

Article 5 Product Liability

1. Without prejudice to Article 4(2), the law applicable to a non-contractual obligation arising out of damage caused by a product shall be:

(a) the law of the country in which the person sustaining the damage had his or her habitual residence when the damage occurred, if the product was marketed in that country; or, failing that,

(b) the law of the country in which the product was acquired, if the product was marketed in that country; or, failing that,

(c) the law of the country in which the damage occurred, if the product was marketed in that country.

However, the law applicable shall be the law of the country in which the person claimed to be liable is habitually resident if he or she could not reasonably foresee the marketing of the product, or a product of the same type, in the country the law of which is applicable under (a), (b) or (c).

2. Where it is clear from all the circumstances of the case that the tort/delict is manifestly more closely connected with a country other than that indicated in paragraph 1, the law of that other country shall apply. A manifestly closer connection with another country might be based in particular on a pre-existing relationship between the parties, such as a contract, that is closely connected with the tort/delict in question.

Article 6 Unfair Competition and Acts Restricting Free Competition

1. The law applicable to a non-contractual obligation arising out of an act of unfair competition shall be the law of the country where competitive relations or the collective interests of consumers are, or are likely to be, affected.

2. Where an act of unfair competition affects exclusively the interests of a specific competitor, Article 4 shall apply.

3.(a) The law applicable to a non-contractual obligation arising out of a restriction of competition shall be the law of the country where the market is, or is likely to be, affected.

(b) When the market is, or is likely to be, affected in more than one country, the person seeking compensation for damage who sues in the court of the domicile of the defendant, may instead choose to base his or her claim on the law of the court seised, provided that the market in that Member State is amongst those directly and substantially affected by the restriction of competition out of which the non-contractual obligation on which the claim is based arises; where the claimant sues, in accordance with the applicable rules on jurisdiction, more than one defendant in that court, he or she can only choose to base his or her claim on the law of that court if the restriction of competition on which the claim against each of these defendants relies directly and substantially affects also the market in the Member State of that court.

4. The law applicable under this Article may not be derogated from by an agreement pursuant to Article 14.

Article 7 Environmental Damage

The law applicable to a non-contractual obligation arising out of environmental damage or damage sustained by persons or property as a result of such damage shall be the law determined pursuant to Article 4(1), unless the person seeking compensation for damage chooses to base his or her claim on the law of the country in which the event giving rise to the damage occurred.

Article 8 Infringement of Intellectual Property Rights

1. The law applicable to a non-contractual obligation arising from an infringement of an intellectual property right shall be the law of the country for which protection is claimed.

2. In the case of a non-contractual obligation arising from an infringement of a unitary Community intellectual property right, the law applicable shall, for any question that is not governed by the relevant Community instrument, be the law of the country in which the act of infringement was committed.

3. The law applicable under this Article may not be derogated from by an agreement pursuant to Article 14.

Article 9 Industrial Action

Without prejudice to Article 4(2), the law applicable to a non-contractual obligation in respect of the liability of a person in the capacity of a worker or an employer or the organisations representing their professional interests for damages caused by an industrial action, pending or carried out, shall be the law of the country where the action is to be, or has been, taken.

CHAPTER III – UNJUST ENRICHMENT, NEGOTIORUM GESTIO AND CULPA IN CONTRAHENDO

Article 10 Unjust Enrichment

1. If a non-contractual obligation arising out of unjust enrichment, including payment of amounts wrongly received, concerns a relationship existing between the parties, such as one

arising out of a contract or a tort/delict, that is closely connected with that unjust enrichment, it shall be governed by the law that governs that relationship.

2. Where the law applicable cannot be determined on the basis of paragraph 1 and the parties have their habitual residence in the same country when the event giving rise to unjust enrichment occurs, the law of that country shall apply.

3. Where the law applicable cannot be determined on the basis of paragraphs 1 or 2, it shall be the law of the country in which the unjust enrichment took place.

4. Where it is clear from all the circumstances of the case that the non-contractual obligation arising out of unjust enrichment is manifestly more closely connected with a country other than that indicated in paragraphs 1, 2 and 3, the law of that other country shall apply.

Article 11 Negotiorum Gestio

1. If a non-contractual obligation arising out of an act performed without due authority in connection with the affairs of another person concerns a relationship existing between the parties, such as one arising out of a contract or a tort/delict, that is closely connected with that non-contractual obligation, it shall be governed by the law that governs that relationship.

2. Where the law applicable cannot be determined on the basis of paragraph 1, and the parties have their habitual residence in the same country when the event giving rise to the damage occurs, the law of that country shall apply.

3. Where the law applicable cannot be determined on the basis of paragraphs 1 or 2, it shall be the law of the country in which the act was performed.

4. Where it is clear from all the circumstances of the case that the non-contractual obligation arising out of an act performed without due authority in connection with the affairs of another person is manifestly more closely connected with a country other than that indicated in paragraphs 1, 2 and 3, the law of that other country shall apply.

Article 12 Culpa in Contrahendo

1. The law applicable to a non-contractual obligation arising out of dealings prior to the conclusion of a contract, regardless of whether the contract was actually concluded or not, shall be the law that applies to the contract or that would have been applicable to it had it been entered into.

2. Where the law applicable cannot be determined on the basis of paragraph 1, it shall be:

(a) the law of the country in which the damage occurs, irrespective of the country in which the event giving rise to the damage occurred and irrespective of the country or countries in which the indirect consequences of that event occurred; or

(b) where the parties have their habitual residence in the same country at the time when the event giving rise to the damage occurs, the law of that country; or

(c) where it is clear from all the circumstances of the case that the non-contractual obligation arising out of dealings prior to the conclusion of a contract is manifestly more closely connected with a country other than that indicated in points (a) and (b), the law of that other country.

Article 13 Applicability of Article 8

For the purposes of this Chapter, Article 8 shall apply to non-contractual obligations arising from an infringement of an intellectual property right.

CHAPTER IV – FREEDOM OF CHOICE

Article 14 Freedom of Choice

1. The parties may agree to submit non-contractual obligations to the law of their choice:

(a) by an agreement entered into after the event giving rise to the damage occurred; or

(b) where all the parties are pursuing a commercial activity, also by an agreement freely negotiated before the event giving rise to the damage occurred.

The choice shall be expressed or demonstrated with reasonable certainty by the circumstances of the case and shall not prejudice the rights of third parties.

2. Where all the elements relevant to the situation at the time when the event giving rise to the damage occurs are located in a country other than the country whose law has been chosen, the choice of the parties shall not prejudice the application of provisions of the law of that other country which cannot be derogated from by agreement.

3. Where all the elements relevant to the situation at the time when the event giving rise to the damage occurs are located in one or more of the Member States, the parties' choice of the law applicable other than that of a Member State shall not prejudice the application of provisions of Community law, where appropriate as implemented in the Member State of the forum, which cannot be derogated from by agreement.

CHAPTER V – COMMON RULES

Article 15 Scope of the Law Applicable

The law applicable to non-contractual obligations under this Regulation shall govern in particular:

(a) the basis and extent of liability, including the determination of persons who may be held liable for acts performed by them;

(b) the grounds for exemption from liability, any limitation of liability and any division of liability;

(c) the existence, the nature and the assessment of damage or the remedy claimed;

(d) within the limits of powers conferred on the court by its procedural law, the measures which a court may take to prevent or terminate injury or damage or to ensure the provision of compensation;

(e) the question whether a right to claim damages or a remedy may be transferred, including by inheritance;

(f) persons entitled to compensation for damage sustained personally;

(g) liability for the acts of another person;

(h) the manner in which an obligation may be extinguished and rules of prescription and limitation, including rules relating to the commencement, interruption and suspension of a period of prescription or limitation.

Article 16 Overriding Mandatory Provisions

Nothing in this Regulation shall restrict the application of the provisions of the law of the forum in a situation where they are mandatory irrespective of the law otherwise applicable to the non-contractual obligation.

Article 17 Rules of Safety and Conduct

In assessing the conduct of the person claimed to be liable, account shall be taken, as a matter of fact and in so far as is appropriate, of the rules of safety and conduct which were in force at the place and time of the event giving rise to the liability.

Article 18 Direct Action Against the Insurer of the Person Liable

The person having suffered damage may bring his or her claim directly against the insurer of the person liable to provide compensation if the law applicable to the non-contractual obligation or the law applicable to the insurance contract so provides.

Article 19 Subrogation

Where a person (the creditor) has a non-contractual claim upon another (the debtor), and a third person has a duty to satisfy the creditor, or has in fact satisfied the creditor in discharge of that duty, the law which governs the third person's duty to satisfy the creditor shall determine whether, and the extent to which, the third person is entitled to exercise against the debtor the rights which the creditor had against the debtor under the law governing their relationship.

Article 20 Multiple Liability

If a creditor has a claim against several debtors who are liable for the same claim, and one of the debtors has already satisfied the claim in whole or in part, the question of that debtor's right to demand compensation from the other debtors shall be governed by the law applicable to that debtor's non-contractual obligation towards the creditor.

Article 21 Formal Validity

A unilateral act intended to have legal effect and relating to a non-contractual obligation shall be formally valid if it satisfies the formal requirements of the law governing the non-contractual obligation in question or the law of the country in which the act is performed.

Article 22 Burden of Proof

1. The law governing a non-contractual obligation under this Regulation shall apply to the extent that, in matters of non-contractual obligations, it contains rules which raise presumptions of law or determine the burden of proof.

2. Acts intended to have legal effect may be proved by any mode of proof recognised by the law of the forum or by any of the laws referred to in Article 21 under which that act is formally valid, provided that such mode of proof can be administered by the forum.

CHAPTER VI – OTHER PROVISIONS

Article 23 Habitual Residence

1. For the purposes of this Regulation, the habitual residence of companies and other bodies, corporate or unincorporated, shall be the place of central administration.

Where the event giving rise to the damage occurs, or the damage arises, in the course of operation of a branch, agency or any other establishment, the place where the branch, agency or any other establishment is located shall be treated as the place of habitual residence.

2. For the purposes of this Regulation, the habitual residence of a natural person acting in the course of his or her business activity shall be his or her principal place of business.

Article 24 Exclusion of Renvoi

The application of the law of any country specified by this Regulation means the application of the rules of law in force in that country other than its rules of private international law.

Article 25 States with More than One Legal System

1. Where a State comprises several territorial units, each of which has its own rules of law in respect of non-contractual obligations, each territorial unit shall be considered as a country for the purposes of identifying the law applicable under this Regulation.

2. A Member State within which different territorial units have their own rules of law in respect of non-contractual obligations shall not be required to apply this Regulation to conflicts solely between the laws of such units.

Article 26 Public Policy of the Forum

The application of a provision of the law of any country specified by this Regulation may be refused only if such application is manifestly incompatible with the public policy (ordre public) of the forum.

Article 27 Relationship with Other Provisions of Community Law

This Regulation shall not prejudice the application of provisions of Community law which, in relation to particular matters, lay down conflict-of-law rules relating to non-contractual obligations.

Article 28 Relationship with Existing International Conventions

1. This Regulation shall not prejudice the application of international conventions to which one or more Member States are parties at the time when this Regulation is adopted and which lay down conflict-of-law rules relating to non-contractual obligations.

2. However, this Regulation shall, as between Member States, take precedence over conventions concluded exclusively between two or more of them in so far as such conventions concern matters governed by this Regulation.

CHAPTER VII – FINAL PROVISIONS

Article 29 List of Conventions

1. By 11 July 2008, Member States shall notify the Commission of the conventions referred to in Article 28(1). After that date, Member States shall notify the Commission of all denunciations of such conventions.

2. The Commission shall publish in the Official Journal of the European Union within six months of receipt:

(i) a list of the conventions referred to in paragraph 1;

(ii) the denunciations referred to in paragraph 1.

Article 30 Review Clause

1. Not later than 20 August 2011, the Commission shall submit to the European Parliament, the Council and the European Economic and Social Committee a report on the application of this Regulation. If necessary, the report shall be accompanied by proposals to adapt this Regulation. The report shall include:

(i) a study on the effects of the way in which foreign law is treated in the different jurisdictions and on the extent to which courts in the Member States apply foreign law in practice pursuant to this Regulation;

(ii) a study on the effects of Article 28 of this Regulation with respect to the Hague Convention of 4 May 1971 on the law applicable to traffic accidents.

2. Not later than 31 December 2008, the Commission shall submit to the European Parliament, the Council and the European Economic and Social Committee a study on the situation in the field of the law applicable to non-contractual obligations arising out of violations of privacy and rights relating to personality, taking into account rules relating to freedom of the press and freedom of expression in the media, and conflict-of-law issues related to Directive 95/46/EC of the European Parliament and of the Council of 24 October 1995 on the protection of individuals with regard to the processing of personal data and on the free movement of such data.

Article 31 Application in Time

This Regulation shall apply to events giving rise to damage which occur after its entry into force.

Article 32 Date of Application

This Regulation shall apply from 11 January 2009, except for Article 29, which shall apply from 11 July 2008.

This Regulation shall be binding in its entirety and directly applicable in the Member States in accordance with the Treaty establishing the European Community.

Done at Strasbourg, 11 July 2007.

9) 1980 United Nations Convention on Contracts for the International Sale of Goods[1]

THE STATES PARTIES TO THIS CONVENTION,

BEARING IN MIND the broad objectives in the resolutions adopted by the sixth special session of the General Assembly of the United Nations on the establishment of a New International Economic Order,

CONSIDERING that the development of international trade on the basis of equality and mutual benefit is an important element in promoting friendly relations among States,

BEING OF THE OPINION that the adoption of uniform rules which govern contracts for the international sale of goods and take into account the different social, economic and legal systems would contribute to the removal of legal barriers in international trade and promote the development of international trade,

HAVE DECREED as follows:

PART I – SPHERE OF APPLICATION AND GENERAL PROVISIONS

CHAPTER I - SPHERE OF APPLICATION

Article 1 [Scope of Application]

(1) This Convention applies to contracts of sale of goods between parties whose places of business are in different States:

(a) when the States are Contracting States; or

(b) when the rules of private international law lead to the application of the law of a Contracting State.

(2) The fact that the parties have their places of business in different States is to be disregarded whenever this fact does not appear either from the contract or from any dealings between, or from information disclosed by, the parties at any time before or at the conclusion of the contract.

(3) Neither the nationality of the parties nor the civil or commercial character of the parties or of the contract is to be taken into consideration in determining the application of this Convention.

Article 2 [Sales Contracts Not Covered]

This Convention does not apply to sales:

(a) of goods bought for personal, family or household use, unless the seller, at any time before or at the conclusion of the contract, neither knew nor ought to have known that the goods were bought for any such use;

(b) by auction;

(c) on execution or otherwise by authority of law;

(d) of stocks, shares, investment securities, negotiable instruments or money;

(e) of ships, vessels, hovercraft or aircraft;

(f) of electricity.

Article 3 [Contracts Involving Works or Services]

(1) Contracts for the supply of goods to be manufactured or produced are to be considered sales unless the party who orders the goods undertakes to supply a substantial part of the materials necessary for such manufacture or production.

(2) This Convention does not apply to contracts in which the preponderant part of the obligations of the party who furnishes the goods consists in the supply of labour or other services.

Article 4 [Scope in Substantive Contract Law]

This Convention governs only the formation of the contract of sale and the rights and obligations of the seller and the buyer arising from such a contract. In particular, except as otherwise expressly provided in this Convention, it is not concerned with:

(a) the validity of the contract or of any of its provisions or of any usage;

(b) the effect which the contract may have on the property in the goods sold.

Article 5 [No Application in Tort Law]

This Convention does not apply to the liability of the seller for death or personal injury caused by the goods to any person.

Article 6 [Priority of Contractual Clauses]

The parties may exclude the application of this Convention or, subject to Article 12, derogate from or vary the effect of any of its provisions.

CHAPTER II - GENERAL PROVISIONS

Article 7 [Interpretation of the CISG]

(1) In the interpretation of this Convention, regard is to be had to its international character and to the need to promote uniformity in its application and the observance of good faith in international trade.

(2) Questions concerning matters governed by this Convention which are not expressly settled in it are to be settled in conformity with the general principles on which it is based or, in the absence of such principles, in conformity with the law applicable by virtue of the rules of private international law.

Article 8 [Interpretation of Conduct and Statements]

(1) For the purposes of this Convention statements made by and other conduct of a party are to be interpreted according to his intent where the other party knew or could not have been unaware what that intent was.

(2) If the preceding paragraph is not applicable, statements made by and other conduct of a party are to be interpreted according to the understanding that a reasonable person of the same kind as the other party would have had in the same circumstances.

(3) In determining the intent of a party or the understanding a reasonable person would have had, due consideration is to be given to all relevant circumstances of the case including the negotiations, any practices which the parties have established between themselves, usages and any subsequent conduct of the parties.

Article 9 [Usages of the Parties and the Industry]

(1) The parties are bound by any usage to which they have agreed and by any practices which they have established between themselves.

(2) The parties are considered, unless otherwise agreed, to have impliedly made applicable to their contract or its formation a usage of which the parties knew or ought to have known and

which in international trade is widely known to, and regularly observed by, parties to contracts of the type involved in the particular trade concerned.

Article 10 [Definition of "Place of Business"]

For the purposes of this Convention:

(a) if a party has more than one place of business, the place of business is that which has the closest relationship to the contract and its performance, having regard to the circumstances known to or contemplated by the parties at any time before or at the conclusion of the contract;

(b) if a party does not have a place of business, reference is to be made to his habitual residence.

Article 11 [Freedom of Form]

A contract of sale need not be concluded in or evidenced by writing and is not subject to any other requirement as to form. It may be proved by any means, including witnesses.

Article 12 [Exceptions to the Freedom of Form]

Any provision of Article 11, Article 29 or Part II of this Convention that allows a contract of sale or its modification or termination by agreement or any offer, acceptance or other indication of intention to be made in any form other than in writing does not apply where any party has his place of business in a Contracting State which has made a declaration under Article 96 of this Convention. The parties may not derogate from or vary the effect or this article.

Article 13 [Definition of Written Form]

For the purposes of this Convention "writing" includes telegram and telex.

PART II – FORMATION OF THE CONTRACT

Article 14 [Offer or Invitation]

(1) A proposal for concluding a contract addressed to one or more specific persons constitutes an offer if it is sufficiently definite and indicates the intention of the offeror to be bound in case of acceptance. A proposal is sufficiently definite if it indicates the goods and expressly or implicitly fixes or makes provision for determining the quantity and the price.

(2) A proposal other than one addressed to one or more specific persons is to be considered merely as an invitation to make offers, unless the contrary is clearly indicated by the person making the proposal.

Article 15 [Effective and Withdrawn Offers]

(1) An offer becomes effective when it reaches the offeree.

(2) An offer, even if it is irrevocable, may be withdrawn if the withdrawal reaches the offeree before or at the same time as the offer.

Article 16 [Revocable and Irrevocable Offers]

(1) Until a contract is concluded an offer may be revoked if the revocation reaches the offeree before he has dispatched an acceptance.

(2) However, an offer cannot be revoked:

(a) if it indicates, whether by stating a fixed time for acceptance or otherwise, that it is irrevocable; or

(b) if it was reasonable for the offeree to rely on the offer as being irrevocable and the offeree has acted in reliance on the offer.

Article 17 [Rejection of Offers]

An offer, even if it is irrevocable, is terminated when a rejection reaches the offeror.

Article 18 [Acceptance of Offers]

(1) A statement made by or other conduct of the offeree indicating assent to an offer is an acceptance. Silence or inactivity does not in itself amount to acceptance.

(2) An acceptance of an offer becomes effective at the moment the indication of assent reaches the offeror. An acceptance is not effective if the indication of assent does not reach the offeror within the time he has fixed or, if no time is fixed, within a reasonable time, due account being taken of the circumstances of the transaction, including the rapidity of the means of communication employed by the offeror. An oral offer must be accepted immediately unless the circumstances indicate otherwise.

(3) However, if, by virtue of the offer or as a result of practices which the parties have established between themselves or of usage, the offeree may indicate assent by performing an act, such as one relating to the dispatch of the goods or payment of the price, without notice to the offeror, the acceptance is effective at the moment the act is performed, provided that the act is performed within the period of time laid down in the preceding paragraph.

Article 19 [Modified Acceptance or Counter-Offer]

(1) A reply to an offer which purports to be an acceptance but contains additions, limitations or other modifications is a rejection of the offer and constitutes a counter-offer.

(2) However, a reply to an offer which purports to be an acceptance but contains additional or different terms which do not materially alter the terms of the offer constitutes an acceptance, unless the offeror, without undue delay, objects orally to the discrepancy or dispatches a notice to that effect. If he does not so object, the terms of the contract are the terms of the offer with the modifications contained in the acceptance.

(3) Additional or different terms relating, among other things, to the price, payment, quality and quantity of the goods, place and time of delivery, extent of one party's liability to the other or the settlement of disputes are considered to alter the terms of the offer materially.

Article 20 [Time Limit for Acceptance]

(1) A period of time for acceptance fixed by the offeror in a telegram or a letter begins to run from the moment the telegram is handed in for dispatch or from the date shown on the letter or, if no such date is shown, from the date shown on the envelope. A period of time for acceptance fixed by the offeror by telephone, telex or other means of instantaneous communication, begins to run from the moment that the offer reaches the offeree.

(2) Official holidays or non-business days occurring during the period for acceptance are included in calculating the period. However, if a notice of acceptance cannot be delivered at the address of the offeror on the last day of the period because that day falls on an official holiday or a non-business day at the place of business of the offeror, the period is extended until the first business day which follows.

Article 21 [Late Acceptance]

(1) A late acceptance is nevertheless effective as an acceptance if without delay the offeror orally so informs the offeree or dispatches a notice to that effect.

(2) If a letter or other writing containing a late acceptance shows that it has been sent in such circumstances that if its transmission had been normal it would have reached the offeror in due time, the late acceptance is effective as an acceptance unless, without delay, the offeror orally informs the offeree that he considers his offer as having lapsed or dispatches a notice to that effect.

Article 22 *[Withdrawal of Acceptance]*

An acceptance may be withdrawn if the withdrawal reaches the offeror before or at the same time as the acceptance would have become effective.

Article 23 [Conclusion of Contract]

A contract is concluded at the moment when an acceptance of an offer becomes effective in accordance with the provisions of this Convention.

Article 24 [Definition of "Reaches"]

For the purposes of this Part of the Convention, an offer, declaration of acceptance or any other indication of intention "reaches" the addressee when it is made orally to him or delivered by any other means to him personally, to his place of business or mailing address or, if he does not have a place of business or mailing address, to his habitual residence.

PART III – SALE OF GOODS

CHAPTER I - GENERAL PROVISIONS

Article 25 [Definition of "Fundamental Breach"]

A breach of contract committed by one of the parties is fundamental if it results in such detriment to the other party as substantially to deprive him of what he is entitled to expect under the contract, unless the party in breach did not foresee and a reasonable person of the same kind in the same circumstances would not have foreseen such a result.

Article 26 [Declaration of Avoidance]

A declaration of avoidance of the contract is effective only if made by notice to the other party.

Article 27 [Delay or Error in Transmission of Communications]

Unless otherwise expressly provided in this Part of the Convention, if any notice, request or other communication is given or made by a party in accordance with this Part and by means appropriate in the circumstances, a delay or error in the transmission of the communication or its failure to arrive does not deprive that party of the right to rely on the communication.

Article 28 [Specific Performance]

If, in accordance with the provisions of this Convention, one party is entitled to require performance of any obligation by the other party, a court is not bound to enter a judgement for specific performance unless the court would do so under its own law in respect of similar contracts of sale not governed by this Convention.

Article 29 [Modification or Termination by Agreement]

(1) A contract may be modified or terminated by the mere agreement of the parties.

(2) A contract in writing which contains a provision requiring any modification or termination by agreement to be in writing may not be otherwise modified or terminated by agreement. However, a party may be precluded by his conduct from asserting such a provision to the extent that the other party has relied on that conduct.

CHAPTER II - OBLIGATIONS OF THE SELLER

Article 30 [Primary Obligations]

The seller must deliver the goods, hand over any documents relating to them and transfer the property in the goods, as required by the contract and this Convention.

Section I. Delivery of the Goods and Handing over of Documents

Article 31 [Place of Delivery] UCC 2 – 308

If the seller is not bound to deliver the goods at any other particular place, his obligation to deliver consists:

(a) if the contract of sale involves carriage of the goods - in handing the goods over to the first carrier for transmission to the buyer;

(b) if, in cases not within the preceding subparagraph, the contract related to specific goods, or unidentified goods to be drawn from a specific stock or to be manufactured or produced, and at the time of the conclusion of the contract the parties knew that the goods were at, or were to be manufactured or produced at, a particular place - in placing the goods at the buyer's disposal at that place;

(c) in other cases - in placing the goods at the buyer's disposal at the place where the seller had his place of business at the time of the conclusion of the contract.

Article 32 [Carriage and Insurance]

(1) If the seller, in accordance with the contract or this Convention, hands the goods over to a carrier and if the goods are not clearly identified to the contract by markings on the goods, by shipping documents or otherwise, the seller must give the buyer notice of the consignment specifying the goods.

(2) If the seller is bound to arrange for carriage of the goods, he must make such contracts as are necessary for carriage to the place fixed by means of transportation appropriate in the circumstances and according to the usual terms for such transportation.

(3) If the seller is not bound to effect insurance in respect of the carriage of the goods, he must, at the buyer's request, provide him with all available information necessary to enable him to effect such insurance.

Article 33 [Time of Delivery]

The seller must deliver the goods:

(a) if a date is fixed by or determinable from the contract, on that date;

(b) if a period of time is fixed by or determinable from the contract, at any time within that period unless circumstances indicate that the buyer is to choose a date; or

(c) in any other case, within a reasonable time after the conclusion of the contract.

Article 34 [Delivery of Related Documents]

If the seller is bound to hand over documents relating to the goods, he must hand them over at the time and place and in the form required by the contract. If the seller has handed over documents before that time, he may, up to that time, cure any lack of conformity in the documents, if the exercise of this right does not cause the buyer unreasonable inconvenience or unreasonable expense. However, the buyer retains any right to claim damages as provided for in this Convention.

Section II. Conformity of the Goods and Third Party Claims

Article 35 [Conformity of Goods to Contract]

(1) The seller must deliver goods which are of the quantity, quality and description required by the contract and which are contained or packaged in the manner required by the contract.

(2) Except where the parties have agreed otherwise, the goods do not conform with the contract unless they:

(a) are fit for the purposes for which goods of the same description would ordinarily be used;

(b) are fit for any particular purpose expressly or impliedly made known to the seller at the time of the conclusion of the contract, except where the circumstances show that the buyer did not rely, or that it was unreasonable for him to rely, on the seller's skill and judgement;

(c) possess the qualities of goods which the seller has held out to the buyer as a sample or model;

(d) are contained or packaged in the manner usual for such goods or, where there is no such manner, in a manner adequate to preserve and protect the goods.

(3) The seller is not liable under subparagraphs (a) to (d) of the preceding paragraph for any lack of conformity of the goods if at the time of the conclusion of the contract the buyer knew or could not have been unaware of such lack of conformity.

Article 36 [Time When Goods Must Be in Conformity]

(1) The seller is liable in accordance with the contract and this Convention for any lack of conformity which exists at the time when the risk passes to the buyer, even though the lack of conformity becomes apparent only after that time.

(2) The seller is also liable for any lack of conformity which occurs after the time indicated in the preceding paragraph and which is due to a breach of any of his obligations, including a breach of any guarantee that for a period of time the goods will remain fit for their ordinary purpose or for some particular purpose or will retain specified qualities or characteristics.

Article 37 [Seller's Right to Cure Defects Before Due Date for Delivery]

If the seller has delivered goods before the date for delivery, he may, up to that date, deliver any missing part or make up any deficiency in the quantity of the goods delivered, or deliver goods in replacement of any non-conforming goods delivered or remedy any lack of conformity in the goods delivered, provided that the exercise of this right does not cause the buyer unreasonable inconvenience or unreasonable expense. However, the buyer retains any right to claim damages as provided for in this Convention.

Article 38 [Buyer's Obligation to Examine Goods]

(1) The buyer must examine the goods, or cause them to be examined, within as short a period as is practicable in the circumstances.

(2) If the contract involves carriage of the goods, examination may be deferred until after the goods have arrived at their destination.

(3) If the goods are redirected in transit or redispatched by the buyer without a reasonable opportunity for examination by him and at the time of the conclusion of the contract the seller knew or ought to have known of the possibility of such redirection or redispatch, examination may be deferred until after the goods have arrived at the new destination.

Article 39 [Buyer's Obligation to Notify Non-Conformity]

(1) The buyer loses the right to rely on a lack of conformity of the goods if he does not give notice to the seller specifying the nature of the lack of conformity within a reasonable time after he has discovered it or ought to have discovered it.

(2) In any event, the buyer loses the right to rely on a lack of conformity of the goods if he does not give the seller notice thereof at the latest within a period of two years from the date on which the goods were actually handed over to the buyer, unless this time-limit is inconsistent with a contractual period of guarantee.

Article 40 [Seller's Knowledge of Non-Conformity]

The seller is not entitled to rely on the provisions of Articles 38 and 39 if the lack of conformity relates to facts of which he knew or could not have been unaware and which he did not disclose to the buyer.

Article 41 [Delivery with Title and Free from Encumbrances]

The seller must deliver goods which are free from any right or claim of a third party, unless the buyer agreed to take the goods subject to that right or claim. However, if such right or claim is based on industrial property or other intellectual property, the seller's obligation is governed by Article 42.

Article 42 [Third Party Industrial or Intellectual Property Rights]

(1) The seller must deliver goods which are free from any right or claim of a third party based on industrial property or other intellectual property, of which at the time of the conclusion of the contract the seller knew or could not have been unaware, provided that the right or claim is based on industrial property or other intellectual property:

(a) under the law of the State where the goods will be resold or otherwise used, if it was contemplated by the parties at the time of the conclusion of the contract that the goods would be resold or otherwise used in that State; or

(b) in any other case, under the law of the State where the buyer has his place of business.

(2) The obligation of the seller under the preceding paragraph does not extend to cases where:

(a) at the time of the conclusion of the contract the buyer knew or could not have been unaware of the right or claim; or

(b) the right or claim results from the seller's compliance with technical drawings, designs, formulae or other such specifications furnished by the buyer.

Article 43 [Buyer's Obligation to Notify Third Party Claims]

(1) The buyer loses the right to rely on the provisions of Article 41 or Article 42 if he does not give notice to the seller specifying the nature of the right or claim of the third party within a reasonable time after he has become aware or ought to have become aware of the right or claim.

(2) The seller is not entitled to rely on the provisions of the preceding paragraph if he knew of the right or claim of the third party and the nature of it.

Article 44 [Exception to Article 39(1) and 43]

Notwithstanding the provisions of paragraph (1) of Article 39 and paragraph (1) of Article 43, the buyer may reduce the price in accordance with Article 50 or claim damages, except for loss of profit, if he has a reasonable excuse for his failure to give the required notice.

Section III. Remedies for Breach of Contract by the Seller

Article 45 [Buyer's Remedies in the Event of Seller's Breach]

(1) If the seller fails to perform any of his obligations under the contract or this Convention, the buyer may:

(a) exercise the rights provided in Articles 46 to 52; [and/or]

(b) claim damages as provided in Articles 74 to 77.

(2) The buyer is not deprived of any right he may have to claim damages by exercising his right to other remedies.

(3) No period of grace may be granted to the seller by a court or arbitral tribunal when the buyer resorts to a remedy for breach of contract.

Article 46 [Priority of the Right to Require Performance]

(1) The buyer may require performance by the seller of his obligations unless the buyer has resorted to a remedy which is inconsistent with this requirement.

(2) If the goods do not conform with the contract, the buyer may require delivery of substitute goods only if the lack of conformity constitutes a fundamental breach of contract and a request for substitute goods is made either in conjunction with notice given under Article 39 or within a reasonable time thereafter.

(3) If the goods do not conform with the contract, the buyer may require the seller to remedy the lack of conformity by repair, unless this is unreasonable having regard to all the circumstances. A request for repair must be made either in conjunction with notice given under Article 39 or within a reasonable time thereafter.

Article 47 [Additional Time Limit for Performance]

(1) The buyer may fix an additional period of time of reasonable length for performance by the seller of his obligations.

(2) Unless the buyer has received notice from the seller that he will not perform within the period so fixed, the buyer may not, during that period, resort to any remedy for breach of contract. However, the buyer is not deprived thereby of any right he may have to claim damages for delay in performance.

Article 48 [Seller's Right to Remedy Performance Even After Date for Delivery]

(1) Subject to Article 49, the seller may, even after the date for delivery, remedy at his own expense any failure to perform his obligations, if he can do so without unreasonable delay and without causing the buyer unreasonable inconvenience or uncertainty of reimbursement by the seller of expenses advanced by the buyer. However, the buyer retains any right to claim damages as provided for in this Convention.

(2) If the seller requests the buyer to make known whether he will accept performance and the buyer does not comply with the request within a reasonable time, the seller may perform within the time indicated in his request. The buyer may not, during that period of time, resort to any remedy which is inconsistent with performance by the seller.

(3) A notice by the seller that he will perform within a specified period of time is assumed to include a request, under the preceding paragraph, that the buyer make known his decision.

(4) A request or notice by the seller under paragraph (2) or (3) of this Article is not effective unless received by the buyer.

Article 49 [Buyer's Right to Avoid]

(1) The buyer may declare the contract avoided:

(a) if the failure by the seller to perform any of his obligations under the contract or this Convention amounts to a fundamental breach of contract; or

(b) in case of non-delivery, if the seller does not deliver the goods within the additional period of time fixed by the buyer in accordance with paragraph (1) of Article 47 or declares that he will not deliver within the period so fixed.

(2) However, in cases where the seller has delivered the goods, the buyer loses the right to declare the contract avoided unless he does so:

(a) in respect of late delivery, within a reasonable time after he has become aware that delivery has been made;

(b) in respect of any breach other than late delivery, within a reasonable time:

  (i) after he knew or ought to have known of the breach;

  (ii) after the expiration of any additional period of time fixed by the buyer in accordance with paragraph (1) of Article 47, or after the seller has declared that he will not perform his obligations within such an additional period; or

  (iii) after the expiration of any additional period of time indicated by the seller in accordance with paragraph (2) of Article 48, or after the buyer has declared that he will not accept performance.

Article 50 [Buyer's Right to Keep Non-Conforming Goods and Reduce Price]

If the goods do not conform with the contract and whether or not the price has already been paid, the buyer may reduce the price in the same proportion as the value that the goods actually delivered had at the time of the delivery bears to the value that conforming goods would have had at that time. However, if the seller remedies any failure to perform his obligations in accordance with Article 37 or Article 48 or if the buyer refuses to accept performance by the seller in accordance with those articles, the buyer may not reduce the price.

Article 51 [Partial Delivery]

(1) If the seller delivers only a part of the goods or if only a part of the goods delivered is in conformity with the contract, Articles 46 to 50 apply in respect of the part which is missing or which does not conform.

(2) The buyer may declare the contract avoided in its entirety only if the failure to make delivery completely or in conformity with the contract amounts to a fundamental breach of the contract.

Article 52 [Early Delivery and Excess Delivery]

(1) If the seller delivers the goods before the date fixed, the buyer may take delivery or refuse to take delivery.

(2) If the seller delivers a quantity of goods greater than that provided for in the contract, the buyer may take delivery or refuse to take delivery of the excess quantity. If the buyer takes delivery of all or part of the excess quantity, he must pay for it at the contract rate.

CHAPTER III - OBLIGATIONS OF THE BUYER

Article 53 [Primary Obligations]

The buyer must pay the price for the goods and take delivery of them as required by the contract and this Convention.

Section I. Payment of the Price

Article 54 [Payment and Payment Formalities]

The buyer's obligation to pay the price includes taking such steps and complying with such formalities as may be required under the contract or any laws and regulations to enable payment to be made.

Article 55 [Determination of Price]

Where a contract has been validly concluded but does not expressly or implicitly fix or make provision for determining the price, the parties are considered, in the absence of any indication to the contrary, to have impliedly made reference to the price generally charged at the time of the conclusion of the contract for such goods sold under comparable circumstances in the trade concerned.

Article 56 [Price Fixed According to Weight]

If the price is fixed according to the weight of the goods, in case of doubt it is to be determined by the net weight.

Article 57 [Place of Payment]

(1) If the buyer is not bound to pay the price at any other particular place, he must pay it to the seller:

(a) at the seller's place of business; or

(b) if the payment is to be made against the handing over of the goods or of documents, at the place where the handing over takes place.

(2) The seller must bear any increases in the expenses incidental to payment which is caused by a change in his place of business subsequent to the conclusion of the contract.

Article 58 [Time of Payment]

(1) If the buyer is not bound to pay the price at any other specific time, he must pay it when the seller places either the goods or documents controlling their disposition at the buyer's disposal in accordance with the contract and this Convention. The seller may make such payment a condition for handing over the goods or documents.

(2) If the contract involves carriage of the goods, the seller may dispatch the goods on terms whereby the goods, or documents controlling their disposition, will not be handed over to the buyer except against payment of the price.

(3) The buyer is not bound to pay the price until he has had an opportunity to examine the goods, unless the procedures for delivery or payment agreed upon by the parties are inconsistent with his having such an opportunity.

Article 59 [Payment Due Without Formal Demand]

The buyer must pay the price on the date fixed by or determinable from the contract and this Convention without the need for any request or compliance with any formality on the part of the seller.

Section II. Taking Delivery

Article 60 [Buyer's Obligation to Take Delivery] Delivery

The buyer's obligation to take delivery consists:

(a) in doing all the acts which could reasonably be expected of him in order to enable the seller to make delivery; and

(b) in taking over the goods.

Section III. Remedies for Breach of Contract by the Buyer

Article 61 [Seller's Remedies in the Event of Buyer's Breach]

(1) If the buyer fails to perform any of his obligations under the contract or this Convention, the seller may:

(a) exercise the rights provided in Articles 62 to 65; [and/or]

(b) claim damages as provided in Articles 74 to 77.

(2) The seller is not deprived of any right he may have to claim damages by exercising his right to other remedies.

(3) No period of grace may be granted to the buyer by a court or arbitral tribunal when the seller resorts to a remedy for breach of contract.

Article 62 [Priority of the Right to Require Performance]

The seller may require the buyer to pay the price, take delivery or perform his other obligations, unless the seller has resorted to a remedy which is inconsistent with this requirement.

Article 63 [Additional Time Limit for Performance]

(1) The seller may fix an additional period of time of reasonable length for performance by the buyer of his obligations.

(2) Unless the seller has received notice from the buyer that he will not perform within the period so fixed, the seller may not, during that period, resort to any remedy for breach of contract. However, the seller is not deprived thereby of any right he may have to claim damages for delay in performance.

Article 64 [Seller's Right to Avoid]

(1) The seller may declare the contract avoided:

(a) if the failure by the buyer to perform any of his obligations under the contract or this Convention amounts to a fundamental breach of contract; or

(b) if the buyer does not, within the additional period of time fixed by the seller in accordance with paragraph (1) of Article 63, perform his obligation to pay the price or take delivery of the goods, or if he declares that he will not do so within the period so fixed.

(2) However, in cases where the buyer has paid the price, the seller loses the right to declare the contract avoided unless he does so:

(a) in respect of late performance by the buyer, before the seller has become aware that performance has been rendered; or

(b) in respect of any breach other than late performance by the buyer, within a reasonable time:

(i) after the seller knew or ought to have known of the breach; or

(ii) after the expiration of any additional period of time fixed by the seller in accordance with paragraph (1) or Article 63, or after the buyer has declared that he will not perform his obligations within such an additional period.

Article 65 [Right and Obligation to Make Specifications]

(1) If under the contract the buyer is to specify the form, measurement or other features of the goods and he fails to make such specification either on the date agreed upon or within a reasonable time after receipt of a request from the seller, the seller may, without prejudice to any other rights he may have, make the specification himself in accordance with the requirements of the buyer that may be known to him.

(2) If the seller makes the specification himself, he must inform the buyer of the details thereof and must fix a reasonable time within which the buyer may make a different specification. If, after receipt of such a communication, the buyer fails to do so within the time so fixed, the specification made by the seller is binding.

CHAPTER IV - PASSING OF RISK

Article 66 [General Rule]

Loss of or damage to the goods after the risk has passed to the buyer does not discharge him from his obligation to pay the price, unless the loss or damage is due to an act or omission of the seller.

Article 67 [Passing of Risk in the Absence of INCOTERM Specification]

(1) If the contract of sale involves carriage of the goods and the seller is not bound to hand them over at a particular place, the risk passes to the buyer when the goods are handed over to the first carrier for transmission to the buyer in accordance with the contract of sale. If the seller is bound to hand the goods over to a carrier at a particular place, the risk does not pass to the buyer until the goods are handed over to the carrier at that place. The fact that the seller is authorized to retain documents controlling the disposition of the goods does not affect the passage of the risk.

(2) Nevertheless, the risk does not pass to the buyer until the goods are clearly identified to the contract, whether by markings on the goods, by shipping documents, by notice given to the buyer or otherwise.

Article 68 [Goods Sold in Transit]

The risk in respect of goods sold in transit passes to the buyer from the time of the conclusion of the contract. However, if the circumstances so indicate, the risk is assumed by the buyer from the time the goods were handed over to the carrier who issued the documents embodying the contract of carriage. Nevertheless, if at the time of the conclusion of the contract of sale the seller knew or ought to have known that the goods had been lost or damaged and did not disclose this to the buyer, the loss or damage is at the risk of the seller.

Article 69 [Passing of Risk When Goods Are Delivered]

(1) In cases not within Articles 67 and 68, the risk passes to the buyer when he takes over the goods or, if he does not do so in due time, from the time when the goods are placed at his disposal and he commits a breach of contract by failing to take delivery.

(2) However, if the buyer is bound to take over the goods at a place other than a place of business of the seller, the risk passes when delivery is due and the buyer is aware of the fact that the goods are placed at his disposal at that place.

(3) If the contract relates to goods not then identified, the goods are considered not to be placed at the disposal of the buyer until they are clearly identified to the contract.

Article 70 [Seller's Breach Unconnected to Loss of Goods]

If the seller has committed a fundamental breach of contract, Articles 67, 68 and 69 do not impair the remedies available to the buyer on account of the breach.

CHAPTER V - PROVISIONS COMMON TO THE OBLIGATIONS OF THE SELLER AND OF THE BUYER

Section I. Anticipatory Breach and Instalment Contracts

Article 71 [Anticipated Problems Prior to Performance]

(1) A party may suspend the performance of his obligations if, after the conclusion of the contract, it becomes apparent that the other party will not perform a substantial part of his obligations as a result of:

(a) a serious deficiency in his ability to perform or in his creditworthiness; or

(b) his conduct in preparing to perform or in performing the contract.

(2) If the seller has already dispatched the goods before the grounds described in the preceding paragraph become evident, he may prevent the handing over of the goods to the buyer even though the buyer holds a document which entitles him to obtain them. The present paragraph relates only to the rights in the goods as between the buyer and the seller.

(3) A party suspending performance, whether before or after dispatch of the goods, must immediately give notice of the suspension to the other party and must continue with performance if the other party provides adequate assurance of his performance.

Article 72 [Preventive Avoidance for Anticipatory Breach]

(1) If prior to the date for performance of the contract it is clear that one of the parties will commit a fundamental breach of contract, the other party may declare the contract avoided.

(2) If time allows, the party intending to declare the contract avoided must give reasonable notice to the other party in order to permit him to provide adequate assurance of his performance.

(3) The requirements of the preceding paragraph do not apply if the other party has declared that he will not perform his obligations.

Article 73 [Problems with Installment Contracts]

(1) In the case of a contract for delivery of goods by instalments, if the failure of one party to perform any of his obligations in respect of any instalment constitutes a fundamental breach of contract with respect to that instalment, the other party may declare the contract avoided with respect to that instalment.

(2) If one party's failure to perform any of his obligations in respect of any instalment gives the other party good grounds to conclude that a fundamental breach of contract will occur with respect to future instalments, he may declare the contract avoided for the future, provided that he does so within a reasonable time.

(3) A buyer who declares the contract avoided in respect of any delivery may, at the same time, declare it avoided in respect of deliveries already made or of future deliveries if, by reason of their interdependence, those deliveries could not be used for the purpose contemplated by the parties at the time of the conclusion of the contract.

Section II. Damages

Article 74 [Calculation of Damages]

Damages for breach of contract by one party consist of a sum equal to the loss, including loss of profit, suffered by the other party as a consequence of the breach. Such damages may not exceed the loss which the party in breach foresaw or ought to have foreseen at the time of the conclusion of the contract, in the light of the facts and matters of which he then knew or ought to have known, as a possible consequence of the breach of contract.

Article 75 [Cover Transaction]

If the contract is avoided and if, in a reasonable manner and within a reasonable time after avoidance, the buyer has bought goods in replacement or the seller has resold the goods, the party claiming damages may recover the difference between the contract price and the price in the substitute transaction as well as any further damages recoverable under Article 74.

Article 76 [Difference Between Contract Price and Current Price as Damage]

(1) If the contract is avoided and there is a current price for the goods, the party claiming damages may, if he has not made a purchase or resale under Article 75, recover the difference between the price fixed by the contract and the current price at the time of avoidance as well as any further damages recoverable under Article 74. If, however, the party claiming damages has

avoided the contract after taking over the goods, the current price at the time of such taking over shall be applied instead of the current price at the time of avoidance.

(2) For the purposes of the preceding paragraph, the current price is the price prevailing at the place where delivery of the goods should have been made or, if there is no current price at that place, the price at such other place as serves as a reasonable substitute, making due allowance for differences in the cost of transporting the goods.

Article 77 [Obligation to Mitigate Losses]

A party who relies on a breach of contract must take such measures as are reasonable in the circumstances to mitigate the loss, including loss of profit, resulting from the breach. If he fails to take such measures, the party in breach may claim a reduction in the damages in the amount by which the loss should have been mitigated.

Section III. Interest

Article 78 [Interest Separate from Damages]

If a party fails to pay the price or any other sum that is in arrears, the other party is entitled to interest on it, without prejudice to any claim for damages recoverable under Article 74.

Section IV. Exemptions

Article 79 [Force Majeure and Third Party Failure] impracticability

(1) A party is not liable for a failure to perform any of his obligations if he proves that the failure was due to an impediment beyond his control and that he could not reasonably be expected to have taken the impediment into account at the time of the conclusion of the contract or to have avoided or overcome it or its consequences.

(2) If the party's failure is due to the failure by a third person whom he has engaged to perform the whole or a part of the contract, that party is exempt from liability only if:

(a) he is exempt under the preceding paragraph; and

(b) the person whom he has so engaged would be so exempt if the provisions of that paragraph were applied to him.

(3) The exemption provided by this Article has effect for the period during which the impediment exists.

(4) The party who fails to perform must give notice to the other party of the impediment and its effect on his ability to perform. If the notice is not received by the other party within a reasonable time after the party who fails to perform knew or ought to have known of the impediment, he is liable for damages resulting from such non-receipt.

(5) Nothing in this Article prevents either party from exercising any right other than to claim damages under this Convention.

Article 80 [Detrimental Act or Omission by the Promisee]

A party may not rely on a failure of the other party to perform, to the extent that such failure was caused by the first party's act or omission.

Section V. Effects of Avoidance

Article 81 [Some Contractual Obligations Survive Avoidance]

(1) Avoidance of the contract releases both parties from their [primary] obligations under it, subject to any damages which may be due. Avoidance does not affect any provision of the contract for the settlement of disputes or any other provision of the contract governing the rights and obligations of the parties consequent upon the avoidance of the contract.

(2) A party who has performed the contract either wholly or in part may claim restitution from the other party of whatever the first party has supplied or paid under the contract. If both parties are bound to make restitution, they must do so concurrently.

Article 82 [Right to Substitute Goods Requires Restitution of Non-Conforming Goods]

(1) The buyer loses the right to declare the contract avoided or to require the seller to deliver substitute goods if it is impossible for him to make restitution of the goods substantially in the condition in which he received them.

(2) The preceding paragraph does not apply:

(a) if the impossibility of making restitution of the goods or of making restitution of the goods substantially in the condition in which the buyer received them is not due to his act or omission;

(b) if the goods or part of the goods have perished or deteriorated as a result of the examination provided for in Article 38; or

(c) if the goods or part of the goods have been sold in the normal course of business or have been consumed or transformed by the buyer in the course of normal use before he discovered or ought to have discovered the lack of conformity.

Article 83 [Independence of Different Remedies]

A buyer who has lost the right to declare the contract avoided or to require the seller to deliver substitute goods in accordance with Article 82 retains all other remedies under the contract and this Convention.

Article 84 [Mutual Restitution of Benefits After Avoidance]

(1) If the seller is bound to refund the price, he must also pay interest on it, from the date on which the price was paid.

(2) The buyer must account to the seller for all benefits which he has derived from the goods or part of them:

(a) if he must make restitution of the goods or part of them; or

(b) if it is impossible for him to make restitution of all or part of the goods or to make restitution of all or part of the goods substantially in the condition in which he received them, but he has nevertheless declared the contract avoided or required the seller to deliver substitute goods.

Section VI. Preservation of the Goods

Article 85 [Preservation by the Seller]

If the buyer is in delay in taking delivery of the goods or, where payment of the price and delivery of the goods are to be made concurrently, if he fails to pay the price, and the seller is either in possession of the goods or otherwise able to control their disposition, the seller must take such steps as are reasonable in the circumstances to preserve them. He is entitled to retain them until he has been reimbursed his reasonable expenses by the buyer.

Article 86 [Preservation by the Buyer]

(1) If the buyer has received the goods and intends to exercise any right under the contract or this Convention to reject them, he must take such steps to preserve them as are reasonable in the circumstances. He is entitled to retain them until he has been reimbursed his reasonable expenses by the seller.

(2) If goods dispatched to the buyer have been placed at his disposal at their destination and he exercises the right to reject them, he must take possession of them on behalf of the seller,

provided that this can be done without payment of the price and without unreasonable inconvenience or unreasonable expense. This provision does not apply if the seller or a person authorized to take charge of the goods on his behalf is present at the destination. If the buyer takes possession of the goods under this paragraph, his rights and obligations are governed by the preceding paragraph.

Article 87 [Preservation by Third Parties]

A party who is bound to take steps to preserve the goods may deposit them in a warehouse of a third person at the expense of the other party provided that the expense incurred is not unreasonable.

Article 88 [Self-Help Sale]

(1) A party who is bound to preserve the goods in accordance with Article 85 or 86 may sell them by any appropriate means if there has been an unreasonable delay by the other party in taking possession of the goods or in taking them back or in paying the price or the cost of preservation, provided that reasonable notice of the intention to sell has been given to the other party.

(2) If the goods are subject to rapid deterioration or their preservation would involve unreasonable expense, a party who is bound to preserve the goods in accordance with Article 85 or 86 must take reasonable measures to sell them. To the extent possible he must give notice to the other party of his intention to sell.

(3) A party selling the goods has the right to retain out of the proceeds of sale an amount equal to the reasonable expenses of preserving the goods and of selling them. He must account to the other party for the balance.

PART IV – FINAL PROVISIONS

Article 89 [Depository]

The Secretary-General of the United Nations is hereby designated as the depositary for this Convention.

Article 90 [Priority of Preceding Conventions]

This Convention does not prevail over any international agreement which has already been or may be entered into and which contains provisions concerning the matters governed by this Convention, provided that the parties have their places of business in States parties to such agreement.

Article 91 [Signature, Ratification, Accession]

(1) This Convention is open for signature at the concluding meeting of the United Nations Conference on Contracts for the International Sale of Goods and will remain open for signature by all States at the Headquarters of the United Nations, New York until 30 September 1981.

(2) This Convention is subject to ratification, acceptance or approval by the signatory States.

(3) This Convention is open for accession by all States which are not signatory States as from the date it is open for signature.

(4) Instruments of ratification, acceptance, approval and accession are to be deposited with the Secretary-General of the United Nations.

Article 92 [Reservation Against Part II or Part III of the Convention]

(1) A Contracting State may declare at the time of signature, ratification, acceptance, approval or accession that it will not be bound by Part II of this Convention or that it will not be bound by Part III of this Convention.

(2) A Contracting State which makes a declaration in accordance with the preceding paragraph in respect of Part II or Part III of this Convention is not to be considered a Contracting State within paragraph (1) of Article 1 of this Convention in respect of matters governed by the Part to which the declaration applies.

Article 93 [Federal State Clause]

(1) If a Contracting State has two or more territorial units in which, according to its constitution, different systems of law are applicable in relation to the matters dealt with in this Convention, it may, at the time of signature, ratification, acceptance, approval or accession, declare that this Convention is to extend to all its territorial units or only to one or more of them, and may amend its declaration by submitting another declaration at any time.

(2) These declarations are to be notified to the depositary and are to state expressly the territorial units to which the Convention extends.

(3) If, by virtue of a declaration under this article, this Convention extends to one or more but not all of the territorial units of a Contracting State, and if the place of business of a party is located in that State, this place of business, for the purposes of this Convention, is considered not to be in a Contracting State, unless it is in a territorial unit to which the Convention extends.

(4) If a Contracting State makes no declaration under paragraph (1) of this article, the Convention is to extend to all territorial units of that State.

Article 94 [Regional Harmonization]

(1) Two or more Contracting States which have the same or closely related legal rules on matters governed by this Convention may at any time declare that the Convention is not to apply to contracts of sale or to their formation where the parties have their places of business in those States. Such declarations may be made jointly or by reciprocal unilateral declarations.

(2) A Contracting State which has the same or closely related legal rules on matters governed by this Convention as one or more non-Contracting States may at any time declare that the Convention is not to apply to contracts of sale or to their formation where the parties have their places of business in those States.

(3) If a State which is the object of a declaration under the preceding paragraph subsequently becomes a Contracting State, the declaration made will, as from the date on which the Convention enters into force in respect of the new Contracting State, have the effect of a declaration made under paragraph (1), provided that the new Contracting State joins in such declaration or makes a reciprocal unilateral declaration.

Article 95 [Reservation Against Article 1(1)(b) of the Convention]

Any State may declare at the time of the deposit of its instrument of ratification, acceptance, approval or accession that it will not be bound by subparagraph (1)(b) of Article 1 of this Convention.

Article 96 [Reservation Against Unwritten Contracts]

A Contracting State whose legislation requires contracts of sale to be concluded in or evidenced by writing may at any time make a declaration in accordance with Article 12 that any provision of Article 11, Article 29, or Part II of this Convention, that allows a contract of sale or its modification or termination by agreement or any offer, acceptance, or other indication of intention to be made in any form other than in writing, does not apply where any party has his place of business in that State.

Article 97 [Formal Requirements for Declarations and Reservations]

(1) Declarations made under this Convention at the time of signature are subject to confirmation upon ratification, acceptance or approval.

(2) Declarations and confirmations of declarations are to be in writing and be formally notified to the depositary.

(3) A declaration takes effect simultaneously with the entry into force of this Convention in respect of the State concerned. However, a declaration of which the depositary receives formal notification after such entry into force takes effect on the first day of the month following the expiration of six months after the date of its receipt by the depositary. Reciprocal unilateral declarations under Article 94 take effect on the first day of the month following the expiration of six months after the receipt of the latest declaration by the depositary.

(4) Any State which makes a declaration under this Convention may withdraw it at any time by a formal notification in writing addressed to the depositary. Such withdrawal is to take effect on the first day of the month following the expiration of six months after the date of the receipt of the notification by the depositary.

(5) A withdrawal of a declaration made under Article 94 renders inoperative, as from the date on which the withdrawal takes effect, any reciprocal declaration made by another State under that article.

Article 98 [Prohibition of Other Reservations]

No reservations are permitted except those expressly authorized in this Convention.

Article 99 [Entry into Force]

(1) [...]

(2) When a State ratifies, accepts, approves or accedes to this Convention [...], this Convention, with the exception of the Part excluded, enters into force in respect of that State, [...] on the first day of the month following the expiration of twelve months after the date of the deposit of its instrument of ratification, acceptance, approval or accession. [...]

Article 100 [Temporal Application]

(1) This Convention applies to the formation of a contract only when the proposal for concluding the contract is made on or after the date when the Convention enters into force in respect of the Contracting States referred to in subparagraph (1)(a) or the Contracting State referred to in subparagraph (1)(b) of Article 1.

(2) This Convention applies only to contracts concluded on or after the date when the Convention enters into force in respect of the Contracting States referred to in subparagraph (1)(a) or the Contracting State referred to in subparagraph (1)(b) of Article 1.

Article 101 [Denounciation]

(1) A Contracting State may denounce this Convention, or Part II or Part III of the Convention, by a formal notification in writing addressed to the depositary.

(2) The denunciation takes effect on the first day of the month following the expiration of twelve months after the notification is received by the depositary. Where a longer period for the denunciation to take effect is specified in the notification, the denunciation takes effect upon the expiration of such longer period after the notification is received by the depositary.

DONE at Vienna, this day of eleventh day of April, one thousand nine hundred and eighty, in a single original, of which the Arabic, Chinese, English, French, Russian and Spanish texts are equally authentic.

IN WITNESS WHEREOF the undersigned plenipotentiaries, being duly authorized by their respective Governments, have signed this Convention.

Entry into force: 1 January 1988

Ratifications and binding effect as of June 2020:

No.	Country	Entry into Force	Reservations
1	Albania	1 Jun 2010	
2	Argentina	1 Jan 1988	Art. 96
3	Armenia	1 Jan 2010	Art. 94, Art. 96
4	Australia	1 Apr 1989	Art. 93
5	Austria	1 Jan 1989	
6	Azerbaijan	1 Jun 2017	
7	Bahrain	1 Oct 2014	
8	Belarus	1 Nov 1990	Art. 96
9	Belgium	1 Nov 1997	
10	Benin	1 Aug 2012	
11	Bosnia-Herzegovina	6 Mar 1992	
12	Brazil	1 Apr 2014	
13	Bulgaria	1 Aug 1991	
14	Burundi	1 Oct 1999	
15	Cameroon	1 Nov 2018	
16	Canada	1 May 1992	
17	Chile	1 Mar 1991	Art. 96
18	China	1 Jan 1988	Art. 95
19	Colombia	1 Aug 2002	
20	Congo	1 Jul 2015	
21	Costa Rica	1 Aug 2018	
22	Croatia	8 Oct 1991	
23	Cuba	1 Dec 1995	
24	Cyprus	1 Apr 2006	
25	Czech Republic	1 Jan 1993	
26	Democratic People's Republic of Korea	1 Apr 2020	Art. 96
27	Denmark	1 Mar 1990	Art. 92 (II) and Art. 94
28	Dominican Republic	1 Jul 2011	
29	Ecuador	1 Feb 1993	
30	Egypt	1 Jan 1988	
31	El Salvador	1 Dec 2007	
32	Estonia	1 Oct 1994	
33	Fiji	1 Jul 2018	
34	Finland	1 Jan 1989	Art. 92 (II) and Art. 94
35	France	1 Jan 1988	
36	Gabon	1 Jan 2006	
37	Georgia	1 Sept 1995	
38	Germany	1 Jan 1991	
39	Greece	1 Feb 1999	
40	Guatemala	1 Jan 2021	

41	Guinea	1 Feb 1992	
42	Guyana	1 Oct 2015	
43	Honduras	1 Nov 2003	
44	Hungary	1 Jan 1988	
45	Iceland	1 Jun 2002	Art. 92 (II) and Art. 94
46	Iraq	1 Apr 1991	
47	Israel	1 Feb 2003	
48	Italy	1 Jan 1988	
49	Japan	1 Aug 2009	
50	Kyrgyzstan	1 Jun 2000	
51	Latvia	1 Aug 1998	
52	Laos	1 Oct 2020	Art. 95
53	Lebanon	1 Dec 2009	
54	Lesotho	1 Jan 1988	
55	Liberia	1 Oct 2006	
56	Liechtenstein	1 May 2020	
57	Lithuania	1 Feb 1996	
58	Luxembourg	1 Feb 1998	
59	Madagascar	1 Oct 2015	
60	Mauritania	1 Sept 2000	
61	Mexico	1 Jan 1989	
62	Mongolia	1 Jan 1999	
63	Montenegro	3 Jun 2006	
64	Netherlands	1 Jan 1992	
65	New Zealand	1 Oct 1995	
66	North Macedonia	17 Nov 1991	
67	Norway	1 Aug 1989	Art. 92 (II) and Art. 94
68	Paraguay	1 Feb 2007	Art. 96
69	Peru	1 Apr 2000	
70	Poland	1 Jun 1996	
71	Republic of Korea	1 Mar 2005	
72	Republic of Moldova	1 Nov 1995	
74	Romania	1 Jun 1992	
75	Russian Federation	1 Sept 1991	Art. 96
76	Saint Vincent & Grenadines	1 Oct 2001	Art. 95
77	San Marino	1 Mar 2003	
78	Serbia	27 Apr 1992	
79	Singapore	1 Mar 1996	Art. 95
80	Slovakia	1 Jan 1993	Art. 95
81	Slovenia	25 Jun 1991	
82	Spain	1 Aug 1991	
83	State of Palestine	1 Jan 2019	
84	Sweden	1 Jan 1989	Art. 92 (II) and Art. 94
85	Switzerland	1 Mar 1991	
86	Syrian Arab Rep.	1 Jan 1988	
87	Turkey	1 Aug 2011	
88	Uganda	1 March 1993	
89	Ukraine	1 Feb 1991	Art. 96

90	United States of America	1 Jan 1988	Art. 95
91	Uruguay	1 Feb 2000	
92	Uzbekistan	1 Dec 1997	
93	Viet Nam	1 Jan 2017	
94	Zambia	1 Jan 1988	

10) 2016 UNIDROIT Principles of International Commercial Contracts[1]

PREAMBLE – Purpose of the Principles

These Principles set forth general rules for international commercial contracts.

They shall be applied when the parties have agreed that their contract be governed by them.(*)

They may be applied when the parties have agreed that their contract be governed by general principles of law, the lex mercatoria or the like.

They may be applied when the parties have not chosen any law to govern their contract.

They may be used to interpret or supplement international uniform law instruments.

They may be used to interpret or supplement domestic law.

They may serve as a model for national and international legislators.

CHAPTER 1 – GENERAL PROVISIONS

Article 1.1 Freedom of Contract

The parties are free to enter into a contract and to determine its content.

Article 1.2 No Form Required

Nothing in these Principles requires a contract, statement or any other act to be made in or evidenced by a particular form. It may be proved by any means, including witnesses.

Article 1.3 Binding Character of Contract

A contract validly entered into is binding upon the parties. It can only be modified or terminated in accordance with its terms or by agreement or as otherwise provided in these Principles.

Article 1.4 Mandatory Rules

Nothing in these Principles shall restrict the application of mandatory rules, whether of national, international or supranational origin, which are applicable in accordance with the relevant rules of private international law.

Article 1.5 Exclusion or Modification by the Parties

The parties may exclude the application of these Principles or derogate from or vary the effect of any of their provisions, except as otherwise provided in the Principles.

Article 1.6 Interpretation and Supplementation of the Principles

(1) In the interpretation of these Principles, regard is to be had to their international character and to their purposes including the need to promote uniformity in their application.

(2) Issues within the scope of these Principles but not expressly settled by them are as far as possible to be settled in accordance with their underlying general principles.

---

1 Reproduced by kind permission of the International Institute for the Unification of Private Law (UNIDROIT). Readers are reminded that the complete text of the *UNIDROIT Principles of International Commercial Contracts 2016* is composed of both black-letter rules and accompanying Comments. The full text is available in book form directly from UNIDROIT and is also available on the UNIDROIT website at https://www.unidroit.org/instruments/commercial-contracts/unidroit-principles-2016. For select case law and bibliography relating to the Principles, see www.unilex.info.

Article 1.7 Good Faith and Fair Dealing

(1) Each party must act in accordance with good faith and fair dealing in international trade.

(2) The parties may not exclude or limit this duty.

Article 1.8 Inconsistent Behaviour

A party cannot act inconsistently with an understanding it has caused the other party to have and upon which that other party reasonably has acted in reliance to its detriment.

Article 1.9 Usages and Practices

(1) The parties are bound by any usage to which they have agreed and by any practices which they have established between themselves.

(2) The parties are bound by a usage that is widely known to and regularly observed in international trade by parties in the particular trade concerned except where the application of such a usage would be unreasonable.

Article 1.10 Notice

(1) Where notice is required it may be given by any means appropriate to the circumstances.

(2) A notice is effective when it reaches the person to whom it is given.

(3) For the purpose of paragraph (2) a notice "reaches" a person when given to that person orally or delivered at that person's place of business or mailing address.

(4) For the purpose of this Article "notice" includes a declaration, demand, request or any other communication of intention.

Article 1.11 Definitions

In these Principles

– "court" includes an arbitral tribunal;
– where a party has more than one place of business the relevant "place of business" is that which has the closest relationship to the contract and its performance, having regard to the circumstances known to or contemplated by the parties at any time before or at the conclusion of the contract;
– "long-term contract" refers to a contract which is to be performed over a period of time and which normally involves, to a varying degree, complexity of the transaction and an ongoing relationship between the parties;
– "obligor" refers to the party who is to perform an obligation and "obligee" refers to the party who is entitled to performance of that obligation;
– "writing" means any mode of communication that preserves a record of the information contained therein and is capable of being reproduced in tangible form.

Article 1.12 Computation of Time Set by Parties

(1) Official holidays or non-business days occurring during a period set by parties for an act to be performed are included in calculating the period.

(2) However, if the last day of the period is an official holiday or a non-business day at the place of business of the party to perform the act, the period is extended until the first business day which follows, unless the circumstances indicate otherwise.

(3) The relevant time zone is that of the place of business of the party setting the time, unless the circumstances indicate otherwise.

CHAPTER 2 – FORMATION AND AUTHORITY OF AGENTS

SECTION 1: FORMATION

Article 2.1.1 Manner of Formation

A contract may be concluded either by the acceptance of an offer or by conduct of the parties that is sufficient to show agreement.

Article 2.1.2 Definition of Offer

A proposal for concluding a contract constitutes an offer if it is sufficiently definite and indicates the intention of the offeror to be bound in case of acceptance.

Article 2.1.3 Withdrawal of Offer

(1) An offer becomes effective when it reaches the offeree.

(2) An offer, even if it is irrevocable, may be withdrawn if the withdrawal reaches the offeree before or at the same time as the offer.

Article 2.1.4 Revocation of Offer

(1) Until a contract is concluded an offer may be revoked if the revocation reaches the offeree before it has dispatched an acceptance.

(2) However, an offer cannot be revoked

(a) if it indicates, whether by stating a fixed time for acceptance or otherwise, that it is irrevocable; or

(b) if it was reasonable for the offeree to rely on the offer as being irrevocable and the offeree has acted in reliance on the offer.

Article 2.1.5 Rejection of Offer

An offer is terminated when a rejection reaches the offeror.

Article 2.1.6 Mode of Acceptance

(1) A statement made by or other conduct of the offeree indicating assent to an offer is an acceptance. Silence or inactivity does not in itself amount to acceptance.

(2) An acceptance of an offer becomes effective when the indication of assent reaches the offeror.

(3) However, if, by virtue of the offer or as a result of practices which the parties have established between themselves or of usage, the offeree may indicate assent by performing an act without notice to the offeror, the acceptance is effective when the act is performed.

Article 2.1.7 Time of Acceptance

An offer must be accepted within the time the offeror has fixed or, if no time is fixed, within a reasonable time having regard to the circumstances, including the rapidity of the means of communication employed by the offeror. An oral offer must be accepted immediately unless the circumstances indicate otherwise.

Article 2.1.8 Acceptance Within a Fixed Period of Time

A period of acceptance fixed by the offeror begins to run from the time that the offer is dispatched. A time indicated in the offer is deemed to be the time of dispatch unless the circumstances indicate otherwise.

Article 2.1.9 Late Acceptance. Delay in Transmission

(1) A late acceptance is nevertheless effective as an acceptance if without undue delay the offeror so informs the offeree or gives notice to that effect.

(2) If a communication containing a late acceptance shows that it has been sent in such circumstances that if its transmission had been normal it would have reached the offeror in due time, the late acceptance is effective as an acceptance unless, without undue delay, the offeror informs the offeree that it considers the offer as having lapsed.

Article 2.1.10 Withdrawal of Acceptance

An acceptance may be withdrawn if the withdrawal reaches the offeror before or at the same time as the acceptance would have become effective.

Article 2.1.11 Modified Acceptance

(1) A reply to an offer which purports to be an acceptance but contains additions, limitations or other modifications is a rejection of the offer and constitutes a counter-offer.

(2) However, a reply to an offer which purports to be an acceptance but contains additional or different terms which do not materially alter the terms of the offer constitutes an acceptance, unless the offeror, without undue delay, objects to the discrepancy. If the offeror does not object, the terms of the contract are the terms of the offer with the modifications contained in the acceptance.

Article 2.1.12 Writings in Confirmation

If a writing which is sent within a reasonable time after the conclusion of the contract and which purports to be a confirmation of the contract contains additional or different terms, such terms become part of the contract, unless they materially alter the contract or the recipient, without undue delay, objects to the discrepancy.

Article 2.1.13 Conclusion of Contract Dependent on Agreement on Specific Matters or in a Particular Form

Where in the course of negotiations one of the parties insists that the contract is not concluded until there is agreement on specific matters or in a particular form, no contract is concluded before agreement is reached on those matters or in that form.

Article 2.1.14 Contract with Terms Deliberately Left Open

(1) If the parties intend to conclude a contract, the fact that they intentionally leave a term to be agreed upon in further negotiations or to be determined by one of the parties or by a third person does not prevent a contract from coming into existence.

(2) The existence of the contract is not affected by the fact that subsequently

(a) the parties reach no agreement on the term;

(b) the party who is to determine the term does not do so; or

(c) the third person does not determine the term,

provided that there is an alternative means of rendering the term definite that is reasonable in the circumstances, having regard to the intention of the parties.

Article 2.1.15 Negotiations in Bad Faith

(1) A party is free to negotiate and is not liable for failure to reach an agreement.

(2) However, a party who negotiates or breaks off negotiations in bad faith is liable for the losses caused to the other party.

(3) It is bad faith, in particular, for a party to enter into or continue negotiations when intending not to reach an agreement with the other party.

Article 2.1.16 Duty of Confidentiality

Where information is given as confidential by one party in the course of negotiations, the other party is under a duty not to disclose that information or to use it improperly for its own purposes, whether or not a contract is subsequently concluded. Where appropriate, the remedy for breach of that duty may include compensation based on the benefit received by the other party.

Article 2.1.17 Merger Clauses

A contract in writing which contains a clause indicating that the writing completely embodies the terms on which the parties have agreed cannot be contradicted or supplemented by evidence of prior statements or agreements. However, such statements or agreements may be used to interpret the writing.

Article 2.1.18 Modification in a Particular Form

A contract in writing which contains a clause requiring any modification or termination by agreement to be in a particular form may not be otherwise modified or terminated. However, a party may be precluded by its conduct from asserting such a clause to the extent that the other party has reasonably acted in reliance on that conduct.

Article 2.1.19 Contracting under Standard Terms

(1) Where one party or both parties use standard terms in concluding a contract, the general rules on formation apply, subject to Articles 2.1.20 - 2.1.22.

(2) Standard terms are provisions which are prepared in advance for general and repeated use by one party and which are actually used without negotiation with the other party.

Article 2.1.20 Surprising Terms

(1) No term contained in standard terms which is of such a character that the other party could not reasonably have expected it, is effective unless it has been expressly accepted by that party.

(2) In determining whether a term is of such a character regard shall be had to its content, language and presentation.

Article 2.1.21 Conflict Between Standard Terms and Non-standard Terms

In case of conflict between a standard term and a term which is not a standard term the latter prevails.

Article 2.1.22 Battle of Forms

Where both parties use standard terms and reach agreement except on those terms, a contract is concluded on the basis of the agreed terms and of any standard terms which are common in substance unless one party clearly indicates in advance, or later and without undue delay informs the other party, that it does not intend to be bound by such a contract.

SECTION 2: AUTHORITY OF AGENTS

Article 2.2.1 Scope of the Section

(1) This Section governs the authority of a person ("the agent") to affect the legal relations of another person ("the principal") by or with respect to a contract with a third party, whether the agent acts in its own name or in that of the principal.

(2) It governs only the relations between the principal or the agent on the one hand, and the third party on the other.

(3) It does not govern an agent's authority conferred by law or the authority of an agent appointed by a public or judicial authority.

Article 2.2.2 Establishment and Scope of the Authority of the Agent

(1) The principal's grant of authority to an agent may be express or implied.

(2) The agent has authority to perform all acts necessary in the circumstances to achieve the purposes for which the authority was granted.

Article 2.2.3 Agency Disclosed

(1) Where an agent acts within the scope of its authority and the third party knew or ought to have known that the agent was acting as an agent, the acts of the agent shall directly affect the legal relations between the principal and the third party and no legal relation is created between the agent and the third party.

(2) However, the acts of the agent shall affect only the relations between the agent and the third party, where the agent with the consent of the principal undertakes to become the party to the contract.

Article 2.2.4 Agency Undisclosed

(1) Where an agent acts within the scope of its authority and the third party neither knew nor ought to have known that the agent was acting as an agent, the acts of the agent shall affect only the relations between the agent and the third party.

(2) However, where such an agent, when contracting with the third party on behalf of a business, represents itself to be the owner of that business, the third party, upon discovery of the real owner of the business, may exercise also against the latter the rights it has against the agent.

Article 2.2.5 Agent Acting Without or Exceeding its Authority

(1) Where an agent acts without authority or exceeds its authority, its acts do not affect the legal relations between the principal and the third party.

(2) However, where the principal causes the third party reasonably to believe that the agent has authority to act on behalf of the principal and that the agent is acting within the scope of that authority, the principal may not invoke against the third party the lack of authority of the agent.

Article 2.2.6 Liability of Agent Acting Without or Exceeding its Authority

(1) An agent that acts without authority or exceeds its authority is, failing ratification by the principal, liable for damages that will place the third party in the same position as if the agent had acted with authority and not exceeded its authority.

(2) However, the agent is not liable if the third party knew or ought to have known that the agent had no authority or was exceeding its authority.

Article 2.2.7 Conflict of Interests

(1) If a contract concluded by an agent involves the agent in a conflict of interests with the principal of which the third party knew or ought to have known, the principal may avoid the contract. The right to avoid is subject to Articles 3.2.9 and 3.2.11 to 3.2.15.

(2) However, the principal may not avoid the contract

(a) if the principal had consented to, or knew or ought to have known of, the agent's involvement in the conflict of interests; or

(b) if the agent had disclosed the conflict of interests to the principal and the latter had not objected within a reasonable time.

Article 2.2.8 Sub-Agency

An agent has implied authority to appoint a sub-agent to perform acts which it is not reasonable to expect the agent to perform itself. The rules of this Section apply to the sub-agency.

Article 2.2.9 Ratification

(1) An act by an agent that acts without authority or exceeds its authority may be ratified by the principal. On ratification the act produces the same effects as if it had initially been carried out with authority.

(2) The third party may by notice to the principal specify a reasonable period of time for ratification. If the principal does not ratify within that period of time it can no longer do so.

(3) If, at the time of the agent's act, the third party neither knew nor ought to have known of the lack of authority, it may, at any time before ratification, by notice to the principal indicate its refusal to become bound by a ratification.

Article 2.2.10 Termination of Authority

(1) Termination of authority is not effective in relation to the third party unless the third party knew or ought to have known of it.

(2) Notwithstanding the termination of its authority, an agent remains authorised to perform the acts that are necessary to prevent harm to the principal's interests.

CHAPTER 3 – VALIDITY

SECTION 1: GENERAL PROVISIONS

Article 3.1.1 Matters Not Covered

This Chapter does not deal with lack of capacity.

Article 3.1.2 Validity of Mere Agreement

A contract is concluded, modified or terminated by the mere agreement of the parties, without any further requirement.

Article 3.1.3 Initial Impossibility

(1) The mere fact that at the time of the conclusion of the contract the performance of the obligation assumed was impossible does not affect the validity of the contract.

(2) The mere fact that at the time of the conclusion of the contract a party was not entitled to dispose of the assets to which the contract relates does not affect the validity of the contract.

Article 3.1.4 Mandatory Character of the Provisions

The provisions on fraud, threat, gross disparity and illegality contained in this Chapter are mandatory.

SECTION 2: GROUNDS FOR AVOIDANCE

Article 3.2.1 Definition of Mistake

Mistake is an erroneous assumption relating to facts or to law existing when the contract was concluded.

Article 3.2.2 Relevant Mistake

(1) A party may only avoid the contract for mistake if, when the contract was concluded, the mistake was of such importance that a reasonable person in the same situation as the party in error would only have concluded the contract on materially different terms or would not have concluded it at all if the true state of affairs had been known, and

(a) the other party made the same mistake, or caused the mistake, or knew or ought to have known of the mistake and it was contrary to reasonable commercial standards of fair dealing to leave the mistaken party in error; or

(b) the other party had not at the time of avoidance reasonably acted in reliance on the contract.

(2) However, a party may not avoid the contract if

(a) it was grossly negligent in committing the mistake; or

(b) the mistake relates to a matter in regard to which the risk of mistake was assumed or, having regard to the circumstances, should be borne by the mistaken party.

Article 3.2.3 Error in Expression or Transmission

An error occurring in the expression or transmission of a declaration is considered to be a mistake of the person from whom the declaration emanated.

Article 3.2.4 Remedies for Non-Performance

A party is not entitled to avoid the contract on the ground of mistake if the circumstances on which that party relies afford, or could have afforded, a remedy for non-performance.

Article 3.2.5 Fraud

A party may avoid the contract when it has been led to conclude the contract by the other party's fraudulent representation, including language or practices, or fraudulent non-disclosure of circumstances which, according to reasonable commercial standards of fair dealing, the latter party should have disclosed.

Article 3.2.6 Threat

A party may avoid the contract when it has been led to conclude the contract by the other party's unjustified threat which, having regard to the circumstances, is so imminent and serious as to leave the first party no reasonable alternative. In particular, a threat is unjustified if the act or omission with which a party has been threatened is wrongful in itself, or it is wrongful to use it as a means to obtain the conclusion of the contract.

Article 3.2.7 Gross Disparity

(1) A party may avoid the contract or an individual term of it if, at the time of the conclusion of the contract, the contract or term unjustifiably gave the other party an excessive advantage. Regard is to be had, among other factors, to

(a) the fact that the other party has taken unfair advantage of the first party's dependence, economic distress or urgent needs, or of its improvidence, ignorance, inexperience or lack of bargaining skill, and

(b) the nature and purpose of the contract.

(2) Upon the request of the party entitled to avoidance, a court may adapt the contract or term in order to make it accord with reasonable commercial standards of fair dealing.

(3) A court may also adapt the contract or term upon the request of the party receiving notice of avoidance, provided that that party informs the other party of its request promptly after receiving such notice and before the other party has reasonably acted in reliance on it. Article 3.2.10(2) applies accordingly.

Article 3.2.8 Third Persons

(1) Where fraud, threat, gross disparity or a party's mistake is imputable to, or is known or ought to be known by, a third person for whose acts the other party is responsible, the contract

may be avoided under the same conditions as if the behaviour or knowledge had been that of the party itself.

(2) Where fraud, threat or gross disparity is imputable to a third person for whose acts the other party is not responsible, the contract may be avoided if that party knew or ought to have known of the fraud, threat or disparity, or has not at the time of avoidance reasonably acted in reliance on the contract.

Article 3.2.9 Confirmation

If the party entitled to avoid the contract expressly or impliedly confirms the contract after the period of time for giving notice of avoidance has begun to run, avoidance of the contract is excluded.

Article 3.2.10 Loss of Right to Avoid

(1) If a party is entitled to avoid the contract for mistake but the other party declares itself willing to perform or performs the contract as it was understood by the party entitled to avoidance, the contract is considered to have been concluded as the latter party understood it. The other party must make such a declaration or render such performance promptly after having been informed of the manner in which the party entitled to avoidance had understood the contract and before that party has reasonably acted in reliance on a notice of avoidance.

(2) After such a declaration or performance the right to avoidance is lost and any earlier notice of avoidance is ineffective.

Article 3.2.11 Notice of Avoidance

The right of a party to avoid the contract is exercised by notice to the other party.

Article 3.2.12 Time Limits

(1) Notice of avoidance shall be given within a reasonable time, having regard to the circumstances, after the avoiding party knew or could not have been unaware of the relevant facts or became capable of acting freely.

(2) Where an individual term of the contract may be avoided by a party under Article 3.2.7, the period of time for giving notice of avoidance begins to run when that term is asserted by the other party.

Article 3.2.13 Partial Avoidance

Where a ground of avoidance affects only individual terms of the contract, the effect of avoidance is limited to those terms unless, having regard to the circumstances, it is unreasonable to uphold the remaining contract.

Article 3.2.14 Retroactive Effect of Avoidance

Avoidance takes effect retroactively.

Article 3.2.15 Restitution

(1) On avoidance either party may claim restitution of whatever it has supplied under the contract, or the part of it avoided, provided that the party concurrently makes restitution of whatever it has received under the contract, or the part of it avoided.

(2) If restitution in kind is not possible or appropriate, an allowance has to be made in money whenever reasonable.

(3) The recipient of the performance does not have to make an allowance in money if the impossibility to make restitution in kind is attributable to the other party.

(4) Compensation may be claimed for expenses reasonably required to preserve or maintain the performance received.

Article 3.2.16 Damages

Irrespective of whether or not the contract has been avoided, the party who knew or ought to have known of the ground for avoidance is liable for damages so as to put the other party in the same position in which it would have been if it had not concluded the contract.

Article 3.2.17 Unilateral Declarations

The provisions of this Chapter apply with appropriate adaptations to any communication of intention addressed by one party to the other.

SECTION 3: ILLEGALITY

Article 3.3.1 Contracts Infringing Mandatory Rules

(1) Where a contract infringes a mandatory rule, whether of national, international or supra-national origin, applicable under Article 1.4 of these Principles, the effects of that infringement upon the contract are the effects, if any, expressly prescribed by that mandatory rule.

(2) Where the mandatory rule does not expressly prescribe the effects of an infringement upon a contract, the parties have the right to exercise such remedies under the contract as in the circumstances are reasonable.

(3) In determining what is reasonable regard is to be had in particular to:

(a) the purpose of the rule which has been infringed;

(b) the category of persons for whose protection the rule exists;

(c) any sanction that may be imposed under the rule infringed;

(d) the seriousness of the infringement;

(e) whether one or both parties knew or ought to have known of the infringement;

(f) whether the performance of the contract necessitates the infringement; and

(g) the parties' reasonable expectations.

Article 3.3.2 Restitution

(1) Where there has been performance under a contract infringing a mandatory rule under Article 3.3.1, restitution may be granted where this would be reasonable in the circumstances.

(2) In determining what is reasonable, regard is to be had, with the appropriate adaptations, to the criteria referred to in Article 3.3.1(3).

(3) If restitution is granted, the rules set out in Article 3.2.15 apply with appropriate adaptations.

CHAPTER 4 – INTERPRETATION

Article 4.1 Intention of the Parties

(1) A contract shall be interpreted according to the common intention of the parties.

(2) If such an intention cannot be established, the contract shall be interpreted according to the meaning that reasonable persons of the same kind as the parties would give to it in the same circumstances.

Article 4.2 Interpretation of Statements and Other Conduct

(1) The statements and other conduct of a party shall be interpreted according to that party's intention if the other party knew or could not have been unaware of that intention.

(2) If the preceding paragraph is not applicable, such statements and other conduct shall be interpreted according to the meaning that a reasonable person of the same kind as the other party would give to it in the same circumstances.

Article 4.3 Relevant Circumstances

In applying Articles 4.1 and 4.2, regard shall be had to all the circumstances, including

(a) preliminary negotiations between the parties;

(b) practices which the parties have established between themselves;

(c) the conduct of the parties subsequent to the conclusion of the contract;

(d) the nature and purpose of the contract;

(e) the meaning commonly given to terms and expressions in the trade concerned;

(f) usages.

Article 4.4 Reference to Contract or Statement as a Whole

Terms and expressions shall be interpreted in the light of the whole contract or statement in which they appear.

Article 4.5 All Terms to Be Given Effect

Contract terms shall be interpreted so as to give effect to all the terms rather than to deprive some of them of effect.

Article 4.6 Contra Proferentem Rule

If contract terms supplied by one party are unclear, an interpretation against that party is preferred.

Article 4.7 Linguistic Discrepancies

Where a contract is drawn up in two or more language versions which are equally authoritative there is, in case of discrepancy between the versions, a preference for the interpretation according to a version in which the contract was originally drawn up.

Article 4.8 Supplying an Omitted Term

(1) Where the parties to a contract have not agreed with respect to a term which is important for a determination of their rights and duties, a term which is appropriate in the circumstances shall be supplied.

(2) In determining what is an appropriate term regard shall be had, among other factors, to

(a) the intention of the parties;

(b) the nature and purpose of the contract;

(c) good faith and fair dealing;

(d) reasonableness.

CHAPTER 5 – CONTENT AND THIRD PARTY RIGHTS

SECTION 1: CONTENT

Article 5.1.1 Express and Implied Obligations

The contractual obligations of the parties may be express or implied.

Article 5.1.2 Implied Obligations

Implied obligations stem from

(a) the nature and purpose of the contract;

(b) practices established between the parties and usages;

(c) good faith and fair dealing;

(d) reasonableness.

Article 5.1.3 Co-operation Between the Parties

Each party shall cooperate with the other party when such co-operation may reasonably be expected for the performance of that party's obligations.

Article 5.1.4 Duty to Achieve a Specific Result. Duty of Best Efforts

(1) To the extent that an obligation of a party involves a duty to achieve a specific result, that party is bound to achieve that result.

(2) To the extent that an obligation of a party involves a duty of best efforts in the performance of an activity, that party is bound to make such efforts as would be made by a reasonable person of the same kind in the same circumstances.

Article 5.1.5 Determination of Kind of Duty Involved

In determining the extent to which an obligation of a party involves a duty of best efforts in the performance of an activity or a duty to achieve a specific result, regard shall be had, among other factors, to

(a) the way in which the obligation is expressed in the contract;

(b) the contractual price and other terms of the contract;

(c) the degree of risk normally involved in achieving the expected result;

(d) the ability of the other party to influence the performance of the obligation.

Article 5.1.6 Determination of Quality of Performance

Where the quality of performance is neither fixed by, nor determinable from, the contract a party is bound to render a performance of a quality that is reasonable and not less than average in the circumstances.

Article 5.1.7 Price Determination

(1) Where a contract does not fix or make provision for determining the price, the parties are considered, in the absence of any indication to the contrary, to have made reference to the price generally charged at the time of the conclusion of the contract for such performance in comparable circumstances in the trade concerned or, if no such price is available, to a reasonable price.

(2) Where the price is to be determined by one party and that determination is manifestly unreasonable, a reasonable price shall be substituted notwithstanding any contract term to the contrary.

(3) Where the price is to be fixed by one party or a third person, and that party or third person does not do so, the price shall be a reasonable price.

(4) Where the price is to be fixed by reference to factors which do not exist or have ceased to exist or to be accessible, the nearest equivalent factor shall be treated as a substitute.

Article 5.1.8 Termination of a Contract for an Indefinite Period

A contract for an indefinite period may be terminated by either party by giving notice a reasonable time in advance. As to the effects of termination in general, and as to restitution, the provisions in Articles 7.3.5 and 7.3.7 apply.

Article 5.1.9 Release by Agreement

(1) An obligee may release its right by agreement with the obligor.

(2) An offer to release a right gratuitously shall be deemed accepted if the obligor does not reject the offer without delay after having become aware of it.

SECTION 2: THIRD PARTY RIGHTS

Article 5.2.1 Contracts in Favour of Third Parties

(1) The parties (the "promisor" and the "promisee") may confer by express or implied agreement a right on a third party (the "beneficiary").

(2) The existence and content of the beneficiary's right against the promisor are determined by the agreement of the parties and are subject to any conditions or other limitations under the agreement.

Article 5.2.2 Third Party Identifiable

The beneficiary must be identifiable with adequate certainty by the contract but need not be in existence at the time the contract is made.

Article 5.2.3 Exclusion and Limitation Clauses

The conferment of rights in the beneficiary includes the right to invoke a clause in the contract which excludes or limits the liability of the beneficiary.

Article 5.2.4 Defences

The promisor may assert against the beneficiary all defences which the promisor could assert against the promisee.

Article 5.2.5 Revocation

The parties may modify or revoke the rights conferred by the contract on the beneficiary until the beneficiary has accepted them or reasonably acted in reliance on them.

Article 5.2.6 Renunciation

The beneficiary may renounce a right conferred on it.

SECTION 3: CONDITIONS

Article 5.3.1 Types of Condition

A contract or a contractual obligation may be made conditional upon the occurrence of a future uncertain event, so that the contract or the contractual obligation only takes effect if the event occurs (suspensive condition) or comes to an end if the event occurs (resolutive condition).

Article 5.3.2 Effect of Conditions

Unless the parties otherwise agree:

(a) the relevant contract or contractual obligation takes effect upon fulfilment of a suspensive condition;

(b) the relevant contract or contractual obligation comes to an end upon fulfilment of a resolutive condition.

Article 5.3.3 Interference with Conditions

(1) If fulfilment of a condition is prevented by a party, contrary to the duty of good faith and fair dealing or the duty of co-operation, that party may not rely on the non-fulfilment of the condition.

(2) If fulfilment of a condition is brought about by a party, contrary to the duty of good faith and fair dealing or the duty of co-operation, that party may not rely on the fulfilment of the condition.

Article 5.3.4 Duty to Preserve Rights

Pending fulfilment of a condition, a party may not, contrary to the duty to act in accordance with good faith and fair dealing, act so as to prejudice the other party's rights in case of fulfilment of the condition.

Article 5.3.5 Restitution in Case of Fulfilment of a Resolutive Condition

(1) On fulfilment of a resolutive condition, the rules on restitution set out in Articles 7.3.6 and 7.3.7 apply with appropriate adaptations.

(2) If the parties have agreed that the resolutive condition is to operate retroactively, the rules on restitution set out in Article 3.2.15 apply with appropriate adaptations.

CHAPTER 6 – PERFORMANCE

SECTION 1: PERFORMANCE IN GENERAL

Article 6.1.1 Time of Performance

A party must perform its obligations:

(a) if a time is fixed by or determinable from the contract, at that time;

(b) if a period of time is fixed by or determinable from the contract, at any time within that period unless circumstances indicate that the other party is to choose a time;

(c) in any other case, within a reasonable time after the conclusion of the contract.

Article 6.1.2 Performance at One Time or in Instalments

In cases under Article 6.1.1(b) or (c), a party must perform its obligations at one time if that performance can be rendered at one time and the circumstances do not indicate otherwise.

Article 6.1.3 Partial Performance

(1) The obligee may reject an offer to perform in part at the time performance is due, whether or not such offer is coupled with an assurance as to the balance of the performance, unless the obligee has no legitimate interest in so doing.

(2) Additional expenses caused to the obligee by partial performance are to be borne by the obligor without prejudice to any other remedy.

Article 6.1.4 Order of Performance

(1) To the extent that the performances of the parties can be rendered simultaneously, the parties are bound to render them simultaneously unless the circumstances indicate otherwise.

(2) To the extent that the performance of only one party requires a period of time, that party is bound to render its performance first, unless the circumstances indicate otherwise.

Article 6.1.5 Earlier Performance

(1) The obligee may reject an earlier performance unless it has no legitimate interest in so doing.

(2) Acceptance by a party of an earlier performance does not affect the time for the performance of its own obligations if that time has been fixed irrespective of the performance of the other party's obligations.

(3) Additional expenses caused to the obligee by earlier performance are to be borne by the obligor, without prejudice to any other remedy.

Article 6.1.6 Place of Performance

(1) If the place of performance is neither fixed by, nor determinable from, the contract, a party is to perform:

(a) a monetary obligation, at the obligee's place of business;

(b) any other obligation, at its own place of business.

(2) A party must bear any increase in the expenses incidental to performance which is caused by a change in its place of business subsequent to the conclusion of the contract.

Article 6.1.7 Payment by Cheque or Other Instrument

(1) Payment may be made in any form used in the ordinary course of business at the place for payment.

(2) However, an obligee who accepts, either by virtue of paragraph (1) or voluntarily, a cheque, any other order to pay or a promise to pay, is presumed to do so only on condition that it will be honoured.

Article 6.1.8 Payment by Funds Transfer

(1) Unless the obligee has indicated a particular account, payment may be made by a transfer to any of the financial institutions in which the obligee has made it known that it has an account.

(2) In case of payment by a transfer the obligation of the obligor is discharged when the transfer to the obligee's financial institution becomes effective.

Article 6.1.9 Currency of Payment

(1) If a monetary obligation is expressed in a currency other than that of the place for payment, it may be paid by the obligor in the currency of the place for payment unless

(a) that currency is not freely convertible; or

(b) the parties have agreed that payment should be made only in the currency in which the monetary obligation is expressed.

(2) If it is impossible for the obligor to make payment in the currency in which the monetary obligation is expressed, the obligee may require payment in the currency of the place for payment, even in the case referred to in paragraph (1)(b).

(3) Payment in the currency of the place for payment is to be made according to the applicable rate of exchange prevailing there when payment is due.

(4) However, if the obligor has not paid at the time when payment is due, the obligee may require payment according to the applicable rate of exchange prevailing either when payment is due or at the time of actual payment.

Article 6.1.10 Currency Not Expressed

Where a monetary obligation is not expressed in a particular currency, payment must be made in the currency of the place where payment is to be made.

Article 6.1.11 Costs of Performance

Each party shall bear the costs of performance of its obligations.

Article 6.1.12 Imputation of Payments

(1) An obligor owing several monetary obligations to the same obligee may specify at the time of payment the debt to which it intends the payment to be applied. However, the payment discharges first any expenses, then interest due and finally the principal.

(2) If the obligor makes no such specification, the obligee may, within a reasonable time after payment, declare to the obligor the obligation to which it imputes the payment, provided that the obligation is due and undisputed.

(3) In the absence of imputation under paragraphs (1) or (2), payment is imputed to that obligation which satisfies one of the following criteria in the order indicated:

(a) an obligation which is due or which is the first to fall due;

(b) the obligation for which the obligee has least security;

(c) the obligation which is the most burdensome for the obligor;

(d) the obligation which has arisen first.

If none of the preceding criteria applies, payment is imputed to all the obligations proportionally.

Article 6.1.13 Imputation of Non-Monetary Obligations

Article 6.1.12 applies with appropriate adaptations to the imputation of performance of non-monetary obligations.

Article 6.1.14 Application for Public Permission

Where the law of a State requires a public permission affecting the validity of the contract or its performance and neither that law nor the circumstances indicate otherwise

(a) if only one party has its place of business in that State, that party shall take the measures necessary to obtain the permission;

(b) in any other case the party whose performance requires permission shall take the necessary measures.

Article 6.1.15 Procedure in Applying for Permission

(1) The party required to take the measures necessary to obtain the permission shall do so without undue delay and shall bear any expenses incurred.

(2) That party shall whenever appropriate give the other party notice of the grant or refusal of such permission without undue delay.

Article 6.1.16 Permission Neither Granted Nor Refused

(1) If, notwithstanding the fact that the party responsible has taken all measures required, permission is neither granted nor refused within an agreed period or, where no period has been agreed, within a reasonable time from the conclusion of the contract, either party is entitled to terminate the contract.

(2) Where the permission affects some terms only, paragraph (1) does not apply if, having regard to the circumstances, it is reasonable to uphold the remaining contract even if the permission is refused.

Article 6.1.17 Permission Refused

(1) The refusal of a permission affecting the validity of the contract renders the contract void. If the refusal affects the validity of some terms only, only such terms are void if, having regard to the circumstances, it is reasonable to uphold the remaining contract.

(2) Where the refusal of a permission renders the performance of the contract impossible in whole or in part, the rules on non-performance apply.

SECTION 2: HARDSHIP

Article 6.2.1 Contract to Be Observed

Where the performance of a contract becomes more onerous for one of the parties, that party is nevertheless bound to perform its obligations subject to the following provisions on hardship.

Article 6.2.2 Definition of Hardship

There is hardship where the occurrence of events fundamentally alters the equilibrium of the contract either because the cost of a party's performance has increased or because the value of the performance a party receives has diminished, and

(a) the events occur or become known to the disadvantaged party after the conclusion of the contract;

(b) the events could not reasonably have been taken into account by the disadvantaged party at the time of the conclusion of the contract;

(c) the events are beyond the control of the disadvantaged party; and

(d) the risk of the events was not assumed by the disadvantaged party.

Article 6.2.3 Effects of Hardship

(1) In case of hardship the disadvantaged party is entitled to request renegotiations. The request shall be made without undue delay and shall indicate the grounds on which it is based.

(2) The request for renegotiation does not in itself entitle the disadvantaged party to withhold performance.

(3) Upon failure to reach agreement within a reasonable time either party may resort to the court.

(4) If the court finds hardship it may, if reasonable,

(a) terminate the contract at a date and on terms to be fixed, or

(b) adapt the contract with a view to restoring its equilibrium.

CHAPTER 7 – NON-PERFORMANCE

SECTION 1: NON-PERFORMANCE IN GENERAL

Article 7.1.1 Non-Performance Defined

Non-performance is failure by a party to perform any of its obligations under the contract, including defective performance or late performance.

Article 7.1.2 Interference by the Other Party

A party may not rely on the non-performance of the other party to the extent that such non-performance was caused by the first party's act or omission or by another event for which the first party bears the risk.

Article 7.1.3 Withholding Performance

(1) Where the parties are to perform simultaneously, either party may withhold performance until the other party tenders its performance.

(2) Where the parties are to perform consecutively, the party that is to perform later may withhold its performance until the first party has performed.

Article 7.1.4 Cure by Non-Performing Party

(1) The non-performing party may, at its own expense, cure any non-performance, provided that

(a) without undue delay, it gives notice indicating the proposed manner and timing of the cure;

(b) cure is appropriate in the circumstances;

(c) the aggrieved party has no legitimate interest in refusing cure; and

(d) cure is effected promptly.

(2) The right to cure is not precluded by notice of termination.

(3) Upon effective notice of cure, rights of the aggrieved party that are inconsistent with the non-performing party's performance are suspended until the time for cure has expired.

(4) The aggrieved party may withhold performance pending cure.

(5) Notwithstanding cure, the aggrieved party retains the right to claim damages for delay as well as for any harm caused or not prevented by the cure.

Article 7.1.5 Additional Period for Performance

(1) In a case of non-performance the aggrieved party may by notice to the other party allow an additional period of time for performance.

(2) During the additional period the aggrieved party may withhold performance of its own reciprocal obligations and may claim damages but may not resort to any other remedy. If it receives notice from the other party that the latter will not perform within that period, or if upon expiry of that period due performance has not been made, the aggrieved party may resort to any of the remedies that may be available under this Chapter.

(3) Where in a case of delay in performance which is not fundamental the aggrieved party has given notice allowing an additional period of time of reasonable length, it may terminate the contract at the end of that period. If the additional period allowed is not of reasonable length it shall be extended to a reasonable length. The aggrieved party may in its notice provide that if the other party fails to perform within the period allowed by the notice the contract shall automatically terminate.

(4) Paragraph (3) does not apply where the obligation which has not been performed is only a minor part of the contractual obligation of the non-performing party.

Article 7.1.6 Exemption Clauses

A clause which limits or excludes one party's liability for non-performance or which permits one party to render performance substantially different from what the other party reasonably expected may not be invoked if it would be grossly unfair to do so, having regard to the purpose of the contract.

Article 7.1.7 Force Majeure

(1) Non-performance by a party is excused if that party proves that the nonperformance was due to an impediment beyond its control and that it could not reasonably be expected to have taken the impediment into account at the time of the conclusion of the contract or to have avoided or overcome it or its consequences.

(2) When the impediment is only temporary, the excuse shall have effect for such period as is reasonable having regard to the effect of the impediment on the performance of the contract.

(3) The party who fails to perform must give notice to the other party of the impediment and its effect on its ability to perform. If the notice is not received by the other party within a reasonable time after the party who fails to perform knew or ought to have known of the impediment, it is liable for damages resulting from such non-receipt.

(4) Nothing in this Article prevents a party from exercising a right to terminate the contract or to withhold performance or request interest on money due.

SECTION 2: RIGHT TO PERFORMANCE

Article 7.2.1 Performance of Monetary Obligation

Where a party who is obliged to pay money does not do so, the other party may require payment.

Article 7.2.2 Performance of Non-Monetary Obligation

Where a party who owes an obligation other than one to pay money does not perform, the other party may require performance, unless

(a) performance is impossible in law or in fact;

(b) performance or, where relevant, enforcement is unreasonably burdensome or expensive;

(c) the party entitled to performance may reasonably obtain performance from another source;

(d) performance is of an exclusively personal character; or

(e) the party entitled to performance does not require performance within a reasonable time after it has, or ought to have, become aware of the non-performance.

Article 7.2.3 Repair and Replacement of Defective Performance

The right to performance includes in appropriate cases the right to require repair, replacement, or other cure of defective performance. The provisions of Articles 7.2.1 and 7.2.2 apply accordingly.

Article 7.2.4 Judicial Penalty

(1) Where the court orders a party to perform, it may also direct that this party pay a penalty if it does not comply with the order.

(2) The penalty shall be paid to the aggrieved party unless mandatory provisions of the law of the forum provide otherwise. Payment of the penalty to the aggrieved party does not exclude any claim for damages.

Article 7.2.5 Change of Remedy

(1) An aggrieved party who has required performance of a non-monetary obligation and who has not received performance within a period fixed or otherwise within a reasonable period of time may invoke any other remedy.

(2) Where the decision of a court for performance of a non-monetary obligation cannot be enforced, the aggrieved party may invoke any other remedy.

SECTION 3: TERMINATION

Article 7.3.1 Right to Terminate the Contract

(1) A party may terminate the contract where the failure of the other party to perform an obligation under the contract amounts to a fundamental non-performance.

(2) In determining whether a failure to perform an obligation amounts to a fundamental non-performance regard shall be had, in particular, to whether

(a) the non-performance substantially deprives the aggrieved party of what it was entitled to expect under the contract unless the other party did not foresee and could not reasonably have foreseen such result;

(b) strict compliance with the obligation which has not been performed is of essence under the contract;

(c) the non-performance is intentional or reckless;

(d) the non-performance gives the aggrieved party reason to believe that it cannot rely on the other party's future performance;

(e) the non-performing party will suffer disproportionate loss as a result of the preparation or performance if the contract is terminated.

(3) In the case of delay the aggrieved party may also terminate the contract if the other party fails to perform before the time allowed it under Article 7.1.5 has expired.

Article 7.3.2 Notice of Termination

(1) The right of a party to terminate the contract is exercised by notice to the other party.

(2) If performance has been offered late or otherwise does not conform to the contract the aggrieved party will lose its right to terminate the contract unless it gives notice to the other party within a reasonable time after it has or ought to have become aware of the offer or of the non-conforming performance.

Article 7.3.3 Anticipatory Non-Performance

Where prior to the date for performance by one of the parties it is clear that there will be a fundamental non-performance by that party, the other party may terminate the contract.

Article 7.3.4 Adequate Assurance of Due Performance

A party who reasonably believes that there will be a fundamental non-performance by the other party may demand adequate assurance of due performance and may meanwhile withhold its own performance. Where this assurance is not provided within a reasonable time the party demanding it may terminate the contract.

Article 7.3.5 Effects of Termination in General

(1) Termination of the contract releases both parties from their obligation to effect and to receive future performance.

(2) Termination does not preclude a claim for damages for non-performance.

(3) Termination does not affect any provision in the contract for the settlement of disputes or any other term of the contract which is to operate even after termination.

Article 7.3.6 Restitution with Respect to Contracts to Be Performed at One Time

(1) On termination of a contract to be performed at one time either party may claim restitution of whatever it has supplied under the contract, provided that such party concurrently makes restitution of whatever it has received under the contract.

(2) If restitution in kind is not possible or appropriate, an allowance has to be made in money whenever reasonable.

(3) The recipient of the performance does not have to make an allowance in money if the impossibility to make restitution in kind is attributable to the other party.

(4) Compensation may be claimed for expenses reasonably required to preserve or maintain the performance received.

Article 7.3.7 Restitution with Respect to Long-Term Contracts

(1) On termination of a long-term contract restitution can only be claimed for the period after termination has taken effect, provided the contract is divisible.

(2) As far as restitution has to be made, the provisions of Article 7.3.6 apply.

SECTION 4: DAMAGES

Article 7.4.1 Right to Damages

Any non-performance gives the aggrieved party a right to damages either exclusively or in conjunction with any other remedies except where the nonperformance is excused under these Principles.

Article 7.4.2 Full Compensation

(1) The aggrieved party is entitled to full compensation for harm sustained as a result of the non-performance. Such harm includes both any loss which it suffered and any gain of which it was deprived, taking into account any gain to the aggrieved party resulting from its avoidance of cost or harm.

(2) Such harm may be non-pecuniary and includes, for instance, physical suffering or emotional distress.

Article 7.4.3 Certainty of Harm

(1) Compensation is due only for harm, including future harm, that is established with a reasonable degree of certainty.

(2) Compensation may be due for the loss of a chance in proportion to the probability of its occurrence.

(3) Where the amount of damages cannot be established with a sufficient degree of certainty, the assessment is at the discretion of the court.

Article 7.4.4 Foreseeability of Harm

The non-performing party is liable only for harm which it foresaw or could reasonably have foreseen at the time of the conclusion of the contract as being likely to result from its non-performance.

Article 7.4.5 Proof of Harm in Case of Replacement Transaction

Where the aggrieved party has terminated the contract and has made a replacement transaction within a reasonable time and in a reasonable manner it may recover the difference between the contract price and the price of the replacement transaction as well as damages for any further harm.

Article 7.4.6 Proof of Harm by Current Price

(1) Where the aggrieved party has terminated the contract and has not made a replacement transaction but there is a current price for the performance contracted for, it may recover the difference between the contract price and the price current at the time the contract is terminated as well as damages for any further harm.

(2) Current price is the price generally charged for goods delivered or services rendered in comparable circumstances at the place where the contract should have been performed or, if there is no current price at that place, the current price at such other place that appears reasonable to take as a reference.

Article 7.4.7 Harm Due in Part to Aggrieved Party

Where the harm is due in part to an act or omission of the aggrieved party or to another event for which that party bears the risk, the amount of damages shall be reduced to the extent that these factors have contributed to the harm, having regard to the conduct of each of the parties.

Article 7.4.8 Mitigation of Harm

(1) The non-performing party is not liable for harm suffered by the aggrieved party to the extent that the harm could have been reduced by the latter party's taking reasonable steps.

(2) The aggrieved party is entitled to recover any expenses reasonably incurred in attempting to reduce the harm.

Article 7.4.9 Interest for Failure to Pay Money

(1) If a party does not pay a sum of money when it falls due the aggrieved party is entitled to interest upon that sum from the time when payment is due to the time of payment whether or not the non-payment is excused.

(2) The rate of interest shall be the average bank short-term lending rate to prime borrowers prevailing for the currency of payment at the place for payment, or where no such rate exists at that place, then the same rate in the State of the currency of payment. In the absence of such a rate at either place the rate of interest shall be the appropriate rate fixed by the law of the State of the currency of payment.

(3) The aggrieved party is entitled to additional damages if the non-payment caused it a greater harm.

Article 7.4.10 Interest on Damages

Unless otherwise agreed, interest on damages for non-performance of non-monetary obligations accrues as from the time of non-performance.

Article 7.4.11 Manner of Monetary Redress

(1) Damages are to be paid in a lump sum. However, they may be payable in instalments where the nature of the harm makes this appropriate.

(2) Damages to be paid in instalments may be indexed.

Article 7.4.12 Currency in Which to Assess Damages

Damages are to be assessed either in the currency in which the monetary obligation was expressed or in the currency in which the harm was suffered, whichever is more appropriate.

Article 7.4.13 Agreed Payment for Non-Performance

(1) Where the contract provides that a party who does not perform is to pay a specified sum to the aggrieved party for such non-performance, the aggrieved party is entitled to that sum irrespective of its actual harm.

(2) However, notwithstanding any agreement to the contrary the specified sum may be reduced to a reasonable amount where it is grossly excessive in relation to the harm resulting from the non-performance and to the other circumstances.

CHAPTER 8 – SET-OFF

Article 8.1 Conditions of Set-Off

(1) Where two parties owe each other money or other performances of the same kind, either of them ("the first party") may set off its obligation against that of its obligee ("the other party") if at the time of set-off,

(a) the first party is entitled to perform its obligation;

(b) the other party's obligation is ascertained as to its existence and amount and performance is due.

(2) If the obligations of both parties arise from the same contract, the first party may also set off its obligation against an obligation of the other party which is not ascertained as to its existence or to its amount.

Article 8.2 Foreign Currency Set-Off

Where the obligations are to pay money in different currencies, the right of set-off may be exercised, provided that both currencies are freely convertible and the parties have not agreed that the first party shall pay only in a specified currency.

Article 8.3 Set-Off by Notice

The right of set-off is exercised by notice to the other party.

Article 8.4 Content of Notice

(1) The notice must specify the obligations to which it relates.

(2) If the notice does not specify the obligation against which set-off is exercised, the other party may, within a reasonable time, declare to the first party the obligation to which set-off relates. If no such declaration is made, the set-off will relate to all the obligations proportionally.

Article 8.5 Effect of Set-Off

(1) Set-off discharges the obligations.

(2) If obligations differ in amount, set-off discharges the obligations up to the amount of the lesser obligation.

(3) Set-off takes effect as from the time of notice.

CHAPTER 9 – ASSIGNMENT OF RIGHTS, TRANSFER OF OBLIGATIONS, ASSIGNMENT OF CONTRACTS

SECTION 1: ASSIGNMENT OF RIGHTS

Article 9.1.1 Definitions

"Assignment of a right" means the transfer by agreement from one person (the "assignor") to another person (the "assignee"), including transfer by way of security, of the assignor's right to payment of a monetary sum or other performance from a third person ("the obligor").

Article 9.1.2 Exclusions

This Section does not apply to transfers made under the special rules governing the transfers:

(a) of instruments such as negotiable instruments, documents of title or financial instruments, or

(b) of rights in the course of transferring a business.

Article 9.1.3 Assignability of Non-Monetary Rights

A right to non-monetary performance may be assigned only if the assignment does not render the obligation significantly more burdensome.

Article 9.1.4 Partial Assignment

(1) A right to the payment of a monetary sum may be assigned partially.

(2) A right to other performance may be assigned partially only if it is divisible, and the assignment does not render the obligation significantly more burdensome.

Article 9.1.5 Future Rights

A future right is deemed to be transferred at the time of the agreement, provided the right, when it comes into existence, can be identified as the right to which the assignment relates.

Article 9.1.6 Rights Assigned Without Individual Specification

A number of rights may be assigned without individual specification, provided such rights can be identified as rights to which the assignment relates at the time of the assignment or when they come into existence.

Article 9.1.7 Agreement Between Assignor and Assignee Sufficient

(1) A right is assigned by mere agreement between the assignor and the assignee, without notice to the obligor.

(2) The consent of the obligor is not required unless the obligation in the circumstances is of an essentially personal character.

Article 9.1.8 Obligor's Additional Costs

The obligor has a right to be compensated by the assignor or the assignee for any additional costs caused by the assignment.

Article 9.1.9 Non-Assignment Clauses

(1) The assignment of a right to the payment of a monetary sum is effective notwithstanding an agreement between the assignor and the obligor limiting or prohibiting such an assignment. However, the assignor may be liable to the obligor for breach of contract.

(2) The assignment of a right to other performance is ineffective if it is contrary to an agreement between the assignor and the obligor limiting or prohibiting the assignment. Nevertheless, the assignment is effective if the assignee, at the time of the assignment, neither knew nor ought to have known of the agreement. The assignor may then be liable to the obligor for breach of contract.

Article 9.1.10 Notice to the Obligor

(1) Until the obligor receives a notice of the assignment from either the assignor or the assignee, it is discharged by paying the assignor.

(2) After the obligor receives such a notice, it is discharged only by paying the assignee.

Article 9.1.11 Successive Assignments

If the same right has been assigned by the same assignor to two or more successive assignees, the obligor is discharged by paying according to the order in which the notices were received.

Article 9.1.12 Adequate Proof of Assignment

(1) If notice of the assignment is given by the assignee, the obligor may request the assignee to provide within a reasonable time adequate proof that the assignment has been made.

(2) Until adequate proof is provided, the obligor may withhold payment.

(3) Unless adequate proof is provided, notice is not effective.

(4) Adequate proof includes, but is not limited to, any writing emanating from the assignor and indicating that the assignment has taken place.

Article 9.1.13 Defences and Rights of Set-Off

(1) The obligor may assert against the assignee all defences that the obligor could assert against the assignor.

(2) The obligor may exercise against the assignee any right of set-off available to the obligor against the assignor up to the time notice of assignment was received.

Article 9.1.14 Rights Related to the Right Assigned

The assignment of a right transfers to the assignee:

(a) all the assignor's rights to payment or other performance under the contract in respect of the right assigned, and

(b) all rights securing performance of the right assigned.

Article 9.1.15 Undertakings of the Assignor

The assignor undertakes towards the assignee, except as otherwise disclosed to the assignee, that:

(a) the assigned right exists at the time of the assignment, unless the right is a future right;

(b) the assignor is entitled to assign the right;

(c) the right has not been previously assigned to another assignee, and it is free from any right or claim from a third party;

(d) the obligor does not have any defences;

(e) neither the obligor nor the assignor has given notice of set-off concerning the assigned right and will not give any such notice;

(f) the assignor will reimburse the assignee for any payment received from the obligor before notice of the assignment was given.

SECTION 2: TRANSFER OF OBLIGATIONS

Article 9.2.1 Modes of Transfer

An obligation to pay money or render other performance may be transferred from one person (the "original obligor") to another person (the "new obligor") either

(a) by an agreement between the original obligor and the new obligor subject to Article 9.2.3, or

(b) by an agreement between the obligee and the new obligor, by which the new obligor assumes the obligation.

Article 9.2.2 Exclusion

This Section does not apply to transfers of obligations made under the special rules governing transfers of obligations in the course of transferring a business.

Article 9.2.3 Requirement of Obligee's Consent to Transfer

The transfer of an obligation by an agreement between the original obligor and the new obligor requires the consent of the obligee.

Article 9.2.4 Advance Consent of Obligee

(1) The obligee may give its consent in advance.

(2) If the obligee has given its consent in advance, the transfer of the obligation becomes effective when a notice of the transfer is given to the obligee or when the obligee acknowledges it.

Article 9.2.5 Discharge of Original Obligor

(1) The obligee may discharge the original obligor.

(2) The obligee may also retain the original obligor as an obligor in case the new obligor does not perform properly.

(3) Otherwise the original obligor and the new obligor are jointly and severally liable.

Article 9.2.6 Third Party Performance

(1) Without the obligee's consent, the obligor may contract with another person that this person will perform the obligation in place of the obligor, unless the obligation in the circumstances has an essentially personal character.

(2) The obligee retains its claim against the obligor.

Article 9.2.7 Defences and Rights of Set-Off

(1) The new obligor may assert against the obligee all defences which the original obligor could assert against the obligee.

(2) The new obligor may not exercise against the obligee any right of set-off available to the original obligor against the obligee.

Article 9.2.8 Rights Related to the Obligation Transferred

(1) The obligee may assert against the new obligor all its rights to payment or other performance under the contract in respect of the obligation transferred.

(2) If the original obligor is discharged under Article 9.2.5(1), a security granted by any person other than the new obligor for the performance of the obligation is discharged, unless that other person agrees that it should continue to be available to the obligee.

(3) Discharge of the original obligor also extends to any security of the original obligor given to the obligee for the performance of the obligation, unless the security is over an asset which is transferred as part of a transaction between the original obligor and the new obligor.

SECTION 3: ASSIGNMENT OF CONTRACTS

Article 9.3.1 Definitions

"Assignment of a contract" means the transfer by agreement from one person (the "assignor") to another person (the "assignee") of the assignor's rights and obligations arising out of a contract with another person (the "other party").

Article 9.3.2 Exclusion

This Section does not apply to the assignment of contracts made under the special rules governing transfers of contracts in the course of transferring a business.

Article 9.3.3 Requirement of Consent of the Other Party

The assignment of a contract requires the consent of the other party.

Article 9.3.4 Advance Consent of the Other Party

(1) The other party may give its consent in advance.

(2) If the other party has given its consent in advance, the assignment of the contract becomes effective when a notice of the assignment is given to the other party or when the other party acknowledges it.

Article 9.3.5 Discharge of the Assignor

(1) The other party may discharge the assignor.

(2) The other party may also retain the assignor as an obligor in case the assignee does not perform properly.

(3) Otherwise the assignor and the assignee are jointly and severally liable.

Article 9.3.6 Defences and Rights of Set-Off

(1) To the extent that the assignment of a contract involves an assignment of rights, Article 9.1.13 applies accordingly.

(2) To the extent that the assignment of a contract involves a transfer of obligations, Article 9.2.7 applies accordingly.

Article 9.3.7 Rights Transferred with the Contract

(1) To the extent that the assignment of a contract involves an assignment of rights, Article 9.1.14 applies accordingly.

(2) To the extent that the assignment of a contract involves a transfer of obligations, Article 9.2.8 applies accordingly.

CHAPTER 10 – LIMITATION PERIODS

Article 10.1 Scope of the Chapter

(1) The exercise of rights governed by the Principles is barred by the expiration of a period of time, referred to as "limitation period", according to the rules of this Chapter.

(2) This Chapter does not govern the time within which one party is required under the Principles, as a condition for the acquisition or exercise of its right, to give notice to the other party or to perform any act other than the institution of legal proceedings.

Article 10.2 Limitation Periods

(1) The general limitation period is three years beginning on the day after the day the obligee knows or ought to know the facts as a result of which the obligee's right can be exercised.

(2) In any event, the maximum limitation period is ten years beginning on the day after the day the right can be exercised.

Article 10.3 Modification of Limitation Periods by the Parties

(1) The parties may modify the limitation periods.

(2) However they may not

(a) shorten the general limitation period to less than one year;

(b) shorten the maximum limitation period to less than four years;

(c) extend the maximum limitation period to more than fifteen years.

Article 10.4 New Limitation Period by Acknowledgement

(1) Where the obligor before the expiration of the general limitation period acknowledges the right of the obligee, a new general limitation period begins on the day after the day of the acknowledgement.

(2) The maximum limitation period does not begin to run again, but may be exceeded by the beginning of a new general limitation period under Article 10.2(1).

Article 10.5 Suspension by Judicial Proceedings

(1) The running of the limitation period is suspended

(a) when the obligee performs any act, by commencing judicial proceedings or in judicial proceedings already instituted, that is recognised by the law of the court as asserting the obligee's right against the obligor;

(b) in the case of the obligor's insolvency when the obligee has asserted its rights in the insolvency proceedings; or

(c) in the case of proceedings for dissolution of the entity which is the obligor when the obligee has asserted its rights in the dissolution proceedings.

(2) Suspension lasts until a final decision has been issued or until the proceedings have been otherwise terminated.

Article 10.6 Suspension by Arbitral Proceedings

(1) The running of the limitation period is suspended when the obligee performs any act, by commencing arbitral proceedings or in arbitral proceedings already instituted, that is recognised by the law of the arbitral tribunal as asserting the obligee's right against the obligor. In the absence of regulations for arbitral proceedings or provisions determining the exact date of the commencement of arbitral proceedings, the proceedings are deemed to commence on the date on which a request that the right in dispute should be adjudicated reaches the obligor.

(2) Suspension lasts until a binding decision has been issued or until the proceedings have been otherwise terminated.

Article 10.7 Alternative Dispute Resolution

The provisions of Articles 10.5 and 10.6 apply with appropriate modifications to other proceedings whereby the parties request a third person to assist them in their attempt to reach an amicable settlement of their dispute.

Article 10.8 Suspension in Case of Force Majeure, Death or Incapacity

(1) Where the obligee has been prevented by an impediment that is beyond its control and that it could neither avoid nor overcome, from causing a limitation period to cease to run under the preceding Articles, the general limitation period is suspended so as not to expire before one year after the relevant impediment has ceased to exist.

(2) Where the impediment consists of the incapacity or death of the obligee or obligor, suspension ceases when a representative for the incapacitated or deceased party or its estate has been appointed or a successor has inherited the respective party's position. The additional one-year period under paragraph (1) applies accordingly.

Article 10.9 Effects of Expiration of Limitation Period

(1) The expiration of the limitation period does not extinguish the right.

(2) For the expiration of the limitation period to have effect, the obligor must assert it as a defence.

(3) A right may still be relied on as a defence even though the expiration of the limitation period for that right has been asserted.

Article 10.10 Right of Set-Off

The obligee may exercise the right of set-off until the obligor has asserted the expiration of the limitation period.

Article 10.11 Restitution

Where there has been performance in order to discharge an obligation, there is no right of restitution merely because the limitation period has expired.

CHAPTER 11 – PLURALITY OF OBLIGORS AND OF OBLIGEES

SECTION 1: PLURALITY OF OBLIGORS

Article 11.1.1 Definitions

When several obligors are bound by the same obligation towards an obligee:

(a) the obligations are joint and several when each obligor is bound for the whole obligation;

(b) the obligations are separate when each obligor is bound only for its share.

Article 11.1.2 Presumption of Joint and Several Obligations

When several obligors are bound by the same obligation towards an obligee, they are presumed to be jointly and severally bound, unless the circumstances indicate otherwise.

Article 11.1.3 Obligee's Rights Against Joint and Several Obligors

When obligors are jointly and severally bound, the obligee may require performance from any one of them, until full performance has been received.

Article 11.1.4 Availability of Defences and Rights of Set-Off

A joint and several obligor against whom a claim is made by the obligee may assert all the defences and rights of set-off that are personal to it or that are common to all the co-obligors, but may not assert defences or rights of set-off that are personal to one or several of the other co-obligors.

Article 11.1.5 Effect of Performance or Set-Off

Performance or set-off by a joint and several obligor or set-off by the obligee against one joint and several obligor discharges the other obligors in relation to the obligee to the extent of the performance or set-off.

Article 11.1.6 Effect of Release or Settlement

(1) Release of one joint and several obligor, or settlement with one joint and several obligor, discharges all the other obligors for the share of the released or settling obligor, unless the circumstances indicate otherwise.

(2) When the other obligors are discharged for the share of the released obligor, they no longer have a contributory claim against the released obligor under Article 11.1.10.

Article 11.1.7 Effect of Expiration or Suspension of Limitation Period

(1) Expiration of the limitation period of the obligee's rights against one joint and several obligor does not affect:

(a) the obligations to the obligee of the other joint and several obligors; or

(b) the rights of recourse between the joint and several obligors under Article 11.1.10.

(2) If the obligee initiates proceedings under Articles 10.5, 10.6 or 10.7 against one joint and several obligor, the running of the limitation period is also suspended against the other joint and several obligors.

Article 11.1.8 Effect of Judgment

(1) A decision by a court as to the liability to the obligee of one joint and several obligor does not affect:

(a) the obligations to the obligee of the other joint and several obligors; or

(b) the rights of recourse between the joint and several obligors under Article 11.1.10.

(2) However, the other joint and several obligors may rely on such a decision, except if it was based on grounds personal to the obligor concerned. In such a case, the rights of recourse between the joint and several obligors under Article 11.1.10 are affected accordingly.

Article 11.1.9 Apportionment Among Joint and Several Obligors

As among themselves, joint and several obligors are bound in equal shares, unless the circumstances indicate otherwise.

Article 11.1.10 Extent of Contributory Claim

A joint and several obligor who has performed more than its share may claim the excess from any of the other obligors to the extent of each obligor's unperformed share.

Article 11.1.11 Rights of the Obligee

(1) A joint and several obligor to whom Article 11.1.10 applies may also exercise the rights of the obligee, including all rights securing their performance, to recover the excess from all or any of the other obligors to the extent of each obligor's unperformed share.

(2) An obligee who has not received full performance retains its rights against the co- obligors to the extent of the unperformed part, with precedence over co-obligors exercising contributory claims.

Article 11.1.12 Defences in Contributory Claims

A joint and several obligor against whom a claim is made by the co-obligor who has performed the obligation:

(a) may raise any common defences and rights of set-off that were available to be asserted by the co-obligor against the obligee ;

(b) may assert defences which are personal to itself;

(c) may not assert defences and rights of set-off which are personal to one or several of the other co-obligors.

Article 11.1.13 Inability to Recover

If a joint and several obligor who has performed more than that obligor's share is unable, despite all reasonable efforts, to recover contribution from another joint and several obligor, the share of the others, including the one who has performed, is increased proportionally.

SECTION 2: PLURALITY OF OBLIGEES

Article 11.2.1 Definitions

When several obligees can claim performance of the same obligation from an obligor:

(a) the claims are separate when each obligee can only claim its share;

(b) the claims are joint and several when each obligee can claim the whole performance;

(c) the claims are joint when all obligees have to claim performance together.

Article 11.2.2 Effects of Joint and Several Claims

Full performance of an obligation in favour of one of the joint and several obligees discharges the obligor towards the other obligees.

Article 11.2.3 Availability of Defences Against Joint and Several Obligees

(1) The obligor may assert against any of the joint and several obligees all the defences and rights of set-off that are personal to its relationship to that obligee or that it can assert against all the co-obligees, but may not assert defences and rights of set-off that are personal to its relationship to one or several of the other co-obligees.

(2) The provisions of Articles 11.1.5, 11.1.6, 11.1.7 and 11.1.8 apply, with appropriate adaptations, to joint and several claims.

Article 11.2.4 Allocation Between Joint and Several Obligees

(1) As among themselves, joint and several obligees are entitled to equal shares, unless the circumstances indicate otherwise.

(2) An obligee who has received more than its share must transfer the excess to the other obligees to the extent of their respective shares.

11) 1974 UN Convention on the Limitation Period in the International Sale of Goods[1]

Preamble

THE STATES PARTIES TO THE PRESENT CONVENTION,

CONSIDERING that international trade is an important factor in the promotion of friendly relations amongst States,

BELIEVING that the adoption of uniform rules governing the limitation period in the international sale of goods would facilitate the development of world trade,

HAVE AGREED as follows:

Part I. Substantive Provisions

SPHERE OF APPLICATION

Article 1

(1) This Convention shall determine when claims of a buyer and a seller against each other arising from a contract of international sale of goods or relating to its breach, termination or invalidity can no longer be exercised by reason of the expiration of a period of time. Such a period of time is hereinafter referred to as "the limitation period".

(2) This Convention shall not affect a particular time-limit within which one party is required, as a condition for the acquisition or exercise of his claim, to give notice to the other party or perform any act other than the institution of legal proceedings.

(3) In this Convention:

(a) "buyer", "seller" and "party" mean persons who buy or sell, or agree to buy or sell, goods, and the successors to and assigns of their rights or obligations under the contract of sale;

(b) "creditor" means a party who asserts a claim, whether or not such a claim is for a sum of money;

(c) "debtor" means a party against whom a creditor asserts a claim;

(d) "breach of contract" means the failure of a party to perform the contract or any performance not in conformity with the contract;

(e) "legal proceedings" includes judicial, arbitral and administrative proceedings;

(f) "person" includes corporation, company, partnership, association or entity, whether private or public, which can sue or be sued;

(g) "writing" includes telegram and telex;

(h) "year" means a year according to the Gregorian calendar.

Article 2

For the purposes of this Convention:

(a) a contract of sale of goods shall be considered international if, at the time of the conclusion of the contract, the buyer and the seller have their places of business in different States;

(b) the fact that the parties have their places of business in different States shall be disregarded whenever this fact does not appear either from the contract or from any dealings

---

1 ©1974, United Nations, 1511 UNTS 99, as amended by the Protocol amending the Convention on the Limitation Period in the International Sale of Goods, all rights reserved.

between, or from information disclosed by, the parties at any time before or at the conclusion of the contract;

(c) where a party to a contract of sale of goods has places of business in more than one State, the place of business shall be that which has the closest relationship to the contract and its performance, having regard to the circumstances known to or contemplated by the parties at the time of the conclusion of the contract;

(d) where a party does not have a place of business, reference shall be made to his habitual residence;

(e) neither the nationality of the parties nor the civil or commercial character of the parties or of the contract shall be taken into consideration.

Article 3[1]

(1) This Convention shall apply only

(a) if, at the time of the conclusion of the contract, the places of business of the parties to a contract of international sale of goods are in Contracting States; or

(b) if the rules of private international law make the law of a Contracting State applicable to the contract of sale.

(2) This Convention shall not apply when the parties have expressly excluded its application.

Article 4[2]

This Convention shall not apply to sales:

(a) of goods bought for personal, family or household use, unless the seller, at any time before or at the conclusion of the contract, neither knew nor ought to have known that the goods were bought for any such use;

(b) by auction;

(c) on execution or otherwise by authority of law;

(d) of stocks, shares, investment securities, negotiable instruments or money;

(e) of ships, vessels, hovercraft or aircraft;

(f) of electricity.

Article 5

This Convention shall not apply to claims based upon:

(a) death of, or personal injury to, any person;

---

1 Text as amended in accordance with Article I of the 1980 Protocol. States that make a declaration under Article 36 bis (Article XII of the 1980 Protocol) will be bound by Article 3 as originally adopted in the Limitation Convention, 1974. Article 3 as originally adopted reads as follows:
"*Article 3*
(1) This Convention shall apply only if, at the time of the conclusion of the contract, the places of business of the parties to a contract of international sale of goods are in Contracting States.
(2) Unless this Convention provides otherwise, it shall apply irrespective of the law which would otherwise be applicable by virtue of the rules of private international law.
(3) This Convention shall not apply when the parties have expressly excluded its application."

2 Text of paragraphs (a) and (e) as amended in accordance with Article II of the 1980 Protocol. Paragraphs (a) and (e) of Article 4 as originally adopted in the Limitation Convention, 1974, prior to its amendment under the 1980 Protocol, read as follows:
"(a) of goods bought for personal, family or household use;
(e) of ships, vessels, or aircraft;".

(b) nuclear damage caused by the goods sold;

(c) a lien, mortgage or other security interest in property;

(d) a judgement or award made in legal proceedings;

(e) a document on which direct enforcement or execution can be obtained in accordance with the law of the place where such enforcement or execution is sought;

(f) a bill of exchange, cheque or promissory note.

Article 6

(1) This Convention shall not apply to contracts in which the preponderant part of the obligations of the seller consists in the supply of labour or other services.

(2) Contracts for the supply of goods to be manufactured or produced shall be considered to be sales, unless the party who orders the goods undertakes to supply a substantial part of the materials necessary for such manufacture or production.

Article 7

In the interpretation and application of the provisions of this Convention, regard shall be had to its international character and to the need to promote uniformity.

THE DURATION AND COMMENCEMENT OF THE LIMITATION PERIOD

Article 8

The limitation period shall be four years.

Article 9

(1) Subject to the provisions of Articles 10, 11 and 12 the limitation period shall commence on the date [on] which the claim accrues.

(2) The commencement of the limitation period shall not be postponed by:

(a) a requirement that the party be given a notice as described in paragraph 2 of Article 1, or

(b) a provision in an arbitration agreement that no right shall arise until an arbitration award has been made.

Article 10

(1) A claim arising from a breach of contract shall accrue on the date on which such breach occurs.

(2) A claim arising from a defect or other lack of conformity shall accrue on the date on which the goods are actually handed over to, or their tender is refused by, the buyer.

(3) A claim based on fraud committed before or at the time of the conclusion of the contract or during its performance shall accrue on the date on which the fraud was or reasonably could have been discovered.

Article 11

If the seller has given an express undertaking relating to the goods which is stated to have effect for a certain period of time, whether expressed in terms of a specific period of time or otherwise, the limitation period in respect of any claim, arising from the undertaking shall commence on the date on which the buyer notifies the seller of the fact on which the claim is based, but not later than on the date of the expiration of the period of the undertaking.

Article 12

(1) If, in circumstances provided for by the law applicable to the contract, one party is entitled to declare the contract terminated before the time for performance is due, and exercises this

right, the limitation period in respect of a claim based on any such circumstances shall commence on the date on which the declaration is made to the other party. If the contract is not declared to be terminated before performance becomes due, the limitation period shall commence on the date on which performance is due.

(2) The limitation period in respect of a claim arising out of a breach by one party of a contract for the delivery of or payment for goods by instalments shall, in relation to each separate instalment, commence on the date on which the particular breach occurs. If, under the law applicable to the contract, one party is entitled to declare the contract terminated by reason of such breach, and exercises this right, the limitation period in respect of all relevant instalments shall commence on the date on which the declaration is made to the other party.

CESSATION AND EXTENSION OF THE LIMITATION PERIOD

Article 13

The limitation period shall cease to run when the creditor performs any act which, under the law of the court where the proceedings are instituted, is recognized as commencing judicial proceedings against the debtor or as asserting his claim in such proceedings already instituted against the debtor, for the purpose of obtaining satisfaction or recognition of his claim.

Article 14

1. Where the parties have agreed to submit to arbitration, the limitation period shall cease to run when either party commences arbitral proceedings in the manner provided for in the arbitration agreement or by the law applicable to such proceedings.

2. In the absence of any such provision, arbitral proceedings shall be deemed to commence on the date on which a request that the claim in dispute be referred to arbitration is delivered at the habitual residence or place of business of the other party or, if he has no such residence or place of business, then at his last known residence or place of business.

Article 15

In any legal proceedings other than those mentioned in Articles 13 and 14, including legal proceedings commenced upon the occurrence of:

(a) the death or incapacity of the debtor,

(b) the bankruptcy or any state of insolvency affecting the whole of the property of the debtor, or

(c) the dissolution or liquidation of a corporation, company, partnership, association or entity when it is the debtor, the limitation period shall cease to run when the creditor asserts his claim in such proceedings for the purpose of obtaining satisfaction or recognition of the claim, subject to the law governing the proceedings.

Article 16

For the purposes of Articles 13, 14 and 15, any act performed by way of counterclaim shall be deemed to have been performed on the same date as the act performed in relation to the claim against which the counterclaim is raised, provided that both the claim and the counterclaim relate to the same contract or to several contracts concluded in the course of the same transaction.

Article 17

(1) Where a claim has been asserted in legal proceedings within the limitation period in accordance with Article 13, 14, 15 or 16, but such legal proceedings have ended without a decision binding on the merits of the claim, the limitation period shall be deemed to have continued to run.

(2) If, at the time such legal proceedings ended, the limitation period has expired or has less than one year to run, the creditor shall be entitled to a period of one year from the date on which the legal proceedings ended.

Article 18

(1) Where legal proceedings have been commenced against one debtor, the limitation period prescribed in this Convention shall cease to run against any other party jointly and severally liable with the debtor, provided that the creditor informs such party in writing within that period that the proceedings have been commenced.

(2) Where legal proceedings have been commenced by a subpurchaser against the buyer, the limitation period prescribed in this Convention shall cease to run in relation to the buyer's claim over against the seller, if the buyer informs the seller in writing within that period that the proceedings have been commenced.

(3) Where the legal proceedings referred to in paragraphs 1 and 2 of this Article have ended, the limitation period in respect of the claim of the creditor or the buyer against the party jointly and severally liable or against the seller shall be deemed not to have ceased running by virtue of paragraphs 1 and 2 of this article, but the creditor or the buyer shall be entitled to an additional year from the date on which the legal proceedings ended, if at that time the limitation period had expired or had less than one year to run.

Article 19

Where the creditor performs, in the State in which the debtor has his place of business and before the expiration of the limitation period, any act, other than the acts described in Articles 13, 14, 15 and 16, which under the law of that State has the effect of recommencing a limitation period, a new limitation period of four years shall commence on the date prescribed by that law.

Article 20

(1) Where the debtor, before the expiration of the limitation period, acknowledges in writing his obligation to the creditor, a new limitation period of four years shall commence to run from the date of such acknowledgement.

(2) Payment of interest or partial performance of an obligation by the debtor shall have the same effect as an acknowledgement under paragraph 1 of this Article if it can reasonably be inferred from such payment or performance that the debtor acknowledges that obligation.

Article 21

Where, as a result of a circumstance which is beyond the control of the creditor and which he could neither avoid nor overcome, the creditor has been prevented from causing the limitation period to cease to run, the limitation period shall be extended so as not to expire before the expiration of one year from the date on which the relevant circumstance ceased to exist.

MODIFICATION OF THE LIMITATION PERIOD BY THE PARTIES

Article 22

(1) The limitation period cannot be modified or affected by any declaration or agreement between the parties, except in the cases provided for in paragraph 2 of this article.

(2) The debtor may at any time during the running of the limitation period extend the period by a declaration in writing to the creditor. This declaration may be renewed.

(3) The provisions of this Article shall not affect the validity of a clause in the contract of sale which stipulates that arbitral proceedings shall be commenced within a shorter period of limi-

tation than that prescribed by this Convention, provided that such clause is valid under the law applicable to the contract of sale.

GENERAL LIMIT OF THE LIMITATION PERIOD

Article 23

Notwithstanding the provisions of this Convention, a limitation period shall in any event expire not later than ten years from the date on which it commenced to run under Articles 9, 10, 11 and 12 of this Convention.

CONSEQUENCES OF THE EXPIRATION OF THE LIMITATION PERIOD

Article 24

Expiration of the limitation period shall be taken into consideration in any legal proceedings only if invoked by a party to such proceedings.

Article 25

(1) Subject to the provisions of paragraph 2 of this Article and of Article 24, no claim shall be recognized or enforced in any legal proceedings commenced after the expiration of the limitation period.

(2) Notwithstanding the expiration of the limitation period, one party may rely on his claim as a defence or for the purpose of set-off against a claim asserted by the other party, provided that in the latter case this may only be done:

(a) if both claims relate to the same contract or to several contracts concluded in the course of the same transaction; or

(b) if the claims could have been set-off at any time before the expiration of the limitation period.

Article 26

Where the debtor performs his obligation after the expiration of the limitation period, he shall not on that ground be entitled in any way to claim restitution even if he did not know at the time when he performed his obligation that the limitation period had expired.

Article 27

The expiration of the limitation period with respect to a principal debt shall have the same effect with respect to an obligation to pay interest on that debt.

CALCULATION OF THE PERIOD

Article 28

(1) The limitation period shall be calculated in such a way that it shall expire at the end of the day which corresponds to the date on which the period commenced to run. If there is no such corresponding date, the period shall expire at the end of the last day of the last month of the limitation period.

(2) The limitation period shall be calculated by reference to the date of the place where the legal proceedings are instituted.

Article 29

Where the last day of the limitation period falls on an official holiday or other dies non juridicus precluding the appropriate legal action in the jurisdiction where the creditor institutes legal proceedings or asserts a claim as envisaged in Article 13, 14 or 15, the limitation period shall be extended so as not to expire until the end of the first day following that official holiday or dies non juridicus on which such proceedings could be instituted or on which such a claim could be asserted in that jurisdiction.

INTERNATIONAL EFFECT

Article 30

The acts and circumstances referred to in Articles 13 through 19 which have taken place in one Contracting State shall have effect for the purposes of this Convention in another Contracting State, provided that the creditor has taken all reasonable steps to ensure that the debtor is informed of the relevant act or circumstances as soon as possible.

Part II. Implementation [...]

Part III. Declarations and Reservations [...]

Article 35

A Contracting State may declare, at the time of the deposit of its instrument of ratification or accession, that it will not apply the provisions of this Convention to actions for annulment of the contract.

Article 36

Any State may declare, at the time of the deposit of its instrument of ratification or accession, that it shall not be compelled to apply the provisions of Article 24 of this Convention.

Article 36 bis (Article XII of the Protocol)

Any State may declare at the time of the deposit of its instrument of accession or its notification under Article 43 bis that it will not be bound by the amendments to Article 3 made by Article I of the 1980 Protocol.[1] A declaration made under this Article shall be in writing and be formally notified to the depositary.

Article 37[2]

This Convention shall not prevail over any international agreement which has already been or may be entered into and which contains provisions concerning the matters governed by this Convention, provided that the seller and buyer have their places of business in States parties to such agreement.

Article 38

(1) A Contracting State which is a party to an existing convention relating to the international sale of goods may declare, at the time of the deposit of its instrument of ratification or accession, that it will apply this Convention exclusively to contracts of international sale of goods as defined in such existing convention.

---

1 Such a State will then be bound by Article 3 of the unamended Convention. For its text, see footnote under Article 3.

2 Text as amended in accordance with Article V of the Protocol. Article 37 as originally adopted in the Limitation Convention, 1974, prior to its amendment under the 1980 Protocol, read as follows:
"Article 37
This Convention shall not prevail over conventions already entered into or which may be entered into, and which contain provisions concerning the matters covered by this Convention, provided that the seller and buyer have their places of business in States parties to such a convention."

(2) Such declaration shall cease to be effective on the first day of the month following the expiration of twelve months after a new convention on the international sale of goods, concluded under the auspices of the United Nations, shall have entered into force.

Article 39

No reservation other than those made in accordance with Articles 34, 35, 36, 36 bis and 38 shall be permitted. [...]

Part IV. Final Clauses [...]

III. Explanatory Note by the UNCITRAL Secretariat on the Convention on the Limitation Period in the International Sale of Goods and the Protocol Amending the Convention on the Limitation Period in the International Sale of Goods

This note has been prepared by the secretariat of the United Nations Commission on International Trade Law for informational purposes; it is not an official commentary on the Convention. [...]

A. Introduction

1. The Convention on the Limitation Period in the International Sale of Goods (New York, 1974) provides uniform international legal rules governing the period of time within which a party under a contract for the international sale of goods must commence legal proceedings against the other party to assert a claim arising from the contract or relating to its breach, termination or invalidity. This period is referred to in the Convention as the "limitation period". The basic aims of the limitation period are to prevent the institution of legal proceedings at such a late date that the evidence relating to the claim is likely to be unreliable or lost and to protect against the uncertainty and injustice that would result if a party were to remain exposed to unasserted claims for an extensive period of time.

2. The Limitation Convention grew out of the work of the United Nations Commission on International Trade Law (UNCITRAL) towards the harmonization and unification of international sales law, which also resulted in the United Nations Convention on Contracts for the International Sale of Goods (Vienna, 1980) (hereinafter referred to as the "United Nations Sales Convention"). During that work it was observed that, while most legal systems limited or prescribed a claim from being asserted after the lapse of a specified period of time, numerous disparities existed among legal systems with respect to the conceptual basis for doing so. As a result there were disparities in the length of the period and in the rules governing the limitation or prescription of claims after that period. Those disparities created difficulties in the enforcement of claims arising from international sales transactions, and thus burdened international trade.

3. In view of those problems UNCITRAL decided to prepare uniform international legal rules on the limitation period in the international sale of goods. On the basis of a draft Convention prepared by UNCITRAL, a diplomatic conference convened in New York by the General Assembly adopted the Limitation Convention on 14 June 1974.

4. The Limitation Convention was amended by a Protocol adopted in 1980 by the diplomatic conference that adopted the United Nations Sales Convention, in order to harmonize the Limitation Convention with the latter Convention, in particular, with regard to scope of application and admissible declarations. As a result, the scope of application of the amended Limitation Convention and that of the United Nations Sales Convention are identical.

5. The Limitation Convention entered into force on 1 August 1988. As of 1 October 2011, 29 States are parties to the unamended Convention and 21 of those 29 States are parties to the amended Convention. The current updated status of the Convention is available on the UNCITRAL website. Authoritative information on the status of the Convention, as well as on related

declarations, including with respect to territorial application and succession of States, may be found on the United Nations Treaty Collection on the Internet.

B. Scope of Application

6. The Convention applies to contracts for the sale of goods between parties whose places of business are in different States if both of those States are Contracting States. Under the 1980 Protocol the Convention also applies if the rules of private international law make the law of a Contracting State applicable to the contract. However, in becoming a party to the Protocol a State may declare that it will not be bound by that provision. Each Contracting State must apply the Convention to contracts concluded on or after the date of the entry into force of the Convention.

7. The application of the Convention is excluded in certain situations. Firstly, the Convention will not apply if the parties to a sales contract expressly exclude its application. This provision gives effect to the basic principle of freedom of contract in the international sale of goods. Secondly, the Convention will not apply in certain cases where matters covered by the Convention are governed by other Conventions. Thirdly, Contracting States are permitted to deposit declarations excluding the application of the Convention in the following situations: two or more Contracting States may exclude the application of the Convention to contracts between parties having their places of business in those States when the States apply to those contracts the same or closely related legal rules. So far, one State has made that declaration. In addition, a State may exclude the application of the Convention to actions for annulment of the contract. No State has thus far availed itself of such a declaration.

8. Since the Convention applies only in respect of international sales contracts, it clarifies whether contracts involving certain services are covered. A contract for the supply of goods to be manufactured or produced is considered to be a sales contract unless the party who orders the goods undertakes to supply a substantial part of the materials necessary for their manufacture or production. Furthermore, when the preponderant part of the obligations of the party who furnishes the goods consists in the supply of labour or other services, the Convention does not apply.

9. The Convention contains a list of types of sales that are excluded from the Convention, either because of the purpose of the sale (goods bought for personal, family or household use (under the 1980 Protocol sales of those goods are covered by the Convention if the seller could not have known that they were bought for such use)), the nature of the sale (sales by auction, on execution or otherwise by law) or the nature of the goods (stocks, shares, investment securities, negotiable instruments, money, ships, vessels, aircraft or electricity (the 1980 Protocol adds hovercraft)).

10. The Convention makes it clear that it applies only to the usual type of commercial claims based on contract. It specifically excludes claims based on death or personal injury; nuclear damage; a lien, mortgage or other security interest; a judgment or award; a document on which direct enforcement or execution can be obtained; and a bill of exchange, cheque or promissory note. The limitation periods for those claims are generally subject to particular rules and it would not necessarily be appropriate to apply in respect of those claims the rules applicable to ordinary commercial contractual claims.

C. Duration and Commencement of Limitation Period

11. The duration of the limitation period under the Convention is four years. The period cannot be modified by agreement of the parties, but it can be extended by a written declaration of the debtor during the running of the period. Also, the contract of sale may stipulate a shorter period

for the commencement of arbitral proceedings, if the stipulation is valid under the law applicable to the contract. Rules are provided as to how the limitation period should be calculated.

12. A limitation period of four years' duration was thought to accomplish the aims of the limitation period and yet to provide an adequate period of time to enable a party to an international sales contract to assert his claim against the other party. Circumstances where an extension or recommencement of the limitation period would be justified are dealt with in particular provisions of the Convention.

13. With respect to the time when the limitation period commences to run, the basic rule is that it commences on the date on which the claim accrues. The Convention establishes when claims for breach of contract, for defects in the goods or other lack of conformity and for fraud are deemed to accrue. Special rules are provided for the commencement of the limitation period in two particular cases: where the seller has given the buyer an express undertaking (such as a warranty or guarantee) relating to the goods which is stated to have effect for a certain period of time, and where a party terminates the contract before the time for performance is due. Rules are also provided in respect of claims arising from the breach of an instalment contract and claims based on circumstances giving rise to a termination of an instalment contract.

D. Cessation and Extension of Limitation Period

14. Having established the time of commencement and the length of the limitation period, the Convention sets forth rules concerning the cessation of the period. The period ceases to run when the claimant commences judicial or arbitral proceedings against the debtor, or when he asserts his claim in existing proceedings. A counterclaim is deemed to have been asserted on the same date as the date when the proceedings in which the counterclaim is asserted were commenced, if the counterclaim and the claim against which it is raised relate to the same contract or to several contracts concluded in the course of the same transaction.

15. Judicial or arbitral proceedings commenced by a claimant within the limitation period might terminate without a binding decision on the merits of the claim, for example, because the court or arbitral tribunal lacks jurisdiction or because of a procedural defect. The creditor would normally be able to pursue his claim by commencing new proceedings. Thus, the Convention provides that if the original proceedings end without a binding decision on the merits the limitation period will be deemed to have continued to run. However, by the time the original proceedings have ended, the limitation period might have expired, or there might remain insufficient time for the claimant to commence new proceedings. To protect the claimant in those cases the Convention grants him an additional period of one year to commence new proceedings.

16. The Convention contains rules to resolve in a uniform manner questions concerning the running of the limitation period in two particular cases. Firstly, it provides that where legal proceedings have been commenced against one party to the sales contract, the limitation period ceases to run against a person jointly and severally liable with him if the claimant informs that person in writing within the limitation period that the proceedings have been commenced. Secondly, it provides that where proceedings have been commenced against a buyer by a party who purchased the goods from him, the limitation period ceases to run in respect of the buyer's recourse claim against the seller if the buyer informs the seller in writing within the limitation period that the proceedings against the buyer have been commenced. Where the proceedings in either of those two cases have ended, the limitation period in respect of the claim against the jointly and severally liable person or against the seller will be deemed to have continued to run without interruption, but there will be an additional year to commence new proceedings if at that time the limitation period has expired or has less than a year to run.

17. One effect of the provision mentioned above relating to the buyer is to enable him to await the outcome of the claim against him before commencing an action against the seller. This

enables the buyer to avoid the trouble and expense of instituting proceedings against the seller and the disruption of their good business relationship if it turns out that the claim against the buyer was not successful.

18. Under the Convention the limitation period recommences in two cases: if the creditor performs in the debtor's State an act that, under the law of that State, has the effect of recommencing a limitation period, or if the debtor acknowledges in writing his obligation to the creditor or pays interest or partially performs the obligation from which his acknowledgement can be inferred.

19. The Convention protects a creditor who was prevented from taking the necessary acts to stop the running of the limitation period in extreme cases. It provides that when the creditor could not take those acts as a result of a circumstance beyond his control and which he could neither avoid nor overcome, the limitation period will be extended so as to expire one year after the date when the circumstance ceased to exist.

E. Overall Limit of Limitation Period

20. Since the limitation period may, under the circumstances noted above, be extended or recommence, the Convention establishes an overall time period of 10 years, from the date on which the limitation period originally commenced to run, beyond which no legal proceedings to assert the claim may be commenced under any circumstances. The theory behind that provision is that enabling proceedings to be brought after that time would be inconsistent with the aims of the Convention in providing a definite limitation period.

F. Consequences of Expiration of Limitation Period

21. The principal consequence of the expiration of the limitation period is that no claim will be recognized or enforced in legal proceedings commenced thereafter. The expiration of the limitation period will not be taken into consideration in legal proceedings unless it is invoked by a party to the proceedings. However, in light of views expressed at the diplomatic conference that adopted the Convention that the limitation or prescription of actions was a matter of public policy and that a court should be able to take the expiration of the limitation period into account on its own initiative, a Contracting State is permitted to declare that it will not apply that provision. No State has thus far made such a declaration.

22. Even after the limitation period has expired a party can in certain situations raise his claim as a defence to or set-off against a claim asserted by the other party.

G. Other Provisions and Final Clauses [...]

H. Complementary Texts

27. The Limitation Convention is complemented by the United Nations Convention on Contracts for the International Sale of Goods (the United Nations Sales Convention, also known as "CISG"). Adopted by a diplomatic conference on 11 April 1980, the United Nations Sales Convention establishes a comprehensive code of legal rules governing the formation of contracts for the international sale of goods, the obligations of the buyer and seller, remedies for breach of contract and other aspects of the contract.

28. The Limitation Convention is also complemented, with respect to the use of electronic communications, by the United Nations Convention on the Use of Electronic Communications in International Contracts, 2005 (the Electronic Communications Convention). The Electronic Communications Convention aims at facilitating the use of electronic communications in international trade by assuring that contracts concluded and other communications exchanged electronically are as valid and enforceable as their traditional paper-based equivalents. In particular, certain formal requirements contained in widely adopted international trade law treaties may

hinder the legal recognition of the use of electronic communications. The Electronic Communications Convention is an enabling treaty whose effect is to remove those formal obstacles by establishing the requirements for functional equivalence between electronic and written form.

Ratifications and binding effect as of June 2020:

No.	Country	Ratification only of the 1974 Convention	Ratification also of the 1980 Protocol
1	Argentina		1 Aug 1988
2	Belarus		1 Aug 1997
3	Belgium		1 Mar 2009
4	Benin	1 Feb 2012	
5	Bosnia and Herzegovina	6 March 1992	
6	Burundi	1 Apr 1999	
7	Côte d´Ivoire		1 Sep 2016
8	Cuba		1 June 1995
9	Czech Republic		1 Jan 1993
10	Dominican Republic		1 Feb 2011
11	Egypt		1 Aug 1988
12	Ghana	1 Aug 1988	
13	Guinea		1 Aug 1991
14	Hungary		1 Aug 1988
15	Liberia		1 Apr 2006
16	Mexico		1 Aug 1988
17	Montenegro		1 Mar 2013
18	Norway	1 Aug 1988	
19	Paraguay		1 Mar 2004
20	Poland		1 Dec 1995
21	Moldova		1 Mar 1998
22	Romania		1 Nov 1992
23	Serbia	27 Apr 1992	
24	Slovakia		1 Jan 1993
25	Slovenia		1 Mar 1996
26	Uganda		1 Sep 1992
27	Ukraine	1 Apr 1994	
28	United States of America		1 Dec 1994
29	Uruguay		1 Nov 1997
30	Zambia		1 Aug 1988

12) UNIFORM COMMERCIAL CODE, USA[1]

U.C.C. – ARTICLE 1 – GENERAL PROVISIONS

PART 1. GENERAL PROVISIONS

§ 1-101. Short Titles

(a) This [Act] may be cited as the Uniform Commercial Code [UCC].

(b) This Article may be cited as [UCC]-General Provisions.

§ 1-102. Scope of Article

This Article applies to a transaction to the extent that it is governed by another Article of the [UCC].

§ 1-103. Construction of [UCC] to Promote its Purposes and Policies: Applicability of Supplemental Principles of Law

(a) The [UCC] must be liberally construed and applied to promote its underlying purposes and policies, which are: (1) to simplify, clarify, and modernize the law governing commercial transactions; (2) to permit the continued expansion of commercial practices through custom, usage, and agreement of the parties; and (3) to make uniform the law among the various jurisdictions.

(b) Unless displaced by the particular provisions of the [UCC], the principles of law and equity, including the law merchant and the law relative to capacity to contract, principal and agent, estoppel, fraud, misrepresentation, duress, coercion, mistake, bankruptcy, and other validating or invalidating cause supplement its provisions.

§ 1-104. Construction Against Implied Repeal

The [UCC] being a general act intended as a unified coverage of its subject matter, no part of it shall be deemed to be impliedly repealed by subsequent legislation if such construction can reasonably be avoided.

§ 1-105. Severability

If any provision or clause of the [UCC] or its application to any person or circumstance is held invalid, the invalidity does not affect other provisions or applications of the [UCC] which can be given effect without the invalid provision or application, and to this end the provisions of the [UCC] are severable.

§ 1-106. Use of Singular and Plural; Gender

In the [UCC], unless the statutory context otherwise requires: (1) words in the singular number include the plural, and those in the plural include the singular; and (2) words of any gender also refer to any other gender.

§ 1-107. Section Captions

Section captions are part of the Uniform Commercial Code.

§ 1-108. Relation to Electronic Signatures in Global and National Commerce Act

This Article modifies, limits, and supersedes the federal Electronic Signatures in Global and National Commerce Act, 15 U.S.C. Section 7001 et seq., except that nothing in this Article modifies, limits, or supersedes Section 7001(c) of that Act or authorizes electronic delivery of any of the notices described in Section 7003(b) of that Act.

PART 2. GENERAL DEFINITIONS AND PRINCIPLES OF INTERPRETATION

§ 1-201. General Definitions

(a) Unless the context otherwise requires, words or phrases defined in this section, or in the additional definitions contained in other articles of the [UCC] that apply to particular articles or parts thereof, have the meanings stated.

(b) Subject to definitions contained in other articles of the [UCC] that apply to particular articles or parts thereof:

(1) "Action", in the sense of a judicial proceeding, includes recoupment, counterclaim, set-off, suit in equity, and any other proceeding in which rights are determined.

(2) "Aggrieved party" means a party entitled to pursue a remedy.

(3) "Agreement", as distinguished from "contract", means the bargain of the parties in fact, as found in their language or inferred from other circumstances, including course of performance, course of dealing, or usage of trade as provided in Section 1-303.

(4) "Bank" means a person engaged in the business of banking and includes a savings bank, savings and loan association, credit union, and trust company.

(5) "Bearer" means a person in possession of a negotiable instrument, document of title, or certificated security that is payable to bearer or indorsed in blank.

(6) "Bill of lading" means a document evidencing the receipt of goods for shipment issued by a person engaged in the business of transporting or forwarding goods.

(7) "Branch" includes a separately incorporated foreign branch of a bank.

(8) "Burden of establishing" a fact means the burden of persuading the trier of fact that the existence of the fact is more probable than its nonexistence.

(9) "Buyer in ordinary course of business" means a person that buys goods in good faith, without knowledge that the sale violates the rights of another person in the goods, and in the ordinary course from a person, other than a pawnbroker, in the business of selling goods of that kind. A person buys goods in the ordinary course if the sale to the person comports with the usual or customary practices in the kind of business in which the seller is engaged or with the seller's own usual or customary practices. A person that sells oil, gas, or other minerals at the wellhead or minehead is a person in the business of selling goods of that kind. A buyer in ordinary course of business may buy for cash, by exchange of other property, or on secured or unsecured credit, and may acquire goods or documents of title under a preexisting contract for sale. Only a buyer that takes possession of the goods or has a right to recover the goods from the seller under Article 2 may be a buyer in ordinary course of business. "Buyer in ordinary course of business" does not include a person that acquires goods in a transfer in bulk or as security for or in total or partial satisfaction of a money debt.

(10) "Conspicuous", with reference to a term, means so written, displayed, or presented that a reasonable person against which it is to operate ought to have noticed it. Whether a term is "conspicuous" or not is a decision for the court. Conspicuous terms include the following: (A) a heading in capitals equal to or greater in size than the surrounding text, or in contrasting type, font, or color to the surrounding text of the same or lesser size; and (B) language in the body of a record or display in larger type than the surrounding text, or in contrasting type, font, or color to the surrounding text of the same size, or set off from surrounding text of the same size by symbols or other marks that call attention to the language.

(11) "Consumer" means an individual who enters into a transaction primarily for personal, family, or household purposes.

(12) "Contract", as distinguished from "agreement", means the total legal obligation that results from the parties' agreement as determined by [the UCC] as supplemented by any other applicable laws.

(13) "Creditor" includes a general creditor, a secured creditor, a lien creditor, and any representative of creditors, including an assignee for the benefit of creditors, a trustee in bankruptcy, a receiver in equity, and an executor or administrator of an insolvent debtor's or assignor's estate.

(14) "Defendant" includes a person in the position of defendant in a counterclaim, cross-claim, or third-party claim.

(15) "Delivery", with respect to an instrument, document of title, or chattel paper, means voluntary transfer of possession.

(16) "Document of title" includes bill of lading, dock warrant, dock receipt, warehouse receipt or order for the delivery of goods, and also any other document which in the regular course of business or financing is treated as adequately evidencing that the person in possession of it is entitled to receive, hold, and dispose of the document and the goods it covers. To be a document of title, a document must purport to be issued by or addressed to a bailee and purport to cover goods in the bailee's possession which are either identified or are fungible portions of an identified mass.

(17) "Fault" means a default, breach, or wrongful act or omission.

(18) "Fungible goods" means: (A) goods of which any unit, by nature or usage of trade, is the equivalent of any other like unit; or (B) goods that by agreement are treated as equivalent.

(19) "Genuine" means free of forgery or counterfeiting.

(20) "Good faith," except as otherwise provided in Article 5, means honesty in fact and the observance of reasonable commercial standards of fair dealing.

(21) "Holder" means: (A) the person in possession of a negotiable instrument that is payable either to bearer or to an identified person that is the person in possession; or (B) the person in possession of a document of title if the goods are deliverable either to bearer or to the order of the person in possession.

(22) "Insolvency proceeding" includes an assignment for the benefit of creditors or other proceeding intended to liquidate or rehabilitate the estate of the person involved.

(23) "Insolvent" means: (A) having generally ceased to pay debts in the ordinary course of business other than as a result of bona fide dispute; (B) being unable to pay debts as they become due; or (C) being insolvent within the meaning of federal bankruptcy law.

(24) "Money" means a medium of exchange currently authorized or adopted by a domestic or foreign government. The term includes a monetary unit of account established by an intergovernmental organization or by agreement between two or more countries.

(25) "Organization" means a person other than an individual.

(26) "Party", as distinguished from "third party", means a person that has engaged in a transaction or made an agreement subject to [the UCC].

(27) "Person" means an individual, corporation, business trust, estate, trust, partnership, limited liability company, association, joint venture, government, governmental subdivision, agency, or instrumentality, public corporation, or any other legal or commercial entity.

(28) "Present value" means the amount as of a date certain of one or more sums payable in the future, discounted to the date certain by use of either an interest rate specified by the parties if that rate is not manifestly unreasonable at the time the transaction is entered into

or, if an interest rate is not so specified, a commercially reasonable rate that takes into account the facts and circumstances at the time the transaction is entered into.

(29) "Purchase" means taking by sale, lease, discount, negotiation, mortgage, pledge, lien, security interest, issue or reissue, gift, or any other voluntary transaction creating an interest in property.

(30) "Purchaser" means a person that takes by purchase.

(31) "Record" means information that is inscribed on a tangible medium or that is stored in an electronic or other medium and is retrievable in perceivable form.

(32) "Remedy" means any remedial right to which an aggrieved party is entitled with or without resort to a tribunal.

(33) "Representative" means a person empowered to act for another, including an agent, an officer of a corporation or association, and a trustee, executor, or administrator of an estate.

(34) "Right" includes remedy.

(35) "Security interest" means an interest in personal property or fixtures which secures payment or performance of an obligation. "Security interest" includes any interest of a consignor and a buyer of accounts, chattel paper, a payment intangible, or a promissory note in a transaction that is subject to Article 9. "Security interest" does not include the special property interest of a buyer of goods on identification of those goods to a contract for sale under Section 2-505, the right of a seller or lessor of goods under Article 2 or 2A to retain or acquire possession of the goods is not a "security interest", but a seller or lessor may also acquire a "security interest" by complying with Article 9. The retention or reservation of title by a seller of goods notwithstanding shipment or delivery to the buyer under Section 2-401 is limited in effect to a reservation of a "security interest." Whether a transaction in the form of a lease creates a "security interest" is determined pursuant to Section 1-203.

(36) "Send" in connection with a writing, record, or notice means: (A) to deposit in the mail or deliver for transmission by any other usual means of communication with postage or cost of transmission provided for and properly addressed and, in the case of an instrument, to an address specified thereon or otherwise agreed, or if there be none to any address reasonable under the circumstances; or (B) in any other way to cause to be received any record or notice within the time it would have arrived if properly sent.

(37) "Signed" includes using any symbol executed or adopted with present intention to adopt or accept a writing.

(38) "State" means a State of the United States, the District of Columbia, Puerto Rico, the United States Virgin Islands, or any territory or insular possession subject to the jurisdiction of the United States.

(39) "Surety" includes a guarantor or other secondary obligor.

(40) "Term" means a portion of an agreement that relates to a particular matter.

(41) "Unauthorized signature" means a signature made without actual, implied, or apparent authority. The term includes a forgery.

(42) "Warehouse receipt" means a receipt issued by a person engaged in the business of storing goods for hire.

(43) "Writing" includes printing, typewriting, or any other intentional reduction to tangible form. "Written" has a corresponding meaning.

§ 1-202. Notice; Knowledge

(a) Subject to subsection (f), a person has "notice" of a fact if the person: (1) has actual knowledge of it; (2) has received a notice or notification of it; or (3) from all the facts and circumstances known to the person at the time in question, has reason to know that it exists.

(b) "Knowledge" means actual knowledge. "Knows" has a corresponding meaning.

(c) "Discover", "learn", or words of similar import refer to knowledge rather than to reason to know.

(d) A person "notifies" or "gives" a notice or notification to another person by taking such steps as may be reasonably required to inform the other person in ordinary course, whether or not the other person actually comes to know of it.

(e) Subject to subsection (f), a person "receives" a notice or notification when: (1) it comes to that person's attention; or (2) it is duly delivered in a form reasonable under the circumstances at the place of business through which the contract was made or at another location held out by that person as the place for receipt of such communications.

(f) Notice, knowledge, or a notice or notification received by an organization is effective for a particular transaction from the time it is brought to the attention of the individual conducting that transaction and, in any event, from the time it would have been brought to the individual's attention if the organization had exercised due diligence. An organization exercises due diligence if it maintains reasonable routines for communicating significant information to the person conducting the transaction and there is reasonable compliance with the routines. Due diligence does not require an individual acting for the organization to communicate information unless the communication is part of the individual's regular duties or the individual has reason to know of the transaction and that the transaction would be materially affected by the information.

§ 1-203. Lease Distinguished from Security Interest

(a) Whether a transaction in the form of a lease creates a lease or security interest is determined by the facts of each case.

(b) A transaction in the form of a lease creates a security interest if the consideration that the lessee is to pay the lessor for the right to possession and use of the goods is an obligation for the term of the lease and is not subject to termination by the lessee, and: (1) the original term of the lease is equal to or greater than the remaining economic life of the goods; (2) the lessee is bound to renew the lease for the remaining economic life of the goods or is bound to become the owner of the goods; (3) the lessee has an option to renew the lease for the remaining economic life of the goods for no additional consideration or for nominal additional consideration upon compliance with the lease agreement; or (4) the lessee has an option to become the owner of the goods for no additional consideration or for nominal additional consideration upon compliance with the lease agreement.

(c) A transaction in the form of a lease does not create a security interest merely because: (1) the present value of the consideration the lessee is obligated to pay the lessor for the right to possession and use of the goods is substantially equal to or is greater than the fair market value of the goods at the time the lease is entered into; (2) the lessee assumes risk of loss of the goods; (3) the lessee agrees to pay, with respect to the goods, taxes, insurance, filing, recording, or registration fees, or service or maintenance costs; (4) the lessee has an option to renew the lease or to become the owner of the goods; (5) the lessee has an option to renew the lease for a fixed rent that is equal to or greater than the reasonably predictable fair market rent for the use of the goods for the term of the renewal at the time the option is to be performed; or (6) the lessee has an option to become the owner of the goods for a fixed price that is equal to or greater than the reasonably predictable fair market value of the goods at the time the option is to be performed.

(d) Additional consideration is nominal if it is less than the lessee's reasonably predictable cost of performing under the lease agreement if the option is not exercised. Additional consideration is not nominal if: (1) when the option to renew the lease is granted to the lessee, the rent is stated to be the fair market rent for the use of the goods for the term of the renewal determined at the time the option is to be performed; or (2) when the option to become the owner of the goods is granted to the lessee, the price is stated to be the fair market value of the goods determined at the time the option is to be performed.

(e) The "remaining economic life of the goods" and "reasonably predictable" fair market rent, fair market value, or cost of performing under the lease agreement must be determined with reference to the facts and circumstances at the time the transaction is entered into.

§ 1-204. Value

Except as otherwise provided in Articles 3, 4, [and] 5, [and 6], a person gives value for rights if the person acquires them: (1) in return for a binding commitment to extend credit or for the extension of immediately available credit, whether or not drawn upon and whether or not a charge-back is provided for in the event of difficulties in collection; (2) as security for, or in total or partial satisfaction of, a preexisting claim; (3) by accepting delivery under a preexisting contract for purchase; or (4) in return for any consideration sufficient to support a simple contract.

§ 1-205. Reasonable Time; Seasonableness

(a) Whether a time for taking an action required by [the UCC] is reasonable depends on the nature, purpose, and circumstances of the action.

(b) An action is taken seasonably if it is taken at or within the time agreed or, if no time is agreed, at or within a reasonable time.

§ 1-206. Presumptions

Whenever [the UCC] creates a "presumption" with respect to a fact, or provides that a fact is "presumed," the trier of fact must find the existence of the fact unless and until evidence is introduced that supports a finding of its nonexistence.

PART 3. TERRITORIAL APPLICABILITY AND GENERAL RULES

§ 1-301. Territorial Applicability; Parties' Power to Choose Applicable Law

(a) In this section:

(1) "Domestic transaction" means a transaction other than an international transaction.

(2) "International transaction" means a transaction that bears a reasonable relation to a country other than the United States.

(b) This section applies to a transaction to the extent that it is governed by another article of the [UCC].

(c) Except as otherwise provided in this section:

(1) an agreement by parties to a domestic transaction that any or all of their rights and obligations are to be determined by the law of this State or of another State is effective, whether or not the transaction bears a relation to the State designated; and

(2) an agreement by parties to an international transaction that any or all of their rights and obligations are to be determined by the law of this State or of another State or country is

effective, whether or not the transaction bears a relation to the State or country designated.

(d) In the absence of an agreement effective under subsection (c), and except as provided in subsections (e) and (g), the rights and obligations of the parties are determined by the law that would be selected by application of this State's conflict of laws principles.

(e) If one of the parties to a transaction is a consumer, the following rules apply:

(1) An agreement referred to in subsection (c) is not effective unless the transaction bears a reasonable relation to the State or country designated.

(2) Application of the law of the State or country determined pursuant to subsection (c) or (d) may not deprive the consumer of the protection of any rule of law governing a matter within the scope of this section, which both is protective of consumers and may not be varied by agreement: (A) of the State or country in which the consumer principally resides, unless subparagraph (B) applies; or (B) if the transaction is a sale of goods, of the State or country in which the consumer both makes the contract and takes delivery of those goods, if such State or country is not the State or country in which the consumer principally resides.

(f) An agreement otherwise effective under subsection (c) is not effective to the extent that application of the law of the State or country designated would be contrary to a fundamental policy of the State or country whose law would govern in the absence of agreement under subsection (d).

(g) To the extent that [the UCC] governs a transaction, if one of the following provisions of [the UCC] specifies the applicable law, that provision governs and a contrary agreement is effective only to the extent permitted by the law so specified: (1) Section 2-402; (2) Sections 2A-105 and 2A-106; (3) Section 4-102; (4) Section 4A-507; (5) Section 5-116; [(6) Section 6-103;] (7) Section 8-110; (8) Sections 9-301 through 9-307.

§ 1-302. Variation by Agreement

(a) Except as otherwise provided in subsection (b) or elsewhere in [the UCC], the effect of provisions of [the UCC] may be varied by agreement.

(b) The obligations of good faith, diligence, reasonableness, and care prescribed by [the UCC] may not be disclaimed by agreement. The parties, by agreement, may determine the standards by which the performance of those obligations is to be measured if those standards are not manifestly unreasonable. Whenever [the UCC] requires an action to be taken within a reasonable time, a time that is not manifestly unreasonable may be fixed by agreement.

(c) The presence in certain provisions of [the UCC] of the phrase "unless otherwise agreed", or words of similar import, does not imply that the effect of other provisions may not be varied by agreement under this section.

§ 1-303. Course of Performance, Course of Dealing, and Usage of Trade

(a) A "course of performance" is a sequence of conduct between the parties to a particular transaction that exists if: (1) the agreement of the parties with respect to the transaction involves repeated occasions for performance by a party; and (2) the other party, with knowledge of the nature of the performance and opportunity for objection to it, accepts the performance or acquiesces in it without objection.

(b) A "course of dealing" is a sequence of conduct concerning previous transactions between the parties to a particular transaction that is fairly to be regarded as establishing a common basis of understanding for interpreting their expressions and other conduct.

(c) A "usage of trade" is any practice or method of dealing having such regularity of observance in a place, vocation, or trade as to justify an expectation that it will be observed with respect to the transaction in question. The existence and scope of such a usage must be proved as facts. If it is established that such a usage is embodied in a trade code or similar record, the interpretation of the record is a question of law.

(d) A course of performance or course of dealing between the parties or usage of trade in the vocation or trade in which they are engaged or of which they are or should be aware is relevant in ascertaining the meaning of the parties' agreement, may give particular meaning to specific terms of the agreement, and may supplement or qualify the terms of the agreement. A usage of trade applicable in the place in which part of the performance under the agreement is to occur may be so utilized as to that part of the performance.

(e) Except as otherwise provided in subsection (f), the express terms of an agreement and any applicable course of performance, course of dealing, or usage of trade must be construed whenever reasonable as consistent with each other. If such a construction is unreasonable: (1) express terms prevail over course of performance, course of dealing, and usage of trade; (2) course of performance prevails over course of dealing and usage of trade; and (3) course of dealing prevails over usage of trade.

(f) Subject to Section 2-209, a course of performance is relevant to show a waiver or modification of any term inconsistent with the course of performance.

(g) Evidence of a relevant usage of trade offered by one party is not admissible unless that party has given the other party notice that the court finds sufficient to prevent unfair surprise to the other party.

§ 1-304. Obligation of Good Faith

Every contract or duty within [the Uniform Commercial Code] imposes an obligation of good faith in its performance and enforcement.

§ 1-305. Remedies to Be Liberally Administered

(a) The remedies provided by [the UCC] must be liberally administered to the end that the aggrieved party may be put in as good a position as if the other party had fully performed but neither consequential or special damages nor penal damages may be had except as specifically provided in [the UCC] or by other rule of law.

(b) Any right or obligation declared by [the UCC] is enforceable by action unless the provision declaring it specifies a different and limited effect.

§ 1-306. Waiver or Renunciation of Claim or Right After Breach

A claim or right arising out of an alleged breach may be discharged in whole or in part without consideration by agreement of the aggrieved party in an authenticated record.

§ 1-307. Prima Facie Evidence by Third-Party Documents

A document in due form purporting to be a bill of lading, policy or certificate of insurance, official weigher's or inspector's certificate, consular invoice, or any other document authorized or required by the contract to be issued by a third party is prima facie evidence of its own authenticity and genuineness and of the facts stated in the document by the third party.

§ 1-308. Performance or Acceptance Under Reservation of Rights

(a) A party that with explicit reservation of rights performs or promises performance or assents to performance in a manner demanded or offered by the other party does not thereby prejudice the rights reserved. Such words as "without prejudice," "under protest," or the like are sufficient.

(b) Subsection (a) does not apply to an accord and satisfaction.

§ 1-309. Option to Accelerate at Will

A term providing that one party or that party's successor in interest may accelerate payment or performance or require collateral or additional collateral "at will" or when the party "deems itself insecure," or words of similar import, means that the party has power to do so only if that party in good faith believes that the prospect of payment or performance is impaired. The burden of establishing lack of good faith is on the party against which the power has been exercised.

§ 1-310. Subordinated Obligations

An obligation may be issued as subordinated to performance of another obligation of the person obligated, or a creditor may subordinate its right to performance of an obligation by agreement with either the person obligated or another creditor of the person obligated. Subordination does not create a security interest as against either the common debtor or a subordinated creditor.

U.C.C. -- ARTICLE 2 – SALES

PART 1. SHORT TITLE, GENERAL CONSTRUCTION AND SUBJECT MATTER

§§2-101. Short Title

This Article shall be known and may be cited as Uniform Commercial Code-Sales.

§2-102. Scope; Certain Security and Other Transactions Excluded From this Article

Unless the context otherwise requires, this Article applies to transactions in goods; it does not apply to any transaction which although in the form of an unconditional contract to sell or present sale is intended to operate only as a security transaction nor does this Article impair or repeal any statute regulating sales to consumers, farmers or other specified classes of buyers.

§2-103. Definitions and Index of Definitions

(1) In this Article unless the context otherwise requires

(a) "Buyer" means a person that buys or contracts to buy goods.

(b) "Good faith" in the case of merchants means honesty in fact and the observance of reasonable commercial standards of fair dealing in the trade.

(c) "Receipt" of goods means taking physical possession of them.

(d) "Seller" means a person who sells or contracts to sell goods.

(2) Other definitions applying to this Article or to specified Parts thereof, and the sections in which they appear are:

"Acceptance". Section 2-606.
"Banker's credit". Section 2-325.
"Between merchants". Section 2-104.
"Cancellation". Section 2-106(4).
"Commercial unit". Section 2-105.
"Confirmed credit". Section 2-325.
"Conforming to contract". Section 2-106.
"Contract for sale". Section 2-106.
"Cover". Section 2-712.
"Entrusting". Section 2-403.
"Financing agency". Section 2-104.
"Future Goods". Section 2-105.
"Goods". Section 2-105.
"Identification". Section 2-501.

"Installment contract". Section 2-612.
"Letter of credit". Section 2-325.
"Lot". Section 2-105.
"Merchant". Section 2-104.
"Overseas". Section 2-323.
"Person in position of Seller". Section 2-707.
"Present sale". Section 2-106.
"Sale". Section 2-106.
"Sale on approval". Section 2-326.
"Sale or return". Section 2-326.
"Termination". Section 2-106.

(3) The following definitions in other Articles apply to this Article:
"Check". Section 3-104.
"Consignee". Section 7-102.
"Consignor". Section 7-102.
"Consumer Goods". Section 9-109.
"Dishonor". Section 3-507.
"Draft". Section 3-104.

(4) In addition Article 1 contains general definitions and principles of construction and interpretation applicable throughout this Article.

§2-104. Definitions: "Merchant"; "Between Merchants"; "Financing Agency"

(1) "Merchant" means a person who deals in goods of the kind or otherwise by his occupation holds himself out as having knowledge or skill peculiar to the practices or goods involved in the transaction or to whom such knowledge or skill may be attributed by his employment of an agent or broker or other intermediary who by his occupation holds himself as having such knowledge or skill.

(2) "Financing agency" means a bank, finance company or other person who in the ordinary course of business makes advances against goods or documents of title or who by arrangement with either the seller or the buyer intervenes in ordinary course to make or collect payment due or claimed under the contract for sale, as by purchasing or paying the seller's draft or making advances against it or by merely taking it for collection whether or not documents of title accompany the draft. "Financing agency" includes also a bank or other person who similarly intervenes between persons who are in the position of seller and buyer in respect to the goods (Section 2-707).

(3) "Between Merchants" means in any transaction with respect to which both parties are chargeable with the knowledge or skill of merchants.

§2-105. Definitions: Transferability; "Goods"; "Future" Goods; "Lot"; "Commercial Unit"

(1) "Goods" means all things (including specially manufactured goods) which are movable at the time of identification to the contract for sale other than the money in which the price is to be paid, investment securities (Article 8) and things in action. "Goods" also includes the unborn young of animals and growing crops and other identified things attached to realty as described in the section on goods to be severed from realty (Section 2-107).

(2) Goods must be both existing and identified before any interest in them can pass. Goods which are not both existing and identified are "future" goods. A purported present sale of future goods or of any interest therein operates as a contract to sell.

(3) There may be a sale of a part interest in existing identified goods.

(4) An undivided share in an identified bulk of fungible goods is sufficiently identified to be sold although the quantity of the bulk is not determined. Any agreed proportion of such a bulk or any

quantity thereof agreed upon by number, weight or other measure may to the extent of the seller's interest in the bulk be sold to the buyer who then becomes an owner in common.

(5) "Lot" means a parcel or a single article which is the subject matter of a separate sale or delivery, whether or not it is sufficient to perform the contract.

(6) "Commercial unit" means such a unit of goods as by commercial usage is a single whole for purposes of sale and division of which materially impairs its character or value on the market or in use. A commercial unit may be a single article (as a machine) or a set of articles (as a suite of furniture or an assortment of sizes) or a quantity (as a bale, gross, or carload) or any other unit treated in use or in the relevant market as a single whole.

§2-106. Definitions: "Contract"; "Agreement"; "Contract for sale"; "Sale"; "Present Sale"; "Conforming" to Contract; "Termination"; "Cancellation"

(1) In this Article unless the context otherwise requires "contract" and "agreement" are limited to those relating to the present or future sale of goods. "Contract for sale" includes both a present sale of goods and a contract to sell goods at a future time. A "sale" consists in the passing of title from the seller to the buyer for a price (Section 2-401). A "present sale" means a sale which is accomplished by the making of the contract.

(2) Goods or conduct including any part of a performance are "conforming" or conform to the contract when they are in accordance with the obligations under the contract.

(3) "Termination" occurs when either party pursuant to a power created by agreement or law puts an end to the contract otherwise than for its breach. On "termination" all obligations which are still executory on both sides are discharged but any right based on prior breach or performance survives.

(4) "Cancellation" occurs when either party puts an end to the contract for breach by the other and its effect is the same as that of "termination" except that the cancelling party also retains any remedy for breach of the whole contract or any unperformed balance.

§2-107. Goods to Be Severed From Realty: Recording

(1) A contract for the sale of minerals or the like (including oil and gas) or a structure or its materials to be removed from realty is a contract for the sale of goods within this Article if they are to be severed by the seller but until severance a purported present sale thereof which is not effective as a transfer of an interest in land is effective only as a contract to sell.

(2) A contract for the sale apart from the land of growing crops or other things attached to realty and capable of severance without material harm thereto but not described in subsection (1) or of timber to be cut is a contract for the sale of goods within this Article whether the subject matter is to be severed by the buyer or by the seller even though it forms part of the realty at the time of contracting, and the parties can by identification effect a present sale before severance.

(3) The provisions of this section are subject to any third party rights provided by the law relating to realty records, and the contract for sale may be executed and recorded as a document transferring an interest in land and shall then constitute notice to third parties of the buyer's rights under the contract for sale.

PART 2. FORM, FORMATION AND READJUSTMENT OF CONTRACT

§2-201. Formal Requirements; Statute of Frauds

(1) Except as otherwise provided in this section a contract for the sale of goods for the price of $500 or more is not enforceable by way of action or defense unless there is some writing sufficient to indicate that a contract for sale has been made between the parties and signed by the party against whom enforcement is sought or by his authorized agent or broker. A writing

is not insufficient because it omits or incorrectly states a term agreed upon but the contract is not enforceable under this paragraph beyond the quantity of goods shown in such writing.

(2) Between merchants if within a reasonable time a writing in confirmation of the contract and sufficient against the sender is received and the party receiving it has reason to know its contents, it satisfies the requirements of subsection (1) against such party unless written notice of objection to its contents is given within 10 days after it is received.

(3) A contract which does not satisfy the requirements of subsection (1) but which is valid in other respects is enforceable

(a) if the goods are to be specially manufactured for the buyer and are not suitable for sale to others in the ordinary course of the seller's business and the seller, before notice of repudiation is received and under circumstances that reasonably indicate that the goods are for the buyer, has made either a substantial beginning of their manufacture or commitments for their procurement; or

(b) if the party against whom enforcement is sought admits in his pleading, testimony or otherwise in court that a contract for sale was made, but the contract is not enforceable under this provision beyond the quantity of goods admitted; or

(c) with respect to goods for which payment has been made and accepted or which have been received and accepted (Sec. 2-606).

§2-202. Final Written Expression: Parol or Extrinsic Evidence

(1) Terms with respect to which the confirmatory memoranda of the parties agree or which are otherwise set forth in a writing intended by the parties as a final expression of their agreement with respect to such terms as are included therein may not be contradicted by evidence of any prior agreement or of a contemporaneous oral agreement but may be explained or supplemented

(a) by course of dealing or usage of trade (Section 1-205) or by course of performance (Section 2-208); and

(b) by evidence of consistent additional terms unless the court finds the writing to have been intended also as a complete and exclusive statement of the terms of the agreement. [...]

§2-204. Formation in General

(1) A contract for sale of goods may be made in any manner sufficient to show agreement, including conduct by both parties which recognizes the existence of such a contract.

(2) An agreement sufficient to constitute a contract for sale may be found even though the moment of its making is undetermined.

(3) Even though one or more terms are left open a contract for sale does not fail for indefiniteness if the parties have intended to make a contract and there is a reasonably certain basis for giving an appropriate remedy.

§2-205. Firm Offers

An offer by a merchant to buy or sell goods in a signed writing which by its terms gives assurance that it will be held open is not revocable, for lack of consideration, during the time stated or if no time is stated for a reasonable time, but in no event may such period of irrevocability exceed three months; but any such term of assurance on a form supplied by the offeree must be separately signed by the offeror.

§2-206. Offer and Acceptance in Formation of Contract

(1) Unless otherwise unambiguously indicated by the language or circumstances

(a) an offer to make a contract shall be construed as inviting acceptance in any manner and by any medium reasonable in the circumstances:

(b) an order or other offer to buy goods for prompt or current shipment shall be construed as inviting acceptance either by a prompt promise to ship or by the prompt or current shipment of conforming or non-conforming goods, but such a shipment of non-conforming goods does not constitute an acceptance if the seller seasonably notifies the buyer that the shipment is offered only as an accommodation to the buyer.

(2) Where the beginning of a requested performance is a reasonable mode of acceptance an offeror who is not notified of acceptance within a reasonable time may treat the offer as having lapsed before acceptance.

§2-207. Additional Terms in Acceptance or Confirmation

(1) A definite and seasonable expression of acceptance or a written confirmation which is sent within a reasonable time operates as an acceptance even though it states terms additional to or different from those offered or agreed upon, unless acceptance is expressly made conditional on assent to the additional or different terms.

(2) The additional terms are to be construed as proposals for addition to the contract. Between merchants such terms become part of the contract unless:

(a) the offer expressly limits acceptance to the terms of the offer;

(b) they materially alter it; or

(c) notification of objection to them has already been given or is given within a reasonable time after notice of them is received.

(3) Conduct by both parties which recognizes the existence of a contract is sufficient to establish a contract for sale although the writings of the parties do not otherwise establish a contract. In such case the terms of the particular contract consist of those terms on which the writings of the parties agree, together with any supplementary terms incorporated under any other provisions of this Act.

§2-208. Course of Performance or Practical Construction

(1) Where the contract for sale involves repeated occasions for performance by either party with knowledge of the nature of the performance and opportunity for objection to it by the other, any course of performance accepted or acquiesced in without objection shall be relevant to determine the meaning of the agreement.

(2) The express terms of the agreement and any such course of performance, as well as any course of dealing and usage of trade, shall be construed whenever reasonable as consistent with each other; but when such construction is unreasonable, express terms shall control course of performance and course of performance shall control both course of dealing and usage of trade (Section 1-205).

(3) Subject to the provisions of the next section on modification and waiver, such course of performance shall be relevant to show a waiver or modification of any term inconsistent with such course of performance.

§2-209. Modification, Rescission and Waiver

(1) An agreement modifying a contract within this Article needs no consideration to be binding.

(2) A signed agreement which excludes modification or rescission except by a signed writing cannot be otherwise modified or rescinded, but except as between merchants such a requirement on a form supplied by the merchant must be separately signed by the other party.

(3) The requirements of the statute of frauds section of this Article (Section 2-201) must be satisfied if the contract as modified is within its provisions.

(4) Although an attempt at modification or rescission does not satisfy the requirements of subsection (2) or (3) it can operate as a waiver.

(5) A party who has made a waiver affecting an executory portion of the contract may retract the waiver by reasonable notification received by the other party that strict performance will be required of any term waived, unless the retraction would be unjust in view of a material change of position in reliance on the waiver.

§2-210. Delegation of Performance; Assignment of Rights

(1) A party may perform his duty through a delegate unless otherwise agreed or unless the other party has a substantial interest in having his original promisor perform or control the acts required by the contract. No delegation of performance relieves the party delegating of any duty to perform or any liability for breach.

(2) Unless otherwise agreed all rights of either seller or buyer can be assigned except where the assignment would materially change the duty of the other party, or increase materially the burden or risk imposed on him by his contract, or impair materially his chance of obtaining return performance. A right to damages for breach of the whole contract or a right arising out of the assignor's due performance of his entire obligation can be assigned despite agreement otherwise.

(3) Unless the circumstances indicate the contrary a prohibition of assignment of "the contract" is to be construed as barring only the delegation to the assignee of the assignor's performance.

(4) An assignment of "the contract" or of "all my rights under the contract" or an assignment in similar general terms is an assignment of rights and unless the language or the circumstances (as in an assignment for security) indicate the contrary, it is a delegation of performance of the duties of the assignor and its acceptance by the assignee constitutes a promise by him to perform those duties. This promise is enforceable by either the assignor or the other party to the original contract.

(5) The other party may treat any assignment which delegates performance as creating reasonable grounds for insecurity and may without prejudice to his rights against the assignor demand assurances from the assignee (Section 2-609).

PART 3. GENERAL OBLIGATION AND CONSTRUCTION OF CONTRACT

§2-301. General Obligations of Parties

The obligation of the seller is to transfer and deliver and that of the buyer is to accept and pay in accordance with the contract.

§2-302. Unconscionable Contract or Term

(1) If the court as a matter of law finds the contract or any clause of the contract to have been unconscionable at the time it was made the court may refuse to enforce the contract, or it may enforce the remainder of the contract without the unconscionable clause, or it may so limit the application of any unconscionable clause as to avoid any unconscionable result.

(2) When it is claimed or appears to the court that the contract or any clause thereof may be unconscionable the parties shall be afforded a reasonable opportunity to present evidence as to its commercial setting, purpose, and effect to aid the court in making the determination.

§2-303. Allocation or Division of Risks

Where this Article allocates a risk or a burden as between the parties "unless otherwise agreed", the agreement may not only shift the allocation but may also divide the risk or burden.

§2-304. Price Payable in Money, Goods, Realty, or Otherwise

(1) The price can be made payable in money or otherwise. If it is payable in whole or in part in goods each party is a seller of the goods which he is to transfer.

(2) Even though all or part of the price is payable in an interest in realty the transfer of the goods and the seller's obligations with reference to them are subject to this Article, but not the transfer of the interest in realty or the transferor's obligations in connection therewith.

§2-305. Open Price Term

(1) The parties if they so intend can conclude a contract for sale even if the price is not settled. In such a case the price is a reasonable price at the time for delivery if

(a) nothing is said as to price; or

(b) the price is left to be agreed by the parties and they fail to agree; or

(c) the price is to be fixed in terms of some agreed market or other standard as set or recorded by a third person or agency and it is not so set or recorded.

(2) A price to be fixed by the seller or by the buyer means a price for him to fix in good faith.

(3) If a price left to be fixed otherwise than by agreement of the parties fails to be fixed through fault of one party the other may at his option treat the contract as cancelled or himself fix a reasonable price.

(4) Where, however, the parties intend not to be bound unless the price be fixed or agreed and it is not fixed or agreed there is no contract. In such a case the buyer must return any goods already received or if unable to do so must pay their reasonable value at the time of delivery and the seller must return any portion of the price paid on account.

§2-306. Output, Requirements and Exclusive Dealings

(1) A term which measures the quantity by the output of the seller or the requirements of the buyer means such actual output or requirements as may occur in good faith, except that no quantity unreasonably disproportionate to any stated estimate or in the absence of a stated estimate to any normal or otherwise comparable prior output or requirements may be tendered or demanded.

(2) A lawful agreement by either the seller or the buyer for exclusive dealing in the kind of goods concerned imposes unless otherwise agreed an obligation by the seller to use best efforts to supply the goods and by the buyer to use best efforts to promote their sale.

§2-307. Delivery in Single Lot or Several Lots

Unless otherwise agreed all goods called for by a contract for sale must be tendered in a single delivery and payment is due only on such tender but where the circumstances give either party the right to make or demand delivery in lots the price if it can be apportioned may be demanded for each lot.

§2-308. Absence of Specified Place for Delivery

Unless otherwise agreed

(a) the place for delivery of goods is the seller's place of business or if he has none his residence; but

(b) in a contract for sale of identified goods which to the knowledge of the parties at the time of contracting are in some other place, that place is the place for their delivery; and

(c) documents of title may be delivered through customary banking channels.

§2-309. Absence of Specific Time Provisions; Notice of Termination

(1) The time for shipment or delivery or any other action under a contract if not provided in this Article or agreed upon shall be a reasonable time.

(2) Where the contract provides for successive performances but is indefinite in duration it is valid for a reasonable time but unless otherwise agreed may be terminated at any time by either party.

(3) Termination of a contract by one party except on the happening of an agreed event requires that reasonable notification be received by the other party and an agreement dispensing with notification is invalid if its operation would be unconscionable.

§2-310. Open Time for Payment or Running of Credit; Authority to Ship Under Reservation

Unless otherwise agreed

(a) payment is due at the time and place at which the buyer is to receive the goods even though the place of shipment is the place of delivery; and

(b) if the seller is authorized to send the goods he may ship them under reservation, and may tender the documents of title, but the buyer may inspect the goods after their arrival before payment is due unless such inspection is inconsistent with the terms of the contract (Section 2-513); and

(c) if delivery is authorized and made by way of documents of title otherwise than by subsection (b) then payment is due at the time and place at which the buyer is to receive delivery of the tangible documents, or (ii) at the time the buyer is to receive the documents regardless of where the goods are to be received; and

(d) where the seller is required or authorized to ship the goods on credit the credit period runs from the time of shipment but post-dating the invoice or delaying its dispatch will correspondingly delay the starting of the credit period.

§2-311. Options and Cooperation Respecting Performance

(1) An agreement for sale which is otherwise sufficiently definite (subsection (3) of Section 2-204) to be a contract is not made invalid by the fact that it leaves particulars of performance to be specified by one of the parties. Any such specification must be made in good faith and within limits set by commercial reasonableness.

(2) Unless otherwise agreed specifications relating to assortment of the goods are at the buyer's option and except as otherwise provided in subsections (1)(c) and (3) of Section 2-319 specifications or arrangements relating to shipment are at the seller's option.

(3) Where such specification would materially affect the other party's performance but is not seasonably made or where one party's cooperation is necessary to the agreed performance of the other but is not seasonably forthcoming, the other party in addition to all other remedies

(a) is excused for any resulting delay in his own performance; and

(b) may also either proceed to perform in any reasonable manner or after the time for a material part of his own performance treat the failure to specify or to cooperate as a breach by failure to deliver or accept the goods.

§2-312. Warranty of Title and Against Infringement; Buyer's Obligation Against Infringement

(1) Subject to subsection (2), there is in a contract for sale a warranty by the seller that

(a) the title conveyed shall be good and its transfer rightful; and

(b) the goods shall be delivered free from any security interest or other lien or encumbrance of which the buyer at the time of contracting has no knowledge.

(2) A warranty under subsection (1) will be excluded or modified only by specific language or by circumstances which give the buyer reason to know that the person selling does not claim title in himself or that he is purporting to sell only such right or title as he or a third person may have.

(3) Unless otherwise agreed a seller who is a merchant regularly dealing in goods of the kind warrants that the goods shall be delivered free of the rightful claim of any third person by way of infringement or the like but a buyer who furnishes specifications to the seller must hold the seller harmless against any such claim which arises out of compliance with the specifications.

§2-313. Express Warranties by Affirmation, Promise, Description, Sample

(1) Express warranties by the seller are created as follows:

(a) Any affirmation of fact or promise made by the seller to the buyer which relates to the goods and becomes part of the basis of the bargain creates an express warranty that the goods shall conform to the affirmation or promise.

(b) Any description of the goods which is made part of the basis of the bargain creates an express warranty that the goods shall conform to the description.

(c) Any sample or model which is made part of the basis of the bargain creates an express warranty that the whole of the goods shall conform to the sample or model.

(2) It is not necessary to the creation of an express warranty that the seller use formal words such as "warrant" or "guarantee" or that he have a specific intention to make a warranty, but an affirmation merely of the value of the goods or a statement purporting to be merely the seller's opinion or commendation of the goods does not create a warranty.

§2-314. Implied Warranty: Merchantability; Usage of Trade

(1) Unless excluded or modified (Section 2-316), a warranty that the goods shall be merchantable is implied in a contract for their sale if the seller is a merchant with respect to goods of that kind. Under this section the serving for value of food or drink to be consumed either on the premises or elsewhere is a sale.

(2) Goods to be merchantable must be at least such as:

(a) pass without objection in the trade under the contract description; and

(b) in the case of fungible goods, are of fair average quality within the description; and

(c) are fit for the ordinary purposes for which goods of that description are used; and

(d) run, within the variations permitted by the agreement, of even kind, quality and quantity within each unit and among all units involved; and

(e) are adequately contained, packaged, and labeled as the agreement may require; and

(f) conform to the promise or affirmations of fact made on the container or label if any.

(3) Unless excluded or modified (Section 2-316) other implied warranties may arise from course of dealing or usage of trade.

§2-315. Implied Warranty: Fitness for Particular Purpose

Where the seller at the time of contracting has reason to know any particular purpose for which the goods are required and that the buyer is relying on the seller's skill or judgment to select or furnish suitable goods, there is unless excluded or modified under the next section an implied warranty that the goods shall be fit for such purpose.

§2-316. Exclusion or Modification of Warranties

(1) Words or conduct relevant to the creation of an express warranty and words or conduct tending to negate or limit warranty shall be construed wherever reasonable as consistent with each other; but subject to the provisions of this Article on parol or extrinsic evidence (Section 2-202), negation or limitation is inoperative to the extent that such construction is unreasonable.

(2) Subject to subsection (3), to exclude or modify the implied warranty of merchantability or any part of it the language must mention merchantability and in case of writing must be conspicuous, and to exclude or modify any implied warranty of fitness the exclusion must be by a writing and conspicuous. Language to exclude all implied warranties of fitness is sufficient if it states, for example, that "There are no warranties which extend beyond the description on the face hereof."

(3) Notwithstanding subsection (2)

(a) unless the circumstances indicate otherwise, all implied warranties are excluded by expressions like "as is", "with all faults" or other language that in common understanding calls the buyer's attention to the exclusion of warranties and makes plain that there is no implied warranty; and

(b) when the buyer before entering into the contract has examined the goods or the sample or model as fully as desired or has refused to examine the goods there is no implied warranty with regard to defects which an examination ought in the circumstances have revealed to him; and

(c) an implied warranty can also be excluded or modified by course of dealing or course of performance or usage of trade.

(4) Remedies for breach of warranty can be limited in accordance with the provisions of this Article on liquidation or limitation of damages and on contractual modification of remedy (Sections 2-718 and 2-719).

§2-317. Cumulation and Conflict of Warranties Express or Implied

Warranties whether express or implied shall be construed as consistent with each other and as cumulative, but if such construction is unreasonable the intention of the parties shall determine which warranty is dominant. In ascertaining that intention the following rules apply:

(a) Exact or technical specifications displace an inconsistent sample or model or general language of description.

(b) A sample from an existing bulk displaces inconsistent general language of description.

(c) Express warranties displace inconsistent implied warranties other than an implied warranty of fitness for a particular purpose.

§2-318. Third Party Beneficiaries of Warranties Express or Implied

Alternative A

A seller's warranty whether express or implied extends to any natural person who is in the family or household of his buyer or who is a guest in his home if it is reasonable to expect that such person may use, consume or be affected by the goods and who is injured in person by breach of the warranty. A seller may not exclude or limit the operation of this section.

Alternative B

A seller's warranty whether express or implied extends to any natural person who may reasonably be expected to use, consume or be affected by the goods and who is injured in person by breach of the warranty. A seller may not exclude or limit the operation of this section.

Alternative C

A seller's warranty whether express or implied extends to any person who may reasonably be expected to use, consume or be affected by the goods and who is injured by breach of the warranty. A seller may not exclude or limit the operation of this section with respect to injury to the person of an individual to whom the warranty extends.

§2-319. F.O.B. and F.A.S. Terms

(1) Unless otherwise agreed the term F.O.B. (which means "free on board") at a named place, even though used only in connection with the stated price, is a delivery term under which

(a) when the term is F.O.B. the place of shipment, the seller must at that place ship the goods in the manner provided in this Article (Section 2-504) and bear the expense and risk of putting them into the possession of the carrier; or

(b) when the term is F.O.B. the place of destination, the seller must at his own expense and risk transport the goods to that place and there tender delivery of them in the manner provided in this Article (Section 2-503);

(c) when under either (a) or (b) the term is also F.O.B. vessel, car or other vehicle, the seller must in addition at his own expense and risk load the goods on board. If the term is F.O.B. vessel the buyer must name the vessel and in an appropriate case the seller must comply with the provisions of this Article on the form of bill of lading (Section 2-323).

(2) Unless otherwise agreed the term F.A.S. vessel (which means "free alongside") at a named port, even though used only in connection with the stated price, is a delivery term under which the seller must

(a) at his own expense and risk deliver the goods alongside the vessel in the manner usual in that port or on a dock designated and provided by the buyer; and

(b) obtain and tender a receipt for the goods in exchange for which the carrier is under a duty to issue a bill of lading.

(3) Unless otherwise agreed in any case falling within subsection (1)(a) or (c) or subsection (2) the buyer must seasonably give any needed instructions for making delivery, including when the term is F.A.S. or F.O.B. the loading berth of the vessel and in an appropriate case its name and sailing date. The seller may treat the failure of needed instructions as a failure of cooperation under this Article (Section 2-311). He may also at his option move the goods in any reasonable manner preparatory to delivery or shipment.

(4) Under the term F.O.B. vessel or F.A.S. unless otherwise agreed the buyer must make payment against tender of the required documents and the seller may not tender nor the buyer demand delivery of the goods in substitution for the documents.

§2-320. C.I.F. and C. & F. Terms

(1) The term C.I.F. means that the price includes in a lump sum the cost of the goods and the insurance and freight to the named destination. The term C. & F. or C.F. means that the price so includes cost and freight to the named destination.

(2) Unless otherwise agreed and even though used only in connection with the stated price and destination, the term C.I.F. destination or its equivalent requires the seller at his own expense and risk to

(a) put the goods into the possession of a carrier at the port for shipment and obtain a negotiable bill or bills of lading covering the entire transportation to the named destination; and

(b) load the goods and obtain a receipt from the carrier (which may be contained in the bill of lading) showing that the freight has been paid or provided for; and

(c) obtain a policy or certificate of insurance, including any war risk insurance, of a kind and on terms then current at the port of shipment in the usual amount, in the currency of the contract, shown to cover the same goods covered by the bill of lading and providing for payment of loss to the order of the buyer or for the account of whom it may concern; but the seller may add to the price the amount of the premium for any such war risk insurance; and

(d) prepare an invoice of the goods and procure any other documents required to effect shipment or to comply with the contract; and

(e) forward and tender with commercial promptness all the documents in due form and with any indorsement necessary to perfect the buyer's rights.

(3) Unless otherwise agreed the term C. & F. or its equivalent has the same effect and imposes upon the seller the same obligations and risks as a C.I.F. term except the obligation as to insurance.

(4) Under the term C.I.F. or C. & F. unless otherwise agreed the buyer must make payment against tender of the required documents and the seller may not tender nor the buyer demand delivery of the goods in substitution for the documents.

§2-321. C.I.F. or C. & F.: "Net Landed Weights"; "Payment on Arrival"; Warranty of Condition on Arrival

Under a contract containing a term C.I.F. or C. & F.

(1) Where the price is based on or is to be adjusted according to "net landed weights", "delivered weights", "out turn" quantity or quality or the like, unless otherwise agreed the seller must reasonably estimate the price. The payment due on tender of the documents called for by the contract is the amount so estimated, but after final adjustment of the price a settlement must be made with commercial promptness.

(2) An agreement described in subsection (1) or any warranty of quality or condition of the goods on arrival places upon the seller the risk of ordinary deterioration, shrinkage and the like in transportation but has no effect on the place or time of identification to the contract for sale or delivery or on the passing of the risk of loss.

(3) Unless otherwise agreed where the contract provides for payment on or after arrival of the goods the seller must before payment allow such preliminary inspection as is feasible; but if the goods are lost delivery of the documents and payment are due when the goods should have arrived.

§2-322. Delivery "Ex-Ship"

(1) Unless otherwise agreed a term for delivery of goods "ex-ship" (which means from the carrying vessel) or in equivalent language is not restricted to a particular ship and requires delivery from a ship which has reached a place at the named port of destination where goods of the kind are usually discharged.

(2) Under such a term unless otherwise agreed

(a) the seller must discharge all liens arising out of the carriage and furnish the buyer with a direction which puts the carrier under a duty to deliver the goods; and

(b) the risk of loss does not pass to the buyer until the goods leave the ship's tackle or are otherwise properly unloaded.

§2-323. Form of Bill of Lading Required in Overseas Shipment; "Overseas"

(1) Where the contract contemplates overseas shipment and contains a term C.I.F. or C. & F. or F.O.B. vessel, the seller unless otherwise agreed must obtain a negotiable bill of lading stating that the goods have been loaded in board or, in the case of a term C.I.F. or C. & F., received for shipment.

(2) Where in a case within subsection (1) a bill of lading has been issued in a set of parts, unless otherwise agreed if the documents are not to be sent from abroad the buyer may demand tender of the full set; otherwise only one part of the bill of lading need be tendered. Even if the agreement expressly requires a full set

(a) due tender of a single part is acceptable within the provisions of this Article on cure of improper delivery (subsection (1) of Section 2-508); and

(b) even though the full set is demanded, if the documents are sent from abroad the person tendering an incomplete set may nevertheless require payment upon furnishing an indemnity which the buyer in good faith deems adequate.

(3) A shipment by water or by air or a contract contemplating such shipment is "overseas" insofar as by usage of trade or agreement it is subject to the commercial, financing or shipping practices characteristic of international deep water commerce.

§2-324. "No Arrival, No Sale" Term

Under a term, "no sale no arrival" or terms of like meaning, unless otherwise agreed,

(a) the seller must properly ship conforming goods and if they arrive by any means he must tender them on arrival but he assumes no obligation that the goods will arrive unless he has caused the non-arrival; and

(b) where without fault of the seller the goods are in part lost or have so deteriorated as no longer to conform to the contract or arrive after the contract time, the buyer may proceed as if there had been casualty to identified goods (Section 2-613).

§2-325. "Letter of Credit" Term; "Confirmed Credit"

(1) Failure of the buyer seasonably to furnish an agreed letter of credit is a breach of the contract for sale.

(2) The delivery to seller of a proper letter of credit suspends the buyer's obligation to pay. If the letter of credit is dishonored, the seller may on seasonable notification to the buyer require payment directly from him.

(3) Unless otherwise agreed the term "letter of credit" or "banker's credit" in a contract for sale means an irrevocable credit issued by a financing agency of good repute and, where the shipment is overseas, of good international repute. The term "confirmed credit" means that the credit must also carry the direct obligation of such an agency which does business in the seller's financial market.

§2-326. Sale on Approval and Sale or Return; Consignment Sales and Rights of Creditors

(1) Unless otherwise agreed, if delivered goods may be returned by the buyer even though they conform to the contract, the transaction is

(a) a "sale on approval" if the goods are delivered primarily for use; and

(b) a "sale or return" if the goods are delivered primarily for resale.

(2) Except as provided in subsection (3), goods held on approval are not subject to the claims of the buyer's creditors until acceptance; goods held on sale or return are subject to such claims while in the buyer's possession.

(3) Where goods are delivered to a person for sale and such person maintains a place of business at which he deals in goods of the kind involved, under a name other than the name of the person making delivery, then with respect to claims of creditors of the person conducting the business the goods are deemed to be on sale or return. The provisions of this subsection are applicable even though an agreement purports to reserve title to the person making delivery until payment or resale or uses such words as "on consignment" or "on memorandum". However, this subsection is not applicable if the person making delivery

(a) complies with an applicable law providing for a consignor's interest or the like to be evidenced by a sign, or

(b) establishes that the person conducting the business is generally known by his creditors to be substantially engaged in selling the goods of others, or

(c) complies with the filing provisions of the Article on Secured Transactions (Article 9).

(4) Any "or return" term of a contract for sale is to be treated as a separate contract for sale within the statute of frauds section of this Article (Section 2-201) and as contradicting the sale aspect of the contract within the provisions of this Article on parol or extrinsic evidence (Section 2-202).

§2-327. Special Incidents of Sale on Approval and Sale or Return

(1) Under a sale on approval unless otherwise agreed

(a) although the goods are identified to the contract the risk of loss and the title do not pass to the buyer until acceptance; and

(b) use of the goods consistent with the purpose of trial is not acceptance but failure seasonably to notify the seller of election to return the goods is acceptance, and if the goods conform to the contract acceptance of any part is acceptance of the whole; and

(c) after due notification of election to return, the return is at the seller's risk and expense but a merchant buyer must follow any reasonable instructions.

(2) Under a sale or return unless otherwise agreed

(a) the option to return extends to the whole or any commercial unit of the goods while in substantially their original condition, but must be exercised seasonably; and

(b) the return is at the buyer's risk and expense.

§2-328. Sale by Auction

(1) In a sale by auction, if goods are put up in lots each lot is the subject of a separate sale.

(2) A sale by auction is complete when the auctioneer so announces by the fall of the hammer or in other customary manner. If a bid is made while the hammer is falling in acceptance of a prior bid the auctioneer may in his discretion reopen the bidding or to declare the goods sold under the bid on which the hammer was falling.

(3) Such a sale is with reserve unless the goods are in explicit terms put up without reserve. In an auction with reserve the auctioneer may withdraw the goods at any time until he announces completion of the sale. In an auction without reserve, after the auctioneer calls for bids on an article or lot, that article or lot cannot be withdrawn unless no bid is made within a reasonable time. In either case a bidder may retract his bid until the auctioneer's announcement of completion of the sale, but a bidder's retraction does not revive any previous bid.

(4) If the auctioneer knowingly receives a bid on the seller's behalf or the seller makes or procures such a bid, and notice has not been given that liberty for such bidding is reserved, the buyer may at his option avoid the sale or take the goods at the price of the last good faith bid prior to the completion of the sale. This subsection shall not apply to any bid at a forced sale.

PART 4. TITLE, CREDITORS AND GOOD FAITH PURCHASERS

§2-401. Passing of Title; Reservation for Security; Limited Application of this Section

Each provision of this Article with regard to the rights, obligations and remedies of the seller, the buyer, purchasers or other third parties applies irrespective of title to the goods except where the provision refers to such title. Insofar as situations are not covered by the other provisions of this Article and matters concerning title become material the following rules apply:

(1) Title to goods cannot pass under a contract for sale prior to their identification to the contract (Section 2-501), and unless otherwise explicitly agreed the buyer acquires by their identification a special property as limited by this Act. Any retention or reservation by the seller of the title (property) in goods shipped or delivered to the buyer is limited in effect to a reservation of a security interest. Subject to these provisions and to the provisions of the Article on Secured Transactions (Article 9), title to goods passes from the seller to the buyer in any manner and on any conditions explicitly agreed on by the parties.

(2) Unless otherwise explicitly agreed title passes to the buyer at the time and place at which the seller completes his performance with reference to the physical delivery of the goods, despite any reservation of a security interest and even though a document of title is to be delivered at a different time or place; and in particular and despite any reservation of a security interest by the bill of lading

(a) if the contract requires or authorizes the seller to send the goods to the buyer but does not require him to deliver them at destination, title passes to the buyer at the time and place of shipment; but

(b) if the contract requires delivery at destination, title passes on tender there.

(3) Unless otherwise explicitly agreed where delivery is to be made without moving the goods,

(a) if the seller is to deliver a document of title, title passes at the time when and the place where he delivers such documents; or

(b) if the goods are at the time of contracting already identified and no documents are to be delivered, title passes at the time and place of contracting.

(4) A rejection or other refusal by the buyer to receive or retain the goods, whether or not justified, or a justified revocation of acceptance revests title to the goods in the seller. Such revesting occurs by operation of law and is not a "sale".

§2-402. Rights of Seller's Creditors Against Sold Goods

(1) Except as provided in subsections (2) and (3), rights of unsecured creditors of the seller with respect to goods which have been identified to a contract for sale are subject to the buyer's rights to recover the goods under this Article (Sections 2-502 and 2-716).

(2) A creditor of the seller may treat a sale or an identification of goods to a contract for sale as void if as against him a retention of possession by the seller is fraudulent under any rule of law of the state where the goods are situated, except that retention of possession in good faith and current course of trade by a merchant-seller for a commercially reasonable time after a sale or identification is not fraudulent.

(3) Nothing in this Article shall be deemed to impair the rights of creditors of the seller

(a) under the provisions of the Article on Secured Transactions (Article 9); or

(b) where identification to the contract or delivery is made not in current course of trade but in satisfaction of or as security for a pre-existing claim for money, security or the like and is made under circumstances which under any rule of law of the state where the goods are situated would apart from this Article constitute the transaction a fraudulent transfer or voidable preference.

§2-403. Power to Transfer; Good Faith Purchase of Goods; "Entrusting"

(1) A purchaser of goods acquires all title which his transferor had or had power to transfer except that a purchaser of a limited interest acquires rights only to the extent of the interest purchased. A person with voidable title has power to transfer a good title to a good faith purchaser for value. When goods have been delivered under a transaction of purchase the purchaser has such power even though

(a) the transferor was deceived as to the identity of the purchaser, or

(b) the delivery was in exchange for a check which is later dishonored, or

(c) it was agreed that the transaction was to be a "cash sale", or

(d) the delivery was procured through fraud punishable as larcenous under the criminal law.

(2) Any entrusting of possession of goods to a merchant that deals in goods of that kind gives him power to transfer all rights of the entruster to a buyer in ordinary course of business.

(3) "Entrusting" includes any delivery and any acquiescence in retention of possession regardless of any condition expressed between the parties to the delivery or acquiescence and regardless of whether the procurement of the entrusting or the possessor's disposition of the goods have been such as to be larcenous under the criminal law.

[Note: If a state adopts the repealer of Article 6-Bulk Transfers (Alternative A), subsec. (4) should read as follows:]

(4) The rights of other purchasers of goods and of lien creditors are governed by the Articles on Secured Transactions (Article 9) and Documents of Title (Article 7).

[Note: If a state adopts Revised Article 6-Bulk Sales (Alternative B), subsec. (4) should read as follows:]

(4) The rights of other purchasers of goods and of lien creditors are governed by the Articles on Secured Transactions (Article 9), Bulk Sales (Article 6) and Documents of Title (Article 7).

PART 5. PERFORMANCE

§2-501. Insurable Interest in Goods; Manner of Identification of Goods

(1) The buyer obtains a special property and an insurable interest in goods by identification of existing goods as goods to which the contract refers even though the goods so identified are non-conforming and he has an option to return or reject them. Such identification can be made at any time and in any manner explicitly agreed to by the parties. In the absence of explicit agreement identification occurs

(a) when the contract is made if it is for the sale of goods already existing and identified;

(b) if the contract is for the sale of future goods other than those described in paragraph (c), when goods are shipped, marked or otherwise designated by the seller as goods to which the contract refers;

(c) when the crops are planted or otherwise become growing crops or the young are conceived if the contract is for the sale of unborn young to be born within twelve months after contracting or for the sale of crops to be harvested within twelve months or the next normal harvest reason after contracting whichever is longer.

(2) The seller retains an insurable interest in goods so long as title to or any security interest in the goods remains in him and where the identification is by the seller alone he may until default or insolvency or notification to the buyer that the identification is final substitute other goods for those identified.

(3) Nothing in this section impairs any insurable interest recognized under any other statute or rule of law.

§2-502. Buyer's Right to Goods on Seller's Insolvency

(1) Subject to subsections (2) and even though the goods have not been shipped a buyer who has paid a part or all of the price of goods in which he has a special property under the provisions of the immediately preceding section may on making and keeping good a tender of any unpaid portion of their price recover them from the seller if the seller becomes insolvent within ten days after receipt of the first installment on their price.

(2) If the identification creating his special property has been made by the buyer he acquires the right to recover the goods only if they conform to the contract for sale.

§2-503. Manner of Seller's Tender of Delivery

(1) Tender of delivery requires that the seller put and hold conforming goods at the buyer's disposition and give the buyer any notification reasonably necessary to enable him to take delivery. The manner, time and place for tender are determined by the agreement and this Article, and in particular

(a) tender must be at a reasonable hour, and if it is of goods they must be kept available for the period reasonably necessary to enable the buyer to take possession; but

(b) unless otherwise agreed the buyer must furnish facilities reasonably suited to the receipt of the goods.

(2) Where the case is within the next section respecting shipment tender requires that the seller comply with its provisions.

(3) Where the seller is required to deliver at a particular destination tender requires that he comply with subsection (1) and also in any appropriate case tender documents as described in subsections (4) and (5) of this section.

(4) Where goods are in the possession of a bailee and are to be delivered without being moved

(a) tender requires that the seller either tender a negotiable document of title covering such goods or procure acknowledgment by the bailee of the buyer's right to possession of the goods; but

(b) tender to the buyer of a non-negotiable document of title or of a written direction to the bailee to deliver is sufficient tender unless the buyer seasonably objects, and receipt by the bailee of notification of the buyer's rights fixes those rights as against the bailee and all third persons; but risk of loss of the goods and of any failure by the bailee to honor the non-negotiable document of title or to obey the direction remains on the seller until the buyer has had a reasonable time to present the document or direction, and a refusal by the bailee to honor the document or to obey the direction defeats the tender.

(5) Where the contract requires the seller to deliver documents

(a) he must tender all such documents in correct form, except as provided in this Article with respect to bills of lading in a set (subsection (2) of Section 2-323); and

(b) tender through customary banking channels is sufficient and dishonor of a draft accompanying the documents constitutes non-acceptance or rejection.

§2-504. Shipment by Seller

Where the seller is required or authorized to send the goods to the buyer and the contract does not require him to deliver them at a particular destination, then unless otherwise agreed he must

(a) put the goods in the possession of such a carrier and make such a contract for their transportation as may be reasonable having regard to the nature of the goods and other circumstances of the case; and

(b) obtain and promptly deliver or tender in due form any document necessary to enable the buyer to obtain possession of the goods or otherwise required by the agreement or by usage of trade; and

(c) promptly notify the buyer of the shipment.

Failure to notify the buyer under paragraph (c) or to make a proper contract under paragraph (a) is a ground for rejection only if material delay or loss ensues.

§2-505. Seller's Shipment Under Reservation

(1) Where the seller has identified goods to the contract by or before shipment:

(a) his procurement of a negotiable bill of lading to his own order or otherwise reserves in him a security interest in the goods. His procurement of the bill to the order of a financing agency or of the buyer indicates in addition only the seller's expectation of transferring that interest to the person named.

(b) a non-negotiable bill of lading to himself or his nominee reserves possession of the goods as security but except in a case of conditional delivery (subsection (2) of Section 2-507) a non-negotiable bill of lading naming the buyer as consignee reserves no security interest even though the seller retains possession or control of the bill of lading.

(2) When shipment by the seller with reservation of a security interest is in violation of the contract for sale it constitutes an improper contract for transportation within the preceding section but impairs neither the rights given to the buyer by shipment and identification of the goods to the contract nor the seller's powers as a holder of a negotiable document of title.

§2-506. Rights of Financing Agency

(1) A financing agency by paying or purchasing for value a draft which relates to a shipment of goods acquires to the extent of the payment or purchase and in addition to its own rights under the draft and any document of title securing it any rights of the shipper in the goods including the right to stop delivery and the shipper's right to have the draft honored by the buyer.

(2) The right to reimbursement of a financing agency which has in good faith honored or purchased the draft under commitment to or authority from the buyer is not impaired by subsequent discovery of defects with reference to any relevant document which was apparently regular on its face.

§2-507. Effect of Seller's Tender; Delivery on Condition

(1) Tender of delivery is a condition to the buyer's duty to accept the goods and, unless otherwise agreed, to his duty to pay for them. Tender entitles the seller to acceptance of the goods and to payment according to the contract.

(2) Where payment is due and demanded on the delivery to the buyer of goods or documents of title, his right as against the seller to retain or dispose of them is conditional upon his making the payment due.

§2-508. Cure by Seller of Improper Tender or Delivery; Replacement

(1) Where any tender or delivery by the seller is rejected because non-conforming and the time for performance has not yet expired, the seller may seasonably notify the buyer of his intention to cure and may then within the contract time make a conforming delivery.

(2) Where the buyer rejects a non-conforming tender which the seller had reasonable grounds to believe would be acceptable with or without money allowance the seller may if he seasonably notifies the buyer have a further reasonable time to substitute a conforming tender.

§2-509. Risk of Loss in the Absence of Breach

(1) Where the contract requires or authorizes the seller to ship the goods by carrier

(a) if it does not require him to deliver them at a particular destination, the risk of loss passes to the buyer when the goods are duly delivered to the carrier even though the shipment is under reservation (Section 2-505); but

(b) if it does require him to deliver them at a particular destination and the goods are there duly tendered while in the possession of the carrier, the risk of loss passes to the buyer when the goods are there duly so tendered as to enable the buyer to take delivery.

(2) Where the goods are held by a bailee to be delivered without being moved, the risk of loss passes to the buyer

(a) on his receipt of a negotiable document of title covering the goods; or

(b) on acknowledgment by the bailee of the buyer's right to possession of the goods; or

(c) after his receipt of a non-negotiable document of title or other written direction to deliver, as provided in subsection (4)(b) of Section 2-503.

(3) In any case not within subsection (1) or (2), the risk of loss passes to the buyer on his receipt of the goods if the seller is a merchant; otherwise the risk passes to the buyer on tender of delivery.

(4) The provisions of this section are subject to contrary agreement of the parties and to the provisions of this Article on sale on approval (Section 2-327) and on effect of breach on risk of loss (Section 2-510).

§2-510. Effect of Breach on Risk of Loss

(1) Where a tender or delivery of goods so fails to conform to the contract as to give a right of rejection the risk of their loss remains on the seller until cure or acceptance.

(2) Where the buyer rightfully revokes acceptance he may to the extent of any deficiency in his effective insurance coverage treat the risk of loss as having rested on the seller from the beginning.

(3) Where the buyer as to conforming goods already identified to the contract for sale repudiates or is otherwise in breach before risk of their loss has passed to him, the seller may to the extent of any deficiency in his effective insurance coverage treat the risk of loss as resting on the buyer for a commercially reasonable time.

§2-511. Tender of Payment by Buyer; Payment by Check

(1) Unless otherwise agreed tender of payment is a condition to the seller's duty to tender and complete any delivery.

(2) Tender of payment is sufficient when made by any means or in any manner current in the ordinary course of business unless the seller demands payment in legal tender and gives any extension of time reasonably necessary to procure it.

(3) Subject to the provisions of this Act on the effect of an instrument on an obligation (Section 3-802), payment by check is conditional and is defeated as between the parties by dishonor of the check on due presentment.

§2-512. Payment by Buyer Before Inspection

(1) Where the contract requires payment before inspection non-conformity of the goods does not excuse the buyer from so making payment unless

(a) the non-conformity appears without inspection; or

(b) despite tender of the required documents the circumstances would justify injunction against honor under the provisions of this Act (Section 5-109(b)).

(2) Payment pursuant to subsection (1) does not constitute an acceptance of goods or impair the buyer's right to inspect or any of his remedies.

§2-513. Buyer's Right to Inspection of Goods

(1) Unless otherwise agreed and subject to subsection (3), where goods are tendered or delivered or identified to the contract for sale, the buyer has a right before payment or acceptance to inspect them at any reasonable place and time and in any reasonable manner. When the seller is required or authorized to send the goods to the buyer, the inspection may be after their arrival.

(2) Expenses of inspection must be borne by the buyer but may be recovered from the seller if the goods do not conform and are rejected.

(3) Unless otherwise agreed and subject to the provisions of this Article on C.I.F. contracts (subsection (3) of Section 2-321), the buyer is not entitled to inspect the goods before payment of the price when the contract provides

(a) for delivery "C.O.D." or on other like terms; or

(b) for payment against documents of title, except where such payment is due only after the goods are to become available for inspection.

(4) A place or method of inspection fixed by the parties is presumed to be exclusive but unless otherwise expressly agreed it does not postpone identification or shift the place for delivery or for passing the risk of loss. If compliance becomes impossible, inspection shall be as provided in this section unless the place or method fixed was clearly intended as an indispensable condition failure of which avoids the contract.

§2-514. When Documents Deliverable on Acceptance; When on Payment

Unless otherwise agreed documents against which a draft is drawn are to be delivered to the drawee on acceptance of the draft if it is payable more than three days after presentment; otherwise, only on payment.

§2-515. Preserving Evidence of Goods in Dispute

In furtherance of the adjustment of any claim or dispute

(a) either party on reasonable notification to the other and for the purpose of ascertaining the facts and preserving evidence has the right to inspect, test and sample the goods including such of them as may be in the possession or control of the other; and

(b) the parties may agree to a third party inspection or survey to determine the conformity or condition of the goods and may agree that the findings shall be binding upon them in any subsequent litigation or adjustment.

PART 6. BREACH, REPUDIATION AND EXCUSE

§2-601. Buyer's Rights on Improper Delivery

Subject to the provisions of this Article on breach in installment contracts (Section 2-612) and unless otherwise agreed under the sections on contractual limitations of remedy (Sections 2-718 and 2-719), if the goods or the tender of delivery fail in any respect to conform to the contract, the buyer may

(a) reject the whole; or

(b) accept the whole; or

(c) accept any commercial unit or units and reject the rest.

§2-602. Manner and Effect of Rightful Rejection

(1) Rejection of goods must be within a reasonable time after their delivery or tender. It is ineffective unless the buyer seasonably notifies the seller.

(2) Subject to the provisions of the two following sections on rejected goods (Sections 2-603 and 2-604),

(a) after rejection any exercise of ownership by the buyer with respect to any commercial unit is wrongful as against the seller; and

(b) if the buyer has before rejection taken physical possession of goods in which he does not have a security interest under the provisions of this Article (subsection (3) of Section 2-711), he is under a duty after rejection to hold them with reasonable care at the seller's disposition for a time sufficient to permit the seller to remove them; but

(c) the buyer has no further obligations with regard to goods rightfully rejected.

(3) The seller's rights with respect to goods wrongfully rejected are governed by the provisions of this Article on seller's remedies in general (Section 2-703).

§2-603. Merchant Buyer's Duties as to Rightfully Rejected Goods

(1) Subject to any security interest in the buyer (subsection (3) of Section 2-711), when the seller has no agent or place of business at the market of rejection a merchant buyer is under a duty after rejection of goods in his possession or control to follow any reasonable instructions received from the seller with respect to the goods and in the absence of such instructions to make reasonable efforts to sell them for the seller's account if they are perishable or threaten to decline in value speedily. Instructions are not reasonable if on demand indemnity for expenses is not forthcoming.

(2) When the buyer sells goods under subsection (1), he is entitled to reimbursement from the seller or out of the proceeds for reasonable expenses of caring for and selling them, and if the expenses include no selling commission then to such commission as is usual in the trade or if there is none to a reasonable sum not exceeding ten per cent on the gross proceeds.

(3) In complying with this section the buyer is held only to good faith and good faith conduct hereunder is neither acceptance nor conversion nor the basis of an action for damages.

§2-604. Buyer's Options as to Salvage of Rightfully Rejected Goods

Subject to the provisions of the immediately preceding section on perishables if the seller gives no instructions within a reasonable time after notification of rejection the buyer may store the rejected goods for the seller's account or reship them to him or resell them for the seller's account with reimbursement as provided in the preceding section. Such action is not acceptance or conversion.

§2-605. Waiver of Buyer's Objections by Failure to Particularize

(1) The buyer's failure to state in connection with rejection a particular defect which is ascertainable by reasonable inspection precludes him from relying on the unstated defect to justify rejection or to establish breach

(a) where the seller could have cured it if stated seasonably; or

(b) between merchants when the seller has after rejection made a request in writing for a full and final written statement of all defects on which the buyer proposes to rely.

(2) Payment against documents made without reservation of rights precludes recovery of the payment for defects apparent on the face of the documents.

§2-606. What Constitutes Acceptance of Goods

(1) Acceptance of goods occurs when the buyer

(a) after a reasonable opportunity to inspect the goods signifies to the seller that the goods are conforming or that he will take or retain them in spite of their non-conformity; or

(b) fails to make an effective rejection (subsection (1) of Section 2-602), but such acceptance does not occur until the buyer has had a reasonable opportunity to inspect them; or

(c) does any act inconsistent with the seller's ownership; but if such act is wrongful as against the seller it is an acceptance only if ratified by him.

(2) Acceptance of a part of any commercial unit is acceptance of that entire unit.

§2-607. Effect of Acceptance; Notice of Breach; Burden of Establishing Breach After Acceptance; Notice of Claim or Litigation to Person Answerable Over

(1) The buyer must pay at the contract rate for any goods accepted.

(2) Acceptance of goods by the buyer precludes rejection of the goods accepted and if made with knowledge of a non-conformity cannot be revoked because of it unless the acceptance was on the reasonable assumption that the non-conformity would be seasonably cured but acceptance does not of itself impair any other remedy provided by this Article for non-conformity.

(3) Where a tender has been accepted

(a) the buyer must within a reasonable time after he discovers or should have discovered any breach notify the seller of breach or be barred from any remedy; and

(b) if the claim is one for infringement or the like (subsection (3) of Section 2-312) and the buyer is sued as a result of such a breach he must so notify the seller within a reasonable time after he receives notice of the litigation or be barred from any remedy over for liability established by the litigation.

(4) The burden is on the buyer to establish any breach with respect to the goods accepted.

(5) Where the buyer is sued for breach of a warranty or other obligation for which his seller is answerable over

(a) he may give his seller written notice of the litigation. If the notice states that the seller may come in and defend and that if the seller does not do so he will be bound in any action against him by his buyer by any determination of fact common to the two litigations, then unless the seller after seasonable receipt of the notice does come in and defend he is so bound.

(b) if the claim is one for infringement or the like (subsection (3) of Section 2-312) the original seller may demand in writing that his buyer turn over to him control of the litigation including settlement or else be barred from any remedy over and if he also agrees to bear all expense and to satisfy any adverse judgment, then unless the buyer after seasonable receipt of the demand does turn over control the buyer is so barred.

(6) The provisions of subsections (3), (4) and (5) apply to any obligation of a buyer to hold the seller harmless against infringement or the like (subsection (3) of Section 2-312).

§2-608. Revocation of Acceptance in Whole or in Part

(1) The buyer may revoke his acceptance of a lot or commercial unit whose non-conformity substantially impairs its value to him if he has accepted it

(a) on the reasonable assumption that its non-conformity would be cured and it has not been seasonably cured; or

(b) without discovery of such non-conformity if his acceptance was reasonably induced either by the difficulty of discovery before acceptance or by the seller's assurances.

(2) Revocation of acceptance must occur within a reasonable time after the buyer discovers or should have discovered the ground for it and before any substantial change in condition of the goods which is not caused by their own defects. It is not effective until the buyer notifies the seller of it.

(3) A buyer who so revokes has the same rights and duties with regard to the goods involved as if he had rejected them.

§2-609. Right to Adequate Assurance of Performance

(1) A contract for sale imposes an obligation on each party that the other's expectation of receiving due performance will not be impaired. When reasonable grounds for insecurity arise with respect to the performance of either party the other may in writing demand adequate assurance of due performance and until he receives such assurance may if commercially reasonable suspend any performance for which he has not already received the agreed return.

(2) Between merchants the reasonableness of grounds for insecurity and the adequacy of any assurance offered shall be determined according to commercial standards.

(3) Acceptance of any improper delivery or payment does not prejudice the aggrieved party's right to demand adequate assurance of future performance.

(4) After receipt of a justified demand failure to provide within a reasonable time not exceeding thirty days such assurance of due performance as is adequate under the circumstances of the particular case is a repudiation of the contract.

§2-610. Anticipatory Repudiation

When either party repudiates the contract with respect to a performance not yet due the loss of which will substantially impair the value of the contract to the other, the aggrieved party may

(a) for a commercially reasonable time await performance by the repudiating party; or

(b) resort to any remedy for breach (Section 2-703 or Section 2-711), even though he has notified the repudiating party that he would await the latter's performance and has urged retraction; and

(c) in either case suspend his own performance or proceed in accordance with the provisions of this Article on the seller's right to identify goods to the contract notwithstanding breach or to salvage unfinished goods (Section 2-704).

§2-611. Retraction of Anticipatory Repudiation

(1) Until the repudiating party's next performance is due he can retract his repudiation unless the aggrieved party has since the repudiation cancelled or materially changed his position or otherwise indicated that he considers the repudiation final.

(2) Retraction may be by any method which clearly indicates to the aggrieved party that the repudiating party intends to perform, but must include any assurance justifiably demanded under the provisions of this Article (Section 2-609).

(3) Retraction reinstates the repudiating party's rights under the contract with due excuse and allowance to the aggrieved party for any delay occasioned by the repudiation.

§2-612. "Installment Contract"; Breach

(1) An "installment contract" is one which requires or authorizes the delivery of goods in separate lots to be separately accepted, even though the contract contains a clause "each delivery is a separate contract" or its equivalent.

(2) The buyer may reject any installment which is non-conforming if the non-conformity substantially impairs the value of that installment and cannot be cured or if the non-conformity is a defect in the required documents; but if the non-conformity does not fall within subsection (3) and the seller gives adequate assurance of its cure the buyer must accept that installment.

(3) Whenever non-conformity or default with respect to one or more installments substantially impairs the value of the whole contract there is a breach of the whole. But the aggrieved party reinstates the contract if he accepts a non-conforming installment without seasonably notifying of cancellation or if he brings an action with respect only to past installments or demands performance as to future installments.

§2-613. Casualty to Identified Goods

Where the contract requires for its performance goods identified when the contract is made, and the goods suffer casualty without fault of either party before the risk of loss passes to the buyer, or in a proper case under a "no arrival, no sale" term (Section 2-324) then

(a) if the loss is total the contract is avoided; and

(b) if the loss is partial or the goods have so deteriorated as no longer to conform to the contract the buyer may nevertheless demand inspection and at his option either treat the contract as avoided or accept the goods with due allowance from the contract price for the deterioration or the deficiency in quantity but without further right against the seller.

§2-614. Substituted Performance

(1) Where without fault of either party the agreed berthing, loading, or unloading facilities fail or an agreed type of carrier becomes unavailable or the agreed manner of delivery otherwise becomes commercially impracticable but a commercially reasonable substitute is available, such substitute performance must be tendered and accepted.

(2) If the agreed means or manner of payment fails because of domestic or foreign governmental regulation, the seller may withhold or stop delivery unless the buyer provides a means or manner of payment which is commercially a substantial equivalent. If delivery has already been taken, payment by the means or in the manner provided by the regulation discharges the buyer's obligation unless the regulation is discriminatory, oppressive or predatory.

§2-615. Excuse by Failure of Presupposed Conditions

Except so far as a seller may have assumed a greater obligation and subject to the preceding section on substituted performance:

(a) Delay in delivery or non-delivery in whole or in part by a seller who complies with paragraphs (b) and (c) is not a breach of his duty under a contract for sale if performance as agreed has been made impracticable by the occurrence of a contingency the non-occurrence of which was a basic assumption on which the contract was made or by compliance in good faith with any applicable foreign or domestic governmental regulation or order whether or not it later proves to be invalid.

(b) Where the causes mentioned in paragraph (a) affect only a part of the seller's capacity to perform, he must allocate production and deliveries among his customers but may at his option include regular customers not then under contract as well as his own requirements for further manufacture. He may so allocate in any manner which is fair and reasonable.

(c) The seller must notify the buyer seasonably that there will be delay or non-delivery and, when allocation is required under paragraph (b), of the estimated quota thus made available for the buyer.

§2-616. Procedure on Notice Claiming Excuse

(1) Where the buyer receives notification of a material or indefinite delay or an allocation justified under the preceding section he may by written notification to the seller as to any delivery concerned, and where the prospective deficiency substantially impairs the value of the whole contract under the provisions of this Article relating to breach of installment contracts (Section 2-612), then also as to the whole,

(a) terminate and thereby discharge any unexecuted portion of the contract; or

(b) modify the contract by agreeing to take his available quota in substitution.

(2) If after receipt of such notification from the seller the buyer fails so to modify the contract within a reasonable time not exceeding thirty days the contract lapses with respect to any deliveries affected.

(3) The provisions of this section may not be negated by agreement except in so far as the seller has assumed a greater obligation under the preceding sections.

PART 7. REMEDIES

§2-701. Remedies for Breach of Collateral Contracts Not Impaired

Remedies for breach of any obligation or promise collateral or ancillary to a contract for sale are not impaired by the provisions of this Article.

§2-702. Seller's Remedies on Discovery of Buyer's Insolvency

(1) Where the seller discovers the buyer to be insolvent he may refuse delivery except for cash including payment for all goods theretofore delivered under the contract, and stop delivery under this Article (Section 2-705).

(2) Where the seller discovers that the buyer has received goods on credit while insolvent he may reclaim the goods upon demand made within a ten days after the receipt, but if misrepresentation of solvency has been made to the particular seller in writing within three months before delivery the ten day limitation does not apply. Except as provided in this subsection the seller may not base a right to reclaim goods on the buyer's fraudulent or innocent misrepresentation of solvency or of intent to pay.

(3) The seller's right to reclaim under subsection (2) is subject to the rights of a buyer in ordinary course or other good faith purchaser under this Article (Section 2-403). Successful reclamation of goods excludes all other remedies with respect to them.

§2-703. Seller's Remedies in General

Where the buyer wrongfully rejects or revokes acceptance of goods or fails to make a payment due on or before delivery or repudiates with respect to a part or the whole, then with respect to any goods directly affected and, if the breach is of the whole contract (Section 2-612), then also with respect to the whole undelivered balance, the aggrieved seller may

(a) withhold delivery of such goods;

(b) stop delivery by any bailee as hereafter provided (Section 2-705);

(c) proceed under the next section respecting goods still unidentified to the contract;

(d) resell and recover damages as hereafter provided (Section 2-706);

(e) recover damages for non-acceptance (Section 2-708) or in a proper case the price (Section 2-709);

(f) cancel.

§2-704. Seller's Right to Identify Goods to the Contract Notwithstanding Breach or to Salvage Unfinished Goods

(1) An aggrieved seller under the preceding section may

(a) identify to the contract conforming goods not already identified if at the time he learned of the breach they are in his possession or control;

(b) treat as the subject of resale goods which have demonstrably been intended for the particular contract even though those goods are unfinished.

(2) Where the goods are unfinished an aggrieved seller may in the exercise of reasonable commercial judgment for the purposes of avoiding loss and of effective realization either complete the manufacture and wholly identify the goods to the contract or cease manufacture and resell for scrap or salvage value or proceed in any other reasonable manner.

§2-705. Seller's Stoppage of Delivery in Transit or Otherwise

(1) The seller may stop delivery of goods in the possession of a carrier or other bailee when he discovers the buyer to be insolvent (Section 2-702) and may stop delivery of carload, truckload, planeload or larger shipments of express or freight when the buyer repudiates or fails to make a payment due before delivery or if for any other reason the seller has a right to withhold or reclaim the goods.

(2) As against such buyer the seller may stop delivery until

(a) receipt of the goods by the buyer; or

(b) acknowledgment to the buyer by any bailee of the goods except a carrier that the bailee holds the goods for the buyer; or

(c) such acknowledgment to the buyer by a carrier by reshipment or as a warehouseman; or

(d) negotiation to the buyer of any negotiable document of title covering the goods.

(3)(a) To stop delivery the seller must so notify as to enable the bailee by reasonable diligence to prevent delivery of the goods.

(b) After such notification the bailee must hold and deliver the goods according to the directions of the seller but the seller is liable to the bailee for any ensuing charges or damages.

(c) If a negotiable document of title has been issued for goods the bailee is not obliged to obey a notification to stop until surrender of the document.

(d) A carrier who has issued a non-negotiable bill of lading is not obliged to obey a notification to stop received from a person other than the consignor.

§2-706. Seller's Resale Including Contract for Resale

(1) Under the conditions stated in Section 2-703 on seller's remedies, the seller may resell the goods concerned or the undelivered balance thereof. Where the resale is made in good faith and in a commercially reasonable manner the seller may recover the difference between the resale price and the contract price together with any incidental damages allowed under the provisions of this Article (Section 2-710), but less expenses saved in consequence of the buyer's breach.

(2) Except as otherwise provided in subsection (3) or unless otherwise agreed resale may be at public or private sale including sale by way of one or more contracts to sell or of identification to an existing contract of the seller. Sale may be as a unit or in parcels and at any time and place and on any terms but every aspect of the sale including the method, manner, time, place and terms must be commercially reasonable. The resale must be reasonably identified as referring to the broken contract, but it is not necessary that the goods be in existence or that any or all of them have been identified to the contract before the breach.

(3) Where the resale is at private sale the seller must give the buyer reasonable notification of his intention to resell.

(4) Where the resale is at public sale

(a) only identified goods can be sold except where there is a recognized market for a public sale of futures in goods of the kind; and

(b) it must be made at a usual place or market for public sale if one is reasonably available and except in the case of goods which are perishable or threaten to decline in value speedily the seller must give the buyer reasonable notice of the time and place of the resale; and

(c) if the goods are not to be within the view of those attending the sale the notification of sale must state the place where the goods are located and provide for their reasonable inspection by prospective bidders; and

(d) the seller may buy.

(5) A purchaser that buys in good faith at a resale takes the goods free of any rights of the original buyer even though the seller fails to comply with one or more of the requirements of this section.

(6) The seller is not accountable to the buyer for any profit made on any resale. A person in the position of a seller (Section 2-707) or a buyer that has rightfully rejected or justifiably revoked acceptance must account for any excess over the amount of his security interest, as hereinafter defined (subsection (3) of Section 2-711).

§2-707. "Person in the Position of a Seller"

(1) A "person in the position of a seller" includes as against a principal an agent who has paid or become responsible for the price of goods on behalf of his principal or anyone who otherwise holds a security interest or other right in goods similar to that of a seller.

(2) A person in the position of a seller may as provided in this Article withhold or stop delivery (Section 2-705) and resell (Section 2-706) and recover incidental damages (Section 2-710).

§2-708. Seller's Damages for Non-Acceptance or Repudiation

(1) Subject to subsection (2) and to the provisions of this Article with respect to proof of market price (Section 2-723), the measure of damages for non-acceptance or repudiation by the buyer is the difference between the market price at the time and place for tender and the unpaid contract price together with any incidental damages provided in this Article (Section 2-710), but less expenses saved in consequence of the buyer's breach.

(2) If the measure of damages provided in subsection (1) is inadequate to put the seller in as good a position as performance would have done then the measure of damages is the profit (including reasonable overhead) which the seller would have made from full performance by the buyer, together with any incidental damages provided in this Article (Section 2-710), due allowance for costs reasonably incurred and due credit for payments or proceeds of resale.

§2-709. Action for the Price

(1) When the buyer fails to pay the price as it becomes due the seller may recover, together with any incidental damages under the next section, the price

(a) of goods accepted or of conforming goods lost or damaged within a commercially reasonable time after risk of their loss has passed to the buyer; and

(b) of goods identified to the contract if the seller is unable after reasonable effort to resell them at a reasonable price or the circumstances reasonably indicate that such effort will be unavailing.

(2) Where the seller sues for the price he must hold for the buyer any goods which have been identified to the contract and are still in his control except that if resale becomes possible he may resell them at any time prior to the collection of the judgment. The net proceeds of any such resale must be credited to the buyer and payment of the judgment entitles him to any goods not resold.

(3) After the buyer has wrongfully rejected or revoked acceptance of the goods or has failed to make a payment due or has repudiated (Section 2-610), a seller who is held not entitled to the price under this section shall nevertheless be awarded damages for non-acceptance under the preceding section.

§2-710. Seller's Incidental Damages

Incidental damages to an aggrieved seller include any commercially reasonable charges, expenses or commissions incurred in stopping delivery, in the transportation, care and custody of goods after the buyer's breach, in connection with return or resale of the goods or otherwise resulting from the breach.

§2-711. Buyer's Remedies in General; Buyer's Security Interest in Rejected Goods

(1) Where the seller fails to make delivery or repudiates or the buyer rightfully rejects or justifiably revokes acceptance then with respect to any goods involved, and with respect to the whole if the breach goes to the whole contract (Section 2-612), the buyer may cancel and whether or not he has done so may in addition to recovering so much of the price as has been paid

(a) "cover" and have damages under the next section as to all the goods affected whether or not they have been identified to the contract; or

(b) recover damages for non-delivery as provided in this Article (Section 2-713).

(2) Where the seller fails to deliver or repudiates the buyer may also

(a) if the goods have been identified recover them as provided in this Article (Section 2-502); or

(b) in a proper case obtain specific performance or replevy the goods as provided in this Article (Section 2-716).

(3) On rightful rejection or justifiable revocation of acceptance a buyer has a security interest in goods in his possession or control for any payments made on their price and any expenses reasonably incurred in their inspection, receipt, transportation, care and custody and may hold such goods and resell them in like manner as an aggrieved seller (Section 2-706).

§2-712. "Cover"; Buyer's Procurement of Substitute Goods

(1) After a breach within the preceding section the buyer may "cover" by making in good faith and without unreasonable delay any reasonable purchase of or contract to purchase goods in substitution for those due from the seller.

(2) The buyer may recover from the seller as damages the difference between the cost of cover and the contract price together with any incidental or consequential damages as hereinafter defined (Section 2-715), but less expenses saved in consequence of the seller's breach.

(3) Failure of the buyer to effect cover within this section does not bar him from any other remedy.

§2-713. Buyer's Damages for Non-Delivery or Repudiation

(1) Subject to the provisions of this Article with respect to proof of market price (Section 2-723), the measure of damages for non-delivery or repudiation by the seller is the difference between the market price at the time when the buyer learned of the breach and the contract

price together with any incidental and consequential damages provided in this Article (Section 2-715), but less expenses saved in consequence of the seller's breach.

(2) Market price is to be determined as of the place for tender or, in cases of rejection after arrival or revocation of acceptance, as of the place of arrival.

§2-714. Buyer's Damages for Breach in Regard to Accepted Goods

(1) Where the buyer has accepted goods and given notification (subsection (3) of Section 2-607) he may recover as damages for any non-conformity of tender the loss resulting in the ordinary course of events from the seller's breach as determined in any manner which is reasonable.

(2) The measure of damages for breach of warranty is the difference at the time and place of acceptance between the value of the goods accepted and the value they would have had if they had been as warranted, unless special circumstances show proximate damages of a different amount.

(3) In a proper case any incidental and consequential damages under the next section may also be recovered.

§2-715. Buyer's Incidental and Consequential Damages

(1) Incidental damages resulting from the seller's breach include expenses reasonably incurred in inspection, receipt, transportation and care and custody of goods rightfully rejected, any commercially reasonable charges, expenses or commissions in connection with effecting cover and any other reasonable expense incident to the delay or other breach.

(2) Consequential damages resulting from the seller's breach include

(a) any loss resulting from general or particular requirements and needs of which the seller at the time of contracting had reason to know and which could not reasonably be prevented by cover or otherwise; and

(b) injury to person or property proximately resulting from any breach of warranty.

§2-716. Buyer's Right to Specific Performance or Replevin

(1) Specific performance may be decreed if the goods are unique or in other proper circumstances.

(2) The decree for specific performance may include such terms and conditions as to payment of the price, damages, or other relief as the court may deem just.

(3) The buyer has a right of replevin for goods identified to the contract if after reasonable effort the buyer is unable to effect cover for such goods or the circumstances reasonably indicate that such effort will be unavailing or if the goods have been shipped under reservation and satisfaction of the security interest in them has been made or tendered.

2-717. Deduction of Damages From the Price

The buyer on notifying the seller of his intention to do so may deduct all or any part of the damages resulting from any breach of the contract from any part of the price still due under the same contract.

§2-718. Liquidation or Limitation of Damages; Deposits

(1) Damages for breach by either party may be liquidated in the agreement but only at an amount which is reasonable in the light of the anticipated or actual harm caused by the breach, the difficulties of proof of loss, and the inconvenience or nonfeasibility of otherwise obtaining an adequate remedy. A term fixing unreasonably large liquidated damages is void as a penalty.

(2) Where the seller justifiably withholds delivery of goods because of the buyer's breach, the buyer is entitled to restitution of any amount by which the sum of the buyer's payments exceeds

(a) the amount to which the seller is entitled by virtue of terms liquidating the seller's damages in accordance with subsection (1), or

(b) in the absence of such terms, twenty per cent of the value of the total performance for which the buyer is obligated under the contract or $500, whichever is smaller.

(3) The buyer's right to restitution under subsection (2) is subject to offset to the extent that the seller establishes

(a) a right to recover damages under the provisions of this Article other than subsection (1), and

(b) the amount or value of any benefits received by the buyer directly or indirectly by reason of the contract.

(4) Where a seller has received payment in goods their reasonable value or the proceeds of their resale shall be treated as payments for the purposes of subsection (2); but if the seller has notice of the buyer's breach before reselling goods received in part performance, his resale is subject to the conditions laid down in this Article on resale by an aggrieved seller (Section 2-706).

§2-719. Contractual Modification or Limitation of Remedy

(1) Subject to the provisions of subsections (2) and (3) of this section and of the preceding section on liquidation and limitation of damages,

(a) the agreement may provide for remedies in addition to or in substitution for those provided in this Article and may limit or alter the measure of damages recoverable under this Article, as by limiting the buyer's remedies to return of the goods and repayment of the price or to repair and replacement of non-conforming goods or parts; and

(b) resort to a remedy as provided is optional unless the remedy is expressly agreed to be exclusive, in which case it is the sole remedy.

(2) Where circumstances cause an exclusive or limited remedy to fail of its essential purpose, remedy may be had as provided in this Act.

(3) Consequential damages may be limited or excluded unless the limitation or exclusion is unconscionable. Limitation of consequential damages for injury to the person in the case of consumer goods is prima facie unconscionable but limitation of damages where the loss is commercial is not.

§2-720. Effect of "Cancellation" or "Rescission" on Claims for Antecedent Breach

Unless the contrary intention clearly appears, expressions of "cancellation" or "rescission" of the contract or the like shall not be construed as a renunciation or discharge of any claim in damages for an antecedent breach.

§2-721. Remedies for Fraud

Remedies for material misrepresentation or fraud include all remedies available under this Article for non-fraudulent breach. Neither rescission or a claim for rescission of the contract for sale nor rejection or return of the goods shall bar or be deemed inconsistent with a claim for damages or other remedy.

§2-722. Who Can Sue Third Parties for Injury to Goods

Where a third party so deals with goods which have been identified to a contract for sale as to cause actionable injury to a party to that contract

(a) a right of action against the third party is in either party to the contract for sale who has title to or a security interest or a special property or an insurable interest in the goods; and if the goods have been destroyed or converted a right of action is also in the party who either bore the risk of loss under the contract for sale or has since the injury assumed that risk as against the other;

(b) if at the time of the injury the party plaintiff did not bear the risk of loss as against the other party to the contract for sale and there is no arrangement between them for disposition of the recovery, his suit or settlement is, subject to his own interest, as a fiduciary for the other party to the contract;

(c) either party may with the consent of the other sue for the benefit of which it may concern.

§2-723. Proof of Market Price: Time and Place

(1) If an action based on anticipatory repudiation comes to trial before the time for performance with respect to some or all of the goods, any damages based on market price (Section 2-708 or Section 2-713) shall be determined according to the price of such goods prevailing at the time when the aggrieved party learned of the repudiation.

(2) If evidence of a price prevailing at the times or places described in this Article is not readily available the price prevailing within any reasonable time before or after the time described or at any other place which in commercial judgment or under usage of trade would serve as a reasonable substitute for the one described may be used, making any proper allowance for the cost of transporting the goods to or from such other place.

(3) Evidence of a relevant price prevailing at a time or place other than the one described in this Article offered by one party is not admissible unless and until he has given the other party such notice as the court finds sufficient to prevent unfair surprise.

§2-724. Admissibility of Market Quotations

Whenever the prevailing price or value of any goods regularly bought and sold in any established commodity market is in issue, reports in official publications or trade journals or in newspapers or periodicals of general circulation published as the reports of such market shall be admissible in evidence. The circumstances of the preparation of such a report may be shown to affect its weight but not its admissibility.

§2-725. Statute of Limitations in Contracts for Sale

(1) An action for breach of any contract for sale must be commenced within four years after the cause of action has accrued. By the original agreement the parties may reduce the period of limitation to not less than one year but may not extend it.

(2) A cause of action accrues when the breach occurs, regardless of the aggrieved party's lack of knowledge of the breach. A breach of warranty occurs when tender of delivery is made, except that where a warranty explicitly extends to future performance of the goods and discovery of the breach must await the time of such performance the cause of action accrues when the breach is or should have been discovered.

(3) Where an action commenced within the time limited by subsection (1) is so terminated as to leave available a remedy by another action for the same breach such other action may be commenced after the expiration of the time limited and within six months after the termination of the first action unless the termination resulted from voluntary discontinuance or from dismissal for failure or neglect to prosecute.

(4) This section does not alter the law on tolling of the statute of limitations nor does it apply to causes of action which have accrued before this Act becomes effective.

U.C.C. – ARTICLE 7 – DOCUMENTS OF TITLE

PART 1. GENERAL

§ 7-101. Short Title

This Article may be cited as Uniform Commercial Code-Documents of Title.

§ 7-102. Definitions and Index of Definitions

(a) In this Article, unless the context otherwise requires:

(1) "Bailee" means a person that by a warehouse receipt, bill of lading, or other document of title acknowledges possession of goods and contracts to deliver them.

(2) "Carrier" means a person that issues a bill of lading.

(3) "Consignee" means a person named in a bill of lading to which or to whose order the bill promises delivery.

(4) "Consignor" means a person named in a bill of lading as the person from which the goods have been received for shipment.

(5) "Delivery order" means a record that contains an order to deliver goods directed to a warehouse, carrier, or other person that in the ordinary course of business issues warehouse receipts or bills of lading.

(6) "Good faith" means honesty in fact and the observance of reasonable commercial standards of fair dealing.

(7) "Goods" means all things that are treated as movable for the purposes of a contract for storage or transportation.

(8) "Issuer" means a bailee that issues a document of title or, in the case of an unaccepted delivery order, the person that orders the possessor of goods to deliver. The term includes a person for which an agent or employee purports to act in issuing a document if the agent or employee has real or apparent authority to issue documents, even if the issuer did not receive any goods, the goods were misdescribed, or in any other respect the agent or employee violated the issuer's instructions.

(9) "Person entitled under the document" means the holder, in the case of a negotiable document of title, or the person to which delivery of the goods is to be made by the terms of, or pursuant to instructions in a record under, a nonnegotiable document of title.

(10) "Record" means information that is inscribed on a tangible medium or that is stored in an electronic or other medium and is retrievable in perceivable form.

(11) "Sign" means, with present intent to authenticate or adopt a record:

  (A) to execute or adopt a tangible symbol; or

  (B) to attach to or logically associate with the record an electronic sound, symbol, or process.

(12) "Shipper" means a person that enters into a contract of transportation with a carrier.

(13) "Warehouse" means a person engaged in the business of storing goods for hire.

(b) Definitions in other articles applying to this Article and the sections in which they appear are:

(1) "Contract for sale", Section 2-106.

(2) "Lessee in ordinary course of business", Section 2A-103.

(3) "Receipt" of goods, Section 2-103.

(c) In addition, Article 1 contains general definitions and principles of construction and interpretation applicable throughout this article.

§ 7-103. Relation of Article to Treaty or Statute

(a) This Article is subject to any treaty or statute of the United States or a regulatory statute of this State to the extent the treaty, statute, or regulatory statute is applicable.

(b) This Article does not repeal or modify any law prescribing the form or contents of a document of title or the services or facilities to be afforded by a bailee, or otherwise regulating a bailee's businesses in respects not specifically treated in this article. However, violation of these laws does not affect the status of a document of title that otherwise complies with the definition of a document of title.

(c) This [Act] modifies, limits, and supersedes the federal Electronic Signatures in Global and National Commerce Act (15 U.S.C. Section 7001, et. seq.) but does not modify, limit, or supersede Section 101(c) of that act (15 U.S.C. Section 7001(c)) or authorize electronic delivery of any of the notices described in Section 103(b) of that act (15 U.S.C. Section 7003(b)).

(d) To the extent there is a conflict between the Uniform Electronic Transactions Act and this article, this Article governs.

§ 7-104. Negotiable and Non-Negotiable Document of Title

(a) A document of title is negotiable if by its terms the goods are to be delivered to bearer or to the order of a named person.

(b) A document of title other than one described in subsection (a) is non-negotiable. A bill of lading that states that the goods are consigned to a named person is not made negotiable by a provision that the goods are to be delivered only against an order in a record signed by the same or another named person.

(c) A document of title is non-negotiable if, at the time it is issued, the document has a conspicuous legend, however expressed, that it is non-negotiable.

§ 7-105. Reissuance in Alternative Medium

(a) Upon request of a person entitled under an electronic document of title, the issuer of the electronic document may issue a tangible document of title as a substitute for the electronic document if:

(1) the person entitled under the electronic document surrenders control of the document to the issuer; and

(2) the tangible document when issued contains a statement that it is issued in substitution for the electronic document.

(b) Upon issuance of a tangible document of title in substitution for an electronic document of title in accordance with subsection (a):

(1) the electronic document ceases to have any effect or validity; and

(2) the person that procured issuance of the tangible document warrants to all subsequent persons entitled under the tangible document that the warrantor was a person entitled under the electronic document when the warrantor surrendered control of the electronic document to the issuer.

(c) Upon request of a person entitled under a tangible document of title, the issuer of the tangible document may issue an electronic document of title as a substitute for the tangible document if:

(1) the person entitled under the tangible document surrenders possession of the document to the issuer; and

(2) the electronic document when issued contains a statement that it is issued in substitution for the tangible document.

(d) Upon issuance of the electronic document of title in substitution for a tangible document of title in accordance with subsection (c):

(1) the tangible document ceases to have any effect or validity; and

(2) the person that procured issuance of the electronic document warrants to all subsequent persons entitled under the electronic document that the warrantor was a person entitled under the tangible document when the warrantor surrendered possession of the tangible document to the issuer.

§ 7-106. Control of Electronic Document of Title

(a) A person has control of an electronic document of title if a system employed for evidencing the transfer of interests in the electronic document reliably establishes that person as the person to which the electronic document was issued or transferred.

(b) A system satisfies subsection (a), and a person is deemed to have control of an electronic document of title, if the document is created, stored, and assigned in such a manner that:

(1) a single authoritative copy of the document exists which is unique, identifiable, and, except as otherwise provided in paragraphs (4), (5), and (6), unalterable;

(2) the authoritative copy identifies the person asserting control as:

(A) the person to which the document was issued; or

(B) if the authoritative copy indicates that the document has been transferred, the person to which the document was most recently transferred;

(3) the authoritative copy is communicated to and maintained by the person asserting control or its designated custodian;

(4) copies or amendments that add or change an identified assignee of the authoritative copy can be made only with the consent of the person asserting control;

(5) each copy of the authoritative copy and any copy of a copy is readily identifiable as a copy that is not the authoritative copy; and

(6) any amendment of the authoritative copy is readily identifiable as authorized or unauthorized.

PART 2. WAREHOUSE RECEIPTS: SPECIAL PROVISIONS

§ 7-201. Person That May Issue a Warehouse Receipt; Storage Under Bond

(a) A warehouse receipt may be issued by any warehouse.

(b) If goods, including distilled spirits and agricultural commodities, are stored under a statute requiring a bond against withdrawal or a license for the issuance of receipts in the nature of warehouse receipts, a receipt issued for the goods is deemed to be a warehouse receipt even if issued by a person that is the owner of the goods and is not a warehouse.

§ 7-202. Form of Warehouse Receipt

(a) A warehouse receipt need not be in any particular form.

(b) Unless a warehouse receipt provides for each of the following, the warehouse is liable for damages caused to a person injured by its omission:

(1) the location of the warehouse facility where the goods are stored;

(2) the date of issue of the receipt;

(3) the unique identification code of the receipt;

(4) a statement whether the goods received will be delivered to the bearer, to a named person, or to a named person or its order;

(5) the rate of storage and handling charges, but if goods are stored under a field warehousing arrangement, a statement of that fact is sufficient on a non-negotiable receipt;

(6) a description of the goods or the packages containing them;

(7) the signature of the warehouse or its agent;

(8) if the receipt is issued for goods that the warehouse owns, either solely, jointly, or in common with others, the fact of that ownership; and

(9) a statement of the amount of advances made and of liabilities incurred for which the warehouse claims a lien or security interest, but if the precise amount of advances made or of liabilities incurred is, at the time of the issue of the receipt, unknown to the warehouse or to its agent that issued the receipt, a statement of the fact that advances have been made or liabilities incurred and the purpose of the advances or liabilities is sufficient.

(c) A warehouse may insert in its receipt any terms that are not contrary to [the UCC] and do not impair its obligation of delivery under Section 7-403 or its duty of care under Section 7-204. Any contrary provisions are ineffective.

§ 7-203. Liability for Nonreceipt or Misdescription

A party to or purchaser for value in good faith of a document of title, other than a bill of lading, that relies upon the description of the goods in the document may recover from the issuer damages caused by the nonreceipt or misdescription of the goods, except to the extent that:

(1) the document conspicuously indicates that the issuer does not know whether all or part of the goods in fact were received or conform to the description, such as a case in which the description is in terms of marks or labels or kind, quantity, or condition, or the receipt or description is qualified by “contents, condition, and quality unknown”, “said to contain”, or words of similar import, if the indication is true; or

(2) the party or purchaser otherwise has notice of the nonreceipt or misdescription.

§ 7-204. Duty of Care; Contractual Limitation of Warehouse’s Liability

(a) A warehouse is liable for damages for loss of or injury to the goods caused by its failure to exercise care with regard to the goods that a reasonably careful person would exercise under similar circumstances. However, unless otherwise agreed, the warehouse is not liable for damages that could not have been avoided by the exercise of that care.

(b) Damages may be limited by a term in the warehouse receipt or storage agreement limiting the amount of liability in case of loss or damage beyond which the warehouse is not liable. Such a limitation is not effective with respect to the warehouse’s liability for conversion to its own use. The warehouse’s liability, on request of the bailor in a record at the time of signing such storage agreement or within a reasonable time after receipt of the warehouse receipt, may be increased on part or all of the goods covered by the storage agreement or the warehouse receipt. In this event, increased rates may be charged based on an increased valuation of the goods.

(c) Reasonable provisions as to the time and manner of presenting claims and commencing actions based on the bailment may be included in the warehouse receipt or storage agreement.

(d) This section does not impair or repeal [Insert reference to any statute that imposes a higher responsibility upon the warehouse or invalidates contractual limitations that would be permissible under this Article.]

§ 7-205. Title Under Warehouse Receipt Defeated in Certain Cases

A buyer in ordinary course of business of fungible goods goods and delivered by a warehouse that is also in the business of buying and selling such goods takes the goods free of any claim under a warehouse receipt even if the receipt is negotiable and has been duly negotiated.

§ 7-206. Termination of Storage at Warehouse's Option

(a) A warehouse, by giving notice to the person on whose account the goods are held and any other person known to claim an interest in the goods, may require payment of any charges and removal of the goods from the warehouse at the termination of the period of storage fixed by the document of title or, if a period is not fixed, within a stated period not less than 30 days after the warehouse gives notice. If the goods are not removed before the date specified in the notice, the warehouse may sell them pursuant to Section 7-210.

(b) If a warehouse in good faith believes that goods are about to deteriorate or decline in value to less than the amount of its lien within the time provided in subsection (a) and Section 7-210, the warehouse may specify in the notice given under subsection (a) any reasonable shorter time for removal of the goods and, if the goods are not removed, may sell them at public sale held not less than one week after a single advertisement or posting.

(c) If, as a result of a quality or condition of the goods of which the warehouse did not have notice at the time of deposit, the goods are a hazard to other property, the warehouse facilities, or other persons, the warehouse may sell the goods at public or private sale without advertisement or posting on reasonable notification to all persons known to claim an interest in the goods. If the warehouse, after a reasonable effort, is unable to sell the goods, it may dispose of them in any lawful manner and does not incur liability by reason of that disposition.

(d) A warehouse shall deliver the goods to any person entitled to them under this Article upon due demand made at any time before sale or other disposition under this section.

(e) A warehouse may satisfy its lien from the proceeds of any sale or disposition under this section but shall hold the balance for delivery on the demand of any person to which the warehouse would have been bound to deliver the goods.

§ 7-207. Goods Must Be Kept Separate; Fungible Goods

(a) Unless the warehouse receipt provides otherwise, a warehouse shall keep separate the goods covered by each receipt so as to permit at all times identification and delivery of those goods. However, different lots of fungible goods may be commingled.

(b) If different lots of fungible goods are commingled, the good are owned in common by the persons entitled thereto and the warehouse is severally liable to each owner for that owner's share. If, because of overissue, a mass of fungible goods is insufficient to meet all the receipts the warehouse has issued against it, the persons entitled include all holders to which overissued receipts have been duly negotiated.

§ 7-208. Altered Warehouse Receipts

If a blank in a negotiable tangible warehouse receipt has been filled in without authority, a good faith purchaser for value and without notice of the lack of authority may treat the insertion as authorized. Any other unauthorized alteration leaves any tangible or electronic warehouse receipt enforceable against the issuer according to its original tenor.

§ 7-209. Lien of Warehouse

(a) A warehouse has a lien against the bailor on the goods covered by a warehouse receipt or storage agreement or on the proceeds thereof in its possession for charges for storage or transportation, including demurrage and terminal charges, insurance, labor, or other charges, present or future, in relation to the goods, and for expenses necessary for preservation of the goods or reasonably incurred in their sale pursuant to law. If the person on whose account the goods are held is liable for similar charges or expenses in relation to other goods whenever deposited and it is stated in the warehouse receipt or storage agreement that a lien is claimed for charges and expenses in relation to other goods, the warehouse also has a lien against the goods covered by the warehouse receipt or storage agreement or on the proceeds thereof in its possession for those charges and expenses, whether or not the other goods have been delivered by the warehouse. However, as against a person to which a negotiable warehouse receipt is duly negotiated, a warehouse's lien is limited to charges in an amount or at a rate specified in the warehouse receipt or, if no charges are so specified, to a reasonable charge for storage of the specific goods covered by the receipt subsequent to the date of the receipt.

(b) The warehouse may also reserve a security interest under Article 9 against the bailor for the maximum amount specified on the receipt for charges other than those specified in subsection (a), such as for money advanced and interest. A security interest is governed by Article 9.

(c) A warehouse's lien for charges and expenses under subsection (a) or a security interest under subsection (b) is also effective against any person that so entrusted the bailor with possession of the goods that a pledge of them by the bailor to a good faith purchaser for value would have been valid. However, the lien or security interest is not effective against a person that before issuance of a document of title had a legal interest or a perfected security interest in the goods and that did not:

(1) deliver or entrust the goods or any document covering the goods to the bailor or the bailor's nominee with actual or apparent authority to ship, store, or sell; or with power to obtain delivery under Section 7-403; or with power of disposition under Sections 2-403, 2A-304(2), 2A-305(2) or 9-320 or other statute or rule of law; or

(2) acquiesce in the procurement by the bailor or its nominee of any document.

(d) A warehouse's lien on household goods for charges and expenses in relation to the goods under subsection (a) is also effective against all persons if the depositor was the legal possessor of the goods at the time of deposit. In this subsection, "household goods" means furniture, furnishings, or personal effects used by the depositor in a dwelling.

(e) A warehouse loses its lien on any goods that it voluntarily delivers or unjustifiably refuses to deliver.

§ 7-210. Enforcement of Warehouse's Lien

(a) Except as otherwise provided in subsection (b), a warehouse's lien may be enforced by public or private sale of the goods, in bulk or in packages, at any time or place and on any terms that are commercially reasonable, after notifying all persons known to claim an interest in the goods. The notification must include a statement of the amount due, the nature of the proposed sale, and the time and place of any public sale. The fact that a better price could have been obtained by a sale at a different time or in a different method from that selected by the warehouse is not of itself sufficient to establish that the sale was not made in a commercially reasonable manner. The warehouse has sold in a commercially reasonable manner if the warehouse sells the goods in the usual manner in any recognized market therefor, sells at the price current in that market at the time of the sale, or has otherwise sold in conformity with commercially reasonable practices among dealers in the type of goods sold. A sale of more goods than apparently necessary to be offered to ensure satisfaction of the obligation is not commercially reasonable, except in cases covered by the preceding sentence.

(b) A warehouse's lien on goods, other than goods stored by a merchant in the course of its business, may be enforced only if the following requirements are satisfied:

(1) All persons known to claim an interest in the goods must be notified.

(2) The notification must include an itemized statement of the claim, a description of the goods subject to the lien, a demand for payment within a specified time not less than 10 days after receipt of the notification, and a conspicuous statement that unless the claim is paid within that time the goods will be advertised for sale and sold by auction at a specified time and place.

(3) The sale must conform to the terms of the notification.

(4) The sale must be held at the nearest suitable place to where the goods are held or stored.

(5) After the expiration of the time given in the notification, an advertisement of the sale must be published once a week for two weeks consecutively in a newspaper of general circulation where the sale is to be held. The advertisement must include a description of the goods, the name of the person on whose account the goods are being held, and the time and place of the sale. The sale must take place at least 15 days after the first publication. If there is no newspaper of general circulation where the sale is to be held, the advertisement must be posted at least 10 days before the sale in not less than six conspicuous places in the neighborhood of the proposed sale.

(c) Before any sale pursuant to this section, any person claiming a right in the goods may pay the amount necessary to satisfy the lien and the reasonable expenses incurred in complying with this section. In that event, the goods may not be sold but must be retained by the warehouse subject to the terms of the receipt and this article.

(d) A warehouse may buy at any public sale held pursuant to this section.

(e) A purchaser in good faith of goods sold to enforce a warehouse's lien takes the goods free of any rights of persons against which the lien was valid, despite the warehouse's noncompliance with this section.

(f) A warehouse may satisfy its lien from the proceeds of any sale pursuant to this section but shall hold the balance, if any, for delivery on demand to any person to which the warehouse would have been bound to deliver the goods.

(g) The rights provided by this section are in addition to all other rights allowed by law to a creditor against a debtor.

(h) If a lien is on goods stored by a merchant in the course of its business, the lien may be enforced in accordance with subsection (a) or (b).

(i) A warehouse is liable for damages caused by failure to comply with the requirements for sale under this section and, in case of willful violation, is liable for conversion.

PART 3. BILLS OF LADING: SPECIAL PROVISIONS

§ 7-301. Liability for Non-Receipt or Misdescription; "Said to Contain"; "Shipper's Load and Count"; Improper Handling

(a) A consignee of a nonnegotiable bill of lading which has given value in good faith, or a holder to which a negotiable bill has been duly negotiated, relying upon the description of the goods in the bill or upon the date shown in the bill, may recover from the issuer damages caused by the misdating of the bill or the nonreceipt or misdescription of the goods, except to the extent that the document of title indicates that the issuer does not know whether any part or all of the goods in fact were received or conform to the description, such as in a case in which the description is in terms of marks or labels or kind, quantity, or condition or the receipt or description is qualified by "contents or condition of contents of packages unknown", "said to contain", "shipper's weight, load and count," or words of similar import, if that indication is true.

(b) If goods are loaded by the issuer of the bill of lading, the issuer shall count the packages of goods if shipped in packages and ascertain the kind and quantity if shipped in bulk and words such as "shipper's weight, load and count," or words of similar import indicating that the description was made by the shipper are ineffective except as to goods concealed by packages.

(c) If bulk goods are loaded by a shipper that makes available to the issuer of the bill of lading adequate facilities for weighing those goods, the issuer shall ascertain the kind and quantity within a reasonable time after receiving the shipper's request in a record to do so. In that case, "shipper's weight" or words of similar import are ineffective.

(d) The issuer, by including in the bill of lading the words "shipper's weight, load and count," or words of similar import, may indicate that the goods were loaded by the shipper, and, if that statement is true, the issuer is not liable for damages caused by the improper loading. However, omission of such words does not imply liability for damages caused by improper loading.

(e) A shipper guarantees to the issuer the accuracy at the time of shipment of the description, marks, labels, number, kind, quantity, condition, and weight, as furnished by the shipper, and the shipper shall indemnify the issuer against damage caused by inaccuracies in those particulars. This right of the issuer to that indemnity does not limit its responsibility or liability under the contract of carriage to any person other than the shipper.

§ 7-302. Through Bills of Lading and Similar Documents of Title

(a) The issuer of a through bill of lading or other document of title embodying an undertaking to be performed in part by a person acting as its agent or by a performing carrier is liable to any person entitled to recover on the document for any breach by the other person or the performing carrier of its obligation under the document. However, to the extent that the bill covers an undertaking to be performed overseas or in territory not contiguous to the continental United States or an undertaking including matters other than transportation, this liability for breach by the other person or the performing carrier may be varied by agreement of the parties.

(b) If goods covered by a through bill of lading or other document of title embodying an undertaking to be performed in part by a person other than the issuer are received by that person, the person is subject, with respect to its own performance while the goods are in its possession, to the obligation of the issuer. The person's obligation is discharged by delivery of the goods to another person pursuant to the document and does not include liability for breach by any other person or by the issuer.

(c) The issuer of a through bill of lading or other document of title described in subsection (a) is entitled to recover from the performing carrier, or other person in possession of the goods when the breach of the obligation under the document occurred:

(1) the amount it may be required to pay to any person entitled to recover on the document for the breach, as may be evidenced by any receipt, judgment, or transcript of judgment, and;

(2) the amount of any expense reasonably incurred by the issuer in defending any action commenced by any person entitled to recover on the document for the breach.

§ 7-303. Diversion; Reconsignment; Change of Instructions

(a) Unless the bill of lading otherwise provides, a carrier may deliver the goods to a person or destination other than that stated in the bill or may otherwise dispose of the goods, without liability for misdelivery, on instructions from:

(1) the holder of a negotiable bill;

(2) the consignor on a nonnegotiable bill even if the consignee has given contrary instructions;

(3) the consignee on a nonnegotiable bill in the absence of contrary instructions from the consignor, if the goods have arrived at the billed destination or if the consignee is in possession of the tangible bill or in control of the electronic bill; or

(4) the consignee on a nonnegotiable bill, if the consignee is entitled as against the consignor to dispose of the goods.

(b) Unless instructions described in subsection (a) are included in a negotiable bill of lading, a person to which the bill is duly negotiated may hold the bailee according to the original terms.

§ 7-304. Tangible Bills of Lading in a Set

(a) Except as customary in international transportation, a tangible bill of lading may not be issued in a set of parts. The issuer is liable for damages caused by violation of this subsection.

(b) If a tangible bill of lading is lawfully issued in a set of parts, each of which contains an identification code and is expressed to be valid only if the goods have not been delivered against any other part, the whole of the parts constitutes one bill.

(c) If a tangible negotiable bill of lading is lawfully issued in a set of parts and different parts are negotiated to different persons, the title of the holder to which the first due negotiation is made prevails as to both the document of title and the goods even if any later holder may have received the goods from the carrier in good faith and discharged the carrier's obligation by surrendering its part.

(d) A person that negotiates or transfers a single part of a tangible bill of lading issued in a set is liable to holders of that part as if it were the whole set.

(e) The bailee is obliged to deliver in accordance with Part 4 against the first presented part of a tangible bill of lading lawfully issued in a set. Delivery in this manner discharges the bailee's obligation on the whole bill.

§ 7-305. Destination Bills

(a) Instead of issuing a bill of lading to the consignor at the place of shipment, a carrier, at the request of the consignor, may procure the bill to be issued at destination or at any other place designated in the request.

(b) Upon request of any person entitled as against a carrier to control the goods while in transit and on surrender of possession or control of any outstanding bill of lading or other receipt covering the goods, the issuer, subject to Section 7-105, may procure a substitute bill to be issued at any place designated in the request.

§ 7-306. Altered Bills of Lading

An unauthorized alteration or filling in of a blank in a bill of lading leaves the bill enforceable according to its original tenor.

§ 7-307. Lien of Carrier

(a) A carrier has a lien on the goods covered by a bill of lading or on the proceeds thereof in its possession for charges after the date of the carrier's receipt of the goods for storage or transportation, including demurrage and terminal charges, and for expenses necessary for preservation of the goods incident to their transportation or reasonably incurred in their sale pursuant to law. However, against a purchaser for value of a negotiable bill of lading, a carrier's lien is limited to charges stated in the bill or the applicable tariffs or, if no charges are stated, a reasonable charge.

(b) A lien for charges and expenses under subsection (a) on goods that the carrier was required by law to receive for transportation is effective against the consignor or any person entitled to the goods unless the carrier had notice that the consignor lacked authority to subject the goods to those charges and expenses. Any other lien under subsection (a) is effective against the consignor and any person that permitted the bailor to have control or possession of the goods unless the carrier had notice that the bailor lacked authority.

(c) A carrier loses its lien on any goods that it voluntarily delivers or unjustifiably refuses to deliver.

§ 7-308. Enforcement of Carrier's Lien

(a) A carrier's lien on goods may be enforced by public or private sale of the goods, in bulk or in packages, at any time or place and on any terms that are commercially reasonable, after notifying all persons known to claim an interest in the goods. The notification must include a statement of the amount due, the nature of the proposed sale, and the time and place of any public sale. The fact that a better price could have been obtained by a sale at a different time or in a different method from that selected by the carrier is not of itself sufficient to establish that the sale was not made in a commercially reasonable manner. The carrier has sold goods in a commercially reasonable manner if the carrier sells the goods in the usual manner in any recognized market therefor, sells at the price current in that market at the time of the sale, or has otherwise sold in conformity with commercially reasonable practices among dealers in the type of goods sold. A sale of more goods than apparently necessary to be offered to ensure satisfaction of the obligation is not commercially reasonable, except in cases covered by the preceding sentence.

(b) Before any sale pursuant to this section, any person claiming a right in the goods may pay the amount necessary to satisfy the lien and the reasonable expenses incurred in complying with this section. In that event, the goods may not be sold but must be retained by the carrier, subject to the terms of the bill of lading and this article.

(c) A carrier may buy at any public sale pursuant to this section.

(d) A purchaser in good faith of goods sold to enforce a carrier's lien takes the goods free of any rights of persons against which the lien was valid, despite the carrier's noncompliance with this section.

(e) A carrier may satisfy its lien from the proceeds of any sale pursuant to this section but shall hold the balance, if any, for delivery on demand to any person to which the carrier would have been bound to deliver the goods.

(f) The rights provided by this section are in addition to all other rights allowed by law to a creditor against a debtor.

(g) A carrier's lien may be enforced pursuant to either subsection (a) or the procedure set forth in Section 7-210(b).

(h) A carrier is liable for damages caused by failure to comply with the requirements for sale under this section and, in case of willful violation, is liable for conversion.

§ 7-309. Duty of Care; Contractual Limitation of Carrier's Liability

(a) A carrier that issues a bill of lading, whether negotiable or nonnegotiable, shall exercise the degree of care in relation to the goods which a reasonably careful person would exercise under similar circumstances. This subsection does not affect any statute, regulation, or rule of law that imposes liability upon a common carrier for damages not caused by its negligence.

(b) Damages may be limited by a term in the bill of lading or in a transportation agreement that the carrier's liability may not exceed a value stated in the bill or transportation agreement if the carrier's rates are dependent upon value and the consignor is afforded an opportunity to declare a higher value and the consignor is advised of the opportunity. However, such a limitation is not effective with respect to the carrier's liability for conversion to its own use.

(c) Reasonable provisions as to the time and manner of presenting claims and commencing actions based on the shipment may be included in a bill of lading or a transportation agreement.

PART 4. WAREHOUSE RECEIPTS AND BILLS OF LADING: GENERAL OBLIGATIONS

§ 7-401. Irregularities in Issue of Receipt or Bill or Conduct of Issuer

The obligations imposed by this Article on an issuer apply to a document of title even if:

(1) the document does not comply with the requirements of this Article or of any other statute, rule, or regulation regarding its issue, form, or content;

(2) the issuer violated laws regulating the conduct of its business;

(3) the goods covered by the document were owned by the bailee when the document was issued; or

(4) the person issuing the document is not a warehouse but the document purports to be a warehouse receipt.

§ 7-402. Duplicate Document of Title; Overissue

A duplicate or any other document of title purporting to cover goods already represented by an outstanding document of the same issuer does not confer any right in the goods, except as provided in the case of tangible bills of lading in a set of parts, overissue of documents for fungible goods, substitutes for lost, stolen, or destroyed documents, or substitute documents issued pursuant to Section 7-105. The issuer is liable for damages caused by its overissue or failure to identify a duplicate document by a conspicuous notation.

§ 7-403. Obligation of Warehouse or Carrier to Deliver; Excuse

(a) A bailee shall deliver the goods to a person entitled under a document of title if the person complies with subsections (b) and (c), unless and to the extent that the bailee establishes any of the following:

(1) delivery of the goods to a person whose receipt was rightful as against the claimant;

(2) damage to or delay, loss, or destruction of the goods for which the bailee is not liable;

(3) previous sale or other disposition of the goods in lawful enforcement of a lien or on a warehouse's lawful termination of storage;

(4) the exercise by a seller of its right to stop delivery pursuant to Section 2-705 or by a lessor of its right to stop delivery pursuant to Section 2A-526;

(5) a diversion, reconsignment, or other disposition pursuant to Section 7-303;

(6) release, satisfaction, or any other fact affording a personal defense against the claimant; or

(7) any other lawful excuse.

(b) A person claiming goods covered by a document of title shall satisfy the bailee's lien if the bailee so requests or the bailee is prohibited by law from delivering the goods until the charges are paid.

(c) Unless a person claiming the goods is one against which the document of title does not confer a right under Section 7-503(a):

(1) the person claiming under a document shall surrender possession or control of any outstanding negotiable document covering the goods for cancellation or indication of partial deliveries; and

(2) the bailee shall cancel the document or conspicuously indicate in the document the partial delivery or be liable to any person to which the document is duly negotiated.

§ 7-404. No Liability for Good Faith Delivery Pursuant to Document of Title

A bailee that in good faith has received goods and delivered or otherwise disposed of the goods according to the terms of a document of title or pursuant to this Article is not liable for the goods even if:

(1) the person from which the bailee received the goods did not have authority to procure the document or to dispose of the goods; or

(2) the person to which the bailee delivered the goods did not have authority to receive the goods.

PART 5. WAREHOUSE RECEIPTS AND BILLS OF LADING: NEGOTIATION AND TRANSFER

§ 7-501. Form of Negotiation and Requirements of Due Negotiation

(a) The following rules apply to a negotiable tangible document of title:

(1) If the document's original terms run to the order of a named person, the document is negotiated by the named person's indorsement and delivery. After the named person's indorsement in blank or to bearer, any person may negotiate the document by delivery alone.

(2) If the document's original terms run to bearer, it is negotiated by delivery alone.

(3) If the document's original terms run to the order of a named person and it is delivered to the named person, the effect is the same as if the document had been negotiated.

(4) Negotiation of the document after it has been indorsed to a named person requires indorsement by the named person as well as delivery.

(5) A document is duly negotiated if it is negotiated in the manner stated in this subsection to a holder that purchases it in good faith, without notice of any defense against or claim to it on the part of any person, and for value, unless it is established that the negotiation is not in the regular course of business or financing or involves receiving the document in settlement or payment of a monetary obligation.

(b) The following rules apply to a negotiable electronic document of title:

(1) If the document's original terms run to the order of a named person or to bearer, the document is negotiated by delivery of the document to another person. Indorsement by the named person is not required to negotiate the document.

(2) If the document's original terms run to the order of a named person and the named person has control of the document, the effect is the same as if the document had been negotiated.

(3) A document is duly negotiated if it is negotiated in the manner stated in this subsection to a holder that purchases it in good faith, without notice of any defense against or claim to it on the part of any person, and for value, unless it is established that the negotiation is

not in the regular course of business or financing or involves taking delivery of the document in settlement or payment of a monetary obligation.

(c) Indorsement of a nonnegotiable document of title neither makes it negotiable nor adds to the transferee's rights.

(d) The naming in a negotiable bill of lading of a person to be notified of the arrival of the goods does not limit the negotiability of the bill or constitute notice to a purchaser of the bill of any interest of that person in the goods.

§ 7-502. Rights Acquired by Due Negotiation

(a) Subject to Sections 7-205 and 7-503, a holder to which a negotiable document of title has been duly negotiated acquires thereby:

(1) title to the document;

(2) title to the goods;

(3) all rights accruing under the law of agency or estoppel, including rights to goods delivered to the bailee after the document was issued; and

(4) the direct obligation of the issuer to hold or deliver the goods according to the terms of the document free of any defense or claim by the issuer except those arising under the terms of the document or under this article. In the case of a delivery order, the bailee's obligation accrues only upon the bailee's acceptance of the delivery order and the obligation acquired by the holder is that the issuer and any indorser will procure the acceptance of the bailee.

(b) Subject to Section 7-503, title and rights acquired by due negotiation are not defeated by any stoppage of the goods represented by the document of title or by surrender of the goods by the bailee and are not impaired even if:

(1) the due negotiation or any prior due negotiation constituted a breach of duty;

(2) any person has been deprived of possession of a negotiable tangible document or control of a negotiable electronic document by misrepresentation, fraud, accident, mistake, duress, loss, theft, or conversion; or

(3) a previous sale or other transfer of the goods or document has been made to a third person.

§ 7-503. Document of Title to Goods Defeated in Certain Cases

(a) A document of title confers no right in goods against a person that before issuance of the document had a legal interest or a perfected security interest in the goods and that did not:

(1) deliver or entrust the goods or any document covering the goods to the bailor or the bailor's nominee with actual or apparent authority to ship, store, or sell; with power to obtain delivery under Section 7-403; or with power of disposition under Section 2-403, 2A-304(2), 2A-305(2), or 9-320 or other statute or rule of law; or

(2) acquiesce in the procurement by the bailor or its nominee of any document.

(b) Title to goods based upon an unaccepted delivery order is subject to the rights of any person to which a negotiable warehouse receipt or bill of lading covering the goods has been duly negotiated. That title may be defeated under Section 7-504 to the same extent as the rights of the issuer or a transferee from the issuer.

(c) Title to goods based upon a bill of lading issued to a freight forwarder is subject to the rights of any person to which a bill issued by the freight forwarder is duly negotiated. However, delivery by the carrier in accordance with Part 4 pursuant to its own bill of lading discharges the carrier's obligation to deliver.

§ 7-504. Rights Acquired in the Absence of Due Negotiation; Effect of Diversion; Stoppage of Delivery

(a) A transferee of a document of title, whether negotiable or non-negotiable, to which the document has been delivered but not duly negotiated, acquires the title and rights that its transferor had or had actual authority to convey.

(b) In the case of a non-negotiable document of title, until but not after the bailee receives notice of the transfer, the rights of the transferee may be defeated:

(1) by those creditors of the transferor that could treat the transfer as void under Section 2-402 or 2A-308;

(2) by a buyer from the transferor in ordinary course of business if the bailee has delivered the goods to the buyer or received notification of the buyer's rights;

(3) by a lessee from the transferor in ordinary course of business if the bailee has delivered the goods to the lessee or received notification of the lessee's rights; or

(4) as against the bailee, by good faith dealings of the bailee with the transferor.

(c) A diversion or other change of shipping instructions by the consignor in a non-negotiable bill of lading which causes the bailee not to deliver the goods to the consignee defeats the consignee's title to the goods if the goods have been delivered to a buyer in ordinary course of business or a lessee in ordinary course of business and in any event defeats the consignee's rights against the bailee.

(d) Delivery of the goods pursuant to a non-negotiable document of title may be stopped by a seller under Section 2-705 or a lessor under Section 2A-526, subject to the requirements of due notification in those sections. A bailee honoring the seller's or lessor's instructions is entitled to be indemnified by the seller or lessor against any resulting loss or expense.

§ 7-505. Indorser Not a Guarantor for Other Parties

The indorsement of a tangible document of title issued by a bailee does not make the indorser liable for any default by the bailee or previous indorsers.

§ 7-506. Delivery Without Indorsement: Right to Compel Indorsement

The transferee of a negotiable tangible document of title has a specifically enforceable right to have its transferor supply any necessary indorsement, but the transfer becomes a negotiation only as of the time the indorsement is supplied.

7-507. Warranties on Negotiation or Transfer of Document of Title

If a person negotiates or delivers a document of title for value, otherwise than as a mere intermediary under Section 7-508, unless otherwise agreed, the transferor warrants to its immediate purchaser only in addition to any warranty made in selling or leasing the goods that:

(1) the document is genuine;

(2) the transferor does not have knowledge of any fact that would impair the document's validity or worth; and

(3) the negotiation or delivery is rightful and fully effective with respect to the title to the document and the goods it represents.

§ 7-508. Warranties of Collecting Bank as to Documents of Title

A collecting bank or other intermediary known to be entrusted with documents of title on behalf of another or with collection of a draft or other claim against delivery of documents warrants by the delivery of the documents only its own good faith and authority even if the collecting bank or other intermediary has purchased or made advances against the claim or draft to be collected.

§ 7-509. Adequate Compliance With Commercial Contract

Whether a document of title is adequate to fulfill the obligations of a contract for sale, a contract for lease, or the conditions of a letter of credit is determined by Article 2, 2A, or 5.

PART 6. WAREHOUSE RECEIPTS AND BILLS OF LADING: MISCELLANEOUS PROVISIONS

§ 7-601. Lost, Stolen, or Destroyed Documents of Title

(a) If a document of title is lost, stolen, or destroyed, a court may order delivery of the goods or issuance of a substitute document and the bailee may without liability to any person comply with the order. If the document was negotiable, a court may not order delivery of the goods or issuance of a substitute document without the claimant's posting security unless it finds that any person that may suffer loss as a result of non-surrender of possession or control of the document is adequately protected against the loss. If the document was nonnegotiable, the court may require security. The court may also order payment of the bailee's reasonable costs and attorney's fees in any action under this subsection.

(b) A bailee that without court order delivers goods to a person claiming under a missing negotiable document of title is liable to any person injured thereby. If the delivery is not in good faith, the bailee is liable for conversion. Delivery in good faith is not conversion if the claimant posts security with the bailee in an amount at least double the value of the goods at the time of posting to indemnify any person injured by the delivery which files a notice of claim within one year after the delivery.

§ 7-602. Attachment of Goods Covered by a Negotiable Document

Unless a document of title was originally issued upon delivery of the goods by a person that did not have power to dispose of them, a lien does not attach by virtue of any judicial process to goods in the possession of a bailee for which a negotiable document of title is outstanding unless possession or control of the document is first surrendered to the bailee or the document's negotiation is enjoined. The bailee may not be compelled to deliver the goods pursuant to process until possession or control of the document is surrendered to the bailee or to the court. A purchaser of the document for value without notice of the process or injunction takes free of the lien imposed by judicial process.

§ 7-603. Conflicting Claims; Interpleader

If more than one person claims title to or possession of the goods, the bailee is excused from delivery until the bailee has a reasonable time to ascertain the validity of the adverse claims or to commence an action for interpleader. The bailee may assert an interpleader either in defending an action for non-delivery of the goods or by original action.

PART 7. MISCELLANEOUS PROVISIONS [...]

13) RESTATEMENT (SECOND) OF CONTRACTS (1981), USA[1]

Table of Contents

Introductory Note

A persistent source of difficulty in the law of contracts is the fact that words often have different meanings to the speaker and to the hearer. Most words are commonly used in more than one sense, and the words used in this Restatement are no exception. It is arguable that the difficulty is increased rather than diminished by an attempt to give a word a single definition and to use it only as defined. But where usage varies widely, definition makes it possible to avoid circumlocution in the statement of rules and to hold ambiguity to a minimum.

In the Restatement, an effort has been made to use only words with connotations familiar to the legal profession, and not to use two or more words to express the same legal concept. Where a word frequently used has a variety of distinct meanings, one meaning has been selected and indicated by definition. But it is obviously impossible to capture in a definition an entire complex institution such as "contract" or "promise." The operative facts necessary or sufficient to create legal relations and the legal relations created by those facts will appear with greater fullness in the succeeding chapters.

Chapter 1. Meaning of Terms

§1 Contract Defined

A contract is a promise or a set of promises for the breach of which the law gives a remedy, or the performance of which the law in some way recognizes as a duty.

§2 Promise; Promisor; Promisee; Beneficiary

(1) A promise is a manifestation of intention to act or refrain from acting in a specified way, so made as to justify a promisee in understanding that a commitment has been made.

(2) The person manifesting the intention is the promisor.

(3) The person to whom the manifestation is addressed is the promisee.

(4) Where performance will benefit a person other than the promisee, that person is a beneficiary.

§3 Agreement Defined; Bargain Defined

An agreement is a manifestation of mutual assent on the part of two or more persons. A bargain is an agreement to exchange promises or to exchange a promise for a performance or to exchange performances.

§4 How a Promise May Be Made

A promise may be stated in words either oral or written, or may be inferred wholly or partly from conduct.

§5 Terms of Promise, Agreement, or Contract

(1) A term of a promise or agreement is that portion of the intention or assent manifested which relates to a particular matter.

(2) A term of a contract is that portion of the legal relations resulting from the promise or set of promises which relates to a particular matter, whether or not the parties manifest an intention to create those relations.

§6 Formal Contracts

The following types of contracts are subject in some respects to special rules that depend on their formal characteristics and differ from those governing contracts in general:

(a) Contracts under seal,

(b) Recognizances,

(c) Negotiable instruments and documents,

(d) Letters of credit.

§7 Voidable Contracts

A voidable contract is one where one or more parties have the power, by a manifestation of election to do so, to avoid the legal relations created by the contract, or by ratification of the contract to extinguish the power of avoidance.

§8 Unenforceable Contracts

An unenforceable contract is one for the breach of which neither the remedy of damages nor the remedy of specific performance is available, but which is recognized in some other way as creating a duty of performance, though there has been no ratification.

Chapter 2. Formation of Contracts – Parties and Capacity

§9 Parties Required

There must be at least two parties to a contract, a promisor and a promisee, but there may be any greater number.

§10 Multiple Promisors and Promisees of the Same Performance

(1) Where there are more promisors than one in a contract, some or all of them may promise the same performance, whether or not there are also promises of separate performances.

(2) Where there are more promisees than one in a contract, a promise may be made to some or all of them as a unit, whether or not the same or another performance is separately promised to one or more of them.

§11 When a Person May Be Both Promisor and Promisee

A contract may be formed between two or more persons acting as a unit and one or more but fewer than all of these persons, acting either singly or with other persons.

§12 Capacity to Contract

(1) No one can be bound by contract who has not legal capacity to incur at least voidable contractual duties. Capacity to contract may be partial and its existence in respect of a particular transaction may depend upon the nature of the transaction or upon other circumstances.

(2) A natural person who manifests assent to a transaction has full legal capacity to incur contractual duties thereby unless he is

(a) under guardianship, or

(b) an infant, or

(c) mentally ill or defective, or

(d) intoxicated.

§13 Persons Affected by Guardianship

A person has no capacity to incur contractual duties if his property is under guardianship by reason of an adjudication of mental illness or defect.

§14 Infants

Unless a statute provides otherwise, a natural person has the capacity to incur only voidable contractual duties until the beginning of the day before the person's eighteenth birthday.

§15 Mental Illness or Defect

(1) A person incurs only voidable contractual duties by entering into a transaction if by reason of mental illness or defect

(a) he is unable to understand in a reasonable manner the nature and consequences of the transaction, or

(b) he is unable to act in a reasonable manner in relation to the transaction and the other party has reason to know of his condition.

(2) Where the contract is made on fair terms and the other party is without knowledge of the mental illness or defect, the power of avoidance under Subsection (1) terminates to the extent that the contract has been so performed in whole or in part or the circumstances have so changed that avoidance would be unjust. In such a case a court may grant relief as justice requires.

§16 Intoxicated Persons

A person incurs only voidable contractual duties by entering into a transaction if the other party has reason to know that by reason of intoxication

(a) he is unable to understand in a reasonable manner the nature and consequences of the transaction, or

(b) he is unable to act in a reasonable manner in relation to the transaction.

Chapter 3. Formation of Contracts – Mutual Assent

Topic 1. In General

§17 Requirement of a Bargain

(1) Except as stated in Subsection (2), the formation of a contract requires a bargain in which there is a manifestation of mutual assent to the exchange and a consideration.

(2) Whether or not there is a bargain a contract may be formed under special rules applicable to formal contracts or under the rules stated in §§82- 94.

Topic 2. Manifestation of Assent in General

§18 Manifestation of Mutual Assent

Manifestation of mutual assent to an exchange requires that each party either make a promise or begin or render a performance.

§19 Conduct as Manifestation of Assent

(1) The manifestation of assent may be made wholly or partly by written or spoken words or by other acts or by failure to act.

(2) The conduct of a party is not effective as a manifestation of his assent unless he intends to engage in the conduct and knows or has reason to know that the other party may infer from his conduct that he assents.

(3) The conduct of a party may manifest assent even though he does not in fact assent. In such cases a resulting contract may be voidable because of fraud, duress, mistake, or other invalidating cause.

§20 Effect of Misunderstanding

(1) There is no manifestation of mutual assent to an exchange if the parties attach materially different meanings to their manifestations and

(a) neither party knows or has reason to know the meaning attached by the other; or

(b) each party knows or each party has reason to know the meaning attached by the other.

(2) The manifestations of the parties are operative in accordance with the meaning attached to them by one of the parties if

(a) that party does not know of any different meaning attached by the other, and the other knows the meaning attached by the first party; or

(b) that party has no reason to know of any different meaning attached by the other, and the other has reason to know the meaning attached by the first party.

§21 Intention to Be Legally Bound

Neither real nor apparent intention that a promise be legally binding is essential to the formation of a contract, but a manifestation of intention that a promise shall not affect legal relations may prevent the formation of a contract.

§22 Mode of Assent: Offer and Acceptance

(1) The manifestation of mutual assent to an exchange ordinarily takes the form of an offer or proposal by one party followed by an acceptance by the other party or parties.

(2) A manifestation of mutual assent may be made even though neither offer nor acceptance can be identified and even though the moment of formation cannot be determined.

§23 Necessity That Manifestations Have Reference to Each Other

It is essential to a bargain that each party manifest assent with reference to the manifestation of the other.

Topic 3. Making of Offers

§24 Offer Defined

An offer is the manifestation of willingness to enter into a bargain, so made as to justify another person in understanding that his assent to that bargain is invited and will conclude it.

§25 Option Contracts

An option contract is a promise which meets the requirements for the formation of a contract and limits the promisor's power to revoke an offer.

§26 Preliminary Negotiations

A manifestation of willingness to enter into a bargain is not an offer if the person to whom it is addressed knows or has reason to know that the person making it does not intend to conclude a bargain until he has made a further manifestation of assent.

§27 Existence of Contract Where Written Memorial is Contemplated

Manifestations of assent that are in themselves sufficient to conclude a contract will not be prevented from so operating by the fact that the parties also manifest an intention to prepare and adopt a written memorial thereof; but the circumstances may show that the agreements are preliminary negotiations.

§28 Auctions

(1) At an auction, unless a contrary intention is manifested,

(a) the auctioneer invites offers from successive bidders which he may accept or reject;

(b) when goods are put up without reserve, the auctioneer makes an offer to sell at any price bid by the highest bidder, and after the auctioneer calls for bids the goods cannot be withdrawn unless no bid is made within a reasonable time;

(c) whether or not the auction is without reserve, a bidder may withdraw his bid until the auctioneer's announcement of completion of the sale, but a bidder's retraction does not revive any previous bid.

(2) Unless a contrary intention is manifested, bids at an auction embody terms made known by advertisement, posting or other publication of which bidders are or should be aware, as modified by any announcement made by the auctioneer when the goods are put up.

§29 To Whom an Offer is Addressed

(1) The manifested intention of the offeror determines the person or persons in whom is created a power of acceptance.

(2) An offer may create a power of acceptance in a specified person or in one or more of a specified group or class of persons, acting separately or together, or in anyone or everyone who makes a specified promise or renders a specified performance.

§30 Form of Acceptance Invited

(1) An offer may invite or require acceptance to be made by an affirmative answer in words, or by performing or refraining from performing a specified act, or may empower the offeree to make a selection of terms in his acceptance.

(2) Unless otherwise indicated by the language or the circumstances, an offer invites acceptance in any manner and by any medium reasonable in the circumstances.

§31 Offer Proposing a Single Contract or a Number of Contracts

An offer may propose the formation of a single contract by a single acceptance or the formation of a number of contracts by successive acceptances from time to time.

§32 Invitation of Promise or Performance

In case of doubt an offer is interpreted as inviting the offeree to accept either by promising to perform what the offer requests or by rendering the performance, as the offeree chooses.

§33 Certainty

(1) Even though a manifestation of intention is intended to be understood as an offer, it cannot be accepted so as to form a contract unless the terms of the contract are reasonably certain.

(2) The terms of a contract are reasonably certain if they provide a basis for determining the existence of a breach and for giving an appropriate remedy.

(3) The fact that one or more terms of a proposed bargain are left open or uncertain may show that a manifestation of intention is not intended to be understood as an offer or as an acceptance.

§34 Certainty and Choice of Terms; Effect of Performance or Reliance

(1) The terms of a contract may be reasonably certain even though it empowers one or both parties to make a selection of terms in the course of performance.

(2) Part performance under an agreement may remove uncertainty and establish that a contract enforceable as a bargain has been formed.

(3) Action in reliance on an agreement may make a contractual remedy appropriate even though uncertainty is not removed.

Topic 4. Duration of the Offeree's Power of Acceptance

§35 The Offeree's Power of Acceptance

(1) An offer gives to the offeree a continuing power to complete the manifestation of mutual assent by acceptance of the offer.

(2) A contract cannot be created by acceptance of an offer after the power of acceptance has been terminated in one of the ways listed in §36.

§36 Methods of Termination of the Power of Acceptance

(1) An offeree's power of acceptance may be terminated by

(a) rejection or counter offer by the offeree, or

(b) lapse of time, or

(c) revocation by the offeror, or

(d) death or incapacity of the offeror or offeree.

(2) In addition, an offeree's power of acceptance is terminated by the non occurrence of any condition of acceptance under the terms of the offer.

§37 Termination of Power of Acceptance Under Option Contract

Notwithstanding §§38- 49, the power of acceptance under an option contract is not terminated by rejection or counter-offer, by revocation, or by death or incapacity of the offeror, unless the requirements are met for the discharge of a contractual duty.

§38 Rejection

(1) An offeree's power of acceptance is terminated by his rejection of the offer, unless the offeror has manifested a contrary intention.

(2) A manifestation of intention not to accept an offer is a rejection unless the offeree manifests an intention to take it under further advisement.

§39 Counter Offers

(1) A counter offer is an offer made by an offeree to his offeror relating to the same matter as the original offer and proposing a substituted bargain differing from that proposed by the original offer.

(2) An offeree's power of acceptance is terminated by his making of a counter offer, unless the offeror has manifested a contrary intention or unless the counter offer manifests a contrary intention of the offeree.

§40 Time When Rejection or Counter Offer Terminates the Power of Acceptance

Rejection or counter offer by mail or telegram does not terminate the power of acceptance until received by the offeror, but limits the power so that a letter or telegram of acceptance started after the sending of an otherwise effective rejection or counter offer is only a counter offer unless the acceptance is received by the offeror before he receives the rejection or counter offer.

§41 Lapse of Time

(1) An offeree's power of acceptance is terminated at the time specified in the offer, or, if no time is specified, at the end of a reasonable time.

(2) What is a reasonable time is a question of fact, depending on all the circumstances existing when the offer and attempted acceptance are made.

(3) Unless otherwise indicated by the language or the circumstances, and subject to the rule stated in §49, an offer sent by mail is seasonably accepted if an acceptance is mailed at any time before midnight on the day on which the offer is received.

§42 Revocation by Communication from Offeror Received by Offeree

An offeree's power of acceptance is terminated when the offeree receives from the offeror a manifestation of an intention not to enter into the proposed contract.

§43 Indirect Communication of Revocation

An offeree's power of acceptance is terminated when the offeror takes definite action inconsistent with an intention to enter into the proposed contract and the offeree acquires reliable information to that effect.

§44 Effect of Deposit on Revocability of Offer

An offeror's power of revocation is not limited by the deposit of money or other property to be forfeited in the event of revocation, but the deposit may be forfeited to the extent that it is not a penalty.

§45 Option Contract Created by Part Performance or Tender

(1) Where an offer invites an offeree to accept by rendering a performance and does not invite a promissory acceptance, an option contract is created when the offeree tenders or begins the invited performance or tenders a beginning of it.

(2) The offeror's duty of performance under any option contract so created is conditional on completion or tender of the invited performance in accordance with the terms of the offer.

§46 Revocation of General Offer

Where an offer is made by advertisement in a newspaper or other general notification to the public or to a number of persons whose identity is unknown to the offeror, the offeree's power of acceptance is terminated when a notice of termination is given publicity by advertisement or other general notification equal to that given to the offer and no better means of notification is reasonably available.

§47 Revocation of Divisible Offer

An offer contemplating a series of independent contracts by separate acceptances may be effectively revoked so as to terminate the power to create future contracts, though one or more of the proposed contracts have already been formed by the offeree's acceptance.

§48 Death or Incapacity of Offeror or Offeree

An offeree's power of acceptance is terminated when the offeree or offeror dies or is deprived of legal capacity to enter into the proposed contract.

§49 Effect of Delay in Communication of Offer

If communication of an offer to the offeree is delayed, the period within which a contract can be created by acceptance is not thereby extended if the offeree knows or has reason to know of the delay, though it is due to the fault of the offeror; but if the delay is due to the fault of the offeror or to the means of transmission adopted by him, and the offeree neither knows nor has reason to know that there has been delay, a contract can be created by acceptance within the period which would have been permissible if the offer had been dispatched at the time that its arrival seems to indicate.

Topic 5. Acceptance of Offers

§50 Acceptance of Offer Defined; Acceptance by Performance; Acceptance by Promise

(1) Acceptance of an offer is a manifestation of assent to the terms thereof made by the offeree in a manner invited or required by the offer.

(2) Acceptance by performance requires that at least part of what the offer requests be performed or tendered and includes acceptance by a performance which operates as a return promise.

(3) Acceptance by a promise requires that the offeree complete every act essential to the making of the promise.

§51 Effect of Part Performance Without Knowledge of Offer

Unless the offeror manifests a contrary intention, an offeree who learns of an offer after he has rendered part of the performance requested by the offer may accept by completing the requested performance.

§52 Who May Accept an Offer

An offer can be accepted only by a person whom it invites to furnish the consideration.

§53 Acceptance by Performance; Manifestation of Intention Not to Accept

(1) An offer can be accepted by the rendering of a performance only if the offer invites such an acceptance.

(2) Except as stated in §69, the rendering of a performance does not constitute an acceptance if within a reasonable time the offeree exercises reasonable diligence to notify the offeror of non acceptance.

(3) Where an offer of a promise invites acceptance by performance and does not invite a promissory acceptance, the rendering of the invited performance does not constitute an acceptance if before the offeror performs his promise the offeree manifests an intention not to accept.

§54 Acceptance by Performance; Necessity of Notification to Offeror

(1) Where an offer invites an offeree to accept by rendering a performance, no notification is necessary to make such an acceptance effective unless the offer requests such a notification.

(2) If an offeree who accepts by rendering a performance has reason to know that the offeror has no adequate means of learning of the performance with reasonable promptness and certainty, the contractual duty of the offeror is discharged unless

(a) the offeree exercises reasonable diligence to notify the offeror of acceptance, or

(b) the offeror learns of the performance within a reasonable time, or

(c) the offer indicates that notification of acceptance is not required.

§55 Acceptance of Non-Promissory Offers

Acceptance by promise may create a contract in which the offeror's performance is completed when the offeree's promise is made.

§56 Acceptance by Promise; Necessity of Notification to Offeror

Except as stated in §69 or where the offer manifests a contrary intention, it is essential to an acceptance by promise either that the offeree exercise reasonable diligence to notify the offeror of acceptance or that the offeror receive the acceptance seasonably.

§57 Effect of Equivocal Acceptance

Where notification is essential to acceptance by promise, the offeror is not bound by an acceptance in equivocal terms unless he reasonably understands it as an acceptance.

§58 Necessity of Acceptance Complying with Terms of Offer

An acceptance must comply with the requirements of the offer as to the promise to be made or the performance to be rendered.

§59 Purported Acceptance Which Adds Qualifications

A reply to an offer which purports to accept it but is conditional on the offeror's assent to terms additional to or different from those offered is not an acceptance but is a counter-offer.

§60 Acceptance of Offer Which States Place, Time or Manner of Acceptance

If an offer prescribes the place, time or manner of acceptance its terms in this respect must be complied with in order to create a contract. If an offer merely suggests a permitted place, time or manner of acceptance, another method of acceptance is not precluded.

§61 Acceptance Which Requests Change of Terms

An acceptance which requests a change or addition to the terms of the offer is not thereby invalidated unless the acceptance is made to depend on an assent to the changed or added terms.

§62 Effect of Performance by Offeree Where Offer Invites Either Performance or Promise

(1) Where an offer invites an offeree to choose between acceptance by promise and acceptance by performance, the tender or beginning of the invited performance or a tender of a beginning of it is an acceptance by performance.

(2) Such an acceptance operates as a promise to render complete performance.

§63 Time When Acceptance Takes Effect

Unless the offer provides otherwise,

(a) an acceptance made in a manner and by a medium invited by an offer is operative and completes the manifestation of mutual assent as soon as put out of the offeree's possession, without regard to whether it ever reaches the offeror; but

(b) an acceptance under an option contract is not operative until received by the offeror.

§ 64 Acceptance by Telephone or Teletype

Acceptance given by telephone or other medium of substantially instantaneous two-way communication is governed by the principles applicable to acceptances where the parties are in the presence of each other.

§65 Reasonableness of Medium of Acceptance

Unless circumstances known to the offeree indicate otherwise, a medium of acceptance is reasonable if it is the one used by the offeror or one customary in similar transactions at the time and place the offer is received.

§66 Acceptance Must Be Properly Dispatched

An acceptance sent by mail or otherwise from a distance is not operative when dispatched, unless it is properly addressed and such other precautions taken as are ordinarily observed to insure safe transmission of similar messages.

§67 Effect of Receipt of Acceptance Improperly Dispatched

Where an acceptance is seasonably dispatched but the offeree uses means of transmission not invited by the offer or fails to exercise reasonable diligence to insure safe transmission, it is treated as operative upon dispatch if received within the time in which a properly dispatched acceptance would normally have arrived.

§68 What Constitutes Receipt of Revocation, Rejection, or Acceptance

A written revocation, rejection, or acceptance is received when the writing comes into the possession of the person addressed, or of some person authorized by him to receive it for him, or when it is deposited in some place which he has authorized as the place for this or similar communications to be deposited for him.

§69 Acceptance by Silence or Exercise of Dominion

(1) Where an offeree fails to reply to an offer, his silence and inaction operate as an acceptance in the following cases only:

(a) Where an offeree takes the benefit of offered services with reasonable opportunity to reject them and reason to know that they were offered with the expectation of compensation.

(b) Where the offeror has stated or given the offeree reason to understand that assent may be manifested by silence or inaction, and the offeree in remaining silent and inactive intends to accept the offer.

(c) Where because of previous dealings or otherwise, it is reasonable that the offeree should notify the offeror if he does not intend to accept.

(2) An offeree who does any act inconsistent with the offeror's ownership of offered property is bound in accordance with the offered terms unless they are manifestly unreasonable. But if the act is wrongful as against the offeror it is an acceptance only if ratified by him.

§70 Effect of Receipt by Offeror of a Late or Otherwise Defective Acceptance

A late or otherwise defective acceptance may be effective as an offer to the original offeror, but his silence operates as an acceptance in such a case only as stated in §69.

Chapter 4. Formation of Contracts – Consideration

Topic 1. The Requirement of Consideration

§71 Requirement of Exchange; Types of Exchange

(1) To constitute consideration, a performance or a return promise must be bargained for.

(2) A performance or return promise is bargained for if it is sought by the promisor in exchange for his promise and is given by the promisee in exchange for that promise.

(3) The performance may consist of

(a) an act other than a promise, or

(b) a forbearance, or

(c) the creation, modification, or destruction of a legal relation.

(4) The performance or return promise may be given to the promisor or to some other person. It may be given by the promisee or by some other person.

§72 Exchange of Promise for Performance

Except as stated in §§73 and 74, any performance which is bargained for is consideration.

§73 Performance of Legal Duty

Performance of a legal duty owed to a promisor which is neither doubtful nor the subject of honest dispute is not consideration; but a similar performance is consideration if it differs from what was required by the duty in a way which reflects more than a pretense of bargain.

§74 Settlement of Claims

(1) Forbearance to assert or the surrender of a claim or defense which proves to be invalid is not consideration unless

(a) the claim or defense is in fact doubtful because of uncertainty as to the facts or the law, or

(b) the forbearing or surrendering party believes that the claim or defense may be fairly determined to be valid.

(2) The execution of a written instrument surrendering a claim or defense by one who is under no duty to execute it is consideration if the execution of the written instrument is bargained for even though he is not asserting the claim or defense and believes that no valid claim or defense exists.

§75 Exchange of Promise for Promise

Except as stated in §§76 and 77, a promise which is bargained for is consideration if, but only if, the promised performance would be consideration.

§76 Conditional Promise

(1) A conditional promise is not consideration if the promisor knows at the time of making the promise that the condition cannot occur.

(2) A promise conditional on a performance by the promisor is a promise of alternative performances within §77 unless occurrence of the condition is also promised.

§77 Illusory and Alternative Promises

A promise or apparent promise is not consideration if by its terms the promisor or purported promisor reserves a choice of alternative performances unless

(a) each of the alternative performances would have been consideration if it alone had been bargained for; or

(b) one of the alternative performances would have been consideration and there is or appears to the parties to be a substantial possibility that before the promisor exercises his choice events may eliminate the alternatives which would not have been consideration.

§78 Voidable and Unenforceable Promises

The fact that a rule of law renders a promise voidable or unenforceable does not prevent it from being consideration.

§79 Adequacy of Consideration; Mutuality of Obligation

If the requirement of consideration is met, there is no additional requirement of

(a) a gain, advantage, or benefit to the promisor or a loss, disadvantage, or detriment to the promisee; or

(b) equivalence in the values exchanged; or

(c) "mutuality of obligation."

§80 Multiple Exchanges

(1) There is consideration for a set of promises if what is bargained for and given in exchange would have been consideration for each promise in the set if exchanged for that promise alone.

(2) The fact that part of what is bargained for would not have been consideration if that part alone had been bargained for does not prevent the whole from being consideration.

§81 Consideration as Motive or Inducing Cause

(1) The fact that what is bargained for does not of itself induce the making of a promise does not prevent it from being consideration for the promise.

(2) The fact that a promise does not of itself induce a performance or return promise does not prevent the performance or return promise from being consideration for the promise.

Topic 2. Contracts Without Consideration

Introductory Note

Bases for enforcement. The rules of this Topic are exceptions to the general requirement of a bargain stated in §17. The elements in a transaction which justify enforcement of a promise which is not part of a bargain are also often present in bargains. The principal substantive bases for enforcement are reliance and unjust enrichment. Also relevant is the extent to which the evidentiary, cautionary, deterrent and channeling functions of formalities are satisfied. [...] Additional justification for the enforcement of some promises is found in the fact that they are preliminary steps toward bargain or are otherwise ancillary to the making or performance of a bargain.

Omitted cases. In the absence of bargain, the factors bearing on the enforcement of promises appear in widely varying combinations, and no general principle has emerged which distinguishes the binding promise from the non-binding. Sections 82- 94 state rules for certain cases which have arisen often enough so that rules have crystallized, and §§ 86 and 90 state general principles with respect to the effect of unjust enrichment and reliance, respectively. In some States, by statute or decision, additional categories of promises are binding without consideration.

Promises conditional on mutual assent and consideration. Sections 82- 94 state the circumstances under which certain types of promises are binding. Where the stated circumstances do not include mutual assent or consideration, those elements are not required by law. But a promise may be in terms conditional on acceptance or performance or return promise by the promisee, and such a condition is effective. See §91. Where such a condition is met, there may be a transaction enforceable as a bargain; if so, limitations stated in §§ 82- 94, relating to enforcement in the absence of bargain, may be inappropriate and inapplicable.

§82 Promise to Pay Indebtedness; Effect on the Statute of Limitations

(1) A promise to pay all or part of an antecedent contractual or quasi contractual indebtedness owed by the promisor is binding if the indebtedness is still enforceable or would be except for the effect of a statute of limitations.

(2) The following facts operate as such a promise unless other facts indicate a different intention:

(a) A voluntary acknowledgment to the obligee, admitting the present existence of the antecedent indebtedness; or

(b) A voluntary transfer of money, a negotiable instrument, or other thing by the obligor to the obligee, made as interest on or part payment of or collateral security for the antecedent indebtedness; or

(c) A statement to the obligee that the statute of limitations will not be pleaded as a defense.

§83 Promise to Pay Indebtedness Discharged in Bankruptcy

An express promise to pay all or part of an indebtedness of the promisor, discharged or dischargeable in bankruptcy proceedings begun before the promise is made, is binding.

§84 Promise to Perform a Duty in Spite of Non-Occurrence of a Condition

(1) Except as stated in Subsection (2), a promise to perform all or part of a conditional duty under an antecedent contract in spite of the non occurrence of the condition is binding, whether the promise is made before or after the time for the condition to occur, unless

(a) occurrence of the condition was a material part of the agreed exchange for the performance of the duty and the promise was under no duty that it occur; or

(b) uncertainty of the occurrence of the condition was an element of the risk assumed by the promisor.

(2) If such a promise is made before the time for the occurrence of the condition has expired and the condition is within the control of the promisee or a beneficiary, the promisor can make his duty again subject to the condition by notifying the promisee or beneficiary of his intention to do so if

(a) the notification is received while there is still a reasonable time to cause the condition to occur under the antecedent terms or an extension given by the promisor; and

(b) reinstatement of the requirement of the condition is not unjust because of a material change of position by the promisee or beneficiary; and

(c) the promise is not binding apart from the rule stated in Subsection (1).

§85 Promise to Perform a Voidable Duty

Except as stated in §93, a promise to perform all or part of an antecedent contract of the promisor, previously voidable by him, but not avoided prior to the making of the promise, is binding.

§86 Promise for Benefit Received

(1) A promise made in recognition of a benefit previously received by the promisor from the promisee is binding to the extent necessary to prevent injustice.

(2) A promise is not binding under Subsection (1)

(a) if the promisee conferred the benefit as a gift or for other reasons the promisor has not been unjustly enriched; or

(b) to the extent that its value is disproportionate to the benefit.

§87 Option Contract

(1) An offer is binding as an option contract if it

(a) is in writing and signed by the offeror, recites a purported consideration for the making of the offer, and proposes an exchange on fair terms within a reasonable time; or

(b) is made irrevocable by statute.

(2) An offer which the offeror should reasonably expect to induce action or forbearance of a substantial character on the part of the offeree before acceptance and which does induce such action or forbearance is binding as an option contract to the extent necessary to avoid injustice.

§88 Guaranty

A promise to be surety for the performance of a contractual obligation, made to the obligee, is binding if

(a) the promise is in writing and signed by the promisor and recites a purported consideration; or

(b) the promise is made binding by statute; or

(c) the promisor should reasonably expect the promise to induce action or forbearance of a substantial character on the part of the promisee or a third person, and the promise does induce such action or forbearance.

§89 Modification of Executory Contract

A promise modifying a duty under a contract not fully performed on either side is binding

(a) if the modification is fair and equitable in view of circumstances not anticipated by the parties when the contract was made; or

(b) to the extent provided by statute; or

(c) to the extent that justice requires enforcement in view of material change of position in reliance on the promise.

§90 Promise Reasonably Inducing Action or Forbearance

(1) A promise which the promisor should reasonably expect to induce action or forbearance on the part of the promisee or a third person and which does induce such action or forbearance is binding if injustice can be avoided only by enforcement of the promise. The remedy granted for breach may be limited as justice requires.

(2) A charitable subscription or a marriage settlement is binding under Subsection (1) without proof that the promise induced action or forbearance.

§91 Effect of Promises Enumerated in §§82 - 90 When Conditional

If a promise within the terms of §§ 82- 90 is in terms conditional or performable at a future time the promisor is bound thereby, but performance becomes due only upon the occurrence of the condition or upon the arrival of the specified time.

§92 To Whom Promises Enumerated in §§ 82-85 Must Be Made

The new promise referred to in §§ 82- 85 is not binding unless it is made to a person who is then an obligee of the antecedent duty.

§93 Promises Enumerated in §§ 82-85 Made in Ignorance of Facts

A promise within the terms of §§ 82- 85 is not binding unless the promisor knew or had reason to know the essential facts of the previous transaction to which the promise relates, but his knowledge of the legal effect of the facts is immaterial.

§94 Stipulations

A promise or agreement with reference to a pending judicial proceeding, made by a party to the proceeding or his attorney, is binding without consideration. By statute or rule of court such an agreement is generally binding only

(a) if it is in writing and signed by the party or attorney, or

(b) if it is made or admitted in the presence of the court, or

(c) to the extent that justice requires enforcement in view of material change of position in reliance on the promise or agreement.

Topic 3. Contracts Under Seal; Writing as a Statutory Substitute for the Seal [...]

Chapter 5. The Statute of Frauds

§110 Classes of Contracts Covered

(1) The following classes of contracts are subject to a statute, commonly called the Statute of Frauds, forbidding enforcement unless there is a written memorandum or an applicable exception:

(a) a contract of an executor or administrator to answer for a duty of his decedent (the executor-administrator provision);

(b) a contract to answer for the duty of another (the suretyship provision);

(c) a contract made upon consideration of marriage (the marriage provision);

(d) a contract for the sale of an interest in land (the land contract provision);

(e) a contract that is not to be performed within one year from the making thereof (the one-year provision).

(2) The following classes of contracts, which were traditionally subject to the Statute of Frauds, are now governed by Statute of Frauds provisions of the Uniform Commercial Code:

(a) a contract for the sale of goods for the price of $500 or more (Uniform Commercial Code § 2-201);

(b) a contract for the sale of securities (Uniform Commercial Code § 8-319);

(c) a contract for the sale of personal property not otherwise covered, to the extent of enforcement by way of action or defense beyond $5,000 in amount or value of remedy (Uniform Commercial Code § 1-206).

(3) In addition the Uniform Commercial Code requires a writing signed by the debtor for an agreement which creates or provides for a security interest in personal property or fixtures not in the possession of the secured party.

(4) Statutes in most states provide that no acknowledgment or promise is sufficient evidence of a new or continuing contract to take a case out of the operation of a statute of limitations unless made in some writing signed by the party to be charged, but that the statute does not alter the effect of any payment of principal or interest.

(5) In many states other classes of contracts are subject to a requirement of a writing.

Topic 1. The Executor-Administrator Provision

§111 Contract of Executor or Administrator

A contract of an executor or administrator to answer personally for a duty of his decedent is within the Statute of Frauds if a similar contract to answer for the duty of a living person would be within the Statute as a contract to answer for the duty of another.

Topic 2. The Suretyship Provision

§112 Requirement of Suretyship

A contract is not within the Statute of Frauds as a contract to answer for the duty of another unless the promisee is an obligee of the other's duty, the promisor is a surety for the other, and the promisee knows or has reason to know of the suretyship relation.

§113 Promises of the Same Performance for the Same Consideration

Where promises of the same performance are made by two persons for a consideration which inures to the benefit of only one of them, the promise of the other is within the Statute of Frauds as a contract to answer for the duty of another, whether or not the promise is in terms conditional on default by the one to whose benefit the consideration inures, unless

(a) the other is not a surety for the one to whose benefit the consideration inures; or

(b) the promises are in terms joint and do not create several duties or joint and several duties; or

(c) the promisee neither knows nor has reason to know that the consideration does not inure to the benefit of both promisors.

§114 Independent Duty of Promisor

A contract to perform or otherwise to satisfy all or part of a duty of a third person to the promisee is not within the Statute of Frauds as a contract to answer for the duty of another if, by the terms of the promise when it is made, performance thereof can involve no more than

(a) the application of funds or property held by the promisor for the purpose, or

(b) performance of any other duty owing, irrespective of his promise, by the promisor to the promisee, or

(c) performance of a duty which is either owing, irrespective of his promise, by the promisor to the third person, or which the promisee reasonably believes to be so owing.

§115 Novation

A contract that is itself accepted in satisfaction of a previously existing duty of a third person to the promisee is not within the Statute of Frauds as a contract to answer for the duty of another.

§116 Main Purpose; Advantage to Surety

A contract that all or part of a duty of a third person to the promisee shall be satisfied is not within the Statute of Frauds as a promise to answer for the duty of another if the consideration for the promise is in fact or apparently desired by the promisor mainly for his own economic advantage, rather than in order to benefit the third person. If, however, the consideration is merely a premium for insurance, the contract is within the Statute.

§117 Promise to Sign a Written Contract of Suretyship

A promise to sign a written contract as a surety for the performance of a duty owed to the promisee or to sign a negotiable instrument for the accommodation of a person other than the promisee is within the Statute of Frauds.

§118 Promise to Indemnify a Surety

A promise to indemnify against liability or loss made to induce the promisee to become a surety is not within the Statute of Frauds as a contract to answer for the duty of another.

§119 Assumption of Duty by Another

A contract not within the Statute of Frauds as a contract to answer for the duty of another when made is not brought within it by a subsequent promise of another person to assume performance of the duty as principal obligor.

§120 Obligations on Negotiable Instruments

(1) An obligation on a negotiable instrument or a guaranty written on the instrument is not within the Statute of Frauds.

(2) A promise to pay a negotiable instrument, made by a party to it who has been or may be discharged by the holder's failure or delay in making presentment or giving notice of dishonor or in making protest, is not within the Statute of Frauds.

§121 Contract of Assignor or Factor

(1) A contract by the assignor of a right that the obligor of the assigned right will perform his duty is not within the Statute of Frauds as a contract to answer for the duty of another.

(2) A contract by an agent with his principal that a purchaser of the principal's goods through the agent will pay their price to the principal is not within the Statute of Frauds as a contract to answer for the duty of another.

§122 Contract to Buy a Right from the Obligee

A contract to purchase a right which the promisee has or may acquire against a third person is not within the Statute of Frauds as a contract to answer for the duty of another.

§123 Contract to Discharge the Promisee's Duty

A contract to discharge a duty owed by the promisee to a third person is not within the Statute of Frauds as a contract to answer for the duty of another.

Topic 3. The Marriage Provision [...]

Topic 4. The Land Contract Provision [...]

Topic 5. The One-Year Provision [...]

Topic 6. Satisfaction of the Statute by a Memorandum

§131 General Requisites of a Memorandum

Unless additional requirements are prescribed by the particular statute, a contract within the Statute of Frauds is enforceable if it is evidenced by any writing, signed by or on behalf of the party to be charged, which

(a) reasonably identifies the subject matter of the contract,

(b) is sufficient to indicate that a contract with respect thereto has been made between the parties or offered by the signer to the other party, and

(c) states with reasonable certainty the essential terms of the unperformed promises in the contract.

§132 Several Writings

The memorandum may consist of several writings if one of the writings is signed and the writings in the circumstances clearly indicate that they relate to the same transaction.

§133 Memorandum Not Made as Such

Except in the case of a writing evidencing a contract upon consideration of marriage, the Statute may be satisfied by a signed writing not made as a memorandum of a contract.

§134 Signature

The signature to a memorandum may be any symbol made or adopted with an intention, actual or apparent, to authenticate the writing as that of the signer.

§135 Who Must Sign

Where a memorandum of a contract within the Statute is signed by fewer than all parties to the contract and the Statute is not otherwise satisfied, the contract is enforceable against the signers but not against the others.

§136 Time of Memorandum

A memorandum sufficient to satisfy the Statute may be made or signed at any time before or after the formation of the contract.

§137 Loss or Destruction of a Memorandum

The loss or destruction of a memorandum does not deprive it of effect under the Statute.

Topic 7. Consequences of Non-Compliance

Introductory Note

The circumstances in which a contract within the Statute of Frauds may have legal effect notwithstanding failure to comply with the Statute are specified in this Topic. The rules stated in this Topic are general in the sense that they are not limited to any particular class of contracts covered by the Statute. These rules for the most part relate to the effect of conduct subsequent to the making of an unenforceable contract, and deal with problems arising from reliance on it. Section 139 states a general principle permitting enforcement based on reliance. Sections 140-42 specify situations where defensive use of a contract is not treated as "enforcement," Sections 143- 45 situations where the contract can be used either to support or resist a claim. Sections 146- 50 deal with the effect of the Statute on transfers of property related to an unenforceable promise, on other promises in the same contract, and on prior contracts.

§138 Unenforceability

Where a contract within the Statute of Frauds is not enforceable against the party to be charged by an action against him, it is not enforceable by a set-off or counterclaim in an action brought by him, or as a defense to a claim by him.

§139 Enforcement by Virtue of Action in Reliance

(1) A promise which the promisor should reasonably expect to induce action or forbearance on the part of the promisee or a third person and which does induce the action or forbearance is enforceable notwithstanding the Statute of Frauds if injustice can be avoided only by enforcement of the promise. The remedy granted for breach is to be limited as justice requires.

(2) In determining whether injustice can be avoided only by enforcement of the promise, the following circumstances are significant:

(a) the availability and adequacy of other remedies, particularly cancellation and restitution;

(b) the definite and substantial character of the action or forbearance in relation to the remedy sought;

(c) the extent to which the action or forbearance corroborates evidence of the making and terms of the promise, or the making and terms are otherwise established by clear and convincing evidence;

(d) the reasonableness of the action or forbearance;

(e) the extent to which the action or forbearance was foreseeable by the promisor.

§140 Defense of Failure to Perform

The Statute of Frauds does not invalidate defenses based on the plaintiff's failure to perform a condition of his claim or defenses based on his present or prospective breach of the contract he seeks to enforce.

§141 Action for Value of Performance Under Unenforceable Contract

(1) In an action for the value of performance under a contract, except as stated in Subsection (2), the Statute of Frauds does not invalidate any defense which would be available if the contract were enforceable against both parties.

(2) Where a party to a contract which is unenforceable against him refuses either to perform the contract or to sign a sufficient memorandum, the other party is justified in suspending any performance for which he has not already received the agreed return, and such a suspension is not a defense in an action for the value of performance rendered before the suspension.

§142 Tort Liability for Acts Under Unenforceable Contract

Where because of the existence of a contract conduct would not be tortious, unenforceability of the contract under the Statute of Frauds does not make the conduct tortious if it occurs without notice of repudiation of the contract.

§143 Unenforceable Contract as Evidence

The Statute of Frauds does not make an unenforceable contract inadmissible in evidence for any purpose other than its enforcement in violation of the Statute.

§144 Effect of Unenforceable Contract as to Third Parties

Only a party to a contract or a transferee or successor of a party to the contract can assert that the contract is unenforceable under the Statute of Frauds.

§145 Effect of Full Performance

Where the promises in a contract have been fully performed by all parties, the Statute of Frauds does not affect the legal relations of the parties.

§146 Rights of Competing Transferees of Property

(1) Where a contract to transfer property or a transfer was unenforceable against the transferor under the Statute of Frauds but subsequently becomes enforceable, the contract or transfer has whatever priority it would have had aside from the Statute of Frauds over an intervening contract by the transferor to transfer the same property to a third person.

(2) If the third person obtains title to the property by an enforceable transaction before the prior contract becomes enforceable, the prior contract is unenforceable against him and does not affect his title.

§147 Contract Containing Multiple Promises

(1) Where performance of the promises in a contract which subject it to the Statute of Frauds is exclusively beneficial to one party, that party by agreeing to forego the performance may render the remainder of the contract enforceable, but this rule does not apply to a contract to transfer property on the promisor's death.

(2) Where the promises in a contract which subject it to the Statute have become enforceable or where the duty to perform them has been discharged by performance or otherwise, the Statute does not prevent enforcement of the remaining promises.

(3) Except as stated in this Section, where some of the unperformed promises in a contract are unenforceable against a party under the Statute of Frauds, all the promises in the contract are unenforceable against him.

§148 Rescission by Oral Agreement

Notwithstanding the Statute of Frauds, all unperformed duties under an enforceable contract may be discharged by an oral agreement of rescission. The Statute may, however, apply to a contract to rescind a transfer of property.

§149 Oral Modification

(1) For the purpose of determining whether the Statute of Frauds applies to a contract modifying but not rescinding a prior contract, the second contract is treated as containing the originally agreed terms as modified. The Statute may, however, apply independently of the original terms to a contract to modify a transfer of property.

(2) Where the second contract is unenforceable by virtue of the Statute of Frauds and there has been no material change of position in reliance on it, the prior contract is not modified.

§150 Reliance on Oral Modification

Where the parties to an enforceable contract subsequently agree that all or part of a duty need not be performed or of a condition need not occur, the Statute of Frauds does not prevent enforcement of the subsequent agreement if reinstatement of the original terms would be unjust in view of a material change of position in reliance on the subsequent agreement.

Chapter 6. Mistake

Introductory Note

The law of contracts supports the finality of transactions lest justifiable expectations be disappointed. This Chapter deals with exceptional situations in which the law departs from this policy favoring finality and allows either avoidance or reformation on the ground of mistake. As §151 makes clear, the word "mistake" is here used to refer to a belief that is not in accord with existing facts, rather than to an act that is the result of such an erroneous belief.

The type of mistake dealt with in this Chapter is one that relates to existing facts that the parties regard as a basis for making an agreement. An important sub-category of such mistake is mistake as to expression, in which the mistake relates to the contents or effect of a writing that expresses an agreement. In general, the appropriate relief for mistake takes the form of avoidance of the contract. Where, however, because of a mistake of both parties as to expression the writing fails to express an agreement that they have reached previously, the appropriate relief ordinarily takes the form of reformation of the writing to make it conform to their intention. To the extent that reformation is available, as it usually will be, to correct the effects of such a mistake, it is the exclusive remedy and avoidance is unnecessary and unavailable. See §152. A mistake of only one party as to expression, however, may be a basis for avoidance under the rule stated in §153. [...]

The basic rule for mistake of both parties is stated in §152. It allows avoidance by the adversely affected party if the mistake was one as to a basic assumption on which the contract was made, if it had a material effect on the agreed exchange of performances, and if he does not bear the risk of the mistake. The situations to which this rule is applicable are often similar to those governed by §266 on existing impracticability or frustration, since those latter situations also involve mistake. However, the justification underlying the two sections is significantly different. Underlying §266 is the notion of unexpected extreme hardship, either through impracticability of performance or frustration of purpose, and the legal consequence is that no duty to render performance arises. Underlying §152 is the notion of an unexpected material imbalance in the exchange, and the legal consequence is merely that the contract is voidable by the party adversely affected. The consequences of impracticability of performance or frustration of purpose are so extreme that it is relatively unusual for a party to agree to perform in spite of mistake that results in such unexpected hardship as would justify his non-performance on one of these grounds. Therefore, §266 provides for an exception only in the relatively narrow case where "the language or the circumstances indicate the contrary." [...] The consequences of a mistake that materially affects the exchange of performances may be, on the contrary, much less extreme. It is, therefore, much more common for a party to undertake to perform in spite of mistake that would justify his avoidance on this ground. (Indeed, in the absence of provision to the contrary and aside from the exceptional cases of supervening impracticability (§261) and frustration (§265), a party generally bears the entire risk of subsequent changes that affect the agreed exchange.) Therefore, §152 provides for an exception, much broader than that in §266, in all cases where the adversely affected party "bears the risk of mistake." The scope of this exception is spelled out in more detail in a separate section, §154, since the notion of allocation of risk plays a much more significant role in connection with the law of mistake than it does in connection with the law of impracticability and frustration.

The basic rule for mistake of only one party is stated in §153. In situations where the rule stated in §153 allows the mistaken party to avoid the contract, avoidance will more clearly disappoint the expectations of the other party, who was not mistaken, than will avoidance under the rule stated in §152, where he too was mistaken. Therefore, the rule stated in §153 is more restrictive than that stated in §152 and generally allows the mistaken party to avoid only in extreme cases where it would be unconscionable to require him to perform, or where the other party had reason to know of the mistake or his fault caused it.

The rules stated in §§152 and 153 tell only whether a contract is voidable (§7) on the ground of mistake. A party wishing to exercise a power of avoidance will usually simply notify the other party of his rescission, offering to return what he has received or the equivalent. He may then either sue for the return of his own performance or the equivalent or set up his rescission as a defense to a suit on the contract. Sometimes he will instead institute direct proceedings for rescission of the contract. In any case there may be limitations on his power of avoidance. The rules governing this power are stated elsewhere (§§380- 85), together with those for contracts voidable on the ground of incapacity (§§12- 16) or misrepresentation, duress or undue influence (Chapter 7).

The basic rule for mistake of both parties as to expression is stated in §155. It allows reformation where the parties are mistaken in thinking that a writing correctly expresses an agreement that they have previously reached. Avoidance is not an appropriate remedy where the mistake can be corrected by reformation. Under the rule stated in §214(d), the parol evidence rule does not prevent reformation in such a case, and, under the rule stated in §156, the Statute of Frauds does not prevent reformation. However, since reformation is a discretionary equitable remedy, the rule stated in §155 tells only when a court "may" grant such relief, leaving open the possibility that it might deny it on equitable grounds. [...]

If there is a mistake of only one party as to expression, avoidance may be an appropriate remedy under the rule stated in §153. See Illustrations 5 and 6 to §153. If, however, his mistake is in believing that a writing correctly expresses a prior agreement and the other party knows that it does not correctly express that agreement, the problem is one of the effect of the latter's failure to disclose this fact. This is dealt with in §§160- 61, together with other instances in which non-disclosure may be tantamount to misrepresentation.

The rules governing all of the situations dealt with in this Chapter have traditionally been marked by flexibility and have conferred considerable discretion on the court. In part, this has been due to the protean character of the situations involved and the circumstance that they are almost inevitably unforeseen by the parties. In part it has been due to the fact that the law of mistake was shaped largely by courts of equity which had broad discretionary powers. This characteristic of flexibility marks the rules stated in this Chapter, as is evidenced by such necessarily imprecise language as "materially" (§152), "unconscionable" (§153), and "bears the risk" (§§152, 153, 154). In addition, §158 makes it clear that if these rules will not suffice to do substantial justice, it is within the discretion of the court to grant relief on such terms as justice requires. Compare §272, which makes this clear in cases of impracticability and frustration.

A number of problems closely related to those dealt with in this Chapter are found elsewhere in the Restatement of this Subject. Some of these, in contrast to those dealt with here, involve the question whether a contract was formed at all. Thus, the effect of misunderstanding, where the parties attach such different meanings to their language or other manifestations that there is no manifestation of mutual assent, is governed by the rule stated in §20. [...] Similarly, the effect of a mistake of the offeree as to the fact of a delay in the transmission of an offer is dealt with in §49, and the effect of a mistake of the offeree as to the terms of the offer, caused by defective transmission, would be determined by analogous principles. As to the effect of a mistake of a party who makes a contract unaware of the death or insanity of the other, see §§15 and 48. Other problems, involving a mistake of one party caused by the fraud or misrepresentation of the other, are dealt with in §161.

Only those aspects of mistake that affect contract law are dealt with in the Restatement of this Subject. Important questions may arise as to money paid or other performance rendered by mistake, for example, under a mistaken belief that such performance is due under an actual or supposed contract. These questions, however, are not dealt with here unless they are inextricably bound up with the enforceability of contract duties, as may be the case for restitution in connection with avoidance of a contract. Similarly, the Restatement of this Subject does not generally cover present transfers, as by assignment or deed. Such matters are, for the most part, left to the Restatement of Restitution. (As to the effect of mistake on equitable remedies, see §364(a).)

Furthermore, for the sake of simplicity, the rules stated in this Chapter have been formulated in terms of the typical contract based on an exchange of consideration by two parties. It does not, therefore, deal exhaustively with situations involving several parties (§9) including intended beneficiaries (§302), promises enforceable because of reliance (§90), promises enforceable because under seal (§95), and other less typical situations. [...]

§151 Mistake Defined

A mistake is a belief that is not in accord with the facts.

§152 When Mistake of Both Parties Makes a Contract Voidable

(1) Where a mistake of both parties at the time a contract was made as to a basic assumption on which the contract was made has a material effect on the agreed exchange of performances,

the contract is voidable by the adversely affected party unless he bears the risk of the mistake under the rule stated in §154.

(2) In determining whether the mistake has a material effect on the agreed exchange of performances, account is taken of any relief by way of reformation, restitution, or otherwise.

§153 When Mistake of One Party Makes a Contract Voidable

Where a mistake of one party at the time a contract was made as to a basic assumption on which he made the contract has a material effect on the agreed exchange of performances that is adverse to him, the contract is voidable by him if he does not bear the risk of the mistake under the rule stated in §154, and

(a) the effect of the mistake is such that enforcement of the contract would be unconscionable, or

(b) the other party had reason to know of the mistake or his fault caused the mistake.

§154 When a Party Bears the Risk of a Mistake

A party bears the risk of a mistake when

(a) The risk is allocated to him by agreement of the parties, or

(b) he is aware, at the time the contract is made, that he has only limited knowledge with respect to the facts to which the mistake relates but treats his limited knowledge as sufficient, or

(c) the risk is allocated to him by the court on the ground that it is reasonable in the circumstances to do so.

§155 When Mistake of Both Parties as to Written Expression Justifies Reformation

Where a writing that evidences or embodies an agreement in whole or in part fails to express the agreement because of a mistake of both parties as to the contents or effect of the writing, the court may at the request of a party reform the writing to express the agreement, except to the extent that rights of third parties such as good faith purchasers for value will be unfairly affected.

§156 Mistake as to Contract Within the Statute of Frauds

If reformation of a writing is otherwise appropriate, it is not precluded by the fact that the contract is within the Statute of Frauds.

§157 Effect of Fault of Party Seeking Relief

A mistaken party's fault in failing to know or discover the facts before making the contract does not bar him from avoidance or reformation under the rules stated in this Chapter, unless his fault amounts to a failure to act in good faith and in accordance with reasonable standards of fair dealing.

§158 Relief Including Restitution; Supplying a Term

(1) In any case governed by the rules stated in this Chapter, either party may have a claim for relief including restitution under the rules stated in § 240 and 376.

(2) In any case governed by the rules stated in this Chapter, if those rules together with the rules stated in Chapter 16 will not avoid injustice, the court may grant relief on such terms as justice requires including protection of the parties' reliance interest.

Chapter 7. Misrepresentation, Duress and Undue Influence

Introductory Note

Contract law has traditionally relied in large part on the premise that the parties should be able to make legally enforceable agreements on their own terms, freely arrived at by the process of bargaining. This premise presupposes that the integrity of the bargaining process has not been impaired by misrepresentation, duress or undue influence.

Topic 1 of this Chapter deals with situations in which a party has been induced to make a contract by a misrepresentation, that is, an assertion, either fraudulent or non-fraudulent, that is not in accord with existing facts. Topic 2 deals with situations in which a party has been influenced to make a contract by improper pressure. This pressure may take the form of duress by physical compulsion or by threat, or may take the form of undue influence.

Only those aspects of these subjects that deal with contract law are treated in the Restatement of this Subject. Important questions may arise, for example, as to the payment of money or other performance induced by misrepresentation, duress or undue influence. These questions are not dealt with here unless they are inextricably bound up with the enforceability of contract duties, as in the case of restitution in connection with avoidance of a contract on one of these grounds. Similarly, the Restatement of this Subject does not generally cover present transfers, as by assignment or deed. Such matters are, for the most part, left to the Restatement of Restitution. Furthermore, for the sake of simplicity, the rules stated in this Chapter have been formulated in terms of the typical contract involving only two parties and supported by consideration and do not deal exhaustively with less typical situations such as those involving several parties (§9) or promises enforceable because of reliance (§90) or because under seal (§95). As to the possibility that misconduct short of that required by the rules stated in this Chapter may nevertheless be sufficient to preclude equitable relief, see §364. As to the effect of unconscionability, see §208.

At most, the rules stated in this Chapter make the contract voidable, rather than giving the aggrieved party the right to a claim for damages. Compare Restatement, Second, Torts chs. 22, 23.

Topic 1. Misrepresentation

Introductory Note

A misrepresentation is an assertion that is not in accord with the facts (§159). Concealment (§160) and in some cases non-disclosure (§161) of a fact are equivalent to such an assertion. A misrepresentation may have three distinct effects under the rules stated in this Chapter. First, in rare cases, it may prevent the formation of any contract at all (§163). Second, it may make a contract voidable (§164). Third, it may be the grounds for a decree reforming the contract (§166). In the case of non-disclosure by a fiduciary, making a contract with his beneficiary, these rules are supplemented by the rule stated in §173.

A misrepresentation may also be the basis for an affirmative claim for liability for misrepresentation under the law of torts. Such liability for misrepresentation is dealt with in the Restatement, Second, Torts. See Restatement, Second, Torts chs. 22, 23. The rules stated there conform generally to those stated here. However, because tort law imposes liability in damages for misrepresentation, while contract law does not, the requirements imposed by contract law are in some instances less stringent. Notably, under tort law a misrepresentation does not give rise to liability for fraudulent misrepresentation unless it is both fraudulent and material, while under contract law a misrepresentation may make a contract voidable if it is either fraudulent or material. [...]

The most common of the three possible effects of a misrepresentation under the rules stated in this Chapter is that of making the resulting contract voidable. In order for this effect to follow, four things must be shown. First, there must have been a misrepresentation (§§159, 160, 161).

Second, the misrepresentation must have been either fraudulent or material (§162). Third, the misrepresentation must have induced the recipient to make the contract (§167). Fourth, the recipient's reliance on the misrepresentation must have been justified. Specific aspects of the last requirement are treated in connection with assertions of opinion (§§168, 169), assertions as to matters of law (§170), assertions of intention (§171), and fault (§172).

Assertions of opinion pose particularly difficult problems. If such an assertion is solely one of opinion and carries with it no assertion of fact beyond one as to the maker's state of mind, the recipient's reliance on it is usually unjustified, since a party is generally expected to form his own opinions as to the proposed bargain. Exceptional situations, where reliance on such an assertion is justified, are enumerated in §169. However, the recipient may properly interpret a statement of a person's opinion as to facts not known to the recipient as more than a statement of opinion only. He may interpret it as, in addition, an assertion that that person knows of facts sufficient to justify him in forming the opinion, or at least that he knows of no facts incompatible with it (§168(2)). To this extent, the recipient may be justified in relying on that assertion, even if reliance on the assertion as one of opinion only would not be justified under the rule stated in §169.

Because a misrepresentation induces the recipient to make a contract while under a mistake, the rules on mistake stated in Chapter 6 also apply to many cases of misrepresentation. However, a mistaken party who can show the elements required for avoidance on the ground of misrepresentation will ordinarily prefer to base his claim on this ground rather than attempting to establish the additional elements required by the law of mistake.

Special rules of law, applicable to particular types of contracts, also supplement or qualify the rules stated in this Topic. Examples include the provisions of the [UCC] relating to warranties in contracts for the sale of goods and those of statutes requiring disclosure in consumer transactions or regulating transactions in securities (see Federal Securities Code, Parts XVI, XVII). These special rules are not dealt with in this Restatement.

§159 Misrepresentation Defined

A misrepresentation is an assertion that is not in accord with the facts.

§160 When Action is Equivalent to an Assertion (Concealment)

Action intended or known to be likely to prevent another from learning a fact is equivalent to an assertion that the fact does not exist.

§161 When Non-Disclosure Is Equivalent to an Assertion

A person's non-disclosure of a fact known to him is equivalent to an assertion that the fact does not exist in the following cases only:

(a) where he knows that disclosure of the fact is necessary to prevent some previous assertion from being a misrepresentation or from being fraudulent or material.

(b) where he knows that disclosure of the fact would correct a mistake of the other party as to a basic assumption on which that party is making the contract and if non-disclosure of the fact amounts to a failure to act in good faith and in accordance with reasonable standards of fair dealing.

(c) where he knows that disclosure of the fact would correct a mistake of the other party as to the contents or effect of a writing, evidencing or embodying an agreement in whole or in part.

(d) where the other person is entitled to know the fact because of a relation of trust and confidence between them.

§162 When a Misrepresentation Is Fraudulent or Material

(1) A misrepresentation is fraudulent if the maker intends his assertion to induce a party to manifest his assent and the maker

(a) knows or believes that the assertion is not in accord with the facts, or

(b) does not have the confidence that he states or implies in the truth of the assertion, or

(c) knows that he does not have the basis that he states or implies for the assertion.

(2) A misrepresentation is material if it would be likely to induce a reasonable person to manifest his assent, or if the maker knows that it would be likely to induce the recipient to do so.

§163 When a Misrepresentation Prevents Formation of a Contract

If a misrepresentation as to the character or essential terms of a proposed contract induces conduct that appears to be a manifestation of assent by one who neither knows nor has reasonable opportunity to know of the character or essential terms of the proposed contract, his conduct is not effective as a manifestation of assent.

§164 When a Misrepresentation Makes a Contract Voidable

(1) If a party's manifestation of assent is induced by either a fraudulent or a material misrepresentation by the other party upon which the recipient is justified in relying, the contract is voidable by the recipient.

(2) If a party's manifestation of assent is induced by either a fraudulent or a material misrepresentation by one who is not a party to the transaction upon which the recipient is justified in relying, the contract is voidable by the recipient, unless the other party to the transaction in good faith and without reason to know of the misrepresentation either gives value or relies materially on the transaction.

§ 165 Cure by Change of Circumstances

If a contract is voidable because of a misrepresentation and, before notice of an intention to avoid the contract, the facts come into accord with the assertion, the contract is no longer voidable unless the recipient has been harmed by relying on the misrepresentation.

§166 When a Misrepresentation as to a Writing Justifies Reformation

If a party's manifestation of assent is induced by the other party's fraudulent misrepresentation as to the contents or effect of a writing evidencing or embodying in whole or in part an agreement, the court at the request of the recipient may reform the writing to express the terms of the agreement as asserted,

(a) if the recipient was justified in relying on the misrepresentation, and

(b) except to the extent that rights of third parties such as good faith purchasers for value will be unfairly affected.

§167 When a Misrepresentation Is an Inducing Cause

A misrepresentation induces a party's manifestation of assent if it substantially contributes to his decision to manifest his assent.

§168 Reliance on Assertions of Opinion

(1) An assertion is one of opinion if it expresses only a belief, without certainty, as to the existence of a fact or expresses only a judgment as to quality, value, authenticity, or similar matters.

(2) If it is reasonable to do so, the recipient of an assertion of a person's opinion as to facts not disclosed and not otherwise known to the recipient may properly interpret it as an assertion

(a) that the facts known to that person are not incompatible with his opinion, or

(b) that he knows facts sufficient to justify him in forming it.

§169 When Reliance on an Assertion of Opinion Is Not Justified

To the extent that an assertion is one of opinion only, the recipient is not justified in relying on it unless the recipient

(a) stands in such a relation of trust and confidence to the person whose opinion is asserted that the recipient is reasonable in relying on it, or

(b) reasonably believes that, as compared with himself, the person whose opinion is asserted has special skill, judgment or objectivity with respect to the subject matter, or

(c) is for some other special reason particularly susceptible to a misrepresentation of the type involved.

§170 Reliance on Assertions as to Matters of Law

If an assertion is one as to a matter of law, the same rules that apply in the case of other assertions determine whether the recipient is justified in relying on it.

§171 When Reliance on an Assertion of Intention Is Not Justified

(1) To the extent that an assertion is one of intention only, the recipient is not justified in relying on it if in the circumstances a misrepresentation of intention is consistent with reasonable standards of dealing.

(2) If it is reasonable to do so, the promisee may properly interpret a promise as an assertion that the promisor intends to perform the promise.

§172 When Fault Makes Reliance Unjustified

A recipient's fault in not knowing or discovering the facts before making the contract does not make his reliance unjustified unless it amounts to a failure to act in good faith and in accordance with reasonable standards of fair dealing.

§173 When Abuse of a Fiduciary Relation Makes a Contract Voidable

If a fiduciary makes a contract with his beneficiary relating to matters within the scope of the fiduciary relation, the contract is voidable by the beneficiary, unless

(a) it is on fair terms, and

(b) all parties beneficially interested manifest assent with full understanding of their legal rights and of all relevant facts that the fiduciary knows or should know.

Topic 2. Duress and Undue Influence

Introductory Note

This Topic deals with improper pressure in the bargaining process, in the form of either duress or undue influence. Duress takes two forms. In one, a person physically compels conduct that appears to be a manifestation of assent by a party who has no intention of engaging in that conduct. The result of this type of duress is that the conduct is not effective to create a contract (§174). In the other, a person makes an improper threat that induces a party who has no reasonable alternative to manifesting his assent. The result of this type of duress is that the contract that is created is voidable by the victim (§ 175). This latter type of duress is in practice the more common and more important. Either type may be exercised by one who is not a party to the contract as well as by one who is, but if the duress is of the latter type, avoidance is precluded if the other party to the transaction has in good faith and without reason to know of the duress either given value or relied materially (§175(2)).

Over the course of centuries, courts have greatly expanded the classes of threats that will be characterized as improper. The rule stated in §176 which determines whether a threat is improper, therefore includes types of pressure commonly known as "economic duress" or "business compulsion."

Undue influence involves unfair persuasion, a milder form of pressure than duress. Such persuasion nevertheless makes the contract voidable if it is exercised on a party who is under the domination of the person exercising it or is, by virtue of his relation with that person, justified in assuming that this person will not act in a manner inconsistent with his welfare. This rule is subject to an exception similar to that applicable to duress where the undue influence is exercised by one who is not a party (§177(2)).

Since duress and undue influence, unlike deceit, are not generally of themselves actionable torts, the victim of duress or undue influence is usually limited to avoidance and does not have an affirmative action for damages. [...]

§174 When Duress by Physical Compulsion Prevents Formation of a Contract

If conduct that appears to be a manifestation of assent by a party who does not intend to engage in that conduct is physically compelled by duress, the conduct is not effective as a manifestation of assent.

§175 When Duress by Threat Makes a Contract Voidable

(1) If a party's manifestation of assent is induced by an improper threat by the other party that leaves the victim no reasonable alternative, the contract is voidable by the victim.

(2) If a party's manifestation of assent is induced by one who is not a party to the transaction, the contract is voidable by the victim unless the other party to the transaction in good faith and without reason to know of the duress either gives value or relies materially on the transaction.

§176 When a Threat Is Improper

(1) A threat is improper if

(a) what is threatened is a crime or a tort, or the threat itself would be a crime or a tort if it resulted in obtaining property,

(b) what is threatened is a criminal prosecution,

(c) what is threatened is the use of civil process and the threat is made in bad faith, or

(d) the threat is a breach of the duty of good faith and fair dealing under a contract with the recipient.

(2) A threat is improper if the resulting exchange is not on fair terms, and

(a) the threatened act would harm the recipient and would not significantly benefit the party making the threat,

(b) the effectiveness of the threat in inducing the manifestation of assent is significantly increased by prior unfair dealing by the party making the threat, or

(c) what is threatened is otherwise a use of power for illegitimate ends.

§177 When Undue Influence Makes a Contract Voidable

(1) Undue influence is unfair persuasion of a party who is under the domination of the person exercising the persuasion or who by virtue of the relation between them is justified in assuming that that person will not act in a manner inconsistent with his welfare.

(2) If a party's manifestation of assent is induced by undue influence by the other party, the contract is voidable by the victim.

(3) If a party's manifestation of assent is induced by one who is not a party to the transaction, the contract is voidable by the victim unless the other party to the transaction in good faith and without reason to know of the undue influence either gives value or relies materially on the transaction.

Chapter 8. Unenforceability on Grounds of Public Policy

Introductory Note

In general, parties may contract as they wish, and courts will enforce their agreements without passing on their substance. Sometimes, however, a court will decide that the interest in freedom of contract is outweighed by some overriding interest of society and will refuse to enforce a promise or other term on grounds of public policy. Such a decision is based on a reluctance to aid the promisee rather than on solicitude for the promisor as such. Two reasons lie behind this reluctance. First, a refusal to enforce the promise may be an appropriate sanction to discourage undesirable conduct, either by the parties themselves or by others. Second, enforcement of the promise may be an inappropriate use of the judicial process in carrying out an unsavory transaction. The decision in a particular case will often turn on a delicate balancing of these considerations against those that favor supporting transactions freely entered into by the parties. This Chapter states the rules by which courts are guided in making such decisions.

These are not, to be sure, the only rules relating to contracts that are based on public policy. The principle of freedom of contract is itself rooted in the notion that it is in the public interest to recognize that individuals have broad powers to order their own affairs by making legally enforceable promises. Similarly, the rules relating to consideration manifest a policy in favor of limiting that enforcement to those promises that are arrived at by bargain. Other rules, such as those that treat of misrepresentation, duress and undue influence, serve to insure that bargaining has taken place in a suitable climate. The policies behind all of these rules are, however, related to the very process by which the promise itself is made. In contrast, the policies with which this Chapter is concerned touch upon matters of substance related to the public welfare rather than aspects of the bargaining process between the parties. Because of the myriad of such policies, this Chapter does not purport to deal in detail with all of the many kinds of promises that may be unenforceable on grounds of public policy. Nor does it catalog promises that are enforceable in spite of arguments to the contrary based on public policy.

Some policies are purely the product of judicial development. No attempt is made here to present a complete catalog of these, although rules are included in three major areas that have often been before the courts, relating to restraint of trade (Topic 2), impairment of family relations (Topic 3), and interference with other protected interests (Topic 4). Other judicially developed policies are dealt with in the Restatements of other subjects. See Restatement, Second, Conflict of Laws §§32, 80 (choice of forum clauses), 187 (choice of law clauses); Restatement of Property, Division IV, Part II (restraints on alienation); Restatement, Second, Property (Landlord and Tenant) §9.1 (property leased for illegal purposes). See also §317(2)(b) of this Restatement (assignments).

Other policies are implemented by courts for the reason that they have been manifested by legislation. Such legislation may vary widely from one jurisdiction to another, and no attempt is made here to deal with questions of its interpretation. The law of the particular jurisdiction must determine whether there has been a violation of a statute of that jurisdiction that, for example, prohibits the conduct of some activity without a license. Once it is decided that the statute has been violated, the rules stated in this Chapter give guidance as to the effect of that violation on any contractual rights claimed by the parties.

For this reason, no detailed rules are included in this Chapter on fields in which legislation has become preeminent. Labor agreements are not touched upon, nor are agreements in restraint of trade except to the limited extent that legislation is not dominant. See Introductory Note to

Topic 2. Older laws prohibiting usury have been supplemented by new ones that focus on consumer transactions, just as older laws prohibiting gambling have been subjected to more modern exceptions. Bargains tending to obstruct the administration of justice or in violation of a public duty have also come under extensive legislative control. Thus penal laws condemn bribery and corrupt influence, perjury and other falsification in official matters, and obstructing governmental operation (see Model Penal Code Arts. 240-42), and legislation has replaced the common law of maintenance and champerty in many states. A particularly important change has been effected by statutes relating to arbitration, which have now been enacted in so many jurisdictions that it seems likely that even in the remaining states, there has been a change in the former judicial attitude of hostility toward agreements to arbitrate future disputes (see Restatement, Second, Conflict of Laws, Introductory Note to Topic 5, Chapter 8). Such agreements are now widely used and serve the public interest by saving court time. The rules stated in this Chapter do not preclude their enforcement, even in the absence of legislation. Because each of these subjects has a heavy legislative ingredient, none is specifically dealt with in this Chapter. They are however, subject to the general rules relating to unenforceability (Topic 1) and restitution (Topic 5), to the extent that the governing legislation does not dictate otherwise.

All of the rules stated in this Chapter are subject to contrary provision by legislation. The possibility of such modification cannot be overlooked, even in areas where legislation is not extensive.

Topic 1. Unenforceability in General

Introductory Note

This Topic states rules that determine when a promise or other term is unenforceable on grounds of public policy. In stating these rules, it avoids the common characterization of such promises or terms as "illegal." This Restatement is concerned with whether a promise is enforceable and not with whether some other sanction has been attached to the act of making or performing it in such a way as to make that act "illegal." The rules stated here are therefore formulated in terms of "unenforceability" rather than "illegality."

They are also broadly formulated to apply to all promises and other terms (§§2(1), 5), including those where there is no agreement or bargain (§3). See Topic 2 of Chapter 4. Even where both parties make promises, the analysis usually begins with the question of the enforceability of one promise or term of it. Sometimes the unenforceability of that promise or term will result in the unenforceability of other promises and the denial of any relief to either party.

The law, however, is not necessarily so severe. In some situations, one party's promise may be enforceable even though the other party's is not. See, for example, §180. In other situations, part of an agreement may be enforceable even though the rest is unenforceable on grounds of public policy. See §§183, 184, 185. Finally, a court may allow restitution under one of the exceptions to the general rule that denies restitution in such cases (Topic 5). In reading the rule stated in §178, it is important to realize not only that it is itself a flexible one, but that it is subject to these mitigating doctrines.

The rules of substantive law stated in this Topic do not turn on niceties of pleading or of proof. Although it is sometimes said that a party's ability to enforce a promise depends on whether he can state his case in his pleadings without disclosing a contravention of public policy, such arbitrary criteria are not satisfactory ones for resolving matters of significant public interest. Even if neither party's pleading or proof reveals the contravention, the court may ordinarily inquire into it and decide the case on the basis of it if it finds it just to do so, subject to any relevant rules of pleading or proof by which it is bound. Those rules are beyond the scope of this Restatement.

Some related problems are dealt with in other parts of this Restatement. Even though enforcement of a promise is not precluded on grounds of public policy, a governmental regulation or order may give rise to a defense based on supervening or even existing impracticability or frustration. [...] A court may decide that, although enforcement of a promise is not precluded on grounds of public policy, the promisee is not entitled to equitable relief such as specific performance. See §365. Or it may avoid the problem of unenforceability by so interpreting the promise that no contravention of public policy is involved. See §§203(a), 207. That a promise that is unenforceable on grounds of public policy may nevertheless be consideration for a return promise, see §78 [...].

§178 When a Term Is Unenforceable on Grounds of Public Policy

(1) A promise or other term of an agreement is unenforceable on grounds of public policy if legislation provides that it is unenforceable or the interest in its enforcement is clearly outweighed in the circumstances by a public policy against the enforcement of such terms.

(2) In weighing the interest in the enforcement of a term, account is taken of

(a) the parties' justified expectations,

(b) any forfeiture that would result if enforcement were denied, and

(c) any special public interest in the enforcement of the particular term.

(3) In weighing a public policy against enforcement of a term, account is taken of

(a) the strength of that policy as manifested by legislation or judicial decisions,

(b) the likelihood that a refusal to enforce the term will further that policy,

(c) the seriousness of any misconduct involved and the extent to which it was deliberate, and

(d) the directness of the connection between that misconduct and the term.

§179 Bases of Public Policies Against Enforcement

A public policy against the enforcement of promises or other terms may be derived by the court from

(a) legislation relevant to such a policy, or

(b) the need to protect some aspect of the public welfare, as is the case for the judicial policies against, for example,

- (i) restraint of trade (§§186- 188),
- (ii) impairment of family relations (§§189- 191), and
- (iii) interference with other protected interests (§§192- 196, 356).

§180 Effect of Excusable Ignorance

If a promisee is excusably ignorant of facts or of legislation of a minor character, of which the promisor is not excusably ignorant and in the absence of which the promise would be enforceable, the promisee has a claim for damages for its breach but cannot recover damages for anything that he has done after he learns of the facts or legislation.

§181 Effect of Failure to Comply with Licensing or Similar Requirement

If a party is prohibited from doing an act because of his failure to comply with a licensing, registration or similar requirement, a promise in consideration of his doing that act or of his promise to do it is unenforceable on grounds of public policy if

(a) the requirement has a regulatory purpose, and

(b) the interest in the enforcement of the promise is clearly outweighed by the public policy behind the requirement.

§182 Effect of Performance if Intended Use Is Improper

If the promisee has substantially performed, enforcement of a promise is not precluded on grounds of public policy because of some improper use that the promisor intends to make of what he obtains unless the promisee

(a) acted for the purpose of furthering the improper use, or

(b) knew of the use and the use involves grave social harm.

§183 When Agreement Is Enforceable as to Agreed Equivalents

If the parties' performances can be apportioned into corresponding pairs of part performances so that the parts of each pair are properly regarded as agreed equivalents and one pair is not offensive to public policy, that portion of the agreement is enforceable by a party who did not engage in serious misconduct.

§184 When Rest of Agreement Is Enforceable

(1) If less than all of an agreement is unenforceable under the rule stated in § 178, a court may nevertheless enforce the rest of the agreement in favor of a party who did not engage in serious misconduct if the performance as to which the agreement is unenforceable is not an essential part of the agreed exchange.

(2) A court may treat only part of a term an unenforceable under the rule stated in Subsection (1) if the party who seeks to enforce the term obtained it in good faith and in accordance with reasonable standards of fair dealing.

§185 Excuse of a Condition on Grounds of Public Policy

To the extent that a term requiring the occurrence of a condition is unenforceable under the rule stated in § 178, a court may excuse the non-occurrence of the condition unless its occurrence was an essential part of the agreed exchange.

Topic 2. Restraint of Trade

Introductory Note

The common law's policy against restraint of trade is one of its oldest and best established. Nevertheless, the statement in this Chapter of the rules that implement that policy is severely circumscribed in two respects.

First, those rules are included only to the extent that they concern the law of contracts. Although activities such as organizing a corporation or refusing to deal with another may be in restraint of trade, they are outside the scope of this Restatement if no promise is involved. However, a promise to organize a corporation or to refuse to deal comes within its purview.

Second, the Restatement does not deal with those aspects of the subject that are largely legislative. See Introductory Note to this Chapter. Promises in restraint of trade are governed by extensive federal and state statutes, under which the promise may not only be unenforceable, as at common law, but may give rise to both civil and criminal responsibility. The substance of that legislation is beyond the scope of this Restatement. With respect to most aspects of the restraint of trade, federal legislation has so completely occupied the field as to make the common law rules of little or no consequence except as they may give meaning to some of the more general terms of that legislation. Examples are the creation of monopoly, the substantial lessening of competition by, for example, tying purchases of one product to another, or the imposition of non-ancillary restraints controlling prices or limiting production. Specific aspects of the subject may also be governed by state statutes.

The first section in this Topic, §186, treats in general terms of promises in restraint of trade and is intended to complement federal and state legislation in those instances in which recourse to a common law rule may be useful. The other two sections, §§187 and 188, are concerned with the one type of promise in restraint of trade that has traditionally been left to be dealt with under judicially developed rules – the promise to refrain from competition. This Topic, like the rest of this Chapter, does not attempt to catalog promises that are enforceable in spite of arguments to the contrary based on public policy.

§186 Promise in Restraint of Trade

(1) A promise is unenforceable on grounds of public policy if it is unreasonably in restraint of trade.

(2) A promise is in restraint of trade if its performance would limit competition in any business or restrict the promisor in the exercise of a gainful occupation.

§187 Non-Ancillary Restraints on Competition

A promise to refrain from competition that imposes a restraint that is not ancillary to an otherwise valid transaction or relationship is unreasonably in restraint of trade.

§188 Ancillary Restraints on Competition

(1) A promise to refrain from competition that imposes a restraint that is ancillary to an otherwise valid transaction or relationship is unreasonably in restraint of trade if

(a) the restraint is greater than is needed to protect the promisee's legitimate interest, or

(b) the promisee's need is outweighed by the hardship to the promisor and the likely injury to the public.

(2) Promises imposing restraints that are ancillary to a valid transaction or relationship include the following:

(a) a promise by the seller of a business not to compete with the buyer in such a way as to injure the value of the business sold;

(b) a promise by an employee or other agent not to compete with his employer or other principal;

(c) a promise by a partner not to compete with the partnership.

Topic 3. Impairment of Family Relations [...]

Topic 4. Interference with Other Protected Interests

Introductory Note

Just as parties are generally free by agreement to impose new duties on each other, they are generally free by agreement to modify existing duties that they owe each other as a matter of law. One party can ordinarily, for example, contract out of his duty to exercise reasonable care with respect to the other party and thereby exonerate himself of liability to him for negligence (§195(2). There are, however, important limitations imposed on grounds of public policy on the parties' power to interfere with such duties. He cannot, for example, exonerate himself of tort liability for harm caused intentionally or recklessly (§195(1)). Other significant limitations relate to a party's duty to refrain from conduct that is tortious (§192), including violation of a fiduciary duty (§193) or interference with a contract (§194). These and related rules are collected in this Topic. They are not intended to be exhaustive. In many instances legislation, such as the [UCC] and consumer protection statutes, prohibits derogation from the rights it creates. See also §356 on liquidated damages and penalties.

§192 Promise Involving Commission of a Tort

A promise to commit a tort or to induce the commission of a tort is unenforceable on grounds of public policy.

§193 Promise Inducing Violation of Fiduciary Duty

A promise by a fiduciary to violate his fiduciary duty or a promise that tends to induce such a violation is unenforceable on grounds of public policy.

§194 Promise Interfering with Contract with Another

A promise that tortiously interferes with performance of a contract with a third person or a tortiously induced promise to commit a breach of contract is unenforceable on grounds of public policy.

§195 Term Exempting from Liability for Harm Caused Intentionally, Recklessly or Negligently

(1) A term exempting a party from tort liability for harm caused intentionally or recklessly is unenforceable on grounds of public policy.

(2) A term exempting a party from tort liability for harm caused negligently is unenforceable on grounds of public policy if

(a) the term exempts an employer from liability to an employee for injury in the course of his employment;

(b) the term exempts one charged with a duty of public service from liability to one to whom that duty is owed for compensation for breach of that duty, or

(c) the other party is similarly a member of a class protected against the class to which the first party belongs.

(3) A term exempting a seller of a product from his special tort liability for physical harm to a user or consumer is unenforceable on grounds of public policy unless the term is fairly bargained for and is consistent with the policy underlying that liability.

§196 Term Exempting from Consequences of Misrepresentation

A term unreasonably exempting a party from the legal consequences of a misrepresentation is unenforceable on grounds of public policy.

Topic 5. Restitution

Introductory Note

Of the cases that raise the question of the unenforceability of promises on grounds of public policy, the hardest are those in which the promisee has performed and not been paid, but is involved in the wrong with the promisor. In deciding whether to enforce the promise, the court faces a dilemma. On the one hand, if it allows the promisee to enforce the promise, it lends its aid to the promisee in spite of his involvement in the wrong. On the other hand, if it refuses to allow the promisee to enforce the promise, it leaves the benefit that he has conferred by performance in the hands of the promisor in spite of his involvement in the wrong. The dilemma is aggravated by the general principle that a court will not aid one wrongdoer by granting him restitution of a benefit conferred upon the other party, even if the other is also a wrongdoer. See §197. But courts have made important exceptions to this general principle out of a desire to avoid unjust enrichment, when consistent with other goals. These exceptions are set out in the following three sections and relate to claims for restitution by one who would otherwise suffer forfeiture that is disproportionate to the contravention of public policy involved (§197), by one who is not equally in the wrong with the other party or is excusably ignorant (§198), and by one who has withdrawn or where the situation is contrary to the public interest (§199). If a claim for restitution is allowed under one of these sections, it is subject to the general rules on restitution stated in §§370- 77. If it is within the power of the court to fashion a form of relief in which the benefit conferred on one wrongdoer is transferred, not to the other wrongdoer, but to an appropriate and innocent third party, the rules stated in this Topic do not prevent it from doing so. As to the effect of public policy on claims in restitution arising out of transactions in which no promise within this Chapter is involved, see Restatement of Restitution §140.

§197 Restitution Generally Unavailable

Except as stated in §§198 and 199, a party has no claim in restitution for performance that he has rendered under or in return for a promise that is unenforceable on grounds of public policy unless denial of restitution would cause disproportionate forfeiture.

§198 Restitution in Favor of Party Who Is Excusably Ignorant or Is Not Equally in the Wrong

A party has a claim in restitution for performance that he has rendered under or in return for a promise that is unenforceable on grounds of public policy if

(a) he was excusably ignorant of the facts or of legislation of a minor character, in the absence of which the promise would be enforceable, or

(b) he was not equally in the wrong with the promisor.

§199 Restitution Where Party Withdraws or Situation Is Contrary to Public Interest

A party has a claim in restitution for performance that he has rendered under or in return for a promise that is unenforceable on grounds of public policy if he did not engage in serious misconduct and

(a) he withdraws from the transaction before the improper purpose has been achieved, or

(b) allowance of the claim would put an end to a continuing situation that is contrary to the public interest.

Chapter 9. The Scope of Contractual Obligations

Introductory Note

The typical contract is a bargain – an agreement in which a promise is exchanged for a consideration; in atypical cases a promise is binding because of its formal characteristics, because of reliance by the promisee, or for some other reason. See §17. The terms of the agreement or promise to a large extent define the obligation created. Certain types of contracts or terms, however, are forbidden or otherwise regulated, and rules of law must fill the gap when the parties have not provided for the situation which arises. Where the parties have adopted a writing as the final expression of all or part of their agreement, interpretation focuses on the writing, and its terms may supersede other manifestations of intention. Whether or not there is a writing, the parties' intention is read in its context, and usages common to the parties are often an important part of the context.

General rules relating to these matters are stated in this chapter. Bargains unenforceable on grounds of public policy, however, are the subject of a separate chapter. See Chapter 8. The scope of a contractual obligation may be determined or affected by the meaning of the promise or agreement (Topic 1), by considerations of fairness and the public interest (Topic 2), by the adoption of a writing (Topic 3), and by usage (Topic 4). Some special rules relating to conditions and their effect on the scope of contractual obligations are stated at the end of this Chapter (Topic 5).

This Chapter analyzes the process of interpreting and applying agreements, stating separately rules with respect to various aspects of the process. Such a separate statement may convey an erroneous impression of the psychological reality of the judicial process in which many elements are typically combined in a single ruling. Nevertheless, where evidence of an oral term is excluded in an action based on a written agreement with simply the imprecise explanation that "the writing speaks for itself," the ruling, when analyzed, may sum up the following determinations: the contract was integrated (§209); the integration was complete (§ 210); the oral term is inconsistent with the written agreement, is within its scope, does not bear on its interpretation, and would not naturally be omitted from the writing (§§ 213- 16).

Topic 1. The Meaning of Agreements

§200 Interpretation of Promise or Agreement

Interpretation of a promise or agreement or a term thereof is the ascertainment of its meaning.

§201 Whose Meaning Prevails

(1) Where the parties have attached the same meaning to a promise or agreement or a term thereof, it is interpreted in accordance with that meaning.

(2) Where the parties have attached different meanings to a promise or agreement or a term thereof, it is interpreted in accordance with the meaning attached by one of them if at the time the agreement was made

(a) that party did not know of any different meaning attached by the other, and the other knew the meaning attached by the first party; or

(b) that party had no reason to know of any different meaning attached by the other, and the other had reason to know the meaning attached by the first party.

(3) Except as stated in this Section, neither party is bound by the meaning attached by the other, even though the result may be a failure of mutual assent.

§202 Rules in Aid of Interpretation

(1) Words and other conduct are interpreted in the light of all the circumstances, and if the principal purpose of the parties is ascertainable it is given great weight.

(2) A writing is interpreted as a whole, and all writings that are part of the same transaction are interpreted together.

(3) Unless a different intention is manifested,

(a) where language has a generally prevailing meaning, it is interpreted in accordance with that meaning;

(b) technical terms and words of art are given their technical meaning when used in a transaction within their technical field.

(4) Where an agreement involves repeated occasions for performance by either party with knowledge of the nature of the performance and opportunity for objection to it by the other, any course of performance accepted or acquiesced in without objection is given great weight in the interpretation of the agreement.

(5) Wherever reasonable, the manifestations of intention of the parties to a promise or agreement are interpreted as consistent with each other and with any relevant course of performance, course of dealing, or usage of trade.

§203 Standards of Preference in Interpretation

In the interpretation of a promise or agreement or a term thereof, the following standards of preference are generally applicable:

(a) an interpretation which gives a reasonable, lawful, and effective meaning to all the terms is preferred to an interpretation which leaves a part unreasonable, unlawful, or of no effect;

(b) express terms are given greater weight than course of performance, course of dealing, and usage of trade, course of performance is given greater weight than course of dealing or usage of trade, and course of dealing is given greater weight than usage of trade;

(c) specific terms and exact terms are given greater weight than general language;

(d) separately negotiated or added terms are given greater weight than standardized terms or other terms not separately negotiated.

§204. Supplying an Omitted Essential Term

When the parties to a bargain sufficiently defined to be a contract have not agreed with respect to a term which is essential to a determination of their rights and duties, a term which is reasonable in the circumstances is supplied by the court.

Topic 2. Considerations of Fairness and the Public Interest

§205 Duty of Good Faith and Fair Dealing

Every contract imposes upon each party a duty of good faith and fair dealing in its performance and its enforcement.

§206 Interpretation Against the Draftsman

In choosing among the reasonable meanings of a promise or agreement or a term thereof, that meaning is generally preferred which operates against the party who supplies the words or from whom a writing otherwise proceeds.

§207 Interpretation Favoring the Public

In choosing among the reasonable meanings of a promise or agreement or a term thereof, a meaning that serves the public interest is generally preferred.

§208. Unconscionable Contract or Term

If a contract or term thereof is unconscionable at the time the contract is made a court may refuse to enforce the contract, or may enforce the remainder of the contract without the unconscionable term, or may so limit the application of any unconscionable term as to avoid any unconscionable result.

Topic 3. Effect of Adoption of a Writing

Introductory Note

The parties to an agreement often reduce all or part of it to writing. Their purpose in so doing is commonly to provide reliable evidence of its making and its terms and to avoid trusting to uncertain memory. Such a purpose is so common that it is often not discussed; it may not even be conscious. In the interest of certainty and security of transactions, the law gives special effect to a writing adopted as a final expression of an agreement. Such a writing is here referred to as an "integrated agreement" (§209).

The principal effects of a binding integrated agreement are to focus interpretation on the meaning of the terms embodied in the writing (§212), to discharge prior inconsistent agreements, and, in a case of complete integration, to discharge prior agreements within its scope regardless of consistency (§213). Evidence of prior agreements and negotiations is admissible for a variety of purposes, but the admissibility of evidence to contradict an integrated agreement or to add to a completely integrated agreement is restricted, and a limit is thus placed on the power of the trier of fact to exercise a dispensing power in the guise of a finding of fact.

The effect of usage on an integrated agreement is treated in Topic 4, §§ 219- 23.

§209 Integrated Agreements

(1) An integrated agreement is a writing or writings constituting a final expression of one or more terms of an agreement.

(2) Whether there is an integrated agreement is to be determined by the court as a question preliminary to determination of a question of interpretation or to application of the parol evidence rule.

(3) Where the parties reduce an agreement to a writing which in view of its completeness and specificity reasonably appears to be a complete agreement, it is taken to be an integrated agreement unless it is established by other evidence that the writing did not constitute a final expression.

§210 Completely and Partially Integrated Agreements

(1) A completely integrated agreement is an integrated agreement adopted by the parties as a complete and exclusive statement of the terms of the agreement.

(2) A partially integrated agreement is an integrated agreement other than a completely integrated agreement.

(3) Whether an agreement is completely or partially integrated is to be determined by the court as a question preliminary to determination of a question of interpretation or to application of the parol evidence rule.

§211 Standardized Agreements

(1) Except as stated in Subsection (3), where a party to an agreement signs or otherwise manifests assent to a writing and has reason to believe that like writings are regularly used to embody terms of agreements of the same type, he adopts the writing as an integrated agreement with respect to the terms included in the writing.

(2) Such a writing is interpreted wherever reasonable as treating alike all those similarly situated, without regard to their knowledge or understanding of the standard terms of the writing.

(3) Where the other party has reason to believe that the party manifesting such assent would not do so if he knew that the writing contained a particular term, the term is not part of the agreement.

§212 Interpretation of Integrated Agreement

(1) The interpretation of an integrated agreement is directed to the meaning of the terms of the writing or writings in the light of the circumstances, in accordance with the rules stated in this Chapter.

(2) A question of interpretation of an integrated agreement is to be determined by the trier of fact if it depends on the credibility of extrinsic evidence or on a choice among reasonable inferences to be drawn from extrinsic evidence. Otherwise a question of interpretation of an integrated agreement is to be determined as a question of law.

§213 Effect of Integrated Agreement on Prior Agreements (Parol Evidence Rule)

(1) A binding integrated agreement discharges prior agreements to the extent that it is inconsistent with them.

(2) A binding completely integrated agreement discharges prior agreements to the extent that they are within its scope.

(3) An integrated agreement that is not binding or that is voidable and avoided does not discharge a prior agreement. But an integrated agreement, even though not binding, may be effective to render inoperative a term which would have been part of the agreement if it had not been integrated.

§214 Evidence of Prior or Contemporaneous Agreements and Negotiations

Agreements and negotiations prior to or contemporaneous with the adoption of a writing are admissible in evidence to establish

(a) that the writing is or is not an integrated agreement;

(b) that the integrated agreement, if any, is completely or partially integrated;

(c) the meaning of the writing, whether or not integrated;

(d) illegality, fraud, duress, mistake, lack of consideration, or other invalidating cause;

(e) ground for granting or denying rescission, reformation, specific performance, or other remedy.

§215 Contradiction of Integrated Terms

Except as stated in the preceding Section, where there is a binding agreement, either completely or partially integrated, evidence of prior or contemporaneous agreements or negotiations is not admissible in evidence to contradict a term of the writing.

§216 Consistent Additional Terms

(1) Evidence of a consistent additional term is admissible to supplement an integrated agreement unless the court finds that the agreement was completely integrated.

(2) An agreement is not completely integrated if the writing omits a consistent additional agreed term which is

(a) agreed to for separate consideration, or

(b) such a term as in the circumstances might naturally be omitted from the writing.

§217 Integrated Agreement Subject to Oral Requirement of a Condition

Where the parties to a written agreement agree orally that performance of the agreement is subject to the occurrence of a stated condition, the agreement is not integrated with respect to the oral condition.

§218 Untrue Recitals; Evidence of Consideration

(1) A recital of a fact in an integrated agreement may be shown to be untrue.

(2) Evidence is admissible to prove whether or not there is consideration for a promise, even though the parties have reduced their agreement to a writing which appears to be a completely integrated agreement.

Topic 4. Scope as Affected by Usage

§219 Usage

Usage is habitual or customary practice.

§220 Usage Relevant to Interpretation

(1) An agreement is interpreted in accordance with a relevant usage if each party knew or had reason to know of the usage and neither party knew or had reason to know that the meaning attached by the other was inconsistent with the usage.

(2) When the meaning attached by one party accorded with a relevant usage and the other knew or had reason to know of the usage, the other is treated as having known or had reason to know the meaning attached by the first party.

§221 Usage Supplementing an Agreement

An agreement is supplemented or qualified by a reasonable usage with respect to agreements of the same type if each party knows or has reason to know of the usage and neither party knows or has reason to know that the other party has an intention inconsistent with the usage.

§222 Usage of Trade

(1) A usage of trade is a usage having such regularity of observance in a place, vocation, or trade as to justify an expectation that it will be observed with respect to a particular agreement. It may include a system of rules regularly observed even though particular rules are changed from time to time.

(2) The existence and scope of a usage of trade are to be determined as questions of fact. If a usage is embodied in a written trade code or similar writing the interpretation of the writing is to be determined by the court as a question of law.

(3) Unless otherwise agreed, a usage of trade in the vocation or trade in which the parties are engaged or a usage of trade of which they know or have reason to know gives meaning to or supplements or qualifies their agreement.

§ 223 Course of Dealing

(1) A course of dealing is a sequence of previous conduct between the parties to an agreement which is fairly to be regarded as establishing a common basis of understanding for interpreting their expressions and other conduct.

(2) Unless otherwise agreed, a course of dealing between the parties gives meaning to or supplements or qualifies their agreement.

Topic 5. Conditions and Similar Events

Introductory Note

The preceding sections of this Chapter have been primarily concerned with duties. This Topic is concerned with conditions. An obligor will often qualify his duty by providing that performance will not become due unless a stated event, which is not certain to occur, does occur. Such an event is called a condition. An obligor may make an event a condition of his duty in order to shift to the obligee the risk of its non-occurrence. In this case the event may be within the control of the obligee (e.g., his furnishing security), or of the obligor (e.g., his satisfaction with the obligee's performance), or of neither (e.g., the accidental destruction of the subject matter). An obligor may also make an event a condition of his duty in order to induce the obligee to cause the event to occur. In this case the event is presumably within the control of the obligee (e.g., his performance within a specified time). And even when the party has not qualified his duty in this way, a court may supply a term (§204) making an event a condition.

When a court determines whether the agreement makes an event a condition, or whether, if the agreement does not, the court itself should supply a term making an event a condition, it follows the general rules already stated in this Chapter. The same rules are used to ascertain the meaning of the agreement (Topic 1), and the same considerations of fairness and the public interest apply (Topic 2); the adoption of a writing has the same consequences (Topic 3; but see §217), and usage has the same effect (Topic 4).

Conditions have, however, traditionally been the subject of a distinctive terminology, and there are some special rules in aid of interpretation with regard to conditions. This Topic deals with this terminology and these rules. The terminology includes the word "condition" itself (§224 and Comment a, the terms "express," "implied in fact" and "constructive" conditions (Comment c to §226), the phrase "excuse of the non-occurrence of a condition" (Comment b to §225), and the terms "condition precedent" and "condition subsequent," which are not used in this Restatement

(Comment e to §224; Comment a to §230). The rules speak to the effect of the non-occurrence of a condition (§225), to whether an event is a condition and, if so, the nature of that event (§§226- 28), and to the excuse of the non-occurrence of a condition to avoid forfeiture (§229). Where performances are to be exchanged under an exchange of promises, a failure of performance by one party may have the same effect as the non-occurrence of a condition, but this matter is covered in Chapter 10 and not in this Topic.

§224 Condition Defined

A condition is an event, not certain to occur, which must occur, unless its non occurrence is excused, before performance under a contract becomes due.

§225 Effects of the Non-Occurrence of a Condition

(1) Performance of a duty subject to a condition cannot become due unless the condition occurs or its non occurrence is excused.

(2) Unless it has been excused, the non occurrence of a condition discharges the duty when the condition can no longer occur.

(3) Non-occurrence of a condition is not a breach by a party unless he is under a duty that the condition occur.

§226 How an Event May Be Made a Condition

An event may be made a condition either by the agreement of the parties or by a term supplied by the court.

§227 Standards of Preference with Regard to Conditions

(1) In resolving doubts as to whether an event is made a condition of an obligor's duty, and as to the nature of such an event, an interpretation is preferred that will reduce the obligee's risk of forfeiture, unless the event is within the obligee's control or the circumstances indicate that he has assumed the risk.

(2) Unless the contract is of a type under which only one party generally undertakes duties, when it is doubtful whether

(a) a duty is imposed on an obligee that an event occur, or

(b) the event is made a condition of the obligor's duty, or

(c) the event is made a condition of the obligor's duty and a duty is imposed on the obligee that the event occur,

the first interpretation is preferred if the event is within the obligee's control.

(3) In case of doubt, an interpretation under which an event is a condition of an obligor's duty is preferred over an interpretation under which the non-occurrence of the event is a ground for discharge of that duty after it has become a duty to perform.

§228 Satisfaction of the Obligor as a Condition

When it is a condition of an obligor's duty that he be satisfied with respect to the obligee's performance or with respect to something else, and it is practicable to determine whether a reasonable person in the position of the obligor would be satisfied, an interpretation is preferred under which the condition occurs if such a reasonable person in the position of the obligor would be satisfied.

§229 Excuse of a Condition to Avoid Forfeiture

To the extent that the non occurrence of a condition would cause disproportionate forfeiture, a court may excuse the non occurrence of that condition unless its occurrence was a material part of the agreed exchange.

§230 Event that Terminates a Duty

(1) Except as stated in Subsection (2), if under the terms of the contract the occurrence of an event is to terminate an obligor's duty of immediate performance or one to pay damages for breach, that duty is discharged if the event occurs.

(2) The obligor's duty is not discharged if occurrence of the event

(a) is the result of a breach by the obligor of his duty of good faith and fair dealing, or

(b) could not have been prevented because of impracticability and continuance of the duty does not subject the obligor to a materially increased burden.

(3) The obligor's duty is not discharged if, before the event occurs, the obligor promises to perform the duty even if the event occurs and does not revoke his promise before the obligee materially changes his position in reliance on it.

Chapter 10. Performance and Non-Performance

Introductory Note

Because contracting parties ordinarily expect that they will perform their obligations, they are usually more explicit in defining those obligations than in stating the consequences of their non-performance. During the course of performance, problems may arise that require a clear definition of the obligations of the parties under the contract and that may make it appropriate for them to adjust those obligations in the light of a situation not contemplated when the contract was made. When such problems arise, the parties should be encouraged to communicate with each other and seek to resolve them without outside intervention. Should their efforts fail, a court may be asked to define their obligations. See §204. This Chapter states rules for this purpose.

In general, these rules are based on fundamental principles of fairness and justice. The provisions of Article 2 of the Uniform Commercial Code that relate to performance and non-performance show the application of these principles to contracts for the sale of goods. They serve therefore both as illustrations of the principles on which the rules stated in this Chapter are based and as sources, by analogy, of those principles. Compare, e.g., §233 with Uniform Commercial Code §2-307, and §251 with Uniform Commercial Code §2-609.

The most important and complex of the rules stated in this Chapter apply to the most significant type of contract, that in which the parties have exchanged promises in the expectation that there will be a subsequent exchange of performances. Rules for identifying contracts of this type are stated in §§231 and 232. The principal objective of the rules applicable to such contracts is to secure the parties' expectation that a subsequent exchange of performances will actually take place.

When a party fails to receive the performance that he expects, the wisest course is ordinarily for the parties to attempt to resolve their differences by negotiations, including clarification of expectations, cure of past defaults, and assurance as to future performance. If these efforts fail, the injured party may pursue his claim in court. It is, of course, always possible to leave a party who is aggrieved by his failure to receive the expected exchange to pursue a claim for damages against the other party. But contracting parties ordinarily bargain for performance rather than for a lawsuit. It is therefore generally fairer to give the injured party, to the extent that it is possible, the right to suspend his own performance and ultimately to refuse it and, if the other party's non-performance is not justified, to claim damages for total breach of contract. This the injured party is permitted to do under §§237 and 238, which make performance, or at least an offer of performance, by the other party a condition of the aggrieved party's remaining duty under the contract.

When the rules stated in these sections apply, their effect is to deny to the other party any right to compensation under the contract itself (as distinguished from any possible claim to restitution) for what he has done. To minimize the risk of forfeiture, they are tempered by provision that only a material failure by the other party operates as the non-occurrence of a condition which justifies the injured party in suspending his own performance and ultimately in treating his duties as discharged. Considerations for determining whether a failure is material and the time after which a material failure discharges the injured party's remaining duties and may also give him a claim for damages for total breach are stated in §§241 and 242. The risk of forfeiture is also reduced by the rule stated in §240, which allows recovery for performance of only a part of what is due subject to any claim for breach as to the remainder, where part performances are agreed equivalents.

In applying these rules it is essential to know the order in which the parties' performances are to be given, so that it can be determined at any particular time whether there has been a material failure by either party with respect to any performance that is due at an earlier time. Where the language or the circumstances indicate the time for performance, that is of course controlling. Otherwise, the rules stated in §§233 and 234 govern. To the extent possible, simultaneous performance by both parties is desirable, since this gives each party the opportunity to withhold his own performance until he is sure that the other party's performance will be forthcoming and requires neither party to finance the transaction before he receives the other's performance.

Other sections in Topic 2 of this Chapter state rules that are applicable to contracts generally and are not limited to performances that are to be exchanged under an exchange of promises. They deal with the effects on contract duties of performance and non-performance (§235), with claims for total and partial breach (§§236, 243), and with the excuse of the non-occurrence of conditions in the course of performance (§§245- 49). Topic 3 deals with prospective non-performance. See Introductory Note to Topic 3.

The rules stated in this Chapter are not intended to apply to performance as a means of acceptance of an offer, including an option contract (§§45, 62), although in some instances the same underlying considerations may apply.

Topic 1. Performances to Be Exchanged Under an Exchange of Promises

§231 Criterion for Determining When Performances Are to Be Exchanged Under an Exchange of Promises

Performances are to be exchanged under an exchange of promises if each promise is at least part of the consideration for the other and the performance of each promise is to be exchanged at least in part for the performance of the other.

§232 When It Is Presumed That Performances Are to Be Exchanged Underan Exchange of Promises

Where the consideration given by each party to a contract consists in whole or in part of promises, all the performances to be rendered by each party taken collectively are treated as performances to be exchanged under an exchange of promises, unless a contrary intention is clearly manifested.

§233 Performance at One Time or in Installments

(1) Where performances are to be exchanged under an exchange of promises, and the whole of one party's performance can be rendered at one time, it is due at one time, unless the language or the circumstances indicate the contrary.

(2) Where only a part of one party's performance is due at one time under Subsection (1), if the other party's performance can be so apportioned that there is a comparable part that can also be rendered at that time, it is due at that time, unless the language or the circumstances indicate the contrary.

§234 Order of Performances

(1) Where all or part of the performances to be exchanged under an exchange of promises can be rendered simultaneously, they are to that extent due simultaneously, unless the language or the circumstances indicate the contrary.

(2) Except to the extent stated in Subsection (1), where the performance of only one party under such an exchange requires a period of time, his performance is due at an earlier time than that of the other party, unless the language or the circumstances indicate the contrary.

Topic 2. Effect of Performance and Non-Performance

§235 Effect of Performance as Discharge and of Non-Performance as Breach

(1) Full performance of a duty under a contract discharges the duty.

(2) When performance of a duty under a contract is due any non-performance is a breach.

§236 Claims for Damages for Total and for Partial Breach

(1) A claim for damages for total breach is one for damages based on all of the injured party's remaining rights to performance.

(2) A claim for damages for partial breach is one for damages based on only part of the injured party's remaining rights to performance.

§237 Effect on Other Party's Duties of a Failure to Render Performance

Except as stated in § 240, it is a condition of each party's remaining duties to render performances to be exchanged under an exchange of promises that there be no uncured material failure by the other party to render any such performance due at an earlier time.

§ 238 Effect on Other Party's Duties of a Failure to Offer Performance

Where all or part of the performances to be exchanged under an exchange of promises are due simultaneously, it is a condition of each party's duties to render such performance that the other party either render or, with manifested present ability to do so, offer performance of his part of the simultaneous exchange.

§239 Effect on Other Party's Duties of a Failure Justified by Non-Occurrence of a Condition

(1) A party's failure to render or to offer performance may, except as stated in Subsection (2), affect the other party's duties under the rules stated in §§237 and 238 even though failure is justified by the non-occurrence of a condition.

(2) The rule stated in Subsection (1) does not apply if the other party assumed the risk that he would have to perform in spite of such a failure.

§240 Part Performances as Agreed Equivalents

If the performances to be exchanged under an exchange of promises can be apportioned into corresponding pairs of part performances so that the parts of each pair are properly regarded as agreed equivalents, a party's performance of his part of such a pair has the same effect on the other's duties to render performance of the agreed equivalent as it would have if only that pair of performances had been promised.

§241 Circumstances Significant in Determining Whether a Failure is Material

In determining whether a failure to render or to offer performance is material, the following circumstances are significant:

(a) the extent to which the injured party will be deprived of the benefit which he reasonably expected;

(b) the extent to which the injured party can be adequately compensated for the part of that benefit of which he will be deprived;

(c) the extent to which the party failing to perform or to offer to perform will suffer forfeiture;

(d) the likelihood that the party failing to perform or to offer to perform will cure his failure, taking account of all the circumstances including any reasonable assurances;

(e) the extent to which the behavior of the party failing to perform or to offer to perform comports with standards of good faith and fair dealing.

§242 Circumstances Significant in Determining When Remaining Duties Are Discharged

In determining the time after which a party's uncured material failure to render or to offer performance discharges the other party's remaining duties to render performance under the rules stated in §237 and 238, the following circumstances are significant:

(a) those stated in §241;

(b) the extent to which it reasonably appears to the injured party that delay may prevent or hinder him in making reasonable substitute arrangements;

(c) the extent to which the agreement provides for performance without delay, but a material failure to perform or to offer to perform on a stated day does not of itself discharge the other party's remaining duties unless the circumstances, including the language of the agreement, indicate that performance or an offer to perform by that day is important.

§243 Effect of a Breach by Non-Performance as Giving Rise to a Claim for Damages for Total Breach

(1) With respect to performances to be exchanged under an exchange of promises, a breach by non performance gives rise to a claim for damages for total breach only if it discharges the injured party's remaining duties to render such performance, other than a duty to render an agreed equivalent under §240.

(2) Except as stated in Subsection (3), a breach by nonperformance accompanied or followed by a repudiation gives rise to a claim for damages for total breach.

(3) Where at the time of the breach the only remaining duties of performance are those of the party in breach and are for the payment of money in installments not related to one another, his breach by non performance as to less than the whole, whether or not accompanied or followed by a repudiation, does not give rise to a claim for damages for total breach.

(4) In any case other than those stated in the preceding subsections, a breach by non performance gives rise to a claim for total breach only if it so substantially impairs the value of the contract to the injured party at the time of the breach that it is just in the circumstances to allow him to recover damages based on all his remaining rights to performance.

§244 Effect of Subsequent Events on Duty to Pay Damages

A party's duty to pay damages for total breach by non-performance is discharged if it appears after the breach that there would have been a total failure by the injured party to perform his return promise.

§245 Effect of a Breach by Non-Performance as Excusing the Non-Occurrence of a Condition

Where a party's breach by non-performance contributes materially to the non-occurrence of a condition of one of his duties, the non-occurrence is excused.

§246 Effect of Acceptance as Excusing the Non-Occurrence of a Condition

(1) Except as stated in Subsection (2), an obligor's acceptance or his retention for an unreasonable time of the obligee's performance, with knowledge of or reason to know of the non-occurrence of a condition of the obligor's duty, operates as a promise to perform in spite of that non-occurrence, under the rules stated in §84.

(2) If at the time of its acceptance or retention the obligee's performance involves such attachment to the obligor's property that removal would cause material loss, the obligor's acceptance or retention of that performance operates as a promise to perform in spite of the non-occurrence of the condition, under the rules stated in §84, only if the obligor with knowledge of or reason to know of the defects manifests assent to the performance.

§247 Effect of Acceptance of Part Performance as Excusing the Subsequent Non-Occurrence of a Condition

An obligor's acceptance of part of the obligee's performance, with knowledge or reason to know of the non-occurrence of a condition of the obligor's duty, operates as a promise to perform in spite of a subsequent non-occurrence of the condition under the rules stated in §84 to the extent that it justifies the obligee in believing that subsequent performances will be accepted in spite of that non-occurrence.

§248 Effect of Insufficient Reason for Rejection as Excusing the Non-Occurrence of a Condition

Where a party rejecting a defective performance or offer of performance gives an insufficient reason for rejection, the non-occurrence of a condition of his duty is excused only if he knew or had reason to know of that non-occurrence and then only to the extent that the giving of an insufficient reason substantially contributes to a failure by the other party to cure.

§249 When Payment Other Than by Legal Tender is Sufficient

Where the payment or offer of payment of money is made a condition of an obligor's duty, payment or offer of payment in any manner current in the ordinary course of business satisfies the requirement unless the obligee demands payment in legal tender and gives any extension of time reasonably necessary to procure it.

Topic 3. Effect of Prospective Non-Performance

Introductory Note

A contracting party expects that the other party will not only perform his duties under the contract when the time for performance comes, but will do nothing substantially to impair this expectation before that time comes. The rules stated in this Topic are designed primarily to afford protection against such impairment.

The first two sections state rules for determining whether there is a repudiation. Section 250 tells when a statement or other voluntary act is a repudiation. Section 251 tells when one party may treat the other party's failure to give assurance as a repudiation. It protects an obligee when, although there has been no repudiation by the obligor, reasonable grounds have nevertheless arisen to believe that the obligor will commit a serious breach. The obligee may demand assurance of due performance, may in a proper case suspend his own performance while he awaits such assurance, and may treat the failure of the obligor to give such assurance as a repudiation.

Section 252 states a special rule that gives the obligee broader protection when it is the obligor's insolvency that gives rise to his belief that the obligor will commit a breach.

Sections 253 and 255 deal with the three possible effects of a repudiation. First, a repudiation may, before any breach by non-performance, give rise to a claim for damages for total breach (§253(1)). (As to when a repudiation coupled with a breach by non-performance gives rise to such a claim, see §243(2).) Second, a repudiation may discharge the other party's remaining duties of performance (§253(2)). Third, a repudiation may excuse the non-occurrence of a condition of the repudiator's duty (§255).

The effect of subsequent events on the repudiator's duty to pay damages is dealt with in §254, while §§256 and 257 deal with the possible effects of subsequent events on the repudiation, itself. Section 256 tells when subsequent events nullify a statement or other event that would otherwise amount to a repudiation under §250 or the basis for a repudiation under §251. Section 257 states that efforts by the injured party to obtain performance in spite of a repudiation do not change its effect.

§250 When a Statement or an Act Is a Repudiation

A repudiation is

(a) a statement by the obligor to the obligee indicating that the obligor will commit a breach that would of itself give the obligee a claim for damages for total breach under §243, or

(b) a voluntary affirmative act which renders the obligor unable or apparently unable to perform without such a breach.

§251 When a Failure to Give Assurance May Be Treated as a Repudiation

(1) Where reasonable grounds arise to believe that the obligor will commit a breach by non performance that would of itself give the obligee a claim for damages for total breach under §243, the obligee may demand adequate assurance of due performance and may, if reasonable, suspend any performance for which he has not already received the agreed exchange until he receives such assurance.

(2) The obligee may treat as a repudiation the obligor's failure to provide within a reasonable time such assurance of due performance as is adequate in the circumstances of the particular case.

§252 Effect of Insolvency

(1) Where the obligor's insolvency gives the obligee reasonable grounds to believe that the obligor will commit a breach under the rule stated in §251, the obligee may suspend any performance for which he has not already received the agreed exchange until he receives assurance in the form of performance itself, an offer of performance, or adequate security.

(2) A person is insolvent who either has ceased to pay his debts in the ordinary course of business or cannot pay his debts as they become due or is insolvent within the meaning of the federal bankruptcy law.

§253 Effect of a Repudiation as a Breach and on Other Party's Duties

(1) Where an obligor repudiates a duty before he has committed a breach by non performance and before he has received all of the agreed exchange for it, his repudiation alone gives rise to a claim for damages for total breach.

(2) Where performances are to be exchanged under an exchange of promises, one party's repudiation of a duty to render performance discharges the other party's remaining duties to render performance.

§254 Effect of Subsequent Events on Duty to Pay Damages

(1) A party's duty to pay damages for total breach by repudiation is discharged if it appears after the breach that there would have been a total failure by the injured party to perform his return promise.

(2) A party's duty to pay damages for total breach by repudiation is discharged if it appears after the breach that the duty that he repudiated would have been discharged by impracticability or frustration before any breach by non-performance.

§255 Effect of a Repudiation as Excusing the Non-Occurrence of a Condition

Where a party's repudiation contributes materially to the non-occurrence of a condition of one of his duties, the non-occurrence is excused.

§256 Nullification of Repudiation or Basis for Repudiation

(1) The effect of a statement as constituting a repudiation under §250 or the basis for a repudiation under §251 is nullified by a retraction of the statement if notification of the retraction comes to the attention of the injured party before he materially changes his position in reliance on the repudiation or indicates to the other party that he considers the repudiation to be final.

(2) The effect of events other than a statement as constituting a repudiation under §250 or the basis for a repudiation under §251 is nullified if, to the knowledge of the injured party, those events have ceased to exist before he materially changes his position in reliance on the repudiation or indicates to the other party that he considers the repudiation to be final.

§257 Effect of Urging Performance in Spite of Repudiation

The injured party does not change the effect of a repudiation by urging the repudiator to perform in spite of his repudiation or to retract his repudiation.

Topic 4. Application of Performances

Introductory Note

If an obligor who owes two or more duties to the same obligee renders a performance that is not sufficient to discharge all of them, it may be important to determine which are discharged. This Topic states rules for the application of performances in that situation. In many states these rules have been modified by statutes governing the application of payments in consumer credit transactions. See, e.g., Uniform Consumer Credit Code §3.303 (1974 ed.), which provides for the application of payments on debts secured by cross-collateral.

The obligor generally has the power to direct application of his performance and often does so explicitly if his intention is not evident from the nature of the performance itself. This rule is stated in §258. Sections 259 and 260 state rules that apply where the obligor has not exercised this power. If the obligor's duties are to render immediate performances of identical character, the obligee generally has the power to apply it as he chooses. If he does not, the performance is applied according to rules of law. In practice the questions dealt with in §§259 and 260 arise almost exclusively in connection with duties to pay money. This is because, even after breach, a duty to pay money continues unchanged, except for the added duty to pay interest, and may still be discharged by payment. However, once a duty to render a performance of another kind has been transformed into a duty to pay damages for total breach, the duty to pay damages cannot be discharged simply by rendering the performance originally called for. Because performances other than payment rarely present questions of the kind dealt with in §§259 and 260, those sections refer only to payment. The principles extend, however, to the occasional instances of other performances of an identical character.

The rules stated in this Topic do not apply to cases in which the obligee accepts a performance different from that owed by the obligor. Rules for those cases are stated in Topic 2 of Chapter 12, Discharge By Assent or Alteration. Nor do the rules stated in this Topic extend to performances that are not rendered voluntarily, such as payments made by the receiver of an insolvent obligor or by the insurer of an obligor under an insurance policy. The rights that an obligor may have to restitution of a payment on grounds such as mistake, misrepresentation or duress at the time of payment are stated in the Restatement of Restitution.

§258 Obligor's Direction of Application

(1) Except as stated in Subsection (2), as between two or more contractual duties owed by an obligor to the same obligee, a performance is applied according to a direction made by the obligor to the obligee at or before the time of performance.

(2) If the obligor is under a duty to a third person to devote a performance to the discharge of a particular duty that the obligor owes to the obligee and the obligee knows or has reason to know this, the obligor's performance is applied to that duty.

§259 Creditor's Application

(1) Except as stated in Subsections (2) and (3), if the debtor has not directed application of a payment as between two or more matured debts, the payment is applied according to a manifestation of intention made within a reasonable time by the creditor to the debtor.

(2) A creditor cannot apply such a payment to a debt if

(a) the debtor could not have directed its application to that debt, or

(b) a forfeiture would result from a failure to apply it to another debt and the creditor knows or has reason to know this, or

(c) the debt is disputed or is unenforceable on grounds of public policy.

(3) If a creditor is owed one such debt in his own right and another in a fiduciary capacity, he cannot, unless empowered to do so by the beneficiary, effectively apply to the debt in his own right a greater proportion of a payment than that borne by the unsecured portion of that debt to the unsecured portions of both claims.

§260 Application of Payments Where Neither Party Exercises His Power

(1) If neither the debtor nor the creditor has exercised his power with respect to the application of a payment as between two or more matured debts, the payment is applied to debts to which the creditor could have applied it with just regard to the interests of third persons, the debtor and the creditor.

(2) In applying payments under the rule stated in Subsection (1), a payment is applied to the earliest matured debt and ratably among debts of the same maturity, except that preference is given

(a) to a debt that the debtor is under a duty to a third person to pay immediately, and

(b) if he is not under such a duty,

(i) to overdue interest rather than principal, and

(ii) to an unsecured or precarious debt rather than one that is secured or certain of payment.

Chapter 11. Impracticability of Performance and Frustration of Purpose

Introductory Note

Contract liability is strict liability. It is an accepted maxim that pacta sunt servanda, contracts are to be kept. The obligor is therefore liable in damages for breach of contract even if he is without fault and even if circumstances have made the contract more burdensome or less desirable than he had anticipated. (As to the effect of hardship on equitable remedies, see §364(b).) The obligor who does not wish to undertake so extensive an obligation may contract for a lesser one by using one of a variety of common clauses: he may agree only to use his "best efforts"; he may restrict his obligation to his output or requirements; he may reserve a right to cancel the contract; he may use a flexible pricing arrangement such as a "cost plus" term; he may insert a force majeure clause; or he may limit his damages for breach. The extent of his obligation then depends on the application of the rules on interpretation stated in Chapter 9, The Scope of Contractual Obligations.

Even where the obligor has not limited his obligation by agreement, a court may grant him relief. An extraordinary circumstance may make performance so vitally different from what was reasonably to be expected as to alter the essential nature of that performance. In such a case the court must determine whether justice requires a departure from the general rule that the obligor bear the risk that the contract may become more burdensome or less desirable. This Chapter is concerned with the principles that guide that determination. The question is generally considered to be one of law rather than fact, for the court rather than the jury. [...] In recent years courts have shown increasing liberality in discharging obligors on the basis of such extraordinary circumstances.

Three distinct grounds for discharge of the obligor's duty must be distinguished. First, the obligor may claim that some circumstance has made his own performance impracticable. The general rule governing impracticability of performance is stated in §261, and three common specific instances of impracticability are dealt with in §§262, 263 and 264. Second, the obligor may claim that some circumstance has so destroyed the value to him of the other party's performance as to frustrate his own purpose in making the contract. The rule governing frustration of purpose is stated in §265. Third, the obligor may claim that he will not receive the agreed exchange for his own performance because some circumstance has discharged the obligee's duty to render that agreed exchange, on the ground of either impracticability or frustration. The general rules on the effect of failure of performance on the other party's duties are stated in Chapter 10 and particularly in §§237 and 238. A special rule for cases in which non-performance is justified by impracticability or frustration is stated in §267.

Usually the impracticability or frustration that is relied upon as a justification for non-performance occurred after the contract was made. The rule stated in §261 applies to such instances of supervening impracticability or frustration. The impracticability or frustration may, however, already have existed, unknown to the obligor, at the time of contracting. The rule stated in §266 applies to such instances of existing impracticability and frustration, and provides for results that are substantially the same as those that would be reached under the rule stated in §261 in analogous cases of supervening impracticability or frustration. The rules stated in §§262, 263 and 264 for specific instances of impracticability apply under §266 as well as under §261. See Chapter 6 for the extent to which rules relating to mistake may also be available to an obligor who seeks to avoid liability on the basis of existing impracticability or frustration.

The rationale behind the doctrines of impracticability and frustration is sometimes said to be that there is an "implied term" of the contract that such extraordinary circumstances will not occur. This Restatement rejects this analysis in favor of that of Uniform Commercial Code §2-615, under which the central inquiry is whether the non-occurrence of the circumstance was a "basic assumption on which the contract was made." [...] In order for the parties to have had such a "basic assumption" it is not necessary for them to have been conscious of alternatives. Where, for example, an artist contracts to paint a painting, it can be said that the death of the artist is an event the non-occurrence of which was a basic assumption on which the contract was made, even though the parties never consciously addressed themselves to that possibility.

Determining whether the non-occurrence of a particular event was or was not a basic assumption involves a judgment as to which party assumed the risk of its occurrence. In contracting for the manufacture and delivery of goods at a price fixed in the contract, for example, the seller assumes the risk of increased costs within the normal range. If, however, a disaster results in an abrupt tenfold increase in cost to the seller, a court might determine that the seller did not assume this risk by concluding that the non-occurrence of the disaster was a "basic assumption" on which the contract was made. In making such determinations, a court will look at all circumstances, including the terms of the contract. The fact that the event was unforeseeable is significant as suggesting that its non-occurrence was a basic assumption. However, the fact that it was foreseeable, or even foreseen, does not, of itself, argue for a contrary conclusion, since the parties may not have thought it sufficiently important a risk to have made it a subject of their bargaining. Another significant factor may be the relative bargaining positions of the parties and the relative ease with which either party could have included a clause. Another may be the effectiveness of the market in spreading such risks as, for example, where the obligor is a middleman who has an opportunity to adjust his prices to cover them.

Under the rationale of this Restatement, the obligor is relieved of his duty because the contract, having been made on a different "basic assumption," is regarded as not covering the case that has arisen. It is an omitted case, falling within a "gap" in the contract. Ordinarily, the just way to deal with the omitted case is to hold that the obligor's duty is discharged, in the case of changed circumstances, or has never arisen, in the case of existing circumstances, and to shift the risk to the obligee. In some cases a party who has already partly performed is entitled to recovery for what he has done under the rule on part performances as agreed equivalents (§240). Even where this is not so, relief may be available in the form of a claim for restitution or expenses incurred in reliance on the contract (§377). These possibilities are dealt with in §272(1). Since the case is properly regarded as an omitted one, however, if none of these techniques will suffice to do substantial justice, it is within the discretion of the court to supply an omitted essential term under the rule stated in §204. This is made clear in §272(2). Other matters dealt with in this Chapter include: the effect on the other party's duties of a prospective non-performance that is justified by impracticability or frustration (§268), temporary impracticability and frustration (§269), partial impracticability (§270), and excuse of a condition by impracticability (§271).

§261 Discharge by Supervening Impracticability

Where, after a contract is made, a party's performance is made impracticable without his fault by the occurrence of an event the non occurrence of which was a basic assumption on which the contract was made, his duty to render that performance is discharged, unless the language or the circumstances indicate the contrary.

§262 Death or Incapacity of Person Necessary for Performance

If the existence of a particular person is necessary for the performance of a duty, his death or such incapacity as makes performance impracticable is an event the non-occurrence of which was a basic assumption on which the contract was made.

§263 Destruction, Deterioration or Failure to Come into Existence of a Thing Necessary for Performance

If the existence of a specific thing is necessary for the performance of a duty, its failure to come into existence, destruction, or such deterioration as makes performance impracticable is an event the non-occurrence of which was a basic assumption on which the contract was made.

§264 Prevention by Governmental Regulation or Order

If the performance of a duty is made impracticable by having to comply with a domestic or foreign governmental regulation or order, that regulation or order is an event the non-occurrence of which was a basic assumption on which the contract was made.

§265 Discharge by Supervening Frustration

Where, after a contract is made, a party's principal purpose is substantially frustrated without his fault by the occurrence of an event the non occurrence of which was a basic assumption on which the contract was made, his remaining duties to render performance are discharged, unless the language or the circumstances indicate the contrary.

§266 Existing Impracticability or Frustration

(1) Where, at the time a contract is made, a party's performance under it is impracticable without his fault because of a fact of which he has no reason to know and the non existence of which is a basic assumption on which the contract is made, no duty to render that performance arises, unless the language or circumstances indicate the contrary.

(2) Where, at the time a contract is made, a party's principal purpose is substantially frustrated without his fault by a fact of which he has no reason to know and the non existence of which is a basic assumption on which the contract is made, no duty of that party to render performance arises, unless the language or circumstances indicate the contrary.

§267 Effect on Other Party's Duties of a Failure Justified by Impracticability or Frustration

(1) A party's failure to render or to offer performance may, except as stated in Subsection (2), affect the other party's duties under the rules stated in §§237 and 238 even though the failure is justified under the rules stated in this Chapter.

(2) The rule stated in Subsection (1) does not apply if the other party assumed the risk that he would have to perform despite such a failure.

§268 Effect on Other Party's Duties of a Prospective Failure Justified by Impracticability or Frustration

(1) A party's prospective failure of performance may, except as stated in Subsection (2), discharge the other party's duties or allow him to suspend performance under the rules stated in §§251(1) and 253(2) even though the failure would be justified under the rules stated in this Chapter.

(2) The rule stated in Subsection (1) does not apply if the other party assumed the risk that he would have to perform in spite of such a failure.

§269 Temporary Impracticability or Frustration

Impracticability of performance or frustration of purpose that is only temporary suspends the obligor's duty to perform while the impracticability or frustration exists but does not discharge his duty or prevent it from arising unless his performance after the cessation of the impracticability or frustration would be materially more burdensome than had there been no impracticability or frustration.

§270 Partial Impracticability

Where only part of an obligor's performance is impracticable, his duty to render the remaining part is unaffected if

(a) it is still practicable for him to render performance that is substantial, taking account of any reasonable substitute performance that he is under a duty to render; or

(b) the obligee, within a reasonable time, agrees to render any remaining performance in full and to allow the obligor to retain any performance that has already been rendered.

§271 Impracticability as Excuse for Non-Occurrence of a Condition

Impracticability excuses the non-occurrence of a condition if the occurrence of the condition is not a material part of the agreed exchange and forfeiture would otherwise result.

§272 Relief Including Restitution; Supplying a Term

(1) In any case governed by the rules stated in this Chapter, either party may have a claim for relief including restitution under the rules stated in §240 and 377.

(2) In any case governed by the rules stated in this Chapter, if those rules together with the rules stated in Chapter 16 will not avoid injustice, the court may grant relief on such terms as justice requires including protection of the parties' reliance interests.

Chapter 12. Discharge by Assent or Alteration

Introductory Note

This Chapter is concerned mainly with the discharge of duties by assent of the obligee. The word "duty," when used in this Chapter without qualifying words, refers not only to contract duties but to other duties as well, and it includes a duty to pay damages for breach of contract or for a tort. It refers to duties that are undisputed as well as those that are disputed, to duties that are liquidated as well as unliquidated, and to duties that are matured as well as unmatured.

Discharge of a duty extinguishes the obligor's duty and terminates the obligee's correlative right and any claim based on that right. Discharge of a duty to pay damages for breach of contract terminates the correlative right including any right to specific performance or other equitable relief. However, discharge of a duty of performance does not of itself extinguish a duty to pay damages for breach or a duty to make restitution.

Courts have generally required consideration or a substitute for consideration to support a discharge by the obligee's assent, even if the discharge is immediate and involves no promise to discharge. Topic 1 deals with this general requirement and the exceptions to it. Topic 2 states rules for substituted performance, substituted contract, accord and account stated. In all but the last of these the obligee receives a substituted performance or promise in satisfaction of the duty, and this furnishes the consideration for the discharge. Topic 3 states rules for rescission, release and covenant not to sue. Here the consideration for the discharge is something other than a substitute performance or promise. Topic 4 deals with discharge of a duty by the obligee's alteration of a writing.

Other methods of discharge. Other Chapters of this Restatement deal with other methods of discharge of contract duties. These include: discharge by performance in full (§§235, 258- 60), discharge on grounds of impracticability or frustration (§§261, 265), discharge by non-occurrence of a condition or the occurrence of a similar event (§§224, 230), discharge by assignment of the correlative right (§317), discharge by the union of a right and duty in the same party (Comment a to §9), and discharge by exercise of a power of avoidance (§7) on grounds of lack of capacity (§§14- 16), mistake (§§152, 153), misrepresentation (§164), a fiduciary relation (§173), duress (§175) or undue influence (§177). Contract provisions giving a power of termination to one or both parties may pose questions of consideration (§77) or interpretation (Chapter 9) that are dealt with in connection with those topics.

Other methods of discharge are beyond the scope of this Restatement. A duty may, for example, be discharged by the running of a statute of limitations or by the operation of the bankruptcy laws and the duty of a surety may be discharged under the laws of suretyship. See Restatement of Security ch. 5. (But see Chapter 13 of this Restatement as to discharge of joint and several promisors.) A duty may be discharged by merger or bar resulting from a judgment or an arbitral award. As to judgments, see Restatement, Second, Judgments §§18, 19.

Topic 1. The Requirement of Consideration

Introductory Note

An obligee's assent to discharge a duty that he is owed may take the form of a promise to discharge that duty in the future or of a present discharge. A promise to discharge the duty must, like any other promise, be supported by consideration or one of its substitutes in order to be enforceable. The common law carried over this requirement to a present discharge, even though it involved no promise. Such a discharge was not effective unless supported by consideration or one of its substitutes. This requirement is stated in §273. It applies to the traditional transactions dealt with in Topics 2 and 3, including discharge by substituted performance or contract, accord, agreement of rescission, release and contract not to sue. It also applies to transactions involving discharge that do not take one of these traditional forms.

The wisdom of applying to a present discharge the rules developed for the enforceability of promises has been questioned, however, particularly since the seal has been deprived of its effect in most states. Exceptions have developed judicially and these are supplemented by statutes in some states. Rules stating these exceptions are also collected in this Topic. Section 274 deals with cancellation, destruction or surrender, an exception applicable to writings that are symbolic or evidentiary of the duty discharged. Sections 275 and 276 deal with assent to discharge duties of return performance and duties to transfer property, two exceptions derived by analogy from the law relating to gifts of tangible property. Section 277 deals with the renunciation of a duty to pay damages for a breach of contract, an exception that is based in part on the Uniform Commercial Code.

Any transaction involving discharge by the obligee's assent, however, is subject to the general rules on effectiveness of assent that are set out in this Restatement. Even if the rule stated in § 273 does not apply, the obligee can set up any of the other defenses generally available to a promisor, such as those based on lack of capacity, mistake, misrepresentation, duress, unconscionability, public policy or the Statute of Frauds. Furthermore, the power of the obligee, even with the assent of the obligor, to vary a duty to an intended beneficiary is limited by the rule stated in §311.

§273 Requirement of Consideration or a Substitute

Except as stated in §§ 274- 77, an obligee's manifestation of assent to a discharge is not effective unless

(a) it is made for consideration,

(b) it is made in circumstances in which a promise would be enforceable without consideration, or

(c) it has induced such action or forbearance as would make a promise enforceable.

§274 Cancellation, Destruction or Surrender of a Writing

An obligee's cancellation, destruction or surrender to the obligor of a writing of a type customarily accepted as a symbol or as evidence of his right discharges without consideration the obligor's duty if it is done with the manifested intention to discharge it.

§275 Assent to Discharge Duty of Return Performance

If a party, before he has fully performed his duty under a contract, manifests to the other party his assent to discharge the other party's duty to render part or all of the agreed exchange, the duty is to that extent discharged without consideration.

§276 Assent to Discharge Duty to Transfer Property

A duty of an obligor in possession of identified personal property to transfer an interest in that property is discharged without consideration if the obligee manifests to the obligor his assent to the discharge of that duty.

§277 Renunciation

(1) A written renunciation signed and delivered by the obligee discharges without consideration a duty arising out of a breach of contract.

(2) A renunciation by the obligee on his acceptance from the obligor of some performance under a contract discharges without consideration a duty to pay damages for a breach that gives rise only to a claim for damages for partial breach of contract.

Topic 2. Substituted Performance, Substituted Contract, Accord and Account Stated

Introductory Note

A duty may be discharged by the obligee's acceptance of either a performance or a contract in substitution for performance of that duty. This may happen in several ways. First, the obligee may accept a substituted performance in present satisfaction of the duty. The rules for discharge by substituted performance are stated in §278. Second, the obligee may accept a promise of a substituted performance in present satisfaction of the duty. The rules for discharge by substituted contracts are stated in §279. A substituted contract in which the obligor or obligee is replaced by a third person is known as a novation and is dealt with in §280. Third, the obligee may bind himself by a contract known as an accord to accept a substituted performance in future satisfaction of the duty. The rules for discharge by accord and satisfaction are stated in §281. The concept of account stated, which results in an admission but not a discharge, is dealt with in §282.

Although much of this terminology is peculiar to the field of discharge, the substantive rules are essentially the same as those generally applicable to the formation of contracts. Under the rules stated in §§279- 281, which speak of a "contract," all of the requirements for enforceability of promises are imported, so that a party may raise such defenses as mistake, misrepresentation, duress and lack of consideration or one of its substitutes. [...]

§278 Substituted Performance

(1) If an obligee accepts in satisfaction of the obligor's duty a performance offered by the obligor that differs from what is due, the duty is discharged.

(2) If an obligee accepts in satisfaction of the obligor's duty a performance offered by a third person, the duty is discharged, but an obligor who has not previously assented to the performance for his benefit may in a reasonable time after learning of it render the discharge inoperative from the beginning by disclaimer.

§279 Substituted Contract

(1) A substituted contract is a contract that is itself accepted by the obligee in satisfaction of the obligor's existing duty.

(2) The substituted contract discharges the original duty and breach of the substituted contract by the obligor does not give the obligee a right to enforce the original duty.

§280 Novation

A novation is a substituted contract that includes as a party one who was neither the obligor nor the obligee of the original duty.

§281 Accord and Satisfaction

(1) An accord is a contract under which an obligee promises to accept a stated performance in satisfaction of the obligor's existing duty. Performance of the accord discharges the original duty.

(2) Until performance of the accord, the original duty is suspended unless there is such a breach of the accord by the obligor as discharges the new duty of the obligee to accept the performance in satisfaction. If there is such a breach, the obligee may enforce either the original duty or any duty under the accord.

(3) Breach of the accord by the obligee does not discharge the original duty, but the obligor may maintain a suit for specific performance of the accord, in addition to any claim for damages for partial breach.

§282 Account Stated

(1) An account stated is a manifestation of assent by debtor and creditor to a stated sum as an accurate computation of an amount due the creditor. A party's retention without objection for an unreasonably long time of a statement of account rendered by the other party is a manifestation of assent.

(2) The account stated does not itself discharge any duty but is an admission by each party of the facts asserted and a promise by the debtor to pay according to its terms.

Topic 3. Agreement of Rescission, Release and Contract Not to Sue

Introductory Note

This Topic deals with three important types of agreements by which duties are discharged. They differ from those in Topic 2 in that they do not involve the obligee's acceptance of either a performance or a contract in substitution for the performance of the duty. They are, however, contractual in nature and must be supported by consideration or one of its substitutes. Agreements of rescission are dealt with in §283, releases in §284 and contracts not to sue in §285.

§283 Agreement of Rescission

(1) An agreement of rescission is an agreement under which each party agrees to discharge all of the other party's remaining duties of performance under an existing contract.

(2) An agreement of rescission discharges all remaining duties of performance of both parties. It is a question of interpretation whether the parties also agree to make restitution with respect to performance that has been rendered.

§284 Release

(1) A release is a writing providing that a duty owed to the maker of the release is discharged immediately or on the occurrence of a condition.

(2) The release takes effect on delivery as stated in §§101- 03 and, subject to the occurrence of any condition, discharges the duty.

§285 Contract Not to Sue

(1) A contract not to sue is a contract under which the obligee of a duty promises never to sue the obligor or a third person to enforce the duty or not to do so for a limited time.

(2) Except as stated in Subsection (3), a contract never to sue discharges the duty and a contract not to sue for a limited time bars an action to enforce the duty during that time.

(3) A contract not to sue one co-obligor bars levy of execution on the property of the promisee during the agreed time but does not bar an action or the recovery of judgment against any co-obligor.

Topic 4. Alteration

Introductory Note

The rules on alteration that developed in order to discourage tampering with writings embodying formal contracts were extended to cover the alteration of writings that are completely or partially integrated agreements under the parol evidence rule (§§209, 210) and of memoranda that are necessary under the Statute of Frauds (§131). The effect of an alteration has been limited, however, so that it results in discharge only if the alteration is both fraudulent and material. In view of the forfeiture that results upon discharge of an obligor if the obligee has already performed, the effect of an alteration may undergo further limitations in the future. See Uniform Commercial Code §§7-208, 7-306, under which even a fraudulent and material alteration of a document of title does not discharge the issuer's duty to deliver the goods according to the original terms of the document. The rules stated here, however, reflect the present state of the law. The effect of an alteration is dealt with in §286 and the effect of assent to or forgiveness of an alteration is dealt with in §287.

§286 Alteration of Writing

(1) If one to whom a duty is owed under a contract alters a writing that is an integrated agreement or that satisfies the Statute of Frauds with respect to that contract, the duty is discharged if the alteration is fraudulent and material.

(2) An alteration is material if it would, if effective, vary any party's legal relations with the maker of the alteration or adversely affect that party's legal relations with a third person. The unauthorized insertion in a blank space in a writing is an alteration.

§287 Assent to or Forgiveness of Alteration

(1) If a party, knowing of an alteration that discharges his duty, manifests assent to the altered terms, his manifestation is equivalent to an acceptance of an offer to substitute those terms.

(2) If a party, knowing of an alteration that discharges his duty, asserts a right under the original contract or otherwise manifests a willingness to remain subject to the original contract or to forgive the alteration, the original contract is revived.

Chapter 13. Joint and Several Promisors and Promisees

Introductory Note

This Chapter deals with the rights and duties created by multiple promises of the same performance, and with the traditional distinctions between "joint," "several," and "joint and several" rights and duties so created. Multiple promises of the same performance are fully recognized by the substantive law. See §10. They are very common and are of great practical importance. But their remedial and procedural consequences are affected by remnants of outworn conceptions only partially corrected by statutory reforms or by judicial decisions made with or without statutory aid.

Promises of the same performance. Whether or not multiple promises have reference to the same performance is entirely a question of interpretation. For example, A and B may each promise to pay C $500, making a total of $1,000; or A and B together may promise to pay C a total of $1,000, each to be fully responsible for the entire payment. Likewise, A may promise C that he will pay C $500 and promise D that he will pay D $500; or he may promise C and D together that he will pay them $1,000. Interpretation determines from whom and to whom the promises run and in what amounts. The rights and duties between the promisors A and B and between the promisees C and D in such cases present distinct questions dealt with only incidentally in this Chapter.

"Joint and several." There is a basic ambiguity in the use of the words "joint" and "several." In one usage, promissory duties are said to be "joint" if two or more promisors promise the same performance, "several" if they promise separate performances, even though similar. In the same way, promises are sometimes said to create "joint" rights if the same performance is promised to more than one promisee, "several" rights if each promisee is promised a different performance. In the second usage, both "joint" and "several" refer to rights and duties created by promises of the same performance. The second usage is more common in judicial and statutory language, and is the usage followed here.

Joinder of parties. Before the procedural reforms of the nineteenth century, common-law pleading was designed to present a single issue between two parties or groups of parties. Parties could be joined in an action only if they had the same interest, and all parties having a "joint" interest had to be joined. From early times the rule requiring joinder of all living joint promisors could be avoided by making the promise "joint and several" in form; and the impact of this and some related rules was mitigated by judicial decision as stated in this Chapter. But the law governing "joint" contractual duties remained unsatisfactory in almost every respect, and even the law of "joint and several" duties was defective.

Topic 1. Joint and Several Promisors

§288 Promises of the Same Performance

(1) Where two or more parties to a contract make a promise or promises to the same promisee, the manifested intention of the parties determines whether they promise that the same performance or separate performances shall be given.

(2) Unless a contrary intention is manifested, a promise by two or more promisors is a promise that the same performance shall be given.

§289 Joint, Several, and Joint and Several Promisors of the Same Performance

(1) Where two or more parties to a contract promise the same performance to the same promisee, each is bound for the whole performance thereof, whether his duty is joint, several, or joint and several.

(2) Where two or more parties to a contract promise the same performance to the same promisee, they incur only a joint duty unless an intention is manifested to create several duties or joint and several duties.

(3) By statute in most states some or all promises which would otherwise create only joint duties create joint and several duties.

§290 Compulsory Joinder of Joint Promisors

(1) By statute in most states where the distinction between joint duties and joint and several duties retains significance, an action can be maintained against one or more promisors who incur only a joint duty, even though other promisors subject to the same duty are not served with process.

(2) In the absence of statute, an action can be maintained against promisors who incur only a joint duty without joinder of those beyond the jurisdiction of the court, the representatives of deceased promisors, or those against whom the duty is not enforceable at the time of suit.

§291 Judgment in an Action Against Co-Promisors

In an action against promisors of the same performance, whether their duties are joint, several, or joint and several, judgment can properly be entered for or against one even though no judgment or a different judgment is entered with respect to another, except that judgment for one and against another is improper where there has been a determination on the merits and the liability of one cannot exist without the liability of the other.

§292 Effect of Judgment for or Against Co-Promisors

(1) A judgment against one or more promisors does not discharge other promisors of the same performance unless joinder of the other promisors is required by the rule stated in § 290. By statute in most states judgment against one promisor does not discharge co-promisors even where such joinder is required.

(2) The effect of judgment for one or more promisors of the same performance is determined by the rules of res judicata relating to suretyship or vicarious liability.

§293 Effect of Performance or Satisfaction on Co-Promisors

Full or partial performance or other satisfaction of the contractual duty of a promisor discharges the duty to the obligee of each other promisor of the same performance to the extent of the amount or value applied to the discharge of the duty of the promisor who renders it.

§294 Effect of Discharge on Co-Promisors

(1) Except as stated in §295, where the obligee of promises of the same performance discharges one promisor by release, rescission or accord and satisfaction,

(a) co-promisors who are bound only by a joint duty are discharged unless the discharged promisor is a surety for the co-promisor;

(b) co-promisors who are bound by joint and several duties or by several duties are not discharged except to the extent required by the law of suretyship.

(2) By statute in many states a discharge of one promisor does not discharge other promisors of the same performance except to the extent required by the law of suretyship.

(3) Any consideration received by the obligee for discharge of one promisor discharges the duty of each other promisor of the same performance to the extent of the amount or value received. An agreement to the contrary is not effective unless it is made with a surety and expressly preserves the duty of his principal.

§295 Effect of Contract Not to Sue; Reservation of Rights

(1) Where the obligee of promises of the same performance contracts not to sue one promisor, the other promisors are not discharged except to the extent required by the law of suretyship.

(2) Words which purport to release or discharge a promisor and also to reserve rights against other promisors of the same performance have the effect of a contract not to sue rather than a release or discharge.

(3) Any consideration received by the obligee for a contract not to sue one promisor discharges the duty of each other promisor of the same performance to the extent of the amount or value received. An agreement to the contrary is not effective unless it is made with a surety and expressly preserves the duty of his principal.

§296 Survivorship of Joint Duties

On the death of one of two or more promisors of the same performance in a contract, the estate of the deceased promisor is bound by the contract, whether the duty was joint, several, or joint and several.

Topic 2. Joint and Several Promisees

§297 Obligees of the Same Promised Performance

(1) Where a party to a contract makes a promise to two or more promisees or for the benefit of two or more beneficiaries, the manifested intention of the parties determines whether he promises the same performance to all, a separate performance to each, or some combination.

(2) Except to the extent that a different intention is manifested or that the interests of the obligees in the performance or in the remedies for breach are distinct, the rights of obligees of the same performance are joint.

§298 Compulsory Joinder of Joint Obligees

(1) In an action based on a joint right created by a promise, the promisor by making appropriate objection can prevent recovery of judgment against him unless there are joined either as plaintiffs or as defendants all the surviving joint obligees.

(2) Except in actions on negotiable instruments and except as stated in § 300, any joint obligee unless limited by agreement may sue in the name of all the joint obligees for the enforcement of the promise by a money judgment.

§299 Discharge by or Tender to One Joint Obligee

Except where the promise is made in a negotiable instrument and except as stated in § 300, any joint obligee, unless limited by agreement, has power to discharge the promisor by receipt of the promised performance or by release or otherwise, and tender to one joint obligee is equivalent to a tender to all.

§300 Effect of Violation of Duty to a Co-Obligee

(1) If an obligee attempts or threatens to discharge the promisor in violation of his duty to a co-obligee of the same performance, the co-obligee may obtain an injunction forbidding the discharge.

(2) A discharge of the promisor by an obligee in violation of his duty to a co-obligee of the same performance is voidable to the extent necessary to protect the co-obligee's interest in the performance, except to the extent that the promisor has given value or otherwise changed his position in good faith and without knowledge or reason to know of the violation.

§301 Survivorship of Joint Rights

On the death of a joint obligee, unless a contrary intention was manifested, the surviving obligees are solely entitled as against the promisor to receive performance, to discharge the promisor, or to sue for the enforcement of the promise by a money judgment. On the death of the last surviving obligee, only his estate is so entitled.

Chapter 14. Contract Beneficiaries

Introductory Note

Historically, the rights of contract beneficiaries have been the subject of doctrinal difficulties in both England and the United States. In both countries, decisions in the latter part of the nineteenth century overruled or limited earlier precedents recognizing such rights. In England, but not in the United States (see §71), the rule was established that consideration must move from the plaintiff. That rule has sometimes been avoided by an artificial holding that the promisee held a contract right in trust for the beneficiary, but it seems to retain some force.

In the United States the principal difficulty was that the beneficiary was not a party to the contract, since the promise was not addressed to him. Some decisions recognized a right only in a "sole" beneficiary or "donee" beneficiary, such as the person to whom the proceeds of a life insurance policy are made payable. Others recognized the beneficiary's right only if the promisor was to satisfy a duty of the promisee to the beneficiary, who was then called a "creditor" beneficiary, or if there was some other relationship between promise and beneficiary.

These difficulties have now been largely resolved in the United States by recognition of the power of promisor and promisee to create rights in a beneficiary by manifesting an intention to do so. Since the terms "donee" beneficiary and "creditor" beneficiary carry overtones of obsolete doctrinal difficulties, they are avoided in the statement of rules in this Chapter. Instead, the terms "intended" beneficiary and "incidental" beneficiary are used to distinguish beneficiaries who have rights from those who do not.

Difficulties of interpretation of course remain. Where the manifested intention is unclear, rules of law may fill the gap. And in some situations overriding social policies may limit the parties' freedom of contract. Thus Uniform Commercial Code §2-318 provides for "third party beneficiaries of warranties express or implied," and includes a provision that "A seller may not exclude or limit the effect of this section." Restatement, Second, Torts §402A deals with the same problem in non-contractual terms. Again, the rights of employees under a collective bargaining agreement are sometimes treated as rights of contract beneficiaries, sometimes as rights based on agency principles, sometimes as rights analogous to the rights of trust beneficiaries. Or the collective bargaining agreement may be treated as establishing a usage incorporated in individual employment contracts, or as analogous to legislation. In any case they are substantially affected by the national labor policy. Such policies are of course beyond the scope of this Restatement.

§302 Intended and Incidental Beneficiaries

(1) Unless otherwise agreed between promisor and promisee, a beneficiary of a promise is an intended beneficiary if recognition of a right to performance in the beneficiary is appropriate to effectuate the intention of the parties and either

(a) the performance of the promise will satisfy an obligation of the promisee to pay money to the beneficiary; or

(b) the circumstances indicate that the promisee intends to give the beneficiary the benefit of the promised performance.

(2) An incidental beneficiary is a beneficiary who is not an intended beneficiary.

§303 Conditional Promises; Promises Under Seal

The statements in this Chapter are applicable to both conditional and unconditional promises and to sealed and unsealed promises.

§304 Creation of Duty to Beneficiary

A promise in a contract creates a duty in the promisor to any intended beneficiary to perform the promise, and the intended beneficiary may enforce the duty.

§305 Overlapping Duties to Beneficiary and Promisee

(1) A promise in a contract creates a duty in the promisor to the promisee to perform the promise even though he also has a similar duty to an intended beneficiary.

(2) Whole or partial satisfaction of the promisor's duty to the beneficiary satisfies to that extent the promisor's duty to the promisee.

§306 Disclaimer by a Beneficiary

A beneficiary who has not previously assented to the promise for his benefit may in a reasonable time after learning of its existence and terms render any duty to himself inoperative from the beginning by disclaimer.

§307 Remedy of Specific Performance

Where specific performance is otherwise an appropriate remedy, either the promisee or the beneficiary may maintain a suit for specific enforcement of a duty owed to an intended beneficiary.

§ 308 Identification of Beneficiaries

It is not essential to the creation of a right in an intended beneficiary that he be identified when a contract containing the promise is made.

§309 Defenses Against the Beneficiary

(1) A promise creates no duty to a beneficiary unless a contract is formed between the promisor and the promisee; and if a contract is voidable or unenforceable at the time of its formation the right of any beneficiary is subject to the infirmity.

(2) If a contract ceases to be binding in whole or in part because of impossibility, illegality, non occurrence of a condition, or present or prospective failure of performance, the right of any beneficiary is to that extent discharged or modified.

(3) Except as stated in Subsections (1) and (2) and in §311 or as provided by the contract, the right of any beneficiary against the promisor is not subject to the promisor's claims or defenses against the promisee or to the promisee's claims or defenses against the beneficiary.

(4) A beneficiary's right against the promisor is subject to any claim or defense arising from his own conduct or agreement.

§310 Remedies of the Beneficiary of a Promise to Pay the Promisee's Debt; Reimbursement of Promisee

(1) Where an intended beneficiary has an enforceable claim against the promisee, he can obtain a judgment or judgments against either the promisee or the promisor or both based on their respective duties to him. Satisfaction in whole or in part of either of these duties, or of a judgment thereon, satisfies to that extent the other duty or judgment, subject to the promisee's right of subrogation.

(2) To the extent that the claim of an intended beneficiary is satisfied from assets of the promisee, the promisee has a right of reimbursement from the promisor, which may be enforced directly and also, if the beneficiary's claim is fully satisfied, by subrogation to the claim of the beneficiary against the promisor, and to any judgment thereon and to any security therefor.

§311 Variation of a Duty to a Beneficiary

(1) Discharge or modification of a duty to an intended beneficiary by conduct of the promisee or by a subsequent agreement between promisor and promisee is ineffective if a term of the promise creating the duty so provides.

(2) In the absence of such a term, the promisor and promisee retain power to discharge or modify the duty by subsequent agreement.

(3) Such a power terminates when the beneficiary, before he receives notification of the discharge or modification, materially changes his position in justifiable reliance on the promise or brings suit on it or manifests assent to it at the request of the promisor or promisee.

(4) If the promisee receives consideration for an attempted discharge or modification of the promisor's duty which is ineffective against the beneficiary, the beneficiary can assert a right to the consideration so received. The promisor's duty is discharged to the extent of the amount received by the beneficiary.

§312 Mistake as to Duty to Beneficiary

The effect of an erroneous belief of the promisor or promisee as to the existence or extent of a duty owed to an intended beneficiary is determined by the rules making contracts voidable for mistake.

§313 Government Contracts

(1) The rules stated in this Chapter apply to contracts with a government or governmental agency except to the extent that application would contravene the policy of the law authorizing the contract or prescribing remedies for its breach.

(2) In particular, a promisor who contracts with a government or governmental agency to do an act for or render a service to the public is not subject to contractual liability to a member of the public for consequential damages resulting from performance or failure to perform unless

(a) the terms of the promise provide for such liability; or

(b) the promisee is subject to liability to the member of the public for the damages and a direct action against the promisor is consistent with the terms of the contract and with the policy of the law authorizing the contract and prescribing remedies for its breach.

§314 Suretyship Defenses

An intended beneficiary who has an enforceable claim against the promisee is affected by the incidents of the suretyship of the promisee from the time he has knowledge of it.

§315 Effect of a Promise of Incidental Benefit

An incidental beneficiary acquires by virtue of the promise no right against the promisor or the promisee.

Chapter 15. Assignment and Delegation

Introductory Note

The subject matter of this Chapter is part of the larger subject of the transfer of intangible property. The historic rule in the common-rule courts of England was that a "chose in action" could not be assigned. The scope of that rule was progressively narrowed by the reception into the common law of doctrines developed in the law merchant and in the courts of equity and by statute. Little remains of it today, but modern rules, both decisional and statutory, must often be read in the light of the development.

The law merchant. The law merchant is a tradition with an international and maritime flavor. It was followed in special merchant tribunals in England; during the seventeenth century it became part of the common law of England. Under its influence mercantile instruments such as the bill of exchange were held transferable by delivery, or by indorsement and delivery, and similar rules have been extended in modern times, by decision and by statute, to documents of title and to investment securities. See Uniform Commercial Code Articles 3, 7, 8. The rules governing such instruments are beyond the scope of this Restatement. See §6.

Law and equity. Also during the seventeenth century, it was established that an assignment could take effect in the common-law courts as a power of attorney enabling the assignee to sue in the assignor's name, and that courts of equity would protect the assignee in cases of death or bankruptcy of the assignor or revocation by him. During the eighteenth century the common-law courts began to give effect to the equitable rights of the assignee. In the United States statutes generally require actions to be brought in the name of the real party in interest, and the assignee of a contract right can sue in his own name without regard to the distinction between actions at law and suits in equity. That distinction is therefore not employed in the statement of rules in this Chapter, although references to the "equitable" character of an assignee's rights can be found in the modern literature on the subject.

§316 Scope of This Chapter

(1) In this Chapter, references to assignment of a right or delegation of a duty or condition, to the obligee or obligor of an assigned right or delegated duty, or to an assignor or assignee, are limited to rights, duties, and conditions arising under a contract or for breach of a contract.

(2) The statements in this Chapter are qualified in some respects by statutory and other rules governing negotiable instruments and documents, relating to interests in land, and affecting other classes of contracts.

Topic 1. What Can Be Assigned or Delegated

§317 Assignment of a Right

(1) An assignment of a right is a manifestation of the assignor's intention to transfer it by virtue of which the assignor's right to performance by the obligor is extinguished in whole or in part and the assignee acquires a right to such performance.

(2) A contractual right can be assigned unless

(a) the substitution of a right of the assignee for the right of the assignor would materially change the duty of the obligor, or materially increase the burden or risk imposed on him by his contract, or materially impair his chance of obtaining return performance, or materially reduce its value to him, or

(b) the assignment is forbidden by statute or is otherwise in operative on grounds of public policy, or

(c) assignment is validly precluded by contract.

§318 Delegation of Performance of Duty

(1) An obligor can properly delegate the performance of his duty to another unless the delegation is contrary to public policy or the terms of his promise.

(2) Unless otherwise agreed, a promise requires performance by a particular person only to the extent that the obligee has a substantial interest in having that person perform or control the acts promised.

(3) Unless the obligee agrees otherwise, neither delegation of performance nor a contract to assume the duty made with the obligor by the person delegated discharges any duty or liability of the delegating obligor.

§319 Delegation of Performance of Condition

(1) Where a performance by a person is made a condition of a duty, performance by a person delegated by his satisfies that requirement unless the delegation is contrary to public policy or the terms of the agreement.

(2) Unless otherwise agreed, an agreement requires performance of a condition by a particular person only to the extent that the obligor has a substantial interest in having that person perform or control the acts required.

§320 Assignment of Conditional Rights

The fact that a right is created by an option contract or is conditional on the performance of a return promise or is otherwise conditional does not prevent its assignment before the condition occurs.

§321 Assignment of Future Rights

(1) Except as otherwise provided by statute, an assignment of a right to payment expected to arise out of an existing employment or other continuing business relationship is effective in the same way as an assignment of an existing right.

(2) Except as otherwise provided by statute and as stated in Subsection (1), a purported assignment of a right expected to arise under a contract not in existence operates only as a promise to assign the right when it arises and as a power to enforce it.

§322 Contractual Prohibition of Assignment

(1) Unless the circumstances indicate the contrary, a contract term prohibiting assignment of "the contract" bars only the delegation to an assignee of the performance by the assignor of a duty or condition.

(2) A contract term prohibiting assignment of rights under the contract, unless a different intention is manifested.

(a) does not forbid assignment of a right to damages for breach of the whole contract or a right arising out of the assignor's due performance of his entire obligation;

(b) gives the obligor a right to damages for breach of the terms forbidding assignment but does not render the assignment ineffective;

(c) is for the benefit of the obligor, and does not prevent the assignee from acquiring rights against the assignor or the obligor from discharging his duty as if there were no such prohibition.

§323 Obligor's Assent to Assignment or Delegation

(1) A term of a contract manifesting an obligor's assent to the future assignment of a right or an obligee's assent to the future delegation of the performance of a duty or condition is effective despite any subsequent objection.

(2) A manifestation of such assent after the formation of a contract is similarly effective if made for consideration or in circumstances in which a promise would be binding without consideration, or if a material change of position takes place in reliance on the manifestation.

Topic 2. Mode of Assignment or Delegation

§324 Mode of Assignment in General

It is essential to an assignment of a right that the obligee manifest an intention to transfer the right to another person without further action or manifestation of intention by the obligee. The manifestation may be made to the other or to a third person on his behalf and, except as provided by statute or by contract, may be made either orally or by a writing.

§325 Order as Assignment

(1) A written order drawn upon an obligor and signed and delivered to another person by the obligee is an assignment if it is conditional on the existence of a duty of the drawee to the drawer to comply with the order and the drawer manifests an intention that a person other than the drawer is to retain the performance.

(2) An order which directs the drawee to render a performance without reference to any duty of the drawee is not of itself an assignment, even though the drawee is under a duty to the

drawer to comply with the order and even though the order indicates a particular account to be debited or any other fund or source from which reimbursement is expected.

§326 Partial Assignment

(1) Except as stated in Subsection (2), an assignment of a part of a right, whether the part is specified as a fraction, as an amount, or otherwise, is operative as to that part to the same extent and in the same manner as if the part had been a separate right.

(2) If the obligor has not contracted to perform separately the assigned part of a right, no legal proceeding can be maintained by the assignor or assignee against the obligor over his objection, unless all the persons entitled to the promised performance are joined in the proceeding, or unless joinder is not feasible and it is equitable to proceed without joinder.

§327 Acceptance or Disclaimer by the Assignee

(1) A manifestation of assent by an assignee to the assignment is essential to make it effective unless

(a) a third person gives consideration for the assignment, or

(b) the assignment is irrevocable by virtue of the delivery of a writing to a third person.

(2) An assignee who has not manifested assent to an assignment may, within a reasonable time after learning of its existence and terms, render it inoperative from the beginning by disclaimer.

§328 Interpretation of Words of Assignment; Effect of Acceptance of Assignment

(1) Unless the language or the circumstances indicate the contrary, as in an assignment for security, an assignment of "the contract" or of "all my rights under the contract" or an assignment in similar general terms is an assignment of the assignor's rights and a delegation of his unperformed duties under the contract.

(2) Unless the language or the circumstances indicate the contrary, the acceptance by an assignee of such an assignment operates as a promise to the assignor to perform the assignor's unperformed duties, and the obligor of the assigned rights is an intended beneficiary of the promise.

Caveat: The Institute expresses no opinion as to whether the rule stated in Subsection (2) applies to an assignment by a purchaser of his rights under a contract for the sale of land.

§329 Repudiation by Assignor and Novation with Assignee

(1) The legal effect of a repudiation by an assignor of his duty to the obligor of the assigned right is not limited by the fact that the assignee is a competent person and has promised to perform the duty.

(2) If the obligor, with knowledge of such a repudiation, accepts any performance from the assignee without reserving his rights against the assignor, a novation arises by which the duty of the assignor is discharged and a similar duty of the assignee is substituted.

§330 Contracts to Assign in the Future, or to Transfer Proceeds to Be Received

(1) A contract to make a future assignment of a right, or to transfer proceeds to be received in the future by the promisor, is not an assignment.

(2) Except as provided by statute, the effect of such a contract on the rights and duties of the obligor and third persons is determined by the rules relating to specific performance of contracts.

Topic 3. Effect Between Assignor and Assignee

§331 Partially Effective Assignments

An assignment may be conditional, revocable, or voidable by the assignor, or unenforceable by virtue of a Statute of Frauds.

§332 Revocability of Gratuitous Assignments

(1) Unless a contrary intention is manifested, a gratuitous assignment is irrevocable if

(a) the assignment is in a writing either signed or under seal that is delivered by the assignor; or

(b) the assignment is accompanied by delivery of a writing of a type customarily accepted as a symbol or as evidence of the right assigned.

(2) Except as stated in this Section, a gratuitous assignment is revocable and the right of the assignee is terminated by the assignor's death or incapacity, by a subsequent assignment by the assignor, or by notification from the assignor received by the assignee or by the obligor.

(3) A gratuitous assignment ceases to be revocable to the extent that before the assignee's right is terminated he obtains

(a) payment or satisfaction of the obligation, or

(b) judgment against the obligor, or

(c) a new contract of the obligor by novation.

(4) A gratuitous assignment is irrevocable to the extent necessary to avoid injustice where the assignor should reasonably expect the assignment to induce action or forbearance by the assignee or a sub assignee and the assignment does induce such action or forbearance.

(5) An assignment is gratuitous unless it is given or taken

(a) in exchange for a performance or return promise that would be consideration for a promise; or

(b) as security for or in total or partial satisfaction of a preexisting debt or other obligation.

§333 Warranties of an Assignor

(1) Unless a contrary intention is manifested, one who assigns or purports to assign a right by assignment under seal or for value warrants to the assignee

(a) that he will do nothing to defeat or impair the value of the assignment and has no knowledge of any fact which would do so;

(b) that the right, as assigned, actually exists and is subject to no limitations or defenses good against the assignor other than those stated or apparent at the time of the assignment;

(c) that any writing evidencing the right which is delivered to the assignee or exhibited to him to induce him to accept the assignment is genuine and what it purports to be.

(2) An assignment does not of itself operate as a warranty that the obligor is solvent or that he will perform his obligation.

(3) An assignor is bound by affirmations and promises to the assignee with reference to the right assigned in the same way and to the same extent that one who transfers goods is bound in like circumstances.

(4) An assignment of a right to a sub assignee does not operate as an assignment of the assignee's rights under his assignor's warranties unless an intention is manifested to assign the rights under the warranties.

Topic 4. Effect on the Obligor's Duty

§334 Variation of Obligor's Duty by Assignment

(1) If the obligor's duty is conditional on the personal cooperation of the original obligee or another person, an assignee's right is subject to the same condition.

(2) If the obligor's duty is conditional on cooperation which the obligee could properly delegate to an agent, the condition may occur if there is similar cooperation by an assignee.

§ 335 Assignment by a Joint Obligee

A joint obligee may effectively assign his right, but the assignee can enforce it only in the same manner and to the same extent as the assignor could have enforced it.

§336 Defenses Against an Assignee

(1) By an assignment the assignee acquires a right against the obligor only to the extent that the obligor is under a duty to the assignor; and if the right of the assignor would be voidable by the obligor or unenforceable against him if no assignment had been made, the right of the assignee is subject to the infirmity.

(2) The right of an assignee is subject to any defense or claim of the obligor which accrues before the obligor receives notification of the assignment, but not to defenses or claims which accrue thereafter except as stated in this Section or as provided by statute.

(3) Where the right of an assignor is subject to discharge or modification in whole or in part by impossibility, illegality, non occurrence of a condition, or present or prospective failure of performance by an obligee, the right of the assignee is to that extent subject to discharge or modification even after the obligor receives notification of the assignment.

(4) An assignee's right against the obligor is subject to any defense or claim arising from his conduct or to which he was subject as a party or a prior assignee because he had notice.

§337 Elimination of Defenses by Subsequent Events

Where the right of an assignor is limited or voidable or unenforceable or subject to discharge or modification, subsequent events which would eliminate the limitation or defense have the same effect on the right of the assignee.

§338 Discharge of an Obligor After Assignment

(1) Except as stated in this Section, notwithstanding an assignment, the assignor retains his power to discharge or modify the duty of the obligor to the extent that the obligor performs or otherwise gives value until but not after the obligor receives notification that the right has been assigned and that performance is to be rendered to the assignee.

(2) So far as an assigned right is conditional on the performance of a return promise, and notwithstanding notification of the assignment, any modification of or substitution for the contract made by the assignor and obligor in good faith and in accordance with reasonable commercial standards is effective against the assignee. The assignee acquires corresponding rights under the modified or substituted contract.

(3) Notwithstanding a defect in the right of an assignee, he has the same power his assignor had to discharge or modify the duty of the obligor to the extent that the obligor gives value or otherwise changes his position in good faith and without knowledge or reason to know of the defect.

(4) Where there is a writing of a type customarily accepted as a symbol or as evidence of the right assigned, a discharge or modification is not effective

(a) against the owner or an assignor having a power of avoidance, unless given by him or by a person in possession of the writing with his consent and any necessary endorsement or assignment;

(b) against a subsequent assignee who takes possession of the writing and gives value in good faith and without knowledge or reason to know of the discharge or modification.

§339 Protection of Obligor in Cases of Adverse Claims

Where a claim adverse to that of an assignee subjects the obligor to a substantial risk beyond that imposed on him by his contract, the obligor will be granted such relief as is equitable in the circumstances.

Topic 5. Priorities Between Assignee and Adverse Claimants

§ 340 Effect of Assignment on Priority and Security

(1) An assignee is entitled to priority of payment from the obligor's insolvent estate to the extent that the assignor would have been so entitled in the absence of assignment.

(2) Where an assignor holds collateral as security for the assigned right and does not effectively transfer the collateral to the assignee, the assignor is a constructive trustee of the collateral for the assignee in accordance with the rules stated for pledges in §§29-34 of the Restatement of Security.

§341 Creditors of an Assignor

(1) Except as provided by statute, the right of an assignee is superior to a judicial lien subsequently obtained against the property of the assignor, unless the assignment is ineffective or revocable or is voidable by the assignor or by the person obtaining the lien or is in fraud of creditors.

(2) Notwithstanding the superiority of the right of an assignee, an obligor who does not receive notification of the assignment until after he has lost his opportunity to assert the assignment as a defense in the proceeding in which the judicial lien was obtained is discharged from his duty to the assignee to the extent of his satisfaction of the lien.

§342 Successive Assignees from the Same Assignor

Except as otherwise provided by statute, the right of an assignee is superior to that of a subsequent assignee of the same right from the same assignor, unless

(a) the first assignment is ineffective or revocable or is voidable by the assignor or by the subsequent assignee; or

(b) the subsequent assignee in good faith and without knowledge or reason to know of the prior assignment gives value and obtains

- (i) payment or satisfaction of the obligation,
- (ii) judgment against the obligor,
- (iii) a new contract with the obligor by novation, or
- (iv) possession of a writing of a type customarily accepted as a symbol or as evidence of the right assigned.

§343 Latent Equities

If an assignor's right against the obligor is held in trust or constructive trust for or subject to a right of avoidance or equitable lien of another than the obligor, an assignee does not so hold it if he gives value and becomes an assignee in good faith and without notice of the right of the other.

Chapter 16. Remedies

Introductory Note

This Chapter deals with remedies that are of special importance in disputes arising out of contracts, including restitution as well as damages and equitable relief. Topic 1 sets out the interests protected by these remedies and enumerates the remedies themselves. The next two topics deal with the enforcement of contracts, by the award of damages under the rules stated in Topic 2 and by specific performance or injunction under the rules in Topic 3. Topic 4 is concerned with restitution when an agreement is, for some reason, not to be enforced under the rules stated in Topics 2 and 3. Finally, Topic 5 deals with those circumstances in which a party is precluded from pursuing a remedy by conduct inconsistent with it.

This Chapter is not exhaustive. It does not treat in detail those forms of relief, such as declaration of the rights of the parties or enforcement of an arbitration award, that are largely statutory and are not limited to contracts cases. See Comments d and e to §345. It does not deal with some specialized remedies, such as reformation of a writing or replevin of property. Nor does it deal with the extent to which a party to a contract is empowered to protect himself or to obtain satisfaction by methods not involving recourse to a court, such as deducting damages that he claims from the price that he owes, retaking goods, or foreclosing on security. See Uniform Commercial Code §§2-717, 9-503, 9-504. Also omitted are the rights of third parties such as those of a good faith purchaser against one who has a power to avoid a contract through which the purchaser derives his title. See Uniform Commercial Code §§2-403, 3-305.

The important role that the institution of contract plays in the economy has drawn the attention of economists to the law of contract remedies. In classic economic theory the mechanism of exchange resulting from bargain is essential to the voluntary reallocation of goods, labor and other resources in a socially desirable manner. However, a party may err in calculating the net benefit to be expected from the performance of a bargain, or circumstances may so change as to disappoint his expectations. A contract that he once thought would be profitable may therefore become unprofitable for him. If the contract is still profitable for the other party, however, a question arises as to whether the reluctant party should be compelled to perform. The answer provided by at least some economic analysis tends to confirm the traditional response of common-law judges in dealing with this question.

The traditional goal of the law of contract remedies has not been compulsion of the promisor to perform his promise but compensation of the promisee for the loss resulting from breach. "Willful" breaches have not been distinguished from other breaches, punitive damages have not been awarded for breach of contract, and specific performance has not been granted where compensation in damages is an adequate substitute for the injured party. In general, therefore, a party may find it advantageous to refuse to perform a contract if he will still have a net gain after he has fully compensated the injured party for the resulting loss.

This traditional response is not without its shortcomings. Its focus on the pecuniary aspects of breach fails to take account of notions of the sanctity of contract and the resulting moral obligation to honor one's promises. The analysis of breach of contract in purely economic terms assumes an ability to measure value with a certainty that is not often possible in the judicial process. The analysis also ignores the "transaction costs" inherent in the bargaining process and in the resolution of disputes, a defect that is especially significant where the amount in controversy is small. However, the main thrust of the preceding economic analysis lends some support to traditional contract doctrine in this area.

Topic 1. In General

§344 Purposes of Remedies

Judicial remedies under the rules stated in this Restatement serve to protect one or more of the following interests of a promisee:

(a) his "expectation interest," which is his interest in having the benefit of his bargain by being put in as good a position as he would have been in had the contract been performed,

(b) his "reliance interest," which is his interest in being reimbursed for loss caused by reliance on the contract by being put in as good a position as he would have been in had the contract not been made, or

(c) his "restitution interest," which is his interest in having restored to him any benefit that he has conferred on the other party.

§345 Judicial Remedies Available

The judicial remedies available for the protection of the interests stated in §344 include a judgment or order

(a) awarding a sum of money due under the contract or as damages,

(b) requiring specific performance of a contract or enjoining its non-performance,

(c) requiring restoration of a specific thing to prevent unjust enrichment,

(d) awarding a sum of money to prevent unjust enrichment,

(e) declaring the rights of the parties, and

(f) enforcing an arbitration award.

Topic 2. Enforcement by Award of Damages

Introductory Note

This Topic contains rules for enforcement of contracts by means of the award of damages. The initial assumption is that the injured party is entitled to full compensation for his actual loss. This is reflected in the general measure of damages set out in §347. However, important limitations including those of avoidability, unforeseeability and uncertainty follow in §§350-53. The limitation of certainty can sometimes be overcome, at least in part, through the use of alternative bases for measuring damages (§348) or through the use of reliance as a measure of damages (§349). Other sections deal with nominal damages (§346), punitive damages (§355) and liquidated damages and penalties (§356). Except for the restrictions imposed by the rule that proscribes the fixing of penalties (§356), parties are free to vary the rules governing damages, subject to the usual limitations on private agreement such as that on unconscionable contracts or terms (§208). Although interest may be awarded as damages under the rule stated in §354, for the sake of simplicity specific references to interest have generally been omitted from the illustrations in this Chapter.

Under the rule stated in §346, a breach of contract ordinarily gives rise to a claim for damages. For the sake of convenience, the term "a claim for damages" is used in other chapters of this Restatement to refer to a right arising out of breach whether or not it includes a right to specific performance or an injunction as well as damages. See, for example, the use of that term in §§243 and 251. Although a claim to the price promised to be paid for something or to a sum of money promised to be repaid is, strictly speaking, not a claim for damages, such money claims are generally enforceable in the same way as those for damages. As to the right of a seller of land to recover the price, see Comment e to §360.

§346 Availability of Damages

(1) The injured party has a right to damages for any breach by a party against whom the contract is enforceable unless the claim for damages has been suspended or discharged.

(2) If the breach caused no loss or if the amount of the loss is not proved under the rules stated in this Chapter, a small sum fixed without regard to the amount of loss will be awarded as nominal damages.

§347 Measure of Damages in General

Subject to the limitations stated in §350 – 53, the injured party has a right to damages based on his expectation interest as measured by

(a) the loss in the value to him of the other party's performance caused by its failure or deficiency, plus

(b) any other loss, including incidental or consequential loss, caused by the breach, less

(c) any cost or other loss that he has avoided by not having to perform.

§348 Alternatives to Loss in Value of Performance

(1) If a breach delays the use of property and the loss in value to the injured party is not proved with reasonable certainty, he may recover damages based on the rental value of the property or on interest on the value of the property.

(2) If a breach results in defective or unfinished construction and the loss in value to the injured party is not proved with sufficient certainty, he may recover damages based on

(a) the diminution in the market price of the property caused by the breach, or

(b) the reasonable cost of completing performance or of remedying the defects if that cost is not clearly disproportionate to the probable loss in value to him.

(3) If a breach is of a promise conditioned on a fortuitous event and it is uncertain whether the event would have occurred had there been no breach, the injured party may recover damages based on the value of the conditional right at the time of breach.

§349 Damages Based on Reliance Interest

As an alternative to the measure of damages stated in §347, the injured party has a right to damages based on his reliance interest, including expenditures made in preparation for performance or in performance, less any loss that the party in breach can prove with reasonable certainty the injured party would have suffered had the contract been performed.

§350 Avoidability as a Limitation on Damages

(1) Except as stated in Subsection (2), damages are not recoverable for loss that the injured party could have avoided without undue risk, burden or humiliation.

(2) The injured party is not precluded from recovery by the rule stated in Subsection (1) to the extent that he has made reasonable but unsuccessful efforts to avoid loss.

§351 Unforeseeability and Related Limitations on Damages

(1) Damages are not recoverable for loss that the party in breach did not have reason to foresee as a probable result of the breach when the contract was made.

(2) Loss may be foreseeable as a probable result of a breach because it follows from the breach

(a) in the ordinary course of events, or

(b) as a result of special circumstances beyond the ordinary course of events, that the party in breach had reason to know.

(3) A court may limit damages for foreseeable loss by excluding recovery for loss of profits, by allowing recovery only for loss incurred in reliance, or otherwise if it concludes that in the circumstances justice so requires in order to avoid disproportionate compensation.

§352 Uncertainty as a Limitation on Damages

Damages are not recoverable for loss beyond an amount that the evidence permits to be established with reasonable certainty.

§353 Loss Due to Emotional Disturbance

Recovery for emotional disturbance will be excluded unless the breach also caused bodily harm or the contract or the breach is of such a kind that serious emotional disturbance was a particularly likely result.

§354 Interest as Damages

(1) If the breach consists of a failure to pay a definite sum in money or to render a performance with fixed or ascertainable monetary value, interest is recoverable from the time for performance on the amount due less all deductions to which the party in breach is entitled.

(2) In any other case, such interest may be allowed as justice requires on the amount that would have been just compensation had it been paid when performance was due.

§355 Punitive Damages

Punitive damages are not recoverable for a breach of contract unless the conduct constituting the breach is also a tort for which punitive damages are recoverable.

§356 Liquidated Damages and Penalties

(1) Damages for breach by either party may be liquidated in the agreement but only at an amount that is reasonable in the light of the anticipated or actual loss caused by the breach and the difficulties of proof of loss. A term fixing unreasonably large liquidated damages is unenforceable on grounds of public policy as a penalty.

(2) A term in a bond providing for an amount of money as a penalty for non-occurrence of the condition of the bond is unenforceable on grounds of public policy to the extent that the amount exceeds the loss caused by such non-occurrence.

Topic 3. Enforcement by Specific Performance and Injunction

Introductory Note

Specific performance and injunction are alternatives to the award of damages as means of enforcing contracts. Specific performance is by definition limited to the enforcement of contract duties. The remedy of injunction is used in many fields of law, but is dealt with here in connection with contracts only. The general availability of these remedies in contract cases is affirmed in §357. The power of the court to shape the remedy is stressed in §358. These remedies originated in courts of equity, and their use is within the discretion of the court and is subject to a number of limitations that are dealt with in §§359- 69. The most significant is the rule that specific performance or an injunction will not be granted if damages are an adequate remedy (§359). This rule, the product of the historical division of jurisdiction between law and equity, has been preserved under the Uniform Commercial Code. See Uniform Commercial Code §2-716(1) and Official Comment; Introductory Note to this Chapter. Nevertheless, there has been an increasing disposition to find that damages are not adequate and the commentary to the Code reflects this "more liberal attitude." Comment 1 to Uniform Commercial Code §2-716. Courts have been increasingly willing to order performance in a wide variety of cases involving output and requirements contracts, contracts for the sale of a business or of an interest in a business represented by shares of stock, and covenants not to compete. Factors that bear on the adequacy of damages are listed in §360. Other limitations on the availability of such equitable relief go to such matters as the need for certainty of terms (§362) and for security as to the completion of the agreed exchange (§363), and to the impact of unfairness (§364), of public policy (§365) and of difficulty of enforcement of the decree (§366). This Chapter does not deal with other equitable remedies such as reformation or cancellation. See Introductory Note to this Chapter and, as to reformation, §§155, 166.

§357 Availability of Specific Performance and Injunction

(1) Subject to the rules stated in §§359- 69, specific performance of a contract duty will be granted in the discretion of the court against a party who has committed or is threatening to commit a breach of the duty.

(2) Subject to the rules stated in §§359- 69, an injunction against breach of a contract duty will be granted in the discretion of the court against a party who has committed or is threatening to commit a breach of the duty if

(a) the duty is one of forbearance, or

(b) the duty is one to act and specific performance would be denied only for reasons that are inapplicable to an injunction.

§358 Form of Order and Other Relief

(1) An order of specific performance or an injunction will be so drawn as best to effectuate the purposes for which the contract was made and on such terms as justice requires. It need not be absolute in form and the performance that it requires need not be identical with that due under the contract.

(2) If specific performance or an injunction is denied as to part of the performance that is due, it may nevertheless be granted as to the remainder.

(3) In addition to specific performance or an injunction, damages and other relief may be awarded in the same proceeding and an indemnity against future harm may be required.

§359 Effect of Adequacy of Damages

(1) Specific performance or an injunction will not be ordered if damages would be adequate to protect the expectation interest of the injured party.

(2) The adequacy of the damage remedy for failure to render one part of the performance due does not preclude specific performance or injunction as to the contract as a whole.

(3) Specific performance or an injunction will not be refused merely because there is a remedy for breach other than damages, but such a remedy may be considered in exercising discretion under the rule stated in §357.

§360 Factors Affecting Adequacy of Damages

In determining whether the remedy in damages would be adequate, the following circumstances are significant:

(a) the difficulty of proving damages with reasonable certainty,

(b) the difficulty of procuring a suitable substitute performance by means of money awarded as damages, and

(c) the likelihood that an award of damages could not be collected.

§361 Effect of Provision for Liquidated Damages

Specific performance or an injunction may be granted to enforce a duty even though there is a provision for liquidated damages for breach of that duty.

§362 Effect of Uncertainty of Terms

Specific performance or an injunction will not be granted unless the terms of the contract are sufficiently certain to provide a basis for an appropriate order.

§363 Effect of Insecurity as to the Agreed Exchange

Specific performance or an injunction may be refused if a substantial part of the agreed exchange for the performance to be compelled is unperformed and its performance is not secured to the satisfaction of the court.

§364 Effect of Unfairness

(1) Specific performance or an injunction will be refused if such relief would be unfair because

(a) the contract was induced by mistake or by unfair practices,

(b) the relief would cause unreasonable hardship or loss to the party in breach or to third persons, or

(c) the exchange is grossly inadequate or the terms of the contract are otherwise unfair.

(2) Specific performance or an injunction will be granted in spite of a term of the agreement if denial of such relief would be unfair because it would cause unreasonable hardship or loss to the party seeking relief or to third persons.

§365 Effect of Public Policy

Specific performance or an injunction will not be granted if the act or forbearance that would be compelled or the use of compulsion is contrary to public policy.

§366 Effect of Difficulty in Enforcement or Supervision

A promise will not be specifically enforced if the character and magnitude of the performance would impose on the court burdens in enforcement or supervision that are disproportionate to the advantages to be gained from enforcement and to the harm to be suffered from its denial.

§367 Contracts for Personal Service or Supervision

(1) A promise to render personal service will not be specifically enforced.

(2) A promise to render personal service exclusively for one employer will not be enforced by an injunction against serving another if its probable result will be to compel a performance involving personal relations the enforced continuance of which is undesirable or will be to leave the employee without other reasonable means of making a living.

§368 Effect of Power of Termination

(1) Specific performance or an injunction will not be granted against a party who can substantially nullify the effect of the order by exercising a power of termination or avoidance.

(2) Specific performance or an injunction will not be denied merely because the party seeking relief has a power to terminate or avoid his duty unless the power could be used, in spite of the order, to deprive the other party of reasonable security for the agreed exchange for his performance.

§369 Effect of Breach by Party Seeking Relief

Specific performance or an injunction may be granted in spite of a breach by the party seeking relief, unless the breach is serious enough to discharge the other party's remaining duties of performance.

Topic 4. Restitution

Introductory Note

Restitution is a common form of relief in contract cases. It has as its objective not the enforcement of contracts through the protection of a party's expectation or reliance interests but the prevention of unjust enrichment through the protection of his restitution interest. See § 344. A party who has received a benefit at the expense of the other party to the agreement is required to account for it, either by returning it in kind or by paying a sum of money. General rules that govern restitution in this context are set out in §§370- 77.

This Chapter does not deal with restitution in general, because that subject is covered by the Restatement of Restitution. This Topic treats restitution in five situations that are closely related to contracts. The first is that in which the other party is in breach and the party seeking restitution has chosen it as an alternative to the enforcement of the contract between them (§373). In the second the party seeking restitution claims the benefit that he has conferred under the contract because he is precluded by his own breach from enforcing the contract (§374). In the third situation the party seeking restitution claims the benefit that he has conferred under the contract because he is precluded from enforcing it against the other party because of the Statute of Frauds (§375). The fourth situation is that in which a party claims restitution upon avoidance of a contract on the ground, for example, of mistake, misrepresentation or duress (§376). The fifth is that in which he claims restitution on the ground that his duty of performance did not arise or was discharged as a result of impracticability of performance, frustration of purpose, non-occurrence of a condition or disclaimer by a beneficiary (§377). A party's right to restitution under an agreement that is unenforceable on grounds of public policy is the subject of Topic 5 of Chapter 8, Unenforceability on Grounds of Public Policy. As to the right to restitution following an agreement of rescission, see Comment c to §283. This Chapter does not deal with restitution for benefits during negotiations that do not result in an agreement or under an agreement that is not enforceable because its terms are not sufficiently certain (§33). See generally Restatement of Restitution §§15, 40, 47, 53.

§370 Requirement That Benefit Be Conferred

A party is entitled to restitution under the rules stated in this Restatement only to the extent that he has conferred a benefit on the other party by way of part performance or reliance.

§371 Measure of Restitution Interest

If a sum of money is awarded to protect a party's restitution interest, it may as justice requires be measured by either

(a) the reasonable value to the other party of what he received in terms of what it would have cost him to obtain it from a person in the claimant's position, or

(b) the extent to which the other party's property has been increased in value or his other interests advanced.

§372 Specific Restitution

(1) Specific restitution will be granted to a party who is entitled to restitution, except that:

(a) specific restitution based on a breach by the other party under the rule stated in § 373 may be refused in the discretion of the court if it would unduly interfere with the certainty of title to land or otherwise cause injustice, and

(b) specific restitution in favor of the party in breach under the rule stated in § 374 will not be granted.

(2) A decree of specific restitution may be made conditional on return of or compensation for anything that the party claiming restitution has received.

(3) If specific restitution, with or without a sum of money, will be substantially as effective as restitution in money in putting the party claiming restitution in the position he was in before rendering any performance, the other party can discharge his duty by tendering such restitution before suit is brought and keeping his tender good.

§373 Restitution When Other Party is in Breach

(1) Subject to the rule stated in Subsection (2), on a breach by non performance that gives rise to a claim for damages for total breach or on a repudiation, the injured party is entitled to restitution for any benefit that he has conferred on the other party by way of part performance or reliance.

(2) The injured party has no right to restitution if he has performed all of his duties under the contract and no performance by the other party remains due other than payment of a definite sum of money for that performance.

§374 Restitution in Favor of Party in Breach

(1) Subject to the rule stated in Subsection (2), if a party justifiably refuses to perform on the ground that his remaining duties of performance have been discharged by the other party's breach, the party in breach is entitled to restitution for any benefit that he has conferred by way of part performance or reliance in excess of the loss that he has caused by his own breach.

(2) To the extent that, under the manifested assent of the parties, a party's performance is to be retained in the case of breach, that party is not entitled to restitution if the value of the performance as liquidated damages is reasonable in the light of the anticipated or actual loss caused by the breach and the difficulties of proof of loss.

§375 Restitution When Contract Is Within Statute of Frauds

A party who would otherwise have a claim in restitution under a contract is not barred from restitution for the reason that the contract is unenforceable by him because of the Statute of Frauds unless the Statute provides otherwise or its purpose would be frustrated by allowing restitution.

§376 Restitution When Contract Is Voidable

A party who has avoided a contract on the ground of lack of capacity, mistake, misrepresentation, duress, undue influence or abuse of a fiduciary relation is entitled to restitution for any benefit that he has conferred on the other party by way of part performance or reliance.

§377 Restitution in Cases of Impracticability, Frustration, Non-Occurrence of Condition or Disclaimer by Beneficiary

A party whose duty of performance does not arise or is discharged as a result of impracticability of performance, frustration of purpose, non occurrence of a condition or disclaimer by a beneficiary is entitled to restitution for any benefit that he has conferred on the other party by way of part performance or reliance.

Topic 5. Preclusion by Election and Affirmance

Introductory Note

Sometimes a party who has a choice of alternative remedies is precluded by his action or inaction from pursuing one of those remedies on the ground that he has "elected" the other. The rules governing this are dealt with in §§ 378 and 379. They reflect the trend against preclusion by election that has resulted from the merger of law and equity and the reform of rules of procedure.

A party who has a power of avoidance on the ground, for example, of mistake, misrepresentation or duress, may be precluded by his action or inaction from exercising it on the ground that he has ratified the contract by affirming it. The rules governing this are dealt with in §§380- 85. This Topic does not contain the substantive rules that determine whether a party has a power of avoidance. Those rules appear in other chapters of this Restatement that deal with the various grounds for avoidance. See §§14-16, 152- 53, 164, 173, 175 and 177.

§378 Election Among Remedies

If a party has more than one remedy under the rules stated in this Chapter, his manifestation of a choice of one of them by bringing suit or otherwise is not a bar to another remedy unless the remedies are inconsistent and the other party materially changes his position in reliance on the manifestation.

§379 Election to Treat Duties of Performance Under Aleatory Contract as Discharged

If a right or duty of the injured party is conditional on an event that is fortuitous or is supposed by the parties to be fortuitous, he cannot treat his remaining duties to render performance as discharged on the ground of the other party's breach by non-performance if he does not manifest to the other party his intention to do so before any adverse change in the situation of the injured party resulting from the occurrence of that event or a material change in the probability of its occurrence.

§380 Loss of Power of Avoidance by Affirmance

(1) The power of a party to avoid a contract for incapacity, duress, undue influence or abuse of a fiduciary relation is lost if, after the circumstances that made the contract voidable have ceased to exist, he manifests to the other party his intention to affirm it or acts with respect to anything that he has received in a manner inconsistent with disaffirmance.

(2) The power of a party to avoid a contract for mistake or misrepresentation is lost if after he knows or has reason to know of the mistake or of the misrepresentation if it is non-fraudulent or knows of the misrepresentation if it is fraudulent, he manifests to the other party his intention to affirm it or acts with respect to anything that he has received in a manner inconsistent with disaffirmance.

(3) If the other party rejects an offer by the party seeking avoidance to return what he has received, the party seeking avoidance if entitled to restitution can, after the lapse of a reasonable time, enforce a lien on what he has received by selling it and crediting the proceeds toward his claim in restitution.

§381 Loss of Power of Avoidance by Delay

(1) The power of a party to avoid a contract for incapacity, duress, undue influence or abuse of a fiduciary relation is lost if, after the circumstances that made it voidable have ceased to exist, he does not within a reasonable time manifest to the other party his intention to avoid it.

(2) The power of a party to avoid a contract for misrepresentation or mistake is lost if after he knows of a fraudulent misrepresentation or knows or has reason to know of a non-fraudulent misrepresentation or mistake he does not within a reasonable time manifest to the other party

his intention to avoid it. The power of a party to avoid a contract for non-fraudulent misrepresentation or mistake is also lost if the contract has been so far performed or the circumstances have otherwise so changed that avoidance would be inequitable and if damages will be adequate compensation.

(3) In determining what is a reasonable time, the following circumstances are significant:

(a) the extent to which the delay enabled or might have enabled the party with the power of avoidance to speculate at the other party's risk;

(b) the extent to which the delay resulted or might have resulted in justifiable reliance by the other party or by third persons;

(c) the extent to which the ground for avoidance was the result of any fault by either party; and

(d) the extent to which the other party's conduct contributed to the delay.

(4) If a right or duty of the party who has the power of avoidance for non-fraudulent misrepresentation or mistake is conditional on an event that is fortuitous or is supposed by the parties to be fortuitous, a manifestation of intention under Subsection (1) or (2) is not effective unless it is made before any adverse change in his situation resulting from the occurrence of that event or a material change in the probability of its occurrence.

§382 Loss of Power to Affirm by Prior Avoidance

(1) If a party has effectively exercised his power of avoidance, a subsequent manifestation of intent to affirm is inoperative unless the other party manifests his assent to affirmance by refusal to accept a return of his performance or otherwise.

(2) A party has not exercised his power of avoidance under the rule stated in Subsection (1) until

(a) he has regained all or a substantial part of what he would be entitled to by way of restitution on avoidance,

(b) he has obtained a final judgment of or based on avoidance, or

(c) the other party has materially relied on or manifested his assent to a statement of disaffirmance.

§383 Avoidance in Part

A contract cannot be avoided in part except that where one or more corresponding pairs of part performances have been fully performed by one or both parties the rest of the contract can be avoided.

§384 Requirement That Party Seeking Restitution Return Benefit

(1) Except as stated in Subsection (2), a party will not be granted restitution unless

(a) he returns or offers to return, conditional on restitution, any interest in property that he has received in exchange in substantially as good condition as when it was received by him, or

(b) the court can assure such return in connection with the relief granted.

(2) The requirement stated in Subsection (1) does not apply to property

(a) that was worthless when received or that has been destroyed or lost by the other party or as a result of its own defects,

(b) that either could not from the time of receipt have been returned or has been used or disposed of without knowledge of the grounds for restitution if justice requires that compensation be accepted in its place and the payment of such compensation can be assured, or

(c) as to which the contract apportions the price if that part of the price is not included in the claim for restitution.

§385 Effect of Power of Avoidance on Duty of Performance or on Duty Arising Out of Breach

(1) Unless an offer to restore performance received is a condition of avoidance, a party has no duty of performance while his power of avoidance exists.

(2) If an offer to restore performance received is a condition of avoidance, a duty to pay damages is terminated by such an offer made before the power of avoidance is lost.

14) 2009 EU Common Frame of Reference[1]

Table of Contents

BOOK I – GENERAL PROVISIONS

I. – 1:101: Intended Field of Application

(1) These rules are intended to be used primarily in relation to contracts and other juridical acts, contractual and non-contractual rights and obligations and related property matters.

(2) They are not intended to be used, or used without modification or supplementation, in relation to rights and obligations of a public law nature or, except where otherwise provided, in relation to:

(a) the status or legal capacity of natural persons;

(b) wills and succession;

(c) family relationships, including matrimonial and similar relationships;

(d) bills of exchange, cheques and promissory notes and other negotiable instruments;

(e) employment relationships;

(f) the ownership of, or rights in security over, immovable property;

(g) the creation, capacity, internal organisation, regulation or dissolution of companies and other bodies corporate or unincorporated;

(h) matters relating primarily to procedure or enforcement.

(3) Further restrictions on intended fields of application are contained in later Books.

I. – 1:102: Interpretation and Development

(1) These rules are to be interpreted and developed autonomously and in accordance with their objectives and the principles underlying them.

(2) They are to be read in the light of any applicable instruments guaranteeing human rights and fundamental freedoms and any applicable constitutional laws.

(3) In their interpretation and development regard should be had to the need to promote:

(a) uniformity of application;

(b) good faith and fair dealing; and

(c) legal certainty.

(4) Issues within the scope of the rules but not expressly settled by them are so far as possible to be settled in accordance with the principles underlying them.

(5) Where there is a general rule and a special rule applying to a particular situation within the scope of the general rule, the special rule prevails in any case of conflict.

I. – 1:103: Good Faith and Fair Dealing

(1) The expression "good faith and fair dealing" refers to a standard of conduct characterised by honesty, openness and consideration for the interests of the other party to the transaction or relationship in question.

(2) It is, in particular, contrary to good faith and fair dealing for a party to act inconsistently with that party's prior statements or conduct when the other party has reasonably relied on them to that other party's detriment.

I. – 1:104: Reasonableness

Reasonableness is to be objectively ascertained, having regard to the nature and purpose of what is being done, to the circumstances of the case and to any relevant usages and practices.

I. – 1:105: "Consumer" and "Business"

(1) A "consumer" means any natural person who is acting primarily for purposes which are not related to his or her trade, business or profession.

(2) A "business" means any natural or legal person, irrespective of whether publicly or privately owned, who is acting for purposes relating to the person's self-employed trade, work or profession, even if the person does not intend to make a profit in the course of the activity.

(3) A person who is within both of the preceding paragraphs is regarded as falling exclusively within paragraph (1) in relation to a rule which would provide protection for that person if that person were a consumer, and otherwise as falling exclusively within paragraph (2).

I. – 1:106: "In Writing" and Similar Expressions

(1) For the purposes of these rules, a statement is "in writing" if it is in textual form and in characters which are directly legible from paper or another tangible durable medium.

(2) "Textual form" means a text which is expressed in alphabetical or other intelligible characters by means of any support which permits reading, recording of the information contained in the text and its reproduction in tangible form.

(3) "Durable medium" means any material on which information is stored so that it is accessible for future reference for a period of time adequate to the purposes of the information, and which allows the unchanged reproduction of this information.

I. – 1:107: "Signature" and Similar Expressions

(1) A reference to a person's signature includes a reference to that person's handwritten signature, electronic signature or advanced electronic signature, and references to anything being signed by a person are to be construed accordingly.

(2) A "handwritten signature" means the name of, or sign representing, a person written by that person's own hand for the purpose of authentication.

(3) An "electronic signature" means data in electronic form which are attached to or logically associated with other electronic data, and which serve as a method of authentication.

(4) An "advanced electronic signature" means an electronic signature which is:

(a) uniquely linked to the signatory;

(b) capable of identifying the signatory;

(c) created using means which can be maintained under the signatory's sole control; and

(d) linked to the data to which it relates in such a manner that any subsequent change of the data is detectable.

(5) In this Article, "electronic" means relating to technology with electrical, digital, magnetic, wireless, optical, electromagnetic, or similar capabilities.

I. – 1:108: Definitions in Annex

(1) The definitions in the Annex apply for all the purposes of these rules unless the context otherwise requires.

(2) Where a word is defined, other grammatical forms of the word have a corresponding meaning.

I. – 1:109: Notice

(1) This Article applies in relation to the giving of notice for any purpose under these rules. "Notice" includes thc communication of information or of a juridical act.

(2) The notice may be given by any means appropriate to the circumstances.

(3) The notice becomes effective when it reaches the addressee, unless it provides for a delayed effect.

(4) The notice reaches the addressee:

(a) when it is delivered to the addressee;

(b) when it is delivered to the addressee's place of business or, where there is no such place of business or the notice does not relate to a business matter, to the addressee's habitual residence;

(c) in the case of a notice transmitted by electronic means, when it can be accessed by the addressee; or

(d) when it is otherwise made available to the addressee at such a place and in such a way that the addressee could reasonably be expected to obtain access to it without undue delay.

(5) The notice has no effect if a revocation of it reaches the addressee before or at the same time as the notice.

(6) Any reference in these rules to a notice given by or to a person includes a notice given by or to an agent of that person who has authority to give or receive it.

(7) In relations between a business and a consumer the parties may not, to the detriment of the consumer, exclude the rule in paragraph (4)(c) or derogate from or vary its effects.

I. – 1:110: Computation of Time

(1) The provisions of this Article apply in relation to the computation of time for any purpose under these rules.

(2) Subject to the following provisions of this Article:

(a) a period expressed in hours starts at the beginning of the first hour and ends with the expiry of the last hour of the period;

(b) a period expressed in days starts at the beginning of the first hour of the first day and ends with the expiry of the last hour of the last day of the period;

(c) a period expressed in weeks, months or years starts at the beginning of the first hour of the first day of the period, and ends with the expiry of the last hour of whichever day in the last week, month or year is the same day of the week, or falls on the same date, as the day from which the period runs; with the qualification that if, in a period expressed in months or in years, the day on which the period should expire does not occur in the last month, it ends with the expiry of the last hour of the last day of that month;

(d) if a period includes part of a month, the month is considered to have thirty days for the purpose of calculating the length of the part.

(3) Where a period is to be calculated from a specified event or action, then:

(a) if the period is expressed in hours, the hour during which the event occurs or the action takes place is not considered to fall within the period in question; and

(b) if the period is expressed in days, weeks, months or years, the day during which the event occurs or the action takes place is not considered to fall within the period in question.

(4) Where a period is to be calculated from a specified time, then:

(a) if the period is expressed in hours, the first hour of the period is considered to begin at the specified time; and

(b) if the period is expressed in days, weeks, months or years, the day during which the specified time arrives is not considered to fall within the period in question.

(5) The periods concerned include Saturdays, Sundays and public holidays, save where these are expressly excepted or where the periods are expressed in working days.

(6) Where the last day of a period expressed otherwise than in hours is a Saturday, Sunday or public holiday at the place where a prescribed act is to be done, the period ends with the expiry of the last hour of the following working day. This provision does not apply to periods calculated retroactively from a given date or event.

(7) Any period of two days or more is regarded as including at least two working days.

(8) Where a person sends another person a document which sets a period of time within which the addressee has to reply or take other action but does not state when the period is to begin, then, in the absence of indications to the contrary, the period is calculated from the date stated as the date of the document or, if no date is stated, from the moment the document reaches the addressee.

(9) In this Article:

(a) "public holiday" with reference to a member state, or part of a member state, of the European Union means any day designated as such for that state or part in a list published in the official journal; and

(b) "working days" means all days other than Saturdays, Sundays and public holidays.

BOOK II – CONTRACTS AND OTHER JURIDICAL ACTS

Chapter 1: General Provisions

II. – 1:101: Meaning of "Contract" and "Juridical Act"

(1) A contract is an agreement which is intended to give rise to a binding legal relationship or to have some other legal effect. It is a bilateral or multilateral juridical act.

(2) A juridical act is any statement or agreement, whether express or implied from conduct, which is intended to have legal effect as such. It may be unilateral, bilateral or multilateral.

II. – 1:102: Party Autonomy

(1) Parties are free to make a contract or other juridical act and to determine its contents, subject to any applicable mandatory rules.

(2) Parties may exclude the application of any of the following rules relating to contracts or other juridical acts, or the rights and obligations arising from them, or derogate from or vary their effects, except as otherwise provided.

(3) A provision to the effect that parties may not exclude the application of a rule or derogate from or vary its effects does not prevent a party from waiving a right which has already arisen and of which that party is aware.

II. – 1:103: Binding Effect

(1) A valid contract is binding on the parties.

(2) A valid unilateral undertaking is binding on the person giving it if it is intended to be legally binding without acceptance.

(3) This Article does not prevent modification or termination of any resulting right or obligation by agreement between the debtor and creditor or as provided by law.

II. – 1:104: Usages and Practices

(1) The parties to a contract are bound by any usage to which they have agreed and by any practice they have established between themselves.

(2) The parties are bound by a usage which would be considered generally applicable by persons in the same situation as the parties, except where the application of such usage would be unreasonable.

(3) This Article applies to other juridical acts with any necessary adaptations.

II. – 1:105: Imputed Knowledge etc.

If a person who with a party's assent was involved in making a contract or other juridical act or in exercising a right or performing an obligation under it:

(a) knew or foresaw a fact, or is treated as having knowledge or foresight of a fact; or

(b) acted intentionally or with any other relevant state of mind this knowledge, foresight or state of mind is imputed to the party.

II. – 1:106: Form

(1) A contract or other juridical act need not be concluded, made or evidenced in writing nor is it subject to any other requirement as to form.

(2) Where a contract or other juridical act is invalid only by reason of noncompliance with a particular requirement as to form, one party (the first party) is liable for any loss suffered by the other (the second party) by acting in the mistaken, but reasonable, belief that it was valid if the first party:

(a) knew it was invalid;

(b) knew or could reasonably be expected to know that the second party was acting to that party's potential prejudice in the mistaken belief that it was valid; and

(c) contrary to good faith and fair dealing, allowed the second party to continue so acting.

II. – 1:107: Mixed Contracts

(1) For the purposes of this Article a mixed contract is a contract which contains:

(a) parts falling within two or more of the categories of contracts regulated specifically in these rules; or

(b) a part falling within one such category and another part falling within the category of contracts governed only by the rules applicable to contracts generally.

(2) Where a contract is a mixed contract then, unless this is contrary to the nature and purpose of the contract, the rules applicable to each relevant category apply, with any appropriate adaptations, to the corresponding part of the contract and the rights and obligations arising from it.

(3) Paragraph (2) does not apply where:

(a) a rule provides that a mixed contract is to be regarded as falling primarily within one category; or

(b) in a case not covered by the preceding sub-paragraph, one part of a mixed contract is in fact so predominant that it would be unreasonable not to regard the contract as falling primarily within one category.

(4) In cases covered by paragraph (3) the rules applicable to the category into which the contract primarily falls (the primary category) apply to the contract and the rights and obligations arising from it. However, rules applicable to any elements of the contract falling within another category apply with any appropriate adaptations so far as is necessary to regulate those elements and provided that they do not conflict with the rules applicable to the primary category.

(5) Nothing in this Article prevents the application of any mandatory rules.

II. – 1:108: Partial Invalidity or Ineffectiveness

Where only part of a contract or other juridical act is invalid or ineffective, the remaining part continues in effect if it can reasonably be maintained without the invalid or ineffective part.

II. – 1:109: Standard Terms

A “standard term” is a term which has been formulated in advance for several transactions involving different parties and which has not been individually negotiated by the parties.

II. – 1:110: Terms “Not Individually Negotiated”

(1) A term supplied by one party is not individually negotiated if the other party has not been able to influence its content, in particular because it has been drafted in advance, whether or not as part of standard terms.

(2) If one party supplies a selection of terms to the other party, a term will not be regarded as individually negotiated merely because the other party chooses that term from that selection.

(3) If it is disputed whether a term supplied by one party as part of standard terms has since been individually negotiated, that party bears the burden of proving that it has been.

(4) In a contract between a business and a consumer, the business bears the burden of proving that a term supplied by the business has been individually negotiated.

(5) In contracts between a business and a consumer, terms drafted by a third person are considered to have been supplied by the business, unless the consumer introduced them to the contract.

Chapter 2: Non-Discrimination

II. – 2:101: Right Not to Be Discriminated Against

A person has a right not to be discriminated against on the grounds of sex or ethnic or racial origin in relation to a contract or other juridical act the object of which is to provide access to, or supply, goods, other assets or services which are available to the public.

II. – 2:102: Meaning of Discrimination

(1) “Discrimination” means any conduct whereby, or situation where, on grounds such as those mentioned in the preceding Article:

(a) one person is treated less favourably than another person is, has been or would be treated in a comparable situation; or

(b) an apparently neutral provision, criterion or practice would place one group of persons at a particular disadvantage when compared to a different group of persons.

(2) Discrimination also includes harassment on grounds such as those mentioned in the preceding Article. “Harassment” means unwanted conduct (including conduct of a sexual nature) which violates a person’s dignity, particularly when such conduct creates an intimidating, hostile, degrading, humiliating or offensive environment, or which aims to do so.

(3) Any instruction to discriminate also amounts to discrimination.

II. – 2:103: Exception

Unequal treatment which is justified by a legitimate aim does not amount to discrimination if the means used to achieve that aim are appropriate and necessary.

II. – 2:104: Remedies

(1) If a person is discriminated against contrary to II. – 2:101 (Right not to be discriminated against) then, without prejudice to any remedy which may be available under Book VI (Non-con-

tractual liability for damage caused to another), the remedies for non-performance of an obligation under Book III, Chapter 3 (including damages for economic and non-economic loss) are available.

(2) Any remedy granted should be proportionate to the injury or anticipated injury; the dissuasive effect of remedies may be taken into account.

II. – 2:105: Burden of Proof

(1) If a person who considers himself or herself discriminated against on one of the grounds mentioned in II. – 2:101 (Right not to be discriminated against) establishes, before a court or another competent authority, facts from which it may be presumed that there has been such discrimination, it falls on the other party to prove that there has been no such discrimination.

(2) Paragraph (1) does not apply to proceedings in which it is for the court or another competent authority to investigate the facts of the case.

Chapter 3: Marketing and Pre-Contractual Duties

Section 1: Information Duties

II. – 3:101: Duty to Disclose Information about Goods, Other Assets and Services

(1) Before the conclusion of a contract for the supply of goods, other assets or services by a business to another person, the business has a duty to disclose to the other person such information concerning the goods, other assets or services to be supplied as the other person can reasonably expect, taking into account the standards of quality and performance which would be normal under the circumstances.

(2) In assessing what information the other person can reasonably expect to be disclosed, the test to be applied, if the other person is also a business, is whether the failure to provide the information would deviate from good commercial practice.

II. – 3:102: Specific Duties for Businesses Marketing to Consumers

(1) Where a business is marketing goods, other assets or services to a consumer, the business has a duty not to give misleading information. Information is misleading if it misrepresents or omits material facts which the average consumer could expect to be given for an informed decision on whether to take steps towards the conclusion of a contract. In assessing what an average consumer could expect to be given, account is to be taken of all the circumstances and of the limitations of the communication medium employed.

(2) Where a business uses a commercial communication which gives the impression to consumers that it contains all the relevant information necessary to make a decision about concluding a contract, the business has a duty to ensure that the communication in fact contains all the relevant information. Where it is not already apparent from the context of the commercial communication, the information to be provided comprises:

(a) the main characteristics of the goods, other assets or services, the identity and address, if relevant, of the business, the price, and any available right of withdrawal;

(b) peculiarities related to payment, delivery, performance and complaint handling, if they depart from the requirements of professional diligence; and

(c) the language to be used for communications between the parties after the conclusion of the contract, if this differs from the language of the commercial communication.

(3) A duty to provide information under this Article is not fulfilled unless all the information to be provided is provided in the same language.

II. – 3:103: Duty to Provide Information When Concluding Contract with a Consumer Who Is at a Particular Disadvantage

(1) In the case of transactions that place the consumer at a significant informational disadvantage because of the technical medium used for contracting, the physical distance between business and consumer, or the nature of the transaction, the business has a duty, as appropriate in the circumstances, to provide clear information about the main characteristics of any goods, other assets or services to be supplied, the price, the address and identity of the business with which the consumer is transacting, the terms of the contract, the rights and obligations of both contracting parties, and any available right of withdrawal or redress procedures. This information must be provided a reasonable time before the conclusion of the contract. The information on the right of withdrawal must, as appropriate in the circumstances, also be adequate in the sense of II. – 5:104 (Adequate information on the right to withdraw).

(2) Where more specific information duties are provided for specific situations, these take precedence over the general information duty under paragraph (1).

(3) The business bears the burden of proof that it has provided the information required by this Article.

II. – 3:104: Information Duties in Real Time Distance Communication

(1) When initiating real time distance communication with a consumer, a business has a duty to provide at the outset explicit information on its name and the commercial purpose of the contact.

(2) Real time distance communication means direct and immediate distance communication of such a type that one party can interrupt the other in the course of the communication. It includes telephone and electronic means such as voice over internet protocol and internet related chat, but does not include communication by electronic mail.

(3) The business bears the burden of proof that the consumer has received the information required under paragraph (1).

(4) If a business has failed to comply with the duty under paragraph (1) and a contract has been concluded as a result of the communication, the other party has a right to withdraw from the contract by giving notice to the business within the period specified in II. – 5:103 (Withdrawal period).

(5) A business is liable to the consumer for any loss caused by a breach of the duty under paragraph (1).

II. – 3:105: Formation by Electronic Means

(1) If a contract is to be concluded by electronic means and without individual communication, a business has a duty to provide information about the following matters before the other party makes or accepts an offer:

(a) the technical steps to be taken in order to conclude the contract;

(b) whether or not a contract document will be filed by the business and whether it will be accessible;

(c) the technical means for identifying and correcting input errors before the other party makes or accepts an offer;

(d) the languages offered for the conclusion of the contract;

(e) any contract terms used.

(2) The business has a duty to ensure that the contract terms referred to in paragraph (1)(e) are available in textual form.

(3) If a business has failed to comply with the duty under paragraph (1) and a contract has been concluded in the circumstances there stated, the other party has a right to withdraw from the contract by giving notice to the business within the period specified in II. – 5:103 (Withdrawal period).

(4) A business is liable to the consumer for any loss caused by a breach of the duty under paragraph (1).

II. – 3:106: Clarity and Form of Information

(1) A duty to provide information imposed on a business under this Chapter is not fulfilled unless the requirements of this Article are satisfied.

(2) The information must be clear and precise, and expressed in plain and intelligible language.

(3) Where rules for specific contracts require information to be provided on a durable medium or in another particular form it must be provided in that way.

(4) In the case of contracts between a business and a consumer concluded at a distance, information about the main characteristics of any goods, other assets or services to be supplied, the price, the address and identity of the business with which the consumer is transacting, the terms of the contract, the rights and obligations of both contracting parties, and any available redress procedures, as may be appropriate in the particular case, must be confirmed in textual form on a durable medium at the time of conclusion of the contract. The information on the right of withdrawal must also be adequate in the sense of II. – 5:104 (Adequate information on the right to withdraw).

II. – 3:107: Information about Price and Additional Charges

Where under this Chapter a business has a duty to provide information about price, the duty is not fulfilled unless what is provided:

(a) includes information about any deposits payable, delivery charges and any additional taxes and duties where these may be indicated separately;

(b) if an exact price cannot be indicated, gives such information on the basis for the calculation as will enable the consumer to verify the price; and

(c) if the price is not payable in one sum, includes information about the payment schedule.

II. – 3:108: Information about Address and Identity of Business

(1) Where under this Chapter a business has a duty to provide information about its address and identity, the duty is not fulfilled unless the information includes:

(a) the name of the business;

(b) any trading names relevant to the contract in question;

(c) the registration number in any official register, and the name of that register;

(d) the geographical address of the business;

(e) contact details;

(f) where the business has a representative in the consumer's state of residence, the address and identity of that representative;

(g) where the activity of the business is subject to an authorisation scheme, the particulars of the relevant supervisory authority; and

(h) where the business exercises an activity which is subject to VAT, the relevant VAT identification number.

(2) For the purpose of II. – 3:103 (Duty to provide information when concluding contract with a consumer who is at a particular disadvantage), the address and identity of the business include only the information indicated in paragraph (1)(a), (c), (d) and (e).

II. – 3:109: Remedies for Breach of Information Duties

(1) If a business has a duty under II. – 3:103 (Duty to provide information when concluding contract with a consumer who is at a particular disadvantage) to provide information to a consumer before the conclusion of a contract from which the consumer has the right to withdraw, the withdrawal period does not commence until all this information has been provided. Regardless of this, the right of withdrawal lapses after one year from the time of the conclusion of the contract.

(2) If a business has failed to comply with any duty imposed by the preceding Articles of this Section and a contract has been concluded, the business has such obligations under the contract as the other party has reasonably expected as a consequence of the absence or incorrectness of the information. Remedies provided under Book III, Chapter 3 apply to non-performance of these obligations.

(3) Whether or not a contract is concluded, a business which has failed to comply with any duty imposed by the preceding Articles of this Section is liable for any loss caused to the other party to the transaction by such failure. This paragraph does not apply to the extent that a remedy is available for non-performance of a contractual obligation under the preceding paragraph.

(4) The remedies provided under this Article are without prejudice to any remedy which may be available under II. – 7:201 (Mistake).

(5) In relations between a business and a consumer the parties may not, to the detriment of the consumer, exclude the application of this Article or derogate from or vary its effects.

Section 2: Duty to Prevent Input Errors and Acknowledge Receipt

II. – 3:201: Correction of Input Errors

(1) A business which intends to conclude a contract by making available electronic means without individual communication for concluding it has a duty to make available to the other party appropriate, effective and accessible technical means for identifying and correcting input errors before the other party makes or accepts an offer.

(2) Where a person concludes a contract in error because of a failure by a business to comply with the duty under paragraph (1) the business is liable for any loss caused to that person by such failure. This is without prejudice to any remedy which may be available under II. – 7:201 (Mistake).

(3) In relations between a business and a consumer the parties may not, to the detriment of the consumer, exclude the application of this Article or derogate from or vary its effects.

II. – 3:202: Acknowledgement of Receipt

(1) A business which offers the facility to conclude a contract by electronic means and without individual communication has a duty to acknowledge by electronic means the receipt of an offer or an acceptance by the other party.

(2) If the other party does not receive the acknowledgement without undue delay, that other party may revoke the offer or withdraw from the contract.

(3) The business is liable for any loss caused to the other party by a breach of the duty under paragraph (1).

(4) In relations between a business and a consumer the parties may not, to the detriment of the consumer, exclude the application of this Article or derogate from or vary its effects.

Section 3: Negotiation and Confidentiality Duties

II. – 3:301: Negotiations Contrary to Good Faith and Fair Dealing

(1) A person is free to negotiate and is not liable for failure to reach an agreement.

(2) A person who is engaged in negotiations has a duty to negotiate in accordance with good faith and fair dealing and not to break off negotiations contrary to good faith and fair dealing. This duty may not be excluded or limited by contract.

(3) A person who is in breach of the duty is liable for any loss caused to the other party by the breach.

(4) It is contrary to good faith and fair dealing, in particular, for a person to enter into or continue negotiations with no real intention of reaching an agreement with the other party.

II. – 3:302: Breach of Confidentiality

(1) If confidential information is given by one party in the course of negotiations, the other party is under a duty not to disclose that information or use it for that party's own purposes whether or not a contract is subsequently concluded.

(2) In this Article, "confidential information" means information which, either from its nature or the circumstances in which it was obtained, the party receiving the information knows or could reasonably be expected to know is confidential to the other party.

(3) A party who reasonably anticipates a breach of the duty may obtain a court order prohibiting it.

(4) A party who is in breach of the duty is liable for any loss caused to the other party by the breach and may be ordered to pay over to the other party any benefit obtained by the breach.

Section 4: Unsolicited Goods or Services

II. – 3:401: No Obligation Arising from Failure to Respond

(1) If a business delivers unsolicited goods to, or performs unsolicited services for, a consumer:

(a) no contract arises from the consumer's failure to respond or from any other action or inaction by the consumer in relation to the goods and services; and

(b) no non-contractual obligation arises from the consumer's acquisition, retention, rejection or use of the goods or receipt of benefit from the services.

(2) Sub-paragraph (b) of the preceding paragraph does not apply if the goods or services were supplied:

(a) by way of benevolent intervention in another's affairs; or

(b) in error or in such other circumstances that there is a right to reversal of an unjustified enrichment.

(3) This Article is subject to the rules on delivery of excess quantity under a contract for the sale of goods.

(4) For the purposes of paragraph (1) delivery occurs when the consumer obtains physical control over the goods.

Section 5: Damages for Breach of Duty under this Chapter

II. – 3:501: Liability for Damages

(1) Where any rule in this Chapter makes a person liable for loss caused to another person by a breach of a duty, the other person has a right to damages for that loss.

(2) The rules on III. – 3:704 (Loss attributable to creditor) and III. – 3:705 (Reduction of loss) apply with the adaptation that the reference to non-performance of the obligation is to be taken as a reference to breach of the duty.

Chapter 4: Formation

Section 1: General Provisions

II. – 4:101: Requirements for the Conclusion of a Contract

A contract is concluded, without any further requirement, if the parties:

(a) intend to enter into a binding legal relationship or bring about some other legal effect; and

(b) reach a sufficient agreement.

II. – 4:102: How Intention Is Determined

The intention of a party to enter into a binding legal relationship or bring about some other legal effect is to be determined from the party's statements or conduct as they were reasonably understood by the other party.

II. – 4:103: Sufficient Agreement

(1) Agreement is sufficient if:

(a) the terms of the contract have been sufficiently defined by the parties for the contract to be given effect; or

(b) the terms of the contract, or the rights and obligations of the parties under it, can be otherwise sufficiently determined for the contract to be given effect.

(2) If one of the parties refuses to conclude a contract unless the parties have agreed on some specific matter, there is no contract unless agreement on that matter has been reached.

II. – 4:104: Merger Clause

(1) If a contract document contains an individually negotiated term stating that the document embodies all the terms of the contract (a merger clause), any prior statements, undertakings or agreements which are not embodied in the document do not form part of the contract.

(2) If the merger clause is not individually negotiated it establishes only a presumption that the parties intended that their prior statements, undertakings or agreements were not to form part of the contract. This rule may not be excluded or restricted.

(3) The parties' prior statements may be used to interpret the contract. This rule may not be excluded or restricted except by an individually negotiated term.

(4) A party may by statements or conduct be precluded from asserting a merger clause to the extent that the other party has reasonably relied on such statements or conduct.

II. – 4:105: Modification in Certain Form Only

(1) A term in a contract requiring any agreement to modify its terms, or to terminate the relationship resulting from it, to be in a certain form establishes only a presumption that any such agreement is not intended to be legally binding unless it is in that form.

(2) A party may by statements or conduct be precluded from asserting such a term to the extent that the other party has reasonably relied on such statements or conduct.

Section 2: Offer and Acceptance

II. – 4:201: Offer

(1) A proposal amounts to an offer if:

(a) it is intended to result in a contract if the other party accepts it; and

(b) it contains sufficiently definite terms to form a contract.

(2) An offer may be made to one or more specific persons or to the public.

(3) A proposal to supply goods from stock, or a service, at a stated price made by a business in a public advertisement or a catalogue, or by a display of goods, is treated, unless the circumstances indicate otherwise, as an offer to supply at that price until the stock of goods, or the business's capacity to supply the service, is exhausted.

II. – 4:202: Revocation of Offer

(1) An offer may be revoked if the revocation reaches the offeree before the offeree has dispatched an acceptance or, in cases of acceptance by conduct, before the contract has been concluded.

(2) An offer made to the public can be revoked by the same means as were used to make the offer.

(3) However, a revocation of an offer is ineffective if:

(a) the offer indicates that it is irrevocable;

(b) the offer states a fixed time for its acceptance; or

(c) it was reasonable for the offeree to rely on the offer as being irrevocable and the offeree has acted in reliance on the offer.

(4) Paragraph (3) does not apply to an offer if the offeror would have a right under any rule in Books II to IV to withdraw from a contract resulting from its acceptance. The parties may not, to the detriment of the offeror, exclude the application of this rule or derogate from or vary its effects.

II. – 4:203: Rejection of Offer

When a rejection of an offer reaches the offeror, the offer lapses.

II. – 4:204: Acceptance

(1) Any form of statement or conduct by the offeree is an acceptance if it indicates assent to the offer.

(2) Silence or inactivity does not in itself amount to acceptance.

II. – 4:205: Time of Conclusion of the Contract

(1) If an acceptance has been dispatched by the offeree the contract is concluded when the acceptance reaches the offeror.

(2) In the case of acceptance by conduct, the contract is concluded when notice of the conduct reaches the offeror.

(3) If by virtue of the offer, of practices which the parties have established between themselves, or of a usage, the offeree may accept the offer by doing an act without notice to the offeror, the contract is concluded when the offeree begins to do the act.

II. – 4:206: Time Limit for Acceptance

(1) An acceptance of an offer is effective only if it reaches the offeror within the time fixed by the offeror.

(2) If no time has been fixed by the offeror the acceptance is effective only if it reaches the offeror within a reasonable time.

(3) Where an offer may be accepted by performing an act without notice to the offeror, the acceptance is effective only if the act is performed within the time for acceptance fixed by the offeror or, if no such time is fixed, within a reasonable time.

II. – 4:207: Late Acceptance

(1) A late acceptance is nonetheless effective as an acceptance if without undue delay the offeror informs the offeree that it is treated as an effective acceptance.

(2) If a letter or other communication containing a late acceptance shows that it has been dispatched in such circumstances that if its transmission had been normal it would have reached the offeror in due time, the late acceptance is effective as an acceptance unless, without undue delay, the offeror informs the offeree that the offer is considered to have lapsed.

II. – 4:208: Modified Acceptance

(1) A reply by the offeree which states or implies additional or different terms which materially alter the terms of the offer is a rejection and a new offer.

(2) A reply which gives a definite assent to an offer operates as an acceptance even if it states or implies additional or different terms, provided these do not materially alter the terms of the offer. The additional or different terms then become part of the contract.

(3) However, such a reply is treated as a rejection of the offer if:

(a) the offer expressly limits acceptance to the terms of the offer;

(b) the offeror objects to the additional or different terms without undue delay; or

(c) the offeree makes the acceptance conditional upon the offeror's assent to the additional or different terms, and the assent does not reach the offeree within a reasonable time.

II. – 4:209: Conflicting Standard Terms

(1) If the parties have reached agreement except that the offer and acceptance refer to conflicting standard terms, a contract is nonetheless formed. The standard terms form part of the contract to the extent that they are common in substance.

(2) However, no contract is formed if one party:

(a) has indicated in advance, explicitly, and not by way of standard terms, an intention not to be bound by a contract on the basis of paragraph (1); or

(b) without undue delay, informs the other party of such an intention.

II. – 4:210: Formal Confirmation of Contract Between Businesses

If businesses have concluded a contract but have not embodied it in a final document, and one without undue delay sends the other a notice in textual form on a durable medium which purports to be a confirmation of the contract but which contains additional or different terms, such terms become part of the contract unless:

(a) the terms materially alter the terms of the contract; or

(b) the addressee objects to them without undue delay.

II. – 4:211: Contracts Not Concluded Through Offer and Acceptance

The rules in this Section apply with appropriate adaptations even though the process of conclusion of a contract cannot be analysed into offer and acceptance.

Section 3: Other Juridical Acts

II. – 4:301: Requirements for a Unilateral Juridical Act

The requirements for a unilateral juridical act are:

(a) that the party doing the act intends to be legally bound or to achieve the relevant legal effect;

(b) that the act is sufficiently certain; and

(c) that notice of the act reaches the person to whom it is addressed or, if the act is addressed to the public, the act is made public by advertisement, public notice or otherwise.

II. – 4:302: How Intention Is Determined

The intention of a party to be legally bound or to achieve the relevant legal effect is to be determined from the party's statements or conduct as they were reasonably understood by the person to whom the act is addressed.

II. – 4:303: Right or Benefit May Be Rejected

Where a unilateral juridical act confers a right or benefit on the person to whom it is addressed, that person may reject it by notice to the maker of the act, provided that is done without undue delay and before the right or benefit has been expressly or impliedly accepted. On such rejection, the right or benefit is treated as never having accrued.

Chapter 5: Right of Withdrawal

Section 1: Exercise and Effect

II. – 5:101: Scope and Mandatory Nature

(1) The provisions in this Section apply where under any rule in Books II to IV a party has a right to withdraw from a contract within a certain period.

(2) The parties may not, to the detriment of the entitled party, exclude the application of the rules in this Chapter or derogate from or vary their effects.

II. – 5:102: Exercise of Right to Withdraw

(1) A right to withdraw is exercised by notice to the other party. No reasons need to be given.

(2) Returning the subject matter of the contract is considered a notice of withdrawal unless the circumstances indicate otherwise.

II. – 5:103: Withdrawal Period

(1) A right to withdraw may be exercised at any time after the conclusion of the contract and before the end of the withdrawal period.

(2) The withdrawal period ends fourteen days after the latest of the following times;

(a) the time of conclusion of the contract;

(b) the time when the entitled party receives from the other party adequate information on the right to withdraw; or

(c) if the subject matter of the contract is the delivery of goods, the time when the goods are received.

(3) The withdrawal period ends no later than one year after the time of conclusion of the contract.

(4) A notice of withdrawal is timely if dispatched before the end of the withdrawal period.

II. – 5:104: Adequate Information on the Right to Withdraw

Adequate information on the right to withdraw requires that the right is appropriately brought to the entitled party's attention, and that the information provides, in textual form on a durable medium and in clear and comprehensible language, information about how the right may be exercised, the withdrawal period, and the name and address of the person to whom the withdrawal is to be communicated.

II. – 5:105: Effects of Withdrawal

(1) Withdrawal terminates the contractual relationship and the obligations of both parties under the contract.

(2) The restitutionary effects of such termination are governed by the rules in Book III, Chapter 3, Section 5, Sub-section 4 (Restitution) as modified by this Article, unless the contract provides otherwise in favour of the withdrawing party.

(3) Where the withdrawing party has made a payment under the contract, the business has an obligation to return the payment without undue delay, and in any case not later than thirty days after the withdrawal becomes effective.

(4) The withdrawing party is not liable to pay:

(a) for any diminution in the value of anything received under the contract caused by inspection and testing;

(b) for any destruction or loss of, or damage to, anything received under the contract, provided the withdrawing party used reasonable care to prevent such destruction, loss or damage.

(5) The withdrawing party is liable for any diminution in value caused by normal use, unless that party had not received adequate notice of the right of withdrawal.

(6) Except as provided in this Article, the withdrawing party does not incur any liability through the exercise of the right of withdrawal.

(7) If a consumer exercises a right to withdraw from a contract after a business has made use of a contractual right to supply something of equivalent quality and price in case what was ordered is unavailable, the business must bear the cost of returning what the consumer has received under the contract.

II. – 5:106: Linked Contracts

(1) If a consumer exercises a right of withdrawal from a contract for the supply of goods, other assets or services by a business, the effects of withdrawal extend to any linked contract.

(2) Where a contract is partially or exclusively financed by a credit contract, they form linked contracts, in particular:

(a) if the business supplying goods, other assets or services finances the consumer's performance;

(b) if a third party which finances the consumer's performance uses the services of the business for preparing or concluding the credit contract;

(c) if the credit contract refers to specific goods, assets or services to be financed with this credit, and if this link between both contracts was suggested by the supplier of the goods, other assets or services, or by the supplier of credit; or

(d) if there is a similar economic link.

(3) The provisions of II. – 5:105 (Effects of withdrawal) apply accordingly to the linked contract.

(4) Paragraph (1) does not apply to credit contracts financing the contracts mentioned in paragraph (2)(f) of the following Article.

Section 2: Particular Rights of Withdrawal

II. – 5:201: Contracts Negotiated Away from Business Premises

(1) A consumer is entitled to withdraw from a contract under which a business supplies goods, other assets or services, including financial services, to the consumer, or is granted a personal security by the consumer, if the consumer's offer or acceptance was expressed away from the business premises.

(2) Paragraph (1) does not apply to:

(a) a contract concluded by means of an automatic vending machine or automated commercial premises;

(b) a contract concluded with telecommunications operators through the use of public payphones;

(c) a contract for the construction and sale of immovable property or relating to other immovable property rights, except for rental;

(d) a contract for the supply of foodstuffs, beverages or other goods intended for everyday consumption supplied to the home, residence or workplace of the consumer by regular roundsmen;

(e) a contract concluded by means of distance communication, but outside of an organised distance sales or service-provision scheme run by the supplier;

(f) a contract for the supply of goods, other assets or services whose price depends on fluctuations in the financial market outside the supplier's control, which may occur during the withdrawal period;

(g) a contract concluded at an auction;

(h) travel and baggage insurance policies or similar short-term insurance policies of less than one month's duration.

(3) If the business has exclusively used means of distance communication for concluding the contract, paragraph (1) also does not apply if the contract is for:

(a) the supply of accommodation, transport, catering or leisure services, where the business undertakes, when the contract is concluded, to supply these services on a specific date or within a specific period;

(b) the supply of services other than financial services if performance has begun, at the consumer's express and informed request, before the end of the withdrawal period referred to in II. – 5:103 (Withdrawal period) paragraph (1);

(c) the supply of goods made to the consumer's specifications or clearly personalised or which, by reason of their nature, cannot be returned or are liable to deteriorate or expire rapidly;

(d) the supply of audio or video recordings or computer software

  (i) which were unsealed by the consumer, or

  (ii) which can be downloaded or reproduced for permanent use, in case of supply by electronic means;

(e) the supply of newspapers, periodicals and magazines;

(f) gaming and lottery services.

(4) With regard to financial services, paragraph (1) also does not apply to contracts that have been fully performed by both parties, at the consumer's express request, before the consumer exercises his or her right of withdrawal.

II. – 5:202: Timeshare Contracts

(1) A consumer who acquires a right to use immovable property under a timeshare contract with a business is entitled to withdraw from the contract.

(2) Where a consumer exercises the right of withdrawal under paragraph (1), the contract may require the consumer to reimburse those expenses which:

(a) have been incurred as a result of the conclusion of and withdrawal from the contract;

(b) correspond to legal formalities which must be completed before the end of the period referred to in II. – 5:103 (Withdrawal period) paragraph (1);

(c) are reasonable and appropriate;

(d) are expressly mentioned in the contract; and

(e) are in conformity with any applicable rules on such expenses.

The consumer is not obliged to reimburse any expenses when exercising the right of withdrawal in the situation covered by paragraph (1) of II. – 3:109 (Remedies for breach of information duties).

(3) The business must not demand or accept any advance payment by the consumer during the period in which the latter may exercise the right of withdrawal. The business is obliged to return any such payment received.

Chapter 6: Representation

II. – 6:101: Scope

(1) This Chapter applies to the external relationships created by acts of representation – that is to say, the relationships between:

(a) the principal and the third party; and

(b) the representative and the third party.

(2) It applies also to situations where a person purports to be a representative without actually being a representative.

(3) It does not apply to the internal relationship between the representative and the principal.

II. – 6:102: Definitions

(1) A "representative" is a person who has authority to affect directly the legal position of another person, the principal, in relation to a third party by acting on behalf of the principal.

(2) The "authority" of a representative is the power to affect the principal's legal position.

(3) The "authorisation" of the representative is the granting or maintaining of the authority.

(4) "Acting without authority" includes acting beyond the scope of the authority granted.

(5) A "third party", in this Chapter, includes the representative who, when acting for the principal, also acts in a personal capacity as the other party to the transaction.

II. – 6:103: Authorisation

(1) The authority of a representative may be granted by the principal or by the law.

(2) The principal's authorisation may be express or implied.

(3) If a person causes a third party reasonably and in good faith to believe that the person has authorised a representative to perform certain acts, the person is treated as a principal who has so authorised the apparent representative.

II. – 6:104: Scope of Authority

(1) The scope of the representative's authority is determined by the grant.

(2) The representative has authority to perform all incidental acts necessary to achieve the purposes for which the authority was granted.

(3) A representative has authority to delegate authority to another person (the delegate) to do acts on behalf of the principal which it is not reasonable to expect the representative to do personally. The rules of this Chapter apply to acts done by the delegate.

II. – 6:105: When Representative's Act Affects Principal's Legal Position

When the representative acts:

(a) in the name of a principal or otherwise in such a way as to indicate to the third party an intention to affect the legal position of a principal; and

(b) within the scope of the representative's authority,

the act affects the legal position of the principal in relation to the third party as if it had been done by the principal. It does not as such give rise to any legal relation between the representative and the third party.

II. – 6:106: Representative Acting in Own Name

When the representative, despite having authority, does an act in the representative's own name or otherwise in such a way as not to indicate to the third party an intention to affect the legal position of a principal, the act affects the legal position of the representative in relation to the third party as if done by the representative in a personal capacity. It does not as such affect the legal position of the principal in relation to the third party unless this is specifically provided for by any rule of law.

II. – 6:107: Person Purporting to Act as Representative but Not Having Authority

(1) When a person acts in the name of a principal or otherwise in such a way as to indicate to the third party an intention to affect the legal position of a principal but acts without authority, the act does not affect the legal position of the purported principal or, save as provided in paragraph (2), give rise to legal relations between the unauthorised person and the third party.

(2) Failing ratification by the purported principal, the person is liable to pay the third party such damages as will place the third party in the same position as if the person had acted with authority.

(3) Paragraph (2) does not apply if the third party knew or could reasonably be expected to have known of the lack of authority.

II. – 6:108: Unidentified Principal

If a representative acts for a principal whose identity is to be revealed later, but fails to reveal that identity within a reasonable time after a request by the third party, the representative is treated as having acted in a personal capacity.

II. – 6:109: Conflict of Interest

(1) If an act done by a representative involves the representative in a conflict of interest of which the third party knew or could reasonably be expected to have known, the principal may

avoid the act according to the provisions of II. – 7:209 (Notice of avoidance) to II. – 7:213 (Partial avoidance).

(2) There is presumed to be a conflict of interest where:

(a) the representative also acted as representative for the third party; or

(b) the transaction was with the representative in a personal capacity.

(3) However, the principal may not avoid the act:

(a) if the representative acted with the principal's prior consent; or

(b) if the representative had disclosed the conflict of interest to the principal and the principal did not object within a reasonable time;

(c) if the principal otherwise knew, or could reasonably be expected to have known, of the representative's involvement in the conflict of interest and did not object within a reasonable time; or

(d) if, for any other reason, the representative was entitled as against the principal to do the act by virtue of IV. D. – 5:101 (Self-contracting) or IV. D. – 5:102 (Double mandate).

II. – 6:110: Several Representatives

Where several representatives have authority to act for the same principal, each of them may act separately.

II. – 6:111: Ratification

(1) Where a person purports to act as a representative but acts without authority, the purported principal may ratify the act.

(2) Upon ratification, the act is considered as having been done with authority, without prejudice to the rights of other persons.

(3) The third party who knows that an act was done without authority may by notice to the purported principal specify a reasonable period of time for ratification. If the act is not ratified within that period ratification is no longer possible.

II. – 6:112: Effect of Ending or Restriction of Authorisation

(1) The authority of a representative continues in relation to a third party who knew of the authority notwithstanding the ending or restriction of the representative's authorisation until the third party knows or can reasonably be expected to know of the ending or restriction.

(2) Where the principal is under an obligation to the third party not to end or restrict the representative's authorisation, the authority of a representative continues notwithstanding an ending or restriction of the authorisation even if the third party knows of the ending or restriction.

(3) The third party can reasonably be expected to know of the ending or restriction if, in particular, it has been communicated or publicised in the same way as the granting of the authority was originally communicated or publicised.

(4) Notwithstanding the ending of authorisation, the representative continues to have authority for a reasonable time to perform those acts which are necessary to protect the interests of the principal or the principal's successors.

Chapter 7: Grounds of Invalidity

Section 1: General Provisions

II. – 7:101: Scope

(1) This Chapter deals with the effects of:

(a) mistake, fraud, threats, or unfair exploitation; and

(b) infringement of fundamental principles or mandatory rules.

(2) It does not deal with lack of capacity.

(3) It applies in relation to contracts and, with any necessary adaptations, other juridical acts.

II. – 7:102: Initial Impossibility or Lack of Right or Authority to Dispose

A contract is not invalid, in whole or in part, merely because at the time it is concluded performance of any obligation assumed is impossible, or because a party has no right or authority to dispose of any assets to which the contract relates.

Section 2: Vitiated Consent or Intention

II. – 7:201: Mistake

(1) A party may avoid a contract for mistake of fact or law existing when the contract was concluded if:

(a) the party, but for the mistake, would not have concluded the contract or would have done so only on fundamentally different terms and the other party knew or could reasonably be expected to have known this; and

(b) the other party;

(i) caused the mistake;

(ii) caused the contract to be concluded in mistake by leaving the mistaken party in error, contrary to good faith and fair dealing, when the other party knew or could reasonably be expected to have known of the mistake;

(iii) caused the contract to be concluded in mistake by failing to comply with a pre-contractual information duty or a duty to make available a means of correcting input errors; or

(iv) made the same mistake.

(2) However a party may not avoid the contract for mistake if:

(a) the mistake was inexcusable in the circumstances; or

(b) the risk of the mistake was assumed, or in the circumstances should be borne, by that party.

II. – 7:202: Inaccuracy in Communication May Be Treated as Mistake

An inaccuracy in the expression or transmission of a statement is treated as a mistake of the person who made or sent the statement.

II. – 7:203: Adaptation of Contract in Case of Mistake

(1) If a party is entitled to avoid the contract for mistake but the other party performs, or indicates a willingness to perform, the obligations under the contract as it was understood by the party entitled to avoid it, the contract is treated as having been concluded as that party understood it. This applies only if the other party performs, or indicates a willingness to perform, without undue delay after being informed of the manner in which the party entitled to avoid it understood the contract and before that party acts in reliance on any notice of avoidance.

(2) After such performance or indication the right to avoid is lost and any earlier notice of avoidance is ineffective.

(3) Where both parties have made the same mistake, the court may at the request of either party bring the contract into accordance with what might reasonably have been agreed had the mistake not occurred.

II. – 7:204: Liability for Loss Caused by Reliance on Incorrect Information

(1) A party who has concluded a contract in reasonable reliance on incorrect information given by the other party in the course of negotiations has a right to damages for loss suffered as a result if the provider of the information:

(a) believed the information to be incorrect or had no reasonable grounds for believing it to be correct; and

(b) knew or could reasonably be expected to have known that the recipient would rely on the information in deciding whether or not to conclude the contract on the agreed terms.

(2) This Article applies even if there is no right to avoid the contract.

II. – 7:205: Fraud

(1) A party may avoid a contract when the other party has induced the conclusion of the contract by fraudulent misrepresentation, whether by words or conduct, or fraudulent non-disclosure of any information which good faith and fair dealing, or any pre-contractual information duty, required that party to disclose.

(2) A misrepresentation is fraudulent if it is made with knowledge or belief that the representation is false and is intended to induce the recipient to make a mistake. A non-disclosure is fraudulent if it is intended to induce the person from whom the information is withheld to make a mistake.

(3) In determining whether good faith and fair dealing required a party to disclose particular information, regard should be had to all the circumstances, including:

(a) whether the party had special expertise;

(b) the cost to the party of acquiring the relevant information;

(c) whether the other party could reasonably acquire the information by other means; and

(d) the apparent importance of the information to the other party.

II. – 7:206: Coercion or Threats

(1) A party may avoid a contract when the other party has induced the conclusion of the contract by coercion or by the threat of an imminent and serious harm which it is wrongful to inflict, or wrongful to use as a means to obtain the conclusion of the contract.

(2) A threat is not regarded as inducing the contract if in the circumstances the threatened party had a reasonable alternative.

II. – 7:207: Unfair Exploitation

(1) A party may avoid a contract if, at the time of the conclusion of the contract:

(a) the party was dependent on or had a relationship of trust with the other party, was in economic distress or had urgent needs, was improvident, ignorant, inexperienced or lacking in bargaining skill; and

(b) the other party knew or could reasonably be expected to have known this and, given the circumstances and purpose of the contract, exploited the first party's situation by taking an excessive benefit or grossly unfair advantage.

(2) Upon the request of the party entitled to avoidance, a court may if it is appropriate adapt the contract in order to bring it into accordance with what might have been agreed had the requirements of good faith and fair dealing been observed.

(3) A court may similarly adapt the contract upon the request of a party receiving notice of avoidance for unfair exploitation, provided that this party informs the party who gave the notice without undue delay after receiving it and before that party has acted in reliance on it.

II. – 7:208: Third Persons

(1) Where a third person for whose acts a party is responsible or who with a party's assent is involved in the making of a contract:

(a) causes a mistake, or knows of or could reasonably be expected to know of a mistake; or

(b) is guilty of fraud, coercion, threats or unfair exploitation, remedies under this Section are available as if the behaviour or knowledge had been that of the party.

(2) Where a third person for whose acts a party is not responsible and who does not have the party's assent to be involved in the making of a contract is guilty of fraud, coercion, threats or unfair exploitation, remedies under this Section are available if the party knew or could reasonably be expected to have known of the relevant facts, or at the time of avoidance has not acted in reliance on the contract.

II. – 7:209: Notice of Avoidance

Avoidance under this Section is effected by notice to the other party.

II. – 7:210: Time

A notice of avoidance under this Section is ineffective unless given within a reasonable time, with due regard to the circumstances, after the avoiding party knew or could reasonably be expected to have known of the relevant facts or became capable of acting freely.

II. – 7:211: Confirmation

If a party who is entitled to avoid a contract under this Section confirms it, expressly or impliedly, after the period of time for giving notice of avoidance has begun to run, avoidance is excluded.

II. – 7:212: Effects of Avoidance

(1) A contract which may be avoided under this Section is valid until avoided but, once avoided, is retrospectively invalid from the beginning.

(2) The question whether either party has a right to the return of whatever has been transferred or supplied under a contract which has been avoided under this Section, or a monetary equivalent, is regulated by the rules on unjustified enrichment.

(3) The effect of avoidance under this Section on the ownership of property which has been transferred under the avoided contract is governed by the rules on the transfer of property.

II. – 7:213: Partial Avoidance

If a ground of avoidance under this Section affects only particular terms of a contract, the effect of an avoidance is limited to those terms unless, giving due consideration to all the circumstances of the case, it is unreasonable to uphold the remaining contract.

II. – 7:214: Damages for Loss

(1) A party who has the right to avoid a contract under this Section (or who had such a right before it was lost by the effect of time limits or confirmation) is entitled, whether or not the contract is avoided, to damages from the other party for any loss suffered as a result of the mistake,

fraud, coercion, threats or unfair exploitation, provided that the other party knew or could reasonably be expected to have known of the ground for avoidance.

(2) The damages recoverable are such as to place the aggrieved party as nearly as possible in the position in which that party would have been if the contract had not been concluded, with the further limitation that, if the party does not avoid the contract, the damages are not to exceed the loss caused by the mistake, fraud, coercion, threats or unfair exploitation.

(3) In other respects the rules on damages for non-performance of a contractual obligation apply with any appropriate adaptation.

II. – 7:215: Exclusion or Restriction of Remedies

(1) Remedies for fraud, coercion, threats and unfair exploitation cannot be excluded or restricted.

(2) Remedies for mistake may be excluded or restricted unless the exclusion or restriction is contrary to good faith and fair dealing.

II. – 7:216: Overlapping Remedies

A party who is entitled to a remedy under this Section in circumstances which afford that party a remedy for non-performance may pursue either remedy.

Section 3: Infringement of Fundamental Principles or Mandatory Rules

II. – 7:301: Contracts Infringing Fundamental Principles

A contract is void to the extent that:

(a) it infringes a principle recognised as fundamental in the laws of the Member States of the European Union; and

(b) nullity is required to give effect to that principle.

II. – 7:302: Contracts Infringing Mandatory Rules

(1) Where a contract is not void under the preceding Article but infringes a mandatory rule of law, the effects of that infringement on the validity of the contract are the effects, if any, expressly prescribed by that mandatory rule.

(2) Where the mandatory rule does not expressly prescribe the effects of an infringement on the validity of a contract, a court may:

(a) declare the contract to be valid;

(b) avoid the contract, with retrospective effect, in whole or in part; or

(c) modify the contract or its effects.

(3) A decision reached under paragraph (2) should be an appropriate and proportional response to the infringement, having regard to all relevant circumstances, including:

(a) the purpose of the rule which has been infringed;

(b) the category of persons for whose protection the rule exists;

(c) any sanction that may be imposed under the rule infringed;

(d) the seriousness of the infringement;

(e) whether the infringement was intentional; and

(f) the closeness of the relationship between the infringement and the contract.

II. – 7:303: Effects of Nullity or Avoidance

(1) The question whether either party has a right to the return of whatever has been transferred or supplied under a contract, or part of a contract, which is void or has been avoided under this Section, or a monetary equivalent, is regulated by the rules on unjustified enrichment.

(2) The effect of nullity or avoidance under this Section on the ownership of property which has been transferred under the void or avoided contract, or part of a contract, is governed by the rules on the transfer of property.

(3) This Article is subject to the powers of the court to modify the contract or its effects.

II. – 7:304: Damages for Loss

(1) A party to a contract which is void or avoided, in whole or in part, under this Section is entitled to damages from the other party for any loss suffered as a result of the invalidity, provided that the first party did not know and could not reasonably be expected to have known, and the other party knew or could reasonably be expected to have known, of the infringement.

(2) The damages recoverable are such as to place the aggrieved party as nearly as possible in the position in which that party would have been if the contract had not been concluded or the infringing term had not been included.

Chapter 8: Interpretation

Section 1: Interpretation of Contracts

II. – 8:101: General Rules

(1) A contract is to be interpreted according to the common intention of the parties even if this differs from the literal meaning of the words.

(2) If one party intended the contract, or a term or expression used in it, to have a particular meaning, and at the time of the conclusion of the contract the other party was aware, or could reasonably be expected to have been aware, of the first party's intention, the contract is to be interpreted in the way intended by the first party.

(3) The contract is, however, to be interpreted according to the meaning which a reasonable person would give to it:

(a) if an intention cannot be established under the preceding paragraphs; or

(b) if the question arises with a person, not being a party to the contract or a person who by law has no better rights than such a party, who has reasonably and in good faith relied on the contract's apparent meaning.

II. – 8:102: Relevant Matters

(1) In interpreting the contract, regard may be had, in particular, to:

(a) the circumstances in which it was concluded, including the preliminary negotiations;

(b) the conduct of the parties, even subsequent to the conclusion of the contract;

(c) the interpretation which has already been given by the parties to terms or expressions which are the same as, or similar to, those used in the contract and the practices they have established between themselves;

(d) the meaning commonly given to such terms or expressions in the branch of activity concerned and the interpretation such terms or expressions may already have received;

(e) the nature and purpose of the contract;

(f) usages; and

(g) good faith and fair dealing.

(2) In a question with a person, not being a party to the contract or a person such as an assignee who by law has no better rights than such a party, who has reasonably and in good faith relied on the contract's apparent meaning, regard may be had to the circumstances mentioned in sub-paragraphs (a) to (c) above only to the extent that those circumstances were known to, or could reasonably be expected to have been known to, that person.

II. – 8:103: Interpretation Against Supplier of Term or Dominant Party

(1) Where there is doubt about the meaning of a term not individually negotiated, an interpretation of the term against the party who supplied it is to be preferred.

(2) Where there is doubt about the meaning of any other term, and that term has been established under the dominant influence of one party, an interpretation of the term against that party is to be preferred.

II. – 8:104: Preference for Negotiated Terms

Terms which have been individually negotiated take preference over those which have not.

II. – 8:105: Reference to Contract as a Whole

Terms and expressions are to be interpreted in the light of the whole contract in which they appear.

II. – 8:106: Preference for Interpretation Which Gives Terms Effect

An interpretation which renders the terms of the contract lawful, or effective, is to be preferred to one which would not.

II. – 8:107: Linguistic Discrepancies

Where a contract document is in two or more language versions none of which is stated to be authoritative, there is, in case of discrepancy between the versions, a preference for the interpretation according to the version in which the contract was originally drawn up.

Section 2: Interpretation of Other Juridical Acts

II. – 8:201: General Rules

(1) A unilateral juridical act is to be interpreted in the way in which it could reasonably be expected to be understood by the person to whom it is addressed.

(2) If the person making the juridical act intended the act, or a term or expression used in it, to have a particular meaning, and at the time of the act the person to whom it was addressed was aware, or could reasonably be expected to have been aware, of the first person's intention, the act is to be interpreted in the way intended by the first person.

(3) The act is, however, to be interpreted according to the meaning which a reasonable person would give to it:

(a) if neither paragraph (1) nor paragraph (2) applies; or

(b) if the question arises with a person, not being the addressee or a person who by law has no better rights than the addressee, who has reasonably and in good faith relied on the contract's apparent meaning.

II. – 8:202: Application of Other Rules by Analogy

The provisions of Section 1, apart from its first Article, apply with appropriate adaptations to the interpretation of a juridical act other than a contract.

Chapter 9: Contents and Effects of Contracts

Section 1: Contents

II. – 9:101: Terms of a Contract

(1) The terms of a contract may be derived from the express or tacit agreement of the parties, from rules of law or from practices established between the parties or usages.

(2) Where it is necessary to provide for a matter which the parties have not foreseen or provided for, a court may imply an additional term, having regard in particular to:

(a) the nature and purpose of the contract;

(b) the circumstances in which the contract was concluded; and

(c) the requirements of good faith and fair dealing.

(3) Any term implied under paragraph (2) should, where possible, be such as to give effect to what the parties, had they provided for the matter, would probably have agreed.

(4) Paragraph (2) does not apply if the parties have deliberately left a matter unprovided for, accepting the consequences of so doing.

II. – 9:102: Certain Pre-Contractual Statements Regarded as Contract Terms

(1) A statement made by one party before a contract is concluded is regarded as a term of the contract if the other party reasonably understood it as being made on the basis that it would form part of the contract terms if a contract were concluded. In assessing whether the other party was reasonable in understanding the statement in that way account may be taken of:

(a) the apparent importance of the statement to the other party;

(b) whether the party was making the statement in the course of business; and

(c) the relative expertise of the parties.

(2) If one of the parties to a contract is a business and before the contract is concluded makes a statement, either to the other party or publicly, about the specific characteristics of what is to be supplied by that business under the contract, the statement is regarded as a term of the contract unless:

(a) the other party was aware when the contract was concluded, or could reasonably be expected to have been so aware, that the statement was incorrect or could not otherwise be relied on as such a term; or

(b) the other party's decision to conclude the contract was not influenced by the statement.

(3) For the purposes of paragraph (2), a statement made by a person engaged in advertising or marketing on behalf of the business is treated as being made by the business.

(4) Where the other party is a consumer then, for the purposes of paragraph (2), a public statement made by or on behalf of a producer or other person in earlier links of the business chain between the producer and the consumer is treated as being made by the business unless the business, at the time of conclusion of the contract, did not know and could not reasonably be expected to have known of it.

(5) In the circumstances covered by paragraph (4) a business which at the time of conclusion of the contract did not know and could not reasonably be expected to have known that the statement was incorrect has a right to be indemnified by the person making the statement for any liability incurred as a result of that paragraph.

(6) In relations between a business and a consumer the parties may not, to the detriment of the consumer, exclude the application of this Article or derogate from or vary its effects.

II. – 9:103: Terms Not Individually Negotiated

(1) Terms supplied by one party and not individually negotiated may be invoked against the other party only if the other party was aware of them, or if the party supplying the terms took reasonable steps to draw the other party's attention to them, before or when the contract was concluded.

(2) If a contract is to be concluded by electronic means, the party supplying any terms which have not been individually negotiated may invoke them against the other party only if they are made available to the other party in textual form.

(3) For the purposes of this Article

(a) "not individually negotiated" has the meaning given by II. – 1:110 (Terms "not individually negotiated"); and

(b) terms are not sufficiently brought to the other party's attention by a mere reference to them in a contract document, even if that party signs the document.

II. – 9:104: Determination of Price

Where the amount of the price payable under a contract cannot be determined from the terms agreed by the parties, from any other applicable rule of law or from usages or practices, the price payable is the price normally charged in comparable circumstances at the time of the conclusion of the contract or, if no such price is available, a reasonable price.

II. – 9:105: Unilateral Determination by a Party

Where the price or any other contractual term is to be determined by one party and that party's determination is grossly unreasonable then, notwithstanding any provision in the contract to the contrary, a reasonable price or other term is substituted.

II. – 9:106: Determination by a Third Person

(1) Where a third person is to determine the price or any other contractual term and cannot or will not do so, a court may, unless this is inconsistent with the terms of the contract, appoint another person to determine it.

(2) If a price or other term determined by a third person is grossly unreasonable, a reasonable price or term is substituted.

II. – 9:107: Reference to a Non-Existent Factor

Where the price or any other contractual term is to be determined by reference to a factor which does not exist or has ceased to exist or to be accessible, the nearest equivalent factor is substituted unless this would be unreasonable in the circumstances, in which case a reasonable price or other term is substituted.

II. – 9:108: Quality

Where the quality of anything to be supplied or provided under the contract cannot be determined from the terms agreed by the parties, from any other applicable rule of law or from usages or practices, the quality required is the quality which the recipient could reasonably expect in the circumstances.

II. – 9:109: Language

Where the language to be used for communications relating to the contract or the rights or obligations arising from it cannot be determined from the terms agreed by the parties, from any other applicable rule of law or from usages or practices, the language to be used is that used for the conclusion of the contract.

Section 2: Simulation

II. – 9:201: Effect of Simulation

(1) When the parties have concluded a contract or an apparent contract and have deliberately done so in such a way that it has an apparent effect different from the effect which the parties intend it to have, the parties' true intention prevails.

(2) However, the apparent effect prevails in relation to a person, not being a party to the contract or apparent contract or a person who by law has no better rights than such a party, who has reasonably and in good faith relied on the apparent effect.

Section 3: Effect of Stipulation in Favour of a Third Party

II. – 9:301: Basic Rules

(1) The parties to a contract may, by the contract, confer a right or other benefit on a third party. The third party need not be in existence or identified at the time the contract is concluded.

(2) The nature and content of the third party's right or benefit are determined by the contract and are subject to any conditions or other limitations under the contract.

(3) The benefit conferred may take the form of an exclusion or limitation of the third party's liability to one of the contracting parties.

II. – 9:302: Rights, Remedies and Defences

Where one of the contracting parties is bound to render a performance to the third party under the contract, then, in the absence of provision to the contrary in the contract:

(a) the third party has the same rights to performance and remedies for non-performance as if the contracting party was bound to render the performance under a binding unilateral undertaking in favour of the third party; and

(b) the contracting party may assert against the third party all defences which the contracting party could assert against the other party to the contract.

II. – 9:303: Rejection or Revocation of Benefit

(1) The third party may reject the right or benefit by notice to either of the contracting parties, if that is done without undue delay after being notified of the right or benefit and before it has been expressly or impliedly accepted. On such rejection, the right or benefit is treated as never having accrued to the third party.

(2) The contracting parties may remove or modify the contractual term conferring the right or benefit if this is done before either of them has given the third party notice that the right or benefit has been conferred. The contract determines whether and by whom and in what circumstances the right or benefit can be revoked or modified after that time.

(3) Even if the right or benefit conferred is by virtue of the contract revocable or subject to modification, the right to revoke or modify is lost if the parties have, or the party having the right to revoke or modify has, led the third party to believe that it is not revocable or subject to modification and if the third party has reasonably acted in reliance on it.

Section 4: Unfair Terms

II. – 9:401: Mandatory Nature of Following Provisions

The parties may not exclude the application of the provisions in this Section or derogate from or vary their effects.

II. – 9:402: Duty of Transparency in Terms Not Individually Negotiated

(1) A person who supplies terms which have not been individually negotiated has a duty to ensure that they are drafted and communicated in plain, intelligible language.

(2) In a contract between a business and a consumer a term which has been supplied by the business in breach of the duty of transparency imposed by paragraph (1) may on that ground alone be considered unfair.

II. – 9:403: Meaning of "Unfair" in Contracts Between a Business and a Consumer

In a contract between a business and a consumer, a term [which has not been individually negotiated] is unfair for the purposes of this Section if it is supplied by the business and if it significantly disadvantages the consumer, contrary to good faith and fair dealing.

II. – 9:404: Meaning of "Unfair" in Contracts Between Non-Business Parties

In a contract between parties neither of whom is a business, a term is unfair for the purposes of this Section only if it is a term forming part of standard terms supplied by one party and significantly disadvantages the other party, contrary to good faith and fair dealing.

II. – 9:405: Meaning of "Unfair" in Contracts Between Businesses

A term in a contract between businesses is unfair for the purposes of this Section only if it is a term forming part of standard terms supplied by one party and of such a nature that its use grossly deviates from good commercial practice, contrary to good faith and fair dealing.

II. – 9:406: Exclusions from Unfairness Test

(1) Contract terms are not subjected to an unfairness test under this Section if they are based on:

(a) provisions of the applicable law;

(b) international conventions to which the Member States are parties, or to which the European Union is a party; or

(c) these rules.

(2) For contract terms which are drafted in plain and intelligible language, the unfairness test extends neither to the definition of the main subject matter of the contract, nor to the adequacy of the price to be paid.

II. – 9:407: Factors to Be Taken into Account in Assessing Unfairness

(1) When assessing the unfairness of a contractual term for the purposes of this Section, regard is to be had to the duty of transparency under II. – 9:402 (Duty of transparency in terms not individually negotiated), to the nature of what is to be provided under the contract, to the circumstances prevailing during the conclusion of the contract, to the other terms of the contract and to the terms of any other contract on which the contract depends.

(2) For the purposes of II. – 9:403 (Meaning of "unfair" in contracts between a business and a consumer) the circumstances prevailing during the conclusion of the contract include the extent to which the consumer was given a real opportunity to become acquainted with the term before the conclusion of the contract.

II. – 9:408: Effects of Unfair Terms

(1) A term which is unfair under this Section is not binding on the party who did not supply it.

(2) If the contract can reasonably be maintained without the unfair term, the other terms remain binding on the parties.

II. – 9:409: Exclusive Jurisdiction Clauses

(1) A term in a contract between a business and a consumer is unfair for the purposes of this Section if it is supplied by the business and if it confers exclusive jurisdiction for all disputes arising under the contract on the court for the place where the business is domiciled.

(2) Paragraph (1) does not apply if the chosen court is also the court for the place where the consumer is domiciled.

II. – 9:410: Terms Which Are Presumed to Be Unfair in Contracts Between a Business and a Consumer

(1) A term in a contract between a business and a consumer is presumed to be unfair for the purposes of this Section if it is supplied by the business and if it:

(a) excludes or limits the liability of a business for death or personal injury caused to a consumer through an act or omission of that business;

(b) inappropriately excludes or limits the remedies, including any right to set-off, available to the consumer against the business or a third party for non-performance by the business of obligations under the contract;

(c) makes binding on a consumer an obligation which is subject to a condition the fulfilment of which depends solely on the intention of the business;

(d) permits a business to keep money paid by a consumer if the latter decides not to conclude the contract, or perform obligations under it, without providing for the consumer to receive compensation of an equivalent amount from the business in the reverse situation;

(e) requires a consumer who fails to perform his or her obligations to pay a disproportionately high amount of damages;

(f) entitles a business to withdraw from or terminate the contractual relationship on a discretionary basis without giving the same right to the consumer, or entitles a business to keep money paid for services not yet supplied in the case where the business withdraws from or terminates the contractual relationship;

(g) enables a business to terminate a contractual relationship of indeterminate duration without reasonable notice, except where there are serious grounds for doing so; this does not affect terms in financial services contracts where there is a valid reason, provided that the supplier is required to inform the other contracting party thereof immediately;

(h) automatically extends a contract of fixed duration unless the consumer indicates otherwise, in cases where such terms provide for an unreasonably early deadline;

(i) enables a business to alter the terms of the contract unilaterally without a valid reason which is specified in the contract; this does not affect terms under which a supplier of financial services reserves the right to change the rate of interest to be paid by, or to, the consumer, or the amount of other charges for financial services without notice where there is a valid reason, provided that the supplier is required to inform the consumer at the earliest opportunity and that the consumer is free to terminate the contractual relationship with immediate effect; neither does it affect terms under which a business reserves the right to alter unilaterally the conditions of a contract of indeterminate duration, provided that the business is required to inform the consumer with reasonable notice, and that the consumer is free to terminate the contractual relationship;

(j) enables a business to alter unilaterally without a valid reason any characteristics of the goods, other assets or services to be provided;

(k) provides that the price of goods or other assets is to be determined at the time of delivery or supply, or allows a business to increase the price without giving the consumer the right to withdraw if the increased price is too high in relation to the price agreed at the conclusion of the contract; this does not affect price-indexation clauses, where lawful, provided that the method by which prices vary is explicitly described;

(l) gives a business the right to determine whether the goods, other assets or services supplied are in conformity with the contract, or gives the business the exclusive right to interpret any term of the contract;

(m) limits the obligation of a business to respect commitments undertaken by its agents, or makes its commitments subject to compliance with a particular formality;

(n) obliges a consumer to fulfil all his or her obligations where the business fails to fulfil its own;

(o) allows a business to transfer its rights and obligations under the contract without the consumer's consent, if this could reduce the guarantees available to the consumer;

(p) excludes or restricts a consumer's right to take legal action or to exercise any other remedy, in particular by referring the consumer to arbitration proceedings which are not covered by legal provisions, by unduly restricting the evidence available to the consumer, or by shifting a burden of proof on to the consumer;

(q) allows a business, where what has been ordered is unavailable, to supply an equivalent without having expressly informed the consumer of this possibility and of the fact that the business must bear the cost of returning what the consumer has received under the contract if the consumer exercises a right to withdraw.

(2) Subparagraphs (g), (i) and (k) do not apply to:

(a) transactions in transferable securities, financial instruments and other products or services where the price is linked to fluctuations in a stock exchange quotation or index or a financial market rate beyond the control of the business;

(b) contracts for the purchase or sale of foreign currency, traveller's cheques or international money orders denominated in foreign currency.

BOOK III – OBLIGATIONS AND CORRESPONDING RIGHTS

Chapter 1: General

III. – 1:101: Scope of Book

This Book applies, except as otherwise provided, to all obligations within the scope of these rules, whether they are contractual or not, and to corresponding rights to performance.

III. – 1:102: Definitions

(1) An obligation is a duty to perform which one party to a legal relationship, the debtor, owes to another party, the creditor.

(2) Performance of an obligation is the doing by the debtor of what is to be done under the obligation or the not doing by the debtor of what is not to be done.

(3) Non-performance of an obligation is any failure to perform the obligation, whether or not excused, and includes delayed performance and any other performance which is not in accordance with the terms regulating the obligation.

(4) An obligation is reciprocal in relation to another obligation if:

(a) performance of the obligation is due in exchange for performance of the other obligation;

(b) it is an obligation to facilitate or accept performance of the other obligation; or

(c) it is so clearly connected to the other obligation or its subject matter that performance of the one can reasonably be regarded as dependent on performance of the other.

(5) The terms regulating an obligation may be derived from a contract or other juridical act, the law or a legally binding usage or practice, or a court order; and similarly for the terms regulating a right.

III. – 1:103: Good Faith and Fair Dealing

(1) A person has a duty to act in accordance with good faith and fair dealing in performing an obligation, in exercising a right to performance, in pursuing or defending a remedy for non-performance, or in exercising a right to terminate an obligation or contractual relationship.

(2) The duty may not be excluded or limited by contract or other juridical act.

(3) Breach of the duty does not give rise directly to the remedies for nonperformance of an obligation but may preclude the person in breach from exercising or relying on a right, remedy or defence which that person would otherwise have.

III. – 1:104: Co-operation

The debtor and creditor are obliged to co-operate with each other when and to the extent that this can reasonably be expected for the performance of the debtor's obligation.

III. – 1:105: Non-Discrimination

Chapter 2 (Non-discrimination) of Book II applies with appropriate adaptations to:

(a) the performance of any obligation to provide access to, or supply, goods, other assets or services which are available to members of the public;

(b) the exercise of a right to performance of any such obligation or the pursuing or defending of any remedy for non-performance of any such obligation; and

(c) the exercise of a right to terminate any such obligation.

III. – 1:106: Conditional Rights and Obligations

(1) The terms regulating a right, obligation or contractual relationship may provide that it is conditional upon the occurrence of an uncertain future event, so that it takes effect only if the event occurs (suspensive condition) or comes to an end if the event occurs (resolutive condition).

(2) Upon fulfilment of a suspensive condition, the relevant right, obligation or relationship takes effect.

(3) Upon fulfilment of a resolutive condition, the relevant right, obligation or relationship comes to an end.

(4) When a party, contrary to the duty of good faith and fair dealing or the obligation to co-operate, interferes with events so as to bring about the fulfilment or non-fulfilment of a condition to that party's advantage, the other party may treat the condition as not having been fulfilled or as having been fulfilled as the case may be.

(5) When a contractual obligation or relationship comes to an end on the fulfilment of a resolutive condition any restitutionary effects are regulated by the rules in Chapter 3, Section 5, Sub-section 4 (Restitution) with appropriate adaptations.

III. – 1:107: Time-Limited Rights and Obligations

(1) The terms regulating a right, obligation or contractual relationship may provide that it is to take effect from or end at a specified time, after a specified period of time or on the occurrence of an event which is certain to occur.

(2) It will take effect or come to an end at the time or on the event without further steps having to be taken.

(3) When a contractual obligation or relationship comes to an end under this Article any restitutionary effects are regulated by the rules in Chapter 3, Section 5, Sub-section 4 (Restitution) with appropriate adaptations.

III. – 1:108: Variation or Termination by Agreement

(1) A right, obligation or contractual relationship may be varied or terminated by agreement at any time.

(2) Where the parties do not regulate the effects of termination, then:

(a) it has prospective effect only and does not affect any right to damages, or a stipulated payment, for non-performance of any obligation performance of which was due before termination;

(b) it does not affect any provision for the settlement of disputes or any other provision which is to operate even after termination; and

(c) in the case of a contractual obligation or relationship any restitutionary effects are regulated by the rules in Chapter 3, Section 5, Sub-section 4 (Restitution) with appropriate adaptations.

III. – 1:109: Variation or Termination by Notice

(1) A right, obligation or contractual relationship may be varied or terminated by notice by either party where this is provided for by the terms regulating it.

(2) Where, in a case involving continuous or periodic performance of a contractual obligation, the terms of the contract do not say when the contractual relationship is to end or say that it will never end, it may be terminated by either party by giving a reasonable period of notice. In assessing whether a period of notice is reasonable, regard may be had to the interval between performances or counter-performances.

(3) Where the parties do not regulate the effects of termination, then:

(a) it has prospective effect only and does not affect any right to damages, or a stipulated payment, for non-performance of any obligation performance of which was due before termination;

(b) it does not affect any provision for the settlement of disputes or any other provision which is to operate even after termination; and

(c) in the case of a contractual obligation or relationship any restitutionary effects are regulated by the rules in Chapter 3, Section 5, Sub-section 4 (Restitution) with appropriate adaptations.

III. – 1:110: Variation or Termination by Court on a Change of Circumstances

(1) An obligation must be performed even if performance has become more onerous, whether because the cost of performance has increased or because the value of what is to be received in return has diminished.

(2) If, however, performance of a contractual obligation or of an obligation arising from a unilateral juridical act becomes so onerous because of an exceptional change of circumstances that it would be manifestly unjust to hold the debtor to the obligation a court may:

(a) vary the obligation in order to make it reasonable and equitable in the new circumstances; or

(b) terminate the obligation at a date and on terms to be determined by the court.

(3) Paragraph (2) applies only if:

(a) the change of circumstances occurred after the time when the obligation was incurred;

(b) the debtor did not at that time take into account, and could not reasonably be expected to have taken into account, the possibility or scale of that change of circumstances;

(c) the debtor did not assume, and cannot reasonably be regarded as having assumed, the risk of that change of circumstances; and

(d) the debtor has attempted, reasonably and in good faith, to achieve by negotiation a reasonable and equitable adjustment of the terms regulating the obligation.

III. – 1:111: Tacit Prolongation

Where a contract provides for continuous or repeated performance of obligations for a definite period and the obligations continue to be performed by both parties after that period has expired, the contract becomes a contract for an indefinite period, unless the circumstances are inconsistent with the tacit consent of the parties to such prolongation.

Chapter 2: Performance

III. – 2:101: Place of Performance

(1) If the place of performance of an obligation cannot be otherwise determined from the terms regulating the obligation it is:

(a) in the case of a monetary obligation, the creditor's place of business;

(b) in the case of any other obligation, the debtor's place of business.

(2) For the purposes of the preceding paragraph:

(a) if a party has more than one place of business, the place of business is that which has the closest relationship to the obligation; and

(b) if a party does not have a place of business, or the obligation does not relate to a business matter, the habitual residence is substituted.

(3) If, in a case to which paragraph (1) applies, a party causes any increase in the expenses incidental to performance by a change in place of business or habitual residence subsequent to the time when the obligation was incurred, that party is obliged to bear the increase.

III. – 2:102: Time of Performance

(1) If the time at which, or a period of time within which, an obligation is to be performed cannot otherwise be determined from the terms regulating the obligation it must be performed within a reasonable time after it arises.

(2) If a period of time within which the obligation is to be performed can be determined from the terms regulating the obligation, the obligation may be performed at any time within that period chosen by the debtor unless the circumstances of the case indicate that the creditor is to choose the time.

(3) Unless the parties have agreed otherwise, a business must perform the obligations incurred under a contract concluded at a distance for the supply of goods, other assets or services to a consumer no later than 30 days after the contract was concluded.

(4) If a business has an obligation to reimburse money received from a consumer for goods, other assets or services supplied, the reimbursement must be made as soon as possible and in any case no later than 30 days after the obligation arose.

III. – 2:103: Early Performance

(1) A creditor may reject an offer to perform before performance is due unless the early performance would not cause the creditor unreasonable prejudice.

(2) A creditor's acceptance of early performance does not affect the time fixed for the performance by the creditor of any reciprocal obligation.

III. – 2:104: Order of Performance

If the order of performance of reciprocal obligations cannot be otherwise determined from the terms regulating the obligations then, to the extent that the obligations can be performed simultaneously, the parties are bound to perform simultaneously unless the circumstances indicate otherwise.

III. – 2:105: Alternative Obligations or Methods of Performance

(1) Where a debtor is bound to perform one of two or more obligations, or to perform an obligation in one of two or more ways, the choice belongs to the debtor, unless the terms regulating the obligations or obligation provide otherwise.

(2) If the party who is to make the choice fails to choose by the time when performance is due, then:

(a) if the delay amounts to a fundamental non-performance, the right to choose passes to the other party;

(b) if the delay does not amount to a fundamental non-performance, the other party may give a notice fixing an additional period of reasonable length within which the party to choose is required to do so. If the latter still fails to do so, the right to choose passes to the other party.

III. – 2:106: Performance Entrusted to Another

A debtor who entrusts performance of an obligation to another person remains responsible for performance.

III. – 2:107: Performance by a Third Person

(1) Where personal performance by the debtor is not required by the terms regulating the obligation, the creditor cannot refuse performance by a third person if:

(a) the third person acts with the assent of the debtor; or

(b) the third person has a legitimate interest in performing and the debtor has failed to perform or it is clear that the debtor will not perform at the time performance is due.

(2) Performance by a third person in accordance with paragraph (1) discharges the debtor except to the extent that the third person takes over the creditor's right by assignment or subrogation.

(3) Where personal performance by the debtor is not required and the creditor accepts performance of the debtor's obligation by a third party in circumstances not covered by paragraph (1) the debtor is discharged but the creditor is liable to the debtor for any loss caused by that acceptance.

III. – 2:108: Method of Payment

(1) Payment of money due may be made by any method used in the ordinary course of business.

(2) A creditor who accepts a cheque or other order to pay or a promise to pay is presumed to do so only on condition that it will be honoured. The creditor may not enforce the original obligation to pay unless the order or promise is not honoured.

III. – 2:109: Currency of Payment

(1) The debtor and the creditor may agree that payment is to be made only in a specified currency.

(2) In the absence of such agreement, a sum of money expressed in a currency other than that of the place where payment is due may be paid in the currency of that place according to the rate of exchange prevailing there at the time when payment is due.

(3) If, in a case falling within the preceding paragraph, the debtor has not paid at the time when payment is due, the creditor may require payment in the currency of the place where payment is due according to the rate of exchange prevailing there either at the time when payment is due or at the time of actual payment.

(4) Where a monetary obligation is not expressed in a particular currency, payment must be made in the currency of the place where payment is to be made.

III. – 2:110: Imputation of Performance

(1) Where a debtor has to perform several obligations of the same nature and makes a performance which does not suffice to extinguish all of the obligations, then subject to paragraph (5), the debtor may at the time of performance notify the creditor of the obligation to which the performance is to be imputed.

(2) If the debtor does not make such a notification the creditor may, within a reasonable time and by notifying the debtor, impute the performance to one of the obligations.

(3) An imputation under paragraph (2) is not effective if it is to an obligation which is not yet due, or is illegal, or is disputed.

(4) In the absence of an effective imputation by either party, and subject to the following paragraph, the performance is imputed to that obligation which satisfies one of the following criteria in the sequence indicated:

(a) the obligation which is due or is the first to fall due;

(b) the obligation for which the creditor has the least security;

(c) the obligation which is the most burdensome for the debtor;

(d) the obligation which has arisen first.

If none of the preceding criteria applies, the performance is imputed proportionately to all the obligations.

(5) In the case of a monetary obligation, a payment by the debtor is to be imputed, first, to expenses, secondly, to interest, and thirdly, to principal, unless the creditor makes a different imputation.

III. – 2:111: Property Not Accepted

(1) A person who has an obligation to deliver or return corporeal property other than money and who is left in possession of the property because of the creditor's failure to accept or retake the property, has an ancillary obligation to take reasonable steps to protect and preserve it.

(2) The debtor may obtain discharge from the obligation to deliver or return and from the ancillary obligation mentioned in the preceding paragraph:

(a) by depositing the property on reasonable terms with a third person to be held to the order of the creditor, and notifying the creditor of this; or

(b) by selling the property on reasonable terms after notice to the creditor, and paying the net proceeds to the creditor.

(3) Where, however, the property is liable to rapid deterioration or its preservation is unreasonably expensive, the debtor has an obligation to take reasonable steps to dispose of it. The debtor may obtain discharge from the obligation to deliver or return by paying the net proceeds to the creditor.

(4) The debtor left in possession is entitled to be reimbursed or to retain out of the proceeds of sale any costs reasonably incurred.

III. – 2:112: Money Not Accepted

(1) Where a creditor fails to accept money properly tendered by the debtor, the debtor may after notice to the creditor obtain discharge from the obligation to pay by depositing the money to the order of the creditor in accordance with the law of the place where payment is due.

(2) Paragraph (1) applies, with appropriate adaptations, to money properly tendered by a third party in circumstances where the creditor is not entitled to refuse such performance.

III. – 2:113: Costs and Formalities of Performance

(1) The costs of performing an obligation are borne by the debtor.

(2) In the case of a monetary obligation the debtor's obligation to pay includes taking such steps and complying with such formalities as may be necessary to enable payment to be made.

III. – 2:114: Extinctive Effect of Performance

Full performance extinguishes the obligation if it is:

(a) in accordance with the terms regulating the obligation; or

(b) of such a type as by law to afford the debtor a good discharge.

Chapter 3: Remedies for Non-Performance

Section 1: General

III. – 3:101: Remedies Available

(1) If an obligation is not performed by the debtor and the non-performance is not excused, the creditor may resort to any of the remedies set out in this Chapter.

(2) If the debtor's non-performance is excused, the creditor may resort to any of those remedies except enforcing specific performance and damages.

(3) The creditor may not resort to any of those remedies to the extent that the creditor caused the debtor's non-performance.

III. – 3:102: Cumulation of Remedies

Remedies which are not incompatible may be cumulated. In particular, a creditor is not deprived of the right to damages by resorting to any other remedy.

III. – 3:103: Notice Fixing Additional Period for Performance

(1) In any case of non-performance of an obligation the creditor may by notice to the debtor allow an additional period of time for performance.

(2) During the additional period the creditor may withhold performance of the creditor's reciprocal obligations and may claim damages, but may not resort to any other remedy.

(3) If the creditor receives notice from the debtor that the debtor will not perform within that period, or if upon expiry of that period due performance has not been made, the creditor may resort to any available remedy.

III. – 3:104: Excuse Due to an Impediment

(1) A debtor's non-performance of an obligation is excused if it is due to an impediment beyond the debtor's control and if the debtor could not reasonably be expected to have avoided or overcome the impediment or its consequences.

(2) Where the obligation arose out of a contract or other juridical act, nonperformance is not excused if the debtor could reasonably be expected to have taken the impediment into account at the time when the obligation was incurred.

(3) Where the excusing impediment is only temporary the excuse has effect for the period during which the impediment exists. However, if the delay amounts to a fundamental non-performance, the creditor may treat it as such.

(4) Where the excusing impediment is permanent the obligation is extinguished. Any reciprocal obligation is also extinguished. In the case of contractual obligations any restitutionary effects of extinction are regulated by the rules in Chapter 3, Section 5, Sub-section 4 (Restitution) with appropriate adaptations.

(5) The debtor has a duty to ensure that notice of the impediment and of its effect on the ability to perform reaches the creditor within a reasonable time after the debtor knew or could reasonably be expected to have known of these circumstances. The creditor is entitled to damages for any loss resulting from the non-receipt of such notice.

III. – 3:105: Term Excluding or Restricting Remedies

(1) A term of a contract or other juridical act which purports to exclude or restrict liability to pay damages for personal injury (including fatal injury) caused intentionally or by gross negligence is void.

(2) A term excluding or restricting a remedy for non-performance of an obligation, even if valid and otherwise effective, having regard in particular to the rules on unfair contract terms in Book II, Chapter 9, Section 4, may nevertheless not be invoked if it would be contrary to good faith and fair dealing to do so.

III. – 3:106: Notices Relating to Non-Performance

(1) If the creditor gives notice to the debtor because of the debtor's nonperformance of an obligation or because such non-performance is anticipated, and the notice is properly dispatched or given, a delay or inaccuracy in the transmission of the notice or its failure to arrive does not prevent it from having effect.

(2) T he notice has effect from the time at which it would have arrived in normal circumstances.

III. – 3:107: Failure to Notify Non-Conformity

(1) If, in the case of an obligation to supply goods, other assets or services, the debtor supplies goods, other assets or services which are not in conformity with the terms regulating the obligation, the creditor may not rely on the lack of conformity unless the creditor gives notice to the debtor within a reasonable time specifying the nature of the lack of conformity.

(2) The reasonable time runs from the time when the goods or other assets are supplied or the service is completed or from the time, if it is later, when the creditor discovered or could reasonably be expected to have discovered the non-conformity.

(3) The debtor is not entitled to rely on paragraph (1) if the failure relates to facts which the debtor knew or could reasonably be expected to have known and which the debtor did not disclose to the creditor.

(4) This Article does not apply where the creditor is a consumer.

III. – 3:108: Business Unable to Fulfil Consumer's Order by Distance Communication

(1) Where a business is unable to perform its obligations under a contract concluded with a consumer by means of distance communication, it is obliged to inform the consumer imme-

diately and refund any sums paid by the consumer without undue delay and in any case within 30 days. The consumer's remedies for non-performance remain unaffected.

(2) The parties may not, to the detriment of the consumer, exclude the application of this Article or derogate from or vary its effects.

Section 2: Cure by Debtor of Non-Conforming Performance

III. – 3:201: Scope

This Section applies where a debtor's performance does not conform to the terms regulating the obligation.

III. – 3:202: Cure by Debtor: General Rules

(1) The debtor may make a new and conforming tender if that can be done within the time allowed for performance.

(2) If the debtor cannot make a new and conforming tender within the time allowed for performance but, promptly after being notified of the lack of conformity, offers to cure it within a reasonable time and at the debtor's own expense, the creditor may not pursue any remedy for non-performance, other than withholding performance, before allowing the debtor a reasonable period in which to attempt to cure the nonconformity.

(3) Paragraph (2) is subject to the provisions of the following Article.

III. – 3:203: When Creditor Need Not Allow Debtor an Opportunity to Cure

The creditor need not, under paragraph (2) of the preceding Article, allow the debtor a period in which to attempt cure if:

(a) failure to perform a contractual obligation within the time allowed for performance amounts to a fundamental non-performance;

(b) the creditor has reason to believe that the debtor's performance was made with knowledge of the non-conformity and was not in accordance with good faith and fair dealing;

(c) the creditor has reason to believe that the debtor will be unable to effect the cure within a reasonable time and without significant inconvenience to the creditor or other prejudice to the creditor's legitimate interests; or

(d) cure would be inappropriate in the circumstances.

III. – 3:204: Consequences of Allowing Debtor Opportunity to Cure

(1) During the period allowed for cure the creditor may withhold performance of the creditor's reciprocal obligations, but may not resort to any other remedy.

(2) If the debtor fails to effect cure within the time allowed, the creditor may resort to any available remedy.

(3) Notwithstanding cure, the creditor retains the right to damages for any loss caused by the debtor's initial or subsequent non-performance or by the process of effecting cure.

III. – 3:205: Return of Replaced Item

(1) Where the debtor has, whether voluntarily or in compliance with an order under III. – 3:302 (Enforcement of non-monetary obligations), remedied a non-conforming performance by replacement, the debtor has a right and an obligation to take back the replaced item at the debtor's expense.

(2) The creditor is not liable to pay for any use made of the replaced item in the period prior to the replacement.

Section 3: Right to Enforce Performance

III. – 3:301: Enforcement of Monetary Obligations

(1) The creditor is entitled to recover money payment of which is due.

(2) Where the creditor has not yet performed the reciprocal obligation for which payment will be due and it is clear that the debtor in the monetary obligation will be unwilling to receive performance, the creditor may nonetheless proceed with performance and may recover payment unless:

(a) the creditor could have made a reasonable substitute transaction without significant effort or expense; or

(b) performance would be unreasonable in the circumstances.

III. – 3:302: Enforcement of Non-Monetary Obligations

(1) The creditor is entitled to enforce specific performance of an obligation other than one to pay money.

(2) Specific performance includes the remedying free of charge of a performance which is not in conformity with the terms regulating the obligation.

(3) Specific performance cannot, however, be enforced where:

(a) performance would be unlawful or impossible;

(b) performance would be unreasonably burdensome or expensive; or

(c) performance would be of such a personal character that it would be unreasonable to enforce it.

(4) The creditor loses the right to enforce specific performance if performance is not requested within a reasonable time after the creditor has become, or could reasonably be expected to have become, aware of the non-performance.

(5) The creditor cannot recover damages for loss or a stipulated payment for non-performance to the extent that the creditor has increased the loss or the amount of the payment by insisting unreasonably on specific performance in circumstances where the creditor could have made a reasonable substitute transaction without significant effort or expense.

III. – 3:303: Damages Not Precluded

The fact that a right to enforce specific performance is excluded under the preceding Article does not preclude a claim for damages.

Section 4: Withholding Performance

III. – 3:401: Right to Withhold Performance of Reciprocal Obligation

(1) A creditor who is to perform a reciprocal obligation at the same time as, or after, the debtor performs has a right to withhold performance of the reciprocal obligation until the debtor has tendered performance or has performed.

(2) A creditor who is to perform a reciprocal obligation before the debtor performs and who reasonably believes that there will be non-performance by the debtor when the debtor's performance becomes due may withhold performance of the reciprocal obligation for as long as the reasonable belief continues. However, the right to withhold performance is lost if the debtor gives an adequate assurance of due performance.

(3) A creditor who withholds performance in the situation mentioned in paragraph (2) has a duty to give notice of that fact to the debtor as soon as is reasonably practicable and is liable for any loss caused to the debtor by a breach of that duty.

(4) The performance which may be withheld under this Article is the whole or part of the performance as may be reasonable in the circumstances.

Section 5: Termination

III. – 3:501: Scope and Definition

(1) This Section applies only to contractual obligations and contractual relationships.

(2) In this Section "termination" means the termination of the contractual relationship in whole or in part and "terminate" has a corresponding meaning.

Sub-section 1: Grounds for Termination

III. – 3:502: Termination for Fundamental Non-Performance

(1) A creditor may terminate if the debtor's non-performance of a contractual obligation is fundamental.

(2) A non-performance of a contractual obligation is fundamental if:

(a) it substantially deprives the creditor of what the creditor was entitled to expect under the contract, as applied to the whole or relevant part of the performance, unless at the time of conclusion of the contract the debtor did not foresee and could not reasonably be expected to have foreseen that result; or

(b) it is intentional or reckless and gives the creditor reason to believe that the debtor's future performance cannot be relied on.

III. – 3:503: Termination After Notice Fixing Additional Time for Performance

(1) A creditor may terminate in a case of delay in performance of a contractual obligation which is not in itself fundamental if the creditor gives a notice fixing an additional period of time of reasonable length for performance and the debtor does not perform within that period.

(2) If the period fixed is unreasonably short, the creditor may terminate only after a reasonable period from the time of the notice.

III. – 3:504: Termination for Anticipated Non-Performance

A creditor may terminate before performance of a contractual obligation is due if the debtor has declared that there will be a non-performance of the obligation, or it is otherwise clear that there will be such a non-performance, and if the non-performance would have been fundamental.

III. – 3:505: Termination for Inadequate Assurance of Performance

A creditor who reasonably believes that there will be a fundamental nonperformance of a contractual obligation by the debtor may terminate if the creditor demands an adequate assurance of due performance and no such assurance is provided within a reasonable time.

Sub-section 2: Scope, Exercise and Loss of Right to Terminate

III. – 3:506: Scope of Right to Terminate

(1) Where the debtor's obligations under the contract are not divisible the creditor may only terminate the contractual relationship as a whole.

(2) Where the debtor's obligations under the contract are to be performed in separate parts or are otherwise divisible, then:

(a) if there is a ground for termination under this Section of a part to which a counter-performance can be apportioned, the creditor may terminate the contractual relationship so far as it relates to that part;

(b) the creditor may terminate the contractual relationship as a whole only if the creditor cannot reasonably be expected to accept performance of the other parts or there is a ground for termination in relation to the contractual relationship as a whole.

III. – 3:507: Notice of Termination

(1) A right to terminate under this Section is exercised by notice to the debtor.

(2) Where a notice under III. – 3:503 (Termination after notice fixing additional time for performance) provides for automatic termination if the debtor does not perform within the period fixed by the notice, termination takes effect after that period or a reasonable length of time from the giving of notice (whichever is longer) without further notice.

III. – 3:508: Loss of Right to Terminate

(1) If performance has been tendered late or a tendered performance otherwise does not conform to the contract the creditor loses the right to terminate under this Section unless notice of termination is given within a reasonable time.

(2) Where the creditor has given the debtor a period of time to cure the non-performance under III. – 3:202 (Cure by debtor: general rules) the time mentioned in paragraph (1) begins to run from the expiry of that period. In other cases that time begins to run from the time when the creditor has become, or could reasonably be expected to have become, aware of the tender or the non-conformity.

(3) A creditor loses a right to terminate by notice under III. – 3:503 (Termination after notice fixing additional time for performance), III. – 3:504 (Termination for anticipated non-performance) or III. – 3:505 (Termination for inadequate assurance of performance) unless the creditor gives notice of termination within a reasonable time after the right has arisen.

Sub-section 3: Effects of Termination

III. – 3:509: Effect on Obligations Under the Contract

(1) On termination under this Section, the outstanding obligations or relevant part of the outstanding obligations of the parties under the contract come to an end.

(2) Termination does not, however, affect any provision of the contract for the settlement of disputes or other provision which is to operate even after termination.

(3) A creditor who terminates under this Section retains existing rights to damages or a stipulated payment for non-performance and in addition has the same right to damages or a stipulated payment for non-performance as the creditor would have had if there had been non-performance of the now extinguished obligations of the debtor. In relation to such extinguished obligations the creditor is not regarded as having caused or contributed to the loss merely by exercising the right to terminate.

Sub-section 4: Restitution

III. – 3:510: Restitution of Benefits Received by Performance

(1) On termination under this Section a party (the recipient) who has received any benefit by the other's performance of obligations under the terminated contractual relationship or terminated part of the contractual relationship is obliged to return it. Where both parties have obligations to return, the obligations are reciprocal.

(2) If the performance was a payment of money, the amount received is to be repaid.

(3) To the extent that the benefit (not being money) is transferable, it is to be returned by transferring it. However, if a transfer would cause unreasonable effort or expense, the benefit may be returned by paying its value.

(4) To the extent that the benefit is not transferable it is to be returned by paying its value in accordance with III. – 3:512 (Payment of value of benefit).

(5) The obligation to return a benefit extends to any natural or legal fruits received from the benefit.

III. – 3:511: When Restitution Not Required

(1) There is no obligation to make restitution under this Sub-section to the extent that conforming performance by one party has been met by conforming performance by the other.

(2) The terminating party may elect to treat performance as non-conforming if what was received by that party is of no, or fundamentally reduced, value to that party because of the other party's non-performance.

(3) Restitution under this Sub-section is not required where the contract was gratuitous.

III. – 3:512: Payment of Value of Benefit

(1) The recipient is obliged to:

(a) pay the value (at the time of performance) of a benefit which is not transferable or which ceases to be transferable before the time when it is to be returned; and

(b) pay recompense for any reduction in the value of a returnable benefit as a result of a change in the condition of the benefit between the time of receipt and the time when it is to be returned.

(2) Where there was an agreed price the value of the benefit is that proportion of the price which the value of the actual performance bears to the value of the promised performance. Where no price was agreed the value of the benefit is the sum of money which a willing and capable provider and a willing and capable recipient, knowing of any non-conformity, would lawfully have agreed.

(3) The recipient's liability to pay the value of a benefit is reduced to the extent that as a result of a non-performance of an obligation owed by the other party to the recipient:

(a) the benefit cannot be returned in essentially the same condition as when it was received; or

(b) the recipient is compelled without compensation either to dispose of it or to sustain a disadvantage in order to preserve it.

(4) The recipient's liability to pay the value of a benefit is likewise reduced to the extent that it cannot be returned in the same condition as when it was received as a result of conduct of the recipient in the reasonable, but mistaken, belief that there was no non-conformity.

III. – 3:513: Use and Improvements

(1) The recipient is obliged to pay a reasonable amount for any use which the recipient makes of the benefit except in so far as the recipient is liable under III. – 3:512 (Payment of value of benefit) paragraph (1) in respect of that use.

(2) A recipient who has improved a benefit which the recipient is obliged under this Section to return has a right to payment of the value of improvements if the other party can readily obtain that value by dealing with the benefit unless:

(a) the improvement was a non-performance of an obligation owed by the recipient to the other party; or

(b) the recipient made the improvement when the recipient knew or could reasonably be expected to know that the benefit would have to be returned.

III. – 3:514: Liabilities Arising after Time When Return Due

(1) The recipient is obliged to:

(a) pay the value (at the time of performance) of a benefit which ceases to be transferable after the time when its return was due; and

(b) pay recompense for any reduction in the value of a returnable benefit as a result of a change in the condition of the benefit after the time when its return was due.

(2) If the benefit is disposed of after the time when return was due, the value to be paid is the value of any proceeds, if this is greater.

(3) Other liabilities arising from non-performance of an obligation to return a benefit are unaffected.

Section 6: Price Reduction

III. – 3:601: Right to Reduce Price

(1) A creditor who accepts a performance not conforming to the terms regulating the obligation may reduce the price. The reduction is to be proportionate to the decrease in the value of what was received by virtue of the performance at the time it was made compared to the value of what would have been received by virtue of a conforming performance.

(2) A creditor who is entitled to reduce the price under the preceding paragraph and who has already paid a sum exceeding the reduced price may recover the excess from the debtor.

(3) A creditor who reduces the price cannot also recover damages for the loss thereby compensated but remains entitled to damages for any further loss suffered.

(4) This Article applies with appropriate adaptations to a reciprocal obligation of the creditor other than an obligation to pay a price.

Section 7: Damages and Interest

III. – 3:701: Right to Damages

(1) The creditor is entitled to damages for loss caused by the debtor's nonperformance of an obligation, unless the non-performance is excused.

(2) The loss for which damages are recoverable includes future loss which is reasonably likely to occur.

(3) "Loss" includes economic and non-economic loss. "Economic loss" includes loss of income or profit, burdens incurred and a reduction in the value of property. "Non-economic loss" includes pain and suffering and impairment of the quality of life.

III. – 3:702: General Measure of Damages

The general measure of damages for loss caused by non-performance of an obligation is such sum as will put the creditor as nearly as possible into the position in which the creditor would have been if the obligation had been duly performed. Such damages cover loss which the creditor has suffered and gain of which the creditor has been deprived.

III. – 3:703: Foreseeability

The debtor in an obligation which arises from a contract or other juridical act is liable only for loss which the debtor foresaw or could reasonably be expected to have foreseen at the time when the obligation was incurred as a likely result of the non-performance, unless the non-performance was intentional, reckless or grossly negligent.

III. – 3:704: Loss Attributable to Creditor

The debtor is not liable for loss suffered by the creditor to the extent that the creditor contributed to the non-performance or its effects.

III. – 3:705: Reduction of Loss

(1) The debtor is not liable for loss suffered by the creditor to the extent that the creditor could have reduced the loss by taking reasonable steps.

(2) The creditor is entitled to recover any expenses reasonably incurred in attempting to reduce the loss.

III. – 3:706: Substitute Transaction

A creditor who has terminated a contractual relationship in whole or in part under Section 5 and has made a substitute transaction within a reasonable time and in a reasonable manner may, in so far as entitled to damages, recover the difference between the value of what would have been payable under the terminated relationship and the value of what is payable under the substitute transaction, as well as damages for any further loss.

III. – 3:707: Current Price

Where the creditor has terminated a contractual relationship in whole or in part under Section 5 and has not made a substitute transaction but there is a current price for the performance, the creditor may, in so far as entitled to damages, recover the difference between the contract price and the price current at the time of termination as well as damages for any further loss.

III. – 3:708: Interest on Late Payments

(1) If payment of a sum of money is delayed, whether or not the nonperformance is excused, the creditor is entitled to interest on that sum from the time when payment is due to the time of payment at the average commercial bank short-term lending rate to prime borrowers prevailing for the currency of payment at the place where payment is due.

(2) The creditor may in addition recover damages for any further loss.

III. – 3:709: When Interest to Be Added to Capital

(1) Interest payable according to the preceding Article is added to the outstanding capital every 12 months.

(2) Paragraph (1) of this Article does not apply if the parties have provided for interest upon delay in payment.

III. – 3:710: Interest in Commercial Contracts

(1) If a business delays the payment of a price due under a contract for the supply of goods, other assets or services without being excused under III. – 3:104 (Excuse due to an impediment), interest is due at the rate specified in paragraph (4), unless a higher interest rate is applicable.

(2) Interest at the rate specified in paragraph (4) starts to run on the day which follows the date or the end of the period for payment provided in the contract. If there is no such date or period, interest at that rate starts to run:

(a) 30 days after the date when the debtor receives the invoice or an equivalent request for payment; or

(b) 30 days after the date of receipt of the goods or services, if the date under (a) is earlier or uncertain, or if it is uncertain whether the debtor has received an invoice or equivalent request for payment.

(3) If conformity of goods or services to the contract is to be ascertained by way of acceptance or verification, the 30 day period under paragraph (2)(b) starts to run on the date of acceptance or verification.

(4) The interest rate for delayed payment is the interest rate applied by the European Central Bank to its most recent main refinancing operation carried out before the first calendar day of the half-year in question ("the reference rate"), plus seven percentage points. For the currency of a Member State which is not participating in the third stage of economic and monetary union, the reference rate is the equivalent rate set by its national central bank.

(5) The creditor may in addition recover damages for any further loss.

III. – 3:711: Unfair Terms Relating to Interest

(1) A term whereby a business pays interest from a date later than that specified in the preceding Article paragraph (2) (a) and (b) and paragraph (3), or at a rate lower than that specified in paragraph (4), is not binding to the extent that this would be unfair.

(2) A term whereby a debtor is allowed to pay the price for goods, other assets or services later than the time when interest starts to run under the preceding Article paragraph (2)(a) and (b) and paragraph (3) does not deprive the creditor of interest to the extent that this would be unfair.

(3) Something is unfair for the purposes of this Article if it grossly deviates from good commercial practice, contrary to good faith and fair dealing.

III. – 3:712: Stipulated Payment for Non-Performance

(1) Where the terms regulating an obligation provide that a debtor who fails to perform the obligation is to pay a specified sum to the creditor for such non-performance, the creditor is entitled to that sum irrespective of the actual loss.

(2) However, despite any provision to the contrary, the sum so specified in a contract or other juridical act may be reduced to a reasonable amount where it is grossly excessive in relation to the loss resulting from the non-performance and the other circumstances.

III. – 3:713: Currency by Which Damages to Be Measured

Damages are to be measured by the currency which most appropriately reflects the creditor's loss.

Chapter 4: Plurality of Debtors and Creditors

Section 1: Plurality of Debtors

III. – 4:101: Scope of Section

This Section applies where two or more debtors are bound to perform one obligation.

III. – 4:102: Solidary, Divided and Joint Obligations

(1) An obligation is solidary when each debtor is bound to perform the obligation in full and the creditor may require performance from any of them until full performance has been received.

(2) An obligation is divided when each debtor is bound to perform only part of the obligation and the creditor may claim from each debtor only performance of that debtor's part.

(3) An obligation is joint when the debtors are bound to perform the obligation together and the creditor may require performance only from all of them together.

III. – 4:103: When Different Types of Obligation Arise

(1) Whether an obligation is solidary, divided or joint depends on the terms regulating the obligation.

(2) If the terms do not determine the question, the liability of two or more debtors to perform the same obligation is solidary. Liability is solidary in particular where two or more persons are liable for the same damage.

(3) The fact that the debtors are not liable on the same terms or grounds does not prevent solidarity.

III. – 4:104: Liability Under Divided Obligations

Debtors bound by a divided obligation are liable in equal shares.

III. – 4:105: Joint Obligations: Special Rule When Money Claimed for Non-Performance

Notwithstanding III. – 4:102 (Solidary, divided and joint obligations) paragraph (3), when money is claimed for non-performance of a joint obligation, the debtors have solidary liability for payment to the creditor.

III. – 4:106: Apportionment Between Solidary Debtors

(1) As between themselves, solidary debtors are liable in equal shares.

(2) If two or more debtors have solidary liability for the same damage, their share of liability as between themselves is equal unless different shares of liability are more appropriate having regard to all the circumstances of the case and in particular to fault or to the extent to which a source of danger for which one of them was responsible contributed to the occurrence or extent of the damage.

III. – 4:107: Recourse Between Solidary Debtors

(1) A solidary debtor who has performed more than that debtor's share has a right to recover the excess from any of the other debtors to the extent of each debtor's unperformed share, together with a share of any costs reasonably incurred.

(2) A solidary debtor to whom paragraph (1) applies may also, subject to any prior right and interest of the creditor, exercise the rights and actions of the creditor, including any supporting security rights, to recover the excess from any of the other debtors to the extent of each debtor's unperformed share.

(3) If a solidary debtor who has performed more than that debtor's share is unable, despite all reasonable efforts, to recover contribution from another solidary debtor, the share of the others, including the one who has performed, is increased proportionally.

III. – 4:108: Performance, Set-off and Merger in Solidary Obligations

(1) Performance or set-off by a solidary debtor or set-off by the creditor against one solidary debtor discharges the other debtors in relation to the creditor to the extent of the performance or set-off.

(2) Merger of debts between a solidary debtor and the creditor discharges the other debtors only for the share of the debtor concerned.

III. – 4:109: Release or Settlement in Solidary Obligations

(1) When the creditor releases, or reaches a settlement with, one solidary debtor, the other debtors are discharged of liability for the share of that debtor.

(2) As between solidary debtors, the debtor who is discharged from that debtor's share is discharged only to the extent of the share at the time of the discharge and not from any supplemen-

tary share for which that debtor may subsequently become liable under III. – 4:107 (Recourse between solidary debtors) paragraph (3).

(3) When the debtors have solidary liability for the same damage the discharge under paragraph (1) extends only so far as is necessary to prevent the creditor from recovering more than full reparation and the other debtors retain their rights of recourse against the released or settling debtor to the extent of that debtor's unperformed share.

III. – 4:110: Effect of Judgment in Solidary Obligations

A decision by a court as to the liability to the creditor of one solidary debtor does not affect:

(a) the liability to the creditor of the other solidary debtors; or

(b) the rights of recourse between the solidary debtors under III. – 4:107 (Recourse between solidary debtors).

III. – 4:111: Prescription in Solidary Obligations

Prescription of the creditor's right to performance against one solidary debtor does not affect:

(a) the liability to the creditor of the other solidary debtors; or

(b) the rights of recourse between the solidary debtors under III. – 4:107 (Recourse between solidary debtors).

III. – 4:112: Opposability of Other Defences in Solidary Obligations

(1) A solidary debtor may invoke against the creditor any defence which another solidary debtor can invoke, other than a defence personal to that other debtor. Invoking the defence has no effect with regard to the other solidary debtors.

(2) A debtor from whom contribution is claimed may invoke against the claimant any personal defence that that debtor could have invoked against the creditor.

Section 2: Plurality of Creditors

III. – 4:201: Scope of Section

This Section applies where two or more creditors have a right to performance under one obligation.

III. – 4:202: Solidary, Divided and Joint Rights

(1) A right to performance is solidary when any of the creditors may require full performance from the debtor and the debtor may perform to any of the creditors.

(2) A right to performance is divided when each creditor may require performance only of that creditor's share and the debtor owes each creditor only that creditor's share.

(3) A right to performance is joint when any creditor may require performance only for the benefit of all the creditors and the debtor must perform to all the creditors.

III. – 4:203: When Different Types of Right Arise

(1) Whether a right to performance is solidary, divided or communal depends on the terms regulating the right.

(2) If the terms do not determine the question, the right of co-creditors is divided.

III. – 4:204: Apportionment in Cases of Divided Rights

In the case of divided rights the creditors have equal shares.

III. – 4:205: Difficulties of Performing in Cases of Joint Rights

If one of the creditors who have joint rights to performance refuses to accept, or is unable to receive, the performance, the debtor may obtain discharge from the obligation by depositing the property or money with a third party according to III. – 2:111 (Property not accepted) or III. – 2:112 (Money not accepted).

III. – 4:206: Apportionment in Cases of Solidary Rights

(1) In the case of solidary rights the creditors have equal shares.

(2) A creditor who has received more than that creditor's share has an obligation to transfer the excess to the other creditors to the extent of their respective shares.

III. – 4:207: Regime of Solidary Rights

(1) A release granted to the debtor by one of the solidary creditors has no effect on the other solidary creditors.

(2) The rules of III. – 4:108 (Performance, set-off and merger in solidary obligations), III. – 4:110 (Effect of judgment in solidary obligations), III. – 4:111 (Prescription in solidary obligations) and III. – 4:112 (Opposability of other defences in solidary obligations) paragraph (1) apply, with appropriate adaptations, to solidary rights to performance.

Chapter 5: Change of Parties

Section 1: Assignment of Rights

Sub-section 1: General

III. – 5:101: Scope of Section

(1) This Section applies to the assignment, by a contract or other juridical act, of a right to performance of an obligation.

(2) It does not apply to the transfer of a financial instrument or investment security where such transfer is required to be by entry in a register maintained by or for the issuer or where there are other requirements for transfer or restrictions on transfer.

III. – 5:102: Definitions

(1) An "assignment" of a right is the transfer of the right from one person (the "assignor") to another person (the "assignee").

(2) An "act of assignment" is a contract or other juridical act which is intended to effect a transfer of the right.

(3) Where part of a right is assigned, any reference in this Section to a right includes a reference to the assigned part of the right.

III. – 5:103: Priority of Provisions on Proprietary Securities and Trusts

(1) In relation to assignments for purposes of security, the provisions of Book IX apply and have priority over the provisions in this Chapter.

(2) In relation to assignments for purposes of a trust, or to or from a trust, the provisions of Book X apply and have priority over the provisions in this Chapter.

Sub-section 2: Requirements for Assignment

III. – 5:104: Basic Requirements

(1) The requirements for an assignment of a right to performance are that:

(a) the right exists;

(b) the right is assignable;

(c) the person purporting to assign the right has the right or authority to transfer it;

(d) the assignee is entitled as against the assignor to the transfer by virtue of a contract or other juridical act, a court order or a rule of law; and

(e) there is a valid act of assignment of the right.

(2) The entitlement referred to in paragraph (1)(d) need not precede the act of assignment.

(3) The same contract or other juridical act may operate as the conferment of an entitlement and as the act of assignment.

(4) Neither notice to the debtor nor the consent of the debtor to the assignment is required.

III. – 5:105: Assignability: General Rule

(1) All rights to performance are assignable except where otherwise provided by law.

(2) A right to performance which is by law accessory to another right is not assignable separately from that right.

III. – 5:106: Future and Unspecified Rights

(1) A future right to performance may be the subject of an act of assignment but the transfer of the right depends on its coming into existence and being identifiable as the right to which the act of assignment relates.

(2) A number of rights to performance may be assigned without individual specification if, at the time when the assignment is to take place in relation to them, they are identifiable as rights to which the act of assignment relates.

III. – 5:107: Assignability in Part

(1) A right to performance of a monetary obligation may be assigned in part.

(2) A right to performance of a non-monetary obligation may be assigned in part only if:

(a) the debtor consents to the assignment; or

(b) the right is divisible and the assignment does not render the obligation significantly more burdensome.

(3) Where a right is assigned in part the assignor is liable to the debtor for any increased costs which the debtor thereby incurs.

III. – 5:108: Assignability: Effect of Contractual Prohibition

(1) A contractual prohibition of, or restriction on, the assignment of a right does not affect the assignability of the right.

(2) However, where a right is assigned in breach of such a prohibition or restriction:

(a) the debtor may perform in favour of the assignor and is discharged by so doing; and

(b) the debtor retains all rights of set-off against the assignor as if the right had not been assigned.

(3) Paragraph (2) does not apply if:

(a) the debtor has consented to the assignment;

(b) the debtor has caused the assignee to believe on reasonable grounds that there was no such prohibition or restriction; or

(c) the assigned right is a right to payment for the provision of goods or services.

(4) The fact that a right is assignable notwithstanding a contractual prohibition or restriction does not affect the assignor's liability to the debtor for any breach of the prohibition or restriction.

III. – 5:109: Assignability: Rights Personal to the Creditor

(1) A right is not assignable if it is a right to a performance which the debtor, by reason of the nature of the performance or the relationship between the debtor and the creditor, could not reasonably be required to render to anyone except that creditor.

(2) Paragraph (1) does not apply if the debtor has consented to the assignment.

III. – 5:110: Act of Assignment: Formation and Validity

(1) Subject to paragraphs (2) and (3), the rules of Book II on the formation and validity of contracts and other juridical acts apply to acts of assignment.

(2) The rules of Book IV.H on the formation and validity of contracts of donation apply to gratuitous acts of assignment.

(3) The rules of Book IX on the formation and validity of security agreements apply to acts of assignment for purposes of security.

III. – 5:111: Right or Authority to Assign

The requirement of right or authority in III. – 5:104 (Basic requirements) paragraph (1)(c) need not be satisfied at the time of the act of assignment but has to be satisfied at the time the assignment is to take place.

Sub-section 3: Undertakings by Assignor

III. – 5:112: Undertakings by Assignor

(1) The undertakings in paragraphs (2) to (6) are included in the act of assignment unless the act of assignment or the circumstances indicate otherwise.

(2) The assignor undertakes that:

(a) the assigned right exists or will exist at the time when the assignment is to take effect;

(b) the assignor is entitled to assign the right or will be so entitled at the time when the assignment is to take effect.

(c) the debtor has no defences against an assertion of the right;

(d) the right will not be affected by any right of set-off available as between the assignor and the debtor; and

(e) the right has not been the subject of a prior assignment to another assignee and is not subject to any right in security in favour of any other person or to any other incumbrance.

(3) The assignor undertakes that any terms of a contract or other juridical act which have been disclosed to the assignee as terms regulating the right have not been modified and are not affected by any undisclosed agreement as to their meaning or effect which would be prejudicial to the assignee.

(4) The assignor undertakes that the terms of any contract or other juridical act from which the right arises will not be modified without the consent of the assignee unless the modification is provided for in the act of assignment or is one which is made in good faith and is of a nature to which the assignee could not reasonably object.

(5) The assignor undertakes not to conclude or grant any subsequent act of assignment of the same right which could lead to another person obtaining priority over the assignee.

(6) The assignor undertakes to transfer to the assignee, or to take such steps as are necessary to complete the transfer of, all transferable rights intended to secure the performance

which are not already transferred by the assignment, and to transfer the proceeds of any non-transferable rights intended to secure the performance.

(7) The assignor does not represent that the debtor has, or will have, the ability to pay.

Sub-section 4: Effects of Assignment

III. – 5:113: New Creditor

As soon as the assignment takes place the assignor ceases to be the creditor and the assignee becomes the creditor in relation to the right assigned.

III. – 5:114: When Assignment Takes Place

(1) An assignment takes place when the requirements of III. – 5:104 (Basic requirements) are satisfied, or at such later time as the act of assignment may provide.

(2) However, an assignment of a right which was a future right at the time of the act of assignment is regarded as having taken place when all requirements other than those dependent on the existence of the right were satisfied.

(3) Where the requirements of III. – 5:104 (Basic requirements) are satisfied in relation to successive acts of assignment at the same time, the earliest act of assignment takes effect unless it provides otherwise.

III. – 5:115: Rights Transferred to Assignee

(1) The assignment of a right to performance transfers to the assignee not only the primary right but also all accessory rights and transferable supporting security rights.

(2) Where the assignment of a right to performance of a contractual obligation is associated with the substitution of the assignee as debtor in respect of any obligation owed by the assignor under the same contract, this Article takes effect subject to III. – 5:302 (Transfer of contractual position).

III. – 5:116: Effect on Defences and Rights of Set-off

(1) The debtor may invoke against the assignee all substantive and procedural defences to a claim based on the assigned right which the debtor could have invoked against the assignor.

(2) The debtor may not, however, invoke a defence against the assignee:

(a) if the debtor has caused the assignee to believe that there was no such defence; or

(b) if the defence is based on breach by the assignor of a prohibition or restriction on assignment.

(3) The debtor may invoke against the assignee all rights of set-off which would have been available against the assignor in respect of rights against the assignor:

(a) existing at the time when the debtor could no longer obtain a discharge by performing to the assignor; or

(b) closely connected with the assigned right.

III. – 5:117: Effect on Place of Performance

(1) Where the assigned right relates to an obligation to pay money at a particular place, the assignee may require payment at any place within the same country or, if that country is a Member State of the European Union, at any place within the European Union, but the assignor is liable to the debtor for any increased costs which the debtor incurs by reason of any change in the place of performance.

(2) Where the assigned right relates to a non-monetary obligation to be performed at a parti cular place, the assignee may not require performance at any other place.

III. – 5:118: Effect of Initial Invalidity, Subsequent Avoidance, Withdrawal, Termination and Revocation

(1) This Article applies where the assignee's entitlement for the purposes of III. – 5:104 (Basic requirements) paragraph (1)(d) arises from a contract or other juridical act (the underlying contract or other juridical act) whether or not it is followed by a separate act of assignment for the purposes of paragraph (1)(e) of that Article.

(2) Where the underlying contract or other juridical act is void from the beginning, no assignment takes place.

(3) Where, after an assignment has taken place, the underlying contract or other juridical act is avoided under Book II, Chapter 7, the right is treated as never having passed to the assignee (retroactive effect on assignment).

(4) Where, after an assignment has taken place, the underlying contract or other juridical act is withdrawn in the sense of Book II, Chapter 5, or the contractual relationship is terminated under any rule of Book III, or a donation is revoked in the sense of Book IV. H Chapter 4, there is no retroactive effect on the assignment.

(5) This Article does not affect any right to recover based on other provisions of these model rules.

Sub-section 5: Protection of Debtor

III. – 5:119: Performance to Person Who Is Not the Creditor

(1) The debtor is discharged by performing to the assignor so long as the debtor has not received a notice of assignment from either the assignor or the assignee and does not know that the assignor is no longer entitled to receive performance.

(2) Notwithstanding that the person identified as the assignee in a notice of assignment received from the assignor is not the creditor, the debtor is discharged by performing in good faith to that person.

(3) Notwithstanding that the person identified as the assignee in a notice of assignment received from a person claiming to be the assignee is not the creditor, the debtor is discharged by performing to that person if the creditor has caused the debtor reasonably and in good faith to believe that the right has been assigned to that person.

III. – 5:120: Adequate Proof of Assignment

(1) A debtor who believes on reasonable grounds that the right has been assigned but who has not received a notice of assignment, may request the person who is believed to have assigned the right to provide a notice of assignment or a confirmation that the right has not been assigned or that the assignor is still entitled to receive payment.

(2) A debtor who has received a notice of assignment which is not in textual form on a durable medium or which does not give adequate information about the assigned right or the name and address of the assignee may request the person giving the notice to provide a new notice which satisfies these requirements.

(3) A debtor who has received a notice of assignment from the assignee but not from the assignor may request the assignee to provide reliable evidence of the assignment. Reliable evidence includes, but is not limited to, any statement in textual form on a durable medium emanating from the assignor indicating that the right has been assigned.

(4) A debtor who has made a request under this Article may withhold performance until the request is met.

Sub-section 6: Priority Rules

III. – 5:121: Competition Between Successive Assignees

(1) Where there are successive purported assignments by the same person of the same right to performance the purported assignee whose assignment is first notified to the debtor has priority over any earlier assignee if at the time of the later assignment the assignee under that assignment neither knew nor could reasonably be expected to have known of the earlier assignment.

(2) The debtor is discharged by paying the first to notify even if aware of competing demands.

III. – 5:122: Competition Between Assignee and Assignor Receiving Proceeds

Where the debtor is discharged under III. – 5:108 (Assignability: effect of contractual prohibition) paragraph (2)(a) or III. – 5:119 (Performance to person who is not the creditor) paragraph (1), the assignee's right against the assignor to the proceeds has priority over the right of a competing claimant so long as the proceeds are held by the assignor and are reasonably identifiable from the other assets of the assignor.

Section 2: Substitution and Addition of Debtors

III. – 5:201: Scope

This Section applies only to the substitution or addition of a new debtor by agreement.

III. – 5:202: Types of Substitution or Addition

(1) A new debtor may be substituted or added:

(a) in such a way that the original debtor is discharged (complete substitution of new debtor);

(b) in such a way that the original debtor is retained as a debtor in case the new debtor does not perform properly (incomplete substitution of new debtor); or

(c) in such a way that the original debtor and the new debtor have solidary liability (addition of new debtor).

(2) If it is clear that there is a new debtor but not clear what type of substitution or addition was intended, the original debtor and the new debtor have solidary liability.

III. – 5:203: Consent of Creditor

(1) The consent of the creditor is required for the substitution of a new debtor, whether complete or incomplete.

(2) The consent of the creditor to the substitution of a new debtor may be given in advance. In such a case the substitution takes effect only when the creditor is given notice by the new debtor of the agreement between the new and the original debtor.

(3) The consent of the creditor is not required for the addition of a new debtor but the creditor, by notice to the new debtor, can reject the right conferred against the new debtor if that is done without undue delay after being informed of the right and before it has been expressly or impliedly accepted. On such rejection the right is treated as never having been conferred.

III. – 5:204: Complete Substitution

A third person may undertake with the agreement of the creditor and the original debtor to be completely substituted as debtor, with the effect that the original debtor is discharged.

III. – 5:205: Effects of Complete Substitution on Defences, Set-off and Security Rights

(1) The new debtor may invoke against the creditor all defences which the original debtor could have invoked against the creditor.

(2) The new debtor may not exercise against the creditor any right of set-off available to the original debtor against the creditor.

(3) The new debtor cannot invoke against the creditor any rights or defences arising from the relationship between the new debtor and the original debtor.

(4) The discharge of the original debtor also extends to any personal or proprietary security provided by the original debtor to the creditor for the performance of the obligation, unless the security is over an asset which is transferred to the new debtor as part of a transaction between the original and the new debtor.

(5) Upon discharge of the original debtor, a security granted by any person other than the new debtor for the performance of the obligation is released, unless that other person agrees that it should continue to be available to the creditor.

III. – 5:206: Incomplete Substitution

A third person may agree with the creditor and with the original debtor to be incompletely substituted as debtor, with the effect that the original debtor is retained as a debtor in case the original debtor does not perform properly.

III. – 5:207: Effects of Incomplete Substitution

(1) The effects of an incomplete substitution on defences and set-off are the same as the effects of a complete substitution.

(2) To the extent that the original debtor is not discharged, any personal or proprietary security provided for the performance of that debtor's obligations is unaffected by the substitution.

(3) So far as not inconsistent with paragraphs (1) and (2) the liability of the original debtor is governed by the rules on the liability of a provider of dependent personal security with subsidiary liability.

III. – 5:208: Addition of New Debtor

A third person may agree with the debtor to be added as a debtor, with the effect that the original debtor and the new debtor have solidary liability.

III. – 5:209: Effects of Addition of New Debtor

(1) Where there is a contract between the new debtor and the creditor, or a separate unilateral juridical act by the new debtor in favour of the creditor, whereby the new debtor is added as a debtor, the new debtor cannot invoke against the creditor any rights or defences arising from the relationship between the new debtor and the original debtor. Where there is no such contract or unilateral juridical act the new debtor can invoke against the creditor any ground of invalidity affecting the agreement with the original debtor.

(2) So far as not inconsistent with paragraph (1), the rules of Book III, Chapter 4, Section 1 (Plurality of debtors) apply.

Section 3: Transfer of Contractual Position

III. – 5:301: Scope

This Section applies only to transfers by agreement.

III. – 5:302: Transfer of Contractual Position

(1) A party to a contractual relationship may agree with a third person, with the consent of the other party to the contractual relationship, that that person is to be substituted as a party to the relationship.

(2) The consent of the other party may be given in advance. In such a case the transfer takes effect only when that party is given notice of it.

(3) To the extent that the substitution of the third person involves a transfer of rights, the provisions of Section 1 of this Chapter on the assignment of rights apply; to the extent that obligations are transferred, the provisions of Section 2 of this Chapter on the substitution of a new debtor apply.

Section 4: Transfer of Rights and Obligations on Agent's Insolvency

III. – 5:401: Principal's Option to Take over Rights in Case of Agent's Insolvency

(1) This Article applies where an agent has concluded a contract with a third party on the instructions of and on behalf of a principal but has done so in such a way that the agent, and not the principal, is a party to the contract.

(2) If the agent becomes insolvent the principal may by notice to the third party and to the agent take over the rights of the agent under the contract in relation to the third party.

(3) The third party may invoke against the principal any defence which the third party could have invoked against the agent and has all the other protections which would be available if the rights had been voluntarily assigned by the agent to the principal.

III. – 5:402: Third Party's Counter-Option

Where the principal has taken over the rights of the agent under the preceding Article, the third party may by notice to the principal and the agent opt to exercise against the principal the rights which the third party has against the agent, subject to any defences which the agent has against the third party.

Chapter 6: Set-Off and Merger

Section 1: Set-off

III. – 6:101: Definition and Scope

(1) "Set-off" is the process by which a person may use a right to performance held against another person to extinguish in whole or in part an obligation owed to that person.

(2) This Chapter does not apply to set-off in insolvency.

III. – 6:102: Requirements for Set-off

If two parties owe each other obligations of the same kind, either party may set off that party's right against the other party's right, if and to the extent that, at the time of set-off:

(a) the performance of the first party is due or, even if it is not due, the first party can oblige the other party to accept performance;

(b) the performance of the other party is due; and

(c) each party has authority to dispose of that party's right for the purpose of the set-off.

III. – 6:103: Unascertained Rights

(1) A debtor may not set off a right which is unascertained as to its existence or value unless the set-off will not prejudice the interests of the creditor.

(2) Where the rights of both parties arise from the same legal relationship it is presumed that the creditor's interests will not be prejudiced.

III. – 6:104: Foreign Currency Set-off

Where parties owe each other money in different currencies, each party may set off that party's right against the other party's right, unless the parties have agreed that the party declaring set-off is to pay exclusively in a specified currency.

III. – 6:105: Set-off by Notice

Set-off is effected by notice to the other party.

III. – 6:106: Two or More Rights and Obligations

(1) Where the party giving notice of set-off has two or more rights against the other party, the notice is effective only if it identifies the right to which it relates.

(2) Where the party giving notice of set-off has to perform two or more obligations towards the other party, the rules on imputation of performance apply with appropriate adaptations.

III. – 6:107: Effect of Set-off

Set-off extinguishes the obligations, as far as they are coextensive, as from the time of notice.

III. – 6:108: Exclusion of Right of Set-off

Set-off cannot be effected:

(a) where it is excluded by agreement;

(b) against a right to the extent that that right is not capable of attachment; and

(c) against a right arising from an intentional wrongful act.

Section 2: Merger of Debts

III. – 6:201: Extinction of Obligations by Merger

(1) An obligation is extinguished if the same person becomes debtor and creditor in the same capacity.

(2) Paragraph (1) does not, however, apply if the effect would be to deprive a third person of a right.

Chapter 7: Prescription

Section 1: General Provision

III. – 7:101: Rights Subject to Prescription

A right to performance of an obligation is subject to prescription by the expiry of a period of time in accordance with the rules in this Chapter.

Section 2: Periods of Prescription and Their Commencement

III. – 7:201: General Period

The general period of prescription is three years.

III. – 7:202: Period for a Right Established by Legal Proceedings

(1) The period of prescription for a right established by judgment is ten years.

(2) The same applies to a right established by an arbitral award or other instrument which is enforceable as if it were a judgment.

III. – 7:203: Commencement

(1) The general period of prescription begins to run from the time when the debtor has to effect performance or, in the case of a right to damages, from the time of the act which gives rise to the right.

(2) Where the debtor is under a continuing obligation to do or refrain from doing something, the general period of prescription begins to run with each breach of the obligation.

(3) The period of prescription set out in III. – 7:202 (Period for a right established by legal proceedings) begins to run from the time when the judgment or arbitral award obtains the effect of res judicata, or the other instrument becomes enforceable, though not before the debtor has to effect performance.

Section 3: Extension of Period

III. – 7:301: Suspension in Case of Ignorance

The running of the period of prescription is suspended as long as the creditor does not know of, and could not reasonably be expected to know of:

(a) the identity of the debtor; or

(b) the facts giving rise to the right including, in the case of a right to damages, the type of damage.

III. – 7:302: Suspension in Case of Judicial and Other Proceedings

(1) The running of the period of prescription is suspended from the time when judicial proceedings to assert the right are begun.

(2) Suspension lasts until a decision has been made which has the effect of res judicata, or until the case has been otherwise disposed of. Where the proceedings end within the last six months of the prescription period without a decision on the merits, the period of prescription does not expire before six months have passed after the time when the proceedings ended.

(3) These provisions apply, with appropriate adaptations, to arbitration proceedings, to mediation proceedings, to proceedings whereby an issue between two parties is referred to a third party for a binding decision and to all other proceedings initiated with the aim of obtaining a decision relating to the right.

(4) Mediation proceedings mean structured proceedings whereby two or more parties to a dispute attempt to reach an agreement on the settlement of their dispute with the assistance of a mediator.

III. – 7:303: Suspension in Case of Impediment Beyond Creditor's Control

(1) The running of the period of prescription is suspended as long as the creditor is prevented from pursuing proceedings to assert the right by an impediment which is beyond the creditor's control and which the creditor could not reasonably have been expected to avoid or overcome.

(2) Paragraph (1) applies only if the impediment arises, or subsists, within the last six months of the prescription period.

(3) Where the duration or nature of the impediment is such that it would be unreasonable to expect the creditor to take proceedings to assert the right within the part of the period of prescription which has still to run after the suspension comes to an end, the period of prescription does not expire before six months have passed after the time when the impediment was removed.

(4) In this Article an impediment includes a psychological impediment.

III. – 7:304: Postponement of Expiry in Case of Negotiations

If the parties negotiate about the right, or about circumstances from which a claim relating to the right might arise, the period of prescription does not expire before one year has passed since the last communication made in the negotiations.

III. – 7:305: Postponement of Expiry in Case of Incapacity

(1) If a person subject to an incapacity is without a representative, the period of prescription of a right held by or against that person does not expire before one year has passed after either the incapacity has ended or a representative has been appointed.

(2) The period of prescription of rights between a person subject to an incapacity and that person's representative does not expire before one year has passed after either the incapacity has ended or a new representative has been appointed.

III. – 7:306: Postponement of Expiry: Deceased's Estate

Where the creditor or debtor has died, the period of prescription of a right held by or against the deceased's estate does not expire before one year has passed after the right can be enforced by or against an heir, or by or against a representative of the estate.

III. – 7:307: Maximum Length of Period

The period of prescription cannot be extended, by suspension of its running or postponement of its expiry under this Chapter, to more than ten years or, in case of rights to damages for personal injuries, to more than thirty years. This does not apply to suspension under III. – 7:302 (Suspension in case of judicial and other proceedings).

Section 4: Renewal of Period

III. – 7:401: Renewal by Acknowledgement

(1) If the debtor acknowledges the right, vis-à-vis the creditor, by part payment, payment of interest, giving of security, or in any other manner, a new period of prescription begins to run.

(2) The new period is the general period of prescription, regardless of whether the right was originally subject to the general period of prescription or the ten year period under III. – 7:202 (Period for a right established by legal proceedings). In the latter case, however, this Article does not operate so as to shorten the ten year period.

III. – 7:402: Renewal by Attempted Execution

The ten year period of prescription laid down in III. – 7:202 (Period for a right established by legal proceedings) begins to run again with each reasonable attempt at execution undertaken by the creditor.

Section 5: Effects of Prescription

III. – 7:501: General Effect

(1) After expiry of the period of prescription the debtor is entitled to refuse performance.

(2) Whatever has been paid or transferred by the debtor in performance of the obligation may not be reclaimed merely because the period of prescription had expired.

III. – 7:502: Effect on Ancillary Rights

The period of prescription for a right to payment of interest, and other rights of an ancillary nature, expires not later than the period for the principal right.

III. – 7:503: Effect on Set-off

A right in relation to which the period of prescription has expired may nonetheless be set off, unless the debtor has invoked prescription previously or does so within two months of notification of set-off.

Section 6: Modification by Agreement

III. – 7:601: Agreements Concerning Prescription

(1) The requirements for prescription may be modified by agreement between the parties, in particular by either shortening or lengthening the periods of prescription.

(2) The period of prescription may not, however, be reduced to less than one year or extended to more than thirty years after the time of commencement set out in III. – 7:203 (Commencement).

Book IV – Specific Contracts and the Rights and Obligations Arising from Them

Part A. Sales

Chapter 1: Scope and Definitions

Section 1: Scope

IV. A. – 1:101: Contracts Covered

(1) This Part of Book IV applies to contracts for the sale of goods and associated consumer guarantees.

(2) It applies with appropriate adaptations to:

(a) contracts for the sale of electricity;

(b) contracts for the sale of stocks, shares, investment securities and negotiable instruments;

(c) contracts for the sale of other forms of incorporeal property, including rights to the performance of obligations, industrial and intellectual property rights and other transferable rights;

(d) contracts conferring, in exchange for a price, rights in information or data, including software and databases;

(e) contracts for the barter of goods or any of the other assets mentioned above.

(3) It does not apply to contracts for the sale or barter of immovable property or rights in immovable property.

IV. A. – 1:102: Goods to Be Manufactured or Produced

A contract under which one party undertakes, for a price, to manufacture or produce goods for the other party and to transfer their ownership to the other party is to be considered as primarily a contract for the sale of the goods.

Section 2: Definitions

IV. A. – 1:201: Goods

In this Part of Book IV:

(a) the word "goods" includes goods which at the time of the conclusion of the contract do not yet exist; and

(b) references to goods, other than in IV. A. – 1:101 (Contracts covered) itself, are to be taken as referring also to the other assets mentioned in paragraph (2) of that Article.

IV. A. – 1:202: Contract for Sale

A contract for the "sale" of goods is a contract under which one party, the seller, undertakes to another party, the buyer, to transfer the ownership of the goods to the buyer, or to a third person, either immediately on conclusion of the contract or at some future time, and the buyer undertakes to pay the price.

IV. A. – 1:203: Contract for Barter

(1) A contract for the "barter" of goods is a contract under which each party undertakes to transfer the ownership of goods, either immediately on conclusion of the contract or at some future time, in return for the transfer of ownership of other goods.

(2) Each party is considered to be the buyer with respect to the goods to be received and the seller with respect to the goods or assets to be transferred.

IV. A. – 1:204: Consumer Contract for Sale

For the purpose of this Part of Book IV, a consumer contract for sale is a contract for sale in which the seller is a business and the buyer is a consumer.

Chapter 2: Obligations of the Seller

Section 1: Overview

IV. A. – 2:101: Overview of Obligations of the Seller

The seller must:

(a) transfer the ownership of the goods;

(b) deliver the goods;

(c) transfer such documents representing or relating to the goods as may be required by the contract; and

(d) ensure that the goods conform to the contract.

Section 2: Delivery of the Goods

IV. A. – 2:201: Delivery

(1) The seller fulfils the obligation to deliver by making the goods, or where it is agreed that the seller need only deliver documents representing the goods, the documents, available to the buyer.

(2) If the contract involves carriage of the goods by a carrier or series of carriers, the seller fulfils the obligation to deliver by handing over the goods to the first carrier for transmission to the buyer and by transferring to the buyer any document necessary to enable the buyer to take over the goods from the carrier holding the goods.

(3) In this Article, any reference to the buyer includes a third person to whom delivery is to be made in accordance with the contract.

IV. A. – 2:202: Place and Time for Delivery

(1) The place and time for delivery are determined by III. – 2:101 (Place of performance) and III. – 2:102 (Time of performance) as modified by this Article.

(2) If the performance of the obligation to deliver requires the transfer of documents representing the goods, the seller must transfer them at such a time and place and in such a form as is required by the contract.

(3) If in a consumer contract for sale the contract involves carriage of goods by a carrier or a series of carriers and the consumer is given a time for delivery, the goods must be received from the last carrier or made available for collection from that carrier by that time.

IV. A. – 2:203: Cure in Case of Early Delivery

(1) If the seller has delivered goods before the time for delivery, the seller may, up to that time, deliver any missing part or make up any deficiency in the quantity of the goods delivered, or deliver goods in replacement of any non-conforming goods delivered or otherwise remedy any lack of conformity in the goods delivered, provided that the exercise of this right does not cause the buyer unreasonable inconvenience or unreasonable expense.

(2) If the seller has transferred documents before the time required by the contract, the seller may, up to that time, cure any lack of conformity in the documents, provided that the exercise of this right does not cause the buyer unreasonable inconvenience or unreasonable expense.

(3) This Article does not preclude the buyer from claiming damages, in accordance with Book III, Chapter 3, Section 7 (Damages and interest), for any loss not remedied by the seller's cure.

IV. A. – 2:204: Carriage of the Goods

(1) If the contract requires the seller to arrange for carriage of the goods, the seller must make such contracts as are necessary for carriage to the place fixed by means of transportation appropriate in the circumstances and according to the usual terms for such transportation.

(2) If the seller, in accordance with the contract, hands over the goods to a carrier and if the goods are not clearly identified to the contract by markings on the goods, by shipping documents or otherwise, the seller must give the buyer notice of the consignment specifying the goods.

(3) If the contract does not require the seller to effect insurance in respect of the carriage of the goods, the seller must, at the buyer's request, provide the buyer with all available information necessary to enable the buyer to effect such insurance.

Section 3: Conformity of the Goods

IV. A. – 2:301: Conformity with the Contract

The goods do not conform with the contract unless they:

(a) are of the quantity, quality and description required by the contract;

(b) are contained or packaged in the manner required by the contract;

(c) are supplied along with any accessories, installation instructions or other instructions required by the contract; and

(d) comply with the remaining Articles of this Section.

IV. A. – 2:302: Fitness for Purpose, Qualities, Packaging

The goods must:

(a) be fit for any particular purpose made known to the seller at the time of the conclusion of the contract, except where the circumstances show that the buyer did not rely, or that it was unreasonable for the buyer to rely, on the seller's skill and judgement;

(b) be fit for the purposes for which goods of the same description would ordinarily be used;

(c) possess the qualities of goods which the seller held out to the buyer as a sample or model;

(d) be contained or packaged in the manner usual for such goods or, where there is no such manner, in a manner adequate to preserve and protect the goods;

(e) be supplied along with such accessories, installation instructions or other instructions as the buyer may reasonably expect to receive; and

(f) possess such qualities and performance capabilities as the buyer may reasonably expect.

IV. A. – 2:303: Statements by Third Persons

The goods must possess the qualities and performance capabilities held out in any statement on the specific characteristics of the goods made about them by a person in earlier links of the business chain, the producer or the producer's representative which forms part of the terms of the contract by virtue of II. – 9:102 (Certain pre-contractual statements regarded as contract terms).

IV. A. – 2:304: Incorrect Installation Under a Consumer Contract for Sale

Where goods supplied under a consumer contract for sale are incorrectly installed, any lack of conformity resulting from the incorrect installation is regarded as a lack of conformity of the goods if:

(a) the goods were installed by the seller or under the seller's responsibility; or

(b) the goods were intended to be installed by the consumer and the incorrect installation was due to a shortcoming in the installation instructions.

IV. A. – 2:305: Third Party Rights or Claims in General

The goods must be free from any right or reasonably well founded claim of a third party. However, if such a right or claim is based on industrial property or other intellectual property, the seller's obligation is governed by the following Article.

IV. A. – 2:306: Third Party Rights or Claims Based on Industrial Property or Other Intellectual Property

(1) The goods must be free from any right or claim of a third party which is based on industrial property or other intellectual property and of which at the time of the conclusion of the contract the seller knew or could reasonably be expected to have known.

(2) However, paragraph (1) does not apply where the right or claim results from the seller's compliance with technical drawings, designs, formulae or other such specifications furnished by the buyer.

IV. A. – 2:307: Buyer's Knowledge of Lack of Conformity

(1) The seller is not liable under IV. A. – 2:302 (Fitness for purpose, qualities, packaging), IV. A. – 2:305 (Third party rights or claims in general) or IV. A. – 2:306 (Third party rights or claims based on industrial property or other intellectual property) if, at the time of the conclusion of the contract, the buyer knew or could reasonably be assumed to have known of the lack of conformity.

(2) The seller is not liable under IV. A. – 2:304 (Incorrect installation under a consumer contract for sale) sub-paragraph (b) if, at the time of the conclusion of the contract, the buyer knew or could reasonably be assumed to have known of the shortcoming in the installation instructions.

IV. A. – 2:308: Relevant Time for Establishing Conformity

(1) The seller is liable for any lack of conformity which exists at the time when the risk passes to the buyer, even if the lack of conformity becomes apparent only after that time.

(2) In a consumer contract for sale, any lack of conformity which becomes apparent within six months of the time when risk passes to the buyer is presumed to have existed at that time unless this is incompatible with the nature of the goods or the nature of the lack of conformity.

(3) In a case governed by IV. A. – 2:304 (Incorrect installation under a consumer contract for sale) any reference in paragraphs (1) or (2) to the time when risk passes to the buyer is to be read as a reference to the time when the installation is complete.

IV. A. – 2:309: Limits on Derogation from Conformity Rights in a Consumer Contract for Sale

In a consumer contract for sale, any contractual term or agreement concluded with the seller before a lack of conformity is brought to the seller's attention which directly or indirectly waives or restricts the rights resulting from the seller's obligation to ensure that the goods conform to the contract is not binding on the consumer.

Chapter 3: Obligations of the Buyer

IV. A. – 3:101: Main Obligations of the Buyer

The buyer must:

(a) pay the price;

(b) take delivery of the goods; and

(c) take over documents representing or relating to the goods as may be required by the contract.

IV. A. – 3:102: Determination of Form, Measurement or Other Features

(1) If under the contract the buyer is to specify the form, measurement or other features of the goods, or the time or manner of their delivery, and fails to make such specification either within the time agreed upon or within a reasonable time after receipt of a request from the seller, the seller may, without prejudice to any other rights, make the specification in accordance with any requirements of the buyer that may be known to the seller.

(2) A seller who makes such a specification must inform the buyer of the details of the specification and must fix a reasonable time within which the buyer may make a different specification. If, after receipt of such a communication, the buyer fails to do so within the time so fixed, the specification made by the seller is binding.

IV. A. – 3:103: Price Fixed by Weight

If the price is fixed according to the weight of the goods, in case of doubt it is to be determined by the net weight.

IV. A. – 3:104: Taking Delivery

The buyer fulfils the obligation to take delivery by:

(a) doing all the acts which could reasonably be expected in order to enable the seller to perform the obligation to deliver; and

(b) taking over the goods, or the documents representing the goods, as required by the contract.

IV. A. – 3:105: Early Delivery and Delivery of Excess Quantity

(1) If the seller delivers all or part of the goods before the time fixed, the buyer may take delivery or, except where acceptance of the tender would not unreasonably prejudice the buyer's interests, refuse to take delivery.

(2) If the seller delivers a quantity of goods greater than that provided for by the contract, the buyer may retain or refuse the excess quantity.

(3) If the buyer retains the excess quantity it is regarded as having been supplied under the contract and must be paid for at the contractual rate.

(4) In a consumer contract for sale paragraph (3) does not apply if the buyer believes on reasonable grounds that the seller has delivered the excess quantity intentionally and without error, knowing that it had not been ordered. In such a case the rules on unsolicited goods apply.

Chapter 4: Remedies

Section 1: Limits on Derogation

IV. A. – 4:101: Limits on Derogation from Remedies for Non-Conformity in a Consumer Contract for Sale

In a consumer contract for sale, any contractual term or agreement concluded with the seller before a lack of conformity is brought to the seller's attention which directly or indirectly waives or restricts the remedies of the buyer provided in Book III, Chapter 3 (Remedies for Non-performance), as modified in this Chapter, in respect of the lack of conformity is not binding on the consumer.

Section 2: Modifications of Buyer's Remedies for Lack of Conformity

IV. A. – 4:201: Termination by Consumer for Lack of Conformity

In a consumer contract for sale, the buyer may terminate the contractual relationship for non-performance under Book III, Chapter 3, Section 5 (Termination) in the case of any lack of conformity, unless the lack of conformity is minor.

IV. A. – 4:202: Limitation of Liability for Damages of Non-Business Sellers

(1) If the seller is a natural person acting for purposes not related to that person's trade, business or profession, the buyer is not entitled to damages for lack of conformity exceeding the contract price.

(2) The seller is not entitled to rely on paragraph (1) if the lack of conformity relates to facts of which the seller, at the time when the risk passed to the buyer, knew or could reasonably be expected to have known and which the seller did not disclose to the buyer before that time.

Section 3: Requirements of Examination and Notification

IV. A. – 4:301: Examination of the Goods

(1) The buyer should examine the goods, or cause them to be examined, within as short a period as is reasonable in the circumstances. Failure to do so may result in the buyer losing, under III. – 3:107 (Failure to notify non-conformity) as supplemented by IV. A. – 4:302 (Notification of lack of conformity), the right to rely on the lack of conformity.

(2) If the contract involves carriage of the goods, examination may be deferred until after the goods have arrived at their destination.

(3) If the goods are redirected in transit, or redispatched by the buyer before the buyer has had a reasonable opportunity to examine them, and at the time of the conclusion of the contract the seller knew or could reasonably be expected to have known of the possibility of such redirection or redispatch, examination may be deferred until after the goods have arrived at the new destination.

(4) This Article does not apply to a consumer contract for sale.

IV. A. – 4:302: Notification of Lack of Conformity

(1) In a contract between two businesses the rule in III. – 3:107 (Failure to notify non-conformity) requiring notification of a lack of conformity within a reasonable time is supplemented by the following rules.

(2) The buyer in any event loses the right to rely on a lack of conformity if the buyer does not give the seller notice of the lack of conformity at the latest within two years from the time at which the goods were actually handed over to the buyer in accordance with the contract.

(3) If the parties have agreed that the goods must remain fit for a particular purpose or for their ordinary purpose during a fixed period of time, the period for giving notice under paragraph (2) does not expire before the end of the agreed period.

(4) Paragraph (2) does not apply in respect of third party claims or rights pursuant to IV. A. – 2:305 (Third party rights or claims in general) and IV. A. – 2:306 (Third party rights or claims based on industrial property or other intellectual property) .

IV. A. – 4:303: Notification of Partial Delivery

The buyer does not have to notify the seller that not all the goods have been delivered, if the buyer has reason to believe that the remaining goods will be delivered.

IV. A. – 4:304: Seller's Knowledge of Lack of Conformity

The seller is not entitled to rely on the provisions of IV. A. – 4:301 (Examination of the goods) or IV. A. – 4:302 (Notification of lack of conformity) if the lack of conformity relates to facts of which the seller knew or could reasonably be expected to have known and which the seller did not disclose to the buyer.

Chapter 5: Passing of Risk

Section 1: General Provisions

IV. A. – 5:101: Effect of Passing of Risk

Loss of, or damage to, the goods after the risk has passed to the buyer does not discharge the buyer from the obligation to pay the price, unless the loss or damage is due to an act or omission of the seller.

IV. A. – 5:102: Time When Risk Passes

(1) The risk passes when the buyer takes over the goods or the documents representing them.

(2) However, if the contract relates to goods not then identified, the risk does not pass to the buyer until the goods are clearly identified to the contract, whether by markings on the goods, by shipping documents, by notice given to the buyer or otherwise.

(3) The rule in paragraph (1) is subject to the Articles in Section 2 of this Chapter.

IV. A. – 5:103: Passing of Risk in a Consumer Contract for Sale

(1) In a consumer contract for sale, the risk does not pass until the buyer takes over the goods.

(2) Paragraph (1) does not apply if the buyer has failed to perform the obligation to take over the goods and the non-performance is not excused under III. – 3:104 (Excuse due to an impediment) in which case IV. A. – 5:201 (Goods placed at buyer's disposal) applies.

(3) Except in so far as provided in the preceding paragraph, Section 2 of this Chapter does not apply to a consumer contract for sale.

(4) The parties may not, to the detriment of the consumer, exclude the application of this Article or derogate from or vary its effects.

Section 2: Special Rules

IV. A. – 5:201: Goods Placed at Buyer's Disposal

(1) If the goods are placed at the buyer's disposal and the buyer is aware of this, the risk passes to the buyer from the time when the goods should have been taken over, unless the buyer was entitled to withhold taking of delivery under III. – 3:401 (Right to withhold performance of reciprocal obligation).

(2) If the goods are placed at the buyer's disposal at a place other than a place of business of the seller, the risk passes when delivery is due and the buyer is aware of the fact that the goods are placed at the buyer's disposal at that place.

IV. A. – 5:202: Carriage of the Goods

(1) This Article applies to any contract of sale which involves carriage of goods.

(2) If the seller is not bound to hand over the goods at a particular place, the risk passes to the buyer when the goods are handed over to the first carrier for transmission to the buyer in accordance with the contract.

(3) If the seller is bound to hand over the goods to a carrier at a particular place, the risk does not pass to the buyer until the goods are handed over to the carrier at that place.

(4) The fact that the seller is authorised to retain documents controlling the disposition of the goods does not affect the passing of the risk.

IV. A. – 5:203: Goods Sold in Transit

(1) This Article applies to any contract of sale which involves goods sold in transit.

(2) The risk passes to the buyer at the time the goods are handed over to the first carrier. However, if the circumstances so indicate, the risk passes to the buyer as from the time of the conclusion of the contract.

(3) If at the time of the conclusion of the contract the seller knew or could reasonably be expected to have known that the goods had been lost or damaged and did not disclose this to the buyer, the loss or damage is at the risk of the seller.

Chapter 6: Consumer Goods Guarantees

IV. A. – 6:101: Definition of a Consumer Goods Guarantee

(1) A consumer goods guarantee means any undertaking of a type mentioned in the following paragraph given to a consumer in connection with a consumer contract for the sale of goods:

(a) by a producer or a person in later links of the business chain; or

(b) by the seller in addition to the seller's obligations as seller of the goods.

(2) The undertaking may be that:

(a) apart from misuse, mistreatment or accident the goods will remain fit for their ordinary purpose for a specified period of time, or otherwise;

(b) the goods will meet the specifications set out in the guarantee document or in associated advertising; or

(c) subject to any conditions stated in the guarantee,

   (i) the goods will be repaired or replaced;

   (ii) the price paid for the goods will be reimbursed in whole or in part; or

   (iii) some other remedy will be provided.

IV. A. – 6:102: Binding Nature of the Guarantee

(1) A consumer goods guarantee, whether contractual or in the form of a unilateral undertaking, is binding in favour of the first buyer, and in the case of a unilateral undertaking is so binding without acceptance notwithstanding any provision to the contrary in the guarantee document or the associated advertising.

(2) If not otherwise provided in the guarantee document, the guarantee is also binding without acceptance in favour of every owner of the goods within the duration of the guarantee.

(3) Any requirement in the guarantee whereby it is conditional on the fulfilment by the guarantee holder of any formal requirement, such as registration or notification of purchase, is not binding on the consumer.

IV. A. – 6:103: Guarantee Document

(1) A person who gives a consumer goods guarantee must (unless such a document has already been provided to the buyer) provide the buyer with a guarantee document which:

(a) states that the buyer has legal rights which are not affected by the guarantee;

(b) points out the advantages of the guarantee for the buyer in comparison with the conformity rules;

(c) lists all the essential particulars necessary for making claims under the guarantee, notably:

– the name and address of the guarantor;

– the name and address of the person to whom any notification is to be made and the procedure by which the notification is to be made;

– any territorial limitations to the guarantee;

(d) is drafted in plain, intelligible language; and

(e) is drafted in the same language as that in which the goods were offered.

(2) The guarantee document must be in textual form on a durable medium and be available and accessible to the buyer.

(3) The validity of the guarantee is not affected by any failure to comply with paragraphs (1) and (2), and accordingly the guarantee holder can still rely on the guarantee and require it to be honoured.

(4) If the obligations under paragraphs (1) and (2) are not observed the guarantee holder may, without prejudice to any right to damages which may be available, require the guarantor to provide a guarantee document which conforms to those requirements.

(5) The parties may not, to the detriment of the consumer, exclude the application of this Article or derogate from or vary its effects.

IV. A. – 6:104: Coverage of the Guarantee

If the guarantee document does not specify otherwise:

(a) the period of the guarantee is 5 years or the estimated life-span of the goods, whichever is shorter;

(b) the guarantor's obligations become effective if, for a reason other than misuse, mistreatment or accident, the goods at any time during the period of the guarantee become unfit for their ordinary purpose or cease to possess such qualities and performance capabilities as the guarantee holder may reasonably expect;

(c) the guarantor is obliged, if the conditions of the guarantee are satisfied, to repair or replace the goods; and

(d) all costs involved in invoking and performing the guarantee are to be borne by the guarantor.

IV. A. – 6:105: Guarantee Limited to Specific Parts

A consumer goods guarantee relating only to a specific part or specific parts of the goods must clearly indicate this limitation in the guarantee document; otherwise the limitation is not binding on the consumer.

IV. A. – 6:106: Exclusion or Limitation of the Guarantor's Liability

The guarantee may exclude or limit the guarantor's liability under the guarantee for any failure of or damage to the goods caused by failure to maintain the goods in accordance with instructions, provided that the exclusion or limitation is clearly set out in the guarantee document.

IV. A. – 6:107: Burden of Proof

(1) Where the guarantee holder invokes a consumer goods guarantee within the period covered by the guarantee the burden of proof is on the guarantor that:

(a) the goods met the specifications set out in the guarantee document or in associated advertisements; and

(b) any failure of or damage to the goods is due to misuse, mistreatment, accident, failure to maintain, or other cause for which the guarantor is not responsible.

(2) The parties may not, to the detriment of the consumer, exclude the application of this Article or derogate from or vary its effects.

IV. A. – 6:108: Prolongation of the Guarantee Period

(1) If any defect or failure in the goods is remedied under the guarantee then the guarantee is prolonged for a period equal to the period during which the guarantee holder could not use the goods due to the defect or failure.

(2) The parties may not, to the detriment of the consumer, exclude the application of this Article or derogate from or vary its effects.

Part B. Lease of Goods

Chapter 1: Scope of Application and General Provisions

IV. B. – 1:101: Lease of Goods

(1) This Part of Book IV applies to contracts for the lease of goods.

(2) A contract for the lease of goods is a contract under which one party, the lessor, undertakes to provide the other party, the lessee, with a temporary right of use of goods in exchange for rent. The rent may be in the form of money or other value.

(3) This Part of Book IV does not apply to contracts where the parties have agreed that ownership will be transferred after a period with right of use even if the parties have described the contract as a lease.

(4) The application of this Part of Book IV is not excluded by the fact that the contract has a financing purpose, the lessor has the role as a financing party, or the lessee has an option to become owner of the goods.

(5) This Part of Book IV regulates only the contractual relationship arising from a contract for lease.

IV. B. – 1:102: Consumer Contract for the Lease of Goods

For the purpose of this Part of Book IV, a consumer contract for the lease of goods is a contract for the lease of goods in which the lessor is a business and the lessee is a consumer.

IV. B. – 1:103: Limits on Derogation from Conformity Rights in a Consumer Contract for Lease

In the case of a consumer contract for the lease of goods, any contractual term or agreement concluded with the lessor before a lack of conformity is brought to the lessor's attention which directly or indirectly waives or restricts the rights resulting from the lessor's obligation to ensure that the goods conform to the contract is not binding on the consumer.

IV. B. – 1:104: Limits on Derogation from Rules on Remedies in a Consumer Contract for Lease

(1) In the case of a consumer contract for the lease of goods the parties may not, to the detriment of the consumer, exclude the application of the rules on remedies in Book III, Chapter 3, as modified in Chapters 3 and 6 of this Part, or derogate from or vary their effects.

(2) Notwithstanding paragraph (1), the parties may agree on a limitation of the lessor's liability for loss related to the lessee's trade, business or profession. Such a term may not, however, be invoked if it would be contrary to good faith and fair dealing to do so.

Chapter 2: Lease Period

IV. B. – 2:101: Start of Lease Period

(1) The lease period starts:

(a) at the time determinable from the terms agreed by the parties;

(b) if a time frame within which the lease period is to start can be determined, at any time chosen by the lessor within that time frame unless the circumstances of the case indicate that the lessee is to choose the time;

(c) in any other case, a reasonable time after the conclusion of the contract, at the request of either party.

(2) The lease period starts at the time when the lessee takes control of the goods if this is earlier than the starting time under paragraph (1).

IV. B. – 2:102: End of Lease Period

(1) A definite lease period ends at the time determinable from the terms agreed by the parties. A definite lease period cannot be terminated unilaterally beforehand by giving notice.

(2) An indefinite lease period ends at the time specified in a notice of termination given by either party.

(3) A notice under paragraph (2) is effective only if the time specified in the notice of termination is in compliance with the terms agreed by the parties or, if no period of notice can be determined from such terms, a reasonable time after the notice has reached the other party.

IV. B. – 2:103: Tacit Prolongation

(1) Where a contract for the lease of goods for a definite period is tacitly prolonged under III. – 1:111 (Tacit prolongation) and where the rent prior to prolongation was calculated so as to take into account amortisation of the cost of the goods by the lessee, the rent payable following prolongation is limited to what is reasonable having regard to the amount already paid.

(2) In the case of a consumer contract for the lease of goods the parties may not, to the detriment of the consumer, exclude the application of paragraph (1) or derogate from or vary its effects.

Chapter 3: Obligations of the Lessor

IV. B. – 3:101: Availability of the Goods

(1) The lessor must make the goods available for the lessee's use at the start of the lease period and at the place determined by III. – 2:101 (Place of performance).

(2) Notwithstanding the rule in the previous paragraph, the lessor must make the goods available for the lessee's use at the lessee's place of business or, as the case may be, at the lessee's habitual residence if the lessor, on the specifications of the lessee, acquires the goods from a supplier selected by the lessee.

(3) The lessor must ensure that the goods remain available for the lessee's use throughout the lease period, free from any right or reasonably based claim of a third party which prevents or is otherwise likely to interfere with the lessee's use of the goods in accordance with the contract.

(4) The lessor's obligations when the goods are lost or damaged during the lease period are regulated by IV. B. – 3:104 (Conformity of the goods during the lease period).

IV. B. – 3:102: Conformity with the Contract at the Start of the Lease Period

(1) The lessor must ensure that the goods conform with the contract at the start of the lease period.

(2) The goods do not conform with the contract unless they:

(a) are of the quantity, quality and description required by the terms agreed by the parties;

(b) are contained or packaged in the manner required by the terms agreed by the parties;

(c) are supplied along with any accessories, installation instructions or other instructions required by the terms agreed by the parties; and

(d) comply with the following Article.

IV. B. – 3:103: Fitness for Purpose, Qualities, Packaging etc.

The goods do not conform with the contract unless they:

(a) are fit for any particular purpose made known to the lessor at the time of the conclusion of the contract, except where the circumstances show that the lessee did not rely, or that it was unreasonable for the lessee to rely, on the lessor's skill and judgement;

(b) are fit for the purposes for which goods of the same description would ordinarily be used;

(c) possess the qualities of goods which the lessor held out to the lessee as a sample or model;

(d) are contained or packaged in the manner usual for such goods or, where there is no such manner, in a manner adequate to preserve and protect the goods;

(e) are supplied along with such accessories, installation instructions or other instructions as the lessee could reasonably expect to receive; and

(f) possess such qualities and performance capabilities as the lessee may reasonably expect.

IV. B. – 3:104: Conformity of the Goods During the Lease Period

(1) The lessor must ensure that throughout the lease period, and subject to normal wear and tear, the goods:

(a) remain of the quantity, quality and description required by the contract; and

(b) remain fit for the purposes of the lease, even where this requires modifications to the goods.

(2) Paragraph (1) does not apply where the rent is calculated so as to take into account the amortisation of the cost of the goods by the lessee.

(3) Nothing in paragraph (1) affects the lessee's obligations under IV. B. – 5:104 (Handling the goods in accordance with the contract) paragraph (1)(c).

IV. B. – 3:105: Incorrect Installation Under a Consumer Contract for the Lease of Goods

Where, under a consumer contract for the lease of goods, the goods are incorrectly installed, any lack of conformity resulting from the incorrect installation is regarded as a lack of conformity of the goods if:

(a) the goods were installed by the lessor or under the lessor's responsibility; or

(b) the goods were intended to be installed by the consumer and the incorrect installation was due to shortcomings in the installation instructions.

IV. B. – 3:106: Obligations on Return of the Goods

The lessor must:

(a) take all the steps which may reasonably be expected in order to enable the lessee to perform the obligation to return the goods; and

(b) accept return of the goods as required by the contract.

Chapter 4: Remedies of the Lessee: Modifications of Normal Rules

IV. B. – 4:101: Lessee's Right to Have Lack of Conformity Remedied

(1) The lessee may have any lack of conformity of the goods remedied, and recover any expenses reasonably incurred, to the extent that the lessee is entitled to enforce specific performance according to III. – 3:302 (Enforcement of non-monetary obligations).

(2) Nothing in the preceding paragraph affects the lessor's right to cure the lack of conformity according to Book III, Chapter 3, Section 2.

IV. B. – 4:102: Rent Reduction

(1) The lessee may reduce the rent for a period in which the value of the lessor's performance is decreased due to delay or lack of conformity, to the extent that the reduction in value is not caused by the lessee.

(2) The rent may be reduced even for periods in which the lessor retains the right to perform or cure according to III. – 3:103 (Notice fixing additional time for performance), III. – 3:202 (Cure by debtor: general rules) paragraph (2) and III. – 3:204 (Consequences of allowing debtor opportunity to cure)).

(3) Notwithstanding the rule in paragraph (1), the lessee may lose the right to reduce the rent for a period according to IV. B. – 4:103 (Notification of lack of conformity).

IV. B. – 4:103: Notification of Lack of Conformity

(1) The lessee cannot resort to remedies for lack of conformity unless notification is given to the lessor. Where notification is not timely, the lack of conformity is disregarded for a period cor-

responding to the unreasonable delay. Notification is always considered timely where it is given within a reasonable time after the lessee has become, or could reasonably be expected to have become, aware of the lack of conformity.

(2) When the lease period has ended the rules in III. – 3:107 (Failure to notify non-conformity) apply.

(3) The lessor is not entitled to rely on the provisions of paragraphs (1) and (2) if the lack of conformity relates to facts of which the lessor knew or could reasonably be expected to have known and which the lessor did not disclose to the lessee.

IV. B. – 4:104: Remedies to Be Directed Towards Supplier of the Goods

(1) This Article applies where:

(a) the lessor, on the specifications of the lessee, acquires the goods from a supplier selected by the lessee;

(b) the lessee, in providing the specifications for the goods and selecting the supplier, does not rely primarily on the skill and judgement of the lessor;

(c) the lessee approves the terms of the supply contract;

(d) the supplier's obligations under the supply contract are owed, by law or by contract, to the lessee as a party to the supply contract or as if the lessee were a party to that contract; and

(e) the supplier's obligations owed to the lessee cannot be varied without the consent of the lessee.

(2) The lessee has no right to enforce performance by the lessor, to reduce the rent or to damages or interest from the lessor, for late delivery or for lack of conformity, unless non-performance results from an act or omission of the lessor.

(3) The provision in paragraph (2) does not preclude:

(a) any right of the lessee to reject the goods, to terminate the lease under Book III, Chapter 3, Section 5 (Termination) or, prior to acceptance of the goods, to withhold rent to the extent that the lessee could have resorted to these remedies as a party to the supply contract; or

(b) any remedy of the lessee where a third party right or reasonably based claim prevents, or is otherwise likely to interfere with, the lessee's continuous use of the goods in accordance with the contract.

(4) The lessee cannot terminate the lessee's contractual relationship with the supplier under the supply contract without the consent of the lessor.

Chapter 5: Obligations of the Lessee

IV. B. – 5:101: Obligation to Pay Rent

(1) The lessee must pay the rent.

(2) Where the rent cannot be determined from the terms agreed by the parties, from any other applicable rule of law or from usages or practices, it is a monetary sum determined in accordance with II. – 9:104 (Determination of price).

(3) The rent accrues from the start of the lease period.

IV. B. – 5:102: Time for Payment

Rent is payable:

(a) at the end of each period for which the rent is agreed;

(b) if the rent is not agreed for certain periods, at the expiry of a definite lease period; or

(c) if no definite lease period is agreed and the rent is not agreed for certain periods, at the end of reasonable intervals.

IV. B. – 5:103: Acceptance of Goods

The lessee must:

(a) take all steps reasonably to be expected in order to enable the lessor to perform the obligation to make the goods available at the start of the lease period; and

(b) take control of the goods as required by the contract.

IV. B. – 5:104: Handling the Goods in Accordance with the Contract

(1) The lessee must:

(a) observe the requirements and restrictions which follow from the terms agreed by the parties;

(b) handle the goods with the care which can reasonably be expected in the circumstances, taking into account the duration of the lease period, the purpose of the lease and the character of the goods; and

(c) take all measures which could ordinarily be expected to become necessary in order to preserve the normal standard and functioning of the goods, in so far as is reasonable, taking into account the duration of the lease period, the purpose of the lease and the character of the goods.

(2) Where the rent is calculated so as to take into account the amortisation of the cost of the goods by the lessee, the lessee must, during the lease period, keep the goods in the condition they were in at the start of the lease period, subject to any wear and tear which is normal for that kind of goods.

IV. B. – 5:105: Intervention to Avoid Danger or Damage to the Goods

(1) The lessee must take such measures for the maintenance and repair of the goods as would ordinarily be carried out by the lessor, if the measures are necessary to avoid danger or damage to the goods, and it is impossible or impracticable for the lessor, but not for the lessee, to ensure these measures are taken.

(2) The lessee has a right against the lessor to indemnification or, as the case may be, reimbursement in respect of an obligation or expenditure (whether of money or other assets) in so far as reasonably incurred for the purposes of the measures.

IV. B. – 5:106: Compensation for Maintenance and Improvements

(1) The lessee has no right to compensation for maintenance of or improvements to the goods.

(2) Paragraph (1) does not exclude or restrict any right the lessee may have to damages or any right the lessee may have under IV. B. – 4:101 (Lessee's right to have lack of conformity remedied), IV. B. – 5:105 (Intervention to avoid danger or damage to the goods) or Book VIII (Acquisition and loss of ownership of goods).

IV. B. – 5:107: Obligation to Inform

(1) The lessee must inform the lessor of any damage or danger to the goods, and of any right or claim of a third party, if these circumstances would normally give rise to a need for action on the part of the lessor.

(2) The lessee must inform the lessor under paragraph (1) within a reasonable time after the lessee first becomes aware of the circumstances and their character.

(3) The lessee is presumed to be aware of the circumstances and their character if the lessee could reasonably be expected to be so aware.

IV. B. – 5:108: Repairs and Inspections of the Lessor

(1) The lessee, if given reasonable notice where possible, must tolerate the carrying out by the lessor of repair work and other work on the goods which is necessary in order to preserve the goods, remove defects and prevent danger. This obligation does not preclude the lessee from reducing the rent in accordance with IV. B. – 4:102 (Rent reduction).

(2) The lessee must tolerate the carrying out of work on the goods which does not fall under paragraph (1), unless there is good reason to object.

(3) The lessee must tolerate inspection of the goods for the purposes indicated in paragraph (1). The lessee must also accept inspection of the goods by a prospective lessee during a reasonable period prior to expiry of the lease.

IV. B. – 5:109: Obligation to Return the Goods

At the end of the lease period the lessee must return the goods to the place where they were made available for the lessee.

Chapter 6: Remedies of the Lessor: Modifications of Normal Rules

IV. B. – 6:101: Limitation of Right to Enforce Payment of Future Rent

(1) Where the lessee has taken control of the goods, the lessor may not enforce payment of future rent if the lessee wishes to return the goods and it would be reasonable for the lessor to accept their return.

(2) The fact that a right to enforce specific performance is excluded under paragraph (1) does not preclude a claim for damages.

IV. B. – 6:102: Reduction of Liability in Consumer Contract for the Lease of Goods

(1) In the case of a consumer contract for the lease of goods, the lessor's right to damages may be reduced to the extent that the loss is mitigated by insurance covering the goods, or to the extent that loss would have been mitigated by insurance, in circumstances where it is reasonable to expect the lessor to take out such insurance.

(2) The rule in paragraph (1) applies in addition to the rules in Book III, Chapter 3, Section 7.

Chapter 7: New Parties and Sublease

IV. B. – 7:101: Change in Ownership and Substitution of Lessor

(1) Where ownership passes from the lessor to a new owner, the new owner of the goods is substituted as a party to the lease if the lessee has possession of the goods at the time ownership passes. The former owner remains subsidiarily liable for the non-performance of the obligations under the contract for lease as a personal security provider.

(2) A reversal of the passing of ownership puts the parties back in their original positions except as regards performance already rendered at the time of reversal.

(3) The rules in the preceding paragraphs apply accordingly where the lessor has acted as holder of a right other than ownership.

IV. B. – 7:102: Assignment of Lessee's Rights to Performance

The lessee's rights to performance of the lessor's obligations under the contract for lease cannot be assigned without the lessor's consent.

IV. B. – 7:103: Sublease

(1) The lessee may not sublease the goods without the lessor's consent.

(2) If consent to a sublease is withheld without good reason, the lessee may terminate the lease by giving a reasonable period of notice.

(3) In the case of a sublease, the lessee remains liable for the performance of the lessee's obligations under the contract for lease.

Part C. Services

Chapter 1: General Provisions

IV. C. – 1:101: Scope

(1) This Part of Book IV applies:

(a) to contracts under which one party, the service provider, undertakes to supply a service to the other party, the client, in exchange for a price; and

(b) with appropriate adaptations, to contracts under which the service provider undertakes to supply a service to the client otherwise than in exchange for a price.

(2) It applies in particular to contracts for construction, processing, storage, design, information or advice, and treatment.

IV. C. – 1:102: Exclusions

This Part does not apply to contracts in so far as they are for transport, insurance, the provision of a security or the supply of a financial product or a financial service.

IV. C. – 1:103: Priority Rules

In the case of any conflict:

(a) the rules in Part IV. D. (Mandate) and Part IV. E. (Commercial agency, franchise and distributorship) prevail over the rules in this Part; and

(b) the rules in Chapters 3 to 8 of this Part prevail over the rules in Chapter 2 of this Part.

Chapter 2: Rules Applying to Service Contracts in General

IV. C. – 2:101: Price

Where the service provider is a business, a price is payable unless the circumstances indicate otherwise.

IV. C. – 2:102: Pre-Contractual Duties to Warn

(1) The service provider is under a pre-contractual duty to warn the client if the service provider becomes aware of a risk that the service requested:

(a) may not achieve the result stated or envisaged by the client;

(b) may damage other interests of the client; or

(c) may become more expensive or take more time than reasonably expected by the client.

(2) The duty to warn in paragraph (1) does not apply if the client:

(a) already knows of the risks referred to in paragraph (1); or

(b) could reasonably be expected to know of them.

(3) If a risk referred to in paragraph (1) materialises and the service provider was in breach of the duty to warn of it, a subsequent change of the service by the service provider under IV. C. – 2:109 (Unilateral variation of the service contract) which is based on the materialisation of the risk is of no effect unless the service provider proves that the client, if duly warned, would have entered into a contract anyway. This is without prejudice to any other remedies, including remedies for mistake, which the client may have.

(4) The client is under a pre-contractual duty to warn the service provider if the client becomes aware of unusual facts which are likely to cause the service to become more expensive or time-consuming than expected by the service provider or to cause any danger to the service provider or others when performing the service.

(5) If the facts referred to under paragraph (4) occur and the service provider was not duly warned, the service provider is entitled to:

(a) damages for the loss the service provider sustained as a consequence of the failure to warn; and

(b) an adjustment of the time allowed for performance of the service.

(6) For the purpose of paragraph (1), the service provider is presumed to be aware of the risks mentioned if they should be obvious from all the facts and circumstances known to the service provider, considering the information which the service provider must collect about the result

stated or envisaged by the client and the circumstances in which the service is to be carried out.

(7) For the purpose of paragraph (2)(b) the client cannot reasonably be expected to know of a risk merely because the client was competent, or was advised by others who were competent, in the relevant field, unless such other person acted as the agent of the client, in which case II. – 1:105 (Imputed knowledge etc.) applies.

(8) For the purpose of paragraph (4), the client is presumed to be aware of the facts mentioned if they should be obvious from all the facts and circumstances known to the client without investigation.

IV. C. – 2:103: Obligation to Co-operate

(1) The obligation of co-operation requires in particular:

(a) the client to answer reasonable requests by the service provider for information in so far as this may reasonably be considered necessary to enable the service provider to perform the obligations under the contract;

(b) the client to give directions regarding the performance of the service in so far as this may reasonably be considered necessary to enable the service provider to perform the obligations under the contract;

(c) the client, in so far as the client is to obtain permits or licences, to obtain these at such time as may reasonably be considered necessary to enable the service provider to perform the obligations under the contract;

(d) the service provider to give the client a reasonable opportunity to determine whether the service provider is performing the obligations under the contract; and

(e) the parties to co-ordinate their respective efforts in so far as this may reasonably be considered necessary to perform their respective obligations under the contract.

(2) If the client fails to perform the obligations under paragraph (1)(a) or (b), the service provider may either withhold performance or base performance on the expectations, preferences and priorities the client could reasonably be expected to have, given the information and directions

which have been gathered, provided that the client is warned in accordance with IV. C. – 2:108 (Contractual obligation of the service provider to warn).

(3) If the client fails to perform the obligations under paragraph (1) causing the service to become more expensive or to take more time than agreed on in the contract, the service provider is entitled to:

(a) damages for the loss the service provider sustained as a consequence of the non-performance; and

(b) an adjustment of the time allowed for supplying the service.

IV. C. – 2:104: Subcontractors, Tools and Materials

(1) The service provider may subcontract the performance of the service in whole or in part without the client's consent, unless personal performance is required by the contract.

(2) Any subcontractor so engaged by the service provider must be of adequate competence.

(3) The service provider must ensure that any tools and materials used for the performance of the service are in conformity with the contract and the applicable statutory rules, and fit to achieve the particular purpose for which they are to be used.

(4) In so far as subcontractors are nominated by the client or tools and materials are provided by the client, the responsibility of the service provider is governed by IV. C. – 2:107 (Directions of the client) and IV. C. – 2:108 (Contractual obligation of the service provider to warn).

IV. C. – 2:105: Obligation of Skill and Care

(1) The service provider must perform the service:

(a) with the care and skill which a reasonable service provider would exercise under the circumstances; and

(b) in conformity with any statutory or other binding legal rules which are applicable to the service.

(2) If the service provider professes a higher standard of care and skill the provider must exercise that care and skill.

(3) If the service provider is, or purports to be, a member of a group of professional service providers for which standards have been set by a relevant authority or by that group itself, the service provider must exercise the care and skill expressed in those standards.

(4) In determining the care and skill the client is entitled to expect, regard is to be had, among other things, to:

(a) the nature, the magnitude, the frequency and the foreseeability of the risks involved in the performance of the service for the client;

(b) if damage has occurred, the costs of any precautions which would have prevented that damage or similar damage from occurring;

(c) whether the service provider is a business;

(d) whether a price is payable and, if one is payable, its amount; and

(e) the time reasonably available for the performance of the service.

(5) The obligations under this Article require in particular the service provider to take reasonable precautions in order to prevent the occurrence of damage as a consequence of the performance of the service.

IV. C. – 2:106: Obligation to Achieve Result

(1) The supplier of a service must achieve the specific result stated or envisaged by the client at the time of the conclusion of the contract,

provided that in the case of a result envisaged but not stated:

(a) the result envisaged was one which the client could reasonably be expected to have envisaged; and

(b) the client had no reason to believe that there was a substantial risk that the result would not be achieved by the service.

(2) In so far as ownership of anything is transferred to the client under the service contract, it must be transferred free from any right or reasonably based claim of a third party. IV. A. – 2:305 (Third party rights or claims in general) and IV. A. – 2:306 (Third party rights or claims based on industrial property or other intellectual property) apply with any appropriate adaptations.

IV. C. – 2:107: Directions of the Client

(1) The service provider must follow all timely directions of the client regarding the performance of the service, provided that the directions:

(a) are part of the contract itself or are specified in any document to which the contract refers; or

(b) result from the realisation of choices left to the client by the contract; or

(c) result from the realisation of choices initially left open by the parties.

(2) If non-performance of one or more of the obligations of the service provider under IV. C. – 2:105 (Obligation of skill and care) or IV. C. – 2:106 (Obligation to achieve result) is the consequence of following a direction which the service provider is obliged to follow under paragraph (1), the service provider is not liable under those Articles, provided that the client was duly warned under IV. C. – 2:108 (Contractual obligation of the service provider to warn).

(3) If the service provider perceives a direction falling under paragraph (1) to be a variation of the contract under IV. C. – 2:109 (Unilateral variation of the service contract) the service provider must warn the client accordingly. Unless the client then revokes the direction without undue delay, the service provider must follow the direction and the direction has effect as a variation of the contract.

IV. C. – 2:108: Contractual Obligation of the Service Provider to Warn

(1) The service provider must warn the client if the service provider becomes aware of a risk that the service requested:

(a) may not achieve the result stated or envisaged by the client at the time of conclusion of the contract;

(b) may damage other interests of the client; or

(c) may become more expensive or take more time than agreed on in the contract either as a result of following information or directions given by the client or collected in preparation for performance, or as a result of the occurrence of any other risk.

(2) The service provider must take reasonable measures to ensure that the client understands the content of the warning.

(3) The obligation to warn in paragraph (1) does not apply if the client:

(a) already knows of the risks referred to in paragraph (1); or

(b) could reasonably be expected to know of them.

(4) If a risk referred to in paragraph (1) materialises and the service provider did not perform the obligation to warn the client of it, a notice of variation by the service provider under IV. C. – 2:109 (Unilateral variation of the service contract) based on the materialisation of that risk is without effect.

(5) For the purpose of paragraph (1), the service provider is presumed to be aware of the risks mentioned if they should be obvious from all the facts and circumstances known to the service provider without investigation.

(6) For the purpose of paragraph (3)(b), the client cannot reasonably be expected to know of a risk merely because the client was competent, or was advised by others who were competent, in the relevant field, unless such other person acted as the agent of the client, in which case II. – 1:105 (Imputed knowledge etc.) applies.

IV. C. – 2:109: Unilateral Variation of the Service Contract

(1) Without prejudice to the client's right to terminate under IV. C. – 2:111 (Client's right to terminate), either party may, by notice to the other party, change the service to be provided, if such a change is reasonable taking into account:

(a) the result to be achieved;

(b) the interests of the client;

(c) the interests of the service provider; and

(d) the circumstances at the time of the change.

(2) A change is regarded as reasonable only if it is:

(a) necessary in order to enable the service provider to act in accordance with IV. C. – 2:105 (Obligation of skill and care) or, as the case may be, IV. C. – 2:106 (Obligation to achieve result);

(b) the consequence of a direction given in accordance with paragraph (1) of IV. C. – 2:107 (Directions of the client) and not revoked without undue delay after receipt of a warning in accordance with paragraph (3) of that Article;

(c) a reasonable response to a warning from the service provider under IV. C. – 2:108 (Contractual obligation of the service provider to warn); or

(d) required by a change of circumstances which would justify a variation of the service provider's obligations under III. – 1:110 (Variation or termination by court on a change of circumstances).

(3) Any additional price due as a result of the change has to be reasonable and is to be determined using the same methods of calculation as were used to establish the original price for the service.

(4) In so far as the service is reduced, the loss of profit, the expenses saved and any possibility that the service provider may be able to use the released capacity for other purposes are to be taken into account in the calculation of the price due as a result of the change.

(5) A change of the service may lead to an adjustment of the time of performance proportionate to the extra work required in relation to the work originally required for the performance of the service and the time span determined for performance of the service.

IV. C. – 2:110: Client's Obligation to Notify Anticipated Non-Conformity

(1) The client must notify the service provider if the client becomes aware during the period for performance of the service that the service provider will fail to perform the obligation under IV. C. – 2:106 (Obligation to achieve result).

(2) The client is presumed to be so aware if from all the facts and circumstances known to the client without investigation the client has reason to be so aware.

(3) If a non-performance of the obligation under paragraph (1) causes the service to become more expensive or to take more time than agreed on in the contract, the service provider is entitled to:

(a) damages for the loss the service provider sustains as a consequence of that failure; and

(b) an adjustment of the time allowed for performance of the service.

IV. C. – 2:111: Client's Right to Terminate

(1) The client may terminate the contractual relationship at any time by giving notice to the service provider.

(2) The effects of termination are governed by III. – 1:109 (Variation or termination by notice) paragraph (3).

(3) When the client was justified in terminating the relationship no damages are payable for so doing.

(4) When the client was not justified in terminating the relationship, the termination is nevertheless effective but, the service provider has a right to damages in accordance with the rules in Book III.

(5) For the purposes of this Article, the client is justified in terminating the relationship if the client:

(a) was entitled to terminate the relationship under the express terms of the contract and observed any requirements laid down in the contract for doing so;

(b) was entitled to terminate the relationship under Book III, Chapter 3, Section 5 (Termination); or

(c) was entitled to terminate the relationship under III. – 1:109 (Variation or termination by notice) paragraph (2) and gave a reasonable period of notice as required by that provision.

Chapter 3: Construction

IV. C. – 3:101: Scope

(1) This Chapter applies to contracts under which one party, the constructor, undertakes to construct a building or other immovable structure, or to materially alter an existing building or other immovable structure, following a design provided by the client.

(2) It applies with appropriate adaptations to contracts under which the constructor undertakes:

(a) to construct a movable or incorporeal thing, following a design provided by the client; or

(b) to construct a building or other immovable structure, to materially alter an existing building or other immovable structure, or to construct a movable or incorporeal thing, following a design provided by the constructor.

IV. C. – 3:102: Obligation of Client to Co-Operate

The obligation of co-operation requires in particular the client to:

(a) provide access to the site where the construction has to take place in so far as this may reasonably be considered necessary to enable the constructor to perform the obligations under the contract; and

(b) provide the components, materials and tools, in so far as they must be provided by the client, at such time as may reasonably be considered necessary to enable the constructor to perform the obligations under the contract.

IV. C. – 3:103: Obligation to Prevent Damage to Structure

The constructor must take reasonable precautions in order to prevent any damage to the structure.

IV. C. – 3:104: Conformity

(1) The constructor must ensure that the structure is of the quality and description required by the contract. Where more than one structure is to be made, the quantity also must be in conformity with the contract.

(2) The structure does not conform to the contract unless it is:

(a) fit for any particular purpose expressly or impliedly made known to the constructor at the time of the conclusion of the contract or at the time of any variation in accordance with IV. C. – 2:109 (Unilateral variation of the service contract) pertaining to the issue in question; and

(b) fit for the particular purpose or purposes for which a structure of the same description would ordinarily be used.

(3) The client is not entitled to invoke a remedy for non-conformity if a direction provided by the client under IV. C. – 2:107 (Directions of the client) is the cause of the non-conformity and the constructor performed the obligation to warn pursuant to IV. C. – 2:108 (Contractual obligation of the service provider to warn).

IV. C. – 3:105: Inspection, Supervision and Acceptance

(1) The client may inspect or supervise the tools and materials used in the construction process, the process of construction and the resulting structure in a reasonable manner and at any reasonable time, but is not bound to do so.

(2) If the parties agree that the constructor has to present certain elements of the tools and materials used, the process or the resulting structure to the client for acceptance, the constructor may not proceed with the construction before having been allowed by the client to do so.

(3) Absence of, or inadequate, inspection, supervision or acceptance does not relieve the constructor wholly or partially from liability. This rule also applies when the client is under a contractual obligation to inspect, supervise or accept the structure or the construction of it.

IV. C. – 3:106: Handing-Over of the Structure

(1) If the constructor regards the structure, or any part of it which is fit for independent use, as sufficiently completed and wishes to transfer control over it to the client, the client must accept such control within a reasonable time after being notified. The client may refuse to accept the control when the structure, or the relevant part of it, does not conform to the contract and such non-conformity makes it unfit for use.

(2) Acceptance by the client of the control over the structure does not relieve the constructor wholly or partially from liability. This rule also applies when the client is under a contractual obligation to inspect, supervise or accept the structure or the construction of it.

(3) This Article does not apply if, under the contract, control is not to be transferred to the client.

IV. C. – 3:107: Payment of the Price

(1) The price or a proportionate part of it is payable when the constructor transfers the control of the structure or a part of it to the client in accordance with the preceding Article.

(2) However, where work remains to be done under the contract on the structure or relevant part of it after such transfer the client may withhold such part of the price as is reasonable until the work is completed.

(3) If, under the contract, control is not to be transferred to the client, the price is payable when the work has been completed, the constructor has so informed the client and the client has had a chance to inspect the structure.

IV. C. – 3:108: Risks

(1) This Article applies if the structure is destroyed or damaged due to an event which the constructor could not have avoided or overcome and the constructor cannot be held accountable for the destruction or damage.

(2) In this Article the "relevant time" is:

(a) where the control of the structure is to be transferred to the client, the time when such control has been, or should have been, transferred in accordance with IV. C. – 3:106 (Handing-over of the structure);

(b) in other cases, the time when the work has been completed and the constructor has so informed the client.

(3) When the situation mentioned in paragraph (1) has been caused by an event occurring before the relevant time and it is still possible to perform:

(a) the constructor still has to perform or, as the case may be, perform again;

(b) the client is only obliged to pay for the constructor's performance under (a);

(c) the time for performance is extended in accordance with paragraph (6) of IV. C. – 2:109 (Unilateral variation of the service contract);

(d) the rules of III. – 3:104 (Excuse due to an impediment) may apply to the constructor's original performance; and

(e) the constructor is not obliged to compensate the client for losses to materials provided by the client.

(4) When the situation mentioned in paragraph (1) has been caused by an event occurring before the relevant time, and it is no longer possible to perform:

(a) the client does not have to pay for the service rendered;

(b) the rules of III. – 3:104 (Excuse due to an impediment) may apply to the constructor's performance; and

(c) the constructor is not obliged to compensate the client for losses to materials provided by the client, but is obliged to return the structure or what remains of it to the client.

(5) When the situation mentioned in paragraph (1) has been caused by an event occurring after the relevant time:

(a) the constructor does not have to perform again; and

(b) the client remains obliged to pay the price.

Chapter 4: Processing

IV. C. – 4:101: Scope

(1) This Chapter applies to contracts under which one party, the processor, undertakes to perform a service on an existing movable or incorporeal thing or to an immovable structure for another party, the client. It does not, however, apply to construction work on an existing building or other immovable structure.

(2) This Chapter applies in particular to contracts under which the processor undertakes to repair, maintain or clean an existing movable or incorporeal thing or immovable structure.

IV. C. – 4:102: Obligation of Client to Co-Operate

The obligation to co-operate requires in particular the client to:

(a) hand over the thing or to give the control of it to the processor, or to give access to the site where the service is to be performed in so far as may reasonably be considered necessary to enable the processor to perform the obligations under the contract; and

(b) in so far as they must be provided by the client, provide the components, materials and tools in time to enable the processor to perform the obligations under the contract.

IV. C. – 4:103: Obligation to Prevent Damage to Thing Being Processed

The processor must take reasonable precautions in order to prevent any damage to the thing being processed.

IV. C. – 4:104: Inspection and Supervision

(1) If the service is to be performed at a site provided by the client, the client may inspect or supervise the tools and material used, the performance of the service and the thing on which the service is performed in a reasonable manner and at any reasonable time, but is not bound to do so.

(2) Absence of, or inadequate inspection or supervision does not relieve the processor wholly or partially from liability. This rule also applies when the client is under a contractual obligation to accept, inspect or supervise the processing of the thing.

IV. C. – 4:105: Return of the Thing Processed

(1) If the processor regards the service as sufficiently completed and wishes to return the thing or the control of it to the client, the client must accept such return or control within a reasonable time after being notified. The client may refuse to accept the return or control when the thing is not fit for use in accordance with the particular purpose for which the client had the service performed, provided that such purpose was made known to the processor or that the processor otherwise has reason to know of it.

(2) The processor must return the thing or the control of it within a reasonable time after being so requested by the client.

(3) Acceptance by the client of the return of the thing or the control of it does not relieve the processor wholly or partially from liability for nonperformance.

(4) If, by virtue of the rules on the acquisition of property, the processor has become the owner of the thing, or a share in it, as a consequence of the performance of the obligations under the contract, the processor must transfer ownership of the thing or share when the thing is returned.

IV. C. – 4:106: Payment of the Price

(1) The price is payable when the processor transfers the thing or the control of it to the client in accordance with IV. C. – 4:105 (Return of the thing processed) or the client, without being entitled to do so, refuses to accept the return of the thing.

(2) However, where work remains to be done under the contract on the thing after such transfer or refusal the client may withhold such part of the price as is reasonable until the work is completed.

(3) If, under the contract, the thing or the control of it is not to be transferred to the client, the price is payable when the work has been completed and the processor has so informed the client.

IV. C. – 4:107: Risks

(1) This Article applies if the thing is destroyed or damaged due to an event which the processor could not have avoided or overcome and the processor cannot be held accountable for the destruction or damage.

(2) If, prior to the event mentioned in paragraph (1), the processor had indicated that the processor regarded the service as sufficiently completed and that the processor wished to return the thing or the control of it to the client:

(a) the processor is not required to perform again; and

(b) the client must pay the price.

The price is due when the processor returns the remains of the thing, if any, or the client indicates that the client does not want the remains. In the latter case, the processor may dispose of the remains at the client's expense. This provision does not apply if the client was entitled to refuse the return of the thing under paragraph (1) of IV. C. – 4:105 (Return of the thing processed).

(3) If the parties had agreed that the processor would be paid for each period which has elapsed, the client is obliged to pay the price for each period which has elapsed before the event mentioned in paragraph (1) occurred.

(4) If, after the event mentioned in paragraph (1), performance of the obligations under the contract is still possible for the processor:

(a) the processor still has to perform or, as the case may be, perform again;

(b) the client is only obliged to pay for the processor's performance under (a); the processor's entitlement to a price under paragraph (3) is not affected by this provision;

(c) the client is obliged to compensate the processor for the costs the processor has to incur in order to acquire materials replacing the materials supplied by the client, unless the client on being so requested by the processor supplies these materials; and

(d) if need be, the time for performance is extended in accordance with paragraph (6) of IV. C. – 2:109 (Unilateral variation of the service contract).

This paragraph is without prejudice to the client's right to terminate the contractual relationship under IV. C. – 2:111 (Client's right to terminate).

(5) If, in the situation mentioned in paragraph (1), performance of the obligations under the contract is no longer possible for the processor:

(a) the client does not have to pay for the service rendered; the processor's entitlement to a price under paragraph (3) is not affected by this provision; and

(b) the processor is obliged to return to the client the thing and the materials supplied by the client or what remains of them, unless the client indicates that the client does not want the remains. In the latter case, the processor may dispose of the remains at the client's expense.

IV. C. – 4:108: Limitation of Liability

In a contract between two businesses, a term restricting the processor's liability for non-performance to the value of the thing, had the service been performed correctly, is presumed to be fair for the purposes of II. – 9:405 (Meaning of "unfair" in contracts between businesses) except to the extent that it restricts liability for damage caused intentionally or by way of grossly negligent behaviour on the part of the processor or any person for whose actions the processor is responsible.

Chapter 5: Storage

IV. C. – 5:101: Scope

(1) This Chapter applies to contracts under which one party, the storer, undertakes to store a movable or incorporeal thing for another party, the client.

(2) This Chapter does not apply to the storage of:

(a) immovable structures;

(b) movable or incorporeal things during transportation; and

(c) money or securities (except in the circumstances mentioned in paragraph (7) of IV. C. – 5:110 (Liability of the hotel-keeper)) or rights.

IV. C. – 5:102: Storage Place and Subcontractors

(1) The storer, in so far as the storer provides the storage place, must provide a place fit for storing the thing in such a manner that the thing can be returned in the condition the client may expect.

(2) The storer may not subcontract the performance of the service without the client's consent.

IV. C. – 5:103: Protection and Use of the Thing Stored

(1) The storer must take reasonable precautions in order to prevent unnecessary deterioration, decay or depreciation of the thing stored.

(2) The storer may use the thing handed over for storage only if the client has agreed to such use.

IV. C. – 5:104: Return of the Thing Stored

(1) Without prejudice to any other obligation to return the thing, the storer must return the thing at the agreed time or, where the contractual relationship is terminated before the agreed time, within a reasonable time after being so requested by the client.

(2) The client must accept the return of the thing when the storage obligation comes to an end and when acceptance of return is properly requested by the storer.

(3) Acceptance by the client of the return of the thing does not relieve the storer wholly or partially from liability for non-performance.

(4) If the client fails to accept the return of the thing at the time provided under paragraph (2), the storer has the right to sell the thing in accordance with III. – 2:111 (Property not accepted), provided that the storer has given the client reasonable warning of the storer's intention to do so.

(5) If, during storage, the thing bears fruit, the storer must hand this fruit over when the thing is returned to the client.

(6) If, by virtue of the rules on the acquisition of ownership, the storer has become the owner of the thing, the storer must return a thing of the same kind and the same quality and quantity and transfer ownership of that thing. This Article applies with appropriate adaptations to the substituted thing.

(7) This Article applies with appropriate adaptations if a third party who has the right or authority to receive the thing requests its return.

IV. C. – 5:105: Conformity

(1) The storage of the thing does not conform with the contract unless the thing is returned in the same condition as it was in when handed over to the storer.

(2) If, given the nature of the thing or the contract, it cannot reasonably be expected that the thing is returned in the same condition, the storage of the thing does not conform with the contract if the thing is not returned in such condition as the client could reasonably expect.

(3) If, given the nature of the thing or the contract, it cannot reasonably be expected that the same thing is returned, the storage of the thing does not conform with the contract if the thing which is returned is not in the same condition as the thing which was handed over for storage, or if it is not of the same kind, quality and quantity, or if ownership of the thing is not transferred in accordance with paragraph (6) of IV. C. – 5:104 (Return of the thing stored).

IV. C. – 5:106: Payment of the Price

(1) The price is payable at the time when the thing is returned to the client in accordance with IV. C. – 5:104 (Return of the thing stored) or the client, without being entitled to do so, refuses to accept the return of the thing.

(2) The storer may withhold the thing until the client pays the price. III. – 3:401 (Right to withhold performance of reciprocal obligation) applies accordingly.

IV. C. – 5:107: Post-Storage Obligation to Inform

After the ending of the storage, the storer must inform the client of:

(a) any damage which has occurred to the thing during storage; and

(b) the necessary precautions which the client must take before using or transporting the thing, unless the client could reasonably be expected to be aware of the need for such precautions.

IV. C. – 5:108: Risks

(1) This Article applies if the thing is destroyed or damaged due to an event which the storer could not have avoided or overcome and if the storer cannot be held accountable for the destruction or damage.

(2) If, prior to the event, the storer had notified the client that the client was required to accept the return of the thing, the client must pay the price. The price is due when the storer returns the remains of the thing, if any, or the client indicates to the storer that the client does not want those remains.

(3) If, prior to the event, the storer had not notified the client that the client was required to accept the return of the thing:

(a) if the parties had agreed that the storer would be paid for each period of time which has elapsed, the client must pay the price for each period which has elapsed before the event occurred;

(b) if further performance of the obligations under the contract is still possible for the storer, the storer is required to continue performance, without prejudice to the client's right to terminate the contractual relationship under IV. C. – 2:111 (Client's right to terminate);

(c) if performance of the obligations under the contract is no longer possible for the storer the client does not have to pay for the service rendered except to the extent that the storer is entitled to a price under subparagraph (a); and the storer must return to the client the remains of the thing unless the client indicates that the client does not want those remains.

(4) If the client indicates to the storer that the client does not want the remains of the thing, the storer may dispose of the remains at the client's expense.

IV. C. – 5:109: Limitation of Liability

In a contract between two businesses, a term restricting the storer's liability for non-performance to the value of the thing is presumed to be fair for the purposes of II. – 9:405 (Meaning of "unfair" in contracts between businesses), except to the extent that it restricts liability for damage caused intentionally or by way of grossly negligent conduct on the part of the storer or any person for whose actions the storer is responsible.

IV. C. – 5:110: Liability of the Hotel-Keeper

(1) A hotel-keeper is liable as a storer for any damage to, or destruction or loss of, a thing brought to the hotel by any guest who stays at the hotel and has sleeping accommodation there.

(2) For the purposes of paragraph (1) a thing is regarded as brought to the hotel:

(a) if it is at the hotel during the time when the guest has the use of sleeping accommodation there;

(b) if the hotel-keeper or a person for whose actions the hotel-keeper is responsible takes charge of it outside the hotel during the period for which the guest has the use of the sleeping accommodation at the hotel; or

(c) if the hotel-keeper or a person for whose actions the hotel-keeper is responsible takes charge of it whether at the hotel or outside it during a reasonable period preceding or following the time when the guest has the use of sleeping accommodation at the hotel.

(3) The hotel-keeper is not liable in so far as the damage, destruction or loss is caused by:

(a) a guest or any person accompanying, employed by or visiting the guest;

(b) an impediment beyond the hotel-keeper's control; or

(c) the nature of the thing.

(4) A term excluding or limiting the liability of the hotel-keeper is unfair for the purposes of Book II, Chapter 9, Section 4 if it excludes or limits liability in a case where the hotel-keeper, or a person for whose actions the hotel-keeper is responsible, causes the damage, destruction or loss intentionally or by way of grossly negligent conduct.

(5) Except where the damage, destruction or loss is caused intentionally or by way of grossly negligent conduct of the hotel-keeper or a person for whose actions the hotel-keeper is responsible, the guest is required to inform the hotel-keeper of the damage, destruction or loss without undue delay. If the guest fails to inform the hotel-keeper without undue delay, the hotel-keeper is not liable.

(6) The hotel-keeper has the right to withhold any thing referred to in paragraph (1) until the guest has satisfied any right the hotel-keeper has against the guest with respect to accommodation, food, drink and solicited services performed for the guest in the hotel-keeper's professional capacity.

(7) This Article does not apply if and to the extent that a separate storage contract is concluded between the hotel-keeper and any guest for any thing brought to the hotel. A separate storage contract is concluded if a thing is handed over for storage to, and accepted for storage by, the hotel-keeper.

Chapter 6: Design

IV. C. – 6:101: Scope

(1) This Chapter applies to contracts under which one party, the designer, undertakes to design for another party, the client:

(a) an immovable structure which is to be constructed by or on behalf of the client; or

(b) a movable or incorporeal thing or service which is to be constructed or performed by or on behalf of the client.

(2) A contract under which one party undertakes to design and to supply a service which consists of carrying out the design is to be considered as primarily a contract for the supply of the subsequent service.

IV. C. – 6:102: Pre-contractual Duty to Warn

The designer's pre-contractual duty to warn requires in particular the designer to warn the client in so far as the designer lacks special expertise in specific problems which require the involvement of specialists.

IV. C. – 6:103: Obligation of Skill and Care

The designer's obligation of skill and care requires in particular the designer to:

(a) attune the design work to the work of other designers who contracted with the client, to enable there to be an efficient performance of all services involved;

(b) integrate the work of other designers which is necessary to ensure that the design will conform to the contract;

(c) include any information for the interpretation of the design which is necessary for a user of the design of average competence (or a specific user made known to the designer at the conclusion of the contract) to give effect to the design;

(d) enable the user of the design to give effect to the design without violation of public law rules or interference based on justified third-party rights of which the designer knows or could reasonably be expected to know; and

(e) provide a design which allows economic and technically efficient realisation.

IV. C. – 6:104: Conformity

(1) The design does not conform to the contract unless it enables the user of the design to achieve a specific result by carrying out the design with the skill and care which could reasonably be expected.

(2) The client is not entitled to invoke a remedy for non-conformity if a direction provided by the client under IV. C. – 2:107 (Directions of the client) is the cause of the non-conformity and the designer performed the obligation to warn under IV. C. – 2:108 (Contractual obligation of the service provider to warn).

IV. C. – 6:105: Handing Over of the Design

(1) In so far as the designer regards the design, or a part of it which is fit for carrying out independently from the completion of the rest of the design, as sufficiently completed and wishes to transfer the design to the client, the client must accept it within a reasonable time after being notified.

(2) The client may refuse to accept the design when it, or the relevant part of it, does not conform to the contract and such non-conformity amounts to a fundamental non-performance.

IV. C. – 6:106: Records

(1) After performance of both parties' other contractual obligations, the designer must, on request by the client, hand over all relevant documents or copies of them.

(2) The designer must store, for a reasonable time, relevant documents which are not handed over. Before destroying the documents, the designer must offer them again to the client.

IV. C. – 6:107: Limitation of Liability

In contracts between two businesses, a term restricting the designer's liability for non-performance to the value of the structure, thing or service which is to be constructed or performed by or on behalf of the client following the design, is presumed to be fair for the purposes of II. – 9:405 (Meaning of "unfair" in contracts between businesses) except to the extent that it restricts liability for damage caused intentionally or by grossly negligent conduct on the part of the designer or any person for whose actions the designer is responsible.

Chapter 7: Information and Advice

IV. C. – 7:101: Scope

(1) This Chapter applies to contracts under which one party, the provider, undertakes to provide information or advice to another party, the client.

(2) This Chapter does not apply in relation to treatment in so far as Chapter 8 (Treatment) contains more specific rules on the obligation to inform.

(3) In the remainder of this Chapter any reference to information includes a reference to advice.

IV. C. – 7:102: Obligation to Collect Preliminary Data

(1) The provider must, in so far as this may reasonably be considered necessary for the performance of the service, collect data about:

(a) the particular purpose for which the client requires the information;

(b) the client's preferences and priorities in relation to the information;

(c) the decision the client can be expected to make on the basis of the information; and

(d) the personal situation of the client.

(2) In case the information is intended to be passed on to a group of persons, the data to be collected must relate to the purposes, preferences, priorities and personal situations that can reasonably be expected from individuals within such a group.

(3) In so far as the provider must obtain data from the client, the provider must explain what the client is required to supply.

IV. C. – 7:103: Obligation to Acquire and Use Expert Knowledge

The provider must acquire and use the expert knowledge to which the provider has or should have access as a professional information provider or adviser, in so far as this may reasonably be considered necessary for the performance of the service.

IV. C. – 7:104: Obligation of Skill and Care

(1) The provider's obligation of skill and care requires in particular the provider to:

(a) take reasonable measures to ensure that the client understands the content of the information;

(b) act with the care and skill that a reasonable information provider would demonstrate under the circumstances when providing evaluative information; and

(c) in any case where the client is expected to make a decision on the basis of the information, inform the client of the risks involved, in so far as such risks could reasonably be expected to influence the client's decision.

(2) When the provider expressly or impliedly undertakes to provide the client with a recommendation to enable the client to make a subsequent decision, the provider must:

(a) base the recommendation on a skilful analysis of the expert knowledge to be collected in relation to the purposes, priorities, preferences and personal situation of the client;

(b) inform the client of alternatives the provider can personally provide relating to the subsequent decision and of their advantages and risks, as compared with those of the recommended decision; and

(c) inform the client of other alternatives the provider cannot personally provide, unless the provider expressly informs the client that only a limited range of alternatives is offered or this is apparent from the situation.

IV. C. – 7:105: Conformity

(1) The provider must provide information which is of the quantity, quality and description required by the contract.

(2) The factual information provided by the information provider to the client must be a correct description of the actual situation described.

IV. C. – 7:106: Records

In so far as this may reasonably be considered necessary, having regard to the interest of the client, the provider must keep records regarding the information provided in accordance with this Chapter and make such records or excerpts from them available to the client on reasonable request.

IV. C. – 7:107: Conflict of Interest

(1) When the provider expressly or impliedly undertakes to provide the client with a recommendation to enable the client to make a subsequent decision, the provider must disclose any possible conflict of interest which might influence the performance of the provider's obligations.

(2) So long as the contractual obligations have not been completely performed, the provider may not enter into a relationship with another party which may give rise to a possible conflict with the interests of the client, without full disclosure to the client and the client's explicit or implicit consent.

IV. C. – 7:108: Influence of Ability of the Client

(1) The involvement in the supply of the service of other persons on the client's behalf or the mere competence of the client does not relieve the provider of any obligation under this Chapter.

(2) The provider is relieved of those obligations if the client already has knowledge of the information or if the client has reason to know of the information.

(3) For the purpose of paragraph (2), the client has reason to know if the information should be obvious to the client without investigation.

IV. C. – 7:109: Causation

If the provider knows or could reasonably be expected to know that a subsequent decision will be based on the information to be provided, and if the client makes such a decision and suffers loss as a result, any non-performance of an obligation under the contract by the provider is presumed to have caused the loss if the client proves that, if the provider had provided all information required, it would have been reasonable for the client to have seriously considered making an alternative decision.

Chapter 8: Treatment

IV. C. – 8:101: Scope

(1) This Chapter applies to contracts under which one party, the treatment provider, undertakes to provide medical treatment for another party, the patient.

(2) It applies with appropriate adaptations to contracts under which the treatment provider undertakes to provide any other service in order to change the physical or mental condition of a person.

(3) Where the patient is not the contracting party, the patient is regarded as a third party on whom the contract confers rights corresponding to the obligations of the treatment provider imposed by this Chapter.

IV. C. – 8:102: Preliminary Assessment

The treatment provider must, in so far as this may reasonably be considered necessary for the performance of the service:

(a) interview the patient about the patient's health condition, symptoms, previous illnesses, allergies, previous or other current treatment and the patient's preferences and priorities in relation to the treatment;

(b) carry out the examinations necessary to diagnose the health condition of the patient; and

(c) consult with any other treatment providers involved in the treatment of the patient.

IV. C. – 8:103: Obligations Regarding Instruments, Medicines, Materials, Installations and Premises

(1) The treatment provider must use instruments, medicines, materials, installations and premises which are of at least the quality demanded by accepted and sound professional practice, which conform to applicable statutory rules, and which are fit to achieve the particular purpose for which they are to be used.

(2) The parties may not, to the detriment of the patient, exclude the application of this Article or derogate from or vary its effects.

IV. C. – 8:104: Obligation of Skill and Care

(1) The treatment provider's obligation of skill and care requires in particular the treatment provider to provide the patient with the care and skill which a reasonable treatment provider exercising and professing care and skill would demonstrate under the given circumstances.

(2) If the treatment provider lacks the experience or skill to treat the patient with the required degree of skill and care, the treatment provider must refer the patient to a treatment provider who can.

(3) The parties may not, to the detriment of the patient, exclude the application of this Article or derogate from or vary its effects.

IV. C. – 8:105: Obligation to Inform

(1) The treatment provider must, in order to give the patient a free choice regarding treatment, inform the patient about, in particular:

(a) the patient's existing state of health;

(b) the nature of the proposed treatment;

(c) the advantages of the proposed treatment;

(d) the risks of the proposed treatment;

(e) the alternatives to the proposed treatment, and their advantages and risks as compared to those of the proposed treatment; and

(f) the consequences of not having treatment.

(2) The treatment provider must, in any case, inform the patient about any risk or alternative which might reasonably influence the patient's decision on whether to give consent to the proposed treatment or not. It is presumed that a risk might reasonably influence that decision if its materialisation would lead to serious detriment to the patient. Unless otherwise provided, the obligation to inform is subject to the provisions of Chapter 7 (Information and Advice).

(3) The information must be provided in a way understandable to the patient.

IV. C. – 8:106: Obligation to Inform in Case of Unnecessary or Experimental Treatment

(1) If the treatment is not necessary for the preservation or improvement of the patient's health, the treatment provider must disclose all known risks.

(2) If the treatment is experimental, the treatment provider must disclose all information regarding the objectives of the experiment, the nature of the treatment, its advantages and risks and the alternatives, even if only potential.

(3) The parties may not, to the detriment of the patient, exclude the application of this Article or derogate from or vary its effects.

IV. C. – 8:107: Exceptions to the Obligation to Inform

(1) Information which would normally have to be provided by virtue of the obligation to inform may be withheld from the patient:

(a) if there are objective reasons to believe that it would seriously and negatively influence the patient's health or life; or

(b) if the patient expressly states a wish not to be informed, provided that the non-disclosure of the information does not endanger the health or safety of third parties.

(2) The obligation to inform need not be performed where treatment must be provided in an emergency. In such a case the treatment provider must, so far as possible, provide the information later.

IV. C. – 8:108: Obligation Not to Treat Without Consent

(1) The treatment provider must not carry out treatment unless the patient has given prior informed consent to it.

(2) The patient may revoke consent at any time.

(3) In so far as the patient is incapable of giving consent, the treatment provider must not carry out treatment unless:

(a) informed consent has been obtained from a person or institution legally entitled to take decisions regarding the treatment on behalf of the patient; or

(b) any rules or procedures enabling treatment to be lawfully given without such consent have been complied with; or

(c) the treatment must be provided in an emergency.

(4) In the situation described in paragraph (3), the treatment provider must not carry out treatment without considering, so far as possible, the opinion of the incapable patient with regard to the treatment and any such opinion expressed by the patient before becoming incapable.

(5) In the situation described in paragraph (3), the treatment provider may carry out only such treatment as is intended to improve the health condition of the patient.

(6) In the situation described in paragraph (2) of IV. C. – 8:106 (Obligation to inform in case of unnecessary or experimental treatment), consent must be given in an express and specific way.

(7) The parties may not, to the detriment of the patient, exclude the application of this Article or derogate from or vary its effects.

IV. C. – 8:109: Records

(1) The treatment provider must create adequate records of the treatment. Such records must include, in particular, information collected in any preliminary interviews, examinations or consultations, information regarding the consent of the patient and information regarding the treatment performed.

(2) The treatment provider must, on reasonable request:

(a) give the patient, or if the patient is incapable of giving consent, the person or institution legally entitled to take decisions on behalf of the patient, access to the records; and

(b) answer, in so far as reasonable, questions regarding the interpretation of the records.

(3) If the patient has suffered injury and claims that it is a result of non-performance by the treatment provider of the obligation of skill and care and the treatment provider fails to comply with paragraph (2), non-performance of the obligation of skill and care and a causal link between such non-performance and the injury are presumed.

(4) The treatment provider must keep the records, and give information about their interpretation, during a reasonable time of at least 10 years after the treatment has ended, depending on the usefulness of these records for the patient or the patient's heirs or representatives and for future treatments. Records which can reasonably be expected to be important after the reasonable time must be kept by the treatment provider after that time. If for any reason the treatment provider ceases activity, the records must be deposited or delivered to the patient for future consultation.

(5) The parties may not, to the detriment of the patient, exclude the application of paragraphs (1) to (4) or derogate from or vary their effects.

(6) The treatment provider may not disclose information about the patient or other persons involved in the patient's treatment to third parties unless disclosure is necessary in order to protect third parties or the public interest. The treatment provider may use the records in an anonymous way for statistical, educational or scientific purposes.

IV. C. – 8:110: Remedies for Non-Performance

With regard to any non-performance of an obligation under a contract for treatment, Book III, Chapter 3 (Remedies for Non-performance) and IV. C. – 2:111 (Client's right to terminate) apply with the following adaptations:

(a) the treatment provider may not withhold performance or terminate the contractual relationship under that Chapter if this would seriously endanger the health of the patient; and

(b) in so far as the treatment provider has the right to withhold performance or to terminate the contractual relationship and is planning to exercise that right, the treatment provider must refer the patient to another treatment provider.

IV. C. – 8:111: Obligations of Treatment-Providing Organisations

(1) If, in the process of performance of the obligations under the treatment contract, activities take place in a hospital or on the premises of another treatment-providing organisation, and the

hospital or that other treatment-providing organisation is not a party to the treatment contract, it must make clear to the patient that it is not the contracting party.

(2) Where the treatment provider cannot be identified, the hospital or treatment-providing organisation in which the treatment took place is treated as the treatment provider unless the hospital or treatment-providing organisation informs the patient, within a reasonable time, of the identity of the treatment provider.

(3) The parties may not, to the detriment of the patient, exclude the application of this Article or derogate from or vary its effects.

Part D. Mandate Contracts

Chapter 1: General Provisions

IV. D. – 1:101: Scope

(1) This Part of Book IV applies to contracts and other juridical acts under which a person, the agent, is authorised and instructed (mandated) by another person, the principal:

(a) to conclude a contract between the principal and a third party or otherwise directly affect the legal position of the principal in relation to a third party;

(b) to conclude a contract with a third party, or do another juridical act in relation to a third party, on behalf of the principal but in such a way that the agent and not the principal is a party to the contract or other juridical act; or

(c) to take steps which are meant to lead to, or facilitate, the conclusion of a contract between the principal and a third party or the doing of another juridical act which would affect the legal position of the principal in relation to a third party.

(2) It applies where the agent undertakes to act on behalf of, and in accordance with the instructions of, the principal and, with appropriate adaptations, where the agent is merely authorised but does not undertake to act, but nevertheless does act.

(3) It applies where the agent is to be paid a price and, with appropriate adaptations, where the agent is not to be paid a price.

(4) It applies only to the internal relationship between the principal and the agent (the mandate relationship). It does not apply to the relationship between the principal and the third party or the relationship (if any) between the agent and the third party.

(5) Contracts to which this Part applies and to which Part C (Services) also applies are to be regarded as falling primarily under this Part.

(6) This Part does not apply to contracts pertaining to investment services and activities as defined by Directive 2004/39/EC, OJ 2004 L 145/1, as subsequently amended or replaced.

IV. D. – 1:102: Definitions

In this Part;

(a) the 'mandate' of the agent is the authorisation and instruction given by the principal as modified by any subsequent direction;

(b) the 'mandate contract' is the contract under which the agent is authorised and instructed to act, and any reference to the mandate contract includes a reference to any other juridical act by which the agent is authorised and instructed to act;

(c) the 'prospective contract' is the contract the agent is authorised and instructed to conclude, negotiate or facilitate, and any reference to the prospective contract includes a reference to any other juridical act which the agent is authorised and instructed to do, negotiate or facilitate;

(d) a mandate for direct representation is a mandate under which the agent is to act in the name of the principal, or otherwise in such a way as to indicate an intention to affect the principal's legal position;

(e) a mandate for indirect representation is a mandate under which the agent is to act in the agent's own name or otherwise in such a way as not to indicate an intention to affect the principal's legal position;

(f) a "direction" is a decision by the principal pertaining to the performance of the obligations under the mandate contract or to the contents of the prospective contract that is given at the time the mandate contract is concluded or, in accordance with the mandate, at a later moment;

(g) the "third party" is the party with whom the prospective contract is to be concluded, negotiated or facilitated by the agent;

(h) the "revocation" of the mandate of the agent is the recall by the principal of the mandate, so that it no longer has effect.

IV. D. – 1:103: Duration of the Mandate Contract

A mandate contract may be concluded:

(a) for an indefinite period of time;

(b) for a fixed period; or

(c) for a particular task.

IV. D. – 1:104: Revocation of the Mandate

(1) Unless the following Article applies, the mandate of the agent can be revoked by the principal at any time by giving notice to the agent.

(2) The termination of the mandate relationship has the effect of a revocation of the mandate of the agent.

(3) The parties may not, to the detriment of the principal, exclude the application of this Article or derogate from or vary its effects, unless the requirements of the following Article are met.

IV. D. – 1:105: Irrevocable Mandate

(1) In derogation of the preceding Article, the mandate of the agent cannot be revoked by the principal if the mandate is given:

(a) in order to safeguard a legitimate interest of the agent other than the interest in the payment of the price; or

(b) in the common interest of the parties to another legal relationship, whether or not these parties are all parties to the mandate contract, and the irrevocability of the mandate of the agent is meant to properly safeguard the interest of one or more of these parties.

(2) The mandate may nevertheless be revoked if:

(a) the mandate is irrevocable under paragraph (1)(a) and:

 (i) the contractual relationship from which the legitimate interest of the agent originates is terminated for non-performance by the agent; or

 (ii) there is a fundamental non-performance by the agent of the obligations under the mandate contract; or

 (iii) there is an extraordinary and serious reason for the principal to terminate under IV. D. – 6:103 (Termination by principal for extraordinary and serious reason); or

(b) the mandate is irrevocable under paragraph (1)(b) and:

(i) the parties in whose interest the mandate is irrevocable have agreed to the revocation of the mandate;

(ii) the relationship referred to in paragraph (1)(b) is terminated;

(iii) the agent commits a fundamental non-performance of the obligations under the mandate contract, provided that the agent is replaced without undue delay by another agent in conformity with the terms regulating the legal relationship between the principal and the other party or parties; or

(iv) there is an extraordinary and serious reason for the principal to terminate under IV. D. – 6:103 (Termination by principal for extraordinary and serious reason), provided that the agent is replaced without undue delay by another agent in conformity with the terms regulating the legal relationship between the principal and the other party or parties.

(3) Where the revocation of the mandate is not allowed under this Article, a notice of revocation is without effect.

(4) This Article does not apply if the mandate relationship is terminated under Chapter 7 of this Part.

Chapter 2: Main Obligations of the Principal

IV. D. – 2:101: Obligation to Co-operate

The obligation to co-operate under III. – 1:104 (Co-operation) requires the principal in particular to:

(a) answer requests by the agent for information in so far as such information is needed to allow the agent to perform the obligations under the mandate contract;

(b) give a direction regarding the performance of the obligations under the mandate contract in so far as this is required under the mandate contract or follows from a request for a direction under IV. D. – 4:102 (Request for a direction).

IV. D. – 2:102: Price

(1) The principal must pay a price if the agent performs the obligations under the mandate contract in the course of a business, unless the principal expected and could reasonably have expected the agent to perform the obligations otherwise than in exchange for a price.

(2) The price is payable when the mandated task has been completed and the agent has given account of that to the principal.

(3) If the parties had agreed on payment of a price for services rendered, the mandate relationship has terminated and the mandated task has not been completed, the price is payable as of the moment the agent has given account of the performance of the obligations under the mandate contract.

(4) When the mandate is for the conclusion of a prospective contract and the principal has concluded the prospective contract directly or another person appointed by the principal has concluded the prospective contract on the principal's behalf, the agent is entitled to the price or a proportionate part of it if the conclusion of the prospective contract can be attributed in full or in part to the agent's performance of the obligations under the mandate contract.

(5) When the mandate is for the conclusion of a prospective contract and the prospective contract is concluded after the mandate relationship has terminated, the principal must pay the price if payment of a price based solely on the conclusion of the prospective contract was agreed and:

(a) the conclusion of the prospective contract is mainly the result of the agent's efforts; and

(b) the prospective contract is concluded within a reasonable period after the mandate relationship has terminated.

IV. D. – 2:103: Expenses Incurred by Agent

(1) When the agent is entitled to a price, the price is presumed to include the reimbursement of the expenses the agent has incurred in the performance of the obligations under the mandate contract.

(2) When the agent is not entitled to a price or when the parties have agreed that the expenses will be paid separately, the principal must reimburse the agent for the expenses the agent has incurred in the performance of the obligations under the mandate contract, when and in so far as the agent acted reasonably when incurring the expenses.

(3) The agent is entitled to reimbursement of expenses under paragraph (2) as from the time when the expenses are incurred and the agent has given account of the expenses.

(4) If the mandate relationship has terminated and the result on which the agent's remuneration is dependent is not achieved, the agent is entitled to reimbursement of reasonable expenses the agent has incurred in the performance of the obligations under the mandate contract. Paragraph (3) applies accordingly.

Chapter 3: Performance by the Agent

Section 1: Main Obligations of Agent

IV. D. – 3:101: Obligation to Act in Accordance with Mandate

At all stages of the mandate relationship the agent must act in accordance with the mandate.

IV. D. – 3:102: Obligation to Act in Interests of Principal

(1) The agent must act in accordance with the interests of the principal, in so far as these have been communicated to the agent or the agent could reasonably be expected to be aware of them.

(2) Where the agent is not sufficiently aware of the principal's interests to enable the agent to properly perform the obligations under the mandate contract, the agent must request information from the principal.

IV. D. – 3:103: Obligation of Skill and Care

(1) The agent has an obligation to perform the obligations under the mandate contract with the care and skill that the principal is entitled to expect under the circumstances.

(2) If the agent professes a higher standard of care and skill the agent has an obligation to exercise that care and skill.

(3) If the agent is, or purports to be, a member of a group of professional agents for which standards exist that have been set by a relevant authority or by that group itself, the agent must exercise the care and skill expressed in these standards.

(4) In determining the care and skill the principal is entitled to expect, regard is to be had, among other things, to:

(a) the nature, the magnitude, the frequency and the foreseeability of the risks involved in the performance of the obligations;

(b) whether the obligations are performed by a non-professional or gratuitously;

(c) the amount of the remuneration for the performance of the obligations; and

(d) the time reasonably available for the performance of the obligations.

Section 2: Consequences of Acting Beyond Mandate

IV. D. – 3:201: Acting Beyond Mandate

(1) The agent may act in a way not covered by the mandate if:

(a) the agent has reasonable ground for so acting on behalf of the principal;

(b) the agent does not have a reasonable opportunity to discover the principal's wishes in the particular circumstances; and

(c) the agent does not know and could not reasonably be expected to know that the act in the particular circumstances is against the principal's wishes.

(2) An act within paragraph (1) has the same consequences as between the agent and the principal as an act covered by the mandate.

IV. D. – 3:202: Consequences of Ratification

Where, in circumstances not covered by the preceding Article, an agent has acted beyond the mandate in concluding a contract on behalf of the principal, ratification of that contract by the principal absolves the agent from liability to the principal, unless the principal without undue delay after ratification notifies the agent that the principal reserves remedies for the non-performance by the agent.

Section 3: Mandate Normally Not Exclusive

IV. D. – 3:301: Exclusivity Not Presumed

The principal is free to conclude, negotiate or facilitate the prospective contract directly or to appoint another agent to do so.

IV. D. – 3:302: Subcontracting

(1) The agent may subcontract the performance of the obligations under the mandate contract in whole or in part without the principal's consent, unless personal performance is required by the contract.

(2) Any subcontractor so engaged by the agent must be of adequate competence.

(3) In accordance with III. – 2:106 (Performance entrusted to another) the agent remains responsible for performance.

Section 4: Obligation to Inform Principal

IV. D. – 3:401: Information About Progress of Performance

During the performance of the obligations under the mandate contract the agent must in so far as is reasonable under the circumstances inform the principal of the existence of, and the progress in, the negotiations or other steps leading to the possible conclusion or facilitation of the prospective contract.

IV. D. – 3:402: Accounting to the Principal

(1) The agent must without undue delay inform the principal of the completion of the mandated task.

(2) The agent must give an account to the principal:

(a) of the manner in which the obligations under the mandate contract have been performed; and

(b) of money spent or received or expenses incurred by the agent in performing those obligations.

(3) Paragraph (2) applies with appropriate modifications if the mandate relationship is terminated in accordance with Chapters 6 and 7 and the obligations under the mandate contract have not been fully performed.

IV. D. – 3:403: Communication of Identity of Third Party

(1) An agent who concludes the prospective contract with a third party must communicate the name and address of the third party to the principal on the principal's demand.

(2) In the case of a mandate for indirect representation paragraph (1) applies only if the agent has become insolvent.

Chapter 4: Directions and Changes

Section 1: Directions

IV. D. – 4:101: Directions Given by Principal

(1) The principal is entitled to give directions to the agent.

(2) The agent must follow directions by the principal.

(3) The agent must warn the principal if the direction:

(a) has the effect that the performance of the obligations under the mandate contract would become significantly more expensive or take significantly more time than agreed upon in the mandate contract; or

(b) is inconsistent with the purpose of the mandate contract or may otherwise be detrimental to the interests of the principal.

(4) Unless the principal revokes the direction without undue delay after having been so warned by the agent, the direction is to be regarded as a change of the mandate contract under IV. D. – 4:201 (Changes of the mandate contract).

IV. D. – 4:102: Request for a Direction

(1) The agent must ask for a direction on obtaining information which requires the principal to make a decision pertaining to the performance of the obligations under the mandate contract or the content of the prospective contract.

(2) The agent must ask for a direction if the mandated task is the conclusion of a prospective contract and the mandate contract does not determine whether the mandate is for direct representation or indirect representation.

IV. D. – 4:103: Consequences of Failure to Give a Direction

(1) If the principal fails to give a direction when required to do so under the mandate contract or under paragraph (1) of IV. D. – 4:102 (Request for a direction), the agent may, in so far as relevant, resort to any of the remedies under Book III, Chapter 3 (Remedies for Non-performance) or base performance upon the expectations, preferences and priorities the principal might reasonably be expected to have, given the information and directions that have been gathered.

(2) Where the agent bases performance upon the expectations, preferences and priorities the principal might reasonably be expected to have, the agent has a right to a proportionate adjustment of the price and of the time allowed or required for the conclusion of the prospective contract.

(3) If the principal fails to give a direction under paragraph (2) of IV. D. – 4:102 (Request for a direction), the agent may choose direct representation or indirect representation or may withhold performance under III. – 3:401 (Right to withhold performance of reciprocal obligation).

(4) The adjusted price that is to be paid under paragraph (2) must be reasonable and is to be determined using the same methods of calculation as were used to establish the original price for the performance of the obligations under the mandate contract.

IV. D. – 4:104: No Time to Ask or Wait for Direction

(1) If the agent is required to ask for a direction under IV. D. – 4:102 (Request for a direction) but needs to act before being able to contact the principal and to ask for a direction, or needs to act before the direction is given, the agent may base performance upon the expectations, preferences and priorities the principal might reasonably be expected to have, given the information and directions that have been gathered.

(2) In the situation referred to in paragraph (1), the agent has a right to a proportionate adjustment of the price and of the time allowed or required for the performance of the obligations under the mandate contract in so far as such an adjustment is reasonable given the circumstances of the case.

Section 2: Changes of the Mandate Contract

IV. D. – 4:201: Changes of the Mandate Contract

(1) The mandate contract is changed if the principal:

(a) significantly changes the mandate of the agent;

(b) does not revoke a direction without undue delay after having been warned in accordance with paragraph (3) of IV. D. – 4:101 (Directions given by principal).

(2) In the case of a change of the mandate contract under paragraph (1) the agent is entitled:

(a) to a proportionate adjustment of the price and of the time allowed or required for the performance of the obligations under the mandate contract; or

(b) to damages in accordance with III. – 3:702 (General measure of damages) to put the agent as nearly as possible into the position in which the agent would have been if the mandate contract had not been changed.

(3) In the case of a change of the mandate contract under paragraph (1) the agent may also terminate the mandate relationship by giving notice of termination for an extraordinary and serious reason under IV. D. – 6:105 (Termination by agent for extraordinary and serious reason), unless the change is minor or is to the agent's advantage.

(4) The adjusted price that is to be paid under paragraph (2)(a) must be reasonable and is to be determined using the same methods of calculation as were used to establish the original price for the performance of the obligations under the mandate contract.

Chapter 5: Conflicts of Interests

IV. D. – 5:101: Self-Contracting

(1) The agent may not become the principal's counterparty to the prospective contract.

(2) The agent may nevertheless become the counterparty if:

(a) this is agreed by the parties in the mandate contract;

(b) the agent has disclosed an intention to become the counterparty and:

  (i) the principal subsequently expresses consent; or

  (ii) the principal does not object to the agent becoming the counterparty after having been requested to indicate consent or a refusal of consent;

(c) the principal otherwise knew, or could reasonably be expected to have known, of the agent becoming the counterparty and the principal did not object within a reasonable time; or

(d) the content of the prospective contract is so precisely determined in the mandate contract that there is no risk that the interests of the principal may be disregarded.

(3) If the principal is a consumer, the agent may only become the counterparty if:

(a) the agent has disclosed that information and the principal has given express consent to the agent becoming the counterparty to the particular prospective contract; or

(b) the content of the prospective contract is so precisely determined in the mandate contract that there is no risk that the interests of the principal may be disregarded.

(4) The parties may not, to the detriment of the principal, exclude the application of paragraph (3) or derogate from or vary its effects.

(5) If the agent has become the counterparty, the agent is not entitled to a price for services rendered as an agent.

IV. D. – 5:102: Double Mandate

(1) The agent may not act as the agent of both the principal and the principal's counterparty to the prospective contract.

(2) The agent may nevertheless act as the agent of both the principal and the counterparty if:

(a) this is agreed by the parties in the mandate contract;

(b) the agent has disclosed an intention to act as the agent of the counterparty and the principal:

(i) subsequently expresses consent; or

(ii) does not object to the agent acting as the agent of the counterparty after having been requested to indicate consent or a refusal of consent;

(c) the principal otherwise knew, or could reasonably be expected to have known, of the agent acting as the agent of the counterparty and the principal did not object within a reasonable time; or

(d) the content of the prospective contract is so precisely determined in the mandate contract that there is no risk that the interests of the principal may be disregarded.

(3) If the principal is a consumer, the agent may only act as the agent of both the principal and of the counterparty if:

(a) the agent has disclosed that information and the principal has given express consent to the agent acting also as the agent of the counterparty to the particular prospective contract; or

(b) the content of the prospective contract is so precisely determined in the mandate contract that there is no risk that the interests of the principal may be disregarded.

(4) The parties may not, to the detriment of the principal, exclude the application of paragraph (3) or derogate from or vary its effects.

(5) If and in so far as the agent has acted in accordance with the previous paragraphs, the agent is entitled to the price.

Chapter 6: Termination by Notice Other than for Non-Performance

IV. D. – 6:101: Termination by Notice in General

(1) Either party may terminate the mandate relationship at any time by giving notice to the other.

(2) For the purposes of paragraph (1), a revocation of the mandate of the agent is treated as termination.

(3) Termination of the mandate relationship is not effective if the mandate of the agent is irrevocable under IV. D. – 1:105 (Irrevocable mandate).

(4) The effects of termination are governed by III. – 1:109 (Variation or termination by notice) paragraph (3).

(5) When the party giving the notice was justified in terminating the relationship no damages are payable for so doing.

(6) When the party giving the notice was not justified in terminating the relationship, the termination is nevertheless effective but the other party is entitled to damages in accordance with the rules in Book III.

(7) For the purposes of this Article the party giving the notice is justified in terminating the relationship if that party:

(a) was entitled to terminate the relationship under the express terms of the contract and observed any requirements laid down in the contract for doing so;

(b) was entitled to terminate the relationship under Book III, Chapter 3, Section 5 (Termination); or

(c) was entitled to terminate the relationship under any other Article of the present Chapter and observed any requirements laid down in such Article for doing so.

IV. D. – 6:102: Termination by Principal When Relationship Is to Last for Indefinite Period or When Mandate Is for a Particular Task

(1) The principal may terminate the mandate relationship at any time by giving notice of reasonable length if the mandate contract has been concluded for an indefinite period or for a particular task.

(2) Paragraph (1) does not apply if the mandate is irrevocable.

(3) The parties may not, to the detriment of the principal, exclude the application of this Article or derogate from or vary its effects, unless the conditions set out under IV. D. – 1:105 (Irrevocable mandate) are met.

IV. D. – 6:103: Termination by Principal for Extraordinary and Serious Reason

(1) The principal may terminate the mandate relationship by giving notice for extraordinary and serious reason.

(2) No period of notice is required.

(3) For the purposes of this Article, the death or incapacity of the person who, at the time of conclusion of the mandate contract, the parties had intended to perform the agent's obligations under the mandate contract, constitutes an extraordinary and serious reason.

(4) This Article applies with appropriate adaptations if the successors of the principal terminate the mandate relationship in accordance with IV. D. – 7:102 (Death of the principal).

(5) The parties may not, to the detriment of the principal or the principal's successors, exclude the application of this Article or derogate from or vary its effects.

IV. D. – 6:104: Termination by Agent When Relationship Is to Last for Indefinite Period or When it Is Gratuitous

(1) The agent may terminate the mandate relationship at any time by giving notice of reasonable length if the mandate contract has been concluded for an indefinite period.

(2) The agent may terminate the mandate relationship by giving notice of reasonable length if the agent is to represent the principal otherwise than in exchange for a price.

(3) The parties may not, to the detriment of the agent, exclude the application of paragraph (1) of this Article or derogate from or vary its effects.

IV. D. – 6:105: Termination by Agent for Extraordinary and Serious Reason

(1) The agent may terminate the mandate relationship by giving notice for extraordinary and serious reason.

(2) No period of notice is required.

(3) For the purposes of this Article an extraordinary and serious reason includes:

(a) a change of the mandate contract under IV. D. – 4:201 (Changes of the mandate contract);

(b) the death or incapacity of the principal; and

(c) the death or incapacity of the person who, at the time of conclusion of the mandate contract, the parties had intended to perform the agent's obligations under the mandate contract.

(4) The parties may not, to the detriment of the agent, exclude the application of this Article or derogate from or vary its effects.

Chapter 7: Other Grounds for Termination

IV. D. – 7:101: Conclusion of Prospective Contract by Principal or Other Agent

(1) If the mandate contract was concluded solely for the conclusion of a specific prospective contract the mandate relationship terminates when the principal or another agent appointed by the principal has concluded the prospective contract.

(2) In such a case, the conclusion of the prospective contract is treated as a notice under IV. D. – 6:101 (Termination by notice in general).

IV. D. – 7:102: Death of the Principal

(1) The death of the principal does not end the mandate relationship.

(2) Both the agent and the successors of the principal may terminate the mandate relationship by giving notice of termination for extraordinary and serious reason under IV. D. – 6:103 (Termination by principal for extraordinary and serious reason) or IV. D. – 6:105 (Termination by agent for extraordinary and serious reason).

IV. D. – 7:103: Death of the Agent

(1) The death of the agent ends the mandate relationship.

(2) The expenses and any other payments due at the time of death remain payable.

Part E. Commercial Agency, Franchise and Distributorship

Chapter 1: General Provisions

Section 1: Scope

IV. E. – 1:101: Contracts Covered

(1) This Part of Book IV applies to contracts for the establishment and regulation of a commercial agency, franchise or distributorship and with appropriate adaptations to other contracts under which a party engaged in business independently is to use skills and efforts to bring another party's products on to the market.

(2) In this Part, "products" includes goods and services.

Section 2: Other General Provisions

IV. E. – 1:201: Priority Rules

In the case of any conflict:

(a) the rules in this Part prevail over the rules in Part D (Mandate); and

(b) the rules in Chapters 3 to 5 of this Part prevail over the rules in Chapter 2 of this Part.

Chapter 2: Rules Applying to All Contracts Within the Scope of this Part

Section 1: Pre-Contractual

IV. E. – 2:101: Pre-contractual Information Duty

A party who is engaged in negotiations for a contract within the scope of this Part has a duty to provide the other party, a reasonable time before the contract is concluded and so far as required by good commercial practice, with such information as is sufficient to enable the other party to decide on a reasonably informed basis whether or not to enter into a contract of the type and on the terms under consideration.

Section 2: Obligations of the Parties

IV. E. – 2:201: Co-Operation

The parties to a contract within the scope of this Part of Book IV must collaborate actively and loyally and co-ordinate their respective efforts in order to achieve the objectives of the contract.

IV. E. – 2:202: Information During the Performance

During the period of the contractual relationship each party must provide the other in due time with all the information which the first party has and the second party needs in order to achieve the objectives of the contract.

IV. E. – 2:203: Confidentiality

(1) A party who receives confidential information from the other must keep such information confidential and must not disclose the information to third parties either during or after the period of the contractual relationship.

(2) A party who receives confidential information from the other must not use such information for purposes other than the objectives of the contract.

(3) Any information which a party already possessed or which has been disclosed to the general public, and any information which must necessarily be disclosed to customers as a result of the operation of the business is not regarded as confidential information for this purpose.

Section 3: Termination of Contractual Relationship

IV. E. – 2:301: Contract for a Definite Period

A party is free not to renew a contract for a definite period. If a party has given notice in due time that it wishes to renew the contract, the contract will be renewed for an indefinite period unless the other party gives that party notice, not later than a reasonable time before the expiry of the contract period, that it is not to be renewed.

IV. E. – 2:302: Contract for an Indefinite Period

(1) Either party to a contract for an indefinite period may terminate the contractual relationship by giving notice to the other.

(2) If the notice provides for termination after a period of reasonable length no damages are payable under IV. E. – 2:303 (Damages for termination with inadequate notice). If the notice provides for immediate termination or termination after a period which is not of reasonable length damages are payable under that Article.

(3) Whether a period of notice is of reasonable length depends, among other factors, on:

(a) the time the contractual relationship has lasted;

(b) reasonable investments made;

(c) the time it will take to find a reasonable alternative; and

(d) usages.

(4) A period of notice of one month for each year during which the contractual relationship has lasted, with a maximum of 36 months, is presumed to be reasonable.

(5) The period of notice for the principal, the franchisor or the supplier is to be no shorter than one month for the first year, two months for the second, three months for the third, four months for the fourth, five months for the fifth and six months for the sixth and subsequent years during which the contractual relationship has lasted. Parties may not exclude the application of this provision or derogate from or vary its effects.

(6) Agreements on longer periods than those laid down in paragraphs (4) and (5) are valid provided that the agreed period to be observed by the principal, franchisor or supplier is no shorter than that to be observed by the commercial agent, the franchisee or the distributor.

(7) In relation to contracts within the scope of this Part, the rules in this Article replace those in paragraph (2) of III. – 1:109 (Variation or termination by notice). Paragraph (3) of that Article governs the effects of termination.

IV. E. – 2:303: Damages for Termination with Inadequate Notice

(1) Where a party terminates a contractual relationship under IV. E. – 2:302 (Contract for an indefinite period) but does not give a reasonable period of notice the other party is entitled to damages.

(2) The general measure of damages is such sum as corresponds to the benefit which the other party would have obtained during the extra period for which the relationship would have lasted if a reasonable period of notice had been given.

(3) The yearly benefit is presumed to be equal to the average benefit which the aggrieved party has obtained from the contract during the previous 3 years or, if the contractual relationship has lasted for a shorter period, during that period.

(4) The general rules on damages for non-performance in Book III, Chapter 3, Section 7 apply with any appropriate adaptations.

IV. E. – 2:304: Termination for Non-Performance

(1) Any term of a contract within the scope of this Part whereby a party may terminate the contractual relationship for non-performance which is not fundamental is without effect.

(2) The parties may not exclude the application of this Article or derogate from or vary its effects.

IV. E. – 2:305: Indemnity for Goodwill

(1) When the contractual relationship comes to an end for any reason (including termination by either party for fundamental non-performance), a party is entitled to an indemnity from the other party for goodwill if and to the extent that:

(a) the first party has significantly increased the other party's volume of business and the other party continues to derive substantial benefits from that business; and

(b) the payment of the indemnity is reasonable.

(2) The grant of an indemnity does not prevent a party from seeking damages under IV. E. – 2:303 (Damages for termination with inadequate notice).

IV. E. – 2:306: Stock, Spare Parts and Materials

If the contract is avoided, or the contractual relationship terminated, by either party, the party whose products are being brought on to the market must repurchase the other party's remaining stock, spare parts and materials at a reasonable price, unless the other party can reasonably resell them.

Section 4: Other General Provisions

IV. E. – 2:401: Right of Retention

In order to secure its rights to remuneration, compensation, damages and indemnity the party who is bringing the products on to the market has a right of retention over the movables of the other party which are in its possession as a result of the contract, until the other party has performed its obligations.

IV. E. – 2:402: Signed Document Available on Request

(1) Each party is entitled to receive from the other, on request, a signed statement in textual form on a durable medium setting out the terms of the contract.

(2) The parties may not exclude the application of this Article or derogate from or vary its effects.

Chapter 3: Commercial Agency

Section 1: General

IV. E. – 3:101: Scope

This Chapter applies to contracts under which one party, the commercial agent, agrees to act on a continuing basis as a self-employed intermediary to negotiate or to conclude contracts on behalf of another party, the principal, and the principal agrees to remunerate the agent for those activities.

Section 2: Obligations of the Commercial Agent

IV. E. – 3:201: Negotiate and Conclude Contracts

The commercial agent must make reasonable efforts to negotiate contracts on behalf of the principal and to conclude the contracts which the agent was instructed to conclude.

IV. E. – 3:202: Instructions

The commercial agent must follow the principal's reasonable instructions, provided they do not substantially affect the agent's independence.

IV. E. – 3:203: Information by Agent During the Performance

The obligation to inform requires the commercial agent in particular to provide the principal with information concerning:

(a) contracts negotiated or concluded;

(b) market conditions;

(c) the solvency of and other characteristics relating to clients.

IV. E. – 3:204: Accounting

(1) The commercial agent must maintain proper accounts relating to the contracts negotiated or concluded on behalf of the principal.

(2) If the agent represents more than one principal, the agent must maintain independent accounts for each principal.

(3) If the principal has important reasons to doubt that the agent maintains proper accounts, the agent must allow an independent accountant to have reasonable access to the agent's books upon the principal's request. The principal must pay for the services of the independent accountant.

Section 3: Obligations of the Principal

IV. E. – 3:301: Commission During the Agency

(1) The commercial agent is entitled to commission on any contract concluded with a client during the period covered by the agency, if:

(a) the contract has been concluded

  (i) as a result of the commercial agent's efforts;

  (ii) with a third party whom the commercial agent has previously acquired as a client for contracts of the same kind; or

  (iii) with a client belonging to a certain geographical area or group of clients with which the commercial agent was entrusted; and

(b) either

  (i) the principal has or should have performed the principal's obligations under the contract; or

  (ii) the client has performed the client's obligations under the contract or justifiably withholds performance.

(2) The parties may not, to the detriment of the commercial agent, exclude the application of paragraph (1)(b)(ii) or derogate from or vary its effects.

IV. E. – 3:302: Commission After the Agency Has Ended

(1) The commercial agent is entitled to commission on any contract concluded with a client after the agency has ended, if:

(a) either

  (i) the contract with the client is mainly the result of the commercial agent's efforts during the period covered by the agency contract, and the contract with the client was concluded within a reasonable period after the agency ended; or

(ii) the requirements of paragraph (1) of IV. E. – 3:301 (Commission during the agency) would have been satisfied except that the contract with the client was not concluded during the period of the agency, and the client's offer reached the principal or the commercial agent before the agency ended; and

(b) either

(i) the principal has or should have performed the principal's obligations under the contract; or

(ii) the client has performed the client's obligations under the contract or justifiably withholds the client's performance.

(2) The parties may not, to the detriment of the commercial agent, exclude the application of paragraph (1)(b)(ii) or derogate from or vary its effects.

IV. E. – 3:303: Conflicting Entitlements of Successive Agents

The commercial agent is not entitled to the commission referred to in IV. E. – 3:301 (Commission during the agency) if a previous commercial agent is entitled to that commission under IV.E– 3:302 (Commission after the agency has ended), unless it is reasonable that the commission is shared between the two commercial agents.

IV. E. – 3:304: When Commission Is to Be Paid

(1) The principal must pay the commercial agent's commission not later than the last day of the month following the quarter in which the agent became entitled to it.

(2) The parties may not, to the detriment of the commercial agent, exclude the application of this Article or derogate from or vary its effects.

IV. E. – 3:305: Entitlement to Commission Extinguished

(1) A contract term whereby the commercial agent's entitlement to commission on a contract concluded with a client is extinguished is valid only if and to the extent that it provides for extinction on the basis that the client's contractual obligations are not performed for a reason for which the principal is not accountable.

(2) Upon the extinguishing of the commercial agent's entitlement to commission, the commercial agent must refund any commission already received.

(3) The parties may not, to the detriment of the commercial agent, exclude the application of paragraph (1) or derogate from or vary its effects.

IV. E. – 3:306: Remuneration

Any remuneration which wholly or partially depends upon the number or value of contracts is presumed to be commission within the meaning of this Chapter.

IV. E. – 3:307: Information by Principal During the Performance

The obligation to inform requires the principal in particular to provide the commercial agent with information concerning:

(a) characteristics of the goods or services; and

(b) prices and conditions of sale or purchase.

IV. E. – 3:308: Information on Acceptance, Rejection and Non-performance

(1) The principal must inform the commercial agent, within a reasonable period, of:

(a) the principal's acceptance or rejection of a contract which the commercial agent has negotiated on the principal's behalf; and

(b) any non-performance of obligations under a contract which the commercial agent has negotiated or concluded on the principal's behalf.

(2) The parties may not, to the detriment of the commercial agent, exclude the application of this Article or derogate from or vary its effects.

IV. E. – 3:309: Warning of Decreased Volume of Contracts

(1) The principal must warn the commercial agent within a reasonable time when the principal foresees that the volume of contracts that the principal will be able to conclude will be significantly lower than the commercial agent could reasonably have expected.

(2) For the purpose of paragraph (1) the principal is presumed to foresee what the principal could reasonably be expected to foresee.

(3) The parties may not, to the detriment of the commercial agent, exclude the application of this Article or derogate from or vary its effects.

IV. E. – 3:310: Information on Commission

(1) The principal must supply the commercial agent in reasonable time with a statement of the commission to which the commercial agent is entitled. This statement must set out how the amount of the commission has been calculated.

(2) For the purpose of calculating commission, the principal must provide the commercial agent upon request with an extract from the principal's books.

(3) The parties may not, to the detriment of the commercial agent, exclude the application of this Article or derogate from or vary its effects.

IV. E. – 3:311: Accounting

(1) The principal must maintain proper accounts relating to the contracts negotiated or concluded by the commercial agent.

(2) If the principal has more than one commercial agent, the principal must maintain independent accounts for each commercial agent.

(3) The principal must allow an independent accountant to have reasonable access to the principal's books upon the commercial agent's request, if:

(a) the principal does not comply with the principal's obligations under paragraphs (1) or (2) of IV. E. – 3:310 (Information on commission); or

(b) the commercial agent has important reasons to doubt that the principal maintains proper accounts.

IV. E. – 3:312: Amount of Indemnity

(1) The commercial agent is entitled to an indemnity for goodwill on the basis of IV. E. – 2:305 (Indemnity for goodwill) amounting to:

(a) the average commission on contracts with new clients and on the increased volume of business with existing clients calculated for the last 12 months, multiplied by:

(b) the number of years the principal is likely to continue to derive benefits from these contracts in the future.

(2) The resulting indemnity must be amended to take account of:

(a) the probable attrition of clients, based on the average rate of migration in the commercial agent's territory; and

(b) the discount required for early payment, based on average interest rates.

(3) In any case, the indemnity must not exceed one year's remuneration, calculated from the commercial agent's average annual remuneration over the preceding five years or, if the contractual relationship has been in existence for less than five years, from the average during the period in question.

(4) The parties may not, to the detriment of the commercial agent, exclude the application of this Article or derogate from or vary its effects.

IV. E. – 3:313: Del Credere Clause

(1) An agreement whereby the commercial agent guarantees that a client will pay the price of the products forming the subject-matter of the contract which the commercial agent has negotiated or concluded (del credere clause) is valid only if and to the extent that the agreement:

(a) is in textual form on a durable medium;

(b) covers particular contracts which were negotiated or concluded by the commercial agent or such contracts with particular clients who are specified in the agreement; and

(c) is reasonable with regard to the interests of the parties.

(2) The commercial agent is entitled to be paid a commission of a reasonable amount on contracts to which the del credere guarantee applies (del credere commission).

Chapter 4: Franchise

Section 1: General

IV. E. – 4:101: Scope

This Chapter applies to contracts under which one party (the franchisor) grants the other party (the franchisee), in exchange for remuneration, the right to conduct a business (franchise business) within the franchisor's network for the purposes of supplying certain products on the franchisee's behalf and in the franchisee's name, and under which the franchisee has the right and the obligation to use the franchisor's tradename or trademark or other intellectual property rights, know-how and business method.

IV. E. – 4:102: Pre-Contractual information

(1) The duty under IV. E. – 2:101 (Pre-contractual information duty) requires the franchisor in particular to provide the franchisee with adequate and timely information concerning:

(a) the franchisor's company and experience;

(b) the relevant intellectual property rights;

(c) the characteristics of the relevant know-how;

(d) the commercial sector and the market conditions;

(e) the particular franchise method and its operation;

(f) the structure and extent of the franchise network;

(g) the fees, royalties or any other periodical payments; and

(h) the terms of the contract.

(2) Even if the franchisor's non-compliance with paragraph (1) does not give rise to a mistake for which the contract could be avoided under II. – 7:201 (Mistake), the franchisee may recover damages in accordance with paragraphs (2) and (3) of II. – 7:214 (Damages for loss), unless the franchisor had reason to believe that the information was adequate or had been given in reasonable time.

(3) The parties may not exclude the application of this Article or derogate from or vary its effects.

IV. E. – 4:103: Co-operation

The parties to a contract within the scope of this Chapter may not exclude the application of IV. E. – 2:201 (Co-operation) or derogate from or vary its effects.

Section 2: Obligations of the Franchisor

IV. E. – 4:201: Intellectual Property Rights

(1) The franchisor must grant the franchisee a right to use the intellectual property rights to the extent necessary to operate the franchise business.

(2) The franchisor must make reasonable efforts to ensure the undisturbed and continuous use of the intellectual property rights.

(3) The parties may not exclude the application of this Article or derogate from or vary its effects.

IV. E. – 4:202: Know-How

(1) Throughout the duration of the contractual relationship the franchisor must provide the franchisee with the know-how which is necessary to operate the franchise business.

(2) The parties may not exclude the application of this Article or derogate from or vary its effects.

IV. E. – 4:203: Assistance

(1) The franchisor must provide the franchisee with assistance in the form of training courses, guidance and advice, in so far as necessary for the operation of the franchise business, without additional charge for the franchisee.

(2) The franchisor must provide further assistance, in so far as reasonably requested by the franchisee, at a reasonable cost.

IV. E. – 4:204: Supply

(1) When the franchisee is obliged to obtain the products from the franchisor, or from a supplier designated by the franchisor, the franchisor must ensure that the products ordered by the franchisee are supplied within a reasonable time, in so far as practicable and provided that the order is reasonable.

(2) Paragraph (1) also applies to cases where the franchisee, although not legally obliged to obtain the products from the franchisor or from a supplier designated by the franchisor, is in fact required to do so.

(3) The parties may not exclude the application of this Article or derogate from or vary its effects.

IV. E. – 4:205: Information by Franchisor During the Performance

The obligation to inform requires the franchisor in particular to provide the franchisee with information concerning:

(a) market conditions;

(b) commercial results of the franchise network;

(c) characteristics of the products;

(d) prices and terms for the supply of products;

(e) any recommended prices and terms for the re-supply of products to customers;

(f) relevant communication between the franchisor and customers in the territory; and

(g) advertising campaigns.

IV. E. – 4:206: Warning of Decreased Supply Capacity

(1) When the franchisee is obliged to obtain the products from the franchisor, or from a supplier designated by the franchisor, the franchisor must warn the franchisee within a reasonable time when the franchisor foresees that the franchisor's supply capacity or the supply capacity of the designated suppliers will be significantly less than the franchisee had reason to expect.

(2) For the purpose of paragraph (1) the franchisor is presumed to foresee what the franchisor could reasonably be expected to foresee.

(3) Paragraph (1) also applies to cases where the franchisee, although not legally obliged to obtain the products from the franchisor or from a supplier designated by the franchisor, is in fact required to do so.

(4) The parties may not, to the detriment of the franchisee, exclude the application of this Article or derogate from or vary its effects.

IV. E. – 4:207: Reputation of Network and Advertising

(1) The franchisor must make reasonable efforts to promote and maintain the reputation of the franchise network.

(2) In particular, the franchisor must design and co-ordinate the appropriate advertising campaigns aiming at the promotion of the franchise network.

(3) The activities of promotion and maintenance of the reputation of the franchise network are to be carried out without additional charge to the franchisee.

Section 3: Obligations of the Franchisee

IV. E. – 4:301: Fees, Royalties and Other Periodical Payments

(1) The franchisee must pay to the franchisor fees, royalties or other periodical payments agreed upon in the contract.

(2) If fees, royalties or any other periodical payments are to be determined unilaterally by the franchisor, II. – 9:105 (Unilateral determination by a party) applies.

IV. E. – 4:302: Information by Franchisee During the Performance

The obligation under IV. E. – 2:202 ((Information during the performance) requires the franchisee in particular to provide the franchisor with information concerning:

(a) claims brought or threatened by third parties in relation to the franchisor's intellectual property rights; and

(b) infringements by third parties of the franchisor's intellectual property rights.

IV. E. – 4:303: Business Method and Instructions

(1) The franchisee must make reasonable efforts to operate the franchise business according to the business method of the franchisor.

(2) The franchisee must follow the franchisor's reasonable instructions in relation to the business method and the maintenance of the reputation of the network.

(3) The franchisee must take reasonable care not to harm the franchise network.

(4) The parties may not exclude the application of this Article or derogate from or vary its effects.

IV. E. – 4:304: Inspection

(1) The franchisee must grant the franchisor reasonable access to the franchisee's premises to enable the franchisor to check that the franchisee is complying with the franchisor's business method and instructions.

(2) The franchise must grant the franchisor reasonable access to the accounting books of the franchisee.

Chapter 5: Distributorship

Section 1: General

IV. E. – 5:101: Scope and Definitions

(1) This Chapter applies to contracts (distribution contracts) under which one party, the supplier, agrees to supply the other party, the distributor, with products on a continuing basis and the distributor agrees to purchase them, or to take and pay for them, and to supply them to others in the distributor's name and on the distributor's behalf.

(2) An exclusive distribution contract is a distribution contract under which the supplier agrees to supply products to only one distributor within a certain territory or to a certain group of customers.

(3) A selective distribution contract is a distribution contract under which the supplier agrees to supply products, either directly or indirectly, only to distributors selected on the basis of specified criteria.

(4) An exclusive purchasing contract is a distribution contract under which the distributor agrees to purchase, or to take and pay for, products only from the supplier or from a party designated by the supplier.

Section 2: Obligations of the Supplier

IV. E. – 5:201: Obligation to Supply

The supplier must supply the products ordered by the distributor in so far as it is practicable and provided that the order is reasonable.

IV. E. – 5:202: Information by Supplier During the Performance

The obligation under IV. E. – 2:202 (Information during the performance) requires the supplier to provide the distributor with information concerning:

(a) the characteristics of the products;

(b) the prices and terms for the supply of the products;

(c) any recommended prices and terms for the re-supply of the products to customers;

(d) any relevant communication between the supplier and customers; and

(e) any advertising campaigns relevant to the operation of the business.

IV. E. – 5:203: Warning by Supplier of Decreased Supply Capacity

(1) The supplier must warn the distributor within a reasonable time when the supplier foresees that the supplier's supply capacity will be significantly less than the distributor had reason to expect.

(2) For the purpose of paragraph (1) the supplier is presumed to foresee what the supplier could reasonably be expected to foresee.

(3) In exclusive purchasing contracts, the parties may not exclude the application of this Article or derogate from or vary its effects.

IV. E. – 5:204: Advertising Materials

The supplier must provide the distributor at a reasonable price with all the advertising materials the supplier has which are needed for the proper distribution and promotion of the products.

IV. E. – 5:205: The Reputation of the Products

The supplier must make reasonable efforts not to damage the reputation of the products.

Section 3: Obligations of the Distributor

IV. E. – 5:301: Obligation to Distribute

In exclusive distribution contracts and selective distribution contracts the distributor must, so far as practicable, make reasonable efforts to promote the products.

IV. E. – 5:302: Information by Distributor During the Performance

In exclusive distribution contracts and selective distribution contracts, the obligation under IV. E. – 2:202 (Information during the performance) requires the distributor to provide the supplier with information concerning:

(a) claims brought or threatened by third parties in relation to the supplier's intellectual property rights; and

(b) infringements by third parties of the supplier's intellectual property rights.

IV. E. – 5:303: Warning by Distributor of Decreased Requirements

(1) In exclusive distribution contracts and selective distribution contracts, the distributor must warn the supplier within a reasonable time when the distributor foresees that the distributor's requirements will be significantly less than the supplier had reason to expect.

(2) For the purpose of paragraph (1) the distributor is presumed to foresee what the distributor could reasonably be expected to foresee.

IV. E. – 5:304: Instructions

In exclusive distribution contracts and selective distribution contracts, the distributor must follow reasonable instructions from the supplier which are designed to secure the proper distribution of the products or to maintain the reputation or the distinctiveness of the products.

IV. E. – 5:305: Inspection

In exclusive distribution contracts and selective distribution contracts, the distributor must provide the supplier with reasonable access to the distributor's premises to enable the supplier to check that the distributor is complying with the standards agreed upon in the contract and with reasonable instructions given.

IV. E. – 5:306: The Reputation of the Products

In exclusive distribution contracts and selective distribution contracts, the distributor must make reasonable efforts not to damage the reputation of the products.

Part F. Loan Contracts

IV.F. – 1:101: Scope

(1) This Part of Book IV applies to loan contracts other than:

(a) those under which a business lends to a consumer; and

(b) those where the loan is made for the purchase or maintenance of immovable property.

(2) A loan contract is a contract by which one party, the lender, is obliged to provide the other party, the borrower, with credit of any amount for a definite or indefinite period (the loan period), in the form of a monetary loan or of an overdraft facility and by which the borrower is obliged to repay the money obtained under the credit, whether or not the borrower is obliged to pay interest or any other kind of remuneration the parties have agreed upon.

(3) A monetary loan is a fixed sum of money which is lent to the borrower and which the borrower agrees to repay either by fixed instalments or by paying the whole sum at the end of the loan period.

(4) An overdraft facility is an option for the borrower to withdraw funds on a fluctuating, limited basis from the borrower's current account in excess of the current balance in the account. Unless otherwise determined, an overdraft facility has a revolving character meaning that the borrower has the possibility to use this facility over and over again.

(5) A contract is not a loan contract merely because it provides for the time of payment of an obligation to pay money to be deferred, unless it requires the borrower to pay interest or any other charge in addition to the price.

(6) The parties may however agree that money due under an existing obligation to pay money will in future be due under a loan contract.

IV.F. – 1:102: Main Obligation of the Lender

(1) The lender is obliged to provide the borrower with credit for the amount, in the manner and for the period determinable from the contract.

(2) If a period of time within which the obligation is to be performed cannot be determined from the terms regulating the obligation, the lender is obliged to make the credit available a reasonable time after the borrower's demand.

IV.F. – 1:103: Obligation of the Borrower to Take up Loan

(1) Where the credit takes the form of a monetary loan, the borrower is obliged to take up the loan in the manner and for the period determinable from the contract.

(2) If the time the borrower is to take up the loan is not determinable from the contract, the borrower is obliged to take up the loan a reasonable time after the lender's demand.

IV.F. – 1:104: Interest

(1) The borrower is obliged to pay interest or any other kind of remuneration according to the terms of the contract.

(2) If the contract does not specify the interest payable, interest is payable unless both parties are consumers.

(3) Interest accrues day by day from the date the borrower takes up the monetary loan or makes use of the overdraft facility but is payable at the end of the loan period or annually, whichever occurs earlier.

(4) Interest payable according to the preceding paragraph is added to the outstanding capital every 12 months.

IV.F. – 1:105: Purpose of the Credit

If the contract restricts use of the credit to a specific purpose, the borrower is obliged, within a reasonable time after the lender's demand, to provide information necessary to enable the lender to verify its use.

IV.F. – 1:106: Repayment and Termination

(1) The borrower is obliged to repay the money obtained under the credit in the manner and at the time determinable from the loan contract. If the time the borrower is to repay the money is not determinable from the contract, the borrower is obliged to repay it a reasonable time after the lender's demand.

(2) The borrower can, by repayment, terminate an overdraft at will.

(3) The borrower can, by repayment, terminate a loan at any time if under the loan contract the borrower does not have to pay interest or any other kind of remuneration which depends on the duration of the credit.

(4) The borrower can, by repayment, terminate at any time the loan under any other type of loan contract with a specified duration. Parties cannot exclude the application of this rule or derogate from or vary its effects.

(5) Where the loan contract has a specified duration of more than 1 year and provides for a fixed interest rate the borrower can terminate by early repayment under paragraph (4) only on giving the lender three months notice.

(6) On early termination under paragraphs (4) or (5) the borrower is obliged to pay all interest due up to the date of repayment and to indemnify the lender for any loss caused by the early termination.

(7) If the loan contract has an unspecified duration then, without prejudice to the borrower's rights under paragraphs (2) and (3), either party can terminate the relationship by giving the other a reasonable period of notice. II. – 1:109 (Variation or termination by notice) applies.

Part G. Personal Security

Chapter 1: Common Rules

IV. G. – 1:101: Definitions

For the purposes of this Part:

(a) a "dependent personal security" is an obligation by a security provider which is assumed in favour of a creditor in order to secure a right to performance of a present or future obligation of the debtor owed to the creditor and performance of which is due only if, and to the extent that, performance of the latter obligation is due;

(b) an "independent personal security" is an obligation by a security provider which is assumed in favour of a creditor for the purposes of security and which is expressly or impliedly declared not to depend upon another person's obligation owed to the creditor;

(c) the "security provider" is the person who assumes the obligations towards the creditor for the purposes of security;

(d) the "debtor" is the person who owes the secured obligation, if any, to the creditor, and, in provisions relating to purported obligations, includes an apparent debtor;

(e) a "co-debtorship for security purposes" is an obligation owed by two or more debtors in which one of the debtors, the security provider, assumes the obligation primarily for purposes of security towards the creditor;

(f) a "global security" is a dependent personal security which is assumed in order to secure a right to performance of all the debtor's obligations towards the creditor or a right to payment of the debit balance of a current account or a security of a similar extent;

(g) "proprietary security" covers security rights in all kinds of assets, whether movable or immovable, corporeal or incorporeal; and

(h) the "secured obligation" is the obligation the right to the performance of which is secured.

IV. G. – 1:102: Scope

(1) This Part applies to any type of voluntarily assumed personal security and, in particular, to:

(a) dependent personal securities, including those assumed by binding comfort letters;

(b) independent personal securities, including those assumed by stand-by letters of credit; and

(c) co-debtorship for security purposes.

(2) This Part does not apply to insurance contracts. In the case of a guarantee insurance, this Part applies only if and in so far as the insurer has issued a document containing a personal security in favour of the creditor.

(3) This Part does not affect the rules on the aval and the security endorsement of negotiable instruments, but does apply to security for obligations resulting from such an aval or security endorsement.

IV. G. – 1:103: Creditor's Acceptance

(1) If the parties intend to create the security by contract, the creditor is regarded as accepting an offer of security as soon as the offer reaches the creditor, unless the offer requires express acceptance, or the creditor without undue delay rejects it or reserves time for consideration.

(2) A personal security can also be assumed by a unilateral undertaking intended to be legally binding without acceptance. The rules of this Part apply with any appropriate adaptations.

IV. G. – 1:104: Co-Debtorship for Security Purposes

A co-debtorship for security purposes is subject to the rules of Chapters 1 and 4 and, subsidiarily, to the rules in Book III, Chapter 4, Section 1 (Plurality of debtors).

IV. G. – 1:105: Several Security Providers: Solidary Liability Towards Creditor

(1) To the extent that several providers of personal security have secured the right to performance of the same obligation or the same part of an obligation or have assumed their undertakings for the same security purpose, each security provider assumes within the limits of that security provider's undertaking to the creditor solidary liability together with the other security providers. This rule also applies if these security providers in assuming their securities have acted independently.

(2) Paragraph (1) applies with appropriate adaptations if proprietary security has been provided by the debtor or a third person in addition to the personal security.

IV. G. – 1:106: Several Security Providers: Internal Recourse

(1) In the cases covered by the preceding Article recourse between several providers of personal security or between providers of personal security and of proprietary security is governed by III. – 4:107 (Recourse between solidary debtors), subject to the following paragraphs.

(2) Subject to paragraph (8), the proportionate share of each security provider for the purposes of that Article is determined according to the rules in paragraphs (3) to (7).

(3) Unless the security providers have otherwise agreed, as between themselves each security provider is liable in the same proportion that the maximum risk assumed by that security provider bore to the total of the maximum risks assumed by all the security providers. The relevant time is that of the creation of the last security.

(4) For personal security, the maximum risk is determined by the agreed maximum amount of the security. In the absence of an agreed maximum amount, the value of the secured right or, if a current account has been secured, the credit limit is decisive. If a secured current account does not have a credit limit, its final balance is decisive.

(5) For proprietary security, the maximum risk is determined by the agreed maximum amount of the security. In the absence of an agreed maximum amount, the value of the assets serving as security is decisive.

(6) If the maximum amount in the case of paragraph (4) first sentence or the maximum amount or the value, respectively, in the case of paragraph (5) is higher than the value of the secured right at the time of creation of the last security, the latter determines the maximum risk.

(7) In the case of an unlimited personal security securing an unlimited credit the maximum risk of other limited personal or proprietary security rights which exceed the final balance of the secured credit is limited to the latter.

(8) The rules in paragraphs (3) to (7) do not apply to proprietary security provided by the debtor and to security providers who, at the time when the creditor was satisfied, were not liable towards the latter.

IV. G. – 1:107: Several Security Providers: Recourse Against Debtor

(1) Any security provider who has satisfied a right of recourse of another security provider is subrogated to this extent to the other security provider's rights against the debtor as acquired under IV. G. – 2:113 (Security provider's rights after performance) paragraphs (1) and (3), including proprietary security rights granted by the debtor. IV. G. – 2:110 (Reduction of creditor's rights) applies with appropriate adaptations.

(2) Where a security provider has recourse against the debtor by virtue of the rights acquired under IV. G. – 2:113 (Security provider's rights after performance) paragraphs (1) and (3) or under the preceding paragraph, including proprietary security rights granted by the debtor, every security provider is entitled to a proportionate share, as defined in IV. G. – 1:106 (Several security providers: internal recourse) paragraph (2) and III. – 4:107 (Recourse between solidary debtors), of the benefits recovered from the debtor. IV. G. – 2:110 (Reduction of creditor's rights) applies with appropriate adaptations.

(3) Unless expressly stated to the contrary, the preceding rules do not apply to proprietary security provided by the debtor.

IV. G. – 1:108: Subsidiary Application of Rules on Solidary Debtors

If and in so far as the provisions of this Part do not apply, the rules on plurality of debtors in III. – 4:107 (Recourse between solidary debtors) to III. – 4:112 (Opposability of other defences in solidary obligations) are subsidiarily applicable.

Chapter 2: Dependent Personal Security

IV. G. – 2:101: Presumption for Dependent Personal Security

(1) Any undertaking to pay, to render any other performance or to pay damages to the creditor by way of security is presumed to give rise to a dependent personal security, unless the creditor shows that it was agreed otherwise.

(2) A binding comfort letter is presumed to give rise to a dependent personal security.

IV. G. – 2:102: Dependence of Security Provider's Obligation

(1) Whether and to what extent performance of the obligation of the provider of a dependent personal security is due, depends upon whether and to what extent performance of the debtor's obligation to the creditor is due.

(2) The security provider's obligation does not exceed the debtor's obligation. This rule does not apply if the debtor's obligations are reduced or discharged:

(a) in an insolvency proceeding;

(b) in any other way caused by the debtor's inability to perform because of insolvency; or

(c) by virtue of law due to events affecting the person of the debtor.

(3) Except in the case of a global security, if an amount has not been fixed for the security and cannot be determined from the agreement of the parties, the security provider's obligation is limited to the value of the secured right at the time the security became effective.

(4) Except in the case of a global security, any agreement between the creditor and the debtor to make performance of the secured obligation due earlier, or to make the obligation more onerous by changing the conditions on which performance is due, or to increase its amount, does not affect the security provider's obligation if the agreement was concluded after the security provider's obligation became effective.

IV. G. – 2:103: Debtor's Defences Available to the Security Provider

(1) As against the creditor, the security provider may invoke any defence of the debtor with respect to the secured obligation, even if the defence is no longer available to the debtor due to acts or omissions of the debtor occurring after the security became effective.

(2) The security provider is entitled to refuse to perform the security obligation if:

(a) the debtor is entitled to withdraw from the contract with the creditor under Book II, Chapter 5 (Right of withdrawal).

(b) the debtor has a right to withhold performance under III. – 3:401 (Right to withhold performance of reciprocal obligation); or

(c) the debtor is entitled to terminate the debtor's contractual relationship with the creditor under Book III, Chapter 3, Section 5 (Termination).

(3) The security provider may not invoke the lack of capacity of the debtor, whether a natural person or a legal entity, or the non-existence of the debtor, if a legal entity, if the relevant facts were known to the security provider at the time when the security became effective.

(4) As long as the debtor is entitled to avoid the contract from which the secured obligation arises on a ground other than those mentioned in the preceding paragraph and has not exercised that right, the security provider is entitled to refuse performance.

(5) The preceding paragraph applies with appropriate adaptations if the secured obligation is subject to set-off.

IV. G. – 2:104: Coverage of Security

(1) The security covers, within its maximum amount, if any, not only the principal secured obligation, but also the debtor's ancillary obligations towards the creditor, especially:

(a) contractual interest and interest due by law on delay in payment;

(b) damages, a penalty or an agreed payment for non-performance by the debtor; and

(c) the reasonable costs of extra-judicial recovery of those items.

(2) The costs of legal proceedings and enforcement proceedings against the debtor are covered, provided the security provider had been informed about the creditor's intention to undertake such proceedings in sufficient time to enable the security provider to avert those costs.

(3) A global security covers only obligations which originated in contracts between the debtor and the creditor.

IV. G. – 2:105: Solidary Liability of Security Provider

Unless otherwise agreed, the liability of the debtor and the security provider is solidary and, accordingly, the creditor has the choice of claiming solidary performance from the debtor or, within the limits of the security, from the security provider.

IV. G. – 2:106: Subsidiary Liability of Security Provider

(1) If so agreed, the security provider may invoke as against the creditor the subsidiary character of the security provider's liability. A binding comfort letter is presumed to establish only subsidiary liability.

(2) Subject to paragraph (3), before demanding performance from the security provider, the creditor must have undertaken appropriate attempts to obtain satisfaction from the debtor and other security providers, if any, securing the same obligation under a personal or proprietary security establishing solidary liability.

(3) The creditor is not required to attempt to obtain satisfaction from the debtor and any other security provider according to the preceding paragraph if and in so far as it is obviously impossible or exceedingly difficult to obtain satisfaction from the person concerned. This exception applies, in particular, if and in so far as an insolvency or equivalent proceeding has been opened against the person concerned or opening of such a proceeding has failed due to insufficient assets, unless a proprietary security provided by that person and for the same obligation is available.

IV. G. – 2:107: Requirement of Notification by Creditor

(1) The creditor is required to notify the security provider without undue delay in case of a non-performance by, or inability to pay of, the debtor as well as of an extension of maturity; this notification must include information about the secured amounts of the principal obligation,

interest and other ancillary obligations owed by the debtor on the date of the notification. An additional notification of a new event of non-performance need not be given before three months have expired since the previous notification. No notification is required if an event of non-performance merely relates to ancillary obligations of the debtor, unless the total amount of all non-performed secured obligations has reached five percent of the outstanding amount of the secured obligation.

(2) In addition, in the case of a global security, the creditor is required to notify the security provider of any agreed increase:

(a) whenever such increase, starting from the creation of the security, reaches 20 percent of the amount that was so secured at that time; and

(b) whenever the secured amount is further increased by 20 percent compared with the secured amount at the date when the last information according to this paragraph was or should have been given.

(3) Paragraphs (1) and (2) do not apply, if and in so far as the security provider knows or could reasonably be expected to know the required information.

(4) If the creditor omits or delays any notification required by this Article the creditor's rights against the security provider are reduced by the extent necessary to prevent the latter from suffering any loss as a result of the omission or delay.

IV. G. – 2:108: Time Limit for Resort to Security

(1) If a time limit has been agreed, directly or indirectly, for resort to a security establishing solidary liability for the security provider, the latter is no longer liable after expiration of the agreed time limit. However, the security provider remains liable if the creditor had requested per-

formance from the security provider after maturity of the secured obligation but before expiration of the time limit for the security.

(2) If a time limit has been agreed, directly or indirectly, for resort to a security establishing subsidiary liability for the security provider, the latter is no longer liable after the expiration of the agreed time limit. However, the security provider remains liable if the creditor:

(a) after maturity of the secured obligation, but before expiration of the time limit, has informed the security provider of an intention to demand performance of the security and of the commencement of appropriate attempts to obtain satisfaction as required according to IV. G. – 2:106 (Subsidiary liability of security provider) paragraphs (2) and (3); and

(b) informs the security provider every six months about the status of these attempts, if so demanded by the security provider.

(3) If performance of the secured obligations falls due upon, or within 14 days before, expiration of the time limit of the security, the request for performance or the information according to paragraphs (1) and (2) may be given earlier than provided for in paragraphs (1) and (2), but no more than 14 days before expiration of the time limit of the security.

(4) If the creditor has taken due measures according to the preceding paragraphs, the security provider's maximum liability is restricted to the amount of the secured obligations as defined in IV. G. – 2:104 (Coverage of security) paragraphs (1) and (2). The relevant time is that at which the agreed time limit expires.

IV. G. – 2:109: Limiting Security Without Time Limit

(1) Where the scope of a security is not limited to obligations arising, or obligations performance of which falls due, within an agreed time limit, the scope of the security may be limited by any party giving notice of at least three months to the other party. The preceding sentence does not apply if the security is restricted to cover specific obligations or obligations arising from specific contracts.

(2) By virtue of the notice, the scope of the security is limited to the secured principal obligations performance of which is due at the date at which the limitation becomes effective and any secured ancillary obligations as defined in IV. G. – 2:104 (Coverage of security) paragraphs (1) and (2).

IV. G. – 2:110: Reduction of Creditor's Rights

(1) If and in so far as due to the creditor's conduct the security provider cannot be subrogated to the creditor's rights against the debtor and to the creditor's personal and proprietary security rights granted by third persons, or cannot be fully reimbursed from the debtor or from third party security providers, if any, the creditor's rights against the security provider are reduced by the extent necessary to prevent the latter from suffering any loss as a result of the creditor's conduct. The security provider has a corresponding right to recover from the creditor if the security provider has already performed.

(2) Paragraph (1) applies only if the creditor's conduct falls short of the standard of care which could be expected of persons managing their affairs with reasonable prudence.

IV. G. – 2:111: Debtor's Relief for the Security Provider

(1) A security provider who has provided a security at the debtor's request or with the debtor's express or presumed consent may request relief by the debtor:

(a) if the debtor has not performed the secured obligation when performance became due;

(b) if the debtor is unable to pay or has suffered a substantial diminution of assets; or

(c) if the creditor has brought an action on the security against the security provider.

(2) Relief may be granted by furnishing adequate security.

IV. G. – 2:112: Notification and Request by Security Provider Before Performance

(1) Before performance to the creditor, the security provider is required to notify the debtor and request information about the outstanding amount of the secured obligation and any defences or counterclaims against it.

(2) If the security provider fails to comply with the requirements in paragraph (1) or neglects to raise defences communicated by the debtor or known to the security provider from other sources, the security provider's rights to recover from the debtor under IV. G. – 2:113 (Security provider's rights after performance) are reduced by the extent necessary to prevent loss to the debtor as a result of such failure or neglect.

(3) The security provider's rights against the creditor remain unaffected.

IV. G. – 2:113: Security Provider's Rights after Performance

(1) The security provider has a right to reimbursement from the debtor if and in so far as the security provider has performed the security obligation. In addition the security provider is subrogated to the extent indicated in the preceding sentence to the creditor's rights against the debtor. The right to reimbursement and rights acquired by subrogation are concurrent.

(2) In case of part performance, the creditor's remaining partial rights against the debtor have priority over the rights to which the security provider has been subrogated.

(3) By virtue of the subrogation under paragraph (1), dependent and independent personal and proprietary security rights are transferred by operation of law to the security provider notwithstanding any contractual restriction or exclusion of transferability agreed by the debtor. Rights against other security providers can be exercised only within the limits of IV. G. – 1:106 (Several security providers: internal recourse).

(4) Where the debtor due to incapacity is not liable to the creditor but the security provider is nonetheless bound by, and performs, the security obligation, the security provider's right to reimbursement from the debtor is limited to the extent of the debtor's enrichment by the transaction with the creditor. This rule applies also if a debtor legal entity has not come into existence.

Chapter 3: Independent Personal Security

IV. G. – 3:101: Scope

(1) The independence of a security is not prejudiced by a mere general reference to an underlying obligation (including a personal security).

(2) The provisions of this Chapter also apply to standby letters of credit.

IV. G. – 3:102: Notification to Debtor by Security Provider

(1) The security provider is required:

(a) to notify the debtor immediately if a demand for performance is received and to state whether or not, in the view of the security provider, performance falls to be made;

(b) to notify the debtor immediately if performance has been made in accordance with a demand; and

(c) to notify the debtor immediately if performance has been refused notwithstanding a demand and to state the reasons for the refusal.

(2) If the security provider fails to comply with the requirements in paragraph (1) the security provider's rights against the debtor under IV. G. – 3:109 (Security provider's rights after perfor-

mance) are reduced by the extent necessary to prevent loss to the debtor as a result of such failure.

IV. G. – 3:103: Performance by Security Provider

(1) The security provider is obliged to perform only if there is, in textual form, a demand for performance which complies exactly with the terms set out in the contract or other juridical act creating the security.

(2) Unless otherwise agreed, the security provider may invoke defences which the security provider has against the creditor.

(3) The security provider must without undue delay and at the latest within seven days of receipt, in textual form, of a demand for performance:

(a) perform in accordance with the demand; or

(b) inform the creditor of a refusal to perform, stating the reasons for the refusal.

IV. G. – 3:104: Independent Personal Security on First Demand

(1) An independent personal security which is expressed as being due upon first demand or which is in such terms that this can unequivocally be inferred, is governed by the rules in the preceding Article, except as provided in the two following paragraphs.

(2) The security provider is obliged to perform only if the creditor's demand is supported by a declaration in textual form by the creditor which expressly confirms that any condition upon which performance of the security becomes due is fulfilled.

(3) Paragraph (2) of the preceding Article does not apply.

IV. G. – 3:105: Manifestly Abusive or Fraudulent Demand

(1) A security provider is not obliged to comply with a demand for performance if it is proved by present evidence that the demand is manifestly abusive or fraudulent.

(2) If the requirements of the preceding paragraph are fulfilled, the debtor may prohibit:

(a) performance by the security provider; and

(b) issuance or utilisation of a demand for performance by the creditor.

IV. G. – 3:106: Security Provider's Right to Reclaim

(1) The security provider has the right to reclaim the benefits received by the creditor if:

(a) the conditions for the creditor's demand were not or subsequently ceased to be fulfilled; or

(b) the creditor's demand was manifestly abusive or fraudulent.

(2) The security provider's right to reclaim benefits is subject to the rules in Book VII (Unjustified Enrichment).

IV. G. – 3:107: Security With or Without Time Limits

(1) If a time limit has been agreed, directly or indirectly, for the resort to a security, the security provider exceptionally remains liable even after expiration of the time limit, provided the creditor had demanded performance according to IV. G. – 3:103 (Performance by security provider) paragraph (1) or IV. G. – 3:104 (Independent personal security on first demand) at a time when the creditor was entitled to do so and before expiration of the time limit for the security. IV. G. – 2:108 (Time limit for resort to security) paragraph (3) applies with appropriate adaptations. The security provider's maximum liability is restricted to the amount which the creditor could have demanded as of the date when the time limit expired.

(2) Where a security does not have an agreed time limit, the security provider may set such a time limit by giving notice of at least three months to the other party. The security provider's liability is restricted to the amount which the creditor could have demanded as of the date set by the security provider. The preceding sentences do not apply if the security is given for specific purposes.

IV. G. – 3:108: Transfer of Security Right

(1) The creditor's right to performance by the security provider can be assigned or otherwise transferred.

(2) However, in the case of an independent personal security on first demand, the right to performance cannot be assigned or otherwise transferred and the demand for performance can be made only by the original creditor, unless the security provides otherwise. This does not prevent transfer of the proceeds of the security.

IV. G. – 3:109: Security Provider's Rights after Performance

IV. G. – 2:113 (Security provider's rights after performance) applies with appropriate adaptations to the rights which the security provider may exercise after performance.

Chapter 4: Special Rules for Personal Security of Consumers

IV. G. – 4:101: Scope of Application

(1) Subject to paragraph (2), this Chapter applies when a security is provided by a consumer.

(2) This Chapter is not applicable if:

(a) the creditor is also a consumer; or

(b) the consumer security provider is able to exercise substantial influence upon the debtor where the debtor is not a natural person.

IV. G. – 4:102: Applicable Rules

(1) A personal security subject to this Chapter is governed by the rules of Chapters 1 and 2, except as otherwise provided in this Chapter.

(2) The parties may not, to the detriment of a security provider, exclude the application of the rules of this Chapter or derogate from or vary their effects.

IV. G. – 4:103: Creditor's Pre-Contractual Duties

(1) Before a security is granted, the creditor has a duty to explain to the intending security provider:

(a) the general effect of the intended security; and

(b) the special risks to which the security provider may according to the information accessible to the creditor be exposed in view of the financial situation of the debtor.

(2) If the creditor knows or has reason to know that due to a relationship of trust and confidence between the debtor and the security provider there is a significant risk that the security provider is not acting freely or with adequate information, the creditor has a duty to ascertain that the security provider has received independent advice.

(3) If the information or independent advice required by the preceding paragraphs is not given at least five days before the security provider signs the offer of security or the contract creating the security, the offer can be revoked or the contract avoided by the security provider within a reasonable time after receipt of the information or the independent advice. For this purpose five days is regarded as a reasonable time unless the circumstances suggest otherwise.

(4) If contrary to paragraph (1) or (2) no information or independent advice is given, the offer can be revoked or the contract avoided by the security provider at any time.

(5) If the security provider revokes the offer or avoids the contract according to the preceding paragraphs, the return of benefits received by the parties is governed by Book VII (Unjustified Enrichment).

IV. G. – 4:104: Form

The contract of security must be in textual form on a durable medium and must be signed by the security provider. A contract of security which does not comply with the requirements of the preceding sentence is void.

IV. G. – 4:105: Nature of Security Provider's Liability

Where this Chapter applies:

(a) an agreement purporting to create a security without a maximum amount, whether a global security or not, is considered as creating a dependent security with a fixed amount to be determined according to IV. G. – 2:102 (Dependence of security provider's obligation) paragraph (3);

(b) the liability of a provider of dependent security is subsidiary within the meaning of IV. G. – 2:106 (Subsidiary liability of security provider), unless expressly agreed otherwise; and

(c) in an agreement purporting to create an independent security, the declaration that it does not depend upon another person's obligation owed to the creditor is disregarded, and accordingly a dependent security is considered as having been created, provided the other requirements of such a security are met.

IV. G. – 4:106: Creditor's Obligations of Annual Information

(1) Subject to the debtor's consent, the creditor has to inform the security provider annually about the secured amounts of the principal obligation, interest and other ancillary obligations owed by the debtor on the date of the information. The debtor's consent, once given, is irrevocable.

(2) IV. G. – 2:107 (Requirement of notification by creditor) paragraphs (3) and (4) apply with appropriate adaptations.

IV. G. – 4:107: Limiting Security with Time Limit

(1) A security provider who has provided a security whose scope is limited to obligations arising, or obligations performance of which falls due, within an agreed time limit may three years after the security became effective limit its effects by giving notice of at least three months to the creditor. The preceding sentence does not apply if the security is restricted to cover specific obligations or obligations arising from specific contracts. The creditor has to inform the debtor immediately on receipt of a notice of limitation of the security by the security provider.

(2) By virtue of the notice, the scope of the security is limited according to IV. G. – 2:109 (Limiting security without time limit) paragraph (2).

Part H. Donation

Chapter 1: Scope and General Provisions

Section 1: Scope and Definitions

IV. H. – 1:101: Contracts Covered

(1) This Part of Book IV applies to contracts for the donation of goods.

(2) A contract for the donation of goods is a contract under which one party, the donor, gratuitously undertakes to transfer the ownership of goods to another party, the donee, and does so with an intention to benefit the donee.

IV. H. – 1:102: Future Goods and Goods to Be Manufactured or Produced

(1) In this Part of Book IV the word "goods" includes goods which at the time of the conclusion of the contract do not yet exist or are to be acquired by the donor.

(2) A contract under which one party undertakes gratuitously, and with an intention to benefit the other party, to manufacture or produce goods for the other party and to transfer their ownership to the other party is to be regarded as primarily a contract for the donation of the goods.

IV. H. – 1:103: Application to Other Assets

(1) This Part applies with appropriate adaptations to:

(a) contracts for the donation of money;

(b) contracts for the donation of electricity;

(c) contracts for the donation of stocks, shares, investment securities and negotiable instruments;

(d) contracts for the donation of other forms of incorporeal property, including rights to the performance of obligations, industrial and intellectual property rights and other transferable rights;

(e) contracts gratuitously conferring rights in information or data, including software and databases.

(2) This Part does not apply to contracts for the donation of immovable property or rights in immovable property.

IV. H. – 1:104: Application to Unilateral Undertakings and Immediate Donations

This Part applies with appropriate adaptations where the donor gratuitously, with an intention to benefit the donee:

(a) unilaterally undertakes to transfer the ownership of goods to the donee; or

(b) immediately transfers the ownership of goods to the donee.

IV. H. – 1:105: Donations Due or Conditional on Death

(1) This Part does not apply where:

(a) performance of the obligation to transfer is due only on the donor's death;

(b) the transfer or obligation to transfer is subject to the suspensive condition of the donor's death; or

(c) the transfer or obligation to transfer is made subject to the resolutive condition of the donee predeceasing the donor.

(2) Paragraph (1) does not apply if the donor renders performance or waives the condition before the donor's death.

Section 2: Gratuitousness and Intention to Benefit

IV. H. – 1:201: Gratuitousness

An undertaking to transfer is gratuitous if it is done without reward.

IV. H. – 1:202: Transactions Which Are Not Entirely Gratuitous

(1) If the party undertaking to transfer receives or is entitled to some reward and the transaction is thereby not entirely gratuitous the contract is regarded primarily as a contract for the donation of goods if:

(a) this party undertakes to transfer with an intention inter alia to benefit the other party; and

(b) the values to be conferred by the performances are regarded by both parties as not substantially equivalent.

(2) If the contract coming under paragraph (1) is void or avoided under these rules but would not be under general rules, III. – 1:110 (Variation or termination by court on a change of circumstances) applies with appropriate adaptations.

(3) If in a case within paragraph (1) a party exercises a right to revoke under this Part, IV. H. – 4:103 (Consequences of revocation) applies to the whole contractual relationship. The other party may prevent the effects of revocation by offering a reasonable reward within a reasonable time after revocation.

IV. H. – 1:203: Intention to Benefit

A donor may be regarded as intending to benefit the donee notwithstanding that the donor:

(a) is under a moral obligation to transfer; or

(b) has a promotional purpose.

Chapter 2: Formation and Validity

IV. H. – 2:101: Form Requirements

A contract for the donation of goods is not valid unless the undertaking of the donor is in textual form on a durable medium signed by the donor. An electronic signature which is not an advanced signature in the sense of I. – 1:107 ("Signature" and similar expressions) paragraph 4, does not suffice in this regard.

IV. H. – 2:102: Exceptions to the Form Requirements

The preceding Article does not apply:

(a) in the case of an immediate delivery of the goods to the donee or an equivalent to such delivery, regardless of whether ownership is transferred;

(b) if the donation is made by a business;

(c) if the undertaking of the donor is declared in a public statement broadcast in the radio or television or published in print and is not excessive in the circumstances.

IV. H. – 2:103: Mistake

A donor may avoid the contract if it was concluded because of a mistake of fact or law although the requirements of II. – 7:201 (Mistake) paragraph (1)(b) are not satisfied.

IV. H. – 2:104: Unfair Exploitation

A donor, who was dependent on, or was the more vulnerable party in a relationship of trust with, the donee, may avoid the contract under II. – 7:207 (Unfair exploitation) unless the donee proves that the donee did not exploit the donor's situation by taking an excessive benefit or grossly unfair advantage.

Chapter 3: Obligations and Remedies

Section 1: Obligations of the Donor

IV. H. – 3:101: Obligations in General

(1) The donor must:

(a) deliver goods which conform with the contract; and

(b) transfer the ownership in the goods as required by the contract.

(2) This Section applies with appropriate adaptations to fruits acquired from the time when the obligation to deliver is due.

IV. H. – 3:102: Conformity of the Goods

(1) The goods do not conform with the contract if they do not possess the qualities which the donee could reasonably expect unless the donee knew of the lack of quality or could reasonably be expected to have known of it when the contract was concluded.

(2) In determining what qualities the donee could reasonably expect, regard is to be had, among other things, to:

(a) the gratuitous nature of the contract;

(b) the purpose of the contract of donation known by, or obvious to, the donee;

(c) whether the transfer or delivery of the goods was immediate;

(d) the value of the goods; and

(e) whether the donor was a business.

(3) The goods do not conform to the contract if they are not of a quantity, quality or description provided for by the terms of the contract.

IV. H. – 3:103: Third Party Rights or Claims

The goods do not conform with the contract if they are not free from any right or reasonably well founded claim of a third party unless the donee knew or could reasonably expected to have known of the third party's right or claim.

Section 2: Remedies of the Donee

IV. H. – 3:201: Application of General Rules

If the donor fails to perform any of the donor's obligations under the contract, the donee has the remedies provided for in Book III, Chapter 3 (Remedies for non-performance) unless otherwise provided in this Section.

IV. H. – 3:202: Restricted Right to Enforce Performance

(1) If the goods do not conform with the contract, the donee may not require replacement or repair under III. – 3:302 (Enforcement of non-monetary obligations).

(2) The donee may not enforce performance under III. – 3:302 (Enforcement of non-monetary obligations) in the case of goods which are to be acquired by the donor.

IV. H. – 3:203: Restitution in Case of Termination

If the donee terminates the contract under Book III, Chapter 3, Section 5 (Termination), III. – 3:511 (When restitution not required) paragraph (3) does not apply.

IV. H. – 3:204: Exclusion of the Right to Damages in Case of Impediment

(1) A donee's right to damages is excluded if the donor's non-performance is due to an impediment and if the donor could not reasonably be expected to have avoided or overcome the impediment or its consequences.

(2) III. – 3:104 (Excuse due to an impediment) paragraphs (3) and (5) apply correspondingly.

(3) In determining what impediment or consequences the donor could reasonably be expected to have avoided or overcome regard is to be had to the gratuitous nature of the contract.

(4) This Article does not affect liability under Book VI (Non-contractual liability arising out of damage caused to another).

IV. H. – 3:205: Measure of Damages

(1) Damages cover loss suffered by the donee acting in the reasonable belief that the donor would fulfil the obligations.

(2) A supplementary sum of damages may be awarded by the court if it is seen as just and reasonable in the circumstances.

(3) In determining what is just and reasonable under paragraph (2), regard is to be had, among other things and apart from the gratuitous nature of the contract:

(a) the declarations and acts of the parties;

(b) the donor's purpose in making the donation; and

(c) the reasonable expectations of the donee.

(4) The total amount of damages under this Article may not exceed such a sum as will put the aggrieved party as nearly as possible into the position in which it would have been if the donor's obligations under the contract had been duly performed.

(5) This Article does not affect liability under Book VI (Non-contractual liability arising out of damage caused to another).

IV. H. – 3:206: Delay in Payment of Money

If payment of a sum of money is delayed, the donee is entitled to interest under III. – 3:708 (Interest on late payments) unless the non-performance is excused under III. – 3:104 (Excuse due to an impediment) or the donee's right to damages is excluded under IV. H. – 3:204 (Exclusion of the right to damages in case of impediment).

Section 3: Obligations of the Donee

IV. H. – 3:301: Obligations to Take Delivery and Accept Transfer

(1) The donee must take delivery and accept the transfer of ownership.

(2) The donee performs the obligation to take delivery and accept transfer by carrying out all the acts which could reasonably be expected of the donee in order to enable the donor to perform the obligations to deliver and transfer.

Section 4: Remedies of the Donor

IV. H. – 3:401: Application of General Rules

If the donee fails to perform any of the donee's obligations under the contract, the donor has the remedies provided for in III. – 2:111 (Property not accepted), III. – 2:112 (Money not accepted) and Book III, Chapter 3 (Remedies for non-performance).

Chapter 4: Revocation by the Donor

Section 1: Revocation in General

IV. H. – 4:101: Irrevocability and its Exceptions

Contracts for the donation of goods are revocable only if a right to revoke is

(a) conferred by the terms of the contract; or

(b) provided for under the rules in this Chapter.

IV. H. – 4:102: Exercise and Scope of the Right to Revoke

(1) The donor's right to revoke is to be exercised by giving notice to the donee.

(2) A declaration of partial revocation is to be understood as a revocation of the whole contract for the donation of goods, if, giving due consideration to all the circumstances of the case, it is unreasonable to uphold the remaining parts.

IV. H. – 4:103: Consequences of Revocation

(1) On revocation under this Chapter, the outstanding obligations of the parties under the contract come to an end. In the case of a partial revocation, the relevant part of the outstanding obligations comes to an end.

(2) On revocation under this Chapter, the donee is obliged to return the goods. Chapters 5 and 6 of Book VII (Unjustified enrichment) apply with appropriate adaptations, unless otherwise provided in this Chapter.

IV. H. – 4:104: Time Limits

The right to revoke under this Chapter expires if notice of revocation is not given within a reasonable time, with due regard to the circumstances, after the donor knew or could reasonably be expected to have known of the relevant facts.

Section 2: Rights of the Donor to Revoke

IV. H. – 4:201: Ingratitude of the Donee

(1) A contract for the donation of goods may be revoked if the donee is guilty of gross ingratitude by intentionally committing a serious wrong against the donor.

(2) Revocation under this Article is excluded if the donor knowing the relevant facts forgives the donee.

(3) For the purpose of paragraph (1) a reasonable time under IV.H–4:104 (Time limits) is at least one year. If the donor dies before the reasonable time has expired, the running of the period is suspended until the person entitled to revoke knows or can reasonably be expected to know of the relevant facts.

(4) For the purpose of paragraph (1) the defence of disenrichment under VII. – 6:101 (Disenrichment) does not apply.

IV. H. – 4:202: Impoverishment of the Donor

(1) A contract for the donation of goods may be revoked if the donor is not in a position to maintain himself or herself out of his or her own patrimony or income.

(2) The donor is not in a position to maintain himself or herself if:

(a) he or she would be entitled to maintenance from another if that other were in a position to provide the maintenance; or

(b) he or she is entitled to social assistance.

(3) The right to revoke is suspended if the donee maintains the donor to the extent that the latter is or would be entitled to under paragraph (2).

(4) A donor who is not in a position to maintain himself or herself in the sense of paragraph (1) or who will imminently be in that situation may withhold performance of any obligations under the contract which have not yet been performed. Paragraph (3) applies correspondingly to the right to withhold performance. If the donor withholds performance, the donee may terminate the contractual relationship.

(5) This Article applies also when the donor's ability to meet maintenance obligations established by rule of law or by court order, or the existence of those obligations, is dependent on effective revocation of a donation.

(6) The right to revoke under this Article may not be restricted or excluded by the parties.

IV. H. – 4:203: Residual Right to Revoke

(1) A contract for the donation of goods may also be revoked to the extent that other essential circumstances upon which it was based have materially changed after the conclusion of the contract, provided that as a result of that change:

(a) the benefit to the donee is manifestly inappropriate or excessive; or

(b) it is manifestly unjust to hold the donor to the donation.

(2) Paragraph (1) applies only if:

(a) the change of circumstances was not so foreseeable at the time of the conclusion of the contract that the donor could reasonably have been expected to provide for it; and

(b) the risk of that change of circumstances was not assumed by the donor.

Book V – Benevolent Intervention in Another's Affairs

Chapter 1: Scope

V. – 1:101: Intervention to Benefit Another

(1) This Book applies where a person, the intervener, acts with the predominant intention of benefiting another, the principal, and:

(a) the intervener has a reasonable ground for acting; or

(b) the principal approves the act without such undue delay as would adversely affect the intervener.

(2) The intervener does not have a reasonable ground for acting if the intervener:

(a) has a reasonable opportunity to discover the principal's wishes but does not do so; or

(b) knows or can reasonably be expected to know that the intervention is against the principal's wishes.

V. – 1:102: Intervention to Perform Another's Duty

Where an intervener acts to perform another person's duty, the performance of which is due and urgently required as a matter of overriding public interest, and the intervener acts with the predominant intention of benefiting the recipient of the performance, the person whose duty the intervener acts to perform is a principal to whom this Book applies.

V. – 1:103: Exclusions

This Book does not apply where the intervener:

(a) is authorised to act under a contractual or other obligation to the principal;

(b) is authorised, other than under this Book, to act independently of the principal's consent; or

(c) is under an obligation to a third party to act.

Chapter 2: Duties of Intervener

V. – 2:101: Duties During Intervention

(1) During the intervention, the intervener must:

(a) act with reasonable care;

(b) except in relation to a principal within V. – 1:102 (Intervention to perform another's duty), act in a manner which the intervener knows or can reasonably be expected to assume accords with the principal's wishes; and

(c) so far as possible and reasonable, inform the principal about the intervention and seek the principal's consent to further acts.

(2) The intervention may not be discontinued without good reason.

V. – 2:102: Reparation for Damage Caused by Breach of Duty

(1) The intervener is liable to make reparation to the principal for damage caused by breach of a duty set out in this Chapter if the damage resulted from a risk which the intervener created, increased or intentionally perpetuated.

(2) The intervener's liability is reduced or excluded in so far as this is fair and reasonable, having regard to, among other things, the intervener's reasons for acting.

(3) An intervener who at the time of intervening lacks full legal capacity is liable to make reparation only in so far as that intervener is also liable to make reparation under Book VI (Non-contractual liability arising out of damage caused to another).

V. – 2:103: Obligations After Intervention

(1) After intervening the intervener must without undue delay report and account to the principal and hand over anything obtained as a result of the intervention.

(2) If at the time of intervening the intervener lacks full legal capacity, the obligation to hand over is subject to the defence which would be available under VII. – 6:101 (Disenrichment).

(3) The remedies for non-performance in Book III, Chapter 3 apply but with the modification that any liability to pay damages or interest is subject to the qualifications in paragraphs (2) and (3) of the preceding Article.

Chapter 3: Rights and Authority of Intervener

V. – 3:101: Right to Indemnification or Reimbursement

The intervener has a right against the principal for indemnification or, as the case may be, reimbursement in respect of an obligation or expenditure (whether of money or other assets) in so far as reasonably incurred for the purposes of the intervention.

V. – 3:102: Right to Remuneration

(1) The intervener has a right to remuneration in so far as the intervention is reasonable and undertaken in the course of the intervener's profession or trade.

(2) The remuneration due is the amount, so far as reasonable, which is ordinarily paid at the time and place of intervention in order to obtain a performance of the kind undertaken. If there is no such amount a reasonable remuneration is due.

V. – 3:103: Right to Reparation

An intervener who acts to protect the principal, or the principal's property or interests, against danger has a right against the principal for reparation for loss caused as a result of personal injury or property damage suffered in acting, if:

(a) the intervention created or significantly increased the risk of such injury or damage; and

(b) that risk, so far as foreseeable, was in reasonable proportion to the risk to the principal.

V. – 3:104: Reduction or Exclusion of Intervener's Rights

(1) The intervener's rights are reduced or excluded in so far as the intervener at the time of acting did not want to demand indemnification, reimbursement, remuneration or reparation, as the case may be.

(2) These rights are also reduced or excluded in so far as this is fair and reasonable, having regard among other things to whether the intervener acted to protect the principal in a situation of joint danger, whether the liability of the principal would be excessive and whether the intervener could reasonably be expected to obtain appropriate redress from another.

V. – 3:105: Obligation of Third Person to Indemnify or Reimburse the Principal

If the intervener acts to protect the principal from damage, a person who would be accountable under Book VI (Non-contractual liability arising out of damage caused to another) for the causation of such damage to the principal is obliged to indemnify or, as the case may be, reimburse the principal's liability to the intervener.

V. – 3:106: Authority of Intervener to Act as Representative of the Principal

(1) The intervener may conclude legal transactions or perform other juridical acts as a representative of the principal in so far as this may reasonably be expected to benefit the principal.

(2) However, a unilateral juridical act by the intervener as a representative of the principal has no effect if the person to whom it is addressed rejects the act without undue delay.

Book VI – Non-Contractual Liability Arising Out of Damage Caused to Another

Chapter 1: Fundamental Provisions

VI. – 1:101: Basic Rule

(1) A person who suffers legally relevant damage has a right to reparation from a person who caused the damage intentionally or negligently or is otherwise accountable for the causation of the damage.

(2) Where a person has not caused legally relevant damage intentionally or negligently that person is accountable for the causation of legally relevant damage only if Chapter 3 so provides.

VI. – 1:102: Prevention

Where legally relevant damage is impending, this Book confers on a person who would suffer the damage a right to prevent it. This right is against a person who would be accountable for the causation of the damage if it occurred.

VI. – 1:103: Scope of Application

VI. – 1:101 (Basic rule) and VI. – 1:102 (Prevention):

(a) apply only in accordance with the following provisions of this Book;

(b) apply to both legal and natural persons, unless otherwise stated;

(c) do not apply in so far as their application would contradict the purpose of other private law rules; and

(d) do not affect remedies available on other legal grounds.

Chapter 2: Legally Relevant Damage

Section 1: General

VI. – 2:101: Meaning of Legally Relevant Damage

(1) Loss, whether economic or non-economic, or injury is legally relevant damage if:

(a) one of the following rules of this Chapter so provides;

(b) the loss or injury results from a violation of a right otherwise conferred by the law; or

(c) the loss or injury results from a violation of an interest worthy of legal protection.

(2) In any case covered only by sub-paragraphs (b) or (c) of paragraph (1) loss or injury constitutes legally relevant damage only if it would be fair and reasonable for there to be a right to reparation or prevention, as the case may be, under VI. – 1:101 (Basic rule) or VI. – 1:102 (Prevention).

(3) In considering whether it would be fair and reasonable for there to be a right to reparation or prevention regard is to be had to the ground of accountability, to the nature and proximity of the damage or impending damage, to the reasonable expectations of the person who suffers or would suffer the damage, and to considerations of public policy.

(4) In this Book:

(a) economic loss includes loss of income or profit, burdens incurred and a reduction in the value of property;

(b) non-economic loss includes pain and suffering and impairment of the quality of life.

Section 2: Particular Instances of Legally Relevant Damage

VI. – 2:201: Personal Injury and Consequential Loss

(1) Loss caused to a natural person as a result of injury to his or her body or health and the injury as such are legally relevant damage.

(2) In this Book:

(a) such loss includes the costs of health care including expenses reasonably incurred for the care of the injured person by those close to him or her; and

(b) personal injury includes injury to mental health only if it amounts to a medical condition.

VI. – 2:202: Loss Suffered by Third Persons as a Result of Another's Personal Injury or Death

(1) Non-economic loss caused to a natural person as a result of another's personal injury or death is legally relevant damage if at the time of injury that person is in a particularly close personal relationship to the injured person.

(2) Where a person has been fatally injured:

(a) legally relevant damage caused to the deceased on account of the injury to the time of death becomes legally relevant damage to the deceased's successors;

(b) reasonable funeral expenses are legally relevant damage to the person incurring them; and

(c) loss of maintenance is legally relevant damage to a natural person whom the deceased maintained or, had death not occurred, would have maintained under statutory provisions or to whom the deceased provided care and financial support.

VI. – 2:203: Infringement of Dignity, Liberty and Privacy

(1) Loss caused to a natural person as a result of infringement of his or her right to respect for his or her dignity, such as the rights to liberty and privacy, and the injury as such are legally relevant damage.

(2) Loss caused to a person as a result of injury to that person's reputation and the injury as such are also legally relevant damage if national law so provides.

VI. – 2:204: Loss upon Communication of Incorrect Information about Another

Loss caused to a person as a result of the communication of information about that person which the person communicating the information knows or could reasonably be expected to know is incorrect is legally relevant damage.

VI. – 2:205: Loss upon Breach of Confidence

Loss caused to a person as a result of the communication of information which, either from its nature or the circumstances in which it was obtained, the person communicating the information knows or could reasonably be expected to know is confidential to the person suffering the loss is legally relevant damage.

VI. – 2:206: Loss upon Infringement of Property or Lawful Possession

(1) Loss caused to a person as a result of an infringement of that person's property right or lawful possession of a movable or immovable thing is legally relevant damage.

(2) In this Article:

(a) loss includes being deprived of the use of property;

(b) infringement of a property right includes destruction of or physical damage to the subject-matter of the right (property damage), disposition of the right, interference with its use and other disturbance of the exercise of the right.

VI. – 2:207: Loss upon Reliance on Incorrect Advice or Information

Loss caused to a person as a result of making a decision in reasonable reliance on incorrect advice or information is legally relevant damage if:

(a) the advice or information is provided by a person in pursuit of a profession or in the course of trade; and

(b) the provider knew or could reasonably be expected to have known that the recipient would rely on the advice or information in making a decision of the kind made.

VI. – 2:208: Loss upon Unlawful Impairment of Business

(1) Loss caused to a person as a result of an unlawful impairment of that person's exercise of a profession or conduct of a trade is legally relevant damage.

(2) Loss caused to a consumer as a result of unfair competition is also legally relevant damage if Community or national law so provides.

VI. – 2:209: Burdens Incurred by the State upon Environmental Impairment

Burdens incurred by the State or designated competent authorities in restoring substantially impaired natural elements constituting the environment, such as air, water, soil, flora and fauna, are legally relevant damage to the State or the authorities concerned.

VI. – 2:210: Loss upon Fraudulent Misrepresentation

(1) Without prejudice to the other provisions of this Section loss caused to a person as a result of another's fraudulent misrepresentation, whether by words or conduct, is legally relevant damage.

(2) A misrepresentation is fraudulent if it is made with knowledge or belief that the representation is false and it is intended to induce the recipient to make a mistake.

VI. – 2:211: Loss upon Inducement of Non-Performance of Obligation

Without prejudice to the other provisions of this Section, loss caused to a person as a result of another's inducement of the non-performance of an obligation by a third person is legally relevant damage only if:

(a) the obligation was owed to the person sustaining the loss; and

(b) the person inducing the non-performance:

    (i) intended the third person to fail to perform the obligation, and

    (ii) did not act in legitimate protection of the inducing person's own interest.

Chapter 3: Accountability

Section 1: Intention and Negligence

VI. – 3:101: Intention

A person causes legally relevant damage intentionally when that person causes such damage either:

(a) meaning to cause damage of the type caused; or

(b) by conduct which that person means to do, knowing that such damage, or damage of that type, will or will almost certainly be caused.

VI. – 3:102: Negligence

A person causes legally relevant damage negligently when that person causes the damage by conduct which either:

(a) does not meet the particular standard of care provided by a statutory provision whose purpose is the protection of the person suffering the damage from that damage; or

(b) does not otherwise amount to such care as could be expected from a reasonably careful person in the circumstances of the case.

VI. – 3:103: Persons Under Eighteen

(1) A person under eighteen years of age is accountable for causing legally relevant damage according to VI. – 3:102 (Negligence) sub-paragraph (b) only in so far as that person does not exercise such care as could be expected from a reasonably careful person of the same age in the circumstances of the case.

(2) A person under seven years of age is not accountable for causing damage intentionally or negligently.

(3) However, paragraphs (1) and (2) do not apply to the extent that:

(a) the person suffering the damage cannot obtain reparation under this Book from another; and

(b) liability to make reparation would be equitable having regard to the financial means of the parties and all other circumstances of the case.

VI. – 3:104: Accountability for Damage Caused by Children or Supervised Persons

(1) Parents or other persons obliged by law to provide parental care for a person under fourteen years of age are accountable for the causation of legally relevant damage where that person under age caused the damage by conduct that would constitute intentional or negligent conduct if it were the conduct of an adult.

(2) An institution or other body obliged to supervise a person is accountable for the causation of legally relevant damage suffered by a third party when:

(a) the damage is personal injury, loss within VI. – 2:202 (Loss suffered by third persons as a result of another's personal injury or death) or property damage;

(b) the person whom the institution or other body is obliged to supervise caused that damage intentionally or negligently or, in the case of a person under eighteen, by conduct that would constitute intention or negligence if it were the conduct of an adult; and

(c) the person whom the institution or other body is obliged to supervise is a person likely to cause damage of that type.

(3) However, a person is not accountable under this Article for the causation of damage if that person shows that there was no defective supervision of the person causing the damage.

Section 2: Accountability Without Intention or Negligence

VI. – 3:201: Accountability for Damage Caused by Employees and Representatives

(1) A person who employs or similarly engages another is accountable for the causation of legally relevant damage suffered by a third person when the person employed or engaged:

(a) caused the damage in the course of the employment or engagement; and

(b) caused the damage intentionally or negligently, or is otherwise accountable for the causation of the damage.

(2) Paragraph (1) applies correspondingly to a legal person in relation to a representative causing damage in the course of their engagement. A representative is a person who is authorised to effect juridical acts on behalf of the legal person by its constitution.

VI. – 3:202: Accountability for Damage Caused by the Unsafe State of an Immovable

(1) A person who independently exercises control over an immovable is accountable for the causation of personal injury and consequential loss, loss within VI. – 2:202 (Loss suffered by third persons as a result of another's personal injury or death), and loss resulting from property damage (other than to the immovable itself) by a state of the immovable which does not ensure such safety as a person in or near the immovable is entitled to expect having regard to the circumstances including:

(a) the nature of the immovable;

(b) the access to the immovable; and

(c) the cost of avoiding the immovable being in that state.

(2) A person exercises independent control over an immovable if that person exercises such control that it is reasonable to impose a duty on that person to prevent legally relevant damage within the scope of this Article.

(3) The owner of the immovable is to be regarded as independently exercising control, unless the owner shows that another independently exercises control.

VI. – 3:203: Accountability for Damage Caused by Animals

A keeper of an animal is accountable for the causation by the animal of personal injury and consequential loss, loss within VI. – 2:202 (Loss suffered by third persons as a result of another's personal injury or death), and loss resulting from property damage.

VI. – 3:204: Accountability for Damage Caused by Defective Products

(1) The producer of a product is accountable for the causation of personal injury and consequential loss, loss within VI. – 2:202 (Loss suffered by third persons as a result of another's personal injury or death), and, in relation to consumers, loss resulting from property damage (other than to the product itself) by a defect in the product.

(2) A person who imported the product into the European Economic Area for sale, hire, leasing or distribution in the course of that person's business is accountable correspondingly.

(3) A supplier of the product is accountable correspondingly if:

(a) the producer cannot be identified; or

(b) in the case of an imported product, the product does not indicate the identity of the importer (whether or not the producer's name is indicated), unless the supplier informs the person suffering the damage, within a reasonable time, of the identity of the producer or the person who supplied that supplier with the product.

(4) A person is not accountable under this Article for the causation of damage if that person shows that:

(a) that person did not put the product into circulation;

(b) it is probable that the defect which caused the damage did not exist at the time when that person put the product into circulation;

(c) that person neither manufactured the product for sale or distribution for economic purpose nor manufactured or distributed it in the course of business;

(d) the defect is due to the product's compliance with mandatory regulations issued by public authorities;

(e) the state of scientific and technical knowledge at the time that person put the product into circulation did not enable the existence of the defect to be discovered; or

(f) in the case of a manufacturer of a component, the defect is attributable to:

(i) the design of the product into which the component has been fitted; or

(ii) instructions given by the manufacturer of the product.

(5) "Producer" means:

(a) in the case of a finished product or a component, the manufacturer;

(b) in the case of raw material, the person who abstracts or wins it; and

(c) any person who, by putting a name, trade mark or other distinguishing feature on the product, gives the impression of being its producer.

(6) "Product" means a movable, even if incorporated into another movable or an immovable, or electricity.

(7) A product is defective if it does not provide the safety which a person is entitled to expect, having regard to the circumstances including:

(a) the presentation of the product;

(b) the use to which it could reasonably be expected that the product would be put; and

(c) the time when the product was put into circulation, but a product is not defective merely because a better product is subsequently put into circulation.

VI. – 3:205: Accountability for Damage Caused by Motor Vehicles

(1) A keeper of a motor vehicle is accountable for the causation of personal injury and consequential loss, loss within VI. – 2:202 (Loss suffered by third persons as a result of another's personal injury or death), and loss resulting from property damage (other than to the vehicle and its freight) in a traffic accident which results from the use of the vehicle.

(2) "Motor vehicle" means any vehicle intended for travel on land and propelled by mechanical power, but not running on rails, and any trailer, whether or not coupled.

VI. – 3:206: Accountability for Damage Caused by Dangerous Substances or Emissions

(1) A keeper of a substance or an operator of an installation is accountable for the causation by that substance or by emissions from that installation of personal injury and consequential loss, loss within VI. – 2:202 (Loss suffered by third persons as a result of another's personal injury or death), loss resulting from property damage, and burdens within VI. – 2:209 (Burdens incurred by the State upon environmental impairment), if:

(a) having regard to their quantity and attributes, at the time of the emission, or, failing an emission, at the time of contact with the substance it is very likely that the substance or emission will cause such damage unless adequately controlled; and

(b) the damage results from the realisation of that danger.

(2) "Substance" includes chemicals (whether solid, liquid or gaseous). Microorganisms are to be treated like substances.

(3) "Emission" includes:

(a) the release or escape of substances;

(b) the conduction of electricity;

(c) heat, light and other radiation;

(d) noise and other vibrations; and

(e) other incorporeal impact on the environment.

(4) "Installation" includes a mobile installation and an installation under construction or not in use.

(5) However, a person is not accountable for the causation of damage under this Article if that person:

(a) does not keep the substance or operate the installation for purposes related to that person's trade, business or profession; or

(b) shows that there was no failure to comply with statutory standards of control of the substance or management of the installation.

VI. – 3:207: Other Accountability for the Causation of Legally Relevant Damage

A person is also accountable for the causation of legally relevant damage if national law so provides where it:

(a) relates to a source of danger which is not within VI. – 3:104 (Accountability for damage caused by children or supervised persons) to VI. – 3:205 (Accountability for damage caused by motor vehicles);

(b) relates to substances or emissions; or

(c) disapplies VI. – 3:204 (Accountability for damage caused by defective products) paragraph (4)(e).

VI. – 3:208: Abandonment

For the purposes of this section, a person remains accountable for an immovable, vehicle, substance or installation which that person abandons until another exercises independent control over it or becomes its keeper or operator. This applies correspondingly, so far as reasonable, in respect of a keeper of an animal.

Chapter 4: Causation

VI. – 4:101: General Rule

(1) A person causes legally relevant damage to another if the damage is to be regarded as a consequence of that person's conduct or the source of danger for which that person is responsible.

(2) In cases of personal injury or death the injured person's predisposition with respect to the type or extent of the injury sustained is to be disregarded.

VI. – 4:102: Collaboration

A person who participates with, instigates or materially assists another in causing legally relevant damage is to be regarded as causing that damage.

VI. – 4:103: Alternative Causes

Where legally relevant damage may have been caused by any one or more of a number of occurrences for which different persons are accountable and it is established that the damage was caused by one of these occurrences but not which one, each person who is accountable for any of the occurrences is rebuttably presumed to have caused that damage.

Chapter 5: Defences

Section 1: Consent or Conduct of the Person Suffering the Damage

VI. – 5:101: Consent and Acting at Own Risk

(1) A person has a defence if the person suffering the damage validly consents to the legally relevant damage and is aware or could reasonably be expected to be aware of the consequences of that consent.

(2) The same applies if the person suffering the damage, knowing the risk of damage of the type caused, voluntarily takes that risk and is to be regarded as accepting it.

VI. – 5:102: Contributory Fault and Accountability

(1) Where the fault of the person suffering the damage contributes to the occurrence or extent of legally relevant damage, reparation is to be reduced according to the degree of such fault.

(2) However, no regard is to be had to:

(a) an insubstantial fault of the person suffering the damage;

(b) fault or accountability whose contribution to the causation of the damage is insubstantial;

(c) the injured person's want of care contributing to that person's personal injury caused by a motor vehicle in a traffic accident, unless that want of care constitutes profound failure to take such care as is manifestly required in the circumstances.

(3) Paragraphs (1) and (2) apply correspondingly where the fault of a person for whom the person suffering the damage is responsible within the scope of VI. – 3:201 (Accountability for

damage caused by employees and representatives) contributes to the occurrence or extent of the damage.

(4) Compensation is to be reduced likewise if and in so far as any other source of danger for which the person suffering the damage is responsible under Chapter 3 (Accountability) contributes to the occurrence or extent of the damage.

VI. – 5:103: Damage Caused by a Criminal to a Collaborator

Legally relevant damage caused unintentionally in the course of committing a criminal offence to another person participating or otherwise collaborating in the offence does not give rise to a right to reparation if this would be contrary to public policy.

Section 2: Interests of Accountable Persons or Third Parties

VI. – 5:201: Authority Conferred by Law

A person has a defence if legally relevant damage is caused with authority conferred by law.

VI. – 5:202: Self-Defence, Benevolent Intervention and Necessity

(1) A person has a defence if that person causes legally relevant damage in reasonable protection of a right or of an interest worthy of legal protection of that person or a third person if the person suffering the legally relevant damage is accountable for endangering the right or interest protected. For the purposes of this paragraph VI. – 3:103 (Persons under eighteen) is to be disregarded.

(2) The same applies to legally relevant damage caused by a benevolent intervener to a principal without breach of the intervener's duties.

(3) Where a person causes legally relevant damage to the patrimony of another in a situation of imminent danger to life, body, health or liberty in order to save the person causing the damage or a third person from that danger and the danger could not be eliminated without causing the damage, the person causing the damage is not liable to make reparation beyond providing reasonable recompense.

VI. – 5:203: Protection of Public Interest

A person has a defence if legally relevant damage is caused in necessary protection of values fundamental to a democratic society, in particular where damage is caused by dissemination of information in the media.

Section 3: Inability to Control

VI. – 5:301: Mental Incompetence

(1) A person who is mentally incompetent at the time of conduct causing legally relevant damage is liable only if this is equitable, having regard to the mentally incompetent person's financial means and all the other circumstances of the case. Liability is limited to reasonable recompense.

(2) A person is to be regarded as mentally incompetent if that person lacks sufficient insight into the nature of his or her conduct, unless the lack of sufficient insight is the temporary result of his or her own misconduct.

VI. – 5:302: Event Beyond Control

A person has a defence if legally relevant damage is caused by an abnormal event which cannot be averted by any reasonable measure and which is not to be regarded as that person's risk.

Section 4: Contractual Exclusion and Restriction of Liability

VI. – 5:401: Contractual Exclusion and Restriction of Liability

(1) Liability for causing legally relevant damage intentionally cannot be excluded or restricted.

(2) Liability for causing legally relevant damage as a result of a profound failure to take such care as is manifestly required in the circumstances cannot be excluded or restricted:

(a) in respect of personal injury (including fatal injury); or

(b) if the exclusion or restriction is otherwise illegal or contrary to good faith and fair dealing.

(3) Liability for damage for the causation of which a person is accountable under VI. – 3:204 (Accountability for damage caused by defective products) cannot be restricted or excluded.

(4) Other liability under this Book can be excluded or restricted unless statute provides otherwise.

Section 5: Loss Within VI. – 2:202 (Loss Suffered by Third Persons as a Result of Another's Personal Injury or Death)

VI. – 5:501: Extension of Defences Against the Injured Person to Third Persons

A defence which may be asserted against a person's right of reparation in respect of that person's personal injury or, if death had not occurred, could have been asserted, may also be asserted against a person suffering loss within VI. – 2:202 (Loss suffered by third persons as a result of another's personal injury or death).

Chapter 6: Remedies

Section 1: Reparation in General

VI. – 6:101: Aim and Forms of Reparation

(1) Reparation is to reinstate the person suffering the legally relevant damage in the position that person would have been in had the legally relevant damage not occurred.

(2) Reparation may be in money (compensation) or otherwise, as is most appropriate, having regard to the kind and extent of damage suffered and all the other circumstances of the case.

(3) Where a tangible object is damaged, compensation equal to its depreciation of value is to be awarded instead of the cost of its repair if the cost of repair unreasonably exceeds the depreciation of value. This rule applies to animals only if appropriate, having regard to the purpose for which the animal was kept.

(4) As an alternative to reinstatement under paragraph (1), but only where this is reasonable, reparation may take the form of recovery from the person accountable for the causation of the legally relevant damage of any advantage obtained by the latter in connection with causing the damage.

VI. – 6:102: De Minimis Rule

Trivial damage is to be disregarded.

VI. – 6:103: Equalisation of Benefits

(1) Benefits arising to the person suffering legally relevant damage as a result of the damaging event are to be disregarded unless it would be fair and reasonable to take them into account.

(2) In deciding whether it would be fair and reasonable to take the benefits into account, regard shall be had to the kind of damage sustained, the nature of the accountability of the person causing the damage and, where the benefits are conferred by a third person, the purpose of conferring those benefits.

VI. – 6:104: Multiple Persons Suffering Damage

Where multiple persons suffer legally relevant damage and reparation to one person will also make reparation to another, Book III, Chapter 4, Section 2 (Plurality of creditors) applies with appropriate adaptation to their rights to reparation.

VI. – 6:105: Solidary Liability

Where several persons are liable for the same legally relevant damage, they are liable solidarily.

VI. – 6:106: Assignment of Right to Reparation

The person suffering the damage may assign a right to reparation, including a right to reparation for non-economic loss.

Section 2: Compensation

VI. – 6:201: Right of Election

The person suffering the damage may choose whether or not to spend compensation on the reinstatement of the damaged interest.

VI. – 6:202: Reduction of Liability

Where it is fair and reasonable to do so, a person may be relieved of liability to compensate, either wholly or in part, if, where the damage is not caused intentionally, liability in full would be disproportionate to the accountability of the person causing the damage or the extent of the damage or the means to prevent it.

VI. – 6:203: Capitalisation and Quantification

(1) Compensation is to be awarded as a lump sum unless a good reason requires periodical payment.

(2) National law determines how compensation for personal injury and non-economic loss is to be quantified.

VI. – 6:204: Compensation for Injury as Such

Injury as such is to be compensated independent of compensation for economic or non-economic loss.

Section 3: Prevention

VI. – 6:301: Right to Prevention

(1) The right to prevention exists only in so far as:

(a) reparation would not be an adequate alternative remedy; and

(b) it is reasonable for the person who would be accountable for the causation of the damage to prevent it from occurring.

(2) Where the source of danger is an object or an animal and it is not reasonably possible for the endangered person to avoid the danger the right to prevention includes a right to have the source of danger removed.

VI. – 6:302: Liability for Loss in Preventing Damage

A person who has reasonably incurred expenditure or sustained other loss in order to prevent that person from suffering an impending damage, or in order to limit the extent or severity of damage suffered, has a right to compensation from the person who would have been accountable for the causation of the damage.

Chapter 7: Ancillary Rules

VI. – 7:101: National Constitutional Laws

The provisions of this Book are to be interpreted and applied in a manner compatible with the constitutional law of the court.

VI. – 7:102: Statutory Provisions

National law determines what legal provisions are statutory provisions.

VI. – 7:103: Public Law Functions and Court Proceedings

This Book does not govern the liability of a person or body arising from the exercise or omission to exercise public law functions or from performing duties during court proceedings.

VI. – 7:104: Liability of Employees, Employers, Trade Unions and Employers' Associations

This Book does not govern the liability of:

(a) employees (whether to co-employees, employers or third parties) arising in the course of employment;

(b) employers to employees arising in the course of employment; and

(c) trade unions and employers' associations arising in the course of an industrial dispute.

VI. – 7:105: Reduction or Exclusion of Liability to Indemnified Persons

If a person is entitled from another source to reparation, whether in full or in part, for that person's damage, in particular from an insurer, fund or other body, national law determines whether or not by virtue of that entitlement liability under this Book is limited or excluded.

Book VII – Unjustified Enrichment

Chapter 1: General

VII. – 1:101: Basic Rule

(1) A person who obtains an unjustified enrichment which is attributable to another's disadvantage is obliged to that other to reverse the enrichment.

(2) This rule applies only in accordance with the following provisions of this Book.

Chapter 2: When Enrichment Is Unjustified

VII. – 2:101: Circumstances in Which an Enrichment Is Unjustified

(1) An enrichment is unjustified unless:

(a) the enriched person is entitled as against the disadvantaged person to the enrichment by virtue of a contract or other juridical act, a court order or a rule of law; or

(b) the disadvantaged person consented freely and without error to the disadvantage.

(2) If the contract or other juridical act, court order or rule of law referred to in paragraph (1)(a) is void or avoided or otherwise rendered ineffective retrospectively, the enriched person is not entitled to the enrichment on that basis.

(3) However, the enriched person is to be regarded as entitled to an enrichment by virtue of a rule of law only if the policy of that rule is that the enriched person is to retain the value of the enrichment.

(4) An enrichment is also unjustified if:

(a) the disadvantaged person conferred it:

(i) for a purpose which is not achieved; or

(ii) with an expectation which is not realised;

(b) the enriched person knew of, or could reasonably be expected to know of, the purpose or expectation; and

(c) the enriched person accepted or could reasonably be assumed to have accepted that the enrichment must be reversed in such circumstances.

VII. – 2:102: Performance of Obligation to Third Person

Where the enriched person obtains the enrichment as a result of the disadvantaged person performing an obligation or a supposed obligation owed by the disadvantaged person to a third person, the enrichment is justified if:

(a) the disadvantaged person performed freely; or

(b) the enrichment was merely the incidental result of performance of the obligation.

VII. – 2:103: Consenting or Performing Freely

(1) If the disadvantaged person's consent is affected by incapacity, fraud, coercion, threats or unfair exploitation, the disadvantaged person does not consent freely.

(2) If the obligation which is performed is ineffective because of incapacity, fraud, coercion threats or unfair exploitation, the disadvantaged person does not perform freely.

Chapter 3: Enrichment and Disadvantage

VII. – 3:101: Enrichment

(1) A person is enriched by:

(a) an increase in assets or a decrease in liabilities;

(b) receiving a service or having work done; or

(c) use of another's assets.

(2) In determining whether and to what extent a person obtains an enrichment, no regard is to be had to any disadvantage which that person sustains in exchange for or after the enrichment.

VII. – 3:102: Disadvantage

(1) A person is disadvantaged by:

(a) a decrease in assets or an increase in liabilities;

(b) rendering a service or doing work; or

(c) another's use of that person's assets.

(2) In determining whether and to what extent a person sustains a disadvantage, no regard is to be had to any enrichment which that person obtains in exchange for or after the disadvantage.

Chapter 4: Attribution

VII. – 4:101: Instances of Attribution

An enrichment is attributable to another's disadvantage in particular where:

(a) an asset of that other is transferred to the enriched person by that other;

(b) a service is rendered to or work is done for the enriched person by that other;

(c) the enriched person uses that other's asset, especially where the enriched person infringes the disadvantaged person's rights or legally protected interests;

(d) an asset of the enriched person is improved by that other; or

(e) the enriched person is discharged from a liability by that other.

VII. – 4:102: Intermediaries

Where one party to a juridical act is an authorised intermediary indirectly representing a principal, any enrichment or disadvantage of the principal which results from the juridical act, or from a performance of obligations under it, is to be regarded as an enrichment or disadvantage of the intermediary.

VII. – 4:103: Debtor's Performance to a Non-Creditor; Onward Transfer in Good Faith

(1) An enrichment is also attributable to another's disadvantage where a debtor confers the enrichment on the enriched person and as a result the disadvantaged person loses a right against the debtor to the same or a like enrichment.

(2) Paragraph (1) applies in particular where a person who is obliged to the disadvantaged person to reverse an unjustified enrichment transfers it to a third person in circumstances in which the debtor has a defence under VII. – 6:101 (Disenrichment).

VII. – 4:104: Ratification of Debtor's Performance to a Non-Creditor

(1) Where a debtor purports to discharge a debt by paying a third person, the creditor may ratify that act.

(2) Ratification extinguishes the creditor's right against the debtor to the extent of the payment with the effect that the third person's enrichment is attributable to the creditor's loss of the claim against the debtor.

(3) As between the creditor and the third person, ratification does not amount to consent to the loss of the creditor's right against the debtor.

(4) This Article applies correspondingly to performances of non-monetary obligations.

(5) Other rules may exclude the application of this Article if an insolvency or equivalent proceeding has been opened against the debtor before the creditor ratifies.

VII. – 4:105: Attribution Resulting from an Act of an Intervener

(1) An enrichment is also attributable to another's disadvantage where a third person uses an asset of the disadvantaged person without authority so that the disadvantaged person is deprived of the asset and it accrues to the enriched person.

(2) Paragraph (1) applies in particular where, as a result of an intervener's interference with or disposition of goods, the disadvantaged person ceases to be owner of the goods and the enriched person becomes owner, whether by juridical act or rule of law.

VII. – 4:106: Ratification of Intervener's Acts

(1) A person entitled to an asset may ratify the act of an intervener who purports to dispose of or otherwise uses that asset in a juridical act with a third person.

(2) The ratified act has the same effect as a juridical act by an authorised intermediary. As between the person ratifying and the intervener, ratification does not amount to consent to the intervener's use of the asset.

VII. – 4:107: Where Type or Value Not Identical

An enrichment may be attributable to another's disadvantage even though the enrichment and disadvantage are not of the same type or value.

Chapter 5: Reversal of Enrichment

VII. – 5:101: Transferable Enrichment

(1) Where the enrichment consists of a transferable asset, the enriched person reverses the enrichment by transferring the asset to the disadvantaged person.

(2) Instead of transferring the asset, the enriched person may choose to reverse the enrichment by paying its monetary value to the disadvantaged person if a transfer would cause the enriched person unreasonable effort or expense.

(3) If the enriched person is no longer able to transfer the asset, the enriched person reverses the enrichment by paying its monetary value to the disadvantaged person.

(4) However, to the extent that the enriched person has obtained a substitute in exchange, the substitute is the enrichment to be reversed if:

(a) the enriched person is in good faith at the time of disposal or loss and the enriched person so chooses; or

(b) the enriched person is not in good faith at the time of disposal or loss, the disadvantaged person so chooses and the choice is not inequitable.

(5) The enriched person is in good faith if that person neither knew nor could reasonably be expected to know that the enrichment was or was likely to become unjustified.

VII. – 5:102: Non-Transferable Enrichment

(1) Where the enrichment does not consist of a transferable asset, the enriched person reverses the enrichment by paying its monetary value to the disadvantaged person.

(2) The enriched person is not liable to pay more than any saving if the enriched person:

(a) did not consent to the enrichment; or

(b) was in good faith.

(3) However, where the enrichment was obtained under an agreement which fixed a price or value for the enrichment, the enriched person is at least liable to pay that sum if the agreement was void or voidable for reasons which were not material to the fixing of the price.

(4) Paragraph (3) does not apply so as to increase liability beyond the monetary value of the enrichment.

VII. – 5:103: Monetary Value of an Enrichment; Saving

(1) The monetary value of an enrichment is the sum of money which a provider and a recipient with a real intention of reaching an agreement would lawfully have agreed as its price. Expenditure of a service provider which the agreement would require the recipient to reimburse is to be regarded as part of the price.

(2) A saving is the decrease in assets or increase in liabilities which the enriched person would have sustained if the enrichment had not been obtained.

VII. – 5:104: Fruits and Use of an Enrichment

(1) Reversal of the enrichment extends to the fruits and use of the enrichment or, if less, any saving resulting from the fruits or use.

(2) However, if the enriched person obtains the fruits or use in bad faith, reversal of the enrichment extends to the fruits and use even if the saving is less than the value of the fruits or use.

Chapter 6: Defences

VII. – 6:101: Disenrichment

(1) The enriched person is not liable to reverse the enrichment to the extent that the enriched person has sustained a disadvantage by disposing of the enrichment or otherwise (disenrichment), unless the enriched person would have been disenriched even if the enrichment had not been obtained.

(2) However, a disenrichment is to be disregarded to the extent that:

(a) the enriched person has obtained a substitute;

(b) the enriched person was not in good faith at the time of disenrichment, unless:

(i) the disadvantaged person would also have been disenriched even if the enrichment had been reversed; or

(ii) the enriched person was in good faith at the time of enrichment, the disenrichment was sustained before performance of the obligation to reverse the enrichment was due and the disenrichment resulted from the realisation of a risk for which the enriched person is not to be regarded as responsible; or

(c) paragraph (3) of VII. – 5:102 (Non-transferable enrichment) applies.

(3) Where the enriched person has a defence under this Article as against the disadvantaged person as a result of a disposal to a third person, any right of the disadvantaged person against that third person is unaffected.

VII. – 6:102: Juridical Acts in Good Faith with Third Parties

The enriched person is also not liable to reverse the enrichment if:

(a) in exchange for that enrichment the enriched person confers another enrichment on a third person; and

(b) the enriched person is still in good faith at that time.

VII. – 6:103: Illegality

Where a contract or other juridical act under which an enrichment is obtained is void or avoided because of an infringement of a fundamental principle (II. – 7:301 (Contracts infringing fundamental principles)) or mandatory rule of law, the enriched person is not liable to reverse the enrichment to the extent that the reversal would contravene the policy underlying the principle or rule.

Chapter 7: Relation to Other Legal Rules

VII. – 7:101: Other Private Law Rights to Recover

(1) The legal consequences of an enrichment which is obtained by virtue of a contract or other juridical act are governed by other rules if those rules grant or exclude a right to reversal of an enrichment, whether on withdrawal, termination, price reduction or otherwise.

(2) This Book does not address the proprietary effect of a right to reversal of an enrichment.

(3) This Book does not affect any other right to recover arising under contractual or other rules of private law.

VII. – 7:102: Concurrent Obligations

(1) Where the disadvantaged person has both:

(a) a claim under this Book for reversal of an unjustified enrichment; and

(b) (i) a claim for reparation for the disadvantage (whether against the enriched person or a third party); or

(ii) a right to recover under other rules of private law as a result of the unjustified enrichment,

the satisfaction of one of the claims reduces the other claim by the same amount.

(2) The same applies where a person uses an asset of the disadvantaged person so that it accrues to another and under this Book:

(a) the user is liable to the disadvantaged person in respect of the use of the asset; and

(b) the recipient is liable to the disadvantaged person in respect of the increase in assets.

VII. – 7:103: Public Law Claims

This Book does not determine whether it applies to enrichments which a person or body obtains or confers in the exercise of public law functions.

Book VIII – Acquisition and Loss of Ownership of Goods

Chapter 1: General Provisions

Section 1: Scope of Application and Relation to Other Provisions

VIII. – 1:101: Scope of Application

(1) This Book applies to the acquisition, loss and protection of ownership of goods and to specific related issues.

(2) This Book does not apply to the acquisition or loss of ownership of goods by:

(a) universal succession, in particular under the law of succession and under company law;

(b) expropriation and forfeiture;

(c) separation from movable or immovable property;

(d) division of co-ownership, unless provided by VIII. – 2:306 (Delivery out of the bulk) or VIII. – 5:202 (Commingling);

(e) survivorship or accrual, unless covered by Chapter 5 of this Book;

(f) real subrogation, unless covered by Chapter 5 of this Book;

(g) occupation;

(h) finding; or

(i) abandonment.

(3) This Book applies to the acquisition and loss of ownership of goods by extrajudicial enforcement in the sense of Book IX or the equivalent. It may be applied, with appropriate adaptations, to the acquisition and loss of ownership of goods by judicial or equivalent enforcement.

(4) This Book does not apply to:

(a) company shares or documents embodying the right to an asset or to the performance of an obligation, except documents containing the undertaking to deliver goods for the purposes of VIII. – 2:105 (Equivalents to delivery) paragraph (4); or

(b) electricity.

(5) This Book applies, with appropriate adaptations, to banknotes and coins that are current legal tender.

VIII. – 1:102: Registration of Goods

(1) Whether ownership and the transfer of ownership in certain categories of goods may be or have to be registered in a public register is determined by national law.

(2) The effects of such registration, as determined by national law, have priority over the respective rules of this Book.

VIII. – 1:103: Priority of Other Provisions

(1) In relation to a transfer, or retention, of ownership for purposes of security, the provisions of Book IX apply and have priority over the provisions in this Book.

(2) In relation to a transfer of ownership for purposes of a trust, or to or from a trust, the provisions of Book X apply and have priority over the provisions in this Book.

VIII. – 1:104: Application of Rules of Books I to III

Where, under the provisions of this Book, proprietary effects are determined by an agreement, Books I to III apply, where appropriate.

Section 2: Definitions

VIII. – 1:201: Goods

"Goods" means corporeal movables. It includes ships, vessels, hovercraft or aircraft, space objects, animals, liquids and gases.

VIII. – 1:202: Ownership

"Ownership" is the most comprehensive right a person, the "owner", can have over property, including the exclusive right, so far as consistent with applicable laws or rights granted by the owner, to use, enjoy, modify, destroy, dispose of and recover the property.

VIII. – 1:203: Co-Ownership

Where "co-ownership" is created under this Book, this means that two or more co-owners own undivided shares in the whole goods and each co-owner can dispose of that co-owner's share by acting alone, unless otherwise provided by the parties.

VIII. – 1:204: Limited Proprietary Rights

Limited proprietary rights in the sense of this Book are:

(a) security rights if characterised or treated as proprietary rights by Book IX or by national law;

(b) rights to use if characterised or treated as proprietary rights by other provisions of these model rules or by national law;

(c) rights to acquire in the sense of VIII. – 2:307 (Contingent right of transferee under retention of ownership) or if characterised or treated as proprietary rights by other provisions of these model rules or by national law;

(d) trust-related rights if characterised or treated as proprietary rights by Book X or by national law.

VIII. – 1:205: Possession

(1) Possession, in relation to goods, means having direct physical control or indirect physical control over the goods.

(2) Direct physical control is physical control which is exercised by the possessor personally or through a possession-agent exercising such control on behalf of the possessor (direct possession).

(3) Indirect physical control is physical control which is exercised by means of another person, a limited-right-possessor (indirect possession).

VIII. – 1:206: Possession by Owner-Possessor

An "owner-possessor" is a person who exercises direct or indirect physical control over the goods with the intention of doing so as, or as if, an owner.

VIII. – 1:207: Possession by Limited-Right-Possessor

(1) A "limited-right-possessor" is a person who exercises physical control over the goods either:

(a) with the intention of doing so in that person's own interest, and under a specific legal relationship with the owner-possessor which gives the limited-right-possessor the right to possess the goods; or

(b) with the intention of doing so to the order of the owner-possessor, and under a specific contractual relationship with the owner-possessor which gives the limited-right-possessor a right to retain the goods until any charges or costs have been paid by the owner-possessor.

(2) A limited-right-possessor may have direct physical control or indirect physical control over the goods.

VIII. – 1:208: Possession Through a Possession-Agent

(1) A "possession-agent" is a person:

(a) who exercises direct physical control over the goods on behalf of an owner-possessor or limited-right-possessor without the intention and specific legal relationship required under VIII. – 1:207 (Possession by limited-right-possessor) paragraph (1); and

(b) to whom the owner-possessor or limited-right-possessor may give binding instructions as to the use of the goods in the interest of the owner-possessor or limited-right-possessor.

(2) A possession-agent may, in particular, be:

(a) an employee of the owner-possessor or limited-right-possessor or a person exercising a similar function; or

(b) a person who is given physical control over the goods by the owner-possessor or limited-right-possessor for practical reasons.

(3) A person is also a possession-agent where that person is accidentally in a position to exercise, and does exercise, direct physical control over the goods for an owner-possessor or limited-right-possessor.

Section 3: Further General Rules

VIII. – 1:301: Transferability

(1) All goods are transferable except where provided otherwise by law. A limitation or prohibition of the transfer of goods by a contract or other juridical act does not affect the transferability of the goods.

(2) Whether or to what extent uncollected fruits of, and accessories or appurtenances to, goods or immovable assets are transferable separately is regulated by national law. Chapter 5 remains unaffected.

Chapter 2: Transfer of Ownership Based on the Transferor's Right or Authority

Section 1: Requirements for Transfer under this Chapter

VIII. – 2:101: Requirements for the Transfer of Ownership in General

(1) The transfer of ownership of goods under this Chapter requires that:

(a) the goods exist;

(b) the goods are transferable;

(c) the transferor has the right or authority to transfer the ownership;

(d) the transferee is entitled as against the transferor to the transfer of ownership by virtue of a contract or other juridical act, a court order or a rule of law; and

(e) there is an agreement as to the time ownership is to pass and the conditions of this agreement are met, or, in the absence of such agreement, delivery or an equivalent to delivery.

(2) For the purposes of paragraph (1)(e) the delivery or equivalent to delivery must be based on, or referable to, the entitlement under the contract or other juridical act, court order or rule of law.

(3) Where the contract or other juridical act, court order or rule of law defines the goods in generic terms, ownership can pass only when the goods are identified to it. Where goods form part of an identified bulk, VIII. – 2:305 (Transfer of goods forming part of a bulk) applies.

(4) Paragraph (1)(e) does not apply where ownership passes under a court order or rule of law at the time determined in it.

VIII. – 2:102: Transferor's Right or Authority

(1) Where the transferor lacks a right or authority to transfer ownership at the time ownership is to pass, the transfer takes place when the right is obtained or the person having the right or authority to transfer has ratified the transfer at a later time.

(2) Upon ratification the transfer produces the same effects as if it had initially been carried out with authority. However, proprietary rights acquired by other persons before ratification remain unaffected.

VIII. – 2:103: Agreement as to the Time Ownership Is to Pass

The point in time when ownership passes may be determined by party agreement, except where registration is necessary to acquire ownership under national law.

VIII. – 2:104: Delivery

(1) For the purposes of this Book, delivery of the goods takes place when the transferor gives up and the transferee obtains possession of the goods in the sense of VIII. – 1:205 (Possession).

(2) If the contract or other juridical act, court order or rule of law involves carriage of the goods by a carrier or a series of carriers, delivery of the goods takes place when the transferor's obligation to deliver is fulfilled and the carrier or the transferee obtains possession of the goods.

VIII. – 2:105: Equivalents to Delivery

(1) Where the goods are already in the possession of the transferee, the retention of the goods on the coming into effect of the entitlement under the contract or other juridical act, court order or rule of law has the same effect as delivery.

(2) Where a third person possesses the goods for the transferor, the same effect as delivery is achieved when the third party receives the transferor's notice of the ownership being transferred to the transferee, or at a later time if so stated in the notice. The same applies where notice is given to a possession-agent in the sense of VIII. – 1:208 (Possession through possession-agent).

(3) The same effect as delivery of the goods is achieved when the transferor gives up and the transferee obtains possession of means enabling the transferee to obtain possession of the goods.

(4) Where a person exercising physical control over goods issues a document containing an undertaking to deliver the goods to the current holder of the document, the transfer of that document is equivalent to delivery of the goods. The document may be an electronic one.

Section 2: Effects

VIII. – 2:201: Effects of the Transfer of Ownership

(1) At the time determined by Section 1, ownership passes within the limits of the transferor's right or authority to dispose, with effect between the parties and with effect against third persons.

(2) The transfer of ownership does not affect rights and obligations between the parties based on the terms of a contract or other juridical act, court order or rule of law, such as:

(a) a right resulting from the passing of risk;

(b) a right to withhold performance;

(c) a right to fruits or benefits, or an obligation to cover costs and charges; or

(d) a right to use or an obligation not to use or otherwise deal with the goods.

(3) The transfer of ownership does not affect rights of or against third parties under other rules of law, such as:

(a) any right of the transferor's creditors to treat the transfer as ineffective arising from the law of insolvency or similar provisions; or

(b) a right to claim reparation under Book VI (Non-contractual liability arising out of damage caused to another) from a third party damaging the goods.

(4) Where ownership has been transferred but the transferor still has a right to withhold delivery of the goods (paragraph (2)(b)), terminating the contractual relationship while exercising the right to withhold performance has retroactive proprietary effect in the sense of the following Article.

VIII. – 2:202: Effect of Initial Invalidity, Subsequent Avoidance, Withdrawal, Termination and Revocation

(1) Where the underlying contract or other juridical act is invalid from the beginning, a transfer of ownership does not take place.

(2) Where, after ownership has been transferred, the underlying contract or other juridical act is avoided under Book II, Chapter 7, ownership is treated as never having passed to the transferee (retroactive proprietary effect).

(3) Where ownership must be re-transferred as a consequence of withdrawal in the sense of Book II, Chapter 5, or termination in the sense of Book III, Chapter 3, or revocation of a donation in the sense of Book IV.H, there is no retroactive proprietary effect nor is ownership re-transferred immediately. VIII. – 2:201 (Effects of the transfer of ownership) paragraph (4) remains unaffected.

(4) This Article does not affect any right to recover the goods based on other provisions of these model rules.

VIII. – 2:203: Transfer Subject to Condition

(1) Where the parties agreed on a transfer subject to a resolutive condition, ownership is re-transferred immediately upon the fulfilment of that condition, subject to the limits of the re-transferor's right or authority to dispose at that time. A retroactive proprietary effect of the re-transfer cannot be achieved by party agreement.

(2) Where the contract or other juridical act entitling to the transfer of ownership is subject to a suspensive condition, ownership passes when the condition is fulfilled.

Section 3: Special Constellations

VIII. – 2:301: Multiple Transfers

(1) Where there are several purported transfers of the same goods by the transferor, ownership is acquired by the transferee who first fulfils all the requirements of Section 1 and, in the case of a later transferee, who neither knew nor could reasonably be expected to know of the earlier entitlement of the other transferee.

(2) A later transferee who first fulfils all the requirements of Section 1 but is not in good faith in the sense of paragraph (1) must restore the goods to the transferor. The transferor's entitlement to recovery of the goods from that transferee may also be exercised by the first transferee.

VIII. – 2:302: Indirect Representation

(1) Where an agent acting under a mandate for indirect representation within the meaning of IV. D. – 1:102 (Definitions) acquires goods from a third party on behalf of the principal, the principal directly acquires the ownership of the goods (representation for acquisition).

(2) Where an agent acting under a mandate for indirect representation within the meaning of IV. D. – 1:102 (Definitions) transfers goods on behalf of the principal to a third party, the third party directly acquires the ownership of the goods (representation for alienation).

(3) The acquisition of ownership of the goods by the principal (paragraph (1)) or by the third party (paragraph (2)) takes place when:

(a) the agent has authority to transfer or receive the goods on behalf of the principal;

(b) there is an entitlement to transfer by virtue of a contract or other juridical act, a court order or a rule of law between the agent and the third party; and

(c) there has been an agreement as to the time ownership is to pass or delivery or an equivalent to delivery in the sense of VIII. – 2:101 (Requirements for the transfer of ownership in general) paragraph (1)(e) between the third party and the agent.

VIII. – 2:303: Passing of Ownership in Case of Direct Delivery in a Chain of Transactions

Where there is a chain of contracts or other juridical acts, court orders or entitlements based on a rule of law for the transfer of ownership of the same goods and delivery or an equivalent to delivery is effected directly between two parties within this chain, ownership passes to the recipient with effect as if it had been transferred from each preceding member of the chain to the next.

VIII. – 2:304: Passing of Ownership of Unsolicited Goods

(1) If a business delivers unsolicited goods to a consumer, the consumer acquires ownership subject to the business's right or authority to transfer ownership. The consumer may reject the acquisition of ownership; for these purposes, II. – 4:303 (Right or benefit may be rejected) applies by way of analogy.

(2) The exceptions provided for in II. – 3:401 (No obligation arising from failure to respond) paragraphs (2) and (3) apply accordingly.

(3) For the purposes of this Article delivery occurs when the consumer obtains physical control over the goods.

VIII. – 2:305: Transfer of Goods Forming Part of a Bulk

(1) For the purposes of this Chapter, "bulk" means a mass or mixture of fungible goods which is identified as contained in a defined space or area.

(2) If the transfer of a specified quantity of an identified bulk fails to take effect because the goods have not yet been identified in the sense of VIII. – 2:101 (Requirements for the transfer of ownership in general) paragraph (3), the transferee acquires co-ownership in the bulk.

(3) The undivided share of the transferee in the bulk at any time is such share as the quantity of goods to which the transferee is entitled out of the bulk as against the transferor bears to the quantity of the goods in the bulk at that time.

(4) Where the sum of the quantities to which the transferees are entitled as against the transferor and, if relevant, of the quantity of the transferor exceeds the total quantity contained in the bulk because the bulk has diminished, the diminution of the bulk is first attributed to the transferor, before being attributed to the transferees in proportion to their individual shares.

(5) Where the transferor purports to transfer more than the total quantity contained in the bulk, the quantity in excess of the total quantity of the bulk to which a transferee is entitled as against the transferor is reflected in the transferee's undivided share in the bulk only if the transferee, acquiring for value, neither knew nor could reasonably be expected to know of this excess. Where, as a result of such purported transfer of a quantity in excess of the bulk to a transferee in good faith and for value, the sum of the quantities to which the transferees are entitled as against the transferor exceeds the total quantity contained in the bulk, the lack of quantity is attributed to the transferees in proportion to their individual shares.

VIII. – 2:306: Delivery out of the Bulk

(1) Each transferee can take delivery of a quantity corresponding to the transferee's undivided share and acquires ownership of that quantity by taking delivery.

(2) Where the delivered quantity exceeds the quantity corresponding to the transferee's undivided share, the transferee acquires ownership of the excess quantity only if the transferee, acquiring for value, neither knew nor could reasonably be expected to know of possible negative consequences of this excess for the other transferees.

VIII. – 2:307: Contingent Right of Transferee Under Retention of Ownership

Where the transferor retains ownership of the goods for the purposes of a "retention of ownership device" in the sense of IX. – 1:103 (Retention of ownership devices: scope), the transferee's right to pay the price under the terms of the contract and the transferee's right to acquire ownership upon payment have effect against the transferor's creditors.

Chapter 3: Good Faith Acquisition of Ownership

VIII. – 3:101: Good Faith Acquisition Through a Person Without Right or Authority to Transfer Ownership

(1) Where the person purporting to transfer the ownership (the transferor) has no right or authority to transfer ownership of the goods, the transferee nevertheless acquires and the former owner loses ownership provided that:

(a) the requirements set out in VIII. – 2:101 (Requirements for the transfer of ownership in general) paragraphs (1)(a), (1)(b), (1)(d), (2) and (3) are fulfilled;

(b) the requirement of delivery or an equivalent to delivery as set out in VIII. – 2:101 (Requirements for the transfer of ownership in general) paragraph (1)(e) is fulfilled;

(c) the transferee acquires the goods for value; and

(d) the transferee neither knew nor could reasonably be expected to know that the transferor had no right or authority to transfer ownership of the goods at the time ownership would pass under VIII. – 2:101 (Requirements for the transfer of ownership in general). The facts from which it follows that the transferee could not reasonably be expected to know of the transferor's lack of right or authority have to be proved by the transferee.

(2) Good faith acquisition in the sense of paragraph (1) does not take place with regard to stolen goods, unless the transferee acquired the goods from a transferor acting in the ordinary

course of business. Good faith acquisition of stolen cultural objects in the sense of VIII. – 4:102 (Cultural objects) is impossible.

(3) Where the transferee is already in possession of the goods, good faith acquisition will take place only if the transferee obtained possession from the transferor.

VIII. – 3:102: Good Faith Acquisition of Ownership Free of Limited Proprietary Rights

(1) Where the goods are encumbered with a limited proprietary right of a third person and the transferor has no right or authority to dispose of the goods free of the third person's right, the transferee nevertheless acquires ownership free of this right provided that:

(a) the transferee acquires ownership in a manner provided for in Chapter 2 or the preceding Article;

(b) the requirement of delivery or an equivalent to delivery as set out in VIII. – 2:101 (Requirements for the transfer of ownership in general) paragraph (1)(e) is fulfilled;

(c) the transferee acquires the goods for value; and

(d) the transferee neither knew nor could reasonably be expected to know that the transferor had no right or authority to transfer ownership of the goods free of the third person's right at the time ownership passes. The facts from which it follows that the transferee could not reasonably be expected to know of the transferor's lack of right or authority have to be proved by the transferee.

(2) Paragraphs (2) and (3) of the preceding Article apply for the purposes of this Article.

(3) Where the goods are transferred by notice as provided for in VIII. – 2:105 (Equivalents to delivery) paragraph (2), the notified person's limited proprietary rights in the goods are not extinguished.

(4) For the purposes of the application of this Article to proprietary security rights, IX. – 6:102 (Loss of proprietary security due to good faith acquisition of ownership) paragraph (2) applies in addition to this Article.

Chapter 4: Acquisition of Ownership by Continuous Possession

Section 1: Requirements for Acquisition of Ownership by Continuous Possession

VIII. – 4:101: Basic Rule

(1) An owner-possessor acquires ownership by continuous possession of goods:

(a) for a period of ten years, provided that the possessor, throughout the whole period, possesses in good faith; or

(b) for a period of thirty years.

(2) For the purposes of paragraph (1)(a):

(a) a person possesses in good faith if, and only if, the person possesses in the belief of being the owner and is reasonably justified in that belief; and

(b) good faith of the possessor is presumed.

(3) Acquisition of ownership by continuous possession is excluded for a person who obtained possession by stealing the goods.

VIII. – 4:102: Cultural Objects

(1) Under this Chapter, acquisition of ownership of goods qualifying as a "cultural object" in the sense of Article 1 (1) of Council Directive 93/7/EEC, regardless of whether the cultural object has been unlawfully removed before or after 1 January 1993, or not removed from the territory of a Member State at all, requires continuous possession of the goods:

(a) for a period of 30 years, provided that the possessor, throughout the whole period, possesses in good faith; or

(b) for a period of 50 years.

(2) Member States may adopt or maintain in force more stringent provisions to ensure a higher level of protection for the owner of cultural objects in the sense of this paragraph or in the sense of national or international regulations.

VIII. – 4:103: Continuous Possession

(1) Involuntary loss of possession does not exclude continuous possession for the purpose of VIII. – 4:101 (Basic rule), provided that possession is recovered within one year or an action which leads to such recovery is instituted within one year.

(2) Where the owner-possessor is in possession of the goods at the beginning and at the end of the period there is a presumption of continuous possession for the whole period.

Section 2: Additional Provisions as to the Period Required for Acquisition of Ownership

VIII. – 4:201: Extension in Case of Incapacity

(1) If an owner who is subject to an incapacity is without a representative when the period required for the acquisition of ownership by another by continuous possession would begin to run, the commencement of the period against that person is suspended until either the incapacity has ended or a representative has been appointed.

(2) If the running of the period has already begun before incapacity occurred, the period does not expire before one year has passed after either incapacity has ended or a representative has been appointed.

(3) The running of the period is suspended where the owner is a person subject to an incapacity and the owner-possessor is that person's representative, as long as this relationship lasts. The period does not expire before one year has passed after either the incapacity has ended or a new representative has been appointed.

VIII. – 4:202: Extension in Case of Impediment Beyond Owner's Control

(1) The running of the period is suspended as long as the owner is prevented from exercising the right to recover the goods by an impediment which is beyond the owner's control and which the owner could not reasonably have been expected to avoid or overcome. The mere fact that the owner does not know where the goods are does not cause suspension under this Article.

(2) Paragraph (1) applies only if the impediment arises, or subsists, within the last six months of the period.

(3) Where the duration or nature of the impediment is such that it would be unreasonable to expect the owner to take proceedings to assert the right to recover the goods within the part of the period which has still to run after the suspension comes to an end, the period does not expire before six months have passed after the time when the impediment was removed.

VIII. – 4:203: Extension and Renewal in Case of Judicial and Other Proceedings

(1) The running of the period is suspended from the time when judicial proceedings are begun against the owner-possessor or a person exercising physical control for the owner-possessor, by or on behalf of the owner, contesting the owner-possessor's ownership or possession. Suspension lasts until a decision has been made which has the effect of res judicata or until the case has otherwise been disposed of. Suspension has effect only in relation to the parties to the judicial proceedings and persons on whose behalf the parties act.

(2) Suspension under paragraph (1) is to be disregarded when the action is dismissed or otherwise unsuccessful. Where the action is dismissed because of incompetence of the court, the period does not expire before six months have passed from this decision.

(3) Where the action is successful, a new period begins to run from the day when the effect of res judicata occurs or the case has otherwise been disposed of in favour of the owner.

(4) These provisions apply, with appropriate adaptations, to arbitration proceedings and to all other proceedings initiated with the aim of obtaining an instrument which is enforceable as if it were a judgment.

VIII. – 4:204: Postponement of Expiry in Case of Negotiations

If the owner and the owner-possessor or a person exercising physical control for the owner-possessor negotiate about the right of ownership, or about circumstances from which acquisition of ownership by the owner-possessor may arise, the period does not expire before six months have passed since the last communication made in the negotiations.

VIII. – 4:205: Ending of Period in Case of Acknowledgement

The period ends when the owner-possessor, or a person exercising physical control for the owner-possessor, acknowledges the owner's right to the goods. A new period begins to run when the former owner-possessor continues to exercise direct or indirect physical control with the intention of doing so as, or as if, an owner.

VIII. – 4:206: Period of a Predecessor to Be Taken into Account

(1) Where one person succeeds another in owner-possession and the requirements set out in this Chapter are fulfilled cumulatively by the predecessor and the successor in possession, the period of the predecessor is taken into account in favour of the successor.

(2) A successor in good faith may take into account the period of a predecessor in bad faith only for acquisition under VIII. – 4:101 (Basic rule) paragraph (1)(b).

Section 3: Effects of Acquisition of Ownership by Continuous Possession

VIII. – 4:301: Acquisition of Ownership

(1) Upon expiry of the period required for the acquisition of ownership by continuous possession the original owner loses and the owner-possessor acquires ownership.

(2) When the owner-possessor knows or can reasonably be expected to know that the goods are encumbered with a limited proprietary right of a third person, this right continues to exist as long as this right is not itself extinguished by expiry of the respective period, or a period of 30 years (VIII. – 4:101 (Basic rule) paragraph (1)(b)) or 50 years (VIII. – 4:102 (Cultural objects) paragraph (1)(b)) has passed.

VIII. – 4:302: Extinction of Rights under Rules on Unjustified Enrichment and Non-Contractual Liability for Damage

Upon acquisition of ownership, the original owner loses all rights to recover the goods and all rights to payment of the monetary value of the goods or for any future use of the goods under the provisions on unjustified enrichment (Book VII) and non-contractual liability for damage (Book VI).

Chapter 5: Production, Combination and Commingling

Section 1: General Provisions

VIII. – 5:101: Party Autonomy and Relation to Other Provisions

(1) The consequences of production, combination or commingling can be regulated by party agreement. The provisions of Section 2 apply where production, combination or commingling takes place:

(a) without the consent of the owner of the material; or

(b) with the consent of the owner of the material, but without a party agreement as to the proprietary consequences.

(2) An agreement in the sense of paragraph (1) may provide for:

(a) proprietary rights as recognised by this Book; and

(b) a right to payment or other performance.

(3) The effects of production, combination and commingling as to goods subject to a retention of ownership device are regulated by Book IX.

(4) Proprietary security rights created under Section 2 of this Chapter are subject to the provisions on proprietary security rights in Book IX, unless provided otherwise in Section 2. Proprietary security rights created by a party agreement under paragraph (1) are subject to the provisions on proprietary security rights in Book IX except as provided otherwise by VIII. – 5:204 (Additional provisions as to proprietary security rights) paragraph (3).

(5) This Chapter does not affect the applicability of the rules on non-contractual liability for damage (Book VI). The rules on benevolent intervention in another's affairs (Book V) have priority over the provisions of this Chapter.

Section 2: Default Rules and Supplementary Provisions

VIII. – 5:201: Production

(1) Where one person, by contributing labour, produces new goods out of material owned by another person, the producer becomes owner of the new goods and the owner of the material is entitled, against the producer, to payment equal to the value of the material at the moment of production, secured by a proprietary security right in the new goods.

(2) Paragraph (1) does not apply where:

(a) the labour contribution is of minor importance; or

(b) the producer knows that the material is owned by another person and that the owner of the material does not consent to the production, unless the value of the labour is much higher than the value of the material.

(3) In the cases covered by paragraph (2) and in cases where no new goods are produced, ownership remains with the owner of the material or, where there is more than one such owner, the attribution of ownership is determined by application of VIII. – 5:202 (Commingling) or VIII. – 5:203 (Combination). The person contributing labour is entitled to the reversal of any enrichment subject to the provisions of Book VII. For the purposes of this paragraph, VII. – 2:101 (Circumstances in which an enrichment is unjustified) paragraph (1)(b) does not exclude the entitlement of a person contributing labour to a reversal of the enrichment.

VIII. – 5:202: Commingling

(1) Where goods owned by different persons are commingled in the sense that it is impossible or economically unreasonable to separate the resulting mass or mixture into its original constituents, but it is possible and economically reasonable to separate the mass or mixture into propor-

tionate quantities, these persons become co-owners of the resulting mass or mixture, each for a share proportionate to the value of the respective part at the moment of commingling.

(2) Each co-owner can separate a quantity equivalent to that co-owner's undivided share out of the mass or mixture.

VIII. – 5:203: Combination

(1) This Article applies where goods owned by different persons are combined in the sense that separation would be impossible or economically unreasonable.

(2) Where one of the component parts is to be regarded as the principal part, the owner of that part acquires sole ownership of the whole, and the owner or the owners of the subordinate parts are entitled, against the sole owner, to payment subject to sentence 2, secured by a proprietary security right in the combined goods. The amount due under sentence 1 is calculated according to the rules on unjustified enrichment (Book VII); or, where the owner of the principal part effects the combination, is equal to the value of the respective subordinate part at the moment of combination.

(3) Where none of the component parts is to be regarded as the principal part, the owners of the component parts become co-owners of the whole, each for a share proportionate to the value of the respective part at the moment of combination. If, in the case of more than two component parts, one component part is of minimal importance in relation to other parts, the owner of this part is entitled, against the co-owners, only to payment proportionate to the value of the respective part at the moment of combination, secured by a proprietary security right in the combined goods.

(4) Paragraph (2) does not apply where the person who owns the principal part effects the combination, knowing that a subordinate part is owned by another person and that the owner of the subordinate part does not consent to combination, unless the value of the principal part is much higher than the value of the subordinate part. The owners of the component parts become co-owners, the shares of the owners of subordinate parts being equal to the value of their respective parts at the moment of combination.

VIII. – 5:204: Additional Provisions as to Proprietary Security Rights

(1) A proprietary security right created under the preceding Articles on production and combination is effective against third persons without requiring possession by, or registration of, the former owner of the material or of the component part.

(2) If the proprietary security right in the new or combined goods is extinguished by a third party's good faith acquisition (Chapter 3), the security right extends to the proceeds of the sale. Paragraph (1) applies accordingly.

(3) A proprietary security right created under the preceding Articles on production and combination takes priority over any other security right which has previously been created, by the producer or by the owner of the principal part, in the new or combined goods. The same applies to equivalent security rights created by agreement between the former owner of the material and the producer, or between the former owner of the subordinate part and the owner of the principal part.

Chapter 6: Protection of Ownership and Protection of Possession

Section 1: Protection of Ownership

VIII. – 6:101: Protection of Ownership

(1) The owner is entitled to obtain or recover possession of the goods from any person exercising physical control over these goods, unless this person has a right to possess the goods in the sense of VIII. – 1:207 (Possession by limited-right-possessor) in relation to the owner.

(2) Where another person interferes with the owner's rights as owner or where such interference is imminent, the owner is entitled to a declaration of ownership and to a protection order.

(3) A protection order is an order which, as the circumstances may require:

(a) prohibits imminent future interference;

(b) orders the cessation of existing interference;

(c) orders the removal of traces of past interference.

VIII. – 6:102: Recovery of Goods after Transfer Based on Invalid or Avoided Contract or Other Juridical Act

(1) Where goods are or have been transferred based on a contract or other juridical act which is invalid or avoided, the transferor may exercise the right of recovery under paragraph (1) of the preceding Article in order to recover physical control of the goods.

(2) Where the obligation of the transferee to restore the goods to the transferor, after a transfer based on an invalid or avoided contract or other juridical act, is one of two reciprocal obligations which have to be performed simultaneously, the transferee may, in accordance with III. – 3:401 (Right to withhold performance of reciprocal obligation), withhold performance of the obligation to restore the goods until the transferor has tendered performance of, or has performed, the transferor's reciprocal obligation.

(3) The preceding paragraphs also apply where the transfer was based on a contract or other juridical act subject to a resolutive condition in the sense of VIII. – 2:203 (Transfer subject to condition) paragraph (1) and this condition is fulfilled.

Section 2: Protection of Mere Possession

VIII. – 6:201: Definition of Unlawful Dispossession and Interference

A person depriving the possessor of possession or interfering with that possession acts "unlawfully" under this Section if the person acts without the consent of the possessor and the dispossession or interference is not permitted by law.

VIII. – 6:202: Self-Help of Possessor

(1) A possessor or a third person may resort to self-help against another person who unlawfully deprives the possessor of possession of the goods, or who otherwise unlawfully interferes with that possession, or whose act of unlawful dispossession or interference is imminent.

(2) The means of self-help are limited to such immediate and proportionate action as is necessary to regain the goods or to stop or prevent the dispossession or interference.

(3) Under the restrictions of paragraphs (1) and (2) self-help may also be directed against an indirect owner-possessor who unlawfully deprives the limited-right-possessor of possession or interferes with that possession in violation of the specific legal relationship between owner-possessor and limited-right-possessor. This rule applies equally to an indirect limited-right-possessor who unlawfully deprives the other limited-right-possessor of possession or interferes with that possession.

(4) Where a person in the exercise of a right of self-help conferred by this Article causes legally relevant damage to the person depriving the possessor of possession or interfering with that possession, VI. – 5:202 (Self-defence, benevolent intervention and necessity) applies.

VIII. – 6:203: Entitlement to Recover as Protection of Mere Possession

(1) Where another person unlawfully deprives an owner-possessor or a limited-right-possessor of possession, the possessor is, within the period of one year, entitled to recover the goods, irrespective of who has the right or better position in terms of VIII. – 6:301 (Entitlement to recover

in case of better possession) to possess the goods. The period of one year starts to run at the time of dispossession.

(2) The right to recover may also be directed against an indirect owner-possessor who unlawfully deprives the limited-right-possessor of possession in violation of the specific legal relationship between them. This rule applies equally to an indirect limited-right-possessor who unlawfully deprives the other limited-right-possessor of possession.

(3) The right to recover is excluded if the person seeking to exercise it unlawfully deprived the other person of possession within the last year.

(4) Where the other person in the sense of paragraph (1) invokes an alleged right or better position in terms of VIII. – 6:301 (Entitlement to recover in case of better possession) to possess the goods as a defence or counter-claim, the obligation to return the goods according to paragraph (1) may be replaced by an obligation to hand the goods over to the court or other competent public authority, or to a third person pursuant to an order of the competent authority.

VIII. – 6:204: Entitlement to Protection Order to Protect Mere Possession

(1) Where another person unlawfully interferes with the possession of goods or such interference or an unlawful dispossession is imminent, the owner-possessor or the limited-right-possessor is, within the period of one year, entitled to a protection order under VIII. – 6:101 (Protection of ownership) paragraph (3), irrespective of who has the right or better position in terms of VIII. – 6:301 (Entitlement to recover in case of better possession) to possess, use or otherwise deal with the goods. The period of one year starts to run from the time when the interference began or, in cases of repeated interferences, from the time when the last interference began.

(2) The protection order may also be directed against an indirect owner-possessor who unlawfully interferes with the possession of a limited-right-possessor in violation of the specific legal relationship between them. This rule applies equally to an indirect limited-right-possessor who unlawfully interferes with the possession of a subsidiary limited-right-possessor in violation of the specific legal relationship between them.

(3) Where the other person in the sense of paragraph (1) invokes an alleged right or better position to possess, use or otherwise deal with the goods as a defence or counter-claim, the court order may be suspended until, or replaced by, a decision on the existence of such alleged right or better position.

Section 3: Protection of Better Possession

VIII. – 6:301: Entitlement to Recover in Case of Better Possession

(1) A former owner-possessor or former limited-right possessor is entitled to recover possession of the goods from another person exercising physical control over them if the former possession was “better” than the current possession of the other person in the sense of paragraph (2).

(2) The former possession is “better” than the current possession if the former possessor is in good faith and has a right to possess, while the other person has no right to possess, the goods. Where both persons are in good faith and have a right to possess the goods, the right derived from the owner prevails over a right derived from an owner-possessor who is not the owner; if this does not apply, the older rightful possession prevails. Where both persons are in good faith, but neither has a right to possess the goods, the current possession prevails.

VIII. – 6:302: Entitlement to Protection Order in Case of Better Possession

Where another person interferes with the possession, or such interference or a dispossession is imminent, the owner-possessor or the limited-right-possessor who is in good faith is entitled to a protection order under VIII. – 6:101 (Protection of ownership) paragraph (3), unless the other person would, in case of dispossession, have a better possession in the sense of VIII. – 6:301 (Entitlement to recover in case of better possession) paragraph (2), or the third person has a better right to use or otherwise deal with the goods than the owner-possessor or limited-right-possessor.

Section 4: Other Remedies

VIII. – 6:401: Non-Contractual Liability

The owner and the limited-right-possessor are entitled to reparation for an infringement of their right of ownership or their right to possess the goods under the terms of VI. – 2:206 (Loss upon infringement of property or lawful possession).

Chapter 7: Consequential Questions on Restitution of Goods

VIII. – 7:101: Scope

(1) This Chapter applies where the situations covered by the subsequent Articles occur while the goods are possessed by a person against whom, at that time, the owner is entitled to obtain or recover possession of the goods.

(2) Where the requirements for the application of Book V are fulfilled, the provisions of that Book apply and have priority over the provisions of this Chapter.

(3) The provisions of Chapter 5 have priority over the provisions of this Chapter.

VIII. – 7:102: Loss of, or Damage to, the Goods During Possession

(1) Where the goods are lost, are destroyed or deteriorate during possession in the sense of VIII. – 7:101 (Scope of application), the rights of the owner resulting from such loss or damage are determined by Book VI.

(2) For the purposes of this Article, intention or negligence as to possessing the goods despite the owner's entitlement to obtain or recover possession suffice to establish accountability in the sense of Book VI, Chapter 3.

VIII. – 7:103: Fruits From, Use of, and Other Benefits Derived from the Goods During Possession

Where the possessor obtains fruits from, makes use of, or derives other benefits from the goods during possession in the sense of VIII. – 7:101 (Scope of application), the rights of the owner resulting from such benefits are determined by Book VII.

VIII. – 7:104: Expenditure on, or Parts Added to, the Goods During Possession

(1) Where the possessor incurs expenditure on, or adds parts to, the goods during possession in the sense of VIII. – 7:101 (Scope of application), the rights of the possessor to reimbursement of such expenditure or for such addition are determined by Book VII.

(2) The possessor is entitled to retain the goods in order to secure the rights referred to in paragraph (1). Sentence 1 does not apply where the possessor knows of the owner's entitlement to obtain or recover possession at the time when expenditure is incurred on, or parts are added to, the goods.

Book IX – Proprietary Security in Movable Assets [omitted]

Book X – Trusts [omitted]

Annex: Definitions

(General notes. These definitions are introduced by I. – 1:108 (Definitions in Annex) which provides that they apply for all the purposes of these rules unless the context otherwise requires and that, where a word is defined, other grammatical forms of the word have a corresponding meaning. For the convenience of the user, where a definition is taken from or derived from a particular Article a reference to that Article is added in brackets after the definition. The list also includes some terms which are frequently used in the rules but which are not defined in any Article. It does not include definitions which do not contain any legal concept but which are only drafting devices for the purposes of a particular Article or group of Articles.)

Accessory An "accessory", in relation to proprietary security, is a corporeal asset that is or becomes closely connected with, or part of, a movable or an immovable, provided it is possible and economically reasonable to separate the accessory without damage from the movable or immovable. (IX. – 1:201)

Acquisition finance device An "acquisition finance device" is (a) a retention of ownership device; (b) where ownership of a sold asset has been transferred to the buyer, those security rights in the asset which secure the right (i) of the seller to payment of the purchase price or (ii) of a lender to repayment of a loan granted to the buyer for payment of the purchase price, if and in so far as this payment is actually made to the seller; and (c) a right of a third person to whom any of the rights under (a) or (b) has been transferred as security for a credit covered by (a) or (b). (IX. – 1:201(3))

Advanced electronic signature An "advanced electronic signature" is an electronic signature which is (a) uniquely linked to the signatory (b) capable of identifying the signatory (c) created using means which can be maintained under the signatory's sole control; and (d) linked to the data to which it relates in such a manner that any subsequent change of the data is detectable. (I. – 1:108(4))

Act of assignment An "act of assignment" of a right is a contract or other juridical act which is intended to effect a transfer of the right. (III. – 5:102(2))

Agent An "agent" is a person who is authorised to act for another.

Assets "Assets" means anything of economic value, including property; rights having a monetary value; and goodwill.

Assignment "Assignment", in relation to a right, means the transfer of the right by one person, the "assignor", to another, "the assignee". (III. – 5:102(1))

Authorisation "Authorisation" is the granting or maintaining of authority. (II. – 6:102(3))

Authority "Authority", in relation to a representative acting for a principal, is the power to affect the principal's legal position. (II. – 6:102(2))

Avoidance "Avoidance" of a juridical act or legal relationship is the process whereby a party or, as the case may be, a court invokes a ground of invalidity so as to make the act or relationship, which has been valid until that point, retrospectively ineffective from the beginning.

Barter, contract for A contract for the "barter" of goods is a contract under which each party undertakes to transfer the ownership of goods, either immediately on conclusion of the contract or at some future time, in return for the transfer of ownership of other goods. (IV. A. – 1:203)

Beneficiary A "beneficiary", in relation to a trust, is a person who, according to the trust terms, has either a right to benefit or an eligibility for benefit from the trust fund. (X. – 1:203(3))

Benevolent intervention in another's affairs "Benevolent intervention in another's affairs" is the process whereby a person, the intervener, acts with the predominant intention of benefiting another, the principal, but without being authorised or bound to do so. (V. – 1:101)

Business "Business" means any natural or legal person, irrespective of whether publicly or privately owned, who is acting for purposes relating to the person's self-employed trade, work or profession, even if the person does not intend to make a profit in the course of the activity. (I. – 1:106(2))

Claim A "claim" is a demand for something based on the assertion of a right.

Claimant A "claimant" is a person who makes, or who has grounds for making, a claim.

Co-debtorship for security purposes A "co-debtorship for security purposes" is an obligation owed by two or more debtors in which one of the debtors, the security provider, assumes the obligation primarily for purposes of security towards the creditor. (IV. G. – 1:101(e))

Commercial agency A "commercial agency" is the legal relationship arising from a contract under which one party, the commercial agent, agrees to act on a continuing basis as a self-employed intermediary to negotiate or to conclude contracts on behalf of another party, the principal, and the principal agrees to remunerate the agent for those activities. (IV. E. – 3:101)

Compensation "Compensation" means reparation in money. (VI. – 6:101(2))

Complete substitution of debtor There is complete substitution of a debtor when a third person is substituted as debtor with the effect that the original debtor is discharged. (III. – 5:203)

Condition A "condition" is a provision which makes a legal relationship or effect depend on the occurrence or non-occurrence of an uncertain future event. A condition may be suspensive or resolutive. (III. – 1:106)

Conduct "Conduct" means voluntary behaviour of any kind, verbal or nonverbal: it includes a single act or a number of acts, behaviour of a negative or passive nature (such as accepting something without protest or not doing something) and behaviour of a continuing or intermittent nature (such as exercising control over something).

Confidential information "Confidential information" means information which, either from its nature or the circumstances in which it was obtained, the party receiving the information knows or could reasonably be expected to know is confidential to the other party. (II. – 2:302(2))

Construction, contract for A contract for construction is a contract under which one party, the constructor, undertakes to construct something for another party, the client, or to materially alter an existing building or other immovable structure for a client. (IV.C–3:101)

Consumer A "consumer" means any natural person who is acting primarily for purposes which are not related to his or her trade, business or profession. (I. – 1:106(1))

Consumer contract for sale A "consumer contract for sale" is a contract for sale in which the seller is a business and the buyer is a consumer. (IV. A. – 1:204)

Contract A "contract" is an agreement which is intended to give rise to a binding legal relationship or to have some other legal effect. It is a bilateral or multilateral juridical act. (II. – 1:101(1))

Contractual obligation A "contractual obligation" is an obligation which arises from a contract, whether from an express term or an implied term or by operation of a rule of law imposing an obligation on a contracting party as such.

Contractual relationship A "contractual relationship" is a legal relationship resulting from a contract.

Co-ownership "Co-ownership", when created under Book VIII, means that two or more co-owners own undivided shares in the whole and each coowner can dispose of that co-owner's share by acting alone, unless otherwise provided by the parties. (Cf. VIII. – 1:203)

Corporeal "Corporeal", in relation to property, means having a physical existence in solid, liquid or gaseous form.

Costs "Costs" includes expenses.

Counter-performance A "counter-performance" is a performance which is due in exchange for another performance.

Court "Court" includes an arbitral tribunal.

Creditor A "creditor" is a person who has a right to performance of an obligation, whether monetary or non-monetary, by another person, the debtor.

Damage "Damage" means any type of detrimental effect.

Damages "Damages" means a sum of money to which a person may be entitled, or which a person may be awarded by a court, as compensation for some specified type of damage.

Debtor A "debtor" is a person who has an obligation, whether monetary or non-monetary, to another person, the creditor.

Default "Default", in relation to proprietary security, means any non-performance by the debtor of the obligation covered by the security; and any other event or set of circumstances agreed by the secured creditor and the security provider as entitling the secured creditor to have recourse to the security. (IX. – 1:201(5))

Defence A "defence" to a claim is a legal objection or a factual argument, other than a mere denial of an element which the claimant has to prove which, if well-founded, defeats the claim in whole or in part.

Delivery "Delivery" to a person, for the purposes of any obligation to deliver goods, means transferring possession of the goods to that person or taking such steps to transfer possession as are required by the terms regulating the obligation. For the purposes of Book VIII (Acquisition and loss of ownership of goods) delivery of the goods takes place only when the transferor gives up and the transferee obtains possession of the goods: if the contract or other juridical act, court order or rule of law under which the transferee is entitled to the transfer of ownership involves carriage of the goods by a carrier or a series of carriers, delivery of the goods takes place when the transferor's obligation to deliver is fulfilled and the carrier or the transferee obtains possession of the goods. (VIII. – 2:104)

Dependent personal security A "dependent personal security" is an obligation by a security provider which is assumed in favour of a creditor in order to secure a present or future obligation of the debtor owed to the creditor and performance of which is due only if, and to the extent that, performance of the latter obligation is due. (IV. G. – 1:101(a))

Design, contract for A contract for design is a contract under which one party, the designer, undertakes to design for another party, the client, an immovable structure which is to be constructed by or on behalf of the client or a movable or incorporeal thing or service which is to be constructed or performed by or on behalf of the client. (IV. C.- 6:101)

Direct physical control Direct physical control is physical control which is exercised by the possessor personally or through a possession-agent exercising such control on behalf of the possessor (direct possession). (VIII. – 1:205)

Discrimination "Discrimination" means any conduct whereby, or situation where, on grounds such as sex or ethnic or racial origin, (a) one person is treated less favourably than another person is, has been or would be treated in a comparable situation; or (b) an apparently neutral provision, criterion or practice would place one group of persons at a particular disadvantage when compared to a different group of persons. (II. – 2:102(1))

Distribution contract A "distribution contract" is a contract under which one party, the supplier, agrees to supply the other party, the distributor, with products on a continuing basis and the distributor agrees to purchase them, or to take and pay for them, and to supply them to others in the distributor's name and on the distributor's behalf. (IV. E. – 5:101(1))

Distributorship A "distributorship" is the legal relationship arising from a distribution contract.

Divided obligation An obligation owed by two or more debtors is a "divided obligation" when each debtor is bound to render only part of the performance and the creditor may require from each debtor only that debtor's part. (III. – 4:102(2))

Divided right A right to performance held by two or more creditors is a "divided right" when the debtor owes each creditor only that creditor's share and each creditor may require performance only of that creditor's share. (III. – 4:202(2))

Donation, contract for A contract for the donation of goods is a contract under which one party, the donor, gratuitously undertakes to transfer the ownership of goods to another party, the donee, and does so with an intention to benefit the donee. (IV. H. – 1:101)

Durable medium A "durable medium" means any material on which information is stored so that it is accessible for future reference for a period of time adequate to the purposes of the information, and which allows the unchanged reproduction of this information. (I. – 1:107(3))

Duty A person has a "duty" to do something if the person is bound to do it or expected to do it according to an applicable normative standard of conduct. A duty may or may not be owed to a specific creditor. A duty is not necessarily an aspect of a legal relationship. There is not necessarily a sanction for breach of a duty. All obligations are duties, but not all duties are obligations.

Economic loss See "Loss".

Electronic "Electronic" means relating to technology with electrical, digital, magnetic, wireless, optical, electromagnetic, or similar capabilities.

Electronic signature An "electronic signature" means data in electronic form which are attached to, or logically associated with, other data and which serve as a method of authentication. (I. – 1:108(3))

Financial assets "Financial assets" are financial instruments and rights to the payment of money. (IX. – 1:201(6))

Financial instruments "Financial instruments" are (a) share certificates and equivalent securities as well as bonds and equivalent debt instruments, if these are negotiable (b) any other securities which are dealt in and which give the right to acquire any such financial instruments or which give rise to cash settlements, except instruments of payment (c) share rights in collective investment undertakings (d) money market instruments and (e) rights in or relating to the foregoing instruments. (IX. – 1:201(7))

Franchise A "franchise" is the legal relationship arising from a contract under which one party, the franchisor, grants the other party, the franchisee, in exchange for remuneration, the right to conduct a business (franchise business) within the franchisor's network for the purposes of supplying certain products on the franchisee's behalf and in the franchisee's name, and whereby the franchisee has the right and the obligation to use the franchisor's trade name or trademark or other intellectual property rights, know-how and business method. (IV. E. – 4:101)

Fraudulent A misrepresentation is fraudulent if it is made with knowledge or belief that it is false and is intended to induce the recipient to make a mistake to the recipient's prejudice. A non-disclosure is fraudulent if it is intended to induce the person from whom the information is withheld to make a mistake to that person's prejudice. (II. – 7:205(2))

Fundamental non-performance A non-performance of a contractual obligation is fundamental if (a) it substantially deprives the creditor of what the creditor was entitled to expect under the contract, as applied to the whole or relevant part of the performance, unless at the time of conclusion of the contract the debtor did not foresee and could not reasonably be expected to have foreseen that result or (b) it is intentional or reckless and gives the creditor reason to believe that the debtor's future performance cannot be relied on. (III. – 3:502(2))

Global security A "global security" is a security which is assumed in order to secure all the debtor's obligations towards the creditor or the debit balance of a current account or a security of a similar extent. (IV.G. – 1:101(f)

Good faith "Good faith" is a mental attitude characterised by honesty and an absence of knowledge that an apparent situation is not the true situation.

Good faith and fair dealing "Good faith and fair dealing" is a standard of conduct characterised by honesty, openness and consideration for the interests of the other party to the transaction or relationship in question. (I. – 1:103)

Goods "Goods" means corporeal movables. It includes ships, vessels, hovercraft or aircraft, space objects, animals, liquids and gases. See also "movables".

Gross negligence There is "gross negligence" if a person is guilty of a profound failure to take such care as is self-evidently required in the circumstances.

Handwritten signature A "handwritten signature" means the name of, or sign representing, a person written by that person's own hand for the purpose of authentication. (I. – 1:108(2))

Harassment "Harassment" means unwanted conduct (including conduct of a sexual nature) which violates a person's dignity, particularly when such conduct creates an intimidating, hostile, degrading, humiliating or offensive environment, or which aims to do so. (II. – 2:102(2))

Immovable property "Immovable property" means land and anything so attached to land as not to be subject to change of place by usual human action.

Incomplete substitution of debtor There is incomplete substitution of a debtor when a third person is substituted as debtor with the effect that the original debtor is retained as a debtor in case the original debtor does not perform properly. (III. – 5:205)

Incorporeal "Incorporeal", in relation to property, means not having a physical existence in solid, liquid or gaseous form.

Indemnify To "indemnify" means to make such payment to a person as will ensure that that person suffers no loss.

Independent personal security An "independent personal security" is an obligation by a security provider which is assumed in favour of a creditor for the purposes of security and which is expressly or impliedly declared not to depend upon another person's obligation owed to the creditor. (IV.G.– 1:101(b))

Indirect physical control Indirect physical control is physical control which is exercised by means of another person, a limited-right-possessor (indirect possession). (VIII. – 1:205)

Individually negotiated See "not individually negotiated" and II. – 1:110.

Ineffective "Ineffective" in relation to a contract or other juridical act means having no effect, whether that state of affairs is temporary or permanent, general or restricted.

Insolvency proceeding An "insolvency proceeding" means a collective judicial or administrative proceeding, including an interim proceeding, in which the assets and affairs of a person who is, or who is believed to be, insolvent are subject to control or supervision by a court or other competent authority for the purpose of reorganisation or liquidation.

Intangibles "Intangibles", in relation to proprietary security, means incorporeal assets and includes uncertificated and indirectly held securities and the undivided share of a co-owner in corporeal assets or in a bulk or a fund. (IX. – 1:201(8))

Interest "Interest" means simple interest without any assumption that it will be capitalised from time to time.

Invalid "Invalid" in relation to a juridical act or legal relationship means that the act or relationship is void or has been avoided.

Joint obligation An obligation owed by two or more debtors is a "joint obligation" when all the debtors are bound to render the performance together and the creditor may require it only from all of them. (III. – 4:102(3))

Joint right A right to performance held by two or more creditors is a "joint right" when the debtor must perform to all the creditors and any creditor may require performance only for the benefit of all. (III. – 4:202(3))

Juridical act A "juridical act" is any statement or agreement, whether express or implied from conduct, which is intended to have legal effect as such. It may be unilateral, bilateral or multilateral. (II. – 1:101(2))

Keeper A keeper, in relation to an animal, vehicle or substance, is the person who has the beneficial use or physical control of it for that person's own benefit and who exercises the right to control it or its use.

Lease A "lease" is the legal relationship arising from a contract under which one party, the lessor, undertakes to provide the other party, the lessee, with a temporary right of use in exchange for rent. (IV. B. – 1:101)

Limited proprietary rights Limited proprietary rights are such rights of the following character as are characterised or treated as proprietary rights by any provision of these model rules or by national law:– (a) security rights (b) rights to use (c) rights to acquire (including a right to acquire in the sense of VIII. – 2:307 (Contingent right of transferee under retention of ownership)) and (d) trust-related rights. (VIII. – 1:204)

Limited-right-possessor A "limited-right-possessor", in relation to goods, is a person who exercises physical control over the goods either (a) with the intention of doing so in that person's own interest, and under a specific legal relationship with the owner-possessor which gives the limited-right-possessor the right to possess the goods or (b) with the intention of doing so to the order of the owner-possessor, and under a specific contractual relationship with the owner-possessor which gives the limited-right-possessor a right to retain the goods until any charges or costs have been paid by the owner-possessor. (VIII. – 1:207)

Loan contract A loan contract is a contract by which one party, the lender, is obliged to provide the other party, the borrower, with credit of any amount for a definite or indefinite period (the loan period), in the form of a monetary loan or of an overdraft facility and by which the borrower is obliged to repay the money obtained under the credit, whether or not the borrower is obliged to pay interest or any other kind of remuneration the parties have agreed upon. (IV. F.– 1:101(2))

Loss "Loss" includes economic and non-economic loss. "Economic loss" includes loss of income or profit, burdens incurred and a reduction in the value of property. "Non-economic loss" includes pain and suffering and impairment of the quality of life. (III. – 3:701(3) and VI. – 2:101(4))

Mandate The "mandate" of an agent is the authorisation and instruction given by the principal, as modified by any subsequent direction, in relation to the facilitation, negotiation or conclusion of a contract or other juridical act with a third party. (IV. D. – 1:102(1)(a))

Mandate for direct representation A "mandate for direct representation" is a mandate under which the agent is to act in the name of the principal, or otherwise in such a way as to indicate an intention to affect the principal's legal position directly. (IV. D. – 1:102(1)(d))

Mandate for indirect representation A "mandate for indirect representation" is a mandate under which the agent is to act in the agent's own name or otherwise in such a way as not to indicate an intention to affect the principal's legal position directly. (IV. D. – 1:102(1)(e))

Merger of debts A "merger of debts" means that the attributes of debtor and creditor are united in the same person in the same capacity. (III. – 6:201)

Merger clause A "merger clause" is a term in a contract document stating that the document embodies all the terms of the contract. (II. – 4:104)

Monetary loan A monetary loan is a fixed sum of money which is lent to the borrower and which the borrower agrees to repay either by fixed instalments or by paying the whole sum at the end of the loan period. (IV. F. – 1:101(3))

Motor vehicle "Motor vehicle" means any vehicle intended for travel on land and propelled by mechanical power, but not running on rails, and any trailer, whether or not coupled. (VI. – 3:205(2))

Movables "Movables" means corporeal and incorporeal property other than immovable property.

Negligence There is "negligence" if a person does not meet the standard of care which could reasonably be expected in the circumstances.

Non-economic loss See "Loss".

Non-performance "Non-performance", in relation to an obligation, means any failure to perform the obligation, whether or not excused. It includes delayed performance and defective performance. (III. – 1:101(3))

Notice "Notice" includes the communication of information or of a juridical act. (I. – 1:105)

Not individually negotiated A term supplied by one party is not individually negotiated if the other party has not been able to influence its content, in particular because it has been drafted in advance, whether or not as part of standard terms. (II. – 1:110)

Obligation An obligation is a duty to perform which one party to a legal relationship, the debtor, owes to another party, the creditor. (III. – 1:101(1))

Overdraft facility An "overdraft facility" is an option for the borrower to withdraw funds on a fluctuating, limited basis from the borrower's current account in excess of the current balance in the account. (IV. F.– 1:101(4))

Owner-possessor An "owner-possessor", in relation to goods, is a person who exercises physical control over the goods with the intention of doing so as, or as if, an owner. ((VIII. – 1:206)

Ownership "Ownership" is the most comprehensive right a person, the owner, can have over property, including the exclusive right, so far as consistent with applicable laws or rights granted by the owner, to use, enjoy, modify, destroy, dispose of and recover the property. (VIII. – 1:202)

Performance "Performance", in relation to an obligation, is the doing by the debtor of what is to be done under the obligation or the not doing by the debtor of what is not to be done. (III. – 1:101(2))

Person "Person" means a natural or legal person.

Physical control "Physical control", in relation to goods, means direct physical control or indirect physical control. (Cf. VIII. – 1:205)

Possession Possession, in relation to goods, means having physical control over the goods. (VIII. – 1:205)

Possession-agent A "possession-agent", in relation to goods, is a person (such as an employee) who exercises direct physical control over the goods on behalf of an owner-possessor or limited-right-possessor (without the intention and specific legal relationship required for that person to be a limited-right-possessor); and to whom the owner-possessor or limited-right-possessor may give binding instructions as to the use of the goods in the interest of the owner-possessor or limited-right-possessor. A person is also a possession-agent where that person is accidentally in a position to exercise, and does exercise, direct physical control over the goods for an owner-possessor or limited-right-possessor. (VIII. – 1:208)

Possessory security right A “possessory security right” is a security right that requires possession of the encumbered corporeal asset by the secured creditor or another person (except the debtor) holding for the secured creditor. (IX. – 1:201(10))

Prescription “Prescription”, in relation to the right to performance of an obligation, is the legal effect whereby the lapse of a prescribed period of time entitles the debtor to refuse performance.

Presumption A “presumption” means that the existence of a known fact or state of affairs allows the deduction that something else should be held true, until the contrary is demonstrated.

Price The “price” is what is due by the debtor under a monetary obligation, in exchange for something supplied or provided, expressed in a currency which the law recognises as such.

Proceeds “Proceeds”, in relation to proprietary security, is every value derived from an encumbered asset, such as value realised by sale, collection or other disposition; damages or insurance payments in respect of defects, damage or loss; civil and natural fruits, including distributions; and proceeds of proceeds. (IX. – 1:201(11))

Processing, contract for A contract for processing is a contract under which one party, the processor, undertakes to perform a service on an existing movable or incorporeal thing or to an immovable structure for another party, the client (except where the service is construction work on an existing building or other immovable structure). (IV. C. – 4:101)

Producer “Producer” includes, in the case of something made, the maker or manufacturer; in the case of raw material, the person who abstracts or wins it; and in the case of something grown, bred or raised, the grower, breeder or raiser. A special definition applies for the purposes of VI. – 3:204.

Property “Property” means anything which can be owned: it may be movable or immovable, corporeal or incorporeal.

Proprietary security A “proprietary security” covers security rights in all kinds of assets, whether movable or immovable, corporeal or incorporeal. (IV.G. – 1:101(g))

Proprietary security, contract for A “contract for proprietary security” is a contract under which a security provider undertakes to grant a security right to the secured creditor; or a secured creditor is entitled to retain a security right when transferring ownership; or a seller, lessor or other supplier of assets is entitled to retain ownership of the supplied assets in order to secure its rights to performance. (IX. – 1:201(4))

Public holiday A “public holiday” with reference to a member state, or part of a member state, of the European Union means any day designated as such for that state or part in a list published in the Official Journal. (I. – 1:110(9))

Ratify “Ratify” means confirm with legal effect.

Reasonable What is “reasonable” is to be objectively ascertained, having regard to the nature and purpose of what is being done, to the circumstances of the case and to any relevant usages and practices. (I. – 1:104)

Reciprocal An obligation is reciprocal in relation to another obligation if (a) performance of the obligation is due in exchange for performance of the other obligation; (b) it is an obligation to facilitate or accept performance of the other obligation; or (c) it is so clearly connected to the other obligation or its subject matter that performance of the one can reasonably be regarded as dependent on performance of the other. (III. – 1:101(4))

Recklessness A person is "reckless" if the person knows of an obvious and serious risk of proceeding in a certain way but nonetheless voluntarily proceeds without caring whether or not the risk materialises.

Rent "Rent" is the money or other value which is due in exchange for a temporary right of use. (IV. B. – 1:101)

Reparation "Reparation" means compensation or another appropriate measure to reinstate the person suffering damage in the position that person would have been in had the damage not occurred. (VI. – 6:101)

Representative A "representative" is a person who has authority to affect the legal position of another person, the principal, in relation to a third party by acting in the name of the principal or otherwise in such a way as to indicate an intention to affect the principal's legal position directly. (II. – 6:102(1))

Requirement A "requirement" is something which is needed before a particular result follows or a particular right can be exercised.

Resolutive A condition is "resolutive" if it causes a legal relationship or effect to come to an end when the condition is satisfied. (III. – 1:106)

Retention of ownership device There is a retention of ownership device when ownership is retained by the owner of supplied assets in order to secure a right to performance of an obligation. (IX. – 1:103)

Revocation "Revocation", means (a) in relation to a juridical act, its recall by a person or persons having the power to recall it, so that it no longer has effect and (b) in relation to something conferred or transferred, its recall, by a person or persons having power to recall it, so that it comes back or must be returned to the person who conferred it or transferred it.

Right "Right", depending on the context, may mean (a) the correlative of an obligation or liability (as in "a significant imbalance in the parties' rights and obligations arising under the contract"); (b) a proprietary right (such as the right of ownership); (c) a personality right (as in a right to respect for dignity, or a right to liberty and privacy); (d) a legally conferred power to bring about a particular result (as in "the right to avoid" a contract); (e) an entitlement to a particular remedy (as in a right to have performance of a contractual obligation judicially ordered) or (f) an entitlement to do or not to do something affecting another person's legal position without exposure to adverse consequences (as in a "right to withhold performance of the reciprocal obligation").

Sale, contract for A contract for the "sale" of goods or other assets is a contract under which one party, the seller, undertakes to another party, the buyer, to transfer the ownership of the goods or other assets to the buyer, or to a third person, either immediately on conclusion of the contract or at some future time, and the buyer undertakes to pay the price. (IV.A. – 1:202)

Security right in movable asset A security right in a movable asset is any limited proprietary right in the asset which entitles the secured creditor to preferential satisfaction of the secured right from the encumbered asset. (IX. – 1:102(1))

Services, contract for A contract for services is a contract under which one party, the service provider, undertakes to supply a service to the other party, the client. (IV. C. – 1:101)

Set-off "Set-off" is the process by which a person may use a right to performance held against another person to extinguish in whole or in part an obligation owed to that person. (III. – 6:101)

Signature "Signature" includes a handwritten signature, an electronic signature or an advanced electronic signature. (I. – 1:108(2))

Solidary obligation An obligation owed by two or more debtors is a "solidary obligation" when all the debtors are bound to render one and the same performance and the creditor may require it from any one of them until there has been full performance. (III. – 4:102(1))

Solidary right A right to performance held by two or more creditors is a "solidary right" when any of the creditors may require full performance from the debtor and the debtor may render performance to any of the creditors. (III. – 4:202(1))

Standard terms "Standard terms" are terms which have been formulated in advance for several transactions involving different parties, and which have not been individually negotiated by the parties. (II. – 1:109)

Storage, contract for A contract for storage is a contract under which one party, the storer, undertakes to store a movable or incorporeal thing for another party, the client. (IV. C. – 5:101)

Subrogation "Subrogation", in relation to rights, is the process by which a person who has made a payment or other performance to another person acquires by operation of law that person's rights against a third person.

Substitution of debtor "Substitution" of a debtor is the process whereby, with the agreement of the creditor, a third party is substituted completely or incompletely for the debtor, the contract remaining in force. (III. – 5:202) See also "complete substitution of debtor" and "incomplete substitution of debtor".

Supply To "supply" goods or other assets means to make them available to another person, whether by sale, gift, barter, lease or other means: to "supply" services means to provide them to another person, whether or not for a price. Unless otherwise stated, "supply" covers the supply of goods, other assets and services.

Suspensive A condition is "suspensive" if it prevents a legal relationship or effect from coming into existence until the condition is satisfied. (III. – 1:106)

Tacit prolongation "Tacit prolongation" is the process whereby, when a contract provides for continuous or repeated performance of obligations for a definite period and the obligations continue to be performed by both parties after that period has expired, the contract becomes a contract for an indefinite period, unless the circumstances are inconsistent with the tacit consent of the parties to such prolongation. (III. – 1:111)

Term "Term" means any provision, express or implied, of a contract or other juridical act, of a law, of a court order or of a legally binding usage or practice: it includes a condition.

Termination "Termination", in relation to an existing right, obligation or legal relationship, means bringing it to an end with prospective effect except in so far as otherwise provided.

Textual form In "textual form", in relation to a statement, means expressed in alphabetical or other intelligible characters by means of any support which permits reading, recording of the information contained in the statement and its reproduction in tangible form. (I. – 1:107(2))

Transfer of contractual position "Transfer of contractual position" is the process whereby, with the agreement of all three parties, a new party replaces an existing party to a contract, taking over the rights, obligations and entire contractual position of that party. (III. – 5:302)

Treatment, contract for A contract for treatment is a contract under which one party, the treatment provider, undertakes to provide medical treatment for another party, the patient, or to provide any other service in order to change the physical or mental condition of a person. (IV. C. – 8:101)

Trust A "trust" is a legal relationship in which a trustee is obliged to administer or dispose of one or more assets (the trust fund) in accordance with the terms governing the relationship (trust terms) to benefit a beneficiary or advance public benefit purposes. (X. – 1:201)

Trustee A "trustee" is a person in whom a trust fund becomes or remains vested when the trust is created or subsequently on or after appointment and who has the obligation set out in the definition of "trust" above. (X. – 1:203(2))

Truster A "truster" is a person who constitutes or intends to constitute a trust by juridical act. (X. – 1:203(1))

Unjustified enrichment An "unjustified enrichment" is an enrichment which is not legally justified.

Valid "Valid", in relation to a juridical act or legal relationship, means that the act or relationship is not void and has not been avoided.

Void "Void", in relation to a juridical act or legal relationship, means that the act or relationship is automatically of no effect from the beginning.

Voidable "Voidable", in relation to a juridical act or legal relationship, means that the act or relationship is subject to a defect which renders it liable to be avoided and hence rendered retrospectively of no effect.

Withdraw A right to "withdraw" from a contract or other juridical act is a right, exercisable only within a limited period, to terminate the legal relationship arising from the contract or other juridical act, without having to give any reason for so doing and without incurring any liability for non-performance of the obligations arising from that contract or juridical act. (II. – 5:101 to II. – 5:105)

Withholding performance "Withholding performance", as a remedy for non-performance of a contractual obligation, means that one party to a contract may decline to render due counter-performance until the other party has tendered performance or has performed. (III. – 3:401)

Working days "Working days" means all days other than Saturdays, Sundays and public holidays. (I. – 1:110(9)(b))

Writing In "writing" means in textual form, on paper or another durable medium and in directly legible characters. (I. – 1:107(1))

15) 2005 United Nations Convention on the Use of Electronic Communications in International Contracts[1]

THE STATES PARTIES TO THIS CONVENTION,

REAFFIRMING their belief that international trade on the basis of equality and mutual benefit is an important element in promoting friendly relations among States,

NOTING that the increased use of electronic communications improves the efficiency of commercial activities, enhances trade connections and allows new access opportunities for previously remote parties and markets, thus playing a fundamental role in promoting trade and economic development, both domestically and internationally,

CONSIDERING that problems created by uncertainty as to the legal value of the use of electronic communications in international contracts constitute an obstacle to international trade,

CONVINCED that the adoption of uniform rules to remove obstacles to the use of electronic communications in international contracts, including obstacles that might result from the operation of existing international trade law instruments, would enhance legal certainty and commercial predictability for international contracts and help States gain access to modern trade routes,

BEING OF THE OPINION that uniform rules should respect the freedom of parties to choose appropriate media and technologies, taking account of the principles of technological neutrality and functional equivalence, to the extent that the means chosen by the parties comply with the purpose of the relevant rules of law,

DESIRING to provide a common solution to remove legal obstacles to the use of electronic communications in a manner acceptable to States with different legal, social and economic systems,

HAVE AGREED as follows:

CHAPTER I. SPHERE OF APPLICATION

Article 1 - Scope of Application

1. This Convention applies to the use of electronic communications in connection with the formation or performance of a contract between parties whose places of business are in different States.

2. The fact that the parties have their places of business in different States is to be disregarded whenever this fact does not appear either from the contract or from any dealings between the parties or from information disclosed by the parties at any time before or at the conclusion of the contract.

3. Neither the nationality of the parties nor the civil or commercial character of the parties or of the contract is to be taken into consideration in determining the application of this Convention.

Article 2 - Exclusions

1. This Convention does not apply to electronic communications relating to any of the following:

(a) Contracts concluded for personal, family or household purposes;

(b) (i) Transactions on a regulated exchange;

(ii) foreign exchange transactions;

---

1 ©2005, United Nations, UNTS Vol. 2898, all rights reserved.

(iii) inter-bank payment systems, inter-bank payment agreements or clearance and settlement systems relating to securities or other financial assets or instruments;

(iv) the transfer of security rights in sale, loan or holding of or agreement to repurchase securities or other financial assets or instruments held with an intermediary.

2. This Convention does not apply to bills of exchange, promissory notes, consignment notes, bills of lading, warehouse receipts or any transferable document or instrument that entitles the bearer or beneficiary to claim the delivery of goods or the payment of a sum of money.

Article 3 - Party Autonomy

The parties may exclude the application of this Convention or derogate from or vary the effect of any of its provisions.

CHAPTER II. GENERAL PROVISIONS

Article 4 - Definitions

For the purposes of this Convention:

(a) "Communication" means any statement, declaration, demand, notice or request, including an offer and the acceptance of an offer, that the parties are required to make or choose to make in connection with the formation or performance of a contract;

(b) "Electronic communication" means any communication that the parties make by means of data messages;

(c) "Data message" means information generated, sent, received or stored by electronic, magnetic, optical or similar means, including, but not limited to, electronic data interchange, electronic mail, telegram, telex or telecopy;

(d) "Originator" of an electronic communication means a party by whom, or on whose behalf, the electronic communication has been sent or generated prior to storage, if any, but it does not include a party acting as an intermediary with respect to that electronic communication;

(e) "Addressee" of an electronic communication means a party who is intended by the originator to receive the electronic communication, but does not include a party acting as an intermediary with respect to that electronic communication;

(f) "Information system" means a system for generating, sending, receiving, storing or otherwise processing data messages;

(g) "Automated message system" means a computer program or an electronic or other automated means used to initiate an action or respond to data messages or performances in whole or in part, without review or intervention by a natural person each time an action is initiated or a response is generated by the system;

(h) "Place of business" means any place where a party maintains a non-transitory establishment to pursue an economic activity other than the temporary provision of goods or services out of a specific location.

Article 5 - Interpretation

1. In the interpretation of this Convention, regard is to be had to its international character and to the need to promote uniformity in its application and the observance of good faith in international trade.

2. Questions concerning matters governed by this Convention which are not expressly settled in it are to be settled in conformity with the general principles on which it is based or, in the absence of such principles, in conformity with the law applicable by virtue of the rules of private international law.

Article 6 - Location of the Parties

1. For the purposes of this Convention, a party's place of business is presumed to be the location indicated by that party, unless another party demonstrates that the party making the indication does not have a place of business at that location.

2. If a party has not indicated a place of business and has more than one place of business, then the place of business for the purposes of this Convention is that which has the closest relationship to the relevant contract, having regard to the circumstances known to or contemplated by the parties at any time before or at the conclusion of the contract.

3. If a natural person does not have a place of business, reference is to be made to the person's habitual residence.

4. A location is not a place of business merely because that is:

(a) where equipment and technology supporting an information system used by a party in connection with the formation of a contract are located; or

(b) where the information system may be accessed by other parties.

5. The sole fact that a party makes use of a domain name or electronic mail address connected to a specific country does not create a presumption that its place of business is located in that country.

Article 7 - Information Requirements

Nothing in this Convention affects the application of any rule of law that may require the parties to disclose their identities, places of business or other information, or relieves a party from the legal consequences of making inaccurate, incomplete or false statements in that regard.

CHAPTER III. USE OF ELECTRONIC COMMUNICATIONS IN INTERNATIONAL CONTRACTS

Article 8 - Legal Recognition of Electronic Communications

1. A communication or a contract shall not be denied validity or enforceability on the sole ground that it is in the form of an electronic communication.

2. Nothing in this Convention requires a party to use or accept electronic communications, but a party's agreement to do so may be inferred from the party's conduct.

Article 9 - Form Requirements

1. Nothing in this Convention requires a communication or a contract to be made or evidenced in any particular form.

2. Where the law requires that a communication or a contract should be in writing, or provides consequences for the absence of a writing, that requirement is met by an electronic communication if the information contained therein is accessible so as to be usable for subsequent reference.

3. Where the law requires that a communication or a contract should be signed by a party, or provides consequences for the absence of a signature, that requirement is met in relation to an electronic communication if:

(a) A method is used to identify the party and to indicate that party's intention in respect of the information contained in the electronic communication; and

(b) The method used is either:

  (i) As reliable as appropriate for the purpose for which the electronic communication was generated or communicated, in the light of all the circumstances, including any relevant agreement; or

(ii) Proven in fact to have fulfilled the functions described in subparagraph (a) above, by itself or together with further evidence.

4. Where the law requires that a communication or a contract should be made available or retained in its original form, or provides consequences for the absence of an original, that requirement is met in relation to an electronic communication if:

(a) There exists a reliable assurance as to the integrity of the information it contains from the time when it was first generated in its final form, as an electronic communication or otherwise; and

(b) Where it is required that the information it contains be made available, that information is capable of being displayed to the person to whom it is to be made available.

5. For the purposes of paragraph 4 (a):

(a) The criteria for assessing integrity shall be whether the information has remained complete and unaltered, apart from the addition of any endorsement and any change that arises in the normal course of communication, storage and display; and

(b) The standard of reliability required shall be assessed in the light of the purpose for which the information was generated and in the light of all the relevant circumstances.

Article 10 - Time and Place of Dispatch and Receipt of Electronic Communications

1. The time of dispatch of an electronic communication is the time when it leaves an information system under the control of the originator or of the party who sent it on behalf of the originator or, if the electronic communication has not left an information system under the control of the originator or of the party who sent it on behalf of the originator, the time when the electronic communication is received.

2. The time of receipt of an electronic communication is the time when it becomes capable of being retrieved by the addressee at an electronic address designated by the addressee. The time of receipt of an electronic communication at another electronic address of the addressee is the time when it becomes capable of being retrieved by the addressee at that address and the addressee becomes aware that the electronic communication has been sent to that address. An electronic communication is presumed to be capable of being retrieved by the addressee when it reaches the addressee's electronic address.

3. An electronic communication is deemed to be dispatched at the place where the originator has its place of business and is deemed to be received at the place where the addressee has its place of business, as determined in accordance with Article 6.

4. Paragraph 2 of this Article applies notwithstanding that the place where the information system supporting an electronic address is located may be different from the place where the electronic communication is deemed to be received under paragraph 3 of this article.

Article 11 - Invitations to Make Offers

A proposal to conclude a contract made through one or more electronic communications which is not addressed to one or more specific parties, but is generally accessible to parties making use of information systems, including proposals that make use of interactive applications for the placement of orders through such information systems, is to be considered as an invitation to make offers, unless it clearly indicates the intention of the party making the proposal to be bound in case of acceptance.

Article 12 - Use of Automated Message Systems for Contract Formation

A contract formed by the interaction of an automated message system and a natural person, or by the interaction of automated message systems, shall not be denied validity or enforceability on the sole ground that no natural person reviewed or intervened in each of the individual actions carried out by the automated message systems or the resulting contract.

Article 13 - Availability of Contract Terms

Nothing in this Convention affects the application of any rule of law that may require a party that negotiates some or all of the terms of a contract through the exchange of electronic communications to make available to the other party those electronic communications which contain the contractual terms in a particular manner, or relieves a party from the legal consequences of its failure to do so.

Article 14 - Error in Electronic Communications

1. Where a natural person makes an input error in an electronic communication exchanged with the automated message system of another party and the automated message system does not provide the person with an opportunity to correct the error, that person, or the party on whose behalf that person was acting, has the right to withdraw the portion of the electronic communication in which the input error was made if:

(a) The person, or the party on whose behalf that person was acting, notifies the other party of the error as soon as possible after having learned of the error and indicates that he or she made an error in the electronic communication; and

(b) The person, or the party on whose behalf that person was acting, has not used or received any material benefit or value from the goods or services, if any, received from the other party.

2. Nothing in this Article affects the application of any rule of law that may govern the consequences of any error other than as provided for in paragraph 1.

CHAPTER IV. FINAL PROVISIONS [...]

Article 17 - Participation by Regional Economic Integration Organizations

1. A regional economic integration organization that is constituted by sovereign States and has competence over certain matters governed by this Convention may similarly sign, ratify, accept, approve or accede to this Convention. The regional economic integration organization shall in that case have the rights and obligations of a Contracting State, to the extent that that organization has competence over matters governed by this Convention. Where the number of Contracting States is relevant in this Convention, the regional economic integration organization shall not count as a Contracting State in addition to its member States that are Contracting States.

2. The regional economic integration organization shall, at the time of signature, ratification, acceptance, approval or accession, make a declaration to the depositary specifying the matters governed by this Convention in respect of which competence has been transferred to that organization by its member States. The regional economic integration organization shall promptly notify the depositary of any changes to the distribution of competence, including new transfers of competence, specified in the declaration under this paragraph.

3. Any reference to a "Contracting State" or "Contracting States" in this Convention applies equally to a regional economic integration organization where the context so requires.

4. This Convention shall not prevail over any conflicting rules of any regional economic integration organization as applicable to parties whose respective places of business are located

in States members of any such organization, as set out by declaration made in accordance with Article 21. [...]

Article 19 - Declarations on the Scope of Application

1. Any Contracting State may declare, in accordance with Article 21, that it will apply this Convention only:

(a) When the States referred to in Article 1, paragraph 1, are Contracting States to this Convention; or

(b) When the parties have agreed that it applies.

2. Any Contracting State may exclude from the scope of application of this Convention the matters it specifies in a declaration made in accordance with Article 21.

Article 20 - Communications Exchanged Under Other International Conventions

1. The provisions of this Convention apply to the use of electronic communications in connection with the formation or performance of a contract to which any of the following international conventions, to which a Contracting State to this Convention is or may become a Contracting State, apply:

- Convention on the Recognition and Enforcement of Foreign Arbitral Awards (New York, 10 June 1958);
- Convention on the Limitation Period in the International Sale of Goods (New York, 14 June 1974) and Protocol thereto (Vienna, 11 April 1980);
- United Nations Convention on Contracts for the International Sale of Goods (Vienna, 11 April 1980);
- United Nations Convention on the Liability of Operators of Transport Terminals in International Trade (Vienna, 19 April 1991);
- United Nations Convention on Independent Guarantees and Stand-by Letters of Credit (New York, 11 December 1995);
- United Nations Convention on the Assignment of Receivables in International Trade (New York, 12 December 2001).

2. The provisions of this Convention apply further to electronic communications in connection with the formation or performance of a contract to which another international convention, treaty or agreement not specifically referred to in paragraph 1 of this article, and to which a Contracting State to this Convention is or may become a Contracting State, applies, unless the State has declared, in accordance with Article 21, that it will not be bound by this paragraph.

3. A State that makes a declaration pursuant to paragraph 2 of this Article may also declare that it will nevertheless apply the provisions of this Convention to the use of electronic communications in connection with the formation or performance of any contract to which a specified international convention, treaty or agreement applies to which the State is or may become a Contracting State.

4. Any State may declare that it will not apply the provisions of this Convention to the use of electronic communications in connection with the formation or performance of a contract to which any international convention, treaty or agreement specified in that State's declaration, to which the State is or may become a Contracting State, applies, including any of the conventions referred to in paragraph 1 of this article, even if such State has not excluded the application of paragraph 2 of this Article by a declaration made in accordance with Article 21.

Article 21 - Procedure and Effects of Declarations

1. Declarations under Article 17, paragraph 4, Article 19, paragraphs 1 and 2, and Article 20, paragraphs 2, 3 and 4, may be made at any time. Declarations made at the time of signature are subject to confirmation upon ratification, acceptance or approval.

2. Declarations and their confirmations are to be in writing and to be formally notified to the depositary.

3. A declaration takes effect simultaneously with the entry into force of this Convention in respect of the State concerned. However, a declaration of which the depositary receives formal notification after such entry into force takes effect on the first day of the month following the expiration of six months after the date of its receipt by the depositary.

4. Any State that makes a declaration under this Convention may modify or withdraw it at any time by a formal notification in writing addressed to the depositary. The modification or withdrawal is to take effect on the first day of the month following the expiration of six months after the date of the receipt of the notification by the depositary.

Article 22 - Reservations

No reservations may be made under this Convention. [...]

DONE at New York this twenty-third day of November two thousand and five, in a single original, of which the Arabic, Chinese, English, French, Russian and Spanish texts are equally authentic.

IN WITNESS WHEREOF the undersigned plenipotentiaries, being duly authorized by their respective Governments, have signed this Convention.

Entry into force: 1 March 2013

Ratifications and binding effect as of April 2020: Azerbaijan (2019); Benin (2020), Cameroon (2018), Congo (2014), Dominican Republic (2013), Fiji (2018); Honduras (2013), Montenegro (2015), Paraguay (2019), Russia (2014); Singapore (2013), Sri Lanka (2016)

16) 1999 Uniform Electronic Transactions Act (UETA), USA[1]

Section 1. Short Title

This [Act] may be cited as the Uniform Electronic Transactions Act.

Section 2. Definitions

In this [Act]:

(1) "Agreement" means the bargain of the parties in fact, as found in their language or inferred from other circumstances and from rules, regulations, and procedures given the effect of agreements under laws otherwise applicable to a particular transaction.

(2) "Automated transaction" means a transaction conducted or performed, in whole or in part, by electronic means or electronic records, in which the acts or records of one or both parties are not reviewed by an individual in the ordinary course in forming a contract, performing under an existing contract, or fulfilling an obligation required by the transaction.

(3) "Computer program" means a set of statements or instructions to be used directly or indirectly in an information processing system in order to bring about a certain result.

(4) "Contract" means the total legal obligation resulting from the parties' agreement as affected by this [Act] and other applicable law.

(5) "Electronic" means relating to technology having electrical, digital, magnetic, wireless, optical, electromagnetic, or similar capabilities.

(6) "Electronic agent" means a computer program or an electronic or other automated means used independently to initiate an action or respond to electronic records or performances in whole or in part, without review or action by an individual.

(7) "Electronic record" means a record created, generated, sent, communicated, received, or stored by electronic means.

(8) "Electronic signature" means an electronic sound, symbol, or process attached to or logically associated with a record and executed or adopted by a person with the intent to sign the record.

(9) "Governmental agency" means an executive, legislative, or judicial agency, department, board, commission, authority, institution, or instrumentality of the federal government or of a State or of a county, municipality, or other political subdivision of a State.

(10) "Information" means data, text, images, sounds, codes, computer programs, software, databases, or the like.

(11) "Information processing system" means an electronic system for creating, generating, sending, receiving, storing, displaying, or processing information.

(12) "Person" means an individual, corporation, business trust, estate, trust, partnership, limited liability company, association, joint venture, governmental agency, public corporation, or any other legal or commercial entity.

(13) "Record" means information that is inscribed on a tangible medium or that is stored in an electronic or other medium and is retrievable in perceivable form.

(14) "Security procedure" means a procedure employed for the purpose of verifying that an electronic signature, record, or performance is that of a specific person or for detecting changes or errors in the information in an electronic record. The term includes a procedure that requires

---

the use of algorithms or other codes, identifying words or numbers, encryption, or callback or other acknowledgment procedures.

(15) "State" means a State of the United States, the District of Columbia, Puerto Rico, the United States Virgin Islands, or any territory or insular possession subject to the jurisdiction of the United States. The term includes an Indian tribe or band, or Alaskan native village, which is recognized by federal law or formally acknowledged by a State.

(16) "Transaction" means an action or set of actions occurring between two or more persons relating to the conduct of business, commercial, or governmental affairs.

Section 3. Scope

(a) Except as otherwise provided in subsection (b), this [Act] applies to electronic records and electronic signatures relating to a transaction.

(b) This [Act] does not apply to a transaction to the extent it is governed by:

(1) a law governing the creation and execution of wills, codicils, or testamentary trusts;

(2) [the Uniform Commercial Code other than Sections 1-107 and 1-206, Article 2, and Article 2A];

(3) [the Uniform Computer Information Transactions Act]; and

(4) [other laws, if any, identified by State].

(c) This [Act] applies to an electronic record or electronic signature otherwise excluded from the application of this [Act] under subsection (b) to the extent it is governed by a law other than those specified in subsection (b).

(d) A transaction subject to this [Act] is also subject to other applicable substantive law.

Section 4. Prospective Application

This [Act] applies to any electronic record or electronic signature created, generated, sent, communicated, received, or stored on or after the effective date of this [Act].

Section 5. Use of Electronic Records and Electronic Signatures; Variation by Agreement

(a) This [Act] does not require a record or signature to be created, generated, sent, communicated, received, stored, or otherwise processed or used by electronic means or in electronic form.

(b) This [Act] applies only to transactions between parties each of which has agreed to conduct transactions by electronic means. Whether the parties agree to conduct a transaction by electronic means is determined from the context and surrounding circumstances, including the parties' conduct.

(c) A party that agrees to conduct a transaction by electronic means may refuse to conduct other transactions by electronic means. The right granted by this subsection may not be waived by agreement.

(d) Except as otherwise provided in this [Act], the effect of any of its provisions may be varied by agreement. The presence in certain provisions of this [Act] of the words "unless otherwise agreed", or words of similar import, does not imply that the effect of other provisions may not be varied by agreement.

(e) Whether an electronic record or electronic signature has legal consequences is determined by this [Act] and other applicable law.

Section 6. Construction and Application

This [Act] must be construed and applied:

(1) to facilitate electronic transactions consistent with other applicable law;

(2) to be consistent with reasonable practices concerning electronic transactions and with the continued expansion of those practices; and

(3) to effectuate its general purpose to make uniform the law with respect to the subject of this [Act] among States enacting it.

Section 7. Legal Recognition of Electronic Records, Electronic Signatures, and Electronic Contracts

(a) A record or signature may not be denied legal effect or enforceability solely because it is in electronic form.

(b) A contract may not be denied legal effect or enforceability solely because an electronic record was used in its formation.

(c) If a law requires a record to be in writing, an electronic record satisfies the law.

(d) If a law requires a signature, an electronic signature satisfies the law.

Section 8. Provision of Information in Writing; Presentation of Records

(a) If parties have agreed to conduct a transaction by electronic means and a law requires a person to provide, send, or deliver information in writing to another person, the requirement is satisfied if the information is provided, sent, or delivered, as the case may be, in an electronic record capable of retention by the recipient at the time of receipt. An electronic record is not capable of retention by the recipient if the sender or its information processing system inhibits the ability of the recipient to print or store the electronic record.

(b) If a law other than this [Act] requires a record (i) to be posted or displayed in a certain manner, (ii) to be sent, communicated, or transmitted by a specified method, or (iii) to contain information that is formatted in a certain manner, the following rules apply:

(1) The record must be posted or displayed in the manner specified in the other law.

(2) Except as otherwise provided in subsection (d)(2), the record must be sent, communicated, or transmitted by the method specified in the other law.

(3) The record must contain the information formatted in the manner specified in the other law.

(c) If a sender inhibits the ability of a recipient to store or print an electronic record, the electronic record is not enforceable against the recipient.

(d) The requirements of this section may not be varied by agreement, but:

(1) to the extent a law other than this [Act] requires information to be provided, sent, or delivered in writing but permits that requirement to be varied by agreement, the requirement under subsection (a) that the information be in the form of an electronic record capable of retention may also be varied by agreement; and

(2) a requirement under a law other than this [Act] to send, communicate, or transmit a record by [first-class mail, postage prepaid] [regular United States mail], may be varied by agreement to the extent permitted by the other law.

Section 9. Attribution and Effect of Electronic Record and Electronic Signature

(a) An electronic record or electronic signature is attributable to a person if it was the act of the person. The act of the person may be shown in any manner, including a showing of the efficacy of any security procedure applied to determine the person to which the electronic record or electronic signature was attributable.

(b) The effect of an electronic record or electronic signature attributed to a person under subsection (a) is determined from the context and surrounding circumstances at the time of its creation, execution, or adoption, including the parties' agreement, if any, and otherwise as provided by law.

Section 10. Effect of Change or Error

If a change or error in an electronic record occurs in a transmission between parties to a transaction, the following rules apply:

(1) If the parties have agreed to use a security procedure to detect changes or errors and one party has conformed to the procedure, but the other party has not, and the nonconforming party would have detected the change or error had that party also conformed, the conforming party may avoid the effect of the changed or erroneous electronic record.

(2) In an automated transaction involving an individual, the individual may avoid the effect of an electronic record that resulted from an error made by the individual in dealing with the electronic agent of another person if the electronic agent did not provide an opportunity for the prevention or correction of the error and, at the time the individual learns of the error, the individual:

(A) promptly notifies the other person of the error and that the individual did not intend to be bound by the electronic record received by the other person;

(B) takes reasonable steps, including steps that conform to the other person's reasonable instructions, to return to the other person or, if instructed by the other person, to destroy the consideration received, if any, as a result of the erroneous electronic record; and

(C) has not used or received any benefit or value from the consideration, if any, received from the other person.

(3) If neither paragraph (1) nor paragraph (2) applies, the change or error has the effect provided by other law, including the law of mistake, and the parties' contract, if any.

(4) Paragraphs (2) and (3) may not be varied by agreement.

Section 11. Notarization and Acknowledgment

If a law requires a signature or record to be notarized, acknowledged, verified, or made under oath, the requirement is satisfied if the electronic signature of the person authorized to perform those acts, together with all other information required to be included by other applicable law, is attached to or logically associated with the signature or record.

Section 12. Retention of Electronic Records; Originals

(a) If a law requires that a record be retained, the requirement is satisfied by retaining an electronic record of the information in the record which:

(1) accurately reflects the information set forth in the record after it was first generated in its final form as an electronic record or otherwise; and

(2) remains accessible for later reference.

(b) A requirement to retain a record in accordance with subsection (a) does not apply to any information the sole purpose of which is to enable the record to be sent, communicated, or received.

(c) A person may satisfy subsection (a) by using the services of another person if the requirements of that subsection are satisfied.

(d) If a law requires a record to be presented or retained in its original form, or provides consequences if the record is not presented or retained in its original form, that law is satisfied by an electronic record retained in accordance with subsection (a).

(e) If a law requires retention of a check, that requirement is satisfied by retention of an electronic record of the information on the front and back of the check in accordance with subsection (a).

(f) A record retained as an electronic record in accordance with subsection (a) satisfies a law requiring a person to retain a record for evidentiary, audit, or like purposes, unless a law enacted after the effective date of this [Act] specifically prohibits the use of an electronic record for the specified purpose.

(g) This section does not preclude a governmental agency of this State from specifying additional requirements for the retention of a record subject to the agency's jurisdiction.

Section 13. Admissibility in Evidence

In a proceeding, evidence of a record or signature may not be excluded solely because it is in electronic form.

Section 14. Automated Transaction

In an automated transaction, the following rules apply:

(1) A contract may be formed by the interaction of electronic agents of the parties, even if no individual was aware of or reviewed the electronic agents' actions or the resulting terms and agreements.

(2) A contract may be formed by the interaction of an electronic agent and an individual, acting on the individual's own behalf or for another person, including by an interaction in which the individual performs actions that the individual is free to refuse to perform and which the individual knows or has reason to know will cause the electronic agent to complete the transaction or performance.

(3) The terms of the contract are determined by the substantive law applicable to it.

Section 15. Time and Place of Sending and Receipt

(a) Unless otherwise agreed between the sender and the recipient, an electronic record is sent when it:

(1) is addressed properly or otherwise directed properly to an information processing system that the recipient has designated or uses for the purpose of receiving electronic records or information of the type sent and from which the recipient is able to retrieve the electronic record;

(2) is in a form capable of being processed by that system; and

(3) enters an information processing system outside the control of the sender or of a person that sent the electronic record on behalf of the sender or enters a region of the information processing system designated or used by the recipient which is under the control of the recipient.

(b) Unless otherwise agreed between a sender and the recipient, an electronic record is received when:

(1) it enters an information processing system that the recipient has designated or uses for the purpose of receiving electronic records or information of the type sent and from which the recipient is able to retrieve the electronic record; and

(2) it is in a form capable of being processed by that system.

(c) Subsection (b) applies even if the place the information processing system is located is different from the place the electronic record is deemed to be received under subsection (d).

(d) Unless otherwise expressly provided in the electronic record or agreed between the sender and the recipient, an electronic record is deemed to be sent from the sender's place of business and to be received at the recipient's place of business. For purposes of this subsection, the following rules apply:

(1) If the sender or recipient has more than one place of business, the place of business of that person is the place having the closest relationship to the underlying transaction.

(2) If the sender or the recipient does not have a place of business, the place of business is the sender's or recipient's residence, as the case may be.

(e) An electronic record is received under subsection (b) even if no individual is aware of its receipt.

(f) Receipt of an electronic acknowledgment from an information processing system described in subsection (b) establishes that a record was received but, by itself, does not establish that the content sent corresponds to the content received.

(g) If a person is aware that an electronic record purportedly sent under subsection (a), or purportedly received under subsection (b), was not actually sent or received, the legal effect of the sending or receipt is determined by other applicable law. Except to the extent permitted by the other law, the requirements of this subsection may not be varied by agreement.

Section 16. Transferable Records

(a) In this section, "transferable record" means an electronic record that:

(1) would be a note under [Article 3 of the Uniform Commercial Code] or a document under [Article 7 of the Uniform Commercial Code] if the electronic record were in writing; and

(2) the issuer of the electronic record expressly has agreed is a transferable record.

(b) A person has control of a transferable record if a system employed for evidencing the transfer of interests in the transferable record reliably establishes that person as the person to which the transferable record was issued or transferred.

(c) A system satisfies subsection (b), and a person is deemed to have control of a transferable record, if the transferable record is created, stored, and assigned in such a manner that:

(1) a single authoritative copy of the transferable record exists which is unique, identifiable, and, except as otherwise provided in paragraphs (4), (5), and (6), unalterable;

(2) the authoritative copy identifies the person asserting control as:

(A) the person to which the transferable record was issued; or

(B) if the authoritative copy indicates that the transferable record has been transferred, the person to which the transferable record was most recently transferred;

(3) the authoritative copy is communicated to and maintained by the person asserting control or its designated custodian;

(4) copies or revisions that add or change an identified assignee of the authoritative copy can be made only with the consent of the person asserting control;

(5) each copy of the authoritative copy and any copy of a copy is readily identifiable as a copy that is not the authoritative copy; and

(6) any revision of the authoritative copy is readily identifiable as authorized or unauthorized.

(d) Except as otherwise agreed, a person having control of a transferable record is the holder, as defined in [Section 1-201(20) of the Uniform Commercial Code], of the transferable record and has the same rights and defenses as a holder of an equivalent record or writing under [the Uniform Commercial Code], including, if the applicable statutory requirements under [Section 3-302(a), 7-501, or 9-308 of the Uniform Commercial Code] are satisfied, the rights and defenses of a holder in due course, a holder to which a negotiable document of title has been duly negotiated, or a purchaser, respectively. Delivery, possession, and indorsement are not required to obtain or exercise any of the rights under this subsection.

(e) Except as otherwise agreed, an obligor under a transferable record has the same rights and defenses as an equivalent obligor under equivalent records or writings under [the Uniform Commercial Code].

(f) If requested by a person against which enforcement is sought, the person seeking to enforce the transferable record shall provide reasonable proof that the person is in control of the transferable record. Proof may include access to the authoritative copy of the transferable record and related business records sufficient to review the terms of the transferable record and to establish the identity of the person having control of the transferable record.

[Section 17. Creation and Retention of Electronic Records and Conversion of Written Records by Governmental Agencies

[Each governmental agency] [The [designated state officer]] of this State shall determine whether, and the extent to which, [it] [a governmental agency] will create and retain electronic records and convert written records to electronic records.]

[Section 18. Acceptance and Distribution of Electronic Records by Governmental Agencies

(a) Except as otherwise provided in Section 12(f), [each governmental agency] [the [designated state officer]] of this State shall determine whether, and the extent to which, [it] [a governmental agency] will send and accept electronic records and electronic signatures to and from other persons and otherwise create, generate, communicate, store, process, use, and rely upon electronic records and electronic signatures.

(b) To the extent that a governmental agency uses electronic records and electronic signatures under subsection (a), the [governmental agency] [designated state officer], giving due consideration to security, may specify:

(1) the manner and format in which the electronic records must be created, generated, sent, communicated, received, and stored and the systems established for those purposes;

(2) if electronic records must be signed by electronic means, the type of electronic signature required, the manner and format in which the electronic signature must be affixed to the electronic record, and the identity of, or criteria that must be met by, any third party used by a person filing a document to facilitate the process;

(3) control processes and procedures as appropriate to ensure adequate preservation, disposition, integrity, security, confidentiality, and auditability of electronic records; and

(4) any other required attributes for electronic records which are specified for corresponding nonelectronic records or reasonably necessary under the circumstances.

(c) Except as otherwise provided in Section 12(f), this [Act] does not require a governmental agency of this State to use or permit the use of electronic records or electronic signatures.]

[Section 19. Interoperability

The [governmental agency] [designated officer] of this State which adopts standards pursuant to Section 18 may encourage and promote consistency and interoperability with similar requirements adopted by other governmental agencies of this and other States and the federal government and nongovernmental persons interacting with governmental agencies of this State.

If appropriate, those standards may specify differing levels of standards from which governmental agencies of this State may choose in implementing the most appropriate standard for a particular application.]

Section 20. Severability Clause

If any provision of this [Act] or its application to any person or circumstance is held invalid, the invalidity does not affect other provisions or applications of this [Act] which can be given effect without the invalid provision or application, and to this end the provisions of this [Act] are severable.

Section 21. Effective Date

This [Act] takes effect ....

17) 2000 Federal E-Sign Act, USA[1]

Title 15. Commerce and Trade

Chapter 96. Electronic Signatures in Global and National Commerce

Subchapter I. Electronic Records and Signatures in Commerce

§ 7001. General Rule of Validity

(a) In general

Notwithstanding any statute, regulation, or other rule of law (other than this subchapter and subchapter II of this chapter), with respect to any transaction in or affecting interstate or foreign commerce --

(1) a signature, contract, or other record relating to such transaction may not be denied legal effect, validity, or enforceability solely because it is in electronic form; and

(2) a contract relating to such transaction may not be denied legal effect, validity, or enforceability solely because an electronic signature or electronic record was used in its formation.

(b) Preservation of rights and obligations

This subchapter does not –

(1) limit, alter, or otherwise affect any requirement imposed by a statute, regulation, or rule of law relating to the rights and obligations of persons under such statute, regulation, or rule of law other than a requirement that contracts or other records be written, signed, or in nonelectronic form; or

(2) require any person to agree to use or accept electronic records or electronic signatures, other than a governmental agency with respect to a record other than a contract to which it is a party.

(c) Consumer disclosures

(1) Consent to electronic records

Notwithstanding subsection (a), if a statute, regulation, or other rule of law requires that information relating to a transaction or transactions in or affecting interstate or foreign commerce be provided or made available to a consumer in writing, the use of an electronic record to provide or make available (whichever is required) such information satisfies the requirement that such information be in writing if --

(A) the consumer has affirmatively consented to such use and has not withdrawn such consent;

(B) the consumer, prior to consenting, is provided with a clear and conspicuous statement--

(i) informing the consumer of (I) any right or option of the consumer to have the record provided or made available on paper or in nonelectronic form, and (II) the right of the consumer to withdraw the consent to have the record provided or made available in an electronic form and of any conditions, consequences (which may include termination of the parties' relationship), or fees in the event of such withdrawal;

---

1 15 U.S. Code Chapter 96, Electronic Signatures in Global and National Commerce Act (E-Sign Act), Pub.L. 106–229, June 30, 2000, 114 Stat. 464.

(ii) informing the consumer of whether the consent applies (I) only to the particular transaction which gave rise to the obligation to provide the record, or (II) to identified categories of records that may be provided or made available during the course of the parties' relationship;

(iii) describing the procedures the consumer must use to withdraw consent as provided in clause (i) and to update information needed to contact the consumer electronically; and

(iv) informing the consumer (I) how, after the consent, the consumer may, upon request, obtain a paper copy of an electronic record, and (II) whether any fee will be charged for such copy;

(C) the consumer --

(i) prior to consenting, is provided with a statement of the hardware and software requirements for access to and retention of the electronic records; and

(ii) consents electronically, or confirms his or her consent electronically, in a manner that reasonably demonstrates that the consumer can access information in the electronic form that will be used to provide the information that is the subject of the consent; and

(D) after the consent of a consumer in accordance with subparagraph (A), if a change in the hardware or software requirements needed to access or retain electronic records creates a material risk that the consumer will not be able to access or retain a subsequent electronic record that was the subject of the consent, the person providing the electronic record--

(i) provides the consumer with a statement of (I) the revised hardware and software requirements for access to and retention of the electronic records, and (II) the right to withdraw consent without the imposition of any fees for such withdrawal and without the imposition of any condition or consequence that was not disclosed under subparagraph (B)(i); and

(ii) again complies with subparagraph (C).

(2) Other rights

(A) Preservation of consumer protections

Nothing in this subchapter affects the content or timing of any disclosure or other record required to be provided or made available to any consumer under any statute, regulation, or other rule of law.

(B) Verification or acknowledgment

If a law that was enacted prior to this chapter expressly requires a record to be provided or made available by a specified method that requires verification or acknowledgment of receipt, the record may be provided or made available electronically only if the method used provides verification or acknowledgment of receipt (whichever is required).

(3) Effect of failure to obtain electronic consent or confirmation of consent

The legal effectiveness, validity, or enforceability of any contract executed by a consumer shall not be denied solely because of the failure to obtain electronic consent or confirmation of consent by that consumer in accordance with paragraph (1)(C)(ii).

(4) Prospective effect

Withdrawal of consent by a consumer shall not affect the legal effectiveness, validity, or enforceability of electronic records provided or made available to that consumer in accordance with paragraph (1) prior to implementation of the consumer's withdrawal of consent. A consumer's withdrawal of consent shall be effective within a reasonable period of time after receipt of the withdrawal by the provider of the record. Failure to comply with paragraph (1)(D) may, at the election of the consumer, be treated as a withdrawal of consent for purposes of this paragraph.

(5) Prior consent

This subsection does not apply to any records that are provided or made available to a consumer who has consented prior to the effective date of this subchapter to receive such records in electronic form as permitted by any statute, regulation, or other rule of law.

(6) Oral communications

An oral communication or a recording of an oral communication shall not qualify as an electronic record for purposes of this subsection except as otherwise provided under applicable law.

(d) Retention of contracts and records

(1) Accuracy and accessibility

If a statute, regulation, or other rule of law requires that a contract or other record relating to a transaction in or affecting interstate or foreign commerce be retained, that requirement is met by retaining an electronic record of the information in the contract or other record that--

(A) accurately reflects the information set forth in the contract or other record; and

(B) remains accessible to all persons who are entitled to access by statute, regulation, or rule of law, for the period required by such statute, regulation, or rule of law, in a form that is capable of being accurately reproduced for later reference, whether by transmission, printing, or otherwise.

(2) Exception

A requirement to retain a contract or other record in accordance with paragraph (1) does not apply to any information whose sole purpose is to enable the contract or other record to be sent, communicated, or received.

(3) Originals

If a statute, regulation, or other rule of law requires a contract or other record relating to a transaction in or affecting interstate or foreign commerce to be provided, available, or retained in its original form, or provides consequences if the contract or other record is not provided, available, or retained in its original form, that statute, regulation, or rule of law is satisfied by an electronic record that complies with paragraph (1).

(4) Checks

If a statute, regulation, or other rule of law requires the retention of a check, that requirement is satisfied by retention of an electronic record of the information on the front and back of the check in accordance with paragraph (1).

(e) Accuracy and ability to retain contracts and other records

Notwithstanding subsection (a), if a statute, regulation, or other rule of law requires that a contract or other record relating to a transaction in or affecting interstate or foreign commerce be in writing, the legal effect, validity, or enforceability of an electronic record of such contract or other record may be denied if such electronic record is not in a form that is capable of being retained and accurately reproduced for later reference by all parties or persons who are entitled to retain the contract or other record.

(f) Proximity

Nothing in this subchapter affects the proximity required by any statute, regulation, or other rule of law with respect to any warning, notice, disclosure, or other record required to be posted, displayed, or publicly affixed.

(g) Notarization and acknowledgment

If a statute, regulation, or other rule of law requires a signature or record relating to a transaction in or affecting interstate or foreign commerce to be notarized, acknowledged, verified, or made under oath, that requirement is satisfied if the electronic signature of the person authorized to perform those acts, together with all other information required to be included by other applicable statute, regulation, or rule of law, is attached to or logically associated with the signature or record.

(h) Electronic agents

A contract or other record relating to a transaction in or affecting interstate or foreign commerce may not be denied legal effect, validity, or enforceability solely because its formation, creation, or delivery involved the action of one or more electronic agents so long as the action of any such electronic agent is legally attributable to the person to be bound.

(i) Insurance

It is the specific intent of the Congress that this subchapter and subchapter II of this chapter apply to the business of insurance.

(j) Insurance agents and brokers

An insurance agent or broker acting under the direction of a party that enters into a contract by means of an electronic record or electronic signature may not be held liable for any deficiency in the electronic procedures agreed to by the parties under that contract if--

(1) the agent or broker has not engaged in negligent, reckless, or intentional tortious conduct;

(2) the agent or broker was not involved in the development or establishment of such electronic procedures; and

(3) the agent or broker did not deviate from such procedures.

§ 7002. Exemption to Preemption

(a) In general

A State statute, regulation, or other rule of law may modify, limit, or supersede the provisions of section 7001 of this title with respect to State law only if such statute, regulation, or rule of law--

(1) constitutes an enactment or adoption of the Uniform Electronic Transactions Act as approved and recommended for enactment in all the States by the National Conference of Commissioners on Uniform State Laws in 1999, except that any exception to the scope of such Act enacted by a State under section 3(b)(4) of such Act shall be preempted to the extent such exception is inconsistent with this subchapter or subchapter II of this chapter, or would not be permitted under paragraph (2)(A)(ii) of this subsection; or

(2)(A) specifies the alternative procedures or requirements for the use or acceptance (or both) of electronic records or electronic signatures to establish the legal effect, validity, or enforceability of contracts or other records, if--

(i) such alternative procedures or requirements are consistent with this subchapter and subchapter II of this chapter; and

(ii) such alternative procedures or requirements do not require, or accord greater legal status or effect to, the implementation or application of a specific technology or technical specification for performing the functions of creating, storing, generating, receiving, communicating, or authenticating electronic records or electronic signatures; and

(B) if enacted or adopted after June 30, 2000, makes specific reference to this chapter.

(b) Exceptions for actions by States as market participants

Subsection (a)(2)(A)(ii) of this section shall not apply to the statutes, regulations, or other rules of law governing procurement by any State, or any agency or instrumentality thereof.

(c) Prevention of circumvention

Subsection (a) of this section does not permit a State to circumvent this subchapter or subchapter II of this chapter through the imposition of nonelectronic delivery methods under section 8(b)(2) of the Uniform Electronic Transactions Act.

§ 7003. Specific Exceptions

(a) Excepted requirements

The provisions of section 7001 of this title shall not apply to a contract or other record to the extent it is governed by --

(1) a statute, regulation, or other rule of law governing the creation and execution of wills, codicils, or testamentary trusts;

(2) a State statute, regulation, or other rule of law governing adoption, divorce, or other matters of family law; or

(3) the Uniform Commercial Code, as in effect in any State, other than sections 1-107 and 1-206 and Articles 2 and 2A.

(b) Additional exceptions

The provisions of section 7001 of this title shall not apply to --

(1) court orders or notices, or official court documents (including briefs, pleadings, and other writings) required to be executed in connection with court proceedings;

(2) any notice of--

(A) the cancellation or termination of utility services (including water, heat, and power);

(B) default, acceleration, repossession, foreclosure, or eviction, or the right to cure, under a credit agreement secured by, or a rental agreement for, a primary residence of an individual;

(C) the cancellation or termination of health insurance or benefits or life insurance benefits (excluding annuities); or

(D) recall of a product, or material failure of a product, that risks endangering health or safety; or

(3) any document required to accompany any transportation or handling of hazardous materials, pesticides, or other toxic or dangerous materials.

(c) Review of exceptions [...]

§ 7006. Definitions

For purposes of this subchapter:

(1) Consumer

The term "consumer" means an individual who obtains, through a transaction, products or services which are used primarily for personal, family, or household purposes, and also means the legal representative of such an individual.

(2) Electronic

The term "electronic" means relating to technology having electrical, digital, magnetic, wireless, optical, electromagnetic, or similar capabilities.

(3) Electronic agent

The term "electronic agent" means a computer program or an electronic or other automated means used independently to initiate an action or respond to electronic records or performances in whole or in part without review or action by an individual at the time of the action or response.

(4) Electronic record

The term "electronic record" means a contract or other record created, generated, sent, communicated, received, or stored by electronic means.

(5) Electronic signature

The term "electronic signature" means an electronic sound, symbol, or process, attached to or logically associated with a contract or other record and executed or adopted by a person with the intent to sign the record.

(6) Federal regulatory agency

The term "Federal regulatory agency" means an agency, as that term is defined in section 552(f) of Title 5.

(7) Information

The term "information" means data, text, images, sounds, codes, computer programs, software, databases, or the like.

(8) Person

The term "person" means an individual, corporation, business trust, estate, trust, partnership, limited liability company, association, joint venture, governmental agency, public corporation, or any other legal or commercial entity.

(9) Record

The term "record" means information that is inscribed on a tangible medium or that is stored in an electronic or other medium and is retrievable in perceivable form.

(10) Requirement

The term "requirement" includes a prohibition.

(11) Self-regulatory organization

The term "self-regulatory organization" means an organization or entity that is not a Federal regulatory agency or a State, but that is under the supervision of a Federal regulatory agency and is authorized under Federal law to adopt and administer rules applicable to its members that are enforced by such organization or entity, by a Federal regulatory agency, or by another self-regulatory organization.

(12) State

The term "State" includes the District of Columbia and the territories and possessions of the United States.

(13) Transaction

The term "transaction" means an action or set of actions relating to the conduct of business, consumer, or commercial affairs between two or more persons, including any of the following types of conduct--

(A) the sale, lease, exchange, licensing, or other disposition of (i) personal property, including goods and intangibles, (ii) services, and (iii) any combination thereof; and

(B) the sale, lease, exchange, or other disposition of any interest in real property, or any combination thereof.

Subchapter II. Transferable Records

§ 7021. Transferable Records

(a) Definitions

For purposes of this section:

(1) Transferable record

The term "transferable record" means an electronic record that --

(A) would be a note under Article 3 of the Uniform Commercial Code if the electronic record were in writing;

(B) the issuer of the electronic record expressly has agreed is a transferable record; and

(C) relates to a loan secured by real property.

A transferable record may be executed using an electronic signature.

(2) Other definitions

The terms "electronic record", "electronic signature", and "person" have the same meanings provided in section 7006 of this title.

(b) Control

A person has control of a transferable record if a system employed for evidencing the transfer of interests in the transferable record reliably establishes that person as the person to which the transferable record was issued or transferred.

(c) Conditions

A system satisfies subsection (b) of this section, and a person is deemed to have control of a transferable record, if the transferable record is created, stored, and assigned in such a manner that--

(1) a single authoritative copy of the transferable record exists which is unique, identifiable, and, except as otherwise provided in paragraphs (4), (5), and (6), unalterable;

(2) the authoritative copy identifies the person asserting control as --

(A) the person to which the transferable record was issued; or

(B) if the authoritative copy indicates that the transferable record has been transferred, the person to which the transferable record was most recently transferred;

(3) the authoritative copy is communicated to and maintained by the person asserting control or its designated custodian;

(4) copies or revisions that add or change an identified assignee of the authoritative copy can be made only with the consent of the person asserting control;

(5) each copy of the authoritative copy and any copy of a copy is readily identifiable as a copy that is not the authoritative copy; and

(6) any revision of the authoritative copy is readily identifiable as authorized or un-authorized.

(d) Status as holder

Except as otherwise agreed, a person having control of a transferable record is the holder, as defined in section 1-201(20) of the Uniform Commercial Code, of the transferable record and has the same rights and defenses as a holder of an equivalent record or writing under the Uniform Commercial Code, including, if the applicable statutory requirements under section 3-302(a), 9-308, or revised section 9-330 of the Uniform Commercial Code are satisfied, the rights and defenses of a holder in due course or a purchaser, respectively. Delivery, possession, and endorsement are not required to obtain or exercise any of the rights under this subsection.

(e) Obligor rights

Except as otherwise agreed, an obligor under a transferable record has the same rights and defenses as an equivalent obligor under equivalent records or writings under the Uniform Commercial Code.

(f) Proof of control

If requested by a person against which enforcement is sought, the person seeking to enforce the transferable record shall provide reasonable proof that the person is in control of the transferable record. Proof may include access to the authoritative copy of the transferable record and related business records sufficient to review the terms of the transferable record and to establish the identity of the person having control of the transferable record.

(g) UCC references

For purposes of this subsection, all references to the Uniform Commercial Code are to the Uniform Commercial Code as in effect in the jurisdiction the law of which governs the transferable record.

Subchapter III. Promotion of International Electronic Commerce

§ 7031. Principles Governing the Use of Electronic Signatures in International Transactions

(a) Promotion of electronic signatures

(1) Required actions

The Secretary of Commerce shall promote the acceptance and use, on an international basis, of electronic signatures in accordance with the principles specified in paragraph (2) and in a manner consistent with section 7001 of this title. The Secretary of Commerce shall take all actions necessary in a manner consistent with such principles to eliminate or reduce, to the maximum extent possible, the impediments to commerce in electronic signatures, for the purpose of facilitating the development of interstate and foreign commerce.

(2) Principles

The principles specified in this paragraph are the following:

(A) Remove paper-based obstacles to electronic transactions by adopting relevant principles from the Model Law on Electronic Commerce adopted in 1996 by the United Nations Commission on International Trade Law.

(B) Permit parties to a transaction to determine the appropriate authentication technologies and implementation models for their transactions, with assurance that those technologies and implementation models will be recognized and enforced.

(C) Permit parties to a transaction to have the opportunity to prove in court or other proceedings that their authentication approaches and their transactions are valid.

(D) Take a nondiscriminatory approach to electronic signatures and authentication methods from other jurisdictions.

(b) Consultation

In conducting the activities required by this section, the Secretary shall consult with users and providers of electronic signature products and services and other interested persons.

(c) Definitions

As used in this section, the terms “electronic record” and “electronic signature” have the same meanings provided in section 7006 of this title.

18) INCOTERMS® 2020

INCOTERMS for Any Mode or Modes of Transport

EXW [Place] INCOTERMS® 2020 — Ex Works
FCA [Place] INCOTERMS® 2020 — Free Carrier
CIP [Place] INCOTERMS® 2020 — Carriage and Insurance Paid to
CPT [Place] INCOTERMS® 2020 — Carriage Paid to
DAP [Place] INCOTERMS® 2020 — Delivered at Place
DPU [Place] INCOTERMS® 2020 — Delivered at Place Unloaded
DDP [Place] INCOTERMS® 2020 — Delivered Duty Paid

INCOTERMS for Maritime Transport

FAS [Place] INCOTERMS® 2020 — Free Alongside Ship
FOB [Place] INCOTERMS® 2020 — Free on Board
CIF [Place] INCOTERMS® 2020 — Cost, Insurance and Freight
CFR [Place] INCOTERMS® 2020 — Cost and Freight

Distribution of Tasks, Risk, and Cost Between Seller S and Buyer B

	EXW	FCA	FAS*	FOB*	CIF*	CFR*	CIP	CPT	DAP	DPU	DDP
packaging	S	S	S	S	S	S	S	S	S	S	S
packing list & invoice	S	S	S	S	S	S	S	S	S	S	S
marking & labeling	S	S	S	S	S	S	S	S	S	S	S
loading onto first carrier	B	S	S	S	S	S	S	S	S	S	S
transport to port of departure	B	S / B	S	S	S	S	S	S	S	S	S
export clearance	B	S / B	S	S	S	S	S	S	S	S	S
loading onto main vessel	B	S / B	B	S	S	S	S	S	S	S	S
freight charges	B	B	B	B	S	S	S	S	S	S	S
insurance	B	B	B	B	S	B	S	B	S	S	S
unloading at destination port	B	B	B	B	B	B	B / S	B / S	B / S	S	S
terminal charges	B	B	B	B	B	B	B / S	B / S	B / S	B	S
import duties & clearance	B	B	B	B	B	B	B	B	B	B	S
delivery to final destination	B	B	B	B	B	B	B	B	B	B	S
unloading at final destination	B	B	B	B	B	B	B	B	B	B	B

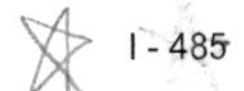

Part Three: The Documentary Sale 2 of 4 – Payment and Financing Contracts

19) 1930 Geneva Convention Providing a Uniform Law for Bills of Exchange and Promissory Notes[1]

TITLE I - Bills of Exchange

CHAPTER I - Issue and Form of a Bill of Exchange

Article 1 [Essential Elements of a Bill of Exchange]

A bill of exchange contains:

1. The term 'bill of exchange' inserted in the body of the instrument and expressed in the language employed in drawing up the instrument;
2. An unconditional order to pay a determinate sum of money;
3. The name of the person who is to pay (drawee);
4. A statement of the time of payment;
5. A statement of the place where payment is to be made;
6. The name of the person to whom or to whose order payment is to be made;
7. A statement of the date and of the place where the bill is issued;
8. The signature of the person who issues the bill (drawer).

Article 2 [Exceptions]

An instrument in which any of the requirements mentioned in the preceding Article is wanting is invalid as a bill of exchange, except in the cases specified in the following paragraphs:

A bill of exchange in which the time of payment is not specified is deemed to be payable at sight.

In default of special mention, the place specified beside the name of the drawee is deemed to be the place of payment, and at the same time the place of the domicile of the drawee.

A bill of exchange which does not mention the place of its issue is deemed to have been drawn in the place mentioned beside the name of the drawer.

Article 3 [Drawer and Drawee]

A bill of exchange may be drawn payable to drawer's order. It may be drawn on the drawer himself. It may be drawn for account of a third person.

Article 4 [Place of Payment]

A bill of exchange may be payable at the domicile of a third person either in the locality where the drawee has his domicile or in another locality.

---

1 League of Nations Treaty Series Vol. 143, p. 257. The more modern *1988 UN Convention on International Bills of Exchange and International Promissory Notes* has not entered into force as of April 2020. It requires at least 10 ratifications and has so far been ratified by 5 States (Guinea, Mexico, Honduras, Gabon, and Liberia) and signed by 3 more (Canada, USA, Russia).

Article 5 [Interest]

When a bill of exchange is payable at sight, or at a fixed period after sight, the drawer may stipulate that the sum payable shall bear interest. In the case of any other bill of exchange, this stipulation is deemed not to be written.

The rate of interest must be specified in the bill; in default of such specification, the stipulation shall be deemed not to be written.

Interest runs from the date of the bill of exchange, unless some other date is specified.

Article 6 [Amount Payable]

When the sum payable by a bill of exchange is expressed in words and also in figures, and there is a discrepancy between the two, the sum denoted by the words is the amount payable. Where the sum payable by a bill of exchange is expressed more than once in words or more than once in figures, and there is a discrepancy, the smaller sum is the sum payable.

Article 7 [Invalid Signatures on a Bill of Exchange]

If a bill of exchange bears signatures of persons incapable of binding themselves by a bill of exchange, or forged signatures, or signatures of fictitious persons, or signatures which for any other reason cannot bind the persons who signed the bill of exchange or on whose behalf it was signed, the obligations of the other persons who signed it are none the less valid.

Article 8 [Unauthorized Signatures on a Bill of Exchange]

Whosoever puts his signature on a bill of exchange as representing a person for whom he had no power to act is bound himself as a party to the bill and, if he pays, has the same rights as the person for whom he purported to act. The same rule applies to a representative who has exceeded his powers.

Article 9 [Obligations of Drawer]

The drawer guarantees both acceptance and payment. He may release himself from guaranteeing acceptance; every stipulation by which he releases himself from the guarantee of payment is deemed not to be written (non écrite).

Article 10

If a bill of exchange, which was incomplete when issued, has been completed otherwise than in accordance with the agreements entered into, the non-observance of such agreements may not be set up against the holder unless he has acquired the bill of exchange in bad faith or, in acquiring it, has been guilty of gross negligence.

CHAPTER II - Endorsement

Article 11 [Transfer of a Bill of Exchange by Endorsement]

Every bill of exchange, even if not expressly drawn to order, may be transferred by means of endorsement.

When the drawer has inserted in a bill of exchange the words 'not to order' or an equivalent expression, the instrument can only be transferred according to the form, and with the effects of an ordinary assignment.

The bill may be endorsed even in favour of the drawee, whether he has accepted or not, or of the drawer, or of any other party to the bill. These persons may re-endorse the bill.

Article 12

An endorsement must be unconditional. Any condition to which it is made subject is deemed not to be written (non écrite). A partial endorsement is null and void. An endorsement 'to bearer' is equivalent to an endorsement in blank.

Article 13

An endorsement must be written on the bill of exchange or on a slip affixed thereto (allonge). It must be signed by the endorser.

The endorsement may leave the beneficiary unspecified or may consist simply of the signature of the endorser (endorsement in blank). In the latter case, the endorsement, to be valid, must be written on the back of the bill of exchange or on the slip attached thereto (allonge).

Article 14

An endorsement transfers all the rights arising out of a bill of exchange. If the endorsement is in blank, the holder may:

1. Fill up the blank either with his own name or with the name of some other person;
2. Re-endorse the bill in blank, or to some other person;
3. Transfer the bill to a third person without filling up the blank, and without endorsing it.

Article 15

In the absence of any contrary stipulation, the endorser guarantees acceptance and payment. He may prohibit any further endorsement; in this case, he gives no guarantee to the persons to whom the bill is subsequently endorsed.

Article 16

The possessor of a bill of exchange is deemed to be the lawful holder if he establishes his title to the bill through an uninterrupted series of endorsements, even if the last endorsement is in blank. In this connection, cancelled endorsements are deemed not to be written (non écrits). When an endorsement in blank is followed by another endorsement, the person who signed this last endorsement is deemed to have acquired the bill by the endorsement in blank.

Where a person has been dispossessed of a bill of exchanged, in any manner whatsoever, the holder who establishes his right thereto in the manner mentioned in the preceding paragraph is not bound to give up the bill unless he has acquired it in bad faith, or unless in acquiring it he has been guilty of gross negligence.

Article 17

Persons sued on a bill of exchange cannot set up against the holder defences founded on their personal relations with the drawer or with previous holders, unless the holder, in acquiring the bill, has knowingly acted to the detriment of the debtor.

Article 18

When an endorsement contains the statements 'value in collection' ('valeur en recouvrement'), 'for collection' ('pour encaissement'), 'by procuration' ('par procuration') or any other phrase implying a simple mandate, the holder may exercise all rights arising out of the bill of exchange, but he can only endorse it in his capacity as agent.

In this case, the parties liable can only set up against the holder defences which could be set up against the endorser.

The mandate contained in an endorsement by procuration does not terminate by reason of the death of the party giving the mandate or by reason of his becoming legally incapable.

Article 19

When an endorsement contains the statements 'value in security' ('valeur en garantie'), 'value in pledge' ('valeur en gage'), or any other statement implying a pledge, the holder may exercise all the rights arising out of the bill of exchange, but an endorsement by him has the effects only of an endorsement by an agent.

The parties liable cannot set up against the holder defences founded on their personal relations with the endorser, unless the holder, in receiving the bill, has knowingly acted to the detriment of the debtor.

Article 20

An endorsement after maturity has the same effects as an endorsement before maturity. Nevertheless an endorsement after protest for non-payment, or after the expiration of the limit of time fixed for drawing up the protest, operates only as an ordinary assignment.

Failing proof to the contrary, an endorsement without date is deemed to have been placed on the bill before the expiration of the limit of time fixed for drawing up the protest.

CHAPTER III - Acceptance

Article 21

Until maturity, a bill of exchange may be presented to the drawee for acceptance at his domicile. either by the holder or by a person who is merely in possession of the bill.

Article 22

In any bill of exchange, the drawer may stipulate that it shall be presented for acceptance with or without fixing a limit of time for presentment.

Except in the case of a bill payable at the address of a third party or in a locality other than that of the domicile of the drawee, or, except in the case of a bill drawn payable at a fixed period after sight, the drawer may prohibit presentment for acceptance.

He may also stipulate that presentment for acceptance shall not take place before a named date.

Unless the drawer has prohibited acceptance, every endorser may stipulate that the bill shall be presented for acceptance, with or without fixing a limit of time for presentment.

Article 23

Bills of exchange payable at a fixed period after sight must be presented for acceptance within one year of their date. The drawer may abridge or extend this period. These periods may be abridged by the endorsers.

Article 24

The drawee may demand that a bill shall be presented to him a second time on the day after the first presentment. Parties interested are not allowed to set up that this demand has not been complied with unless this request is mentioned in the protest.

The holder is not obliged to surrender to the drawee a bill presented for acceptance.

Article 25

An acceptance is written on the bill of exchange. It is expressed by the word 'accepted' or any other equivalent term. It is signed by the drawee. The simple signature of the drawee on the face of the bill constitutes an acceptance.

When the bill is payable at a certain time after sight, or when it must be presented for acceptance within a certain limit of time in accordance with a special stipulation the acceptance must be dated as of the day when the acceptance is given unless the holder requires it shall be dated as of the day of presentment. If it is undated, the holder, in order to preserve his right of recourse against the endorsers and the drawer, must authenticate the omission by a protest drawn up within the proper time.

Article 26

An acceptance is unconditional, but the drawee may restrict it to part of the sum payable. Every other modification introduced by an acceptance into the tenor of the bill of exchange operates as a refusal to accept. Nevertheless, the acceptor is bound according to the terms of his acceptance.

Article 27

When the drawer of a bill has indicated a place of payment other than the domicile of the drawee without specifying a third party at whose address payment must be made, the drawee may name such third party at the time of acceptance. In default of this indication, the acceptor is deemed to have undertaken to pay the bill himself at the place of payment.

If a bill is payable at the domicile of the drawee, the latter may in his acceptance indicate an address in the same place where payment is to be made.

Article 28

By accepting, the drawee undertakes to pay the bill of exchange at its maturity. In default of payment, the holder, even if he is the drawer, has a direct action on the bill of exchange against the acceptor for all that can be demanded in accordance with Articles 48 and 49.

Article 29

Where the drawee who has put his acceptance on a bill has cancelled it before restoring the bill, acceptance is deemed to be refused. Failing proof to the contrary, the cancellation is deemed to have taken place before the bill was restored.

Nevertheless, if the drawee has notified his acceptance in writing to the holder or to any party who has signed the bill, he is liable to such parties according to the terms of his acceptance.

CHAPTER IV - 'Avals'

Article 30

Payment of a bill of exchange may be guaranteed by an 'aval' as to the whole or part of its amount.

This guarantee may be given by a third person or even by a person who has signed as a party to the bill.

Article 31

The 'aval' is given either on the bill itself or on an 'allonge'.

It is expressed by the words 'good as aval' ('bon pour aval') or by any other equivalent formula. It is signed by the giver of the 'aval'.

It is deemed to be constituted by the mere signature of the giver of the 'aval' placed on the face of the bill, except in the case of the signature of the drawee or of the drawer.

An 'aval' must specify for whose account it is given. In default of this it is deemed to be given for the drawer.

Article 32

The giver of an 'aval' is bound in the same manner as the person for whom he has become guarantor.

His undertaking is valid even when the liability which he has guaranteed is inoperative for any reason other than defect of form.

He has, when he pays a bill of exchange, the rights arising out of the bill of exchange against the person guaranteed and against those who are liable to the latter on the bill of exchange.

CHAPTER V - Maturity

Article 33

A bill of exchange may be drawn payable:

- at sight;
- at a fixed period after sight;
- at a fixed period after date;
- at a fixed date.

Bills of exchange at other maturities or payable by instalments are null and void.

Article 34

A bill of exchange at sight is payable on presentment. It must be presented for payment within a year of its date. The drawer may abridge or extend this period. These periods may be abridged by the endorsers.

The drawer may prescribe that a bill of exchange payable at sight must not be presented for payment before a named date. In this case, the period for presentation begins from the said date.

Article 35

The maturity of a bill of exchange payable at a fixed period after sight is determined either by the date of the acceptance or by the date of the protest.

In the absence of the protest, an undated acceptance is deemed, so far as regards the acceptor, to have been given on the last day of the limit of time for presentment for acceptance.

Article 36

Where a bill of exchange is drawn at one or more months after date or after sight, the bill matures on the corresponding date of the month when payment must be made. If there be no corresponding date, the bill matures on the last day of this month.

When a bill of exchange is drawn at one or more months and a-half after date or sight, entire months must first be calculated.

If the maturity is fixed at the commencement, in the middle (mid-January or mid-February, etc.,) or at the end of the month, the first, fifteenth or last day of the month is to be understood.

The expressions 'eight days' or 'fifteen days' indicate not one or two weeks, but a period of eight or fifteen actual days.

The expression 'half-month' means a period of fifteen days.

Article 37

When a bill of exchange is payable on a fixed day in a place where the calendar is different from the calendar in the place of issue, the day of maturity is deemed to be fixed according to the calendar of the place of payment.

When a bill of exchange drawn between two places having different calendars is payable at a fixed period after date, the day of issue is referred to the corresponding day of the calendar in the place of payment, and the maturity is fixed accordingly.

The time for presenting bills of exchange is calculated in accordance with the rules of the preceding paragraph.

These rules do not apply if a stipulation in the bill or even the simple terms of the instrument indicate an intention to adopt some different rule.

Bills of exchange at other maturities or payable by instalments are null and void.

CHAPTER VI - Payment

Article 38

The holder of a bill of exchange payable on a fixed day or at a fixed period after date or after sight must present the bill for payment either on the day on which it is payable or on one of the two business days which follow.

The presentment of a bill of exchange at a clearing-house is equivalent to a presentment for payment.

Article 39

The drawee who pays a bill of exchange may require that it shall be given up to him receipted by the holder.

The holder may not refuse partial payment.

In case of partial payment the drawee may require that mention of this payment shall be made on the bill, and that a receipt therefor shall be given to him.

Article 40 [Payment Before Maturity]

The holder of a bill of exchange cannot be compelled to receive a payment thereof before maturity.

The drawee who pays before maturity does so at his own risk and peril. He who pays at maturity is validly discharged, unless he has been guilty of fraud or gross negligence. He is bound to verify the regularity of the series of endorsements, but not the signature of the endorsers.

Article 41 [Currency of Payment]

When a bill of exchange is drawn payable in a currency which is not that of the place of payment, the sum payable may be paid in the currency of the country, according to its value on the date of maturity. If the debtor is in default, the holder may at his option demand that the amount of the bill be paid in the currency of the country according to the rate on the day of maturity or the day of payment.

The usages of the place of payment determine the value of foreign currency. Nevertheless, the drawer may stipulate that the sum payable shall be calculated according to a rate expressed in the bill.

The foregoing rules shall not apply to the case in which the drawer has stipulated that payment must be made in a certain specified currency (stipulation for effective payment in foreign currency).

If the amount of the bill of exchange is specified in a currency having the same denomination, but a different value in the country of issue and the country of payment, reference is deemed to be made to the currency of the place of payment.

Article 42

When a bill of exchange is not presented for payment within the limit of time fixed by Article 38, every debtor is authorised to deposit the amount with the competent authority at the charge, risk and peril of the holder.

CHAPTER VII - Recourse for Non-Acceptance or Non-Payment

Article 43

The holder may exercise his right of recourse against the endorsers, the drawer and the other parties liable:

At maturity: If payment has not been made;

Even before maturity;

1. If there has been total or partial refusal to accept;
2. In the event of the bankruptcy (faillite) of the drawee, whether he has accepted or not, or in the event of a stoppage of payment on his part, even when not declared by a judgement, or when execution has been levied against his goods without result;
3. In the event of the bankruptcy (faillite) of the drawer of a non-acceptable bill.

Article 44

Default of acceptance or on payment must be evidenced by an authentic act (protest for non-acceptance or non-payment).

Protest for non-acceptance must be made within the limit of time fixed for presentment for acceptance. If in the case contemplated by Article 24, paragraph 1, the first presentment takes place on the last day of that time, the protest may nevertheless be drawn up on the next day.

Protest for non-payment of a bill of exchange payable on a fixed day or at a fixed period after date or sight must be made on one of the two business days following the day on which the bill is payable. In the case of a bill payable at sight, the protest must be drawn up under the conditions specified in the foregoing paragraph for the drawing up of a protest for non-acceptance.

Protest for non-acceptance dispenses with presentment for payment and protest for non-payment.

If there is a stoppage of payment on the part of the drawee, whether he has accepted or not, or if execution has been levied against his goods without result, the holder cannot exercise his right of recourse until after presentment of the bill to the drawee for payment and after the protest has been drawn up.

If the drawee, whether he accepted or not, is declared bankrupt (faillite déclarée), or in the event of the declared bankruptcy of the drawer of a non-acceptable bill, the production of the judgement declaring the bankruptcy suffices to enable the holder to exercise his right of recourse.

Article 45

The holder must give notice of non-acceptance or non-payment to his endorser and to the drawer within the four business days which follow the day for protest or, in case of a stipulation 'retour sans frais', the day for presentment. Every endorser must, within the two business days following the day on which he receives notice, notify his endorser of the notice he has received, mentioning the names and addresses of those who have given the previous notices, and so on through the series until the drawer is reached. The periods mentioned above run from the receipt of the preceding notice.

When, in conformity with the preceding paragraph, notice is given to a person who has signed a bill of exchange, the same notice must be given within the same limit of time to his avaliseur.

Where an endorser either has not specified his address or has specified it in an illegible manner, it is sufficient that notice should be given to the preceding endorser.

A person who must give notice may give it in any form whatever, even by simply returning the bill of exchange.

He must prove that he has given notice within the time allowed. This time-limit shall be regarded as having been observed if a letter giving the notice has been posted within the prescribed time.

A person who does not give notice within the limit of time mentioned above does not forfeit his rights. He is responsible for the injury, if any, caused by his negligence, but the damages shall not exceed the amount of the bill of exchange.

Article 46

The drawer, an endorser, or a person guaranteeing payment by aval (avaliseur) may, by the stipulation 'retour sans frais', 'sans protêt', or any other equivalent expression written on the instrument and signed, release the holder from having a protest of non-acceptance or non-payment drawn up in order to exercise his right of recourse.

This stipulation does not release the holder from presenting the bill within the prescribed time, or from the notices he has to give. The burden of proving the non-observance of the limits of time lies on the person who seeks to set it up against the holder.

If the stipulation is written by the drawer, it is operative in respect of all persons who have signed the bill; if it is written by an endorser or an avaliseur, it is operative only in respect of such endorser or avaliseur. If, in spite of the stipulation written by the drawer, the holder has the protest drawn up, he must bear the expenses thereof. When the stipulation emanates from an endorser or avaliseur, the costs of the protest, if one is drawn up, may be recovered from all the persons who have signed the bill.

Article 47 [Joint and Several Liability]

All drawers, acceptors, endorsers or guarantors by aval of a bill of exchange are jointly and severally liable to the holder. The holder has the right of proceeding against all these persons individually or collectively without being required to observe the order in which they have become bound.

The same right is possessed by any person signing the bill who has taken it up and paid it.

Proceedings against one of the parties liable do not prevent proceedings against the others, even though they may be subsequent to the party first proceeded against.

Article 48

The holder may recover from the person against whom he exercises his right of recourse:

1. The amount of the unaccepted or unpaid bill of exchange with interest, if interest has been stipulated for;
2. Interest at the rate of 6 per cent from the date of maturity;
3. The expenses of protest and of the notices given as well as other expenses.

If the right of recourse is exercised before maturity, the amount of the bill shall be subject to a discount. This discount shall be calculated according to the official rate of discount (bank-rate) ruling on the date when recourse is exercised at the place of domicile of the holder.

Article 49

A party who takes up and pays a bill of exchange can recover from the parties liable to him:

1. The entire sum which he has paid;
2. Interest on the said sum calculated at the rate of 6 per cent, starting from the day when he made payment;
3. Any expenses which he has incurred.

Article 50

Every party liable against whom a right of recourse is or may be exercised, can require against payment, that the bill shall be given up to him with the protest and a receipted account.

Every endorser who has taken up and paid a bill of exchange may cancel his own endorsement and those of subsequent endorsers.

Article 51

In the case of the exercise of the right of recourse after a partial acceptance, the party who pays the sum in respect of which the bill has not been accepted can require that this payment shall be specified on the bill and that he shall be given a receipt therefor. The holder must also give him a certified copy of the bill, together with the protest, in order to enable subsequent recourse to be exercised.

Article 52

Every person having the right of recourse may, in the absence of agreement to the contrary, reimburse himself by means of a fresh bill (redraft) to be drawn at sight on one of the parties liable to him and payable at the domicile of that party.

The redraft includes, in addition to the sums mentioned in Articles 48 and 49, brokerage and the cost of stamping the redraft.

If the redraft is drawn by the holder, the sum payable is fixed according to the rate for a sight bill drawn at the place where the original bill was payable upon the party liable at the place of his domicile. If the redraft is drawn by an endorser, the sum payable is fixed according to the rate for a sight bill drawn at the place where the drawer of the redraft is domiciled upon the place of domicile of the party liable.

Article 53

After the expiration of the limits of time fixed:

- for the presentment of a bill of exchange drawn at sight or at a fixed period after sight;
- for drawing up the protest for non-acceptance or non-payment;
- for presentment for payment in the case of a stipulation retour sans frais,

the holder loses his rights of recourse against the endorsers, against the drawer and against the other parties liable, with the exception of the acceptor.

In default of presentment for acceptance within the limit of time stipulated by the drawer, the holder loses his right of recourse for non-payment, as well as for non-acceptance, unless it appears from the terms of the stipulation that the drawer only meant to release himself from the guarantee of acceptance.

If the stipulation for a limit of time for presentment is contained in an endorsement, the endorser alone can avail himself of it.

Article 54 [Legal Obstacle and Force Majeure]

Should the presentment of the bill of exchange or the drawing up of the protest within the prescribed limits of time be prevented by an insurmountable obstacle (legal prohibition (prescription légale) by any State or other case of vis major), these limits of time shall be extended. The holder is bound to give notice without delay of the case of vis major to his endorser and to specify this notice, which he must date and sign, on the bill or on an allonge; in other respects the provisions of Article 45 shall apply.

When vis major has terminated the holder must without delay present the bill of exchange for acceptance or payment and, if need be, draw up the protest. If vis major continues to operate beyond thirty days after maturity, recourse may be exercised, and neither presentment nor the drawing up of a protest shall be necessary.

In the case of bills of exchange drawn at sight or at a fixed period after sight, the time-limit of thirty days shall run from the date on which the holder, even before the expiration of the time for presentment, has given notice of vis major to his endorser. In the case of bill of exchange drawn at a certain time after sight, the above time-limit of thirty days shall be added to the period after sight specified in the bill of exchange.

Facts which are purely personal to the holder or to the person whom he has entrusted with the presentment of the bill or drawing up of the bill or drawing up of the protest are not deemed to constitute cases of vis major.

CHAPTER VIII - Intervention for Honour

I. General Provisions

Article 55

The drawer, an endorser, or a person giving an aval may specify a person who is to accept or pay in case of need.

A bill of exchange may, subject as hereinafter mentioned, be accepted or paid by a person who intervenes for the honour of any debtor against whom a right of recourse exists.

The person intervening may be a third party, even the drawee, or, save the acceptor, a party already liable on the bill of exchange.

The person intervening is bound to give, within two business days, notice of his intervention to the party for whose honour he has intervened. In default, he is responsible for the injury, if any, due to his negligence, but the damages shall not exceed the amount of the bill of exchange.

2. Acceptance by Intervention (for Honour)

Article 56

There may be acceptance by intervention in all cases where the holder has a right of recourse before maturity on a bill which is capable of acceptance.

When the bill of exchange indicates a person who is designated to accept or pay it in case of need at the place of payment, the holder may not exercise his rights of recourse before maturity against the person naming such referee in case of need and against subsequent signatories, unless he has presented the bill of exchange to the referee in case of need and until, if acceptance is refused by the latter, this refusal has been authenticated by a protest.

In other cases of intervention the holder may refuse an acceptance by intervention. Nevertheless, if he allows it, he loses his right of recourse before maturity against the person on whose behalf such acceptance was given and against subsequent signatories.

Article 57

Acceptance by intervention is specified on the bill of exchange. It is signed by the person intervening. It mentions the person for whose honour it has been given and, in default of such mention, the acceptance is deemed to have been given for the honour of the drawer.

Article 58

The acceptor by intervention is liable to the holder and to the endorsers subsequent to the party for whose honour he intervened, in the same manner as such party.

Notwithstanding an acceptance by intervention, the party for whose honour it has been given and the parties liable to him may require the holder, in exchange for payment of the sum mentioned in Article 48, to deliver the bill, the protest, and a receipted account, if any.

3. Payment by Intervention

Article 59

Payment by intervention may take place in all cases where, either at maturity or before maturity, the holder has a right of recourse on the bill.

Payment must include the whole amount payable by the party for whose honour it is made.

It must be made at the latest on the day following the last day allowed for drawing up the protest for non-payment.

Article 60

If a bill of exchange has been accepted by persons intervening who are domiciled in the place of payment, or if persons domiciled therein have been named as referees in case of need, the holder must present the bill to all these persons and, if necessary, have a protest for non-payment drawn up at latest on the day following the last day allowed for drawing up the protest.

In default of protest within this limit of time, the party who has named the referee in case of need, or for whose account the bill has been accepted, and the subsequent endorsers are discharged.

Article 61

The holder who refuses payment by intervention loses his right of recourse against any persons who would have been discharged thereby.

Article 62

Payment by intervention must be authenticated by a receipt given on the bill of exchange mentioning the person for whose honour payment has been made. In default of such mention, payment is deemed to have been made for the honour of the drawer.

The bill of exchange and the protest, if any, must be given up to the person paying by intervention.

Article 63

The person paying by intervention acquires the rights arising out of the bill of exchange against the party for whose honour he has paid and against persons who are liable to the latter on the bill of exchange. Nevertheless, he cannot re-endorse the bill of exchange.

Endorsers subsequent to the party for whose honour payment has been made are discharged.

In case of competition for payment by intervention, the payment which effects the greater number of releases has the preference. Any person who, with a knowledge of the facts, intervenes in a manner contrary to this rule, loses his right of recourse against those who would have been discharged.

CHAPTER IX - Parts of a Set and Copies

1. Parts of a Set

Article 64

A bill of exchange can be drawn in a set of two or more identical parts. These parts must be numbered in the body of the instrument itself; in default, each part is considered as a separate bill of exchange.

Every holder of a bill which does not specify that it has been drawn as a sole bill may, at his own expense, require the delivery of two or more parts. For this purpose he must apply to his immediate endorser, who is bound to assist him in proceeding against his own endorser, and so on in the series until the drawer is reached. The endorsers are bound to reproduce their endorsements on the new parts of the set.

Article 65

Payment made on one part of a set operates as a discharge, even though there is no stipulation that this payment annuls the effect on the other parts. Nevertheless, the drawee is liable on each accepted part which he has not recovered.

An endorser who has transferred parts of a set to different persons, as well as subsequent endorsers, are liable on all the parts bearing their signature which have not been restored.

Article 66

A party who has sent one part for acceptance must indicate on the other parts the name of the person in whose hands this part is to be found. That person is bound to give it up to the lawful holder of another part.

If he refuses, the holder cannot exercise his right of recourse until he has had a protest drawn us specifying:

1. That the part sent for acceptance has not been given up to him on demand;
2. that acceptance or payment could not be obtained on another of parts.

2. Copies

Article 67

Every holder of a bill of exchange has the right to make copies of it. A copy must reproduce the original exactly, with the endorsements and all other statements to be found therein. It must specify where the copy ends. It may be endorsed and guaranteed by aval in the same manner and with the same effects as the original.

Article 68

A copy must specify the person in possession of the original instrument. The latter is bound to hand over the said instrument to the lawful holder of the copy.

If he refuses, the holder may not exercise his right of recourse against the persons who have endorsed the copy or guaranteed it by aval until he has had a protest drawn up specifying that the original has not been given up to him on his demand.

Where the original instrument, after the last endorsement before the making of the copy contains a clause 'commencing from here an endorsement is only valid if made on the copy' or some equivalent formula, a subsequent endorsement on the original is null and void.

CHAPTER X - Alterations

Article 69

In case of alteration of the text of a bill of exchange, parties who have signed subsequent to the alteration are bound according to the terms of the altered text; parties who have signed before the alteration are bound according to the terms of the original text.

CHAPTER XI - Limitation of Actions

Article 70

All actions arising out of a bill of exchange against the acceptor are barred after three years, reckoned from the date of maturity.

Actions by the holder against the endorsers and against the drawer are barred after one year from the date of a protest drawn up within proper time, or from the date of maturity where there is a stipulation retour sans frais.

Actions by endorsers against each other and against the drawer are barred after six months, reckoned from the day when the endorser took up and paid the bill or from the day when he himself was sued.

Article 71

Interruption of the period of limitation is only effective against the person in respect of whom the period has been interrupted.

CHAPTER XII - General Provisions

Article 72

Payment of a bill of exchange which falls due on a legal holiday (jour férié légal) cannot be demanded until the next business day. So, too, all other proceedings relating to a bill of exchange, in particular presentment for acceptance and protest, can only be taken on a business day.

Where any of these proceedings must be taken within a certain limit of time the last day of which is a legal holiday (jour férié légal), the limit of time is extended until the first business day which follows the expiration of that time. Intermediate holidays (jours fériés) are included in computing limits of time.

Article 73

Legal or contractual limits of time do not include the day on which the period commences.

Article 74

No days of grace, whether legal or judicial, are permitted.

TITLE II - Promissory Notes

Article 75 [Essential Elements of a Promissory Note]

A promissory note contains:

1. The term 'promissory note' inserted in the body of the instrument and expressed in the language employed in drawing up the instrument;
2. An unconditional promise to pay a determinate sum of money;
3. A statement of the time of payment;
4. A statement of the place where payment is to be made;
5. The name of the person to whom or to whose order payment is to be made;
6. A statement of the date and of the place where the promissory note is issued;
7. The signature of the person who issues the instrument (maker).

Article 76 [Exceptions]

An instrument in which any of the requirements mentioned in the preceding Article are wanting is invalid as a promissory note except in the cases specified in the following paragraphs.

A promissory note in which the time of payment is not specified is deemed to be payable at sight.

In default of special mention, the place where the instrument is made is deemed to be the place of payment and at the same time the place of the domicile of the maker.

A promissory note which does not mention the place of its issue is deemed to have been made in the place mentioned beside the name of the maker.

Article 77

The following provisions relating to bills of exchange apply to promissory notes so far as they are not inconsistent with the nature of these instruments, viz:

- Endorsement (Article 11 to 20);
- Time of payment (Articles 33 to 37);
- Payment (Articles 38 to 42);
- Recourse in case of non-payment (Articles 43 to 50, 52 to 54);
- Payment by intervention (Articles 55, 59 to 63);
- Copies (Articles 67 and 68);
- Alterations (Article 69);
- Limitation of actions (Articles 70 and 71);
- Holidays, computation of limits of time and prohibition of days of grace (Articles 72, 73 and 74).

The following provisions are also applicable to a promissory note: The provisions concerning a bill of exchange payable at the address of a third party or in a locality other than that of the domicile of the drawee (Articles 4 and 27): stipulation for interest (Article 5); discrepancies as regards the sum payable (Article 6); the consequences of signature under the conditions mentioned in Article 7, the consequences of signature by a person who acts without authority or who exceeds his authority (Article 8); and provisions concerning a bill of exchange in blank (Article 10).

The following provisions are also applicable to a promissory note: Provisions relating to guarantee by aval (Articles 30-32); in the case provided for in Article 31, last paragraph, if the aval does not specify on whose behalf it has been given, it is deemed to have been given on behalf of the maker of the promissory note.

Article 78

The maker of a promissory note is bound in the same manner as an acceptor of a bill of exchange.

Promissory notes payable at a certain time after sight must be presented for the visa of the maker within the limits of time fixed by Article 23. The limit of time runs from the date of which marks the commencement of the period of time after sight. [...]

Entry into Force: 1 January 1934

Ratification and Binding Effect as of April 2020: Austria (1934), Azerbaijan (2000), Belarus (1998), Belgium (1934), Brazil (1942), Denmark (1934), Finland (1934), France (1936), Germany (1934), Greece (1934), Hungary (1964), Italy (1934), Japan (1934), Kazakhstan (1995), Kyrgyzstan (2003), Lithuania (1997), Luxembourg (1963), Monaco (1934), Netherlands (1934), Norway (1934), Poland (1936), Portugal (1934), Sweden (1934), Switzerland (1934), Ukraine (1999), USSR (1936).

20) Uniform Customs and Practice for Documentary Credits (UCP 600)[1]

Article 1 Application of UCP

The Uniform Customs and Practice for Documentary Credits, 2007 Revision, ICC Publication no. 600 ("UCP") are rules that apply to any documentary credit ("credit") (including, to the extent to which they may be applicable, any standby letter of credit) when the text of the credit expressly indicates that it is subject to these rules. They are binding on all parties thereto unless expressly modified or excluded by the credit.

Article 2 Definitions

For the purpose of these rules:

Advising bank means the bank that advises the credit at the request of the issuing bank.

Applicant means the party on whose request the credit is issued.

Banking day means a day on which a bank is regularly open at the place at which an act subject to these rules is to be performed.

Beneficiary means the party in whose favour a credit is issued.

Complying presentation means a presentation that is in accordance with the terms and conditions of the credit, the applicable provisions of these rules and international standard banking practice.

Confirmation means a definite undertaking of the confirming bank, in addition to that of the issuing bank, to honour or negotiate a complying presentation.

Confirming bank means the bank that adds its confirmation to a credit upon the issuing bank's authorization or request.

Credit means any arrangement, however named or described, that is irrevocable and thereby constitutes a definite undertaking of the issuing bank to honour a complying presentation.

Honour means:

a. to pay at sight if the credit is available by sight payment.

b. to incur a deferred payment undertaking and pay at maturity if the credit is available by deferred payment.

c. to accept a bill of exchange ("draft") drawn by the beneficiary and pay at maturity if the credit is available by acceptance.

Issuing bank means the bank that issues a credit at the request of an applicant or on its own behalf.

Negotiation means the purchase by the nominated bank of drafts (drawn on a bank other than the nominated bank) and/or documents under a complying presentation, by advancing or agreeing to advance funds to the beneficiary on or before the banking day on which reimbursement is due to the nominated bank.

Nominated bank means the bank with which the credit is available or any bank in the case of a credit available with any bank.

Presentation means either the delivery of documents under a credit to the issuing bank or nominated bank or the documents so delivered.

Presenter means a beneficiary, bank or other party that makes a presentation.

Article 3 Interpretations

For the purpose of these rules:

Where applicable, words in the singular include the plural and in the plural include the singular.

A credit is irrevocable even if there is no indication to that effect.

A document may be signed by handwriting, facsimile signature, perforated signature, stamp, symbol or any other mechanical or electronic method of authentication.

A requirement for a document to be legalized, visaed, certified or similar will be satisfied by any signature, mark, stamp or label on the document which appears to satisfy that requirement.

Branches of a bank in different countries are considered to be separate banks.

Terms such as "first class', 'well known', "qualified", "independent", "official", "competent" or 'local" used to describe the issuer of a document allow any issuer except the beneficiary to issue that document.

Unless required to be used in a document, words such as "prompt", "immediately" or "as soon as possible" will be disregarded.

The expression "on or about" or similar will be interpreted as a stipulation that an event is to occur during a period of five calendar days before until five calendar days after the specified date, both start and end dates included.

The words "to', "until', "till", "from" and "between" when used to determine a period of shipment include the date or dates mentioned, and the words "before' and "after" exclude the date mentioned.

The words "from" and "after" when used to determine a maturity date exclude the date mentioned.

The terms "first half" and "second half" of a month shall be construed respectively as the 1st to the 15th and the 16th to the last day of the month, all dates inclusive.

The terms "beginning", "middle" and "end" of a month shall be construed respectively as the 1st to the 10th, the 11th to the 20th and the 21st to the last day of the month, all dates inclusive.

Article 4 Credits v. Contracts

a. A credit by its nature is a separate transaction from the sale or other contract on which it may be based. Banks are in no way concerned with or bound by such contract, even if any reference whatsoever to it is included in the credit. Consequently, the undertaking of a bank to honour, to negotiate or to fulfil any other obligation under the credit is not subject to claims or defences by the applicant resulting from its relationships with the issuing bank or the beneficiary.

A beneficiary can in no case avail itself of the contractual relationships existing between banks or between the applicant and the issuing bank.

b. An issuing bank should discourage any attempt by the applicant to include, as an integral part of the credit, copies of the underlying contract, proforma invoice and the like.

Article 5 Documents v. Goods, Services or Performance

Banks deal with documents and not with goods, services or performance to which the documents may relate.

Article 6 Availability, Expiry Date and Place for Presentation

a. A credit must state the bank with which it is available or whether it is available with any bank.

A credit available with a nominated bank is also available with the issuing bank.

b. A credit must state whether it is available by sight payment, deferred payment, acceptance or negotiation.

c. A credit must not be issued available by a draft drawn on the applicant.

d. **i**. A credit must state an expiry date for presentation. An expiry date stated for honour or negotiation will be deemed to be an expiry date for presentation.

ii. The place of the bank with which the credit is available is the place for presentation. The place for presentation under a credit available with any bank is that of any bank. A place for presentation other than that of the issuing bank is in addition to the place of the issuing bank.

e. Except as provided in sub-article 29 (a), a presentation by or on behalf of the beneficiary must be made on or before the expiry date.

Article 7 Issuing Bank Undertaking

a. Provided that the stipulated documents are presented to the nominated bank or to the issuing bank and that they constitute a complying presentation, the issuing bank must honour if the credit is available by:

i. sight payment, deferred payment or acceptance with the issuing bank;

ii. sight payment with a nominated bank and that nominated bank does not pay;

iii. deferred payment with a nominated bank and that nominated bank does not incur its deferred payment undertaking or, having incurred its deferred payment undertaking, does not pay at maturity;

iv. acceptance with a nominated bank and that nominated bank does not accept a draft drawn on it or, having accepted a draft drawn on it, does not pay at maturity;

v. negotiation with a nominated bank and that nominated bank does not negotiate.

b. An issuing bank is irrevocably bound to honour as of the time it issues the credit.

c. An issuing bank undertakes to reimburse a nominated bank that has honoured or negotiated a complying presentation and forwarded the documents to the issuing bank. Reimbursement for the amount of a complying presentation under a credit available by acceptance or deferred payment is due at maturity, whether or not the nominated bank prepaid or purchased before maturity. An issuing bank's undertaking to reimburse a nominated bank is independent of the issuing bank's undertaking to the beneficiary.

Article 8 Confirming Bank Undertaking

a. Provided that the stipulated documents are presented to the confirming bank or to any other nominated bank and that they constitute a complying presentation, the confirming bank must:

i. honour, if the credit is available by

aa. sight payment, deferred payment or acceptance with the confirming bank;

bb. sight payment with another nominated bank and that nominated bank does not pay;

cc. deferred payment with another nominated bank and that nominated bank does not incur its deferred payment undertaking or, having incurred its deferred payment undertaking, does not pay at maturity;

dd. acceptance with another nominated bank and that nominated bank does not accept a draft drawn on it or, having accepted a draft drawn on it, does not pay at maturity;

ee. negotiation with another nominated bank and that nominated bank does not negotiate.

ii. negotiate, without recourse, if the credit is available by negotiation with the confirming bank.

b. A confirming bank is irrevocably bound to honour or negotiate as of the time it adds its confirmation to the credit.

c. A confirming bank undertakes to reimburse another nominated bank that has honoured or negotiated a complying presentation and forwarded the documents to the confirming bank. Reimbursement for the amount of a complying presentation under a credit available by acceptance or deferred payment is due at maturity, whether or not another nominated bank prepaid or purchased before maturity. A confirming bank's undertaking to reimburse another nominated bank is independent of the confirming bank's undertaking to the beneficiary.

d. If a bank is authorized or requested by the issuing bank to confirm a credit but is not prepared to do so, it must inform the issuing bank without delay and may advise the credit without confirmation.

Article 9 Advising of Credits and Amendments

a. A credit and any amendment may be advised to a beneficiary through an advising bank. An advising bank that is not a confirming bank advises the credit and any amendment without any undertaking to honour or negotiate.

b. By advising the credit or amendment, the advising bank signifies that it has satisfied itself as to the apparent authenticity of the credit or amendment and that the advice accurately reflects the terms and conditions of the credit or amendment received.

c. An advising bank may utilize the services of another bank ("second advising bank") to advise the credit and any amendment to the beneficiary. By advising the credit or amendment, the second advising bank signifies that it has satisfied itself as to the apparent authenticity of the advice it has received and that the advice accurately reflects the terms and conditions of the credit or amendment received.

d. A bank utilizing the services of an advising bank or second advising bank to advise a credit must use the same bank to advise any amendment thereto.

e. If a bank is requested to advise a credit or amendment but elects not to do so, it must so inform, without delay, the bank from which the credit, amendment or advice has been received.

f. If a bank is requested to advise a credit or amendment but cannot satisfy itself as to the apparent authenticity of the credit, the amendment or the advice, it must so inform, without delay, the bank from which the instructions appear to have been received. If the advising bank or second advising bank elects nonetheless to advise the credit or amendment, it must inform the beneficiary or second advising bank that it has not been able to satisfy itself as to the apparent authenticity of the credit, the amendment or the advice.

Article 10 Amendments

a. Except as otherwise provided by Article 38, a credit can neither be amended nor cancelled without the agreement of the issuing bank, the confirming bank, if any, and the beneficiary.

b. An issuing bank is irrevocably bound by an amendment as of the time it issues the amendment. A confirming bank may extend its confirmation to an amendment and will be irrevocably bound as of the time it advises the amendment. A confirming bank may, however, choose to advise an amendment without extending its confirmation and, if so, it must inform the issuing bank without delay and inform the beneficiary in its advice.

c. The terms and conditions of the original credit (or a credit incorporating previously accepted amendments) will remain in force for the beneficiary until the beneficiary communicates its acceptance of the amendment to the bank that advised such amendment. The beneficiary should give notification of acceptance or rejection of an amendment. If the beneficiary fails to give such notification, a presentation that complies with the credit and to any not yet accepted amendment will be deemed to be notification of acceptance by the beneficiary of such amendment. As of that moment the credit will be amended.

d. A bank that advises an amendment should inform the bank from which it received the amendment of any notification of acceptance or rejection.

e. Partial acceptance of an amendment is not allowed and will be deemed to be notification of rejection of the amendment.

f. A provision in an amendment to the effect that the amendment shall enter into force unless rejected by the beneficiary within a certain time shall be disregarded.

Article 11 Teletransmitted and Pre-Advised Credits and Amendments

a. An authenticated teletransmission of a credit or amendment will be deemed to be the operative credit or amendment, and any subsequent mail confirmation shall be disregarded.

If a teletransmission states "full details to follow" (or words of similar effect), or states that the mail confirmation is to be the operative credit or amendment, then the teletransmission will not be deemed to be the operative credit or amendment. The issuing bank must then issue the operative credit or amendment without delay in terms not inconsistent with the teletransmission.

b. A preliminary advice of the issuance of a credit or amendment ("pre-advice") shall only be sent if the issuing bank is prepared to issue the operative credit or amendment. An issuing bank that sends a pre-advice is irrevocably committed to issue the operative credit or amendment, without delay, in terms not inconsistent with the pre-advice.

Article 12 Nomination

a. Unless a nominated bank is the confirming bank, an authorization to honour or negotiate does not impose any obligation on that nominated bank to honour or negotiate, except when expressly agreed to by that nominated bank and so communicated to the beneficiary.

b. By nominating a bank to accept a draft or incur a deferred payment undertaking, an issuing bank authorizes that nominated bank to prepay or purchase a draft accepted or a deferred payment undertaking incurred by that nominated bank.

c. Receipt or examination and forwarding of documents by a nominated bank that is not a confirming bank does not make that nominated bank liable to honour or negotiate, nor does it constitute honour or negotiation.

Article 13 Bank-to-Bank Reimbursement Arrangements

a. If a credit states that reimbursement is to be obtained by a nominated bank ("claiming bank") claiming on another party ("reimbursing bank"), the credit must state if the reimbursement is subject to the ICC rules for bank-to-bank reimbursements in effect on the date of issuance of the credit.

b. If a credit does not state that reimbursement is subject to the ICC rules for bank-to-bank reimbursements, the following apply:

i. An issuing bank must provide a reimbursing bank with a reimbursement authorization that conforms with the availability stated in the credit. The reimbursement authorization should not be subject to an expiry date.

ii. A claiming bank shall not be required to supply a reimbursing bank with a certificate of compliance with the terms and conditions of the credit.

iii. An issuing bank will be responsible for any loss of interest, together with any expenses incurred, if reimbursement is not provided on first demand by a reimbursing bank in accordance with the terms and conditions of the credit.

iv. A reimbursing bank's charges are for the account of the issuing bank. However, if the charges are for the account of the beneficiary, it is the responsibility of an issuing bank to so indicate in the credit and in the reimbursement authorization. If a reimbursing bank's charges are for the account of the beneficiary, they shall be deducted from the amount due to a claiming bank when reimbursement is made. If no reimbursement is made, the reimbursing bank's charges remain the obligation of the issuing bank.

c. An issuing bank is not relieved of any of its obligations to provide reimbursement if reimbursement is not made by a reimbursing bank on first demand.

Article 14 Standard for Examination of Documents

a. A nominated bank acting on its nomination, a confirming bank, if any, and the issuing bank must examine a presentation to determine, on the basis of the documents alone, whether or not the documents appear on their face to constitute a complying presentation.

b. A nominated bank acting on its nomination, a confirming bank, if any, and the issuing bank shall each have a maximum of five banking days following the day of presentation to determine if a presentation is complying. This period is not curtailed or otherwise affected by the occurrence on or after the date of presentation of any expiry date or last day for presentation.

c. A presentation including one or more original transport documents subject to articles 19, 20, 21, 22, 23, 24 or 25 must be made by or on behalf of the beneficiary not later than 21 calendar days after the date of shipment as described in these rules, but in any event not later than the expiry date of the credit.

d. Data in a document, when read in context with the credit, the document itself and international standard banking practice, need not be identical to, but must not conflict with, data in that document, any other stipulated document or the credit.

e. In documents other than the commercial invoice, the description of the goods, services or performance, if stated, may be in general terms not conflicting with their description in the credit.

f. If a credit requires presentation of a document other than a transport document, insurance document or commercial invoice, without stipulating by whom the document is to be issued or its data content, banks will accept the document as presented if its content appears to fulfil the function of the required document and otherwise complies with sub-article 14 (d).

g. A document presented but not required by the credit will be disregarded and may be returned to the presenter.

h. If a credit contains a condition without stipulating the document to indicate compliance with the condition, banks will deem such condition as not stated and will disregard it.

i. A document may be dated prior to the issuance date of the credit, but must not be dated later than its date of presentation.

j. When the addresses of the beneficiary and the applicant appear in any stipulated document, they need not be the same as those stated in the credit or in any other stipulated document, but must be within the same country as the respective addresses mentioned in the credit. Contact details (telefax, telephone, email and the like) stated as part of the beneficiary's and the applicant's address will be disregarded. However, when the address and contact details of the applicant appear as part of the consignee or notify party details on a transport document subject to articles 19, 20, 21, 22, 23, 24 or 25, they must be as stated in the credit.

k. The shipper or consignor of the goods indicated on any document need not be the beneficiary of the credit.

l. A transport document may be issued by any party other than a carrier, owner, master or charterer provided that the transport document meets the requirements of articles 19, 20, 21, 22, 23 or 24 of these rules.

Article 15 Complying Presentation

a. When an issuing bank determines that a presentation is complying, it must honour.

b. When a confirming bank determines that a presentation is complying, it must honour or negotiate and forward the documents to the issuing bank.

c. When a nominated bank determines that a presentation is complying and honours or negotiates, it must forward the documents to the confirming bank or issuing bank.

Article 16 Discrepant Documents, Waiver and Notice

a. When a nominated bank acting on its nomination, a confirming bank, if any, or the issuing bank determines that a presentation does not comply, it may refuse to honour or negotiate.

b. When an issuing bank determines that a presentation does not comply, it may in its sole judgement approach the applicant for a waiver of the discrepancies. This does not, however, extend the period mentioned in sub-article 14 (b).

c. When a nominated bank acting on its nomination, a confirming bank, if any, or the issuing bank decides to refuse to honour or negotiate, it must give a single notice to that effect to the presenter.

The notice must state:

i. that the bank is refusing to honour or negotiate; and

ii. each discrepancy in respect of which the bank refuses to honour or negotiate; and

iii. aa. that the bank is holding the documents pending further instructions from the presenter; or

bb. that the issuing bank is holding the documents until it receives a waiver from the applicant and agrees to accept it, or receives further instructions from the presenter prior to agreeing to accept a waiver; or

cc. that the bank is returning the documents; or

dd. that the bank is acting in accordance with instructions previously received from the presenter.

d. The notice required in sub-article 16 (c) must be given by telecommunication or, if that is not possible, by other expeditious means no later than the close of the fifth banking day following the day of presentation.

e. A nominated bank acting on its nomination, a confirming bank, if any, or the issuing bank may, after providing notice required by sub-article 16 (c) (iii) (a) or (b), return the documents to the presenter at any time.

f. If an issuing bank or a confirming bank fails to act in accordance with the provisions of this article, it shall be precluded from claiming that the documents do not constitute a complying presentation.

g. When an issuing bank refuses to honour or a confirming bank refuses to honour or negotiate and has given notice to that effect in accordance with this article, it shall then be entitled to claim a refund, with interest, of any reimbursement made.

Article 17 Original Documents and Copies

a. At least one original of each document stipulated in the credit must be presented.

b. A bank shall treat as an original any document bearing an apparently original signature, mark, stamp, or label of the issuer of the document, unless the document itself indicates that it is not an original.

c. Unless a document indicates otherwise, a bank will also accept a document as original if it:

i. appears to be written, typed, perforated or stamped by the document issuer's hand; or

ii. appears to be on the document issuer's original stationery; or

iii. states that it is original, unless the statement appears not to apply to the document presented.

d. If a credit requires presentation of copies of documents, presentation of either originals or copies is permitted.

e. If a credit requires presentation of multiple documents by using terms such as "in duplicate", "in two fold" or "in two copies", this will be satisfied by the presentation of at least one original and the remaining number in copies, except when the document itself indicates otherwise.

Article 18 Commercial Invoice

a. A commercial invoice:

i. must appear to have been issued by the beneficiary (except as provided in Article 38);

ii. must be made out in the name of the applicant (except as provided in sub-article 38 (g));

iii. must be made out in the same currency as the credit; and

iv. need not be signed.

b. A nominated bank acting on its nomination, a confirming bank, if any, or the issuing bank may accept a commercial invoice issued for an amount in excess of the amount permitted by the credit, and its decision will be binding upon all parties, provided the bank in question has not honoured or negotiated for an amount in excess of that permitted by the credit.

c. The description of the goods, services or performance in a commercial invoice must correspond with that appearing in the credit.

Article 19 Transport Document Covering at Least Two Different Modes of Transport

a. A transport document covering at least two different modes of transport (multimodal or combined transport document), however named, must appear to:

i. indicate the name of the carrier and be signed by:

- the carrier or a named agent for or on behalf of the carrier, or
- the master or a named agent for or on behalf of the master.

Any signature by the carrier, master or agent must be identified as that of the carrier, master or agent.

Any signature by an agent must indicate whether the agent has signed for or on behalf of the carrier or for or on behalf of the master.

ii. indicate that the goods have been dispatched, taken in charge or shipped on board at the place stated in the credit, by:

– pre-printed wording, or

– a stamp or notation indicating the date on which the goods have been dispatched, taken in charge or shipped on board.

The date of issuance of the transport document will be deemed to be the date of dispatch, taking in charge or shipped on board, and the date of shipment. However, if the transport document indicates, by stamp or notation, a date of dispatch, taking in charge or shipped on board, this date will be deemed to be the date of shipment.

iii. indicate the place of dispatch, taking in charge or shipment and the place of final destination stated in the credit, even if:

aa. the transport document states, in addition, a different place of dispatch, taking in charge or shipment or place of final destination, or

bb. the transport document contains the indication "intended" or similar qualification in relation to the vessel, port of loading or port of discharge.

iv. be the sole original transport document or, if issued in more than one original, be the full set as indicated on the transport document.

v. contain terms and conditions of carriage or make reference to another source containing the terms and conditions of carriage (short form or blank back transport document). Contents of terms and conditions of carriage will not be examined.

vi. contain no indication that it is subject to a charter party.

b. For the purpose of this article, transhipment means unloading from one means of conveyance and reloading to another means of conveyance (whether or not in different modes of transport) during the carriage from the place of dispatch, taking in charge or shipment to the place of final destination stated in the credit.

c. **i.** A transport document may indicate that the goods will or may be transhipped provided that the entire carriage is covered by one and the same transport document.

ii. A transport document indicating that transhipment will or may take place is acceptable, even if the credit prohibits transhipment.

Article 20 Bill of Lading

a. A bill of lading, however named, must appear to:

i. indicate the name of the carrier and be signed by:

– the carrier or a named agent for or on behalf of the carrier, or

– the master or a named agent for or on behalf of the master.

Any signature by the carrier, master or agent must be identified as that of the carrier, master or agent.

Any signature by an agent must indicate whether the agent has signed for or on behalf of the carrier or for or on behalf of the master.

ii. indicate that the goods have been shipped on board a named vessel at the port of loading stated in the credit by:

– pre-printed wording, or

– an on board notation indicating the date on which the goods have been shipped on board.

The date of issuance of the bill of lading will be deemed to be the date of shipment unless the bill of lading contains an on board notation indicating the date of shipment, in which case the date stated in the on board notation will be deemed to be the date of shipment.

If the bill of lading contains the indication "intended vessel" or similar qualification in relation to the name of the vessel, an on board notation indicating the date of shipment and the name of the actual vessel is required.

iii. indicate shipment from the port of loading to the port of discharge stated in the credit.

If the bill of lading does not indicate the port of loading stated in the credit as the port of loading, or if it contains the indication "intended" or similar qualification in relation to the port of loading, an on board notation indicating the port of loading as stated in the credit, the date of shipment and the name of the vessel is required. This provision applies even when loading on board or shipment on a named vessel is indicated by preprinted wording on the bill of lading.

iv. be the sole original bill of lading or, if issued in more than one original, be the full set as indicated on the bill of lading.

v. contain terms and conditions of carriage or make reference to another source containing the terms and conditions of carriage (short form or blank back bill of lading). Contents of terms and conditions of carriage will not be examined.

vi. contain no indication that it is subject to a charter party.

b. For the purpose of this article, transhipment means unloading from one vessel and reloading to another vessel during the carriage from the port of loading to the port of discharge stated in the credit.

c. **i.** A bill of lading may indicate that the goods will or may be transshipped provided that the entire carriage is covered by one and the same bill of lading.

ii. A bill of lading indicating that transhipment will or may take place is acceptable, even if the credit prohibits transhipment, if the goods have been shipped in a container, trailer or LASH barge as evidenced by the bill of lading.

d. Clauses in a bill of lading stating that the carrier reserves the right to tranship will be disregarded.

Article 21 Non-Negotiable Sea Waybill

a. A non-negotiable sea waybill, however named, must appear to:

i. indicate the name of the carrier and be signed by:

- the carrier or a named agent for or on behalf of the carrier, or
- the master or a named agent for or on behalf of the master.

Any signature by the carrier, master or agent must be identified as that of the carrier, master or agent.

Any signature by an agent must indicate whether the agent has signed for or on behalf of the carrier or for or on behalf of the master.

ii. indicate that the goods have been shipped on board a named vessel at the port of loading stated in the credit by:

- pre-printed wording, or
- an on board notation indicating the date on which the goods have been shipped on board.

The date of issuance of the non-negotiable sea waybill will be deemed to be the date of shipment unless the non-negotiable sea waybill contains an on board notation indicating the date of shipment, in which case the date stated in the on board notation will be deemed to be the date of shipment.

If the non-negotiable sea waybill contains the indication "intended vessel" or similar qualification in relation to the name of the vessel, an on board notation indicating the date of shipment and the name of the actual vessel is required.

iii. indicate shipment from the port of loading to the port of discharge stated in the credit.

If the non-negotiable sea waybill does not indicate the port of loading stated in the credit as the port of loading, or if it contains the indication "intended" or similar qualification in relation to the port of loading, an on board notation indicating the port of loading as stated in the credit, the date of shipment and the name of the vessel is required. This provision applies even when loading on board or shipment on a named vessel is indicated by pre-printed wording on the non-negotiable sea waybill.

iv. be the sole original non-negotiable sea waybill or, if issued in more than one original, be the full set as indicated on the non-negotiable sea waybill.

v. contain terms and conditions of carriage or make reference to another source containing the terms and conditions of carriage (short form or blank back non-negotiable sea waybill). Contents of terms and conditions of carriage will not be examined.

vi. contain no indication that it is subject to a charter party.

b. For the purpose of this article, transhipment means unloading from one vessel and reloading to another vessel during the carriage from the port of loading to the port of discharge stated in the credit.

c. **i.** A non-negotiable sea waybill may indicate that the goods will or may be transhipped provided that the entire carriage is covered by one and the same non-negotiable sea waybill.

ii. A non-negotiable sea waybill indicating that transhipment will or may take place is acceptable, even if the credit prohibits transhipment, if the goods have been shipped in a container, trailer or LASH barge as evidenced by the non-negotiable sea waybill.

d. Clauses in a non-negotiable sea waybill stating that the carrier reserves the right to tranship will be disregarded.

Article 22 Charter Party Bill of Lading

a. A bill of lading, however named, containing an indication that it is subject to a charter party (charter party bill of lading), must appear to:

i. be signed by:

- the master or a named agent for or on behalf of the master, or
- the owner or a named agent for or on behalf of the owner, or
- the charterer or a named agent for or on behalf of the charterer.

Any signature by the master, owner, charterer or agent must be identified as that of the master, owner, charterer or agent.

Any signature by an agent must indicate whether the agent has signed for or on behalf of the master, owner or charterer.

An agent signing for or on behalf of the owner or charterer must indicate the name of the owner or charterer.

ii. indicate that the goods have been shipped on board a named vessel at the port of loading stated in the credit by:

- pre-printed wording, or

– an on board notation indicating the date on which the goods have been shipped on board.

The date of issuance of the charter party bill of lading will be deemed to be the date of shipment unless the charter party bill of lading contains an on board notation indicating the date of shipment, in which case the date stated in the on board notation will be deemed to be the date of shipment.

iii. indicate shipment from the port of loading to the port of discharge stated in the credit. The port of discharge may also be shown as a range of ports or a geographical area, as stated in the credit.

iv. be the sole original charter party bill of lading or, if issued in more than one original, be the full set as indicated on the charter party bill of lading.

b. A bank will not examine charter party contracts, even if they are required to be presented by the terms of the credit.

Article 23 Air Transport Document

a. An air transport document, however named, must appear to:

i. indicate the name of the carrier and be signed by:

– the carrier, or

– a named agent for or on behalf of the carrier.

Any signature by the carrier or agent must be identified as that of the carrier or agent.

Any signature by an agent must indicate that the agent has signed for or on behalf of the carrier.

ii. indicate that the goods have been accepted for carriage.

iii. indicate the date of issuance. This date will be deemed to be the date of shipment unless the air transport document contains a specific notation of the actual date of shipment, in which case the date stated in the notation will be deemed to be the date of shipment.

Any other information appearing on the air transport document relative to the flight number and date will not be considered in determining the date of shipment.

iv. indicate the airport of departure and the airport of destination stated in the credit.

v. be the original for consignor or shipper, even if the credit stipulates a full set of originals.

vi. contain terms and conditions of carriage or make reference to another source containing the terms and conditions of carriage. Contents of terms and conditions of carriage will not be examined.

b. For the purpose of this article, transhipment means unloading from one aircraft and reloading to another aircraft during the carriage from the airport of departure to the airport of destination stated in the credit.

c. **i.** An air transport document may indicate that the goods will or may be transhipped, provided that the entire carriage is covered by one and the same air transport document.

ii. An air transport document indicating that transhipment will or may take place is acceptable, even if the credit prohibits transhipment.

Article 24 Road, Rail or Inland Waterway Transport Documents

a. A road, rail or inland waterway transport document, however named, must appear to:

i. indicate the name of the carrier and:

– be signed by the carrier or a named agent for or on behalf of the carrier, or

– indicate receipt of the goods by signature, stamp or notation by the carrier or a named agent for or on behalf of the carrier.

Any signature, stamp or notation of receipt of the goods by the carrier or agent must be identified as that of the carrier or agent.

Any signature, stamp or notation of receipt of the goods by the agent must indicate that the agent has signed or acted for or on behalf of the carrier.

If a rail transport document does not identify the carrier, any signature or stamp of the railway company will be accepted as evidence of the document being signed by the carrier.

ii. indicate the date of shipment or the date the goods have been received for shipment, dispatch or carriage at the place stated in the credit. Unless the transport document contains a dated reception stamp, an indication of the date of receipt or a date of shipment, the date of issuance of the transport document will be deemed to be the date of shipment.

iii. indicate the place of shipment and the place of destination stated in the credit.

b. **i.** A road transport document must appear to be the original for consignor or shipper or bear no marking indicating for whom the document has been prepared.

ii. A rail transport document marked "duplicate" will be accepted as an original.

iii. A rail or inland waterway transport document will be accepted as an original whether marked as an original or not.

c. In the absence of an indication on the transport document as to the number of originals issued, the number presented will be deemed to constitute a full set.

d. For the purpose of this article, transhipment means unloading from one means of conveyance and reloading to another means of conveyance, within the same mode of transport, during the carriage from the place of shipment, dispatch or carriage to the place of destination stated in the credit.

e. **i.** A road, rail or inland waterway transport document may indicate that the goods will or may be transhipped provided that the entire carriage is covered by one and the same transport document.

ii. A road, rail or inland waterway transport document indicating that transhipment will or may take place is acceptable, even if the credit prohibits transhipment.

Article 25 Courier Receipt, Post Receipt or Certificate of Posting

a. A courier receipt, however named, evidencing receipt of goods for transport, must appear to:

i. indicate the name of the courier service and be stamped or signed by the named courier service at the place from which the credit states the goods are to be shipped; and

ii. indicate a date of pick-up or of receipt or wording to this effect. This date will be deemed to be the date of shipment.

b. A requirement that courier charges are to be paid or prepaid may be satisfied by a transport document issued by a courier service evidencing that courier charges are for the account of a party other than the consignee.

c. A post receipt or certificate of posting, however named, evidencing receipt of goods for transport, must appear to be stamped or signed and dated at the place from which the credit states the goods are to be shipped. This date will be deemed to be the date of shipment.

Article 26 "On Deck", "Shipper's Load and Count", "Said by Shipper to Contain" and Charges Additional to Freight

a. A transport document must not indicate that the goods are or will be loaded on deck. A clause on a transport document stating that the goods may be loaded on deck is acceptable.

b. A transport document bearing a clause such as "shipper's load and count" and "said by shipper to contain" is acceptable.

c. A transport document may bear a reference, by stamp or otherwise, to charges additional to the freight.

Article 27 Clean Transport Document

A bank will only accept a clean transport document. A clean transport document is one bearing no clause or notation expressly declaring a defective condition of the goods or their packaging. The word "clean" need not appear on a transport document, even if a credit has a requirement for that transport document to be "clean on board".

Article 28 Insurance Document and Coverage

a. An insurance document, such as an insurance policy, an insurance certificate or a declaration under an open cover, must appear to be issued and signed by an insurance company, an underwriter or their agents or their proxies.

Any signature by an agent or proxy must indicate whether the agent or proxy has signed for or on behalf of the insurance company or underwriter.

b. When the insurance document indicates that it has been issued in more than one original, all originals must be presented.

c. Cover notes will not be accepted.

d. An insurance policy is acceptable in lieu of an insurance certificate or a declaration under an open cover.

e. The date of the insurance document must be no later than the date of shipment, unless it appears from the insurance document that the cover is effective from a date not later than the date of shipment.

f. **i.** The insurance document must indicate the amount of insurance coverage and be in the same currency as the credit.

ii. A requirement in the credit for insurance coverage to be for a percentage of the value of the goods, of the invoice value or similar is deemed to be the minimum amount of coverage required.

If there is no indication in the credit of the insurance coverage required, the amount of insurance coverage must be at least 110% of the CIF or CIP value of the goods.

When the CIF or CIP value cannot be determined from the documents, the amount of insurance coverage must be calculated on the basis of the amount for which honour or negotiation is requested or the gross value of the goods as shown on the invoice, whichever is greater.

iii. The insurance document must indicate that risks are covered at least between the place of taking in charge or shipment and the place of discharge or final destination as stated in the credit.

g. A credit should state the type of insurance required and, if any, the additional risks to be covered. An insurance document will be accepted without regard to any risks that are not covered if the credit uses imprecise terms such as "usual risks" or "customary risks".

h. When a credit requires insurance against "all risks" and an insurance document is presented containing any "all risks" notation or clause, whether or not bearing the heading "all risks", the insurance document will be accepted without regard to any risks stated to be excluded.

i. An insurance document may contain reference to any exclusion clause.

j. An insurance document may indicate that the cover is subject to a franchise or excess (deductible).

Article 29 Extension of Expiry Date or Last Day for Presentation

a. If the expiry date of a credit or the last day for presentation falls on a day when the bank to which presentation is to be made is closed for reasons other than those referred to in Article 36, the expiry date or the last day for presentation, as the case may be, will be extended to the first following banking day.

b. If presentation is made on the first following banking day, a nominated bank must provide the issuing bank or confirming bank with a statement on its covering schedule that the presentation was made within the time limits extended in accordance with sub-article 29 (a).

c. The latest date for shipment will not be extended as a result of sub-article 29 (a).

Article 30 Tolerance in Credit Amount, Quantity and Unit Prices

a. The words "about" or "approximately" used in connection with the amount of the credit or the quantity or the unit price stated in the credit are to be construed as allowing a tolerance not to exceed 10% more or 10% less than the amount, the quantity or the unit price to which they refer.

b. A tolerance not to exceed 5% more or 5% less than the quantity of the goods is allowed, provided the credit does not state the quantity in terms of a stipulated number of packing units or individual items and the total amount of the drawings does not exceed the amount of the credit.

c. Even when partial shipments are not allowed, a tolerance not to exceed 5% less than the amount of the credit is allowed, provided that the quantity of the goods, if stated in the credit, is shipped in full and a unit price, if stated in the credit, is not reduced or that sub-article 30 (b) is not applicable. This tolerance does not apply when the credit stipulates a specific tolerance or uses the expressions referred to in sub-article 30 (a).

Article 31 Partial Drawings or Shipments

a. Partial drawings or shipments are allowed.

b. A presentation consisting of more than one set of transport documents evidencing shipment commencing on the same means of conveyance and for the same journey, provided they indicate the same destination, will not be regarded as covering a partial shipment, even if they indicate different dates of shipment or different ports of loading, places of taking in charge or dispatch. If the presentation consists of more than one set of transport documents, the latest date of shipment as evidenced on any of the sets of transport documents will be regarded as the date of shipment.

A presentation consisting of one or more sets of transport documents evidencing shipment on more than one means of conveyance within the same mode of transport will be regarded as covering a partial shipment, even if the means of conveyance leave on the same day for the same destination.

c. A presentation consisting of more than one courier receipt, post receipt or certificate of posting will not be regarded as a partial shipment if the courier receipts, post receipts or certificates of posting appear to have been stamped or signed by the same courier or postal service at the same place and date and for the same destination.

Article 32 Instalment Drawings or Shipments

If a drawing or shipment by instalments within given periods is stipulated in the credit and any instalment is not drawn or shipped within the period allowed for that instalment, the credit ceases to be available for that and any subsequent instalment.

Article 33 Hours of Presentation

A bank has no obligation to accept a presentation outside of its banking hours.

Article 34 Disclaimer on Effectiveness of Documents

A bank assumes no liability or responsibility for the form, sufficiency, accuracy, genuineness, falsification or legal effect of any document, or for the general or particular conditions stipulated in a document or superimposed thereon; nor does it assume any liability or responsibility for the description, quantity, weight, quality, condition, packing, delivery, value or existence of the goods, services or other performance represented by any document, or for the good faith or acts or omissions, solvency, performance or standing of the consignor, the carrier, the forwarder, the consignee or the insurer of the goods or any other person.

Article 35 Disclaimer on Transmission and Translation

A bank assumes no liability or responsibility for the consequences arising out of delay, loss in transit, mutilation or other errors arising in the transmission of any messages or delivery of letters or documents, when such messages, letters or documents are transmitted or sent according to the requirements stated in the credit, or when the bank may have taken the initiative in the choice of the delivery service in the absence of such instructions in the credit.

If a nominated bank determines that a presentation is complying and forwards the documents to the issuing bank or confirming bank, whether or not the nominated bank has honoured or negotiated, an issuing bank or confirming bank must honour or negotiate, or reimburse that nominated bank, even when the documents have been lost in transit between the nominated bank and the issuing bank or confirming bank, or between the confirming bank and the issuing bank.

A bank assumes no liability or responsibility for errors in translation or interpretation of technical terms and may transmit credit terms without translating them.

Article 36 Force Majeure

A bank assumes no liability or responsibility for the consequences arising out of the interruption of its business by Acts of God, riots, civil commotions, insurrections, wars, acts of terrorism, or by any strikes or lockouts or any other causes beyond its control.

A bank will not, upon resumption of its business, honour or negotiate under a credit that expired during such interruption of its business.

Article 37 Disclaimer for Acts of an Instructed Party

a. A bank utilizing the services of another bank for the purpose of giving effect to the instructions of the applicant does so for the account and at the risk of the applicant.

b. An issuing bank or advising bank assumes no liability or responsibility should the instructions it transmits to another bank not be carried out, even if it has taken the initiative in the choice of that other bank.

c. A bank instructing another bank to perform services is liable for any commissions, fees, costs or expenses ("charges") incurred by that bank in connection with its instructions.

If a credit states that charges are for the account of the beneficiary and charges cannot be collected or deducted from proceeds, the issuing bank remains liable for payment of charges.

A credit or amendment should not stipulate that the advising to a beneficiary is conditional upon the receipt by the advising bank or second advising bank of its charges.

d. The applicant shall be bound by and liable to indemnify a bank against all obligations and responsibilities imposed by foreign laws and usages.

Article 38 Transferable Credits

a. A bank is under no obligation to transfer a credit except to the extent and in the manner expressly consented to by that bank.

b. For the purpose of this article:

Transferable credit means a credit that specifically states it is "transferable". A transferable credit may be made available in whole or in part to another beneficiary ("second beneficiary") at the request of the beneficiary ("first beneficiary").

Transferring bank means a nominated bank that transfers the credit or, in a credit available with any bank, a bank that is specifically authorized by the issuing bank to transfer and that transfers the credit. An issuing bank may be a transferring bank.

Transferred credit means a credit that has been made available by the transferring bank to a second beneficiary.

c. Unless otherwise agreed at the time of transfer, all charges (such as commissions, fees, costs or expenses) incurred in respect of a transfer must be paid by the first beneficiary.

d. A credit may be transferred in part to more than one second beneficiary provided partial drawings or shipments are allowed.

A transferred credit cannot be transferred at the request of a second beneficiary to any subsequent beneficiary. The first beneficiary is not considered to be a subsequent beneficiary.

e. Any request for transfer must indicate if and under what conditions amendments may be advised to the second beneficiary. The transferred credit must clearly indicate those conditions.

f. If a credit is transferred to more than one second beneficiary, rejection of an amendment by one or more second beneficiary does not invalidate the acceptance by any other second beneficiary, with respect to which the transferred credit will be amended accordingly. For any second beneficiary that rejected the amendment, the transferred credit will remain unamended.

g. The transferred credit must accurately reflect the terms and conditions of the credit, including confirmation, if any, with the exception of:

- the amount of the credit,
- any unit price stated therein,
- the expiry date,
- the period for presentation, or
- the latest shipment date or given period for shipment,

any or all of which may be reduced or curtailed.

The percentage for which insurance cover must be effected may be increased to provide the amount of cover stipulated in the credit or these articles.

The name of the first beneficiary may be substituted for that of the applicant in the credit.

If the name of the applicant is specifically required by the credit to appear in any document other than the invoice, such requirement must be reflected in the transferred credit.

h. The first beneficiary has the right to substitute its own invoice and draft, if any, for those of a second beneficiary for an amount not in excess of that stipulated in the credit, and upon such substitution the first beneficiary can draw under the credit for the difference, if any, between its invoice and the invoice of a second beneficiary.

i. If the first beneficiary is to present its own invoice and draft, if any, but fails to do so on first demand, or if the invoices presented by the first beneficiary create discrepancies that did not exist in the presentation made by the second beneficiary and the first beneficiary fails to correct them on first demand, the transferring bank has the right to present the documents as received from the second beneficiary to the issuing bank, without further responsibility to the first beneficiary.

j. The first beneficiary may, in its request for transfer, indicate that honour or negotiation is to be effected to a second beneficiary at the place to which the credit has been transferred, up to and including the expiry date of the credit. This is without prejudice to the right of the first beneficiary in accordance with sub-article 38 (h).

k. Presentation of documents by or on behalf of a second beneficiary must be made to the transferring bank.

Article 39 Assignment of Proceeds

The fact that a credit is not stated to be transferable shall not affect the right of the beneficiary to assign any proceeds to which it may be or may become entitled under the credit, in accordance with the provisions of applicable law. This Article relates only to the assignment of proceeds and not to the assignment of the right to perform under the credit.

21) Uniform Customs and Practice for Documentary Credits for Electronic Presentation (e-UCP 600)[1]

Preliminary Considerations

The mode of presentation to the nominated bank, confirming bank, if any, or the issuing bank, by or on behalf of the beneficiary, of electronic records alone or in combination with paper documents, is outside the scope of the eUCP.

The mode of presentation to the applicant, by the issuing bank, of electronic records alone or in combination with paper documents, is outside the scope of the eUCP.

Where not defined or modified in the eUCP, definitions given in UCP 600 will continue to apply.

Before agreeing to issue, advise, confirm, amend or transfer an eUCP credit, banks should satisfy themselves that they can examine the required electronic records in a presentation made thereunder.

Article e1 Scope of the Uniform Customs and Practice for Documentary Credits (UCP 600) Supplement for Electronic Presentations ("eUCP")

a. The eUCP supplements the Uniform Customs and Practice for Documentary Credits (2007 Revision, ICC Publication No. 600) ("UCP") in order to accommodate presentation of electronic records alone or in combination with paper documents.

b. The eUCP shall apply where the credit indicates that it is subject to the eUCP ("eUCP credit").

c. This version is Version 2.0. An eUCP credit must indicate the applicable version of the eUCP. If not indicated, it is subject to the latest version in effect on the date the eUCP credit is issued or, if made subject to the eUCP by an amendment accepted by the beneficiary, the date of that amendment.

d. An eUCP credit must indicate the physical location of the issuing bank.

In addition, it must also indicate the physical location of any nominated bank and, if different to the nominated bank, the physical location of the confirming bank, if any, when such location is known to the issuing bank at the time of issuance. If the physical location of any nominated bank and/or confirming bank is not indicated in the credit, such bank must indicate its physical location to the beneficiary no later than the time of advising or confirming the credit or, in the case of a credit available with any bank, and where another bank willing to act on the nomination to honour or negotiate is not the advising or confirming bank, at the time of agreeing to act on its nomination.

Article e2 Relationship of the eUCP to the UCP

a. An eUCP credit is also subject to the UCP without express incorporation of the UCP.

b. Where the eUCP applies, its provisions shall prevail to the extent that they would produce a result different from the application of the UCP.

c. If an eUCP credit allows the beneficiary to choose between presentation of paper documents or electronic records and it chooses to present only paper documents, the UCP alone shall apply to that presentation. If only paper documents are permitted under an eUCP credit, the UCP alone shall apply.

Article e3 Definitions

a. Where the following terms are used in the UCP, for the purpose of applying the UCP to an electronic record presented under an eUCP credit, the term:

i. Appear on their face and the like shall apply to examination of the data content of an electronic record.

ii. Document shall include an electronic record.

iii. Place for presentation of an electronic record means an electronic address of a data processing system.

iv. Presenter means the beneficiary, or any party acting on behalf of the beneficiary who makes a presentation to a nominated bank, confirming bank, if any, or to the issuing bank directly.

v. Sign and the like shall include an electronic signature.

vi. Superimposed, notation or stamped means data content whose supplementary character is apparent in an electronic record.

b. The following terms used in the eUCP shall have the following meaning:

i. Data corruption means any distortion or loss of data that renders the electronic record, as it was presented, unreadable in whole or in part.

ii. Data processing system means a computerised or an electronic or any other automated means used to process and manipulate data, initiate an action or respond to data messages or performances in whole or in part.

iii. Electronic record means data created, generated, sent, communicated, received or stored by electronic means, including, where appropriate, all information logically associated with or otherwise linked together so as to become part of the record, whether generated contemporaneously or not, that is:

- capable of being authenticated as to the apparent identity of a sender and the apparent source of the data contained in it, and as to whether it has remained complete and unaltered, and
- capable of being examined for compliance with the terms and conditions of the eUCP credit.

iv. Electronic signature means a data process attached to or logically associated with an electronic record and executed or adopted by a person in order to identify that person and to indicate that person's authentication of the electronic record.

v. Format means the data organisation in which the electronic record is expressed or to which it refers.

vi. Paper document means a document in a paper form.

vii. Received means when an electronic record enters a data processing system, at the place for presentation indicated in the eUCP credit, in a format capable of being accepted by that system. Any acknowledgement of receipt generated by that system does not imply that the electronic record has been viewed, examined, accepted or refused under an eUCP credit.

viii. Re-present or re-presented means to substitute or replace an electronic record already presented.

Article e4 Electronic Records and Paper Documents v. Good, Services or Performance

Banks do not deal with the goods, services or performance to which an electronic record or paper document may relate.

Article e5 Format

An eUCP credit must indicate the format of each electronic record. If the format of an electronic record is not indicated, it may be presented in any format.

Article e6 Presentation

a. i. An eUCP credit must indicate a place for presentation of electronic records.

ii. An eUCP credit requiring or allowing presentation of both electronic records and paper documents must, in addition to the place for presentation of the electronic records, also indicate a place for presentation of the paper documents.

b. Electronic records may be presented separately and need not be presented at the same time.

c. i. When one or more electronic records are presented alone or in combination with paper documents, the presenter is responsible for providing a notice of completeness to the nominated bank, confirming bank, if any, or to the issuing bank, where a presentation is made directly. The receipt of the notice of completeness will act as notification that the presentation is complete and that the period for examination of the presentation is to commence.

ii. The notice of completeness may be given as an electronic record or paper document and must identify the eUCP credit to which it relates.

iii. Presentation is deemed not to have been made if the notice of completeness is not received.

iv. When a nominated bank, whether acting on its nomination or not, forwards or makes available electronic records to a confirming bank or issuing bank, a notice of completeness need not be sent.

d. i. Each presentation of an electronic record under an eUCP credit must identify the eUCP credit under which it is presented. This may be by specific reference thereto in the electronic record itself, or in metadata attached or superimposed thereto, or by identification in the covering letter or schedule that accompanies the presentation.

ii. Any presentation of an electronic record not so identified may be treated as not received.

e. i. If the bank to which presentation is to be made is open but its system is unable to receive a transmitted electronic record on the stipulated expiry date and/or the last day for presentation, as the case may be, the bank will be deemed to be closed and the expiry date and/or last day for presentation shall be extended to the next banking day on which such bank is able to receive an electronic record.

ii. In this event, the nominated bank must provide the confirming bank or issuing bank, if any, with a statement on its covering schedule that the presentation of electronic records was made within the time limits extended in accordance with sub-article e6 (e) (i).

iii. If the only electronic record remaining to be presented is the notice of completeness, it may be given by telecommunication or by paper document and will be deemed timely, provided that it is sent before the bank is able to receive an electronic record.

f. An electronic record that cannot be authenticated is deemed not to have been presented.

Article e7 Examination

a. i. The period for the examination of documents commences on the banking day following the day on which the notice of completeness is received by the nominated bank, confirming bank, if any, or by the issuing bank, where a presentation is made directly.

ii. If the time for presentation of documents or the notice of completeness is extended, as provided in sub-article e6 (e) (i), the time for the examination of documents commences on the next banking day following the day on which the bank to which presentation is to be made is able to receive the notice of completeness, at the place for presentation.

b. i. If an electronic record contains a hyperlink to an external system or a presentation indicates that the electronic record may be examined by reference to an external system, the electronic record at the hyperlink or the external system shall be deemed to constitute an integral part of the electronic record to be examined.

ii. The failure of the external system to provide access to the required electronic record at the time of examination shall constitute a discrepancy, except as provided in sub-article e7 (d) (ii).

c. The inability of a nominated bank acting on its nomination, a confirming bank, if any, or the issuing bank, to examine an electronic record in a format required by an eUCP credit or, if no format is required, to examine it in the format presented is not a basis for refusal.

d. i. The forwarding of electronic records by a nominated bank, whether or not it is acting on its nomination to honour or negotiate, signifies that it has satisfied itself as to the apparent authenticity of the electronic records.

ii. In the event that a nominated bank determines that a presentation is complying and forwards or makes available those electronic records to the confirming bank or issuing bank, whether or not the nominated bank has honoured or negotiated, an issuing bank or confirming bank must honour or negotiate, or reimburse that nominated bank, even when a specified hyperlink or external system does not allow the issuing bank or confirming bank to examine one or more electronic records that have been made available between the nominated bank and the issuing bank or confirming bank, or between the confirming bank and the issuing bank.

Article e8 Notice of Refusal

If a nominated bank acting on its nomination, a confirming bank, if any, or the issuing bank, provides a notice of refusal of a presentation which includes electronic records and does not receive instructions from the party to which notice of refusal is given for the disposition of the electronic records within 30 calendar days from the date the notice of refusal is given, the bank shall return any paper documents not previously returned to that party, but may dispose of the electronic records in any manner deemed appropriate without any responsibility.

Article e9 Originals and Copies

Any requirements for presentation of one or more originals or copies of an electronic record is satisfied by the presentation of one electronic record.

Article e10 Date of Issuance

An electronic record must provide evidence of its date of issuance.

Article e11 Transport

If an electronic record evidencing transport does not indicate a date of shipment or dispatch or taking in charge or a date the goods were accepted for carriage, the date of issuance of the electronic record will be deemed to be the date of shipment or dispatch or taking in charge or the date the goods were accepted for carriage. However, if the electronic record bears a notation that evidences the date of shipment or dispatch or taking in charge or the date the goods were accepted for carriage, the date of the notation will be deemed to be the date of shipment or dispatch or taking in charge or the date the goods were accepted for carriage. Such a notation showing additional data content need not be separately signed or otherwise authenticated.

Article e12 Corruption of an Electronic Record After Presentation

a. If an electronic record that has been received by a nominated bank acting on its nomination or not, confirming bank, if any, or the issuing bank, appears to have been affected by a data corruption, the bank may inform the presenter and may request it to be re-presented.

b. If a bank makes such a request:

i. the time for examination is suspended and resumes when the electronic record is re-presented; and

ii. if the nominated bank is not a confirming bank, it must provide any confirming bank and the issuing bank with notice of the request for the electronic record to be re-presented and inform it of the suspension; but

iii. if the same electronic record is not re-presented within 30 calendar days, or on or before the expiry date and/or last day for presentation, whichever occurs first, the bank may treat the electronic record as not presented.

Article e13 Additional Disclaimer of Liability for Presentation of Electronic Records under eUCP

a. By satisfying itself as to the apparent authenticity of an electronic record, a bank assumes no liability for the identity of the sender, source of the information, or its complete and unaltered character other than that which is apparent in the electronic record received by the use of a data processing system for the receipt, authentication, and identification of electronic records.

b. A bank assumes no liability or responsibility for the consequences arising out of the unavailability of a data processing system other than its own.

Article e14 Force Majeure

A bank assumes no liability or responsibility for the consequences arising out of the interruption of its business, including but not limited to its inability to access a data processing system, or a failure of equipment, software or communications network, caused by Acts of God, riots, civil commotions, insurrections, wars, acts of terrorism, cyberattacks, or by any strikes or lockouts or any other causes, including failure of equipment, software or communications networks, beyond its control.

22) 1995 United Nations Convention on Independent Guarantees and Stand-by Letters of Credit[1]

CHAPTER I. SCOPE OF APPLICATION

Article 1 - Scope of Application

(1) This Convention applies to an international undertaking referred to in Article 2:

(a) If the place of business of the guarantor/issuer at which the undertaking is issued is in a Contracting State, or

(b) If the rules of private international law lead to the application of the law of a Contracting State, unless the undertaking excludes the application of the Convention.

(2) This Convention applies also to an international letter of credit not falling within Article 2 if it expressly states that it is subject to this Convention.

(3) The provisions of articles 21 and 22 apply to international undertakings referred to in Article 2 independently of paragraph (1) of this article.

Article 2 - Undertaking

(1) For the purposes of this Convention, an undertaking is an independent commitment, known in international practice as an independent guarantee or as a stand-by letter of credit, given by a bank or other institution or person ("guarantor/issuer") to pay to the beneficiary a certain or determinable amount upon simple demand or upon demand accompanied by other documents, in conformity with the terms and any documentary conditions of the undertaking, indicating, or from which it is to be inferred, that payment is due because of a default in the performance of an obligation, or because of another contingency, or for money borrowed or advanced, or on account of any mature indebtedness undertaken by the principal/applicant or another person.

(2) The undertaking may be given:

(a) At the request or on the instruction of the customer ("principal/applicant") of the guarantor/issuer;

(b) On the instruction of another bank, institution or person ("instructing party") that acts at the request of the customer ("principal/applicant") of that instructing party; or

(c) On behalf of the guarantor/issuer itself.

(3) Payment may be stipulated in the undertaking to be made in any form, including:

(a) Payment in a specified currency or unit of account;

(b) Acceptance of a bill of exchange (draft);

(c) Payment on a deferred basis;

(d) Supply of a specified item of value.

(4) The undertaking may stipulate that the guarantor/issuer itself is the beneficiary when acting in favour of another person.

Article 3 - Independence of Undertaking

For the purposes of this Convention, an undertaking is independent where the guarantor/issuer's obligation to the beneficiary is not:

1

(a) dependent upon the existence or validity of any underlying transaction, or upon any other undertaking (including stand-by letters of credit or independent guarantees to which confirmations or counter-guarantees relate); or

(b) subject to any term or condition not appearing in the undertaking, or to any future, uncertain act or event except presentation of documents or another such act or event within a guarantor/issuer's sphere of operations.

Article 4 - Internationality of Undertaking

(1) An undertaking is international if the places of business, as specified in the undertaking, of any two of the following persons are in different States: guarantor/issuer, beneficiary, principal/applicant, instructing party, confirmer.

(2) For the purposes of the preceding paragraph:

(a) If the undertaking lists more than one place of business for a given person, the relevant place of business is that which has the closest relationship to the undertaking;

(b) If the undertaking does not specify a place of business for a given person but specifies its habitual residence, that residence is relevant for determining the international character of the undertaking.

CHAPTER II. INTERPRETATION

Article 5 - Principles of Interpretation

In the interpretation of this Convention, regard is to be had to its international character and to the need to promote uniformity in its application and the observance of good faith in the international practice of independent guarantees and stand-by letters of credit.

Article 6 - Definitions

For the purposes of this Convention and unless otherwise indicated in a provision of this Convention or required by the context:

(a) "Undertaking" includes "counter-guarantee" and "confirmation of an undertaking";

(b) "Guarantor/issuer" includes "counter-guarantor" and "confirmer";

(c) "Counter-guarantee" means an undertaking given to the guarantor/issuer of another undertaking by its instructing party and providing for payment upon simple demand or upon demand accompanied by other documents, in conformity with the terms and any documentary conditions of the undertaking, indicating, or from which it is to be inferred, that payment under that other undertaking has been demanded from, or made by, the person issuing that other undertaking;

(d) "Counter-guarantor" means the person issuing a counter-guarantee;

(e) "Confirmation" of an undertaking means an undertaking added to that of the guarantor/issuer, and authorized by the guarantor/issuer, providing the beneficiary with the option of demanding payment from the confirmer instead of from the guarantor/issuer, upon simple demand or upon demand accompanied by other documents, in conformity with the terms and any documentary conditions of the confirmed undertaking, without prejudice to the beneficiary's right to demand payment from the guarantor/issuer;

(f) "Confirmer" means the person adding a confirmation to an undertaking;

(g) "Document" means a communication made in a form that provides a complete record thereof.

CHAPTER III. FORM AND CONTENT OF UNDERTAKING

Article 7 - Issuance, Form and Irrevocability of Undertaking

(1) Issuance of an undertaking occurs when and where the undertaking leaves the sphere of control of the guarantor/issuer concerned.

(2) An undertaking may be issued in any form which preserves a complete record of the text of the undertaking and provides authentication of its source by generally accepted means or by a procedure agreed upon by the guarantor/issuer and the beneficiary.

(3) From the time of issuance of an undertaking, a demand for payment may be made in accordance with the terms and conditions of the undertaking, unless the undertaking stipulates a different time.

(4) An undertaking is irrevocable upon issuance, unless it stipulates that it is revocable.

Article 8 - Amendment

(1) An undertaking may not be amended except in the form stipulated in the undertaking or, failing such stipulation, in a form referred to in paragraph (2) of Article 7.

(2) Unless otherwise stipulated in the undertaking or elsewhere agreed by the guarantor/ issuer and the beneficiary, an undertaking is amended upon issuance of the amendment if the amendment has previously been authorized by the beneficiary.

(3) Unless otherwise stipulated in the undertaking or elsewhere agreed by the guarantor/issuer and the beneficiary, where any amendment has not previously been authorized by the beneficiary, the undertaking is amended only when the guarantor/issuer receives a notice of acceptance of the amendment by the beneficiary in a form referred to in paragraph (2) of Article 7.

(4) An amendment of an undertaking has no effect on the rights and obligations of the principal/ applicant (or an instructing party) or of a confirmer of the undertaking unless such person consents to the amendment.

Article 9 - Transfer of Beneficiary's Right to Demand Payment

(1) The beneficiary's right to demand payment may be transferred only if authorized in the undertaking, and only to the extent and in the manner authorized in the undertaking.

(2) If an undertaking is designated as transferable without specifying whether or not the consent of the guarantor/issuer or another authorized person is required for the actual transfer, neither the guarantor/issuer nor any other authorized person is obliged to effect the transfer except to the extent and in the manner expressly consented to by it.

Article 10 - Assignment of Proceeds

(1) Unless otherwise stipulated in the undertaking or elsewhere agreed by the guarantor/issuer and the beneficiary, the beneficiary may assign to another person any proceeds to which it may be, or may become, entitled under the undertaking.

(2) If the guarantor/issuer or another person obliged to effect payment has received a notice originating from the beneficiary, in a form referred to in paragraph (2) of Article 7, of the beneficiary's irrevocable assignment, payment to the assignee discharges the obligor, to the extent of its payment, from its liability under the undertaking.

Article 11 - Cessation of Right to Demand Payment

(1) The right of the beneficiary to demand payment under the undertaking ceases when:

(a) The guarantor/issuer has received a statement by the beneficiary of release from liability in a form referred to in paragraph (2) of Article 7;

(b) The beneficiary and the guarantor/issuer have agreed on the termination of the undertaking in the form stipulated in the undertaking or, failing such stipulation, in a form referred to in paragraph (2) of Article 7;

(c) The amount available under the undertaking has been paid, unless the undertaking provides for the automatic renewal or for an automatic increase of the amount available or otherwise provides for continuation of the undertaking;

(d) The validity period of the undertaking expires in accordance with the provisions of Article 12.

(2) The undertaking may stipulate, or the guarantor/issuer and the beneficiary may agree elsewhere, that return of the document embodying the undertaking to the guarantor/issuer, or a procedure functionally equivalent to the return of the document in the case of the issuance of the undertaking in non-paper form, is required for the cessation of the right to demand payment, either alone or in conjunction with one of the events referred to in subparagraphs (a) and (b) of paragraph (1) of this article. However, in no case shall retention of any such document by the beneficiary after the right to demand payment ceases in accordance with subparagraph (c) or (d) of paragraph (1) of this Article preserve any rights of the beneficiary under the undertaking.

Article 12 - Expiry

The validity period of the undertaking expires:

(a) At the expiry date, which may be a specified calendar date or the last day of a fixed period of time stipulated in the undertaking, provided that, if the expiry date is not a business day at the place of business of the guarantor/issuer at which the undertaking is issued, or of another person or at another place stipulated in the undertaking for presentation of the demand for payment, expiry occurs on the first business day which follows;

(b) If expiry depends according to the undertaking on the occurrence of an act or event not within the guarantor/issuer's sphere of operations, when the guarantor/issuer is advised that the act or event has occurred by presentation of the document specified for that purpose in the undertaking or, if no such document is specified, of a certification by the beneficiary of the occurrence of the act or event;

(c) If the undertaking does not state an expiry date, or if the act or event on which expiry is stated to depend has not yet been established by presentation of the required document and an expiry date has not been stated in addition, when six years have elapsed from the date of issuance of the undertaking.

CHAPTER IV. RIGHTS, OBLIGATIONS AND DEFENCES

Article 13 - Determination of Rights and Obligations

(1) The rights and obligations of the guarantor/issuer and the beneficiary arising from the undertaking are determined by the terms and conditions set forth in the undertaking, including any rules, general conditions or usages specifically referred to therein, and by the provisions of this Convention.

(2) In interpreting terms and conditions of the undertaking and in settling questions that are not addressed by the terms and conditions of the undertaking or by the provisions of this Convention, regard shall be had to generally accepted international rules and usages of independent guarantee or stand-by letter of credit practice.

Article 14 - Standard of Conduct and Liability of Guarantor/Issuer

(1) In discharging its obligations under the undertaking and this Convention, the guarantor/issuer shall act in good faith and exercise reasonable care having due regard to generally

accepted standards of international practice of independent guarantees or stand-by letters of credit.

(2) A guarantor/issuer may not be exempted from liability for its failure to act in good faith or for any grossly negligent conduct.

Article 15 - Demand

(1) Any demand for payment under the undertaking shall be made in a form referred to in paragraph (2) of Article 7 and in conformity with the terms and conditions of the undertaking.

(2) Unless otherwise stipulated in the undertaking, the demand and any certification or other document required by the undertaking shall be presented, within the time that a demand for payment may be made, to the guarantor/issuer at the place where the undertaking was issued.

(3) The beneficiary, when demanding payment, is deemed to certify that the demand is not in bad faith and that none of the elements referred to in subparagraphs (a), (b) and (c) of paragraph (1) of Article 19 are present.

Article 16 - Examination of Demand and Accompanying Documents

(1) The guarantor/issuer shall examine the demand and any accompanying documents in accordance with the standard of conduct referred to in paragraph (1) of Article 14. In determining whether documents are in facial conformity with the terms and conditions of the undertaking, and are consistent with one another, the guarantor/issuer shall have due regard to the applicable international standard of independent guarantee or stand-by letter of credit practice.

(2) Unless otherwise stipulated in the undertaking or elsewhere agreed by the guarantor/issuer and the beneficiary, the guarantor/issuer shall have reasonable time, but not more than seven business days following the day of receipt of the demand and any accompanying documents, in which to:

(a) Examine the demand and any accompanying documents;

(b) Decide whether or not to pay;

(c) If the decision is not to pay, issue notice thereof to the beneficiary.

The notice referred to in subparagraph (c) above shall, unless otherwise stipulated in the undertaking or elsewhere agreed by the guarantor/issuer and the beneficiary, be made by teletransmission or, if that is not possible, by other expeditious means and indicate the reason for the decision not to pay.

Article 17 - Payment

(1) Subject to Article 19, the guarantor/issuer shall pay against a demand made in accordance with the provisions of Article 15. Following a determination that a demand for payment so conforms, payment shall be made promptly, unless the undertaking stipulates payment on a deferred basis, in which case payment shall be made at the stipulated time.

(2) Any payment against a demand that is not in accordance with the provisions of Article 15 does not prejudice the rights of the principal/applicant.

Article 18 - Set-Off

Unless otherwise stipulated in the undertaking or elsewhere agreed by the guarantor/issuer and the beneficiary, the guarantor/issuer may discharge the payment obligation under the undertaking by availing itself of a right of set-off, except with any claim assigned to it by the principal/applicant or the instructing party.

Article 19 - Exception to Payment Obligation

(1) If it is manifest and clear that:

(a) Any document is not genuine or has been falsified;

(b) No payment is due on the basis asserted in the demand and the supporting documents; or

(c) Judging by the type and purpose of the undertaking, the demand has no conceivable basis, the guarantor/issuer, acting in good faith, has a right, as against the beneficiary, to withhold payment.

(2) For the purposes of subparagraph (c) of paragraph (1) of this article, the following are types of situations in which a demand has no conceivable basis:

(a) The contingency or risk against which the undertaking was designed to secure the beneficiary has undoubtedly not materialized;

(b) The underlying obligation of the principal/applicant has been declared invalid by a court or arbitral tribunal, unless the undertaking indicates that such contingency falls within the risk to be covered by the undertaking;

(c) The underlying obligation has undoubtedly been fulfilled to the satisfaction of the beneficiary;

(d) Fulfilment of the underlying obligation has clearly been prevented by wilful misconduct of the beneficiary;

(e) In the case of a demand under a counter-guarantee, the beneficiary of the counter-guarantee has made payment in bad faith as guarantor/issuer of the undertaking to which the counter-guarantee relates.

(3) In the circumstances set out in subparagraphs (a), (b) and (c) of paragraph (1) of this article, the principal/applicant is entitled to provisional court measures in accordance with Article 20.

CHAPTER V. PROVISIONAL COURT MEASURES

Article 20 - Provisional Court Measures

(1) Where, on an application by the principal/applicant or the instructing party, it is shown that there is a high probability that, with regard to a demand made, or expected to be made, by the beneficiary, one of the circumstances referred to in subparagraphs (a), (b) and (c) of paragraph (1) of Article 19 is present, the court, on the basis of immediately available strong evidence, may:

(a) Issue a provisional order to the effect that the beneficiary does not receive payment, including an order that the guarantor/issuer hold the amount of the undertaking, or

(b) Issue a provisional order to the effect that the proceeds of the undertaking paid to the beneficiary are blocked, taking into account whether in the absence of such an order the principal/ applicant would be likely to suffer serious harm.

(2) The court, when issuing a provisional order referred to in paragraph (1) of this article, may require the person applying therefor to furnish such form of security as the court deems appropriate.

(3) The court may not issue a provisional order of the kind referred to in paragraph (1) of this Article based on any objection to payment other than those referred to in subparagraphs (a), (b) and (c) of paragraph (1) of Article 19, or use of the undertaking for a criminal purpose.

CHAPTER VI. CONFLICT OF LAWS

Article 21 - Choice of Applicable Law

The undertaking is governed by the law the choice of which is:

(a) Stipulated in the undertaking or demonstrated by the terms and conditions of the undertaking; or

(b) Agreed elsewhere by the guarantor/issuer and the beneficiary.

Article 22 - Determination of Applicable Law

Failing a choice of law in accordance with Article 21, the undertaking is governed by the law of the State where the guarantor/issuer has that place of business at which the undertaking was issued.

CHAPTER VII. FINAL CLAUSES

Article 23 - Depositary

The Secretary-General of the United Nations is the depositary of this Convention.

Article 24 - Signature, Ratification, Acceptance, Approval, Accession

(1) This Convention is open for signature by all States at the Headquarters of the United Nations, New York, until 11 December 1997.

(2) This Convention is subject to ratification, acceptance or approval by the signatory States.

(3) This Convention is open to accession by all States which are not signatory States as from the date it is open for signature.

(4) Instruments of ratification, acceptance, approval and accession are to be deposited with the Secretary-General of the United Nations.

Article 25 - Application to Territorial Units

(1) If a State has two or more territorial units in which different systems of law are applicable in relation to the matters dealt with in this Convention, it may, at the time of signature, ratification, acceptance, approval or accession, declare that this Convention is to extend to all its territorial units or only one or more of them, and may at any time substitute another declaration for its earlier declaration.

(2) These declarations are to state expressly the territorial units to which the Convention extends.

(3) If, by virtue of a declaration under this article, this Convention does not extend to all territorial units of a State and the place of business of the guarantor/issuer or of the beneficiary is located in a territorial unit to which the Convention does not extend, this place of business is considered not to be in a Contracting State.

(4) If a State makes no declaration under paragraph (1) of this article, the Convention is to extend to all territorial units of that State.

Article 26 - Effect of Declaration

(1) Declarations made under Article 25 at the time of signature are subject to confirmation upon ratification, acceptance or approval.

(2) Declarations and confirmations of declarations are to be in writing and to be formally notified to the depositary.

(3) A declaration takes effect simultaneously with the entry into force of this Convention in respect of the State concerned. However, a declaration of which the depositary receives formal

notification after such entry into force takes effect on the first day of the month following the expiration of six months after the date of its receipt by the depositary.

(4) Any State which makes a declaration under Article 25 may withdraw it at any time by a formal notification in writing addressed to the depositary. Such withdrawal takes effect on the first day of the month following the expiration of six months after the date of the receipt of the notification of the depositary.

Article 27 - Reservations

No reservations may be made to this Convention.

Article 28 - Entry into Force

(1) This Convention enters into force on the first day of the month following the expiration of one year from the date of the deposit of the fifth instrument of ratification, acceptance, approval or accession.

(2) For each State which becomes a Contracting State to this Convention after the date of the deposit of the fifth instrument of ratification, acceptance, approval or accession, this Convention enters into force on the first day of the month following the expiration of one year after the date of the deposit of the appropriate instrument on behalf of that State.

(3) This Convention applies only to undertakings issued on or after the date when the Convention enters into force in respect of the Contracting State referred to in subparagraph (a) or the Contracting State referred to in subparagraph (b) of paragraph (1) of Article 1.

Article 29 - Denunciation

(1) A Contracting State may denounce this Convention at any time by means of a notification in writing addressed to the depositary.

(2) The denunciation takes effect on the first day of the month following the expiration of one year after the notification is received by the depositary. Where a longer period is specified in the notification, the denunciation takes effect upon the expiration of such longer period after the notification is received by the depositary.

DONE at New York, this eleventh day of December one thousand nine hundred and ninety-five, in a single original, of which the Arabic, Chinese, English, French, Russian and Spanish texts are equally authentic.

IN WITNESS WHEREOF the undersigned plenipotentiaries, being duly authorized by their respective Governments, have signed the present Convention.

Entry into force: 1 January 2000

Ratifications and binding effect as of April 2020: Belarus (2003), Ecuador (2000), El Salvador (2000), Gabon (2006), Kuwait (2000), Liberia (2006), Panama (2000), Tunisia (2000)

23) INTERNATIONAL STANDBY PRACTICES (ISP98)[1]

RULE 1: GENERAL PROVISIONS

Scope, Application, Definitions, and Interpretation of These Rules

1.01 Scope and Application

(a) These Rules are intended to be applied to standby letters of credit (including performance, financial, and direct pay standby letters of credit).

(b) A standby letter of credit or other similar undertaking, however named or described, whether for domestic or international use, may be made subject to these Rules by express reference to them.

(c) An undertaking subject to these Rules may expressly modify or exclude their application.

(d) An undertaking subject to these Rules is hereinafter referred to as a "standby".

1.02 Relationship to Law and Other Rules

(a) These Rules supplement the applicable law to the extent not prohibited by that law.

(b) These Rules supersede conflicting provisions in any other rules of practice to which a standby letter of credit is also made subject.

1.03 Interpretative Principles

These Rules shall be interpreted as mercantile usage with regard for:

(a) integrity of standbys as reliable and efficient undertakings to pay;

(b) practice and terminology of banks and businesses in day-to-day transactions;

(c) consistency within the worldwide system of banking operations and commerce; and

(d) worldwide uniformity in their interpretation and application.

1.04 Effect of the Rules

Unless the context otherwise requires, or unless expressly modified or excluded, these Rules apply as terms and conditions incorporated into a standby, confirmation, advice, nomination, amendment, transfer, request for issuance, or other agreement of:

(i) the issuer;

(ii) the beneficiary to the extent it uses the standby;

(iii) any advisor;

(iv) any confirmer;

(v) any person nominated in the standby who acts or agrees to act; and

(vi) the applicant who authorizes issuance of the standby or otherwise agrees to the application of these Rules.

1.05 Exclusion of Matters Related to Due Issuance and Fraudulent or Abusive Drawing

These Rules do not define or otherwise provide for:

(a) power or authority to issue a standby;

(b) formal requirements for execution of a standby (e.g. a signed writing); or

(c) defenses to honour based on fraud, abuse, or similar matters.

These matters are left to applicable law.

General Principles

1.06 Nature of Standbys

(a) A standby is an irrevocable, independent, documentary, and binding undertaking when issued and need not so state.

(b) Because a standby is irrevocable, an issuer's obligations under a standby cannot be amended or cancelled by the issuer except as provided in the standby or as consented to by the person against whom the amendment or cancellation is asserted.

(c) Because a standby is independent, the enforceability of an issuer's obligations under a standby does not depend on:

(i) the issuer's right or ability to obtain reimbursement from the applicant;

(ii) the beneficiary's right to obtain payment from the applicant;

(iii) a reference in the standby to any reimbursement agreement or underlying transaction; or

(iv) the issuer's knowledge of performance or breach of any reimbursement agreement or underlying transaction.

(d) Because a standby is documentary, an issuer's obligations depend on the presentation of documents and an examination of required documents on their face.

(e) Because a standby or amendment is binding when issued, it is enforceable against an issuer whether or not the applicant authorized its issuance, the issuer received a fee, or the beneficiary received or relied on the standby or the amendment.

1.07 Independence of the Issuer-Beneficiary Relationship

An issuer's obligations toward the beneficiary are not affected by the issuer's rights and obligations toward the applicant under any applicable agreement, practice, or law.

1.08 Limits to Responsibilities

An issuer is not responsible for:

(a) performance or breach of any underlying transaction;

(b) accuracy, genuineness, or effect of any document presented under the standby;

(c) action or omission of others even if the other person is chosen by the issuer or nominated person; or

(d) observance of law or practice other than that chosen in the standby or applicable at the place of issuance.

Terminology

1.09 Defined Terms

In addition to the meanings given in standard banking practice and applicable law, the following terms have or include the meanings indicated below:

(a) Definitions

"Applicant" is a person who applies for issuance of a standby or for whose account it is issued, and includes (i) a person applying in its own name but for the account of another person or (ii) an issuer acting for its own account.

"Beneficiary" is a named person who is entitled to draw under a standby. See Rule 1.11(c)(ii).

"Business day" means a day on which the place of business at which the relevant act is to be performed is regularly open; and

"Banking day" means a day on which the relevant bank is regularly open at the place at which the relevant act is to be performed.

"Confirmer" is a person who, upon an issuer's nomination to do so, adds to the issuer's undertaking its own undertaking to honour a standby. See Rule 1.11(c)(i).

"Demand" means, depending on the context, either a request to honour a standby or a document that makes such request.

"Document" means a draft, demand, document of title, investment security, invoice, certificate of default, or any other representation of fact, law, right, or opinion, that upon presentation (whether in a paper or electronic medium), is capable of being examined for compliance with the terms and conditions of a standby.

"Drawing" means, depending on the context, either a demand presented or a demand honoured.

"Expiration date" means the latest day for a complying presentation provided in a standby.

"Person" includes a natural person, partnership, corporation, limited liability company, government agency, bank, trustee, and any other legal or commercial association or entity.

"Presentation" means, depending on the context, either the act of delivering documents for examination under a standby or the documents so delivered.

"Presenter" is a person who makes a presentation as or on behalf of a beneficiary or nominated person.

"Signature" includes any symbol executed or adopted by a person with a present intent to authenticate a document.

(b) Cross references

"Amendment"	—	Rule 2.06
"Advice"	—	Rule 2.05
"Approximately" ("About" or "Circa")	—	Rule 3.08(f)
"Assignment of Proceeds"	—	Rule 6.06
"Automatic amendment"	—	Rule 2.06(a)
"Copy"	—	Rule 4.15(d)
"Cover instructions"	—	Rule 5.08
"Honour"	—	Rule 2.01
"Issuer"	—	Rule 2.01
"Multiple presentations"	—	Rule 3.08(b)
"Nominated person"	—	Rule 2.04
"Non-documentary conditions"	—	Rule 4.11
"Original"	—	Rule 4.15(b) and (c)
"Partial drawing"	—	Rule 3.08(a)
"Standby"	—	Rule 1.01(d)
"Transfer"	—	Rule 6.01
"Transferee beneficiary"	—	Rule 1.11*(c)*(ii)
"Transfer by operation of law"	—	Rule 6.11

(c) Electronic presentations

The following terms in a standby providing for or permitting electronic presentation shall have the following meanings unless the context otherwise requires:

"Electronic record" means:

(i) a record (information that is inscribed on a tangible medium or that is stored in an electronic or other medium and is retrievable in perceivable form);

(ii) communicated by electronic means to a system for receiving, storing, re-transmitting, or otherwise processing information (data, text, images, sounds, codes, computer programs, software, databases, and the like); and

(iii) capable of being authenticated and then examined for compliance with the terms and conditions of the standby.

"Authenticate" means to verify an electronic record by generally accepted procedure or methodology in commercial practice:

(i) the identity of a sender or source, and

(ii) the integrity of or errors in the transmission of information content.

The criteria for assessing the integrity of information in an electronic record is whether the information has remained complete and unaltered, apart from the addition of any endorsement and any change which arises in the normal course of communication, storage, and display.

"Electronic signature" means letters, characters, numbers, or other symbols in electronic form, attached to or logically associated with an electronic record that are executed or adopted by a party with present intent to authenticate an electronic record.

"Receipt" occurs when:

(i) an electronic record enters in a form capable of being processed by the information system designated in the standby, or

(ii) an issuer retrieves an electronic record sent to an information system other than that designated by the issuer.

1.10 Redundant or Otherwise Undesirable Terms

(a) A standby should not or need not state that it is:

(i) unconditional or abstract (if it does, it signifies merely that payment under it is conditioned solely on presentation of specified documents);

(ii) absolute (if it does, it signifies merely that it is irrevocable);

(iii) primary (if it does, it signifies merely that it is the independent obligation of the issuer);

(iv) payable from the issuer's own funds (if it does, it signifies merely that payment under it does not depend on the availability of applicant funds and is made to satisfy the issuer's own independent obligation);

(v) clean or payable on demand (if it does, it signifies merely that it is payable upon presentation of a written demand or other documents specified in the standby).

(b) A standby should not use the term "and/or" (if it does it means either or both).

(c) The following terms have no single accepted meaning:

(i) and shall be disregarded: "callable", "divisible", "fractionable", "indivisible", and "transmissible".

(ii) and shall be disregarded unless their context gives them meaning: "assignable", "evergreen", "reinstate", and "revolving".

1.11 Interpretation of These Rules

(a) These Rules are to be interpreted in the context of applicable standard practice.

(b) In these Rules, "standby letter of credit" refers to the type of independent undertaking for which these Rules were intended, whereas "standby" refers to an undertaking subjected to these Rules.

(c) Unless the context otherwise requires:

(i) "Issuer" includes a "confirmer" as if the confirmer were a separate issuer and its confirmation were a separate standby issued for the account of the issuer;

(ii) "Beneficiary" includes a person to whom the named beneficiary has effectively transferred drawing rights ("transferee beneficiary");

(iii) "Including" means "including but not limited to";

(iv) "A or B" means "A or B or both"; "either A or B" means "A or B, but not both"; and "A and B" means "both A and B";

(v) Words in the singular number include the plural, and in the plural include the singular; and

(vi) Words of the neuter gender include any gender.

(d)(i) Use of the phrase "unless a standby otherwise states" or the like in a rule emphasizes that the text of the standby controls over the rule;

(ii) Absence of such a phrase in other rules does not imply that other rules have priority over the text of the standby;

(iii) Addition of the term "expressly" or "clearly" to the phrase "unless a standby otherwise states" or the like emphasizes that the rule should be excluded or modified only by wording in the standby that is specific and unambiguous; and

(iv) While the effect of all of these Rules may be varied by the text of the standby, variations of the effect of some of these Rules may disqualify the standby as an independent undertaking under applicable law.

(e) The phrase "stated in the standby" or the like refers to the actual text of a standby (whether as issued or effectively amended) whereas the phrase "provided in the standby" or the like refers to both the text of the standby and these Rules as incorporated.

RULE 2: OBLIGATIONS

2.01 Undertaking to Honour by Issuer and Any Confirmer to Beneficiary

(a) An issuer undertakes to the beneficiary to honour a presentation that appears on its face to comply with the terms and conditions of the standby in accordance with these Rules supplemented by standard standby practice.

(b) An issuer honours a complying presentation made to it by paying the amount demanded of it at sight, unless the standby provides for honour:

(i) by acceptance of a draft drawn by the beneficiary on the issuer, in which case the issuer honours by:

- timely accepting the draft; and
- thereafter paying the holder of the draft on presentation of the accepted draft on or after its maturity.

(ii) by deferred payment of a demand made by the beneficiary on the issuer, in which case the issuer honours by:

- timely incurring a deferred payment obligation; and
- thereafter paying at maturity.

(iii) by negotiation, in which case the issuer honours by paying the amount demanded at sight without recourse.

(c) An issuer acts in a timely manner if it pays at sight, accepts a draft, or undertakes a deferred payment obligation (or if it gives notice of dishonour) within the time permitted for examining the presentation and giving notice of dishonour.

(d)(i) A confirmer undertakes to honour a complying presentation made to it by paying the amount demanded of it at sight or, if the standby so states, by another method of honour consistent with the issuer's undertaking.

(ii) If the confirmation permits presentation to the issuer, then the confirmer undertakes also to honour upon the issuer's wrongful dishonour by performing as if the presentation had been made to the confirmer.

(iii) If the standby permits presentation to the confirmer, then the issuer undertakes also to honour upon the confirmer's wrongful dishonour by performing as if the presentation had been made to the issuer.

(e) An issuer honours by paying in immediately available funds in the currency designated in the standby unless the standby states it is payable by:

(i) payment of a monetary unit of account, in which case the undertaking is to pay in that unit of account; or

(ii) delivery of other items of value, in which case the undertaking is to deliver those items.

2.02 Obligation of Different Branches, Agencies, or Other Offices

For the purposes of these Rules, an issuer's branch, agency, or other office acting or undertaking to act under a standby in a capacity other than as issuer is obligated in that capacity only and shall be treated as a different person.

2.03 Conditions to Issuance

A standby is issued when it leaves an issuer's control unless it clearly specifies that it is not then "issued" or "enforceable". Statements that a standby is not "available", "operative", "effective", or the like do not affect its irrevocable and binding nature at the time it leaves the issuer's control.

2.04 Nomination

(a) A standby may nominate a person to advise, receive a presentation, effect a transfer, confirm, pay, negotiate, incur a deferred payment obligation, or accept a draft.

(b) Nomination does not obligate the nominated person to act except to the extent that the nominated person undertakes to act.

(c) A nominated person is not authorized to bind the person making the nomination.

2.05 Advice of Standby or Amendment

(a) Unless an advice states otherwise, it signifies that:

(i) the advisor has checked the apparent authenticity of the advised message in accordance with standard letter of credit practice; and

(ii) the advice accurately reflects what has been received.

(b) A person who is requested to advise a standby and decides not to do so should notify the requesting party.

2.06 When an Amendment Is Authorized and Binding

(a) If a standby expressly states that it is subject to "automatic amendment" by an increase or decrease in the amount available, an extension of the expiration date, or the like, the amendment is effective automatically without any further notification or consent beyond that expressly provided for in the standby. (Such an amendment may also be referred to as becoming effective "without amendment".)

(b) If there is no provision for automatic amendment, an amendment binds:

(i) the issuer when it leaves the issuer's control; and

(ii) the confirmer when it leaves the confirmer's control, unless the confirmer indicates that it does not confirm the amendment.

(c) If there is no provision for automatic amendment:

(i) the beneficiary must consent to the amendment for it to be binding;

(ii) the beneficiary's consent must be made by an express communication to the person advising the amendment unless the beneficiary presents documents which comply with the standby as amended and which would not comply with the standby prior to such amendment; and

(iii) an amendment does not require the applicant's consent to be binding on the issuer, the confirmer, or the beneficiary.

(d) Consent to only part of an amendment is a rejection of the entire amendment.

2.07 Routing of Amendments

(a) An issuer using another person to advise a standby must advise all amendments to that person.

(b) An amendment or cancellation of a standby does not affect the issuer's obligation to a nominated person that has acted within the scope of its nomination before receipt of notice of the amendment or cancellation.

(c) Non-extension of an automatically extendable (renewable) standby does not affect an issuer's obligation to a nominated person who has acted within the scope of its nomination before receipt of a notice of non-extension.

RULE 3: PRESENTATION

3.01 Complying Presentation Under a Standby

A standby should indicate the time, place and location within that place, person to whom, and medium in which presentation should be made. If so, presentation must be so made in order to comply. To the extent that a standby does not so indicate, presentation must be made in accordance with these Rules in order to be complying.

3.02 What Constitutes a Presentation?

The receipt of a document required by and presented under a standby constitutes a presentation requiring examination for compliance with the terms and conditions of the standby even if not all of the required documents have been presented.

3.03 Identification of Standby

(a) A presentation must identify the standby under which the presentation is made.

(b) A presentation may identify the standby by stating the complete reference number of the standby and the name and location of the issuer or by attaching the original or a copy of the standby.

(c) If the issuer cannot determine from the face of a document received that it should be processed under a standby or cannot identify the standby to which it relates, presentation is deemed to have been made on the date of identification.

3.04 Where and to Whom Complying Presentation Made?

(a) To comply, a presentation must be made at the place and any location at that place indicated in the standby or provided in these Rules.

(b) If no place of presentation to the issuer is indicated in the standby, presentation to the issuer must be made at the place of business from which the standby was issued.

(c) If a standby is confirmed, but no place for presentation is indicated in the confirmation, presentation for the purpose of obligating the confirmer (and the issuer) must be made at the place of business of the confirmer from which the confirmation was issued or to the issuer.

(d) If no location at a place of presentation is indicated (such as department, floor, room, station, mail stop, post office box, or other location), presentation may be made to:

(i) the general postal address indicated in the standby;

(ii) any location at the place designated to receive deliveries of mail or documents; or

(iii) any person at the place of presentation actually or apparently authorized to receive it.

3.05 When Timely Presentation Made?

(a) A presentation is timely if made at any time after issuance and before expiry on the expiration date.

(b) A presentation made after the close of business at the place of presentation is deemed to have been made on the next business day.

3.06 Complying Medium of Presentation

(a) To comply, a document must be presented in the medium indicated in the standby.

(b) Where no medium is indicated, to comply a document must be presented as a paper document, unless only a demand is required, in which case:

(i) a demand that is presented via S.W.I.F.T., tested telex, or other similar authenticated means by a beneficiary that is a S.W.I.F.T. participant or a bank complies; otherwise

(ii) a demand that is not presented as a paper document does not comply unless the issuer permits, in its sole discretion, the use of that medium.

(c) A document is not presented as a paper document if it is communicated by electronic means even if the issuer or nominated person receiving it generates a paper document from it.

(d) Where presentation in an electronic medium is indicated, to comply a document must be presented as an electronic record capable of being authenticated by the issuer or nominated person to whom it is presented.

3.07 Separateness of Each Presentation

(a) Making a non-complying presentation, withdrawing a presentation, or failing to make any one of a number of scheduled or permitted presentations does not waive or otherwise prejudice the right to make another timely presentation or a timely re-presentation whether or not the standby prohibits partial or multiple drawings or presentations.

(b) Wrongful dishonour of a complying presentation does not constitute dishonour of any other presentation under a standby or repudiation of the standby.

(c) Honour of a non-complying presentation, with or without notice of its non-compliance, does not waive requirements of a standby for other presentations.

3.08 Partial Drawing and Multiple Presentations; Amount of Drawings

(a) A presentation may be made for less than the full amount available ("partial drawing").

(b) More than one presentation ("multiple presentations") may be made.

(c) The statement "partial drawings prohibited" or a similar expression means that a presentation must be for the full amount available.

(d) The statement "multiple drawings prohibited" or a similar expression means that only one presentation may be made and honoured but that it may be for less than the full amount available.

(e) If a demand exceeds the amount available under the standby, the drawing is discrepant. Any document other than the demand stating an amount in excess of the amount demanded is not discrepant for that reason.

(f) Use of "approximately", "about", "circa", or a similar word permits a tolerance not to exceed 10 per cent more or 10 per cent less of the amount to which such word refers.

3.09 Extend or Pay

A beneficiary's request to extend the expiration date of the standby or, alternatively, to pay the amount available under it:

(a) is a presentation demanding payment under the standby, to be examined as such in accordance with these Rules; and

(b) implies that the beneficiary:

(i) consents to the amendment to extend the expiry date to the date requested;

(ii) requests the issuer to exercise its discretion to seek the approval of the applicant and to issue that amendment;

(iii) upon issuance of that amendment, retracts its demand for payment; and

(iv) consents to the maximum time available under these Rules for examination and notice of dishonour.

3.10 No Notice of Receipt of Presentation

An issuer is not required to notify the applicant of receipt of a presentation under the standby.

3.11 Issuer Waiver and Applicant Consent to Waiver of Presentation Rules

In addition to other discretionary provisions in a standby or these Rules, an issuer may, in its sole discretion, without notice to or consent of the applicant and without effect on the applicant's obligations to the issuer, waive:

(a) the following Rules and any similar terms stated in the standby which are primarily for the issuer's benefit or operational convenience:

(i) treatment of documents received, at the request of the presenter, as having been presented at a later date (Rule 3.02);

(ii) identification of a presentation to the standby under which it is presented (Rule 3.03(a));

(iii) where and to whom presentation is made (Rule 3.04(b), (c), and (d)), except the country of presentation stated in the standby; or

(iv) treatment of a presentation made after the close of business as if it were made on the next business day (Rule 3.05(b)).

(b) the following Rule but not similar terms stated in the standby:

(i) a required document dated after the date of its stated presentation (Rule 4.06); or

(ii) the requirement that a document issued by the beneficiary be in the language of the standby (Rule 4.04).

(c) the following Rule relating to the operational integrity of the standby only in so far as the bank is in fact dealing with the true beneficiary:

-- acceptance of a demand in an electronic medium (Rule 3.06(b)).

Waiver by the confirmer requires the consent of the issuer with respect to paragraphs (b) and (c) of this Rule.

3.12 Original Standby Lost, Stolen, Mutilated, or Destroyed

(a) If an original standby is lost, stolen, mutilated, or destroyed, the issuer need not replace it or waive any requirement that the original be presented under the standby.

(b) If the issuer agrees to replace an original standby or to waive a requirement for its presentation, it may provide a replacement or copy to the beneficiary without affecting the applicant's obligations to the issuer to reimburse, but, if it does so, the issuer must mark the replacement or copy as such. The issuer may, in its sole discretion, require indemnities satisfactory to it from the beneficiary and assurances from nominated persons that no payment has been made.

Closure on Expiry Date

3.13 Expiration Date on a Non-Business Day

(a) If the last day for presentation stated in a standby (whether stated to be the expiration date or the date by which documents must be received) is not a business day of the issuer or nominated person where presentation is to be made, then presentation made there on the first following business day shall be deemed timely.

(b) A nominated person to whom such a presentation is made must so notify the issuer.

3.14 Closure on a Business Day and Authorization of Another Reasonable Place for Presentation

(a) If on the last business day for presentation the place for presentation stated in a standby is for any reason closed and presentation is not timely made because of the closure, then the last day for presentation is automatically extended to the day occurring thirty calendar days after the place for presentation re-opens for business, unless the standby otherwise provides.

(b) Upon or in anticipation of closure of the place of presentation, an issuer may authorize another reasonable place for presentation in the standby or in a communication received by the beneficiary. If it does so, then

(i) presentation must be made at that reasonable place; and

(ii) if the communication is received fewer than thirty calendar days before the last day for presentation and for that reason presentation is not timely made, the last day for presentation is automatically extended to the day occurring thirty calendar days after the last day for presentation.

RULE 4: EXAMINATION

4.01 Examination for Compliance

(a) Demands for honour of a standby must comply with the terms and conditions of the standby.

(b) Whether a presentation appears to comply is determined by examining the presentation on its face against the terms and conditions stated in the standby as interpreted and supplemented by these Rules which are to be read in the context of standard standby practice.

4.02 Non-Examination of Extraneous Documents

Documents presented which are not required by the standby need not be examined and, in any event, shall be disregarded for purposes of determining compliance of the presentation. They may without responsibility be returned to the presenter or passed on with the other documents presented.

4.03 Examination for Inconsistency

An issuer or nominated person is required to examine documents for inconsistency with each other only to the extent provided in the standby.

4.04 Language of Documents

The language of all documents issued by the beneficiary is to be that of the standby.

4.05 Issuer of Documents

Any required document must be issued by the beneficiary unless the standby indicates that the document is to be issued by a third person or the document is of a type that standard standby practice requires to be issued by a third person.

4.06 Date of Documents

The issuance date of a required document may be earlier but not later than the date of its presentation.

4.07 Required Signature on a Document

(a) A required document need not be signed unless the standby indicates that the document must be signed or the document is of a type that standard standby practice requires be signed.

(b) A required signature may be made in any manner that corresponds to the medium in which the signed document is presented.

(c) Unless a standby specifies:

(i) the name of a person who must sign a document, any signature or authentication will be regarded as a complying signature.

(ii) the status of a person who must sign, no indication of status is necessary.

(d) If a standby specifies that a signature must be made by:

(i) a named natural person without requiring that the signer's status be identified, a signature complies that appears to be that of the named person;

(ii) a named legal person or government agency without identifying who is to sign on its behalf or its status, any signature complies that appears to have been made on behalf of the named legal person or government agency; or

(iii) a named natural person, legal person, or government agency requiring the status of the signer be indicated, a signature complies which appears to be that of the named natural person, legal person, or government agency and indicates its status.

4.08 Demand Document Implied

If a standby does not specify any required document, it will still be deemed to require a documentary demand for payment.

4.09 Identical Wording and Quotation Marks

If a standby requires:

(a) a statement without specifying precise wording, then the wording in the document presented must appear to convey the same meaning as that required by the standby;

(b) specified wording by the use of quotation marks, blocked wording, or an attached exhibit or form, the typographical errors in spelling, punctuation, spacing, or the like that are apparent when read in context are not required to be duplicated and blank lines or spaces for data may be completed in any manner not inconsistent with the standby; or

(c) specified wording by the use of quotation marks, blocked wording, or an attached exhibit or form, and also provides that the specified wording be "exact" or "identical", then the wording in the documents presented must duplicate the specified wording, including typographical errors in spelling, punctuation, spacing and the like, as well as blank lines and spaces for data must be exactly reproduced.

4.10 Applicant Approval

A standby should not specify that a required document be issued, signed, or counter-signed by the applicant. However, if the standby includes such a requirement, the issuer may not waive the requirement and is not responsible for the applicant's withholding of the document or signature.

4.11 Non-Documentary Terms or Conditions

(a) A standby term or condition which is non-documentary must be disregarded whether or not it affects the issuer's obligation to treat a presentation as complying or to treat the standby as issued, amended, or terminated.

(b) Terms or conditions are non-documentary if the standby does not require presentation of a document in which they are to be evidenced and if their fulfillment cannot be determined by the issuer from the issuer's own records or within the issuer's normal operations.

(c) Determinations from the issuer's own records or within the issuer's normal operations include determinations of:

(i) when, where, and how documents are presented or otherwise delivered to the issuer;

(ii) when, where, and how communications affecting the standby are sent or received by the issuer, beneficiary, or any nominated person;

(iii) amounts transferred into or out of accounts with the issuer; and

(iv) amounts determinable from a published index (e.g. if a standby provides for determining amounts of interest accruing according to published interest rates).

(d) An issuer need not re-compute a beneficiary's computations under a formula stated or referenced in a standby except to the extent that the standby so provides.

4.12 Formality of Statements in Documents

(a) A required statement need not be accompanied by a solemnity, officialization, or any other formality.

(b) If a standby provides for the addition of a formality to a required statement by the person making it without specifying form or content, the statement complies if it indicates that it was declared, averred, warranted, attested, sworn under oath, affirmed, certified, or the like.

(c) If a standby provides for a statement to be witnessed by another person without specifying form or content, the witnessed statement complies if it appears to contain a signature of a person other than the beneficiary with an indication that the person is acting as a witness.

(d) If a standby provides for a statement to be counter-signed, legalized, visaed, or the like by a person other than the beneficiary acting in a governmental, judicial, corporate, or other representative capacity without specifying form or content, the statement complies if it contains the signature of a person other than the beneficiary and includes an indication of that person's representative capacity and the organization on whose behalf the person has acted.

4.13 No Responsibility to Identify Beneficiary

Except to the extent that a standby requires presentation of an electronic record:

(a) a person honouring a presentation has no obligation to the applicant to ascertain the identity of any person making a presentation or any assignee of proceeds;

(b) payment to a named beneficiary, transferee, an acknowledged assignee, successor by operation of law, to an account or account number stated in the standby or in a cover instruction from the beneficiary or nominated person fulfils the obligation under the standby to effect payment.

4.14 Name of Acquired or Merged Issuer or Confirmer

If the issuer or confirmer is reorganized, merged, or changes its name, any required reference by name to the issuer or confirmer in the documents presented may be to it or its successor.

4.15 Original, Copy, and Multiple Documents

(a) A presented document must be an original.

(b) Presentation of an electronic record, where an electronic presentation is permitted or required, is deemed to be an "original".

(c)(i) A presented document is deemed to be an original unless it appears on its face to have been reproduced from an original.

(ii) A document which appears to have been reproduced from an original is deemed to be an original if the signature or authentication appears to be original.

(d) A standby that requires presentation of a "copy" permits presentation of either an original or copy unless the standby states that only a copy be presented or otherwise addresses the disposition of all originals.

(e) If multiples of the same document are requested, only one must be an original unless:

(i) "duplicate originals" or "multiple originals" are requested in which case all must be originals; or

(ii) "two copies", "two-fold", or the like are requested in which case either originals or copies may be presented.

Standby Document Types

4.16 Demand for Payment

(a) A demand for payment need not be separate from the beneficiary's statement or other required document.

(b) If a separate demand is required, it must contain:

(i) a demand for payment from the beneficiary directed to the issuer or nominated person;

(ii) a date indicating when the demand was issued;

(iii) the amount demanded; and

(iv) the beneficiary's signature.

(c) A demand may be in the form of a draft or other instruction, order, or request to pay. If a standby requires presentation of a "draft" or "bill of exchange", that draft or bill of exchange need not be in negotiable form unless the standby so states.

4.17 Statement of Default or Other Drawing Event

If a standby requires a statement, certificate, or other recital of a default or other drawing event and does not specify content, the document complies if it contains:

(a) a representation to the effect that payment is due because a drawing event described in the standby has occurred;

(b) a date indicating when it was issued; and

(c) the beneficiary's signature.

4.18 Negotiable Documents

If a standby requires presentation of a document that is transferable by endorsement and delivery without stating whether, how, or to whom endorsement must be made, then the document may be presented without endorsement, or, if endorsed, the endorsement may be in blank and, in any event, the document may be issued or negotiated with or without recourse.

4.19 Legal or Judicial Documents

If a standby requires presentation of a government-issued document, a court order, an arbitration award, or the like, a document or a copy is deemed to comply if it appears to be:

(i) issued by a government agency, court, tribunal, or the like;

(ii) suitably titled or named;

(iii) signed;

(iv) dated; and

(v) originally certified or authenticated by an official of a government agency, court, tribunal, or the like.

4.20 Other Documents

(a) If a standby requires a document other than one whose content is specified in these Rules without specifying the issuer, data content, or wording, a document complies if it appears to be appropriately titled or to serve the function of that type of document under standard standby practice.

(b) A document presented under a standby is to be examined in the context of standby practice under these Rules even if the document is of a type (such as a commercial invoice, transport documents, insurance documents or the like) for which the Uniform Customs and Practice for Documentary Credits contains detailed rules.

4.21 Request to Issue Separate Undertaking

If a standby requests that the beneficiary of the standby issue its own separate undertaking to another (whether or not the standby recites the text of that undertaking):

(a) the beneficiary receives no rights other than its rights to draw under the standby even if the issuer pays a fee to the beneficiary for issuing the separate undertaking;

(b) neither the separate undertaking nor any documents presented under it need be presented to the issuer; and

(c) if originals or copies of the separate undertaking or documents presented under it are received by the issuer although not required to be presented as a condition to honour of the standby:

(i) the issuer need not examine, and, in any event, shall disregard their compliance or consistency with the standby, with the beneficiary's demand under the standby, or with the beneficiary's separate undertaking; and

(ii) the issuer may without responsibility return them to the presenter or forward them to the applicant with the presentation.

RULE 5: NOTICE, PRECLUSION, AND DISPOSITION OF DOCUMENTS

5.01 Timely Notice of Dishonour

(a) Notice of dishonour must be given within a time after presentation of documents which is not unreasonable.

(i) Notice given within three business days is deemed to be not unreasonable and beyond seven business days is deemed to be unreasonable.

(ii) Whether the time within which notice is given is unreasonable does not depend upon an imminent deadline for presentation.

(iii) The time for calculating when notice of dishonour must be given begins on the business day following the business day of presentation.

(iv) Unless a standby otherwise expressly states a shortened time within which notice of dishonour must be given, the issuer has no obligation to accelerate its examination of a presentation.

(b)(i) The means by which a notice of dishonour is to be given is by telecommunication, if available, and, if not, by another available means which allows for prompt notice.

(ii) If notice of dishonour is received within the time permitted for giving the notice, then it is deemed to have been given by prompt means.

(c) Notice of dishonour must be given to the person from whom the documents were received (whether the beneficiary, nominated person, or person other than a delivery person) except as otherwise requested by the presenter.

5.02 Statement of Grounds for Dishonour

A notice of dishonour shall state all discrepancies upon which dishonour is based.

5.03 Failure to Give Timely Notice of Dishonour

(a) Failure to give notice of a discrepancy in a notice of dishonour within the time and by the means specified in the standby or these rules precludes assertion of that discrepancy in any document containing the discrepancy that is retained or re-presented, but does not preclude assertion of that discrepancy in any different presentation under the same or a separate standby.

(b) Failure to give notice of dishonour or acceptance or acknowledgement that a deferred payment undertaking has been incurred obligates the issuer to pay at maturity.

5.04 Notice of Expiry

Failure to give notice that a presentation was made after the expiration date does not preclude dishonour for that reason.

5.05 Issuer Request for Applicant Waiver Without Request by Presenter

If the issuer decides that a presentation does not comply and if the presenter does not otherwise instruct, the issuer may, in its sole discretion, request the applicant to waive non-compliance or otherwise to authorize honour within the time available for giving notice of dishonour but without extending it. Obtaining the applicant's waiver does not obligate the issuer to waive non-compliance.

5.06 Issuer Request for Applicant Waiver upon Request of Presenter

If, after receipt of notice of dishonour, a presenter requests that the presented documents be forwarded to the issuer or that the issuer seek the applicant's waiver:

(a) no person is obligated to forward the discrepant documents or seek the applicant's waiver;

(b) the presentation to the issuer remains subject to these Rules unless departure from them is expressly consented to by the presenter; and

(c) if the documents are forwarded or if a waiver is sought:

(i) the presenter is precluded from objecting to the discrepancies notified to it by the issuer;

(ii) the issuer is not relieved from examining the presentation under these Rules;

(iii) the issuer is not obligated to waive the discrepancy even if the applicant waives it; and

(iv) the issuer must hold the documents until it receives a response from the applicant or is requested by the presenter to return the documents, and if the issuer receives no such response or request within ten business days of its notice of dishonour, it may return the documents to the presenter.

5.07 Disposition of Documents

Dishonoured documents must be returned, held, or disposed of as reasonably instructed by the presenter. Failure to give notice of the disposition of documents in the notice of dishonour does not preclude the issuer from asserting any defense otherwise available to it against honour.

5.08 Cover Instructions/Transmittal Letter

(a) Instructions accompanying a presentation made under a standby may be relied on to the extent that they are not contrary to the terms or conditions of the standby, the demand, or these Rules.

(b) Representations made by a nominated person accompanying a presentation may be relied upon to the extent that they are not contrary to the terms or conditions of a standby or these Rules.

(c) Notwithstanding receipt of instructions, an issuer or nominated person may pay, give notice, return the documents, or otherwise deal directly with the presenter.

(d) A statement in the cover letter that the documents are discrepant does not relieve the issuer from examining the presentation for compliance.

5.09 Applicant Notice of Objection

(a) An applicant must timely object to an issuer's honour of a noncomplying presentation by giving timely notice by prompt means.

(b) An applicant acts timely if it objects to discrepancies by sending a notice to the issuer stating the discrepancies on which the objection is based within a time after the applicant's receipt of the documents which is not unreasonable.

(c) Failure to give a timely notice of objection by prompt means precludes assertion by the applicant against the issuer of any discrepancy or other matter apparent on the face of the documents received by the applicant, but does not preclude assertion of that objection to any different presentation under the same or a different standby.

RULE 6: TRANSFER, ASSIGNMENT, AND TRANSFER BY OPERATION OF LAW

Transfer of Drawing Rights

6.01 Request to Transfer Drawing Rights

Where a beneficiary requests that an issuer or nominated person honour a drawing from another person as if that person were the beneficiary, these Rules on transfer of drawing rights ("transfer") apply.

6.02 When Drawing Rights Are Transferable

(a) A standby is not transferable unless it so states.

(b) A standby that states that it is transferable without further provision means that drawing rights:

(i) may be transferred in their entirety more than once;

(ii) may not be partially transferred; and

(iii) may not be transferred unless the issuer (including the confirmer) or another person specifically nominated in the standby agrees to and effects the transfer requested by the beneficiary.

6.03 Conditions to Transfer

An issuer of a transferable standby or a nominated person need not effect a transfer unless:

(a) it is satisfied as to the existence and authenticity of the original standby; and

(b) the beneficiary submits or fulfils:

(i) a request in a form acceptable to the issuer or nominated person including the effective date of the transfer and the name and address of the transferee;

(ii) the original standby;

(iii) verification of the signature of the person signing for the beneficiary;

(iv) verification of the authority of the person signing for the beneficiary;

(v) payment of the transfer fee; and

(vi) any other reasonable requirements.

6.04 Effect of Transfer on Required Documents

Where there has been a transfer of drawing rights in their entirety:

(a) a draft or demand must be signed by the transferee beneficiary; and

(b) the name of the transferee beneficiary may be used in place of the name of the transferor beneficiary in any other required document.

6.05 Reimbursement for Payment Based on a Transfer

An issuer or nominated person paying under a transfer pursuant to Rule 6.03*(a)*, *(b)*(i), and *(b)*(ii) is entitled to reimbursement as if it had made payment to the beneficiary.

Acknowledgement of Assignment of Proceeds

6.06 Assignment of Proceeds

Where an issuer or nominated person is asked to acknowledge a beneficiary's request to pay an assignee all or part of any proceeds of the beneficiary's drawing under the standby, these Rules on acknowledgement of an assignment of proceeds apply except where applicable law otherwise requires.

6.07 Request for Acknowledgement

(a) Unless applicable law otherwise requires, an issuer or nominated person

(i) is not obligated to give effect to an assignment of proceeds which it has not acknowledged; and

(ii) is not obligated to acknowledge the assignment.

(b) If an assignment is acknowledged:

(i) the acknowledgement confers no rights with respect to the standby to the assignee who is only entitled to the proceeds assigned, if any, and whose rights may be affected by amendment or cancellation; and

(ii) the rights of the assignee are subject to:

(a) the existence of any net proceeds payable to the beneficiary by the person making the acknowledgement;

(b) rights of nominated persons and transferee beneficiaries;

(c) rights of other acknowledged assignees; and

(d) any other rights or interests that may have priority under applicable law.

6.08 Conditions to Acknowledgement of Assignment of Proceeds

An issuer or nominated person may condition its acknowledgement on receipt of:

(a) the original standby for examination or notation;

(b) verification of the signature of the person signing for the beneficiary;

(c) verification of the authority of the person signing for the beneficiary;

(d) an irrevocable request signed by the beneficiary for acknowledgement of the assignment that includes statements, covenants, indemnities, and other provisions which may be contained in the issuer's or nominated person's required form requesting acknowledgement of assignment, such as:

(i) the identity of the affected drawings if the standby permits multiple drawings;

(ii) the full name, legal form, location, and mailing address of the beneficiary and the assignee;

(iii) details of any request affecting the method of payment or delivery of the standby proceeds;

(iv) limitation on partial assignments and prohibition of successive assignments;

(v) statements regarding the legality and relative priority of the assignment; or

(vi) right of recovery by the issuer or nominated person of any proceeds received by the assignee that are recoverable from the beneficiary;

(e) payment of a fee for the acknowledgement; and

(f) fulfilment of other reasonable requirements.

6.09 Conflicting Claims to Proceeds

If there are conflicting claims to proceeds, then payment to an acknowledged assignee may be suspended pending resolution of the conflict.

6.10 Reimbursement for Payment Based on an Assignment

An issuer or nominated person paying under an acknowledged assignment pursuant to Rule 6.08(a) and (b) is entitled to reimbursement as if it had made payment to the beneficiary. If the beneficiary is a bank, the acknowledgement may be based solely upon an authenticated communication.

Transfer by Operation of Law

6.11 Transferee by Operation of Law

Where an heir, personal representative, liquidator, trustee, receiver, successor corporation, or similar person who claims to be designated by law to succeed to the interests of a beneficiary presents documents in its own name as if it were the authorized transferee of the beneficiary, these Rules on transfer by operation of law apply.

6.12 Additional Document in Event of Drawing in Successor's Name

A claimed successor may be treated as if it were an authorized transferee of a beneficiary's drawing rights in their entirety if it presents an additional document or documents which appear to be issued by a public official or representative (including a judicial officer) and indicate:

(a) that the claimed successor is the survivor of a merger, consolidation, or similar action of a corporation, limited liability company, or other similar organization;

(b) that the claimed successor is authorized or appointed to act on behalf of the named beneficiary or its estate because of an insolvency proceeding;

(c) that the claimed successor is authorized or appointed to act on behalf of the named beneficiary because of death or incapacity; or

(d) that the name of the named beneficiary has been changed to that of the claimed successor.

6.13 Suspension of Obligations upon Presentation by Successor

An issuer or nominated person which receives a presentation from a claimed successor which complies in all respects except for the name of the beneficiary:

(a) may request in a manner satisfactory as to form and substance:

(i) a legal opinion;

(ii) an additional document referred to in Rule 6.12 (Additional document in event of drawing in successor's name) from a public official;

(iii) statements, covenants, and indemnities regarding the status of the claimed successor as successor by operation of law;

(iv) payment of fees reasonably related to these determinations; and

(v) anything which may be required for a transfer under Rule 6.03 (Conditions to transfer) or an acknowledgement of assignment of proceeds under Rule 6.08 (Conditions to acknowledgement of assignment of proceeds);

but such documentation shall not constitute a required document for purposes of expiry of the standby.

(b) Until the issuer or nominated person receives the requested documentation, its obligation to honour or give notice of dishonour is suspended, but any deadline for presentation of required documents is not thereby extended.

6.14 Reimbursement for Payment Based on a Transfer by Operation of Law

An issuer or nominated person paying under a transfer by operation of law pursuant to Rule 6.12 (Additional document in event of drawing in successor's name) is entitled to reimbursement as if it had made payment to the beneficiary.

RULE 7: CANCELLATION

7.01 When an Irrevocable Standby Is Cancelled or Terminated

A beneficiary's rights under a standby may not be cancelled without its consent. Consent may be evidenced in writing or by an action such as return of the original standby in a manner which implies that the beneficiary consents to cancellation. A beneficiary's consent to cancellation is irrevocable when communicated to the issuer.

7.02 Issuer's Discretion Regarding a Decision to Cancel

Before acceding to a beneficiary's authorization to cancel and treating the standby as cancelled for all purposes, an issuer may require in a manner satisfactory as to form and substance:

(a) the original standby;

(b) verification of the signature of the person signing for the beneficiary;

(c) verification of the authorization of the person signing for the beneficiary;

(d) a legal opinion;

(e) an irrevocable authority signed by the beneficiary for cancellation that includes statements, covenants, indemnities, and similar provisions contained in a required form;

(f) satisfaction that the obligation of any confirmer has been cancelled;

(g) satisfaction that there has not been a transfer or payment by any nominated person; and

(h) any other reasonable measure.

RULE 8: REIMBURSEMENT OBLIGATIONS

8.01 Right to Reimbursement

(a) Where payment is made against a complying presentation in accordance with these Rules, reimbursement must be made by:

(i) an applicant to an issuer requested to issue a standby; and

(ii) an issuer to a person nominated to honour or otherwise give value.

(b) An applicant must indemnify the issuer against all claims, obligations, and responsibilities (including attorney's fees) arising out of:

(i) the imposition of law or practice other than that chosen in the standby or applicable at the place of issuance;

(ii) the fraud, forgery, or illegal action of others; or

(iii) the issuer's performance of the obligations of a confirmer that wrongfully dishonours a confirmation.

(c) This Rule supplements any applicable agreement, course of dealing, practice, custom or usage providing for reimbursement or indemnification on lesser or other grounds.

8.02 Charges for Fees and Costs

(a) An applicant must pay the issuer's charges and reimburse the issuer for any charges that the issuer is obligated to pay to persons nominated with the applicant's consent to advise, confirm, honour, negotiate, transfer, or to issue a separate undertaking.

(b) An issuer is obligated to pay the charges of other persons:

(i) if they are payable in accordance with the terms of the standby; or

(ii) if they are the reasonable and customary fees and expenses of a person requested by the issuer to advise, honour, negotiate, transfer, or to issue a separate undertaking, and they are unrecovered and unrecoverable from the beneficiary or other presenter because no demand is made under the standby.

8.03 Refund of Reimbursement

A nominated person that obtains reimbursement before the issuer timely dishonours the presentation must refund the reimbursement with interest if the issuer dishonours. The refund does not preclude the nominated person's wrongful dishonour claims.

8.04 Bank-to-Bank Reimbursement

Any instruction or authorization to obtain reimbursement from another bank is subject to the International Chamber of Commerce standard rules for bank-to-bank reimbursements.

RULE 9: TIMING

9.01 Duration of Standby

A standby must:

(a) contain an expiry date; or

(b) permit the issuer to terminate the standby upon reasonable prior notice or payment.

9.02 Effect of Expiration on Nominated Person

The rights of a nominated person that acts within the scope of its nomination are not affected by the subsequent expiry of the standby.

9.03 Calculation of Time

(a) A period of time within which an action must be taken under these Rules begins to run on the first business day following the business day when the action could have been undertaken at the place where the action should have been undertaken.

(b) An extension period starts on the calendar day following the stated expiry date even if either day falls on a day when the issuer is closed.

9.04 Time of Day of Expiration

If no time of day is stated for expiration, it occurs at the close of business at the place of presentation.

9.05 Retention of Standby

Retention of the original standby does not preserve any rights under the standby after the right to demand payment ceases.

RULE 10: SYNDICATION/PARTICIPATION

10.01 Syndication

If a standby with more than one issuer does not state to whom presentation may be made, presentation may be made to any issuer with binding effect on all issuers.

10.02 Participation

(a) Unless otherwise agreed between an applicant and an issuer, the issuer may sell participations in the issuer's rights against the applicant and any presenter and may disclose relevant applicant information in confidence to potential participants.

(b) An issuer's sale of participations does not affect the obligations of the issuer under the standby or create any rights or obligations between the beneficiary and any participant.

24) Uniform Rules for Demand Guarantees (URDG 758)[1]

Article 1 - Application of URDG

a. The Uniform Rules for Demand Guarantees ("URDG") apply to any demand guarantee or counter-guarantee that expressly indicates it is subject to them. They are binding on all parties to the demand guarantee or counter-guarantee except so far as the demand guarantee or counter-guarantee modifies or excludes them.

b. Where, at the request of a counter-guarantor, a demand guarantee is issued subject to the URDG, the counter-guarantee shall also be subject to the URDG unless the counter-guarantee excludes the URDG. However, a demand guarantee does not become subject to the URDG merely because the counter-guarantee is subject to the URDG.

c. Where, at the request or with the agreement of the instructing party, a demand guarantee or counter-guarantee is issued subject to the URDG, the instructing party is deemed to have accepted the rights and obligations expressly ascribed to it in these rules.

d. Where a demand guarantee or counter-guarantee issued on or after 1 July 2010 states that it is subject to the URDG without stating whether the 1992 version or the 2010 revision is to apply or indicating the publication number, the demand guarantee or counter-guarantee shall be subject to the URDG 2010 revision.

Article 2 - Definitions

In these rules:

advising party means the party that advises the guarantee at the request of the guarantor;

applicant means the party indicated in the guarantee as having its obligation under the underlying relationship supported by the guarantee. The applicant may or may not be the instructing party;

application means the request for the issue of the guarantee;

authenticated, when applied to an electronic document, means that the party to whom that document is presented is able to verify the apparent identity of the sender and whether the data received have remained complete and unaltered;

beneficiary means the party in whose favour a guarantee is issued;

business day means a day on which the place of business where an act of a kind subject to these rules is to be performed is regularly open for the performance of such an act;

charges mean any commissions, fees, costs or expenses due to any party acting under a guarantee governed by these rules;

complying demand means a demand that meets the requirements of a complying presentation;

complying presentation under a guarantee means a presentation that is in accordance with, first, the terms and conditions of that guarantee, second, these rules so far as consistent with those terms and conditions and, third, in the absence of a relevant provision in the guarantee or these rules, international standard demand guarantee practice;

counter-guarantee means any signed undertaking, however named or described, that is given by the counter-guarantor to another party to procure the issue by that other party of a guarantee

---

or another counter-guarantee, and that provides for payment upon the presentation of a complying demand under the counter-guarantee issued in favour of that party;

counter-guarantor means the party issuing a counter-guarantee, whether in favour of a guarantor or another counter-guarantor, and includes a party acting for its own account;

demand means a signed document by the beneficiary demanding payment under a guarantee;

demand guarantee or **guarantee** means any signed undertaking, however named or described, providing for payment on presentation of a complying demand;

document means a signed or unsigned record of information, in paper or in electronic form, that is capable of being reproduced in tangible form by the person to whom it is presented. Under these rules, a document includes a demand and a supporting statement;

expiry means the expiry date or the expiry event or, if both are specified, the earlier of the two;

expiry date means the date specified in the guarantee on or before which a presentation may be made;

expiry event means an event which under the terms of the guarantee results in its expiry, whether immediately or within a specified time after the event occurs, for which purpose the event is deemed to occur only:

a. when a document specified in the guarantee as indicating the occurrence of the event is presented to the guarantor, or

b. if no such document is specified in the guarantee, when the occurrence of the event becomes determinable from the guarantor's own records.

guarantee, see demand guarantee;

guarantor means the party issuing a guarantee, and includes a party acting for its own account;

guarantor's own records means records of the guarantor showing amounts credited to or debited from accounts held with the guarantor, provided the record of those credits or debits enables the guarantor to identify the guarantee to which they relate;

instructing party means the party, other than the counter-guarantor, who gives instructions to issue a guarantee or counter-guarantee and is responsible for indemnifying the guarantor or, in the case of a counter-guarantee, the counter-guarantor. The instructing party may or may not be the applicant;

presentation means the delivery of a document under a guarantee to the guarantor or the document so delivered. It includes a presentation other than for a demand, for example, a presentation for the purpose of triggering the expiry of the guarantee or a variation of its amount;

presenter means a person who makes a presentation as or on behalf of the beneficiary or the applicant, as the case may be;

signed, when applied to a document, a guarantee or a counter-guarantee, means that an original of the same is signed by or on behalf of its issuer, whether by an electronic signature that can be authenticated by the party to whom that document, guarantee or counter-guarantee is presented or by handwriting, facsimile signature, perforated signature, stamp, symbol or other mechanical method;

supporting statement means the statement referred to in either Article 15 (a) or Article 15 (b);

underlying relationship means the contract, tender conditions or other relationship between the applicant and the beneficiary on which the guarantee is based.

Article 3 - Interpretation

In these rules;

a. Branches of a guarantor in different countries are considered to be separate entities.

b. Except where the context otherwise requires, a guarantee includes a counter-guarantee and any amendment to either, a guarantor includes a counter-guarantor, and a beneficiary includes the party in whose favour a counter-guarantee is issued.

c. Any requirement for presentation of one or more originals or copies of an electronic document is satisfied by the presentation of one electronic document.

d. When used with a date or dates to determine the start, end or duration of any period, the terms (I.) "from", "to", "until", "till" and "between", include; and (ii.) "before" and "after" exclude, the date or dates mentioned.

e. The term "within", when used in connection with a period after a given date or event, excludes that date or the date of that event but includes the last date of that period.

f. Terms such as "first class", "well-known", "qualified", "independent", "official", "competent" or "local" when used to describe the issuer of a document allow any issuer except the beneficiary or the applicant to issue that document.

Article 4 - Issue and Effectiveness

a. A guarantee is issued when it leaves the control of the guarantor.

b. A guarantee is irrevocable on issue even if it does not state this.

c. The beneficiary may present a demand from the time of issue of the guarantee or such later time or event as the guarantee provides.

Article 5 - Independence of Guarantee and Counter-Guarantee

a. A guarantee is by its nature independent of the underlying relationship and the application, and the guarantor is in no way concerned with or bound by such relationship. A reference in the guarantee to the underlying relationship for the purpose of identifying it does not change the independent nature of the guarantee. The undertaking of a guarantor to pay under the guarantee is not subject to claims or defences arising from any relationship other than a relationship between the guarantor and the beneficiary.

b. A counter-guarantee is by its nature independent of the guarantee, the underlying relationship, the application and any other counter-guarantee to which it relates, and the counter-guarantor is in no way concerned with or bound by such relationship. A reference in the counter-guarantee to the underlying relationship for the purpose of identifying it does not change the independent nature of the counter-guarantee. The undertaking of a counter-guarantor to pay under the counter-guarantee is not subject to claims or defences arising from any relationship other than a relationship between the counter-guarantor and the guarantor or other counter-guarantor to whom the counter-guarantee is issued.

Article 6 - Documents v. Goods, Services or Performance

Guarantors deal with documents and not with goods, services or performance to which the documents may relate.

Article 7 - Non-Documentary Conditions

A guarantee should not contain a condition other than a date or the lapse of a period without specifying a document to indicate compliance with that condition. If the guarantee does not specify any such document and the fulfilment of the condition cannot be determined from the guarantor's own records or from an index specified in the guarantee, then the guarantor will deem such condition as not stated and will disregard it except for the purpose of determining whether data that may appear in a document specified in and presented under the guarantee do not conflict with data in the guarantee.

Article 8 - Content of Instructions and Guarantees

All instructions for the issue of guarantees and guarantees themselves should be clear and precise and should avoid excessive detail. It is recommended that all guarantees specify:

a. the applicant;

b. the beneficiary;

c. the guarantor;

d. a reference number or other information identifying the underlying relationship;

e. a reference number or other information identifying the issued guarantee or in the case of a counter-guarantee, the issued counter-guarantee;

f. the amount or maximum amount payable and the currency in which it is payable;

g. the expiry of the guarantee;

h. any terms for demanding payment;

i. whether a demand or other document shall be presented in paper and/or electronic form;

j. the language of any document specified in the guarantee; and

k. the party liable for the payment of any charges.

Article 9 - Application Not Taken Up

Where, at the tame of receipt of the application, the guarantor is not prepared or is unable to issue the guarantee, the guarantor should without delay so inform the party that gave the guarantor its instructions.

Article 10 - Advising of Guarantee or Amendment

a. A guarantee may be advised to a beneficiary through an advising party. By advising a guarantee, whether directly or by utilizing the services of another party ("second advising party"), the advising party signifies to the beneficiary and, if applicable, to the second advising party, that it has satisfied itself as to the apparent authenticity of the guarantee and that the advice accurately reflects the terms and conditions of the guarantee as received by the advising party.

b. By advising a guarantee, the second advising party signifies to the beneficiary that it has satisfied itself as to the apparent authenticity of the advice it has received and that the advice accurately reflects the terms and conditions of the guarantee as received by the second advising party.

c. An advising party or a second advising party advises a guarantee without any additional representation or any undertaking whatsoever to the beneficiary.

d. If a party is requested to advise a guarantee or an amendment but is not prepared or is unable to do so, it should without delay so inform the party from whom it received that guarantee, amendment or advice.

e. If a party is requested to advise a guarantee, and agrees to do so, but cannot satisfy itself as to the apparent authenticity of that guarantee or advice, it shall without delay so inform the party from whom the instructions appear to have been received. If the advising party or second advising party elects nonetheless to advise that guarantee, it shall inform the beneficiary or second advising party that it has not been able to satisfy itself as to the apparent authenticity of the guarantee or the advice.

f. A guarantor using the services of an advising party or a second advising party, as well as an advising party using the services of a second advising party, to advise a guarantee should whenever possible use the same party to advise any amendment to that guarantee.

Article 11 - Amendments

a. Where, at the time of receipt of instructions for the issue of an amendment to the guarantee, the guarantor for whatever reason is not prepared or is unable to issue that amendment, the guarantor shall without delay so inform the party that gave the guarantor its instructions.

b. An amendment made without the beneficiary's agreement is not binding on the beneficiary. Nevertheless the guarantor is irrevocably bound by an amendment from the time it issues the amendment, unless and until the beneficiary rejects that amendment.

c. Except where made in accordance with the terms of the guarantee, the beneficiary may reject an amendment of the guarantee at any time until it notifies its acceptance of the amendment or makes a presentation that complies only with the guarantee as amended.

d. An advising party shall without delay inform the party from which it has received the amendment of the beneficiary's notification of acceptance or rejection of that amendment.

e. Partial acceptance of an amendment is not allowed and will be deemed to be notification of rejection of the amendment.

f. A provision in an amendment to the effect that the amendment shall take effect unless rejected within a certain time shall be disregarded.

Article 12 - Extent of Guarantor's Liability Under Guarantee

A guarantor is liable to the beneficiary only in accordance with, first, the terms and conditions of the guarantee and, second, these rules so far as consistent with those terms and conditions, up to the guarantee amount.

Article 13 - Variation of Amount of Guarantee

A guarantee may provide for the reduction or the increase of its amount on specified dates or on the occurrence of a specified event which under the terms of the guarantee results in the variation of its amount, and for this purpose the event is deemed to have occurred only:

a. when a document specified in the guarantee as indicating the occurrence of the event is presented to the guarantor, or

b. if no such document is specified in the guarantee, when the occurrence of the event becomes determinable from the guarantor's own records or from an index specified in the guarantee.

Article 14 - Presentation

a. A presentation shall be made to the guarantor:

i. at the place of issue, or such other place as is specified in the guarantee and,

ii. on or before expiry.

b. A presentation has to be complete unless it indicates that it is to be completed later. In that case, it shall be completed before expiry.

c. Where the guarantee indicates that a presentation is to be made in electronic form, the guarantee should specify the format, the system for data delivery and the electronic address for that presentation. If the guarantee does not so specify, a document may be presented in any electronic format that allows it to be authenticated or in paper form. An electronic document that cannot be authenticated is deemed not to have been presented.

d. Where the guarantee indicates that a presentation is to be made in paper form through a particular mode of delivery but does not expressly exclude the use of another mode, the use of another mode of delivery by the presenter shall be effective if the presentation is received at the place and by the time indicated in paragraph (a) of this article.

e. Where the guarantee does not indicate whether a presentation is to be made in electronic or paper form, any presentation shall be made in paper form.

f. Each presentation shall identify the guarantee under which it is made, such as by stating the guarantor's reference number for the guarantee. If it does not, the time for examination indicated in Article 20 shall start on the date of identification. Nothing in this paragraph shall result in an extension of the guarantee or limit the requirement in Article 15 (a) or (b) for any separately presented documents also to identify the demand to which they relate.

g. Except where the guarantee otherwise provides, documents issued by or on behalf of the applicant or the beneficiary, including any demand or supporting statement, shall be in the language of the guarantee. Documents issued by any other person may be in any language.

Article 15 - Requirements for Demand

a. A demand under the guarantee shall be supported by such other documents as the guarantee specifies, and in any event by a statement, by the beneficiary, indicating in what respect the applicant is in breach of its obligations under the underlying relationship. This statement may be in the demand or in a separate signed document accompanying or identifying the demand.

b. A demand under the counter-guarantee shall in any event be supported by a statement, by the party to whom the counter-guarantee was issued, indicating that such party has received a complying demand under the guarantee or counter-guarantee issued by that party. This statement may be in the demand or in a separate signed document accompanying or identifying the demand.

c. The requirement for a supporting statement in paragraph(a) or (b) of this Article applies except to the extent the guarantee or counter-guarantee expressly excludes this requirement. Exclusion terms such as "The supporting statement under Article 15[(a)] [(b)] is excluded" satisfy the requirement of this paragraph.

d. Neither the demand nor the supporting statement may be dated before the date when the beneficiary is entitled to present a demand. Any other document may be dated before that date. Neither the demand, nor the supporting statement, nor any other document may be dated later than the date of its presentation.

Article 16 - Information About Demand

The guarantor shall without delay inform the instructing party or, where applicable, the counter-guarantor of any demand under the guarantee and of any request, as an alternative, to extend the expiry of the guarantee. The counter-guarantor shall without delay inform the instructing party of any demand under the counter-guarantee and of any request, as an alternative, to extend the expiry of the counter-guarantee.

Article 17 - Partial Demand and Multiple Demands; Amount of Demands

a. A demand may be made for less than the full amount available ("partial demand").

b. More than one demand ("multiple demands") may be made.

c. The expression "multiple demands prohibited" or a similar expression means that only one demand covering all or part of the amount available may be made.

d. Where the guarantee provides that only one demand may be made, and that demand is rejected, another demand can be made on or before expiry of the guarantee.

e. A demand is a non-complying demand if:

i. it is for more than the amount available under the guarantee, or

ii. any supporting statement or other documents required by the guarantee indicate amounts that in total are less than the amount demanded.

Conversely, any supporting statement or other document indicating an amount that is more than the amount demanded does not make the demand a non-complying demand.

Article 18 - Separateness of Each Demand

a. Making a demand that is not a complying demand or withdrawing a demand does not waive or otherwise prejudice the right to make another timely demand, whether or not the guarantee prohibits partial or multiple demands.

b. Payment of a demand that is not a complying demand does not waive the requirement for other demands to be complying demands.

Article 19 - Examination

a. The guarantor shall determine, on the basis of a presentation alone, whether it appears on its face to be a complying presentation.

b. Data in a document required by the guarantee shall be examined in context with that document, the guarantee and these rules. Data need not be identical to, but shall not conflict with, data in that document, any other required document or the guarantee.

c. If the guarantee requires presentation of a document without stipulating whether it needs to be signed, by whom it is to be issued or signed, or its data content, then:

i. the guarantor will accept the document as presented if its content appears to fulfil the function of the document required by the guarantee and otherwise complies with Article 19 (b), and

ii. if the document is signed, any signature will be accepted and no indication of name or position of the signatory is necessary.

d. If a document that is not required by the guarantee or referred to in these rules is presented, it will be disregarded and may be returned to the presenter.

e. The guarantor need not re-calculate a beneficiary's calculations under a formula stated or referenced in a guarantee.

f. The guarantor shall consider a requirement for a document to be legalised, visaed, certified or similar as satisfied by any signature, mark, stamp or label on the document which appears to satisfy that requirement.

Article 20 - Time for Examination of Demand; Payment

a. If a presentation of a demand does not indicate that it is to be completed later, the guarantor shall, within five business days following the day of presentation, examine that demand and determine if it is a complying demand. This period is not shortened or otherwise affected by the expiry of the guarantee on or after the date of presentation. However, if the presentation indicates that it is to be completed later, it need not be examined until it is completed.

b. When the guarantor determines that a demand is complying, it shall pay.

c. Payment is to be made at the branch or office of the guarantor or counter-guarantor that issued the guarantee or counter-guarantee or such other place as may be indicated in that guarantee or counter-guarantee ("place for payment").

Article 21 - Currency of Payment

a. The guarantor shall pay a complying demand in the currency specified in the guarantee.

b. If, on any date on which a payment is to be made under the guarantee:

i. the guarantor is unable to make payment in the currency specified in the guarantee due to an impediment beyond its control; or

ii. it is illegal under the law of the place for payment to make payment in the specified currency,

the guarantor shall make payment in the currency of the place for payment even if the guarantee indicates that payment can only be made in the currency specified in the guarantee. The instructing party or, in the case of a counter-guarantee, the counter-guarantor, shall be bound by a payment made in such currency. The guarantor or counter-guarantor may elect to be reimbursed either in the currency in which payment was made or in the currency specified in the guarantee or, as the case may be, the counter-guarantee.

c. Payment or reimbursement in the currency of the place for payment under paragraph (b) is to be made according to the applicable rate of exchange prevailing there when payment or reimbursement is due. However, if the guarantor has not paid at the time when payment is due, the beneficiary may require payment according to the applicable rate of exchange prevailing either when payment was due or at the time of actual payment.

Article 22 - Transmission of Copies of Complying Demand

The guarantor shall without delay transmit a copy of the complying demand and of any related documents to the instructing party or, where applicable, to the counter-guarantor for transmission to the instructing party. However, neither the counter-guarantor nor the instructing party, as the case may be, may withhold payment or reimbursement pending such transmission.

Article 23 - Extend or Pay

a. Where a complying demand includes, as an alternative, a request to extend the expiry, the guarantor may suspend payment for a period not exceeding 30 calendar days following its receipt of the demand.

b. Where, following such suspension, the guarantor makes a complying demand under the counter-guarantee that includes, as an alternative, a request to extend the expiry, the counter-guarantor may suspend payment for a period not exceeding four calendar days less than the period during which payment of the demand under the guarantee was suspended.

c. The guarantor shall without delay inform the instructing party or, in the case of a counter-guarantee, the counter-guarantor, of the period of suspension of payment under the guarantee. The counter-guarantor shall then inform the instructing party of such suspension and of any suspension of payment under the counter-guarantee. Complying with this Article satisfies the information duty under Article 16.

d. The demand for payment is deemed to be withdrawn if the period of extension requested in that demand or otherwise agreed by the party making that demand is granted within the time provided under paragraph (a) or (b) of this article. If no such period of extension is granted, the complying demand shall be paid without the need to present any further demand.

e. The guarantor or counter-guarantor may refuse to grant any extension even if instructed to do so and shall then pay.

f. The guarantor or counter-guarantor shall without delay inform the party from whom it has received its instructions of its decision to extend under paragraph (d) or to pay.

g. The guarantor and the counter-guarantor assume no liability for any payment suspended in accordance with this article.

Article 24 - Non-Complying Demand, Waiver and Notice

a. When the guarantor determines that a demand under the guarantee is not a complying demand, it may reject that demand or, in its sole judgement, approach the instructing party, or in the case of a counter-guarantee, the counter-guarantor, for a waiver of the discrepancies.

b. When the counter-guarantor determines that a demand under the counter-guarantee is not a complying demand, it may reject that demand or, in its sole judgement, approach the instructing party for a waiver of the discrepancies.

c. Nothing in paragraphs (a) or (b) of this Article shall extend the period mentioned in Article 20 or dispense with the requirements of Article 16. Obtaining the waiver of the counter-guarantor or of the instructing party does not oblige the guarantor or the counter-guarantor to waive any discrepancy.

d. When the guarantor rejects a demand, it shall give a single notice to that effect to the presenter of the demand. The notice shall state:

i. that the guarantor is rejecting the demand, and

ii. each discrepancy for which the guarantor rejects the demand.

e. The notice required by paragraph (d) of this Article shall be sent without delay but not later than the close of the fifth business day following the day of presentation.

f. A guarantor failing to act in accordance with paragraphs (d)or (e) of this Article shall be precluded from claiming that the demand and any related documents do not constitute a complying demand.

g. The guarantor may at any time, after providing the notice required in paragraph (d) of this article, return any documents presented in paper form to the presenter and dispose of the electronic records in any manner that it considers appropriate without incurring any responsibility.

h. For the purpose of paragraphs (d), (f) and (g) of this article, guarantor includes counter-guarantor.

Article 25 - Reduction and Termination

a. The amount payable under the guarantee shall be reduced by any amount:

i. paid under the guarantee,

ii. resulting from the application of Article 13, or

iii. indicated in the beneficiary's signed partial release from liability under the guarantee.

b. Whether or not the guarantee document is returned to the guarantor, the guarantee shall terminate:

i. on expiry,

ii. when no amount remains payable under it, or

iii. on presentation to the guarantor of the beneficiary's signed release from liability under the guarantee.

c. If the guarantee or the counter-guarantee states neither an expiry date nor an expiry event, the guarantee shall terminate after the lapse of three years from the date of issue and the counter-guarantee shall terminate 30 calendar days after the guarantee terminates.

d. If the expiry date of a guarantee falls on a day that is not a business day at the place for presentation of the demand, the expiry date is extended to the first following business day at that place.

e. Where, to the knowledge of the guarantor, the guarantee terminates as a result of any of the reasons indicated in paragraph (b) above, but other than because of the advent of the expiry date, the guarantor shall without delay so inform the instructing party or, where applicable, the counter-guarantor and, in that case, the counter-guarantor shall so inform the instructing party.

Article 26 - Force Majeure

a. In this article, "force majeure" means acts of God, riots, civil commotions, insurrections, wars, acts of terrorism or any causes beyond the control of the guarantor or counter-guarantor that interrupt its business as it relates to acts of a kind subject to these rules.

b. Should the guarantee expire at a time when presentation or payment under that guarantee is prevented by force majeure:

i. each of the guarantee and any counter-guarantee shall be extended for a period of 30 calendar days from the date on which it would otherwise have expired, and the guarantor shall as soon as practicable inform the instructing party or, in the case of a counter-guarantee, the counter-guarantor, of the force majeure and the extension, and the counter-guarantor shall so inform the instructing party;

ii. the running of the time for examination under Article 20 of a presentation made but not yet examined before the force majeure shall be suspended until the resumption of the guarantor's business; and

iii. a complying demand under the guarantee presented before the force majeure but not paid because of the force majeure shall be paid when the force majeure ceases even if that guarantee has expired, and in this situation the guarantor shall be entitled to present a demand under the counter-guarantee within 30 calendar days after cessation of the force majeure even if the counter-guarantee has expired.

c. Should the counter-guarantee expire at a time when presentation or payment under that counter-guarantee is prevented by force majeure:

i. the counter-guarantee shall be extended for a period of 30 calendar days from the date on which the counter-guarantor informs the guarantor of the cessation of the force majeure. The counter-guarantor shall then inform the instructing party of the force majeure and the extension;

ii. the running of the time for examination under Article 20 of a presentation made but not yet examined before the force majeure shall be suspended until the resumption of the counter-guarantor's business; and

iii. a complying demand under the counter-guarantee presented before the force majeure but not paid because of the force majeure shall be paid when the force majeure ceases even if that counter-guarantee has expired.

d. The instructing party shall be bound by any extension, suspension or payment under this article.

e. The guarantor and the counter-guarantor assume no further liability for the consequences of the force majeure.

Article 27 - Disclaimer on Effectiveness of Documents

The guarantor assumes no liability or responsibility for:

a. the form, sufficiency, accuracy, genuineness, falsification, or legal effect of any signature or document presented to it;

b. the general or particular statements made in, or superimposed on, document presented to it;

c. the description, quantity, weight, quality, condition, packing, delivery, value or existence of the goods, services or other performance or data represented by or referred to in any document presented to it; or

d. the good faith, acts, omissions, solvency, performance or standing of any person issuing or referred to in any other capacity in any document presented to it.

Article 28 - Disclaimer on Transmission and Translation

a. The guarantor assumes no liability or responsibility for the consequences of delay, loss in transit, mutilation or other errors arising in the transmission of any document, if that document is transmitted or sent according to the requirements stated in the guarantee, or when the guarantor may have taken the initiative in the choice of the delivery service in the absence of instructions to that effect.

b. The guarantor assumes no liability or responsibility for errors in translation or interpretation of technical terms and may transmit all or any part of the guarantee text without translating it.

Article 29 - Disclaimer for Acts of Another Party

A guarantor using the services of another party for the purpose of giving effect to the instructions of an instructing party or counter-guarantor does so for the account and at the risk of that instructing party or counter-guarantor.

Article 30 - Limits on Exemption from Liability

Articles 27 to 29 shall not exempt a guarantor from liability or responsibility for its failure to act in good faith.

Article 31 - Indemnity for Foreign Laws and Usages

The instructing party or, in the case of a counter-guarantee, the counter-guarantor, shall indemnify the guarantor against all obligations and responsibilities imposed by foreign laws and usages, including where those foreign laws and usages impose terms into the guarantee or the counter-guarantee that override its specified terms. The instructing party shall indemnify the counter-guarantor that has indemnified the guarantor under this article.

Article 32 - Liability for Charges

a. A party instructing another party to perform services under these rules is liable to pay that party's charges for carrying out its instructions.

b. If a guarantee states that charges are for the account of the beneficiary and those charges cannot be collected, the instructing party is liable to pay those charges. If a counter-guarantee states that charges relating to the guarantee are for the account of the beneficiary and those charges cannot be collected, the counter-guarantor remains liable to the guarantor, and the instructing party to the counter-guarantor, to pay those charges.

c. Neither the guarantor nor any advising party should stipulate that the guarantee, or any advice or amendment of it, is conditional upon the receipt by the guarantor or any advising party of its charges.

Article 33 - Transfer of Guarantee and Assignment of Proceeds

a. A guarantee is transferable only if it specifically states that it is "transferable", in which case it may be transferred more than once for the full amount available at the time of transfer. A counter-guarantee is not transferable.

b. Even if a guarantee specifically states that it is transferable, the guarantor is not obliged to give effect to a request to transfer that guarantee after its issue except to the extent and in the manner expressly consented to by the guarantor.

c. A transferable guarantee means a guarantee that may be made available by the guarantor to a new beneficiary ("transferee") at the request of the existing beneficiary ("transferor").

d. The following provisions apply to the transfer of a guarantee:

i. a transferred guarantee shall include all amendments to which the transferor and guarantor have agreed as of the date of transfer; and

ii. a guarantee can only be transferred where, in addition to the conditions stated in paragraphs (a), (b) and (d)(i) of this article, the transferor has provided a signed statement to the guarantor that the transferee has acquired the transferor's rights and obligations in the underlying relationship.

e. Unless otherwise agreed at the time of transfer, the transferor shall pay all charges incurred for the transfer.

f. Under a transferred guarantee, a demand and any supporting statement shall be signed by the transferee. Unless the guarantee provides otherwise, the name and the signature of the transferee may be used in place of the name and signature of the transferor in any other document.

g. Whether or not the guarantee states that it is transferable, and subject to the provisions of the applicable law:

i. the beneficiary may assign any proceeds to which it may be or may become entitled under the guarantee;

ii. however, the guarantor shall not be obliged to pay an assignee of these proceeds unless the guarantor has agreed to do so.

Article 34 - Governing Law

a. Unless otherwise provided in the guarantee, its governing law shall be that of the location of the guarantor's branch or office that issued the guarantee.

b. Unless otherwise provided in the counter-guarantee, its governing law shall be that of the location of the counter-guarantor's branch or office that issued the counter-guarantee.

Article 35 - Jurisdiction

a. Unless otherwise provided in the guarantee, any dispute between the guarantor and the beneficiary relating to the guarantee shall be settled exclusively by the competent court of the country of the location of the guarantor's branch or office that issued the guarantee.

b. Unless otherwise provided in the counter-guarantee, any dispute between the counter-guarantor and the guarantor relating to the counter-guarantee shall be settled exclusively by the competent court of the country of the location of the counter-guarantor's branch or office that issued the counter-guarantee.

ICC

25) UNIFORM RULES FOR CONTRACT BONDS (URCB 524)[1]

Article 1 Scope and Application

(a) These Rules shall be known as the "Uniform Rules for Contract Bonds" and shall apply to any Bond which states that these Rules shall apply, or otherwise incorporates these Rules by reference and, for such purposes, it shall suffice that the Bond incorporates a reference to these Rules and the publication number.

(b) If there shall be any conflict in the construction or operation of the obligations of any parties under a Bond between the provisions of these Rules and such Bond, or mandatory provisions of the Applicable Law regulating the same, the provisions of the Bond or, as the case may be, the mandatory provisions of the Applicable Law shall prevail.

Article 2 Definitions

In these Rules, words or expressions shall bear the meanings set out below and be construed accordingly

Advance Payment Bond – A Bond given by the Guarantor in favour of the Beneficiary to secure the repayment of any sum or sums advanced by the Beneficiary to the Principal under or for the purposes of the Contract, where such sum or sums is or are advanced before the carrying out of works, the performance of services or the supply or provision of any goods pursuant to such Contract.

Beneficiary – The party in whose favour a Bond is issued or provided.

Bond – Any bond, guarantee or other instrument in writing issued or executed by the Guarantor in favour of the Beneficiary pursuant to which the Guarantor undertakes on Default, either:

(i) to pay or satisfy any claim or entitlement to payment of damages, compensation or other financial relief up to the Bond Amount; or

(ii) to pay or satisfy such claim or entitlement up to the Bond Amount or at the Guarantor's option to perform or execute the Contract or any Contractual Obligation.

In either case where the liability of the Guarantor shall be accessory to the liability of the Principal under the Contract or such Contractual Obligation and such expression shall without limitation include Advance Payment Bonds, Maintenance Bonds, Performance Bonds, Retention Bonds and Tender Bonds.

Bond Amount – The sum inserted in the Bond as the maximum aggregate liability of the Guarantor as amended, varied or reduced from time to time or, following the payment of any amount in satisfaction or partial satisfaction of a claim under any Bond, such lesser sum as shall be calculated by deducting from the sum inserted in the Bond the amount of any such payment.

Contract – Any written agreement between the Principal and the Beneficiary for the carrying out of works, the performance of services or the supply or provision of any goods.

Contractual Obligation – Any duty, obligation or requirement imposed by a clause, paragraph, section, term, condition, provision or stipulation contained in or forming part of a Contract or tender.

Default – Any breach, default or failure to perform any Contractual Obligation which shall give rise to a claim for performance, damages, compensation or other financial remedy by the Beneficiary and which is established pursuant to paragraph j of Article 7.

Expiry Date – Either (a) the date fixed or the date of the event on which the obligations of the Guarantor under the Bond are expressed to expire or (b) if no such date is stipulated, the date determined in accordance with Article 4.

Guarantor – Any Person who shall issue or execute a Bond on behalf of a Principal.

Maintenance Bond – A Bond to secure Contractual Obligations relating to the maintenance of works or goods following the physical completion or the provision thereof, pursuant to a Contract.

Performance Bond – A Bond to secure the performance of any Contract or Contractual Obligation.

Person – Any company, corporation, firm, association, body, individual or any legal entity whatsoever.

Principal – Any Person who (i) either (a) submits a tender for the purpose of entering into a Contract with the Beneficiary or (b) enters into a Contract with the Beneficiary and (ii) assumes primary liability for all Contractual Obligations thereunder.

Retention Bond – A Bond to secure the payment of any sum or sums paid or released to the Principal by the Beneficiary before the date for payment or release thereof contained in the Contract.

Tender Bond – A Bond in respect of a tender to secure the payment of any loss or damage suffered or incurred by the Beneficiary arising out of the failure by the Principal to enter into a Contract or provide a Performance Bond or other Bond pursuant to such tender.

Writing and Written – Shall include any authenticated tele-transmissions or tested electronic data interchange ("EDI") message equivalent thereto.

Article 3 Form of Bond and Liability of the Guarantor to the Beneficiary

(a) The Bond should stipulate:

(i) The Principal.

(ii) The Beneficiary.

(iii) The Guarantor.

(iv) The Contract.

(v) Where the Bond does not extend to the whole of the Contract, the precise Contractual Obligation or Obligations to which the Bond relates.

(vi) The Bond Amount.

(vii) Any provisions for the reduction of the Bond Amount.

(viii) The date when the Bond becomes effective (defined in these rules as the "Effective Date").

(ix) Whether the Guarantor shall be entitled at its option to perform or execute the Contract or any Contractual Obligation.

(x) The Expiry Date.

(xi) The names, addresses, telex and/or telefax numbers and contact references of the Beneficiary, the Guarantor and the Principal.

(xii) Whether sub-paragraph i of Article 7(j) is to apply and the name of the third party to be nominated thereunder for the purpose of Article 7 below (claims procedure).

(xiii) How disputes or differences between the Beneficiary, the Principal and the Guarantor in relation to the Bond are to be settled.

(b) The liability of the Guarantor to the Beneficiary under the Bond is accessory to the liability of the Principal to the Beneficiary under the Contract and shall arise upon Default. The Contract is deemed to be incorporated into and form part of the Bond. The liability of the Guarantor shall not exceed the Bond Amount.

(c) Save for any reduction of the Bond Amount under the terms of the Bond or the Contract and subject to Article 4, the liability of the Guarantor shall not be reduced or discharged by reason of any partial performance of the Contract or any Contractual Obligation.

(d) All defences, remedies, cross claims, counter-claims and other rights or entitlements to relief which the Principal may have against the Beneficiary under the Contract, or which may otherwise be available to the Principal in respect of the subject matter thereof, shall be available to the Guarantor in respect of any Default in addition to and without limiting any defence under or arising out of the Bond.

Article 4 Release and Discharge of Guarantor

(a) Subject to any contrary provision in the Bond and the provisions of paragraph (b) of this Article 4, the Expiry Date shall be six months from the latest date for the performance of the Contract or the relevant Contractual Obligations thereunder, as the case may be.

(b) Subject to any contrary provision of the Bond, the Expiry Date for the purposes of an Advance Payment Bond, a Maintenance Bond, a Retention Bond and a Tender Bond shall be as follows:

(i) In the case of an Advance Payment Bond, the date on which the Principal shall have carried out works, supplied goods or services or otherwise performed Contractual Obligations having a value as certified or otherwise determined pursuant to the Contract equal to or exceeding the Bond Amount.

(ii) In the case of a Maintenance Bond, six months after either the date stipulated by the Contract or, if no date has been specified for the termination of the Principal's maintenance obligations, the last day of the applicable warranty period or defects liability period under the Contract.

(iii) In the case of a Retention Bond, six months after the date stipulated by the Contract for the payment, repayment or release of any retention monies.

(iv) In the case of a Tender Bond, six months after the latest date set out in the tender documents or conditions for the submission of tenders.

(c) Where the Expiry Date falls on a day which is not a Business Day, the Expiry Date shall be the first following Business Day. For the purpose of these Rules "Business Day" shall mean any day on which the offices of the Guarantor shall ordinarily be open for business.

(d) A Bond shall terminate and, without prejudice to any term, provision, agreement or stipulation of the Bond, any other agreement or the Applicable Law providing for earlier release or discharge, the liability of the Guarantor shall be discharged absolutely and the Guarantor shall be released upon the Expiry Date whether or not the Bond shall be returned to the Guarantor, save in respect of any claim served in accordance with Article 7.

(e) Notwithstanding the provisions of paragraph (d) of this Article 4, the Bond may be cancelled at any time by the return of the Bond itself to the Guarantor or by the service upon and delivery or transmission to the Guarantor of a release in writing duly signed by an authorized representative of the Beneficiary, whether or not accompanied by the Bond and/or any amendment or amendments thereto.

(f) The Guarantor shall promptly inform the Principal of any payment made under or pursuant to the Bond and of the cancellation, release or discharge thereof or any reduction in the Bond Amount where the same shall not already have been communicated.

Article 5 Return of the Bond

The Bond shall immediately after release or discharge under these Rules be returned to the Guarantor, and the retention or possession of the Bond following such release or discharge shall not of itself operate to confer any right or entitlement thereunder upon the Beneficiary.

Article 6 Amendments and Variations to and of the Contract and the Bond and Extensions of Time

(a) The Bond shall, subject to the Bond Amount and the Expiry Date, apply to the Contract as amended or varied by the Principal and the Beneficiary from time to time.

(b) A Tender Bond shall be valid only in respect of the works and contract particulars set out or described in the tender documents at the Effective Date, and shall not apply beyond the Expiry Date or in any case where there shall be any substantial or material variation of or amendment to the original tender after the Effective Date, unless the Guarantor shall confirm, in the same manner as set out in paragraph c of this Article 6, that the Tender Bond so applies or the Expiry Date has been extended.

(c) Any amendment to a Bond, including without limitation the increase of the Bond Amount or the alteration of the Expiry Date, shall be in writing duly signed or executed by authorized representatives of each of the Beneficiary, the Principal and the Guarantor.

Article 7 Submission of Claims and Claims Procedure

(a) A claim under a Bond shall be in writing and shall be served upon the Guarantor on or before the Expiry Date and by no later than the close of the Business Day at the Guarantor's principal place of business set out in the Bond, on the Expiry Date.

(b) A claim submitted by authenticated tele-transmission, EDI, telex or other means of telefax facsimile or electronic transmission shall be deemed to be received on the arrival of such transmission.

(c) A claim delivered to the Guarantor's principal place of business set out in the Bond shall, subject to proof of delivery, be deemed to be served on the date of such delivery.

(d) A claim served or transmitted by post shall, subject to satisfactory proof of delivery by the Beneficiary, be deemed to be served upon actual receipt thereof by the Guarantor.

(e) The Beneficiary shall, when giving notice of any claim by telefax or other tele-transmission or EDI, also send a copy of such claim by post.

(f) Any claim shall state brief details of the Contract to identify the same, state that there has been a breach or default and set out the circumstances of such breach or default and any request for payment, performance or execution.

(g) Upon receipt of a claim from the Beneficiary, the Guarantor shall send notice in writing to the Principal of such claim as soon as reasonably practicable and before either (a) making any payment in satisfaction or partial satisfaction of the same or (b) performing the Contract or any part thereof pursuant to a Contractual Obligation.

(h) The Beneficiary shall, upon written request by the Guarantor, supply to the Guarantor such further information as the Guarantor may reasonably request to enable it to consider the claim, and shall provide copies of any correspondence or other documents relating to the Contract or the performance of any Contractual Obligations and allow the Guarantor, its employees, agents or representatives to inspect any works, goods or services carried out or supplied by the Principal.

(i) A claim shall not be honoured unless

(i) A Default has occurred; and

(ii) The claim has been made and served in accordance with the provisions of paragraphs (a) to (f) of Article 7 on or before the Expiry Date.

(j) Notwithstanding any dispute or difference between the Principal and the Beneficiary in relation to the performance of the Contract or any Contractual Obligation, a Default shall be deemed to be established for the purposes of these Rules:

(i) upon issue of a certificate of Default by a third party (who may without limitation be an independent architect or engineer or a Pre-Arbitral referee of the ICC) if the Bond so provides and the service of such certificate or a certified copy thereof upon the Guarantor, or

(ii) if the Bond does not provide for the issue of a certificate by a third party, upon the issue of a certificate of Default by the Guarantor, or

(iii) by the final judgement, order or award of a court or tribunal of competent jurisdiction, and the issue of a certificate of Default under paragraph (i) or (ii) shall not restrict the rights of the parties to seek or require the determination of any dispute or difference arising under the Contract or the Bond or the review of any certificate of Default or payment made pursuant thereto by a court or tribunal of competent jurisdiction.

(k) A copy of any certificate of Default issued under (j) (i) or (ii) shall be given by the Guarantor to the Principal and the Beneficiary forthwith.

(l) The Guarantor shall consider any claim expeditiously and, if such claim is rejected, shall immediately give notice thereof to the Beneficiary by authenticated tele-transmission or other telefax, facsimile transmission, telex, cable or EDI, confirming the same by letter, setting out the grounds for such refusal including any defences or other matters raised under paragraph (d) of Article 3.

Article 8 Jurisdiction and Settlement of Disputes

(a) The Applicable Law shall be the law of the country selected by the parties to govern the operation of the Bond and, in the absence of any express choice of law, shall be the law governing the Contract and any dispute or difference arising under these Rules in relation to a Bond shall be determined in accordance with the Applicable Law.

(b) All disputes arising between the Beneficiary, the Principal and the Guarantor or any of them in relation to a Bond governed by these Rules shall, unless otherwise agreed, be finally settled under the Rules of Conciliation and Arbitration of the International Chamber of Commerce by one or more arbitrators appointed in accordance with the said Rules.

(c) If the Bond shall exclude the operation of the arbitration provisions of this Article 8, any dispute between the parties to the Bond shall be determined by the courts of the country nominated in the Bond, or, if there is no such nomination, the competent court of the Guarantor's principal place of business or, at the option of the Beneficiary, the competent court of the country in which the branch of the Guarantor which issued the Bond is situated.

26) Uniform Rules for Collections (URC 522)[1]

Article 1 Application of URC 522

a The Uniform Rules for Collections, 1995 Revision, ICC Publication No. 522, shall apply to all collections as defined in Article 2 where such rules are incorporated into the text of the "collection instruction" referred to in Article 4 and are binding on all parties thereto unless otherwise expressly agreed or contrary to the provisions of a national, state or local law and/or regulation which cannot be departed from.

b Banks shall have no obligation to handle either a collection or any collection instruction or subsequent related instructions.

c If a bank elects, for any reason, not to handle a collection or any related instructions received by it, it must advise the party from whom it received the collection or the instructions by telecommunication or, if that is not possible, by other expeditious means, without delay.

Article 2 Definition of Collection

For the purposes of these Articles:

a "Collection" means the handling by banks of documents as defined in sub-Article 2(b), in accordance with instructions received, in order to:

1 obtain payment and/or acceptance, or

2 deliver documents against payment and/or against acceptance, or

3 deliver documents on other terms and conditions.

b "Documents" means financial documents and/or commercial documents:

1 "Financial documents" means bills of exchange, promissory notes, cheques, or other similar instruments used for obtaining the payment of money;

2 "Commercial documents" means invoices, transport documents, documents of title or other similar documents, or any other documents whatsoever, not being financial documents.

c "Clean collection" means collection of financial documents not accompanied by commercial documents.

d "Documentary collection" means collection of:

1 Financial documents accompanied by commercial documents;

2 Commercial documents not accompanied by financial documents.

Article 3 Parties to a Collection

a For the purposes of these Articles the "parties thereto" are:

1 the "principal" who is the party entrusting the handling of a collection to a bank;

2 the "remitting bank" which is the bank to which the principal has entrusted the handling of a collection;

3 the "collecting bank" which is any bank, other than the remitting bank, involved in processing the collection;

---

1 © International Chamber of Commerce (ICC). Reproduced with permission of the ICC. The text reproduced here is valid at the time of reproduction [August 2020]. As amendments may from time to time be made to the text, please refer to the website https://iccwbo.org/ for the latest version and for more information on ICC documents and services.

4 the “presenting bank” which is the collecting bank making presentation to the drawee.

b The “drawee” is the one to whom presentation is to be made in accordance with the collection instruction.

Article 4 Collection Instruction

a 1 All documents sent for collection must be accompanied by a collection instruction indicating that the collection is subject to URC 522 and giving complete and precise instructions. Banks are only permitted to act upon the instructions given in such collection instruction, and in accordance with these Rules.

2 Banks will not examine documents in order to obtain instructions.

3 Unless otherwise authorised in the collection instruction, banks will disregard any instructions from any party/bank other than the party/bank from whom they received the collection.

b A collection instruction should contain the following items of information, as appropriate.

1 Details of the bank from which the collection was received including full name, postal and SWIFT addresses, telex, telephone, facsimile numbers and reference.

2 Details of the principal including full name, postal address, and if applicable telex, telephone and facsimile numbers.

3 Details of the drawee including full name, postal address, or the domicile at which presentation is to be made and if applicable telex, telephone and facsimile numbers.

4 Details of the presenting bank, if any, including full name, postal address, and if applicable telex, telephone and facsimile numbers.

5 Amount(s) and currency(ies) to be collected.

6 List of documents enclosed and the numerical count of each document.

7 a. Terms and conditions upon which payment and/or acceptance is to be obtained.

b. Terms of delivery of documents against:

1) payment and/or acceptance

2) other terms and conditions

It is the responsibility of the party preparing the collection instruction to ensure that the terms for the delivery of documents are clearly and unambiguously stated, otherwise banks will not be responsible for any consequences arising therefrom.

8 Charges to be collected, indicating whether they may be waived or not.

9 Interest to be collected, if applicable, indicating whether it may be waived or not, including:

a. rate of interest

b. interest period

c. basis of calculation (for example 360 or 365 days in a year) as applicable.

10 Method of payment and form of payment advice.

11 Instructions in case of non-payment, non-acceptance and/or noncompliance with other instructions.

c 1 Collection instructions should bear the complete address of the drawee or of the domicile at which the presentation is to be made. If the address is incomplete or incorrect, the collecting bank may, without any liability and responsibility on its part, endeavour to ascertain the proper address.

2 The collecting bank will not be liable or responsible for any ensuing delay as a result of an incomplete/incorrect address being provided.

Article 5 Presentation

a For the purposes of these Articles, presentation is the procedure whereby the presenting bank makes the documents available to the drawee as instructed.

b The collection instruction should state the exact period of time within which any action is to be taken by the drawee.

Expressions such as "first", "prompt", "immediate", and the like should not be used in connection with presentation or with reference to any period of time within which documents have to be taken up or for any other action that is to be taken by the drawee. If such terms are used banks will disregard them.

c Documents are to be presented to the drawee in the form in which they are received, except that banks are authorised to affix any necessary stamps, at the expense of the party from whom they received the collection unless otherwise instructed, and to make any necessary endorsements or place any rubber stamps or other identifying marks or symbols customary to or required for the collection operation.

d For the purpose of giving effect to the instructions of the principal, the remitting bank will utilise the bank nominated by the principal as the collecting bank. In the absence of such nomination, the remitting bank will utilise any bank of its own, or another bank's choice in the country of payment or acceptance or in the country where other terms and conditions have to be complied with.

e The documents and collection instruction may be sent directly by the remitting bank to the collecting bank or through another bank as intermediary.

f If the remitting bank does not nominate a specific presenting bank, the collecting bank may utilise a presenting bank of its choice.

Article 6 Sight/Acceptance

In the case of documents payable at sight the presenting bank must make presentation for payment without delay. In the case of documents payable at a tenor other than sight the presenting bank must, where acceptance is called for, make presentation for acceptance without delay, and where payment is called for, make presentation for payment not later than the appropriate maturity date.

Article 7 Release of Commercial Documents

Documents Against Acceptance (D/A) vs. Documents Against Payment (D/P)

a Collections should not contain bills of exchange payable at a future date with instructions that commercial documents are to be delivered against payment.

b If a collection contains a bill of exchange payable at a future date, the collection instruction should state whether the commercial documents are to be released to the drawee against acceptance (D/A) or against payment (D/P).

In the absence of such statement commercial documents will be released only against payment and the collecting bank will not be responsible for any consequences arising out of any delay in the delivery of documents.

c If a collection contains a bill of exchange payable at a future date and the collection instruction indicates that commercial documents are to be released against payment, documents will be released only against such payment and the collecting bank will not be responsible for any consequences arising out of any delay in the delivery of documents.

Article 8 Creation of Documents

Where the remitting bank instructs that either the collecting bank or the drawee is to create documents (bills of exchange, promissory notes, trust receipts, letters of undertaking or other documents) that were not included in the collection, the form and wording of such documents shall be provided by the remitting bank, otherwise the collecting bank shall not be liable or responsible for the form and wording of any such document provided by the collecting bank and/or the drawee.

Article 9 Good Faith and Reasonable Care

Banks will act in good faith and exercise reasonable care.

Article 10 Documents vs. Goods, Services, Performances

a Goods should not be despatched directly to the address of a bank or consigned to or to the order of a bank without prior agreement on the part of that bank.

Nevertheless, in the event that goods are despatched directly to the address of a bank or consigned to or to the order of a bank for release to a drawee against payment or acceptance or upon other terms and conditions without prior agreement on the part of that bank, such bank shall have no obligation to take delivery of the goods, which remain at the risk and responsibility of the party despatching the goods.

b Banks have no obligation to take any action in respect of the goods to which a documentary collection relates, including storage and insurance of the goods even when specific instructions are given to do so. Banks will only take such action if, when, and to the extent that they agree to do so in each case. Notwithstanding the provisions of sub-Article 1(c) this rule applies even in the absence of any specific advice to this effect by the collecting bank.

c Nevertheless, in the case that banks take action for the protection of the goods, whether instructed or not, they assume no liability or responsibility with regard to the fate and/or condition of the goods and/or for any acts and/or omissions on the part of any third parties entrusted with the custody and/or protection of the goods. However, the collecting bank must advise without delay the bank from which the collection instruction was received of any such action taken.

d Any charges and/or expenses incurred by banks in connection with any action taken to protect the goods will be for the account of the party from whom they received the collection.

e 1 Notwithstanding the provisions of sub-Article 10(a), where the goods are consigned to or to the order of the collecting bank and the drawee has honoured the collection by payment, acceptance or other terms and conditions, and the collecting bank arranges for the release of the goods, the remitting bank shall be deemed to have authorised the collecting bank to do so.

2 Where a collecting bank on the instructions of the remitting bank or in terms of sub-Article 10(e)i, arranges for the release of the goods, the remitting bank shall indemnify such collecting bank for all damages and expenses incurred.

Article 11 Disclaimer for Acts of an Instructed Party

a Banks utilising the services of another bank or other banks for the purpose of giving effect to the instructions of the principal, do so for the account and at the risk of such principal.

b Banks assume no liability or responsibility should the instructions they transmit not be carried out, even if they have themselves taken the initiative in the choice of such other bank(s).

c A party instructing another party to perform services shall be bound by and liable to indemnify the instructed party against all obligations and responsibilities imposed by foreign laws and usages.

Article 12 Disclaimer on Documents Received

a Banks must determine that the documents received appear to be as listed in the collection instruction and must advise by telecommunication or, if that is not possible, by other expeditious means, without delay, the party from whom the collection instruction was received of any documents missing, or found to be other than listed.

Banks have no further obligation in this respect.

b If the documents do not appear to be listed, the remitting bank shall be precluded from disputing the type and number of documents received by the collecting bank.

c Subject to sub-Article 5(c) and sub-Articles 12(a) and 12(b) above, banks will present documents as received without further examination.

Article 13 Disclaimer on Effectiveness of Documents

Banks assume no liability or responsibility for the form, sufficiency, accuracy, genuineness, falsification or legal effect of any document(s), or for the general and/or particular conditions stipulated in the document(s) or superimposed thereon; nor do they assume any liability or responsibility for the description, quantity, weight, quality, condition, packing, delivery, value or existence of the goods represented by any document(s), or for the good faith or acts and/or omissions, solvency, performance or standing of the consignors, the carriers, the forwarders, the consignees or the insurers of the goods, or any other person whomsoever.

Article 14 Disclaimer on Delays, Loss in Transit and Translation

a Banks assume no liability or responsibility for the consequences arising out of delay and/or loss in transit of any message(s), letter(s) or document(s), or for delay, mutilation or other error(s) arising in transmission of any telecommunication or for error(s) in translation and/or interpretation of technical terms.

b Banks will not be liable or responsible for any delays resulting from the need to obtain clarification of any instructions received.

Article 15 Force Majeure

Banks assume no liability or responsibility for consequences arising out of the interruption of their business by Acts of God, riots, civil commotions, insurrections, wars, or any other causes beyond their control or by strikes or lockouts.

Article 16 Payment Without Delay

a Amounts collected (less charges and/or disbursements and/or expenses where applicable) must be made available without delay to the party from whom the collection instruction was received in accordance with the terms and conditions of the collection instruction.

b Notwithstanding the provisions of sub-Article 1(c), and unless otherwise agreed, the collecting bank will effect payment of the amount collected in favour of the remitting bank only.

Article 17 Payment in Local Currency

In the case of documents payable in the currency of the country of payment (local currency), the presenting bank must, unless otherwise instructed in the collection instruction, release the documents to the drawee against payment in local currency only if such currency is immediately available for disposal in the manner specified in the collection instruction.

Article 18 Payment in Foreign Currency

In the case of documents payable in a currency other than that of the country of payment (foreign currency), the presenting bank must, unless otherwise instructed in the collection instruction, release the documents to the drawee against payment in the designated foreign currency only if such foreign currency can immediately be remitted in accordance with the instructions given in the collection instruction.

Article 19 Partial Payments

a In respect of clean collections, partial payments may be accepted if and to the extent to which and on the conditions on which partial payments are authorised by the law in force in the place of payment. The financial document(s) will be released to the drawee only when full payment thereof has been received.

b In respect of documentary collections, partial payments will only be accepted if specifically authorised in the collection instruction. However, unless otherwise instructed, the presenting bank will release the documents to the drawee only after full payment has been received, and the presenting bank will not be responsible for any consequences arising out of any delay in the delivery of documents.

c In all cases partial payments will be accepted only subject to compliance with the provisions of either Article 17 or Article 18 as appropriate.

Partial payment, if accepted, will be dealt with in accordance with the provisions of Article 16.

Article 20 Interest

a If the collection instruction specifies that interest is to be collected and the drawee refuses to pay such interest, the presenting bank may deliver the document(s) against payment or acceptance or on other terms and conditions as the case may be, without collecting such interest, unless sub-Article 20(c) applies.

b Where such interest is to be collected, the collection instruction must specify the rate of interest, interest period and basis of calculation.

c Where the collection instruction expressly states that interest may not be waived and the drawee refuses to pay such interest the presenting bank will not deliver documents and will not be responsible for any consequences arising out of any delay in the delivery of document(s).

When payment of interest has been refused, the presenting bank must inform by telecommunication or, if that is not possible, by other expeditious means without delay the bank from which the collection instruction was received.

Article 21 Charges and Expenses

a If the collection instruction specifies that collection charges and/or expenses are to be for account of the drawee and the drawee refuses to pay them, the presenting bank may deliver the document(s) against payment or acceptance or on other terms and conditions as the case may be, without collecting charges and/or expenses, unless sub-Article 21(b) applies.

Whenever collection charges and/or expenses are so waived they will be for the account of the party from whom the collection was received and may be deducted from the proceeds.

b Where the collection instruction expressly states that charges and/or expenses may not be waived and the drawee refuses to pay such charges and/or expenses, the presenting bank will not deliver documents and will not be responsible for any consequences arising out of any delay in the delivery of the document(s). When payment of collection charges and/or expenses has been refused the presenting bank must inform by telecommunication or, if that is not possible, by other expeditious means without delay the bank from which the collection instruction was received.

c In all cases where in the express terms of a collection instruction or under these Rules, disbursements and/or expenses and/or collection charges are to be borne by the principal, the collecting bank(s) shall be entitled to recover promptly outlays in respect of disbursements, expenses and charges from the bank from which the collection instruction was received, and the remitting bank shall be entitled to recover promptly from the principal any amount so paid out by it, together with its own disbursements, expenses and charges, regardless of the fate of the collection.

d Banks reserve the right to demand payment of charges and/or expenses in advance from the party from whom the collection instruction was received, to cover costs in attempting to carry out any instructions, and pending receipt of such payment also reserve the right not to carry out such instructions.

Article 22 Acceptance

The presenting bank is responsible for seeing that the form of the acceptance of a bill of exchange appears to be complete and correct, but is not responsible for the genuineness of any signature or for the authority of any signatory to sign the acceptance.

Article 23 Promissory Notes and Other Instruments

The presenting bank is not responsible for the genuineness of any signature or for the authority of any signatory to sign a promissory note, receipt, or other instruments.

Article 24 Protest

The collection instruction should give specific instructions regarding protest (or other legal process in lieu thereof), in the event of non-payment or non-acceptance.

In the absence of such specific instructions, the banks concerned with the collection have no obligation to have the document(s) protested (or subjected to other legal process in lieu thereof) for non-payment or non-acceptance.

Any charges and/or expenses incurred by banks in connection with such protest, or other legal process, will be for the account of the party from whom the collection instruction was received.

Article 25 Case-of-Need

If the principal nominates a representative to act as case-of-need in the event of non-payment and/or non-acceptance the collection instruction should clearly and fully indicate the powers of such case-of-need. In the absence of such indication banks will not accept any instructions from the case-of-need.

Article 26 Advices

Collecting banks are to advise fate in accordance with the following rules:

a FORM OF ADVICE

All advices or information from the collecting bank to the bank from which the collection instruction was received, must bear appropriate details including, in all cases, the latter bank's reference as stated in the collection instruction.

b METHOD OF ADVICE

It shall be the responsibility of the remitting bank to instruct the collecting bank regarding the method by which the advices detailed in sub-Articles (c)i, (c)ii and (c)iii are to be given. In the absence of such instructions, the collecting bank will send the relative advices by the method of its choice at the expense of the bank from which the collection instruction was received.

c 1 ADVICE OF PAYMENT

The collecting bank must send without delay advice of payment to the bank from which the collection instruction was received, detailing the amount or amounts collected, charges and/or disbursements and/or expenses deducted, where appropriate, and method of disposal of the funds.

c 2 ADVICE OF ACCEPTANCE

The collecting bank must send without delay advice of acceptance to the bank from which the collection instruction was received.

c 3 ADVICE OF NON-PAYMENT AND/OR NON-ACCEPTANCE

The presenting bank should endeavour to ascertain the reasons for non-payment and/or non-acceptance and advise accordingly, without delay, the bank from which it received the collection instruction.

The presenting bank must send without delay advice of non-payment and/or advice of non-acceptance to the bank from which it received the collection instruction.

On receipt of such advice the remitting bank must give appropriate instructions as to the further handling of the documents. If such instructions are not received by the presenting bank within 60 days after its advice of non-payment and/or non-acceptance, the documents may be returned to the bank from which the collection instruction was received without any further responsibility on the part of the presenting bank.

27) Uniform Rules for Collections (URC 522) Supplement for Electronic Presentation (eURC)[1]

Preliminary Considerations

The mode of presentation to the remitting bank, by or on behalf of the principal, of electronic records alone or in combination with paper documents, is outside the scope of the eURC.

The mode of presentation to the drawee, by the collecting or presenting bank, of electronic records alone or in combination with paper documents, is outside the scope of the eURC.

Where not defined or modified in the eURC, definitions given in URC 522 will continue to apply.

Article e1 Application of the eURC

a. A collection instruction should only indicate that it is subject to the Uniform Rules for Collections (URC 522) Supplement for Electronic Presentation ("eURC") where a prior arrangement exists between the remitting bank and the collecting or presenting bank, for the presentation of electronic records alone or in combination with paper documents.

b. Such prior arrangement should specify:

i. the format in which each electronic record will be issued and presented; and

ii. the place for presentation, to the collecting or presenting bank.

Article e2 Scope of the eURC

a. The eURC supplements the Uniform Rules for Collections (1995 Revision, ICC Publication No. 522) ("URC") in order to accommodate presentation of electronic records alone or in combination with paper documents.

b. The eURC shall apply where a collection instruction indicates that it is subject to the eURC ("eURC collection instruction").

c. This version is Version 1.0. An eURC collection instruction must indicate the applicable version of the eURC. If not indicated, it is subject to the version in effect on the date the eURC collection instruction is issued or, if made subject to the eURC by an amendment, the date of that amendment.

Article e3 Relationship of the eURC to the URC

a. An eURC collection instruction is also subject to the URC without express incorporation of the URC.

b. Where the eURC applies, its provisions shall prevail to the extent that they would produce a result different from the application of the URC.

c. Where an eURC collection instruction is issued but the presentation consists of only paper documents, the URC alone shall apply.

Article e4 Definitions

a. Where the following terms are used in the URC, for the purpose of applying the URC to an electronic record presented under an eURC collection instruction, the term:

i. "advices" includes electronic records originating from a data processing system;

1 © International Chamber of Commerce (ICC). Reproduced with permission of the ICC. The text reproduced here is valid at the time of reproduction [August 2020]. As amendments may from time to time be made to the text, please refer to the website https://iccwbo.org/ for the latest version and for more information on ICC documents and services.

ii. "collection instruction" shall include an instruction originating from a data processing system;

iii. "document" shall include an electronic record;

iv. "place for presentation" of an electronic record means an electronic address of a data processing system;

v. "sign" and the like shall include an electronic signature;

vi. "superimposed" means data content whose supplementary character is apparent in an electronic record.

b. The following terms used in the eURC shall have the following meaning:

i. "data corruption" means any distortion or loss of data that renders the electronic record, as it was presented, unreadable in whole or in part;

ii. "data processing system" means a computerised or an electronic or any other automated means used to process and manipulate data, initiate an action or respond to data messages or performances in whole or in part;

iii. "electronic record" means data created, generated, sent, communicated, received or stored by electronic means including, where appropriate, all information logically associated with or otherwise linked together so as to become part of the record, whether generated contemporaneously or not, that is:

   a. capable of being authenticated as to the apparent identity of a sender and the apparent source of the data contained in it, and as to whether it has remained complete and unaltered, and

   b. capable of being viewed to ensure that it represents the type and/or description of the electronic record listed on the eURC collection instruction;

iv. "electronic signature" means a data process attached to or logically associated with an electronic record and executed or adopted by a person in order to identify that person and to indicate that person's authentication of the electronic record;

v. "format" means the data organisation in which the electronic record is expressed or to which it refers;

vi. "paper document" means a document in a paper form;

vii. "presenter" means the principal or a party that makes a presentation on behalf of the principal;

viii. "received" means when an electronic record enters a data processing system, at the agreed place for presentation, in a format capable of being accepted by that system. Any acknowledgement of receipt generated by that system is not to be construed that the electronic record has been authenticated and/or viewed under the eURC collection instruction;

ix. "re-present" means to substitute or replace an electronic record already presented.

Article e5 Electronic Records and Paper Documents v. Goods, Services or Performance

Banks do not deal with the goods, services or performance to which an electronic record or paper document may relate.

Article e6 Format

a. An eURC collection instruction must indicate the format of each electronic record.

b i. The format of each electronic record must be as previously arranged between the remitting bank and the collecting or presenting bank, as required by sub-article e1 (b).

ii. An electronic record received in a format that has not previously been agreed may be treated as not received, and the collecting or presenting bank must inform the remitting bank accordingly.

Article e7 Presentation

a. When electronic records alone are presented under an eURC collection instruction, these must be accessible to a collecting or presenting bank at the time the collecting or presenting bank receives the eURC collection instruction.

b. When electronic records, in combination with paper documents, are presented by the remitting bank under an eURC collection instruction, all the electronic records referred to in the eURC collection instruction must be accessible to the collecting or presenting bank at the time the collecting or presenting bank receives the eURC collection instruction enclosing the paper documents.

c. An electronic record that cannot be authenticated is deemed not to have been presented.

d i. The remitting bank is responsible for ensuring that each presentation of an electronic record, and any presentation of paper documents, identifies the eURC collection instruction under which presentation is being made. For electronic records this may be by specific reference thereto in the electronic record itself, or in metadata attached or superimposed thereto, or by identification in the eURC collection instruction itself.

ii. Any electronic record or paper document not so identified may be treated as not received.

Article e8 Advice of Non-Payment or Non-Acceptance

If a collecting or presenting bank receives an eURC collection instruction and issues an advice of nonpayment and/or non-acceptance to the bank from which it received the collection instruction and does not receive instructions from such bank for the disposition of the electronic records within 60 calendar days from the date the advice of non-payment and/or nonacceptance is given, the collecting or presenting bank may dispose of the electronic records in any manner deemed appropriate without any responsibility.

Article e9 Determination of a Due Date

When settlement under an eURC collection instruction is due a number of days after the date of shipment or dispatch of the goods, or a number of days after any other date appearing in an electronic record, an eURC collection instruction must indicate the due date.

Article e10 Release of Electronic Records

a. An eURC collection instruction must indicate the manner in which electronic records may be accessed by the drawee.

b. When electronic records are presented in combination with paper documents, and one of those paper documents is a bill of exchange that is to be accepted by the drawee, the electronic records and paper documents are to be released against acceptance of the bill of exchange (D/A) and the eURC collection instruction must indicate the manner in which those electronic records may be accessed by the drawee.

Article e11 Data Corruption of an Electronic Record

a. If an electronic record that has been received by a bank appears to have been corrupted, the remitting bank may inform the presenter, or the collecting or presenting bank may inform the remitting bank, and may request it to re-present the electronic record.

b. If a collecting or presenting bank makes such a request and the presenter or remitting bank does not re-present the electronic record within 30 calendar days, the collecting or presenting bank may treat the electronic record as not presented and may dispose of the electronic records in any manner deemed appropriate without any responsibility.

Article e12 Additional Disclaimer of Liability for Presentation of Electronic Records under eURC

a. By satisfying itself as to the apparent authenticity of an electronic record, a bank assumes no liability for the identity of the sender, source of the information, or its complete and unaltered character other than that which is apparent in the electronic record received by the use of a data processing system for the receipt, authentication, and identification of electronic records.

b. A bank assumes no liability or responsibility for the consequences arising out of the unavailability of a data processing system other than its own.

Article e13 Force Majeure

A bank assumes no liability or responsibility for the consequences arising out of the interruption of its business, including but not limited to its inability to access a data processing system, or a failure of equipment, software or communications network, caused by Acts of God, riots, civil commotions, insurrections, wars, acts of terrorism, cyberattacks, or by any strikes or lockouts or any other causes, including failure of equipment, software or communications networks, beyond its control.

28) U.C.C. – ARTICLE 3 – NEGOTIABLE INSTRUMENTS (2002), USA[1]

Part 1. General Provisions and Definitions

§3-101. Short Title

This Article may be cited as Uniform Commercial Code – Negotiable Instruments.

§3-102. Subject Matter

(a) This Article applies to negotiable instruments. It does not apply to money, to payment orders governed by Article 4A, or to securities governed by Article 8.

(b) If there is conflict between this Article and Article 4 or 9, Articles 4 and 9 govern.

(c) Regulations of the Board of Governors of the Federal Reserve System and operating circulars of the Federal Reserve Banks supersede any inconsistent provision of this Article to the extent of the inconsistency.

§3-103. Definitions

(a) In this Article:

(1) "Acceptor" means a drawee who has accepted a draft.

(2) "Consumer account" means an account established by an individual primarily for personal, family, or household purposes.

(3) "Consumer transaction" means a transaction in which an individual incurs an obligation primarily for personal, family, or household purposes.

(4) "Drawee" means a person ordered in a draft to make payment.

(5) "Drawer" means a person who signs or is identified in a draft as a person ordering payment.

(6) [reserved]

(7) "Maker" means a person who signs or is identified in a note as a person undertaking to pay.

(8) "Order" means a written instruction to pay money signed by the person giving the instruction. The instruction may be addressed to any person, including the person giving the instruction, or to one or more persons jointly or in the alternative but not in succession. An authorization to pay is not an order unless the person authorized to pay is also instructed to pay.

(9) "Ordinary care" in the case of a person engaged in business means observance of reasonable commercial standards, prevailing in the area in which the person is located, with respect to the business in which the person is engaged. In the case of a bank that takes an instrument for processing for collection or payment by automated means, reasonable commercial standards do not require the bank to examine the instrument if the failure to examine does not violate the bank's prescribed procedures and the bank's procedures do not vary unreasonably from general banking usage not disapproved by this Article or Article 4.

(10) "Party" means a party to an instrument.

---

1 Uniform Commercial Code,

(11) "Principal obligor," with respect to an instrument, means the accommodated party or any other party to the instrument against whom a secondary obligor has recourse under this article.

(12) "Promise" means a written undertaking to pay money signed by the person undertaking to pay. An acknowledgment of an obligation by the obligor is not a promise unless the obligor also undertakes to pay the obligation.

(13) "Prove" with respect to a fact means to meet the burden of establishing the fact (Section 1-201(b)(8)).

(14) [reserved]

(15) "Remitter" means a person who purchases an instrument from its issuer if the instrument is payable to an identified person other than the purchaser.

(16) "Remotely-created consumer item" means an item drawn on a consumer account, which is not created by the payor bank and does not bear a handwritten signature purporting to be the signature of the drawer.

(17) "Secondary obligor," with respect to an instrument, means (a) an indorser or an accommodation party, (b) a drawer having the obligation described in Section 3-414(d), or (c) any other party to the instrument that has recourse against another party to the instrument pursuant to Section 3-116(b).

(b) Other definitions applying to this Article and the sections in which they appear are:

"Acceptance" Section 3-409
"Accommodated party" Section 3-419
"Accommodation party" Section 3-419
"Account" Section 4-104
"Alteration" Section 3-407
"Anomalous indorsement" Section 3-205
"Blank indorsement" Section 3-205
"Cashier's check" Section 3-104
"Certificate of deposit" Section 3-104
"Certified check" Section 3-409
"Check" Section 3-104
"Consideration" Section 3-303
"Draft" Section 3-104
"Holder in due course" Section 3-302
"Incomplete instrument" Section 3-115
"Indorsement" Section 3-204
"Indorser" Section 3-204
"Instrument" Section 3-104
"Issue" Section 3-105
"Issuer" Section 3-105
"Negotiable instrument" Section 3-104
"Negotiation" Section 3-201
"Note" Section 3-104
"Payable at a definite time" Section 3-108
"Payable on demand" Section 3-108
"Payable to bearer" Section 3-109
"Payable to order" Section 3-109
"Payment" Section 3-602
"Person entitled to enforce" Section 3-301

"Presentment" Section 3-501
"Reacquisition" Section 3-207
"Special indorsement" Section 3-205
"Teller's check" Section 3-104
"Transfer of instrument" Section 3-203
"Traveler's check" Section 3-104
"Value" Section 3-303

(c) The following definitions in other Articles apply to this Article:

"Banking day" Section 4-104
"Clearing house" Section 4-104
"Collecting bank" Section 4-105
"Depositary bank" Section 4-105
"Documentary draft" Section 4-104
"Intermediary bank" Section 4-105
"Item" Section 4-104
"Payor bank" Section 4-105
"Suspends payments" Section 4-104

(d) In addition, Article 1 contains general definitions and principles of construction and interpretation applicable throughout this Article.

§3-104. Negotiable Instrument

(a) Except as provided in subsections (c) and (d), "negotiable instrument" means an unconditional promise or order to pay a fixed amount of money, with or without interest or other charges described in the promise or order, if it:

(1) is payable to bearer or to order at the time it is issued or first comes into possession of a holder;

(2) is payable on demand or at a definite time; and

(3) does not state any other undertaking or instruction by the person promising or ordering payment to do any act in addition to the payment of money, but the promise or order may contain (i) an undertaking or power to give, maintain, or protect collateral to secure payment, (ii) an authorization or power to the holder to confess judgment or realize on or dispose of collateral, or (iii) a waiver of the benefit of any law intended for the advantage or protection of an obligor.

(b) "Instrument" means a negotiable instrument.

(c) An order that meets all of the requirements of subsection (a), except paragraph (1), and otherwise falls within the definition of "check" in subsection (f) is a negotiable instrument and a check.

(d) A promise or order other than a check is not an instrument if, at the time it is issued or first comes into possession of a holder, it contains a conspicuous statement, however expressed, to the effect that the promise or order is not negotiable or is not an instrument governed by this Article.

(e) An instrument is a "note" if it is a promise and is a "draft" if it is an order. If an instrument falls within the definition of both "note" and "draft," a person entitled to enforce the instrument may treat it as either.

(f) "Check" means (i) a draft, other than a documentary draft, payable on demand and drawn on a bank or (ii) a cashier's check or teller's check. An instrument may be a check even though it is described on its face by another term, such as "money order."

(g) "Cashier's check" means a draft with respect to which the drawer and drawee are the same bank or branches of the same bank.

(h) "Teller's check" means a draft drawn by a bank (i) on another bank, or (ii) payable at or through a bank.

(i) "Traveler's check" means an instrument that (i) is payable on demand, (ii) is drawn on or payable at or through a bank, (iii) is designated by the term "traveler's check" or by a substantially similar term, and (iv) requires, as a condition to payment, a countersignature by a person whose specimen signature appears on the instrument.

(j) "Certificate of deposit" means an instrument containing an acknowledgment by a bank that a sum of money has been received by the bank and a promise by the bank to repay the sum of money. A certificate of deposit is a note of the bank.

§3-105. Issue of Instrument

(a) "Issue" means the first delivery of an instrument by the maker or drawer, whether to a holder or nonholder, for the purpose of giving rights on the instrument to any person.

(b) An unissued instrument, or an unissued incomplete instrument that is completed, is binding on the maker or drawer, but nonissuance is a defense. An instrument that is conditionally issued or is issued for a special purpose is binding on the maker or drawer, but failure of the condition or special purpose to be fulfilled is a defense.

(c) "Issuer" applies to issued and unissued instruments and means a maker or drawer of an instrument.

§3-106. Unconditional Promise or Order

(a) Except as provided in this section, for the purposes of Section 3-104(a), a promise or order is unconditional unless it states (i) an express condition to payment, (ii) that the promise or order is subject to or governed by another record, or (iii) that rights or obligations with respect to the promise or order are stated in another record. A reference to another record does not of itself make the promise or order conditional.

(b) A promise or order is not made conditional (i) by a reference to another record for a statement of rights with respect to collateral, prepayment, or acceleration, or (ii) because payment is limited to resort to a particular fund or source.

(c) If a promise or order requires, as a condition to payment, a countersignature by a person whose specimen signature appears on the promise or order, the condition does not make the promise or order conditional for the purposes of Section 3-104(a). If the person whose specimen signature appears on an instrument fails to countersign the instrument, the failure to countersign is a defense to the obligation of the issuer, but the failure does not prevent a transferee of the instrument from becoming a holder of the instrument.

(d) If a promise or order at the time it is issued or first comes into possession of a holder contains a statement, required by applicable statutory or administrative law, to the effect that the rights of a holder or transferee are subject to claims or defenses that the issuer could assert against the original payee, the promise or order is not thereby made conditional for the purposes of Section 3-104(a); but if the promise or order is an instrument, there cannot be a holder in due course of the instrument.

§3-107. Instrument Payable in Foreign Money

Unless the instrument otherwise provides, an instrument that states the amount payable in foreign money may be paid in the foreign money or in an equivalent amount in dollars calculated by using the current bank-offered spot rate at the place of payment for the purchase of dollars on the day on which the instrument is paid.

§3-108. Payable on Demand or at Definite Time

(a) A promise or order is "payable on demand" if it (i) states that it is payable on demand or at sight, or otherwise indicates that it is payable at the will of the holder, or (ii) does not state any time of payment.

(b) A promise or order is "payable at a definite time" if it is payable on elapse of a definite period of time after sight or acceptance or at a fixed date or dates or at a time or times readily ascertainable at the time the promise or order is issued, subject to rights of (i) prepayment, (ii) acceleration, (iii) extension at the option of the holder, or (iv) extension to a further definite time at the option of the maker or acceptor or automatically upon or after a specified act or event.

(c) If an instrument, payable at a fixed date, is also payable upon demand made before the fixed date, the instrument is payable on demand until the fixed date and, if demand for payment is not made before that date, becomes payable at a definite time on the fixed date.

§3-109. Payable to Bearer or to Order

(a) A promise or order is payable to bearer if it:

(1) states that it is payable to bearer or to the order of bearer or otherwise indicates that the person in possession of the promise or order is entitled to payment;

(2) does not state a payee; or

(3) states that it is payable to or to the order of cash or otherwise indicates that it is not payable to an identified person.

(b) A promise or order that is not payable to bearer is payable to order if it is payable (i) to the order of an identified person or (ii) to an identified person or order. A promise or order that is payable to order is payable to the identified person.

(c) An instrument payable to bearer may become payable to an identified person if it is specially indorsed pursuant to Section 3-205(a). An instrument payable to an identified person may become payable to bearer if it is indorsed in blank pursuant to Section 3-205(b).

§3-110. Identification of Person to Whom Instrument is Payable

(a) The person to whom an instrument is initially payable is determined by the intent of the person, whether or not authorized, signing as, or in the name or behalf of, the issuer of the instrument. The instrument is payable to the person intended by the signer even if that person is identified in the instrument by a name or other identification that is not that of the intended person. If more than one person signs in the name or behalf of the issuer of an instrument and all the signers do not intend the same person as payee, the instrument is payable to any person intended by one or more of the signers.

(b) If the signature of the issuer of an instrument is made by automated means, such as a check- writing machine, the payee of the instrument is determined by the intent of the person who supplied the name or identification of the payee, whether or not authorized to do so.

(c) A person to whom an instrument is payable may be identified in any way, including by name, identifying number, office, or account number. For the purpose of determining the holder of an instrument, the following rules apply:

(1) If an instrument is payable to an account and the account is identified only by number, the instrument is payable to the person to whom the account is payable. If an instrument is payable to an account identified by number and by the name of a person, the instrument is payable to the named person, whether or not that person is the owner of the account identified by number.

(2) If an instrument is payable to:

(i) a trust, an estate, or a person described as trustee or representative of a trust or estate, the instrument is payable to the trustee, the representative, or a successor of either, whether or not the beneficiary or estate is also named;

(ii) a person described as agent or similar representative of a named or identified person, the instrument is payable to the represented person, the representative, or a successor of the representative;

(iii) a fund or organization that is not a legal entity, the instrument is payable to a representative of the members of the fund or organization; or

(iv) an office or to a person described as holding an office, the instrument is payable to the named person, the incumbent of the office, or a successor to the incumbent.

(d) If an instrument is payable to two or more persons alternatively, it is payable to any of them and may be negotiated, discharged, or enforced by any or all of them in possession of the instrument. If an instrument is payable to two or more persons not alternatively, it is payable to all of them and may be negotiated, discharged, or enforced only by all of them. If an instrument payable to two or more persons is ambiguous as to whether it is payable to the persons alternatively, the instrument is payable to the persons alternatively.

§3-111. Place of Payment

Except as otherwise provided for items in Article 4, an instrument is payable at the place of payment stated in the instrument. If no place of payment is stated, an instrument is payable at the address of the drawee or maker stated in the instrument. If no address is stated, the place of payment is the place of business of the drawee or maker. If a drawee or maker has more than one place of business, the place of payment is any place of business of the drawee or maker chosen by the person entitled to enforce the instrument. If the drawee or maker has no place of business, the place of payment is the residence of the drawee or maker.

§3-112. Interest

(a) Unless otherwise provided in the instrument, (i) an instrument is not payable with interest, and (ii) interest on an interest-bearing instrument is payable from the date of the instrument.

(b) Interest may be stated in an instrument as a fixed or variable amount of money or it may be expressed as a fixed or variable rate or rates. The amount or rate of interest may be stated or described in the instrument in any manner and may require reference to information not contained in the instrument. If an instrument provides for interest, but the amount of interest payable cannot be ascertained from the description, interest is payable at the judgment rate in effect at the place of payment of the instrument and at the time interest first accrues.

§3-113. Date of Instrument

(a) An instrument may be antedated or postdated. The date stated determines the time of payment if the instrument is payable at a fixed period after date. Except as provided in Section 4-401(c), an instrument payable on demand is not payable before the date of the instrument.

(b) If an instrument is undated, its date is the date of its issue or, in the case of an unissued instrument, the date it first comes into possession of a holder.

§3-114. Contradictory Terms of Instrument

If an instrument contains contradictory terms, typewritten terms prevail over printed terms, handwritten terms prevail over both, and words prevail over numbers.

§3-115. Incomplete Instrument

(a) "Incomplete instrument" means a signed writing, whether or not issued by the signer, the contents of which show at the time of signing that it is incomplete but that the signer intended it to be completed by the addition of words or numbers.

(b) Subject to subsection (c), if an incomplete instrument is an instrument under Section 3-104, it may be enforced according to its terms if it is not completed, or according to its terms as augmented by completion. If an incomplete instrument is not an instrument under Section 3-104, but, after completion, the requirements of Section 3-104 are met, the instrument may be enforced according to its terms as augmented by completion.

(c) If words or numbers are added to an incomplete instrument without authority of the signer, there is an alteration of the incomplete instrument under Section 3-407.

(d) The burden of establishing that words or numbers were added to an incomplete instrument without authority of the signer is on the person asserting the lack of authority.

§3-116. Joint and Several Liability; Contribution

(a) Except as otherwise provided in the instrument, two or more persons who have the same liability on an instrument as makers, drawers, acceptors, indorsers who indorse as joint payees, or anomalous indorsers are jointly and severally liable in the capacity in which they sign.

(b) Except as provided in Section 3-419(e) or by agreement of the affected parties, a party having joint and several liability who pays the instrument is entitled to receive from any party having the same joint and several liability contribution in accordance with applicable law.

§3-117. Other Agreements Affecting Instrument

Subject to applicable law regarding exclusion of proof of contemporaneous or previous agreements, the obligation of a party to an instrument to pay the instrument may be modified, supplemented, or nullified by a separate agreement of the obligor and a person entitled to enforce the instrument, if the instrument is issued or the obligation is incurred in reliance on the agreement or as part of the same transaction giving rise to the agreement. To the extent an obligation is modified, supplemented, or nullified by an agreement under this section, the agreement is a defense to the obligation.

§3-118. Statute of Limitations

(a) Except as provided in subsection (e), an action to enforce the obligation of a party to pay a note payable at a definite time must be commenced within six years after the due date or dates stated in the note or, if a due date is accelerated, within six years after the accelerated due date.

(b) Except as provided in subsection (d) or (e), if demand for payment is made to the maker of a note payable on demand, an action to enforce the obligation of a party to pay the note must be commenced within six years after the demand. If no demand for payment is made to the maker, an action to enforce the note is barred if neither principal nor interest on the note has been paid for a continuous period of 10 years.

(c) Except as provided in subsection (d), an action to enforce the obligation of a party to an unaccepted draft to pay the draft must be commenced within three years after dishonor of the draft or 10 years after the date of the draft, whichever period expires first.

(d) An action to enforce the obligation of the acceptor of a certified check or the issuer of a teller's check, cashier's check, or traveler's check must be commenced within three years after demand for payment is made to the acceptor or issuer, as the case may be.

(e) An action to enforce the obligation of a party to a certificate of deposit to pay the instrument must be commenced within six years after demand for payment is made to the maker, but if the instrument states a due date and the maker is not required to pay before that date, the six-year period begins when a demand for payment is in effect and the due date has passed.

(f) An action to enforce the obligation of a party to pay an accepted draft, other than a certified check, must be commenced (i) within six years after the due date or dates stated in the draft or acceptance if the obligation of the acceptor is payable at a definite time, or (ii) within six years after the date of the acceptance if the obligation of the acceptor is payable on demand.

(g) Unless governed by other law regarding claims for indemnity or contribution, an action (i) for conversion of an instrument, for money had and received, or like action based on conversion, (ii) for breach of warranty, or (iii) to enforce an obligation, duty, or right arising under this Article and not governed by this section must be commenced within three years after the [cause of action] accrues.

§3-119. Notice of Right to Defend Action

In an action for breach of an obligation for which a third person is answerable over pursuant to this Article or Article 4, the defendant may give the third person notice of the litigation in a record, and the person notified may then give similar notice to any other person who is answerable over. If the notice states (i) that the person notified may come in and defend and (ii) that failure to do so will bind the person notified in an action later brought by the person giving the notice as to any determination of fact common to the two litigations, the person notified is so bound unless after seasonable receipt of the notice the person notified does come in and defend.

Part 2. Negotiation, Transfer, and Indorsement

§3-201. Negotiation

(a) "Negotiation" means a transfer of possession, whether voluntary or involuntary, of an instrument by a person other than the issuer to a person who thereby becomes its holder.

(b) Except for negotiation by a remitter, if an instrument is payable to an identified person, negotiation requires transfer of possession of the instrument and its indorsement by the holder. If an instrument is payable to bearer, it may be negotiated by transfer of possession alone.

§3-202. Negotiation Subject to Rescission

(a) Negotiation is effective even if obtained (i) from an infant, a corporation exceeding its powers, or a person without capacity, (ii) by fraud, duress, or mistake, or (iii) in breach of duty or as part of an illegal transaction.

(b) To the extent permitted by other law, negotiation may be rescinded or may be subject to other remedies, but those remedies may not be asserted against a subsequent holder in due course or a person paying the instrument in good faith and without knowledge of facts that are a basis for rescission or other remedy.

§3-203. Transfer of an Instrument; Rights Acquired by Transfer

(a) An instrument is transferred when it is delivered by a person other than its issuer for the purpose of giving to the person receiving delivery the right to enforce the instrument.

(b) Transfer of an instrument, whether or not the transfer is a negotiation, vests in the transferee any right of the transferor to enforce the instrument, including any right as a holder in due course, but the transferee cannot acquire rights of a holder in due course by a transfer, directly or indirectly, from a holder in due course if the transferee engaged in fraud or illegality affecting the instrument.

(c) Unless otherwise agreed, if an instrument is transferred for value and the transferee does not become a holder because of lack of indorsement by the transferor, the transferee has a specifically enforceable right to the unqualified indorsement of the transferor, but negotiation of the instrument does not occur until the indorsement is made.

(d) If a transferor purports to transfer less than the entire instrument, negotiation of the instrument does not occur. The transferee obtains no rights under this Article and has only the rights of a partial assignee.

§3-204. Indorsement

(a) "Indorsement" means a signature, other than that of a signer as maker, drawer, or acceptor, that alone or accompanied by other words is made on an instrument for the purpose of (i) negotiating the instrument, (ii) restricting payment of the instrument, or (iii) incurring indorser's liability on the instrument, but regardless of the intent of the signer, a signature and its accompanying words is an indorsement unless the accompanying words, terms of the instrument, place of the signature, or other circumstances unambiguously indicate that the signature was made for a purpose other than indorsement. For the purpose of determining whether a signature is made on an instrument, a paper affixed to the instrument is a part of the instrument.

(b) "Indorser" means a person who makes an indorsement.

(c) For the purpose of determining whether the transferee of an instrument is a holder, an indorsement that transfers a security interest in the instrument is effective as an unqualified indorsement of the instrument.

(d) If an instrument is payable to a holder under a name that is not the name of the holder, indorsement may be made by the holder in the name stated in the instrument or in the holder's name or both, but signature in both names may be required by a person paying or taking the instrument for value or collection.

§3-205. Special Indorsement; Blank Indorsement; Anomalous Indorsement

(a) If an indorsement is made by the holder of an instrument, whether payable to an identified person or payable to bearer, and the indorsement identifies a person to whom it makes the instrument payable, it is a "special indorsement." When specially indorsed, an instrument becomes payable to the identified person and may be negotiated only by the indorsement of that person. The principles stated in Section 3-110 apply to special indorsements.

(b) If an indorsement is made by the holder of an instrument and it is not a special indorsement, it is a "blank indorsement." When indorsed in blank, an instrument becomes payable to bearer and may be negotiated by transfer of possession alone until specially indorsed.

(c) The holder may convert a blank indorsement that consists only of a signature into a special indorsement by writing, above the signature of the indorser, words identifying the person to whom the instrument is made payable.

(d) "Anomalous indorsement" means an indorsement made by a person who is not the holder of the instrument. An anomalous indorsement does not affect the manner in which the instrument may be negotiated.

§3-206. Restrictive Indorsement

(a) An indorsement limiting payment to a particular person or otherwise prohibiting further transfer or negotiation of the instrument is not effective to prevent further transfer or negotiation of the instrument.

(b) An indorsement stating a condition to the right of the indorsee to receive payment does not affect the right of the indorsee to enforce the instrument. A person paying the instrument or taking it for value or collection may disregard the condition, and the rights and liabilities of that person are not affected by whether the condition has been fulfilled.

(c) If an instrument bears an indorsement (i) described in Section 4-201(b), or (ii) in blank or to a particular bank using the words "for deposit," "for collection," or other words indicating a purpose of having the instrument collected by a bank for the indorser or for a particular account, the following rules apply:

(1) A person, other than a bank, who purchases the instrument when so indorsed converts the instrument unless the amount paid for the instrument is received by the indorser or applied consistently with the indorsement.

(2) A depositary bank that purchases the instrument or takes it for collection when so indorsed converts the instrument unless the amount paid by the bank with respect to the instrument is received by the indorser or applied consistently with the indorsement.

(3) A payor bank that is also the depositary bank or that takes the instrument for immediate payment over the counter from a person other than a collecting bank converts the instrument unless the proceeds of the instrument are received by the indorser or applied consistently with the indorsement.

(4) Except as otherwise provided in paragraph (3), a payor bank or intermediary bank may disregard the indorsement and is not liable if the proceeds of the instrument are not received by the indorser or applied consistently with the indorsement.

(d) Except for an indorsement covered by subsection (c), if an instrument bears an indorsement using words to the effect that payment is to be made to the indorsee as agent, trustee, or other fiduciary for the benefit of the indorser or another person, the following rules apply:

(1) Unless there is notice of breach of fiduciary duty as provided in Section 3-307, a person who purchases the instrument from the indorsee or takes the instrument from the indorsee for collection or payment may pay the proceeds of payment or the value given for the instrument to the indorsee without regard to whether the indorsee violates a fiduciary duty to the indorser.

(2) A subsequent transferee of the instrument or person who pays the instrument is neither given notice nor otherwise affected by the restriction in the indorsement unless the transferee or payor knows that the fiduciary dealt with the instrument or its proceeds in breach of fiduciary duty.

(e) The presence on an instrument of an indorsement to which this section applies does not prevent a purchaser of the instrument from becoming a holder in due course of the instrument unless the purchaser is a converter under subsection (c) or has notice or knowledge of breach of fiduciary duty as stated in subsection (d).

(f) In an action to enforce the obligation of a party to pay the instrument, the obligor has a defense if payment would violate an indorsement to which this section applies and the payment is not permitted by this section.

§3-207. Reacquisition

Reacquisition of an instrument occurs if it is transferred to a former holder, by negotiation or otherwise. A former holder who reacquires the instrument may cancel indorsements made after the reacquirer first became a holder of the instrument. If the cancellation causes the instrument to be payable to the reacquirer or to bearer, the reacquirer may negotiate the instrument. An indorser whose indorsement is canceled is discharged, and the discharge is effective against any subsequent holder.

Part 3. Enforcement of Instruments

§3-301. Person Entitled to Enforce Instrument

"Person entitled to enforce" an instrument means (i) the holder of the instrument, (ii) a nonholder in possession of the instrument who has the rights of a holder, or (iii) a person not in possession of the instrument who is entitled to enforce the instrument pursuant to Section 3-309 or 3-418(d). A person may be a person entitled to enforce the instrument even though the person is not the owner of the instrument or is in wrongful possession of the instrument.

§3-302. Holder in Due Course

(a) Subject to subsection (c) and Section 3-106(d), "holder in due course" means the holder of an instrument if:

(1) the instrument when issued or negotiated to the holder does not bear such apparent evidence of forgery or alteration or is not otherwise so irregular or incomplete as to call into question its authenticity; and

(2) the holder took the instrument (i) for value, (ii) in good faith, (iii) without notice that the instrument is overdue or has been dishonored or that there is an uncured default with respect to payment of another instrument issued as part of the same series, (iv) without notice that the instrument contains an unauthorized signature or has been altered, (v) without notice of any claim to the instrument described in Section 3-306, and (vi) without notice that any party has a defense or claim in recoupment described in Section 3-305(a).

(b) Notice of discharge of a party, other than discharge in an insolvency proceeding, is not notice of a defense under subsection (a), but discharge is effective against a person who became a holder in due course with notice of the discharge. Public filing or recording of a document does not of itself constitute notice of a defense, claim in recoupment, or claim to the instrument.

(c) Except to the extent a transferor or predecessor in interest has rights as a holder in due course, a person does not acquire rights of a holder in due course of an instrument taken (i) by legal process or by purchase in an execution, bankruptcy, or creditor's sale or similar proceeding, (ii) by purchase as part of a bulk transaction not in ordinary course of business of the transferor, or (iii) as the successor in interest to an estate or other organization.

(d) If, under Section 3-303(a)(1), the promise of performance that is the consideration for an instrument has been partially performed, the holder may assert rights as a holder in due course of the instrument only to the fraction of the amount payable under the instrument equal to the value of the partial performance divided by the value of the promised performance.

(e) If (i) the person entitled to enforce an instrument has only a security interest in the instrument and (ii) the person obliged to pay the instrument has a defense, claim in recoupment, or claim to the instrument that may be asserted against the person who granted the security interest, the person entitled to enforce the instrument may assert rights as a holder in due course only to an amount payable under the instrument which, at the time of enforcement of the instrument, does not exceed the amount of the unpaid obligation secured.

(f) To be effective, notice must be received at a time and in a manner that gives a reasonable opportunity to act on it.

(g) This section is subject to any law limiting status as a holder in due course in particular classes of transactions.

§3-303. Value and Consideration

(a) An instrument is issued or transferred for value if:

(1) the instrument is issued or transferred for a promise of performance, to the extent the promise has been performed;

(2) the transferee acquires a security interest or other lien in the instrument other than a lien obtained by judicial proceeding;

(3) the instrument is issued or transferred as payment of, or as security for, an antecedent claim against any person, whether or not the claim is due;

(4) the instrument is issued or transferred in exchange for a negotiable instrument; or

(5) the instrument is issued or transferred in exchange for the incurring of an irrevocable obligation to a third party by the person taking the instrument.

(b) "Consideration" means any consideration sufficient to support a simple contract. The drawer or maker of an instrument has a defense if the instrument is issued without consideration. If an instrument is issued for a promise of performance, the issuer has a defense to the extent performance of the promise is due and the promise has not been performed. If an instrument is issued for value as stated in subsection (a), the instrument is also issued for consideration.

§3-304. Overdue Instrument

(a) An instrument payable on demand becomes overdue at the earliest of the following times:

(1) on the day after the day demand for payment is duly made;

(2) if the instrument is a check, 90 days after its date; or

(3) if the instrument is not a check, when the instrument has been outstanding for a period of time after its date which is unreasonably long under the circumstances of the particular case in light of the nature of the instrument and usage of the trade.

(b) With respect to an instrument payable at a definite time the following rules apply:

(1) If the principal is payable in installments and a due date has not been accelerated, the instrument becomes overdue upon default under the instrument for nonpayment of an installment, and the instrument remains overdue until the default is cured.

(2) If the principal is not payable in installments and the due date has not been accelerated, the instrument becomes overdue on the day after the due date.

(3) If a due date with respect to principal has been accelerated, the instrument becomes overdue on the day after the accelerated due date.

(c) Unless the due date of principal has been accelerated, an instrument does not become overdue if there is default in payment of interest but no default in payment of principal.

§3-305. Defenses and Claims in Recoupment

(a) Except as otherwise provided in this section, the right to enforce the obligation of a party to pay an instrument is subject to the following:

(1) a defense of the obligor based on (i) infancy of the obligor to the extent it is a defense to a simple contract, (ii) duress, lack of legal capacity, or illegality of the transaction which, under other law, nullifies the obligation of the obligor, (iii) fraud that induced the obligor to sign the instrument with neither knowledge nor reasonable opportunity to learn of its character or its essential terms, or (iv) discharge of the obligor in insolvency proceedings;

(2) a defense of the obligor stated in another section of this Article or a defense of the obligor that would be available if the person entitled to enforce the instrument were enforcing a right to payment under a simple contract; and

(3) a claim in recoupment of the obligor against the original payee of the instrument if the claim arose from the transaction that gave rise to the instrument; but the claim of the

obligor may be asserted against a transferee of the instrument only to reduce the amount owing on the instrument at the time the action is brought.

(b) The right of a holder in due course to enforce the obligation of a party to pay the instrument is subject to defenses of the obligor stated in subsection (a)(1), but is not subject to defenses of the obligor stated in subsection (a)(2) or claims in recoupment stated in subsection (a)(3) against a person other than the holder.

(c) Except as stated in subsection (d), in an action to enforce the obligation of a party to pay the instrument, the obligor may not assert against the person entitled to enforce the instrument a defense, claim in recoupment, or claim to the instrument (Section 3-306) of another person, but the other person's claim to the instrument may be asserted by the obligor if the other person is joined in the action and personally asserts the claim against the person entitled to enforce the instrument. An obligor is not obliged to pay the instrument if the person seeking enforcement of the instrument does not have rights of a holder in due course and the obligor proves that the instrument is a lost or stolen instrument.

(d) In an action to enforce the obligation of an accommodation party to pay an instrument, the accommodation party may assert against the person entitled to enforce the instrument any defense or claim in recoupment under subsection (a) that the accommodated party could assert against the person entitled to enforce the instrument, except the defenses of discharge in insolvency proceedings, infancy, and lack of legal capacity.

(e) In a consumer transaction, if law other than this article requires that an instrument include a statement to the effect that the rights of a holder or transferee are subject to a claim or defense that the issuer could assert against the original payee, and the instrument does not include such a statement:

(1) the instrument has the same effect as if the instrument included such a statement;

(2) the issuer may assert against the holder or transferee all claims and defenses that would have been available if the instrument included such a statement; and (3) the extent to which claims may be asserted against the holder or transferee is determined as if the instrument included such a statement.

(f) This section is subject to law other than this article that establishes a different rule for consumer transactions.

Part 4. Liability of Parties

§3-401. Signature

(a) A person is not liable on an instrument unless (i) the person signed the instrument, or (ii) the person is represented by an agent or representative who signed the instrument and the signature is binding on the represented person under Section 3-402.

(b) A signature may be made (i) manually or by means of a device or machine, and (ii) by the use of any name, including a trade or assumed name, or by a word, mark, or symbol executed or adopted by a person with present intention to authenticate a writing.

§3-402. Signature by Representative

(a) If a person acting, or purporting to act, as a representative signs an instrument by signing either the name of the represented person or the name of the signer, the represented person is bound by the signature to the same extent the represented person would be bound if the signature were on a simple contract. If the represented person is bound, the signature of the representative is the "authorized signature of the represented person" and the represented person is liable on the instrument, whether or not identified in the instrument.

(b) If a representative signs the name of the representative to an instrument and the signature is an authorized signature of the represented person, the following rules apply:

(1) If the form of the signature shows unambiguously that the signature is made on behalf of the represented person who is identified in the instrument, the representative is not liable on the instrument.

(2) Subject to subsection (c), if (i) the form of the signature does not show unambiguously that the signature is made in a representative capacity or (ii) the represented person is not identified in the instrument, the representative is liable on the instrument to a holder in due course that took the instrument without notice that the representative was not intended to be liable on the instrument. With respect to any other person, the representative is liable on the instrument unless the representative proves that the original parties did not intend the representative to be liable on the instrument.

(c) If a representative signs the name of the representative as drawer of a check without indication of the representative status and the check is payable from an account of the represented person who is identified on the check, the signer is not liable on the check if the signature is an authorized signature of the represented person.

§3-403. Unauthorized Signature

(a) Unless otherwise provided in this Article or Article 4, an unauthorized signature is ineffective except as the signature of the unauthorized signer in favor of a person who in good faith pays the instrument or takes it for value. An unauthorized signature may be ratified for all purposes of this Article.

(b) If the signature of more than one person is required to constitute the authorized signature of an organization, the signature of the organization is unauthorized if one of the required signatures is lacking.

(c) The civil or criminal liability of a person who makes an unauthorized signature is not affected by any provision of this Article which makes the unauthorized signature effective for the purposes of this Article.

§3-404. Impostors; Fictitious Parties

(a) If an impostor, by use of the mails or otherwise, induces the issuer of an instrument to issue the instrument to the impostor, or to a person acting in concert with the impostor, by impersonating the payee of the instrument or a person authorized to act for the payee, an indorsement of the instrument by any person in the name of the payee is effective as the indorsement of the payee in favor of a person who, in good faith, pays the instrument or takes it for value or for collection.

(b) If (i) a person whose intent determines to whom an instrument is payable (Section 3-110(a) or (b)) does not intend the person identified as payee to have any interest in the instrument, or (ii) the person identified as payee of an instrument is a fictitious person, the following rules apply until the instrument is negotiated by special indorsement:

(1) Any person in possession of the instrument is its holder.

(2) An indorsement by any person in the name of the payee stated in the instrument is effective as the indorsement of the payee in favor of a person who, in good faith, pays the instrument or takes it for value or for collection.

(c) Under subsection (a) or (b), an indorsement is made in the name of a payee if (i) it is made in a name substantially similar to that of the payee or (ii) the instrument, whether or not indorsed, is deposited in a depositary bank to an account in a name substantially similar to that of the payee.

(d) With respect to an instrument to which subsection (a) or (b) applies, if a person paying the instrument or taking it for value or for collection fails to exercise ordinary care in paying or taking the instrument and that failure substantially contributes to loss resulting from payment of the instrument, the person bearing the loss may recover from the person failing to exercise ordinary care to the extent the failure to exercise ordinary care contributed to the loss.

§3-405. Employer's Responsibility for Fraudulent Indorsement by Employee

(a) In this section:

(1) "Employee" includes an independent contractor and employee of an independent contractor retained by the employer.

(2) "Fraudulent indorsement" means (i) in the case of an instrument payable to the employer, a forged indorsement purporting to be that of the employer, or (ii) in the case of an instrument with respect to which the employer is the issuer, a forged indorsement purporting to be that of the person identified as payee.

(3) "Responsibility" with respect to instruments means authority (i) to sign or indorse instruments on behalf of the employer, (ii) to process instruments received by the employer for bookkeeping purposes, for deposit to an account, or for other disposition, (iii) to prepare or process instruments for issue in the name of the employer, (iv) to supply information determining the names or addresses of payees of instruments to be issued in the name of the employer, (v) to control the disposition of instruments to be issued in the name of the employer, or (vi) to act otherwise with respect to instruments in a responsible capacity. "Responsibility" does not include authority that merely allows an employee to have access to instruments or blank or incomplete instrument forms that are being stored or transported or are part of incoming or outgoing mail, or similar access.

(b) For the purpose of determining the rights and liabilities of a person who, in good faith, pays an instrument or takes it for value or for collection, if an employer entrusted an employee with responsibility with respect to the instrument and the employee or a person acting in concert with the employee makes a fraudulent indorsement of the instrument, the indorsement is effective as the indorsement of the person to whom the instrument is payable if it is made in the name of that person. If the person paying the instrument or taking it for value or for collection fails to exercise ordinary care in paying or taking the instrument and that failure substantially contributes to loss resulting from the fraud, the person bearing the loss may recover from the person failing to exercise ordinary care to the extent the failure to exercise ordinary care contributed to the loss.

(c) Under subsection (b), an indorsement is made in the name of the person to whom an instrument is payable if (i) it is made in a name substantially similar to the name of that person or (ii) the instrument, whether or not indorsed, is deposited in a depositary bank to an account in a name substantially similar to the name of that person.

§3-406. Negligence Contributing to Forged Signature or Alteration of Instrument

(a) A person whose failure to exercise ordinary care substantially contributes to an alteration of an instrument or to the making of a forged signature on an instrument is precluded from asserting the alteration or the forgery against a person who, in good faith, pays the instrument or takes it for value or for collection.

(b) Under subsection (a), if the person asserting the preclusion fails to exercise ordinary care in paying or taking the instrument and that failure substantially contributes to loss, the loss is allocated between the person precluded and the person asserting the preclusion according to the extent to which the failure of each to exercise ordinary care contributed to the loss.

(c) Under subsection (a), the burden of proving failure to exercise ordinary care is on the person asserting the preclusion. Under subsection (b), the burden of proving failure to exercise ordinary care is on the person precluded.

§3-407. Alteration

(a) "Alteration" means (i) an unauthorized change in an instrument that purports to modify in any respect the obligation of a party, or (ii) an unauthorized addition of words or numbers or other change to an incomplete instrument relating to the obligation of a party.

(b) Except as provided in subsection (c), an alteration fraudulently made discharges a party whose obligation is affected by the alteration unless that party assents or is precluded from asserting the alteration. No other alteration discharges a party, and the instrument may be enforced according to its original terms.

(c) A payor bank or drawee paying a fraudulently altered instrument or a person taking it for value, in good faith and without notice of the alteration, may enforce rights with respect to the instrument (i) according to its original terms, or (ii) in the case of an incomplete instrument altered by unauthorized completion, according to its terms as completed.

§3-408. Drawee Not Liable on Unaccepted Draft

A check or other draft does not of itself operate as an assignment of funds in the hands of the drawee available for its payment, and the drawee is not liable on the instrument until the drawee accepts it.

§3-409. Acceptance of Draft; Certified Check

(a) "Acceptance" means the drawee's signed agreement to pay a draft as presented. It must be written on the draft and may consist of the drawee's signature alone. Acceptance may be made at any time and becomes effective when notification pursuant to instructions is given or the accepted draft is delivered for the purpose of giving rights on the acceptance to any person.

(b) A draft may be accepted although it has not been signed by the drawer, is otherwise incomplete, is overdue, or has been dishonored.

(c) If a draft is payable at a fixed period after sight and the acceptor fails to date the acceptance, the holder may complete the acceptance by supplying a date in good faith.

(d) "Certified check" means a check accepted by the bank on which it is drawn. Acceptance may be made as stated in subsection (a) or by a writing on the check which indicates that the check is certified. The drawee of a check has no obligation to certify the check, and refusal to certify is not dishonor of the check.

§3-410. Acceptance Varying Draft

(a) If the terms of a drawee's acceptance vary from the terms of the draft as presented, the holder may refuse the acceptance and treat the draft as dishonored. In that case, the drawee may cancel the acceptance.

(b) The terms of a draft are not varied by an acceptance to pay at a particular bank or place in the United States, unless the acceptance states that the draft is to be paid only at that bank or place.

(c) If the holder assents to an acceptance varying the terms of a draft, the obligation of each drawer and indorser that does not expressly assent to the acceptance is discharged.

§3-411. Refusal to Pay Cashier's Checks, Teller's Checks, and Certified Checks

(a) In this section, "obligated bank" means the acceptor of a certified check or the issuer of a cashier's check or teller's check bought from the issuer.

(b) If the obligated bank wrongfully (i) refuses to pay a cashier's check or certified check, (ii) stops payment of a teller's check, or (iii) refuses to pay a dishonored teller's check, the person asserting the right to enforce the check is entitled to compensation for expenses and loss of interest resulting from the nonpayment and may recover consequential damages if the obligated bank refuses to pay after receiving notice of particular circumstances giving rise to the damages.

(c) Expenses or consequential damages under subsection (b) are not recoverable if the refusal of the obligated bank to pay occurs because (i) the bank suspends payments, (ii) the obligated bank asserts a claim or defense of the bank that it has reasonable grounds to believe is available against the person entitled to enforce the instrument, (iii) the obligated bank has a reasonable doubt whether the person demanding payment is the person entitled to enforce the instrument, or (iv) payment is prohibited by law.

§3-412. Obligation of Issuer of Note or Cashier's Check

The issuer of a note or cashier's check or other draft drawn on the drawer is obliged to pay the instrument (i) according to its terms at the time it was issued or, if not issued, at the time it first came into possession of a holder, or (ii) if the issuer signed an incomplete instrument, according to its terms when completed, to the extent stated in Sections 3-115 and 3-407. The obligation is owed to a person entitled to enforce the instrument or to an indorser who paid the instrument under Section 3-415.

§3-413. Obligation of Acceptor

(a) The acceptor of a draft is obliged to pay the draft (i) according to its terms at the time it was accepted, even though the acceptance states that the draft is payable "as originally drawn" or equivalent terms, (ii) if the acceptance varies the terms of the draft, according to the terms of the draft as varied, or (iii) if the acceptance is of a draft that is an incomplete instrument, according to its terms when completed, to the extent stated in Sections 3-115 and 3-407. The obligation is owed to a person entitled to enforce the draft or to the drawer or an indorser who paid the draft under Section 3-414 or 3-415.

(b) If the certification of a check or other acceptance of a draft states the amount certified or accepted, the obligation of the acceptor is that amount. If (i) the certification or acceptance does not state an amount, (ii) the amount of the instrument is subsequently raised, and (iii) the instrument is then negotiated to a holder in due course, the obligation of the acceptor is the amount of the instrument at the time it was taken by the holder in due course.

§3-414. Obligation of Drawer

(a) This section does not apply to cashier's checks or other drafts drawn on the drawer.

(b) If an unaccepted draft is dishonored, the drawer is obliged to pay the draft (i) according to its terms at the time it was issued or, if not issued, at the time it first came into possession of a holder, or (ii) if the drawer signed an incomplete instrument, according to its terms when completed, to the extent stated in Sections 3-115 and 3-407. The obligation is owed to a person entitled to enforce the draft or to an indorser who paid the draft under Section 3-415.

(c) If a draft is accepted by a bank, the drawer is discharged, regardless of when or by whom acceptance was obtained.

(d) If a draft is accepted and the acceptor is not a bank, the obligation of the drawer to pay the draft if the draft is dishonored by the acceptor is the same as the obligation of an indorser under Section 3-415(a) and (c).

(e) If a draft states that it is drawn "without recourse" or otherwise disclaims liability of the drawer to pay the draft, the drawer is not liable under subsection (b) to pay the draft if the draft is not a check. A disclaimer of the liability stated in subsection (b) is not effective if the draft is a check.

(f) If (i) a check is not presented for payment or given to a depositary bank for collection within 30 days after its date, (ii) the drawee suspends payments after expiration of the 30-day period without paying the check, and (iii) because of the suspension of payments, the drawer is deprived of funds maintained with the drawee to cover payment of the check, the drawer to the extent deprived of funds may discharge its obligation to pay the check by assigning to the person entitled to enforce the check the rights of the drawer against the drawee with respect to the funds.

§3-415. Obligation of Indorser

(a) Subject to subsections (b), (c), and (d) and to Section 3-419(d), if an instrument is dishonored, an indorser is obliged to pay the amount due on the instrument (i) according to the terms of the instrument at the time it was indorsed, or (ii) if the indorser indorsed an incomplete instrument, according to its terms when completed, to the extent stated in Sections 3-115 and 3-407. The obligation of the indorser is owed to a person entitled to enforce the instrument or to a subsequent indorser who paid the instrument under this section.

(b) If an indorsement states that it is made "without recourse" or otherwise disclaims liability of the indorser, the indorser is not liable under subsection (a) to pay the instrument.

(c) If notice of dishonor of an instrument is required by Section 3-503 and notice of dishonor complying with that section is not given to an indorser, the liability of the indorser under subsection (a) is discharged.

(d) If a draft is accepted by a bank after an indorsement is made, the liability of the indorser under subsection (a) is discharged.

(e) If an indorser of a check is liable under subsection (a) and the check is not presented for payment, or given to a depositary bank for collection, within 30 days after the day the indorsement was made, the liability of the indorser under subsection (a) is discharged.

§3-416. Transfer Warranties

(a) A person who transfers an instrument for consideration warrants to the transferee and, if the transfer is by indorsement, to any subsequent transferee that:

(1) the warrantor is a person entitled to enforce the instrument;

(2) all signatures on the instrument are authentic and authorized;

(3) the instrument has not been altered;

(4) the instrument is not subject to a defense or claim in recoupment of any party which can be asserted against the warrantor; and

(5) the warrantor has no knowledge of any insolvency proceeding commenced with respect to the maker or acceptor or, in the case of an unaccepted draft, the drawer; and

(6) with respect to a remotely-created consumer item, that the person on whose account the item is drawn authorized the issuance of the item in the amount for which the item is drawn.

(b) A person to whom the warranties under subsection (a) are made and who took the instrument in good faith may recover from the warrantor as damages for breach of warranty an amount equal to the loss suffered as a result of the breach, but not more than the amount of the instrument plus expenses and loss of interest incurred as a result of the breach.

(c) The warranties stated in subsection (a) cannot be disclaimed with respect to checks. Unless notice of a claim for breach of warranty is given to the warrantor within 30 days after the claimant has reason to know of the breach and the identity of the warrantor, the liability of the warrantor under subsection (b) is discharged to the extent of any loss caused by the delay in giving notice of the claim.

(d) A [cause of action] for breach of warranty under this section accrues when the claimant has reason to know of the breach.

§3-417. Presentment Warranties

(a) If an unaccepted draft is presented to the drawee for payment or acceptance and the drawee pays or accepts the draft, (i) the person obtaining payment or acceptance, at the time of presentment, and (ii) a previous transferor of the draft, at the time of transfer, warrant to the drawee making payment or accepting the draft in good faith that:

(1) the warrantor is, or was, at the time the warrantor transferred the draft, a person entitled to enforce the draft or authorized to obtain payment or acceptance of the draft on behalf of a person entitled to enforce the draft;

(2) the draft has not been altered;

(3) the warrantor has no knowledge that the signature of the drawer of the draft is unauthorized;

(4) with respect to any remotely-created consumer item, that the person on whose account the item is drawn authorized the issuance of the item in the amount for which the item is drawn.

(b) A drawee making payment may recover from any warrantor damages for breach of warranty equal to the amount paid by the drawee less the amount the drawee received or is entitled to receive from the drawer because of the payment. In addition, the drawee is entitled to compensation for expenses and loss of interest resulting from the breach. The right of the drawee to recover damages under this subsection is not affected by any failure of the drawee to exercise ordinary care in making payment. If the drawee accepts the draft, breach of warranty is a defense to the obligation of the acceptor. If the acceptor makes payment with respect to the draft, the acceptor is entitled to recover from any warrantor for breach of warranty the amounts stated in this subsection.

(c) If a drawee asserts a claim for breach of warranty under subsection (a) based on an unauthorized indorsement of the draft or an alteration of the draft, the warrantor may defend by proving that the indorsement is effective under Section 3-404 or 3-405 or the drawer is precluded under Section 3-406 or 4-406 from asserting against the drawee the unauthorized indorsement or alteration.

(d) If (i) a dishonored draft is presented for payment to the drawer or an indorser or (ii) any other instrument is presented for payment to a party obliged to pay the instrument, and (iii) payment is received, the following rules apply:

(1) The person obtaining payment and a prior transferor of the instrument warrant to the person making payment in good faith that the warrantor is, or was, at the time the warrantor transferred the instrument, a person entitled to enforce the instrument or authorized to obtain payment on behalf of a person entitled to enforce the instrument.

(2) The person making payment may recover from any warrantor for breach of warranty an amount equal to the amount paid plus expenses and loss of interest resulting from the breach.

(e) The warranties stated in subsections (a) and (d) cannot be disclaimed with respect to checks. Unless notice of a claim for breach of warranty is given to the warrantor within 30 days after the claimant has reason to know of the breach and the identity of the warrantor, the liability of the warrantor under subsection (b) or (d) is discharged to the extent of any loss caused by the delay in giving notice of the claim.

(f) A [cause of action] for breach of warranty under this section accrues when the claimant has reason to know of the breach.

§3-418. Payment or Acceptance by Mistake

(a) Except as provided in subsection (c), if the drawee of a draft pays or accepts the draft and the drawee acted on the mistaken belief that (i) payment of the draft had not been stopped pursuant to Section 4-403 or (ii) the signature of the drawer of the draft was authorized, the drawee may recover the amount of the draft from the person to whom or for whose benefit payment was made or, in the case of acceptance, may revoke the acceptance. Rights of the drawee under this subsection are not affected by failure of the drawee to exercise ordinary care in paying or accepting the draft.

(b) Except as provided in subsection (c), if an instrument has been paid or accepted by mistake and the case is not covered by subsection (a), the person paying or accepting may, to the extent permitted by the law governing mistake and restitution, (i) recover the payment from the person to whom or for whose benefit payment was made or (ii) in the case of acceptance, may revoke the acceptance.

(c) The remedies provided by subsection (a) or (b) may not be asserted against a person who took the instrument in good faith and for value or who in good faith changed position in reliance on the payment or acceptance. This subsection does not limit remedies provided by Section 3-417 or 4-407.

(d) Notwithstanding Section 4-215, if an instrument is paid or accepted by mistake and the payor or acceptor recovers payment or revokes acceptance under subsection (a) or (b), the instrument is deemed not to have been paid or accepted and is treated as dishonored, and the person from whom payment is recovered has rights as a person entitled to enforce the dishonored instrument.

§3-419. Instruments Signed for Accommodation

(a) If an instrument is issued for value given for the benefit of a party to the instrument ("accommodated party") and another party to the instrument ("accommodation party") signs the instrument for the purpose of incurring liability on the instrument without being a direct beneficiary of the value given for the instrument, the instrument is signed by the accommodation party "for accommodation."

(b) An accommodation party may sign the instrument as maker, drawer, acceptor, or indorser and, subject to subsection (d), is obliged to pay the instrument in the capacity in which the accommodation party signs. The obligation of an accommodation party may be enforced notwithstanding any statute of frauds and whether or not the accommodation party receives consideration for the accommodation.

(c) A person signing an instrument is presumed to be an accommodation party and there is notice that the instrument is signed for accommodation if the signature is an anomalous indorsement or is accompanied by words indicating that the signer is acting as surety or guarantor with respect to the obligation of another party to the instrument. Except as provided in Section 3-605, the obligation of an accommodation party to pay the instrument is not affected by the fact that the person enforcing the obligation had notice when the instrument was taken by that person that the accommodation party signed the instrument for accommodation.

(d) If the signature of a party to an instrument is accompanied by words indicating unambiguously that the party is guaranteeing collection rather than payment of the obligation of another party to the instrument, the signer is obliged to pay the amount due on the instrument to a person entitled to enforce the instrument only if (i) execution of judgment against the other party has been returned unsatisfied, (ii) the other party is insolvent or in an insolvency proceeding, (iii) the other party cannot be served with process, or (iv) it is otherwise apparent that payment cannot be obtained from the other party.

(e) If the signature of a party to an instrument is accompanied by words indicating that the party guarantees payment or the signer signs the instrument as an accommodation party in some other manner that does not unambiguously indicate an intention to guarantee collection rather than payment, the signer is obliged to pay the amount due on the instrument to a person entitled to enforce the instrument in the same circumstances as the accommodated party would be obliged, without prior resort to the accommodated party by the person entitled to enforce the instrument.

(f) An accommodation party who pays the instrument is entitled to reimbursement from the accommodated party and is entitled to enforce the instrument against the accommodated party. In proper circumstances, an accommodation party may obtain relief that requires the accommodated party to perform its obligations on the instrument. An accommodated party that pays the instrument has no right of recourse against, and is not entitled to contribution from, an accommodation party.

§3-420. Conversion of Instrument

(a) The law applicable to conversion of personal property applies to instruments. An instrument is also converted if it is taken by transfer, other than a negotiation, from a person not entitled to enforce the instrument or a bank makes or obtains payment with respect to the instrument for a person not entitled to enforce the instrument or receive payment. An action for conversion of an instrument may not be brought by (i) the issuer or acceptor of the instrument or (ii) a payee or indorsee who did not receive delivery of the instrument either directly or through delivery to an agent or a co-payee.

(b) In an action under subsection (a), the measure of liability is presumed to be the amount payable on the instrument, but recovery may not exceed the amount of the plaintiff's interest in the instrument.

(c) A representative, other than a depositary bank, who has in good faith dealt with an instrument or its proceeds on behalf of one who was not the person entitled to enforce the instrument is not liable in conversion to that person beyond the amount of any proceeds that it has not paid out.

Part 5. Dishonor

§3-501. Presentment

(a) "Presentment" means a demand made by or on behalf of a person entitled to enforce an instrument (i) to pay the instrument made to the drawee or a party obliged to pay the instrument or, in the case of a note or accepted draft payable at a bank, to the bank, or (ii) to accept a draft made to the drawee.

(b) The following rules are subject to Article 4, agreement of the parties, and clearing-house rules and the like:

(1) Presentment may be made at the place of payment of the instrument and must be made at the place of payment if the instrument is payable at a bank in the United States; may be made by any commercially reasonable means, including an oral, written, or electronic communication; is effective when the demand for payment or acceptance is received by the person to whom presentment is made; and is effective if made to any one of two or more makers, acceptors, drawees, or other payors.

(2) Upon demand of the person to whom presentment is made, the person making presentment must (i) exhibit the instrument, (ii) give reasonable identification and, if presentment is made on behalf of another person, reasonable evidence of authority to do so, and (iii) sign a receipt on the instrument for any payment made or surrender the instrument if full payment is made.

(3) Without dishonoring the instrument, the party to whom presentment is made may (i) return the instrument for lack of a necessary indorsement, or (ii) refuse payment or acceptance for failure of the presentment to comply with the terms of the instrument, an agreement of the parties, or other applicable law or rule.

(4) The party to whom presentment is made may treat presentment as occurring on the next business day after the day of presentment if the party to whom presentment is made has established a cut-off hour not earlier than 2 p.m. for the receipt and processing of instruments presented for payment or acceptance and presentment is made after the cut-off hour.

§3-502. Dishonor

(a) Dishonor of a note is governed by the following rules:

(1) If the note is payable on demand, the note is dishonored if presentment is duly made to the maker and the note is not paid on the day of presentment.

(2) If the note is not payable on demand and is payable at or through a bank or the terms of the note require presentment, the note is dishonored if presentment is duly made and the note is not paid on the day it becomes payable or the day of presentment, whichever is later.

(3) If the note is not payable on demand and paragraph (2) does not apply, the note is dishonored if it is not paid on the day it becomes payable.

(b) Dishonor of an unaccepted draft other than a documentary draft is governed by the following rules:

(1) If a check is duly presented for payment to the payor bank otherwise than for immediate payment over the counter, the check is dishonored if the payor bank makes timely return of the check or sends timely notice of dishonor or nonpayment under Section 4-301 or 4-302, or becomes accountable for the amount of the check under Section 4-302.

(2) If a draft is payable on demand and paragraph (1) does not apply, the draft is dishonored if presentment for payment is duly made to the drawee and the draft is not paid on the day of presentment.

(3) If a draft is payable on a date stated in the draft, the draft is dishonored if (i) presentment for payment is duly made to the drawee and payment is not made on the day the draft becomes payable or the day of presentment, whichever is later, or (ii) presentment for acceptance is duly made before the day the draft becomes payable and the draft is not accepted on the day of presentment.

(4) If a draft is payable on elapse of a period of time after sight or acceptance, the draft is dishonored if presentment for acceptance is duly made and the draft is not accepted on the day of presentment.

(c) Dishonor of an unaccepted documentary draft occurs according to the rules stated in subsection (b)(2), (3), and (4), except that payment or acceptance may be delayed without dishonor until no later than the close of the third business day of the drawee following the day on which payment or acceptance is required by those paragraphs.

(d) Dishonor of an accepted draft is governed by the following rules:

(1) If the draft is payable on demand, the draft is dishonored if presentment for payment is duly made to the acceptor and the draft is not paid on the day of presentment.

(2) If the draft is not payable on demand, the draft is dishonored if presentment for payment is duly made to the acceptor and payment is not made on the day it becomes payable or the day of presentment, whichever is later.

(e) In any case in which presentment is otherwise required for dishonor under this section and presentment is excused under Section 3-504, dishonor occurs without presentment if the instrument is not duly accepted or paid.

(f) If a draft is dishonored because timely acceptance of the draft was not made and the person entitled to demand acceptance consents to a late acceptance, from the time of acceptance the draft is treated as never having been dishonored.

§3-503. Notice of Dishonor

(a) The obligation of an indorser stated in Section 3-415(a) and the obligation of a drawer stated in Section 3-414(d) may not be enforced unless (i) the indorser or drawer is given notice of dishonor of the instrument complying with this section or (ii) notice of dishonor is excused under Section 3-504(b).

(b) Notice of dishonor may be given by any person; may be given by any commercially reasonable means, including an oral, written, or electronic communication; and is sufficient if it reasonably identifies the instrument and indicates that the instrument has been dishonored or has not been paid or accepted. Return of an instrument given to a bank for collection is sufficient notice of dishonor.

(c) Subject to Section 3-504(c), with respect to an instrument taken for collection by a collecting bank, notice of dishonor must be given (i) by the bank before midnight of the next banking day following the banking day on which the bank receives notice of dishonor of the instrument, or (ii) by any other person within 30 days following the day on which the person receives notice of dishonor. With respect to any other instrument, notice of dishonor must be given within 30 days following the day on which dishonor occurs.

§3-504. Excused Presentment and Notice of Dishonor

(a) Presentment for payment or acceptance of an instrument is excused if (i) the person entitled to present the instrument cannot with reasonable diligence make presentment, (ii) the maker or acceptor has repudiated an obligation to pay the instrument or is dead or in insolvency proceedings, (iii) by the terms of the instrument presentment is not necessary to enforce the obligation of indorsers or the drawer, (iv) the drawer or indorser whose obligation is being enforced has waived presentment or otherwise has no reason to expect or right to require that the instrument be paid or accepted, or (v) the drawer instructed the drawee not to pay or accept the draft or the drawee was not obligated to the drawer to pay the draft.

(b) Notice of dishonor is excused if (i) by the terms of the instrument notice of dishonor is not necessary to enforce the obligation of a party to pay the instrument, or (ii) the party whose obligation is being enforced waived notice of dishonor. A waiver of presentment is also a waiver of notice of dishonor.

(c) Delay in giving notice of dishonor is excused if the delay was caused by circumstances beyond the control of the person giving the notice and the person giving the notice exercised reasonable diligence after the cause of the delay ceased to operate.

§3-505. Evidence of Dishonor

(a) The following are admissible as evidence and create a presumption of dishonor and of any notice of dishonor stated:

(1) a document regular in form as provided in subsection (b) which purports to be a protest;

(2) a purported stamp or writing of the drawee, payor bank, or presenting bank on or accompanying the instrument stating that acceptance or payment has been refused unless reasons for the refusal are stated and the reasons are not consistent with dishonor;

(3) a book or record of the drawee, payor bank, or collecting bank, kept in the usual course of business which shows dishonor, even if there is no evidence of who made the entry.

(b) A protest is a certificate of dishonor made by a United States consul or vice consul, or a notary public or other person authorized to administer oaths by the law of the place where dishonor occurs. It may be made upon information satisfactory to that person. The protest must identify the instrument and certify either that presentment has been made or, if not made, the reason why it was not made, and that the instrument has been dishonored by nonacceptance or nonpayment. The protest may also certify that notice of dishonor has been given to some or all parties.

Part 6. Discharge and Payment

§3-601. Discharge and Effect of Discharge

(a) The obligation of a party to pay the instrument is discharged as stated in this Article or by an act or agreement with the party which would discharge an obligation to pay money under a simple contract.

(b) Discharge of the obligation of a party is not effective against a person acquiring rights of a holder in due course of the instrument without notice of the discharge.

§3-602. Payment

(a) Subject to subsection (b), an instrument is paid to the extent payment is made (i) by or on behalf of a party obliged to pay the instrument, and (ii) to a person entitled to enforce the instrument. To the extent of the payment, the obligation of the party obliged to pay the instrument is discharged even though payment is made with knowledge of a claim to the instrument under Section 3-306 by another person.

(b) Subject to subsection (e) a note is paid to the extent payment is made by or on behalf of a party obliged to pay the note to a person that formerly was entitled to enforce the note only if at the time of the payment the party obliged to pay has not received adequate notification that the note has been transferred and that payment is to be made to the transferee. A notification is adequate only if it is signed by the transferor or the transferee; reasonably identifies the transferred note; and provides an address at which payments subsequently can be made. Upon request, a transferee shall seasonably furnish reasonable proof that the note has been transferred. Unless the transferee complies with the request, a payment to the person that formerly was entitled to enforce the note is effective for purposes of subsection (c) even if the party obliged to pay the note has received a notification under this paragraph.

(c) Subject to subsection (e), to the extent of a payment under subsections (a) and (b), the obligation of the party obliged to pay the instrument is discharged even though payment is made with knowledge of a claim to the instrument under Section 3-306 by another person.

(d) Subject to subsection (e), a transferee, or any party that has acquired rights in the instrument directly or indirectly from a transferee, including any such party that has rights as a holder in due course, is deemed to have notice of any payment that is made under subsection (b) after the date that the note is transferred to the transferee but before the party obliged to pay the note receives adequate notification of the transfer.

(e) The obligation of a party to pay the instrument is not discharged under subsections (a) through (d) if:

(1) a claim to the instrument under Section 3-306 is enforceable against the party receiving payment and (i) payment is made with knowledge by the payor that payment is prohibited by injunction or similar process of a court of competent jurisdiction, or (ii) in the case of an instrument other than a cashier's check, teller's check, or certified check, the party making payment accepted, from the person having a claim to the instrument, indemnity against loss resulting from refusal to pay the person entitled to enforce the instrument; or

(2) the person making payment knows that the instrument is a stolen instrument and pays a person it knows is in wrongful possession of the instrument.

(f) As used in this section, "signed," with respect to a record that is not a writing, includes the attachment to or logical association with the record of an electronic symbol, sound, or process to or with the record with the present intent to adopt or accept the record.

§3-603. Tender of Payment

(a) If tender of payment of an obligation to pay an instrument is made to a person entitled to enforce the instrument, the effect of tender is governed by principles of law applicable to tender of payment under a simple contract.

(b) If tender of payment of an obligation to pay an instrument is made to a person entitled to enforce the instrument and the tender is refused, there is discharge, to the extent of the amount of the tender, of the obligation of an indorser or accommodation party having a right of recourse with respect to the obligation to which the tender relates.

(c) If tender of payment of an amount due on an instrument is made to a person entitled to enforce the instrument, the obligation of the obligor to pay interest after the due date on the amount tendered is discharged. If presentment is required with respect to an instrument and the obligor is able and ready to pay on the due date at every place of payment stated in the instrument, the obligor is deemed to have made tender of payment on the due date to the person entitled to enforce the instrument.

§3-604. Discharge by Cancellation or Renunciation

(a) A person entitled to enforce an instrument, with or without consideration, may discharge the obligation of a party to pay the instrument (i) by an intentional voluntary act, such as surrender of the instrument to the party, destruction, mutilation, or cancellation of the instrument, cancellation or striking out of the party's signature, or the addition of words to the instrument indicating discharge, or (ii) by agreeing not to sue or otherwise renouncing rights against the party by a signed record.

(b) Cancellation or striking out of an indorsement pursuant to subsection (a) does not affect the status and rights of a party derived from the indorsement.

(c) As used in this section, "signed," with respect to a record that is not a writing, includes the attachment to or logical association with the record of an electronic symbol, sound, or process to or with the record with the present intent to adopt or accept the record.

§3-605. Discharge of Secondary Obligors

(a) If a person entitled to enforce an instrument releases the obligation of a principal obligor in whole or in part, and another party to the instrument is a secondary obligor with respect to the obligation of that principal obligor, the following rules apply:

(1) Any obligations of the principal obligor to the secondary obligor with respect to any previous payment by the secondary obligor are not affected. Unless the terms of the release preserve the secondary obligor's recourse, the principal obligor is discharged, to the extent of the release, from any other duties to the secondary obligor under this article.

(2) Unless the terms of the release provide that the person entitled to enforce the instrument retains the right to enforce the instrument against the secondary obligor, the secondary obligor is discharged to the same extent as the principal obligor from any unperformed portion of its obligation on the instrument. If the instrument is a check and the obligation of the secondary obligor is based on an indorsement of the check, the secondary obligor is discharged without regard to the language or circumstances of the discharge or other release.

(3) If the secondary obligor is not discharged under paragraph (2), the secondary obligor is discharged to the extent of the value of the consideration for the release, and to the extent that the release would otherwise cause the secondary obligor a loss.

(b) If a person entitled to enforce an instrument grants a principal obligor an extension of the time at which one or more payments are due on the instrument and another party to the instrument is a secondary obligor with respect to the obligation of that principal obligor, the following rules apply:

(1) Any obligations of the principal obligor to the secondary obligor with respect to any previous payment by the secondary obligor are not affected. Unless the terms of the extension preserve the secondary obligor's recourse, the extension correspondingly extends the time for performance of any other duties owed to the secondary obligor by the principal obligor under this article.

(2) The secondary obligor is discharged to the extent that the extension would otherwise cause the secondary obligor a loss.

(3) To the extent that the secondary obligor is not discharged under paragraph (2), the secondary obligor may perform its obligations to a person entitled to enforce the instrument as if the time for payment had not been extended or, unless the terms of the extension provide that the person entitled to enforce the instrument retains the right to enforce the instrument against the secondary obligor as if the time for payment had not been extended, treat the time for performance of its obligations as having been extended correspondingly.

(c) If a person entitled to enforce an instrument agrees, with or without consideration, to a modification of the obligation of a principal obligor other than a complete or partial release or an extension of the due date and another party to the instrument is a secondary obligor with respect to the obligation of that principal obligor, the following rules apply:

(1) Any obligations of the principal obligor to the secondary obligor with respect to any previous payment by the secondary obligor are not affected. The modification correspondingly modifies any other duties owed to the secondary obligor by the principal obligor under this article.

(2) The secondary obligor is discharged from any unperformed portion of its obligation to the extent that the modification would otherwise cause the secondary obligor a loss.

(3) To the extent that the secondary obligor is not discharged under paragraph (2), the secondary obligor may satisfy its obligation on the instrument as if the modification had not occurred, or treat its obligation on the instrument as having been modified correspondingly.

(d) If the obligation of a principal obligor is secured by an interest in collateral, another party to the instrument is a secondary obligor with respect to that obligation, and a person entitled to enforce the instrument impairs the value of the interest in collateral, the obligation of the secondary obligor is discharged to the extent of the impairment. The value of an interest in collateral is impaired to the extent the value of the interest is reduced to an amount less than the amount of the recourse of the secondary obligor, or the reduction in value of the interest causes an increase in the amount by which the amount of the recourse exceeds the value of the interest.

For purposes of this subsection, impairing the value of an interest in collateral includes failure to obtain or maintain perfection or recordation of the interest in collateral, release of collateral without substitution of collateral of equal value or equivalent reduction of the underlying obligation, failure to perform a duty to preserve the value of collateral owed, under Article 9 or other law, to a debtor or other person secondarily liable, and failure to comply with applicable law in disposing of or otherwise enforcing the interest in collateral.

(e) A secondary obligor is not discharged under subsection (a)(3), (b), (c), or (d) unless the person entitled to enforce the instrument knows that the person is a secondary obligor or has notice under Section 3-419(c) that the instrument was signed for accommodation.

(f) A secondary obligor is not discharged under this section if the secondary obligor consents to the event or conduct that is the basis of the discharge, or the instrument or a separate agreement of the party provides for waiver of discharge under this section specifically or by general language indicating that parties waive defenses based on suretyship or impairment of collateral. Unless the circumstances indicate otherwise, consent by the principal obligor to an act that would lead to a discharge under this section constitutes consent to that act by the secondary obligor if the secondary obligor controls the principal obligor or deals with the person entitled to enforce the instrument on behalf of the principal obligor.

(g) A release or extension preserves a secondary obligor's recourse if the terms of the release or extension provide that the person entitled to enforce the instrument retains the right to enforce the instrument against the secondary obligor; and the recourse of the secondary obligor continues as though the release or extension had not been granted.

(h) Except as otherwise provided in subsection (i), a secondary obligor asserting discharge under this section has the burden of persuasion both with respect to the occurrence of the acts alleged to harm the secondary obligor and loss or prejudice caused by those acts.

(i) If the secondary obligor demonstrates prejudice caused by an impairment of its recourse, and the circumstances of the case indicate that the amount of loss is not reasonably susceptible of calculation or requires proof of facts that are not ascertainable, it is presumed that the act impairing recourse caused a loss or impairment equal to the liability of the secondary obligor on the instrument. In that event, the burden of persuasion as to any lesser amount of the loss is on the person entitled to enforce the instrument.

U.C.C. – Article 4 – Bank Deposits and Collections (2002)

PART 1. GENERAL PROVISIONS AND DEFINITIONS

§4-101. Short Title

This Article may be cited as Uniform Commercial Code – Bank Deposits and Collections.

§4-102. Applicability

(a) To the extent that items within this Article are also within Articles 3 and 8, they are subject to those Articles. If there is conflict, this Article governs Article 3, but Article 8 governs this Article.

(b) The liability of a bank for action or non-action with respect to an item handled by it for purposes of presentment, payment, or collection is governed by the law of the place where the bank is located. In the case of action or non-action by or at a branch or separate office of a bank, its liability is governed by the law of the place where the branch or separate office is located.

§4-103. Variation by Agreement; Measure of Damages; Action Constituting Ordinary Care

(a) The effect of the provisions of this Article may be varied by agreement, but the parties to the agreement cannot disclaim a bank's responsibility for its lack of good faith or failure to exercise ordinary care or limit the measure of damages for the lack or failure. However, the parties may determine by agreement the standards by which the bank's responsibility is to be measured if those standards are not manifestly unreasonable.

(b) Federal Reserve regulations and operating circulars, clearing-house rules, and the like have the effect of agreements under subsection (a), whether or not specifically assented to by all parties interested in items handled.

(c) Action or non-action approved by this Article or pursuant to Federal Reserve regulations or operating circulars is the exercise of ordinary care and, in the absence of special instructions, action or non-action consistent with clearing-house rules and the like or with a general banking usage not disapproved by this Article, is prima facie the exercise of ordinary care.

(d) The specification or approval of certain procedures by this Article is not disapproval of other procedures that may be reasonable under the circumstances.

(e) The measure of damages for failure to exercise ordinary care in handling an item is the amount of the item reduced by an amount that could not have been realized by the exercise of ordinary care. If there is also bad faith it includes any other damages the party suffered as a proximate consequence.

§4-104. Definitions and Index of Definitions

(a) In this Article, unless the context otherwise requires:

(1) "Account" means any deposit or credit account with a bank, including a demand, time, savings, passbook, share draft, or like account, other than an account evidenced by a certificate of deposit;

(2) "Afternoon" means the period of a day between noon and midnight;

(3) "Banking day" means the part of a day on which a bank is open to the public for carrying on substantially all of its banking functions;

(4) "Clearing house" means an association of banks or other payors regularly clearing items;

(5) "Customer" means a person having an account with a bank or for whom a bank has agreed to collect items, including a bank that maintains an account at another bank;

(6) "Documentary draft" means a draft to be presented for acceptance or payment if specified documents, certificated securities (Section 8-102) or instructions for uncertificated securities (Section 8-102), or other certificates, statements, or the like are to be received by the drawee or other payor before acceptance or payment of the draft;

(7) "Draft" means a draft as defined in Section 3-104 or an item, other than an instrument, that is an order.

(8) "Drawee" means a person ordered in a draft to make payment.

(9) "Item" means an instrument or a promise or order to pay money handled by a bank for collection or payment. The term does not include a payment order governed by Article 4A or a credit or debit card slip;

(10) "Midnight deadline" with respect to a bank is midnight on its next banking day following the banking day on which it receives the relevant item or notice or from which the time for taking action commences to run, whichever is later;

(11) "Settle" means to pay in cash, by clearing-house settlement, in a charge or credit or by remittance, or otherwise as agreed. A settlement may be either provisional or final.

(12) "Suspends payments" with respect to a bank means that it has been closed by order of the supervisory authorities, that a public officer has been appointed to take it over, or that it ceases or refuses to make payments in the ordinary course of business.

(b) Other definitions applying to this Article and the sections in which they appear are:

"Agreement for electronic presentment" Section 4-110
"Collecting bank" Section 4-105
"Depositary bank" Section 4-105
"Intermediary bank" Section 4-105
"Payor bank" Section 4-105
"Presenting bank" Section 4-105
"Presentment notice" Section 4-110

(c) "Control" as provided in Section 7-106 and the following definitions in other Articles apply to this Article:

"Acceptance" Section 3-409
"Alteration" Section 3-407
"Cashier's check" Section 3-104
"Certificate of deposit" Section 3-104
"Certified check" Section 3-409
"Check" Section 3-104
"Holder in due course" Section 3-302
"Instrument" Section 3-104
"Notice of dishonor" Section 3-503
"Order" Section 3-103
"Ordinary care" Section 3-103
"Person entitled to enforce" Section 3-301
"Presentment" Section 3-501
"Promise" Section 3-103
"Prove" Section 3-103
"Record" Section 3-103
"Remotely-Created consumer item" Section 3-103
"Teller's check" Section 3-104
"Unauthorized signature" Section 3-403

(d) In addition, Article 1 contains general definitions and principles of construction and interpretation applicable throughout this Article.

§4-105. "Bank"; "Depositary Bank"; "Payor Bank"; "Intermediary Bank"; "Collecting Bank"; "Presenting Bank"

In this Article :

(1) "Bank" means a person engaged in the business of banking, including a savings bank, savings and loan association, credit union, or trust company.

(2) "Depositary bank" means the first bank to take an item even though it is also the payor bank, unless the item is presented for immediate payment over the counter;

(3) "Payor bank" means a bank that is the drawee of a draft;

(4) "Intermediary bank" means a bank to which an item is transferred in course of collection except the depositary or payor bank;

(5) "Collecting bank" means a bank handling an item for collection except the payor bank;

(6) "Presenting bank" means a bank presenting an item except a payor bank.

§4-106. Payable Through or Payable at Bank; Collecting Bank

(a) If an item states that it is "payable through" a bank identified in the item, (i) the item designates the bank as a collecting bank and does not by itself authorize the bank to pay the item, and (ii) the item may be presented for payment only by or through the bank.

Alternative A

(b) If an item states that it is "payable at" a bank identified in the item, the item is equivalent to a draft drawn on the bank.

Alternative B

(b) If an item states that it is "payable at" a bank identified in the item, (i) the item designates the bank as a collecting bank and does not by itself authorize the bank to pay the item, and (ii) the item may be presented for payment only by or through the bank.

(c) If a draft names a nonbank drawee and it is unclear whether a bank named in the draft is a co-drawee or a collecting bank, the bank is a collecting bank.

§4-107. Separate Office of Bank

A branch or separate office of a bank is a separate bank for the purpose of computing the time within which and determining the place at or to which action may be taken or notice or orders must be given under this Article and under Article 3.

§4-108. Time of Receipt of Items

(a) For the purpose of allowing time to process items, prove balances, and make the necessary entries on its books to determine its position for the day, a bank may fix an afternoon hour of 2 P.M. or later as a cutoff hour for the handling of money and items and the making of entries on its books.

(b) An item or deposit of money received on any day after a cutoff hour so fixed or after the close of the banking day may be treated as being received at the opening of the next banking day.

§4-109. Delays

(a) Unless otherwise instructed, a collecting bank in a good faith effort to secure payment of a specific item drawn on a payor other than a bank, and with or without the approval of any person involved, may waive, modify, or extend time limits imposed or permitted by this [Act] for a period not exceeding two additional banking days without discharge of drawers or indorsers or liability to its transferor or a prior party.

(b) Delay by a collecting bank or payor bank beyond time limits prescribed or permitted by this [Act] or by instructions is excused if (i) the delay is caused by interruption of communication or computer facilities, suspension of payments by another bank, war, emergency conditions, failure of equipment, or other circumstances beyond the control of the bank, and (ii) the bank exercises such diligence as the circumstances require.

§4-110. Electronic Presentment

(a) "Agreement for electronic presentment" means an agreement, clearing-house rule, or Federal Reserve regulation or operating circular, providing that presentment of an item may be made by transmission of an image of an item or information describing the item ("presentment notice") rather than delivery of the item itself. The agreement may provide for procedures governing retention, presentment, payment, dishonor, and other matters concerning items subject to the agreement.

(b) Presentment of an item pursuant to an agreement for presentment is made when the presentment notice is received.

(c) If presentment is made by presentment notice, a reference to "item" or "check" in this Article means the presentment notice unless the context otherwise indicates.

§4-111. Statute of Limitations

An action to enforce an obligation, duty, or right arising under this Article must be commenced within three years after the [cause of action] accrues.

PART 2. COLLECTION OF ITEMS: DEPOSITARY AND COLLECTING BANKS

§4-201. Status of Collecting Bank as Agent and Provisional Status of Credits; Applicability of Article; Item Indorsed "Pay Any Bank"

(a) Unless a contrary intent clearly appears and before the time that a settlement given by a collecting bank for an item is or becomes final, the bank, with respect to the item, is an agent or sub-agent of the owner of the item and any settlement given for the item is provisional. This provision applies regardless of the form of indorsement or lack of indorsement and even though credit given for the item is subject to immediate withdrawal as of right or is in fact withdrawn; but the continuance of ownership of an item by its owner and any rights of the owner to proceeds of the item are subject to rights of a collecting bank, such as those resulting from outstanding advances on the item and rights of recoupment or setoff. If an item is handled by banks for purposes of presentment, payment, collection, or return, the relevant provisions of this Article apply even though action of the parties clearly establishes that a particular bank has purchased the item and is the owner of it.

(b) After an item has been indorsed with the words "pay any bank" or the like, only a bank may acquire the rights of a holder until the item has been:

(1) returned to the customer initiating collection; or

(2) specially indorsed by a bank to a person who is not a bank.

§4-202. Responsibility for Collection or Return; When Action Timely

(a) A collecting bank must exercise ordinary care in:

(1) presenting an item or sending it for presentment;

(2) sending notice of dishonor or nonpayment or returning an item other than a documentary draft to the bank's transferor after learning that the item has not been paid or accepted, as the case may be;

(3) settling for an item when the bank receives final settlement; and

(4) notifying its transferor of any loss or delay in transit within a reasonable time after discovery thereof.

(b) A collecting bank exercises ordinary care under subsection (a) by taking proper action before its midnight deadline following receipt of an item, notice, or settlement. Taking proper action within a reasonably longer time may constitute the exercise of ordinary care, but the bank has the burden of establishing timeliness.

(c) Subject to subsection (a)(1), a bank is not liable for the insolvency, neglect, misconduct, mistake, or default of another bank or person or for loss or destruction of an item in the possession of others or in transit.

§4-203. Effect of Instructions

Subject to Article 3 concerning conversion of instruments (Section 3-420) and restrictive indorsements (Section 3-206), only a collecting bank's transferor can give instructions that affect the bank or constitute notice to it, and a collecting bank is not liable to prior parties for any action taken pursuant to the instructions or in accordance with any agreement with its transferor.

§4-204. Methods of Sending and Presenting; Sending Directly to Payor Bank

(a) A collecting bank shall send items by a reasonably prompt method, taking into consideration relevant instructions, the nature of the item, the number of those items on hand, the cost of collection involved, and the method generally used by it or others to present those items.

(b) A collecting bank may send:

(1) an item directly to the payor bank;

(2) an item to a nonbank payor if authorized by its transferor; and

(3) an item other than documentary drafts to a nonbank payor, if authorized by Federal Reserve regulation or operating circular, clearing-house rule, or the like.

(c) Presentment may be made by a presenting bank at a place where the payor bank or other payor has requested that presentment be made.

§4-205. Depositary Bank Holder of Unindorsed Item

If a customer delivers an item to a depositary bank for collection:

(1) the depositary bank becomes a holder of the item at the time it receives the item for collection if the customer at the time of delivery was a holder of the item, whether or not the customer indorses the item, and, if the bank satisfies the other requirements of Section 3-302, it is a holder in due course; and

(2) the depositary bank warrants to collecting banks, the payor bank or other payor, and the drawer that the amount of the item was paid to the customer or deposited to the customer's account.

§4-206. Transfer Between Banks

Any agreed method that identifies the transferor bank is sufficient for the item's further transfer to another bank.

§4-207. Transfer Warranties

(a) A customer or collecting bank that transfers an item and receives a settlement or other consideration warrants to the transferee and to any subsequent collecting bank that:

(1) the warrantor is a person entitled to enforce the item;

(2) all signatures on the item are authentic and authorized;

(3) the item has not been altered;

(4) the item is not subject to a defense or claim in recoupment (Section 3-305(a)) of any party that can be asserted against the warrantor; and

(5) the warrantor has no knowledge of any insolvency proceeding commenced with respect to the maker or acceptor or, in the case of an unaccepted draft, the drawer; and

(6) with respect to any remotely-created consumer item, that the person on whose account the item is drawn authorized the issuance of the item in the amount for which the item is drawn.

(b) If an item is dishonored, a customer or collecting bank transferring the item and receiving settlement or other consideration is obliged to pay the amount due on the item (i) according to the terms of the item at the time it was transferred, or (ii) if the transfer was of an incomplete item, according to its terms when completed as stated in Sections 3-115 and 3-407. The obligation of a transferor is owed to the transferee and to any subsequent collecting bank that takes the item in good faith. A transferor cannot disclaim its obligation under this subsection by an indorsement stating that it is made "without recourse" or otherwise disclaiming liability.

(c) A person to whom the warranties under subsection (a) are made and who took the item in good faith may recover from the warrantor as damages for breach of warranty an amount equal to the loss suffered as a result of the breach, but not more than the amount of the item plus expenses and loss of interest incurred as a result of the breach.

(d) The warranties stated in subsection (a) cannot be disclaimed with respect to checks. Unless notice of a claim for breach of warranty is given to the warrantor within 30 days after the claimant has reason to know of the breach and the identity of the warrantor, the warrantor is discharged to the extent of any loss caused by the delay in giving notice of the claim.

(e) A cause of action for breach of warranty under this section accrues when the claimant has reason to know of the breach.

§4-208. Presentment Warranties

(a) If an unaccepted draft is presented to the drawee for payment or acceptance and the drawee pays or accepts the draft, (i) the person obtaining payment or acceptance, at the time of presentment, and (ii) a previous transferor of the draft, at the time of transfer, warrant to the drawee that pays or accepts the draft in good faith that:

(1) the warrantor is, or was, at the time the warrantor transferred the draft, a person entitled to enforce the draft or authorized to obtain payment or acceptance of the draft on behalf of a person entitled to enforce the draft;

(2) the draft has not been altered; and

(3) the warrantor has no knowledge that the signature of the purported drawer of the draft is unauthorized; and

(4) with respect to any remotely-created consumer item, that the person on whose account the item is drawn authorized the issuance of the item in the amount for which the item is drawn.

(b) A drawee making payment may recover from a warrantor damages for breach of warranty equal to the amount paid by the drawee less the amount the drawee received or is entitled to receive from the drawer because of the payment. In addition, the drawee is entitled to compensation for expenses and loss of interest resulting from the breach. The right of the drawee to recover damages under this subsection is not affected by any failure of the drawee to exercise ordinary care in making payment. If the drawee accepts the draft (i) breach of warranty is a defense to the obligation of the acceptor, and (ii) if the acceptor makes payment with respect to the draft, the acceptor is entitled to recover from a warrantor for breach of warranty the amounts stated in this subsection.

(c) If a drawee asserts a claim for breach of warranty under subsection (a) based on an unauthorized indorsement of the draft or an alteration of the draft, the warrantor may defend by proving that the indorsement is effective under Section 3-404 or 3-405 or the drawer is precluded under Section 3-406 or 4-406 from asserting against the drawee the unauthorized indorsement or alteration.

(d) If (i) a dishonored draft is presented for payment to the drawer or an indorser or (ii) any other item is presented for payment to a party obliged to pay the item, and the item is paid, the person obtaining payment and a prior transferor of the item warrant to the person making payment in good faith that the warrantor is, or was, at the time the warrantor transferred the item, a person entitled to enforce the item or authorized to obtain payment on behalf of a person entitled to enforce the item. The person making payment may recover from any warrantor for breach of warranty an amount equal to the amount paid plus expenses and loss of interest resulting from the breach.

(e) The warranties stated in subsections (a) and (d) cannot be disclaimed with respect to checks. Unless notice of a claim for breach of warranty is given to the warrantor within 30 days after the claimant has reason to know of the breach and the identity of the warrantor, the warrantor is discharged to the extent of any loss caused by the delay in giving notice of the claim.

(f) A cause of action for breach of warranty under this section accrues when the claimant has reason to know of the breach.

§4-209. Encoding and Retention Warranties

(a) A person who encodes information on or with respect to an item after issue warrants to any subsequent collecting bank and to the payor bank or other payor that the information is correctly encoded. If the customer of a depositary bank encodes, that bank also makes the warranty.

(b) A person who undertakes to retain an item pursuant to an agreement for electronic presentment warrants to any subsequent collecting bank and to the payor bank or other payor that retention and presentment of the item comply with the agreement. If a customer of a depositary bank undertakes to retain an item, that bank also makes this warranty.

(c) A person to whom warranties are made under this section and who took the item in good faith may recover from the warrantor as damages for breach of warranty an amount equal to the loss suffered as a result of the breach, plus expenses and loss of interest incurred as a result of the breach.

§4-210. Security Interest of Collecting Bank in Items, Accompanying Documents and Proceeds

(a) A collecting bank has a security interest in an item and any accompanying documents or the proceeds of either:

(1) in case of an item deposited in an account, to the extent to which credit given for the item has been withdrawn or applied;

(2) in case of an item for which it has given credit available for withdrawal as of right, to the extent of the credit given, whether or not the credit is drawn upon or there is a right of charge-back; or

(3) if it makes an advance on or against the item.

(b) If credit given for several items received at one time or pursuant to a single agreement is withdrawn or applied in part, the security interest remains upon all the items, any accompanying documents or the proceeds of either. For the purpose of this section, credits first given are first withdrawn.

(c) Receipt by a collecting bank of a final settlement for an item is a realization on its security interest in the item, accompanying documents, and proceeds. So long as the bank does not receive final settlement for the item or give up possession of the item or possession or control of the accompanying documents for purposes other than collection, the security interest continues to that extent and is subject to Article 9, but:

(1) no security agreement is necessary to make the security interest enforceable (Section 9-203(b)(3)(A));

(2) no filing is required to perfect the security interest; and

(3) the security interest has priority over conflicting perfected security interests in the item, accompanying documents, or proceeds.

§4-211. When Bank Gives Value for Purposes of Holder in Due Course

For purposes of determining its status as a holder in due course, a bank has given value to the extent it has a security interest in an item, if the bank otherwise complies with the requirements of Section 3-302 on what constitutes a holder in due course.

§4-212. Presentment by Notice of Item Not Payable By, Through, or at Bank; Liability of Drawer or Indorser

(a) Unless otherwise instructed, a collecting bank may present an item not payable by, through, or at a bank by sending to the party to accept or pay a record providing notice that the bank holds the item for acceptance or payment. The notice must be sent in time to be received on or before the day when presentment is due and the bank must meet any requirement of the party to accept or pay under Section 3-501 by the close of the bank's next banking day after it knows of the requirement.

(b) If presentment is made by notice and payment, acceptance, or request for compliance with a requirement under Section 3-501 is not received by the close of business on the day after maturity or, in the case of demand items, by the close of business on the third banking day after notice was sent, the presenting bank may treat the item as dishonored and charge any drawer or indorser by sending it notice of the facts.

§4-213. Medium and Time of Settlement by Bank

(a) With respect to settlement by a bank, the medium and time of settlement may be prescribed by Federal Reserve regulations or circulars, clearing-house rules, and the like, or agreement. In the absence of such prescription:

(1) the medium of settlement is cash or credit to an account in a Federal Reserve bank of or specified by the person to receive settlement; and

(2) the time of settlement, is:

  (i) with respect to tender of settlement by cash, a cashier's check, or teller's check, when the cash or check is sent or delivered;

  (ii) with respect to tender of settlement by credit in an account in a Federal Reserve Bank, when the credit is made;

  (iii) with respect to tender of settlement by a credit or debit to an account in a bank, when the credit or debit is made or, in the case of tender of settlement by authority to charge an account, when the authority is sent or delivered; or

  (iv) with respect to tender of settlement by a funds transfer, when payment is made pursuant to Section 4A-406(a) to the person receiving settlement.

(b) If the tender of settlement is not by a medium authorized by subsection (a) or the time of settlement is not fixed by subsection (a), no settlement occurs until the tender of settlement is accepted by the person receiving settlement.

(c) If settlement for an item is made by cashier's check or teller's check and the person receiving settlement, before its midnight deadline:

(1) presents or forwards the check for collection, settlement is final when the check is finally paid; or

(2) fails to present or forward the check for collection, settlement is final at the midnight deadline of the person receiving settlement.

(d) If settlement for an item is made by giving authority to charge the account of the bank giving settlement in the bank receiving settlement, settlement is final when the charge is made by the bank receiving settlement if there are funds available in the account for the amount of the item.

§4-214. Right of Charge-back or Refund; Liability of Collecting Bank; Return of Item

(a) If a collecting bank has made provisional settlement with its customer for an item and fails by reason of dishonor, suspension of payments by a bank, or otherwise to receive settlement for the item which is or becomes final, the bank may revoke the settlement given by it, charge back the amount of any credit given for the item to its customer's account, or obtain refund from its customer, whether or not it is able to return the item, if by its midnight deadline or within a longer reasonable time after it learns the facts it returns the item or sends notification of the facts. If the return or notice is delayed beyond the bank's midnight deadline or a longer reasonable time after it learns the facts, the bank may revoke the settlement, charge back the credit, or obtain refund from its customer, but it is liable for any loss resulting from the delay. These rights to revoke, charge back, and obtain refund terminate if and when a settlement for the item received by the bank is or becomes final.

(b) A collecting bank returns an item when it is sent or delivered to the bank's customer or transferor or pursuant to its instructions.

(c) A depositary bank that is also the payor may charge back the amount of an item to its customer's account or obtain refund in accordance with the section governing return of an item received by a payor bank for credit on its books (Section 4-301).

(d) The right to charge back is not affected by:

(1) previous use of a credit given for the item; or

(2) failure by any bank to exercise ordinary care with respect to the item, but a bank so failing remains liable.

(e) A failure to charge back or claim refund does not affect other rights of the bank against the customer or any other party.

(f) If credit is given in dollars as the equivalent of the value of an item payable in foreign money, the dollar amount of any charge-back or refund must be calculated on the basis of the bank-offered spot rate for the foreign money prevailing on the day when the person entitled to the charge-back or refund learns that it will not receive payment in ordinary course.

§4-215. Final Payment of Item by Payor Bank; When Provisional Debits and Credits Become Final; When Certain Credits Become Available for Withdrawal

(a) An item is finally paid by a payor bank when the bank has first done any of the following:

(1) paid the item in cash;

(2) settled for the item without having a right to revoke the settlement under statute, clearing-house rule, or agreement; or

(3) made a provisional settlement for the item and failed to revoke the settlement in the time and manner permitted by statute, clearing-house rule, or agreement.

(b) If provisional settlement for an item does not become final, the item is not finally paid.

(c) If provisional settlement for an item between the presenting and payor banks is made through a clearing house or by debits or credits in an account between them, then to the extent that provisional debits or credits for the item are entered in accounts between the presenting and payor banks or between the presenting and successive prior collecting banks seriatim, they become final upon final payment of the items by the payor bank.

(d) If a collecting bank receives a settlement for an item which is or becomes final, the bank is accountable to its customer for the amount of the item and any provisional credit given for the item in an account with its customer becomes final.

(e) Subject to (i) applicable law stating a time for availability of funds and (ii) any right of the bank to apply the credit to an obligation of the customer, credit given by a bank for an item in a customer's account becomes available for withdrawal as of right:

(1) if the bank has received a provisional settlement for the item, when the settlement becomes final and the bank has had a reasonable time to receive return of the item and the item has not been received within that time;

(2) if the bank is both the depositary bank and the payor bank, and the item is finally paid, at the opening of the bank's second banking day following receipt of the item.

(f) Subject to applicable law stating a time for availability of funds and any right of a bank to apply a deposit to an obligation of the depositor, a deposit of money becomes available for withdrawal as of right at the opening of the bank's next banking day after receipt of the deposit.

§4-216. Insolvency and Preference

(a) If an item is in or comes into the possession of a payor or collecting bank that suspends payment and the item has not been finally paid, the item must be returned by the receiver, trustee, or agent in charge of the closed bank to the presenting bank or the closed bank's customer.

(b) If a payor bank finally pays an item and suspends payments without making a settlement for the item with its customer or the presenting bank which settlement is or becomes final, the owner of the item has a preferred claim against the payor bank.

(c) If a payor bank gives or a collecting bank gives or receives a provisional settlement for an item and thereafter suspends payments, the suspension does not prevent or interfere with the settlement's becoming final if the finality occurs automatically upon the lapse of certain time or the happening of certain events .

(d) If a collecting bank receives from subsequent parties settlement for an item, which settlement is or becomes final and the bank suspends payments without making a settlement for the item with its customer which settlement is or becomes final, the owner of the item has a preferred claim against the collecting bank.

PART 3. COLLECTION OF ITEMS: PAYOR BANKS

§4-301. Deferred Posting; Recovery of Payment by Return of Items; Time of Dishonor; Return of Items by Payor Bank

(a) If a payor bank settles for a demand item other than a documentary draft presented otherwise than for immediate payment over the counter before midnight of the banking day of receipt, the payor bank may revoke the settlement and recover the settlement if, before it has made final payment and before its midnight deadline, it

(1) returns the item;

(2) returns an image of the item, if the party to which the return is made has entered into an agreement to accept an image as a return of the item; and the image is returned in accordance with that agreement;

(3) sends a record providing notice of dishonor or nonpayment if the item is unavailable for return.

(b) If a demand item is received by a payor bank for credit on its books, it may return the item or send notice of dishonor and may revoke any credit given or recover the amount thereof withdrawn by its customer, if it acts within the time limit and in the manner specified in subsection (a).

(c) Unless previous notice of dishonor has been sent, an item is dishonored at the time when for purposes of dishonor it is returned or notice sent in accordance with this section.

(d) An item is returned:

(1) as to an item presented through a clearing house, when it is delivered to the presenting or last collecting bank or to the clearing house or is sent or delivered in accordance with clearing- house rules; or

(2) in all other cases, when it is sent or delivered to the bank's customer or transferor or pursuant to instructions.

§4-302. Payor Bank's Responsibility for Late Return of Item

(a) If an item is presented to and received by a payor bank, the bank is accountable for the amount of:

(1) a demand item, other than a documentary draft, whether properly payable or not, if the bank, in any case in which it is not also the depositary bank, retains the item beyond midnight of the banking day of receipt without settling for it or, whether or not it is also the depositary bank, does not pay or return the item or send notice of dishonor until after its midnight deadline; or

(2) any other properly payable item unless, within the time allowed for acceptance or payment of that item, the bank either accepts or pays the item or returns it and accompanying documents.

(b) The liability of a payor bank to pay an item pursuant to subsection (a) is subject to defenses based on breach of a presentment warranty (Section 4-208) or proof that the person seeking enforcement of the liability presented or transferred the item for the purpose of defrauding the payor bank.

§4-303. When Items Subject to Notice, Stop-Payment Order, Legal Process, or Setoff; Order in Which Items May Be Charged or Certified

(a) Any knowledge, notice, or stop-payment order received by, legal process served upon, or setoff exercised by a payor bank comes too late to terminate, suspend, or modify the bank's right or duty to pay an item or to charge its customer's account for the item if the knowledge, notice, stop-payment order, or legal process is received or served and a reasonable time for the bank to act thereon expires or the setoff is exercised after the earliest of the following:

(1) the bank accepts or certifies the item;

(2) the bank pays the item in cash;

(3) the bank settles for the item without having a right to revoke the settlement under statute, clearing-house rule, or agreement;

(4) the bank becomes accountable for the amount of the item under Section 4-302 dealing with the payor bank's responsibility for late return of items; or

(5) with respect to checks, a cutoff hour no earlier than one hour after the opening of the next banking day after the banking day on which the bank received the check and no later than the close of that next banking day or, if no cutoff hour is fixed, the close of the next banking day after the banking day on which the bank received the check.

(b) Subject to subsection (a), items may be accepted, paid, certified, or charged to the indicated account of its customer in any order.

PART 4. RELATIONSHIP BETWEEN PAYOR BANK AND ITS CUSTOMER

§4-401. When Bank May Charge Customer's Account

(a) A bank may charge against the account of a customer an item that is properly payable from that account even though the charge creates an overdraft. An item is properly payable if it is authorized by the customer and is in accordance with any agreement between the customer and bank.

(b) A customer is not liable for the amount of an overdraft if the customer neither signed the item nor benefited from the proceeds of the item.

(c) A bank may charge against the account of a customer a check that is otherwise properly payable from the account, even though payment was made before the date of the check, unless the customer has given notice to the bank of the postdating describing the check with reasonable certainty. The notice is effective for the period stated in Section 4-403(b) for stop-payment orders, and must be received at such time and in such manner as to afford the bank a reasonable opportunity to act on it before the bank takes any action with respect to the check described in Section 4-303. If a bank charges against the account of a customer a check before the date stated in the notice of postdating, the bank is liable for damages for the loss resulting from its act. The loss may include damages for dishonor of subsequent items under Section 4-402.

(d) A bank that in good faith makes payment to a holder may charge the indicated account of its customer according to:

(1) the original terms of the altered item; or

(2) the terms of the completed item, even though the bank knows the item has been completed unless the bank has notice that the completion was improper.

§4-402. Bank's Liability to Customer for Wrongful Dishonor; Time of Determining Insufficiency of Account

(a) Except as otherwise provided in this Article, a payor bank wrongfully dishonors an item if it dishonors an item that is properly payable, but a bank may dishonor an item that would create an overdraft unless it has agreed to pay the overdraft.

(b) A payor bank is liable to its customer for damages proximately caused by the wrongful dishonor of an item. Liability is limited to actual damages proved and may include damages for an arrest or prosecution of the customer or other consequential damages. Whether any consequential damages are proximately caused by the wrongful dishonor is a question of fact to be determined in each case.

(c) A payor bank's determination of the customer's account balance on which a decision to dishonor for insufficiency of available funds is based may be made at any time between the time the item is received by the payor bank and the time that the payor bank returns the item or gives notice in lieu of return, and no more than one determination need be made. If, at the election of the payor bank, a subsequent balance determination is made for the purpose of reevaluating the bank's decision to dishonor the item, the account balance at that time is determinative of whether a dishonor for insufficiency of available funds is wrongful.

§4-403. Customer's Right to Stop Payment; Burden of Proof of Loss

(a) A customer or any person authorized to draw on the account if there is more than one person may stop payment of any item drawn on the customer's account or close the account by an order to the bank describing the item or account with reasonable certainty received at a time and in a manner that affords the bank a reasonable opportunity to act on it before any action by the bank with respcct to the item described in Section 4-303. If the signature of more than one person is required to draw on an account, any of these persons may stop payment or close the account.

(b) A stop-payment order is effective for six months, but it lapses after 14 calendar days if the original order was oral and was not confirmed in a record within that period. A stop-payment order may be renewed for additional six-month periods by a record given to the bank within a period during which the stop-payment order is effective.

(c) The burden of establishing the fact and amount of loss resulting from the payment of an item contrary to a stop-payment order or order to close an account is on the customer. The loss from payment of an item contrary to a stop-payment order may include damages for dishonor of subsequent items under Section 4-402.

§4-404. Bank Not Obliged to Pay Check More than Six Months Old

A bank is under no obligation to a customer having a checking account to pay a check, other than a certified check, which is presented more than six months after its date, but it may charge its customer's account for a payment made thereafter in good faith.

§4-405. Death or Incompetence of Customer

(a) A payor or collecting bank's authority to accept, pay, or collect an item or to account for proceeds of its collection, if otherwise effective, is not rendered ineffective by incompetence of a customer of either bank existing at the time the item is issued or its collection is undertaken if the bank does not know of an adjudication of incompetence. Neither death nor incompetence of a customer revokes the authority to accept, pay, collect, or account until the bank knows of the fact of death or of an adjudication of incompetence and has reasonable opportunity to act on it.

(b) Even with knowledge, a bank may for 10 days after the date of death pay or certify checks drawn on or before that date unless ordered to stop payment by a person claiming an interest in the account.

§4-406. Customer's Duty to Discover and Report Unauthorized Signature or Alteration

(a) A bank that sends or makes available to a customer a statement of account showing payment of items for the account shall either return or make available to the customer the items paid or provide information in the statement of account sufficient to allow the customer reasonably to identify the items paid. The statement of account provides sufficient information if the item is described by item number, amount, and date of payment.

(b) If the items are not returned to the customer, the person retaining the items shall either retain the items or, if the items are destroyed, maintain the capacity to furnish legible copies of the items until the expiration of seven years after receipt of the items. A customer may request an item from the bank that paid the item, and that bank must provide in a reasonable time either the item or, if the item has been destroyed or is not otherwise obtainable, a legible copy of the item.

(c) If a bank sends or makes available a statement of account or items pursuant to subsection (a), the customer must exercise reasonable promptness in examining the statement or the items to determine whether any payment was not authorized because of an alteration of an item or because a purported signature by or on behalf of the customer was not authorized. If, based on the statement or items provided, the customer should reasonably have discovered the unauthorized payment, the customer must promptly notify the bank of the relevant facts.

(d) If the bank proves that the customer failed, with respect to an item, to comply with the duties imposed on the customer by subsection (c), the customer is precluded from asserting against the bank:

(1) the customer's unauthorized signature or any alteration on the item, if the bank also proves that it suffered a loss by reason of the failure; and

(2) the customer's unauthorized signature or alteration by the same wrongdoer on any other item paid in good faith by the bank if the payment was made before the bank received notice from the customer of the unauthorized signature or alteration and after the customer had been afforded a reasonable period of time, not exceeding 30 days, in which to examine the item or statement of account and notify the bank.

(e) If subsection (d) applies and the customer proves that the bank failed to exercise ordinary care in paying the item and that the failure substantially contributed to loss, the loss is allocated between the customer precluded and the bank asserting the preclusion according to the extent to which the failure of the customer to comply with subsection (c) and the failure of the bank to exercise ordinary care contributed to the loss. If the customer proves that the bank did not pay the item in good faith, the preclusion under subsection (d) does not apply.

(f) Without regard to care or lack of care of either the customer or the bank, a customer who does not within one year after the statement or items are made available to the customer (subsection (a)) discover and report the customer's unauthorized signature on or any alteration on the item is precluded from asserting against the bank the unauthorized signature or alteration. If there is a preclusion under this subsection, the payor bank may not recover for breach of warranty under Section 4-208 with respect to the unauthorized signature or alteration to which the preclusion applies.

§4-407. Payor Bank's Right to Subrogation on Improper Payment

If a payor bank has paid an item over the order of the drawer or maker to stop payment, or after an account has been closed, or otherwise under circumstances giving a basis for objection by the drawer or maker, to prevent unjust enrichment and only to the extent necessary to prevent loss to the bank by reason of its payment of the item, the payor bank is subrogated to the rights

(1) of any holder in due course on the item against the drawer or maker;

(2) of the payee or any other holder of the item against the drawer or maker either on the item or under the transaction out of which the item arose; and

(3) of the drawer or maker against the payee or any other holder of the item with respect to the transaction out of which the item arose.

PART 5. COLLECTION OF DOCUMENTARY DRAFTS

§4-501. Handling of Documentary Drafts; Duty to Send for Presentment and to Notify Customer of Dishonor

A bank that takes a documentary draft for collection shall present or send the draft and accompanying documents for presentment and, upon learning that the draft has not been paid or accepted in due course, shall seasonably notify its customer of the fact even though it may have discounted or bought the draft or extended credit available for withdrawal as of right.

§4-502. Presentment of "On Arrival" Drafts

If a draft or the relevant instructions require presentment "on arrival", "when goods arrive" or the like, the collecting bank need not present until in its judgment a reasonable time for arrival of the goods has expired. Refusal to pay or accept because the goods have not arrived is not dishonor; the bank must notify its transferor of the refusal but need not present the draft again until it is instructed to do so or learns of the arrival of the goods.

§4-503. Responsibility of Presenting Bank for Documents and Goods; Report of Reasons for Dishonor; Referee in Case of Need

Unless otherwise instructed and except as provided in Article 5, a bank presenting a documentary draft:

(1) must deliver the documents to the drawee on acceptance of the draft if it is payable more than three days after presentment; otherwise, only on payment; and

(2) upon dishonor, either in the case of presentment for acceptance or presentment for payment, may seek and follow instructions from any referee in case of need designated in the draft or, if the presenting bank does not choose to utilize the referee's services, it must use diligence and good faith to ascertain the reason for dishonor, must notify its transferor of the dishonor and of the results of its effort to ascertain the reasons therefor, and must request instructions.

However the presenting bank is under no obligation with respect to goods represented by the documents except to follow any reasonable instructions seasonably received; it has a right to reimbursement for any expense incurred in following instructions and to prepayment of or indemnity for those expenses.

§4-504. Privilege of Presenting Bank to Deal with Goods; Security Interest for Expenses

(a) A presenting bank that, following the dishonor of a documentary draft, has seasonably requested instructions but does not receive them within a reasonable time may store, sell, or otherwise deal with the goods in any reasonable manner.

(b) For its reasonable expenses incurred by action under subsection (a), the presenting bank has a lien upon the goods or their proceeds, which may be foreclosed in the same manner as an unpaid seller's lien.

U.C.C. – ARTICLE 4A – FUNDS TRANSFERS (2012)

PART 1. SUBJECT MATTER AND DEFINITIONS

§ 4A-101. Short Title

This Article may be cited as Uniform Commercial Code--Funds Transfers.

§ 4A-102. Subject Matter

Except as otherwise provided in Section 4A-108, this Article applies to funds transfers defined in Section 4A-104.

§ 4A-103. Payment Order - Definitions

(a) In this Article:

(1) "Payment order" means an instruction of a sender to a receiving bank, transmitted orally, electronically, or in writing, to pay, or to cause another bank to pay, a fixed or determinable amount of money to a beneficiary if:

(i) the instruction does not state a condition to payment to the beneficiary other than time of payment,

(ii) the receiving bank is to be reimbursed by debiting an account of, or otherwise receiving payment from, the sender, and

(iii) the instruction is transmitted by the sender directly to the receiving bank or to an agent, funds-transfer system, or communication system for transmittal to the receiving bank.

(2) "Beneficiary" means the person to be paid by the beneficiary's bank.

(3) "Beneficiary's bank" means the bank identified in a payment order in which an account of the beneficiary is to be credited pursuant to the order or which otherwise is to make payment to the beneficiary if the order does not provide for payment to an account.

(4) "Receiving bank" means the bank to which the sender's instruction is addressed.

(5) "Sender" means the person giving the instruction to the receiving bank.

(b) If an instruction complying with subsection (a)(1) is to make more than one payment to a beneficiary, the instruction is a separate payment order with respect to each payment.

(c) A payment order is issued when it is sent to the receiving bank.

§ 4A-104. Funds Transfer - Definitions

In this Article:

(a) "Funds transfer" means the series of transactions, beginning with the originator's payment order, made for the purpose of making payment to the beneficiary of the order. The term includes any payment order issued by the originator's bank or an intermediary bank intended to carry out the originator's payment order. A funds transfer is completed by acceptance by the beneficiary's bank of a payment order for the benefit of the beneficiary of the originator's payment order.

(b) "Intermediary bank" means a receiving bank other than the originator's bank or the beneficiary's bank.

(c) "Originator" means the sender of the first payment order in a funds transfer.

(d) "Originator's bank" means (i) the receiving bank to which the payment order of the originator is issued if the originator is not a bank, or (ii) the originator if the originator is a bank.

§ 4A-105. Other Definitions

(a) In this Article:

(1) "Authorized account" means a deposit account of a customer in a bank designated by the customer as a source of payment of payment orders issued by the customer to the bank. If a customer does not so designate an account, any account of the customer is an authorized account if payment of a payment order from that account is not inconsistent with a restriction on the use of that account.

(2) "Bank" means a person engaged in the business of banking and includes a savings bank, savings and loan association, credit union, and trust company. A branch or separate office of a bank is a separate bank for purposes of this Article.

(3) "Customer" means a person, including a bank, having an account with a bank or from whom a bank has agreed to receive payment orders.

(4) "Funds-transfer business day" of a receiving bank means the part of a day during which the receiving bank is open for the receipt, processing, and transmittal of payment orders and cancellations and amendments of payment orders.

(5) "Funds-transfer system" means a wire transfer network, automated clearing house, or other communication system of a clearing house or other association of banks through which a payment order by a bank may be transmitted to the bank to which the order is addressed.

(6) [reserved]

(7) "Prove" with respect to a fact means to meet the burden of establishing the fact (Section 1-201(b)(8)).

(b) Other definitions applying to this Article and the sections in which they appear are:

"Acceptance"	– Section 4A-209
"Beneficiary"	– Section 4A-103
"Beneficiary's bank"	– Section 4A-103
"Executed"	– Section 4A-301

"Execution date"	– Section 4A-301
"Funds transfer"	– Section 4A-104
"Funds-transfer system rule"	– Section 4A-501
"Intermediary bank"	– Section 4A-104
"Originator"	– Section 4A-104
"Originator's bank"	– Section 4A-104
"Payment by beneficiary's bank to beneficiary"	– Section 4A-405
"Payment by originator to beneficiary"	– Section 4A-406
"Payment by sender to receiving bank"	– Section 4A-403
"Payment date"	– Section 4A-401
"Payment order"	– Section 4A-103
"Receiving bank"	– Section 4A-103
"Security procedure"	– Section 4A-201
"Sender"	– Section 4A-103

(c) The following definitions in Article 4 apply to this Article:

"Clearing house"	– Section 4-104
"Item"	– Section 4-104
"Suspends payments"	– Section 4-104

(d) In addition Article 1 contains general definitions and principles of construction and interpretation applicable throughout this Article.

§ 4A-106. Time Payment Order Is Received

(a) The time of receipt of a payment order or communication cancelling or amending a payment order is determined by the rules applicable to receipt of a notice stated in Section 1-202. A receiving bank may fix a cut-off time or times on a funds-transfer business day for the receipt and processing of payment orders and communications cancelling or amending payment orders. Different cut-off times may apply to payment orders, cancellations, or amendments, or to different categories of payment orders, cancellations, or amendments. A cut-off time may apply to senders generally or different cut-off times may apply to different senders or categories of payment orders. If a payment order or communication cancelling or amending a payment order is received after the close of a funds-transfer business day or after the appropriate cut-off time on a funds-transfer business day, the receiving bank may treat the payment order or communication as received at the opening of the next funds-transfer business day.

(b) If this Article refers to an execution date or payment date or states a day on which a receiving bank is required to take action, and the date or day does not fall on a funds-transfer business day, the next day that is a funds-transfer business day is treated as the date or day stated, unless the contrary is stated in this Article.

§ 4A-107. Federal Reserve Regulations and Operating Circulars

Regulations of the Board of Governors of the Federal Reserve System and operating circulars of the Federal Reserve Banks supersede any inconsistent provision of this Article to the extent of the inconsistency.

§ 4A-108. Exclusion of Consumer Transactions Governed by Federal Law

This Article does not apply to a funds transfer any part of which is governed by the Electronic Fund Transfer Act of 1978 (Title XX, Public Law 95-630, 92 Stat. 3728, 15 U.S.C. § 1693 et seq.) as amended from time to time.

PART 2. ISSUE AND ACCEPTANCE OF PAYMENT ORDER

§ 4A-201. Security Procedure

"Security procedure" means a procedure established by agreement of a customer and a receiving bank for the purpose of (i) verifying that a payment order or communication amending or cancelling a payment order is that of the customer, or (ii) detecting error in the transmission or the content of the payment order or communication. A security procedure may require the use of algorithms or other codes, identifying words or numbers, encryption, callback procedures, or similar security devices. Comparison of a signature on a payment order or communication with an authorized specimen signature of the customer is not by itself a security procedure.

§ 4A-202. Authorized and Verified Payment Orders

(a) A payment order received by the receiving bank is the authorized order of the person identified as sender if that person authorized the order or is otherwise bound by it under the law of agency.

(b) If a bank and its customer have agreed that the authenticity of payment orders issued to the bank in the name of the customer as sender will be verified pursuant to a security procedure, a payment order received by the receiving bank is effective as the order of the customer, whether or not authorized, if (i) the security procedure is a commercially reasonable method of providing security against unauthorized payment orders, and (ii) the bank proves that it accepted the payment order in good faith and in compliance with the security procedure and any written agreement or instruction of the customer restricting acceptance of payment orders issued in the name of the customer. The bank is not required to follow an instruction that violates a written agreement with the customer or notice of which is not received at a time and in a manner affording the bank a reasonable opportunity to act on it before the payment order is accepted.

(c) Commercial reasonableness of a security procedure is a question of law to be determined by considering the wishes of the customer expressed to the bank, the circumstances of the customer known to the bank, including the size, type, and frequency of payment orders normally issued by the customer to the bank, alternative security procedures offered to the customer, and security procedures in general use by customers and receiving banks similarly situated. A security procedure is deemed to be commercially reasonable if (i) the security procedure was chosen by the customer after the bank offered, and the customer refused, a security procedure that was commercially reasonable for that customer, and (ii) the customer expressly agreed in writing to be bound by any payment order, whether or not authorized, issued in its name and accepted by the bank in compliance with the security procedure chosen by the customer.

(d) The term "sender" in this Article includes the customer in whose name a payment order is issued if the order is the authorized order of the customer under subsection (a), or it is effective as the order of the customer under subsection (b).

(e) This section applies to amendments and cancellations of payment orders to the same extent it applies to payment orders.

(f) Except as provided in this section and in Section 4A-203(a)(1), rights and obligations arising under this section or Section 4A-203 may not be varied by agreement.

§ 4A-203. Unenforceability of Certain Verified Payment Orders

(a) If an accepted payment order is not, under Section 4A-202(a), an authorized order of a customer identified as sender, but is effective as an order of the customer pursuant to Section 4A-202(b), the following rules apply:

(1) By express written agreement, the receiving bank may limit the extent to which it is entitled to enforce or retain payment of the payment order.

(2) The receiving bank is not entitled to enforce or retain payment of the payment order if the customer proves that the order was not caused, directly or indirectly, by a person (i) entrusted at any time with duties to act for the customer with respect to payment orders or the security procedure, or (ii) who obtained access to transmitting facilities of the customer or who obtained, from a source controlled by the customer and without authority of the receiving bank, information facilitating breach of the security procedure, regardless of how the information was obtained or whether the customer was at fault. Information includes any access device, computer software, or the like.

(b) This section applies to amendments of payment orders to the same extent it applies to payment orders.

§ 4A-204. Refund of Payment and Duty of Customer to Report with Respect to Unauthorized Payment Order

(a) If a receiving bank accepts a payment order issued in the name of its customer as sender which is (i) not authorized and not effective as the order of the customer under Section 4A-202, or (ii) not enforceable, in whole or in part, against the customer under Section 4A-203, the bank shall refund any payment of the payment order received from the customer to the extent the bank is not entitled to enforce payment and shall pay interest on the refundable amount calculated from the date the bank received payment to the date of the refund. However, the customer is not entitled to interest from the bank on the amount to be refunded if the customer fails to exercise ordinary care to determine that the order was not authorized by the customer and to notify the bank of the relevant facts within a reasonable time not exceeding 90 days after the date the customer received notification from the bank that the order was accepted or that the customer's account was debited with respect to the order. The bank is not entitled to any recovery from the customer on account of a failure by the customer to give notification as stated in this section.

(b) Reasonable time under subsection (a) may be fixed by agreement as stated in Section 1-204(1), but the obligation of a receiving bank to refund payment as stated in subsection (a) may not otherwise be varied by agreement.

§ 4A-205. Erroneous Payment Orders

(a) If an accepted payment order was transmitted pursuant to a security procedure for the detection of error and the payment order (i) erroneously instructed payment to a beneficiary not intended by the sender, (ii) erroneously instructed payment in an amount greater than the amount intended by the sender, or (iii) was an erroneously transmitted duplicate of a payment order previously sent by the sender, the following rules apply:

(1) If the sender proves that the sender or a person acting on behalf of the sender pursuant to Section 4A-206 complied with the security procedure and that the error would have been detected if the receiving bank had also complied, the sender is not obliged to pay the order to the extent stated in paragraphs (2) and (3).

(2) If the funds transfer is completed on the basis of an erroneous payment order described in clause (i) or (iii) of subsection (a), the sender is not obliged to pay the order and the receiving bank is entitled to recover from the beneficiary any amount paid to the beneficiary to the extent allowed by the law governing mistake and restitution.

(3) If the funds transfer is completed on the basis of a payment order described in clause (ii) of subsection (a), the sender is not obliged to pay the order to the extent the amount received by the beneficiary is greater than the amount intended by the sender. In that case, the receiving bank is entitled to recover from the beneficiary the excess amount received to the extent allowed by the law governing mistake and restitution.

(b) If (i) the sender of an erroneous payment order described in subsection (a) is not obliged to pay all or part of the order, and (ii) the sender receives notification from the receiving bank that the order was accepted by the bank or that the sender's account was debited with respect to the order, the sender has a duty to exercise ordinary care, on the basis of information available to the sender, to discover the error with respect to the order and to advise the bank of the relevant facts within a reasonable time, not exceeding 90 days, after the bank's notification was received by the sender. If the bank proves that the sender failed to perform that duty, the sender is liable to the bank for the loss the bank proves it incurred as a result of the failure, but the liability of the sender may not exceed the amount of the sender's order.

(c) This section applies to amendments to payment orders to the same extent it applies to payment orders.

§ 4A-206. Transmission of Payment Order Through Funds-Transfer or Other Communication System

(a) If a payment order addressed to a receiving bank is transmitted to a funds-transfer system or other third-party communication system for transmittal to the bank, the system is deemed to be an agent of the sender for the purpose of transmitting the payment order to the bank. If there is a discrepancy between the terms of the payment order transmitted to the system and the terms of the payment order transmitted by the system to the bank, the terms of the payment order of the sender are those transmitted by the system. This section does not apply to a funds-transfer system of the Federal Reserve Banks.

(b) This section applies to cancellations and amendments of payment orders to the same extent it applies to payment orders.

§ 4A-207. Misdescription of Beneficiary

(a) Subject to subsection (b), if, in a payment order received by the beneficiary's bank, the name, bank account number, or other identification of the beneficiary refers to a nonexistent or unidentifiable person or account, no person has rights as a beneficiary of the order and acceptance of the order cannot occur.

(b) If a payment order received by the beneficiary's bank identifies the beneficiary both by name and by an identifying or bank account number and the name and number identify different persons, the following rules apply:

(1) Except as otherwise provided in subsection (c), if the beneficiary's bank does not know that the name and number refer to different persons, it may rely on the number as the proper identification of the beneficiary of the order. The beneficiary's bank need not determine whether the name and number refer to the same person.

(2) If the beneficiary's bank pays the person identified by name or knows that the name and number identify different persons, no person has rights as beneficiary except the person paid by the beneficiary's bank if that person was entitled to receive payment from the originator of the funds transfer. If no person has rights as beneficiary, acceptance of the order cannot occur.

(c) If (i) a payment order described in subsection (b) is accepted, (ii) the originator's payment order described the beneficiary inconsistently by name and number, and (iii) the beneficiary's bank pays the person identified by number as permitted by subsection (b)(1), the following rules apply:

(1) If the originator is a bank, the originator is obliged to pay its order.

(2) If the originator is not a bank and proves that the person identified by number was not entitled to receive payment from the originator, the originator is not obliged to pay its order unless the originator's bank proves that the originator, before acceptance of the origi-

nator's order, had notice that payment of a payment order issued by the originator might be made by the beneficiary's bank on the basis of an identifying or bank account number even if it identifies a person different from the named beneficiary. Proof of notice may be made by any admissible evidence. The originator's bank satisfies the burden of proof if it proves that the originator, before the payment order was accepted, signed a writing stating the information to which the notice relates.

(d) In a case governed by subsection (b)(1), if the beneficiary's bank rightfully pays the person identified by number and that person was not entitled to receive payment from the originator, the amount paid may be recovered from that person to the extent allowed by the law governing mistake and restitution as follows:

(1) If the originator is obliged to pay its payment order as stated in subsection (c), the originator has the right to recover.

(2) If the originator is not a bank and is not obliged to pay its payment order, the originator's bank has the right to recover.

§ 4A-208. Misdescription of Intermediary Bank or Beneficiary's Bank

(a) This subsection applies to a payment order identifying an intermediary bank or the beneficiary's bank only by an identifying number.

(1) The receiving bank may rely on the number as the proper identification of the intermediary or beneficiary's bank and need not determine whether the number identifies a bank.

(2) The sender is obliged to compensate the receiving bank for any loss and expenses incurred by the receiving bank as a result of its reliance on the number in executing or attempting to execute the order.

(b) This subsection applies to a payment order identifying an intermediary bank or the beneficiary's bank both by name and an identifying number if the name and number identify different persons.

(1) If the sender is a bank, the receiving bank may rely on the number as the proper identification of the intermediary or beneficiary's bank if the receiving bank, when it executes the sender's order, does not know that the name and number identify different persons. The receiving bank need not determine whether the name and number refer to the same person or whether the number refers to a bank. The sender is obliged to compensate the receiving bank for any loss and expenses incurred by the receiving bank as a result of its reliance on the number in executing or attempting to execute the order.

(2) If the sender is not a bank and the receiving bank proves that the sender, before the payment order was accepted, had notice that the receiving bank might rely on the number as the proper identification of the intermediary or beneficiary's bank even if it identifies a person different from the bank identified by name, the rights and obligations of the sender and the receiving bank are governed by subsection (b)(1), as though the sender were a bank. Proof of notice may be made by any admissible evidence. The receiving bank satisfies the burden of proof if it proves that the sender, before the payment order was accepted, signed a writing stating the information to which the notice relates.

(3) Regardless of whether the sender is a bank, the receiving bank may rely on the name as the proper identification of the intermediary or beneficiary's bank if the receiving bank, at the time it executes the sender's order, does not know that the name and number identify different persons. The receiving bank need not determine whether the name and number refer to the same person.

(4) If the receiving bank knows that the name and number identify different persons, reliance on either the name or the number in executing the sender's payment order is a breach of the obligation stated in Section 4A-302(a)(1).

§ 4A-209. Acceptance of Payment Order

(a) Subject to subsection (d), a receiving bank other than the beneficiary's bank accepts a payment order when it executes the order.

(b) Subject to subsections (c) and (d), a beneficiary's bank accepts a payment order at the earliest of the following times:

(1) when the bank (i) pays the beneficiary as stated in Section 4A-405(a) or 4A-405(b), or (ii) notifies the beneficiary of receipt of the order or that the account of the beneficiary has been credited with respect to the order unless the notice indicates that the bank is rejecting the order or that funds with respect to the order may not be withdrawn or used until receipt of payment from the sender of the order;

(2) when the bank receives payment of the entire amount of the sender's order pursuant to Section 4A-403(a)(1) or 4A-403(a)(2); or

(3) the opening of the next funds-transfer business day of the bank following the payment date of the order if, at that time, the amount of the sender's order is fully covered by a withdrawable credit balance in an authorized account of the sender or the bank has otherwise received full payment from the sender, unless the order was rejected before that time or is rejected within (i) one hour after that time, or (ii) one hour after the opening of the next business day of the sender following the payment date if that time is later. If notice of rejection is received by the sender after the payment date and the authorized account of the sender does not bear interest, the bank is obliged to pay interest to the sender on the amount of the order for the number of days elapsing after the payment date to the day the sender receives notice or learns that the order was not accepted, counting that day as an elapsed day. If the withdrawable credit balance during that period falls below the amount of the order, the amount of interest payable is reduced accordingly.

(c) Acceptance of a payment order cannot occur before the order is received by the receiving bank. Acceptance does not occur under subsection (b)(2) or (b)(3) if the beneficiary of the payment order does not have an account with the receiving bank, the account has been closed, or the receiving bank is not permitted by law to receive credits for the beneficiary's account.

(d) A payment order issued to the originator's bank cannot be accepted until the payment date if the bank is the beneficiary's bank, or the execution date if the bank is not the beneficiary's bank. If the originator's bank executes the originator's payment order before the execution date or pays the beneficiary of the originator's payment order before the payment date and the payment order is subsequently canceled pursuant to Section 4A-211(b), the bank may recover from the beneficiary any payment received to the extent allowed by the law governing mistake and restitution.

§ 4A-210. Rejection of Payment Order

(a) A payment order is rejected by the receiving bank by a notice of rejection transmitted to the sender orally, electronically, or in writing. A notice of rejection need not use any particular words and is sufficient if it indicates that the receiving bank is rejecting the order or will not execute or pay the order. Rejection is effective when the notice is given if transmission is by a means that is reasonable in the circumstances. If notice of rejection is given by a means that is not reasonable, rejection is effective when the notice is received. If an agreement of the sender and receiving bank establishes the means to be used to reject a payment order, (i) any means complying with the agreement is reasonable and (ii) any means not complying is not reasonable unless no significant delay in receipt of the notice resulted from the use of the noncomplying means.

(b) This subsection applies if a receiving bank other than the beneficiary's bank fails to execute a payment order despite the existence on the execution date of a withdrawable credit balance in an authorized account of the sender sufficient to cover the order. If the sender does not receive notice of rejection of the order on the execution date and the authorized account of the sender does not bear interest, the bank is obliged to pay interest to the sender on the amount of the order for the number of days elapsing after the execution date to the earlier of the day the order is canceled pursuant to Section 4A-211(d) or the day the sender receives notice or learns that the order was not executed, counting the final day of the period as an elapsed day. If the withdrawable credit balance during that period falls below the amount of the order, the amount of interest is reduced accordingly.

(c) If a receiving bank suspends payments, all unaccepted payment orders issued to it are deemed rejected at the time the bank suspends payments.

(d) Acceptance of a payment order precludes a later rejection of the order. Rejection of a payment order precludes a later acceptance of the order.

§ 4A-211. Cancellation and Amendment of Payment Order

(a) A communication of the sender of a payment order cancelling or amending the order may be transmitted to the receiving bank orally, electronically, or in writing. If a security procedure is in effect between the sender and the receiving bank, the communication is not effective to cancel or amend the order unless the communication is verified pursuant to the security procedure or the bank agrees to the cancellation or amendment.

(b) Subject to subsection (a), a communication by the sender cancelling or amending a payment order is effective to cancel or amend the order if notice of the communication is received at a time and in a manner affording the receiving bank a reasonable opportunity to act on the communication before the bank accepts the payment order.

(c) After a payment order has been accepted, cancellation or amendment of the order is not effective unless the receiving bank agrees or a funds-transfer system rule allows cancellation or amendment without agreement of the bank.

(1) With respect to a payment order accepted by a receiving bank other than the beneficiary's bank, cancellation or amendment is not effective unless a conforming cancellation or amendment of the payment order issued by the receiving bank is also made.

(2) With respect to a payment order accepted by the beneficiary's bank, cancellation or amendment is not effective unless the order was issued in execution of an unauthorized payment order, or because of a mistake by a sender in the funds transfer which resulted in the issuance of a payment order (i) that is a duplicate of a payment order previously issued by the sender, (ii) that orders payment to a beneficiary not entitled to receive payment from the originator, or (iii) that orders payment in an amount greater than the amount the beneficiary was entitled to receive from the originator. If the payment order is canceled or amended, the beneficiary's bank is entitled to recover from the beneficiary any amount paid to the beneficiary to the extent allowed by the law governing mistake and restitution.

(d) An unaccepted payment order is canceled by operation of law at the close of the fifth funds-transfer business day of the receiving bank after the execution date or payment date of the order.

(e) A canceled payment order cannot be accepted. If an accepted payment order is canceled, the acceptance is nullified and no person has any right or obligation based on the acceptance.

Amendment of a payment order is deemed to be cancellation of the original order at the time of amendment and issue of a new payment order in the amended form at the same time.

(f) Unless otherwise provided in an agreement of the parties or in a funds-transfer system rule, if the receiving bank, after accepting a payment order, agrees to cancellation or amendment of the order by the sender or is bound by a funds-transfer system rule allowing cancellation or amendment without the bank's agreement, the sender, whether or not cancellation or amendment is effective, is liable to the bank for any loss and expenses, including reasonable attorney's fees, incurred by the bank as a result of the cancellation or amendment or attempted cancellation or amendment.

(g) A payment order is not revoked by the death or legal incapacity of the sender unless the receiving bank knows of the death or of an adjudication of incapacity by a court of competent jurisdiction and has reasonable opportunity to act before acceptance of the order.

(h) A funds-transfer system rule is not effective to the extent it conflicts with subsection (c)(2).

§ 4A-212. Liability and Duty of Receiving Bank Regarding Unaccepted Payment Order

If a receiving bank fails to accept a payment order that it is obliged by express agreement to accept, the bank is liable for breach of the agreement to the extent provided in the agreement or in this Article, but does not otherwise have any duty to accept a payment order or, before acceptance, to take any action, or refrain from taking action, with respect to the order except as provided in this Article or by express agreement. Liability based on acceptance arises only when acceptance occurs as stated in Section 4A-209, and liability is limited to that provided in this Article. A receiving bank is not the agent of the sender or beneficiary of the payment order it accepts, or of any other party to the funds transfer, and the bank owes no duty to any party to the funds transfer except as provided in this Article or by express agreement.

PART 3. EXECUTION OF SENDER'S PAYMENT ORDER BY RECEIVING BANK

§ 4A-301. Execution and Execution Date

(a) A payment order is "executed" by the receiving bank when it issues a payment order intended to carry out the payment order received by the bank. A payment order received by the beneficiary's bank can be accepted but cannot be executed.

(b) "Execution date" of a payment order means the day on which the receiving bank may properly issue a payment order in execution of the sender's order. The execution date may be determined by instruction of the sender but cannot be earlier than the day the order is received and, unless otherwise determined, is the day the order is received. If the sender's instruction states a payment date, the execution date is the payment date or an earlier date on which execution is reasonably necessary to allow payment to the beneficiary on the payment date.

§ 4A-302. Obligations of Receiving Bank in Execution of Payment Order

(a) Except as provided in subsections (b) through (d), if the receiving bank accepts a payment order pursuant to Section 4A-209(a), the bank has the following obligations in executing the order:

(1) The receiving bank is obliged to issue, on the execution date, a payment order complying with the sender's order and to follow the sender's instructions concerning (i) any intermediary bank or funds-transfer system to be used in carrying out the funds transfer, or (ii) the means by which payment orders are to be transmitted in the funds transfer. If the originator's bank issues a payment order to an intermediary bank, the originator's bank is obliged to instruct the intermediary bank according to the instruction of the originator. An intermediary bank in the funds transfer is similarly bound by an instruction given to it by the sender of the payment order it accepts.

(2) If the sender's instruction states that the funds transfer is to be carried out telephonically or by wire transfer or otherwise indicates that the funds transfer is to be carried out by the most expeditious means, the receiving bank is obliged to transmit its payment order by the most expeditious available means, and to instruct any intermediary bank accordingly. If a sender's instruction states a payment date, the receiving bank is obliged to transmit its payment order at a time and by means reasonably necessary to allow payment to the beneficiary on the payment date or as soon thereafter as is feasible.

(b) Unless otherwise instructed, a receiving bank executing a payment order may (i) use any funds-transfer system if use of that system is reasonable in the circumstances, and (ii) issue a payment order to the beneficiary's bank or to an intermediary bank through which a payment order conforming to the sender's order can expeditiously be issued to the beneficiary's bank if the receiving bank exercises ordinary care in the selection of the intermediary bank. A receiving bank is not required to follow an instruction of the sender designating a funds-transfer system to be used in carrying out the funds transfer if the receiving bank, in good faith, determines that it is not feasible to follow the instruction or that following the instruction would unduly delay completion of the funds transfer.

(c) Unless subsection (a)(2) applies or the receiving bank is otherwise instructed, the bank may execute a payment order by transmitting its payment order by first class mail or by any means reasonable in the circumstances. If the receiving bank is instructed to execute the sender's order by transmitting its payment order by a particular means, the receiving bank may issue its payment order by the means stated or by any means as expeditious as the means stated.

(d) Unless instructed by the sender, (i) the receiving bank may not obtain payment of its charges for services and expenses in connection with the execution of the sender's order by issuing a payment order in an amount equal to the amount of the sender's order less the amount of the charges, and (ii) may not instruct a subsequent receiving bank to obtain payment of its charges in the same manner.

§ 4A-303. Erroneous Execution of Payment Order

(a) A receiving bank that (i) executes the payment order of the sender by issuing a payment order in an amount greater than the amount of the sender's order, or (ii) issues a payment order in execution of the sender's order and then issues a duplicate order, is entitled to payment of the amount of the sender's order under Section 4A-402(c) if that subsection is otherwise satisfied. The bank is entitled to recover from the beneficiary of the erroneous order the excess payment received to the extent allowed by the law governing mistake and restitution.

(b) A receiving bank that executes the payment order of the sender by issuing a payment order in an amount less than the amount of the sender's order is entitled to payment of the amount of the sender's order under Section 4A-402(c) if (i) that subsection is otherwise satisfied and (ii) the bank corrects its mistake by issuing an additional payment order for the benefit of the beneficiary of the sender's order. If the error is not corrected, the issuer of the erroneous order is entitled to receive or retain payment from the sender of the order it accepted only to the extent of the amount of the erroneous order. This subsection does not apply if the receiving bank executes the sender's payment order by issuing a payment order in an amount less than the amount of the sender's order for the purpose of obtaining payment of its charges for services and expenses pursuant to instruction of the sender.

(c) If a receiving bank executes the payment order of the sender by issuing a payment order to a beneficiary different from the beneficiary of the sender's order and the funds transfer is completed on the basis of that error, the sender of the payment order that was erroneously executed and all previous senders in the funds transfer are not obliged to pay the payment orders they issued. The issuer of the erroneous order is entitled to recover from the beneficiary of the order the payment received to the extent allowed by the law governing mistake and restitution.

§ 4A-304. Duty of Sender to Report Erroneously Executed Payment Order

If the sender of a payment order that is erroneously executed as stated in Section 4A-303 receives notification from the receiving bank that the order was executed or that the sender's account was debited with respect to the order, the sender has a duty to exercise ordinary care to determine, on the basis of information available to the sender, that the order was erroneously executed and to notify the bank of the relevant facts within a reasonable time not exceeding 90 days after the notification from the bank was received by the sender. If the sender fails to perform that duty, the bank is not obliged to pay interest on any amount refundable to the sender under Section 4A-402(d) for the period before the bank learns of the execution error. The bank is not entitled to any recovery from the sender on account of a failure by the sender to perform the duty stated in this section.

§ 4A-305. Liability for Late or Improper Execution or Failure to Execute Payment Order

(a) If a funds transfer is completed but execution of a payment order by the receiving bank in breach of Section 4A-302 results in delay in payment to the beneficiary, the bank is obliged to pay interest to either the originator or the beneficiary of the funds transfer for the period of delay caused by the improper execution. Except as provided in subsection (c), additional damages are not recoverable.

(b) If execution of a payment order by a receiving bank in breach of Section 4A-302 results in (i) non-completion of the funds transfer, (ii) failure to use an intermediary bank designated by the originator, or (iii) issuance of a payment order that does not comply with the terms of the payment order of the originator, the bank is liable to the originator for its expenses in the funds transfer and for incidental expenses and interest losses, to the extent not covered by subsection (a), resulting from the improper execution. Except as provided in subsection (c), additional damages are not recoverable.

(c) In addition to the amounts payable under subsections (a) and (b), damages, including consequential damages, are recoverable to the extent provided in an express written agreement of the receiving bank.

(d) If a receiving bank fails to execute a payment order it was obliged by express agreement to execute, the receiving bank is liable to the sender for its expenses in the transaction and for incidental expenses and interest losses resulting from the failure to execute. Additional damages, including consequential damages, are recoverable to the extent provided in an express written agreement of the receiving bank, but are not otherwise recoverable.

(e) Reasonable attorney's fees are recoverable if demand for compensation under subsection (a) or (b) is made and refused before an action is brought on the claim. If a claim is made for breach of an agreement under subsection (d) and the agreement does not provide for damages, reasonable attorney's fees are recoverable if demand for compensation under subsection (d) is made and refused before an action is brought on the claim.

(f) Except as stated in this section, the liability of a receiving bank under subsections (a) and (b) may not be varied by agreement.

PART 4. PAYMENT

§ 4A-401. Payment Date

"Payment date" of a payment order means the day on which the amount of the order is payable to the beneficiary by the beneficiary's bank. The payment date may be determined by instruction of the sender but cannot be earlier than the day the order is received by the beneficiary's bank and, unless otherwise determined, is the day the order is received by the beneficiary's bank.

§ 4A-402. Obligation of Sender to Pay Receiving Bank

(a) This section is subject to Sections 4A-205 and 4A-207.

(b) With respect to a payment order issued to the beneficiary's bank, acceptance of the order by the bank obliges the sender to pay the bank the amount of the order, but payment is not due until the payment date of the order.

(c) This subsection is subject to subsection (e) and to Section 4A-303. With respect to a payment order issued to a receiving bank other than the beneficiary's bank, acceptance of the order by the receiving bank obliges the sender to pay the bank the amount of the sender's order. Payment by the sender is not due until the execution date of the sender's order. The obligation of that sender to pay its payment order is excused if the funds transfer is not completed by acceptance by the beneficiary's bank of a payment order instructing payment to the beneficiary of that sender's payment order.

(d) If the sender of a payment order pays the order and was not obliged to pay all or part of the amount paid, the bank receiving payment is obliged to refund payment to the extent the sender was not obliged to pay. Except as provided in Sections 4A-204 and 4A-304, interest is payable on the refundable amount from the date of payment.

(e) If a funds transfer is not completed as stated in subsection (c) and an intermediary bank is obliged to refund payment as stated in subsection (d) but is unable to do so because not permitted by applicable law or because the bank suspends payments, a sender in the funds transfer that executed a payment order in compliance with an instruction, as stated in Section 4A-302(a)(1), to route the funds transfer through that intermediary bank is entitled to receive or retain payment from the sender of the payment order that it accepted. The first sender in the funds transfer that issued an instruction requiring routing through that intermediary bank is subrogated to the right of the bank that paid the intermediary bank to refund as stated in subsection (d).

(f) The right of the sender of a payment order to be excused from the obligation to pay the order as stated in subsection (c) or to receive refund under subsection (d) may not be varied by agreement.

§ 4A-403. Payment by Sender to Receiving Bank

(a) Payment of the sender's obligation under Section 4A-402 to pay the receiving bank occurs as follows:

(1) If the sender is a bank, payment occurs when the receiving bank receives final settlement of the obligation through a Federal Reserve Bank or through a funds-transfer system.

(2) If the sender is a bank and the sender (i) credited an account of the receiving bank with the sender, or (ii) caused an account of the receiving bank in another bank to be credited, payment occurs when the credit is withdrawn or, if not withdrawn, at midnight of the day on which the credit is withdrawable and the receiving bank learns of that fact.

(3) If the receiving bank debits an account of the sender with the receiving bank, payment occurs when the debit is made to the extent the debit is covered by a withdrawable credit balance in the account.

(b) If the sender and receiving bank are members of a funds-transfer system that nets obligations multilaterally among participants, the receiving bank receives final settlement when settlement is complete in accordance with the rules of the system. The obligation of the sender to pay the amount of a payment order transmitted through the funds-transfer system may be satisfied, to the extent permitted by the rules of the system, by setting off and applying against the sender's obligation the right of the sender to receive payment from the receiving bank of the amount of any other payment order transmitted to the sender by the receiving bank through the funds-transfer system. The aggregate balance of obligations owed by each sender to each receiving bank in the funds-transfer system may be satisfied, to the extent permitted by the rules of the system, by setting off and applying against that balance the aggregate balance of obligations owed to the sender by other members of the system. The aggregate balance is determined after the right of setoff stated in the second sentence of this subsection has been exercised.

(c) If two banks transmit payment orders to each other under an agreement that settlement of the obligations of each bank to the other under Section 4A-402 will be made at the end of the day or other period, the total amount owed with respect to all orders transmitted by one bank shall be set off against the total amount owed with respect to all orders transmitted by the other bank. To the extent of the setoff, each bank has made payment to the other.

(d) In a case not covered by subsection (a), the time when payment of the sender's obligation under Section 4A-402(b) or 4A-402(c) occurs is governed by applicable principles of law that determine when an obligation is satisfied.

§ 4A-404. Obligation of Beneficiary's Bank to Pay and Give Notice to Beneficiary

(a) Subject to Sections 4A-211(e), 4A-405(d), and 4A-405(e), if a beneficiary's bank accepts a payment order, the bank is obliged to pay the amount of the order to the beneficiary of the order. Payment is due on the payment date of the order, but if acceptance occurs on the payment date after the close of the funds-transfer business day of the bank, payment is due on the next funds-transfer business day. If the bank refuses to pay after demand by the beneficiary and receipt of notice of particular circumstances that will give rise to consequential damages as a result of nonpayment, the beneficiary may recover damages resulting from the refusal to pay to the extent the bank had notice of the damages, unless the bank proves that it did not pay because of a reasonable doubt concerning the right of the beneficiary to payment.

(b) If a payment order accepted by the beneficiary's bank instructs payment to an account of the beneficiary, the bank is obliged to notify the beneficiary of receipt of the order before midnight of the next funds-transfer business day following the payment date. If the payment order does not instruct payment to an account of the beneficiary, the bank is required to notify the beneficiary only if notice is required by the order. Notice may be given by first class mail or any other means reasonable in the circumstances. If the bank fails to give the required notice, the bank is obliged to pay interest to the beneficiary on the amount of the payment order from the day notice should have been given until the day the beneficiary learned of receipt of the payment order by the bank. No other damages are recoverable. Reasonable attorney's fees are also recoverable if demand for interest is made and refused before an action is brought on the claim.

(c) The right of a beneficiary to receive payment and damages as stated in subsection (a) may not be varied by agreement or a funds-transfer system rule. The right of a beneficiary to be notified as stated in subsection (b) may be varied by agreement of the beneficiary or by a funds-transfer system rule if the beneficiary is notified of the rule before initiation of the funds transfer.

§ 4A-405. Payment by Beneficiary's Bank to Beneficiary

(a) If the beneficiary's bank credits an account of the beneficiary of a payment order, payment of the bank's obligation under Section 4A-404(a) occurs when and to the extent (i) the beneficiary is notified of the right to withdraw the credit, (ii) the bank lawfully applies the credit to a debt of the beneficiary, or (iii) funds with respect to the order are otherwise made available to the beneficiary by the bank.

(b) If the beneficiary's bank does not credit an account of the beneficiary of a payment order, the time when payment of the bank's obligation under Section 4A-404(a) occurs is governed by principles of law that determine when an obligation is satisfied.

(c) Except as stated in subsections (d) and (e), if the beneficiary's bank pays the beneficiary of a payment order under a condition to payment or agreement of the beneficiary giving the bank the right to recover payment from the beneficiary if the bank does not receive payment of the order, the condition to payment or agreement is not enforceable.

(d) A funds-transfer system rule may provide that payments made to beneficiaries of funds transfers made through the system are provisional until receipt of payment by the beneficiary's bank of the payment order it accepted. A beneficiary's bank that makes a payment that is provisional under the rule is entitled to refund from the beneficiary if (i) the rule requires that both the beneficiary and the originator be given notice of the provisional nature of the payment before the funds transfer is initiated, (ii) the beneficiary, the beneficiary's bank and the originator's bank agreed to be bound by the rule, and (iii) the beneficiary's bank did not receive payment of the payment order that it accepted. If the beneficiary is obliged to refund payment to the beneficiary's bank, acceptance of the payment order by the beneficiary's bank is nullified and no payment by the originator of the funds transfer to the beneficiary occurs under Section 4A-406.

(e) This subsection applies to a funds transfer that includes a payment order transmitted over a funds-transfer system that (i) nets obligations multilaterally among participants, and (ii) has in effect a loss-sharing agreement among participants for the purpose of providing funds necessary to complete settlement of the obligations of one or more participants that do not meet their settlement obligations. If the beneficiary's bank in the funds transfer accepts a payment order and the system fails to complete settlement pursuant to its rules with respect to any payment order in the funds transfer, (i) the acceptance by the beneficiary's bank is nullified and no person has any right or obligation based on the acceptance, (ii) the beneficiary's bank is entitled to recover payment from the beneficiary, (iii) no payment by the originator to the beneficiary occurs under Section 4A-406, and (iv) subject to Section 4A-402(e), each sender in the funds transfer is excused from its obligation to pay its payment order under Section 4A-402(c) because the funds transfer has not been completed.

§ 4A-406. Payment by Originator to Beneficiary; Discharge of Underlying Obligation

(a) Subject to Sections 4A-211(e), 4A-405(d), and 4A-405(e), the originator of a funds transfer pays the beneficiary of the originator's payment order (i) at the time a payment order for the benefit of the beneficiary is accepted by the beneficiary's bank in the funds transfer and (ii) in an amount equal to the amount of the order accepted by the beneficiary's bank, but not more than the amount of the originator's order.

(b) If payment under subsection (a) is made to satisfy an obligation, the obligation is discharged to the same extent discharge would result from payment to the beneficiary of the same amount in money, unless (i) the payment under subsection (a) was made by a means prohibited by the contract of the beneficiary with respect to the obligation, (ii) the beneficiary, within a reasonable time after receiving notice of receipt of the order by the beneficiary's bank, notified the originator of the beneficiary's refusal of the payment, (iii) funds with respect to the order were not withdrawn by the beneficiary or applied to a debt of the beneficiary, and (iv) the beneficiary would suffer a loss that could reasonably have been avoided if payment had been made by a means complying with the contract. If payment by the originator does not result in discharge under this section, the originator is subrogated to the rights of the beneficiary to receive payment from the beneficiary's bank under Section 4A-404(a).

(c) For the purpose of determining whether discharge of an obligation occurs under subsection (b), if the beneficiary's bank accepts a payment order in an amount equal to the amount of the originator's payment order less charges of one or more receiving banks in the funds transfer, payment to the beneficiary is deemed to be in the amount of the originator's order unless upon demand by the beneficiary the originator does not pay the beneficiary the amount of the deducted charges.

(d) Rights of the originator or of the beneficiary of a funds transfer under this section may be varied only by agreement of the originator and the beneficiary.

PART 5. MISCELLANEOUS PROVISIONS

§ 4A-501. Variation by Agreement and Effect of Funds-Transfer System Rule

(a) Except as otherwise provided in this Article, the rights and obligations of a party to a funds transfer may be varied by agreement of the affected party.

(b) "Funds-transfer system rule" means a rule of an association of banks (i) governing transmission of payment orders by means of a funds-transfer system of the association or rights and obligations with respect to those orders, or (ii) to the extent the rule governs rights and obligations between banks that are parties to a funds transfer in which a Federal Reserve Bank, acting as an intermediary bank, sends a payment order to the beneficiary's bank. Except as otherwise provided in this Article, a funds-transfer system rule governing rights and obligations between participating banks using the system may be effective even if the rule conflicts with this Article and indirectly affects another party to the funds transfer who does not consent to the rule. A funds-transfer system rule may also govern rights and obligations of parties other than participating banks using the system to the extent stated in Sections 4A-404(c), 4A-405(d), and 4A-507(c).

§ 4A-502. Creditor Process Served on Receiving Bank; Set-off by Beneficiary's Bank

(a) As used in this section, "creditor process" means levy, attachment, garnishment, notice of lien, sequestration, or similar process issued by or on behalf of a creditor or other claimant with respect to an account.

(b) This subsection applies to creditor process with respect to an authorized account of the sender of a payment order if the creditor process is served on the receiving bank. For the purpose of determining rights with respect to the creditor process, if the receiving bank accepts the payment order the balance in the authorized account is deemed to be reduced by the amount of the payment order to the extent the bank did not otherwise receive payment of the order, unless the creditor process is served at a time and in a manner affording the bank a reasonable opportunity to act on it before the bank accepts the payment order.

(c) If a beneficiary's bank has received a payment order for payment to the beneficiary's account in the bank, the following rules apply:

(1) The bank may credit the beneficiary's account. The amount credited may be set off against an obligation owed by the beneficiary to the bank or may be applied to satisfy creditor process served on the bank with respect to the account.

(2) The bank may credit the beneficiary's account and allow withdrawal of the amount credited unless creditor process with respect to the account is served at a time and in a manner affording the bank a reasonable opportunity to act to prevent withdrawal.

(3) If creditor process with respect to the beneficiary's account has been served and the bank has had a reasonable opportunity to act on it, the bank may not reject the payment order except for a reason unrelated to the service of process.

(d) Creditor process with respect to a payment by the originator to the beneficiary pursuant to a funds transfer may be served only on the beneficiary's bank with respect to the debt owed by that bank to the beneficiary. Any other bank served with the creditor process is not obliged to act with respect to the process.

§ 4A-503. Injunction or Restraining Order with Respect to Funds Transfer

For proper cause and in compliance with applicable law, a court may restrain (i) a person from issuing a payment order to initiate a funds transfer, (ii) an originator's bank from executing the payment order of the originator, or (iii) the beneficiary's bank from releasing funds to the beneficiary or the beneficiary from withdrawing the funds. A court may not otherwise restrain a person from issuing a payment order, paying or receiving payment of a payment order, or otherwise acting with respect to a funds transfer.

§ 4A-504. Order in Which Items and Payment Orders May Be Charged to Account; Order of Withdrawals from Account

(a) If a receiving bank has received more than one payment order of the sender or one or more payment orders and other items that are payable from the sender's account, the bank may charge the sender's account with respect to the various orders and items in any sequence.

(b) In determining whether a credit to an account has been withdrawn by the holder of the account or applied to a debt of the holder of the account, credits first made to the account are first withdrawn or applied.

§ 4A-505. Preclusion of Objection to Debit of Customer's Account

If a receiving bank has received payment from its customer with respect to a payment order issued in the name of the customer as sender and accepted by the bank, and the customer received notification reasonably identifying the order, the customer is precluded from asserting that the bank is not entitled to retain the payment unless the customer notifies the bank of the customer's objection to the payment within one year after the notification was received by the customer.

§ 4A-506. Rate of Interest

(a) If, under this Article, a receiving bank is obliged to pay interest with respect to a payment order issued to the bank, the amount payable may be determined (i) by agreement of the sender and receiving bank, or (ii) by a funds-transfer system rule if the payment order is transmitted through a funds-transfer system.

(b) If the amount of interest is not determined by an agreement or rule as stated in subsection (a), the amount is calculated by multiplying the applicable Federal Funds rate by the amount on which interest is payable, and then multiplying the product by the number of days for which interest is payable. The applicable Federal Funds rate is the average of the Federal Funds rates published by the Federal Reserve Bank of New York for each of the days for which interest is payable divided by 360. The Federal Funds rate for any day on which a published rate is not available is the same as the published rate for the next preceding day for which there is a published rate. If a receiving bank that accepted a payment order is required to refund payment to the sender of the order because the funds transfer was not completed, but the failure to complete was not due to any fault by the bank, the interest payable is reduced by a percentage equal to the reserve requirement on deposits of the receiving bank.

§ 4A-507. Choice of Law

(a) The following rules apply unless the affected parties otherwise agree or subsection (c) applies:

(1) The rights and obligations between the sender of a payment order and the receiving bank are governed by the law of the jurisdiction in which the receiving bank is located.

(2) The rights and obligations between the beneficiary's bank and the beneficiary are governed by the law of the jurisdiction in which the beneficiary's bank is located.

(3) The issue of when payment is made pursuant to a funds transfer by the originator to the beneficiary is governed by the law of the jurisdiction in which the beneficiary's bank is located.

(b) If the parties described in each paragraph of subsection (a) have made an agreement selecting the law of a particular jurisdiction to govern rights and obligations between each other, the law of that jurisdiction governs those rights and obligations, whether or not the payment order or the funds transfer bears a reasonable relation to that jurisdiction.

(c) A funds-transfer system rule may select the law of a particular jurisdiction to govern (i) rights and obligations between participating banks with respect to payment orders transmitted or processed through the system, or (ii) the rights and obligations of some or all parties to a funds transfer any part of which is carried out by means of the system. A choice of law made pursuant to clause (i) is binding on participating banks. A choice of law made pursuant to clause (ii) is binding on the originator, other sender, or a receiving bank having notice that the funds-transfer system might be used in the funds transfer and of the choice of law by the system when the originator, other sender, or receiving bank issued or accepted a payment order. The beneficiary of a funds transfer is bound by the choice of law if, when the funds transfer is initiated, the beneficiary has notice that the funds-transfer system might be used in the funds transfer and of the choice of law by the system. The law of a jurisdiction selected pursuant to this subsection may govern, whether or not that law bears a reasonable relation to the matter in issue.

(d) In the event of inconsistency between an agreement under subsection (b) and a choice-of-law rule under subsection (c), the agreement under subsection (b) prevails.

(e) If a funds transfer is made by use of more than one funds-transfer system and there is inconsistency between choice-of-law rules of the systems, the matter in issue is governed by the law of the selected jurisdiction that has the most significant relationship to the matter in issue.

U.C.C. – ARTICLE 5 – LETTERS OF CREDIT (1995)

§ 5-101. Short Title

This Article shall be known and may be cited as Uniform Commercial Code-Letters of Credit.

§ 5-102. Definitions

(a) In this article:

(1) "Adviser" means a person who, at the request of the issuer, a confirmer, or another adviser, notifies or requests another adviser to notify the beneficiary that a letter of credit has been issued, confirmed, or amended.

(2) "Applicant" means a person at whose request or for whose account a letter of credit is issued. The term includes a person who requests an issuer to issue a letter of credit on behalf of another if the person making the request undertakes an obligation to reimburse the issuer.

(3) "Beneficiary" means a person who under the terms of a letter of credit is entitled to have its complying presentation honored. The term includes a person to whom drawing rights have been transferred under a transferable letter of credit.

(4) "Confirmer" means a nominated person who undertakes, at the request or with the consent of the issuer, to honor a presentation under a letter of credit issued by another.

(5) "Dishonor" of a letter of credit means failure timely to honor or to take an interim action, such as acceptance of a draft, that may be required by the letter of credit.

(6) "Document" means a draft or other demand, document of title, investment security, certificate, invoice, or other record, statement, or representation of fact, law, right, or opinion (i) which is presented in a written or other medium permitted by the letter of credit or, unless prohibited by the letter of credit, by the standard practice referred to in Section 5-108(e) and (ii) which is capable of being examined for compliance with the terms and conditions of the letter of credit. A document may not be oral.

(7) "Good faith" means honesty in fact in the conduct or transaction concerned.

(8) "Honor" of a letter of credit means performance of the issuer's undertaking in the letter of credit to pay or deliver an item of value. Unless the letter of credit otherwise provides, "honor" occurs (i) upon payment,(ii) if the letter of credit provides for acceptance, upon acceptance of a draft and, at maturity, its payment, or(iii) if the letter of credit provides for incurring a deferred obligation, upon incurring the obligation and, at maturity, its performance.

(9) "Issuer" means a bank or other person that issues a letter of credit, but does not include an individual who makes an engagement for personal, family, or household purposes.

(10) "Letter of credit" means a definite undertaking that satisfies the requirements of Section 5-104 by an issuer to a beneficiary at the request or for the account of an applicant or, in the case of a financial institution, to itself or for its own account, to honor a documentary presentation by payment or delivery of an item of value.

(11) "Nominated person" means a person whom the issuer (i) designates or authorizes to pay, accept, negotiate, or otherwise give value under a letter of credit and (ii) undertakes by agreement or custom and practice to reimburse.

(12) "Presentation" means delivery of a document to an issuer or nominated person for honor or giving of value under a letter of credit.

(13) "Presenter" means a person making a presentation as or on behalf of a beneficiary or nominated person.

(14) "Record" means information that is inscribed on a tangible medium, or that is stored in an electronic or other medium and is retrievable in perceivable form.

(15) "Successor of a beneficiary" means a person who succeeds to substantially all of the rights of a beneficiary by operation of law, including a corporation with or into which the beneficiary has been merged or consolidated, an administrator, executor, personal representative, trustee in bankruptcy, debtor in possession, liquidator, and receiver.

(b) Definitions in other Articles applying to this Article and the sections in which they appear are:

"Accept" or "Acceptance"	– Section 3-409
"Value"	– Sections 3-303, 4-211

(c) Article 1 contains certain additional general definitions and principles of construction and interpretation applicable throughout this article.

§ 5-103. Scope

(a) This Article applies to letters of credit and to certain rights and obligations arising out of transactions involving letters of credit.

(b) The statement of a rule in this Article does not by itself require, imply, or negate application of the same or a different rule to a situation not provided for, or to a person not specified, in this article.

(c) With the exception of this subsection, subsections (a) and (d), Sections 5-102(a)(9) and (10), 5-106(d), and 5-114(d), and except to the extent prohibited in Sections 1-302 and 5-117(d), the effect of this Article may be varied by agreement or by a provision stated or incorporated by reference in an undertaking. A term in an agreement or undertaking generally excusing liability or generally limiting remedies for failure to perform obligations is not sufficient to vary obligations prescribed by this article.

(d) Rights and obligations of an issuer to a beneficiary or a nominated person under a letter of credit are independent of the existence, performance, or nonperformance of a contract or arrangement out of which the letter of credit arises or which underlies it, including contracts or arrangements between the issuer and the applicant and between the applicant and the beneficiary.

§ 5-104. Formal Requirements

A letter of credit, confirmation, advice, transfer, amendment, or cancellation may be issued in any form that is a record and is authenticated (i) by a signature or (ii) in accordance with the agreement of the parties or the standard practice referred to in Section 5-108(e).

§ 5-105. Consideration

Consideration is not required to issue, amend, transfer, or cancel a letter of credit, advice, or confirmation.

§ 5-106. Issuance, Amendment, Cancellation, and Duration

(a) A letter of credit is issued and becomes enforceable according to its terms against the issuer when the issuer sends or otherwise transmits it to the person requested to advise or to the beneficiary. A letter of credit is revocable only if it so provides.

(b) After a letter of credit is issued, rights and obligations of a beneficiary, applicant, confirmer, and issuer are not affected by an amendment or cancellation to which that person has not consented except to the extent the letter of credit provides that it is revocable or that the issuer may amend or cancel the letter of credit without that consent.

(c) If there is no stated expiration date or other provision that determines its duration, a letter of credit expires one year after its stated date of issuance or, if none is stated, after the date on which it is issued.

(d) A letter of credit that states that it is perpetual expires five years after its stated date of issuance, or if none is stated, after the date on which it is issued.

§ 5-107. Confirmer, Nominated Person, and Adviser

(a) A confirmer is directly obligated on a letter of credit and has the rights and obligations of an issuer to the extent of its confirmation. The confirmer also has rights against and obligations to the issuer as if the issuer were an applicant and the confirmer had issued the letter of credit at the request and for the account of the issuer.

(b) A nominated person who is not a confirmer is not obligated to honor or otherwise give value for a presentation.

(c) A person requested to advise may decline to act as an adviser. An adviser that is not a confirmer is not obligated to honor or give value for a presentation. An adviser undertakes to the issuer and to the beneficiary accurately to advise the terms of the letter of credit, confirmation, amendment, or advice received by that person and undertakes to the beneficiary to check the apparent authenticity of the request to advise. Even if the advice is inaccurate, the letter of credit, confirmation, or amendment is enforceable as issued.

(d) A person who notifies a transferee beneficiary of the terms of a letter of credit, confirmation, amendment, or advice has the rights and obligations of an adviser under subsection (c). The terms in the notice to the transferee beneficiary may differ from the terms in any notice to the transferor beneficiary to the extent permitted by the letter of credit, confirmation, amendment, or advice received by the person who so notifies.

§ 5-108. Issuer's Rights and Obligations

(a) Except as otherwise provided in Section 5-109, an issuer shall honor a presentation that, as determined by the standard practice referred to in subsection (e), appears on its face strictly to comply with the terms and conditions of the letter of credit. Except as otherwise provided in Section 5-113 and unless otherwise agreed with the applicant, an issuer shall dishonor a presentation that does not appear so to comply.

(b) An issuer has a reasonable time after presentation, but not beyond the end of the seventh business day of the issuer after the day of its receipt of documents:

(1) to honor,

(2) if the letter of credit provides for honor to be completed more than seven business days after presentation, to accept a draft or incur a deferred obligation, or

(3) to give notice to the presenter of discrepancies in the presentation.

(c) Except as otherwise provided in subsection (d), an issuer is precluded from asserting as a basis for dishonor any discrepancy if timely notice is not given, or any discrepancy not stated in the notice if timely notice is given.

(d) Failure to give the notice specified in subsection (b) or to mention fraud, forgery, or expiration in the notice does not preclude the issuer from asserting as a basis for dishonor fraud or forgery as described in Section 5-109(a) or expiration of the letter of credit before presentation.

(e) An issuer shall observe standard practice of financial institutions that regularly issue letters of credit. Determination of the issuer's observance of the standard practice is a matter of interpretation for the court. The court shall offer the parties a reasonable opportunity to present evidence of the standard practice.

(f) An issuer is not responsible for:

(1) the performance or nonperformance of the underlying contract, arrangement, or transaction,

(2) an act or omission of others, or

(3) observance or knowledge of the usage of a particular trade other than the standard practice referred to in subsection (e).

(g) If an undertaking constituting a letter of credit under Section 5-102(a)(10) contains nondocumentary conditions, an issuer shall disregard the nondocumentary conditions and treat them as if they were not stated.

(h) An issuer that has dishonored a presentation shall return the documents or hold them at the disposal of, and send advice to that effect to, the presenter.

(i) An issuer that has honored a presentation as permitted or required by this article:

(1) is entitled to be reimbursed by the applicant in immediately available funds not later than the date of its payment of funds;

(2) takes the documents free of claims of the beneficiary or presenter;

(3) is precluded from asserting a right of recourse on a draft under Sections 3-414 and 3-415;

(4) except as otherwise provided in Sections 5-110 and 5-117, is precluded from restitution of money paid or other value given by mistake to the extent the mistake concerns discrepancies in the documents or tender which are apparent on the face of the presentation; and

(5) is discharged to the extent of its performance under the letter of credit unless the issuer honored a presentation in which a required signature of a beneficiary was forged.

§ 5-109. Fraud and Forgery

(a) If a presentation is made that appears on its face strictly to comply with the terms and conditions of the letter of credit, but a required document is forged or materially fraudulent, or honor of the presentation would facilitate a material fraud by the beneficiary on the issuer or applicant:

(1) the issuer shall honor the presentation, if honor is demanded by (i) a nominated person who has given value in good faith and without notice of forgery or material fraud, (ii) a confirmer who has honored its confirmation in good faith, (iii) a holder in due course of a draft drawn under the letter of credit which was taken after acceptance by the issuer or nominated person, or (iv) an assignee of the issuer's or nominated person's deferred obligation that was taken for value and without notice of forgery or material fraud after the obligation was incurred by the issuer or nominated person; and

(2) the issuer, acting in good faith, may honor or dishonor the presentation in any other case.

(b) If an applicant claims that a required document is forged or materially fraudulent or that honor of the presentation would facilitate a material fraud by the beneficiary on the issuer or applicant, a court of competent jurisdiction may temporarily or permanently enjoin the issuer from honoring a presentation or grant similar relief against the issuer or other persons only if the court finds that:

(1) the relief is not prohibited under the law applicable to an accepted draft or deferred obligation incurred by the issuer;

(2) a beneficiary, issuer, or nominated person who may be adversely affected is adequately protected against loss that it may suffer because the relief is granted;

(3) all of the conditions to entitle a person to the relief under the law of this State have been met; and

(4) on the basis of the information submitted to the court, the applicant is more likely than not to succeed under its claim of forgery or material fraud and the person demanding honor does not qualify for protection under subsection (a)(1).

§ 5-110. Warranties

(a) If its presentation is honored, the beneficiary warrants:

(1) to the issuer, any other person to whom presentation is made, and the applicant that there is no fraud or forgery of the kind described in Section 5-109(a); and

(2) to the applicant that the drawing does not violate any agreement between the applicant and beneficiary or any other agreement intended by them to be augmented by the letter of credit.

(b) The warranties in subsection (a) are in addition to warranties arising under Article 3, 4, 7, and 8 because of the presentation or transfer of documents covered by any of those articles.

§ 5-111. Remedies

(a) If an issuer wrongfully dishonors or repudiates its obligation to pay money under a letter of credit before presentation, the beneficiary, successor, or nominated person presenting on its own behalf may recover from the issuer the amount that is the subject of the dishonor or repudiation. If the issuer's obligation under the letter of credit is not for the payment of money, the claimant may obtain specific performance or, at the claimant's election, recover an amount equal to the value of performance from the issuer. In either case, the claimant may also recover incidental but not consequential damages. The claimant is not obligated to take action to avoid damages that might be due from the issuer under this subsection. If, although not obligated to do so, the claimant avoids damages, the claimant's recovery from the issuer must be reduced by the amount of damages avoided. The issuer has the burden of proving the amount of damages avoided. In the case of repudiation the claimant need not present any document.

(b) If an issuer wrongfully dishonors a draft or demand presented under a letter of credit or honors a draft or demand in breach of its obligation to the applicant, the applicant may recover damages resulting from the breach, including incidental but not consequential damages, less any amount saved as a result of the breach.

(c) If an adviser or nominated person other than a confirmer breaches an obligation under this Article or an issuer breaches an obligation not covered in subsection (a) or (b), a person to whom the obligation is owed may recover damages resulting from the breach, including incidental but not consequential damages, less any amount saved as a result of the breach. To the extent of the confirmation, a confirmer has the liability of an issuer specified in this subsection and subsections (a) and (b).

(d) An issuer, nominated person, or adviser who is found liable under subsection (a), (b), or (c) shall pay interest on the amount owed thereunder from the date of wrongful dishonor or other appropriate date.

(e) Reasonable attorney's fees and other expenses of litigation must be awarded to the prevailing party in an action in which a remedy is sought under this article.

(f) Damages that would otherwise be payable by a party for breach of an obligation under this Article may be liquidated by agreement or undertaking, but only in an amount or by a formula that is reasonable in light of the harm anticipated.

§ 5-112. Transfer of Letter of Credit

(a) Except as otherwise provided in Section 5-113, unless a letter of credit provides that it is transferable, the right of a beneficiary to draw or otherwise demand performance under a letter of credit may not be transferred.

(b) Even if a letter of credit provides that it is transferable, the issuer may refuse to recognize or carry out a transfer if:

(1) the transfer would violate applicable law; or

(2) the transferor or transferee has failed to comply with any requirement stated in the letter of credit or any other requirement relating to transfer imposed by the issuer which is within the standard practice referred to in Section 5-108(e) or is otherwise reasonable under the circumstances.

§ 5-113. Transfer by Operation of Law

(a) A successor of a beneficiary may consent to amendments, sign and present documents, and receive payment or other items of value in the name of the beneficiary without disclosing its status as a successor.

(b) A successor of a beneficiary may consent to amendments, sign and present documents, and receive payment or other items of value in its own name as the disclosed successor of the beneficiary. Except as otherwise provided in subsection (e), an issuer shall recognize a disclosed successor of a beneficiary as beneficiary in full substitution for its predecessor upon compliance with the requirements for recognition by the issuer of a transfer of drawing rights by operation of law under the standard practice referred to in Section 5-108(e) or, in the absence of such a practice, compliance with other reasonable procedures sufficient to protect the issuer.

(c) An issuer is not obliged to determine whether a purported successor is a successor of a beneficiary or whether the signature of a purported successor is genuine or authorized.

(d) Honor of a purported successor's apparently complying presentation under subsection (a) or (b) has the consequences specified in Section 5-108(i) even if the purported successor is not the successor of a beneficiary. Documents signed in the name of the beneficiary or of a disclosed successor by a person who is neither the beneficiary nor the successor of the beneficiary are forged documents for the purposes of Section 5-109.

(e) An issuer whose rights of reimbursement are not covered by subsection (d) or substantially similar law and any confirmer or nominated person may decline to recognize a presentation under subsection (b).

(f) A beneficiary whose name is changed after the issuance of a letter of credit has the same rights and obligations as a successor of a beneficiary under this section.

§ 5-114. Assignment of Proceeds

(a) In this section, "proceeds of a letter of credit" means the cash, check, accepted draft, or other item of value paid or delivered upon honor or giving of value by the issuer or any nominated person under the letter of credit. The term does not include a beneficiary's drawing rights or documents presented by the beneficiary.

(b) A beneficiary may assign its right to part or all of the proceeds of a letter of credit. The beneficiary may do so before presentation as a present assignment of its right to receive proceeds contingent upon its compliance with the terms and conditions of the letter of credit.

(c) An issuer or nominated person need not recognize an assignment of proceeds of a letter of credit until it consents to the assignment.

(d) An issuer or nominated person has no obligation to give or withhold its consent to an assignment of proceeds of a letter of credit, but consent may not be unreasonably withheld if the assignee possesses and exhibits the letter of credit and presentation of the letter of credit is a condition to honor.

(e) Rights of a transferee beneficiary or nominated person are independent of the beneficiary's assignment of the proceeds of a letter of credit and are superior to the assignee's right to the proceeds.

(f) Neither the rights recognized by this section between an assignee and an issuer, transferee beneficiary, or nominated person nor the issuer's or nominated person's payment of proceeds to an assignee or a third person affect the rights between the assignee and any person other than the issuer, transferee beneficiary, or nominated person. The mode of creating and perfecting a security interest in or granting an assignment of a beneficiary's rights to proceeds is governed by Article 9 or other law. Against persons other than the issuer, transferee beneficiary, or nominated person, the rights and obligations arising upon the creation of a security interest or other assignment of a beneficiary's right to proceeds and its perfection are governed by Article 9 or other law.

§ 5-115. Statute of Limitations

An action to enforce a right or obligation arising under this Article must be commenced within one year after the expiration date of the relevant letter of credit or one year after the [claim for relief] [cause of action] accrues, whichever occurs later. A [claim for relief] [cause of action] accrues when the breach occurs, regardless of the aggrieved party's lack of knowledge of the breach.

§ 5-116. Choice of Law and Forum

(a) The liability of an issuer, nominated person, or adviser for action or omission is governed by the law of the jurisdiction chosen by an agreement in the form of a record signed or otherwise authenticated by the affected parties in the manner provided in Section 5-104 or by a provision in the person's letter of credit, confirmation, or other undertaking. The jurisdiction whose law is chosen need not bear any relation to the transaction.

(b) Unless subsection (a) applies, the liability of an issuer, nominated person, or adviser for action or omission is governed by the law of the jurisdiction in which the person is located. The person is considered to be located at the address indicated in the person's undertaking. If more than one address is indicated, the person is considered to be located at the address from which the person's undertaking was issued. For the purpose of jurisdiction, choice of law, and recognition of interbranch letters of credit, but not enforcement of a judgment, all branches of a bank are considered separate juridical entities and a bank is considered to be located at the place where its relevant branch is considered to be located under this subsection.

(c) Except as otherwise provided in this subsection, the liability of an issuer, nominated person, or adviser is governed by any rules of custom or practice, such as the Uniform Customs and Practice for Documentary Credits, to which the letter of credit, confirmation, or other undertaking is expressly made subject. If (i) this Article would govern the liability of an issuer, nominated person, or adviser under subsection (a) or (b), (ii) the relevant undertaking incorporates rules of custom or practice, and (iii) there is conflict between this Article and those rules as applied to that undertaking, those rules govern except to the extent of any conflict with the nonvariable provisions specified in Section 5-103(c).

(d) If there is conflict between this Article and Article 3, 4, 4A, or 9, this Article governs.

(e) The forum for settling disputes arising out of an undertaking within this Article may be chosen in the manner and with the binding effect that governing law may be chosen in accordance with subsection (a).

§ 5-117. Subrogation of Issuer, Applicant, and Nominated Person

(a) An issuer that honors a beneficiary's presentation is subrogated to the rights of the beneficiary to the same extent as if the issuer were a secondary obligor of the underlying obligation owed to the beneficiary and of the applicant to the same extent as if the issuer were the secondary obligor of the underlying obligation owed to the applicant.

(b) An applicant that reimburses an issuer is subrogated to the rights of the issuer against any beneficiary, presenter, or nominated person to the same extent as if the applicant were the secondary obligor of the obligations owed to the issuer and has the rights of subrogation of the issuer to the rights of the beneficiary stated in subsection (a).

(c) A nominated person who pays or gives value against a draft or demand presented under a letter of credit is subrogated to the rights of:

(1) the issuer against the applicant to the same extent as if the nominated person were a secondary obligor of the obligation owed to the issuer by the applicant;

(2) the beneficiary to the same extent as if the nominated person were a secondary obligor of the underlying obligation owed to the beneficiary; and

(3) the applicant to same extent as if the nominated person were a secondary obligor of the underlying obligation owed to the applicant.

(d) Notwithstanding any agreement or term to the contrary, the rights of subrogation stated in subsections (a) and (b) do not arise until the issuer honors the letter of credit or otherwise pays and the rights in subsection (c) do not arise until the nominated person pays or otherwise gives value. Until then, the issuer, nominated person, and the applicant do not derive under this section present or prospective rights forming the basis of a claim, defense, or excuse.

§ 5-118. Security Interest of Issuer or Nominated Person

(a) An issuer or nominated person has a security interest in a document presented under a letter of credit and any identifiable proceeds of the collateral to the extent that the issuer or nominated person honors or gives value for the presentation.

(b) Subject to subsection (c), as long as and to the extent that an issuer or nominated person has not been reimbursed or has not otherwise recovered the value given with respect to a security interest in a document under subsection (a), the security interest continues and is subject to Article 9, but:

(1) a security agreement is not necessary to make the security interest enforceable under Section 9-203(b)(3);

(2) if the document is presented in a medium other than a written or other tangible medium, the security interest is perfected; and

(3) if the document is presented in a written or other tangible medium and is not a certificated security, chattel paper, a document of title, an instrument, or a letter of credit, so long as the debtor does not have possession of the document, the security interest is perfected and has priority over a conflicting security interest in the document.

TRANSITION PROVISIONS [...]

Part Four: Documentary Sale 3 of 4 – Shipping Contracts

29) 1924 International Convention for the Unification of Certain Rules of Law Relating to Bills of Lading ("Hague Rules")

The [Contracting Parties],

HAVING RECOGNIZED the utility of fixing by agreement certain uniform rules of law relating to bills of lading,

HAVE DECIDED to conclude a convention with this object and have appointed the following Plenipotentiaries:

WHO, duly authorized thereto, have agreed as follows:

Article 1 [Definitions]

In this Convention the following words are employed with the meanings set out below:

(a) "Carrier" includes the owner or the charterer who enters into a contract of carriage with a shipper.

(b) "Contract of carriage" applies only to contracts of carriage covered by a bill of lading or any similar document of title, in so far as such document relates to the carriage of goods by sea, including any bill of lading or any similar document as aforesaid issued under or pursuant to a charter party from the moment at which such bill of lading or similar document of title regulates the relations between a carrier and a holder of the same.

(c) "Goods" includes goods, wares, merchandise and articles of every kind whatsoever except live animals and cargo which by the contract of carriage in stated as being carried on deck and is so carried.

(d) "Ship" means any vessel used for the carriage of goods by sea.

(e) "Carriage of goods" covers the period from the time when the goods are loaded on to the time they are discharged from the ship.

Article 2 [Scope]

Subject to the provisions of Article 6, under every contract of carriage of goods by sea the carrier, in relation to the loading, handling, stowage, carriage, custody, care and discharge of such goods, shall be subject to the responsibilities and liabilities, and entitled to the rights and immunities hereinafter set forth.

Article 3 [Responsibilities of the Carrier]

1. The carrier shall be bound before and at the beginning of the voyage to exercise due diligence to:

(a) Make the ship seaworthy.

(b) Properly man, equip and supply the ship.

(c) Make the holds, refrigerating and cool chambers, and all other parts of the ship in which goods are carried, fit and safe for their reception, carriage and preservation.

2. Subject to the provisions of Article 4, the carrier shall properly and carefully load, handle, stow, carry, keep, care for, and discharge the goods carried.

3. After receiving the goods into his charge the carrier or the master or agent of the carrier shall, on demand of the shipper, issue to the shipper a bill of lading showing among other things:

(a) The leading marks necessary for identification of the goods as the same are furnished in writing by the shipper before the loading of such goods starts, provided such marks are stamped or otherwise shown clearly upon the goods if uncovered, or on the cases or coverings in which such goods are contained, in such a manner as should ordinarily remain legible until the end of the voyage.

(b) Either the number of packages or pieces, or the quantity, or weight, as the case may be, as furnished in writing by the shipper.

(c) The apparent order and condition of the goods.

Provided that no carrier, master or agent of the carrier shall be bound to state or show in the bill of lading any marks, number, quantity, or weight which he has reasonable ground for suspecting not accurately to represent the goods actually received, or which he has had no reasonable means of checking.

4. Such a bill of lading shall be prima facie evidence of the receipt by the carrier of the goods as therein described in accordance with paragraph 3(a), (b) and (c).

5. The shipper shall be deemed to have guaranteed to the carrier the accuracy at the time of shipment of the marks, number, quantity and weight, as furnished by him, and the shipper shall indemnity the carrier against all loss, damages and expenses arising or resulting from inaccuracies in such particulars. The right of the carrier to such indemnity shall in no way limit his responsibility and liability under the contract of carriage to any person other than the shipper.

6. Unless notice of loss or damage and the general nature of such loss or damage be given in writing to the carrier or his agent at the port of discharge before or at the time of the removal of the goods into the custody of the person entitled to delivery thereof under the contract of carriage, or, if the loss or damage be not apparent, within three days, such removal shall be prima facie evidence of the delivery by the carrier of the goods as described in the bill of lading. If the loss or damage is not apparent, the notice must be given within three days of the delivery of the goods.

The notice in writing need not be given if the state of the goods has, at the time of their receipt, been the subject of joint survey or inspection.

In any event the carrier and the ship shall be discharged from all liability in respect of loss or damage unless suit is brought within one year after delivery of the goods or the date when the goods should have been delivered.

In the case of any actual or apprehended loss or damage the carrier and the receiver shall give all reasonable facilities to each other for inspecting and tallying the goods.

7. After the goods are loaded the bill of lading to be issued by the carrier, master, or agent of the carrier, to the shipper shall, if the shipper so demands, be a "shipped" bill of lading, provided that if the shipper shall have previously taken up any document of title to such goods, he shall surrender the same as against the issue of the "shipped" bill of lading, but at the option of the carrier such document of title may be noted at the port of shipment by the carrier, master, or agent with the name or names of the ship or ships upon which the goods have been shipped and the date or dates of shipment, and when so noted, if it shows the particulars mentioned in paragraph 3 of Article 3, shall for the purpose of this Article be deemed to constitute a "shipped" bill of lading.

8. Any clause, covenant, or agreement in a contract of carriage relieving the carrier or the ship from liability for loss or damage to, or in connexion with, goods arising from negligence, fault, or failure in the duties and obligations provided in this Article or lessening such liability otherwise than as provided in this Convention, shall be null and void and of no effect. A benefit of insurance in favour of the carrier or similar clause shall be deemed to be a clause relieving the carrier from liability.

Article 4 *[Limitations of Carrier Liability]*

1. Neither the carrier nor the ship shall be liable for loss or damage arising or resulting from unseaworthiness unless caused by want of due diligence on the part of the carrier to make the ship seaworthy and to secure that the ship is properly manned, equipped and supplied, and to make the holds, refrigerating and cool chambers and all other parts of the ship in which goods are carried fit and safe for their reception, carriage and preservation in accordance with the provisions of paragraph 1 of Article 3. Whenever loss or damage has resulted from unseaworthiness the burden of proving the exercise of due diligence shall be on the carrier or other person claiming exemption under this Article.

2. Neither the carrier nor the ship shall be responsible for loss or damage arising or resulting from:

(a) Act, neglect, or default of the master, mariner, pilot, or the servants of the carrier in the navigation or in the management of the ship.

(b) Fire, unless caused by the actual fault or privity of the carrier.

(c) Perils, dangers and accidents of the sea or other navigable waters.

(d) Act of God.

(e) Act of war.

(f) Act of public enemies.

(g) Arrest or restraint of princes, rulers or people, or seizure under legal process.

(h) Quarantine restrictions.

(i) Act or omission of the shipper or owner of the goods, his agent or representative.

(j) Strikes or lockouts or stoppage or restraint of labour from whatever cause, whether partial or general.

(k) Riots and civil commotions.

(l) Saving or attempting to save life or property at sea.

(m) Wastage in bulk or weight or any other loss or damage arising from inherent defect, quality or vice of the goods.

(n) Insufficiency of packing.

(o) Insufficiency or inadequacy of marks.

(p) Latent defects not discoverable by due diligence.

(q) Any other cause arising without the actual fault or privity of the carrier, or without the actual fault or neglect of the agents or servants of the carrier, but the burden of proof shall be on the person claiming the benefit of this exception to show that neither the actual fault or privity of the carrier nor the fault or neglect of the agents or servants of the carrier contributed to the loss or damage.

3. The shipper shall not be responsible for loss or damage sustained by the carrier or the ship arising or resulting from any cause without the act, fault or neglect of the shipper, his agents or his servants.

4. Any deviation in saving or attempting to save life or property at sea or any reasonable deviation shall not be deemed to be an infringement or breach of this Convention or of the contract of carriage, and the carrier shall not be liable for any loss or damage resulting therefrom.

5. Neither the carrier nor the ship shall in any event be or become liable for any loss or damage to or in connexion with goods in an amount exceeding 100 pounds sterling per package

or unit, or the equivalent of that sum in other currency unless the nature and value of such goods have been declared by the shipper before shipment and inserted in the bill of lading.

This declaration if embodied in the bill of lading shall be prima facie evidence, but shall not be binding or conclusive on the carrier.

By agreement between the carrier, master or agent of the carrier and the shipper another maximum amount than that mentioned in this paragraph may be fixed, provided that such maximum shall not be less than the figure above named.

Neither the carrier nor the ship shall be responsible in any event for loss or damage to, or in connexion with, goods if the nature or value thereof has been knowingly misstated by the shipper in the bill of lading.

6. Goods of an inflammable, explosive or dangerous nature to the shipment whereof the carrier, master or agent of the carrier has not consented with knowledge of their nature and character, may at any time before discharge be landed at any place, or destroyed or rendered innocuous by the carrier without compensation and the shipper of such goods shall be liable for all damage and expenses directly or indirectly arising out of or resulting from such shipment. If any such goods shipped with such knowledge and consent shall become a danger to the ship or cargo, they may in like manner be landed at any place, or destroyed or rendered innocuous by the carrier without liability on the part of the carrier except to general average, if any.

Article 5 [Priority of Provisions in the Bill of Lading]

A carrier shall be at liberty to surrender in whole or in part all or any of his rights and immunities or to increase any of his responsibilities and obligations under this Convention, provided such surrender or increase shall be embodied in the bill of lading issued to the shipper.

The provisions of this Convention shall not be applicable to charter parties, but if bills of lading are issued in the case of a ship under a charter party they shall comply with the terms of this Convention. Nothing in these rules shall be held to prevent the insertion in a bill of lading of any lawful provision regarding general average.

Article 6 [Priority of Contracts of Carriage]

Notwithstanding the provisions of the preceding Articles, a carrier, master or agent of the carrier and a shipper shall in regard to any particular goods be at liberty to enter into any agreement in any terms as to the responsibility and liability of the carrier for such goods, and as to the rights and immunities of the carrier in respect of such goods, or his obligation as to seaworthiness, so far as this stipulation is not contrary to public policy, or the care or diligence of his servants or agents in regard to the loading, handling, stowage, carriage, custody, care and discharge of the goods carried by sea, provided that in this case no bill of lading has been or shall be issued and that the terms agreed shall be embodied in a receipt which shall be a non-negotiable document and shall be marked as such.

Any agreement so entered into shall have full legal effect.

Provided that this Article shall not apply to ordinary commercial shipments made in the ordinary course of trade, but only to other shipments where the character or condition of the property to be carried or the circumstances, terms and conditions under which the carriage is to be performed are such as reasonably to justify a special agreement.

Article 7 [Priority of Other Agreements]

Nothing herein contained shall prevent a carrier or a shipper from entering into any agreement, stipulation, condition, reservation or exemption as to the responsibility and liability of the carrier or the ship for the loss or damage to, or in connexion with, the custody and care and handling of goods prior to the loading on, and subsequent to, the discharge from the ship on which the goods are carried by sea.

Article 8 [Priority of Statutory Provisions]

The provisions of this Convention shall not affect the rights and obligations of the carrier under any statute for the time being in force relating to the limitation of the liability of owners of sea-going vessels.

Article 9 [Monetary Units]

The monetary units mentioned in this Convention are to be taken to be gold value.

Those contracting States in which the pound sterling is not a monetary unit reserve to themselves the right of translating the sums indicated in this Convention in terms of pound sterling into terms of their own monetary system in round figures.

The national laws may reserve to the debtor the right of discharging his debt in national currency according to the rate of exchange prevailing on the day of the arrival of the ship at the port of discharge of the goods concerned.

Article 10 [Application to all Bills of Lading]

The provisions of this Convention shall apply to all bills of lading issued in any of the contracting States.

Article 11 [Ratification and Entry into Force]

After an interval of not more than two years from the day on which the Convention is signed, the Belgian Government shall place itself in communication with the Governments of the High Contracting Parties which have declared themselves prepared to ratify the Convention, with a view to deciding whether it shall be put into force. The ratifications shall be deposited at Brussels at a date to be fixed by agreement among the said Governments. The first deposit of ratifications shall be recorded in a procès- verbal signed by the representatives of the Powers which take part therein and by the Belgian Minister of Foreign Affairs.

The subsequent deposit of ratifications shall be made by means of a written notification, addressed to the Belgian Government and accompanied by the instrument of ratification.

A duly certified copy of the procès-verbal relating to the first deposit of ratifications, of the notifications referred to in the previous paragraph, and also of the instruments of ratification accompanying them, shall be immediately sent by the Belgian Government through the diplomatic channel to the Powers who have signed this Convention or who have acceded to it. In the cases contemplated in the preceding paragraph, the said Government shall inform them at the same time of the date on which it received the notification.

Article 12 [Accession]

Non-signatory States may accede to the present Convention whether or not they have been represented at the International Conference at Brussels.

A State which desires to accede shall notify its intention in writing to the Belgian Government, forwarding to it the document of accession, which shall be deposited in the archives of the said Government.

The Belgian Government shall immediately forward to all the States which have signed or acceded to the Convention a duly certified copy of the notification and of the act of accession, mentioning the date on which it received the notification.

Article 13 [Territorial Application]

The High Contracting Parties may at the time of signature, ratification or accession declare that their acceptance of the present Convention does not include any or all of the self-governing dominions, or of the colonies, overseas possessions, protectorates or territories under their sovereignty or authority, and they may subsequently accede separately on behalf of any self-governing dominion, colony, overseas possession, protectorate or territory excluded in their declaration. They may also denounce the Convention separately in accordance with its provisions in respect of any self-governing dominion, or any colony, overseas possession, protectorate or territory under their sovereignty or authority.

Article 14 [Entry into Force]

The present Convention shall take effect, in the case of the States which have taken part in the first deposit of ratifications, one year after the date of the protocol recording such deposit.

As respects the States which ratify subsequently or which accede, and also in cases in which the Convention is subsequently put into effect in accordance with Article 13, it shall take effect six months after the notifications specified in paragraph 2 of Article 11 and paragraph 2 of Article 12 have been received by the Belgian Government.

Article 15 [Denounciation]

In the event of one of the contracting States wishing to denounce the present Convention, the denunciation shall be notified in writing to the Belgian Government, which shall immediately communicate a duly certified copy of the notification to all the other States, informing them of the date on which it was received.

The denunciation shall only operate in respect of the State which made the notification, and on the expiry of one year after the notification has reached the Belgian Government.

Article 16 [Amendments]

Any one of the contracting States shall have the right to call for a fresh conference with a view to considering possible amendments.

A State which would exercise this right should notify its intention to the other States through the Belgian Government, which would make arrangements for convening the Conference.

DONE at Brussels, in a single copy, August 25th, 1924.

PROTOCOL OF SIGNATURE

At the time of signing the International Convention for the Unification of Certain Rules of Law relating to Bills of Lading the Plenipotentiaries whose signatures appear below have adopted this Protocol, which will have the same force and the same value as if its provisions were inserted in the text of the Convention to which it relates.

The High Contracting Parties may give effect to this Convention either by giving it the force of law or by including in their national legislation in a form appropriate to that legislation the rules adopted under this Convention.

They may reserve the right:

1. To prescribe that in the cases referred to in paragraph 2(c) to (p) of Article 4 the holder of a bill of lading shall be entitled to establish responsibility for loss or damage arising from the personal fault of the carrier or the fault of his servants which are not covered by paragraph (a).

2. To apply Article 6 in so far as the national coasting trade is concerned to all classes of goods without taking account of the restriction set out in the last paragraph of that Article.

DONE at Brussels, in single copy, August 25th, 1924.

Entry into force: 2 June 1931

Ratification and binding effect as of April 2020: Algeria, Angola, Antigua and Barbuda, Argentina, Bahamas, Barbados, Belize, Bolivia, Bosnia and Herzegovina, Congo, Croatia, Cuba, Cyprus, Fiji, Gambia, Ghana, Grenada, Guyana, Iran, Ireland, Israel, Ivory Coast, Jamaica, Kenya, Kiribati, Kuwait, Macedonia, Madagascar, Mauritius, Monaco, Montenegro, Nauru, Netherlands, Nigeria, Papua New Guinea, Paraguay, Peru, Portugal, St. Kitts and Nevis, St. Lucia, St. Vincent, Salomon Islands, Serbia, Seychelles, Slovenia, Somalia, Trinidad and Tobago, Turkey, Tuvalu, United Kingdom, United States of America[1]

1 The following countries apply parallel national laws without having ratified the Rules: India, Malaysia, Taiwan.

30) The Hague-Visby Rules

The Hague Rules as Amended by the Brussels Protocol of 1968

Article I [Definitions]

In these Rules the following words are employed, with the meanings set out below:

(a) 'Carrier' includes the owner or the charterer who enters into a contract of carriage with a shipper.

(b) 'Contract of carriage' applies only to contracts of carriage covered by a bill of lading or any similar document of title, in so far as such document relates to the carriage of goods by sea, including any bill of lading or any similar document as aforesaid issued under or pursuant to a charter party from the moment at which such bill of lading or similar document of title regulates the relations between a carrier and a holder of the same.

(c) 'Goods' includes goods, wares, merchandise, and articles of every kind whatsoever except live animals and cargo which by the contract of carriage is stated as being carried on deck and is so carried.

(d) 'Ship' means any vessel used for the carriage of goods by sea.

(e) 'Carriage of goods' covers the period from the time when the goods are loaded on to the time they are discharged from the ship.

Article II [Scope and Purpose]

Subject to the provisions of Article VI, under every contract of carriage of goods by sea the carrier, in relation to the loading, handling, stowage, carriage, custody, care and discharge of such goods, shall be subject to the responsibilities and liabilities and entitled to the rights and immunities hereinafter set forth.

Article III [Responsibilities of the Carrier]

1. The carrier shall be bound before and at the beginning of the voyage to exercise due diligence to:

(a) Make the ship seaworthy;

(b) Properly man, equip and supply the ship;

(c) Make the holds, refrigerating and cool chambers, and all other parts of the ship in which goods are carried, fit and safe for their reception, carriage and preservation.

2. Subject to the provisions of Article IV, the carrier shall properly and carefully load, handle, stow, carry, keep, care for, and discharge the goods carried.

3. After receiving the goods into his charge the carrier or the master or agent of the carrier shall, on demand of the shipper, issue to the shipper a bill of lading showing among other things:

(a) The leading marks necessary for identification of the goods as the same are furnished in writing by the shipper before the loading of such goods starts, provided such marks are stamped or otherwise shown clearly upon the goods if uncovered, or on the cases or coverings in which such goods are contained, in such a manner as should ordinarily remain legible until the end of the voyage.

(b) Either the number of packages or pieces, or the quantity, or weight, as the case may be, as furnished in writing by the shipper.

(c) The apparent order and condition of the goods.

Provided that no carrier, master or agent of the carrier shall be bound to state or show in the bill of lading any marks, number, quantity or weight which he has reasonable ground for suspecting not accurately to represent the goods actually received, or which he has had no reasonable means of checking.

4. Such a bill of lading shall be prima facie evidence of the receipt by the carrier of the goods as therein described in accordance with paragraph 3 (a), (b) and (c). However, proof to the contrary shall not be admissible when the bill of lading has been transferred to a third party acting in good faith.

5. The shipper shall be deemed to have guaranteed to the carrier the accuracy at the time of shipment of the marks, number, quantity and weight, as furnished by him, and the shipper shall indemnify the carrier against all loss, damages and expenses arising or resulting from inaccuracies in such particulars. The right of the carrier to such indemnity shall in no way limit his responsibility and liability under the contract of carriage to any person other than the shipper.

6. Unless notice of loss or damage and the general nature of such loss or damage be given in writing to the carrier or his agent at the port of discharge before or at the time of the removal of the goods into the custody of the person entitled to delivery thereof under the contract of carriage, or, if the loss or damage be not apparent, within three days, such removal shall be prima facie evidence of the delivery by the carrier of the goods as described in the bill of lading.

The notice in writing need not be given if the state of the goods has, at the time of their receipt, been the subject of joint survey or inspection.

Subject to paragraph 6bis the carrier and the ship shall in any event be discharged from all liability whatsoever in respect of the goods, unless suit is brought within one year of their delivery or of the date when they should have been delivered. This period, may however, be extended if the parties so agree after the cause of action has arisen.

In the case of any actual or apprehended loss or damage the carrier and the receiver shall give all reasonable facilities to each other for inspecting and tallying the goods.

6bis. An action for indemnity against a third person may be brought even after the expiration of the year provided for in the preceding paragraph if brought within the time allowed by the law of the Court seized of the case. However, the time allowed shall be not less than three months, commencing from the day when the person bringing such action for indemnity has settled the claim or has been served with process in the action against himself.

7. After the goods are loaded the bill of lading to be issued by the carrier, master, or agent of the carrier, to the shipper shall, if the shipper so demands be a 'shipped' bill of lading, provided that if the shipper shall have previously taken up any document of title to such goods, he shall surrender the same as against the issue of the 'shipped' bill of lading, but at the option of the carrier such document of title may be noted at the port of shipment by the carrier, master, or agent with the name or names of the ship or ships upon which the goods have been shipped and the date or dates of shipment, and when so noted, if it shows the particulars mentioned in paragraph 3 of Article III, shall for the purpose of this Article be deemed to constitute a 'shipped' bill of lading.

8. Any clause, covenant, or agreement in a contract of carriage relieving the carrier or the ship from liability for loss or damage to, or in connection with, goods arising from negligence, fault, or failure in the duties and obligations provided in this Article or lessening such liability otherwise than as provided in these Rules, shall be null and void and of no effect. A benefit of insurance in favour of the carrier or similar clause shall be deemed to be a clause relieving the carrier from liability.

Article IV [Limitation of Carrier Liability]

1. Neither the carrier nor the ship shall be liable for loss or damage arising or resulting from unseaworthiness unless caused by want of due diligence on the part of the carrier to make the

ship seaworthy, and to secure that the ship is properly manned, equipped and supplied, and to make the holds, refrigerating and cool chambers and all other parts of the ship in which goods are carried fit and safe for their reception, carriage and preservation in accordance with the provisions of paragraph 1 of Article III. Whenever loss or damage has resulted from unseaworthiness the burden of proving the exercise of due diligence shall be on the carrier or other person claiming exemption under this article.

2. Neither the carrier nor the ship shall be responsible for loss or damage arising or resulting from:

(a) Act, neglect, or default of the master, mariner, pilot, or the servants of the carrier in the navigation or in the management of the ship.

(b) Fire, unless caused by the actual fault or privity of the carrier.

(c) Perils, dangers and accidents of the sea or other navigable waters.

(d) Act of God.

(e) Act of war.

(f) Act of public enemies.

(g) Arrest or restraint of princes, rulers or people, or seizure under legal process.

(h) Quarantine restrictions.

(i) Act or omission of the shipper or owner of the goods, his agent or representative.

(j) Strikes or lockouts or stoppage or restraint of labour from whatever cause, whether partial or general.

(k) Riots and civil commotions.

(l) Saving or attempting to save life or property at sea.

(m) Wastage in bulk of weight or any other loss or damage arising from inherent defect, quality or vice of the goods.

(n) Insufficiency of packing.

(o) Insufficiency or inadequacy of marks.

(p) Latent defects not discoverable by due diligence.

(q) Any other cause arising without the actual fault or privity of the carrier, or without the fault or neglect of the agents or servants of the carrier, but the burden of proof shall be on the person claiming the benefit of this exception to show that neither the actual fault or privity of the carrier nor the fault or neglect of the agents or servants of the carrier contributed to the loss or damage.

3. The shipper shall not be responsible for loss or damage sustained by the carrier or the ship arising or resulting from any cause without the act, fault or neglect of the shipper, his agents or his servants.

4. Any deviation in saving or attempting to save life or property at sea or any reasonable deviation shall not be deemed to be an infringement or breach of these Rules or of the contract of carriage, and the carrier shall not be liable for any loss or damage resulting therefrom.

5.(a) Unless the nature and value of such goods have been declared by the shipper before shipment and inserted in the bill of lading, neither the carrier nor the ship shall in any event be or become liable for any loss or damage to or in connection with the goods in an amount exceeding the equivalent of 666.67 units of account per package or unit or units of account per kilo of gross weight of the goods lost or damaged, whichever is the higher.

(b) The total amount recoverable shall be calculated by reference to the value of such goods at the place and time at which the goods are discharged from the ship in accordance with the contract or should have been so discharged.

The value of the goods shall be fixed according to the commodity exchange price, or, if there be no such price, according to the current market price, or, if there be no commodity exchange price or current market price, by reference to the normal value of goods of the same kind and quality.

(c) Where a container, pallet or similar article of transport is used to consolidate goods, the number of packages or units enumerated in the bill of lading as packed in such article of transport shall be deemed the number of packages or units for the purpose of this paragraph as far as these packages or units are concerned. Except as aforesaid such article of transport shall be considered the package or unit.

(d) The unit of account mentioned in this Article is the special drawing right as defined by the International Monetary Fund. The amounts mentioned in sub-paragraph (a) of this paragraph shall be converted into national currency on the basis of the value of that currency on a date to be determined by the law of the Court seized of the case.

(e) Neither the carrier nor the ship shall be entitled to the benefit of the limitation of liability provided for in this paragraph if it is proved that the damage resulted from an act or omission of the carrier done with intent to cause damage, or recklessly and with knowledge that damage would probably result.

(f) The declaration mentioned in sub-paragraph (a) of this paragraph, if embodied in the bill of lading, shall be prima facie evidence, but shall not be binding or conclusive on the carrier.

(g) By agreement between the carrier, master or agent of the carrier and the shipper other maximum amounts than those mentioned in sub-paragraph (a) of this paragraph may be fixed, provided that no maximum amount so fixed shall be less than the appropriate maximum mentioned in that sub-paragraph.

(h) Neither the carrier nor the ship shall be responsible in any event for loss or damage to, or in connection with, goods if the nature or value thereof has been knowingly misstated by the shipper in the bill of lading.

6. Goods of an inflammable, explosive or dangerous nature to the shipment whereof the carrier, master or agent of the carrier has not consented with knowledge of their nature and character, may at any time before discharge be landed at any place, or destroyed or rendered innocuous by the carrier without compensation and the shipper of such goods shall be liable for all damages and expenses directly or indirectly arising out of or resulting from such shipment. If any such goods shipped with such knowledge and consent shall become a danger to the ship or cargo, they may in like manner be landed at any place, or destroyed or rendered innocuous by the carrier without liability on the part of the carrier except to general average, if any.

Article IV bis [Himalaya Clause]

1. The defences and limits of liability provided for in these Rules shall apply in any action against the carrier in respect of loss or damage to goods covered by a contract of carriage whether the action be founded in contract or in tort.

2. If such an action is brought against a servant or agent of the carrier (such servant or agent not being an independent contractor), such servant or agent shall be entitled to avail himself of the defences and limits of liability which the carrier is entitled to invoke under these Rules.

3. The aggregate of the amounts recoverable from the carrier, and such servants and agents, shall in no case exceed the limit provided for in these Rules.

4. Nevertheless, a servant or agent of the carrier shall not be entitled to avail himself of the provisions of this article, if it is proved that the damage resulted from an act or omission of the servant or agent done with intent to cause damage or recklessly and with knowledge that damage would probably result.

Article V [Freedom of Contract]

A carrier shall be at liberty to surrender in whole or in part all or any of his rights and immunities or to increase any of his responsibilities and obligations under these Rules, provided such surrender or increase shall be embodied in the bill of lading issued to the shipper. The provisions of these Rules shall not be applicable to charter parties, but if bills of lading are issued in the case of a ship under a charter party they shall comply with the terms of these Rules. Nothing in these Rules shall be held to prevent the insertion in a bill of lading of any lawful provision regarding general average.

Article VI [Liability Agreements for Particular Goods Outside the Bill of Lading]

Notwithstanding the provisions of the preceding articles, a carrier, master or agent of the carrier and a shipper shall in regard to any particular goods be at liberty to enter into any agreement in any terms as to the responsibility and liability of the carrier for such goods, and as to the rights and immunities of the carrier in respect of such goods, or his obligation as to seaworthiness, so far as this stipulation is not contrary to public policy, or the care or diligence of his servants or agents in regard to the loading, handling, stowage, carriage, custody, care and discharge of the goods carried by sea, provided that in this case no bill of lading has been or shall be issued and that the terms agreed shall be embodied in a receipt which shall be a non-negotiable document and shall be marked as such.

An agreement so entered into shall have full legal effect.

Provided that this Article shall not apply to ordinary commercial shipments made in the ordinary course of trade, but only to other shipments where the character or condition of the property to be carried or the circumstances, terms and conditions under which the carriage is to be performed are such as reasonably to justify a special agreement.

Article VII [Warehouse to Warehouse Coverage]

Nothing herein contained shall prevent a carrier or a shipper from entering into any agreement, stipulation, condition, reservation or exemption as to the responsibility and liability of the carrier or the ship for the loss or damage to, or in connection with, the custody and care and handling of goods prior to the loading on, and subsequent to the discharge from, the ship on which the goods are carried by sea.

Article VIII [Priority of Mandatory Statutory Provisions]

The provisions of these Rules shall not affect the rights and obligations of the carrier under any statute for the time being in force relating to the limitation of the liability of owners of sea-going vessels.

Article IX [Exception for Nuclear Accidents]

These Rules shall not affect the provisions of any international Convention or national law governing liability for nuclear damage.

Article X [Scope of Application]

The provisions of these Rules shall apply to every bill of lading relating to the carriage of goods between ports in two different States if

(a) the bill of lading is issued in a contracting State, or

(b) the carriage is from a port in a contracting State, or

(c) the contract contained in or evidenced by the bill of lading provides that these Rules or legislation of any State giving effect to them are to govern the contract;

whatever may be the nationality of the ship, the carrier, the shipper, the consignee, or any other interested person.

Each Contracting State shall apply the provisions of this Convention to the bills of lading mentioned above.

This Article shall not prevent a Contracting State from applying the Rules of this Convention to bills of lading not included in the preceding paragraphs.

[Article 11 to 16 on ratification, accession, denunciation, and review omitted.]

Entry into force: 1977

Ratification and binding effect as of April 2020: Australia, Belgium, Canada, Denmark, Ecuador, Finland, France, Greece, Italy, Japan, Latvia, Luxembourg, Netherlands, New Zealand, Norway, Poland, Singapore, Spain, Sri Lanka, Sweden, Switzerland, Syria, Tonga, United Kingdom[1]

1 The following countries apply parallel national rules without having ratified the Rules: Germany, Liberia, South Africa.

31) 1978 UNITED NATIONS CONVENTION ON THE CARRIAGE OF GOODS BY SEA ("HAMBURG RULES")[1]

Preamble

THE STATES PARTIES TO THIS CONVENTION,

HAVING RECOGNIZED the desirability of determining by agreement certain rules relating to the carriage of goods by sea,

HAVE DECIDED to conclude a Convention for this purpose and have thereto agreed as follows:

PART I - GENERAL PROVISIONS

Article 1 Definitions

In this Convention:

1. "Carrier" means any person by whom or in whose name a contract of carriage of goods by sea has been concluded with a shipper.

2. "Actual carrier" means any person to whom the performance of the carriage of the goods, or of part of the carriage, has been entrusted by the carrier, and includes any other person to whom such performance has been entrusted.

3. "Shipper" means any person by whom or in whose name or on whose behalf a contract of carriage of goods by sea has been concluded with a carrier, or any person by whom or in whose name or on whose behalf the goods are actually delivered to the carrier in relation to the contract of carriage by sea.

4. "Consignee" means the person entitled to take delivery of the goods.

5. "Goods" includes live animals; where the goods are consolidated in a container, pallet or similar article of transport or where they are packed, "goods" includes such article of transport or packaging if supplied by the shipper.

6. "Contract of carriage by sea" means any contract whereby the carrier undertakes against payment of freight to carry goods by sea from one port to another; however, a contract which involves carriage by sea and also carriage by some other means is deemed to be a contract of carriage by sea for the purposes of this Convention only in so far as it relates to the carriage by sea.

7. "Bill of lading" means a document which evidences a contract of carriage by sea and the taking over or loading of the goods by the carrier, and by which the carrier undertakes to deliver the goods against surrender of the document. A provision in the document that the goods are to be delivered to the order of a named person, or to order, or to bearer, constitutes such an undertaking.

8. "Writing" includes, inter alia, telegram and telex.

Article 2 Scope of Application

1. The provisions of this Convention are applicable to all contracts of carriage by sea between two different States, if:

(a) the port of loading as provided for in the contract of carriage by sea is located in a Contracting State, or

(b) the port of discharge as provided for in the contract of carriage by sea is located in a Contracting State, or

(c) one of the optional ports of discharge provided for in the contract of carriage by sea is the actual port of discharge and such port is located in a Contracting State, or

(d) the bill of lading or other document evidencing the contract of carriage by sea is issued in a Contracting State, or

(e) the bill of lading or other document evidencing the contract of carriage by sea provides that the provisions of this Convention or the legislation of any State giving effect to them are to govern the contract.

2. The provisions of this Convention are applicable without regard to the nationality of the ship, the carrier, the actual carrier, the shipper, the consignee or any other interested person.

3. The provisions of this Convention are not applicable to charter-parties. However, where a bill of lading is issued pursuant to a charter-party, the provisions of the Convention apply to such a bill of lading if it governs the relation between the carrier and the holder of the bill of lading, not being the charterer.

4. If a contract provides for future carriage of goods in a series of shipments during an agreed period, the provisions of this Convention apply to each shipment. However, where a shipment is made under a charter-party, the provisions of paragraph 3 of this Article apply.

Article 3 Interpretation of the Convention

In the interpretation and application of the provisions of this Convention regard shall be had to its international character and to the need to promote uniformity.

PART II - LIABILITY OF THE CARRIER

Article 4 Period of Responsibility

1. The responsibility of the carrier for the goods under this Convention covers the period during which the carrier is in charge of the goods at the port of loading, during the carriage and at the port of discharge.

2. For the purpose of paragraph 1 of this article, the carrier is deemed to be in charge of the goods

(a) from the time he has taken over the goods from:

  (i) the shipper, or a person acting on his behalf; or

  (ii) an authority or other third party to whom, pursuant to law or regulations applicable at the port of loading, the goods must be handed over for shipment;

(b) until the time he has delivered the goods:

  (i) by handing over the goods to the consignee; or

  (ii) in cases where the consignee does not receive the goods from the carrier, by placing them at the disposal of the consignee in accordance with the contract or with the law or with the usage of the particular trade, applicable at the port of discharge; or

  (iii) by handing over the goods to an authority or other third party to whom, pursuant to law or regulations applicable at the port of discharge, the goods must be handed over.

3. In paragraphs 1 and 2 of this article, reference to the carrier or to the consignee means, in addition to the carrier or the consignee, the servants or agents, respectively of the carrier or the consignee.

Article 5 Basis of Liability

1. The carrier is liable for loss resulting from loss of or damage to the goods, as well as from delay in delivery, if the occurrence which caused the loss, damage or delay took place while the

goods were in his charge as defined in Article 4, unless the carrier proves that he, his servants or agents took all measures that could reasonably be required to avoid the occurrence and its consequences.

2. Delay in delivery occurs when the goods have not been delivered at the port of discharge provided for in the contract of carriage by sea within the time expressly agreed upon or, in the absence of such agreement, within the time which it would be reasonable to require of a diligent carrier, having regard to the circumstances of the case.

3. The person entitled to make a claim for the loss of goods may treat the goods as lost if they have not been delivered as required by Article 4 within 60 consecutive days following the expiry of the time for delivery according to paragraph 2 of this article.

4.(a) The carrier is liable

(i) for loss of or damage to the goods or delay in delivery caused by fire, if the claimant proves that the fire arose from fault or neglect on the part of the carrier, his servants or agents;

(ii) for such loss, damage or delay in delivery which is proved by the claimant to have resulted from the fault or neglect of the carrier, his servants or agents, in taking all measures that could reasonably be required to put out the fire and avoid or mitigate its consequences.

(b) In case of fire on board the ship affecting the goods, if the claimant or the carrier so desires, a survey in accordance with shipping practices must be held into the cause and circumstances of the fire, and a copy of the surveyor's report shall be made available on demand to the carrier and the claimant.

5. With respect to live animals, the carrier is not liable for loss, damage or delay in delivery resulting from any special risks inherent in that kind of carriage. If the carrier proves that he has complied with any special instructions given to him by the shipper respecting the animals and that, in the circumstances of the case, the loss, damage or delay in delivery could be attributed to such risks, it is presumed that the loss, damage or delay in delivery was so caused, unless there is proof that all or a part of the loss, damage or delay in delivery resulted from fault or neglect on the part of the carrier, his servants or agents.

6. The carrier is not liable, except in general average, where loss, damage or delay in delivery resulted from measures to save life or from reasonable measures to save property at sea.

7. Where fault or neglect on the part of the carrier, his servants or agents combines with another cause to produce loss, damage or delay in delivery the carrier is liable only to the extent that the loss, damage or delay in delivery is attributable to such fault or neglect, provided that the carrier proves the amount of the loss, damage or delay in delivery not attributable thereto.

Article 6 Limits of Liability

1.(a) The liability of the carrier for loss resulting from loss of or damage to goods according to the provisions of Article 5 is limited to an amount equivalent to 835 units of account per package or other shipping unit or 2.5 units of account per kilogramme of gross weight of the goods lost or damaged, whichever is the higher.

(b) The liability of the carrier for delay in delivery according to the provisions of Article 5 is limited to an amount equivalent to two and a half times the freight payable for the goods delayed, but not exceeding the total freight payable under the contract of carriage of goods by sea.

(c) In no case shall the aggregate liability of the carrier, under both subparagraphs (a) and (b) of this paragraph, exceed the limitation which would be established under subparagraph

(a) of this paragraph for total loss of the goods with respect to which such liability was incurred.

2. For the purpose of calculating which amount is the higher in accordance with paragraph 1(a) of this article, the following rules apply:

(a) Where a container, pallet or similar article of transport is used to consolidate goods, the package or other shipping units enumerated in the bill of lading, if issued, or otherwise in any other document evidencing the contract of carriage by sea, as packed in such article of transport are deemed packages or shipping units. Except as aforesaid the goods in such article of transport are deemed one shipping unit.

(b) In cases where the article of transport itself has been lost or damaged, that article of transport, if not owned or otherwise supplied by the carrier, is considered one separate shipping unit.

3. Unit of account means the unit of account mentioned in Article 26.

4. By agreement between the carrier and the shipper, limits of liability exceeding those provided for in paragraph 1 may be fixed.

Article 7 Application to Non-Contractual Claims

1. The defences and limits of liability provided for in this Convention apply in any action against the carrier in respect of loss or damage to the goods covered by the contract of carriage by sea, as well as of delay in delivery whether the action is founded in contract, in tort or otherwise.

2. If such an action is brought against a servant or agent of the carrier, such servant or agent, if he proves that he acted within the scope of his employment, is entitled to avail himself of the defences and limits of liability which the carrier is entitled to invoke under this Convention.

3. Except as provided in Article 8, the aggregate of the amounts recoverable from the carrier and from any persons referred to in paragraph 2 of this Article shall not exceed the limits of liability provided for in this Convention.

Article 8 Loss of Right to Limit Responsibility

1. The carrier is not entitled to the benefit of the limitation of liability provided for in Article 6 if it is proved that the loss, damage or delay in delivery resulted from an act or omission of the carrier done with the intent to cause such loss, damage or delay, or recklessly and with knowledge that such loss, damage or delay would probably result.

2. Notwithstanding the provisions of paragraph 2 of Article 7, a servant or agent of the carrier is not entitled to the benefit of the limitation of liability provided for in Article 6 if it is proved that the loss, damage or delay in delivery resulted from an act or omission of such servant or agent, done with the intent to cause such loss, damage or delay, or recklessly and with knowledge that such loss, damage or delay would probably result.

Article 9 Deck Cargo

1. The carrier is entitled to carry the goods on deck only if such carriage is in accordance with an agreement with the shipper or with the usage of the particular trade or is required by statutory rules or regulations.

2. If the carrier and the shipper have agreed that the goods shall or may be carried on deck, the carrier must insert in the bill of lading or other document evidencing the contract of carriage by sea a statement to that effect. In the absence of such a statement the carrier has the burden of proving that an agreement for carriage on deck has been entered into; however, the carrier

is not entitled to invoke such an agreement against a third party, including a consignee, who has acquired the bill of lading in good faith.

3. Where the goods have been carried on deck contrary to the provisions of paragraph 1 of this Article or where the carrier may not under paragraph 2 of this Article invoke an agreement for carriage on deck, the carrier, notwithstanding the provisions of paragraph 1 of Article 5, is liable for loss of or damage to the goods, as well as for delay in delivery, resulting solely from the carriage on deck, and the extent of his liability is to be determined in accordance with the provisions of Article 6 or Article 8 of this Convention, as the case may be.

4. Carriage of goods on deck contrary to express agreement for carriage under deck is deemed to be an act or omission of the carrier within the meaning of Article 8.

Article 10 Liability of the Carrier and Actual Carrier

1. Where the performance of the carriage or part thereof has been entrusted to an actual carrier, whether or not in pursuance of a liberty under the contract of carriage by sea to do so, the carrier nevertheless remains responsible for the entire carriage according to the provisions of this Convention. The carrier is responsible, in relation to the carriage performed by the actual carrier, for the acts and omissions of the actual carrier and of his servants and agents acting within the scope of their employment.

2. All the provisions of this Convention governing the responsibility of the carrier also apply to the responsibility of the actual carrier for the carriage performed by him. The provisions of paragraphs 2 and 3 of Article 7 and of paragraph 2 of Article 8 apply if an action is brought against a servant or agent of the actual carrier.

3. Any special agreement under which the carrier assumes obligations not imposed by this Convention or waives rights conferred by this Convention affects the actual carrier only if agreed to by him expressly and in writing. Whether or not the actual carrier has so agreed, the carrier nevertheless remains bound by the obligations or waivers resulting from such special agreement.

4. Where and to the extent that both the carrier and the actual carrier are liable, their liability is joint and several.

5. The aggregate of the amounts recoverable from the carrier, the actual carrier and their servants and agents shall not exceed the limits of liability provided for in this Convention.

6. Nothing in this Article shall prejudice any right of recourse as between the carrier and the actual carrier.

Article 11 Through Carriage

1. Notwithstanding the provisions of paragraph 1 of Article 10, where a contract of carriage by sea provides explicitly that a specified part of the carriage covered by the said contract is to be performed by a named person other than the carrier, the contract may also provide that the carrier is not liable for loss, damage or delay in delivery caused by an occurrence which takes place while the goods are in the charge of the actual carrier during such part of the carriage. Nevertheless, any stipulation limiting or excluding such liability is without effect if no judicial proceedings can be instituted against the actual carrier in a court competent under paragraph 1 or 2 of Article 21. The burden of proving that any loss, damage or delay in delivery has been caused by such an occurrence rests upon the carrier.

2. The actual carrier is responsible in accordance with the provisions of paragraph 2 of Article 10 for loss, damage or delay in delivery caused by an occurrence which takes place while the goods are in his charge.

PART III - LIABILITY OF THE SHIPPER

Article 12 General Rule

The shipper is not liable for loss sustained by the carrier or the actual carrier, or for damage sustained by the ship, unless such loss or damage was caused by the fault or neglect of the shipper, his servants or agents. Nor is any servant or agent of the shipper liable for such loss or damage unless the loss or damage was caused by fault or neglect on his part.

Article 13 Special Rules on Dangerous Goods

1. The shipper must mark or label in a suitable manner dangerous goods as dangerous.

2. Where the shipper hands over dangerous goods to the carrier or an actual carrier, as the case may be, the shipper must inform him of the dangerous character of the goods and, if necessary, of the precautions to be taken. If the shipper fails to do so and such carrier or actual carrier does not otherwise have knowledge of their dangerous character:

(a) the shipper is liable to the carrier and any actual carrier for the loss resulting from the shipment of such goods, and

(b) the goods may at any time be unloaded, destroyed or rendered innocuous, as the circumstances may require, without payment of compensation.

3. The provisions of paragraph 2 of this Article may not be invoked by any person if during the carriage he has taken the goods in his charge with knowledge of their dangerous character.

4. If, in cases where the provisions of paragraph 2, subparagraph (b), of this Article do not apply or may not be invoked, dangerous goods become an actual danger to life or property, they may be unloaded, destroyed or rendered innocuous, as the circumstances may require, without payment of compensation except where there is an obligation to contribute in general average or where the carrier is liable in accordance with the provisions of Article 5.

PART IV - TRANSPORT DOCUMENTS

Article 14 Issue of Bill of Lading

1. When the carrier or the actual carrier takes the goods in his charge, the carrier must, on demand of the shipper, issue to the shipper a bill of lading.

2. The bill of lading may be signed by a person having authority from the carrier. A bill of lading signed by the master of the ship carrying the goods is deemed to have been signed on behalf of the carrier.

3. The signature on the bill of lading may be in handwriting, printed in facsimile, perforated, stamped, in symbols, or made by an other mechanical or electronic means, if not inconsistent with the law of the country where the bill of lading is issued.

Article 15 Contents of Bill of Lading

1. The bill of lading must include, inter alia, the following particulars:

(a) the general nature of the goods, the leading marks necessary for identification of the goods, an express statement, if applicable, as to the dangerous character of the goods, the number of packages or pieces, and the weight of the goods or their quantity otherwise expressed, all such particulars as furnished by the shipper;

(b) the apparent condition of the goods;

(c) the name and principal place of business of the carrier;

(d) the name of the shipper;

(e) the consignee if named by the shipper;

(f) the port of loading under the contract of carriage by sea and the date on which the goods were taken over by the carrier at the port of loading;

(g) the port of discharge under the contract of carriage by sea;

(h) the number of originals of the bill of lading, if more than one;

(i) the place of issuance of the bill of lading;

(j) the signature of the carrier or a person acting on his behalf;

(k) the freight to the extent payable by the consignee or other indication that freight is payable by him;

(l) the statement referred to in paragraph 3 of Article 23;

(m) the statement, if applicable, that the goods shall or may be carried on deck;

(n) the date or the period of delivery of the goods at the port of discharge if expressly agreed upon between the parties; and

(o) any increased limit or limits of liability where agreed in accordance with paragraph 4 of Article 6.

2. After the goods have been loaded on board, if the shipper so demands, the carrier must issue to the shipper a "shipped" bill of lading which, in addition to the particulars required under paragraph 1 of this article, must state that the goods are on board a named ship or ships, and the date or dates of loading. If the carrier has previously issued to the shipper a bill of lading or other document of title with respect to any of such goods, on request of the carrier, the shipper must surrender such document in exchange for a "shipped" bill of lading. The carrier may amend any previously issued document in order to meet the shipper's demand for a "shipped" bill of lading if, as amended, such document includes all the information required to be contained in a "shipped" bill of lading.

3. The absence in the bill of lading of one or more particulars referred to in this Article does not affect the legal character of the document as a bill of lading provided that it nevertheless meets the requirements set out in paragraph 7 of Article 1.

Article 16 Bills of Lading: Reservations and Evidentiary Effect

1. If the bill of lading contains particulars concerning the general nature, leading marks, number of packages or pieces, weight or quantity of the goods which the carrier or other person issuing the bill of lading on his behalf knows or has reasonable grounds to suspect do not accurately represent the goods actually taken over or, where a "shipped" bill of lading is issued, loaded, or if he had no reasonable means of checking such particulars, the carrier or such other person must insert in the bill of lading a reservation specifying these inaccuracies, grounds of suspicion or the absence of reasonable means of checking.

2. If the carrier or other person issuing the bill of lading on his behalf fails to note on the bill of lading the apparent condition of the goods, he is deemed to have noted on the bill of lading that the goods were in apparent good condition.

3. Except for particulars in respect of which and to the extent to which a reservation permitted under paragraph 1 of this Article has been entered:

(a) the bill of lading is prima facie evidence of the taking over or, where a "shipped" bill of lading is issued, loading, by the carrier of the goods as described in the bill of lading; and

(b) proof to the contrary by the carrier is not admissible if the bill of lading has been transferred to a third party, including a consignee, who in good faith has acted in reliance on the description of the goods therein.

4. A bill of lading which does not, as provided in paragraph 1, subparagraph (k) of Article 15, set forth the freight or otherwise indicate that freight is payable by the consignee or does not set forth demurrage incurred at the port of loading payable by the consignee, is prima facie evidence that no freight or such demurrage is payable by him. However, proof to the contrary by the carrier is not admissible when the bill of lading has been transferred to a third party, including a consignee, who in good faith has acted in reliance on the absence in the bill of lading of any such indication.

Article 17 Guarantees by the Shipper

1. The shipper is deemed to have guaranteed to the carrier the accuracy of particulars relating to the general nature of the goods, their marks, number, weight and quantity as furnished by him for insertion in the bill of lading. The shipper must indemnify the carrier against the loss resulting from inaccuracies in such particulars. The shipper remains liable even if the bill of lading has been transferred by him. The right of the carrier to such indemnity in no way limits his liability under the contract of carriage by sea to any person other than the shipper.

2. Any letter of guarantee or agreement by which the shipper undertakes to indemnify the carrier against loss resulting from the issuance of the bill of lading by the carrier, or by a person acting on his behalf, without entering a reservation relating to particulars furnished by the shipper for insertion in the bill of lading, or to the apparent condition of the goods, is void and of no effect as against any third party, including a consignee, to whom the bill of lading has been transferred.

3. Such letter of guarantee or agreement is valid as against the shipper unless the carrier or the person acting on his behalf, by omitting the reservation referred to in paragraph 2 of this article, intends to defraud a third party, including a consignee, who acts in reliance on the description of the goods in the bill of lading. In the latter case, if the reservation omitted relates to particulars furnished by the shipper for insertion in the bill of lading, the carrier has no right of indemnity from the shipper pursuant to paragraph 1 of this article.

4. In the case of intended fraud referred to in paragraph 3 of this Article the carrier is liable, without the benefit of the limitation of liability provided for in this Convention, for the loss incurred by a third party, including a consignee, because he has acted in reliance on the description of the goods in the bill of lading.

Article 18 Documents Other than Bills of Lading

Where a carrier issues a document other than a bill of lading to evidence the receipt of the goods to be carried, such a document is prima facie evidence of the conclusion of the contract of carriage by sea and the taking over by the carrier of the goods as therein described.

PART V - CLAIMS AND ACTIONS

Article 19 Notice of Loss, Damage or Delay

1. Unless notice of loss or damage, specifying the general nature of such loss or damage, is given in writing by the consignee to the carrier not later than the working day after the day when the goods were handed over to the consignee, such handing over is prima facie evidence of the delivery by the carrier of the goods as described in the document of transport or, if no such document has been issued, in good condition.

2. Where the loss or damage is not apparent, the provisions of paragraph 1 of this Article apply correspondingly if notice in writing is not given within 15 consecutive days after the day when the goods were handed over to the consignee.

3. If the state of the goods at the time they were handed over to the consignee has been the subject of a joint survey or inspection by the parties, notice in writing need not be given of loss or damage ascertained during such survey or inspection.

4. In the case of any actual or apprehended loss or damage the carrier and the consignee must give all reasonable facilities to each other for inspecting and tallying the goods.

5. No compensation shall be payable for loss resulting from delay in delivery unless a notice has been given in writing to the carrier within 60 consecutive days after the day when the goods were handed over to the consignee.

6. If the goods have been delivered by an actual carrier, any notice given under this Article to him shall have the same effect as if it had been given to the carrier, and any notice given to the carrier shall have effect as if given to such actual carrier.

7. Unless notice of loss or damage, specifying the general nature of the loss or damage, is given in writing by the carrier or actual carrier to the shipper not later than 90 consecutive days after the occurrence of such loss or damage or after the delivery of the goods in accordance with paragraph 2 of Article 4, whichever is later, the failure to give such notice is prima facie evidence that the carrier or the actual carrier has sustained no loss or damage due to the fault or neglect of the shipper, his servants or agents.

8. For the purpose of this article, notice given to a person acting on the carrier's or the actual carrier's behalf, including the master or the officer in charge of the ship, or to a person acting on the shipper's behalf is deemed to have been given to the carrier, to the actual carrier or to the shipper, respectively.

Article 20 Limitation of Actions

1. Any action relating to carriage of goods under this Convention is time-barred if judicial or arbitral proceedings have not been instituted within a period of two years.

2. The limitation period commences on the day on which the carrier has delivered the goods or part thereof or, in cases where no goods have been delivered, on the last day on which the goods should have been delivered.

3. The day on which the limitation period commences is not included in the period.

4. The person against whom a claim is made may at any time during the running of the limitation period extend that period by a declaration in writing to the claimant. This period may be further extended by another declaration or declarations.

5. An action for indemnity by a person held liable may be instituted even after the expiration of the limitation period provided for in the preceding paragraphs if instituted within the time allowed by the law of the State where proceedings are instituted. However, the time allowed shall not be less than 90 days commencing from the day when the person instituting such action for indemnity has settled the claim or has been served with process in the action against himself.

Article 21 Jurisdiction

1. In judicial proceedings relating to carriage of goods under this Convention the plaintiff, at his option, may institute an action in a court which, according to the law of the State where the court is situated, is competent and within the jurisdiction of which is situated one of the following places:

(a) the principal place of business or, in the absence thereof, the habitual residence of the defendant; or

(b) the place where the contract was made provided that the defendant has there a place of business, branch or agency through which the contract was made; or

(c) the port of loading or the port of discharge; or

(d) any additional place designated for that purpose in the contract of carriage by sea.

2.(a) Notwithstanding the preceding provisions of this article, an action may be instituted in the courts of any port or place in a Contracting State at which the carrying vessel or any other vessel of the same ownership may have been arrested in accordance with applicable rules of the law of that State and of international law. However, in such a case, at the petition of the defendant, the claimant must remove the action, at his choice, to one of the jurisdictions referred to in paragraph 1 of this Article for the determination of the claim, but before such removal the defendant must furnish security sufficient to ensure payment of any judgement that may subsequently be awarded to the claimant in the action.

(b) All questions relating to the sufficiency or otherwise of the security shall be determined by the court of the port or place of the arrest.

3. No judicial proceedings relating to carriage of goods under this Convention may be instituted in a place not specified in paragraph 1 or 2 of this article. The provisions of this paragraph do not constitute an obstacle to the jurisdiction of the Contracting States for provisional or protective measures.

4.(a) Where an action has been instituted in a court competent under paragraph 1 or 2 of this Article or where judgement has been delivered by such a court, no new action may be started between the same parties on the same grounds unless the judgement of the court before which the first action was instituted is not enforceable in the country in which the new proceedings are instituted;

(b) for the purpose of this Article the institution of measures with a view to obtaining enforcement of a judgement is not to be considered as the starting of a new action;

(c) for the purpose of this article, the removal of an action to a different court within the same country, or to a court in another country, in accordance with paragraph 2(a) of this article, is not to be considered as the starting of a new action.

5. Notwithstanding the provisions of the preceding paragraphs, an agreement made by the parties, after a claim under the contract of carriage by sea has arisen, which designates the place where the claimant may institute an action, is effective.

Article 22 Arbitration

1. Subject to the provisions of this article, parties may provide by agreement evidenced in writing that any dispute that may arise relating to carriage of goods under this Convention shall be referred to arbitration.

2. Where a charter-party contains a provision that disputes arising thereunder shall be referred to arbitration and a bill of lading issued pursuant to the charter-party does not contain a special annotation providing that such provision shall be binding upon the holder of the bill of lading, the carrier may not invoke such provision as against a holder having acquired the bill of lading in good faith.

3. The arbitration proceedings shall, at the option of the claimant, be instituted at one of the following places:

(a) a place in a State within whose territory is situated:

   (i) the principal place of business of the defendant or, in the absence thereof, the habitual residence of the defendant; or

   (ii) the place where the contract was made, provided that the defendant has there a place of business, branch or agency through which the contract was made; or

   (iii) the port of loading or the port of discharge; or

(b) any place designated for that purpose in the arbitration clause or agreement.

4. The arbitrator or arbitration tribunal shall apply the rules of this Convention.

5. The provisions of paragraphs 3 and 4 of this Article are deemed to be part of every arbitration clause or agreement, and any term of such clause or agreement which is inconsistent therewith is null and void.

6. Nothing in this Article affects the validity of an agreement relating to arbitration made by the parties after the claim under the contract of carriage by sea has arisen.

PART VI - SUPPLEMENTARY PROVISIONS

Article 23 Contractual Stipulations

1. Any stipulation in a contract of carriage by sea, in a bill of lading, or in any other document evidencing the contract of carriage by sea is null and void to the extent that it derogates, directly or indirectly, from the provisions of this Convention. The nullity of such a stipulation does not affect the validity of the other provisions of the contract or document of which it forms a part. A clause assigning benefit of insurance of the goods in favour of the carrier, or any similar clause, is null and void.

2. Notwithstanding the provisions of paragraph 1 of this article, a carrier may increase his responsibilities and obligations under this Convention.

3. Where a bill of lading or any other document evidencing the contract of carriage by sea is issued, it must contain a statement that the carriage is subject to the provisions of this Convention which nullify any stipulation derogating therefrom to the detriment of the shipper or the consignee.

4. Where the claimant in respect of the goods has incurred loss as a result of a stipulation which is null and void by virtue of the present article, or as a result of the omission of the statement referred to in paragraph 3 of this article, the carrier must pay compensation to the extent required in order to give the claimant compensation in accordance with the provisions of this Convention for any loss of or damage to the goods as well as for delay in delivery. The carrier must, in addition, pay compensation for costs incurred by the claimant for the purpose of exercising his right, provided that costs incurred in the action where the foregoing provision is invoked are to be determined in accordance with the law of the State where proceedings are instituted.

Article 24 General Average

1. Nothing in this Convention shall prevent the application of provisions in the contract of carriage by sea or national law regarding the adjustment of general average.

2. With the exception of Article 20, the provisions of this Convention relating to the liability of the carrier for loss of or damage to the goods also determine whether the consignee may refuse contribution in general average and the liability of the carrier to indemnify the consignee in respect of any such contribution made or any salvage paid.

Article 25 Other Conventions

1. This Convention does not modify the rights or duties of the carrier, the actual carrier and their servants and agents, provided for in international conventions or national law relating to the limitation of liability of owners of seagoing ships.

2. The provisions of articles 21 and 22 of this Convention do not prevent the application of the mandatory provisions of any other multilateral convention already in force at the date of this Convention [March 31, 1978] relating to matters dealt with in the said articles, provided that the dispute arises exclusively between parties having their principal place of business in States members of such other convention. However, this paragraph does not affect the application of paragraph 4 of Article 22 of this Convention.

3. No liability shall arise under the provisions of this Convention for damage caused by a nuclear incident if the operator of a nuclear installation is liable for such damage:

(a) under either the Paris Convention of 29 July 1960 on Third Party Liability in the Field of Nuclear Energy as amended by the Additional Protocol of 28 January 1964 or the Vienna Convention of 21 May 1963 on Civil Liability for Nuclear Damage, or

(b) by virtue of national law governing the liability for such damage, provided that such law is in all respects as favourable to persons who may suffer damage as either the Paris or Vienna Conventions.

4. No liability shall arise under the provisions of this Convention for any loss of or damage to or delay in delivery of luggage for which the carrier is responsible under any international convention or national law relating to the carriage of passengers and their luggage by sea.

5. Nothing contained in this Convention prevents a Contracting State from applying any other international convention which is already in force at the date of this Convention and which applies mandatorily to contracts of carriage of goods primarily by a mode of transport other than transport by sea. This provision also applies to any subsequent revision or amendment of such international convention.

Article 26 Unit of Account

1. The unit of account referred to in Article 6 of this Convention is the Special Drawing Right as defined by the International Monetary Fund. The amounts mentioned in Article 6 are to be converted into the national currency of a State according to the value of such currency at the date of judgement or the date agreed upon by the parties. The value of a national currency, in terms of the Special Drawing Right, of a Contracting State which is a member of the International Monetary Fund is to be calculated in accordance with the method of valuation applied by the International Monetary Fund in effect at the date in question for its operations and transactions. The value of a national currency in terms of the Special Drawing Right of a Contracting State which is not a member of the International Monetary Fund is to be calculated in a manner determined by that State.

2. Nevertheless, those States which are not members of the International Monetary Fund and whose law does not permit the application of the provisions of paragraph 1 of this Article may, at the time of signature, or at the time of ratification, acceptance, approval or accession or at any time thereafter, declare that the limits of liability provided for in this Convention to be applied in their territories shall be fixed as:

12,500 monetary units per package or other shipping unit or 37.5 monetary units per kilogramme of gross weight of the goods.

3. The monetary unit referred to in paragraph 2 of this Article corresponds to sixty-five and a half milligrammes of gold of millesimal fineness nine hundred. The conversion of the amounts referred to in paragraph 2 into the national currency is to be made according to the law of the State concerned.

4. The calculation mentioned in the last sentence of paragraph 1 and the conversion mentioned in paragraph 3 of this Article is to be made in such a manner as to express in the national currency of the Contracting State as far as possible the same real value for the amounts in Article 6 as is expressed there in units of account. Contracting States must communicate to the depositary the manner of calculation pursuant to paragraph 1 of this article, or the result of the conversion mentioned in paragraph 3 of this article, as the case may be, at the time of signature or when depositing their instruments of ratification, acceptance, approval or accession, or when availing themselves of the option provided for in paragraph 2 of this Article and whenever there is a change in the manner of such calculation or in the result of such conversion.

PART VII - FINAL CLAUSES

Article 27 Depositary [...]

Article 28 Signature, Ratification, Acceptance, Approval, Accession [...]

Article 29 Reservations

No reservations may be made to this Convention.

Article 30 Entry into Force

1. This Convention enters into force on the first day of the month following the expiration of one year from the date of deposit of the 20th instrument of ratification, acceptance, approval or accession.

2. For each State which becomes a Contracting State to this Convention after the date of deposit of the 20th instrument of ratification, acceptance approval or accession, this Convention enters into force on the first day of the month following the expiration of one year after the deposit of the appropriate instrument on behalf of that State.

3. Each Contracting State shall apply the provisions of this Convention to contracts of carriage by sea concluded on or after the date of the entry into force of this Convention in respect of that State.

Article 31 Denunciation of Other Conventions

1. Upon becoming a Contracting State to this Convention, any State party to the International Convention for the Unification of Certain Rules relating to Bills of Lading signed at Brussels on 25 August 1924 (["the Hague Rules"]) must notify the Government of Belgium as the depositary of the 1924 Convention of its denunciation of the said Convention with a declaration that the denunciation is to take effect as from the date when this Convention enters into force in respect of that State.

2. Upon the entry into force of this Convention under paragraph 1 of Article 30, the depositary of this Convention must notify the Government of Belgium as the depositary of the 1924 Convention of the date of such entry into force, and of the names of the Contracting States in respect of which the Convention has entered into force.

3. The provisions of paragraphs 1 and 2 of this Article apply correspondingly in respect of States parties to the Protocol signed on 23 February 1968 to amend the International Convention for the Unification of Certain Rules relating to Bills of Lading signed at Brussels on 25 August 1924 [the "Hague-Visby Rules"].

4. Notwithstanding Article 2 of this Convention, for the purposes of paragraph 1 of this article, a Contracting State may, if it deems it desirable, defer the denunciation of the 1924 Convention and of the 1924 Convention as modified by the 1968 Protocol for a maximum period of five years from the entry into force of this Convention. It will then notify the Government of Belgium of its intention. During this transitory period, it must apply to the Contracting States this Convention to the exclusion of any other one.

Article 32 Revision and Amendment

1. At the request of not less than one-third of the Contracting States to this Convention, the depositary shall convene a conference of the Contracting States for revising or amending it.

2. Any instrument of ratification, acceptance, approval or accession deposited after the entry into force of an amendment to this Convention, is deemed to apply to the Convention as amended.

Article 33 Revision of the Limitation Amounts and Unit of Account or Monetary Unit

1. Notwithstanding the provisions of Article 32, a conference only for the purpose of altering the amount specified in Article 6 and paragraph 2 of Article 26, or of substituting either or both of the units defined in paragraphs 1 and 3 of Article 26 by other units is to be convened by the depositary in accordance with paragraph 2 of this article. An alteration of the amounts shall be made only because of a significant change in their real value.

2. A revision conference is to be convened by the depositary when not less than one-fourth of the Contracting States so request.

3. Any decision by the conference must be taken by a two-thirds majority of the participating States. The amendment is communicated by the depositary to all the Contracting States for acceptance and to all the States signatories of the Convention for information.

4. Any amendment adopted enters into force on the first day of the month following one year after its acceptance by two-thirds of the Contracting States. Acceptance is to be effected by the deposit of a formal instrument to that effect, with the depositary.

5. After entry into force of an amendment a Contracting State which has accepted the amendment is entitled to apply the Convention as amended in its relations with Contracting States which have not within six months after the adoption of the amendment notified the depositary that they are not bound by the amendment.

6. Any instrument of ratification, acceptance, approval or accession deposited after the entry into force of an amendment to this Convention, is deemed to apply to the Convention as amended.

Article 34 Denunciation

1. A Contracting State may denounce this Convention at any time by means of a notification in writing addressed to the depositary.

2. The denunciation takes effect on the first day of the month following the expiration of one year after the notification is received by the depositary. Where a longer period is specified in the notification, the denunciation takes effect upon the expiration of such longer period after the notification is received by the depositary.

DONE at Hamburg, this thirty-first day of March one thousand nine hundred and seventy-eight, in a single original, of which the Arabic, Chinese, English, French, Russian and Spanish texts are equally authentic. [...]

COMMON UNDERSTANDING ADOPTED BY THE UNITED NATIONS CONFERENCE ON THE CARRIAGE OF GOODS BY SEA

It is the common understanding that the liability of the carrier under this Convention is based on the principle of presumed fault or neglect. This means that, as a rule, the burden of proof rests on the carrier but, with respect to certain cases, the provisions of the Convention modify this rule.

Entry into force: 1 November 1992

Ratifications and binding effect as of April 2020: Albania (2007), Austria (1994), Barbados (1992), Botswana (1992), Burkina Faso (1992), Burundi (1999), Cameroon (1994), Chile (1992), Czech Republic (1996), Dominican Republic (2008), Egypt (1992), Gambia (1997), Georgia (1997), Guinea (1992), Hungary (1992), Jordan (2002), Kazakhstan (2009), Kenya (1992), Lebanon (1992), Lesotho (1992), Liberia (2006), Malawi (1992), Morocco (1992), Nigeria (1992), Paraguay (2006), Romania (1992), Senegal (1992), Sierra Leone (1992), St. Vincent and the

Grenadines (2001), Syria (2003), Tanzania (1992), Tunisia (1992), Uganda (1992), Zambia (1992)[1]

---

1 The following countries have signed but not yet ratified the Convention as of April 2020: Brazil, Democratic Republic of Congo, Denmark, Ecuador, Finland, France, Germany, Ghana, Holy See, Madagascar, Mexico, Norway, Pakistan, Panama, Philippines, Portugal, Singapore, Slovakia, Sweden, United States of America, and Venezuela.

32) 2009 United Nations Convention on Contracts for the International Carriage of Goods Wholly or Partly by Sea ("Rotterdam Rules")[1]

THE GENERAL ASSEMBLY,

RECALLING its resolution 2205 (XXI) of 17 December 1966, by which it established the United Nations Commission on International Trade Law with a mandate to further the progressive harmonization and unification of the law of international trade and in that respect to bear in mind the interests of all peoples, in particular those of developing countries, in the extensive development of international trade,

CONCERNED that the current legal regime governing the international carriage of goods by sea lacks uniformity and fails to adequately take into account modern transport practices, including containerization, door-to-door transport contracts and the use of electronic transport documents,

NOTING that the development of international trade on the basis of equality and mutual benefit is an important element in promoting friendly relations among States,

CONVINCED that the adoption of uniform rules to modernize and harmonize the rules that govern the international carriage of goods involving a sea leg would enhance legal certainty, improve efficiency and commercial predictability in the international carriage of goods and reduce legal obstacles to the flow of international trade among all States,

BELIEVING that the adoption of uniform rules to govern international contracts of carriage wholly or partly by sea will promote legal certainty, improve the efficiency of international carriage of goods and facilitate new access opportunities for previously remote parties and markets, thus playing a fundamental role in promoting trade and economic development, both domestically and internationally,

NOTING that shippers and carriers do not have the benefit of a binding and balanced universal regime to support the operation of contracts of carriage involving various modes of transport,

RECALLING that, at its thirty-fourth and thirty-fifth sessions, in 2001 and 2002, the Commission decided to prepare an international legislative instrument governing door-to-door transport operations that involve a sea leg,

RECOGNIZING that all States and interested international organizations were invited to participate in the preparation of the draft Convention on Contracts for the International Carriage of Goods Wholly or Partly by Sea and in the forty-first session of the Commission, either as members or as observers, with a full opportunity to speak and make proposals, [...]

1. COMMENDS the United Nations Commission on International Trade Law for preparing the draft Convention on Contracts for the International Carriage of Goods Wholly or Partly by Sea;

2. ADOPTS the United Nations Convention on Contracts for the International Carriage of Goods Wholly or Partly by Sea, contained in the annex to the present resolution;

3. AUTHORIZES a ceremony for the opening for signature to be held on 23 September 2009 in Rotterdam, the Netherlands, and recommends that the rules embodied in the Convention be known as the "Rotterdam Rules";

4. CALLS UPON all Governments to consider becoming party to the Convention.

67th plenary meeting 11 December 2008

1

Annex

UNITED NATIONS CONVENTION ON CONTRACTS FOR THE INTERNATIONAL CARRIAGE OF GOODS WHOLLY OR PARTLY BY SEA

THE STATES PARTIES TO THIS CONVENTION,

REAFFIRMING their belief that international trade on the basis of equality and mutual benefit is an important element in promoting friendly relations among States,

CONVINCED that the progressive harmonization and unification of international trade law, in reducing or removing legal obstacles to the flow of international trade, significantly contributes to universal economic cooperation among all States on a basis of equality, equity and common interest, and to the well-being of all peoples,

RECOGNIZING the significant contribution of the International Convention for the Unification of Certain Rules of Law relating to Bills of Lading, signed in Brussels on 25 August 1924, and its Protocols, and of the United Nations Convention on the Carriage of Goods by Sea, signed in Hamburg on 31 March 1978, to the harmonization of the law governing the carriage of goods by sea,

MINDFUL of the technological and commercial developments that have taken place since the adoption of those conventions and of the need to consolidate and modernize them,

Noting that shippers and carriers do not have the benefit of a binding universal regime to support the operation of contracts of maritime carriage involving other modes of transport,

BELIEVING that the adoption of uniform rules to govern international contracts of carriage wholly or partly by sea will promote legal certainty, improve the efficiency of international carriage of goods and facilitate new access opportunities for previously remote parties and markets, thus playing a fundamental role in promoting trade and economic development, both domestically and internationally,

HAVE AGREED as follows:

Chapter 1 General Provisions

Article 1 Definitions

For the purposes of this Convention:

1. "Contract of carriage" means a contract in which a carrier, against the payment of freight, undertakes to carry goods from one place to another. The contract shall provide for carriage by sea and may provide for carriage by other modes of transport in addition to the sea carriage.

2. "Volume contract" means a contract of carriage that provides for the carriage of a specified quantity of goods in a series of shipments during an agreed period of time. The specification of the quantity may include a minimum, a maximum or a certain range.

3. "Liner transportation" means a transportation service that is offered to the public through publication or similar means and includes transportation by ships operating on a regular schedule between specified ports in accordance with publicly available timetables of sailing dates.

4. "Non-liner transportation" means any transportation that is not liner transportation.

5. "Carrier" means a person that enters into a contract of carriage with a shipper.

6.(a) "Performing party" means a person other than the carrier that performs or undertakes to perform any of the carrier's obligations under a contract of carriage with respect to the receipt, loading, handling, stowage, carriage, care, unloading or delivery of the goods, to the extent that such person acts, either directly or indirectly, at the carrier's request or under the carrier's supervision or control.

(b) “Performing party” does not include any person that is retained, directly or indirectly, by a shipper, by a documentary shipper, by the controlling party or by the consignee instead of by the carrier.

7. “Maritime performing party” means a performing party to the extent that it performs or undertakes to perform any of the carrier’s obligations during the period between the arrival of the goods at the port of loading of a ship and their departure from the port of discharge of a ship. An inland carrier is a maritime performing party only if it performs or undertakes to perform its services exclusively within a port area.

8. “Shipper” means a person that enters into a contract of carriage with a carrier.

9. “Documentary shipper” means a person, other than the shipper, that accepts to be named as “shipper” in the transport document or electronic transport record.

10. “Holder” means:

(a) A person that is in possession of a negotiable transport document; and (i) if the document is an order document, is identified in it as the shipper or the consignee, or is the person to which the document is duly endorsed; or (ii) if the document is a blank endorsed order document or bearer document, is the bearer thereof; or

(b) The person to which a negotiable electronic transport record has been issued or transferred in accordance with the procedures referred to in Article 9, paragraph 1.

11. “Consignee” means a person entitled to delivery of the goods under a contract of carriage or a transport document or electronic transport record.

12. “Right of control” of the goods means the right under the contract of carriage to give the carrier instructions in respect of the goods in accordance with chapter 10.

13. “Controlling party” means the person that pursuant to Article 51 is entitled to exercise the right of control.

14. “Transport document” means a document issued under a contract of carriage by the carrier that:

(a) Evidences the carrier’s or a performing party’s receipt of goods under a contract of carriage; and

(b) Evidences or contains a contract of carriage.

15. “Negotiable transport document” means a transport document that indicates, by wording such as “to order” or “negotiable” or other appropriate wording recognized as having the same effect by the law applicable to the document, that the goods have been consigned to the order of the shipper, to the order of the consignee, or to bearer, and is not explicitly stated as being “non-negotiable” or “not negotiable”.

16. “Non-negotiable transport document” means a transport document that is not a negotiable transport document.

17. “Electronic communication” means information generated, sent, received or stored by electronic, optical, digital or similar means with the result that the information communicated is accessible so as to be usable for subsequent reference.

18. “Electronic transport record” means information in one or more messages issued by electronic communication under a contract of carriage by a carrier, including information logically associated with the electronic transport record by attachments or otherwise linked to the electronic transport record contemporaneously with or subsequent to its issue by the carrier, so as to become part of the electronic transport record, that:

(a) Evidences the carrier’s or a performing party’s receipt of goods under a contract of carriage; and

(b) Evidences or contains a contract of carriage.

19. "Negotiable electronic transport record" means an electronic transport record:

(a) That indicates, by wording such as "to order", or "negotiable", or other appropriate wording recognized as having the same effect by the law applicable to the record, that the goods have been consigned to the order of the shipper or to the order of the consignee, and is not explicitly stated as being "non-negotiable" or "not negotiable"; and

(b) The use of which meets the requirements of Article 9, paragraph 1.

20. "Non-negotiable electronic transport record" means an electronic transport record that is not a negotiable electronic transport record.

21. The "issuance" of a negotiable electronic transport record means the issuance of the record in accordance with procedures that ensure that the record is subject to exclusive control from its creation until it ceases to have any effect or validity.

22. The "transfer" of a negotiable electronic transport record means the transfer of exclusive control over the record.

23. "Contract particulars" means any information relating to the contract of carriage or to the goods (including terms, notations, signatures and endorsements) that is in a transport document or an electronic transport record.

24. "Goods" means the wares, merchandise, and articles of every kind whatsoever that a carrier undertakes to carry under a contract of carriage and includes the packing and any equipment and container not supplied by or on behalf of the carrier.

25. "Ship" means any vessel used to carry goods by sea.

26. "Container" means any type of container, transportable tank or flat, swapbody, or any similar unit load used to consolidate goods, and any equipment ancillary to such unit load.

27. "Vehicle" means a road or railroad cargo vehicle.

28. "Freight" means the remuneration payable to the carrier for the carriage of goods under a contract of carriage.

29. "Domicile" means (*a*) a place where a company or other legal person or association of natural or legal persons has its (i) statutory seat or place of incorporation or central registered office, whichever is applicable, (ii) central administration or (iii) principal place of business, and (*b*) the habitual residence of a natural person.

30. "Competent court" means a court in a Contracting State that, according to the rules on the internal allocation of jurisdiction among the courts of that State, may exercise jurisdiction over the dispute.

Article 2 Interpretation of this Convention

In the interpretation of this Convention, regard is to be had to its international character and to the need to promote uniformity in its application and the observance of good faith in international trade.

Article 3 Form Requirements

The notices, confirmation, consent, agreement, declaration and other communications referred to in articles 19, paragraph 2; 23, paragraphs 1 to 4; 36, subparagraphs 1 (*b*), (*c*) and (*d*); 40, subparagraph 4 (*b*); 44; 48, paragraph 3; 51, subparagraph 1 (*b*); 59, paragraph 1; 63; 66; 67, paragraph 2; 75, paragraph 4; and 80, paragraphs 2 and 5, shall be in writing. Electronic communications may be used for these purposes, provided that the use of such means is with the consent of the person by which it is communicated and of the person to which it is communicated.

Article 4 Applicability of Defences and Limits of Liability

1. Any provision of this Convention that may provide a defence for, or limit the liability of, the carrier applies in any judicial or arbitral proceeding, whether founded in contract, in tort, or otherwise, that is instituted in respect of loss of, damage to, or delay in delivery of goods covered by a contract of carriage or for the breach of any other obligation under this Convention against:

(a) The carrier or a maritime performing party;

(b) The master, crew or any other person that performs services on board the ship; or

(c) Employees of the carrier or a maritime performing party.

2. Any provision of this Convention that may provide a defence for the shipper or the documentary shipper applies in any judicial or arbitral proceeding, whether founded in contract, in tort, or otherwise, that is instituted against the shipper, the documentary shipper, or their subcontractors, agents or employees.

Chapter 2 Scope of Application

Article 5 General Scope of Application

1. Subject to Article 6, this Convention applies to contracts of carriage in which the place of receipt and the place of delivery are in different States, and the port of loading of a sea carriage and the port of discharge of the same sea carriage are in different States, if, according to the contract of carriage, any one of the following places is located in a Contracting State:

(a) The place of receipt;

(b) The port of loading;

(c) The place of delivery; or

(d) The port of discharge.

2. This Convention applies without regard to the nationality of the vessel, the carrier, the performing parties, the shipper, the consignee, or any other interested parties.

Article 6 Specific Exclusions

1. This Convention does not apply to the following contracts in liner transportation:

(a) Charter parties; and

(b) Other contracts for the use of a ship or of any space thereon.

2. This Convention does not apply to contracts of carriage in non-liner transportation except when:

(a) There is no charter party or other contract between the parties for the use of a ship or of any space thereon; and

(b) A transport document or an electronic transport record is issued.

Article 7 Application to Certain Parties

Notwithstanding Article 6, this Convention applies as between the carrier and the consignee, controlling party or holder that is not an original party to the charter party or other contract of carriage excluded from the application of this Convention. However, this Convention does not apply as between the original parties to a contract of carriage excluded pursuant to Article 6.

Chapter 3 Electronic Transport Records

Article 8 Use and Effect of Electronic Transport Records

Subject to the requirements set out in this Convention:

(a) Anything that is to be in or on a transport document under this Convention may be recorded in an electronic transport record, provided the issuance and subsequent use of an electronic transport record is with the consent of the carrier and the shipper; and

(b) The issuance, exclusive control, or transfer of an electronic transport record has the same effect as the issuance, possession, or transfer of a transport document.

Article 9 Procedures for Use of Negotiable Electronic Transport Records

1. The use of a negotiable electronic transport record shall be subject to procedures that provide for:

(a) The method for the issuance and the transfer of that record to an intended holder;

(b) An assurance that the negotiable electronic transport record retains its integrity;

(c) The manner in which the holder is able to demonstrate that it is the holder; and

(d) The manner of providing confirmation that delivery to the holder has been effected, or that, pursuant to articles 10, paragraph 2, or 47, subparagraphs 1 (a) (ii) and (c), the electronic transport record has ceased to have any effect or validity.

2. The procedures in paragraph 1 of this Article shall be referred to in the contract particulars and be readily ascertainable.

Article 10 Replacement of Negotiable Transport Document or Negotiable Electronic Transport Record

1. If a negotiable transport document has been issued and the carrier and the holder agree to replace that document by a negotiable electronic transport record:

(a) The holder shall surrender the negotiable transport document, or all of them if more than one has been issued, to the carrier;

(b) The carrier shall issue to the holder a negotiable electronic transport record that includes a statement that it replaces the negotiable transport document; and

(c) The negotiable transport document ceases thereafter to have any effect or validity.

2. If a negotiable electronic transport record has been issued and the carrier and the holder agree to replace that electronic transport record by a negotiable transport document:

(a) The carrier shall issue to the holder, in place of the electronic transport record, a negotiable transport document that includes a statement that it replaces the negotiable electronic transport record; and

(b) The electronic transport record ceases thereafter to have any effect or validity.

Chapter 4 Obligations of the Carrier

Article 11 Carriage and Delivery of the Goods

The carrier shall, subject to this Convention and in accordance with the terms of the contract of carriage, carry the goods to the place of destination and deliver them to the consignee.

Article 12 Period of Responsibility of the Carrier

1. The period of responsibility of the carrier for the goods under this Convention begins when the carrier or a performing party receives the goods for carriage and ends when the goods are delivered.

2.(a) If the law or regulations of the place of receipt require the goods to be handed over to an authority or other third party from which the carrier may collect them, the period of responsibility of the carrier begins when the carrier collects the goods from the authority or other third party.

(b) If the law or regulations of the place of delivery require the carrier to hand over the goods to an authority or other third party from which the consignee may collect them, the period of responsibility of the carrier ends when the carrier hands the goods over to the authority or other third party.

3. For the purpose of determining the carrier's period of responsibility, the parties may agree on the time and location of receipt and delivery of the goods, but a provision in a contract of carriage is void to the extent that it provides that:

(a) The time of receipt of the goods is subsequent to the beginning of their initial loading under the contract of carriage; or

(b) The time of delivery of the goods is prior to the completion of their final unloading under the contract of carriage.

Article 13 Specific Obligations

1. The carrier shall during the period of its responsibility as defined in Article 12, and subject to Article 26, properly and carefully receive, load, handle, stow, carry, keep, care for, unload and deliver the goods.

2. Notwithstanding paragraph 1 of this article, and without prejudice to the other provisions in chapter 4 and to chapters 5 to 7, the carrier and the shipper may agree that the loading, handling, stowing or unloading of the goods is to be performed by the shipper, the documentary shipper or the consignee. Such an agreement shall be referred to in the contract particulars.

Article 14 Specific Obligations Applicable to the Voyage by Sea

The carrier is bound before, at the beginning of, and during the voyage by sea to exercise due diligence to:

(a) Make and keep the ship seaworthy;

(b) Properly crew, equip and supply the ship and keep the ship so crewed, equipped and supplied throughout the voyage; and

(c) Make and keep the holds and all other parts of the ship in which the goods are carried, and any containers supplied by the carrier in or upon which the goods are carried, fit and safe for their reception, carriage and preservation.

Article 15 Goods That May Become a Danger

Notwithstanding articles 11 and 13, the carrier or a performing party may decline to receive or to load, and may take such other measures as are reasonable, including unloading, destroying, or rendering goods harmless, if the goods are, or reasonably appear likely to become during the carrier's period of responsibility, an actual danger to persons, property or the environment.

Article 16 Sacrifice of the Goods During the Voyage by Sea

Notwithstanding articles 11, 13, and 14, the carrier or a performing party may sacrifice goods at sea when the sacrifice is reasonably made for the common safety or for the purpose of preserving from peril human life or other property involved in the common adventure.

Chapter 5 Liability of the Carrier for Loss, Damage or Delay

Article 17 Basis of Liability

1. The carrier is liable for loss of or damage to the goods, as well as for delay in delivery, if the claimant proves that the loss, damage, or delay, or the event or circumstance that caused

or contributed to it took place during the period of the carrier's responsibility as defined in chapter 4.

2. The carrier is relieved of all or part of its liability pursuant to paragraph 1 of this Article if it proves that the cause or one of the causes of the loss, damage, or delay is not attributable to its fault or to the fault of any person referred to in Article 18.

3. The carrier is also relieved of all or part of its liability pursuant to paragraph 1 of this Article if, alternatively to proving the absence of fault as provided in paragraph 2 of this article, it proves that one or more of the following events or circumstances caused or contributed to the loss, damage, or delay:

(a) Act of God;

(b) Perils, dangers, and accidents of the sea or other navigable waters;

(c) War, hostilities, armed conflict, piracy, terrorism, riots, and civil commotions;

(d) Quarantine restrictions; interference by or impediments created by governments, public authorities, rulers, or people including detention, arrest, or seizure not attributable to the carrier or any person referred to in Article 18;

(e) Strikes, lockouts, stoppages, or restraints of labour;

(f) Fire on the ship;

(g) Latent defects not discoverable by due diligence;

(h) Act or omission of the shipper, the documentary shipper, the controlling party, or any other person for whose acts the shipper or the documentary shipper is liable pursuant to Article 33 or 34;

(i) Loading, handling, stowing, or unloading of the goods performed pursuant to an agreement in accordance with Article 13, paragraph 2, unless the carrier or a performing party performs such activity on behalf of the shipper, the documentary shipper or the consignee;

(j) Wastage in bulk or weight or any other loss or damage arising from inherent defect, quality, or vice of the goods;

(k) Insufficiency or defective condition of packing or marking not performed by or on behalf of the carrier;

(l) Saving or attempting to save life at sea;

(m) Reasonable measures to save or attempt to save property at sea;

(n) Reasonable measures to avoid or attempt to avoid damage to the environment; or

(o) Acts of the carrier in pursuance of the powers conferred by articles 15 and 16.

4. Notwithstanding paragraph 3 of this article, the carrier is liable for all or part of the loss, damage, or delay:

(a) If the claimant proves that the fault of the carrier or of a person referred to in Article 18 caused or contributed to the event or circumstance on which the carrier relies; or

(b) If the claimant proves that an event or circumstance not listed in paragraph 3 of this Article contributed to the loss, damage, or delay, and the carrier cannot prove that this event or circumstance is not attributable to its fault or to the fault of any person referred to in Article 18.

5. The carrier is also liable, notwithstanding paragraph 3 of this article, for all or part of the loss, damage, or delay if:

(a) The claimant proves that the loss, damage, or delay was or was probably caused by or contributed to by (i) the unseaworthiness of the ship; (ii) the improper crewing, equipping, and supplying of the ship; or (iii) the fact that the holds or other parts of the ship in which the goods are carried, or any containers supplied by the carrier in or upon which the goods are carried, were not fit and safe for reception, carriage, and preservation of the goods; and

(b) The carrier is unable to prove either that: (i) none of the events or circumstances referred to in subparagraph 5 (*a*) of this Article caused the loss, damage, or delay; or (ii) it complied with its obligation to exercise due diligence pursuant to Article 14.

6. When the carrier is relieved of part of its liability pursuant to this article, the carrier is liable only for that part of the loss, damage or delay that is attributable to the event or circumstance for which it is liable pursuant to this article.

Article 18 Liability of the Carrier for Other Persons

The carrier is liable for the breach of its obligations under this Convention caused by the acts or omissions of:

(a) Any performing party;

(b) The master or crew of the ship;

(c) Employees of the carrier or a performing party; or

(d) Any other person that performs or undertakes to perform any of the carrier's obligations under the contract of carriage, to the extent that the person acts, either directly or indirectly, at the carrier's request or under the carrier's supervision or control.

Article 19 Liability of Maritime Performing Parties

1. A maritime performing party is subject to the obligations and liabilities imposed on the carrier under this Convention and is entitled to the carrier's defences and limits of liability as provided for in this Convention if:

(*a*) The maritime performing party received the goods for carriage in a Contracting State, or delivered them in a Contracting State, or performed its activities with respect to the goods in a port in a Contracting State; and

(*b*) The occurrence that caused the loss, damage or delay took place: (i) during the period between the arrival of the goods at the port of loading of the ship and their departure from the port of discharge from the ship; (ii) while the maritime performing party had custody of the goods; or (iii) at any other time to the extent that it was participating in the performance of any of the activities contemplated by the contract of carriage.

2. If the carrier agrees to assume obligations other than those imposed on the carrier under this Convention, or agrees that the limits of its liability are higher than the limits specified under this Convention, a maritime performing party is not bound by this agreement unless it expressly agrees to accept such obligations or such higher limits.

3. A maritime performing party is liable for the breach of its obligations under this Convention caused by the acts or omissions of any person to which it has entrusted the performance of any of the carrier's obligations under the contract of carriage under the conditions set out in paragraph 1 of this article.

4. Nothing in this Convention imposes liability on the master or crew of the ship or on an employee of the carrier or of a maritime performing party.

Article 20 Joint and Several Liability

1. If the carrier and one or more maritime performing parties are liable for the loss of, damage to, or delay in delivery of the goods, their liability is joint and several but only up to the limits provided for under this Convention.

2. Without prejudice to Article 61, the aggregate liability of all such persons shall not exceed the overall limits of liability under this Convention.

Article 21 Delay

Delay in delivery occurs when the goods are not delivered at the place of destination provided for in the contract of carriage within the time agreed.

Article 22 Calculation of Compensation

1. Subject to Article 59, the compensation payable by the carrier for loss of or damage to the goods is calculated by reference to the value of such goods at the place and time of delivery established in accordance with Article 43.

2. The value of the goods is fixed according to the commodity exchange price or, if there is no such price, according to their market price or, if there is no commodity exchange price or market price, by reference to the normal value of the goods of the same kind and quality at the place of delivery.

3. In case of loss of or damage to the goods, the carrier is not liable for payment of any compensation beyond what is provided for in paragraphs 1 and 2 of this Article except when the carrier and the shipper have agreed to calculate compensation in a different manner within the limits of chapter 16.

Article 23 Notice in Case of Loss, Damage or Delay

1. The carrier is presumed, in absence of proof to the contrary, to have delivered the goods according to their description in the contract particulars unless notice of loss of or damage to the goods, indicating the general nature of such loss or damage, was given to the carrier or the performing party that delivered the goods before or at the time of the delivery, or, if the loss or damage is not apparent, within seven working days at the place of delivery after the delivery of the goods.

2. Failure to provide the notice referred to in this Article to the carrier or the performing party shall not affect the right to claim compensation for loss of or damage to the goods under this Convention, nor shall it affect the allocation of the burden of proof set out in Article 17.

3. The notice referred to in this Article is not required in respect of loss or damage that is ascertained in a joint inspection of the goods by the person to which they have been delivered and the carrier or the maritime performing party against which liability is being asserted.

4. No compensation in respect of delay is payable unless notice of loss due to delay was given to the carrier within twenty-one consecutive days of delivery of the goods.

5. When the notice referred to in this Article is given to the performing party that delivered the goods, it has the same effect as if that notice was given to the carrier, and notice given to the carrier has the same effect as a notice given to a maritime performing party.

6. In the case of any actual or apprehended loss or damage, the parties to the dispute shall give all reasonable facilities to each other for inspecting and tallying the goods and shall provide access to records and documents relevant to the carriage of the goods.

Chapter 6 Additional Provisions Relating to Particular Stages of Carriage

Article 24 Deviation

When pursuant to applicable law a deviation constitutes a breach of the carrier's obligations, such deviation of itself shall not deprive the carrier or a maritime performing party of any defence or limitation of this Convention, except to the extent provided in Article 61.

Article 25 Deck Cargo on Ships

1. Goods may be carried on the deck of a ship only if:

(a) Such carriage is required by law;

(b) They are carried in or on containers or vehicles that are fit for deck carriage, and the decks are specially fitted to carry such containers or vehicles; or

(c) The carriage on deck is in accordance with the contract of carriage, or the customs, usages or practices of the trade in question.

2. The provisions of this Convention relating to the liability of the carrier apply to the loss of, damage to or delay in the delivery of goods carried on deck pursuant to paragraph 1 of this article, but the carrier is not liable for loss of or damage to such goods, or delay in their delivery, caused by the special risks involved in their carriage on deck when the goods are carried in accordance with subparagraphs 1 (*a*) or (*c*) of this article.

3. If the goods have been carried on deck in cases other than those permitted pursuant to paragraph 1 of this article, the carrier is liable for loss of or damage to the goods or delay in their delivery that is exclusively caused by their carriage on deck, and is not entitled to the defences provided for in Article 17.

4. The carrier is not entitled to invoke subparagraph 1 (*c*) of this Article against a third party that has acquired a negotiable transport document or a negotiable electronic transport record in good faith, unless the contract particulars state that the goods may be carried on deck.

5. If the carrier and shipper expressly agreed that the goods would be carried under deck, the carrier is not entitled to the benefit of the limitation of liability for any loss of, damage to or delay in the delivery of the goods to the extent that such loss, damage, or delay resulted from their carriage on deck.

Article 26 Carriage Preceding or Subsequent to Sea Carriage

When loss of or damage to goods, or an event or circumstance causing a delay in their delivery, occurs during the carrier's period of responsibility but solely before their loading onto the ship or solely after their discharge from the ship, the provisions of this Convention do not prevail over those provisions of another international instrument that, at the time of such loss, damage or event or circumstance causing delay:

(a) Pursuant to the provisions of such international instrument would have applied to all or any of the carrier's activities if the shipper had made a separate and direct contract with the carrier in respect of the particular stage of carriage where the loss of, or damage to goods, or an event or circumstance causing delay in their delivery occurred;

(b) Specifically provide for the carrier's liability, limitation of liability, or time for suit; and

(c) Cannot be departed from by contract either at all or to the detriment of the shipper under that instrument.

Chapter 7 Obligations of the Shipper to the Carrier

Article 27 Delivery for Carriage

1. Unless otherwise agreed in the contract of carriage, the shipper shall deliver the goods ready for carriage. In any event, the shipper shall deliver the goods in such condition that they will withstand the intended carriage, including their loading, handling, stowing, lashing and securing, and unloading, and that they will not cause harm to persons or property.

2. The shipper shall properly and carefully perform any obligation assumed under an agreement made pursuant to Article 13, paragraph 2.

3. When a container is packed or a vehicle is loaded by the shipper, the shipper shall properly and carefully stow, lash and secure the contents in or on the container or vehicle, and in such a way that they will not cause harm to persons or property.

Article 28 Cooperation of the Shipper and the Carrier in Providing Information and Instructions

The carrier and the shipper shall respond to requests from each other to provide information and instructions required for the proper handling and carriage of the goods if the information is in the requested party's possession or the instructions are within the requested party's reasonable ability to provide and they are not otherwise reasonably available to the requesting party.

Article 29 Shipper's Obligation to Provide Information, Instructions and Documents

1. The shipper shall provide to the carrier in a timely manner such information, instructions and documents relating to the goods that are not otherwise reasonably available to the carrier, and that are reasonably necessary:

(a) For the proper handling and carriage of the goods, including precautions to be taken by the carrier or a performing party; and

(b) For the carrier to comply with law, regulations or other requirements of public authorities in connection with the intended carriage, provided that the carrier notifies the shipper in a timely manner of the information, instructions and documents it requires.

2. Nothing in this Article affects any specific obligation to provide certain information, instructions and documents related to the goods pursuant to law, regulations or other requirements of public authorities in connection with the intended carriage.

Article 30 Basis of Shipper's Liability to the Carrier

1. The shipper is liable for loss or damage sustained by the carrier if the carrier proves that such loss or damage was caused by a breach of the shipper's obligations under this Convention.

2. Except in respect of loss or damage caused by a breach by the shipper of its obligations pursuant to articles 31, paragraph 2, and 32, the shipper is relieved of all or part of its liability if the cause or one of the causes of the loss or damage is not attributable to its fault or to the fault of any person referred to in Article 34.

3. When the shipper is relieved of part of its liability pursuant to this article, the shipper is liable only for that part of the loss or damage that is attributable to its fault or to the fault of any person referred to in Article 34.

Article 31 Information for Compilation of Contract Particulars

1. The shipper shall provide to the carrier, in a timely manner, accurate information required for the compilation of the contract particulars and the issuance of the transport documents or electronic transport records, including the particulars referred to in Articlc 36, paragraph 1; the name of the party to be identified as the shipper in the contract particulars; the name of the

consignee, if any; and the name of the person to whose order the transport document or electronic transport record is to be issued, if any.

2. The shipper is deemed to have guaranteed the accuracy at the time of receipt by the carrier of the information that is provided according to paragraph 1 of this article. The shipper shall indemnify the carrier against loss or damage resulting from the inaccuracy of such information.

Article 32 Special Rules on Dangerous Goods

When goods by their nature or character are, or reasonably appear likely to become, a danger to persons, property or the environment:

(a) The shipper shall inform the carrier of the dangerous nature or character of the goods in a timely manner before they are delivered to the carrier or a performing party. If the shipper fails to do so and the carrier or performing party does not otherwise have knowledge of their dangerous nature or character, the shipper is liable to the carrier for loss or damage resulting from such failure to inform; and

(b) The shipper shall mark or label dangerous goods in accordance with any law, regulations or other requirements of public authorities that apply during any stage of the intended carriage of the goods. If the shipper fails to do so, it is liable to the carrier for loss or damage resulting from such failure.

Article 33 Assumption of Shipper's Rights and Obligations by the Documentary Shipper

1. A documentary shipper is subject to the obligations and liabilities imposed on the shipper pursuant to this chapter and pursuant to Article 55, and is entitled to the shipper's rights and defences provided by this chapter and by chapter 13.

2. Paragraph 1 of this Article does not affect the obligations, liabilities, rights or defences of the shipper.

Article 34 Liability of the Shipper for Other Persons

The shipper is liable for the breach of its obligations under this Convention caused by the acts or omissions of any person, including employees, agents and subcontractors, to which it has entrusted the performance of any of its obligations, but the shipper is not liable for acts or omissions of the carrier or a performing party acting on behalf of the carrier, to which the shipper has entrusted the performance of its obligations.

Chapter 8 Transport Documents and Electronic Transport Records

Article 35 Issuance of the Transport Document or the Electronic Transport Record

Unless the shipper and the carrier have agreed not to use a transport document or an electronic transport record, or it is the custom, usage or practice of the trade not to use one, upon delivery of the goods for carriage to the carrier or performing party, the shipper or, if the shipper consents, the documentary shipper, is entitled to obtain from the carrier, at the shipper's option:

(a) A non-negotiable transport document or, subject to Article 8, subparagraph (a), a non-negotiable electronic transport record; or

(b) An appropriate negotiable transport document or, subject to Article 8, subparagraph (*a*), a negotiable electronic transport record, unless the shipper and the carrier have agreed not to use a negotiable transport document or negotiable electronic transport record, or it is the custom, usage or practice of the trade not to use one.

Article 36 Contract Particulars

1. The contract particulars in the transport document or electronic transport record referred to in Article 35 shall include the following information, as furnished by the shipper:

(a) A description of the goods as appropriate for the transport;

(b) The leading marks necessary for identification of the goods;

(c) The number of packages or pieces, or the quantity of goods; and

(d) The weight of the goods, if furnished by the shipper.

2. The contract particulars in the transport document or electronic transport record referred to in Article 35 shall also include:

(a) A statement of the apparent order and condition of the goods at the time the carrier or a performing party receives them for carriage;

(b) The name and address of the carrier;

(c) The date on which the carrier or a performing party received the goods, or on which the goods were loaded on board the ship, or on which the transport document or electronic transport record was issued; and

(d) If the transport document is negotiable, the number of originals of the negotiable transport document, when more than one original is issued.

3. The contract particulars in the transport document or electronic transport record referred to in Article 35 shall further include:

(a) The name and address of the consignee, if named by the shipper;

(b) The name of a ship, if specified in the contract of carriage;

(c) The place of receipt and, if known to the carrier, the place of delivery; and

(d) The port of loading and the port of discharge, if specified in the contract of carriage.

4. For the purposes of this article, the phrase "apparent order and condition of the goods" in subparagraph 2 (*a*) of this Article refers to the order and condition of the goods based on:

(a) A reasonable external inspection of the goods as packaged at the time the shipper delivers them to the carrier or a performing party; and

(b) Any additional inspection that the carrier or a performing party actually performs before issuing the transport document or electronic transport record.

Article 37 Identity of the Carrier

1. If a carrier is identified by name in the contract particulars, any other information in the transport document or electronic transport record relating to the identity of the carrier shall have no effect to the extent that it is inconsistent with that identification.

2. If no person is identified in the contract particulars as the carrier as required pursuant to Article 36, subparagraph 2 (*b*), but the contract particulars indicate that the goods have been loaded on board a named ship, the registered owner of that ship is presumed to be the carrier, unless it proves that the ship was under a bareboat charter at the time of the carriage and it identifies this bareboat charterer and indicates its address, in which case this bareboat charterer is presumed to be the carrier. Alternatively, the registered owner may rebut the presumption of being the carrier by identifying the carrier and indicating its address. The bareboat charterer may rebut any presumption of being the carrier in the same manner.

3. Nothing in this Article prevents the claimant from proving that any person other than a person identified in the contract particulars or pursuant to paragraph 2 of this Article is the carrier.

Article 38 Signature

1. A transport document shall be signed by the carrier or a person acting on its behalf.

2. An electronic transport record shall include the electronic signature of the carrier or a person acting on its behalf. Such electronic signature shall identify the signatory in relation to the electronic transport record and indicate the carrier's authorization of the electronic transport record.

Article 39 Deficiencies in the Contract Particulars

1. The absence or inaccuracy of one or more of the contract particulars referred to in Article 36, paragraphs 1, 2 or 3, does not of itself affect the legal character or validity of the transport document or of the electronic transport record.

2. If the contract particulars include the date but fail to indicate its significance, the date is deemed to be:

(a) The date on which all of the goods indicated in the transport document or electronic transport record were loaded on board the ship, if the contract particulars indicate that the goods have been loaded on board a ship; or

(b) The date on which the carrier or a performing party received the goods, if the contract particulars do not indicate that the goods have been loaded on board a ship.

3. If the contract particulars fail to state the apparent order and condition of the goods at the time the carrier or a performing party receives them, the contract particulars are deemed to have stated that the goods were in apparent good order and condition at the time the carrier or a performing party received them.

Article 40 Qualifying the Information Relating to the Goods in the Contract Particulars

1. The carrier shall qualify the information referred to in Article 36, paragraph 1, to indicate that the carrier does not assume responsibility for the accuracy of the information furnished by the shipper if:

(a) The carrier has actual knowledge that any material statement in the transport document or electronic transport record is false or misleading; or

(b) The carrier has reasonable grounds to believe that a material statement in the transport document or electronic transport record is false or misleading.

2. Without prejudice to paragraph 1 of this article, the carrier may qualify the information referred to in Article 36, paragraph 1, in the circumstances and in the manner set out in paragraphs 3 and 4 of this Article to indicate that the carrier does not assume responsibility for the accuracy of the information furnished by the shipper.

3. When the goods are not delivered for carriage to the carrier or a performing party in a closed container or vehicle, or when they are delivered in a closed container or vehicle and the carrier or a performing party actually inspects them, the carrier may qualify the information referred to in Article 36, paragraph 1, if:

(a) The carrier had no physically practicable or commercially reasonable means of checking the information furnished by the shipper, in which case it may indicate which information it was unable to check; or

(b) The carrier has reasonable grounds to believe the information furnished by the shipper to be inaccurate, in which case it may include a clause providing what it reasonably considers accurate information.

4. When the goods are delivered for carriage to the carrier or a performing party in a closed container or vehicle, the carrier may qualify the information referred to in:

(a) Article 36, subparagraphs 1 (a), (b), or (c), if:

(i) The goods inside the container or vehicle have not actually been inspected by the carrier or a performing party; and

(ii) Neither the carrier nor a performing party otherwise has actual knowledge of its contents before issuing the transport document or the electronic transport record; and

(b) Article 36, subparagraph 1 (*d*), if:

(i) Neither the carrier nor a performing party weighed the container or vehicle, and the shipper and the carrier had not agreed prior to the shipment that the container or vehicle would be weighed and the weight would be included in the contract particulars; or

(ii) There was no physically practicable or commercially reasonable means of checking the weight of the container or vehicle.

Article 41 Evidentiary Effect of the Contract Particulars

Except to the extent that the contract particulars have been qualified in the circumstances and in the manner set out in Article 40:

(a) A transport document or an electronic transport record is prima facie evidence of the carrier's receipt of the goods as stated in the contract particulars;

(b) Proof to the contrary by the carrier in respect of any contract particulars shall not be admissible, when such contract particulars are included in:

(i) A negotiable transport document or a negotiable electronic transport record that is transferred to a third party acting in good faith; or

(ii) A non-negotiable transport document that indicates that it must be surrendered in order to obtain delivery of the goods and is transferred to the consignee acting in good faith;

(*c*) Proof to the contrary by the carrier shall not be admissible against a consignee that in good faith has acted in reliance on any of the following contract particulars included in a non-negotiable transport document or a non-negotiable electronic transport record:

(i) The contract particulars referred to in Article 36, paragraph 1, when such contract particulars are furnished by the carrier;

(ii) The number, type and identifying numbers of the containers, but not the identifying numbers of the container seals; and

(iii) The contract particulars referred to in Article 36, paragraph 2.

Article 42 "Freight Prepaid"

If the contract particulars contain the statement "freight prepaid" or a statement of a similar nature, the carrier cannot assert against the holder or the consignee the fact that the freight has not been paid. This Article does not apply if the holder or the consignee is also the shipper.

Chapter 9 Delivery of the Goods

Article 43 Obligation to Accept Delivery

When the goods have arrived at their destination, the consignee that demands delivery of the goods under the contract of carriage shall accept delivery of the goods at the time or within the time period and at the location agreed in the contract of carriage or, failing such agreement, at the time and location at which, having regard to the terms of the contract, the customs, usages or practices of the trade and the circumstances of the carriage, delivery could reasonably be expected.

Article 44 Obligation to Acknowledge Receipt

On request of the carrier or the performing party that delivers the goods, the consignee shall acknowledge receipt of the goods from the carrier or the performing party in the manner that is customary at the place of delivery. The carrier may refuse delivery if the consignee refuses to acknowledge such receipt.

Article 45 Delivery When No Negotiable Transport Document or Negotiable Electronic Transport Record Is Issued

When neither a negotiable transport document nor a negotiable electronic transport record has been issued:

(a) The carrier shall deliver the goods to the consignee at the time and location referred to in Article 43. The carrier may refuse delivery if the person claiming to be the consignee does not properly identify itself as the consignee on the request of the carrier;

(b) If the name and address of the consignee are not referred to in the contract particulars, the controlling party shall prior to or upon the arrival of the goods at the place of destination advise the carrier of such name and address;

(c) Without prejudice to Article 48, paragraph 1, if the goods are not deliverable because (i) the consignee, after having received a notice of arrival, does not, at the time or within the time period referred to in Article 43, claim delivery of the goods from the carrier after their arrival at the place of destination, (ii) the carrier refuses delivery because the person claiming to be the consignee does not properly identify itself as the consignee, or (iii) the carrier is, after reasonable effort, unable to locate the consignee in order to request delivery instructions, the carrier may so advise the controlling party and request instructions in respect of the delivery of the goods. If, after reasonable effort, the carrier is unable to locate the controlling party, the carrier may so advise the shipper and request instructions in respect of the delivery of the goods. If, after reasonable effort, the carrier is unable to locate the shipper, the carrier may so advise the documentary shipper and request instructions in respect of the delivery of the goods;

(d) The carrier that delivers the goods upon instruction of the controlling party, the shipper or the documentary shipper pursuant to subparagraph (*c*) of this Article is discharged from its obligations to deliver the goods under the contract of carriage.

Article 46 Delivery When a Non-Negotiable Transport Document That Requires Surrender Is Issued

When a non-negotiable transport document has been issued that indicates that it shall be surrendered in order to obtain delivery of the goods:

(a) The carrier shall deliver the goods at the time and location referred to in Article 43 to the consignee upon the consignee properly identifying itself on the request of the carrier and surrender of the non-negotiable document. The carrier may refuse delivery if the person claiming to be the consignee fails to properly identify itself on the request of the carrier, and shall refuse delivery if the non-negotiable document is not surrendered. If more than one original of the non-negotiable document has been issued, the surrender of one original will suffice and the other originals cease to have any effect or validity;

(b) Without prejudice to Article 48, paragraph 1, if the goods are not deliverable because (i) the consignee, after having received a notice of arrival, does not, at the time or within the time period referred to in Article 43, claim delivery of the goods from the carrier after their arrival at the place of destination, (ii) the carrier refuses delivery because the person claiming to be the consignee does not properly identify itself as the consignee or does not surrender the document, or (iii) the carrier is, after reasonable effort, unable to locate the consignee in order to request delivery instructions, the carrier may so advise the shipper and request instructions in respect of the delivery of the goods. If, after reasonable effort, the carrier is unable to locate the shipper, the carrier may so advise the documentary shipper and request instructions in respect of the delivery of the goods;

(c) The carrier that delivers the goods upon instruction of the shipper or the documentary shipper pursuant to subparagraph (*b*) of this Article is discharged from its obligation to deliver the goods under the contract of carriage, irrespective of whether the non-negotiable transport document has been surrendered to it.

Article 47 Delivery When a Negotiable Transport Document or Negotiable Electronic Transport Record Is Issued

1. When a negotiable transport document or a negotiable electronic transport record has been issued:

(a) The holder of the negotiable transport document or negotiable electronic transport record is entitled to claim delivery of the goods from the carrier after they have arrived at the place of destination, in which event the carrier shall deliver the goods at the time and location referred to in Article 43 to the holder:

(i) Upon surrender of the negotiable transport document and, if the holder is one of the persons referred to in Article 1, subparagraph 10 (a) (i), upon the holder properly identifying itself; or

(ii) Upon demonstration by the holder, in accordance with the procedures referred to in Article 9, paragraph 1, that it is the holder of the negotiable electronic transport record;

(b) The carrier shall refuse delivery if the requirements of subparagraph (a) (i) or (a) (ii) of this paragraph are not met;

(c) If more than one original of the negotiable transport document has been issued, and the number of originals is stated in that document, the surrender of one original will suffice and the other originals cease to have any effect or validity. When a negotiable electronic transport record has been used, such electronic transport record ceases to have any effect or validity upon delivery to the holder in accordance with the procedures required by Article 9, paragraph 1.

2. Without prejudice to Article 48, paragraph 1, if the negotiable transport document or the negotiable electronic transport record expressly states that the goods may be delivered without the surrender of the transport document or the electronic transport record, the following rules apply:

(a) If the goods are not deliverable because (i) the holder, after having received a notice of arrival, does not, at the time or within the time period referred to in Article 43, claim delivery of the goods from the carrier after their arrival at the place of destination, (ii) the carrier refuses delivery because the person claiming to be a holder does not properly identify itself as one of the persons referred to in Article 1, subparagraph 10 (*a*) (i), or (iii) the carrier is, after reasonable effort, unable to locate the holder in order to request delivery instructions, the carrier may so advise the shipper and request instructions in respect of the delivery of the goods. If, after reasonable effort, the carrier is unable to locate the shipper, the carrier may so advise the documentary shipper and request instructions in respect of the delivery of the goods;

(b) The carrier that delivers the goods upon instruction of the shipper or the documentary shipper in accordance with subparagraph 2 (a) of this Article is discharged from its obligation to deliver the goods under the contract of carriage to the holder, irrespective of whether the negotiable transport document has been surrendered to it, or the person claiming delivery under a negotiable electronic transport record has demonstrated, in accordance with the procedures referred to in Article 9, paragraph 1, that it is the holder;

(c) The person giving instructions under subparagraph 2 (a) of this Article shall indemnify the carrier against loss arising from its being held liable to the holder under subparagraph 2 (e) of this article. The carrier may refuse to follow those instructions if the person fails to provide adequate security as the carrier may reasonably request;

(d) A person that becomes a holder of the negotiable transport document or the negotiable electronic transport record after the carrier has delivered the goods pursuant to subparagraph 2 (b) of this article, but pursuant to contractual or other arrangements made before such delivery acquires rights against the carrier under the contract of carriage, other than the right to claim delivery of the goods;

(e) Notwithstanding subparagraphs 2 (*b*) and 2 (*d*) of this article, a holder that becomes a holder after such delivery, and that did not have and could not reasonably have had knowledge of such delivery at the time it became a holder, acquires the rights incorporated in the negotiable transport document or negotiable electronic transport record. When the contract particulars state the expected time of arrival of the goods, or indicate how to obtain information as to whether the goods have been delivered, it is presumed that the holder at the time that it became a holder had or could reasonably have had knowledge of the delivery of the goods.

Article 48 Goods Remaining Undelivered

1. For the purposes of this article, goods shall be deemed to have remained undelivered only if, after their arrival at the place of destination:

(a) The consignee does not accept delivery of the goods pursuant to this chapter at the time and location referred to in Article 43;

(b) The controlling party, the holder, the shipper or the documentary shipper cannot be found or does not give the carrier adequate instructions pursuant to articles 45, 46 and 47;

(c) The carrier is entitled or required to refuse delivery pursuant to articles 44, 45, 46 and 47;

(d) The carrier is not allowed to deliver the goods to the consignee pursuant to the law or regulations of the place at which delivery is requested; or

(e) The goods are otherwise undeliverable by the carrier.

2. Without prejudice to any other rights that the carrier may have against the shipper, controlling party or consignee, if the goods have remained undelivered, the carrier may, at the risk and expense of the person entitled to the goods, take such action in respect of the goods as circumstances may reasonably require, including:

(a) To store the goods at any suitable place;

(b) To unpack the goods if they are packed in containers or vehicles, or to act otherwise in respect of the goods, including by moving them; and

(c) To cause the goods to be sold or destroyed in accordance with the practices or pursuant to the law or regulations of the place where the goods are located at the time.

3. The carrier may exercise the rights under paragraph 2 of this Article only after it has given reasonable notice of the intended action under paragraph 2 of this Article to the person stated in the contract particulars as the person, if any, to be notified of the arrival of the goods at the place of destination, and to one of the following persons in the order indicated, if known to the carrier: the consignee, the controlling party or the shipper.

4. If the goods are sold pursuant to subparagraph 2 (*c*) of this article, the carrier shall hold the proceeds of the sale for the benefit of the person entitled to the goods, subject to the deduc-

tion of any costs incurred by the carrier and any other amounts that are due to the carrier in connection with the carriage of those goods.

5. The carrier shall not be liable for loss of or damage to goods that occurs during the time that they remain undelivered pursuant to this Article unless the claimant proves that such loss or damage resulted from the failure by the carrier to take steps that would have been reasonable in the circumstances to preserve the goods and that the carrier knew or ought to have known that the loss or damage to the goods would result from its failure to take such steps.

Article 49 Retention of Goods

Nothing in this Convention affects a right of the carrier or a performing party that may exist pursuant to the contract of carriage or the applicable law to retain the goods to secure the payment of sums due.

Chapter 10 Rights of the Controlling Party

Article 50 Exercise and Extent of Right of Control

1. The right of control may be exercised only by the controlling party and is limited to:

(a) The right to give or modify instructions in respect of the goods that do not constitute a variation of the contract of carriage;

(b) The right to obtain delivery of the goods at a scheduled port of call or, in respect of inland carriage, any place en route; and

(c) The right to replace the consignee by any other person including the controlling party.

2. The right of control exists during the entire period of responsibility of the carrier, as provided in Article 12, and ceases when that period expires.

Article 51 Identity of the Controlling Party and Transfer of the Right of Control

1. Except in the cases referred to in paragraphs 2, 3 and 4 of this article:

(a) The shipper is the controlling party unless the shipper, when the contract of carriage is concluded, designates the consignee, the documentary shipper or another person as the controlling party;

(b) The controlling party is entitled to transfer the right of control to another person. The transfer becomes effective with respect to the carrier upon its notification of the transfer by the transferor, and the transferee becomes the controlling party; and

(c) The controlling party shall properly identify itself when it exercises the right of control.

2. When a non-negotiable transport document has been issued that indicates that it shall be surrendered in order to obtain delivery of the goods:

(a) The shipper is the controlling party and may transfer the right of control to the consignee named in the transport document by transferring the document to that person without endorsement. If more than one original of the document was issued, all originals shall be transferred in order to effect a transfer of the right of control; and

(b) In order to exercise its right of control, the controlling party shall produce the document and properly identify itself. If more than one original of the document was issued, all originals shall be produced, failing which the right of control cannot be exercised.

3. When a negotiable transport document is issued:

(a) The holder or, if more than one original of the negotiable transport document is issued, the holder of all originals is the controlling party;

(b) The holder may transfer the right of control by transferring the negotiable transport document to another person in accordance with Article 57. If more than one original of that document was issued, all originals shall be transferred to that person in order to effect a transfer of the right of control; and

(c) In order to exercise the right of control, the holder shall produce the negotiable transport document to the carrier, and if the holder is one of the persons referred to in Article 1, subparagraph 10 (a) (i), the holder shall properly identify itself. If more than one original of the document was issued, all originals shall be produced, failing which the right of control cannot be exercised.

4. When a negotiable electronic transport record is issued:

(a) The holder is the controlling party;

(b) The holder may transfer the right of control to another person by transferring the negotiable electronic transport record in accordance with the procedures referred to in Article 9, paragraph 1; and

(c) In order to exercise the right of control, the holder shall demonstrate, in accordance with the procedures referred to in Article 9, paragraph 1, that it is the holder.

Article 52 Carrier's Execution of Instructions

1. Subject to paragraphs 2 and 3 of this article, the carrier shall execute the instructions referred to in Article 50 if:

(a) The person giving such instructions is entitled to exercise the right of control;

(b) The instructions can reasonably be executed according to their terms at the moment that they reach the carrier; and

(c) The instructions will not interfere with the normal operations of the carrier, including its delivery practices.

2. In any event, the controlling party shall reimburse the carrier for any reasonable additional expense that the carrier may incur and shall indemnify the carrier against loss or damage that the carrier may suffer as a result of diligently executing any instruction pursuant to this article, including compensation that the carrier may become liable to pay for loss of or damage to other goods being carried.

3. The carrier is entitled to obtain security from the controlling party for the amount of additional expense, loss or damage that the carrier reasonably expects will arise in connection with the execution of an instruction pursuant to this article. The carrier may refuse to carry out the instructions if no such security is provided.

4. The carrier's liability for loss of or damage to the goods or for delay in delivery resulting from its failure to comply with the instructions of the controlling party in breach of its obligation pursuant to paragraph 1 of this Article shall be subject to articles 17 to 23, and the amount of the compensation payable by the carrier shall be subject to articles 59 to 61.

Article 53 Deemed Delivery

Goods that are delivered pursuant to an instruction in accordance with Article 52, paragraph 1, are deemed to be delivered at the place of destination, and the provisions of chapter 9 relating to such delivery apply to such goods.

Article 54 Variations to the Contract of Carriage

1. The controlling party is the only person that may agree with the carrier to variations to the contract of carriage other than those referred to in Article 50, subparagraphs 1 (*b*) and (*c*).

2. Variations to the contract of carriage, including those referred to in Article 50, subparagraphs 1 (*b*) and (*c*), shall be stated in a negotiable transport document or in a non-negotiable

transport document that requires surrender, or incorporated in a negotiable electronic transport record, or, upon the request of the controlling party, shall be stated in a non-negotiable transport document or incorporated in a non-negotiable electronic transport record. If so stated or incorporated, such variations shall be signed in accordance with Article 38.

Article 55 Providing Additional Information, Instructions or Documents to Carrier

1. The controlling party, on request of the carrier or a performing party, shall provide in a timely manner information, instructions or documents relating to the goods not yet provided by the shipper and not otherwise reasonably available to the carrier that the carrier may reasonably need to perform its obligations under the contract of carriage.

2. If the carrier, after reasonable effort, is unable to locate the controlling party or the controlling party is unable to provide adequate information, instructions or documents to the carrier, the shipper shall provide them. If the carrier, after reasonable effort, is unable to locate the shipper, the documentary shipper shall provide such information, instructions or documents.

Article 56 Variation by Agreement

The parties to the contract of carriage may vary the effect of articles 50, subparagraphs 1 (b) and (c), 50, paragraph 2, and 52. The parties may also restrict or exclude the transferability of the right of control referred to in Article 51, subparagraph 1 (b).

Chapter 11 Transfer of Rights

Article 57 When a Negotiable Transport Document or Negotiable Electronic Transport Record Is Issued

1. When a negotiable transport document is issued, the holder may transfer the rights incorporated in the document by transferring it to another person:

(a) Duly endorsed either to such other person or in blank, if an order document; or

(b) Without endorsement, if: (i) a bearer document or a blank endorsed document; or (ii) a document made out to the order of a named person and the transfer is between the first holder and the named person.

2. When a negotiable electronic transport record is issued, its holder may transfer the rights incorporated in it, whether it be made out to order or to the order of a named person, by transferring the electronic transport record in accordance with the procedures referred to in Article 9, paragraph 1.

Article 58 Liability of Holder

1. Without prejudice to Article 55, a holder that is not the shipper and that does not exercise any right under the contract of carriage does not assume any liability under the contract of carriage solely by reason of being a holder.

2. A holder that is not the shipper and that exercises any right under the contract of carriage assumes any liabilities imposed on it under the contract of carriage to the extent that such liabilities are incorporated in or ascertainable from the negotiable transport document or the negotiable electronic transport record.

3. For the purposes of paragraphs 1 and 2 of this article, a holder that is not the shipper does not exercise any right under the contract of carriage solely because:

(a) It agrees with the carrier, pursuant to Article 10, to replace a negotiable transport document by a negotiable electronic transport record or to replace a negotiable electronic transport record by a negotiable transport document; or

(b) It transfers its rights pursuant to Article 57.

Chapter 12 Limits of Liability

Article 59 Limits of Liability

1. Subject to articles 60 and 61, paragraph 1, the carrier's liability for breaches of its obligations under this Convention is limited to 875 units of account per package or other shipping unit, or 3 units of account per kilogram of the gross weight of the goods that are the subject of the claim or dispute, whichever amount is the higher, except when the value of the goods has been declared by the shipper and included in the contract particulars, or when a higher amount than the amount of limitation of liability set out in this Article has been agreed upon between the carrier and the shipper.

2. When goods are carried in or on a container, pallet or similar article of transport used to consolidate goods, or in or on a vehicle, the packages or shipping units enumerated in the contract particulars as packed in or on such article of transport or vehicle are deemed packages or shipping units. If not so enumerated, the goods in or on such article of transport or vehicle are deemed one shipping unit.

3. The unit of account referred to in this Article is the Special Drawing Right as defined by the International Monetary Fund. The amounts referred to in this Article are to be converted into the national currency of a State according to the value of such currency at the date of judgement or award or the date agreed upon by the parties. The value of a national currency, in terms of the Special Drawing Right, of a Contracting State that is a member of the International Monetary Fund is to be calculated in accordance with the method of valuation applied by the International Monetary Fund in effect at the date in question for its operations and transactions. The value of a national currency, in terms of the Special Drawing Right, of a Contracting State that is not a member of the International Monetary Fund is to be calculated in a manner to be determined by that State.

Article 60 Limits of Liability for Loss Caused by Delay

Subject to Article 61, paragraph 2, compensation for loss of or damage to the goods due to delay shall be calculated in accordance with Article 22 and liability for economic loss due to delay is limited to an amount equivalent to two and one-half times the freight payable on the goods delayed. The total amount payable pursuant to this Article and Article 59, paragraph 1, may not exceed the limit that would be established pursuant to Article 59, paragraph 1, in respect of the total loss of the goods concerned.

Article 61 Loss of the Benefit of Limitation of Liability

1. Neither the carrier nor any of the persons referred to in Article 18 is entitled to the benefit of the limitation of liability as provided in Article 59, or as provided in the contract of carriage, if the claimant proves that the loss resulting from the breach of the carrier's obligation under this Convention was attributable to a personal act or omission of the person claiming a right to limit done with the intent to cause such loss or recklessly and with knowledge that such loss would probably result.

2. Neither the carrier nor any of the persons mentioned in Article 18 is entitled to the benefit of the limitation of liability as provided in Article 60 if the claimant proves that the delay in delivery resulted from a personal act or omission of the person claiming a right to limit done with the intent to cause the loss due to delay or recklessly and with knowledge that such loss would probably result.

Chapter 13 Time for Suit

Article 62 Period of Time for Suit

1. No judicial or arbitral proceedings in respect of claims or disputes arising from a breach of an obligation under this Convention may be instituted after the expiration of a period of two years.

2. The period referred to in paragraph 1 of this Article commences on the day on which the carrier has delivered the goods or, in cases in which no goods have been delivered or only part of the goods have been delivered, on the last day on which the goods should have been delivered. The day on which the period commences is not included in the period.

3. Notwithstanding the expiration of the period set out in paragraph 1 of this article, one party may rely on its claim as a defence or for the purpose of set-off against a claim asserted by the other party.

Article 63 Extension of Time for Suit

The period provided in Article 62 shall not be subject to suspension or interruption, but the person against which a claim is made may at any time during the running of the period extend that period by a declaration to the claimant. This period may be further extended by another declaration or declarations.

Article 64 Action for Indemnity

An action for indemnity by a person held liable may be instituted after the expiration of the period provided in Article 62 if the indemnity action is instituted within the later of:

(a) The time allowed by the applicable law in the jurisdiction where proceedings are instituted; or

(b) Ninety days commencing from the day when the person instituting the action for indemnity has either settled the claim or been served with process in the action against itself, whichever is earlier.

Article 65 Actions Against the Person Identified as the Carrier

An action against the bareboat charterer or the person identified as the carrier pursuant to Article 37, paragraph 2, may be instituted after the expiration of the period provided in Article 62 if the action is instituted within the later of:

(a) The time allowed by the applicable law in the jurisdiction where proceedings are instituted; or

(b) Ninety days commencing from the day when the carrier has been identified, or the registered owner or bareboat charterer has rebutted the presumption that it is the carrier, pursuant to Article 37, paragraph 2.

Chapter 14 Jurisdiction

Article 66 Actions Against the Carrier

Unless the contract of carriage contains an exclusive choice of court agreement that complies with Article 67 or 72, the plaintiff has the right to institute judicial proceedings under this Convention against the carrier:

(a) In a competent court within the jurisdiction of which is situated one of the following places:

(i) The domicile of the carrier;

(ii) The place of receipt agreed in the contract of carriage;

(iii) The place of delivery agreed in the contract of carriage; or

(iv) The port where the goods are initially loaded on a ship or the port where the goods are finally discharged from a ship; or

(b) In a competent court or courts designated by an agreement between the shipper and the carrier for the purpose of deciding claims against the carrier that may arise under this Convention.

Article 67 Choice of Court Agreements

1. The jurisdiction of a court chosen in accordance with Article 66, subparagraph *b*), is exclusive for disputes between the parties to the contract only if the parties so agree and the agreement conferring jurisdiction:

(a) Is contained in a volume contract that clearly states the names and addresses of the parties and either (i) is individually negotiated or (ii) contains a prominent statement that there is an exclusive choice of court agreement and specifies the sections of the volume contract containing that agreement; and

(b) Clearly designates the courts of one Contracting State or one or more specific courts of one Contracting State.

2. A person that is not a party to the volume contract is bound by an exclusive choice of court agreement concluded in accordance with paragraph 1 of this Article only if:

(a) The court is in one of the places designated in Article 66, subparagraph (a);

(b) That agreement is contained in the transport document or electronic transport record;

(c) That person is given timely and adequate notice of the court where the action shall be brought and that the jurisdiction of that court is exclusive; and

(d) The law of the court seized recognizes that that person may be bound by the exclusive choice of court agreement.

Article 68 Actions Against the Maritime Performing Party

The plaintiff has the right to institute judicial proceedings under this Convention against the maritime performing party in a competent court within the jurisdiction of which is situated one of the following places:

(a) The domicile of the maritime performing party; or

(b) The port where the goods are received by the maritime performing party, the port where the goods are delivered by the maritime performing party or the port in which the maritime performing party performs its activities with respect to the goods.

Article 69 No Additional Bases of Jurisdiction

Subject to articles 71 and 72, no judicial proceedings under this Convention against the carrier or a maritime performing party may be instituted in a court not designated pursuant to Article 66 or 68.

Article 70 Arrest and Provisional or Protective Measures

Nothing in this Convention affects jurisdiction with regard to provisional or protective measures, including arrest. A court in a State in which a provisional or protective measure was taken does not have jurisdiction to determine the case upon its merits unless:

(a) The requirements of this chapter are fulfilled; or

(b) An international convention that applies in that State so provides.

Article 71 Consolidation and Removal of Actions

1. Except when there is an exclusive choice of court agreement that is binding pursuant to Article 67 or 72, if a single action is brought against both the carrier and the maritime performing party arising out of a single occurrence, the action may be instituted only in a court designated pursuant to both Article 66 and Article 68. If there is no such court, such action may be instituted in a court designated pursuant to Article 68, subparagraph (*b*), if there is such a court.

2. Except when there is an exclusive choice of court agreement that is binding pursuant to Article 67 or 72, a carrier or a maritime performing party that institutes an action seeking a declaration of non-liability or any other action that would deprive a person of its right to select the forum pursuant to Article 66 or 68 shall, at the request of the defendant, withdraw that action once the defendant has chosen a court designated pursuant to Article 66 or 68, whichever is applicable, where the action may be recommenced.

Article 72 Agreement After a Dispute Has Arisen and Jurisdiction When the Defendant Has Entered an Appearance

1. After a dispute has arisen, the parties to the dispute may agree to resolve it in any competent court.

2. A competent court before which a defendant appears, without contesting jurisdiction in accordance with the rules of that court, has jurisdiction.

Article 73 Recognition and Enforcement

1. A decision made in one Contracting State by a court having jurisdiction under this Convention shall be recognized and enforced in another Contracting State in accordance with the law of such latter Contracting State when both States have made a declaration in accordance with Article 74.

2. A court may refuse recognition and enforcement based on the grounds for the refusal of recognition and enforcement available pursuant to its law.

3. This chapter shall not affect the application of the rules of a regional economic integration organization that is a party to this Convention, as concerns the recognition or enforcement of judgements as between member States of the regional economic integration organization, whether adopted before or after this Convention.

Article 74 Application of Chapter 14

The provisions of this chapter shall bind only Contracting States that declare in accordance with Article 91 that they will be bound by them.

Chapter 15 Arbitration

Article 75 Arbitration Agreements

1. Subject to this chapter, parties may agree that any dispute that may arise relating to the carriage of goods under this Convention shall be referred to arbitration.

2. The arbitration proceedings shall, at the option of the person asserting a claim against the carrier, take place at:

(a) Any place designated for that purpose in the arbitration agreement; or

(b) Any other place situated in a State where any of the following places is located:

   (i) The domicile of the carrier;

   (ii) The place of receipt agreed in the contract of carriage;

   (iii) The place of delivery agreed in the contract of carriage; or

(iv) The port where the goods are initially loaded on a ship or the port where the goods are finally discharged from a ship.

3. The designation of the place of arbitration in the agreement is binding for disputes between the parties to the agreement if the agreement is contained in a volume contract that clearly states the names and addresses of the parties and either:

(a) Is individually negotiated; or

(b) Contains a prominent statement that there is an arbitration agreement and specifies the sections of the volume contract containing the arbitration agreement.

4. When an arbitration agreement has been concluded in accordance with paragraph 3 of this article, a person that is not a party to the volume contract is bound by the designation of the place of arbitration in that agreement only if:

(a) The place of arbitration designated in the agreement is situated in one of the places referred to in subparagraph 2 (b) of this article;

(b) The agreement is contained in the transport document or electronic transport record;

(c) The person to be bound is given timely and adequate notice of the place of arbitration; and

(d) Applicable law permits that person to be bound by the arbitration agreement.

5. The provisions of paragraphs 1, 2, 3 and 4 of this Article are deemed to be part of every arbitration clause or agreement, and any term of such clause or agreement to the extent that it is inconsistent therewith is void.

Article 76 Arbitration Agreement in Non-Liner Transportation

1. Nothing in this Convention affects the enforceability of an arbitration agreement in a contract of carriage in non-liner transportation to which this Convention or the provisions of this Convention apply by reason of:

(*a*) The application of Article 7; or

(*b*) The parties' voluntary incorporation of this Convention in a contract of carriage that would not otherwise be subject to this Convention.

2. Notwithstanding paragraph 1 of this article, an arbitration agreement in a transport document or electronic transport record to which this Convention applies by reason of the application of Article 7 is subject to this chapter unless such a transport document or electronic transport record:

(*a*) Identifies the parties to and the date of the charter party or other contract excluded from the application of this Convention by reason of the application of Article 6; and

(*b*) Incorporates by specific reference the clause in the charter party or other contract that contains the terms of the arbitration agreement.

Article 77 Agreement to Arbitrate After a Dispute Has Arisen

Notwithstanding the provisions of this chapter and chapter 14, after a dispute has arisen the parties to the dispute may agree to resolve it by arbitration in any place.

Article 78 Application of Chapter 15

The provisions of this chapter shall bind only Contracting States that declare in accordance with Article 91 that they will be bound by them.

Chapter 16 Validity of Contractual Terms

Article 79 General Provisions

1. Unless otherwise provided in this Convention, any term in a contract of carriage is void to the extent that it:

(*a*) Directly or indirectly excludes or limits the obligations of the carrier or a maritime performing party under this Convention;

(*b*) Directly or indirectly excludes or limits the liability of the carrier or a maritime performing party for breach of an obligation under this Convention; or

(*c*) Assigns a benefit of insurance of the goods in favour of the carrier or a person referred to in Article 18.

2. Unless otherwise provided in this Convention, any term in a contract of carriage is void to the extent that it:

(*a*) Directly or indirectly excludes, limits or increases the obligations under this Convention of the shipper, consignee, controlling party, holder or documentary shipper; or

(*b*) Directly or indirectly excludes, limits or increases the liability of the shipper, consignee, controlling party, holder or documentary shipper for breach of any of its obligations under this Convention.

Article 80 Special Rules for Volume Contracts

1. Notwithstanding Article 79, as between the carrier and the shipper, a volume contract to which this Convention applies may provide for greater or lesser rights, obligations and liabilities than those imposed by this Convention.

2. A derogation pursuant to paragraph 1 of this Article is binding only when:

(a) The volume contract contains a prominent statement that it derogates from this Convention;

(b) The volume contract is (i) individually negotiated or (ii) prominently specifies the sections of the volume contract containing the derogations;

(c) The shipper is given an opportunity and notice of the opportunity to conclude a contract of carriage on terms and conditions that comply with this Convention without any derogation under this article; and

(d) The derogation is neither (i) incorporated by reference from another document nor (ii) included in a contract of adhesion that is not subject to negotiation.

3. A carrier's public schedule of prices and services, transport document, electronic transport record or similar document is not a volume contract pursuant to paragraph 1 of this article, but a volume contract may incorporate such documents by reference as terms of the contract.

4. Paragraph 1 of this Article does not apply to rights and obligations provided in articles 14, subparagraphs (*a*) and (*b*), 29 and 32 or to liability arising from the breach thereof, nor does it apply to any liability arising from an act or omission referred to in Article 61.

5. The terms of the volume contract that derogate from this Convention, if the volume contract satisfies the requirements of paragraph 2 of this article, apply between the carrier and any person other than the shipper provided that:

(a) Such person received information that prominently states that the volume contract derogates from this Convention and gave its express consent to be bound by such derogations; and

(b) Such consent is not solely set forth in a carrier's public schedule of prices and services, transport document or electronic transport record.

6. The party claiming the benefit of the derogation bears the burden of proof that the conditions for derogation have been fulfilled.

Article 81 Special Rules for Live Animals and Certain Other Goods

Notwithstanding Article 79 and without prejudice to Article 80, the contract of carriage may exclude or limit the obligations or the liability of both the carrier and a maritime performing party if:

(a) The goods are live animals, but any such exclusion or limitation will not be effective if the claimant proves that the loss of or damage to the goods, or delay in delivery, resulted from an act or omission of the carrier or of a person referred to in Article 18, done with the intent to cause such loss of or damage to the goods or such loss due to delay or done recklessly and with knowledge that such loss or damage or such loss due to delay would probably result; or

(b) The character or condition of the goods or the circumstances and terms and conditions under which the carriage is to be performed are such as reasonably to justify a special agreement, provided that such contract of carriage is not related to ordinary commercial shipments made in the ordinary course of trade and that no negotiable transport document or negotiable electronic transport record is issued for the carriage of the goods.

Chapter 17 Matters Not Governed by this Convention

Article 82 International Conventions Governing the Carriage of Goods by Other Modes of Transport

Nothing in this Convention affects the application of any of the following international conventions in force at the time this Convention enters into force, including any future amendment to such conventions, that regulate the liability of the carrier for loss of or damage to the goods:

(a) Any convention governing the carriage of goods by air to the extent that such convention according to its provisions applies to any part of the contract of carriage;

(b) Any convention governing the carriage of goods by road to the extent that such convention according to its provisions applies to the carriage of goods that remain loaded on a road cargo vehicle carried on board a ship;

(c) Any convention governing the carriage of goods by rail to the extent that such convention according to its provisions applies to carriage of goods by sea as a supplement to the carriage by rail; or

(d) Any convention governing the carriage of goods by inland waterways to the extent that such convention according to its provisions applies to a carriage of goods without trans-shipment both by inland waterways and sea.

Article 83 Global Limitation of Liability

Nothing in this Convention affects the application of any international convention or national law regulating the global limitation of liability of vessel owners.

Article 84 General Average

Nothing in this Convention affects the application of terms in the contract of carriage or provisions of national law regarding the adjustment of general average.

Article 85 Passengers and Luggage

This Convention does not apply to a contract of carriage for passengers and their luggage.

Article 86 Damage Caused by Nuclear Incident

No liability arises under this Convention for damage caused by a nuclear incident if the operator of a nuclear installation is liable for such damage: [...]

Chapter 18 Final Clauses

Article 87 Depositary

The Secretary-General of the United Nations is hereby designated as the depositary of this Convention.

Article 88 Signature, Ratification, Acceptance, Approval or Accession

1. This Convention is open for signature by all States at Rotterdam, the Netherlands, on 23 September 2009, and thereafter at the Headquarters of the United Nations in New York.

2. This Convention is subject to ratification, acceptance or approval by the signatory States.

3. This Convention is open for accession by all States that are not signatory States as from the date it is open for signature.

4. Instruments of ratification, acceptance, approval and accession are to be deposited with the Secretary-General of the United Nations.

Article 89 Denunciation of Other Conventions

1. A State that ratifies, accepts, approves or accedes to this Convention and is a party to the International Convention for the Unification of certain Rules of Law relating to Bills of Lading signed at Brussels on 25 August 1924, to the Protocol to amend the International Convention for the Unification of certain Rules of Law relating to Bills of Lading, signed at Brussels on 23 February 1968, or to the Protocol to amend the International Convention for the Unification of certain Rules of Law relating to Bills of Lading as Modified by the Amending Protocol of 23 February 1968, signed at Brussels on 21 December 1979, shall at the same time denounce that Convention and the protocol or protocols thereto to which it is a party by notifying the Government of Belgium to that effect, with a declaration that the denunciation is to take effect as from the date when this Convention enters into force in respect of that State.

2. A State that ratifies, accepts, approves or accedes to this Convention and is a party to the United Nations Convention on the Carriage of Goods by Sea concluded at Hamburg on 31 March 1978 shall at the same time denounce that Convention by notifying the Secretary-General of the United Nations to that effect, with a declaration that the denunciation is to take effect as from the date when this Convention enters into force in respect of that State.

3. For the purposes of this article, ratifications, acceptances, approvals and accessions in respect of this Convention by States parties to the instruments listed in paragraphs 1 and 2 of this Article that are notified to the depositary after this Convention has entered into force are not effective until such denunciations as may be required on the part of those States in respect of these instruments have become effective. The depositary of this Convention shall consult with the Government of Belgium, as the depositary of the instruments referred to in paragraph 1 of this article, so as to ensure necessary coordination in this respect.

Article 90 Reservations

No reservation is permitted to this Convention.

Article 91 Procedure and Effect of Declarations

1. The declarations permitted by articles 74 and 78 may be made at any time. The initial declarations permitted by Article 92, paragraph 1, and Article 93, paragraph 2, shall be made

at the time of signature, ratification, acceptance, approval or accession. No other declaration is permitted under this Convention.

2. Declarations made at the time of signature are subject to confirmation upon ratification, acceptance or approval.

3. Declarations and their confirmations are to be in writing and to be formally notified to the depositary.

4. A declaration takes effect simultaneously with the entry into force of this Convention in respect of the State concerned. However, a declaration of which the depositary receives formal notification after such entry into force takes effect on the first day of the month following the expiration of six months after the date of its receipt by the depositary.

5. Any State that makes a declaration under this Convention may withdraw it at any time by a formal notification in writing addressed to the depositary. The withdrawal of a declaration, or its modification where permitted by this Convention, takes effect on the first day of the month following the expiration of six months after the date of the receipt of the notification by the depositary.

Article 92 Effect in Domestic Territorial Units

1. If a Contracting State has two or more territorial units in which different systems of law are applicable in relation to the matters dealt with in this Convention, it may, at the time of signature, ratification, acceptance, approval or accession, declare that this Convention is to extend to all its territorial units or only to one or more of them, and may amend its declaration by submitting another declaration at any time.

2. These declarations are to be notified to the depositary and are to state expressly the territorial units to which the Convention extends.

3. When a Contracting State has declared pursuant to this Article that this Convention extends to one or more but not all of its territorial units, a place located in a territorial unit to which this Convention does not extend is not considered to be in a Contracting State for the purposes of this Convention.

4. If a Contracting State makes no declaration pursuant to paragraph 1 of this article, the Convention is to extend to all territorial units of that State.

Article 93 Participation by Regional Economic Integration Organizations

1. A regional economic integration organization that is constituted by sovereign States and has competence over certain matters governed by this Convention may similarly sign, ratify, accept, approve or accede to this Convention. The regional economic integration organization shall in that case have the rights and obligations of a Contracting State, to the extent that that organization has competence over matters governed by this Convention. When the number of Contracting States is relevant in this Convention, the regional economic integration organization does not count as a Contracting State in addition to its member States which are Contracting States.

2. The regional economic integration organization shall, at the time of signature, ratification, acceptance, approval or accession, make a declaration to the depositary specifying the matters governed by this Convention in respect of which competence has been transferred to that organization by its member States. The regional economic integration organization shall promptly notify the depositary of any changes to the distribution of competence, including new transfers of competence, specified in the declaration pursuant to this paragraph.

3. Any reference to a "Contracting State" or "Contracting States" in this Convention applies equally to a regional economic integration organization when the context so requires.

Article 94 Entry into Force

1. This Convention enters into force on the first day of the month following the expiration of one year after the date of deposit of the twentieth instrument of ratification, acceptance, approval or accession.

2. For each State that becomes a Contracting State to this Convention after the date of the deposit of the twentieth instrument of ratification, acceptance, approval or accession, this Convention enters into force on the first day of the month following the expiration of one year after the deposit of the appropriate instrument on behalf of that State.

3. Each Contracting State shall apply this Convention to contracts of carriage concluded on or after the date of the entry into force of this Convention in respect of that State.

Article 95 Revision and Amendment

1. At the request of not less than one third of the Contracting States to this Convention, the Secretary-General of the United Nations shall convene a conference of the Contracting States for revising or amending it.

2. Any instrument of ratification, acceptance, approval or accession deposited after the entry into force of an amendment to this Convention is deemed to apply to the Convention as amended.

Article 96 Denunciation of this Convention

1. A Contracting State may denounce this Convention at any time by means of a notification in writing addressed to the depositary.

2. The denunciation takes effect on the first day of the month following the expiration of one year after the notification is received by the depositary. If a longer period is specified in the notification, the denunciation takes effect upon the expiration of such longer period after the notification is received by the depositary.

DONE at New York, this eleventh day of December two thousand and eight, in a single original, of which the Arabic, Chinese, English, French, Russian and Spanish texts are equally authentic.

IN WITNESS WHEREOF the undersigned plenipotentiaries, being duly authorized by their respective Governments, have signed this Convention.

Entry into force: not yet in force

Ratification as of April 2020: Benin (2019), Cameroon (2017), Congo (2014), Spain (2011), Togo (2012)[1]

---

1 The Convention has been signed but not yet ratified as of April 2020 by the following countries: Armenia, Democratic Republic of the Congo, Denmark, France, Gabon, Ghana, Greece, Guinea, Guinea-Bissau, Luxembourg, Madagascar, Mali, Netherlands, Niger, Nigeria, Norway, Poland, Senegal, Sweden, Switzerland, and the United States of America.

33) 1936 CARRIAGE OF GOODS BY SEA ACT ("COGSA") USA[1]

§ 1300. Bills of Lading Subject to Chapter

Every bill of lading or similar document of title which is evidence of a contract for the carriage of goods by sea to or from ports of the United States, in foreign trade, shall have effect subject to the provisions of this chapter.

§ 1301. Definitions

When used in this chapter--

(a) The term "carrier" includes the owner or the charterer who enters into a contract of carriage with a shipper.

(b) The term "contract of carriage" applies only to contracts of carriage covered by a bill of lading or any similar document of title, insofar as such document relates to the carriage of goods by sea, including any bill of lading or any similar document as aforesaid issued under or pursuant to a charter party from the moment at which such bill of lading or similar document of title regulates the relations between a carrier and a holder of the same.

(c) The term "goods" includes goods, wares, merchandise, and articles of every kind whatsoever, except live animals and cargo which by the contract of carriage is stated as being carried on deck and is so carried.

(d) The term "ship" means any vessel used for the carriage of goods by sea.

(e) The term "carriage of goods" covers the period from the time when the goods are loaded on to the time when they are discharged from the ship.

§ 1302. Duties and Rights of Carrier

Subject to the provisions of section 1306 of this Appendix, under every contract of carriage of goods by sea, the carrier in relation to the loading, handling, stowage, carriage, custody, care, and discharge of such goods, shall be subject to the responsibilities and liabilities and entitled to the rights and immunities set forth in sections 1303 and 1304 of this Appendix.

§ 1303. Responsibilities and Liabilities of Carrier and Ship

(1) Seaworthiness

The carrier shall be bound, before and at the beginning of the voyage, to exercise due diligence to--

(a) Make the ship seaworthy;

(b) Properly man, equip, and supply the ship;

(c) Make the holds, refrigerating and cooling chambers, and all other parts of the ship in which goods are carried, fit and safe for their reception, carriage, and preservation.

(2) Cargo

The carrier shall properly and carefully load, handle, stow, carry, keep, care for, and discharge the goods carried.

(3) Contents of bill

After receiving the goods into his charge the carrier, or the master or agent of the carrier, shall, on demand of the shipper, issue to the shipper a bill of lading showing among other things--

---

1 16 April 1936, ch. 229, title I, 49 Stat. 1208.

(a) The leading marks necessary for identification of the goods as the same are furnished in writing by the shipper before the loading of such goods starts, provided such marks are stamped or otherwise shown clearly upon the goods if uncovered, or on the cases or coverings in which such goods are contained, in such a manner as should ordinarily remain legible until the end of the voyage.

(b) Either the number of packages or pieces, or the quantity or weight, as the case may be, as furnished in writing by the shipper.

(c) The apparent order and condition of the goods: Provided, That no carrier, master, or agent of the carrier, shall be bound to state or show in the bill of lading any marks, number, quantity, or weight which he has reasonable ground for suspecting not accurately to represent the goods actually received, or which he has had no reasonable means of checking.

(4) Bill as prima facie evidence

Such a bill of lading shall be prima facie evidence of the receipt by the carrier of the goods as therein described in accordance with paragraphs (3)(a), (b), and (c), of this section: Provided, That nothing in this chapter shall be construed as repealing or limiting the application of any part of chapter 801 of title 49. [49 U.S. Code Subtitle X – Miscellaneous, Chapter 801–Bills of Lading]

(5) Guaranty of statements

The shipper shall be deemed to have guaranteed to the carrier the accuracy at the time of shipment of the marks, number, quantity, and weight, as furnished by him; and the shipper shall indemnify the carrier against all loss, damages, and expenses arising or resulting from inaccuracies in such particulars. The right of the carrier to such indemnity shall in no way limit his responsibility and liability under the contract of carriage to any person other than the shipper.

(6) Notice of loss or damage; limitation of actions

Unless notice of loss or damage and the general nature of such loss or damage be given in writing to the carrier or his agent at the port of discharge before or at the time of the removal of the goods into the custody of the person entitled to delivery thereof under the contract of carriage, such removal shall be prima facie evidence of the delivery by the carrier of the goods as described in the bill of lading. If the loss or damage is not apparent, the notice must be given within three days of the delivery.

Said notice of loss or damage may be endorsed upon the receipt for the goods given by the person taking delivery thereof.

The notice in writing need not be given if the state of the goods has at the time of their receipt been the subject of joint survey or inspection.

In any event the carrier and the ship shall be discharged from all liability in respect of loss or damage unless suit is brought within one year after delivery of the goods or the date when the goods should have been delivered: Provided, That if a notice of loss or damage, either apparent or concealed, is not given as provided for in this section, that fact shall not affect or prejudice the right of the shipper to bring suit within one year after the delivery of the goods or the date when the goods should have been delivered.

In the case of any actual or apprehended loss or damage the carrier and the receiver shall give all reasonable facilities to each other for inspecting and tallying the goods.

(7) "Shipped" bill of lading

After the goods are loaded the bill of lading to be issued by the carrier, master, or agent of the carrier to the shipper shall, if the shipper so demands, be a "shipped" bill of lading: Provided, That if the shipper shall have previously taken up any document of title to such goods, he shall surrender the same as against the issue of the "shipped" bill of lading, but at the option of the carrier such document of title may be noted at the port of shipment by the carrier, master, or agent with the name or names of the ship or ships upon which the goods have been shipped and the date or dates of shipment, and when so noted the same shall for the purpose of this section be deemed to constitute a "shipped" bill of lading.

(8) Limitation of liability for negligence

Any clause, covenant, or agreement in a contract of carriage relieving the carrier or the ship from liability for loss or damage to or in connection with the goods, arising from negligence, fault, or failure in the duties and obligations provided in this section, or lessening such liability otherwise than as provided in this chapter, shall be null and void and of no effect. A benefit of insurance in favor of the carrier, or similar clause, shall be deemed to be a clause relieving the carrier from liability.

§ 1304. Rights and Immunities of Carrier and Ship

(1) Unseaworthiness

Neither the carrier nor the ship shall be liable for loss or damage arising or resulting from unseaworthiness unless caused by want of due diligence on the part of the carrier to make the ship seaworthy, and to secure that the ship is properly manned, equipped, and supplied, and to make the holds, refrigerating and cool chambers, and all other parts of the ship in which goods are carried fit and safe for their reception, carriage, and preservation in accordance with the provisions of paragraph (1) of section 1303 of this Appendix. Whenever loss or damage has resulted from unseaworthiness, the burden of proving the exercise of due diligence shall be on the carrier or other persons claiming exemption under this section.

(2) Uncontrollable causes of loss

Neither the carrier nor the ship shall be responsible for loss or damage arising or resulting from--

(a) Act, neglect, or default of the master, mariner, pilot, or the servants of the carrier in the navigation or in the management of the ship;

(b) Fire, unless caused by the actual fault or privity of the carrier;

(c) Perils, dangers, and accidents of the sea or other navigable waters;

(d) Act of God;

(e) Act of war;

(f) Act of public enemies;

(g) Arrest or restraint of princes, rulers, or people, or seizure under legal process;

(h) Quarantine restrictions;

(i) Act or omission of the shipper or owner of the goods, his agent or representative;

(j) Strikes or lockouts or stoppage or restraint of labor from whatever cause, whether partial or general: Provided, That nothing herein contained shall be construed to relieve a carrier from responsibility for the carrier's own acts;

(k) Riots and civil commotions;

(l) Saving or attempting to save life or property at sea;

(m) Wastage in bulk or weight or any other loss or damage arising from inherent defect, quality, or vice of the goods;

(n) Insufficiency of packing;

(o) Insufficiency or inadequacy of marks;

(p) Latent defects not discoverable by due diligence; and

(q) Any other cause arising without the actual fault and privity of the carrier and without the fault or neglect of the agents or servants of the carrier, but the burden of proof shall be on the person claiming the benefit of this exception to show that neither the actual fault or privity of the carrier nor the fault or neglect of the agents or servants of the carrier contributed to the loss or damage.

(3) Freedom from negligence

The shipper shall not be responsible for loss or damage sustained by the carrier or the ship arising or resulting from any cause without the act, fault, or neglect of the shipper, his agents, or his servants.

(4) Deviations

Any deviation in saving or attempting to save life or property at sea, or any reasonable deviation shall not be deemed to be an infringement or breach of this chapter or of the contract of carriage, and the carrier shall not be liable for any loss or damage resulting therefrom: Provided, however, That if the deviation is for the purpose of loading or unloading cargo or passengers it shall, prima facie, be regarded as unreasonable.

(5) Amount of liability; valuation of cargo

Neither the carrier nor the ship shall in any event be or become liable for any loss or damage to or in connection with the transportation of goods in an amount exceeding $500 per package lawful money of the United States, or in case of goods not shipped in packages, per customary freight unit, or the equivalent of that sum in other currency, unless the nature and value of such goods have been declared by the shipper before shipment and inserted in the bill of lading. This declaration, if embodied in the bill of lading, shall be prima facie evidence, but shall not be conclusive on the carrier.

By agreement between the carrier, master, or agent of the carrier, and the shipper another maximum amount than that mentioned in this paragraph may be fixed: Provided, That such maximum shall not be less than the figure above named. In no event shall the carrier be liable for more than the amount of damage actually sustained.

Neither the carrier nor the ship shall be responsible in any event for loss or damage to or in connection with the transportation of the goods if the nature or value thereof has been knowingly and fraudulently misstated by the shipper in the bill of lading.

(6) Inflammable, explosive, or dangerous cargo

Goods of an inflammable, explosive, or dangerous nature to the shipment whereof the carrier, master or agent of the carrier, has not consented with knowledge of their nature and character, may at any time before discharge be landed at any place or destroyed or rendered innocuous by the carrier without compensation, and the shipper of such goods shall be liable for all damages and expenses directly or indirectly arising out of or resulting from such shipment. If any such goods shipped with such knowledge and consent shall become a danger to the ship or cargo, they may in like manner be landed at any place, or destroyed or rendered innocuous by the carrier without liability on the part of the carrier except to general average, if any.

§ 1305. Surrender of Rights; Increase of Liabilities; Charter Parties; General Average

A carrier shall be at liberty to surrender in whole or in part all or any of his rights and immunities or to increase any of his responsibilities and liabilities under this chapter, provided such surrender or increase shall be embodied in the bill of lading issued to the shipper.

The provisions of this chapter shall not be applicable to charter parties; but if bills of lading are issued in the case of a ship under a charter party, they shall comply with the terms of this chapter. Nothing in this chapter shall be held to prevent the insertion in a bill of lading of any lawful provision regarding general average.

§ 1306. Special Agreement as to Particular Goods

Notwithstanding the provisions of sections 1303 to 1305 of this Appendix, a carrier, master or agent of the carrier, and a shipper shall, in regard to any particular goods be at liberty to enter into any agreement in any terms as to the responsibility and liability of the carrier for such goods, and as to the rights and immunities of the carrier in respect of such goods, or his obligation as to seaworthiness (so far as the stipulation regarding seaworthiness is not contrary to public policy), or the care or diligence of his servants or agents in regard to the loading, handling, stowage, carriage, custody, care, and discharge of the goods carried by sea: Provided, That in this case no bill of lading has been or shall be issued and that the terms agreed shall be embodied in a receipt which shall be a nonnegotiable document and shall be marked as such.

Any agreement so entered into shall have full legal effect: Provided, That this section shall not apply to ordinary commercial shipments made in the ordinary course of trade but only to other shipments where the character or condition of the property to be carried or the circumstances, terms, and conditions under which the carriage is to be performed are such as reasonably to justify a special agreement.

§ 1307. Agreement as to Liability Prior to Loading or After Discharge

Nothing contained in this chapter shall prevent a carrier or a shipper from entering into any agreement, stipulation, condition, reservation, or exemption as to the responsibility and liability of the carrier or the ship for the loss or damage to or in connection with the custody and care and handling of goods prior to the loading on and subsequent to the discharge from the ship on which the goods are carried by sea.

§ 1308. Rights and Liabilities Under Other Provisions

The provisions of this chapter shall not affect the rights and obligations of the carrier under the provisions of the Shipping Act, 1916 [as amended ...] or under the provisions of any other enactment for the time being in force relating to the limitation of the liability of the owners of seagoing vessels.

§ 1309. Discrimination Between Competing Shippers

Nothing contained in this chapter shall be construed as permitting a common carrier by water to discriminate between competing shippers similarly placed in time and circumstances, either (a) with respect to their right to demand and receive bills of lading subject to the provisions of this chapter; or (b) when issuing such bills of lading, either in the surrender of any of the carrier's rights and immunities or in the increase of any of the carrier's responsibilities and liabilities pursuant to section 1305 of this Appendix; or (c) in any other way prohibited by the Shipping Act, 1916, as amended [46 App. U.S.C. 801 et seq.].

§ 1310. Weight of Bulk Cargo

Where under the customs of any trade the weight of any bulk cargo inserted in the bill of lading is a weight ascertained or accepted by a third party other than the carrier or the shipper, and the fact that the weight is so ascertained or accepted is stated in the bill of lading, then, notwithstanding anything in this chapter, the bill of lading shall not be deemed to be prima facie evidence against the carrier of the receipt of goods of the weight so inserted in the bill of lading, and the accuracy thereof at the time of shipment shall not be deemed to have been guaranteed by the shipper.

§ 1311. Liabilities Before Loading and After Discharge; Effect on Other Laws

Nothing in this chapter shall be construed as superseding any part of sections 190 to 196 of this Appendix, or of any other law which would be applicable in the absence of this chapter, insofar as they relate to the duties, responsibilities, and liabilities of the ship or carrier prior to the time when the goods are loaded on or after the time they are discharged from the ship.

§ 1312. Scope of Chapter; "United States"; "Foreign Trade"

This chapter shall apply to all contracts for carriage of goods by sea to or from ports of the United States in foreign trade. As used in this chapter the term "United States" includes its districts, territories, and possessions. The term "foreign trade" means the transportation of goods between the ports of the United States and ports of foreign countries. Nothing in this chapter shall be held to apply to contracts for carriage of goods by sea between any port of the United States or its possessions, and any other port of the United States or its possessions: Provided, however, That any bill of lading or similar document of title which is evidence of a contract for the carriage of goods by sea between such ports, containing an express statement that it shall be subject to the provisions of this chapter, shall be subjected hereto as fully as if subject hereto by the express provisions of this chapter: Provided further, That every bill of lading or similar document of title which is evidence of a contract for the carriage of goods by sea from ports of the United States, in foreign trade, shall contain a statement that it shall have effect subject to the provisions of this chapter.

§ 1313. Suspension of Provisions by President

Upon the certification of the Secretary of Transportation that the foreign commerce of the United States in its competition with that of foreign nations is prejudiced by the provisions, or any of them, of sections 1301 to 1308 of this Appendix, or by the laws of any foreign country or countries relating to the carriage of goods by sea, the President of the United States may, from time to time, by proclamation, suspend any or all provisions of said sections for such periods of time or indefinitely as may be designated in the proclamation. The President may at any time rescind such suspension of said sections, and any provisions thereof which may have been suspended shall thereby be reinstated and again apply to contracts thereafter made for the carriage of goods by sea. Any proclamation of suspension or rescission of any such suspension shall take effect on a date named therein, which date shall be not less than ten days from the issue of the proclamation.

Any contract for the carriage of goods by sea, subject to the provisions of this chapter, effective during any period when sections 1301 to 1308 of this Appendix, or any part thereof, are suspended, shall be subject to all provisions of law now or hereafter applicable to that part of said sections which may have thus been suspended.

§ 1314. Effective Date; Retroactive Effect

This chapter shall take effect ninety days after April 16, 1936; but nothing in this chapter shall apply during a period not to exceed one year following April 16, 1936, to any contract for the carriage of goods by sea, made before April 16, 1936, nor to any bill of lading or similar document of title issued, whether before or after such date in pursuance of any such contract as aforesaid.

§ 1315. Short Title

This chapter may be cited as the "Carriage of Goods by Sea Act."

34) 1917 Federal Bill of Lading Act, USA[1]

§ 80101. Definitions

In this chapter –

(1) "consignee" means the person named in a bill of lading as the person to whom the goods are to be delivered.

(2) "consignor" means the person named in a bill of lading as the person from whom the goods have been received for shipment.

(3) "goods" means merchandise or personal property that has been, is being, or will be transported.

(4) "holder" means a person having possession of, and a property right in, a bill of lading.

(5) "order" means an order by indorsement on a bill of lading.

(6) "purchase" includes taking by mortgage or pledge.

§ 80102. Application

This chapter applies to a bill of lading when the bill is issued by a common carrier for the transportation of goods –

(1) between a place in the District of Columbia and another place in the District of Columbia;

(2) between a place in a territory or possession of the United States and another place in the same territory or possession;

(3) between a place in a State and a place in another State;

(4) between a place in a State and a place in the same State through another State or a foreign country; or

(5) from a place in a State to a place in a foreign country.

§ 80103. Negotiable and Non-Negotiable Bills

(a) Negotiable bills. –

(1) A bill of lading is negotiable if the bill –

 (A) states that the goods are to be delivered to the order of a consignee; and

 (B) does not contain on its face an agreement with the shipper that the bill is not negotiable.

(2) Inserting in a negotiable bill of lading the name of a person to be notified of the arrival of the goods --

 (A) does not limit its negotiability; and

 (B) is not notice to the purchaser of the goods of a right the named person has to the goods.

(b) Non-negotiable bills. –

(1) A bill of lading is non-negotiable if the bill states that the goods are to be delivered to a consignee. The indorsement of a non-negotiable bill does not –

 (A) make the bill negotiable; or

 (B) give the transferee any additional right.

---

1 49 U.S. Code Chapter 801 – Bills of Lading, originally adopted in 1916 as the Pomerene Act.

(2) A common carrier issuing a non-negotiable bill of lading must put "non-negotiable" or "not negotiable" on the bill. This paragraph does not apply to an informal memorandum or acknowledgment.

§ 80104. Form and Requirements for Negotiation

(a) General rules. –

(1) A negotiable bill of lading may be negotiated by indorsement. An indorsement may be made in blank or to a specified person. If the goods are deliverable to the order of a specified person, then the bill must be indorsed by that person.

(2) A negotiable bill of lading may be negotiated by delivery when the common carrier, under the terms of the bill, undertakes to deliver the goods to the order of a specified person and that person or a subsequent indorsee has indorsed the bill in blank.

(3) A negotiable bill of lading may be negotiated by a person possessing the bill, regardless of the way in which the person got possession, if –

(A) a common carrier, under the terms of the bill, undertakes to deliver the goods to that person; or

(B) when the bill is negotiated, it is in a form that allows it to be negotiated by delivery.

(b) Validity not affected. – The validity of a negotiation of a bill of lading is not affected by the negotiation having been a breach of duty by the person making the negotiation, or by the owner of the bill having been deprived of possession by fraud, accident, mistake, duress, loss, theft, or conversion, if the person to whom the bill is negotiated, or a person to whom the bill is subsequently negotiated, gives value for the bill in good faith and without notice of the breach of duty, fraud, accident, mistake, duress, loss, theft, or conversion.

(c) Negotiation by seller, mortgagor, or pledgor to person without notice. -- When goods for which a negotiable bill of lading has been issued are in a common carrier's possession, and the person to whom the bill has been issued retains possession of the bill after selling, mortgaging, or pledging the goods or bill, the subsequent negotiation of the bill by that person to another person receiving the bill for value, in good faith, and without notice of the prior sale, mortgage, or pledge has the same effect as if the first purchaser of the goods or bill had expressly authorized the subsequent negotiation.

§ 80105. Title and Rights Affected by Negotiation

(a) Title. – When a negotiable bill of lading is negotiated --

(1) the person to whom it is negotiated acquires the title to the goods that --

(A) the person negotiating the bill had the ability to convey to a purchaser in good faith for value; and

(B) the consignor and consignee had the ability to convey to such a purchaser; and

(2) the common carrier issuing the bill becomes obligated directly to the person to whom the bill is negotiated to hold possession of the goods under the terms of the bill the same as if the carrier had issued the bill to that person.

(b) Superiority of rights. – When a negotiable bill of lading is negotiated to a person for value in good faith, that person's right to the goods for which the bill was issued is superior to a seller's lien or to a right to stop the transportation of the goods. This subsection applies whether the negotiation is made before or after the common carrier issuing the bill receives notice of the seller's claim. The carrier may deliver the goods to an unpaid seller only if the bill first is surrendered for cancellation.

(c) Mortgagee and lien holder rights not affected. – Except as provided in subsection (b) of this section, this chapter does not limit a right of a mortgagee or lien holder having a mortgage or lien on goods against a person that purchased for value in good faith from the owner, and got possession of the goods immediately before delivery to the common carrier.

§ 80106. Transfer Without Negotiation

(a) Delivery and agreement. – The holder of a bill of lading may transfer the bill without negotiating it by delivery and agreement to transfer title to the bill or to the goods represented by it. Subject to the agreement, the person to whom the bill is transferred has title to the goods against the transferor.

(b) Compelling indorsement. – When a negotiable bill of lading is transferred for value by delivery without being negotiated and indorsement of the transferor is essential for negotiation, the transferee may compel the transferor to indorse the bill unless a contrary intention appears. The negotiation is effective when the indorsement is made.

(c) Effect of notification. –

(1) When a transferee notifies the common carrier that a nonnegotiable bill of lading has been transferred under subsection (a) of this section, the carrier is obligated directly to the transferee for any obligations the carrier owed to the transferor immediately before the notification. However, before the carrier is notified, the transferee's title to the goods and right to acquire the obligations of the carrier may be defeated by --

(A) garnishment, attachment, or execution on the goods by a creditor of the transferor; or

(B) notice to the carrier by the transferor or a purchaser from the transferor of a later purchase of the goods from the transferor.

(2) A common carrier has been notified under this subsection only if --

(A) an officer or agent of the carrier, whose actual or apparent authority includes acting on the notification, has been notified; and

(B) the officer or agent has had time, exercising reasonable diligence, to communicate with the agent having possession or control of the goods.

§ 80107. Warranties and Liability

(a) General rule. – Unless a contrary intention appears, a person negotiating or transferring a bill of lading for value warrants that --

(1) the bill is genuine;

(2) the person has the right to transfer the bill and the title to the goods described in the bill;

(3) the person does not know of a fact that would affect the validity or worth of the bill; and

(4) the goods are merchantable or fit for a particular purpose when merchantability or fitness would have been implied if the agreement of the parties had been to transfer the goods without a bill of lading.

(b) Security for debt. – A person holding a bill of lading as security for a debt and in good faith demanding or receiving payment of the debt from another person does not warrant by the demand or receipt –

(1) the genuineness of the bill; or

(2) the quantity or quality of the goods described in the bill.

(c) Duplicates. – A common carrier issuing a bill of lading, on the face of which is the word "duplicate" or another word indicating that the bill is not an original bill, is liable the same as a person that represents and warrants that the bill is an accurate copy of an original bill properly issued. The carrier is not otherwise liable under the bill.

(d) Indorser liability.--Indorsement of a bill of lading does not make the indorser liable for failure of the common carrier or a previous indorser to fulfill its obligations.

§ 80108. Alterations and Additions

An alteration or addition to a bill of lading after its issuance by a common carrier, without authorization from the carrier in writing or noted on the bill, is void. However, the original terms of the bill are enforceable.

§ 80109. Liens Under Negotiable Bills

A common carrier issuing a negotiable bill of lading has a lien on the goods covered by the bill for --

(1) charges for storage, transportation, and delivery (including demurrage and terminal charges), and expenses necessary to preserve the goods or incidental to transporting the goods after the date of the bill; and

(2) other charges for which the bill expressly specifies a lien is claimed to the extent the charges are allowed by law and the agreement between the consignor and carrier.

§ 80110. Duty to Deliver Goods

(a) General rules. – Except to the extent a common carrier establishes an excuse provided by law, the carrier must deliver goods covered by a bill of lading on demand of the consignee named in a nonnegotiable bill or the holder of a negotiable bill for the goods when the consignee or holder –

(1) offers in good faith to satisfy the lien of the carrier on the goods;

(2) has possession of the bill and, if a negotiable bill, offers to indorse and give the bill to the carrier; and

(3) agrees to sign, on delivery of the goods, a receipt for delivery if requested by the carrier.

(b) Persons to whom goods may be delivered. – Subject to section 80111 of this title, a common carrier may deliver the goods covered by a bill of lading to –

(1) a person entitled to their possession;

(2) the consignee named in a non-negotiable bill; or

(3) a person in possession of a negotiable bill if –

  (A) the goods are deliverable to the order of that person; or

  (B) the bill has been indorsed to that person or in blank by the consignee or another indorsee.

(c) Common carrier claims of title and possession. – A claim by a common carrier that the carrier has title to goods or right to their possession is an excuse for non-delivery of the goods only if the title or right is derived from –

(1) a transfer made by the consignor or consignee after the shipment; or

(2) the carrier's lien.

(d) Adverse claims. – If a person other than the consignee or the person in possession of a bill of lading claims title to or possession of goods and the common carrier knows of the claim, the carrier is not required to deliver the goods to any claimant until the carrier has had a reasonable time to decide the validity of the adverse claim or to bring a civil action to require all claimants to interplead.

(e) Interpleader. – If at least 2 persons claim title to or possession of the goods, the common carrier may --

(1) bring a civil action to interplead all known claimants to the goods; or

(2) require those claimants to interplead as a defense in an action brought against the carrier for non-delivery.

(f) Third person claims not a defense. – Except as provided in subsections (b), (d), and (e) of this section, title or a right of a third person is not a defense to an action brought by the consignee of a nonnegotiable bill of lading or by the holder of a negotiable bill against the common carrier for failure to deliver the goods on demand unless enforced by legal process.

§ 80111. Liability for Delivery of Goods

(a) General rules. – A common carrier is liable for damages to a person having title to, or right to possession of, goods when –

(1) the carrier delivers the goods to a person not entitled to their possession unless the delivery is authorized under section 80110(b)(2) or (3) of this title;

(2) the carrier makes a delivery under section 80110(b)(2) or (3) of this title after being requested by or for a person having title to, or right to possession of, the goods not to make the delivery; or

(3) at the time of delivery under section 80110(b)(2) or (3) of this title, the carrier has information it is delivering the goods to a person not entitled to their possession.

(b) Effectiveness of request or information. – A request or information is effective under subsection (a)(2) or (3) of this section only if --

(1) an officer or agent of the carrier, whose actual or apparent authority includes acting on the request or information, has been given the request or information; and

(2) the officer or agent has had time, exercising reasonable diligence, to stop delivery of the goods.

(c) Failure to take and cancel bills. – Except as provided in subsection (d) of this section, if a common carrier delivers goods for which a negotiable bill of lading has been issued without taking and canceling the bill, the carrier is liable for damages for failure to deliver the goods to a person purchasing the bill for value in good faith whether the purchase was before or after delivery and even when delivery was made to the person entitled to the goods. The carrier also is liable under this paragraph if part of the goods are delivered without taking and canceling the bill or plainly noting on the bill that a partial delivery was made and generally describing the goods or the remaining goods kept by the carrier.

(d) Exceptions to liability. – A common carrier is not liable for failure to deliver goods to the consignee or owner of the goods or a holder of the bill if --

(1) a delivery described in subsection (c) of this section was compelled by legal process;

(2) the goods have been sold lawfully to satisfy the carrier's lien;

(3) the goods have not been claimed; or

(4) the goods are perishable or hazardous.

§ 80112. Liability Under Negotiable Bills Issued in Parts, Sets, or Duplicates

(a) Parts and sets. – A negotiable bill of lading issued in a State for the transportation of goods to a place in the 48 contiguous States or the District of Columbia may not be issued in parts or sets. A common carrier issuing a bill in violation of this subsection is liable for damages for failure to deliver the goods to a purchaser of one part for value in good faith even though the purchase occurred after the carrier delivered the goods to a holder of one of the other parts.

(b) Duplicates. – When at least 2 negotiable bills of lading are issued in a State for the same goods to be transported to a place in the 48 contiguous States or the District of Columbia, the word "duplicate" or another word indicating that the bill is not an original must be put plainly on the face of each bill except the original. A common carrier violating this subsection is liable for damages caused by the violation to a purchaser of the bill for value in good faith as an original bill even though the purchase occurred after the carrier delivered the goods to the holder of the original bill.

§ 80113. Liability for Nonreceipt, Misdescription, and Improper Loading

(a) Liability for non-receipt and misdescription. – Except as provided in this section, a common carrier issuing a bill of lading is liable for damages caused by non-receipt by the carrier of any part of the goods by the date shown in the bill or by failure of the goods to correspond with the description contained in the bill. The carrier is liable to the owner of goods transported under a nonnegotiable bill (subject to the right of stoppage in transit) or to the holder of a negotiable bill if the owner or holder gave value in good faith relying on the description of the goods in the bill or on the shipment being made on the date shown in the bill.

(b) Non-liability of carriers. – A common carrier issuing a bill of lading is not liable under subsection (a) of this section –

(1) when the goods are loaded by the shipper;

(2) when the bill –

   (A) describes the goods in terms of marks or labels, or in a statement about kind, quantity, or condition; or

   (B) is qualified by "contents or condition of contents of packages unknown", "said to contain", "shipper's weight, load, and count", or words of the same meaning; and

(3) to the extent the carrier does not know whether any part of the goods were received or conform to the description.

(c) Liability for improper loading. – A common carrier issuing a bill of lading is not liable for damages caused by improper loading if --

(1) the shipper loads the goods; and

(2) the bill contains the words "shipper's weight, load, and count", or words of the same meaning indicating the shipper loaded the goods.

(d) Carrier's duty to determine kind, quantity, and number. –

(1) When bulk freight is loaded by a shipper that makes available to the common carrier adequate facilities for weighing the freight, the carrier must determine the kind and quantity of the freight within a reasonable time after receiving the written request of the shipper to make the determination. In that situation, inserting the words "shipper's weight" or words of the same meaning in the bill of lading has no effect.

(2) When goods are loaded by a common carrier, the carrier must count the packages of goods, if package freight, and determine the kind and quantity, if bulk freight. In that situation, inserting in the bill of lading or in a notice, receipt, contract, rule, or tariff, the words "shipper's weight, load, and count" or words indicating that the shipper described and loaded the goods, has no effect except for freight concealed by packages.

§ 80114. Lost, Stolen, and Destroyed Negotiable Bills

(a) Delivery on court order and surety bond. – If a negotiable bill of lading is lost, stolen, or destroyed, a court of competent jurisdiction may order the common carrier to deliver the goods if the person claiming the goods gives a surety bond, in an amount approved by the court, to indemnify the carrier or a person injured by delivery against liability under the outstanding original bill. The court also may order payment of reasonable costs and attorney's fees to the carrier. A voluntary surety bond, without court order, is binding on the parties to the bond.

(b) Liability to holder. – Delivery of goods under a court order under subsection (a) of this section does not relieve a common carrier from liability to a person to whom the negotiable bill has been or is negotiated for value without notice of the court proceeding or of the delivery of the goods.

§ 80115. Limitation on Use of Judicial Process to Obtain Possession of Goods from Common Carriers

(a) Attachment and levy. – Except when a negotiable bill of lading was issued originally on delivery of goods by a person that did not have the power to dispose of the goods, goods in the possession of a common carrier for which a negotiable bill has been issued may be attached through judicial process or levied on in execution of a judgment only if the bill is surrendered to the carrier or its negotiation is enjoined.

(b) Delivery. – A common carrier may be compelled by judicial process to deliver goods under subsection (a) of this section only when the bill is surrendered to the carrier or impounded by the court.

§ 80116. Criminal Penalty

A person shall be fined under title 18, imprisoned for not more than 5 years, or both, if the person – (1) violates this chapter with intent to defraud; or

(2) knowingly or with intent to defraud –

- (A) falsely makes, alters, or copies a bill of lading subject to this chapter;
- (B) utters, publishes, or issues a falsely made, altered, or copied bill subject to this chapter; or
- (C) negotiates or transfers for value a bill containing a false statement.

35) 1929 Convention for the Unification of Certain Rules Relating to International Carriage by Air ("Warsaw Convention")[1]

CHAPTER I - SCOPE - DEFINITIONS

Article 1

1. This Convention applies to all international carriage of persons, luggage or goods performed by aircraft for reward. It applies equally to gratuitous carriage by aircraft performed by an air transport undertaking.

2. For the purposes of this Convention the expression "international carriage" means any carriage in which, according to the contract made by the parties, the place of departure and the place of destination, whether or not there be a break in the carriage or a transhipment, are situated either within the territories of two High Contracting Parties, or within the territory of a single High Contracting Party, if there is an agreed stopping place within a territory subject to the sovereignty, suzerainty, mandate or authority of another Power, even though that Power is not a party to this Convention. A carriage without such an agreed stopping place between territories subject to the sovereignty, suzerainty, mandate or authority of the same High Contracting Party is not deemed to be international for the purposes of this Convention.

3. A carriage to be performed by several successive air carriers is deemed, for the purposes of this Convention, to be one undivided carriage, if it has been regarded by the parties as a single operation, whether it had been agreed upon under the form of a single contract or of a series of contracts, and it does not lose its international character merely because one contract or a series of contracts is to be performed entirely within a territory subject to the sovereignty, suzerainty, mandate or authority of the same High Contracting Party.

Article 2

1. This Convention applies to carriage performed by the State or by legally constituted public bodies provided it falls within the conditions laid down in Article 1.

2. This Convention does not apply to carriage performed under the terms of any international postal Convention.

CHAPTER II - DOCUMENTS OF CARRIAGE

Section I - Passenger Ticket

Article 3

1. For the carriage of passengers the carrier must deliver a passenger ticket which shall contain the following particulars:

(a) the place and date of issue;

(b) the place of departure and of destination;

(c) the agreed stopping places, provided that the carrier may reserve the right to alter the stopping places in case of necessity, and that if he exercises that right, the alteration shall not have the effect of depriving the carriage of its international character;

(d) the name and address of the carrier or carriers;

(e) a statement that the carriage is subject to the rules relating to liability established by this Convention.

---

2. The absence, irregularity or loss of the passenger ticket does not affect the existence or the validity of the contract of carriage, which shall none the less be subject to the rules of this Convention. Nevertheless, if the carrier accepts a passenger without a passenger ticket having been delivered he shall not be entitled to avail himself of those provisions of this Convention which exclude or limit his liability.

Section II - Luggage Ticket

Article 4

1. For the carriage of luggage, other than small personal objects of which the passenger takes charge himself, the carrier must deliver a luggage ticket.

2. The luggage ticket shall be made out in duplicate, one part for the passenger and the other part for the carrier.

3. The luggage ticket shall contain the following particulars:

(a) the place and date of issue;

(b) the place of departure and of destination;

(c) the name and address of the carrier or carriers;

(d) the number of the passenger ticket;

(e) a statement that delivery of the luggage will be made to the bearer of the luggage ticket;

(f) the number and weight of the packages;

(g) the amount of the value declared in accordance with Article 22(2);

(h) a statement that the carriage is subject to the rules relating to liability established by this Convention.

4. The absence, irregularity or loss of the luggage ticket does not affect the existence or the validity of the contract of carriage, which shall none the less be subject to the rules of this Convention. Nevertheless, if the carrier accepts luggage without a luggage ticket having been delivered, or if the luggage ticket does not contain the particulars set out at (d), (f) and (h) above, the carrier shall not be entitled to avail himself of those provisions of the Convention which exclude or limit his liability.

Section III - Air Consignment Note

Article 5

1. Every carrier of goods has the right to require the consignor to make out and hand over to him a document called an "air consignment note"; every consignor has the right to require the carrier to accept this document.

2. The absence, irregularity or loss of this document does not affect the existence or the validity of the contract of carriage which shall, subject to the provisions of Article 9, be none the less governed by the rules of this Convention.

Article 6

1. The air consignment note shall be made out by the consignor in three original parts and be handed over with the goods.

2. The first part shall be marked "for the carrier," and shall be signed by the consignor. The second part shall be marked "for the consignee"; it shall be signed by the consignor and by the carrier and shall accompany the goods. The third part shall be signed by the carrier and handed by him to the consignor after the goods have been accepted.

3. The carrier shall sign on acceptance of the goods.

4. The signature of the carrier may be stamped; that of the consignor may be printed or stamped.

5. If, at the request of the consignor, the carrier makes out the air consignment note, he shall be deemed, subject to proof to the contrary, to have done so on behalf of the consignor.

Article 7

The carrier of goods has the right to require the consignor to make out separate consignment notes when there is more than one package.

Article 8

The air consignment note shall contain the following particulars:-

(a) the place and date of its execution;

(b) the place of departure and of destination;

(c) the agreed stopping places, provided that the carrier may reserve the right to alter the stopping places in case of necessity, and that if he exercises that right the alteration shall not have the effect of depriving the carriage of its international character;

(d) the name and address of the consignor;

(e) the name and address of the first carrier;

(f) the name and address of the consignee, if the case so requires;

(g) the nature of the goods;

(h) the number of the packages, the method of packing and the particular marks or numbers upon them;

(i) the weight, the quantity and the volume or dimensions of the goods;

(j) the apparent condition of the goods and of the packing;

(k) the freight, if it has been agreed upon, the date and place of payment, and the person who is to pay it;

(l) if the goods are sent for payment on delivery, the price of the goods, and, if the case so requires, the amount of the expenses incurred;

(m) the amount of the value declared in accordance with Article 22 (2);

(n) the number of parts of the air consignment note;

(o) the documents handed to the carrier to accompany the air consignment note;

(p) the time fixed for the completion of the carriage and a brief note of the route to be followed, if these matters have been agreed upon;

(q) a statement that the carriage is subject to the rules relating to liability established by this Convention.

Article 9

If the carrier accepts goods without an air consignment note having been made out, or if the air consignment note does not contain all the particulars set out in Article 8(a) to (i) inclusive and (q), the carrier shall not be entitled to avail himself of the provisions of this Convention which exclude or limit his liability.

Article 10

1. The consignor is responsible for the correctness of the particulars and statements relating to the goods which he inserts in the air consignment note.

2. The consignor will be liable for all damage suffered by the carrier or any other person by reason of the irregularity, incorrectness or incompleteness of the said particulars and statements.

Article 11

1. The air consignment note is prima facie evidence of the conclusion of the contract, of the receipt of the goods and of the conditions of carriage.

2. The statements in the air consignment note relating to the weight, dimensions and packing of the goods, as well as those relating to the number of packages, are prima facie evidence of the facts stated; those relating to the quantity, volume and condition of the goods do not constitute evidence against the carrier except so far as they both have been, and are stated in the air consignment note to have been, checked by him in the presence of the consignor, or relate to the apparent condition of the goods.

Article 12

1. Subject to his liability to carry out all his obligations under the contract of carriage, the consignor has the right to dispose of the goods by withdrawing them at the aerodrome of departure or destination, or by stopping them in the course of the journey on any landing, or by calling for them to be delivered at the place of destination or in the course of the journey to a person other than the consignee named in the air consignment note, or by requiring them to be returned to the aerodrome of departure. He must not exercise this right of disposition in such a way as to prejudice the carrier or other consignors and he must repay any expenses occasioned by the exercise of this right.

2. If it is impossible to carry out the orders of the consignor the carrier must so inform him forthwith.

3. If the carrier obeys the orders of the consignor for the disposition of the goods without requiring the production of the part of the air consignment note delivered to the latter, he will be liable, without prejudice to his right of recovery from the consignor, for any damage which may be caused thereby to any person who is lawfully in possession of that part of the air consignment note.

4. The right conferred on the consignor ceases at the moment when that of the consignee begins in accordance with Article 13. Nevertheless, if the consignee declines to accept the consignment note or the goods, or if he cannot be communicated with, the consignor resumes his right of disposition.

Article 13

1. Except in the circumstances set out in the preceding Article, the consignee is entitled, on arrival of the goods at the place of destination, to require the carrier to hand over to him the air consignment note and to deliver the goods to him, on payment of the charges due and on complying with the conditions of carriage set out in the air consignment note.

2. Unless it is otherwise agreed, it is the duty of the carrier to give notice to the consignee as soon as the goods arrive.

3. If the carrier admits the loss of the goods, or if the goods have not arrived at the expiration of seven days after the date on which they ought to have arrived, the consignee is entitled to put into force against the carrier the rights which flow from the contract of carriage.

Article 14

The consignor and the consignee can respectively enforce all the rights given them by Articles 12 and 13, each in his own name, whether he is acting in his own interest or in the interest of another, provided that he carries out the obligations imposed by the contract.

Article 15

1. Articles 12, 13 and 14 do not affect either the relations of the consignor or the consignee with each other or the mutual relations of third parties whose rights are derived either from the consignor or from the consignee.

2. The provisions of Articles 12, 13 and 14 can only be varied by express provision in the air consignment note.

Article 16

1. The consignor must furnish such information and attach to the air consignment note such documents as are necessary to meet the formalities of customs, octroi or police before the goods can be delivered to the consignee. The consignor is liable to the carrier for any damage occasioned by the absence, insufficiency or irregularity of any such information or documents, unless the damage is due to the fault of the carrier or his agents.

2. The carrier is under no obligation to enquire into the correctness or sufficiency of such information or documents.

CHAPTER III - LIABILITY OF THE CARRIER

Article 17

The carrier is liable for damage sustained in the event of the death or wounding of a passenger or any other bodily injury suffered by a passenger, if the accident which caused the damage so sustained took place on board the aircraft or in the course of any of the operations of embarking or disembarking.

Article 18

1. The carrier is liable for damage sustained in the event of the destruction or loss of, or of damage to, any registered luggage or any goods, if the occurrence which caused the damage so sustained took place during the carriage by air.

2. The carriage by air within the meaning of the preceding paragraph comprises the period during which the luggage or goods are in charge of the carrier, whether in an aerodrome or on board an aircraft, or, in the case of a landing outside an aerodrome, in any place whatsoever.

3. The period of the carriage by air does not extend to any carriage by land, by sea or by river performed outside an aerodrome. If, however, such a carriage takes place in the performance of a contract for carriage by air, for the purpose of loading, delivery or transshipment, any damage is presumed, subject to proof to the contrary, to have been the result of an event which took place during the carriage by air.

Article 19

The carrier is liable for damage occasioned by delay in the carriage by air of passengers, luggage or goods.

Article 20

1. The carrier is not liable if he proves that he and his agents have taken all necessary measures to avoid the damage or that it was impossible for him or them to take such measures.

2. In the carriage of goods and luggage the carrier is not liable if he proves that the damage was occasioned by negligent pilotage or negligence in the handling of the aircraft or in navigation

and that, in all other respects, he and his agents have taken all necessary measures to avoid the damage.

Article 21

If the carrier proves that the damage was caused by or contributed to by the negligence of the injured person the Court may, in accordance with the provisions of its own law, exonerate the carrier wholly or partly from his liability.

Article 22

1. In the carriage of passengers the liability of the carrier for each passenger is limited to the sum of 125,000 francs. Where, in accordance with the law of the Court seised of the case, damages may be awarded in the form of periodical payments, the equivalent capital value of the said payments shall not exceed 125,000 francs. Nevertheless, by special contract, the carrier and the passenger may agree to a higher limit of liability.

2. In the carriage of registered luggage and of goods, the liability of the carrier is limited to a sum of 250 francs per kilogram, unless the consignor has made, at the time when the package was handed over to the carrier, a special declaration of the value at delivery and has paid a supplementary sum if the case so requires. In that case the carrier will be liable to pay a sum not exceeding the declared sum, unless he proves that that sum is greater than the actual value to the consignor at delivery.

3. As regards objects of which the passenger takes charge himself the liability of the carrier is limited to 5,000 francs per passenger.

4. The sums mentioned above shall be deemed to refer to the French franc consisting of 65 milligrams gold of millesimal fineness 900. These sums may be converted into any national currency in round figures.

Article 23

Any provision tending to relieve the carrier of liability or to fix a lower limit than that which is laid down in this Convention shall be null and void, but the nullity of any such provision does not involve the nullity of the whole contract, which shall remain subject to the provisions of this Convention.

Article 24

1. In the cases covered by Articles 18 and 19 any action for damages, however founded, can only be brought subject to the conditions and limits set out in this Convention.

2. In the cases covered by Article 17 the provisions of the preceding paragraph also apply, without prejudice to the questions as to who are the persons who have the right to bring suit and what are their respective rights.

Article 25

1. The carrier shall not be entitled to avail himself of the provisions of this Convention which exclude or limit his liability, if the damage is caused by his wilful misconduct or by such default on his part as, in accordance with the law of the Court seised of the case, is considered to be equivalent to wilful misconduct.

2. Similarly the carrier shall not be entitled to avail himself of the said provisions, if the damage is caused as aforesaid by any agent of the carrier acting within the scope of his employment.

Article 26

1. Receipt by the person entitled to delivery of luggage or goods without complaint is prima facie evidence that the same have been delivered in good condition and in accordance with the document of carriage.

2. In the case of damage, the person entitled to delivery must complain to the carrier forthwith after the discovery of the damage, and, at the latest, within three days from the date of receipt in the case of luggage and seven days from the date of receipt in the case of goods. In the case of delay the complaint must be made at the latest within fourteen days from the date on which the luggage or goods have been placed at his disposal.

3. Every complaint must be made in writing upon the document of carriage or by separate notice in writing despatched within the times aforesaid.

4. Failing complaint within the times aforesaid, no action shall lie against the carrier, save in the case of fraud on his part.

Article 27

In the case of the death of the person liable, an action for damages lies in accordance with the terms of this Convention against those legally representing his estate.

Article 28

1. An action for damages must be brought, at the option of the plaintiff, in the territory of one of the High Contracting Parties, either before the Court having jurisdiction where the carrier is ordinarily resident, or has his principal place of business, or has an establishment by which the contract has been made or before the Court having jurisdiction at the place of destination.

2. Questions of procedure shall be governed by the law of the Court seised of the case.

Article 29

1. The right to damages shall be extinguished if an action is not brought within two years, reckoned from the date of arrival at the destination, or from the date on which the aircraft ought to have arrived, or from the date on which the carriage stopped.

2. The method of calculating the period of limitation shall be determined by the law of the Court seised of the case.

Article 30

1. In the case of carriage to be performed by various successive carriers and falling within the definition set out in the third paragraph of Article 1, each carrier who accepts passengers, luggage or goods is subjected to the rules set out in this Convention, and is deemed to be one of the contracting parties to the contract of carriage in so far as the contract deals with that part of the carriage which is performed under his supervision.

2. In the case of carriage of this nature, the passenger or his representative can take action only against the carrier who performed the carriage during which the accident or the delay occurred, save in the case where, by express agreement, the first carrier has assumed liability for the whole journey.

3. A s regards luggage or goods, the passenger or consignor will have a right of action against the first carrier, and the passenger or consignee who is entitled to delivery will have a right of action against the last carrier, and further, each may take action against the carrier who performed the carriage during which the destruction, loss, damage or delay took place. These carriers will be jointly and severally liable to the passenger or to the consignor or consignee.

CHAPTER IV - PROVISIONS RELATING TO COMBINED CARRIAGE

Article 31

1. In the case of combined carriage performed partly by air and partly by any other mode of carriage, the provisions of this Convention apply only to the carriage by air, provided that the carriage by air falls within the terms of Article 1.

2. Nothing in this Convention shall prevent the parties in the case of combined carriage from inserting in the document of air carriage conditions relating to other modes of carriage, provided that the provisions of this Convention are observed as regards the carriage by air.

CHAPTER V - GENERAL AND FINAL PROVISIONS

Article 32

Any clause contained in the contract and all special agreements entered into before the damage occurred by which the parties purport to infringe the rules laid down by this Convention, whether by deciding the law to be applied, or by altering the rules as to jurisdiction, shall be null and void. Nevertheless for the carriage of goods arbitration clauses are allowed, subject to this Convention, if the arbitration is to take place within one of the jurisdictions referred to in the first paragraph of Article 28.

Article 33

Nothing contained in this Convention shall prevent the carrier either from refusing to enter into any contract of carriage, or from making regulations which do not conflict with the provisions of this Convention.

Article 34

This Convention does not apply to international carriage by air performed by way of experimental trial by air navigation undertakings with the view to the establishment of a regular line of air navigation, nor does it apply to carriage performed in extraordinary circumstances outside the normal scope of an air carrier's business.

Article 35

The expression "days" when used in this Convention means current days not working days.

Articles 36 - 41 [dealing with ratification etc. omitted]

This Convention done at Warsaw on the 12th October, 1929, shall remain open for signature until the 31st January, 1930.

Additional Protocol (With reference to Article 2)

The High Contracting Parties reserve to themselves the right to declare at the time of ratification or of accession that the first paragraph of Article 2 of this Convention shall not apply to international carriage by air performed directly by the State, its colonies, protectorates or mandated territories or by any other territory under its sovereignty, suzerainty or authority."

Entry into force: 13 February 1933

Ratifications and binding effect as of April 2020: 1929 Convention: 152 Member States; 1955 Hague Protocol to Amend the 1929 Convention (amendments not reproduced here): 137 Member States

36) 1999 CONVENTION FOR THE UNIFICATION OF CERTAIN RULES FOR INTERNATIONAL CARRIAGE BY AIR ("MONTREAL CONVENTION")[1]

THE STATES PARTIES TO THIS CONVENTION

RECOGNIZING the significant contribution of the Convention for the Unification of Certain Rules relating to International Carriage by Air signed in Warsaw on 12 October 1929, hereinafter referred to as the "Warsaw Convention", and other related instruments to the harmonization of private international air law;

RECOGNIZING the need to modernize and consolidate the Warsaw Convention and related instruments;

RECOGNIZING the importance of ensuring protection of the interests of consumers in international carriage by air and the need for equitable compensation based on the principle of restitution;

REAFFIRMING the desirability of an orderly development of international air transport operations and the smooth flow of passengers, baggage and cargo in accordance with the principles and objectives of the Convention on International Civil Aviation, done at Chicago on 7 December 1944;

CONVINCED that collective State action for further harmonization and codification of certain rules governing international carriage by air through a new Convention is the most adequate means of achieving an equitable balance of interests;

HAVE AGREED AS FOLLOWS:

Chapter 1 - General Provisions

Article 1 - Scope of Application

1. This Convention applies to all international carriage of persons, baggage or cargo performed by aircraft for reward. It applies equally to gratuitous carriage by aircraft performed by an air transport undertaking.

2. For the purposes of this Convention, the expression "international carriage" means any carriage in which, according to the agreement between the parties, the place of departure and the place of destination, whether or not there be a break in the carriage or a transhipment, are situated either within the territories of two States Parties, or within the territory of a single State Party if there is an agreed stopping place within the territory of another State, even if that State is not a State Party.

Carriage between two points within the territory of a single State Party without an agreed stopping place within the territory of another State is not international carriage for the purposes of this Convention.

3. Carriage to be performed by several successive carriers is deemed, for the purposes of this Convention, to be one undivided carriage if it has been regarded by the parties as a single operation, whether it had been agreed upon under the form of a single contract or of a series of contracts, and it does not lose its international character merely because one contract or a series of contracts is to be performed entirely within the territory of the same State.

4. This Convention applies also to carriage as set out in Chapter V, subject to the terms contained therein.

---

1 This Convention replaces the Warsaw Convention once ratified by all Contracting States.

Article 2 - Carriage Performed by State and Carriage of Postal Items

1. This Convention applies to carriage performed by the State or by legally constituted public bodies provided it falls within the conditions laid down in Article 1.

2. In the carriage of postal items, the carrier shall be liable only to the relevant postal administration in accordance with the rules applicable to the relationship between the carriers and the postal administrations.

3. Except as provided in paragraph 2 of this Article, the provisions of this Convention shall not apply to the carriage of postal items.

Chapter II - Documentation and Duties of the Parties Relating to the Carriage of Passengers, Baggage and Cargo

Article 3 - Passengers and Baggage

1. In respect of carriage of passengers, an individual or collective document of carriage shall be delivered containing:

(a) an indication of the places of departure and destination;

(b) if the places of departure and destination are within the territory of a single State Party, one or more agreed stopping places being within the territory of another State, an indication of at least one such stopping place.

2. Any other means which preserves the information indicated in paragraph 1 may be substituted for the delivery of the document referred to in that paragraph. If any such other means is used, the carrier shall offer to deliver to the passenger a written statement of the information so preserved.

3. The carrier shall deliver to the passenger a baggage identification tag for each piece of checked baggage.

4. The passenger shall be given written notice to the effect that where this Convention is applicable it governs and may limit the liability of carriers in respect of death or injury and for destruction or loss of, or damage to, baggage, and for delay.

5. Non-compliance with the provisions of the foregoing paragraphs shall not affect the existence or the validity of the contract of carriage, which shall, nonetheless, be subject to the rules of this Convention including those relating to limitation of liability.

Article 4 - Cargo

1. In respect of the carriage of cargo, an air waybill shall be delivered.

2. Any other means which preserves a record of the carriage to be performed may be substituted for the delivery of an air waybill. If such other means are used, the carrier shall, if so requested by the consignor, deliver to the consignor a cargo receipt permitting identification of the consignment and access to the information contained in the record preserved by such other means.

Article 5 - Contents of Air Waybill or Cargo Receipt

The air waybill or the cargo receipt shall include:

(a) an indication of the places of departure and destination;

(b) if the places of departure and destination are within the territory of a single State Party, one or more agreed stopping places being within the territory of another State, an indication of at least one such stopping place; and

(c) an indication of the weight of the consignment.

Article 6 - Document Relating to the Nature of the Cargo

The consignor may be required, if necessary, to meet the formalities of customs, police and similar public authorities to deliver a document indicating the nature of the cargo. This provision creates for the carrier no duty, obligation or liability resulting therefrom.

Article 7 - Description of Air Waybill

1. The air waybill shall be made out by the consignor in three original parts.

2. The first part shall be marked “for the carrier”; it shall be signed by the consignor. The second part shall be marked “for the consignee”; it shall be signed by the consignor and by the carrier. The third part shall be signed by the carrier who shall hand it to the consignor after the cargo has been accepted.

3. The signature of the carrier and that of the consignor may be printed or stamped.

4. If, at the request of the consignor, the carrier makes out the air waybill, the carrier shall be deemed, subject to proof to the contrary, to have done so on behalf of the consignor.

Article 8 - Documentation for Multiple Packages

When there is more than one package:

(a) the carrier of cargo has the right to require the consignor to make out separate air waybills;

(b) the consignor has the right to require the carrier to deliver separate cargo receipts when the other means referred to in paragraph 2 of Article 4 are used.

Article 9 - Non-Compliance with Documentary Requirements

Non-compliance with the provisions of Articles 4 to 8 shall not affect the existence or the validity of the contract of carriage, which shall, nonetheless, be subject to the rules of this Convention including those relating to limitation of liability.

Article 10 - Responsibility for Particulars of Documentation

1. The consignor is responsible for the correctness of the particulars and statements relating to the cargo inserted by it or on its behalf in the air waybill or furnished by it or on its behalf to the carrier for insertion in the cargo receipt or for insertion in the record preserved by the other means referred to in paragraph 2 of Article 4. The foregoing shall also apply where the person acting on behalf of the consignor is also the agent of the carrier.

2. The consignor shall indemnify the carrier against all damage suffered by it, or by any other person to whom the carrier is liable, by reason of the irregularity, incorrectness or incompleteness of the particulars and statements furnished by the consignor or on its behalf.

3. Subject to the provisions of paragraphs 1 and 2 of this Article, the carrier shall indemnify the consignor against all damage suffered by it, or by any other person to whom the consignor is liable, by reason of the irregularity, incorrectness or incompleteness of the particulars and statements inserted by the carrier or on its behalf in the cargo receipt or in the record preserved by the other means referred to in paragraph 2 of Article 4.

Article 11 - Evidentiary Value of Documentation

1. The air waybill or the cargo receipt is prima facie evidence of the conclusion of the contract, of the acceptance of the cargo and of the conditions of carriage mentioned therein.

2. Any statements in the air waybill or the cargo receipt relating to the weight, dimensions and packing of the cargo, as well as those relating to the number of packages, are prima facie evidence of the facts stated; those relating to the quantity, volume and condition of the cargo do not constitute evidence against the carrier except so far as they both have been, and are stated

in the air waybill or the cargo receipt to have been, checked by it in the presence of the consignor, or relate to the apparent condition of the cargo.

Article 12 - Right of Disposition of Cargo

1. Subject to its liability to carry out all its obligations under the contract of carriage, the consignor has the right to dispose of the cargo by withdrawing it at the airport of departure or destination, or by stopping it in the course of the journey on any landing, or by calling for it to be delivered at the place of destination or in the course of the journey to a person other than the consignee originally designated, or by requiring it to be returned to the airport of departure. The consignor must not exercise this right of disposition in such a way as to prejudice the carrier or other consignors and must reimburse any expenses occasioned by the exercise of this right.

2. If it is impossible to carry out the instructions of the consignor, the carrier must so inform the consignor forthwith.

3. If the carrier carries out the instructions of the consignor for the disposition of the cargo without requiring the production of the part of the air waybill or the cargo receipt delivered to the latter, the carrier will be liable, without prejudice to its right of recovery from the consignor, for any damage which may be caused thereby to any person who is lawfully in possession of that part of the air waybill or the cargo receipt.

4. The right conferred on the consignor ceases at the moment when that of the consignee begins in accordance with Article 13. Nevertheless, if the consignee declines to accept the cargo, or cannot be communicated with, the consignor resumes its right of disposition.

Article 13 - Delivery of the Cargo

1. Except when the consignor has exercised its right under Article 12, the consignee is entitled, on arrival of the cargo at the place of destination, to require the carrier to deliver the cargo to it, on payment of the charges due and on complying with the conditions of carriage.

2. Unless it is otherwise agreed, it is the duty of the carrier to give notice to the consignee as soon as the cargo arrives.

3. If the carrier admits the loss of the cargo, or if the cargo has not arrived at the expiration of seven days after the date on which it ought to have arrived, the consignee is entitled to enforce against the carrier the rights which flow from the contract of carriage.

Article 14 - Enforcement of the Rights of Consignor and Consignee

The consignor and the consignee can respectively enforce all the rights given to them by Articles 12 and 13, each in its own name, whether it is acting in its own interest or in the interest of another, provided that it carries out the obligations imposed by the contract of carriage.

Article 15 - Relations of Consignor and Consignee or Mutual Relations of Third Parties

1. Articles 12, 13 and 14 do not affect either the relations of the consignor and the consignee with each other or the mutual relations of third parties whose rights are derived either from the consignor or from the consignee.

2. The provisions of Articles 12, 13 and 14 can only be varied by express provision in the air waybill or the cargo receipt.

Article 16 - Formalities of Customs, Police or Other Public Authorities

1. The consignor must furnish such information and such documents as are necessary to meet the formalities of customs, police and any other public authorities before the cargo can be delivered to the consignee. The consignor is liable to the carrier for any damage occasioned by

the absence, insufficiency or irregularity of any such information or documents, unless the damage is due to the fault of the carrier, its servants or agents.

2. The carrier is under no obligation to enquire into the correctness or sufficiency of such information or documents.

Chapter III - Liability of the Carrier and Extent of Compensation for Damage

Article 17 - Death and Injury of Passengers - Damage to Baggage

1. The carrier is liable for damage sustained in case of death or bodily injury of a passenger upon condition only that the accident which caused the death or injury took place on board the aircraft or in the course of any of the operations of embarking or disembarking.

2. The carrier liable for damage sustained in case of destruction or loss of, or of damage to, checked baggage upon condition only that the event which caused the destruction, loss or damage took place on board the aircraft or during any period within which the checked baggage was in the charge of the carrier. However, the carrier is not liable if and to the extent that the damage resulted from the inherent defect, quality or vice of the baggage. In the case of unchecked baggage, including personal items, the carrier is liable if the damage resulted from its fault or that of its servants or agents.

3. If the carrier admits the loss of the checked baggage, or if the checked baggage has not arrived at the expiration of twenty-one days after the date on which it ought to have arrived, the passenger is entitled to enforce against the carrier the rights which flow from the contract of carriage.

4. Unless otherwise specified, in this Convention the term "baggage" means both checked baggage and unchecked baggage.

Article 18 - Damage to Cargo

1. The carrier is liable for damage sustained in the event of the destruction or loss of or damage to, cargo upon condition only that the event which caused the damage so sustained took place during the carriage by air.

2. However, the carrier is not liable if and to the extent it proves that the destruction, or loss of, or damage to, the cargo resulted from one or more of the following:

(a) inherent defect, quality or vice of that cargo;

(b) defective packing of that cargo performed by a person other than the carrier or its servants or agents;

(c) an act of war or an armed conflict;

(d) an act of public authority carried out in connection with the entry, exit or transit of the cargo.

3. The carriage by air within the meaning of paragraph 1 of this Article comprises the period during which the cargo is in the charge of the carrier.

4. The period of the carriage by air does not extend to any carriage by land, by sea or by inland waterway performed outside an airport. If, however, such carriage takes place in the performance of a contract for carriage by air, for the purpose of loading, delivery or transhipment, any damage is presumed, subject to proof to the contrary, to have been the result of an event which took place during the carriage by air. If a carrier, without the consent of the consignor, substitutes carriage by another mode of transport for the whole or part of a carriage intended by the agreement between the parties to be carriage by air, such carriage by another mode of transport is deemed to be within the period of carriage by air.

Article 19 - Delay

The carrier is liable for damage occasioned by delay in the carriage by air of passengers, baggage or cargo. Nevertheless, the carrier shall not be liable for damage occasioned by delay if it proves that it and its servants and agents took all measures that could reasonably be required to avoid the damage or that it was impossible for it or them to take such measures.

Article 20 - Exoneration

If the carrier proves that the damage was caused or contributed to by the negligence or other wrongful act or omission of the person claiming compensation, or the person from whom he or she derives his or her rights, the carrier shall be wholly or partly exonerated from its liability to the claimant to the extent that such negligence or wrongful act or omission caused or contributed to the damage. When by reason of death or injury of a passenger compensation is claimed by a person other than the passenger, the carrier shall likewise be wholly or partly exonerated from its liability to the extent that it proves that the damage was caused or contributed to by the negligence or other wrongful act or omission of that passenger. This Article applies to all the liability provisions in this Convention, including paragraph 1 of Article 21.

Article 21 - Compensation in Case of Death or Injury of Passengers

1. For damages arising under paragraph 1 of Article 17 not exceeding 100,000 Special Drawing Rights for each passenger, the carrier shall not be able to exclude or limit its liability.

2. The carrier shall not be liable for damages arising under paragraph 1 of Article 17 to the extent that they exceed for each passenger 100,000 Special Drawing Rights if the carrier proves that:

(a) such damage was not due to the negligence or other wrongful act or omission of the carrier or its servants or agents; or

(b) such damage was solely due to the negligence or other wrongful act or omission of a third party.

Article 22 - Limits of Liability in Relation to Delay, Baggage and Cargo

1. In the case of damage caused by delay as specified in Article 19 in the carriage of persons, the liability of the carrier for each passenger is limited to 4,150 Special Drawing Rights.

2. In the carriage of baggage, the liability of the carrier in the case of destruction, loss, damage or delay is limited to 1,000 Special Drawing Rights for each passenger unless the passenger has made, at the time when the checked baggage was handed over to the carrier, a special declaration of interest in delivery at destination and has paid a supplementary sum if the case so requires. In that case the carrier will be liable to pay a sum not exceeding the declared sum, unless it proves that the sum is greater than the passenger's actual interest in delivery at destination.

3. In the carriage of cargo, the liability of the carrier in the case of destruction, loss, damage or delay is limited to a sum of 17 Special Drawing Rights per kilogram, unless the consignor has made, at the time when the package was handed over to the carrier, a special declaration of interest in delivery at destination and has paid a supplementary sum if the case so requires. In that case the carrier will be liable to pay a sum not exceeding the declared sum, unless it proves that the sum is greater than the consignor's actual interest in delivery at destination.

4. In the case of destruction, loss, damage or delay of part of the cargo, or of any object contained therein, the weight to be taken into consideration in determining the amount to which the carrier's liability is limited shall be only the total weight of the package or packages concerned.

Nevertheless, when the destruction, loss, damage or delay of a part of the cargo, or of an object contained therein, affects the value of other packages covered by the same air waybill, or the same receipt or, if they were not issued, by the same record preserved by the other means referred to in paragraph 2 of Article 4, the total weight of such package or packages shall also be taken into consideration in determining the limit of liability.

5. The foregoing provisions of paragraphs 1 and 2 of this Article shall not apply if it is proved that the damage resulted from an act or omission of the carrier, its servants or agents, done with intent to cause damage or recklessly and with knowledge that damage would probably result; provided that, in the case of such act or omission of a servant or agent, it is also proved that such servant or agent was acting within the scope of its employment.

6. The limits prescribed in Article 21 and in this Article shall not prevent the court from awarding, in accordance with its own law, in addition, the whole or part of the court costs and of the other expenses of the litigation incurred by the plaintiff, including interest. The foregoing provision shall not apply if the amount of the damages awarded, excluding court costs and other expenses of the litigation, does not exceed the sum which the carrier has offered in writing to the plaintiff within a period of six months from the date of the occurrence causing the damage, or before the commencement of the action, if that is later.

Article 23 - Conversion of Monetary Units

1. The sums mentioned in terms of Special Drawing Right in this Convention shall be deemed to refer to the Special Drawing Right as defined by the International Monetary Fund. Conversion of the sums into national currencies shall, in case of judicial proceedings, be made according to the value of such currencies in terms of the Special Drawing Right at the date of the judgement. The value of a national currency, in terms of the Special Drawing Right, of a State Party which is a Member of the International Monetary Fund, shall be calculated in accordance with the method of valuation applied by the International Monetary Fund, in effect at the date of the judgement, for its operations and transactions. The value of a national currency, in terms of the Special Drawing Right, of a State Party which is not a Member of the International Monetary Fund, shall be calculated in a manner determined by that State.

2. Nevertheless, those States which are not Members of the International Monetary Fund and whose law does not permit the application of the provisions of paragraph 1 of this Article may, at the time of ratification or accession or at any time thereafter, declare that the limit of liability of the carrier prescribed in Article 21 is fixed at a sum of 1,500,000 monetary units per passenger in judicial proceedings in their territories; 62,500 monetary units per passenger with respect to paragraph 1 of Article 22; 15,000 monetary units per passenger with respect to paragraph 2 of Article 22; and 250 monetary units per kilogram with respect to paragraph 3 of Article 22. This monetary unit corresponds to sixty-five and a half milligrams of gold of millesimal fineness nine hundred. These sums may be converted into the national currency concerned in round figures. The conversion of these sums into national currency shall be made according to the law of the State concerned.

3. The calculation mentioned in the last sentence of paragraph I of this Article and the conversion method mentioned in paragraph 2 of this Article shall be made in such manner as to express in the national currency of the State Party as far as possible the same real value for the amounts in Articles 21 and 22 as would result from the application of the first three sentences of paragraph 1 of this Article. States Parties shall communicate to the depositary the manner of calculation pursuant to paragraph 1 of this Article, or the result of the conversion in paragraph 2 of this Article as the case may be, when depositing an instrument of ratification, acceptance, approval of or accession to this Convention and whenever there is a change in either.

Article 24 - Review of Limits

1. Without prejudice to the provisions of Article 25 of this Convention and subject to paragraph 2 below, the limits of liability prescribed in Articles 21, 22 and 23 shall be reviewed by the Depositary at five-year intervals, the first such review to take place at the end of the fifth year following the date of entry into force of this Convention, or if the Convention does not enter into force within five years of the date it is first open for signature, within the first year of its entry into force, by reference to an inflation factor which corresponds to the accumulated rate of inflation since the previous revision or in the first instance since the date of entry into force of the Convention. The measure of the rate of inflation to be used in determining the inflation factor shall be the weighted average of the annual rates of increase or decrease in the Consumer Price Indices of the States whose currencies comprise the Special Drawing Right mentioned in paragraph 1 of Article 23.

2. If the review referred to in the preceding paragraph concludes that the inflation factor has exceeded 10 percent, the Depositary shall notify States Parties of a revision of the limits of liability. Any such revision shall become effective six months after its notification to the States Parties. If within three months after its notification to the States Parties a majority of the States Parties register their disapproval, the revision shall not become effective and the Depositary shall refer the matter to a meeting of the States Parties. The Depositary shall immediately notify all States Parties of the coming into force of any revision.

3. Notwithstanding paragraph 1 of this Article, the procedure referred to in paragraph 2 of this Article shall be applied at any time provided that one-third of the States Parties express a desire to that effect and upon condition that the inflation factor referred to in paragraph 1 has exceeded 30 percent since the previous revision or since the date of entry into force of this Convention if there has been no previous revision. Subsequent reviews using the procedure described in paragraph 1 of this Article will take place at five-year intervals starting at the end of the fifth year following the date of the reviews under the present paragraph.

Article 25 - Stipulation on Limits

A carrier may stipulate that the contract of carriage shall be subject to higher limits of liability than those provided for in this Convention or to no limits of liability whatsoever.

Article 26 - Invalidity of Contractual Provisions

Any provision tending to relieve the carrier of liability or to fix a lower limit than that which is laid down in this Convention shall be null and void, but the nullity of any such provision does not involve the nullity of the whole contract, which shall remain subject to the provisions of this Convention.

Article 27 - Freedom to Contract

Nothing contained in this Convention shall prevent the carrier from refusing to enter into any contract of carriage, from waiving any defences available under the Convention, or from laying down conditions which do not conflict with the provisions of this Convention.

Article 28 - Advance Payments

In the case of aircraft accidents resulting in death or injury of passengers, the carrier shall, if required by its national law, make advance payments without delay to a natural person or persons who are entitled to claim compensation in order to meet the immediate economic needs of such persons. Such advance payments shall not constitute a recognition of liability and may be offset against any amounts subsequently paid as damages by the carrier.

Article 29 - Basis of Claims

In the carriage of passengers, baggage and cargo, any action for damages, however founded, whether under this Convention or in contract or in tort or otherwise, can only be brought subject to the conditions and such limits of liability as are set out in this Convention without prejudice to the question as to who are the persons who have the right to bring suit and what are their respective rights. In any such action, punitive, exemplary or any other non-compensatory damages shall not be recoverable.

Article 30 - Servants, Agents - Aggregation of Claims

1. If an action is brought against a servant or agent of the carrier arising out of damage to which the Convention relates, such servant or agent, if they prove that they acted within the scope of their employment, shall be entitled to avail themselves of the conditions and limits of liability which the carrier itself is entitled to invoke under this Convention.

2. The aggregate of the amounts recoverable from the carrier, its servants and agents, in that case, shall not exceed the said limits.

3. Save in respect of the carriage of cargo, the provisions of paragraphs 1 and 2 of this Article shall not apply if it is proved that the damage resulted from an act or omission of the servant or agent done with intent to cause damage or recklessly and with knowledge that damage would probably result.

Article 31 - Timely Notice of Complaints

1. Receipt by the person entitled to delivery of checked baggage or cargo without complaint is prima facie evidence that the same has been delivered in good condition and in accordance with the document of carriage or with the record preserved by the other means referred to in paragraph 2 of Article 3 and paragraph 2 of Article 4.

2. In the case of damage, the person entitled to delivery must complain to the carrier forthwith after the discovery of the damage, and, at the latest, within seven days from the date of receipt in the case of checked baggage and fourteen days from the date of receipt in the case of cargo. In the case of delay, the complaint must be made at the latest within twenty-one days from the date on which the baggage or cargo have been placed at his or her disposal.

3. Every complaint must be made in writing and given or dispatched within the times aforesaid.

4. If no complaint is made within the times aforesaid, no action shall lie against the carrier, save in the case of fraud on its part.

Article 32 - Death of Person Liable

In the case of the death of the person liable, an action for damages lies in accordance with the terms of this Convention against those legally representing his or her estate.

Article 33 - Jurisdiction

1. An action for damages must be brought, at the option of the plaintiff, in the territory of one of the States Parties, either before the court of the domicile of the carrier or of its principal place of business, or where it has a place of business through which the contract has been made or before the court at the place of destination.

2. In respect of damage resulting from the death or injury of a passenger, an action may be brought before one of the courts mentioned in paragraph 1 of this Article, or in the territory of a State Party in which at the time of the accident the passenger has his or her principal and permanent residence and to or from which the carrier operates services for the carriage of passen-

gers by air, either on its own aircraft or on another carrier's aircraft pursuant to a commercial agreement, and in which that carrier conducts its business of carriage of passengers by air from premises leased or owned by the carrier itself or by another carrier with which it has a commercial agreement.

3. For the purposes of paragraph 2,

(a) "commercial agreement" means an agreement, other than an agency agreement, made between carriers and relating to the provision of their joint services for carriage of passengers by air;

(b) "principal and permanent residence" means the one fixed and permanent abode of the passenger at the time of the accident. The nationality of the passenger shall not be the determining factor in this regard.

4. Questions of procedure shall be governed by the law of the court seized of the case.

Article 34 - Arbitration

1. Subject to the provisions of this Article, the parties to the contract of carriage for cargo may stipulate that any dispute relating to the liability of the carrier under this Convention shall be settled by arbitration. Such agreement shall be in writing.

2. The arbitration proceedings shall, at the option of the claimant, take place within one of the jurisdictions referred to in Article 33.

3. The arbitrator or arbitration tribunal shall apply the provisions of this Convention.

4. The provisions of paragraphs 2 and 3 of this Article shall be deemed to be part of every arbitration clause or agreement, and any term of such clause or agreement which is inconsistent therewith shall be null and void.

Article 35 - Limitation of Actions

1. The right to damages shall be extinguished if an action is not brought within a period of two years, reckoned from the date of arrival at the destination, or from the date on which the aircraft ought to have arrived, or from the date on which the carriage stopped.

2. The method of calculating that period shall be determined by the law of the court seized of the case.

Article 36 - Successive Carriage

1. In the case of carriage to be performed by various successive carriers and falling within the definition set out in paragraph 3 of Article 1, each carrier which accepts passengers, baggage or cargo is subject to the rules set out in this Convention and is deemed to be one of the parties to the contract of carriage in so far as the contract deals with that part of the carriage which is performed under its supervision.

2. In the case of carriage of this nature, the passenger or any person entitled to compensation in respect of him or her can take action only against the carrier which performed the carriage during which the accident or the delay occurred, save in the case where, by express agreement, the first carrier has assumed liability for the whole journey.

3. As regards baggage or cargo, the passenger or consignor will have a right of action against the first carrier, and the passenger or consignee who is entitled to delivery will have a right of action against the last carrier, and further, each may take action against the carrier which performed the carriage during which the destruction, loss, damage or delay took place. These carriers will be jointly and severally liable to the passenger or to the consignor or consignee.

Article 37 - Right of Recourse Against Third Parties

Nothing in this Convention shall prejudice the question whether a person liable for damage in accordance with its provisions has a right of recourse against any other person.

Chapter IV - Combined Carriage

Article 38 - Combined Carriage

1. In the case of combined carriage performed partly by air and partly by any other mode of carriage, the provisions of this Convention shall, subject to paragraph 4 of Article 18, apply only to the carriage by air, provided that the carriage by air falls within the terms of Article 1.

2. Nothing in this Convention shall prevent the parties in the case of combined carriage from inserting in the document of air carriage conditions relating to other modes of carriage, provided that the provisions of this Convention are observed as regards the carriage by air.

Chapter V - Carriage by Air Performed by a Person Other than the Contracting Carrier

Article 39 - Contracting Carrier - Actual Carrier

The provisions of this Chapter apply when a person (hereinafter referred to as "the contracting carrier") as a principal makes a contract of carriage governed by this Convention with a passenger or consignor or with a person acting on behalf of the passenger or consignor, and another person (hereinafter referred to as "the actual carrier") performs, by virtue of authority from the contracting carrier, the whole or part of the carriage, but is not with respect to such part a successive carrier within the meaning of this Convention. Such authority shall be presumed in the absence of proof to the contrary.

Article 40 - Respective Liability of Contracting and Actual Carriers

If an actual carrier performs the whole or part of carriage which, according to the contract referred to in Article 39, is governed by this Convention, both the contracting carrier and the actual carrier shall, except as otherwise provided in this Chapter, be subject to the rules of this Convention, the former for the whole of the carriage contemplated in the contract, the latter solely for the carriage which it performs.

Article 41 - Mutual Liability

1. The acts and omissions of the actual carrier and of its servants and agents acting within the scope of their employment shall, in relation to the carriage performed by the actual carrier, be deemed to be also those of the contracting carrier.

2. The acts and omissions of the contracting carrier and of its servants and agents acting within the scope of their employment shall, in relation to the carriage performed by the actual carrier, be deemed to be also those of the actual carrier. Nevertheless, no such act or omission shall subject the actual carrier to liability exceeding the amounts referred to in Articles 21, 22, 23 and 24. Any special agreement under which the contracting carrier assumes obligations not imposed by this Convention or any waiver of rights or defences conferred by this Convention or any special declaration of interest in delivery at destination contemplated in Article 22 shall not affect the actual carrier unless agreed to by it.

Article 42 - Addressee of Complaints and Instructions

Any complaint to be made or instruction to be given under this Convention to the carrier shall have the same effect whether addressed to the contracting carrier or to the actual carrier. Nevertheless, instructions referred to in Article 12 shall only be effective if addressed to the contracting carrier.

Article 43 - Servants and Agents

In relation to the carriage performed by the actual carrier, any servant or agent of that carrier or of the contracting carrier shall, if they prove that they acted within the scope of their employment, be entitled to avail themselves of the conditions and limits of liability which are applicable under this Convention to the carrier whose servant or agent they are, unless it is proved that they acted in a manner that prevents the limits of liability from being invoked in accordance with this Convention.

Article 44 - Aggregation of Damages

In relation to the carriage performed by the actual carrier, the aggregate of the amounts recoverable from that carrier and the contracting carrier, and from their servants and agents acting within the scope of their employment, shall not exceed the highest amount which could be awarded against either the contracting carrier or the actual carrier under this Convention, but none of the persons mentioned shall be liable for a sum in excess of the limit applicable to that person.

Article 45 - Addressee of Claims

In relation to the carriage performed by the actual carrier, an action for damages may be brought, at the option of the plaintiff, against that carrier or the contracting carrier, or against both together or separately. If the action is brought against only one of those carriers, that carrier shall have the right to require the other carrier to be joined in the proceedings, the procedure and effects being governed by the law of the court seized of the case.

Article 46 - Additional Jurisdiction

Any action for damages contemplated in Article 45 must be brought, at the option of the plaintiff, in the territory of one of the States Parties, either before a court in which an action may be brought against the contracting carrier, as provided in Article 33, or before the court having jurisdiction at the place where the actual carrier has its domicile or its principal place of business.

Article 47 - Invalidity of Contractual Provisions

Any contractual provision tending to relieve the contracting carrier or the actual carrier of liability under this Chapter or to fix a lower limit than that which is applicable according to this Chapter shall be null and void, but the nullity of any such provision does not involve the nullity of the whole contract, which shall remain subject to the provisions of this Chapter.

Article 48 - Mutual Relations of Contracting and Actual Carriers

Except as provided in Article 45, nothing in this Chapter shall affect the rights and obligations of the carriers between themselves, including any right of recourse or indemnification.

Chapter VI - Other Provisions

Article 49 - Mandatory Application

Any clause contained in the contract of carriage and all special agreements entered into before the damage occurred by which the parties purport to infringe the rules laid down by this Convention, whether by deciding the law to be applied, or by altering the rules as to jurisdiction, shall be null and void.

Article 50 - Insurance

States Parties shall require their carriers to maintain adequate insurance covering their liability under this Convention. A carrier may be required by the State Party into which it operates to furnish evidence that it maintains adequate insurance covering its liability under this Convention.

Article 51 - Carriage Performed in Extraordinary Circumstances

The provisions of Articles 3 to 5, 7 and 8 relating to the documentation of carriage shall not apply in the case of carriage performed in extraordinary circumstances outside the normal scope of a carrier's business.

Article 52 - Definition of Days

The expression "days" when used in this Convention means calendar days, not working days.

Chapter VII - Final Clauses

Article 53 - Signature, Ratification and Entry into Force

1. This Convention shall be open for signature in Montreal on 28 May 1999 by States participating in the International Conference on Air Law held at Montreal from 10 to 28 May 1999. After 28 May 1999, the Convention shall be open to all States for signature at the headquarters of the International Civil Aviation Organization in Montreal until it enters into force in accordance with paragraph 6 of this Article.

2. This Convention shall similarly be open for signature by Regional Economic Integration Organisations. For the purpose of this Convention, a "Regional Economic Integration Organisation" means any organisation which is constituted by sovereign States of a given region which has competence in respect of certain matters governed by this Convention and has been duly authorized to sign and to ratify, accept, approve or accede to this Convention. A reference to a "State Party" or "States Parties" in this Convention, otherwise than in paragraph 2 of Article 1, paragraph 1(b) of Article 3, paragraph (b) of Article 5, Articles 23, 33, 46 and paragraph (b) of Article 57, applies equally to a Regional Economic Integration Organisation. For the purpose of Article 24, the references to "a majority of the States Parties" and "one-third of the States Parties" shall not apply to a Regional Economic Integration Organisation.

3. This Convention shall be subject to ratification by States and by Regional Economic Integration Organisations which have signed it.

4. Any State or Regional Economic Integration Organisation which does not sign this Convention may accept, approve or accede to it at any time.

5. Instruments of ratification, acceptance, approval or accession shall be deposited with the International Civil Aviation Organization, which is hereby designated the Depositary.

6. This Convention shall enter into force on the sixtieth day following the date of deposit of the thirtieth instrument of ratification, acceptance, approval or accession with the Depositary between the States which have deposited such instrument. An instrument deposited by a Regional Economic Integration Organisation shall not be counted for the purpose of this paragraph.

7. For other States and for other Regional Economic Integration Organisations, this Convention shall take effect sixty days following the date of deposit of the instrument of ratification, acceptance, approval or accession.

8. The Depositary shall promptly notify all signatories and States Parties of:

(a) each signature of this Convention and date thereof;

(b) each deposit of an instrument of ratification, acceptance, approval or accession and date thereof;

(c) the date of entry into force of this Convention;

(d) the date of the coming into force of any revision of the limits of liability established under this Convention;

(e) any denunciation under Article 54.

Article 54 - Denunciation

1. Any State Party may denounce this Convention by written notification to the Depositary.

2. Denunciation shall take effect one hundred and eighty days following the date on which notification is received by the Depositary.

Article 55 - Relationship with Other Warsaw Convention Instruments

This Convention shall prevail over any rules which apply to international carriage by air:

1. between States Parties to this Convention by virtue of those States commonly being Party to

(a) the Convention for the Unification of Certain Rules relating to International Carriage by Air signed at Warsaw on 12 October 1929 (hereinafter called the Warsaw Convention);

(b) the Protocol to amend the Convention for the Unification of Certain Rules relating to International Carriage by Air signed at Warsaw on 12 October 1929, done at The Hague on 28 September 1955 (hereinafter called The Hague Protocol);

(c) the Convention, Supplementary to the Warsaw Convention, for the Unification of Certain Rules relating to International Carriage by Air Performed by a Person other than the Contracting Carrier, signed at Guadalajara on 18 September 1961 (hereinafter called the Guadalajara Convention);

(d) the Protocol to amend the Convention for the Unification of Certain Rules relating to International Carriage by Air signed at Warsaw on 12 October 1929 as amended by the Protocol done at The Hague on 28 September 1955, signed at Guatemala City on 8 March 1971 (hereinafter called the Guatemala City Protocol);

(e) Additional Protocol Nos. 1 to 3 and Montreal Protocol No. 4 to amend the Warsaw Convention as amended by The Hague Protocol or the Warsaw Convention as amended by both The Hague Protocol and the Guatemala City Protocol, signed at Montreal on 25 September 1975 (hereinafter called the Montreal Protocols); or

2. within the territory of any single State Party to this Convention by virtue of that State being Party to one or more of the instruments referred to in sub-paragraphs (a) to (e) above.

Article 56 - States with More than One System of Law

1. If a State has two or more territorial units in which different systems of law are applicable in relation to matters dealt with in this Convention, it may at the time of signature, ratification, acceptance, approval or accession declare that this Convention shall extend to all its territorial units or only to one or more of them and may modify this declaration by submitting another declaration at any time.

2. Any such declaration shall be notified to the Depositary and shall state expressly the territorial units to which the Convention applies.

3. In relation to a State Party which has made such a declaration:

(a) references in Article 23 to “national currency” shall be construed as referring to the currency of the relevant territorial unit of that State; and

(b) the reference in Article 28 to “national law” shall be construed as referring to the law of the relevant territorial unit of that State.

Article 57 - Reservations

No reservation may be made to this Convention except that a State Party may at any time declare by a notification addressed to the Depositary that this Convention shall not apply to:

(a) international carriage by air performed and operated directly by that State Party for non-commercial purposes in respect to its functions and duties as a sovereign State; and/or

(b) the carriage of persons, cargo and baggage for its military authorities on aircraft registered in or leased by that State Party, the whole capacity of which has been reserved by or on behalf of such authorities.

IN WITNESS WHEREOF the undersigned Plenipotentiaries, having been duly authorized, have signed this Convention.

DONE at Montreal on the 28th day of May of the year one thousand nine hundred and ninety-nine in the English, Arabic, Chinese, French, Russian and Spanish languages, all texts being equally authentic. This Convention shall remain deposited in the archives of the International Civil Aviation Organization, and certified copies thereof shall be transmitted by the Depositary to all States Parties to this Convention, as well as to all States Parties to the Warsaw Convention, The Hague Protocol, the Guadalajara Convention, the Guatemala City Protocol and the Montreal Protocols.

Entry into force: 4 November 2003

Ratification and binding effect as of April 2020: 136 Member States

Part Five: The Documentary Sale 4 of 4 – Insurance Contracts

37) 1906 Marine Insurance Act, as Amended, United Kingdom[1]

1906 Chapter 41 6 Edw 7

MARINE INSURANCE

s. 1 Marine Insurance Defined

A contract of marine insurance is a contract whereby the insurer undertakes to indemnify the assured, in manner and to the extent thereby agreed, against marinelosses, that is to say, the losses incident to marine adventure.

s. 2 Mixed Sea and Land Risks

(1) A contract of marine insurance may, by its express terms, or by usage of trade, be extended so as to protect the assured against losses on inland waters or on any land risk which may be incidental to any sea voyage.

(2) Where a ship in course of building, or the launch of a ship, or any adventure analogous to a marine adventure, is covered by a policy in the form of a marine policy, the provisions of this Act, in so far as applicable, shall apply thereto; but, except as by this section provided, nothing in this Act shall alter or affect any rule of law applicable to any contract of insurance other than a contract of marine insurance as by this Act defined.

s. 3 Marine Adventure and Maritime Perils Defined

(1) Subject to the provisions of this Act, every lawful marine adventure may be the subject of a contract of marine insurance.

(2) In particular there is a marine adventure where—

(a) Any ship goods or other moveables are exposed to maritime perils. Such property is in this Act referred to as "insurable property";

(b) The earning or acquisition of any freight, passage money, commission, profit, or other pecuniary benefit, or the security for any advances, loan, or disbursements, is endangered by the exposure of insurable property to maritime perils;

(c) Any liability to a third party may be incurred by the owner of, or other person interested in or responsible for, insurable property, by reason of maritime perils.

"Maritime perils" means the perils consequent on, or incidental to, the navigation of the sea, that is to say, perils of the seas, fire, war perils, pirates, rovers, thieves, captures, seisures, restraints, and detainments of princes and peoples, jettisons, barratry, and any other perils, either of the like kind or which may be designated by the policy.

INSURABLE INTEREST

s. 4 Avoidance of Wagering or Gaming Contracts

(1) Every contract of marine insurance by way of gaming or wagering is void.

(2) A contract of marine insurance is deemed to be a gaming or wagering contract—

(a) Where the assured has not an insurable interest as defined by this Act, and the contract is entered into with no expectation of acquiring such an interest; or

---

1 Available at http://www.legislation.gov.uk/ukpga/Edw7/6/41/contents; last amended by the Insurance Act 2015.

(b) Where the policy is made "interest or no interest," or "without further proof of interest than the policy itself," or "without benefit of salvage to the insurer," or subject to any other like term:

Provided that, where there is no possibility of salvage, a policy may be effected without benefit of salvage to the insurer.

s. 5 Insurable Interest Defined

(1) Subject to the provisions of this Act, every person has an insurable interest who is interested in a marine adventure.

(2) In particular a person is interested in a marine adventure where he stands in any legal or equitable relation to the adventure or to any insurable property at risk therein, in consequence of which he may benefit by the safety or due arrival of insurable property, or may be prejudiced by its loss, or by damage thereto, or by the detention thereof, or may incur liability in respect thereof.

s. 6 When Interest Must Attach

(1) The assured must be interested in the subject-matter insured at the time of the loss though he need not be interested when the insurance is effected:

Provided that where the subject-matter is insured "lost or not lost," the assured may recover although he may not have acquired his interest until after the loss, unless at the time of effecting the contract of insurance the assured was aware of the loss, and the insurer was not.

(2) Where the assured has no interest at the time of the loss, he cannot acquire interest by any act or election after he is aware of the loss.

s. 7 Defeasible or Contingent Interest

(1) A defeasible interest is insurable, as also is a contingent interest.

(2) In particular, where the buyer of goods has insured them, he has an insurable interest, notwithstanding that he might, at his election, have rejected the goods, or have treated them as at the seller's risk, by reason of the latter's delay in making delivery or otherwise.

s. 8 Partial Interest

A partial interest of any nature is insurable.

s. 9 Re-Insurance

(1) The insurer under a contract of marine insurance has an insurable interest in his risk, and may re-insure in respect of it.

(2) Unless the policy otherwise provides, the original assured has no right or interest in respect of such re-insurance.

s. 10 Bottomry

The lender of money on bottomry or respondentia has an insurable interest in respect of the loan.

s. 11 Master's and Seamen's Wages

The master or any member of the crew of a ship has an insurable interest in respect of his wages.

s. 12 Advance Freight

In the case of advance freight, the person advancing the freight has an insurable interest, in so far as such freight is not repayable in case of loss.

s. 13 Charges of Insurance

The assured has an insurable interest in the charges of any insurance which he may effect.

s. 14 Quantum of Interest

(1) Where the subject-matter insured is mortgaged, the mortgagor has an insurable interest in the full value thereof, and the mortgagee has an insurable interest in respect of any sum due or to become due under the mortgage.

(2) A mortgagee, consignee, or other person having an interest in the subject-matter insured may insure on behalf and for the benefit of other persons interested as well as for his own benefit.

(3) The owner of insurable property has an insurable interest in respect of the full value thereof, notwithstanding that some third person may have agreed, or be liable, to indemnify him in case of loss.

s. 15 Assignment of Interest

Where the assured assigns or otherwise parts with his interest in the subject-matter insured, he does not thereby transfer to the assignee his rights under the contract of insurance, unless there be an express or implied agreement with the assignee to that effect.

But the provisions of this section do not affect a transmission of interest by operation of law.

INSURABLE VALUE

s. 16 Measure of Insurable Value

Subject to any express provision or valuation in the policy, the insurable value of the subject-matter insured must be ascertained as follows:—

(1) In insurance on ship, the insurable value is the value, at the commencement of the risk, of the ship, including her outfit, provisions and stores for the officers and crew, money advanced for seamen's wages, and other disbursements (if any) incurred to make the ship fit for the voyage or adventure contemplated by the policy, plus the charges of insurance upon the whole: The insurable value, in the case of a steamship, includes also the machinery, boilers, and coals and engine stores if owned by the assured, and, in the case of a ship engaged in a special trade, the ordinary fittings requisite for that trade:

(2) In insurance on freight, whether paid in advance or otherwise, the insurable value is the gross amount of the freight at the risk of the assured, plus the charges of insurance:

(3) In insurance on goods or merchandise, the insurable value is the prime cost of the property insured, plus the expenses of and incidental to shipping and the charges of insurance upon the whole:

(4) In insurance on any other subject-matter, the insurable value is the amount at the risk of the assured when the policy attaches, plus the charges of insurance.

DISCLOSURE AND REPRESENTATIONS

s. 17 Insurance Is uberrimæ fidei

A contract of marine insurance is a contract based upon the utmost good faith [and, if the utmost good faith be not observed by either party, the contract may be avoided by the other party.][1]

[s. 18 Disclosure by Assured] [1]

1 The passages in brackets were deleted by the Insurance Act of 2015 (UK).

[s. 19 Disclosure by Agent Effecting Insurance] [1]

[s. 20 Representations Pending Negotiation of Contract] [1]

s. 21 When Contract Is Deemed to Be Concluded

A contract of marine insurance is deemed to be concluded when the proposal of the assured is accepted by the insurer, whether the policy be then issued or not; and, for the purpose of showing when the proposal was accepted, reference may be made to the slip or covering note or other customary memorandum of the contract.

THE POLICY

s. 22 Contract must Be Embodied in Policy

Subject to the provisions of any statute, a contract of marine insurance is inadmissible in evidence unless it is embodied in a marine policy in accordance with this Act. The policy may be executed and issued either at the time when the contract is concluded, or afterwards.

s. 23 What Policy Must Specify

A marine policy must specify—

(1) The name of the assured, or of some person who effects the insurance on his behalf:

(2) . . . . [repealed by Finance Act of 1959 (UK)]

s. 24 Signature of Insurer

(1) A marine policy must be signed by or on behalf of the insurer, provided that in the case of a corporation the corporate seal may be sufficient, but nothing in this section shall be construed as requiring the subscription of a corporation to be under seal.

(2) Where a policy is subscribed by or on behalf of two or more insurers, each subscription, unless the contrary be expressed, constitutes a distinct contract with the assured.

s. 25 Voyage and Time Policies

(1) Where the contract is to insure the subject-matter "at and from," or from one place to another or others, the policy is called a "voyage policy," and where the contract is to insure the subject-matter for a definite period of time the policy is called a "time policy." A contract for both voyage and time may be included in the same policy.

(2) . . . . [repealed by Finance Act of 1959 (UK)]

s. 26 Designation of Subject-Matter

(1) The subject-matter insured must be designated in a marine policy with reasonable certainty.

(2) The nature and extent of the interest of the assured in the subject-matter insured need not be specified in the policy.

(3) Where the policy designates the subject-matter insured in general terms, it shall be construed to apply to the interest intended by the assured to be covered.

(4) In the application of this section regard shall be had to any usage regulating the designation of the subject-matter insured.

s. 27 Valued Policy

(1) A policy may be either valued or unvalued.

(2) A valued policy is a policy which specifies the agreed value of the subject-matter insured.

(3) Subject to the provisions of this Act, and in the absence of fraud, the value fixed by the policy is, as between the insurer and assured, conclusive of the insurable value of the subject intended to be insured, whether the loss be total or partial.

(4) Unless the policy otherwise provides, the value fixed by the policy is not conclusive for the purpose of determining whether there has been a constructive total loss.

s. 28 Unvalued Policy

An unvalued policy is a policy which does not specify the value of the subject-matter insured, but, subject to the limit of the sum insured, leaves the insurable value to be subsequently ascertained, in the manner herein-before specified.

s. 29 Floating Policy by Ship or Ships

(1) A floating policy is a policy which describes the insurance in general terms, and leaves the name of the ship or ships and other particulars to be defined by subsequent declaration.

(2) The subsequent declaration or declarations may be made by indorsement on the policy, or in other customary manner.

(3) Unless the policy otherwise provides, the declarations must be made in the order of dispatch or shipment. They must, in the case of goods, comprise all consignments within the terms of the policy, and the value of the goods or other property must be honestly stated, but an omission or erroneous declaration may be rectified even after loss or arrival, provided the omission or declaration was made in good faith.

(4) Unless the policy otherwise provides, where a declaration of value is not made until after notice of loss or arrival, the policy must be treated as an unvalued policy as regards the subject-matter of that declaration.

s. 30 Construction of Terms in Policy

(1) A policy may be in the form in the First Schedule to this Act.[1]

(2) Subject to the provisions of this Act, and unless the context of the policy otherwise requires, the terms and expressions mentioned in the First Schedule to this Act shall be construed as having the scope and meaning in that schedule assigned to them.

s. 31 Premium to Be Arranged

(1) Where an insurance is effected at a premium to be arranged, and no arrangement is made, a reasonable premium is payable.

(2) Where an insurance is effected on the terms that an additional premium is to be arranged in a given event, and that event happens but no arrangement is made, then a reasonable additional premium is payable.

DOUBLE INSURANCE

s. 32 Double Insurance

(1) Where two or more policies are effected by or on behalf of the assured on the same adventure and interest or any part thereof, and the sums insured exceed the indemnity allowed by this Act, the assured is said to be over-insured by double insurance.

(2) Where the assured is over-insured by double insurance—

---

1 The so-called "SG Policy" traces its origins as far back as the 15th century. It was the dominant form of policy until it was replaced in 1982 by the Institute Cargo Clauses. The Institute Cargo Clauses can be found in the Documents Collection at p. I - 789.

(a) The assured, unless the policy otherwise provides, may claim payment from the insurers in such order as he may think fit, provided that he is not entitled to receive any sum in excess of the indemnity allowed by this Act;

(b) Where the policy under which the assured claims is a valued policy, the assured must give credit as against the valuation for any sum received by him under any other policy without regard to the actual value of the subject-matter insured;

(c) Where the policy under which the assured claims is an unvalued policy he must give credit, as against the full insurable value, for any sum received by him under any other policy:

(d) Where the assured receives any sum in excess of the indemnity allowed by this Act, he is deemed to hold such sum in trust for the insurers, according to their right of contribution among themselves.

WARRANTIES, &C.

s. 33 Nature of Warranty

(1) A warranty, in the following sections relating to warranties, means a promissory warranty, that is to say, a warranty by which the assured undertakes that some particular thing shall or shall not be done, or that some condition shall be fulfilled, or whereby he affirms or negatives the existence of a particular state of facts.

(2) A warranty may be express or implied.

(3) A warranty, as above defined, is a condition which must be exactly complied with, whether it be material to the risk or not. [If it be not so complied with, then, subject to any express provision in the policy, the insurer is discharged from liability as from the date of the breach of warranty, but without prejudice to any liability incurred by him before that date.][1]

[s. 34 When Breach of Warranty Excused] [1]

s. 35 Express Warranties

(1) An express warranty may be in any form of words from which the intention to warrant is to be inferred.

(2) An express warranty must be included in, or written upon, the policy, or must be contained in some document incorporated by reference into the policy.

(3) An express warranty does not exclude an implied warranty, unless it be inconsistent therewith.

s. 36 Warranty of Neutrality

(1) Where insurable property, whether ship or goods, is expressly warranted neutral, there is an implied condition that the property shall have a neutral character at the commencement of the risk, and that, so far as the assured can control the matter, its neutral character shall be preserved during the risk.

(2) Where a ship is expressly warranted "neutral" there is also an implied condition that, so far as the assured can control the matter, she shall be properly documented, that is to say, that she shall carry the necessary papers to establish her neutrality, and that she shall not falsify or suppress her papers, or use simulated papers. If any loss occurs through breach of this condition, the insurer may avoid the contract.

---

1 The passage in brackets was deleted by the Insurance Act of 2015 (UK).

s. 37 No Implied Warranty of Nationality

There is no implied warranty as to the nationality of a ship, or that her nationality shall not be changed during the risk.

s. 38 Warranty of Good Safety

Where the subject-matter insured is warranted "well" or "in good safety" on a particular day, it is sufficient if it be safe at any time during that day.

s. 39 Warranty of Seaworthiness of Ship

(1) In a voyage policy there is an implied warranty that at the commencement of the voyage the ship shall be seaworthy for the purpose of the particular adventure insured.

(2) Where the policy attaches while the ship is in port, there is also an implied warranty that she shall, at the commencement of the risk, be reasonably fit to encounter the ordinary perils of the port.

(3) Where the policy relates to a voyage which is performed in different stages, during which the ship requires different kinds of or further preparation or equipment, there is an implied warranty that at the commencement of each stage the ship is seaworthy in respect of such preparation or equipment for the purposes of that stage.

(4) A ship is deemed to be seaworthy when she is reasonably fit in all respects to encounter the ordinary perils of the seas of the adventure insured.

(5) In a time policy there is no implied warranty that the ship shall be seaworthy at any stage of the adventure, but where, with the privity of the assured, the ship is sent to sea in an unseaworthy state, the insurer is not liable for any loss attributable to unseaworthiness.

s. 40 No Implied Warranty That Goods Are Seaworthy

(1) In a policy on goods or other moveables there is no implied warranty that the goods or moveables are seaworthy.

(2) In a voyage policy on goods or other moveables there is an implied warranty that at the commencement of the voyage the ship is not only seaworthy as a ship, but also that she is reasonably fit to carry the goods or other moveables to the destination contemplated by the policy.

s. 41 Warranty of Legality

There is an implied warranty that the adventure insured is a lawful one, and that, so far as the assured can control the matter, the adventure shall be carried out in a lawful manner.

THE VOYAGE

s. 42 Implied Condition as to Commencement of Risk

(1) Where the subject-matter is insured by a voyage policy "at and from" or "from" a particular place, it is not necessary that the ship should be at that place when the contract is concluded, but there is an implied condition that the adventure shall be commenced within a reasonable time, and that if the adventure be not so commenced the insurer may avoid the contract.

(2) The implied condition may be negatived by showing that the delay was caused by circumstances known to the insurer before the contract was concluded, or by showing that he waived the condition.

s. 43 Alteration of Port of Departure

Where the place of departure is specified by the policy, and the ship instead of sailing from that place sails from any other place, the risk does not attach.

s. 44 Sailing for Different Destination

Where the destination is specified in the policy, and the ship, instead of sailing for that destination, sails for any other destination, the risk does not attach.

s. 45 Change of Voyage

(1) Where, after the commencement of the risk, the destination of the ship is voluntarily changed from the destination contemplated by the policy, there is said to be a change of voyage.

(2) Unless the policy otherwise provides, where there is a change of voyage, the insurer is discharged from liability as from the time of change, that is to say, as from the time when the determination to change it is manifested; and it is immaterial that the ship may not in fact have left the course of voyage contemplated by the policy when the loss occurs.

s. 46 Deviation

(1) Where a ship, without lawful excuse, deviates from the voyage contemplated by the policy, the insurer is discharged from liability as from the time of deviation, and it is immaterial that the ship may have regained her route before any loss occurs.

(2) There is a deviation from the voyage contemplated by the policy—

(a) Where the course of the voyage is specifically designated by the policy, and that course is departed from; or

(b) Where the course of the voyage is not specifically designated by the policy, but the usual and customary course is departed from.

(3) The intention to deviate is immaterial; there must be a deviation in fact to discharge the insurer from his liability under the contract.

s. 47 Several Ports of Discharge

(1) Where several ports of discharge are specified by the policy, the ship may proceed to all or any of them, but, in the absence of any usage or sufficient cause to the contrary, she must proceed to them, or such of them as she goes to, in the order designated by the policy. If she does not there is a deviation.

(2) Where the policy is to "ports of discharge," within a given area, which are not named, the ship must, in the absence of any usage or sufficient cause to the contrary, proceed to them, or such of them as she goes to, in their geographical order. If she does not there is a deviation.

s. 48 Delay in Voyage

In the case of a voyage policy, the adventure insured must be prosecuted throughout its course with reasonable dispatch, and, if without lawful excuse it is not so prosecuted, the insurer is discharged from liability as from the time when the delay became unreasonable.

s. 49 Excuses for Deviation or Delay

(1) Deviation or delay in prosecuting the voyage contemplated by the policy is excused—

(a) Where authorised by any special term in the policy; or

(b) Where caused by circumstances beyond the control of the master and his employer; or

(c) Where reasonably necessary in order to comply with an express or implied warranty; or

(d) Where reasonably necessary for the safety of the ship or subject-matter insured; or

(e) For the purpose of saving human life, or aiding a ship in distress where human life may be in danger; or

(f) Where reasonably necessary for the purpose of obtaining medical or surgical aid for any person on board the ship; or

(g) Where caused by the barratrous conduct of the master or crew, if barratry be one of the perils insured against.

(2) When the cause excusing the deviation or delay ceases to operate, the ship must resume her course, and prosecute her voyage, with reasonable dispatch.

ASSIGNMENT OF POLICY

s. 50 When and How Policy Is Assignable

(1) A marine policy is assignable unless it contains terms expressly prohibiting assignment. It may be assigned either before or after loss.

(2) Where a marine policy has been assigned so as to pass the beneficial interest in such policy, the assignee of the policy is entitled to sue thereon in his own name; and the defendant is entitled to make any defence arising out of the contract which he would have been entitled to make if the action had been brought in the name of the person by or on behalf of whom the policy was effected.

(3) A marine policy may be assigned by indorsement thereon or in other customary manner.

s. 51 Assured Who Has No Interest Cannot Assign

Where the assured has parted with or lost his interest in the subject-matter insured, and has not, before or at the time of so doing, expressly or impliedly agreed to assign the policy, any subsequent assignment of the policy is inoperative:

Provided that nothing in this section affects the assignment of a policy after loss.

THE PREMIUM

s. 52 When Premium Payable

Unless otherwise agreed, the duty of the assured or his agent to pay the premium, and the duty of the insurer to issue the policy to the assured or his agent, are concurrent conditions, and the insurer is not bound to issue the policy until payment or tender of the premium.

s. 53 Policy Effected Through Broker

(1) Unless otherwise agreed, where a marine policy is effected on behalf of the assured by a broker, the broker is directly responsible to the insurer for the premium, and the insurer is directly responsible to the assured for the amount which may be payable in respect of losses, or in respect of returnable premium.

(2) Unless otherwise agreed, the broker has, as against the assured, a lien upon the policy for the amount of the premium and his charges in respect of effecting the policy; and, where he has dealt with the person who employs him as a principal, he has also a lien on the policy in respect of any balance on any insurance account which may be due to him from such person, unless when the debt was incurred he had reason to believe that such person was only an agent.

s. 54 Effect of Receipt on Policy

Where a marine policy effected on behalf of the assured by a broker acknowledges the receipt of the premium, such acknowledgement is, in the absence of fraud, conclusive as between the insurer and the assured, but not as between the insurer and broker.

LOSS AND ABANDONMENT

s. 55 Included and Excluded Losses

(1) Subject to the provisions of this Act, and unless the policy otherwise provides, the insurer is liable for any loss proximately caused by a peril insured against, but, subject as aforesaid, he is not liable for any loss which is not proximately caused by a peril insured against.

(2) In particular—

(a) The insurer is not liable for any loss attributable to the wilful misconduct of the assured, but, unless the policy otherwise provides, he is liable for any loss proximately caused by a peril insured against, even though the loss would not have happened but for the misconduct or negligence of the master or crew;

(b) Unless the policy otherwise provides, the insurer on ship or goods is not liable for any loss proximately caused by delay, although the delay be caused by a peril insured against;

(c) Unless the policy otherwise provides, the insurer is not liable for ordinary wear and tear, ordinary leakage and breakage, inherent vice or nature of the subject-matter insured, or for any loss proximately caused by rats or vermin, or for any injury to machinery not proximately caused by maritime perils.

s. 56 Partial and Total Loss

(1) A loss may be either total or partial. Any loss other than a total loss, as hereinafter defined, is a partial loss.

(2) A total loss may be either an actual total loss, or a constructive total loss.

(3) Unless a different intention appears from the terms of the policy, an insurance against total loss includes a constructive, as well as an actual, total loss.

(4) Where the assured brings an action for a total loss and the evidence proves only a partial loss, he may, unless the policy otherwise provides, recover for a partial loss.

(5) Where goods reach their destination in specie, but by reason of obliteration of marks, or otherwise, they are incapable of identification, the loss, if any, is partial, and not total.

s. 57 Actual Total Loss

(1) Where the subject-matter insured is destroyed, or so damaged as to cease to be a thing of the kind insured, or where the assured is irretrievably deprived thereof, there is an actual total loss.

(2) In the case of an actual total loss no notice of abandonment need be given.

s. 58 Missing Ship

Where the ship concerned in the adventure is missing, and after the lapse of a reasonable time no news of her has been received, an actual total loss may be presumed.

s. 59 Effect of Transhipment, &c

Where, by a peril insured against, the voyage is interrupted at an intermediate port or place, under such circumstances as, apart from any special stipulation in the contract of affreightment, to justify the master in landing and reshipping the goods or other moveables, or in transhipping them, and sending them on to their destination, the liability of the insurer continues, notwithstanding the landing or transhipment.

s. 60 Constructive Total Loss Defined

(1) Subject to any express provision in the policy, there is a constructive total loss where the subject-matter insured is reasonably abandoned on account of its actual total loss appearing to

be unavoidable, or because it could not be preserved from actual total loss without an expenditure which would exceed its value when the expenditure had been incurred.

(2) In particular, there is a constructive total loss—

(i) Where the assured is deprived of the possession of his ship or goods by a peril insured against, and (a) it is unlikely that he can recover the ship or goods, as the case may be, or (b) the cost of recovering the ship or goods, as the case may be, would exceed their value when recovered; or

(ii) In the case of damage to a ship, where she is so damaged by a peril insured against that the cost of repairing the damage would exceed the value of the ship when repaired.

In estimating the cost of repairs, no deduction is to be made in respect of general average contributions to those repairs payable by other interests, but account is to be taken of the expense of future salvage operations and of any future general average contributions to which the ship would be liable if repaired; or

(iii) In the case of damage to goods, where the cost of repairing the damage and forwarding the goods to their destination would exceed their value on arrival.

s. 61 Effect of Constructive Total Loss

Where there is a constructive total loss the assured may either treat the loss as a partial loss, or abandon the subject-matter insured to the insurer and treat the loss as if it were an actual total loss.

s. 62 Notice of Abandonment

(1) Subject to the provisions of this section, where the assured elects to abandon the subject-matter insured to the insurer, he must give notice of abandonment. If he fails to do so the loss can only be treated as a partial loss.

(2) Notice of abandonment may be given in writing, or by word of mouth, or partly in writing and partly by word of mouth, and may be given in any terms which indicate the intention of the assured to abandon his insured interest in the subject-matter insured unconditionally to the insurer.

(3) Notice of abandonment must be given with reasonable diligence after the receipt of reliable information of the loss, but where the information is of a doubtful character the assured is entitled to a reasonable time to make inquiry.

(4) Where notice of abandonment is properly given, the rights of the assured are not prejudiced by the fact that the insurer refuses to accept the abandonment.

(5) The acceptance of an abandonment may be either express or implied from the conduct of the insurer. The mere silence of the insurer after notice is not an acceptance.

(6) Where notice of abandonment is accepted the abandonment is irrevocable. The acceptance of the notice conclusively admits liability for the loss and the sufficiency of the notice.

(7) Notice of abandonment is unnecessary where, at the time when the assured receives information of the loss, there would be no possibility of benefit to the insurer if notice were given to him.

(8) Notice of abandonment may be waived by the insurer.

(9) Where an insurer has re-insured his risk, no notice of abandonment need be given by him.

s. 63 Effect of Abandonment

(1) Where there is a valid abandonment the insurer is entitled to take over the interest of the assured in whatever may remain of the subject-matter insured, and all proprietary rights incidental thereto.

(2) Upon the abandonment of a ship, the insurer thereof is entitled to any freight in course of being earned, and which is earned by her subsequent to the casualty causing the loss, less the expenses of earning it incurred after the casualty; and, where the ship is carrying the owner's goods, the insurer is entitled to a reasonable remuneration for the carriage of them subsequent to the casualty causing the loss.

PARTIAL LOSSES
(INCLUDING SALVAGE AND GENERAL AVERAGE AND PARTICULAR CHARGES)

s. 64 Particular Average Loss

(1) A particular average loss is a partial loss of the subject-matter insured, caused by a peril insured against, and which is not a general average loss.

(2) Expenses incurred by or on behalf of the assured for the safety or preservation of the subject-matter insured, other than general average and salvage charges, are called particular charges. Particular charges are not included in particular average.

s. 65 Salvage Charges

(1) Subject to any express provision in the policy, salvage charges incurred in preventing a loss by perils insured against may be recovered as a loss by those perils.

(2) "Salvage charges" means the charges recoverable under maritime law by a salvor independently of contract. They do not include the expenses of services in the nature of salvage rendered by the assured or his agents, or any person employed for hire by them, for the purpose of averting a peril insured against. Such expenses, where properly incurred, may be recovered as particular charges or as a general average loss, according to the circumstances under which they were incurred.

s. 66 General Average Loss

(1) A general average loss is a loss caused by or directly consequential on a general average act. It includes a general average expenditure as well as a general average sacrifice.

(2) There is a general average act where any extraordinary sacrifice or expenditure is voluntarily and reasonably made or incurred in time of peril for the purpose of preserving the property imperilled in the common adventure.

(3) Where there is a general average loss, the party on whom it falls is entitled, subject to the conditions imposed by maritime law, to a rateable contribution from the other parties interested, and such contribution is called a general average contribution.

(4) Subject to any express provision in the policy, where the assured has incurred a general average expenditure, he may recover from the insurer in respect of the proportion of the loss which falls upon him; and, in the case of a general average sacrifice, he may recover from the insurer in respect of the whole loss without having enforced his right of contribution from the other parties liable to contribute.

(5) Subject to any express provision in the policy, where the assured has paid, or is liable to pay, a general average contribution in respect of the subject insured, he may recover therefor from the insurer.

(6) In the absence of express stipulation, the insurer is not liable for any general average loss or contribution where the loss was not incurred for the purpose of avoiding, or in connexion with the avoidance of, a peril insured against.

(7) Where ship, freight, and cargo, or any two of those interests, are owned by the same assured, the liability of the insurer in respect of general average losses or contributions is to be determined as if those subjects were owned by different persons.

MEASURE OF INDEMNITY

s. 67 Extent of Liability of Insurer for Loss

(1) The sum which the assured can recover in respect of a loss on a policy by which he is insured, in the case of an unvalued policy to the full extent of the insurable value, or, in the case of a valued policy to the full extent of the value fixed by the policy is called the measure of indemnity.

(2) Where there is a loss recoverable under the policy, the insurer, or each insurer if there be more than one, is liable for such proportion of the measure of indemnity as the amount of his subscription bears to the value fixed by the policy in the case of a valued policy, or to the insurable value in the case of an unvalued policy.

s. 68 Total Loss

Subject to the provisions of this Act and to any express provision in the policy, where there is a total loss of the subject-matter insured,—

(1) If the policy be a valued policy, the measure of indemnity is the sum fixed by the policy:

(2) If the policy be an unvalued policy, the measure of indemnity is the insurable value of the subject-matter insured.

s. 69 Partial Loss of Ship

Where a ship is damaged, but is not totally lost, the measure of indemnity, subject to any express provision in the policy, is as follows:—

(1) Where the ship has been repaired, the assured is entitled to the reasonable cost of the repairs, less the customary deductions, but not exceeding the sum insured in respect of any one casualty:

(2) Where the ship has been only partially repaired, the assured is entitled to the reasonable cost of such repairs, computed as above, and also to be indemnified for the reasonable depreciation, if any, arising from the unrepaired damage, provided that the aggregate amount shall not exceed the cost of repairing the whole damage, computed as above:

(3) Where the ship has not been repaired, and has not been sold in her damaged state during the risk, the assured is entitled to be indemnified for the reasonable depreciation arising from the unrepaired damage, but not exceeding the reasonable cost of repairing such damage, computed as above.

s. 70 Partial Loss of Freight

Subject to any express provision in the policy, where there is a partial loss of freight, the measure of indemnity is such proportion of the sum fixed by the policy in the case of a valued policy, or of the insurable value in the case of an unvalued policy, as the proportion of freight lost by the assured bears to the whole freight at the risk of the assured under the policy.

s. 71 Partial Loss of Goods, Merchandise, &c

Where there is a partial loss of goods, merchandise, or other moveables, the measure of indemnity, subject to any express provision in the policy, is as follows:—

(1) Where part of the goods, merchandise or other moveables insured by a valued policy is totally lost, the measure of indemnity is such proportion of the sum fixed by the policy as the insurable value of the part lost bears to the insurable value of the whole, ascertained as in the case of an unvalued policy:

(2) Where part of the goods, merchandise, or other moveables insured by an unvalued policy is totally lost, the measure of indemnity is the insurable value of the part lost, ascertained as in case of total loss:

(3) Where the whole or any part of the goods or merchandise insured has been delivered damaged at its destination, the measure of indemnity is such proportion of the sum fixed by the policy in the case of a valued policy, or of the insurable value in the case of an unvalued policy, as the difference between the gross sound and damaged values at the place of arrival bears to the gross sound value:

(4) "Gross value" means the wholesale price, or, if there be no such price, the estimated value, with, in either case, freight, landing charges, and duty paid beforehand; provided that, in the case of goods or merchandise customarily sold in bond, the bonded price is deemed to be the gross value. "Gross proceeds" means the actual price obtained at a sale where all charges on sale are paid by the sellers.

s. 72 Apportionment of Valuation

(1) Where different species of property are insured under a single valuation, the valuation must be apportioned over the different species in proportion to their respective insurable values, as in the case of an unvalued policy. The insured value of any part of a species is such proportion of the total insured value of the same as the insurable value of the part bears to the insurable value of the whole, ascertained in both cases as provided by this Act.

(2) Where a valuation has to be apportioned, and particulars of the prime cost of each separate species, quality, or description of goods cannot be ascertained, the division of the valuation may be made over the net arrived sound values of the different species, qualities, or descriptions of goods.

s. 73 General Average Contributions and Salvage Charges

(1) Subject to any express provision in the policy, where the assured has paid, or is liable for, any general average contribution, the measure of indemnity is the full amount of such contribution, if the subject-matter liable to contribution is insured for its full contributory value; but, if such subject-matter be not insured for its full contributory value, or if only part of it be insured, the indemnity payable by the insurer must be reduced in proportion to the under insurance, and where there has been a particular average loss which constitutes a deduction from the contributory value, and for which the insurer is liable, that amount must be deducted from the insured value in order to ascertain what the insurer is liable to contribute.

(2) Where the insurer is liable for salvage charges the extent of his liability must be determined on the like principle.

s. 74 Liabilities to Third Parties

Where the assured has effected an insurance in express terms against any liability to a third party, the measure of indemnity, subject to any express provision in the policy, is the amount paid or payable by him to such third party in respect of such liability.

s. 75 General Provisions as to Measure of Indemnity

(1) Where there has been a loss in respect of any subject-matter not expressly provided for in the foregoing provisions of this Act, the measure of indemnity shall be ascertained, as nearly as may be, in accordance with those provisions, in so far as applicable to the particular case.

(2) Nothing in the provisions of this Act relating to the measure of indemnity shall affect the rules relating to double insurance, or prohibit the insurer from disproving interest wholly or in part, or from showing that at the time of the loss the whole or any part of the subject-matter insured was not at risk under the policy.

s. 76 Particular Average Warranties

(1) Where the subject-matter insured is warranted free from particular average, the assured cannot recover for a loss of part, other than a loss incurred by a general average sacrifice, unless the contract contained in the policy be apportionable; but, if the contract be apportionable, the assured may recover for a total loss of any apportionable part.

(2) Where the subject-matter insured is warranted free from particular average, either wholly or under a certain percentage, the insurer is nevertheless liable for salvage charges, and for particular charges and other expenses properly incurred pursuant to the provisions of the suing and labouring clause in order to avert a loss insured against.

(3) Unless the policy otherwise provides, where the subject-matter insured is warranted free from particular average under a specified percentage, a general average loss cannot be added to a particular average loss to make up the specified percentage.

(4) For the purpose of ascertaining whether the specified percentage has been reached, regard shall be had only to the actual loss suffered by the subject-matter insured. Particular charges and the expenses of and incidental to ascertaining and proving the loss must be excluded.

s. 77 Successive Losses

(1) Unless the policy otherwise provides, and subject to the provisions of this Act, the insurer is liable for successive losses, even though the total amount of such losses may exceed the sum insured.

(2) Where, under the same policy, a partial loss, which has not been repaired or otherwise made good, is followed by a total loss, the assured can only recover in respect of the total loss:

Provided that nothing in this section shall affect the liability of the insurer under the suing and labouring clause.

s. 78 Suing and Labouring Clause

(1) Where the policy contains a suing and labouring clause, the engagement thereby entered into is deemed to be supplementary to the contract of insurance, and the assured may recover from the insurer any expenses properly incurred pursuant to the clause, notwithstanding that the insurer may have paid for a total loss, or that the subject-matter may have been warranted free from particular average, either wholly or under a certain percentage.

(2) General average losses and contributions and salvage charges, as defined by this Act, are not recoverable under the suing and labouring clause.

(3) Expenses incurred for the purpose of averting or diminishing any loss not covered by the policy are not recoverable under the suing and labouring clause.

(4) It is the duty of the assured and his agents, in all cases, to take such measures as maybe reasonable for the purpose of averting or minimising a loss.

RIGHTS OF INSURER ON PAYMENT

s. 79 Right of Subrogation

(1) Where the insurer pays for a total loss, either of the whole, or in the case of goods of any apportionable part, of the subject-matter insured, he thereupon becomes entitled to take over the interest of the assured in whatever may remain of the subject-matter so paid for, and he is

thereby subrogated to all the rights and remedies of the assured in and in respect of that subject-matter as from the time of the casualty causing the loss.

(2) Subject to the foregoing provisions, where the insurer pays for a partial loss, he acquires no title to the subject-matter insured, or such part of it as may remain, but he is thereupon subrogated to all rights and remedies of the assured in and in respect of the subject-matter insured as from the time of the casualty causing the loss, in so far as the assured has been indemnified, according to this Act, by such payment for the loss.

s. 80 Right of Contribution

(1) Where the assured is over-insured by double insurance, each insurer is bound, as between himself and the other insurers, to contribute rateably to the loss in proportion to the amount for which he is liable under his contract.

(2) If any insurer pays more than his proportion of the loss, he is entitled to maintain an action for contribution against the other insurers, and is entitled to the like remedies as a surety who has paid more than his proportion of the debt.

s. 81 Effect of Under Insurance

Where the assured is insured for an amount less than the insurable value or, in the case of a valued policy, for an amount less than the policy valuation, he is deemed to be his own insurer in respect of the uninsured balance.

RETURN OF PREMIUM

s. 82 Enforcement of Return

Where the premium or a proportionate part thereof is, by this Act, declared to be returnable,—

(a) If already paid, it may be recovered by the assured from the insurer; and

(b) If unpaid, it may be retained by the assured or his agent.

s. 83 Return by Agreement

Where the policy contains a stipulation for the return of the premium, or a proportionate part thereof, on the happening of a certain event, and that event happens, the premium, or, as the case may be, the proportionate part thereof, is thereupon returnable to the assured.

s. 84 Return for Failure of Consideration

(1) Where the consideration for the payment of the premium totally fails, and there has been no fraud or illegality on the part of the assured or his agents, the premium is thereupon returnable to the assured.

(2) Where the consideration for the payment of the premium is apportionable and there is a total failure of any apportionable part of the consideration, a proportionate part of the premium is, under the like conditions, thereupon returnable to the assured.

(3) In particular—

(a) Where the policy is void, or is avoided by the insurer as from the commencement of the risk, the premium is returnable, provided that there has been no fraud or illegality on the part of the assured; but if the risk is not apportionable, and has once attached, the premium is not returnable:

(b) Where the subject-matter insured, or part thereof, has never been imperilled, the premium, or, as the case may be, a proportionate part thereof, is returnable:

Provided that where the subject-matter has been insured "lost or not lost" and has arrived in safety at the time when the contract is concluded, the premium is not returnable unless, at such time, the insurer knew of the safe arrival.

(c) Where the assured has no insurable interest throughout the currency of the risk, the premium is returnable, provided that this rule does not apply to a policy effected by way of gaming or wagering;

(d) Where the assured has a defeasible interest which is terminated during the currency of the risk, the premium is not returnable;

(e) Where the assured has over-insured under an unvalued policy, a proportionate part of the premium is returnable;

(f) Subject to the foregoing provisions, where the assured has over-insured by double insurance, a proportionate part of the several premiums is returnable:

Provided that, if the policies are effected at different times, and any earlier policy has at any time borne the entire risk, or if a claim has been paid on the policy in respect of the full sum insured thereby, no premium is returnable in respect of that policy, and when the double insurance is effected knowingly by the assured no premium is returnable.

MUTUAL INSURANCE

s. 85 Modification of Act in Case of Mutual Insurance

(1) Where two or more persons mutually agree to insure each other against marine losses there is said to be a mutual insurance.

(2) The provisions of this Act relating to the premium do not apply to mutual insurance, but a guarantee, or such other arrangement as may be agreed upon, may be substituted for the premium.

(3) The provisions of this Act, in so far as they may be modified by the agreement of the parties, may in the case of mutual insurance be modified by the terms of the policies issued by the association, or by the rules and regulations of the association.

(4) Subject to the exceptions mentioned in this section, the provisions of this Act apply to a mutual insurance.

SUPPLEMENTAL

s. 86 Ratification by Assured

Where a contract of marine insurance is in good faith effected by one person on behalf of another, the person on whose behalf it is effected may ratify the contract even after he is aware of a loss.

s. 87 Implied Obligations Varied by Agreement or Usage

(1) Where any right, duty, or liability would arise under a contract of marine insurance by implication of law, it may be negatived or varied by express agreement, or by usage, if the usage be such as to bind both parties to the contract.

(2) The provisions of this section extend to any right, duty, or liability declared by this Act which may be lawfully modified by agreement.

s. 88 Reasonable Time, &c. a Question of Fact

Where by this Act any reference is made to reasonable time, reasonable premium, or reasonable diligence, the question what is reasonable is a question of fact.

s. 89 Slip as Evidence

Where there is a duly stamped policy, reference may be made, as heretofore, to the slip or covering note, in any legal proceeding.

s. 90 Interpretation of Terms

In this Act, unless the context or subject-matter otherwise requires,

- "Action" includes counter-claim and set off:
- "Freight" includes the profit derivable by a shipowner from the employment of his ship to carry his own goods or moveables, as well as freight payable by a third party, but does not include passage money:
- "Moveables" means any moveable tangible property, other than the ship, and includes money, valuable securities, and other documents:
- "Policy" means a marine policy.

s. 91 Savings

(1) Nothing in this Act, or in any repeal effected thereby, shall affect— [...]

(2) The rules of the common law including the law merchant, save in so far as they are inconsistent with the express provisions of this Act, shall continue to apply to contracts of marine insurance.

[...]

s. 94 Short Title

This Act may be cited as the Marine Insurance Act 1906.

38) 2016 York-Antwerp Rules[1]

Rule of Interpretation

In the adjustment of general average the following Rules shall apply to the exclusion of any law and practice inconsistent therewith.

Except as provided by the Rule Paramount and the numbered Rules, general average shall be adjusted according to the lettered Rules.

Rule Paramount

In no case shall there be any allowance for sacrifice or expenditure unless reasonably made or incurred.

Rule A

1. There is a general average act when, and only when, any extraordinary sacrifice or expenditure is intentionally and reasonably made or incurred for the common safety for the purpose of preserving from peril the property involved in a common maritime adventure.

2. General average sacrifices and expenditures shall be borne by the different contributing interests on the basis hereinafter provided.

Rule B

1. There is a common maritime adventure when one or more vessels are towing or pushing another vessel or vessels, provided that they are all involved in commercial activities and not in a salvage operation.

When measures are taken to preserve the vessels and their cargoes, if any, from a common peril, these Rules shall apply.

2. If the vessels are in common peril and one is disconnected either to increase the disconnecting vessel's safety alone, or the safety of all vessels in the common maritime adventure, the disconnection will be a general average act.

3. Where vessels involved in a common maritime adventure resort to a port or place of refuge, allowances under these Rules may be made in relation to each of the vessels. Subject to the provisions of paragraphs 3 and 4 of Rule G, allowances in general average shall cease at the time that the common maritime adventure comes to an end.

Rule C

1. Only such losses, damages or expenses which are the direct consequence of the general average act shall be allowed as general average.

2. In no case shall there be any allowance in general average for losses, damages or expenses incurred in respect of damage to the environment or in consequence of the escape or release of pollutant substances from the property involved in the common maritime adventure.

3. Demurrage, loss of market, and any loss or damage sustained or expense incurred by reason of delay, whether on the voyage or subsequently, and any indirect loss whatsoever, shall not be allowed as general average.

Rule D

Rights to contribution in general average shall not be affected, though the event which gave rise to the sacrifice or expenditure may have been due to the fault of the parties to the common

1 © Comité Maritime Internationale (CIM), 2004.

maritime adventure, but this shall not prejudice any remedies or defences which may be open against or to that party in respect of such fault.

Rule E

1. The onus of proof is upon the party claiming in general average to show that the loss or expense claimed is properly allowable as general average.

2. All parties to the common maritime adventure shall, as soon as possible, supply particulars of value in respect of their contributory interest and, if claiming in general average, shall give notice in writing to the average adjuster of the loss or expense in respect of which they claim contribution, and supply evidence in support thereof.

3. Failing notification, or if any party does not supply particulars in support of a notified claim, within 12 months of the termination of the common maritime adventure or payment of the expense, the average adjuster shall be at liberty to estimate the extent of the allowance on the basis of the information available to the adjuster. Particulars of value shall be provided within 12 months of the termination of the common maritime adventure, failing which the average adjuster shall be at liberty to estimate the contributory value on the same basis. Such estimates shall be communicated to the party in question in writing. Estimates may only be challenged within two months of receipt of the communication and only on the grounds that they are manifestly incorrect.

4. Any party to the common maritime adventure pursuing a recovery from a third party in respect of sacrifice or expenditure claimed in general average, shall so advise the average adjuster and, in the event that a recovery is achieved, shall supply to the average adjuster full particulars of the recovery within two months of receipt of the recovery.

Rule F

Any additional expense incurred in place of another expense, which would have been allowable as general average shall be deemed to be general average and so allowed without regard to the saving, if any, to other interests, but only up to the amount of the general average expense avoided.

Rule G

1. General average shall be adjusted as regards both loss and contribution upon the basis of values at the time and place when and where the common maritime adventure ends.

2. This rule shall not affect the determination of the place at which the average statement is to be prepared.

3. When a ship is at any port or place in circumstances which would give rise to an allowance in general average under the provisions of Rules X and XI, and the cargo or part thereof is forwarded to destination by other means, rights and liabilities in general average shall, subject to cargo interests being notified if practicable, remain as nearly as possible the same as they would have been in the absence of such forwarding, as if the common maritime adventure had continued in the original ship for so long as justifiable under the contract of carriage and the applicable law.

4. The proportion attaching to cargo of the allowances made in general average by reason of applying the third paragraph of this Rule shall be limited to the cost which would have been borne by the owners of cargo if the cargo had been forwarded at their expense. This limit shall not apply to any allowances made under Rule F.

Rule I – Jettison of Cargo

No jettison of cargo shall be allowed as general average, unless such cargo is carried in accordance with the recognised custom of the trade.

Rule II – Loss or Damage by Sacrifices for the Common Safety

Loss of or damage to the property involved in the common maritime adventure by or in consequence of a sacrifice made for the common safety, and by water which goes down a ship's hatches opened or other opening made for the purpose of making a jettison for the common safety, shall be allowed as general average.

Rule III – Extinguishing Fire on Shipboard

Damage done to a ship and cargo, or either of them, by water or otherwise, including damage by beaching or scuttling a burning ship, in extinguishing a fire on board the ship, shall be allowed as general average; except that no allowance shall be made for damage by smoke however caused or by heat of the fire.

Rule IV -- Cutting Away Wreck

Loss or damage sustained by cutting away wreck or parts of the ship which have been previously carried away or are effectively lost by accident shall not be allowed as general average.

Rule V – Voluntary Stranding

When a ship is intentionally run on shore for the common safety, whether or not she might have been driven on shore, the consequent loss or damage to the property involved in the common maritime adventure shall be allowed in general average.

Rule VI – Salvage Remuneration

(a) Expenditure incurred by the parties to the common maritime adventure in the nature of salvage, whether under contract or otherwise, shall be allowed in general average provided that the salvage operations were carried out for the purpose of preserving from peril the property involved in the common maritime adventure and subject to the provisions of paragraphs (b), (c) and (d).

(b) Notwithstanding (a) above, where the parties to the common maritime adventure have separate contractual or legal liability to salvors, salvage shall only be allowed should any of the following arise:

(i) there is a subsequent accident or other circumstances resulting in loss or damage to property during the voyage that results in significant differences between salved and contributory values,

(ii) there are significant general average sacrifices,

(iii) salved values are manifestly incorrect and there is a significantly incorrect apportionment of salvage expenses,

(iv) any of the parties to the salvage has paid a significant proportion of salvage due from another party,

(v) a significant proportion of the parties have satisfied the salvage claim on substantially different terms, no regard being had to interest, currency correction or legal costs of either the salvor or the contributing interest.

(c) Salvage expenditures referred to in paragraph (a) above shall include any salvage remuneration in which the skill and efforts of the salvors in preventing or minimising damage to the environment such as is referred to in Article 13 paragraph 1(b) of the International Convention on Salvage, 1989 have been taken into account.

(d) Special compensation payable to a salvor by the shipowner under Article 14 of the International Convention on Salvage, 1989 to the extent specified in paragraph 4 of that Article or under any other provision similar in substance (such as SCOPIC) shall not be allowed in general average and shall not be considered a salvage expenditure as referred to in paragraph (a) of this Rule.

Rule VII – Damage to Machinery and Boilers

Damage caused to any machinery and boilers of a ship which is ashore and in a position of peril, in endeavouring to refloat, shall be allowed in general average when shown to have arisen from an actual intention to float the ship for the common safety at the risk of such damage; but where a ship is afloat no loss or damage caused by working the propelling machinery and boilers shall in any circumstances be allowed as general average.

Rule VIII – Expenses Lightening a Ship When Ashore, and Consequent Damage

When a ship is ashore and cargo and ship's fuel and stores or any of them are discharged as a general average act, the extra cost of lightening, lighter hire and reshipping (if incurred), and any loss or damage to the property involved in the common maritime adventure in consequence thereof, shall be allowed as general average.

Rule IX – Cargo, Ship's Materials and Stores Used for Fuel

Cargo, ship's materials and stores, or any of them, necessarily used for fuel for the common safety at a time of peril shall be allowed as general average, but when such an allowance is made for the cost of ship's materials and stores the general average shall be credited with the estimated cost of the fuel which would otherwise have been consumed in prosecuting the intended voyage.

Rule X – Expenses at Port of Refuge, etc.

(a) (i) When a ship shall have entered a port or place of refuge or shall have returned to her port or place of loading in consequence of accident, sacrifice or other extraordinary circumstances which render that necessary for the common safety, the expenses of entering such port or place shall be allowed as general average; and when she shall have sailed thence with her original cargo, or a part of it, the corresponding expenses of leaving such port or place consequent upon such entry or return shall likewise be allowed as general average.

(ii) When a ship is at any port or place of refuge and is necessarily removed to another port or place of refuge because repairs cannot be carried out in the first port or place, the provisions of this Rule shall be applied to the second port or place as if it were a port or place of refuge and the cost of such removal including temporary repairs and towage shall be allowed as general average. The provisions of Rule XI shall be applied to the prolongation of the voyage occasioned by such removal.

(b) (i) The cost of handling on board or discharging cargo, fuel or stores, whether at a port or place of loading, call or refuge, shall be allowed as general average when the handling or discharge was necessary for the common safety or to enable damage to the ship caused by sacrifice or accident to be repaired, if the repairs were necessary for the safe prosecution of the voyage, except in cases where the damage to the ship is discovered at a port or place of loading or call without any accident or other extraordinary circumstances connected with such damage having taken place during the voyage.

(ii) The cost of handling on board or discharging cargo, fuel or stores shall not be allowable as general average when incurred solely for the purpose of restowage due to shifting during the voyage, unless such restowage is necessary for the common safety.

(c) Whenever the cost of handling or discharging cargo, fuel or stores is allowable as general average, the costs of storage, including insurance if reasonably incurred, reloading and stowing of such cargo, fuel or stores shall likewise be allowed as general average. The provisions of Rule XI shall be applied to the extra period of detention occasioned by such reloading or restowing.

(d) When the ship is condemned or does not proceed on her original voyage, storage expenses shall be allowed as general average only up to the date of the ship's condemnation or of the abandonment of the voyage or up to the date of completion of discharge of cargo if the condemnation or abandonment takes place before that date.

Rule XI – Wages and Maintenance of Crew and Other Expenses Putting in to and at a Port of Refuge, etc.

(a) Wages and maintenance of master, officers and crew reasonably incurred and fuel and stores consumed during the prolongation of the voyage occasioned by a ship entering a port or place of refuge or returning to her port or place of loading shall be allowed as general average when the expenses of entering such port or place are allowable as general average in accordance with Rule X(a).

(b) (i) When a ship shall have entered or been detained in any port or place in consequence of accident, sacrifice or other extra-ordinary circumstances which render that entry or detention necessary for the common safety, or to enable damage to the ship caused by sacrifice or accident to be repaired, if the repairs were necessary for the safe prosecution of the voyage, the wages and maintenance of the master, officers and crew reasonably incurred during the extra period of detention in such port or place until the ship shall or should have been made ready to proceed upon her voyage, shall be allowed in general average.

(ii) Fuel and stores consumed during the extra period of detention shall be allowed as general average, except such fuel and stores as are consumed in effecting repairs not allowable in general average.

(iii) Port charges incurred during the extra period of detention shall likewise be allowed as general average except such charges as are incurred solely by reason of repairs not allowable in general average.

(iv) Provided that when damage to the ship is discovered at a port or place of loading or call without any accident or other extraordinary circumstance connected with such damage having taken place during the voyage, then the wages and maintenance of master, officers and crew and fuel and stores consumed and port charges incurred during the extra detention for repairs to damages so discovered shall not be allowable as general average, even if the repairs are necessary for the safe prosecution of the voyage.

(v) When the ship is condemned or does not proceed on her original voyage, the wages and maintenance of the master, officers and crew and fuel and stores consumed and port charges shall be allowed as general average only up to the date of the ship's condemnation or of the abandonment of the voyage or up to the date of completion of discharge of cargo if the condemnation or abandonment takes place before that date.

(c) (i) For the purpose of these Rules wages shall include all payments made to or for the benefit of the master, officers and crew, whether such payments be imposed by law upon the shipowners or be made under the terms of articles of employment.

(ii) For the purpose of these Rules, port charges shall include all customary or additional expenses incurred for the common safety or to enable a vessel to enter or remain at a port of refuge or call in the circumstances outlined in Rule XI(b)(i).

(d) The cost of measures undertaken to prevent or minimise damage to the environment shall be allowed in general average when incurred in any or all of the following circumstances:

(i) as part of an operation performed for the common safety which, had it been undertaken by a party outside the common maritime adventure, would have entitled such party to a salvage reward;

(ii) as a condition of entry into or departure from any port or place in the circumstances prescribed in Rule X(a);

(iii) as a condition of remaining at any port or place in the circumstances prescribed in Rule XI(b), provided that when there is an actual escape or release of pollutant substances, the cost of any additional measures required on that account to prevent or minimise pollution or environmental damage shall not be allowed as general average;

(iv) necessarily in connection with the handling on board, discharging, storing or reloading of cargo, fuel or stores whenever the cost of those operations is allowable as general average.

Rule XII – Damage to Cargo in Discharging, etc.

Damage to or loss of cargo, fuel or stores sustained in consequence of their handling, discharging, storing, reloading and stowing shall be allowed as general average, when and only when the cost of those measures respectively is allowed as general average.

Rule XIII – Deductions from Cost of Repairs

(a) Repairs to be allowed in general average shall not be subject to deductions in respect of "new for old" where old material or parts are replaced by new unless the ship is over fifteen years old in which case there shall be a deduction of one third. The deductions shall be regulated by the age of the ship from the 31st December of the year of completion of construction to the date of the general average act, except for insulation, life and similar boats, communications and navigational apparatus and equipment, machinery and boilers for which the deductions shall be regulated by the age of the particular parts to which they apply.

(b) The deductions shall be made only from the cost of the new material or parts when finished and ready to be installed in the ship. No deduction shall be made in respect of provisions, stores, anchors and chain cables. Drydock and slipway dues and costs of shifting the ship shall be allowed in full.

(c) The costs of cleaning, painting or coating of bottom shall not be allowed in general average unless the bottom has been painted or coated within the 24 months preceding the date of the general average act in which case one half of such costs shall be allowed.

Rule XIV – Temporary Repairs

(a) Where temporary repairs are effected to a ship at a port of loading, call or refuge, for the common safety, or of damage caused by general average sacrifice, the cost of such repairs shall be allowed as general average.

(b) Where temporary repairs of accidental damage are effected in order to enable the common maritime adventure to be completed, the cost of such repairs shall be allowed as general average without regard to the saving, if any, to other interests, but only up to the saving in expense which would have been incurred and allowed in general average if such repairs had not been effected there.

(c) No deductions "new for old" shall be made from the cost of temporary repairs allowable as general average.

Rule XV – Loss of Freight

Loss of freight arising from damage to or loss of cargo shall be allowed as general average, either when caused by a general average act, or when the damage to or loss of cargo is so allowed.

Deduction shall be made from the amount of gross freight lost, of the charges which the owner thereof would have incurred to earn such freight, but has, in consequence of the sacrifice, not incurred.

Rule XVI – Amount to Be Allowed for Cargo Lost or Damaged by Sacrifice

(a) (i) The amount to be allowed as general average for damage to or loss of cargo sacrificed shall be the loss which has been sustained thereby based on the value at the time of discharge, ascertained from the commercial invoice rendered to the receiver or if there is no such invoice from the shipped value. Such commercial invoice may be deemed by the average adjuster to reflect the value at the time of discharge irrespective of the place of final delivery under the contract of carriage.

(ii) The value at the time of discharge shall include the cost of insurance and freight except insofar as such freight is at the risk of interests other than the cargo.

(b) When cargo so damaged is sold and the amount of the damage has not been otherwise agreed, the loss to be allowed in general average shall be the difference between the net proceeds of sale and the net sound value as computed in the first paragraph of this Rule.

Rule XVII – Contributory Values

(a) (i) The contribution to a general average shall be made upon the actual net values of the property at the termination of the common maritime adventure except that the value of cargo shall be the value at the time of discharge, ascertained from the commercial invoice rendered to the receiver or if there is no such invoice from the shipped value. Such commercial invoice may be deemed by the average adjuster to reflect the value at the time of discharge irrespective of the place of final delivery under the contract of carriage.

(ii) The value of the cargo shall include the cost of insurance and freight unless and insofar as such freight is at the risk of interests other than the cargo, deducting therefrom any loss or damage suffered by the cargo prior to or at the time of discharge. Any cargo may be excluded from contributing to general average should the average adjuster consider that the cost of including it in the adjustment would be likely to be disproportionate to its eventual contribution.

(iii) The value of the ship shall be assessed without taking into account the beneficial or detrimental effect of any demise or time charterparty to which the ship may be committed.

(b) To these values shall be added the amount allowed as general average for property sacrificed, if not already included, deduction being made from the freight and passage money at risk of such charges and crew's wages as would not have been incurred in earning the freight had the ship and cargo been totally lost at the date of the general average act and have not been allowed as general average; deduction being also made from the value of the property of all extra charges incurred in respect thereof subsequently to the general average act, except such charges as are allowed in general average or fall upon the ship by virtue of an award for special compensation under Article 14 of the International Convention on Salvage, 1989 or under any other provision similar in substance. Where payment for salvage services has not been allowed as general average by reason of paragraph (b) of Rule VI, deductions in respect of payment for salvage services shall be limited to the amount paid to the salvors including interest and salvors' costs.

(c) In the circumstances envisaged in the third paragraph of Rule G, the cargo and other property shall contribute on the basis of its value upon delivery at original destination unless sold or otherwise disposed of short of that destination, and the ship shall contribute upon its actual net value at the time of completion of discharge of cargo.

(d) Where cargo is sold short of destination, however, it shall contribute upon the actual net proceeds of sale, with the addition of any amount allowed as general average.

(e) Mails, passengers' luggage, personal effects and accompanied private motor vehicles shall not contribute to general average.

Rule XVIII – Damage to Ship

The amount to be allowed as general average for damage or loss to the ship, her machinery and/or gear caused by a general average act shall be as follows:

(a) When repaired or replaced,

The actual reasonable cost of repairing or replacing such damage or loss, subject to deductions in accordance with Rule XIII;

(b) When not repaired or replaced,

The reasonable depreciation arising from such damage or loss, but not exceeding the estimated cost of repairs. But where the ship is an actual total loss or when the cost of repairs of the damage would exceed the value of the ship when repaired, the amount to be allowed as general average shall be the difference between the estimated sound value of the ship after deducting therefrom the estimated cost of repairing damage which is not general average and the value of the ship in her damaged state which may be measured by the net proceeds of sale, if any.

Rule XIX – Undeclared or Wrongfully Declared Cargo

(a) Damage or loss caused to goods loaded without the knowledge of the shipowner or his agent or to goods wilfully misdescribed at time of shipment shall not be allowed as general average, but such goods shall remain liable to contribute, if saved.

(b) Damage or loss caused to goods which have been wrongfully declared on shipment at a value which is lower than their real value, any general average loss or damage shall be allowed on the basis of their declared value, but such goods shall contribute upon their actual value.

Rule XX – Provision of Funds

(a) The capital loss sustained by the owners of goods sold for the purpose of raising funds to defray general average disbursements shall be allowed in general average.

(b) The cost of insuring average disbursements shall also be allowed in general average.

Rule XXI – Interest on Losses Allowed in General Average

(a) Interest shall be allowed on expenditure, sacrifices and allowances in general average until three months after the date of issue of the general average adjustment, due allowance being made for any payment on account by the contributory interests or from the general average deposit fund.

(b) The rate for calculating interest accruing during each calendar year shall be the 12-month ICE LIBOR for the currency in which the adjustment is prepared, as announced on the first banking day of that calendar year, increased by four percentage points. If the adjustment is prepared in a currency for which no ICE LIBOR is announced, the rate shall be the 12-month US Dollar ICE LIBOR, increased by four percentage points.

Rule XXII – Treatment of Cash Deposits

(a) Where cash deposits have been collected in respect of general average, salvage or special charges, such sums shall be remitted forthwith to the average adjuster who shall deposit the sums into a special account, earning interest where possible, in the name of the average adjuster.

(b) The special account shall be constituted in accordance with the law regarding client or third party funds applicable in the domicile of the average adjuster. The account shall be held separately from the average adjuster's own funds, in trust or in compliance with similar rules of law providing for the administration of the funds of third parties.

(c) The sums so deposited, together with accrued interest, if any, shall be held as security for payment to the parties entitled thereto, of the general average, salvage or special charges in respect of which the deposits have been collected. Payments on account or refunds of deposits may only be made when such payments are certified in writing by the average adjuster and notified to the depositor requesting their approval. Upon the receipt of the depositor's approval, or in the absence of such approval within a period of 90 days, the average adjuster may deduct the amount of the payment on account or the final contribution from the deposit.

(d) All deposits and payments or refunds shall be without prejudice to the ultimate liability of the parties.

Rule XXIII – Time Bar for Contributions to General Average

(a) Subject always to any mandatory rule on time limitation contained in any applicable law:

(i) Any rights to general average contribution including any rights to claim under general average bonds and guarantees, shall be extinguished unless an action is brought by the party claiming such contribution within a period of one year after the date upon which the general average adjustment is issued. However, in no case shall such an action be brought after six years from the date of the termination of the common maritime adventure.

(ii) These periods may be extended if the parties so agree after the termination of the common maritime adventure.

(b) This Rule shall not apply as between the parties to the general average and their respective insurers.

39) UNCTAD Model Clauses on Marine Hull and Cargo Insurance[1]

Marine Hull Insurance [omitted]

Cargo Insurance

All Risks Cover

A. COVERAGE

1. This insurance covers all risks of physical loss of or damage to the insured cargo, unless the insurer proves that one of the exclusions in Part B applies.

2. This insurance also covers loss of or damage to the insured cargo caused by any act of any governmental authority to prevent or minimize pollution resulting from damage to the carrying vessel, provided such act of govern mental authority has not resulted from want of due diligence by the assured.

B. GENERAL EXCLUSIONS

3. This insurance does not cover:

3.1 loss, damage, liability or expense caused by:

3.1.1 war, hostilities or warlike acts;

3.1.2 civil war, revolution, rebellion, insurrection, or civil strife arising therefrom;

3.1.3 mines, torpedoes, bombs or other weapons of war;

3.1.4 capture, seizure other than by pirates, masters, officers or crew, arrest, restraint or detainment, and the consequences thereof or any attempt thereat;

3.1.5 sabotage or terrorism committed from a political motive;

3.1.6 detonation of an explosive caused by any person acting maliciously or from a political motive;

3.1.7 strikes, lock-outs or other similar labour disturbances;

3.1.8 civil commotions, riots or other similar events; or

3.1.9 confiscation, requisition, or other similar measures taken or attempted by any government or other similar organization assuming or wielding power;

3.2 loss, damage, liability or expense resulting from the personal act or omission of the assured done with the intent to cause such loss, damage, liability or expense, or recklessly and with knowledge that such loss, damage, liability or expense would probably result;

3.3 ordinary leakage, ordinary loss in weight or volume, or any other ordinary loss of or damage to the insured cargo;

3.4 loss, damage, liability or expense caused by insufficiency or unsuitability of packing or preparation of the insured cargo;

3.5 loss, damage, liability or expense caused by inadequacy or unsuitability of the stowage of the insured cargo in a container or liftvan where such stowage is carried out prior to attachment of this insurance;

3.6.1 loss, damage, liability or expense caused by

3.6.1.1 unseaworthiness of vessel or craft, or

3.6.1.2 unfitness of vessel, craft, conveyance, container or liftvan for the safe carriage of the insured cargo,

where the assured knew of or had recklessly refrained from obtaining knowledge of such unseaworthiness or unfitness by the time the insured cargo was loaded therein.

3.6.2 This exclusion 3.6 shall not be invoked against a party claiming under this insurance to whom the insurance has been assigned and who has bought the insured cargo in good faith without notice of such unseaworthiness or unfitness;

3.7 loss, damage, liability or expense caused by inherent vice or nature of the insured cargo;

3.8 loss, damage, liability or expense caused by delay, even though the delay is caused by a peril insured against, except liability or expense payable under clause S (the General Average and Salvage Clause);

3.9 Alternative A: loss, damage, liability or expense caused by insolvency or financial default of the owners, managers, charterers or operators of the vessel;

Alternative B

3.9.1 loss, damage, liability or expense caused by insolvency or financial default of the owners, managers, charterers or operators of the vessel, where the assured has failed to take all necessary and prudent measures to establish, or to ensure that his agents establish, the financial reliability of those parties.

3.9.2 This exclusion 3.9 shall not be invoked against a party claiming under this insurance to whom the insurance has been assigned and who has bought the insured cargo in good faith without notice of such insolvency or financial default and without notice that the original assured has failed to take such measures.

3.10 Additional exclusion clause (if expressly agreed by the parties): loss, damage, liability or expense caused by piracy.

3.11 Additional exclusion clause (if expressly agreed by the parties): loss, damage, liability or expense arising directly or indirectly from or in connection with nuclear, radioactive or similar material or from the use of or accidents in nuclear installations or reactors.

C. ADDITIONAL COVERAGE

4. Both to Blame Clause

Where the insured cargo is shipped under a contract of carriage or affreightment containing a "Both to Blame Collision" Clause, the insurer also agrees, as to all losses covered by this insurance, to indemnify the assured for the insured cargo's proportion of any amount up to the sum insured which the assured may be liable to pay to the shipowner or carrier under such clause. In the event of any claim by the shipowner or carrier under the said clause, the assured agrees to notify the insurer who shall have the right, at his own cost and expense, to defend the assured against such claim.

5. General Average and Salvage Clause

5.1 This insurance covers the insured cargo's proportion of general average, salvage and/or salvage charges, adjusted or determined according to the contract of carriage or affreightment and/or the governing law and practice. In case of general average sacrifice of the insured cargo, the assured has the right to recover in respect of the whole of such loss.

5.2 No claim under this clause shall in any case be allowed unless the general average act or salvage was undertaken to avoid, or in connection with the avoidance of, a peril insured against.

5.3 Where all the contributing interests are owned by the assured, the provisions of the York-Antwerp Rules, 1974, or similar provisions of other rules if expressly agreed, shall be applied as if the interests were owned by different persons, and the insurer shall pay the insured cargo's proportion as so calculated.

6. Sue and Labour and Forwarding Charges Clause

6.1 Where there has been loss of or damage to the cargo from a peril insured against, or where the cargo is in danger from such a peril, and as a result reasonable expenditure is incurred by the assured in order to avert or minimize a loss which would be recoverable under this insurance, the insurer shall pay to the assured the expenditure incurred.

6.2 Where, as a result of the operation of a peril insured against, the transit is terminated at a port or place other than the destination to which the cargo is insured hereunder, the insurer will reimburse the assured for any extra charges properly and reasonably incurred in unloading, storing and forwarding the cargo to that destination.

6.3 This clause shall not apply to general average, salvage or salvage charges.

6.4 The insurer's liability under this clause is in addition to his liability under the other provisions of this insurance, but shall not exceed an amount equal to the sum insured hereunder in respect of the cargo.

D. PERIOD OF COVERAGE

7. Commencement and Duration

The insurance commences from the time the insured cargo leaves the ware house or place of storage at the place named in this insurance for the commencement of the transit and shall continue during the ordinary course of transit.

8. Termination

This insurance shall terminate

8.1 on delivery of the insured cargo to the consignee's or other final warehouse or place of storage at the destination named in the insurance; or

8.2 Alternative A: on delivery of the insured cargo to any other warehouse or place of storage, whether prior to or at the destination named in the insurance, which the assured chooses to use either

8.2.1 for storage other than in the ordinary course of transit, or

8.2.2 for allocation or distribution; or

8.2 Alternative B: on any taking of delivery of the insured cargo by the assured, the shipper, the consignee or their representatives or other authorized persons before the time when the insurance would otherwise terminate as stipulated in 8.1 above; or

8.3 when ... days have elapsed after completion of discharge of the insured cargo from the oversea vessel at the final port or place of discharge;

8.4 when the insured cargo has been discharged from the oversea vessel at the final port or place of discharge, and transit commences to a destination other than that named in this insurance; whichever shall first occur.

9. Continuation

9.1 The insurance shall remain in force, subject to termination as provided by clauses 8 and 9.2, during delay beyond the control of the assured, any deviation, forced discharge, reshipment or transhipment, and during any variation of the adventure arising from the exercise of a liberty granted to shipowners or charterers under the contract of carriage or affreightment.

9.2 When, owing to circumstances beyond the control of the assured, the contract of carriage or affreightment is terminated at a port or place other than the destination named therein, or the transit is otherwise terminated before delivery of the insured cargo as provided for in clause 8 above, this insurance shall also terminate unless prompt notice is given to the insurer and continuation of cover is requested. In that case this insurance shall remain in force, subject to an additional premium if required by the insurer, either

9.2.1 until the insured cargo is sold and delivered at such port or place or, unless otherwise specially agreed, until the expiry of ... days after its arrival at such port or place, whichever shall first occur, or

9.2.2 if the insured cargo is forwarded within the above ... day period (or any agreed extension thereof) to the destination named in this insurance or to any other destination, until terminated in accordance with clause 8 above.

E. MEASURE OF INDEMNITY

10. General Rules

10.1 Agreed and insurable value

10.1. 1 Where an agreed value is stated in this insurance this agreed value shall be conclusive between the assured and the insurer as to the value of the insured cargo in the absence of fraud.

10.1.2 Where there is no agreed value, the insurable value of the cargo is

Alternative A: the commercial invoice value or, if there is no such invoice, the market value of the cargo at the time and place of commencement of the cover, plus

10.1.2.1 if not already included, freight and other expenses incidental to the transport, customs duties, insurance costs, and

10.1.2.2 an expected profit of ... %

Alternative B: the market value at the place of destination at the time of the arrival of the cargo or, if the cargo does not arrive, at the time it should have arrived at the place of destination.

10.1. 3 Where there is no agreed value and the term "agreed value" is used in other provisions of this insurance, this term shall be deemed also to cover the insurable value, as defined in 10.1.2 above.

10.2 Sum insured

The insurer's total liability under Part A and clauses 4 and 5 of Part C shall be limited to the sum insured. A separate limit shall apply to claims under clause 6 of Part C as provided therein.

10.3 Under- and over-insurance

10.3. 1 Where the sum insured is less than the agreed value, the insurer is only liable to pay that proportion of any loss covered by this insurance that the sum insured bears to the agreed value.

10.3. 2 Where the sum insured is higher than the agreed value, the assured may not recover more than the agreed value.

10.4 Under-valuation

Alternative A: Where the assured has a claim under Part C, clauses 5 and/or 6, the indemnity payable under this insurance shall not be reduced by reason of the agreed value being less than the actual or contributory value of the insured cargo.

Alternative B

10.4. 1 Where the assured has a claim under Part C, clause 5, of this insurance other than for general average sacrifice of the cargo, and the agreed value is less than the full contributory value of the cargo, the insurer shall only pay such proportion of general average, salvage and salvage charges as the agreed value bears to the full contributory value.

10.4. 2 Where the cargo has suffered damage covered by this insurance and such damage constitutes a deduction from the contributory value, the same amount must be deducted from the agreed value when determining whether the agreed value is less than the contributory value.

10.5 Co-insurance

Where two or more insurers are liable under this insurance,

10.5. 1 each insurer is liable only for his proportion of the claim, which is the proportion that his subscription bears to the sum insured, and shall on no account be held jointly liable with his co-insurers.

10.5.2

Alternative A : each insurer agrees to be subject to the jurisdiction of the courts applicable to the leading insurer for all disputes under this insurance. The leading insurer is authorized by his co-insurers to accept and conduct legal proceedings on their behalf.

Alternative B: No provision.

11. Total Losses

11.1 A claim for loss by a peril insured against may be for a total loss, as herein defined, or otherwise for a partial loss.

11.2 Actual total loss occurs where the insured cargo is destroyed or so damaged as to cease to be a thing of the kind insured or where the assured is irretrievably deprived of the cargo.

11.3 Presumed total loss occurs where the carrying vessel is missing with the insured cargo and no news of the vessel or the cargo has been received within a reasonable time but not to exceed ... months.

11.4 Constructive total loss occurs:

11.4. 1 where the assured has been deprived of the free use and disposal of the insured cargo, and

11.4.1.1 it is unlikely that he will be able to recover it within a reasonable time but not to exceed ... months, or

11.4.1.2 he could not recover it without incurring an expenditure which would exceed its value on recovery;

11.4. 2 where the insured cargo has been damaged and it cannot be repaired or reconditioned and forwarded to its destination without:

11.4.2.1 becoming an actual total loss before arrival, or

11.4.2.2 incurring an expenditure which would exceed its value on arrival.

11.5 Where there is a valid claim for a total loss recoverable under this insurance, the amount payable by the insurer is the sum insured in respect of the cargo.

12. Abandonment

12.1 Where the assured elects to claim for a constructive total loss rather than for a partial loss, or where there is a presumed total loss, the assured shall with reasonable diligence notify the insurer that he wishes to abandon what remains of the cargo to the insurer.

12.2 Unless otherwise directed by applicable law, no notice of abandonment need be given if, at the time when the assured receives reliable information of the loss, there would be no possibility of benefit to the insurer if notice were given to him or where the insurer has expressly waived the need for such notice.

12.3 Notice of abandonment may be expressed in any terms which indicate the intention of the assured unconditionally to abandon his interest in the cargo to the insurer. The insurer shall advise the assured whether he accepts or rejects the notice of abandonment within a reasonable time from the date on which the notice is tendered.

12.4 Where notice of abandonment is given as provided herein, the rights of the assured shall not be prejudiced by the refusal of the insurer to accept the abandonment.

12.5 Where notice of abandonment is accepted, the abandonment is irrevocable and the acceptance of the notice of abandonment conclusively admits liability for the loss and the sufficiency of the notice. Upon acceptance of abandonment, the insurer may, if he so wishes, take over whatever may remain of the cargo, with all the rights and obligations attached thereto.

13. Partial Losses

13.1 Total loss of part: Where part of the cargo is totally lost, the assured is entitled to be indemnified for such proportion of the agreed value, if a value has been agreed, or of the insurable value, if no value has been agreed, as the insurable value of the part lost bears to the insurable value of the whole.

13.2 Damage

13.2. 1 Where the whole or any part of the cargo has been delivered damaged at its destination, the assured is entitled to be indemnified for such proportion of the agreed value, if a value has been agreed, or of the insurable value, if no value has been agreed, as the difference between the gross sound and damaged values at the place of destination bears to the gross sound value.

13.2. 2 If the assured chooses to recondition or to repair any part of the cargo which has been delivered damaged at its destination he may, alternatively, claim the reasonable cost of such reconditioning or repair at the time of arrival at its destination.

F. INSURABLE INTEREST

14.1 In order to recover under this insurance the assured must have an insurable interest in the insured cargo at the time of the loss.

14.2 Subject to 14.1 above, the assured shall be entitled to recover in respect of a loss occurring during the transit covered by this insurance, notwithstanding that the loss occurred before the contract of insurance was concluded, unless the assured was aware of the loss and the insurer was not.

CARGO INSURANCE - Intermediate Cover

A. COVERAGE

1. This insurance covers physical loss of or damage to the insured cargo caused by

1.1 vessel or craft being stranded, grounded, sunk or capsized;

1.2 collision or contact of vessel, craft or conveyance with any external object other than water;

1.3 derailment, overturning or falling of the transport conveyance;

1.4 explosion, fire or smoke emanating from that fire;

1.5 general average sacrifice;

1.6 jettison or washing overboard;

1.7 earthquake, volcanic eruption, lightning, or similar natural calamities;

1.8 entry of sea, lake or river water into the vessel, craft, hold, conveyance, container, liftvan or place of storage;

1.9 discharge of all or part of the cargo on the vessel or craft at a port of distress;

1.10 total loss of any package lost overboard or dropped whilst loading on to, or unloading from, vessel or craft.

2. This insurance also covers loss of or damage to the insured cargo caused by any act of any governmental authority to prevent or minimize pollution resulting from damage to the carrying vessel, provided that such act of governmental authority has not resulted from want of due diligence by the assured.

B. GENERAL EXCLUSIONS

3. This insurance does not cover:

3.1 loss, damage, liability or expense caused by:

3.1.1 war, hostilities or warlike acts;

3.1.2 civil war, revolution, rebellion, insurrection, or civil strife arising therefrom;

3.1.3 mines, torpedoes, bombs or other weapons of war;

3.1.4 capture, seizure other than by pirates, masters, officers or crew, arrest, restraint or detainment, and the consequences thereof or any attempt thereat;

3.1.5 sabotage or terrorism committed from a political motive;

3.1.6 detonation of an explosive caused by any person acting maliciously or from a political motive;

3.1.7 strikes, lock-outs or other similar labour disturbances;

3.1.8 civil commotions, riots or other similar events;

3.1.9 confiscation, requisition, or other similar measures taken or attempted by any government or other similar organization assuming or wielding power; or

3.1.1 0 deliberate damage to or deliberate destruction of the insured cargo or any part thereof by the wrongful act of any person or persons;

3.2 loss, damage, liability or expense resulting from the personal act or omission of the assured done with the intent to cause such loss, damage, liability or expense, or recklessly and with knowledge that such loss, damage, liability or expense would probably result;

3.3 ordinary leakage, ordinary loss in weight or volume, or any other ordinary loss of or damage to the insured cargo;

3.4 loss, damage, liability or expense caused by insufficiency or unsuitability of packing or preparation of the insured cargo;

3.5 loss, damage, liability or expense caused by inadequacy or unsuitability of the stowage of the insured cargo in a container or liftvan where such stowage is carried out prior to attachment of this insurance;

3.6.1 loss, damage, liability or expense caused by

3.6.1.1 unseaworthiness of vessel or craft, or

3.6.1.2 unfitness of vessel, craft, conveyance, container or liftvan for the safe carriage of the insured cargo, where the assured knew of or had recklessly refrained from obtaining knowledge of such unseaworthiness of unfitness by the time the insured cargo was loaded therein.

3.6.2 This exclusion 3.6 shall not be invoked against a party claiming under this insurance to whom the insurance has been assigned and who has bought the insured cargo in good faith without notice of such unseaworthiness or unfitness;

3.7 loss, damage, liability or expense caused by inherent vice or nature of the insured cargo;

3.8 loss, damage, liability or expense caused by delay, even though the delay is caused by a peril insured against, except liability or expense payable under clause 5 (the General Average and Salvage Clause);

3.9

Alternative A: loss, damage liability or expense caused by insolvency or financial default of the owners, managers, charterers or operators of the vessel;

Alternative B

3.9.1 loss, damage, liability or expense caused by insolvency or financial default of the owners, managers, charterers or operators of the vessel, where the assured has failed to take all necessary and prudent measures to establish, or to ensure that his agents establish, the financial reliability of those parties.

3.9.2 This exclusion 3.9 shall not be invoked against a party claiming under this insurance to whom the insurance has been assigned and who has bought the insured cargo in good faith without notice of such insolvency or financial default and without notice that the original assured has failed to take such measures.

3.10 Additional exclusion clause (if expressly agreed by the parties): loss, damage, liability or expense caused by piracy.

3.11 Additional exclusion clause (if expressly agreed by the parties): loss, damage, liability or expense arising directly or indirectly from or in connection with nuclear, radioactive or similar material or from the use of or accidents in nuclear installations or reactors.

C. ADDITIONAL COVERAGE

4. Both to Blame Clause

Where the insured cargo is shipped under a contract of carriage or affreightment containing a "Both to Blame Collision" Clause, the insurer also agrees, as to all losses covered by this insurance, to indemnify the assured for the insured cargo's proportion of any amount up to the sum insured which the assured may be liable to pay to the shipowner or carrier under such clause. In the event of any claim by the shipowner or carrier under the said clause the assured agrees to notify the insurer who shall have the right, at his own cost and expense, to defend the assured against such claim.

5. General Average and Salvage Clause

5.1 This insurance covers the insured cargo's proportion of general average, salvage and/or salvage charges, adjusted or determined according to the contract of carriage or affreightment and/or the governing law and practice. In case of general average sacrifice of the insured cargo, the assured has the right to recover in respect of the whole of such loss.

5.2 No claim under this clause shall in any case be allowed unless the general average act or salvage was undertaken to avoid or in connection with the avoidance of, a peril insured against.

5.3 Where all the contributing interests are owned by the assured the provisions of the York-Antwerp Rules, 1974, or similar provisions of other rules if expressly agreed, shall be applied as if the interests were owned by different persons, and the insurer shall pay the insured cargo's proportion as so calculated.

6. Sue and Labour and Forwarding Charges Clause

6.1 Where there has been loss of or damage to the cargo from a peril insured against, or where the cargo is in danger from such a peril, and as a result reasonable expenditure is incurred by the assured in order to avert or minimize a loss which would be recoverable under this insurance, the insurer shall pay to the assured the expenditure incurred.

6.2 Where, as a result of the operation of a peril insured against the transit is terminated at a port or place other than the destination to which the cargo is insured hereunder, the insurer will reimburse the assured for any extra charges properly and reasonably incurred in unloading, storing and forwarding the cargo to that destination.

6.3 This clause shall not apply to general average, salvage or salvage charges.

6.4 The insurer's liability under this clause is in addition to his liability under the other provisions of this insurance, but shall not exceed an amount equal to the sum insured hereunder in respect of the cargo.

D. PERIOD OF COVERAGE

7. Commencement and Duration

The insurance commences from the time the insured cargo leaves the warehouse or place of storage at the place named in this insurance for the commencement of the transit and shall continue during the ordinary course of transit.

8. Termination

This insurance shall terminate

8.1 on delivery of the insured cargo to the consignee's or other final warehouse or place of storage at the destination named in the insurance; or

8.2 Alternative A: on delivery of the insured cargo to any other warehouse or place of storage, whether prior to or at the destination named in the insurance, which the assured chooses to use either

8.2.1 for storage other than in the ordinary course of transit, or

8.2.2 for allocation or distribution; or

Alternative B: on any taking of delivery of the insured cargo by the assured, the shipper, the consignee or their representatives or other authorized persons before the time when the insurance would otherwise terminate as stipulated in 8.1 above; or

8.3 when ... days have elapsed after completion of discharge of the insured cargo from the oversea vessel at the final port or place of discharge;

8.4 when the insured cargo has been discharged from the oversea vessel at the final port or place of discharge, and transit commences to a destination other than that named in this insurance; whichever shall first occur.

9. Continuation

9.1 The insurance shall remain in force, subject to termination as provided by clauses 8 and 9.2, during delay beyond the control of the assured, any deviation, forced discharge, reshipment or transhipment, and during any variation of the adventure arising from the exercise of a liberty granted to shipowners or charterers under the contract of carriage or affreightment.

9.2 When, owing to circumstances beyond the control of the assured, the contract of carriage or affreightment is terminated at a port or place other than the destination named therein, or the transit is otherwise terminated before delivery of the insured cargo as provided for in clause 8 above, this insurance shall also terminate unless prompt notice is given to the insurer and continuation of cover is requested. In that case this insurance shall remain in force, subject to an additional premium if required by the insurer, either

9.2.1 until the insured cargo is sold and delivered at such port or place or, unless otherwise specially agreed, until the expiry of ... days after its arrival at such port or place, whichever shall first occur, or

9.2.2 if the insured cargo is forwarded within the above ... day period (or any agreed extension thereof) to the destination named in this insurance or to any other destination, until terminated in accordance with clause 8 above.

E. MEASURE OF INDEMNITY

10. General Rules

10.1 Agreed and insurable value

10.1. 1 Where an agreed value is stated in this insurance this agreed value shall be conclusive between the assured and the insurer as to the value of the insured cargo in the absence of fraud.

10.1. 2 Where there is no agreed value, the insurable value of the cargo is

Alternative A: the commercial invoice value or, if there is no such invoice, the market value of the cargo at the time and place of commencement of the cover, plus

10.1.2.1 if not already included, freight and other expenses incidental to the transport, customs duties, insurance costs, and

10.1.2.2 an expected profit of ... %.

Alternative B: the market value at the place of destination at the time of the arrival of the cargo or, if the cargo does not arrive, at the time it should have arrived at the place of destination.

10.1. 3 Where there is no agreed value and the term "agreed value" is used in other provisions of this insurance, this term shall be deemed also to cover the insurable value, as defined in 10.1.2 above.

10.2 Sum insured

The insurer's total liability under Part A and clauses 4 and 5 of Part C shall be limited to the sum insured. A separate limit shall apply to claims under clause 6 of Part C as provided therein.

10.3 Under- and over-insurance

10.3. 1 Where the sum insured is less than the agreed value, the insurer is only liable to pay that proportion of any loss covered by this insurance that the sum insured bears to the agreed value.

10.3. 3 Where the sum insured is higher than the agreed value, the assured may not recover more than the agreed value.

10.4 Under-valuation

Alternative A: Where the assured has a claim under Part C, clauses 5 and/or 6, the indemnity payable under this insurance shall not be reduced by reason of the agreed value being less than the actual or contributory value of the insured cargo.

Alternative B

10.4. 1 Where the assured has a claim under Part C, clause 5, of this insurance other than for general average sacrifice of the cargo, and the agreed value is less than the full contributory value of the cargo, the insurer shall only pay such proportion of general average, salvage and salvage charges as the agreed value bears to the full contributory value.

10.4. 2 Where the cargo has suffered damage covered by this insurance and such damage constitutes a deduction from the contributory value, the same amount must be deducted from the agreed value when determining whether the agreed value is less than the contributory value.

10.5 Co-insurance: Where two or more insurers are liable under this insurance,

10.5. 1 each insurer is liable only for his proportion of the claim, which is the proportion that his subscription bears to the sum insured, and shall on no account be held jointly liable with his co-insurers.

10.5. 2 Alternative A: each insurer agrees to be subject to the jurisdiction of the courts applicable to the leading insurer for all disputes under this insurance. The leading insurer is authorized by his co-insurers to accept and conduct legal proceedings on their behalf.

Alternative B: No provision

11. Total Losses

11.1 A claim for loss by a peril insured against may be for a total loss, as herein defined, or otherwise for a partial loss.

11.2 Actual total loss occurs where the insured cargo is destroyed or so damaged as to cease to be a thing of the kind insured or where the assured is irretrievably deprived of the cargo.

11.3 Presumed total loss occurs where the carrying vessel is missing with the insured cargo and no news of the vessel or the cargo has been received within a reasonable time but not to exceed ... months.

11.4 Constructive total loss occurs:

11.4. 1 where the assured has been deprived of the free use and disposal of the insured cargo, and

11.4.1.1 it is unlikely that he will be able to recover it within a reasonable time but not to exceed ... months, or

11.4.1.2 he could not recover it without incurring an expenditure which would exceed its value on recovery;

11.4. 2 where the insured cargo has been damaged and it cannot be repaired or reconditioned and forwarded to its destination without:

11.4.2.1 becoming an actual total loss before arrival, or

11.4.2.2 incurring an expenditure which would exceed its value on arrival.

11.5 Where there is a valid claim for a total loss recoverable under this insurance, the amount payable by the insurer is the sum insured in respect of the cargo.

12. Abandonment

12.1 Where the assured elects to claim for a constructive total loss rather than for a partial loss, or where there is a presumed total loss, the assured shall with reasonable diligence notify the insurer that he wishes to abandon what remains of the cargo to the insurer.

12.2 Unless otherwise directed by applicable law, no notice of abandonment need be given if, at the time when the assured receives reliable information of the loss, there would be no possibility of benefit to the insurer if notice were given to him or where the insurer has expressly waived the need for such notice.

12.3 Notice of abandonment may be expressed in any terms which indicate the intention of the assured unconditionally to abandon his interest in the cargo to the insurer. The insurer shall advise the assured whether he accepts or rejects the notice of abandonment within a reasonable time from the date on which the notice is tendered.

12.4 Where notice of abandonment is given as provided herein, the rights of the assured shall not be prejudiced by the refusal of the insurer to accept the abandonment.

12.5 Where notice of abandonment is accepted, the abandonment is irrevocable and the acceptance of the notice of abandonment conclusively admits liability for the loss and the sufficiency of the notice. Upon acceptance of abandonment, the insurer may, if he so wishes, take over whatever may remain of the cargo, with all the rights and obligations attached thereto.

13. Partial Losses

13.1 Total loss of part: Where part of the cargo is totally lost, the assured is entitled to be indemnified for such proportion of the agreed value, if a value has been agreed, or of the insurable value, if no value has been agreed, as the insurable value of the part lost bears to the insurable value of the whole.

13.2 Damage

13.2. 1 Where the whole or any part of the cargo has been delivered damaged at its destination, the assured is entitled to be indemnified for such proportion of the agreed value, if a value has been agreed, or of the insurable value, if no value has been agreed, as the difference between the gross sound and damaged values at the place of destination bears to the gross sound value.

13.2. 2 If the assured chooses to recondition or to repair any part of the cargo which has been delivered damaged at its destination, he may, alternatively, claim the reasonable cost of such reconditioning or repair at the time of arrival at its destination.

F. INSURABLE INTEREST

14.1 In order to recover under this insurance the assured must have an insurable interest in the insured cargo at the time of the loss.

14.2 Subject to 14.1 above, the assured shall be entitled to recover in respect of a loss occurring during the transit covered by this insurance, notwithstanding that the loss occurred before the contract of insurance was concluded, unless the assured was aware of the loss and the insurer was not.

CARGO INSURANCE - Restricted Cover

A. COVERAGE

1. This insurance covers physical loss of or damage to the insured cargo caused by

1.1 vessel or craft being stranded, grounded, sunk or capsized;

1.2 collision or contact of vessel, craft or conveyance with any external object other than water;

1.3 derailment, overturning or falling of the transport conveyance;

1.4 explosion, fire or smoke emanating from that fire;

1.5 general average sacrifice;

1.6 jettison;

1.7 discharge of all or part of the cargo on the vessel or craft at a port of distress.

2. This insurance also covers loss of or damage to the insured cargo caused by any act of any governmental authority to prevent or minimize pollution resulting from damage to the carry-

ing vessel, provided that such act of governmental authority has not resulted from want of due diligence by the assured.

B. GENERAL EXCLUSIONS

3. This insurance does not cover:

3.1 loss, damage, liability or expense caused by:

3.1.1 war, hostilities or warlike acts;

3.1.2 civil war, revolution, rebellion, insurrection, or civil strife arising therefrom;

3.1.3 mines, torpedoes, bombs or other weapons of war;

3.1.4 capture, seizure other than by pirates, masters, officers or crew, arrest, restraint or detainment, and the consequences thereof or any attempt thereat;

3.1.5 sabotage or terrorism committed from a political motive;

3.1.6 detonation of an explosive caused by any person acting maliciously or from a political motive;

3.1.7 strikes, lock-outs or other similar labour disturbances;

3.1.8 civil commotions, riots or other similar events;

3.1.9 confiscation, requisition, or other similar measures taken or attempted by any government or other similar organization assuming or wielding power; or

3.1.10 deliberate damage to or deliberate destruction of the insured cargo or any part thereof by the wrongful act of any person or persons;

3.2 loss, damage, liability or expense resulting from the personal act or omission of the assured done with the intent to cause such loss, damage, liability or expense, or recklessly and with knowledge that such loss, damage, liability or expense would probably result;

3.3 ordinary leakage, ordinary loss in weight or volume, or any other ordinary loss of or damage to the insured cargo;

3.4 loss, damage, liability or expense caused by insufficiency or unsuitability of packing or preparation of the insured cargo;

3.5 loss, damage, liability or expense caused by inadequacy or unsuitability of the stowage of the insured cargo in a container or liftvan where such stowage is carried out prior to attachment of this insurance;

3.6.1 loss damage, liability or expense caused by

3.6.1.1 unseaworthiness of vessel or craft, or

3.6.1.2 unfitness of vessel, craft, conveyance, container or liftvan for the safe carriage of the insured cargo, where the assured knew of or had recklessly refrained from obtaining knowledge of such unseaworthiness of unfitness by the time the insured cargo was loaded therein.

3.6.2 This exclusion 3.6 shall not be invoked against a party claiming under this insurance to whom the insurance has been assigned and who has bought the insured cargo in good faith without notice of such unseaworthiness or unfitness;

3.7 loss, damage, liability or expense caused by inherent vice or nature of the insured cargo;

3.8 loss, damage, liability or expense caused by delay, even though the delay is caused by a peril insured against, except liability or expense payable under clause 5 (the General Average and Salvage Clause);

3.9 Alternative A: loss, damage, liability or expense caused by insolvency or financial default of the owners, managers, charterers or operators of the vessel;

Alternative B

3.9.1 loss, damage, liability or expense caused by insolvency or financial default of the owners, managers, charterers or operators of the vessel, where the assured has failed to take all necessary and prudent measures to establish, or to ensure that his agents establish, the financial reliability of those parties.

3.9.2 This exclusion 3.9 shall not be invoked against a party claiming under this insurance to whom the insurance has been assigned and who has bought the insured cargo in good faith without notice of such insolvency or financial default and without notice that the original assured has failed to take such measures.

3.10 Additional exclusion clause (if expressly agreed by the parties): loss, damage, liability or expense caused by piracy.

3.11 Additional exclusion clause (if expressly agreed by the parties): loss, damage, liability or expense arising directly or indirectly from or in connection with nuclear, radioactive or similar material or from the use of or accidents in nuclear installations or reactors.

C. ADDITIONAL COVERAGE

4. Both to Blame Clause

Where the insured cargo is shipped under a contract of carriage or affreightment containing a "Both to Blame Collision" Clause, the insurer also agrees, as to all losses covered by this insurance, to indemnify the assured for the insured cargo's proportion of any amount up to the sum insured which the assured may be liable to pay to the shipowner or carrier under such clause. In the event of any claim by the shipowner or carrier under the said clause, the assured agrees to notify the insurer who shall have the right, at his own cost and expense, to defend the assured against such claim.

5. General Average and Salvage Clause

5.1 This insurance covers the insured cargo's proportion of general average, salvage and/or salvage charges, adjusted or determined according to the contract of carriage or affreightment and/or the governing law and practice. In case of general average sacrifice of the insured cargo. the assured has the right to recover in respect of the whole of such loss.

5.2 No claim under this clause shall in any case be allowed unless the general average act or salvage was undertaken to avoid, or in connection with the avoidance of, a peril insured against.

5.3 Where all the contributing interests are owned by the assured, the provisions of the York-Antwerp Rules, 1974, or similar provisions of other rules if expressly agreed, shall be applied as if the interests were owned by different persons, and the insurer shall pay the insured cargo's proportion as so calculated.

6. Sue and Labour and Forwarding Charges Clause

6.1 Where there has been loss of or damage to the cargo from a peril insured against, or where the cargo is in danger from such a peril, and as a result reasonable expenditure is incurred by the assured in order to avert or minimize a loss which would be recoverable under this insurance, the insurer shall pay to the assured the expenditure incurred.

6.2 Where, as a result of the operation of a peril insured against, the transit is terminated at a port or place other than the destination to which the cargo is insured hereunder, the insurer will reimburse the assured for any extra charges properly and reasonably incurred in unloading, storing and forwarding the cargo to that destination.

6.3 This clause shall not apply to general average, salvage or salvage charges.

6.4 The insurer's liability under this clause is in addition to his liability under the other provisions of this insurance, but shall not exceed an amount equal to the sum insured hereunder in respect of the cargo.

D. PERIOD OF COVERAGE

7. Commencement and Duration

The insurance commences from the time the insured cargo leaves the ware house or place of storage at the place named in this insurance for the commencement of the transit and shall continue during the ordinary course of transit.

8. Termination

This insurance shall terminate

8.1 on delivery of the insured cargo to the consignee's or other final warehouse or place of storage at the destination named in the insurance; or

8.2 Alternative A: on delivery of the insured cargo to any other warehouse or place of storage, whether prior to or at the destination named in the insurance, which the assured chooses to use either

8.2.1 for storage other than in the ordinary course of transit, or

8.2.2 for allocation or distribution; or

8.2 Alternative B: on any taking of delivery of the insured cargo by the assured, the shipper, the consignee or their representatives or other authorized persons before the time when the insurance would otherwise terminate as stipulated in 8.1 above; or

8.3 when ... days have elapsed after completion of discharge of the insured cargo from the oversea vessel at the final port or place of discharge;

8.4 when the insured cargo has been discharged from the oversea vessel at the final port or place of discharge, and transit commences to a destination other than that named in this insurance; whichever shall first occur.

9. Continuation

9.1 The insurance shall remain in force, subject to termination as provided by clauses 8 and 9.2, during delay beyond the control of the assured, any deviation, forced discharge, reshipment or transhipment, and during any variation of the adventure arising from the exercise of a liberty granted to shipowners or charterers under the contract of carriage or affreightment.

9.2 When, owing to circumstances beyond the control of the assured, the contract of carriage or affreightment is terminated at a port or place other than the destination named therein, or the transit is otherwise terminated before delivery of the insured cargo as provided for in clause 8 above, this insurance shall also terminate unless prompt notice is given to the insurer and continuation of cover is requested. In that case this insurance shall remain in force, subject to an additional premium if required by the insurer, either

9.2.1 until the insured cargo is sold and delivered at such port or place or, unless otherwise specially agreed, until the expiry of ... days after its arrival at such port or place, whichever shall first occur, or

9.2.2 if the insured cargo is forwarded within the above ... day period (or any agreed extension thereof) to the destination named in this insurance or to any other destination, until terminated in accordance with clause 8 above.

E. MEASURE OF INDEMNITY

10. General Rules

10.1 Agreed and insurable value

10.1. 1 Where an agreed value is stated in this insurance this agreed value shall be conclusive between the assured and the insurer as to the value of the insured cargo in the absence of fraud.

10.1. 2 Where there is no agreed value, the insurable value of the cargo is

Alternative A: the commercial invoice value or, if there is no such invoice, the market value of the cargo at the time and place of commencement of the cover, plus

10.1.2.1 if not already included, freight and other expenses incidental to the transport, customs duties, insurance costs, and

10.1.2.2 an expected profit of ... %.

Alternative B: the market value at the place of destination at the time of the arrival of the cargo or, if the cargo does not arrive, at the time it should have arrived at the place of destination.

10.1. 3 Where there is no agreed value and the term “agreed value” is used in other provisions of this insurance, this term shall be deemed also to cover the insurable value, as defined in 10.1.2 above.

10.2 Sum insured

The insurer’s total liability under Part A and clauses 4 and 5 of Part C shall be limited to the sum insured. A separate limit shall apply to claims under clause 6 of Part C as provided therein.

10.3 Under- and over-insurance

10.3. 1 Where the sum insured is less than the agreed value, the insurer is only liable to pay that proportion of any loss covered by this insurance that the sum insured bears to the agreed value.

10.3. 2 Where the sum insured is higher than the agreed value, the assured may not recover more than the agreed value.

10.4 Under-valuation

Alternative A: Where the assured has a claim under Part C, clauses 5 and/or 6, the indemnity payable under this insurance shall not be reduced by reason of the agreed value being less than the actual or contributory value of the insured cargo.

Alternative B

10.4. 1 Where the assured has a claim under Part C, clause 5, of this insurance other than for general average sacrifice of the cargo, and the agreed value is less than the full contributory value of the cargo, the insurer shall only pay such proportion of general average, salvage and salvage charges as the agreed value bears to the full contributory value.

10.4. 2 Where the cargo has suffered damage covered by this insurance and such damage constitutes a deduction from the contributory value, the same amount must be deducted from the agreed value when determining whether the agreed value is less than the contributory value.

10.5 Co-insurance: Where two or more insurers are liable under this insurance,

10.5. 1 each insurer is liable only for his proportion of the claim, which is the proportion that his subscription bears to the sum insured, and shall on no account be held jointly liable with his co-insurers.

10.5. 2 Alternative A: each insurer agrees to be subject to the jurisdiction of the courts applicable to the leading insurer for all disputes under this insurance. The leading insurer is authorized by his co-insurers to accept and conduct legal proceedings on their behalf.

Alternative B: No provision

11. Total Losses

11.1 A claim for loss by a peril insured against may be for a total loss, as herein defined, or otherwise for a partial loss.

11.2 Actual total loss occurs where the insured cargo is destroyed or so damaged as to cease to be a thing of the kind insured or where the assured is irretrievably deprived of the cargo.

11.3 Presumed total loss occurs where the carrying vessel is missing with the insured cargo and no news of the vessel or the cargo has been received within a reasonable time but not to exceed ... months.

11.4 Constructive total loss occurs:

11.4. 1 where the assured has been deprived of the free use and disposal of the insured cargo, and

11.4.1.1 it is unlikely that he will be able to recover it within a reasonable time but not to exceed ... months, or

11.4.1.2 he could not recover it without incurring an expenditure which would exceed its value on recovery;

11.4. 2 where the insured cargo has been damaged and it cannot be repaired or reconditioned and forwarded to its destination without:

11.4.2.1 becoming an actual total loss before arrival, or

11.4.2.2 incurring an expenditure which would exceed its value on arrival.

11.5 Where there is a valid claim for a total loss recoverable under this insurance, the amount payable by the insurer is the sum insured in respect of the cargo.

12. Abandonment

12.1 Where the assured elects to claim for a constructive total loss rather than for a partial loss, or where there is a presumed total loss, the assured shall with reasonable diligence notify the insurer that he wishes to abandon what remains of the cargo to the insurer.

12.2 Unless otherwise directed by applicable law, no notice of abandonment need be given if, at the time when the assured receives reliable information of the loss, there would be no possibility of benefit to the insurer if notice were given to him or where the insurer has expressly waived the need for such notice.

12.3 Notice of abandonment may be expressed in any terms which indicate the intention of the assured unconditionally to abandon his interest in the cargo to the insurer. The insurer shall advise the assured whether he accepts or rejects the notice of abandonment within a reasonable time from the date on which the notice is tendered.

12.4 Where notice of abandonment is given as provided herein, the rights of the assured shall not be prejudiced by the refusal of the insurer to accept the abandonment.

12.5 Where notice of abandonment is accepted, the abandonment is irrevocable and the acceptance of the notice of abandonment conclusively admits liability for the loss and the sufficiency of the notice. Upon acceptance of abandonment, the insurer may, if he so wishes, take over whatever may remain of the cargo, with all the rights and obligations attached thereto.

13. Partial Losses

13.1 Total loss of part: Where part of the cargo is totally lost, the assured is entitled to be indemnified for such proportion of the agreed value, if a value has been agreed, or of the insurable value, if no value has been agreed, as the insurable value of the part lost bears to the insurable value of the whole.

13.2 Damage

13.2. 1 Where the whole or any part of the cargo has been delivered damaged at its destination, the assured is entitled to be indemnified for such proportion of the agreed value, if a value has been agreed, or of the insurable value, if no value has been agreed, as the difference between the gross sound and damaged values at the place of destination bears to the gross sound value.

13.2. 2 If the assured chooses to recondition or to repair any part of the cargo which has been delivered damaged at its destination, he may, alternatively, claim the reasonable cost of such reconditioning or repair at the time of arrival at its destination.

F. INSURABLE INTEREST

14.1 In order to recover under this insurance the assured must have an insurable interest in the insured cargo at the time of the loss.

14.2 Subject to 14.1 above, the assured shall be entitled to recover in respect of a loss occurring during the transit covered by this insurance, notwithstanding that the loss occurred before the contract of insurance was concluded, unless the assured was aware of the loss and the insurer was not.

40) 2009 INSTITUTE CARGO CLAUSES A + C[1]

Most insurance contracts purchased on the London market are subject to the Institute Cargo Clauses. These are general terms for the insurance contract (the back of the contract), which are incorporated by reference on the front of the contract. Similar to the UNCTAD Model Clauses (above, p. I - 771), and the American Institute Cargo Clauses (below, p. I - 800), different levels of protection are available:

A for “All Risks” is the most comprehensive standard cover available. To be sure, although this level of cover is called “all risks”, it does not cover all conceivable risks and there are still a number of exclusions. However, if a client requires even broader cover, such a contract would have to be specifically negotiated and will be substantially more expensive.

B for “Intermediate Cover” is a mid-level protection contract.

C for “Restricted” or “Minimum Cover” is the lowest level standard cover available. If a client wants to accept further restrictions or exclusions, such a contract would have to be specifically negotiated and might not be substantially cheaper.

There are also more specialized standard term packages available from the Joint Cargo Committee, for example Institute Cargo Clauses (Air), Institute War Clauses, and Institute Strikes Clauses.

The choice between “All Risks” and a lesser cover should generally be made by the party carrying the risk of loss of or damage to the cargo. In the absence of specific and different contractual arrangements, this would be the buyer if the INCOTERM® is EXW or an F-term, since the risk already passes before the main maritime voyage. Conversely, the risk is still born by the seller if a D-term is used. If the contract provides for a C-term, and in particular the widely popular CIF, the risk still passes upon loading of the cargo onto the vessel for the main maritime voyage. However, under CIF and CIP, the insurance contract has to be made and paid for by the seller on behalf of the buyer. Under INCOTERMS 2020®, the seller only has to purchase level C cover if CIF was agreed. By contrast, the seller has to purchase level A cover if CIP was agreed. This is not widely known but potentially important.

To facilitate comparison between the two most commonly used packages A and C, the provisions will be presented on facing pages, i.e. the All Risks A Clauses will be on the left or even numbered pages and the Restricted or Minimum Cover C Clauses will be on the right or odd numbered pages.

Institute Cargo Clauses A = All Risks

RISKS COVERED

Risks

1. This insurance covers all risks of loss of or damage to the subject-matter insured except as excluded by the provisions of Clauses 4, 5, 6 and 7 below.

General Average

2. This insurance covers general average and salvage charges, adjusted or determined according to the contract of carriage and/or the governing law and practice, incurred to avoid or in connection with the avoidance of loss from any cause except those excluded in Clauses 4, 5, 6 and 7 below.

"Both to Blame Collision Clause"

3. This insurance indemnifies the Assured, in respect of any risk insured herein, against liability incurred under any Both to Blame Collision Clause in the contract of carriage. In the event of any claim by carriers under the said Clause, the Assured agree to notify the Insurers who shall have the right, at their own cost and expense, to defend the Assured against such claim.

EXCLUSIONS

4. In no case shall this insurance cover

4.1 loss damage or expense attributable to wilful misconduct of the Assured

4.2 ordinary leakage, ordinary loss in weight or volume, or ordinary wear and tear of the subject-matter insured

4.3 loss damage or expense caused by insufficiency or unsuitability of packing or preparation of the subject-matter insured to withstand the ordinary incidents of the insured transit where such packing or preparation is carried out by the Assured or their employees or prior to the attachment of this insurance (for the purpose of these Clauses "packing" shall be deemed to include stowage in a container and "employees" shall not include independent contractors)

4.4 loss damage or expense caused by inherent vice or nature of the subject-matter insured

4.5 loss damage or expense caused by delay, even though the delay be caused by a risk insured against (except expenses payable under Clause 2 above)

4.6 loss damage or expense caused by insolvency or financial default of the owners managers charterers or operators of the vessel where, at the time of loading of the subject-matter insured on board the vessel, the Assured are aware, or in the ordinary course of business should be aware, that such insolvency or financial default could prevent the normal prosecution of the voyage.

This exclusion shall not apply where the contract of insurance has been assigned to the party claiming hereunder who has bought or agreed to buy the subject-matter insured in good faith under a binding contract.

Institute Cargo Clauses C = Minimum Cargo Insurance

RISKS COVERED

Risks

1. This insurance covers, except as excluded by the provisions of Clauses 4, 5, 6 and 7 below,
1.1 loss of or damage to the subject-matter insured reasonably attributable to
1.1.1 fire or explosion
1.1.2 vessel or craft being stranded grounded sunk or capsized
1.1.3 overturning or derailment of land conveyance
1.1.4 collision or contact of vessel craft or conveyance with any external object other than water
1.1.5 discharge of cargo at a port of distress,
1.2 loss of or damage to the subject-matter insured caused by
1.2.1 general average sacrifice
1.2.2 jettison.

General Average

2. This insurance covers general average and salvage charges, adjusted or determined according to the contract of carriage and/or the governing law and practice, incurred to avoid or in connection with the avoidance of loss from any cause except those excluded in Clauses 4, 5, 6 and 7 below.

"Both to Blame Collision Clause"

3. This insurance indemnifies the Assured, in respect of any risk insured herein, against liability incurred under any Both to Blame Collision Clause in the contract of carriage. In the event of any claim by carriers under the said Clause, the Assured agree to notify the Insurers who shall have the right, at their own cost and expense, to defend the Assured against such claim.

EXCLUSIONS

4. In no case shall this insurance cover

4.1 loss damage or expense attributable to wilful misconduct of the Assured

4.2 ordinary leakage, ordinary loss in weight or volume, or ordinary wear and tear of the subject-matter insured

4.3 loss damage or expense caused by insufficiency or unsuitability of packing or preparation of the subject-matter insured to withstand the ordinary incidents of the insured transit where such packing or preparation is carried out by the Assured or their employees or prior to the attachment of this insurance (for the purpose of these Clauses "packing" shall be deemed to include stowage in a container and "employees" shall not include independent contractors)

4.4 loss damage or expense caused by inherent vice or nature of the subject-matter insured

4.5 loss damage or expense caused by delay, even though the delay be caused by a risk insured against (except expenses payable under Clause 2 above)

4.6 loss damage or expense caused by insolvency or financial default of the owners managers charterers or operators of the vessel where, at the time of loading of the subject-matter insured on board the vessel, the Assured are aware, or in the ordinary course of business should be aware, that such insolvency or financial default could prevent the normal prosecution of the voyage.

This exclusion shall not apply where the contract of insurance has been assigned to the party claiming hereunder who has bought or agreed to buy the subject-matter insured in good faith under a binding contract.

Institute Cargo Clauses A = All Risks (contd)

4.7 loss damage or expense directly or indirectly caused by or arising from the use of any weapon or device employing atomic or nuclear fission and/or fusion or other like reaction or radioactive force or matter.

5.1 In no case shall this insurance cover loss damage or expense arising from

5.1.1 unseaworthiness of vessel or craft or unfitness of vessel or craft for the safe carriage of the subject-matter insured, where the Assured are privy to such unseaworthiness or unfitness, at the time the subject-matter insured is loaded therein

5.1.2 unfitness of container or conveyance for the safe carriage of the subject-matter insured, where loading therein or thereon is carried out prior to attachment of this insurance or by the Assured or their employees and they are privy to such unfitness at the time of loading.

5.2 Exclusion 5.1.1 above shall not apply where the contract of insurance has been assigned to the party claiming hereunder who has bought or agreed to buy the subject-matter insured in good faith under a binding contract.

5.3 The Insurers waive any breach of the implied warranties of seaworthiness of the ship and fitness of the ship to carry the subject-matter insured to destination.

6. In no case shall this insurance cover loss damage or expense caused by

6.1 war civil war revolution rebellion insurrection, or civil strife arising therefrom, or any hostile act by or against a belligerent power

6.2 capture seizure arrest restraint or detainment (piracy excepted), and the consequences thereof or any attempt thereat

6.3 derelict mines torpedoes bombs or other derelict weapons of war.

7. In no case shall this insurance cover loss damage or expense

7.1 caused by strikers, locked-out workmen, or persons taking part in labour disturbances, riots or civil commotions

7.2 resulting from strikes, lock-outs, labour disturbances, riots or civil commotions

7.3 caused by any act of terrorism being an act of any person acting on behalf of, or in connection with, any organisation which carries out activities directed towards the overthrowing or influencing, by force or violence, of any government whether or not legally constituted

7.4 caused by any person acting from a political, ideological or religious motive.

DURATION

Transit Clause

8.1 Subject to Clause 11 below, this insurance attaches from the time the subject-matter insured is first moved in the warehouse or at the place of storage (at the place named in the contract of insurance) for the purpose of the immediate loading into or onto the carrying vehicle or other conveyance for the commencement of transit, continues during the ordinary course of transit and terminates either

8.1.1 on completion of unloading from the carrying vehicle or other conveyance in or at the final warehouse or place of storage at the destination named in the contract of insurance,

Institute Cargo Clauses C = Minimum Cargo Insurance (contd)

4.7 deliberate damage to or deliberate destruction of the subject-matter insured or any part thereof by the wrongful act of any person or persons

4.8 loss damage or expense directly or indirectly caused by or arising from the use of any weapon or device employing atomic or nuclear fission and/or fusion or other like reaction or radioactive force or matter.

5.1 In no case shall this insurance cover loss damage or expense arising from

5.1.1 unseaworthiness of vessel or craft or unfitness of vessel or craft for the safe carriage of the subject-matter insured, where the Assured are privy to such unseaworthiness or unfitness, at the time the subject-matter insured is loaded therein

5.1.2 unfitness of container or conveyance for the safe carriage of the subject-matter insured, where loading therein or thereon is carried out prior to attachment of this insurance or by the Assured or their employees and they are privy to such unfitness at the time of loading.

5.2 Exclusion 5.1.1 above shall not apply where the contract of insurance has been assigned to the party claiming hereunder who has bought or agreed to buy the subject-matter insured in good faith under a binding contract.

5.3 The Insurers waive any breach of the implied warranties of seaworthiness of the ship and fitness of the ship to carry the subject-matter insured to destination.

6. In no case shall this insurance cover loss damage or expense caused by

6.1 war civil war revolution rebellion insurrection, or civil strife arising therefrom, or any hostile act by or against a belligerent power

6.2 capture seizure arrest restraint or detainment, and the consequences thereof or any attempt thereat

6.3 derelict mines torpedoes bombs or other derelict weapons of war.

7. In no case shall this insurance cover loss damage or expense

7.1 caused by strikers, locked-out workmen, or persons taking part in labour disturbances, riots or civil commotions

7.2 resulting from strikes, lock-outs, labour disturbances, riots or civil commotions

7.3 caused by any act of terrorism being an act of any person acting on behalf of, or in connection with, any organisation which carries out activities directed towards the overthrowing or influencing, by force or violence, of any government whether or not legally constituted

7.4 caused by any person acting from a political, ideological or religious motive.

Duration

Transit Clause

8.1 Subject to Clause 11 below, this insurance attaches from the time the subject-matter insured is first moved in the warehouse or at the place of storage (at the place named in the contract of insurance) for the purpose of the immediate loading into or onto the carrying vehicle or other conveyance for the commencement of transit, continues during the ordinary course of transit and terminates either

8.1.1 on completion of unloading from the carrying vehicle or other conveyance in or at the final warehouse or place of storage at the destination named in the contract of insurance,

Institute Cargo Clauses A = All Risks (contd)

8.1.2 on completion of unloading from the carrying vehicle or other conveyance in or at any other warehouse or place of storage, whether prior to or at the destination named in the contract of insurance, which the Assured or their employees elect to use either for storage other than in the ordinary course of transit or for allocation or distribution, or

8.1.3 when the Assured or their employees elect to use any carrying vehicle or other conveyance or any container for storage other than in the ordinary course of transit or

8.1.4 on the expiry of 60 days after completion of discharge overside of the subject-matter insured from the oversea vessel at the final port of discharge, whichever shall first occur.

8.2 If, after discharge overside from the oversea vessel at the final port of discharge, but prior to termination of this insurance, the subject-matter insured is to be forwarded to a destination other than that to which it is insured, this insurance, whilst remaining subject to termination as provided in Clauses 8.1.1 to 8.1.4, shall not extend beyond the time the subject-matter insured is first moved for the purpose of the commencement of transit to such other destination.

8.3 This insurance shall remain in force (subject to termination as provided for in Clauses 8.1.1 to 8.1.4 above and to the provisions of Clause 9 below) during delay beyond the control of the Assured, any deviation, forced discharge, reshipment or transhipment and during any variation of the adventure arising from the exercise of a liberty granted to carriers under the contract of carriage.

Termination of Contract of Carriage

9. If owing to circumstances beyond the control of the Assured either the contract of carriage is terminated at a port or place other than the destination named therein or the transit is otherwise terminated before unloading of the subject-matter insured as provided for in Clause 8 above, then this insurance shall also terminate unless prompt notice is given to the Insurers and continuation of cover is requested when this insurance shall remain in force, subject to an additional premium if required by the Insurers, either

9.1 until the subject-matter insured is sold and delivered at such port or place, or, unless otherwise specially agreed, until the expiry of 60 days after arrival of the subject-matter insured at such port or place, whichever shall first occur, or

9.2 if the subject-matter insured is forwarded within the said period of 60 days (or any agreed extension thereof) to the destination named in the contract of insurance or to any other destination, until terminated in accordance with the provisions of Clause 8 above.

Change of Voyage

10.1 Where, after attachment of this insurance, the destination is changed by the Assured, this must be notified promptly to Insurers for rates and terms to be agreed. Should a loss occur prior to such agreement being obtained cover may be provided but only if cover would have been available at a reasonable commercial market rate on reasonable market terms.

10.2 Where the subject-matter insured commences the transit contemplated by this insurance (in accordance with Clause 8.1), but, without the knowledge of the Assured or their employees the ship sails for another destination, this insurance will nevertheless be deemed to have attached at commencement of such transit.

Institute Cargo Clauses C = Minimum Cargo Insurance (contd)

8.1.2 on completion of unloading from the carrying vehicle or other conveyance in or at any other warehouse or place of storage, whether prior to or at the destination named in the contract of insurance, which the Assured or their employees elect to use either for storage other than in the ordinary course of transit or for allocation or distribution, or

8.1.3 when the Assured or their employees elect to use any carrying vehicle or other conveyance or any container for storage other than in the ordinary course of transit or

8.1.4 on the expiry of 60 days after completion of discharge overside of the subject-matter insured from the oversea vessel at the final port of discharge, whichever shall first occur.

8.2 If, after discharge overside from the oversea vessel at the final port of discharge, but prior to termination of this insurance, the subject-matter insured is to be forwarded to a destination other than that to which it is insured, this insurance, whilst remaining subject to termination as provided in Clauses 8.1.1 to 8.1.4, shall not extend beyond the time the subject-matter insured is first moved for the purpose of the commencement of transit to such other destination.

8.3 This insurance shall remain in force (subject to termination as provided for in Clauses 8.1.1 to 8.1.4 above and to the provisions of Clause 9 below) during delay beyond the control of the Assured, any deviation, forced discharge, reshipment or transhipment and during any variation of the adventure arising from the exercise of a liberty granted to carriers under the contract of carriage.

Termination of Contract of Carriage

9. If owing to circumstances beyond the control of the Assured either the contract of carriage is terminated at a port or place other than the destination named therein or the transit is otherwise terminated before unloading of the subject-matter insured as provided for in Clause 8 above, then this insurance shall also terminate unless prompt notice is given to the Insurers and continuation of cover is requested when this insurance shall remain in force, subject to an additional premium if required by the Insurers, either

9.1 until the subject-matter insured is sold and delivered at such port or place, or, unless otherwise specially agreed, until the expiry of 60 days after arrival of the subject-matter insured at such port or place, whichever shall first occur, or

9.2 if the subject-matter insured is forwarded within the said period of 60 days (or any agreed extension thereof) to the destination named in the contract of insurance or to any other destination, until terminated in accordance with the provisions of Clause 8 above.

Change of Voyage

10.1 Where, after attachment of this insurance, the destination is changed by the Assured, this must be notified promptly to Insurers for rates and terms to be agreed. Should a loss occur prior to such agreement being obtained cover may be provided but only if cover would have been available at a reasonable commercial market rate on reasonable market terms.

10.2 Where the subject-matter insured commences the transit contemplated by this insurance (in accordance with Clause 8.1), but, without the knowledge of the Assured or their employees the ship sails for another destination, this insurance will nevertheless be deemed to have attached at commencement of such transit.

Institute Cargo Clauses A = All Risks (contd)

CLAIMS

Insurable Interest

11.1 In order to recover under this insurance the Assured must have an insurable interest in the subject-matter insured at the time of the loss.

11.2 Subject to Clause 11.1 above, the Assured shall be entitled to recover for insured loss occurring during the period covered by this insurance, notwithstanding that the loss occurred before the contract of insurance was concluded, unless the Assured were aware of the loss and the Insurers were not.

Forwarding Charges

12. Where, as a result of the operation of a risk covered by this insurance, the insured transit is terminated at a port or place other than that to which the subject-matter insured is covered under this insurance, the Insurers will reimburse the Assured for any extra charges properly and reasonably incurred in unloading storing and forwarding the subject-matter insured to the destination to which it is insured.

This Clause 12, which does not apply to general average or salvage charges, shall be subject to the exclusions contained in Clauses 4, 5, 6 and 7 above, and shall not include charges arising from the fault negligence insolvency or financial default of the Assured or their employees.

Constructive Total Loss

13. No claim for Constructive Total Loss shall be recoverable hereunder unless the subject-matter insured is reasonably abandoned either on account of its actual total loss appearing to be unavoidable or because the cost of recovering, reconditioning and forwarding the subject-matter insured to the destination to which it is insured would exceed its value on arrival.

Increased Value

14.1 If any Increased Value insurance is effected by the Assured on the subject-matter insured under this insurance the agreed value of the subject-matter insured shall be deemed to be increased to the total amount insured under this insurance and all Increased Value insurances covering the loss, and liability under this insurance shall be in such proportion as the sum insured under this insurance bears to such total amount insured.

In the event of claim the Assured shall provide the Insurers with evidence of the amounts insured under all other insurances.

14.2 Where this insurance is on Increased Value the following clause shall apply:

The agreed value of the subject-matter insured shall be deemed to be equal to the total amount insured under the primary insurance and all Increased Value insurances covering the loss and effected on the subject-matter insured by the Assured, and liability under this insurance shall be in such proportion as the sum insured under this insurance bears to such total amount insured.

In the event of claim the Assured shall provide the Insurers with evidence of the amounts insured under all other insurances.

Institute Cargo Clauses C = Minimum Cargo Insurance (contd)

CLAIMS

Insurable Interest

11.1 In order to recover under this insurance the Assured must have an insurable interest in the subject-matter insured at the time of the loss.

11.2 Subject to Clause 11.1 above, the Assured shall be entitled to recover for insured loss occurring during the period covered by this insurance, notwithstanding that the loss occurred before the contract of insurance was concluded, unless the Assured were aware of the loss and the Insurers were not.

Forwarding Charges

12. Where, as a result of the operation of a risk covered by this insurance, the insured transit is terminated at a port or place other than that to which the subject-matter insured is covered under this insurance, the Insurers will reimburse the Assured for any extra charges properly and reasonably incurred in unloading storing and forwarding the subject-matter insured to the destination to which it is insured.

This Clause 12, which does not apply to general average or salvage charges, shall be subject to the exclusions contained in Clauses 4, 5, 6 and 7 above, and shall not include charges arising from the fault negligence insolvency or financial default of the Assured or their employees.

Constructive Total Loss

13. No claim for Constructive Total Loss shall be recoverable hereunder unless the subject-matter insured is reasonably abandoned either on account of its actual total loss appearing to be unavoidable or because the cost of recovering, reconditioning and forwarding the subject-matter insured to the destination to which it is insured would exceed its value on arrival.

Increased Value

14.1 If any Increased Value insurance is effected by the Assured on the subject-matter insured under this insurance the agreed value of the subject-matter insured shall be deemed to be increased to the total amount insured under this insurance and all Increased Value insurances covering the loss, and liability under this insurance shall be in such proportion as the sum insured under this insurance bears to such total amount insured.

In the event of claim the Assured shall provide the Insurers with evidence of the amounts insured under all other insurances.

14.2 Where this insurance is on Increased Value the following clause shall apply:

The agreed value of the subject-matter insured shall be deemed to be equal to the total amount insured under the primary insurance and all Increased Value insurances covering the loss and effected on the subject-matter insured by the Assured, and liability under this insurance shall be in such proportion as the sum insured under this insurance bears to such total amount insured.

In the event of claim the Assured shall provide the Insurers with evidence of the amounts insured under all other insurances.

Institute Cargo Clauses A = All Risks (contd)

BENEFIT OF INSURANCE

15. This insurance

15.1 covers the Assured which includes the person claiming indemnity either as the person by or on whose behalf the contract of insurance was effected or as an assignee,

15.2 shall not extend to or otherwise benefit the carrier or other bailee.

MINIMISING LOSSES

Duty of Assured

16. It is the duty of the Assured and their employees and agents in respect of loss recoverable hereunder

16.1 to take such measures as may be reasonable for the purpose of averting or minimising such loss, and

16.2 to ensure that all rights against carriers, bailees or other third parties are properly preserved and exercised

and the Insurers will, in addition to any loss recoverable hereunder, reimburse the Assured for any charges properly and reasonably incurred in pursuance of these duties.

Waiver

17. Measures taken by the Assured or the Insurers with the object of saving, protecting or recovering the subject-matter insured shall not be considered as a waiver or acceptance of abandonment or otherwise prejudice the rights of either party.

AVOIDANCE OF DELAY

18. It is a condition of this insurance that the Assured shall act with reasonable despatch in all circumstances within their control.

LAW AND PRACTICE

19. This insurance is subject to English law and practice.

NOTE: Where a continuation of cover is requested under Clause 9, or a change of destination is notified under Clause 10, there is an obligation to give prompt notice to the Insurers and the right to such cover is dependent upon compliance with this obligation.

Institute Cargo Clauses C = Minimum Cargo Insurance (contd)

BENEFIT OF INSURANCE

15. This insurance

15.1 covers the Assured which includes the person claiming indemnity either as the person by or on whose behalf the contract of insurance was effected or as an assignee,

15.2 shall not extend to or otherwise benefit the carrier or other bailee.

MINIMISING LOSSES

Duty of Assured

16. It is the duty of the Assured and their employees and agents in respect of loss recoverable hereunder

16.1 to take such measures as may be reasonable for the purpose of averting or minimising such loss, and

16.2 to ensure that all rights against carriers, bailees or other third parties are properly preserved and exercised

and the Insurers will, in addition to any loss recoverable hereunder, reimburse the Assured for any charges properly and reasonably incurred in pursuance of these duties.

Waiver

17. Measures taken by the Assured or the Insurers with the object of saving, protecting or recovering the subject-matter insured shall not be considered as a waiver or acceptance of abandonment or otherwise prejudice the rights of either party.

AVOIDANCE OF DELAY

18. It is a condition of this insurance that the Assured shall act with reasonable despatch in all circumstances within their control.

LAW AND PRACTICE

19. This insurance is subject to English law and practice.

NOTE: Where a continuation of cover is requested under Clause 9, or a change of destination is notified under Clause 10, there is an obligation to give prompt notice to the Insurers and the right to such cover is dependent upon compliance with this obligation.

41) 2004 American Institute Cargo Clauses A "All Risks"[1]

1. AVERAGE TERMS

The following average terms shall apply:

"All Risks"

A. Unless otherwise specified below, this policy insures against "All Risks" of physical loss or damage from any external cause irrespective of percentage, but excluding nevertheless the risks of War, Strikes, Riots, Seizure, Detention and other risks excluded by the Nuclear/Radio-active Contamination Exclusions Clause, the F.C & S. (Free of Capture and Seizure) Warranty and the S.R. & C.C. (Strikes, Riots and Civil Commotions) Warranty of this policy, excepting to the extent that such risks are specifically covered by endorsement.

"On Deck" Bill of Lading FPA Terms

B. Insured property while shipped on deck of an ocean vessel subject to an "On Deck" bill of lading is warranted free from Particular Average unless caused by the vessel being stranded, sunk or burnt, but notwithstanding this Warranty the Company is to pay any physical loss of or damage to the insured property which may reasonably be attributed to fire, collision or contact of the vessel and/or craft and/or conveyance with any external substance (ice included) other than water, or to discharge of cargo at a port of distress.

2. ADDITIONAL COVERAGES

This policy shall also cover the following contributions and/or expenses:

General Average & Salvage Charges

A. General Average contribution and Salvage Charges determined to be due from or in respect to insured property.

Landing, Warehouse & Forwarding Charges

B. Landing, warehousing, forwarding and special charges incurred by reason of perils insured against.

Brands & Trademarks

C. Expenses to remove Brands and Trademarks pursuant to the Brands and Trademarks provisions of the Loss Adjustment Clauses.

"Both to Blame"

D. Where insured property is shipped under a Bill of Lading containing the so-called "Both to Blame Collision" Clause the Company agrees as to all losses covered by this insurance, to indemnify the Assured for this policy's proportion of any amount (not exceeding the amount insured) which the Assured may be legally bound to pay to the shipowners under such clause. In the event that such liability is asserted the Assured agrees to notify the Company as promptly as possible and the Company shall have the right, at its own cost and expense, to defend the Assured against such claim.

Sue & Labor Charges

E. Charges reasonably incurred pursuant to the duty set forth below, whether said efforts are successful or not:

---

1 ©2004, American Institute of Marine Underwriters (AIMU), all rights reserved.

In the event of loss or misfortune, it is the duty of the Assured and any assignee of the Assured's rights hereunder to take all reasonable measures to avert or minimize loss insured against by this policy and to ensure that all rights against third parties are preserved and exercised.

The Company shall be liable in full for the charges incurred under this Clause whether the combined amount of physical loss or damage and Sue and Labor Charges exceeded the applicable policy limit or not.

Craft/Lighter Charges

F. Including transit by craft, raft or lighter to or from the vessel. Each craft, raft or lighter to be deemed a separate insurance. The Assured are not to be prejudiced by any agreement exempting lightermen from liability.

3. EXCLUSIONS

The following exclusions shall apply unless modified or superseded elsewhere herein or endorsed hereon:

Basic Exclusions

A. This policy does not cover:

(1) Ordinary leakage, ordinary loss in weight or volume, or ordinary wear and tear.

(2) Loss, damage, or expense:

   (a) Attributable to willful misconduct of the Assured;

   (b) caused by inherent vice or nature of the insured property;

   (c) arising from insolvency or financial default of the owners, managers, charterers, or operators of the vessel;

   (d) resulting from insufficiency or unsuitability of packing or preparation of the insured property for the intended voyage. For the purposes of this clause, "packing" shall be deemed to include stowage into an overseas container but only when such stowage is carried out prior to the commencement of the insured voyage or when performed by the Assured or his representative.

4. PARAMOUNT WARRANTIES

Subject to the following Paramount Warranties which shall not be modified or superseded by any other provisions included herein or stamped or endorsed hereon unless such other provision refers specifically to the risks excluded by these Warranties and expressly assumes the said risks:

F.C. & S. Warranty

A. Notwithstanding anything herein contained to the contrary, this insurance is warranted free from:

(1) all consequences of capture, seizure, arrest, restraint, detainment, confiscation, preemption, requisition, nationalization, and the consequences thereof or any attempt thereat, whether in time of peace or war and whether lawful or otherwise;

(2) all loss or damage or expense, whether in time of peace or war, caused by:

   (a) any weapon of war employing atomic or nuclear fission and/or fusion and/or reaction or radioactive force or matter or

   (b) any mine or torpedo;

(3) all consequences of hostilities or warlike operations (whether there be a declaration of war or not), but this Warranty shall not exclude collision or contact with rockets or similar missiles (other than weapons of war) or with any fixed or floating object (other than a mine or torpedo),

stranding, heavy weather, fire or explosion unless caused directly (and independently of the nature of the voyage or service which the vessel concerned or, in the case of collision, any other vessel involved therein, is performing) by a hostile act by or against a belligerent power, and for the purposes of this Warranty "power" includes any authority maintaining naval, military, or air forces in association with a power;

(4) all consequences of civil war, revolution, rebellion, insurrection, or civil strife arising therefrom, or from the consequences of the imposition of martial law, military or usurped power, or piracy.

S.R. & C.C. Warranty

B. Warranted free from loss, damage, or expense caused by or resulting from:

(1) strikes, lockouts, labor disturbances, riots, civil commotions, or the acts of any person or persons, taking part in any such occurrences or disorders;

(2) vandalism, sabotage, or malicious act, which shall be deemed also to encompass the act or acts of one or more persons, whether or not agents of a sovereign power, carried out for political, terroristic or ideological purposes and whether any loss, damage or expense resulting therefrom is accidental or intentional.

Delay Warranty

C. Warranted free of claim for loss of market or for loss, damage, expense or deterioration arising from delay, whether caused by a peril insured against or otherwise.

Nuclear/Radioactive Contamination Exclusion Warranty

D. Warranted that this policy shall not apply to any loss, damage or expenses due to or arising out of, whether directly or indirectly, nuclear reaction, radiation or radioactive contamination, regardless of how it was caused. However, subject to all provisions of this policy, if this policy insures against fire, then direct physical damage to the insured property located within the United States or any territory of the United States or Puerto Rico by fire directly caused by the above excluded perils, is insured, provided that the nuclear reaction, radiation, or radioactive contamination was not caused, whether directly or indirectly, by any of the perils excluded by the F.C. & S. Warranty of this policy. Nothing in this clause shall be construed to cover any loss, damage or expense caused by nuclear reaction, radiation or radioactive contamination arising directly or indirectly from the fire mentioned above.

5. ADDITIONAL CONDITIONS

The following additional clauses shall also apply:

Seaworthiness

A. The seaworthiness of the vessel operating as a common carrier is hereby admitted as between the Assured and the Company and the wrongful act or misconduct of the shipowner or his servants causing a loss is not to defeat the recovery by an innocent Assured if the loss in the absence of such wrongful act or misconduct would have been a loss recoverable on this policy. With leave to sail with or without pilots, and to tow and assist vessels or craft in all situations, and to be towed. The Assured is not to be prejudiced by the presence of the negligence clause and/or latent defect clause in the Bill(s) of Lading and/or Charter Party.

Carrier Clause

B. Warranted that this insurance shall not inure, directly or indirectly, to the benefit of any carrier or bailee.

Economic & Trade Sanctions

C. Whenever coverage provided by this policy would be in violation of any U.S. economic or trade sanctions such as, but not limited to, those sanctions administered and enforced by the U.S. Treasury Department's Office of Foreign Assets Control ("OFAC"), such coverage shall be null and void.

Similarly, any coverage relating to or referred to in any certificates or other evidences of insurance or any claim that would be in violation of U.S. economic or trade sanctions as described above shall also be null and void.

6. DURATION OF RISK

The following conditions apply regarding the duration of risk:

Transit Clause

A. (1) This insurance attaches from the time the insured property leaves the warehouse, or is delivered alongside or on board the overseas conveyance in accordance with the obligation of the Assured under the terms of sale, for the commencement of transit and continues until:

(a) insured property is delivered to the Consignee's or other final warehouse or place of storage at the intended destination; or

(b) the insured property is delivered to any other warehouse or place of storage, whether prior to or at the intended destination, which the Assured (including any shipper, assignee, consignee or claimant that has control of the insured property at the relevant time) elects to use either:

i. for storage other than in the ordinary course of transit; or

ii. for allocation or distribution; or

(c) the expiring of 60 days (30 days on air shipments) after completion of discharge from the overseas vessel (or aircraft), whichever shall first occur. In the event of delay in excess of the limits specified in (c) above arising from circumstances beyond the control of the Assured, held covered at a premium to be named for an additional 30 days provided the Assured gives notice thereof to the Company as promptly as possible but in any event prior to the expiry of the original 60 days (30 days on air shipments) period.

(2) (a) This insurance specially to cover the insured property during deviation, delay, forced discharge, re-shipment, transshipment and any other variation of the adventure arising from the exercise of a liberty granted to the shipowner or charterer under the contract of affreightment.

(b) In the event of the exercise of any liberty granted to the shipowner or charterer under the contract of affreightment whereby such contract is terminated at a port or place other than the original insured destination, this insurance continues until the insured property is sold and delivered at such port or place; or, if the insured property be not sold but is forwarded to the original insured destination or to any other destination this insurance continues until the insured property has been sold and delivered to the warehouse or place of storage as provided in section 1.

(3) If while this insurance is still in force and before the expiry of 15 days from midnight on the day on which the discharge overside of the insured property from the overseas vessel at the final port of discharge is completed, the insured property is re-sold (not being a sale within the terms of Section 2(b)) and is to be forwarded to a destination other than that covered by this insurance, the insured property is covered hereunder while deposited at such port of discharge until again in transit or until expiry of the aforementioned 15 days whichever shall first occur. If a sale is

effected after the expiry of the aforementioned 15 days while this insurance is still in force the protection afforded hereunder shall cease as from the time of the sale.

(4) Held covered at a premium to be named in case of change of voyage or of any omission or error in the description of the interest, vessel or voyage.

(5) It is a condition of this insurance that there shall be no interruption or suspension of transit unless due to circumstances beyond the control of the Assured, Assignee, Consignee or Claimant and the Assured, Assignee, Consignee or Claimant shall act with reasonable dispatch in all circumstances within their control.

(6) It is agreed that insured property taken out of transit upon instructions of surveyors appointed by or on behalf of the Company for the purpose of establishment of loss or damage, shall be held covered, subject to the original terms and conditions applying to such shipment, without payment of additional premium or advice to the Company, during such interruption or suspension of transit until disposed of by delivery to and acceptance by the original Consignee or by sale to others or otherwise, provided that during such interruption or suspension of transit the Assured complies with the surveyors' instructions.

Shipments Returned or Refused

B. In the event of refusal or inability of the Assured, or Consignee, to accept delivery of insured property, this policy is extended to cover such insured property, subject to the original insuring terms, during delay and/or return or until otherwise disposed of, provided the Assured reports the facts of such situations to the Company as soon as they have knowledge of such an occurrence and pays additional premium if required.

Consolidation/Deconsolidation

C. This policy is extended to cover the insured property temporarily stopped in transit for the purpose of consolidation or deconsolidation in or from overseas containers for not exceeding 30 days whether the said stoppage in transit is within the control of the Assured or not. Held covered at an additional premium to be named for an additional 30 days provided the Assured gives notice thereof to the Company as promptly as possible but in any event prior to the expiry of the original 30 day period.

7. LOSS ADJUSTMENT CLAUSES

The following loss adjustment clauses shall apply:

Constructive Total Loss

A. No recovery for a Constructive Total Loss shall be paid hereunder unless the insured property is reasonably abandoned on account of its actual total loss appearing to be unavoidable, or because it cannot be preserved from actual total loss without an expenditure which would exceed its value if the expenditure had been incurred.

Partial Loss

B. In case of partial loss or damage insured against by this policy, a separation of sound and damaged insured property shall be made and the amount of loss determined by:

(1) an agreed percentage of depreciation, in which event the Assured shall receive such percentage of the insured value of the damaged insured property, or, if there is no agreement;

(2) sale of the damaged insured property, in which event the Assured shall receive the difference between the insured value of the damaged insured property sold and the proceeds of sale.

General Average & Salvage Charges

C. General Average contributions and Salvage Charges shall be payable according to United States laws and usage and/or as per foreign statement and/or as per York Antwerp Rules (as prescribed in whole or in part) if in accordance with the Contract of Affreightment.

Machinery Clause

D. When the insured property includes a machine consisting when complete for sale or use of several parts, then, in case of loss or damage covered by this insurance to any part of such machine, the Company shall be liable only for the proportion of the insured value of the part lost or damaged, or at the Assured's option, for the cost and expense, including labor and forwarding charges, of replacing or repairing the lost or damaged part, excluding loss, if any, sustained by payment of additional duty unless the full duty is included in the amount insured; but in no event shall the Company be liable for more than the insured value of the complete machine.

Labels Clause

E. In case of damage affecting labels, capsules, or wrappers, the Company, if liable therefor under the terms of this policy, shall not be liable for more than an amount sufficient to pay the cost of replacing the labels, capsules or wrappers and the cost of reconditioning the insured property, but in no event shall the Company be liable for more than the insured value of the damaged insured property.

Brands & Trademarks

F. In case of damage by a peril insured against to insured property bearing a brand or trademark associated with the Assured, the damage value shall be ascertained after removal of such markings. Where removal is impracticable, the Company and the Assured shall consult as to how the loss may best be minimized; however, the Assured shall have the option of destroying the damaged insured property upon payment to the Company of the value which could have been realized by the sale of the insured property in its damaged condition.

Subrogation

G. It is a condition of this insurance that upon payment of any loss the Company shall be subrogated to all rights of the Assured against third parties with respect to such loss.

It is a further condition of this insurance that if the Assured or any Claimant impairs or diminishes the rights to which the Company would be subrogated upon payment, the Company may deduct from such payment a sum equal to the estimated recovery lost by reason of the Assured's or Claimant's action or inaction.

Notice of Loss

H. It is a condition of the Company's liability that the Assured, Assignee, Consignee or Claimant promptly report any loss or damage which may give rise to a claim hereunder. Notice may be given to any office of the Company or to the Company's claim or survey representative near the place where the insured property is or was destined. If no claim or survey representative of the Company is at or near such place, notice may be given to the nearest representative of the American Institute of Marine Underwriters, or if no such representative is available, to the nearest Lloyd's agent.

Payment of Loss

I. In case of loss, such loss to be paid no later than thirty days after satisfactory proof of loss and satisfactory proof of interest in the insured property has been established by the Company (the amount of the premium, if unpaid, being first deducted). Proofs of loss to be submitted to the representative of the Company, if there be one at the place such proofs are taken. If there be no such representative the correspondent of the American Institute of Marine Underwriters may authenticate said proofs or in the absence of such correspondent, the nearest Lloyd's agent. Where such proofs have been established by the Company and the final amount of loss cannot be determined within said 30 days, the Company may advance an amount, to be agreed upon, pending final adjustment of the claim. Any amount advanced in excess of the final claim amount to be refunded to the Company by the Assured.

Notice of Suit

J. No suit or action on this policy shall be sustainable in any Court of Law or Equity unless the Assured shall have complied in full with all the terms and conditions of this insurance, nor unless same shall be commenced within twelve (12) months after the loss, provided that where such limitation of time is prohibited by the laws of the State wherein this policy is issued, then no such suit or action shall be sustainable unless commenced within the shortest limitation of time permitted by the laws of such State.

Choice of Law

K. It is agreed that this policy and its endorsement(s) is a contract of marine insurance protecting against marine risks and has been applied for, priced and underwritten as such, and the law applicable to any interpretation of this policy and the rights and obligations of the Company and the Assured hereunder shall be US federal maritime common law or, in the absence of US federal maritime common law, the law of the state of New York, irrespective of any principles of choice of law.

8. OPERATING CLAUSES

The following operating clauses shall apply:

Reports of Shipments

A. It is a condition of this insurance that the Assured report to the Company all shipments of insured property or other insured interests coming within the terms hereof within thirty days after the end of the month in which all details of insured shipments or other insured interests become known to the Assured, unless otherwise agreed. Premium for all reported shipments or other insured interests shall be paid by the Assured at rates as agreed. The Company, however, being entitled to all premium as agreed whether interests have been reported or not. Willful failure to make such reports shall render this policy voidable at the Company's option as of the date it would have attached to the unreported shipment or other insured interest. However, unintentional error or omission or delay in making any such report shall not void this insurance provided the same be reported to the Company as soon as known to the Assured.

Inspections of Records

B. The Company or a person appointed by the Company may examine the books and records of the Assured as far as they relate to the subject matter of this insurance at any time while this insurance is in force and for twelve months after termination.

Special Cargo Policies

C. When the Company supplies Special Cargo Policies or Certificates to the Assured, such action authorizes the Assured to utilize such Special Cargo Policies or Certificates to provide evidence of insurance to third parties, subject to the following restrictions:

(1) Special Cargo Policies or Certificates may be used only in connection with shipments to which this Open Policy attaches.

(2) Terms, conditions, and values entered upon a Special Cargo Policy or Certificate by the Assured must conform to Open Policy terms applicable to the shipment for which the Special

Cargo Policy or Certificate is utilized unless the Company's written agreement to other terms is obtained.

(3) Copies of all Special Cargo Policies or Certificates utilized by the Assured must be sent to the Company promptly upon issuance.

(4) In the event a Special Cargo Policy or Certificate is spoiled or voided, the original and any duplicate are to be returned to the Company.

By utilizing a Special Cargo Policy or Certificate, the Assured agrees to reimburse the Company, if by reason of any omission or insertions made by the Assured or their authorized representative upon such Special Cargo Policy or Certificate, the Company is obligated to pay a claim not covered by this policy or an amount in excess of what this policy undertakes to pay.

Other Insurance

D. As respects each shipment or other insured interest:

(1) This insurance shall be deemed void to the extent of any insurance procured by any carrier or other bailee which is available to the beneficiary hereof or will be so available if this insurance is voided.

(2) If the Assured or others (excepting any carrier or other bailee) shall have procured other ocean marine insurance attaching earlier than the attachment hereunder, then this insurance shall be liable only to the extent of any deficiency in such prior insurance as compared to the insured value hereunder.

(3) If the Assured or others (excepting any carrier or other bailee) shall have procured other ocean marine insurance attaching later than the attachment hereunder, then this insurance shall be liable up to the insured value hereunder without any claim to contribution.

(4) If the Assured or others (excepting any carrier or other bailee) shall have procured other ocean marine insurance attaching simultaneous with insurance hereunder, then this insurance shall be liable, only for the pro rata share of any claim that the insured value hereunder bears to the total amount available from all insurance.

(5) If the Company is relieved of any liability by the operation of this clause it shall, nevertheless, retain all premium. In consideration of such premium the Company guarantees prompt payment of claims covered by this insurance. The Company further insures against any difference in conditions which make the other insurance less favorable to the Assured than insurance hereunder.

Also published by the Council on International Law and Politics

International Business and Trade Law:

Talia Einhorn & Frank Emmert: International Business Transactions – Documents, 2nd rev. ed., Chicago 2013, ISBN 978-09858156-2-2

Joseph E. Miller: Changing Our Approach to Changing the World – Encouraging and Enhancing American Engagement in International Philanthropy Through Tax Law Reform, Chicago 2013, ISBN 978-09858156-3-9

Frank Emmert (ed.): Corporate Social Responsibility in Comparative Perspective, Chicago 2014, ISBN 978-09858156-4-6

Frank Emmert (ed.): World Trade and Investment Law – Documents, Indianapolis 2018, ISBN 978-0-9858156-7-7

Csongor István Nagy (ed.), Investment Arbitration and National Interest, Indianapolis 2018, ISBN 978-0-9858156-8-4

Frank Emmert (ed.): International Business Transactions – Documents, Vol. II – Dispute Settlement Documents, Indianapolis 2020, ISBN 978-1-950137-01-5

Islamic Law Library:

Ahmed M. El Demery: The Arab Charter of Human Rights – A Voice for Sharia in the Modern World, with a Foreword by Prof. M. Cherif Bassiouni, Chicago 2015, ISBN 978-0985815653

Ahmed A. Altawyan: International Commercial Arbitration in Saudi Arabia, Indianapolis 2018, ISBN 978-0-9858156-9-1

Rakan F. Alharbi: The Development of Saudi Women's Rights – Theory, Practice, Challenges, and Solutions – a Critical and Analytical Study of the Impact of Cultural Norms on the Recognition of Women's Rights of Employment and Freedom of Movement, Indianapolis 2020 (forthcoming)

Mohammad M. Bayoumi Ibrahim: Women's Rights Under International, American, Islamic and Egyptian Law: An Irresolvable Conflict?, Indianapolis 2020 (forthcoming)

All publications of the Council on International Law and Politics are available on Amazon and from leading booksellers.

Made in the USA
Monee, IL
18 August 2021